THE COMMUNICATION DISORDERS
CASEBOOK
Learning by Example

Second Edition

THE COMMUNICATION DISORDERS
CASEBOOK
Learning by Example

Second Edition

Shelly S. Chabon, PhD, CCC-SLP
Ellen R. Cohn, PhD, CCC-SLP
Dorian Lee-Wilkerson, PhD, CCC-SLP

PLURAL
PUBLISHING
INC.

9177 Aero Drive, Suite B
San Diego, CA 92123

email: information@pluralpublishing.com
website: https://www.pluralpublishing.com

Typeset in 10/13 Stone Informal by Flanagan's Publishing Services, Inc.
Printed in United States of America by Integrated Books International

For permission to use material from this text, contact us by
Telephone: (866) 758-7251
Fax: (888) 758-7255
email: permissions@pluralpublishing.com

Every attempt has been made to contact the copyright holders for material originally printed in another source. If any have been inadvertently overlooked, the publisher will gladly make the necessary arrangements at the first opportunity.

This book was previously published by Pearson Education, Inc.

Library of Congress Cataloging-in-Publication Data:
Names: Chabon, Shelly S., editor. | Cohn, Ellen R. (Speech therapist)
   editor. | Lee-Wilkerson, Dorian, editor.
Title: The communication disorders casebook : learning by example / [edited
   by] Shelly S. Chabon, Ellen R. Cohn, Dorian Lee-Wilkerson.
Description: Second edition. | San Diego, CA : Plural Publishing, Inc.,
   [2025] | a Preceded by: The communication disorders casebook / [edited
   by] Shelly S. Chabon, Ellen R. Cohn. Upper Saddle River, N.J. :
   Pearson, c2011. | Includes bibliographical references.
Identifiers: LCCN 2023008619 (print) | LCCN 2023008620 (ebook) | ISBN
   9781635504095 (paperback) | ISBN 1635504090 (paperback) | ISBN
   9781635504101 (ebook)
Subjects: MESH: Communication Disorders | Case Reports
Classification: LCC RC425 (print) | LCC RC425 (ebook) | NLM WL 340.2 |
   DDC 616.85/5—dc23/eng/20230412
LC record available at https://lccn.loc.gov/2023008619
LC ebook record available at https://lccn.loc.gov/2023008620

CONTENTS

Part III. School-Age Child Cases

LITERACY

LITERACY/PHONOLOGY

SWALLOWING

VOICE

Part IV. Adult Cases

APHASIA

APHASIA

APHASIA

APHASIA

APHASIA

ABOUT THE EDITORS

Shelly S. Chabon, PhD, CCC-SLP, is the Vice Provost for Academic Personnel and Dean of Interdisciplinary General Education at Portland State University. Dr. Chabon formerly served as PSU's Associate Dean of Humanities and Social Sciences, as well as Chair and Professor in the Department of Speech and Hearing Sciences. She is a Fellow of the American Speech-Language-Hearing Association (ASHA), recipient of the Dorothy Dreyer award for Volunteerism, the Certificate of Recognition for Outstanding Contributions in Higher Education, the Honors of the Association, and was the 2012 ASHA President. Dr. Chabon served as a member of several ASHA committees and councils and as Chair of the ASHA Board of Ethics.

Ellen R. Cohn, PhD, CCC-SLP, ASHA Fellow, is a part-time faculty member in the Department of Communication at the University of Pittsburgh and University of Maryland Global Campus, teaching health communication and other applied communication courses in remote formats. At the University of Pittsburgh, she served as Associate Dean for Instruction and Interim Director, Rehabilitation Science Undergraduate Program, School of Health and Rehabilitation Sciences; and professor, Department of Communication Science and Disorders. Cohn has been Editor of the *International Journal of Telerehabilitation* since 2008 and was founding Coordinator of ASHA SIG #18 on Telepractice. She has coproduced books about videofluoroscopy in cleft palate; telerehabilitation, communication as culture, diversity in higher education, tele-AAC, fundamentals of AAC, and diversity in remote learning and is coeditor of this casebook's first edition. Cohn is a life member of the American Cleft Palate-Craniofacial Association and a faculty fellow of Pitt's McGowan Institute on Regenerative Medicine.

Dorian Lee-Wilkerson, PhD, CCC-SLP, is Associate Professor at Hampton University. She has had over 30 years of clinical and higher education experience. She has published and presented in the areas of scholarship of teaching and learning, cultural competence, and childhood language disorders. She is an ASHA Fellow, has served on ASHA's Multicultural Issues Board, and is a recipient of the Excellence in Diversity Award from CAPCSD.

PREFACE
Casebook Songs

Introducing Our Book

The Communication Disorders Casebook: Learning by Example is intentionally different from most textbooks in communication sciences and disorders in both breadth and depth. The book includes an unusually broad examination of individuals with a variety of communication disorders. In-depth case reports describe real-life examples of clinical encounters between clinicians and the clients they serve, with references to historically significant and current literature and discussion of scientific evidence, clinicians' experiences, and clients' preferences.

We hope that the book will serve many audiences, including students, practicing clinicians, colleagues from other health care professions, and consumers of speech-language pathology and audiology services. An accompanying **Instructor's Manual**, which poses provocative questions concerning each case, offers additional resources and includes a test bank. A PowerPoint presentation is also included for each case, to stimulate students' critical thinking.

This book brings together a remarkably diverse and gifted group of scholars and clinicians. The cases themselves involve individuals across the age range. The text contains 61 cases divided into four sections by age group (infant/toddler, preschool, school age, and adult). Each situation depicts a unique relationship between at least two partners: a client and a clinician. Each author shares his or her story so that readers can learn about individuals with communication disorders and how they are evaluated and treated from the perspectives of those who provide services. The first chapter describes the common elements of each case study.

Our collective approach is decidedly client centered and challenges readers to give weight to both the art and science of our profession. We trust you will agree that the therapeutic relationship that develops between a clinician and client (and/ or the client's family) is enhanced by a spirit of mutual respect and collaboration and a focus on solutions and quality of life.

Reaching Back—Before We Look Ahead

To set the stage for your reading of the case studies, we ask you to think back to the first person you met with atypical speech and/or hearing. Can you recall the details of that interaction, the individual's communication characteristics, and how you felt? How did this person function within his or her day-to-day environment? What impact did this person have on your decision to enter or interact with our profession? We will each share one of our stories.

Shelly: I have a number of clients whom I remember with affection and gratitude. I will begin at the beginning, with my first client as a new graduate student. My "clinical assignment" (I will call him Bill) was a college freshman who stuttered. This young man was a basketball star and was over 6'6" tall. As someone who is not quite 5' and who had never worked with a person who stuttered, I felt intimidated by his height and the severity of his speech disorder and concerned about how I could help, given my limited experience. Each time Bill spoke, he diverted his eye contact, his face turned red, and he started to perspire, apparently because of the effort required to communicate.

It seemed as if he stuttered on every word. I wanted to politely excuse myself, but his gentleness and his determination "to get rid of 'this' before it ruins everything" changed my mind and my life. I read all I could find on stuttering, talked with professors and supervisors, and observed my fellow student clinicians. I also decided to accompany Bill to some of his classes and even a few basketball game practices so I could see and hear his communication outside of the clinic room. He worked hard and seemed extremely motivated to change. We shared in the success of his becoming stutter-free and of the partnership that led him down a new path. During treatment, he spoke of the pain and frustration he felt as a person who stuttered. He continually expressed his appreciation to me for what had been achieved. I am not sure I ever told him just how much he meant to me. Perhaps I didn't know. So, "thank you, Bill. You had a profound and lasting impact on me as a person and a professional."

Ellen: My first memories of a person with an atypical speech disorder date to the late 1950s, when I was no more than 3 years old. Like Shelly and Dorian, I am profoundly grateful for the lessons learned. Walking hand-in-hand with my dad on the way to buy a new toy at the five-and-dime store, we passed by a man whose loud voice and appearance truly startled me. My father whispered, "Don't be scared, that's Cookie." He warmly acknowledged Cookie and introduced me to him.

Cookie, as he was affectionately known by almost all who lived in our small New Jersey seaside town, was a man with multiple disabilities. He was largely edentulous and had a very hoarse voice and limited, difficult-to-understand speech. By traditional clinical standards, Cookie's speech and expressive language would indeed be considered disordered. In addition, Cookie walked with a severe gait disturbance and one arm appeared contracted. Cookie's vocal quality attracted attention and was jarring to listen to—initially frightening small children. That is, however, only part of the story. Cookie was known by first name and was beloved and since remembered by many of the residents. Cookie held a full-time job in which he used his voice to sell a product. With a smile for all, each day Cookie stood near the five-and-dime store on Broadway Avenue and called out "aper, aper" to sell *The Daily Record*.

U.S. Poet Laureate (1997–2000) Robert Pinsky, PhD, also a native of Long Branch, New Jersey, immortalized Cookie in his collection of poetry, *The Figured Wheel: New and Collected Poems, 1966–1996*. Pinsky vividly celebrated Cookie and his hoarse voice within the fabric of a small town's "song" in the title of his poem "A Long Branch Song." As in any good case report, Pinsky succinctly described Cookie's voice, unique communication style, and employment: "The hoarse voice of Cookie, hawking / *The Daily Record* for thirty-five years" (Pinsky, 1996, p. 148).

Later, U.S. Representative Frank Pallone entered "A Long Branch Song," additional Pinsky poems, and his own recollection of Cookie in the 1997 U.S. Congressional Record (H.R.R., 1997-05-06).

How many of us can say that we are affectionately remembered by our first name (and a distinctive voice) by several generations of one small town, were celebrated by both a U.S. poet laureate and a U.S. congressman, and featured in the preface of a book on communication science and disorders? Cookie's story embodies our commitment to the importance of looking beyond a diagnosis. We must always interpret the impact of our clients' communication capacities on their hopes and dreams as they relate to their family and friends, workplaces, and communities. It is important to create the possibilities for joyful human communication in the context of accepting environments that de-emphasize the prefix *dis-* in the term *disability*.

Dorian: One client that I remember well was suspected of having a speech and language delay and I was asked to see her for a screening and possible full evaluation. Her name was Isabelle, and she was a charming 4-year-old attending the local Head Start program. She eagerly walked over to meet me as requested by one of her classroom teachers. Before I could formally introduce myself, she asked me my name and wanted to know what the "speech teacher" did. I told her my name and briefly described my job. She responded with the biggest smile, told me her name was Isabelle, and happily accompanied me on a short walk to the small room reserved for special programs, leaving behind her envious playmates. Isabelle made herself comfortable at the table and waited for me to position my materials and myself at the table. Once I settled at the table, I asked Isabelle to tell me something wonderful about herself and family. That captivating smile appeared, and Isabelle told me the most delightful stories. Stories about her parents, her four sisters, her grandmother, the two cats, and the aunts, uncles, and cousins who visited frequently for birthday parties and holidays. Needless to say, I was stumped to find one speech or language behavior that caused her teachers to be concerned.

When I asked the teachers their concerns (the lead teacher and two classroom aides), they all said the same: Isabelle's dialect is too strong. She will not excel academically speaking that way.

Isabelle was bright, confident, and loquacious. I did not want to change that, but I also wanted Isabelle's teachers to have the same confidence in her that she had in herself. At the time, in the very late 1970s, I am not sure that my decision was the right one, but I decided to work with Isabelle, giving her second dialect instruction. We played games talking in different voices: the voices for school and grownups and the voices for home, play, and peers. I also gave the teachers information about the dialects of American English. While I never convinced those teachers that the dialect one speaks is not reflective of intelligence or a predictor of academic performance, I frequently think back to Isabelle, the child who showed me that intelligence and academic ability is expressed using many different speech and language forms.

61 More Stories

Remembering Isabelle, Cookie, and Bill and the thousands of clients we have collectively had the privilege to know, we have written this book to underscore the importance of putting the person first. We trust you will enjoy meeting the clients and gifted clinicians within these 61 case studies and that you will be enriched by their collective "songs."

Shelly S. Chabon, PhD, CCC-SLP
Ellen R. Cohn, PhD, CCC-SLP
Dorian Lee-Wilkerson, PhD, CCC-SLP

Authors' Note

Cookie is referred to by his real name, as the author did not engage in a clinical interaction with him. He has been previously publicly named in newspapers, a book, and the U.S. Congressional Record.

References

Pallone, F. (1997, May 5). America's 39th Poet Laureate Robert Pinsky. *C-SPAN Congressional Chronicle.* http://www.c-spanarchives.org/congress/?q=node/77531&id=6819033

Pinsky, R. A. "Long Branch Song." In *The figured wheel: New and collected poems 1966–1996* (p. 148). Farrar, Straus and Giroux.

ACKNOWLEDGMENTS

To our dear families and friends: We are immensely grateful for your sustaining love, encouragement, and understanding. You are our true sources of strength, laughter, and pride.

To our authors: Thank you to our esteemed colleagues for entrusting these outstanding cases to us. As coeditors of this text, we continue to learn from your humility, experiences with, and insights about the clinical decision-making process. This edition has benefited greatly from your updates, ideas, and degree of compassion and cooperation.

To our second edition publisher: Our gratitude to Plural Publishing, Inc., especially Kaitlin Nadal and Valerie Johns, for your trust, guidance, and expert editorial support.

To our first edition publisher: Our appreciation to Pearson Education, Inc., for bringing the first edition to life in 2011, and then in 2021, for enabling publication of the second edition by Plural Publishing, Inc.

To our project assistants: We could not have asked for better project assistants: Bhavani Ganesh for your early work and Brandy Bell and Katelyn Tabler for your ongoing help and attention to the many details and parts of this project that enabled us to complete it with grace and on time.

CONTRIBUTORS

Shamine Alves is a senior at Hampton University majoring in Communicative Sciences and Disorders and minoring in Psychology. She is from the Atlanta Metropolitan area and has been a musician for 13 years. Shamine is a McNair Scholar and a member of the Hampton University Marching Force. Her passion for music has connected her to the field of audiology, which she plans to pursue after graduating from Hampton University.

Noma B. Anderson, PhD, is Dean of the College of Nursing and Health Sciences at the University of Vermont. She is a speech-language pathologist with areas of expertise in multicultural aspects of communication sciences and disorders, health and educational disparities, language acquisition, and microaggressions. She has served ASHA as President and Vice President for Academic Affairs and has been Deputy Director of the National Black Association for Speech-Language and Hearing. She is a Fellow and recipient of Association Honors from ASHA. Her degrees are from the Hampton Institute (BA), Emerson College (MS), and University of Pittsburgh (PhD).

Steven M. Barlow, PhD, ASHA F/H, is a Corwin Moore Professor and served as Chair of the Department of Special Education and Communication Disorders at the University of Nebraska and Associate Director of the Center for Brain-Biology-Behavior. He has been awarded more than 30 U.S. and international patents for device and software innovations for assessment of somatosensory and motor function in orofacial and limb systems. Dr. Barlow has led several major NIH projects since 1987, resulting in the development of the medical device technology known as the NTrainer (FDA approved in 2008) used by NICUs to promote ororhythmic suck pattern generation and oral feeding skills in preterm infants.

Christina A. Baumgartner, MS, CCC-SLP, is the Executive Director of Therapy Operations at the Rehabilitation Hospital of Indiana (RHI). Prior to joining RHI, Christina served in various leadership roles in the health care industry including director of the Speech, Language and Learning Clinic at Northwestern University, Evanston, IL, and manager of the Speech-Language Pathology Department at the University of Kansas Hospital, Kansas City, KS. She has extensive clinical experience as a medical speech-language pathologist with a specialty in acquired communication, cognitive, and swallowing disorders. Christina earned her MS in medical speech pathology from Rush University and completed doctoral coursework at the University of Colorado–Boulder.

Gabriella Billups, BS, is a graduate student attending Hampton University, where she is pursuing her master's in Communicative Sciences and Disorders. She is a recipient of the National NSSLHA Excellence in Speech-Language Pathology Award and is a 2022 participant in the ASHA Minority Student Leadership Program. Gabriella intends to open a private practice while promoting early language and literacy programs in her community and apply to a doctoral program to further research in the field of speech-language pathology. Gabriella is a member of the National Student Speech Language and Hearing Association (NSSLHA) and the National Black Association for Speech Language Pathology (NBASLH).

Arpita Bose, PhD, primarily focuses her research on extending our theoretical understanding of the interplay between cognitive, linguistic, and speech motor processes during language production (in normal and neurologically impaired speakers such as those with dementia, aphasia, apraxia of speech, and Parkinson's disease) and subsequently implementing those findings to develop better intervention strategies for language production deficits in neurologically impaired populations. Using methodologies and approaches from various disciplines (for example, psycholinguistics, experimental psychology, neuroscience, and speech and language therapy), she has strived to bridge the gap between theoretical and applied research in language processing and its disorders.

Mindy S. Bridges, MS, CCC-SLP, is a clinical speech-language pathologist and a doctoral candidate in the Department of Speech-Language-Hearing at the University of Kansas. Her research interests include the connection between language and reading disorders, early identification of children at risk for disabilities, and the use of response to intervention practices in school settings.

Danielle Brimo, PhD, CCC-SLP, is Associate Professor and Graduate Program Director of the Davies School of COSD at Texas Christian University. The overarching goal of her research is to explore the language and literacy skills of school-age children with and without language and reading impairments. Her primary line of research investigates how syntax contributes to school-age children's spoken language, written language, and reading comprehension.

Paul M. Brueggeman, AuD, CCC-A, has been working in the field of audiology for over 24 years, with the last 8 at Sound Decision Hearing in Sioux Falls, SD. In this capacity, his clinical work has continued to focus on children and adults with hearing loss. His clinical and research focus has consistently centered upon adult education principles, pediatric hearing issues, and psychosocial counseling in communication disorders. Throughout his career, Paul has helped children and adults with hearing loss improve their lives through proper hearing aid fittings and counseling.

Telina P. Caudill, MS, CCC-SLP, ATP, is the lead speech-language pathologist at the Veterans' Hospital Assistive Technology Program in Tampa, FL. She developed the program in 2009 and has facilitated the four CARF accreditations. She is a SME in AAC, ATC, and tele-AAC. She has presented at 25+ regional and national lectures, guest lectured at the USF graduate program, and authored/coauthored two textbook chapters. She was presented with the Rick L. Bollinger Clinician of the Year Award in 2017.

Erin Clark, MS, CCC-SLP, is an Assistant Professor and Clinic Director in the Speech-Language Pathology Program at Indiana University of Pennsylvania (IUP). She received her BS and MS from Indiana University of Pennsylvania. Mrs. Clark maintains both a professional and personal interest in audiology/aural rehabilitation. She teaches the undergraduate aural rehabilitation course, supervises the graduate-level hearing clinic at IUP, and serves as the faculty supervisor for the IUP Chapter of the Audiology Student Association. In addition, Mrs. Clark is the parent of a child with hearing loss.

Terese Conrad, MA, CCC-SLP, is a Clinical Professor in the Communication Sciences and Disorders Department at Wichita State University in Wichita, Kansas. She provides supervision to undergraduate and graduate students working with clients with complex and/or limited language. Teaching responsibilities include the graduate course: Augmentative and Alternative Communication. Terese has been a practicing clinician for 30 years, providing assessment, treatment, support, and training for children and adults presenting with communication disorders related to autism spectrum disorders in addition to other developmental disabilities.

Suzanne Coyle, MA, CCC-SLP, is Executive Director of Stroke Comeback Center, a nonprofit organization in the Washington, DC area that is committed to supporting stroke survivors and their families throughout their recoveries. She completed her undergraduate and graduate studies at Miami University in Oxford, OH, and received a Nonprofit Management Executive Certificate from Georgetown University. Prior to her current role, she spent 20 years working with adults with neurogenic communication disorders in the outpatient rehabilitation setting. Her research interests include aphasia group treatment and quality of life after stroke.

Sena Crutchley, MA, CCC-SLP, a graduate of UNC Greensboro, is currently an Associate Professor and Clinical Educator in the UNC Greensboro Department of Communication Sciences and Disorders. She brings to gender-affirming care a background in theater and voice, expertise in multicultural issues in speech-language pathology, and 22 years of experience as an SLP in a variety of clinical settings. Sena now leads the Gender Affirming Voice and Communication Program at UNC Greensboro and has presented and is published in the area of gender-affirming care.

Michael de Riesthal, PhD, CCC-SLP, is Associate Professor in the Department of Hearing and Speech Sciences at Vanderbilt University Medical Center (VUMC) and Director of Pi Beta Phi Rehabilitation Institute. He mentors clinicians and graduate students in clinical practice and research, and he serves as the lead speech-language pathologist in the Multidisciplinary Traumatic Brain Injury Clinic (TBI) and Huntington's Disease Clinic at VUMC. Dr. de Riesthal teaches graduate-level courses on aphasia, TBI, and motor speech disorders. His research has focused on clinical outcomes following TBI, cognitive-communication and motor speech changes in Huntington's disease, and assessment and prognosis for aphasia.

Jodelle F. Deem, PhD, CCC-SLP, is Associate Professor Emeritus in the Department of Communication Sciences and Disorders at the University of Kentucky. Dr. Deem is the former Director of the Program in Communication Sciences and Disorders in the United Kingdom. Her scholarly interests included assessment and management of adult voice disorders as well as assessment and management of swallowing disorders and motor speech disorders in adults. She is coauthor of *Manual of Voice Therapy* (2nd ed., with Lynda Miller, 2000).

Aimee Dietz, PhD, CCC-SLP, RYT-200, is Professor and Department Chair at Georgia State University. She is a speech-language pathologist at heart and is dedicated to training the next generation of academic researchers and clinicians, as well as improving outcomes for people with aphasia. Her research focuses on using AAC as a language recovery tool and identifying associated neurobiomarkers. In recent years, she has cultivated a new line of research that seeks to understand how mind-body practices, including adapted yoga, might be harnessed to build resilience and coping for people with poststroke aphasia and their cosurvivors.

Roxann Diez Gross, PhD, CCC-SLP, ASHA Fellow, has over 35 years of clinical experience. She is a consultant and clinical specialist for Swallowing Diagnostics, Inc., Parkland, FL. She has served as principal investigator on several research grants that she has been awarded. Her research in the area of respiratory and swallowing interactions has resulted in multiple peer-reviewed and invited publications, as well as frequent invitations to lecture both nationally and internationally. Her research study that developed a method and apparatus for quantifying pharyngeal residue was granted a U.S. patent (#7,555,329 B2).

Leo Dunham, MS, CCC-SLP, is currently working for Choice Rehabilitation at Autumn Hill Therapy and Living Center and Brighton Ridge Therapy and Living Center as a Speech-Language Pathologist and as Director of Rehabilitation. He obtained his master's degree from Rockhurst University in Kansas City, MO. Speech-language pathology is his second career, as he spent almost 30 years working in mechanical design and engineering. Leo earned a law degree from the University of Kansas in 1987. His experience has been focused on dysphagia, voice, aphasia, and cognitive communication disorders in skilled nursing environments.

Manaswita Dutta, PhD, CCC-SLP, is Assistant Professor at the Department of Speech and Hearing Sciences at Portland State University. Her research interests include understanding the nature of cognitive-linguistic changes that occur as a result of aging and neurological impairments such as stroke, traumatic brain injury, dementia, and epilepsy. More specifically, her research examines the relationship between nonlinguistic cognitive functions (e.g., attention, executive functioning) and language and its impact on functional communication and psychosocial outcomes of individuals with acquired neurogenic communication disorders. Her recent work focuses on the improvement and standardization of spoken discourse assessment in aphasia and bilingual dementia.

Lea Helen Evans, PhD, CCC-SLP, is a speech-language pathologist. Her specializations are in child language development and child language disorders. She has most recently been a clinical professor through the School of Medicine at Vanderbilt University Medical Center, where she taught in the area of articulation development and disorders, provided direct clinical care, provided managerial support by supervision of a cadre of speech-language pathologists, and supervised graduate students. Previously, she taught, lectured, and supervised in the areas of child language development, child language disorders, articulation development and disorders, and multicultural language differences at the University of Mississippi and Mississippi University for Women. She received her bachelor's degree from Lambuth University, her master's degree from the University of Mississippi, and her doctorate from the University of Tennessee.

Michelle Flippin, PhD, CCC-SLP, is Assistant Professor in Communicative Disorders at the University of Rhode Island. In her research, Dr. Flippin examines the development of social communication in children with neurodevelopmental disorders. She is particularly interested in the role of parents in optimizing children's communicative development and father-implemented social communication intervention.

Diane Garcia, SLP, is a Speech-Language Pathologist in the Palm Springs Unified School District in the sunny California desert. She was previously on the faculty at the University of Redlands, where she supervised the speech sound disorders clinic and taught undergraduate and graduate courses. Diane is the coauthor of *Phonological Treatment of Speech Sound Disorders in Children: A Practical Guide*.

Her areas of expertise and research include assessment and remediation of articulation, motor speech, and phonological disorders in children.

Karen J. Golding-Kushner, PhD, has specialized in speech associated with craniofacial disorders and VPI for over 45 years. An ASHA Fellow, she was NJSHA's 2022 recipient of the Distinguished Clinical Achievement Award. She has authored over 25 chapters and articles, as well as three books on clefting and VCFS/22q, one of which was translated into Japanese. She has made over 100 international presentations, was founding Associate Coordinator of ASHA SIG 18 (Telepractice), and is a charter member of ASHA SIG 5 (Craniofacial). She owns Golding-Kushner Consulting, LLC and is a consultant for the Virtual Center for VCFS and Other Craniofacial Disorders.

Brian A. Goldstein, PhD, CCC-SLP, is the Chief Academic Officer and Executive Dean at the University of St. Augustine for Health Sciences, San Marcos, CA. He is the former editor of *Language, Speech, and Hearing Services in Schools*, is a Fellow of the American Speech-Language-Hearing Association (ASHA), and received the Certificate of Recognition for Special Contribution in Multicultural Affairs from ASHA.

Howard Goldstein, PhD, CCC-SLP, is Associate Dean of Research and Professor of Communication Sciences and Disorders at University of South Florida. His research has sought to enhance the language, social, and literacy development of children with developmental disabilities and students in high-poverty schools at high risk for language and reading disabilities. His contributions to the field were recognized as an ASHA Fellow in 1989 and Honors of the Association in 2016 and AAAS Fellow in 2020.

Sue Grogan-Johnson, PhD, CCC/SLP, is Professor in Speech-Language Pathology at Kent State University, Kent, OH. She teaches courses in pediatric and adult language disorders and directs the school-based telepractice project at the university. She presents on topics related to school-age language disorders and telepractice, and her research interests are in the area of the application of telepractice to school-age populations.

Sue T. Hale, MCD, CCC-SLP (Retired), was Director of Clinical Education and Associate Professor in the Department of Hearing and Speech Sciences at Vanderbilt University Medical Center until her retirement in 2016. An ASHA Honors recipient and Fellow, she served as the 2009 President of the American Speech-Language-Hearing Association. She has extensive previous ASHA service on councils and committees in the areas of clinical and academic standards and professional ethics. Prior to retirement, she taught and lectured in the areas of professional ethics, counseling, and clinical supervision. She received her bachelor's and master's degrees from the University of Mississippi.

Nerissa Hall, PhD, CCC-SLP, is cofounder/director of Commūnicāre, LLC and the SLLC at Tate Behavioral. Her focus is augmentative and alternative communication and tele-AAC, working primarily with school-aged individuals. She has presented nationally regarding AAC and tele-AAC. Nerissa has served as a LEND Fellow and adjunct faculty at Elms, Cambridge College, and UMass-Amherst. She coedited *Tele-AAC: Augmentative and Alternative Communication Through Telepractice* and *Fundamentals of AAC: A Case-Based Approach to Enhancing Communication*, and is passionate about advancing the field to ensure meaningful outcomes for individuals using AAC and the teams that support them.

Meredith Harold, PhD, CCC-SLP, a former speech-language pathologist and university faculty member, is currently CEO of The Informed SLP. She leads a team of over 50 scientists and clinicians in reading and translating our field's latest clinical practice research, then delivers this to practicing SLPs in a format compatible with busy and patient-centered clinical practice. She is President of the Kansas Speech-Language-Hearing Association, member of ASHA's CRISP Committee, and a frequent collaborator on many speech-language pathology podcasts and social media channels.

Gail Harris-Schmidt, PhD, CCC-SLP, is Professor Emeritus (Retired) and former Chair of the Department of Communication Sciences and Disorders at Saint Xavier University in Chicago. She received her BA in Psychology and MA in Speech-Language Pathology from Vanderbilt University and her PhD in Learning Disabilities from Northwestern University. She is a member of the Scientific and Clinical Advisory Committee of the National Fragile X Foundation, for which she wrote sections of the Foundation website (http://www.fragilex.org). She is coauthor, with Dr. Dale Fast, of "The Source for Fragile X Syndrome" and "Fragile X Syndrome: Genetics, Characteristics, and Educational Implications" (in *Advances in Special Education*, Vol. 11, 1998). She has copresented numerous workshops at the national, state, and local levels on the causes and characteristics of and intervention for children with fragile X syndrome.

Pamela Hart, PhD, CCC-SLP, serves as Department Chair and Professor of Communication Sciences and Disorders at Rockhurst University. Dr. Hart's research interests include language and literacy outcomes of individuals with complex communication needs, program evaluation in communication sciences and disorders, and technology applications to assessment and intervention in speech-language pathology. As a CSD student mentor, Dr. Hart is committed to the development of reflective, evidence-based practitioners.

Brooke Hatfield, MS, CCC-SLP, is Associate Director of Health Care Services in Speech-Language Pathology at the American Speech-Language-Hearing Association. After completing her master's at Vanderbilt University in 1998, she worked with adults with neurogenic communication disorders in the Washington, DC area until joining ASHA in 2017. Her research and professional interests include augmentative and alternative communication, group-based services, and social determinants of health.

Victoria S. Henbest, PhD, CCC-SLP, is Assistant Professor at the University of South Alabama, where she provides clinical education and teaches graduate-level courses on school-age language/literacy and augmentative/alternative communication. She earned her master's degree from Missouri

State University and a PhD from the University of South Carolina. Dr. Henbest has clinical experience in the public school and university settings. Her research on children's linguistic awareness skills and word-level literacy has been published in scientific journals.

Sally Hewat, PhD, BappSci (Speech Path), CPSP, is Vice President of Clinical Services at OST Therapy, a national company providing allied health services to children throughout China. Sally believes in the transformative power of human connection that is enabled through one's ability to communicate, and her clinical interest and expertise is focused on development of innovative approaches to support people with communication difficulties worldwide. With a career in the higher education sector spanning 20+ years, Sally is recognized internationally as an innovative academic leader in transnational education and the preparation of speech pathology students for practice. Her work has been recognized through numerous university, national, and international community awards, and in 2021, she was awarded the Elizabeth Usher Memorial prize by Speech Pathology Australia.

Lindsey Hiebert, PhD, CCC-SLP, is a Postdoctoral Research Fellow at the University of Delaware. She earned a PhD in Communication Sciences and Disorders from the University of Texas at Dallas and a Clinical Master's in Speech-Language Pathology. She is a fluent Spanish speaker and obtained a Bachelor of Arts degree in Spanish Language and Literature. Her research interests include bilingual language development, disorders, and intervention in preschool and school-age children, stemming from her extensive clinical work with culturally and linguistically diverse populations. Her publications to date include longitudinal observations of language and reading development in Spanish-English bilingual children across 3 or more years.

Barbara W. Hodson, PhD, CCC-SLP, is Professor Emerita in the Department of Communication Sciences and Disorders at Wichita State University in Wichita, KS. An ASHA Fellow, she is a Board Recognized Specialist in Child Language and received the Frank Kleffner Clinical Career Award in 2004 and ASHA Honors of the Association in 2009. Her major professional interests include clinical phonology, metaphonology, and early literacy.

Tiffany P. Hogan, PhD, CCC-SLP, is a clinical speech-language pathologist and Professor in the Department of Communication Sciences and Disorders at MGH Institute of Health Professions. Dr. Hogan studies the genetic, neurologic, and behavioral links between oral and written language development, with a focus on comorbid speech, language, and literacy disorders.

Emily M. Homer, CCC-SLP, is known nationally for helping school districts, state organizations, and school teams to establish swallowing and feeding procedures. She is an ASHA Fellow (2018) and received the Louis M. DiCarlo (1999) award for her work with school-based swallowing and feeding services. She focuses on utilizing a team approach to establish and maintain safe, efficient, and enjoyable mealtimes for children at school. She has published *Management of Swallowing and Feeding Disorders in Schools*, and she has numerous articles focused on providing swallowing and feeding services in the schools in peer-reviewed journals.

Karen Hux, PhD, CCC-SLP, received her doctorate in speech-language pathology at Northwestern University in Evanston, IL. She is the Director of Research at Quality Living, Inc., Omaha, NE, and a professor emeritus of the University of Nebraska–Lincoln. At Quality Living, she coordinates, performs, and disseminates research about rehabilitation practices pertinent to people with acquired neurological disorders.

Cynthia H. Jacobsen, PhD, CCC-SLP, is an ASHA Fellow (RETD). She served as Director of the Cleft Palate Clinic and Hearing and Speech Clinics at Children's Mercy Hospital, Kansas City for 34 years. Dr. Jacobsen is a Life Member of the American Cleft Palate-Craniofacial Association.

Kathy J. Jakielski, PhD, CCC-SLP, is Professor Emeritus of Communication Sciences and Disorders at Augustana College in Rock Island, IL, and an ASHA Fellow. She specializes in the diagnosis and treatment of children with speech sound disorders, focusing on childhood apraxia of speech (CAS). She is coauthor of *Phonetic Science for Clinical Practice* and *Phonetic Science for Clinical Practice: A Transcription and Application Workbook* (Plural Publishing, 2018) and author of *Building Speech and Quantifying Complexity*, a toolkit for treating children with CAS and other severe disorders of speech.

Shatonda S. Jones, PhD, CCC-SLP, CBIST, is a tenured Associate Professor in the Department of Communication Sciences and Disorders at Rockhurst University in Kansas City, MO. Dr. Jones specializes in adult and geriatric populations with neurogenic communication and swallowing disorders. Her research interests are varied and include diffusion and dissemination of health information and community and individual preparedness and response to health threats, edutainment, vowel erosion, and use of accessible technology in the clinic.

Patricia Kearns, PT, completed her undergraduate education at Doane College and received her master's degree in physical therapy from the University of Nebraska Medical Center. After practicing both in Nebraska and Arizona, Ms. Kearns joined Quality Living, Inc., in 2001 as a physical therapist. In 2011, Patricia was named President and CEO of Quality Living.

Dorothy "Beth" Kelly, MS, CCC-SLP, is Assistive Technology/Augmentative and Alternative Communication (AAC) Liaison in St. Tammany Parish schools. She served as the dysphagia case manager with students from elementary through high school, arranging Safe Eating Plans for them and monitoring their progress. She has presented with her colleagues on dysphagia, oral motor, and augmentative communication in her district. Her work with patients contributed to the study "Benefits of Thickened Feeds in Previously Healthy Infants With Respiratory Syncytial Viral Bronchiolitis" (in *Pediatric Pulmonology*, Vol. 31, 2001). She is currently pursuing her clinical doctorate at Rocky Mountain University of Health Professions.

Gail B. Kempster, PhD, is Associate Professor Emerita at Rush University, having earned her doctoral degree at Northwestern University. In addition to teaching and research, Dr. Kempster continued working with individuals with voice disorders for most of her career. Her most widely known work is as one of the authors of the 2009 CAPE-V (Consensus Auditory-Perceptual Analysis of Voice) protocol, which was published in *Laryngoscope* and documented as one of the 21 most influential papers in laryngology since the year 2000.

Ann W. Kummer, PhD, CCC-SLP, retired as Senior Director of Speech-Language Pathology at Cincinnati Children's Hospital. She is Professor Emeritus of the University of Cincinnati College of Medicine. She has presented hundreds of national and international lectures and published over 60 peer-reviewed articles and 30 book chapters. She is also the author of the text entitled *Cleft Palate and Craniofacial Conditions* (4th ed., 2020), which includes an online course. Dr. Kummer is an ASHA Fellow and received Honors of ASHA in 2017.

Joanne P. Lasker, PhD, is an Associate Professor in the Department of Communication Sciences and Disorders at Emerson College. She investigates the assessment and treatment of people with neurogenic communication disorders who may benefit from augmentative and alternative communication (AAC), specifically, people living with aphasia. Joanne has served as Chair of the Department of Communication Sciences and Disorders, the Graduate Program Director for the On-Campus Master's Program, and the founding Graduate Program Director for the Speech@ Emerson Online Master's program. She is the winner of the 2019 Spirit of Emerson Award and the 2022 Emerson College Alumni Award for Teaching Innovation.

Darchayla Lewis is a graduating senior studying Communicative Sciences and Disorders with a minor in Spanish at Hampton University. She is a 2021 recipient of an ASHA SPARC award and a 2021 summer intern of the SURIEA program through the Acoustical Society of America.

Erin E. G. Lundblom, PhD, CCC-SLP, is Associate Professor and the Director, Clinical Education in Speech-Language Pathology at the University of Pittsburgh. Lundblom teaches both undergraduate and graduate courses related to clinical service delivery and pediatric communication disorders. Before joining higher education, Lundblom worked in various clinical settings, including educational and health care. Lundblom's areas of clinical interest encompass child language development, the importance of early intervention, and the provision of school-based language and literacy services, including service delivery options. She also enjoys exploring higher education pedagogy, such as best practices in adult teaching and learning.

Verity MacMillan, BappSci (Speech Path), Hons, is a speech-language pathologist who works at the South-Western Sydney Stuttering Unit, a unit within South Western Sydney Local Health District. She is an affiliate of the Ingham Institute of Applied Medical Research and an honorary clinical fellow at the Australian Stuttering Research Centre, the University of Technology Sydney. Verity treats people who stutter of all ages and provides clinical guidance to speech pathologists nationally. She has published research in scientific journals and presented research at international conferences. Verity is a member of the Lidcombe Program Trainers Consortium and the Continuing Professional Education in Stuttering Consortium.

Karissa J. Marble-Flint, PhD, CCC-SLP, is Assistant Professor in the Communication Sciences and Disorders Department at Wichita State University in Wichita, KS. She teaches graduate-level coursework in language and literacy, speech sound disorders, and critical thinking and an undergraduate course in early language development. Her major research and clinical interest area is written language assessment and intervention. Dr. Marble-Flint is the director of the Literacy in Kansas (LinKS) Lab, where she coordinates a summer literacy camp for struggling readers and writers, and she supervises graduate students conducting language-literacy evaluations and research projects.

Cynthia McCormick Richburg, PhD, CCC-A, is Professor in the Communication Sciences and Disorders Department at Wichita State University in Wichita, KS. She received her BA, MA, and PhD from the University of Tennessee in Knoxville. She is coauthor of *School-Based Audiology* (2012, Plural Publishing) and *Children with Audiological Needs: From Identification to Aural Rehabilitation* (2014, Butte). She is currently editor of ASHA's Special Interest Group 9 Perspectives (Pediatric Hearing and Hearing Disorders) and is the AuD Program Coordinator at Wichita State. Dr. Richburg teaches several courses and continues to evaluate children in the university's clinic.

Vicki McCready, MA, CCC-SLP (ret.), was Professor and Director of the Speech and Hearing Center in the Department of Communication Sciences and Disorders at the University of North Carolina Greensboro. She has over 40 years of experience in supervision and clinical education and supervised trans women clients since 2004. She has published and presented extensively in the areas of supervision and clinical education. She became an ASHA Fellow in 1998 and received ASHA's Dorothy Dreyer award for volunteerism in 2012.

Miechelle McKelvey, PhD, CCC-SLP, is the Department Chair at the University of Nebraska Kearney. Her area of research is assessment and treatment of augmentative and alternative communication with adults with acquired neurogenic disorders, specifically adults with aphasia and amyotrophic lateral sclerosis. Her research group, AAC CAP, has developed AAC assessment protocols for four populations: aphasia, ALS, autism, and cerebral palsy.

Deanna K. Meinke, PhD, CCC-A, received her undergraduate degree in communication disorders from Colorado State University and a master's degree in Audiology from Northern Illinois University. She holds a PhD in Audiology from the University of Colorado and is currently a Winchester Distinguished Professor in the Audiology and Speech-Language Sciences program at the University of Northern Colorado. Her research focuses on the early detection and prevention of noise-induced hearing loss. She is a past president of the National Hearing Conservation Association and is Co-Director of the Dangerous Decibels® program. Her favorite sound is the call of the sandhill crane at dawn echoing through a mountain valley.

Ross G. Menzies, PhD, is a clinical psychologist with an interest in anxiety-related disorders, the role of existential issues in psychopathology, the mental health of those who stutter, and applications of cognitive behaviour therapy (CBT). He has developed CBT packages for adolescents and adults who stutter and adapted them for Internet presentation. Ross has produced more than 200 manuscripts, including 10 books, and was the President and Convenor of the 8th World Congress of Behavioural and Cognitive Therapies in 2016. He is a previous National President of the Australian Association for CBT and a founding Board member of the World Confederation of CBT.

Deborah Moncrieff, PhD, CCC-A, researches auditory disorders across the life span, with particular emphasis on the negative impact of auditory disorders on communication, language, learning, and reading. She studies the prevalence and impact of auditory disorders in both children and adults. In order to enhance the clinical diagnosis of APD, she has worked to develop and gather normative data on new tests for the clinical assessment of APD. She has also developed a therapeutic approach for remediating children with a binaural integration type of APD (sometimes referred to as an integration deficit), characterized by a unilateral ear deficit during tests of dichotic listening. To better understand the neurophysiology of normal and disordered auditory processing, she is using electrophysiologic methods to explore neural activation patterns within ascending auditory pathways in children with APD. She has also used functional MRI techniques to characterize levels of brain activation during dichotic listening tasks.

Mariateresa (Teri) H. Muñoz, SLPD, CCC-SLP, is Clinical Assistant Professor at Florida International University. She has over 30 years of experience as a speech-language pathologist and special education instructor combined. Her clinical practice and research areas include early childhood language development and intervention, bilingual language disorders, augmentative and alternative communication (AAC), special education, and speech-language and feeding disorders, including avoidant/restrictive feeding intake disorder. Dr. Muñoz is the president and founder of St. Therese's Roses of Hope, Pediatric (and adult) Center, Inc., a nonprofit organization providing evaluative and therapeutic services in speech-language and feeding disorders across the life span.

Kelley Nelson-Strouts, MA, CCC-SLP, is a clinical speech-language pathologist and doctoral candidate in the Department of Speech-Language-Hearing at the University of Kansas. Her primary research interests include the connection between morphology and reading, as well as the use of assessment procedures appropriate for diverse populations.

Sue O'Brian, PhD, is a speech pathologist with many years of clinical and research experience with adults and children who stutter. She has published approximately 100 papers in professional journals and contributed to several books in the area of stuttering. Her particular interests involve the measurement of stuttering, the development of internet treatment programs for stuttering, and research in the Camperdown Program for adults who stutter. Sue is founding member of the Camperdown Program Trainers Consortium and has presented many workshops both locally and internationally for this program and the Lidcombe Program.

Mark Onslow, PhD, is a speech-language pathologist. He is the Foundation Director of the Australian Stuttering Research Centre. His research interests are the epidemiology of early stuttering, mental health of those who stutter, measurement of stuttering, and the nature and treatment of stuttering. Mark is a member of the international Lidcombe Program Trainers Consortium and is in constant demand as a speaker internationally. He has authored more than 200 publications in peer-reviewed scientific journals. He has published 6 books and 37 book chapters. Mark was joint recipient of the American Speech-Language-Hearing Association Kawana Award for Lifetime Achievement in Publication.

Kristin M. Pelczarski, PhD, CCC-SLP, is Associate Professor at Kansas State University, where she teaches graduate and undergraduate classes on stuttering, professional issues, and speech sound disorders, and is also a clinical supervisor. Her research investigates stuttering and the language planning deficits associated with stuttering using eye-tracking methodology. She uses eye gaze movements and pupil dilation to investigate the underlying linguistic mechanisms that contribute to stuttering. She has published several journal articles, coauthored chapters on stuttering therapy, and has presented her research at the local, national, and international conferences.

Beate Peter, PhD, CCC-SLP, is Associate Professor in the College of Health Solutions at Arizona State University. Her research focuses on the genetic etiologies of communication disorders, downstream effects on brain structures and functions, and characteristic behavioral biomarkers, for instance, fine and gross motor dyscoordination in the presence of genetically influenced childhood apraxia of speech. She initiated and launched the Babble Boot Camp©, the first clinical trial of a proactive intervention designed to mitigate or prevent speech and language disorders in infants at predictable risk for these disorders based on their genotypes.

Sheila R. Pratt, PhD, CCC-SLP, is Professor in the Department of Communication Science and Disorders at the University of Pittsburgh. She teaches courses in auditory rehabilitation and speech perception. Her research focuses on the diagnosis and treatment of communication disorders that occur secondary to hearing loss and brain injury in children and adults.

Erin Redle Sizemore, PhD, CCC-SLP, is Associate Professor and Department Chairperson in the Speech, Language, and Hearing Sciences Department at Mount St. Joseph University in Cincinnati, OH. Her teaching, research, and clinical interests focus on topics related to early intervention, including early speech and language development, pediatric feeding and swallowing disorders, and the impact of intrauterine opioid exposure on children. She is a graduate of the Cincinnati Children's Quality Scholars Program, the ASHA Leadership Development Program, and the Early Childhood Personnel Center Leadership Program. Erin currently serves on the Ohio Early Intervention Comprehensive System of Personnel Development Advisory Workgroup.

Christina Rizzo Tatreau, BCBA, LABA, founded Tate Behavioral with the goal of bringing high-quality ABA services to Massachusetts. As CEO, Christina oversees Tate Behavioral, as well as Tate Learning Center, a highly specialized school for students with complex learning and communication needs. Christina holds a BA from Clark University, has an MFA from Bennington College, and completed her coursework in Applied Behavior Analysis at the Florida Institute of Technology. A former writer, her clinical passions are applied verbal behavior, social skills instruction, and schedules of reinforcement. Christina placed on the *Forbes* NEXT1000 2021 list, a designation honoring small business entrepreneurs redefining the American dream.

Jenny A. Roberts, PhD, is Professor in the Department of Speech-Language-Hearing Sciences at Hofstra University. She became interested in the language development of internationally adopted children while working as an SLP in the late 1990s. At that time, there was little published research available for determining what might be typical language development in the population of internationally adopted children. In 2000, she began collaborating with colleagues, some of whom had adopted children of their own, and together they conducted several studies on the language development of children adopted from China. She is the proud mother of a beautiful daughter and aunt of two beautiful nieces, all of whom are adopted from China.

Richard A. Roberts, PhD, CCC-A, is Associate Professor and Vice Chair of Clinical Operations for the Department of Hearing and Speech Sciences at the Vanderbilt Bill Wilkerson Center. His primary research interests include various topics related to assessment and management of vestibular dysfunction. Dr. Roberts has served on the Board of Directors of the Alabama Academy of Audiology, the American Academy of Audiology, and as a Trustee of the American Academy of Audiology Foundation. He was recently recognized by the American Academy of Audiology with the 2020 Clinical Excellence in Audiology award.

Wilder M. Roberts, AuD, CCC-A, is Assistant Professor at the University of South Alabama, where she provides clinical education with speciality areas of pediatric audiology, amplification, pediatric (re)habilitation, educational audiology, and cochlear implants. She earned her BS in Deaf Education and her MS in Audiology from the University of Montevallo and her AuD from the University of Florida. She has worked in both educational and university settings. She has presented her work at local, state, and national levels.

Kathleen Scaler Scott, PhD, CCC-SLP, BCS-F, is a practicing speech-language pathologist, Board Certified Fluency Specialist, and Associate Professor of Speech-Language Pathology at Monmouth University, NJ. Her research interests are largely in cluttering, atypical disfluency, fluency, and concomitant disorders. Dr. Scaler Scott has spoken nationally and internationally on the topics of fluency and social pragmatic disorders. She was the first Coordinator of the International Cluttering Association and is the recipient of the 2018 Deso Weiss Award for Excellence in the Field of Cluttering and the 2018 Professional of the Year award from the National Stuttering Association.

Michele Schmerbauch, MS, CCC-SLP, graduated from the University of Nebraska–Lincoln in 2005. She has been a speech-language pathologist at Mayo Clinic Health System–Eau Claire for the past 15 years. Her professional interests include working with individuals poststroke, TBI, and degenerative disorders. She is passionate about helping people throughout the life span communicate to maintain social closeness with others while continuing to advocate for themselves and make their needs known.

Diane M. Scott, PhD, CCC-A, is a Full Professor in the Department of Communication Sciences and Disorders in the College of Health and Sciences at North Carolina Central University in Durham, NC. She has been working in audiology for 40 years. She has served in academia for most of her career. Dr. Scott served as the director of the American Speech-Language-Hearing Association (ASHA) Office of Multicultural Affairs. She was also on the ASHA Multicultural Issues Board and the ASHA Board of Ethics.

Kathleen A. Scott, PhD, is Professor Emeritus in the Department of Speech-Language Hearing Sciences at Hofstra University. Her doctoral dissertation was on the spoken and written language skills of school-age children adopted from China. She has made several presentations and written articles concerning the language development of internationally developed children. She is the proud aunt of two beautiful nephews adopted from Guatemala.

Jeff Searl, PhD, is Professor at Michigan State University in the Department of Communicative Sciences and Disorders. His teaching, research, and clinical interests are laryngeal voice disorders, head and neck cancer, and cleft of the lip/palate. He has published and presented extensively in these areas. Dr. Searl has had an active clinical career spanning nearly 30 years, providing diagnostic and therapy services to children and adults with voice, resonance, and speech disorders. Dr. Searl has been recognized for his contributions by the International Association of Laryngectomees and selection as a Fellow of the American Speech-Language-Hearing Association.

Trisha L. Self, PhD, CCC-SLP, BCS-CL, is Associate Professor and the Paul M. Cassat Distinguished Chair in the Communication Sciences and Disorders Department at Wichita State University in Wichita, KS. She teaches courses, supervises, and conducts research in ASD. She is a Board Certified

Child Language Specialist with over 30 years of experience working with children demonstrating complex communication needs, including ASD. She is the coordinator of the Autism Interdisciplinary Diagnostic and Treatment Team Lab at WSU.

Amee P. Shah, PhD, CCC-SLP, is Professor of Health Science and Director of the Cross-Cultural Speech, Language and Acoustics Lab at Stockton University, NJ. She is an award-winning ASHA-certified Speech-Language Pathologist and Speech Scientist, working on building evidence-based best practices for multicultural populations through her research, education, and leadership. Her work has helped enhance the individual experiences for her clients as well as transform organizational culture in varied industries such as corporations, universities, police and first responders, and hospitals. She has developed and published frameworks, proven methods, and technology to assess and enhance cross-cultural communication as well as emotional intelligence.

Stacey Sheedy, BAppSci (Speech Path), Hons, is a speech pathologist who works at the Southwestern Sydney Stuttering Unit, a unit within South Western Sydney Local Health District. She is an affiliate of the Ingham Institute of Applied Medical Research and an honorary clinical fellow at the Australian Stuttering Research Centre, the University of Technology Sydney. Stacey treats people who stutter of all ages and provides clinical guidance to speech pathologists nationally. She has published research in scientific journals and presented research at international conferences. Stacey is a member of the Lidcombe Program Trainers Consortium and the Continuing Professional Education in Stuttering Consortium.

Rosalee C. Shenker, PhD, CCC-SLP, is the Founding Executive Director of the Montreal Fluency Centre and a member of the Lidcombe Program Trainers Consortium. She has specialized in fluency disorders for over 40 years, teaching a graduate course at McGill University, providing clinical training and mentoring for speech pathologists, as well as invited presentations and workshops nationally and internationally. Rosalee has pub-

lished in peer-reviewed journals and contributed chapters on stuttering to various textbooks. Her most recent work emphasizes the treatment of bilingual children who stutter, as well as evidence-based stuttering treatment of school-age children.

Kiiya Shibata, MS, CCC-SLP, completed her master's degree in Communicative Disorders at San Francisco State University in 2015. She worked in acute medical, inpatient rehabilitation, and outpatient settings before narrowing her clinical focus to primary progressive aphasia (PPA) and other neurodegenerative diseases impacting communication. In 2021, she returned for her PhD in the Department of Hearing and Speech Sciences at Vanderbilt University, with a focus on equitable clinical management of individuals with PPA and their families.

Robert J. Shprintzen, PhD, CCC-SLP, is President of The Virtual Center for Velo-Cardio-Facial Syndrome, Inc. (http://www.vcfscenter.org). A Fellow of the American Speech-Language-Hearing Association (ASHA), he received ASHA's Outstanding Clinical Achievement Award. ASHA's highest award, Honors of the Association, followed in 2013. He has published 232 journal articles, 40 chapters, and 7 textbooks. He is past Editor of *The Cleft Palate-Craniofacial Journal*. In 1985, he was among the youngest faculty members ever promoted to the rank of Full Professor at the Albert Einstein College of Medicine. Dr. Shprintzen is credited with delineating four genetic syndromes that bear his name in the medical literature.

Jeff Snell, PhD, completed his doctorate in Psychology at the University of Southern Mississippi with a specialization in clinical psychology. In 1998, Dr. Snell joined the staff at Quality Living, Inc., where he has since served as Director of Psychology and Neuropsychology and works with individuals with neurological injuries and chronic pain. Dr. Snell presents regularly to clinical, insurance, case management, and advocacy audiences throughout the United States. At Quality Living, Dr. Snell brings talent and experience in developing compensatory strategies that are critical to the long-term success of clients and their families.

Carolyn (Carney) Sotto, PhD, CCC-SLP, is Professor and Undergraduate Program Director in the Department of Communication Sciences & Disorders at the University of Cincinnati. She teaches graduate/undergraduate students on campus and online in the areas of speech sound disorders, phonetics, assessment, psychometrics, child language, and literacy. Carney was awarded Fellow of ASHA in 2018. She was awarded the Scholar-Mentor Award by the National Black Association Speech Language Hearing (NBASLH) in 2022. Carney is a past President of the Ohio Speech-Language-Hearing Association (OSLHA) and was awarded Fellow and Honors of OSLHA. She is a faculty advisor for UC NSSLHA and Multicultural Concerns in CSD (MC2).

Tamsen St Clare, PhD, is a clinical psychologist with a special interest in treating anxiety and obsessive-compulsive disorders. She is currently working exclusively in private practice but was formerly the Clinical Director of the University of Sydney's Anxiety Disorders Clinic and the Head of the Anxiety Treatment and Research Unit at Westmead Hospital. She has been involved in the development and evaluation of treatment programs for speech-related anxiety in adults who stutter and has published several peer-reviewed articles on this topic.

Kenneth O. St. Louis, PhD, Emeritus Professor of speech-language pathology at West Virginia University, taught and treated fluency disorders for 45 years. His research has culminated in more than 200 publications and 425 presentations. He is an ASHA Fellow and recipient of the Deso Weiss Award for Excellence in Cluttering, WVU's Benedum Distinguished Scholar Award, and WVU's Heebink Award for Outstanding Service. He founded the International Project of Attitudes Toward Human Attributes and has collaborated with more than 300 colleagues internationally to measure public attitudes toward stuttering. He has also presented and published widely on cluttering and stories of stuttering.

Linia Starlet Willis, SLPD, CCC-SLP, is a 2007 graduate of James Madison University. She attained her Master of Arts degree from Hampton University in 2009. She earned her Clinical Doctorate in Speech Language Pathology (SLPD) from Northwestern University in 2020. Dr. Willis promotes medical speech pathology utilizing evidence-based practice through an interdisciplinary lens. She is passionate about helping people with swallowing disorders and neurogenic deficits. Her research interests and background include oral health and hygiene and meeting community reintegration challenges related to speech and language after COVID-19.

Julie A. G. Stierwalt, PhD, is a Consultant in the Division of Speech Pathology, Department of Neurology and Associate Professor in the Mayo Clinic College of Medicine at the Mayo Clinic in Rochester, MN. In this capacity, she provides diagnostic and treatment services for individuals with speech, language, cognitive, and/or swallowing impairment across acute care, outpatient and specialty clinic settings. She maintains an active research agenda across these topic areas as well. In 2009, she was named Fellow of the American Speech-Language-Hearing Association.

Kathy H. Strattman, PhD, is Associate Professor Emerita in the Department of Communication Sciences and Disorders at Wichita State University in Wichita, KS. She is an ASHA Fellow and Board Recognized Specialist in Child Language. She taught undergraduate and graduate courses in speech sound and language development and treatment for disorders of preschool and school-age children. Her research and clinical interests are in the areas of language and literacy development and intervention.

Jessica R. Sullivan, PhD, is the Interim Department Chair and Assistant Professor in the Communicative Sciences and Disorders Department at Hampton University. Dr. Sullivan is an affiliated research scientist at Haskins Laboratories at Yale University. Dr. Sullivan has served on numerous committees and boards with professional organizations. She received her BA in 1996 from Louisiana State University and Master's in Deaf Education from Lamar University in 2000. She received her PhD in Communication Sciences at the University of Texas at Dallas in 2010. Dr. Sullivan has received numerous awards, honors, and grants, including a SBIR from the NIH/NIDCD.

Shurita Thomas-Tate, PhD, CCC-SLP, is Associate Professor of Speech-Language Pathology in the Department of Communication Sciences and Disorders at Missouri State University. She is the founder/director of Ujima Language and Literacy, a nonprofit organization that exists to connect, empower, and advocate for children and families. She has been recognized and honored for her commitment to community engagement, literacy, and diversity/equity/inclusion. Her passion for supporting the holistic development of children drives her involvement in numerous organizations focusing on issues such as poverty, education, and foster care. Dr. Thomas-Tate currently serves on the Board of Education for Springfield, Missouri R–12 Schools.

Janelle Johnson Ward, MHS, CCC-SLP, graduated with a master's degree from the University of Missouri–Columbia. During her career as a speech-language pathologist, she worked both in school and rehabilitation settings with children and adults. Most of her work life has been spent serving young adults who had sustained traumatic brain injury. Currently, Janelle spends her days as a taxi driver and logistics manager for her three children.

Amy L. Weiss, PhD, CCC-SLP, is Professor Emerita at the University of Rhode Island, where she served on the faculty in the Department of Communicative Disorders for 16 years before retiring in 2020. Her clinical, teaching, and research interests focused on child language learning and disorders as well as stuttering in both children and adults. She is currently living in western North Carolina, where she spends her time reading, volunteering, appreciating Appalachian music up close, and buying too many pairs of earrings.

Kristy S. E. Weissling, SLPD, CCC-SLP, is Professor of Practice at the University of Nebraska–Lincoln, where she is program director and clinic coordinator. Her research and teaching focuses on intervention and assessment of aphasia, TBI, dementia, other acquired neurogenic communication disorders, and AAC for individuals with complex communication needs.

Lauraine L. Wells, AuD, is a board-certified audiologist and Lead Regulatory Affairs Specialist with 3M Personal Safety Division working with hearing protection and hearing conservation standards and regulatory issues globally. Previously, Dr. Wells was an occupational audiology consultant and a clinical audiologist at the University of Northern Colorado. Dr. Wells earned her AuD degree from Salus University and a Master of Science degree from the University of Arizona. She has served professional organizations, including the Council for Accreditation in Occupational Hearing Conservation and the National Hearing Conservation Association. Currently, she is co-coordinator of the NORA Cross Sector for Hearing Loss Prevention and serves on the Safe-in-Sound award expert committee.

Tammy Wigginton, MS, BRS-S, CCC-SLP, is a member of the Dysphagia Research Society, an International Association of Laryngectomee Alaryngeal Speech Instructor, a Lee Silverman certified clinician, and a board-certified specialist in swallowing disorders. She is a frequent conference lecturer on the topics of dysphagia and evaluation and treatment of communication and swallowing disorders associated with head and neck cancer. She has a special interest in medical bioethics as it relates to the care and management of patients with swallowing disorders and head and neck cancers.

Diane L. Williams, PhD, CCC-SLP, BCS-CL, is Professor and Head of the Department of Communication Sciences and Disorders at Pennsylvania State University. She has over 40 years of clinical experience with children and adults with a range of developmental language disorders. Dr. Williams conducts research in autism spectrum disorders (ASD) with an emphasis on the processes of language, cognition, and memory. She has authored numerous peer-reviewed publications, book chapters, and a book on the neurobiological basis of language disorders and frequently presents on how what she has learned from her research informs her clinical practice as a speech-language pathologist.

Judith Maige Wingate, PhD, CCC-SLP, is Professor and Chair of the Department of Communication Sciences and Disorders at Jacksonville University. Dr. Wingate received a BA in music therapy from Charleston Southern University, MS in speech-language pathology from the University of South Florida, and a PhD in voice and voice disorders from the University of Florida. She worked as a voice specialist for the University of Florida from 1996 to 2013. Her research interests include occupational voice problems, singing voice, and clinical outcomes in voice therapy. She is the author of *Healthy Singing*, a vocal health book for singers and their teachers.

Carla Wood, PhD, CCC-SLP, is Professor and the Director of the School of Communication Science and Disorders at Florida State University. Her teaching and research engagement focus on child language development and disorders, with specific emphasis on language and literacy interventions for underserved students from culturally and linguistically diverse backgrounds. She has been a certified speech-language pathologist for over 25 years, which included working in elementary schools and early intervention.

J. Scott Yaruss, PhD, CCC-SLP, BCS-F, F-ASHA, is Professor of Communicative Sciences and Disorders at Michigan State University and President of Stuttering Therapy Resources. His NIH-funded research examines the variability of stuttering and the impact of stuttering on people's lives. He has published more than 110 peer-reviewed manuscripts and more than 250 other papers on stuttering and stuttering therapy, as well as several clinical resources, including the Overall Assessment of the Speaker's Experience of Stuttering (OASES), Early Childhood Stuttering: A Practical Guide, School-Age Stuttering Therapy: A Practi-

cal Guide, and the Minimizing Bullying program (http://www.StutteringTherapyResources.com).

Scott R. Youmans, PhD, CCC-SLP, is Associate Professor and Chair in the Department of Communication Sciences and Disorders at Pace University. He obtained his BS from the College of Saint Rose, his MEd from North Carolina Central University, and his PhD from Florida State University. Dr. Youmans has had clinical experience in schools, rehabilitation centers, outpatient clinics, nursing homes, consulting, and private practice; however, the majority of his clinical career has been spent as an acute care, hospital-based speech-language pathologist. His clinical specializations include adults with acquired, neurogenic communication and swallowing disorders and following laryngectomy. Dr. Youmans teaches in the areas of dysphagia and motor speech disorders. His research publications and presentations are in the area of adult, acquired, neurogenic communication disorders and swallowing.

Emily Zimmerman, PhD, CCC-SLP, is Associate Professor and the Associate Chair of Research and Innovation in the Department of Communication Sciences & Disorders at Northeastern University. She directs the Speech & Neurodevelopment Lab, which examines the cross section of sucking, feeding, and speech emergence across environmental, maternal, physiological, and genetic factors. Dr. Zimmerman is the Principal Investigator on several NIH grants, examining these themes across several patient populations and diverse communities.

Robyn A. Ziolkowski, PhD, CCC-SLP, is the Principal of Seminole Elementary School in Okeechobee, Florida. Her research interests include early intervention, literacy and language development, and reading disabilities. She was named Principal of the Year in Okeechobee, FL, in 2022. She has 20+ years of experience in educational settings in administration and working with children with reading disabilities and communication disorders.

We dedicate this text to the children and adults with communication challenges represented in this book who inspire us to do our best and to our students for the pleasure of their dialogue, discovery, and decency.

MAKING THE CASE FOR CASE-BASED LEARNING

Ellen R. Cohn, Shelly Chabon, and Dorian Lee-Wilkerson

An Overview

For three decades as a physician, I looked to traditional sources to assist me in my thinking about patients; textbooks and medical journals, mentors and colleagues with deeper or more varied clinical experience; students and residents who posed challenging questions. But after writing this book, I realized that I can have another vital partner who helps improve my thinking, a partner who may, with a few pertinent and focused questions, protect me from the cascade of cognitive pitfalls that cause misguided care. That partner is present in the moment when flesh-and-blood decision-making occurs. That partner is my patient or her family member or friend who seeks to know what is in my mind, how I am thinking. And by opening my mind I can more clearly recognize its reach and its limits, its understanding of my patient's physical problems and emotional needs. There is no better way to care for those who need my caring.

—Groopman (2007, p. 269)

The Communication Disorders Casebook: Learning by Example is a book about some of the many special people with communication problems and those who are privileged to serve them. It provides students, faculty, and practicing clinicians with relevant "real-life" examples of clinical encounters between clinicians and clients. Why did we perceive a need for this text? While there are many excellent resources in communication sciences and disorders, few books present rich, relatable, and diverse case studies across a broad spectrum of settings, client ages, and communication disorder types. These cases illustrate the importance of asking "a few pertinent and focused questions" (Groopman, 2007), seeking to reconcile the perspectives of all involved and accepting that there are likely to be multiple truths in determining clinical origins and options for families and their loved ones.

We envisioned several audiences for this book, with a shared interest in the use of case studies, as an experiential education strategy that provides both foundational knowledge and awareness of its utility in clinical work.

1. *Prospective students* who are considering undergraduate and/or graduate study in communication sciences and disorders might read this book to expand their views of the discipline by gaining the perspectives of practicing clinicians.
2. *Undergraduate and graduate students* in communication sciences and disorders might apply these "real-life" cases to their classroom studies.
3. *New clinicians* might use this book to assist them in developing a framework for clinical decision-making.
4. *University faculty members and practicing clinicians* may wish to acquire new understanding of parts of the field they might not typically encounter and gain sophisticated perspectives from experienced clinicians related to their current practice.

We also expect that some *persons with communication disorders and their families* may read specific cases to gain insights concerning their personal communication challenges.

The cases described in this book are intentionally varied in terms of the client's age, complexity and type of communication disorders, diagnostic and treatment approaches, and length of treatment. The body of work, however, is unified as follows. Consistent with our clinical philosophies, we have adopted a "client"-centered approach, wherein a real or fictional person (sometimes a composite of individuals seen over an author's years of clinical practice) is the central focus of each chapter. Of course, one chapter on the topic of a speech or hearing disorder cannot represent the entire universe of people with that particular disorder. These are not presented as "textbook cases." Two individuals who share a common diagnosis are not likely to be otherwise identical. We do expect, however, that the background information and clinical reasoning the authors provide will elucidate each topic area and that questions generated and methods considered may be of relevance to the treatment of other individuals.

Readers of the book may use it to expand their *knowledge* of a wide range of communication disorders in both children and adults as well as to increase their *skill* in applying that knowledge to solve a clinical problem. They may relate to the individuals described on the pages that follow on an *affective* level, resulting in empathy and a quality of understanding and caring about the individuals featured. We believe that this combination of *facts and feelings* may well increase readers' application, retention, and generalization of the content. We also hope that review of these cases will encourage readers to "think like speech-language pathologists." That is, reading about the experiences of the clients and clinicians featured in this text will provide an appreciation for the opportunities and the challenges involved in the practice of speech-language pathology.

Some of these cases describe treatment approaches that are supported empirically. Others reflect the wisdom of practice and insights accumulated from clinical careers filled with tested and reasoned discoveries. All offer a balanced, multidimensional context in which the complexities and ambiguities of the clinical relationship are evident and clinical decisions realized. In short, we believe

that readers will benefit from the lessons learned and shared by the authors.

The text is divided into four sections by client age group (infant/toddler, preschool, school age, adult). It contains 61 cases selected to exemplify both the diversity of our services and the uniqueness of those we serve. A broad review of all of these cases will uncover a variety of methodological approaches to the treatment of individuals with communication disorders. Some of these approaches could not have been foreseen a decade ago. Others have a long tradition in our profession. An examination of a single case will reveal the practical application of the array of methodological possibilities. Each individual case is presented in depth and includes the following common elements:

- Conceptual knowledge areas: contains information needed to adequately interpret and resolve the case
- Short introductory paragraph: establishes the problem to be considered
- Background information: provides the historical information necessary to understand the case, summarizes recent developments and significant milestones leading to the clinical challenges, and identifies the pertinent facts
- Evaluative findings: allows authors to discuss a professional hypothesis and possible courses of treatment, in consideration of best data, clinical judgment, and individual patient needs, priorities, and desires
- Description of course of treatment: details the procedures followed for the chosen treatment option, including analysis of patients' responses to the intervention
- Further recommendations: allows for clinician "wrap-up" and review of treatment results as well as reworking of initial hypothesis and/or suggestions for maintaining positive effects of treatment
- Reference section: lists all sources used within the text for the interest and aid of the reader for close or further study

What Is a Case Study?

Each case study in this text is a comprehensive, realistic account of a person with a communication problem that illustrates the decision-making process used to develop, implement, and evaluate clinical services provided by a speech-language pathologist or audiologist. Each case offers a narrative description of the facts, beliefs, feelings, and experiences of the people involved.

What Value Does a Case-Based Approach Bring?

Nohria (2021), in an article about graduate education, noted that the use of case studies in teaching increases student confidence and makes a very strong impact on student learning. The use of a case-based approach by Nohria provides a framework for how to prepare for clinical practicum and ultimately how to prepare for clinical and professional work beyond school.

Nohria lists six key skills students achieve through the use of case studies. These include (1) ways to collaborate, (2) recognizing and correcting bias, (3) advocacy for clients and the profession, (4) critical thinking about key facts and distracting backgrounds, (5) decision-making, and (6) sustaining curiosity about the field.

Case studies make learning more visible, assisting students with seeing what and how learning objectives are met (Columbia University in the City of New York, Office of the Provost, n.d.). They help students connect theory with clinical practice. Case-based instruction naturally integrates consideration of language and cultural factors, preparing students to engage in culturally responsive practice and to continually seek to increase their cultural competence. Case-based instruction also sheds light on the value of engaging in interprofessional practice.

This text is based on the observation that speech-language pathologists need strong theoretical knowledge in *combination with* scientific and clinical skill to make culturally relevant and ethically responsive clinical judgments. It can provide a forum for both the theoretical and the practical aspects, the art and science, of clinical work. Ideally, readers will be moved by a particular case to challenge its theoretical foundation, to ask questions about their own and others' clinical positions, to examine the contexts for the clinical actions, and to consider all of the possible consequences of the professional decisions. One way that this can be accomplished is through the use of questions designed to assess understanding of concepts and theories, their relationship to previous knowledge and experience, and their application to future work. How and why were particular hypotheses formulated? How were evaluation results interpreted, and how were the interpretations applied? How and why did the authors choose particular approaches to intervention? As professionals, we are often distinguished by these types of questions as they inform our scholarship as well as our practices.

Questioning is at the core of science and thus is also central to our clinical success. Asking the right questions guides us to make well-reasoned clinical decisions. So how do you, the reader, know what questions to ask? What types of questions will help you to "realize your potential to learn" (Bain, 2004) from these case studies and lead to an approach of clinical decision-making that is clear and understandable? Chabon and Lee-Wilkerson (2006) described a learning framework, adapted from Fink (2003), which offers a prospective organization for such questions. King (1995) provided some "generic question stems," or exemplars, and the level of thinking reflected in each. Lemoncello (2009) adapted King's work and created a "Critical Thinking Template" to facilitate case analyses. Using Ferguson's (2008) position to adopt "a critical perspective" will also guide the reader to ask questions about the cases that reflect consideration of social, cultural, and linguistic factors. The following are a few examples of questions relevant to the clinical decision-making process that were formulated based on these earlier writings and incorporated into the learning stages proposed by Fink (2003). When we ask these questions of ourselves, they can serve as a mechanism for applying acquired knowledge and skills in new contexts. They foster an ethic of inquiry that shapes the clinical decision-making process reflected by the clinicians and writers included in this text.

Question Framework

Foundational Knowledge: *What do you know about the client in the case study you read?*

These questions involve the recall of information, facts, and concepts at a level that invites explanation:

- What are all of the relevant facts and the existing sociocultural context?
- What are the key physical/emotional/ neurological factors that are impaired?
- Who are the key people involved?
- What activities are limited for the client because of their communication abilities or inabilities?

Skill in Application of Knowledge: *How can the information you read be used?*

These questions lead to making decisions, solving problems, and performing clinical tasks:

- Did the client's communication or swallowing improve with treatment and, if so, in what ways?
- How did the clinician know that the treatment approach was or was not successful?
- What was measured and how was it measured?

Skill in the Integration of Knowledge: *How does the information you read relate to what you knew before?*

These questions involve analysis and synthesis, and they reflect connections with previous learning and experiences:

- What are the strengths and weaknesses of the treatment approach(es) used and assessment methods selected?
- What are some of the differences between this disorder and other similar or related disorders?
- What are the differences between the treatment approach(es) used and other similar or related approaches?
- Was there consensus between the client/ family's and clinician's account of the case?
- Is adequate use made of previous research and observations?
- Are the inferences drawn clear, sound, and appropriate?
- How does the information compare with your previous knowledge about or experience with this disorder and/or the treatment of this disorder?

Skill in Acknowledgment of the Human Dimension: *Why is what you read important to you and to those you serve? How does what you read confirm or alter your attitudes about the client, family, and you as a clinician?*

These questions lead to increased insight about self and others:

- In considering the family's account of the case:
  - What do they believe caused the problem?

- What were their hopes/fears about the progression and length of the treatment?
- What are their expectations about the outcome?
- How might the client's perceptions affect the outcomes of the case?
- Who will be the client's supports throughout and following treatment?
  - How might the clinician's perceptions of family support affect their choice of treatment approach?
- How did the problems described affect the client's and the client's family's daily life and the interaction between the client and their significant others?
- How will cultural/social factors support or inhibit the treatment?
- How will personal traits of the clinician support/inhibit the treatment?
- Whose interests were served and whose were ignored?
- Does the approach selected reflect an objective attitude? Does the approach take the client's perspective into account?

Skill in Assessing the Relevance of Knowledge: *Why is what you read important?*

These questions examine the reasons that underlie or support methods or actions and result in meaningful reflection and self-assessment:

- How does the action taken reflect current criteria, standards, and theory?
- Why do you believe the clinician selected the particular treatment/assessment method?
- What are some alternative treatment options/assessment methods?
- What are the primary reasons for the current outcome?
- Would you use the same treatment/assessment method? Why or why not?

Skill in Self-Directed Learning: *How do you plan to use what you read about in this case?*

These questions lead to active engagement in independent scholarship and reflective practice that continues beyond the reading of a particular case or cases.

- What factors might have led to a different outcome? Why?
- How could the information provided in the case be applied to other clients?
- Are there unanswered questions/concerns?
- How can the treatment program be duplicated and continued by other clinicians/researchers?
- How can you or other professionals evaluate the treatment described in your own practice?
- How do the outcomes in the current case study compare to other related cases reported in the literature?
- What evidence is available to refute or confirm the approaches taken?

What Is New in This Edition

The secret of the care of the patients is in caring for the patient.

—Peabody, Harvard University, 1925

Most of the cases in this edition have been updated consistent with F. W. Peabody's enduring philosophy as well as more recent clinical discussions and discoveries. The cases have also been updated to reflect the influences of online instruction and learning, teletherapy, interprofessional education and practice, and inclusive practices. Instructor resources have also been updated to promote collaborative and interactive learning, to foster inclusion and belonging among students, to enhance scholarship, to generate productive dialogue of theory and practice, and to assist students and practicing clinicians to consider clinical behaviors and to evaluate their possible effectiveness (Dwight, 2022) across clinical sites. Further, the instructor resources provide guidance in how to use the cases to demonstrate and promote understanding of the ways cultural and linguistic characteristics and values influence interpretation of case data and decision-making (Dantuma, 2021) and to facilitate the development of four cardinal attitudes of successful audiologists and speech-language pathologists, as first proposed by Sutherland-Cornett and Chabon in 1988 and expanded on by Wendy Papir-Bernstein (2017). These attitudes include a scientific attitude, a therapeutic attitude, a professional attitude, and a leadership attitude. Finally, the test bank has been updated to reinforce key concepts and to provide additional practice with test taking.

References

Bain, K. (2004). *What the best college teachers do.* Harvard University Press.

Chabon, S., & Lee-Wilkerson, D. (2006). Instructor's manual and test bank for Anderson and Shames. In *Human communication disorders: An introduction* (7th ed.). Pearson Education.

Columbia University in the City of New York, Office of the Provost. (n.d.). Retrieved December 18, 2022, from https://ctl.columbia.edu/resources-and-technology/resources/case-method/

Dantuma, T. (2021). *Professional competencies in speech-language pathology and audiology.* Jones and Bartlett Learning.

Dwight, D. (2022). *Here's how to do therapy: Hands-on core skills in speech-language pathology* (3rd ed.). Plural Publishing.

Ferguson, A. (2008). *Expert practice: A critical discourse.* Plural Publishing.

Fink, L. D. (2003). *Creating significant learning experiences.* Jossey-Bass.

Groopman, J. E. (2007). *How doctors think.* Houghton Mifflin.

King, A. (1995). Designing the instructional process to enhance critical thinking across the curriculum. *Teaching of Psychology, 22,* 1.

Lemoncello, R. (2009). *Critical thinking template* [handout]. Author.

Nohria, N. (2021). What the case study method really teaches. *Harvard Business Review, Business Education.* https://hbr.org/2021/12/what-the-case-study-method-really-teaches

Papir-Berstein, W. (2017). *The practitioner's path in speech-language pathology: The art of school-based practice.* Plural Publishing.

Peabody, F. W. (1925). The care of the patient. *JAMA, 88,* 877–882, 1927.

Sutherland-Cornett, B. S., & Chabon, S. (1988). *The clinical practice of speech-language pathology.* Charles E. Merrill Publishing.

Part I
INFANT OR TODDLER CASES

AUTISM

CASE 1

Anne: Developing a Communication Assessment and Treatment Plan for a Toddler Diagnosed With Autism Spectrum Disorder: Special Considerations

Trisha L. Self and Terese Conrad

Conceptual Knowledge Areas

This case study challenges readers to consider their knowledge of development from birth to age 3 years in the specific areas of cognition, receptive/expressive language, play, oral-motor and sensory-motor skills, self-regulation, and nutrition.

Most infants have an innate drive to learn language and socialize with others (Janzen & Zenko, 2012). In fact, when children's learning systems are developing typically, these skills are acquired automatically without being taught. For children on the autism spectrum, however, early learning strategies, communication skills, and early social skills typically do not develop without intervention (Brien & Prelock, 2021).

Early in the developmental process, children on the autism spectrum demonstrate difficulties attending to people. They tend to avoid interactions with others and thus experience fewer opportunities to hear language and practice reciprocal communication. Additionally, because children with an autism spectrum disorder (ASD) typically are not intrinsically motivated to participate in and/or initiate social interactions, they do not engage in the conventional play activities toddlers often use to learn about their environment and the early rules for social engagement (Brien & Prelock, 2021; Janzen & Zenko, 2012). Children on the autism spectrum often demonstrate difficulties with modulating, processing, and integrating sensory information. These sensory challenges often affect a child's desire to engage in social interactions and thus his or her ability to benefit from naturally occurring learning situations (Ebert, 2020).

The following case study involves a young female child who was referred to a university-based speech-language-hearing clinic by a developmental pediatrician. The child was reported to have delayed speech, language, cognitive, and social skills. She had a history of ear infections, and her nutrition intake was poor. The physician had informed the parents that the child was demonstrating early signs of an autism spectrum disorder.

Description of the Case

Background Information

At age 1 year 10 months, Anne was referred to a university speech-language-hearing clinic (SLHC) by a developmental pediatrician. The pediatrician was concerned, as were the child's parents, that Anne's receptive and expressive language skills were significantly delayed. The pediatrician also recommended the family seek a highly structured early intervention program within the community. Upon referral to the university SLHC, the family was asked to complete a case history prior to being scheduled for a speech-language evaluation. Review of the case history and other evaluations provided by the family revealed the following developmental information.

Past Medical History

Anne was born to a 25-year-old female at 40 weeks' gestation. There was no reported use of alcohol, tobacco, and/or drugs during the pregnancy. At birth, Anne weighed 7 lb 10 oz and was 19 in. long. She responded immediately to breastfeeding and continued to do so without difficulty.

Her mother reported that Anne had chronic ear infections, which were not responsive to antibiotic treatment. Prior to receiving pressure equalization (PE) tubes at approximately 17 months of age, Anne had stopped responding to most sounds, her balance was generally poor, and she had not yet started walking. After receiving the PE tubes, she responded more readily to certain sounds and her balance quickly improved. Not long after the tubes were placed, she began walking.

Anne had otherwise been a healthy child. She had no known drug allergies, and her immunizations were current.

Developmental History

Anne began to roll over at approximately 6 months of age, sat independently at 7 months, crawled at about 9 months, and began walking at 17 months (almost immediately after PE tubes had been placed). Anne's mother reported that Anne began to imitate "mama" and "dada" at about 15 months but would not say those words spontaneously until she was approximately 19 months old. Her mother also reported that Anne babbled at times and imitated a few other words (car, dog).

To communicate her wants/needs, Anne's mother indicated that her daughter would walk to the desired object and stand near it; sometimes she would knock on it and/or attempt to obtain the item on her own. Anne did not use any distal pointing, nor did she use other typical gestures to obtain a desired item/activity.

Her mother reported that Anne was able to respond appropriately to simple questions, such as "Where's your cup?" "Where's your shoe?" and "Where's your brother?" by moving to and/or retrieving the labeled object/person. Additionally, when someone said, "Ready to go outside?" she moved to the door, or when someone said, "Let's go for a ride," she moved toward the garage door. Anne followed an individual's gestural line of regard when items of interest were pointed out and accompanied by information such as "There's a bird." If she was not interested in the object, she was nonresponsive.

Anne liked to assemble puzzles, roll cars, stack Duplos™, and flip through magazines. She was able to roll a car back and forth with an adult. Anne did not initiate her own play but would "play" if an adult initiated it. If Anne got excited during play, she would flap her hands and rock back and forth.

Anne was able to feed herself and drank from an open-mouthed cup. She reportedly ate a variety of foods, as long as the foods did not require much chewing.

At bedtime, Anne allowed someone to brush her teeth and tolerated being given a bath but would not independently wash herself. She did not resist being dressed and, at times, would attempt to assist her parents during this process.

Anne's mother reported that a particular blanket was the greatest source of comfort for her daughter. When Anne held her blanket, it seemed as though she was in another world. She did not respond to activity and/or sound. Because of this, Anne's mother limited the time she was able to access the blanket. She was only allowed to have it during nap times, at bedtime, and when they went out of the house for errands and appointments.

When Anne was approximately 16 months of age, her mother became concerned that she was not walking and her communication skills appeared to be delayed. She took her daughter to a local hospital for an evaluation of her communication and motor skills. At the time of the evaluation, Anne's skills were considered well below normal limits. Her speech and language skills were, reportedly, 7 to 10 months delayed. Her eye contact and joint attention skills were observed to be poor. She was essentially nonverbal. She demonstrated repetitive hand and finger movements and did not tolerate change. She did not play appropriately with toys (often mouthing them or engaging in perseverative movements back and forth). Following the evaluation, Anne began to receive physical therapy and speech-language treatment until insurance would no longer support payment.

Family History/Social History

Anne lived with her mother, father, and brother. Her mother, Amy, was 27 years old, had a college degree, and stayed at home with Anne during the day. Anne's father, Jerrod, was 36 years old and was employed as a computer technician. Anne's brother was 3 years old and appeared to be developing typically. The parents indicated that there had been a history of developmental differences on both sides of their family. Amy reported that she had a 16-year-old cousin who had been diagnosed with high-functioning autism. Jerrod reported having a sister who was socially challenged but had no formal diagnosis.

Medical Diagnostic History

At age 1 year 8 months, Anne was evaluated by a developmental pediatrician. The child's mother reported that she continued to be concerned that Anne was not expressing her needs, had delays in her speech, and did not respond consistently to her name.

During the evaluation, Anne did not separate easily from her mother. A neurodevelopmental evaluation revealed that Anne had low muscle tone in both her upper and lower extremities. She was, however, walking independently at the time of the evaluation.

Anne did not want to participate in many activities with the examiner as she demonstrated stranger anxiety during most of the examination. She did respond favorably when cars were presented and moved from her mother's lap to roll them back and forth repeatedly across the floor. She also enjoyed moving a ball back and forth while lying on the floor to watch the rolling movement. She demonstrated excitement when the examiner blew bubbles by flapping her hands. She did not, however, make any attempts to request more. Anne would not respond when the examiner repeatedly called her name and would not establish joint attention with activities presented by her mother or the examiner.

Reason for Referral

At the time of evaluation, the developmental pediatrician indicated that Anne had significant speech and language delays and poor joint attention and social interaction skills. She was also reported to have stereotypic behaviors. Although the mother was told that Anne demonstrated early signs of an autism spectrum disorder, the doctor indicated that a specific diagnosis might not be reliable prior to 2 years of age.

Based on the findings of the diagnostic evaluation, the developmental pediatrician recommended that the parents seek early intervention services along with individual speech-language treatment. Additionally, he recommended that Anne be tested for fragile X syndrome and have high-resolution chromosome testing completed. After her second birthday, it was recommended that the family return to his office in consultation with a psychologist to reassess the status of the autism spectrum disorder characteristics using the Autism Diagnostic Observation System-2 (ADOS-2; Lord et al., 2012).

Following the completion of this examination, the parents contacted the local university SLHC for an evaluation with the intent to schedule Anne to receive speech-language intervention.

Findings of the Evaluation

At age 1 year 9 months, Anne was first brought to the university SLHC by her mother. Based on the information reported in the case history and the medical documentation received from the developmental pediatrician, it was determined that it would be beneficial to design Anne's sessions to provide diagnostic therapy. The purpose of this plan was to develop a baseline for Anne's receptive and expressive skills and to determine an appropriate communication system based on her abilities and her communication needs (Ricco & Prickett, 2019).

Diagnostic Therapy Findings

Anne's ability to initially participate in treatment sessions was inconsistent. She demonstrated a great deal of difficulty transitioning from the waiting room to the treatment room, even when her mother provided her physical support and remained in the treatment room throughout the session.

Anne tended to have more success during treatment when she was reinforced with highly motivational toys (toys with wheels) that she could operate independently while lying on the floor and watching the wheels move back and forth. When she was presented with toys that required assistance from an adult to appropriately activate them (open containers, turn knobs), she would engage in the following behaviors: turn/move away from the adult, refuse to participate, drop to the floor, whine, cry, crawl under furniture, and hide her face. Additionally, Anne would throw items (that were not intended to be thrown) in an apparent attempt to protest engaging with that particular item. Typically, when Anne was frustrated, she would cry, retrieve her blanket, and attempt to get her mother to pick her up. When her mother immediately picked her up, Anne's crying subsided quickly. If her mother did not readily respond and pick her up, the behavior would escalate and the crying continued for several minutes. When Anne came to treatment without her blanket, her ability to participate functionally in any portion of the session decreased and the whining and crying behaviors increased.

Treatment Options Considered

Initial Treatment Plan

Prior to completing the diagnostic treatment period, it had been anticipated that Anne's treatment goals would include encouraging her to

tolerate hand-over-hand assistance during play activities, spontaneously indicating preferences by choosing one item out of a field of three, and spontaneously requesting an item by exchanging an object/symbol/representation of the item with an adult. Based on the results of the diagnostic therapy sessions as described above, her goals were revised. More importantly, the following modifications were incorporated in an attempt to decrease excess stimulation, reduce stress created by the environment, and encourage Anne to focus and participate.

Physical Modifications

Current evidence for children with ASD (UNC School of Medicine, n.d.) suggests that, when necessary, the physical environment of the treatment room be modified so that unnecessary visual stimulation (decorations on the walls, excess furniture) is eliminated, sensory stimulation that might be distracting/irritating (bright lights, extra treatment materials) is reduced, and preferred motivators to assist with transitions between and within treatment activities are incorporated, thus creating a structured, positive working/playing atmosphere for the child.

To create this type of environment for Anne, the following modifications were implemented. To assist with Anne's transition from the waiting room to the treatment room, a "texture walk" (path of differing textures) was created. This path, approximately 30 feet long, contained a variety of textured pieces (bubble wrap, carpet mats, smooth/silky textures) lined up along the carpeted hallway. Anne was encouraged and assisted to remove her shoes and socks prior to proceeding down the path. Often, Anne stopped and rubbed her feet on certain textures. These textures were also incorporated into the session so she could access them as needed during treatment. Typically, Anne did not need physical assistance to transition down the hallway; only occasional verbal encouragement was needed to keep her moving forward.

The lights in this hallway were turned off; only natural lighting was used as Anne moved from the waiting room to the treatment room.

Additionally, her sessions were conducted without overhead fluorescent lighting. The room was lit by the lighting that came through the window naturally in the treatment room.

The furniture in the treatment room was limited. Needed chairs were placed against the walls and only a large tub that was approximately table height for Anne was placed in the center of the room. Other tubs containing additional treatment items were placed near the wall and out of the direct visual line. The large tub contained two to three highly preferred items. Anne was encouraged to choose one toy and engage in functional play for a period of time. When she was finished with the toy, she was encouraged to place it in a finished basket (with a lid), rather than throwing it when she was frustrated and/or wanted to switch activities.

Anne's blanket was available for her to access, when needed, at each session. She often carried it into the therapy room and dropped it when she became interested in activities in the treatment room. The blanket was left in an area that was visible to her throughout the session. The amount of time she spent holding, touching, and/or cuddling in the blanket was tracked (Ebert, 2020).

Course of Treatment

With type of environment established, Anne's goals were revised to encourage her to participate in therapy activities without exhibiting off-task behavior (crying, dropping to the floor) while interacting with the clinicians, to choose one preferred item (with minimal prompting) from a field of two, and to spontaneously request an item by touching a container, which held a desired item or a digital picture representing that item.

Analysis of Client's Response to Treatment

Once the physical environment was modified and Anne's treatment goals were revised, her inappropriate behaviors (crying, whining, throwing, hid-

ing, etc.) were reduced. After approximately 2.5 months, Anne was participating and interacting appropriately during 90% of the session (45-minute sessions were scheduled two times per week; baseline, 9%). She was making choices from a field of two items (one preferred, one foil) with 83% accuracy (baseline, 0%). She began to request an item by touching a container or a representational digital picture with 66% accuracy (baseline, 0%).

The following semester, the modifications used previously were incorporated into Anne's treatment. Although Anne's off-task behaviors had decreased from the past semester, they continued to disrupt her ability to participate at maximal levels throughout treatment sessions. She continued to demonstrate a "need" to hold preferred toys throughout an entire session and would cry/whine during some transitions between activities. After several sessions, the clinicians began to identify additional motivators for Anne. Soon, she began to work without needing to hold her preferred toys. Additionally, she began to respond favorably to a visual work schedule and was eventually able to transition from the waiting room to the treatment room and between activities without incident (UNC School of Medicine, n.d.).

Anne's goals for this semester included touching an object/color photo to request a preferred item, selecting a picture and choosing the appropriate corresponding item when presented with a choice of two-color pictures/photos representing preferred items/activities, and finally, exchanging a picture/photo with a communication partner to request a preferred item/activity (Alsayedhassan et al., 2021). Initially, Anne's baseline score was 0% for all targeted objectives; by the end of the semester (approximately 3 months; two 45-minute sessions/week), she achieved 90% accuracy or above on all three objectives. Anne also began to spontaneously produce some intelligible and approximated verbalizations (e.g., "no"; "ball"; "block"; /bu/; /mo/) during various activities.

Because Anne achieved her targeted goals, an additional goal was added to improve her turn-taking skills during play-based activities. Initially, Anne was not able to take turns; by the end of the semester, she was able to take her turn at the appropriate time with minimal verbal prompts 96% of the time during highly preferred activities.

Further Recommendations

It was recommended that future treatment focus on developing appropriate communicative means/acts to assist Anne with making requests and indicating protest/rejection. Additionally, it was recommended that Anne be encouraged to use and practice appropriate means/acts via a Picture Exchange Communication System (PECS) (Frost & Bondy, 2002) to communicate with different communication partners in a variety of contexts/activities.

Authors' Note

This information was based on a hypothetical case.

References

Alsayedhassan, B., Lee, J., Banda, D. R., Kim, Y., & Griffin-Shirley, N. (2021). Practitioners' perceptions of the picture exchange communication system for children with autism. *Disability and Rehabilitation, 43*(2), 211–216. https://doi.org/10.1080/09638288.2019.1620878

Brien, A. R., & Prelock, P. A. (2021). Language and communication in ASD: Implications for intervention. In P. A. Prelock & R. J. McCauley (Eds.), *Treatment of autism spectrum disorder: Evidence-based intervention strategies for communication and social interactions* (2nd ed., pp. 51–80). Paul H. Brookes.

Ebert, C. (2020). *The learning to learn program: Assessment and therapy strategies for early intervention providers serving young children with autism spectrum disorder, suspected autism, and social communication delays.* Summit Speech Therapy.

Frost, L., & Bondy, A. (2002). *The picture exchange communication system training manual* (2nd ed.). Pyramid Educational Consultants, Inc.

Janzen, J. E., & Zenko, C.B. (2012). *Understanding the nature of autism: A guide to the autism spectrum disorders* (3rd ed.). Hammill Institute on Disabilities.

Lord, C., Rutter, M., DiLavore, P. C., Risi, S., Gotham, K., & Bishop, S. (2012). *Autism Diagnostic Observation Schedule* (2nd ed.). Western Psychological Services.

Riccio, C. A., & Prickett, C. S. (2019). Autism-focused assessment and program planning. In J. B. Ganz & R. L. Simpson (Eds.), *Interventions for individuals with autism spectrum disorder and complex communication needs* (pp. 21–43). Paul H. Brookes.

UNC School of Medicine. (n.d.). *Services across the lifespan for individuals with autism spectrum disorder: TEACCH Autism Program.* https://teacch.com/structured-teaching-teacch-staff/

CLEFT PALATE

CASE 2
Nancy: A Toddler With Cleft Lip and Palate: Early Therapy

Cynthia H. Jacobsen

Conceptual Knowledge Areas

A speech-language pathologist (SLP) working with families of children with cleft lip and palate may provide counsel and support when a child is born and convey optimism regarding a child's future. They also teach parents how to implement a home program to stimulate early communication development.

The SLP may meet with the family within a few months after a child's birth. During initial visits, the SLP discusses the impact of cleft lip and palate on hearing, speech, and language development. The SLP explains the effect of a cleft on speech and hearing, as well as provides suggestions to parents to encourage oral sound play and to ignore speech sounds that are made in the nose or throat. The SLP teaches parents how to reinforce sounds and to systematically increase sound variety through playful structured parent-child interaction. The SLP selects sounds that are easy to produce such as /w/, /m/, /n/, /l/, and /b/ and teaches parents to practice consonant vowel syllables such as "baba," "lala," and "wewe." Detailed therapy activities for infants and toddlers with cleft lip and palate are available (Golding-Kushner, 2001; Peterson-Falzone et al., 2016).

The SLP listens to parent concerns and observes parent-child interaction. One goal in the first months is to reflect on family concerns in "living room language," maintaining a nonjudgmental attitude. There will be many opportunities to observe the family to discern how well the family is coping with the many demands placed on them. The SLP encourages the family to talk to the primary care physician and cleft team member as concerns arise.

The SLP needs to know the effects of cleft lip and palate on speech production. Children with cleft palate have speech errors that may be due to several sources, including deviant oral structure and function, deviant phonology, and conductive hearing loss. It is essential for the SLP to diagnose problems accurately to provide correct treatment. This case describes a child who had speech errors due to both velopharyngeal insufficiency and deviant phonology. The child did not have obligatory speech errors, made from faulty anatomical structures, but she did have compensatory speech errors due to the lack of velopharyngeal closure.

Cleft Palate

A cleft is an abnormal opening in an anatomical structure. Clefts occur when tissues fail to fuse during early embryologic development. A cleft lip is an opening in the lip and can occur on one or both sides of the mouth, often involving the alveolar ridge. A cleft palate is an opening in the palate, which functions as the roof of the mouth and the floor of the nose. When a baby has a bilateral cleft lip and palate, the lip and maxillary alveolar process are cleft under both nostrils and the central portion of the lip is misaligned. The columella, the central structure of the nose, is usually absent or displaced. There are clefts through the alveolar ridge, affecting dentition. The soft and the hard palate are cleft on both sides of the nasal septum (Kummer, 2020).

A child with a cleft lip and palate is best treated by a team of specialists with expertise in the care of children with clefting. American Cleft Palate-Craniofacial Association–approved teams demonstrate that they meet the Standards for Approval of Cleft Palate and Craniofacial Teams to ensure quality of patient care (American Cleft Palate Craniofacial Association, 2019). A team allows for systematic and comprehensive planning in the long-term care of a child. A cleft palate team has at least four members, including a coordinator, SLP, surgeon, and orthodontist. The surgeon manages the reconstruction of facial defects, such as those of the nose, lip, and palate. The otolaryngologist addresses concerns of the ears and larynx. There is at least one and possibly several dental specialists. Dental health professionals provide consultation at team visits and make recommendations to community dentists and orthodontists. A pediatric dentist cares for teeth, an orthodontist corrects the placement and positioning of the teeth, a prosthodontist constructs oral appliances if needed, and a surgeon might operate on the upper and/or lower jaws and mouth. Team SLPs diagnose and often treat children with speech disorders. Audiologists evaluate hearing and manage hearing loss. A genetic counselor or geneticist assesses whether the cleft is part of a syndrome (i.e., a group of symptoms that consistently occur together). A dietitian or nurse monitors growth and development and instructs parents on feeding a child efficiently and with sufficient calories. Nursing staff serve as the liaison between parents and surgeons and provide education before and after surgery. Mental health specialists and social workers help families to access resources and deal with the adjustment to the birth of a child with facial differences. The child's pediatrician or primary care physician provides ongoing medical care.

A cleft palate affects tongue position in the mouth. In an infant with normal anatomy, the tongue makes a seal against the palate and elevates to squeeze the nipple against the hard palate as the lips create a seal. The tongue then sweeps backward and increases the space in the anterior oral cavity. The milk is expressed from the nipple by a combined action of the tongue squeezing out the contents of the breast or bottle nipple with negative pressure created in the oral cavity by sucking the milk into the mouth. When there is a cleft palate, the oral cavity and the nasal cavity are continuous, preventing the infant from creating negative pressure. Because the infant with a cleft palate needs to interrupt sucking in order to take breaths, the infant cannot coordinate breathing and drinking and there is often nasal regurgitation (Sidoti & Shprintzen, 1995). Most infants with clefts are able to feed and gain weight with adjustments to bottle feeding.

Repair of the palate usually occurs between 9 and 12 months of age unless there are significant airway issues (Kummer, 2020). Prior to the repair, the baby has been practicing speech with the oral and nasal cavities joined together. The tongue position of an infant with a cleft may be in the cleft or to the side, resulting in an incorrect tongue resting position from which babbling occurs. The infant lacks intraoral air pressure to play with sounds in a typical manner. Sounds may not be made in the correct locations, or compensatory tongue placements and constrictions at the level of the pharynx or larynx may result as the baby attempts to close off the oral cavity from the nasal cavity. The baby may also experience conductive hearing loss, which can affect the ability to hear and say sounds (Peterson-Falzone et al., 2016).

Babies with cleft lip and palate make fewer consonants and fewer multisyllabic productions than noncleft babies. Babies with cleft palate appear to be delayed in the onset of babbling and may avoid making sounds that require alveolar and palatal contact. They often make consonants that don't require high intraoral air pressure, such as nasals (/m/, /n/), glides (/w/, /y/), and glottals (/h/). Palatal and alveolar consonants are not heard until after palatal repair (Golding-Kushner, 2001; Peterson-Falzone et al., 2016). Although it is possible for some children to catch up in speech sound usage by preschool years, many continue to have misarticulations (Hardin-Jones & Jones, 2005).

It can be beneficial to prevent the development of speech problems, rather than to treat them after they occur. The focus of early parent training should be on normal speech and language development and to reduce the likelihood of abnormal compensatory errors as a habit pattern. A compensatory articulation error is a maladaptive speech error that may be an attempt by an infant or child with an open palate and/or velopharyngeal insufficiency (VPI) to create the acoustic event of the sound at a place in the vocal tract where this is possible (Golding-Kushner, 2001). This is to be distinguished from obligatory speech errors, where there is clearly a direct relationship between anatomy and the speech error, such as a malocclusion affecting tongue-tip sounds such as /t/ and /s/.

Description of the Case

Background Information

History and Newborn Team Visit

Following a full-term uneventful pregnancy, Nancy was born with a bilateral cleft lip and palate. There was no prior family history of cleft palate, although a sibling had received speech therapy. The family was intact with no psychosocial concerns. Nancy was first seen in a team-approved Cleft Palate Clinic at age 9 days. Although she passed her newborn hearing screening, the otolaryngologist on the team recommended monitoring the ears for possible otitis media. A speech-language pathologist (SLP) counseled the family on the effects of a cleft palate on speech development and resonance and instructed the parents on methods for language stimulation. A dietitian provided feeding instruction while a dentist fabricated a feeding appliance to cover a wide cleft of the hard palate. The team member who provides feeding instruction varies by team. Nancy was fed using the Medela Special-Needs Feeder (http://www.medela.us/), a newborn feeding device that allows parents to control liquid flow, due to a one-way valve (https://acpa-cpf.org). With parent education in child positioning, bottle usage, and length of time to feed, Nancy

learned to feed well and she gained weight (Turner et al., 2001).

Medical Care and Concerns: First Year

Between the first visit at 9 days and the next team visit at 12 months, Nancy was followed by the otolaryngologist and the surgeon. The surgeon repaired the bilateral cleft lip at 3 months. Following episodes of chronic otitis media, bilateral myringotomy with tubes was performed by the otolaryngologist at 8 months of age.

Second Team Visit

At 12 months of age, Nancy returned for a team visit. Hearing was within normal limits. The dietitian noted that the child was growing and gaining weight. Routine oral home care was in place. The nurse recommended that Nancy be weaned from the bottle in preparation for palatal surgery at age 13 months.

A formal assessment and a parent report of speech and overall development were obtained. Parents reported that the child's motor and play skills were developing nicely. The child said her first word at 8 months. Due to limited sound usage, the parents taught "baby signs." Nancy began to use sign language at 9 months. She was beginning to make two-word combinations; however, she usually combined a word with a gesture or sign to communicate. Nancy spontaneously used signs for "please," "thank you," and "more" and demonstrated pretend play. She was social, had an excellent attention span, followed verbal commands, identified pictures in books, and imitated motor requests.

Although Nancy's overall development was excellent, she had a very limited inventory of speech sounds. Nancy said /m/, /n/, and /h/ and occasionally /p/. She could say these sounds at the beginning and ends of syllables and repeat two syllables containing the same consonant such as "mama." She made nasal consonants (/m/, /n/) for plosive sounds such as /t/, /d/. Parent education was provided regarding compensatory speech errors. The parents were told to encourage oral sound productions and to avoid reinforcement of compensatory sounds with glottal and pharyngeal placements. It was recommended that Nancy return for a speech reevaluation in 6 months and for a complete team assessment at 2 years of age.

Findings of the Evaluation

18-Month Speech and Language Evaluation

Language Development. Language development was assessed with the Receptive-Expressive Emergent Language Test (Brown et al., 2020) and the Sequenced Inventory of Communication Development (Hedrick et al., 1984). Language comprehension and expression were within normal limits. Nancy had a speaking vocabulary of 20 words and engaged in two-word combinations. She usually communicated through single-word approximations, signs, and gestures.

Speech Mechanism Examination. Nancy closed her lips while playing, during cup drinking, and when saying words. The symmetry and continuity of lips were good. Nancy moved her lips and tongue adequately for speech sound production. She protruded and elevated the tongue tip and tongue blade in imitation. Additional observations included an intact hard palate with a high-arched palatal vault; the soft palate appeared short with minimal movement.

Resonance. Speech was characterized by moderate hypernasality and suspected nasal air emissions. Nasal grimacing and snorting were observed. Nasal grimacing, snorting, and growls signaled that Nancy was trying to valve the velopharyngeal opening in the throat and nose.

Articulation. The SLP obtained a speech sample including words spoken during play and after single-word imitation. The SLP used phonetic transcription of errors and then documented the size of the sound inventory, sound types, and constraints on producing sounds. She compared Nancy's sound development to the sound develop-ment of normal children of the same age and sex. She noted maladaptive compensatory misarticulations such as sounds made by closing the glottis (glottal stop). The SLP classified the error types, such as substitution (including compensatory), omission, distortion, or voicing. She listened for the presence and degree of hypernasality and the presence of nasal air emission, while she watched facial movements for nasal grimacing. She also related perceptual speech information with examination of the child's mouth. She noted no obligatory speech errors.

Nancy produced the /m/, /n/, /l/, /h/, and /p/ sounds. The /p/ sound lacked plosion. Oral pressure for sounds was not obtained during imitation. For example, Nancy said "nani" for /Barney/, "huni" for /honey/, "mi" or "pi" for /please/, and "memi" for /baby/. Nancy showed reduced sound productions. In 15 utterances, she marked consonants with 8 /n/ sounds, 12 /m/ sounds, 3 /h/ sounds, and 1 /p/ sound. Vowels were accurate. The lack of stop consonants such as /b/, /p/, and /d/ signaled a cleft-related speech disorder.

Nancy's list of sounds and sound substitutions suggested that she lacked velopharyngeal closure to produce oral sounds such as /b/, /d/, and /g/. In addition, she was omitting sounds that did not require strong intraoral pressure, such as /w/. As Nancy continued to develop, it appeared that her speech problems were due to two separate sources, one structural and one phonological in nature. Phonological speech errors are linguistically based, such as consonant harmony (i.e., the child changes one consonant in a word to be the same as another) (Golding-Kushner, 2001).

Course of Treatment

Speech Therapy 18 to 24 Months

The SLP showed Nancy's parents how to encourage oral sound play and to ignore nasal and pharyngeal sounds. Parents were told to play speech games that involved one or two consonants at a time with the goal of increasing the frequency of making or imitating sounds. During game time, parents used a mirror and held toys near the mouth to help Nancy increase oral sounds and to learn that mouth movements required oral airflow. The parents paired toy use with key words containing target sounds. With systematic, frequent imitation of oral-motor movements and speech, Nancy increased imitation. For example, an oral airflow activity was puffing up the cheeks with air and then tapping the cheek to release air through the lips in small pops. Props such as cotton balls, pinwheels, and blowing toys, though not used to improve articulation, demonstrated the movement that occurred when air came out of the mouth. Speech activities included saying words with targeted sounds combined with actions. Parents spoke key words such as "pop," "ball," and "baby" in interactive play. Gestures and speech were combined to teach the pairing of speech and action, such as feeding a doll with a spoon and saying "mmmm," or petting a toy lamb and saying "baaa." Parents identified a few key words and actions to use at home. For example, Nancy had a favorite toy puppy and she looked for it saying "puppy." She practiced a hopping game to say "hop" as she hopped to target picture cards, and she said "up" to stack cups for "up" for the final /p/ sound. Parents made a booklet of target words such as "baby," "mommy," "daddy," "bunny," and "puppy," to practice sounds and the sequencing of CVCV syllables (consonant-vowel). Parents rewarded oral sound productions even if sounds were unavoidably nasal in quality. Parents and the SLP modeled the placement for /t/ and /d/ and at times used visible and exaggerated sound productions to teach the idea that sound was made in the mouth with elevation of the tip of the tongue. The SLP instructed parents to teach the postvocalic /p/ as in /up/ in order to prevent the use of /h/ or glottal stop following the vowel. As mastery of one or two oral consonants was achieved, other consonants were taught in the syllable final position, such as /b/ or /d/ (e.g., "cub," "bed"). Parents were told that frequent, systematic practice of selected targeted sounds was essential to achieve mastery.

Nancy received 18 therapy sessions between 18 and 24 months of age with the following initial goals: to imitate /p/ and /b/ in isolation and in consonant-vowel syllables, such as "bee" and "pie," and to say /b/ and /p/ in vowel-consonant combinations such as "pop" and "up." Correct placement was achieved; however, productions were made with mild to moderate nasal air emission. Subsequent goals included correct placement for /t/, /d/, /k/, and /g/ with oral airflow. A goal to use lingual-alveolar placement for /t/ and /d/ resulted in 75% correct placement for /t/. Placement for /k/ and /g/ sounds was not obtained. Correct placement was verified when Nancy's nose was occluded. Nancy could not produce any fricative sounds when stimulated (/f/, /s/, /z/) but substituted the /h/ consonant whenever a fricative was attempted. Since the placement was at the level of the glottis, this compensatory error was likely to persist even after Nancy's velopharyngeal insufficiency was corrected. Because Nancy had moderate hypernasality and nasal air emission, nasopharyngoscopy was recommended. Although nasopharyngoscopy is typically scheduled after age 3 years (Kummer, 2020), Nancy's parents were eager to know the specific nature of the velopharyngeal insufficiency to obtain early secondary surgery. The SLP thought that Nancy could cooperate with the procedure. After repeated ear infections, the otolaryngologist removed a blocked left ear tube and replaced ear tubes at 20 months.

Analysis of Client's Response to Intervention

2-Year Cleft Team Visit Findings

At the 2-year team visit, hearing was normal, height and weight were normal, and there were no other health concerns. The dentist reported that there was a posterior crossbite and an extra tooth in the area of the cleft. The SLP documented normal language, severe articulation disorder, moderate hypernasality, and nasal air emission. The surgeon noted a bilateral alveolar cleft and a nasoalveolar fistula. He observed the short palate. The treatment plan was to continue speech therapy, complete nasopharyngoscopy, and obtain routine dental care.

Nasopharyngoscopy is an imaging technique in which a flexible fiber-optic endoscope is inserted into the nasal passage to view the velopharyngeal mechanism during speech. The scope allows visualization of the movement of the soft palate as well as movement of lateral and posterior pharyngeal walls. Nancy cried during part of the scoping, but the SLP and plastic surgeon were able to view the velopharyngeal port while Nancy was speaking. There was leakage of air into the nasal cavity across the entire palate. Slight symmetrical palatal movement and slight lateral pharyngeal wall movement were observed. The team diagnosed moderate to severe velopharyngeal insufficiency. The surgeon recommended a Furlow Z-plasty operation to lengthen the soft palate as well as a sphincter pharyngoplasty to reduce the size of the velopharyngeal space. Most cleft team centers report a 20% to 30% rate of velopharyngeal insufficiency in children with cleft palate. As a result, the children require secondary palatal surgery (Kummer, 2020). The team also recommended that Nancy remain in once-weekly speech therapy prior to surgery to maintain correct articulatory placement and to avoid compensatory errors such as pharyngeal stops.

Although the goal of speech therapy prior to surgery was to maintain correct placement for sounds, Nancy also showed a severe phonological disorder (Golding-Kushner, 2001). She continued to front velars so that "key" became "tea," stopped fricatives so that "fun" became "pun," glided liquids so that "light" became "white," and stopped the affricate "ch" so that "chair" because "tair." She reduced consonant clusters so that "play" became "pay" and omitted final consonants.

Following 4 months of once-weekly therapy (18 therapy sessions), Nancy imitated all /b/ and /p/ consonants in consonant-vowel (CV) syllables with the nose occluded as in "bee" and "pie" and half of /b/ and /p/ in consonant-vowel-consonant words such as "bib" or "pop." She was able to make lingual-alveolar contact for /t/ and /d/ in some positions of words as well as to produce an oral air stream for /f/ and /s/, although sound productions were /p/ for /f/ and /h/ for /s/ at 100%. Nancy still scored at the first percentile when retested on the Goldman-Fristoe Test of Articulation (Goldman & Fristoe, 2015).

Team Care and Follow-Up Over the Next Several Years

Speech and Velopharyngeal Functioning. Velopharyngeal closure was obtained following secondary palatal surgery at age 28 months. Within several months after surgery, Nancy produced syllable final consonants such as /p/, /m/, /n,/ /b/, /k/, /l/, /v/, and /z/ but continued to demonstrate a severe phonological disorder. Therapy then focused on the ability to produce speech sounds across syllable positions and in words, phrases, and sentences, which yielded an increase in intelligibility. Nancy continued in speech therapy for 226 sessions, and a parent home program was provided. Nancy completed therapy at age 5 years with a residual mild to moderate articulation disorder. School-based therapy subsequently corrected dentalized productions of lingual-alveolar sounds (t, d, ch, j) and lateralized /s/ on /s/ clusters such as /sl/. After 2 years of school-based speech therapy, Nancy was at age and grade level in all areas of communication and academics.

Hearing. Within normal limits.

Sleep. At age 3 years, Nancy was referred for a sleep study because of nighttime awakenings, daytime naps, and a noisy sound when falling asleep. A pediatric sleep study is an evaluation that analyzes a child's sleeping habits in the controlled setting of a sleep lab. The sleep study was normal and the problems spontaneously resolved.

Nutrition. At age 3 years, most of Nancy's calories came from liquids, which was not normal. With a dietitian's assistance, parents changed the diet and Nancy grew and gained weight normally.

Dental. At age 7 years, a community dentist began expansion of the alveolar arch and the posterior crossbite was corrected. With a bilateral cleft lip and palate, there can be a difference in the size of the maxilla and the mandible, where the maxilla is smaller. As a result, the curve of the row of teeth in each jaw is not aligned, causing a lateral misalignment of the dental arches. Posterior crossbite, a malocclusion, is an inadequate transversal relationship of the two dental arches.

Surgery. Following dental arch expansion, the surgeon repaired a nasoalveolar fistula and completed alveolar bone grafting to provide adequate bone within the alveolar cleft. A fistula is an abnormal opening between two organs that do not normally connect. An alveolar bone graft is a surgery to insert bone into the alveolar cleft at an appropriate time to allow eruption and retention of the permanent dentition (Kummer, 2020).

Psychosocial. Nancy had many friends and did well in school.

Author's Note

The family gave permission to share this case. Many thanks to Sally Helton, MS, CCC-SLP, for treating the patient described.

References

American Cleft Palate-Craniofacial Association. (2012). *Feeding your baby.* http://www.cleftline.org/parents-individuals/feeding-your-baby/

American Cleft Palate-Craniofacial Association. (2019). *Standards for approval of cleft palate and craniofacial teams.* http://www.acpa-cpf.org/team_care/standards/

Brown, V. L, Bzoch, K. R., & League, R. (2020). *Receptive-Expressive Emergent Language Test* (4th ed.). Pro-Ed.

Golding-Kushner, K. J. (2001). *Therapy techniques for cleft palate speech and related disorders.* Singular Publishing Group.

Goldman, R., & Fristoe, M. (2015). *Goldman-Fristoe Test of Articulation* (3rd ed.). Pearson.

Hardin-Jones, M. A., & Jones, D. L. (2005). Speech production of preschoolers with cleft palate. *Cleft Palate-Craniofacial Journal, 42*(1), 7–13. https://doi.org/10.1597/03-134.1

Hedrick, D., Prather, E., & Tobin, A. (1984). *Sequenced Inventory of Communication Development.* University of Washington Press; Western Psychological Services.

Kummer, A. W. (2020). *Cleft palate and craniofacial conditions: A comprehensive guide to clinical management* (4th ed.). Jones and Bartlett Learning.

Medela Inc. (2020). Mini-Special Needs Feeder. https://www.medela.us, item #6100093S.

Peterson-Falzone, S. J., Trost-Cardamone, J., Karnell, M. P., & Hardin-Jones, M. A. (2016). *The clinician's guide to treating cleft palate speech* (e-Book). Elsevier Health Sciences.

Sidoti, E. J., & Shprintzen, R. J. (1995). Pediatric care and feeding of the newborn with a cleft. In R. J. Shprintzen & J. Bardach (Eds.), *Cleft palate speech management: A multidisciplinary approach* (pp. 63–73). Mosby.

Turner, L., Jacobsen, C., Humenczuk, M., Singhal, V., Moore, D., & Bell, H. (2001). Feeding efficiency and caloric intake in breast milk fed cleft lip and palate infants with and without prosthetic appliance and lactation education. *Cleft Palate-Craniofacial Journal, 38*(5), 519–524. https://doi.org/10.1597/1545-1569_2001_038_0519_teolea_2.0.co_2

DEVELOPMENTAL DELAY
CASE 3
Ben: A Toddler With Delayed Speech and Developmental Milestones
Erin Redle Sizemore and Carolyn (Carney) Sotto

Conceptual Knowledge Areas

When evaluating young children, clinicians are frequently challenged to differentially diagnose an expressive language delay (sometimes called a "late talker") from a child who may have a true speech or language disorder. Currently, no gold standard exists regarding the identification and differential diagnosis of early language delays. What appears to be limited expressive output in an otherwise typical toddler may be the result of an expressive language delay or may reflect a delay or disorder in the child's speech production/phonological system. Clinicians must observe the complex interaction of expressive language and phonological development to make an informed diagnosis.

To acquire language, a child must assign representation to the lexicon and extract relevant phonological properties of such words for language production. The association between lexical and phonological development was observed in children with precocious language development as well as in children with delayed language development (Stoel-Gammon, 2011). Children with large vocabularies utilize a greater variety of sounds and sound combinations, while children who generate only a few words produce a more limited number of sounds and sound combinations (Sotto et al., 2014; Storkel & Morrisette, 2002). The relationship between phonological and lexical development is also supported by research on late talkers. In a study of children identified as late talkers, children with 10 or more words

and a larger phonemic repertoire at the initial assessment made more progress than the second group of late talkers with fewer than 10 words and a smaller phonemic repertoire (Thal et al., 1995). Similar findings were reported by Williams and Elbert (2003). Experimental evidence also demonstrates that the severity of a phonological delay at 2 years is predictive of the potential risk of continuing with a language delay at 3 years of age (Carson et al., 2003). However, these particular findings are limited as they are based on the reassessment of only 13 of the original 28 participants available for follow-up assessment. The number of different consonants a child uses in words is clearly associated with expressive language development (McCune & Vihman, 2001; Rescorla & Ratner, 1996). Although the magnitude of the phonetic inventory alone is not predictive when attempting to differentiate delayed from deviant language development (Williams & Elbert, 2003), it should be considered in making a clinical recommendation.

Early Phonological Development

Early phonological development is governed by physiologic factors and reflects both speech and language development (Locke, 2004; Smith & Goffman, 2004). One of the earliest developmental speech milestones, the onset of canonical babbling (consonant-vowel elements), is linked to later language outcomes (McGillion et al., 2017). Infants who are delayed in producing well-formed syllables in canonical babbling had smaller expressive vocabularies at 18, 24, and 30 months when compared to infants who demonstrated canonical babbling by 11 to 12 months of age (Oller et al., 1999). Both the placement and manner of sound production are important considerations in early phonological development. Bilabials and stops are the most prevalent sound classes reported in the early language/phonology literature, most likely due to their ease of production (Crowe & McLeod, 2020; Locke, 2004). Although these are generally accepted to be the most commonly produced consonants, the clinician should not ignore the presence or absence of other manners of production or variations in placement. Fricatives are generally considered a later developing sound class (Crowe & McLeod, 2020; Goldman & Fristoe, 2015; Shriberg, 1993), but there are data to support observations that toddlers produce this manner of phonemes (Gildersleeve-Neumann et al., 2000; Sotto et al., 2014). Clinicians may want to attend to the presence or absence of fricative production in children with potential speech and language delays. Fricatives are needed for production of several syntactical markers as children develop language and are motorically more difficult to produce than other phonemes. Therefore, when weighting factors that may make a child a late versus a delayed talker, the presence of fricatives in the repertoire may be a marker for the motor control necessary to incorporate the phonological, morphological, and syntactical rules of language with motor components of speech production.

Description of the Case

This case is about a child who was evaluated at a pediatric hospital in a U.S. metropolitan city. The evaluation was conducted by a licensed and certified speech-language pathologist.

Reason for Referral

Ben, a 24-month-old male, was referred by his pediatrician for a speech and language evaluation. Ben's parents were concerned that he was not talking as much as his brother did at the same age. Additionally, some of Ben's motor development was "slow," prompting his parents to seek a physical therapy assessment when Ben was 13 months old.

Background Information

Pertinent History

Ben was accompanied to the evaluation by his mother and father, who both actively participated in the interview and assessment process.

Neonatal History. Ben's neonatal history was unremarkable. His parents could not remember his specific Apgar scores. He was discharged without any noted complications.

Medical History. Ben was initially referred to early intervention by his pediatrician because he was not walking at 12 months; he subsequently learned to walk at 14 months (still grossly within the typical range) and the physical therapist (PT) diagnosed him with congenital hypotonia. He was also referred to occupational therapy and pediatric neurology. The PT was concerned regarding the hypotonia and wanted to rule out any significant underlying causes. The pediatric neurologist conducted a thorough clinical assessment as well as magnetic resonance imaging (MRI) of the brain and spine; bilateral electromyography testing including the hands, arms, legs, and feet; and a 1-hour electroencephalogram (EEG). Other than presenting with mild to moderate low tone, Ben's neurological system appeared to be unremarkable.

The parents reported he had one prior ear infection and was successfully treated with antibiotics. A complete audiological assessment was completed at 23 months by a pediatric audiologist, and hearing was within normal limits. There was no history of speech and language delays in the immediate or extended family.

Developmental History. Motor milestones were delayed with independent sitting reported at 8 months, crawling at 11 months, and walking at

14 months. Following his initial occupational and physical therapy evaluations, Ben was enrolled in both physical and occupational therapy and continued these therapies monthly. At 24 months, his parents reported he was still a "clumsy" walker and frequently fell. He did not yet display hand dominance.

Based on parental report, speech and language milestones were also delayed. The clinician linked questions about development to major holidays to assist in determining the time frame of several developmental milestones. Since Ben's birthday was in early January, the clinician targeted speech and language milestones at his first Passover (approximately 3–4 months old), summer vacations (approximately 6 months old), and around Hanukah (almost 12 months old). Using this technique, the parents were able to recall specific examples of Ben's speech and language skills. They reported that he was cooing at 4 months and babbling from the summertime through his first birthday. Ben produced his first true word, "dada," on a summer vacation (approximately 18 months old). He slowly developed a vocabulary of approximately 11 words including mama, dada, baba/bottle, uh-oh, no, wawa/water, sa/Sammie (family dog), ga/Grant (brother), i/eat, di/drink, and hi. He also frequently "jabbered" (unintelligible utterances of connected consonant and vowel sounds with varying intonational patterns) in a conversational manner but without true words.

By report, Ben understood "everything" and pointed to items named, family members when named, and to indicate something he wanted. His mother stated he sometimes became frustrated when she could not figure out what he was pointing to on the pantry shelves or in the refrigerator. His parents read to him frequently, and he engaged with books by pointing to objects and actions, following print left to right, pretending to "read" with jabbering, and turning pages.

Treatment History. Ben began monthly occupational and physical therapy through his local early intervention provider. He was referred for a speech and language evaluation through Part C early intervention, but this has not yet been completed.

Social History. Ben's older brother, who was 4 years, 1 month, had no developmental delays. Ben played with his brother and several cousins on a regular basis and engaged well with other children of all ages. Both parents had a college education (mother was a preschool teacher, father an attorney) and they read to their children daily. As an infant, his maternal grandmother provided childcare when the parents were at work, and Ben is now transitioning to center-based care.

Findings of the Evaluation

Ben's communication was assessed using the Rossetti Infant-Toddler Language Scale (Rossetti, 2006) and through clinical observations. All other skills assessed by the Rossetti scale, including gestures, play, and language comprehension, were within normal limits.

Expressive Language

Expressive language skills were delayed with skills solid at 12 to 15 months and scattering up to 15 to 18 months as assessed using the Rossetti scale. These results were supported by clinical observations and an attempted conversational speech and language sample. Although Ben did not use connected words, it is always best practice for the clinician to attempt to collect, transcribe, and analyze speech and language productions within a natural context of the child's own language (vocabulary, grammar) and running speech (sounds, prosody). He imitated "mama," "dada," and several unintelligible utterances of connected consonant and vowel sounds with varying intonational patterns with clear communicative intent (jabbering).

Receptive Language

As measured by the Rossetti scale, Ben's receptive language was within normal limits. Additionally, he followed novel one-step directions and simple two-step directions. He demonstrated age-appropriate understanding of several words expected at his age through pointing to the specified objects, actions, and early concepts in books and photos.

Phonological Development

The Arizona Articulation and Phonology Scale, Fourth Revision (Arizona-4) (Fudala & Stegall, 2017) was attempted to assess consonants and vowels in various word positions. Standard scores were not obtained as Ben could not name or imitate names of most of the stimulus pictures. Based on parents' report and the observed limited word productions and vocalizations, Ben's phonemic repertoire included /m, d, b, n, s, g, h, w/. Vowel errors were not noted. His syllable structure in words was primarily consonant-vowel (CV) with some CVCV observed; he did not produce final consonants in words. He was, however, able to string together longer sequences of consonants and vowels (e.g., CVCVCV, CVCVCVC) in jabbering.

Gestures and Play. Ben's scores on the Rossetti subscales for Gestures and Play were within normal limits. Informally, he used several gestures to communicate, including waving, pointing, and a "thumbs-up," which mom reported was consistent with his use of gestures at home. Additionally, he demonstrated an appropriate use of toys, and his parents reported he frequently engaged in parallel play with this brother and has even started to share toys.

Other Clinical Observations. Ben's interaction/pragmatic skills were informally judged to be within normal limits. Following a brief familiarization period, he engaged well with the examiner, demonstrated both nonverbal and verbal turn-taking in play, and interacted appropriately with his parents. Consistent and appropriate eye contact was noted.

Vocal quality and resonance were clinically judged to be within normal limits for the limited productions observed.

Oral Mechanism Examination

Formal and comprehensive oral mechanism assessments are extremely difficult to complete in children similar to Ben's age due to the limited ability to follow complex directions, as well as apprehension of strangers approaching the oral cavity. Ben's oral-facial structures appeared symmetrical. His oral-facial tone was low-normal to mildly hypotonic and was consistent with the tone throughout his body. The strength of his articulators seemed adequate for speech production. During play, he was able to imitate puckering for kissing and sticking his tongue out at someone. An intraoral assessment could not be completed. Ben was able to produce stop consonants (b, d), and his parents did not report food or liquids coming out of his nose when eating and drinking. Although these factors do not necessarily exclude the potential for velopharyngeal incompetence or a submucous cleft, they reflect adequate velopharyngeal structure and function for speech production. Overall, oral-motor strength and function appeared adequate for speech production.

Examiners' Impressions

Based on the results of this evaluation, Ben presented with moderately delayed expressive language skills and severely delayed phonological development. His expressive communication appeared to be most impaired by his difficulty putting sounds together into words, most likely due to his small phonemic repertoire. The clinician was faced with determining if Ben's limited vocabulary was due to an isolated early expressive language delay or reflective of a more global speech and language disorder.

The following factors were considered:

1. With the exception of expressive language and phonology, all other essential linguistic foundations, including receptive language, gestures, pragmatics, and play, were within normal limits. This suggests he had the foundation for language but was not producing age-appropriate expressive language.
2. Ben produced sounds utilizing almost all articulatory placements (bilabial, alveolar, velar, glottal) and different manners (stop, glide, fricative), yet the number of consonants he produced was very limited. Overall, his

phonological development appeared to be delayed as he continued to display syllable structure processes (e.g., final consonant deletion, syllable reduction). Although these processes may be observed in 2-year-old children, there is some evidence to suggest these processes are minimizing/reducing. Additionally, he did not mark any final consonants.

3. Ben's mother asked questions about childhood apraxia of speech (CAS). Although the examiner did not mention CAS, the family was aware of this terminology from a family friend. The examiner discussed the difficulty with a correct differential diagnosis of CAS in very young children. Ben did demonstrate a few characteristics that may be consistent with CAS, including limited syllable structures and an overall motor coordination problem. However, the parents reported Ben was a vocal child, and his babbling was similar to his brother's; this is not consistent with historical reports of children with CAS (Overby et al., 2020). His vowel repertoire was varied, and vowel errors were not noted in his spontaneous productions. Additionally, prosodic variation was noted in longer utterances and consonant errors were consistent. Ben also correctly produced a fricative in a word, which requires more advanced speech motor control. Differential diagnosis of CAS in children under 3 years of age can be difficult, especially if a child exhibits very limited expressive language (American Speech-Language-Hearing Association, 2007).

Parental Counseling

The family was counseled regarding the results of the evaluation and their options for treatment. They expressed understanding of the results and discussed both the diagnosis and the efficacy of the proposed treatment approaches with the clinician. Ben's mother, a preschool teacher, was concerned about his future literacy development. Additionally, Ben was scheduled to begin a new daycare facility in a few weeks, and the parents wanted to ensure a smooth transition.

Treatment Options Considered

The SLP presented the family with options regarding Ben's treatment. Speech and language intervention for language-delayed toddlers generally improves both linguistic and phonological complexity (Girolametto et al., 1997; Munro et al., 2021). Although the "wait-and-see" approach may be an option presented by some early childhood professionals, SLPs support that earlier identification and intervention is more likely to yield better outcomes (Capone Singleton, 2018). Given Ben's young age, speech therapy could be provided in an outpatient setting or through early intervention Part C services.

Course of Treatment

The long-term goal for Ben's speech and language therapy was to improve his expressive language skills to an age-appropriate level. The short-term goals included:

1. Increasing the number of different words and word approximations produced
2. Increasing the number of different phonemes and the complexity of syllable structures produced
3. Reinforcing strategies to promote vocabulary development (e.g., expansion), modeling target sound awareness and production, and integrating early literacy activities (e.g., book reading) into daily routines

Analysis of the Client's Response to Intervention

Ben made consistent progress in treatment. After 6 months of speech-language therapy, his vocabulary grew by approximately 75 words, including approximating some rote multiword phrases such as "thank you," "what's that," and "I don't know." He is not yet producing true spontaneous two-word combinations but could imitate these with a direct model (e.g., "want cookie"). His spontaneous phonemic repertoire increased to include /n, m, d, b, g, k, p, t, s, z, w, h/ and his syllable structures included CV, VC, CVCV, VCVC, CVC, and CVCVC. All other language skills, including receptive language, play, and pragmatics, continued to grow to age level. Additionally, his parents reported he was consistently using spoken language to interact with his brother during play and demonstrated more emergent literacy skills (e.g., book handling). Ben's parents reliably implemented speech and language-building strategies recommended by their SLP in daily routines, greatly enhancing his language development.

Further Recommendations

Ben should continue with speech-language pathology services to address phonological and expressive language skills, including multiword combinations. Additionally, Ben would benefit from including emergent literacy activities into treatment and home carryover activities. The strong collaboration between Ben's family and SLP will continue to maximize his opportunity for success.

Authors' Note

This was a fictional case based upon the performance of several children the authors had evaluated.

References

American Speech-Language-Hearing Association. (2007). *Childhood apraxia of speech* [Technical report]. http://www.asha.org/docs/html/TR2007-00278.html

Capone Singleton, N. (2018, February). Late talkers: Why the wait-and-see approach is outdated. *Pediatric Clinics of North America, 65*(1), 13–29.

Carson, C., Klee, T., Carson, D., & Hime, L. (2003). Phonological profiles of 2-year-olds with delayed language development: Predicting clinical outcomes at age 3. *American Journal of Speech-Language Pathology, 12*, 28–39.

Crowe, K., & McLeod, S. (2020). Children's English consonant acquisition in the United States: A review. *American Journal of Speech-Language Pathology, 29*, 2155–2169. https://doi.org/10.1044/2020_AJSLP-19-00168

Fudala, J., & Stegall, S. (2017). *The Arizona Articulation and Phonology Scale, Fourth Revision.* Western Psychological Services.

Gildersleeve-Neumann, C. E., Davis, B. L., & MacNeilage, P. F. (2000). Contingencies governing the production of fricatives, affricates, and liquids in babbling. *Applied Psycholinguistics, 21*, 341–363.

Girolametto, L., Pearce, P. S., & Weitzman, E. (1997). Effects of lexical intervention on the phonology of late talkers. *Journal of Speech, Language and Hearing Research, 40*(2), 338–348.

Goldman, R., Fristoe, M., & Williams, K. (2000). *Goldman-Fristoe Test of Articulation, Second Edition: Supplemental Developmental Norms.* American Guidance Service.

Locke, J. L. (2004). How do infants come to control the organs of speech? In B. Maasen, R. Kent, H. Peters, P. van Lieshout, & W. Hulstijn (Eds.), *Speech motor control in normal and disordered speech* (pp. 175–190). Oxford University Press.

McCune, L., & Vihman, M. M. (2001). Early phonetic and lexical development: A productivity approach. *Journal of Speech, Language, and Hearing Research, 44*(3), 670–684.

McGillion, M., Herbert, J. S., Pine, J., Vihman, M., dePaolis, R., Keren-Portnoy, T., & Matthews, D. (2017). What paves the way to conventional language? The predictive value of babble, pointing, and socioeconomic status. *Child Development, 88*(1), 156–166.

Munro, N., Baker, E., Masso, S., Carson, L., Lee, T., Wong, A. M. Y., & Stokes, S. (2021). Vocabulary acquisition and usage for late talkers treatment: Effect on expressive vocabulary and phonology. *Journal of Speech, Language, and Hearing Research, 64*(7), 2682–2697.

Oller, D. K., Eilers, R. E., Neal, A. R., & Schwartz, H. K. (1999). Precursors to speech in infancy: The prediction of speech and language disorders. *Journal of Communication Disorders, 32*(4), 223–245.

Overby, M., Belardi, K., & Schreiber, J. (2020). A retrospective video analysis of canonical babbling and volubility in infants later diagnoses with childhood apraxia of speech. *Clinical Linguistics and Phonetics, 34*(7), 634–651.

Paul, R., & Jennings, P. (1992). Phonological behavior in toddlers with slow expressive language development. *Journal of Speech and Hearing Research, 35*, 99–107.

Prather, E., Hedrick, D., & Kern, C. (1975). Articulation development in children aged two to four years. *Journal of Speech and Hearing Disorders, 40,* 179–191.

Rescorla, L., & Ratner, N. (1996). Phonetic profiles of toddlers with specific expressive language impairment (SLI-E). *Journal of Speech, Language, and Hearing Research, 39,* 153–156.

Rossetti, L. (2006). *The Rossetti Infant-Toddler Language Scale.* LinguiSystems.

Sander, E. K. (1972). When are speech sounds learned? *Journal of Speech and Hearing Disorders, 37,* 55–63.

Smith, A., & Goffman, L. (2004). Interaction of motor and language factors in the development of speech production. In B. Maasen, R. Kent, H. Peters, P. van Lieshout, & W. Hulstijn (Eds.), *Speech motor control in normal and disordered speech* (pp. 227–252). Oxford University Press.

Sotto, C., Redle, E. E., Bandaranayake, D., Neils-Stunjas, J., & Creaghead, N. (2014). Fricatives at 18 months as a measure for predicting vocabulary and grammar at 24 and 30 months. *Journal of Communication Disorders, 49,* 1–12.

Stoel-Gammon, C. (2011). Relationships between lexical and phonological development in young children. *Journal of Child Language, 38*(1), 1–34.

Storkel, H., & Morrisette, M. (2002). The lexicon and phonology: Interactions in language acquisition. *Language, Speech, and Hearing Services in Schools, 33,* 24–37.

Thal, D., Oroz, M., & McCaw, V. (1995). Phonological and lexical development in normal and late-talking toddlers. *Applied Psycholinguistics, 16,* 407–424.

Williams, A. L., & Elbert, M. (2003). A prospective longitudinal study of phonological development in late talkers. *Language, Speech, and Hearing Services in the Schools, 34,* 138–153.

HEARING

CASE 4

Abby: The Move From Identification to Implantation for a Child With Progressive Sensorineural Hearing Loss Caused by a Connexin 26 Mutation

Cynthia McCormick Richburg and Erin Clark

Conceptual Knowledge Areas

Connexin 26 is a protein found in the GJB2 gene (gap junction protein beta 2). This protein is necessary for cells to communicate with each other, and when there is not enough Connexin 26 protein, the potassium levels within the cochlea become too high and cause damage. Connexin 26 mutations are responsible for approximately 50% of nonsyndromic hearing loss. The hearing loss resulting from this mutation can be congenital or late-onset and progressive (Chan & Chang, 2014).

If each parent is an identified carrier of the GJB2/Connexin 26 gene, their baby will have a one in four chance of being born with an autosomal recessive sensorineural hearing loss. Connexin 26 (Cx26) mutations are responsible for hearing loss in 1 to 3 of every 1,000 births and cause various auditory phenotypes ranging from profound congenital deafness at birth to mild, progressive hearing loss in late childhood (Huculak et al., 2006; Wingard & Zhao, 2015).

To ensure children with sensorineural hearing losses (SNHL) are identified as early as possible, states and territories have implemented Early

Hearing Detection and Intervention (EHDI) programs. Protocols established by EDHI programs are written to ensure all infants are screened for hearing loss (known as universal hearing screening) preferably before the age of 1 month. For infants who fail their screening, follow-up protocols are written to ensure that the infants receive diagnostic audiologic evaluations, ideally before 3 months of age. The ultimate goal for EDHI programs is to enroll infants identified with permanent SNHL into early intervention services before the age of 6 months (The Joint Committee on Infant Hearing, 2019).

Intervention services include amplification with hearing aids and stimulation with cochlear implants. Hearing aids are considered medical devices and, as such, are regulated by the U.S. Food and Drug Administration (American Speech-Language-Hearing Association [ASHA], n.d.-b). These devices amplify sound from the listening environment and therefore require medical clearance from a pediatrician or physician (21 C.F.R. § 801.421; Food and Drug Administration, 2020). Although these amplifying devices can help to detect sound, damage within the cochlear structures means that a child is not guaranteed the ability to comprehend speech and language fully. When children with severe to profound SNHL receive limited benefit from binaural amplification and obtain scores of ≤30% on the (Multisyllabic) Lexical Neighborhood Test ([M]LNT; Kirk et al., 1995), they become candidates for cochlear implantation.

Cochlear implantation has been a safe and reliable treatment for children with severe to profound hearing loss since the 1980s (ASHA, 2003). The primary benefit of these medical devices in children is early access to sound, which leads to the acquisition of listening skills and promotes development of spoken language. While outcomes following cochlear implantation are highly variable and difficult to predict, one factor that is cited as beneficial in pediatric cases is early cochlear implantation. Sharma and Campbell (2011) suggest that the sensitive period for optimal central auditory development ends at approximately the age of 7 years. Other important variables for best outcomes with cochlear implant (CI) use include

compliance factors, such as time and consistency of use, timely follow-up with service providers, and (re)habilitation from specialized clinicians (ASHA, n.d.-a; Sharma et al., 2020).

Description of the Case

This case describes an infant with congenital, progressive, sensorineural hearing loss caused by a Connexin 26 gene mutation. The loss was first identified through an auditory brainstem response (ABR) hearing screening at birth and definitively diagnosed with a diagnostic ABR assessment at age 4 weeks. The infant was referred for otologic diagnosis, and the parents were given information regarding early intervention eligibility immediately. By the age of 4 years, the child had experienced two threshold shifts, making her a candidate for consideration for cochlear implantation. At the age of 6 years, this child successfully obtained listening, speech, and language skills to support transitioning to mainstream education for second grade.

Background Information and Reason for Referral

Abby was the firstborn child to her parents, Valerie and Jack, who lived in an urban area of central Pennsylvania. Jack and Valerie were young, educated professionals. Valerie was a licensed speech-language pathologist (SLP), and Jack was in law school at the time of Abby's birth. Valerie's pregnancy was typical, and Abby was delivered at Harrisburg Hospital at 40 weeks' gestation, weighing 8 pounds. This hospital provided newborn hearing screenings to every baby according to Pennsylvania's Infant Hearing Education, Assessment, Reporting and Referral Act (Act 89 of 2001; IHEARR, 2001). Abby underwent and failed two ABR screenings prior to discharge from the hospital. At that time, her parents were instructed to bring Abby back a week later for a third outpatient ABR screening. Upon failing this third screening, Abby was referred to an audiologist at Select Medical Audiology (a clinic associated with a different hospital) for a complete diagnostic evaluation.

Because of Valerie's professional background, ensuring that Abby returned for the diagnostic appointment that was set for 4 weeks after birth was a priority to the family. Although Valerie was employed, the family's insurance did not cover any of Abby's audiological testing or services. At the diagnostic evaluation that confirmed Abby's hearing loss, it was recommended that the family apply for Medicaid with the state of Pennsylvania. Within 1 month of applying, Abby's testing and services were covered by Medicaid.

Findings of the Evaluation

Initial Diagnostic Evaluations

When Abby was 4 weeks old, Valerie and Jack brought Abby to Select Medical Audiology, where they reported no family history of childhood hearing loss on either side. The child's parents indicated that Abby startled to loud sounds, which made them question the results of the hearing screening.

Abby's audiologist started the evaluation with tympanometry using a 1000 Hz tone due to Abby's age. No middle ear pathology was identified, and the testing progressed to diagnostic distortion product otoacoustic emissions (DPOAE), which were absent bilaterally. Because Valerie was an SLP, she immediately knew that Abby had hearing loss. Auditory brainstem response threshold testing was performed using 500 and 2000 Hz tone bursts to obtain threshold information for both ears. Due to waveforms being identified at 500 Hz in the mild range and 2000 Hz in the moderate range, it was determined that Abby's hearing loss was sloping in configuration, but no worse than moderate. Acoustic reflex testing, performed on each ear, revealed elevated acoustic reflexes at 500 Hz but absent reflexes at 1000 and 2000 Hz. These results were consistent with the absent DPOAEs and ABR waveforms in the mild to moderate range. Due to normal middle ear

results, the hearing loss was confirmed as being sensorineural.

Because Abby's audiologist knew that Valerie was an SLP, she described the test results using appropriate professional terminology but then repeated the information for Jack using laymen's terms. Valerie knew that immediate amplification was needed to support age-appropriate development of receptive and expressive language, appropriate articulatory acquisition, and psychosocial skills. Valerie knew that academic performance would be negatively impacted if they did not seek amplification.

The audiologist indicated that because of her diagnosis, Abby qualified automatically for early intervention services. Earmolds were taken that day in anticipation of receiving a pair of loaner hearing aids within the next 2 weeks. In addition, Abby was referred to an otolaryngologist for further medical testing to potentially determine the etiology of the hearing loss. Medical testing included an electrocardiogram (EKG) to rule out the heart conditions known to exist with Jervell and Lange-Nielsen syndrome, a urinalysis to rule out Alport syndrome, and genetic testing. Abby's test results were negative for the aforementioned syndromes, but her genetic test revealed that Abby was positive for Connexin 26.

Interventions

Audiologic Management: Birth to 2 Years

At 7 weeks of age, Abby was amplified with loaner behind-the-ear (BTE) Oticon hearing aids. She wore those hearing aids for approximately 2 months before receiving her own pair of the same aids. Over the next several months, Abby experienced multiple middle ear infections that ultimately led to bilateral pressure equalization (PE) tubes at 8 months of age. Abby continued with monthly molding and audiologic assessment during this time. At 15 months, there was concern that Abby's hearing sensitivity had decreased. Therefore, another ABR was administered at 18 months and confirmed the shift in hearing from a mild sloping to moderate loss to a moderate sloping to moderately-severe loss bilaterally.

Related Services and Language Interventions: Birth to 2 Years

From the outset, the family's mode of communication with Abby was Total Communication (TC) and Simultaneous Communication (Sim-Comm; refer to Hands & Voices, n.d., for descriptions of these modes of communication). The rationale for this was to provide Abby with multiple modality inputs to support language development. Despite qualifying from birth, Abby's family first requested early intervention services when she was 9 months old. This consult was initiated because there was a discrepancy between Abby's performance in the daycare environment and at home with respect to expressive and receptive language performance. However, due to the waitlist, the evaluation did not take place until Abby was 12 months old. The first service provider to be involved was the Teacher of the Deaf/Hard of Hearing (TOD/HOH), who primarily saw Abby in the daycare. When Abby was approximately 15 months old, the TOD/HOH recommended to initiate the services of an SLP. The TOD/HOH recommended selecting an SLP with Cued Speech experience in order to provide Abby with access to the richness of spoken English that is not easily translated to American Sign Language (ASL; refer to ASHA, n.d-a, for descriptions of these modes of communication).

Audiologic Management: 2 to 4 Years

When Abby was 27 months old, the family moved to western Pennsylvania to pursue job opportunities. As a result, Abby changed service providers, including her otolaryngologist and audiologist, to specialists at the University of Pittsburgh Medical Center (UPMC) Children's Hospital. At the age of 3 years, 1 month, it was determined that Abby was not getting enough gain from her current hearing aids. As a result, Abby was transitioned to larger, more powerful Oticon hearing aids. When she was 3 years, 6 months old, her

new service providers recommended that Abby be evaluated for a cochlear implant (CI). This evaluation required consultation with a cochlear implant team, including an audiologist, an otolaryngologist, a speech-language pathologist, and a neuropsychologist. Following the audiometric evaluation, the audiologist immediately identified her as an appropriate candidate for a CI. It was determined that Abby's right ear, identified as her worse ear with respect to thresholds and discrimination ability, should be the implanted ear. The CI surgery was scheduled for May 2019. In April 2019, another shift in hearing thresholds was identified, changing Abby's hearing sensitivity to the severe-to-profound range. Despite initial reservations, this final threshold shift confirmed Valerie and Jack's decision to pursue the cochlear implant.

Related Services and Language Interventions: 2 to 4 Years

During this time frame, early intervention services were transferred from Cumberland County to Indiana County upon the family's move. It was there that an itinerant TOD/HOH recommended that the family tour the Western Pennsylvania School for the Deaf (WPSD) in Pittsburgh to see if they thought it would be a good fit for Abby. Following her third birthday, Abby started at WPSD's Children's Center part-time and then transitioned to full-time during the next academic year. In addition to speech-language pathology services and support from a TOD/HOH, Abby received simultaneous instruction in English and ASL.

Audiologic Management: 4 to 6 Years

Abby underwent a CI surgery in May 2019. She received her hook-up and turn-on for the Nucleus 7 Sound Processor in late June, with two subsequent mappings in July. Abby continued regular audiologic assessment and management for both the CI and hearing aid from her audiologist. Abby quickly demonstrated a transition in preference from her hearing aid to her CI. Discussions regarding a second CI were placed on hold in the height of the COVID-19 pandemic. However, during the evaluation in July 2021, speech discrimination tasks comparing performance between her CI and hearing aid reignited discussions of a second CI surgery. Abby's aided speech perception was completed using the Lexical Neighborhood Test easy word list in the recorded format at 50 dB HL. Abby correctly scored 32% of the words and 42% of the phonemes with her hearing aid alone. With the CI alone, Abby correctly scored 96% of the words and 96% of the phonemes. As a result of these findings, the family opted to pursue a second CI in December 2021. Initial hook-up and turn-on with the Kanso 2 Digital Sound Processor were completed in January 2022 with mappings finalized 6 weeks later.

Related Services and Language Interventions: 4 to 6 Years

Abby received intensive aural (re)habilitation services through WPSD and UPMC Children's Hospital of Pittsburgh provided at WPSD following each CI surgery. Aural (re)habilitation services included transitioning from closed-set to open-set options, isolating listening skills through each CI independently, and working on developing listening skills in the presence of background noise.

Analysis of Client's Response to Intervention

Early identification, management, and service provision contributed to Abby's developmental success, academic achievements, and appropriate psychosocial development. Consequently, Abby is scheduled to transition to mainstream education during the 2022 to 2023 academic year with the supports of an interpreter, speech-language pathologist, and TOD/HOH.

Authors' Note

This case is based on assessment and intervention outcomes of an actual child with Connexin 26. Informed consent was obtained from both parents.

References

American Speech-Language-Hearing Association. (n.d.-a). *Cochlear implants practice portal.* https://www.asha.org/practice-portal/professional-issues/cochlear-implants/#collapse_1

American Speech-Language-Hearing Association. (n.d.-b). *Hearing aids for children practice portal.* https://www.asha.org/practice-portal/professional-issues/hearing-aids-for-children/

American Speech-Language-Hearing Association. (2003). *Cochlear implants* [Technical report]. https://www.asha.org/policy/tr2004-00041/#sec1.2

Chan, D. K., & Chang, K. W. (2014). GJB2-associated hearing loss: Systematic review of worldwide prevalence, genotype, and auditory phenotype. *Laryngoscope, 124,* E34–E53.

Food and Drug Administration. (2020, April). Title 21 C.F.R. § 801.421; Hearing aid devices; Conditions for sale. https://www.govinfo.gov/content/pkg/CFR-2020-title21-vol8/xml/CFR-2020-title21-vol8-sec801-421.xml

Hands & Voices. (n.d.). *Communication considerations: Total communication.* https://www.handsandvoices.org/comcon/articles/totalcom.htm

Huculak, C., Bruyere, H., Nelson, T., Kozak, F., & Langlois, S. (2006). V371 connexin 26 allele in patients with sensorineural hearing loss: Evidence of its pathogenicity. *American Journal of Medical Genetics Part A, 140*(22), 2394–2400. https://doi.org/10.1002/ajmg.a.31486

Infant Hearing Education, Assessment, Reporting and Referral Act (IHEARR; 2001, November). https://www.legis.state.pa.us/cfdocs/legis/li/uconsCheck.cfm?yr=2001&sessInd=0&act=89

The Joint Committee on Infant Hearing. (2019). Year 2019 position statement: Principles and guidelines for early hearing detection and intervention programs. *Journal of Early Hearing Detection and Intervention, 4*(2), 1–44. https://doi.org/10.15142/fptk-b748

Kirk, K., Pisoni, D., & Osberger, M. (1995). Lexical effects on spoken word recognition by pediatric cochlear implant users. *Ear and Hearing, 16,* 470–481.

Sharma, A., & Campbell, J. (2011). A sensitive period for cochlear implantation in deaf children. *Journal of Maternal Fetal Neonatal Medicine, 24*(1), 151–153. https://doi.org/10.3109/14767058.2011.607614

Sharma, S. D., Cushing, S. L., Papsin, B. C., & Gordon, K. A. (2020). Hearing and speech benefits of cochlear implantation in children: A review of the literature. *International Journal of Pediatric Otorhinolaryngology,*

133, 109984. https://doi.org/10.1016/j.ijporl.2020.10 9984

Wingard, J. C., & Zhao, H.-B. (2015). Cellular and deafness mechanisms underlying Connexin mutation-induced hearing loss—a common hereditary deafness. *Frontiers in Cellular Neuroscience, 9*(202). https://doi .org/10.3389/fncel.2015.00202

FRAGILE X SYNDROME
CASE 5
Jake: The Move From Early Intervention to Early Childhood Education for a Child With Fragile X Syndrome
Gail Harris-Schmidt

Conceptual Knowledge Areas

This case is designed for those with both some knowledge of and interest in young children with speech and language disorders due to genetic syndromes, such as fragile X syndrome. Some knowledge of Early Intervention (EI) and Early Childhood Education (ECE) is helpful, but not required, to fully appreciate the complexities of this case. Understanding and awareness of interdisciplinary service provision is also useful.

Fragile X syndrome is the most common inherited cause of intellectual disabilities. Women may be carriers of a mutation in the FMR1 gene, which is located on the X chromosome, without exhibiting cognitive or linguistic characteristics of the syndrome. Such characteristics may appear clinically in both their male and female offspring. Boys with the full mutation typically have cognitive impairments. These can range from mild learning disabilities to severe cognitive disabilities. Boys with fragile X also often have speech, language, and developmental delays; attention and behavioral issues; low muscle tone; and sensory overload problems. Many boys with fragile X have some autistic-like characteristics, and some are diagnosed with autism (Hagerman & Hagerman, 2002). Girls with the fragile X mutation usually have milder symptoms, as they have a second X chromosome, unaffected by the fragile X gene.

Description of the Case

The EI and ECE teams in a suburban public school began working with Jake and his parents, as Jake was about to turn 3 years of age and transition into Early Childhood Special Education. The ECE team consisted of Jake's parents, a school psychologist, a school social worker, a speech-language pathologist (SLP), a physical therapist (PT), and an occupational therapist (OT).

Background Information

Jake was the first child of a suburban, middle-class, college-educated couple. His father (Will) was a high school history teacher and his mother (Jenny) a part-time school nurse. Jake's mother was pregnant with a second child at the time of the initial ECE evaluation.

Jake was born full-term without complications after an uneventful pregnancy. He weighed 7 pounds 5 ounces at birth and was 21 inches long. There were no initial concerns about Jake's medical status, and he was discharged after 1 day in the hospital. Jake's mother had difficulty nursing him, as he had a weak sucking reflex. She began bottle feeding when he lost weight during his first few weeks and tried a variety of nipples to aid his sucking. Jake was a somewhat "floppy" baby (with low muscle tone), but his parents assumed that he would gain more muscular control as he developed. He had prominent ears, which the parents found endearing.

As Jake approached his first birthday, his parents became more concerned about his development. He was very "high strung" and irritable, and he had problems sleeping and eating. His parents tried soy milk, thinking that he might have lactose intolerance, but Jake remained fussy, both as he ate and afterward. He was late in holding his head up and sitting, and he had not yet begun to crawl. He rarely cooed or babbled and made no attempts to imitate syllables. Jake had already had three ear infections before his first birthday; consequently, throughout his second year, the pediatrician monitored his ears carefully and finally referred the family to an ear, nose, and throat specialist. Jake's hearing was tested periodically from 12 months on. Tympanometry performed at 15 and 18 months of age revealed bilateral fluid. Pressure equalization tubes were inserted at 18 months. One tube was subsequently replaced, while the other (original) tube was still intact at the time he entered ECE. Jake's parents attributed some of his speech and language delays to the ear infections, and the pediatrician assured them that Jake would "catch up."

During his second year, Jake had difficulty making eye contact and did not display the joint attention to books and toys that his parents saw with other children his age. He often fixated on TV shows or toddler DVDs and screamed until they were shown repeatedly. He continued to be "high strung" and flapped his hands when overstimulated. He chewed on his clothing and occasionally on his hand. Jenny and Will expressed concerns

to their pediatrician about Jake's lack of sociability and raised the possibility that Jake might be displaying some symptoms of autism. The pediatrician did not think that Jake displayed autistic characteristics and stated that it was far too early to be considering such a diagnosis.

Jake began to walk at 19 months and said his first word at 23 months ("Bu" for "Burt" of *Sesame Street*). He had not slept through the night during his first 2 years. He was an extremely picky and messy eater; he often stuffed food into his mouth until it was overly full and then spit it out. He continued to drink from a bottle. Often the only way his parents could get him back to sleep at night was by giving him a bottle of juice.

Reason for Referral

By his second birthday, Jake's parents were concerned enough about his developmental delays to seek a referral from their pediatrician for a developmental evaluation with the EI providers in their area. The EI team conducted a play-based evaluation in Jake's home when he was 24 months old. Jake's mother completed the interview and the MacArthur-Bates Communicative Development Inventories: Words and Gestures (Fenson et al., 2015a); the SLP at first considered giving the parents the more age-appropriate MacArthur-Bates Words and Sentences (Fenson et al., 2015b) inventory to complete but decided against it once she saw how limited Jake's language was. Even with the questions designed for those 8 to 16 months old, his mother indicated concerns in all areas.

Jenny reported that Jake's receptive language skills were better than his expressive skills. He could recognize and point to pictures in books and characters in TV shows and movies and could recognize family names (e.g., Mommy, Daddy, Grandma, Grandpa) and find the appropriate person. He knew and could point to a variety of animals and match their sounds to the animal's name. The SLP attempted some play-based interactions but had difficulty getting Jake to cooperate. She observed oral-motor skills, but neither she nor the OT could conduct a complete oral-motor exam due to his resistance. The OT observed his overall low muscle tone, hypersensitivity to touch, and strong reactions to loud sounds.

Early Intervention

Jake qualified for EI services based upon developmental delays of more than 30% in at least two areas (the requirements of the state in which the family lived). Since he qualified on the basis of speech-language and fine motor delays, with some less severe gross motor delays, an Individual Family Service Plan (IFSP) was developed.

A home-based and center-based program was initiated. The SLP and OT provided therapy simultaneously at home once weekly and worked with the parents on language stimulation, oral-motor activities, and sensory integration/calming techniques. Jenny and Will also attended a series of parent education programs based upon the "It Takes Two to Talk" Hanen Program (Weitzman, 2017) designed for parents of children with language delays.

Once each week, Jake and his mother attended a center-based EI class at a local Easter Seals agency, where a small group of parents and children met for language and motor stimulation activities. The SLP used picture cues with Jake to help him learn the routines of the sessions. She found that he responded very well to visual cueing and to routines. He began to anticipate and cooperate with the sequence of activities in the center-based program. If routines and schedules changed, he became agitated. During some sessions, he became extremely overstimulated and uncooperative and tried to bite or hit other children.

The SLP tried a Picture Exchange Communication System (PECS; Frost & Bondy, 2002) and attempted to teach Jake sign language to help him make his wants and needs known; however, as he approached his third birthday, Jake had not made much progress. His parents were somewhat resistant to the use of any type of augmentative or alternative communication (AAC) system, as they continued to hope that Jake would become more verbal. Jake made some gains throughout the year, increasing his expressive vocabulary to five words and improving his receptive vocabulary and understanding of simple one-step commands.

When Jake was 33 months old (2 years, 9 months), his parents received a letter from Jenny's cousin Sara. Her 5-year-old son, who had many developmental delays, had recently been diagnosed with fragile X syndrome. Sara had tested positive as a carrier of fragile X, with the premutation of the syndrome. Both of her parents were tested, and Sara's father (Jenny's uncle) was found to be a carrier, with a premutation and no effects. As a man cannot inherit the X chromosome from his father (fathers pass the Y chromosome, but not the X, to all sons), the fragile X gene was traced back to Sara's and Jenny's grandmother. This meant that any of the grandmother's children (including Jenny's father) might also be a carrier of the fragile X gene. Jenny and Will were devastated to learn the news of the genetic mutation in the family and sought testing for Jake and themselves. Since a father cannot pass the fragile X gene to his son, Will realized that he did not need to be tested. Jake and Jenny were tested through a blood sample sent to a large medical center with a genetic testing facility. Jake was found to have the full mutation of fragile X syndrome; Jenny was found to be a carrier, a person with the genetic repeat pattern in the premutation range.

At the time of the testing, Jenny was pregnant with their second child. She learned that she had a 50/50 chance of passing the fragile X gene to her unborn child, as she had both eggs with the fragile X marker and unaffected eggs. She elected to have genetic testing and learned that her second child, a girl, did not carry the fragile X gene.

At the time of the transition to Early Childhood Education, Will and Jenny were still reeling from news of the fragile X diagnosis. They had thought that Jake's numerous, recurring ear infections or other factors might be causing his difficulties and hoped that intervention would help him "grow out" of his delays. Jenny was feeling extremely guilty for being a "silent carrier" of a genetic disorder, although her husband was very supportive and assured her that it was no one's "fault." It was at this time that Jake began the evaluations for ECE programming, and his parents faced choices about the most appropriate setting for Jake's needs and goals.

Findings of the Evaluation: Early Childhood Education Evaluation

Jake was first assessed in his home with his mother and father present. Observations, language sampling, checklists, the Peabody Picture Vocabulary Test-5 (Dunn & Dunn, 2018), and the Rossetti Infant-Toddler Language Scale (Rossetti, 2006) were used to complete the assessment. The Preschool Language Scale–Fifth Edition (Zimmerman et al., 2011) was attempted, but Jake's attention was minimal, and little was gained from the items sampled. He was unable to comprehend many of the tasks or complete the expressive tasks.

On the Peabody Picture Vocabulary Test-5, Form B (PPVT-5), Jake received a standard score of 65, more than two standard deviations below the mean. Even with the first few pictures, he had some difficulty comprehending what to do and maintaining attention to the task, and the SLP often had to point to each of the four pictures in order to get him to scan them all. She believed that inattention interfered enough that the test score might have been quite minimal and not totally valid.

On the Rossetti Infant-Toddler Language Scale (Rossetti, 2006), Jake demonstrated receptive language skills in the 9- to 12-month range, with some scatter skills at the 12- to 15-month range. Most language comprehension items were either reported or observed in those ranges. The SLP and OT observed Jake in play with his parents and attempted to interest him in some of the toys they had brought. Observations of play and nonverbal communication skills revealed strong attachment skills to familiar people but great difficulty with unfamiliar people. His joint attention to objects with both his parents and the SLP and OT was poor, and they often had to move an object in front of his face to get him to attend to it. He used some intentional gestures to get objects that he wanted, and he showed some functional use of objects in play, especially in imitation. He did not play with objects in a creative way but sometimes banged or shook them. Results of developmental testing placed Jake below his age range for play, when compared to his peer group. His short attention span and frequent outbursts contributed to his difficulty in play skills.

Expressive scores fell in the 6- to 9-month range, with some scatter skills in the 9- to 12-month and 12- to 15-month ranges. Jake used five words expressively (no, me, do/go, mo/more, bu [Burt]), and his mother reported five additional words that she had heard. Informal play-based assessment revealed no two-word combinations. Jake imitated words in play scripts, such as bop/pop, bi/big, and boo/book. These were limited to his current phonetic inventory (/p/, /b/, /m/, /n/, /t/, /d/). He vocalized in order to express his desire to change tasks. He expressed frustration when he was not understood by refusing to attempt the word again. The SLP noted that Jake had very poor eye contact and problems with joint attention.

It was difficult to conduct a thorough oral-motor exam, as Jake demonstrated much resistance to being touched around the face and mouth. The SLP had asked his mother to bring in a variety of food and drinks and attempted to get him to eat pudding, chew a cookie or bagel, and drink from various cups. The SLP noted that he had a high, narrow palate and low muscle tone in his oral musculature. Related to poor mouth closure, lip competence, including rounding and retraction, was weak. Jaw strength and grading for chewing and feeding were also affected. Jake demonstrated an immature feeding pattern consisting of munching and sucking foods, as well as swallowing without chewing to completion. According to his parents, Jake was picky about the foods he would eat. In the evaluation, he preferred crunchy and soft foods. Jake's parents reported that he still drank from a bottle at bedtime and a sippy cup during the day. At the time of the evaluation, Jake could not drink from a juice box. Observation of Jake's use of a straw revealed a sucking pattern resting the straw on the tongue blade, rather than using lip rounding and closure to seal and move the liquid up and into the oral cavity for swallowing. No choking was observed in the evaluation, but his parents reported some choking when he stuffed his mouth with too much food.

The OT concurred with the sensory concerns and found Jake to be a child with hyperarousal, sensory overload issues, and an extremely short attention span. Fine motor skills were found to be well below his age range, with some sensory issues noted. Gross motor skills were found to be below the range for his age, with most difficulty seen in motor planning. Jake demonstrated motor planning difficulties in his speech, as well as with his body in space. His parents reported that he tripped a lot at home.

The social worker interviewed both of Jake's parents and found a very loving, resilient, and caring couple who were deeply concerned about their little boy and his development. She sought out materials from the National Fragile X Foundation (fragilex.org) and the FRAXA Research Foundation (fraxa.org) both for the school team and for Jake's parents. She referred them to a local Fragile X Resource Group, so that they would be able to talk with other parents and find support there.

The school psychologist attempted to administer a preschool intelligence test at the special education center but had great difficulty given Jake's short attention span and anxiety. She believed there were cognitive delays but could not report any scores or results.

Findings of the Evaluation: Results and Diagnostic Hypothesis

It was determined that Jake had speech, language, and oral-motor delays consistent with fragile X syndrome. He was also diagnosed with sensory and motor delays affecting his level of arousal, eating and sleeping patterns, and fine motor skills. A report of his cognitive abilities was not included in the summary. Jake was diagnosed with "developmental delay" with speech-language delay as a secondary diagnosis.

Treatment Options Considered

The team worked to develop an appropriate Individualized Educational Plan (IEP) for Jake's move to an ECE program. His goals clearly required collaborative programming, utilizing the expertise of a variety of professionals. The team immediately ruled out speech-language and occupational therapy services as a nonattending student (that is, one with no other daily program) as inappropriate. They also ruled out a program designed for young children with profound disabilities, as Jake's IEP goals could not be met appropriately in a setting designed for children with much more involved needs.

Two different settings were discussed. There was some disagreement among team members about the most appropriate placement for Jake. One of the settings was in a "blended" classroom in a local public school; the classroom included some at-risk children (not diagnosed with special education classifications) along with children who had a variety of special education classifications (Down syndrome, hearing loss, language delay, phonological delay, autistic spectrum disorders). An early childhood special education teacher taught the half-day class with twice-a-week services from an SLP and an OT, as well as two classroom paraprofessionals. The SLP and OT were present on opposite days and did not provide services together. They did attempt to collaborate by phone and e-mail and help each other with appropriate language/sensory activities. The classroom was very "language rich," lively, and busy. The walls were all decorated in bright colors, and the noise level was often high.

The second placement discussed was a half-day, more structured special education class designed for children who had moderate-to-severe disorders. The program was housed in a special education center with other classes for children in special education from age 3 years through Grade 8. All eight children in the class had multiple needs. Some were nonverbal and used augmentative communication (AAC) devices. Others had physical disabilities with cognitive delays. A nurse was on staff, along with an early childhood special education teacher, SLP, OT, and PT. The SLP, OT, and PT were in attendance for an hour each day of the 4-day a week program. Their services overlapped, and they often coordinated lessons that targeted integrated movement and language activities. On Friday of each week, staff members made home visits to work with parents and children in their own homes. An expert in AAC was a program consultant and visited weekly. The classroom was also language-rich, but more structured and calmer than the first one. The room contained a "quiet area," with a small pop-up tent, beanbag chairs, picture books, and calming music on tapes. There was a small gym nearby, with a ball pit, swings, mats, and a trampoline for sensory activities.

Will and Jenny visited both classrooms and determined that the "blended" classroom provided opportunities for Jake to interact with and imitate more verbal peers and to have good role models for play. The SLP agreed and also recommended the blended classroom. She believed that Jake would benefit from the stimulating language environment there. She also felt that the SLP and OT could design some calming activities for Jake, which could be implemented even when they were not in the classroom at the same time. She believed that the SLP in the blended classroom could consult with the AAC specialist at the special education center to design more helpful ways to augment Jake's expressive language.

The OT had concerns about the "blended" classroom, as he considered it to be overwhelming to the senses. He believed Jake might have more behavioral problems because of the visual and auditory hyperstimulation. He thought that Jake would get more individual attention in a quiet, structured setting, with easy access to calming spaces and activities. He stated that with more staff available and more opportunities for collaborative programming, Jake would make better progress. He felt that Jake could be included in other settings later.

The school psychologist agreed with the OT as she had seen Jake's behavioral and anxiety issues in her attempts to complete an assessment. She believed that if some of the attention and behavior issues could be treated, then Jake might be able to move out of the special education center into a setting that offered more mainstreaming.

Description of Course of Treatment

Ultimately, the team decided to place Jake in the blended classroom with access to more verbal chil-

dren. He turned 3 years of age in July and began the program in late August. Jake's baby sister had been born in the prior spring, and Jenny took a maternity leave. At home, she followed up on suggestions from the school faculty, sent an electronic notebook back and forth each day to communicate, and was a very collaborative member of Jake's ECE team.

Analysis of Client's Response to Intervention

Jake had great difficulty at first with the transition to the new setting and a longer morning, particularly without his mother present. He was scheduled to take the special education bus to school. However, Jenny drove him, as his resistance to the transportation was so strong. He had several "meltdowns" during the first weeks and had to be taken by his one-on-one aide for walks to a quiet place. His behavior continued to be an issue throughout the year, as sensory overload often preceded an aggressive outburst. The staff became better at noticing the antecedents to a behavioral crisis (e.g., becoming red in the face, flapping his hands, or chewing on his clothing) and tried to intercede before Jake would hit or bite another person or himself.

The staff gradually found various ways to calm Jake and help him make it through the morning. The early childhood teacher was excellent at using visual cues for the entire class, and she made sure to go through the picture schedule each day. If there were changes in the schedule, she discussed them with Jenny in advance, so that both of them could work with picture cues to prepare Jake for the day. She provided many visual cues in her teaching, and Jake responded well to them. With both Jake and a child diagnosed with autism in her class, she became more sensitive to the noise level and overload issues in the classroom.

The OT designed a "sensory diet," which included a variety of deep-pressure activities (e.g., wall pushups, rolling in a blanket). She also provided him with a weighted vest during some activities, which seemed to provide the sensory input he needed to calm him. She and the SLP communicated by e-mail and tried to design some activities that would help Jake meet multiple goals in both speech/language and sensory motor areas. She found that Jake enjoyed puzzles and was very good with putting 10- to 20-piece puzzles together. She worked to integrate language into his puzzle time, as she labeled pieces and made comments about their placements (e.g., "Oh, it's under the swing").

The SLP integrated sensory activities into her goals and activities, as she worked in four different areas: (1) Receptive goals included a focus on increasing Jake's comprehension of vocabulary in thematic units and completion of one-step directions. (2) Expressive goals in language and articulation were aimed at increasing his phonetic inventories and his expressive vocabulary. She used many pictures, storyboards, and low-tech AAC devices to help him develop additional ways to express himself. (3) Oral-motor and feeding goals centered on increasing Jake's awareness of and strengthening his oral musculature. (4) Social-pragmatic goals included fostering turn-taking, requesting items, and initiating play. A few simple signs (such as "more") helped him to communicate some wants and needs.

At the end of the school year, his standard score on the Peabody Picture Vocabulary Test-5 (Dunn & Dunn, 2018) increased by 7 points. He did especially well with words that included his interests (transportation and animals) and added receptive vocabulary from all the thematic units of the year. He also comprehended directions utilizing simple prepositions.

His progress in expressive speech was not as good. He added 20 single words but did not increase his sound repertoire. For example, he labeled five new items as "ba": ball, baby, bottle, big, and bear. He could differentiate the items and clearly knew what they were receptively, but his pronunciation was very unclear. Jake made gains in using gestures more expressively and meaningfully.

Jake made some progress in oral-motor areas. He began to drink from a straw that had been cut in half (he could not use the narrow juice box straws), and he could blow bubbles. His eating was still messy. However, his family and the school staff worked on controlling how much he should have on his plate, so that he would not overstuff his mouth and choke.

Social-pragmatic and play skills remained difficult, although Jake would cooperate in structured interactions. He preferred the adult teachers to his classmates and did not make overtures to play unless prompted with very specific directions. He would cooperate in routines, such as going around the snack table to hand out napkins, but continued to have difficulty with eye contact or any verbalization while accomplishing such tasks. He preferred to play alone and often stacked blocks or scooped sand repetitively. During center times, the SLP tried to work with him by playing in a parallel way with comments (self-talk) about what she was doing. She also worked to have another child play near him, while she engaged them both in an activity.

Further Recommendations

At the end-of-the-year annual review and IEP update, the team again discussed the option of moving Jake to the special education classroom housed in the special education center. Jake's parents were pleased with the blended setting and believed that he was making progress. They still hoped that more expressive language and calmer behavior was possible.

The SLP believed that some aspects of the alternative classroom might be beneficial for Jake, including the consultation of the AAC technology expert and the amount of time that the SLP and OT were simultaneously in the classroom. However, she and the others agreed that Jake was making progress, and the team decided to keep Jake in the same placement for another year.

Author's Note

The client, "Jake," is fictional, based upon children with fragile X syndrome seen by the author.

References

Dunn, L., & Dunn, D. (2018). *Peabody Picture Vocabulary Test* (5th ed.). AGS Corporation.

Fenson, L., Marchman, V., Thal, D., Dale, P., Reznick, S., & Bates, E. (2007a). *MacArthur-Bates Communicative Development Inventories: Words and Gestures* (2nd ed.). Brookes Publishing.

Fenson, L., Marchman, V., Thal, D., Dale, P., Reznick, S., & Bates, E. (2007b). *MacArthur-Bates Communicative Development Inventories: Words and Sentences* (2nd ed.). Brookes Publishing.

Frost, L., & Bondy, A. (2002). *The Picture Exchange Communication System training manual* (2nd ed.). Pyramid Educational Consultants.

Hagerman, R., & Hagerman, P. (2002). *Fragile X syndrome: Diagnosis, treatment, and research* (3rd ed.). Johns Hopkins University Press.

Rossetti, L. (2006). *The Rossetti Infant-Toddler Scales.* Brookes Publishing.

Weitzman, E. (2017). *It takes two to talk: The Hanen program for parents.* The Hanen Centre.

Zimmerman, I., Steiner, V., & Pond, R. (2011). *Preschool Language Scale-5.* Pearson.

PRENATAL ALCOHOL/DRUG EXPOSURE
CASE 6
Sybil: Prenatal Alcohol and/or Drug Exposure
Dorian Lee-Wilkerson and Gabriella Billups

Conceptual Knowledge Areas

Prenatal substance exposure continues to be major public health concern. The Substance Abuse and Mental Health Services Administration (SAMHSA, 2020) reported that 15.8% of the U.S. population (38.7 million people) had a substance use disorder. Of that 15.8%, between 8% and 11% of pregnant women aged 15 to 44 had used alcohol, illicit drugs, or tobacco products in the past month. The most commonly used substance among pregnant women in this age group was marijuana.

For over 30 years, researchers have demonstrated the negative effects of prenatal alcohol and/or drug exposure on child development. While more is known about the prenatal effects of the use of alcohol, tobacco, and marijuana than about the prenatal effects of exposure to opioid use, all of these substances are known to increase a child's risk for cognitive and language impair-

ments and behavioral problems (Boggess & Risher, 2022; Chu et al., 2020).

Fetal alcohol spectrum disorders (FASDs) include a wide range of physical, mental, and behavioral characteristics that are associated with maternal use of alcohol during pregnancy. The most severe form of FASD is fetal alcohol syndrome (Wilhoit et al., 2017). During 2018 to 2020, a little over 13% of adults in the United States reported drinking while pregnant, and 5.2% reported binge drinking while pregnant (Gosdin et al., 2022). It is well known that there is no known safe amount of alcohol consumption during pregnancy and that FASD is linked to drinking alcohol during pregnancy. The Centers for Disease Control reports that Fetal Alcohol Syndrome (FAS) occurs in 0.2 to 1.5 per 1,000 live births. Children with FAS usually present with abnormal facial features and growth deficiencies. Children with FAS may also exhibit attention deficits, memory impairments, learning disability, visual disturbances, hearing impairment, and/or speech and language impairment. In addition to FAS, FASDs include alcohol-related birth defects (ARBDs) and alcohol-related neurodevelopmental disorders (ARNDs). The reported prevalence rate for ARBDs and ARNDs combined is three times higher than the rate of FAS. Children with ARBDs may have defects of the skeletal and major organ systems along with some behavioral and cognitive problems. Children with ARND may experience neurological impairments affecting vision, hearing, motor movements, balance, cognition, behavior, and sensory integration (Hagan et al., 2016; Wilhoit et al., 2017).

FASD places a child at risk for school failure, substance abuse, mental illness, poor employment history, and involvement in the criminal justice system (CDC, n.d.-a). According to the Centers for Disease Control, a child with FASD may experience one or more of the following characteristics: small for gestational age, small stature, facial abnormalities, poor coordination, mental retardation, lower than average IQ scores, learning disabilities, hyperactivity, sleep disturbances, poor reasoning and judgment, and speech-language delays. Additional outcomes of prenatal drug exposure include atypical social interactions, minimal play strategies, poor self-regulation, feeding disabilities, poor fine motor development, poor gross motor development, irritability, and attention deficits. These children may also evidence auditory processing deficits and visual processing deficits (Dodge et al., 2019).

The National Institute on Drug Abuse (NIDA) has supported numerous studies and compiled a summary of 24 current investigations that examined the long-term effects of prenatal drug exposure (NIDA Notes, 2004), including cocaine, marijuana, opiates, ecstasy, methamphetamine, and tobacco. One of the largest studies in this group was the Maternal Lifestyle Study (Lester et al., 2004) that reported the outcomes of 1,388 one-month-old infants born with prenatal drug exposure. These infants were found to experience poor quality of movement and regulation, lower arousal, higher excitability, hypertonia, and nonoptimal reflexes. Other studies since that time have reported similar findings (Boggess & Risher, 2022; Chu et al., 2020).

Evidence supporting the likelihood that the effects of prenatal drug exposure may persist beyond early childhood continues to grow. Rivkin et al. (2008) found reductions in the cortical gray matter of participating adolescents, as well as evidence of an additive effect. That is, the adolescents who were exposed to a greater variety of drugs and alcohol prenatally had greater reductions in brain volume when compared with their peers who were reportedly exposed to a single drug. Landi et al. (2017) reported depressed reading and language scores among adolescents with a history of prenatal cocaine exposure. Geng et al. (2018) found evidence of the persistence of the effects of prenatal exposure to drugs on the memory of adolescents. Guille and Aujla (2019) found that prenatal exposure to marijuana was associated with deficits in executive and intellectual function in school-age children and adolescents.

There is also research showing that the effects of intrauterine alcohol and drug exposure are compounded by the association of additional risk factors such as poor nutrition, inadequate prenatal care, limited social supports, unsafe home environments, and unstable lifestyles (Chu et al., 2020). Bakhireva et al. (2018) noted that women who drink or use drugs during pregnancy often use multiple substances that can include combinations of alcohol, marijuana, tobacco, cocaine, and/or other illicit drugs.

Coggins et al. (2007) observed that children with a history of alcohol and drug exposure live in a state of "double jeopardy." Children suffering with the effects of prenatal drug and alcohol exposure are more likely to be born to single mothers living in poverty. They are more likely to be born to mothers who did not complete high school and to mothers and fathers who are or have been involved in the criminal justice system.

For many children, drug exposure and its associated risks do not end at birth. Wymore et al. (2021) examined the breast milk of 25 participating mothers, 12 of whom reported to have abstained from marijuana use during and after pregnancy and 13 who reported to continue with marijuana use during and after pregnancy. All 25 were found to have evidence of marijuana in their breast milk.

Children with prenatal drug and alcohol exposure, born to parents who continue use after the child's birth, are placed at greater risk for developmental delay because of adverse environmental factors such as poor parenting and/or multiple foster care placements (Marcellus & Badry, 2021). Children with histories of alcohol and drug exposure living with parents who continue use are also more likely to experience neglect, verbal abuse, physical abuse, and/or involvement with Child Protective Services than their nonexposed counterparts (CDC, n.d.-b).

Children exposed to maternal prenatal drug use may also suffer adverse medical outcomes, such as premature birth, low birthweight, small for gestational age, failure to thrive, infectious diseases, and sudden infant death syndrome (Dodge et al., 2019).

Despite all of the aforementioned potential risks, it is difficult to predict the developmental outcomes of children born with prenatal exposure to drugs and alcohol. Some children will present with pronounced signs and symptoms of exposure at birth (e.g., children with FAS). Others may not exhibit signs until they enter school and are faced with cognitively demanding tasks. Researchers have shown that biological factors such as frequency of exposure, amount and type of exposure, and genetic susceptibility will interact with environmental factors such as family income, family lifestyle, employment history, and educational background to produce the disparate clinical profiles that define this population. No one factor can reliably predict a profile that is associated with prenatal exposure to drugs and alcohol (Deutsch et al., 2020). The following case presents an opportunity to examine the speech and language patterns of a child in light of her history of prenatal exposure to drugs and alcohol, her social and developmental history, and her present status, and to use this information to plan for follow-up care as she progresses in school.

Description of the Case

At the time of the application to the university speech and hearing clinic's summer program, Sybil was 7 years, 9 months old. She was enrolled in a public school in the second grade and receives school speech therapy services.

Background Information

Sybil lives with her maternal grandparents. At the time of the assessment, neither the grandparents nor Sybil had contact with her biological parents. The grandparents stated that they had no knowledge of where their daughter (i.e., Sybil's mother) was living or how she was doing. They also did not know much about their granddaughter's biological father.

On the case history questionnaire, they indicated that Sybil's biological father was 40 and had completed high school but did not know what he did for a living. The grandparents also stated that they were deeply concerned about Sybil's mother because they had not heard from her in over 2 years. Their daughter began experimenting with drugs in high school, became pregnant, and dropped out of school in the 10th grade. The child from this first pregnancy was raised by his paternal grandparents and is currently attending a local community college. The grandparents also reported that their daughter had been treated for cocaine addiction at least twice before Sybil's birth. Unfortunately, she was not able to maintain recovery. Their daughter became pregnant with Sybil, her second child, when she was 28 years of age and experiencing a relapse. Their daughter reportedly stopped drinking alcohol and taking cocaine and marijuana, as well as stopped smoking when she discovered that she was pregnant with Sybil. This occurred during the second trimester of the pregnancy. She gave birth to Sybil when she was 29 years of age. Sybil, however, tested positive for exposure to cocaine, marijuana, and tobacco at birth.

The grandparents also indicated that their daughter and her boyfriend, Sybil's father, enrolled in drug and alcohol treatment after Sybil's birth and cared for her for 2 years, with their help. Both parents subsequently experienced a relapse and lost custody of Sybil. The grandparents became Sybil's legal guardians when she turned 3 years of age.

Sybil's grandmother works as a housekeeper and her grandfather works as a long-distance truck driver. They described their income level as low-to-middle socioeconomic status (SES) and they own their home. They have raised four children and continued to despair over the plight of their oldest child, Sybil's mother. Their other three children are doing well with family and careers. Besides Sybil, the grandparents have five other grandchildren who live out of state with their parents.

The grandparents reported that Sybil's medical history was unremarkable with the exceptions of prenatal polydrug exposure and typical cases of tonsillitis and bronchitis at ages 3 and 4 years, respectively. They could not accurately report about Sybil's attainment of developmental milestones but noted that they enrolled her in a special preschool program because of a referral made by Sybil's pediatrician at age 3 years, 3 months. Sybil's pediatrician made the referral because of delays in gross motor skills and speech development.

Sybil had experienced school failure in spelling, reading, and mathematics. She liked school and enjoyed reading. She was an active child and demonstrated difficulty in managing her moods when she experienced frustration. Sybil often responded poorly to parental discipline.

Reason for Referral

Sybil was referred to the 6-week summer clinic by her school speech-language pathologist to help her maintain the skills she had achieved during the school year and to facilitate additional growth.

Findings of the Evaluation

Sybil's speech and language skills were evaluated 1 week prior to the start of the 6-week summer session. She was age 7 years, 10 months at the time of testing. Sybil demonstrated speech delay for the sounds /tʃ, r, l/ and for consonantal blends. The Goldman-Fristoe Test of Articulation 3 (Goldman & Fristoe, 2015) revealed the following errors: ʃ/tʃ, w/r substitutions in blends and omission of /l/ in blends. Stimulability for all errors was noted at word level.

Sybil demonstrated specific language impairment at the time of testing. She obtained a listening comprehension score of 6 years, 7 months and an oral expression score of 5 years, 4 months on the Oral and Written Language Scales (OWLS; Carrow-Woolfolk, 1995). Informal testing revealed difficulty with following one-part, two-part, and three-part directions, responding appropriately to "wh" questions and incorrect use of verb tenses in phrases and sentences. Sybil also did not maintain attention to all language tasks and showed behavioral signs of frustration when the examiner attempted to return her attention to the tasks.

Sybil's hearing was screened in an audiometric booth at 20 db HL, bilaterally for the frequencies of 500, 1000, 2000, 4000, and 8000 Hz. She passed the screening. The oral mechanism screening examination produced unremarkable findings with the exception of the diadochokinetic tasks. Rapid movements for single syllables, two syllables, and three syllables were all below age-expected rates.

Treatment Options Considered

Treatment options for speech delay included use of Minimal Pairs Contrast Training (Bernthal & Bankson, 2004) to target sounds using a linguistic approach and Van Riper's traditional (Bernthal & Bankson, 2004) approach to target sounds using a motor approach. Minimal Pairs Contrast Training was considered because Sybil demonstrated stimulability, suggesting that her errors were linguistic in nature. Stimulability was confined, however, to word level. Baseline testing revealed that as the complexity of the phonetic context increased, Sybil's motor control and stimulability for correction decreased. Van Riper's traditional approach proved to be a better choice of treatment because it provided practice in syllables and nonsense words to enhance motor control. Also, baseline testing showed that Sybil was able to detect errors in the clinician's speech and her own speech. These data suggested minimal need for perceptual training.

Treatment options for the language impairment included use of drill play and modeling, focused stimulation, facilitative play, and script therapy. Drill play and modeling were used to teach verb tense targets, response to "wh" questions, and following directions. Drill play was used briefly (5–10 minutes) at the beginning of sessions, because Sybil preferred to be engaged in physical activities that involved small groups of people. Facilitative play was used to provide practice for targets taught through drill but was discontinued because Sybil had difficulty transitioning from one activity to the next. Focused stimulation and script therapy were more effective in providing practiced use of language and speech targets, because the start and end points of each activity could be clearly established by the clinician. The techniques of modeling, utterance expansion, and utterance extension were incorporated during focused stimulation and whenever the opportunity occurred.

Course of Treatment

Treatment was provided 3 hours a day for 4 days a week for a period of 6 weeks during the summer session, yielding a total of 72 hours of therapy. Each goal was targeted every day and included in periods of individual and group treatments.

The goals for the 6-week summer session included:

1. To spontaneously produce /tʃ/ in all word positions at sentence level while engaged in play and structured activities at an 80% accuracy level
2. To spontaneously produce /r/ and /l/ blends in words while engaged in play and structured activities at an 80% level of accuracy
3. To spontaneously respond to "wh" questions while engaged in play and structured activities at a 90% accuracy level
4. To spontaneously respond to one-step and two-step instructions while engaged in play and structured activities at a 90% accuracy level

5. To spontaneously express present, past, and future tenses of irregular verbs while engaged in play and structured activities at an 80% accuracy level

Forty-five minutes of each day were devoted to individual speech training using Van Riper's traditional approach that included perceptual training, production in isolation, production in nonsense syllables, production in words, production in phrases, production in sentences, and production in conversation.

Forty minutes of each day were devoted to individual language training using drill play and modeling, focused stimulation, script therapy, and free play.

Forty-five minutes were used for group practice of speech and language targets using focused stimulation, modeling, and utterance expansion and utterance extension techniques. In the group sessions, four to five clients along with their student clinicians targeted speech and language goals using art projects, dramatic play, preliteracy and literacy tasks, and field trips.

The remaining 45 minutes were used for parent training, free play, rest and bathroom breaks, transitioning from one session to the next, and snacks.

Daily tallies of performances were kept and formal progress measures were gathered at the end of 3 weeks and at the end of 6 weeks.

Analysis of the Client's Response to Intervention

Sybil made progress in treatment. Posttherapy testing at the end of the 6-week session showed that Sybil spontaneously produced /tʃ/ in all word positions in sentences with 85% accuracy and /r/ and /l/ blends in words with 95% accuracy. She responded to "wh" questions with 75% accuracy. Sybil responded to one-step commands with 100% accuracy and to two-step commands with 80% accuracy. Her accuracy for use of present, past, and future tenses of irregular verbs was also good. She used the present, past, and future tenses of the verb "to be" with 90% accuracy, the verb "to have" in the present and future tenses with 75% accuracy and the past tense with 60% accuracy, and the verb "to go" in the present and future tenses with 80% accuracy and in the past tense with 70% accuracy.

Further Recommendations

Sybil will most likely continue to benefit from speech-language pathology services to improve speech intelligibility, language comprehension, and language expression. The impact of these benefits will most likely be seen in academic performance and self-regulation.

Authors' Note

Sybil's case represents a compilation of several cases seen in the Hampton University Speech-Language-Hearing Clinic. The authors thank Mrs. Cheryl H. Freeman for assisting with the development of the case profile.

References

Bakhireva, L. N., Shrestha, S., Garrison, L., Leeman, L., Rayburn, W. F., & Stephen, J. M. (2018). Prevalence of alcohol use in pregnant women with substance use disorder. *Drug and Alcohol Dependency, 187*, 305–310. https://10.1016/j.drugalcdep.2018.02.025

Bernthal, J., & Bankson, N. (2004). *Articulation and phonological disorders* (5th ed.). Pearson.

Boggess, T., & Risher, W. C. (2022) Clinical and basic research investigations into the long-term effects of prenatal opioid exposure on brain development. *Journal of Neuroscience Research, 100*(1), 396–409. https://doi.org/10.1002/jnr.24642

Carrow-Woolfolk, E. (1995). *Oral and Written Language Scales (OWLS)*. American Guidance Service.

Centers for Disease Control and Prevention. (n.d.-a). *Fetal alcohol spectrum disorders (FASDs)*. https://www.cdc.gov/ncbddd/fasd/data.html

Centers for Disease Control and Prevention. (n.d.-b). *FASD awareness*. https://www.cdc.gov/ncbddd/fasd/FASD-Awareness.html

Chu, E. K., Smith, L. M., Derauf, C., Newman, E., Neal, C. R., Arria, A. M., . . . Lester, B. M. (2020). Behavior problems during early childhood in children with prenatal methamphetamine exposure. *Pediatrics, 146*(6), e20190270. https://doi.org/10.1542/peds.2019-0270

Coggins, T., Timler, G., & Olswang, L. (2007). A state of double jeopardy: Impact of prenatal alcohol exposure and adverse environments on the social communicative abilities of school-age children with fetal alcohol syndrome. *Language, Speech and Hearing Services in Schools, 38*, 117–127. https://doi.org/10.1044/0161-1461(2007/012)

Deutsch, S., Donahue, J., Parker, T. Hossain, J., & Jong, A. (2020). Factors associated with child-welfare involvement among prenatally substance-exposed infants. *Journal of Pediatrics, 222*, 35–44. https://doi.org/10.1016/j.jpeds.2020.03.036

Dodge, N. C., Jacobson, J. L., & Jacobson, S. W. (2019). Effects of fetal substance exposure on offspring substance use. *Pediatric Clinics of North America, 66*(6), 1149–1161. https://doi.org/10.1016/j.pcl.2019.08.010

Geng, F., Salmeron, B. J., Ross, T. Black, M., & Riggins, T. (2018). Long-term effects of prenatal drug exposure on the neural correlates of memory at encoding and retrieval. *Neurotoxicology and Teratology, 65*, 70–77. https://doi.org/10.1016/j.ntt.2017.10.008

Goldman, R., & Fristoe, M. (2015). *Goldman-Fristoe Test of Articulation 3*. Pearson Assessments.

Gosdin, L., Deputy, N., Kim, S., Dang, E., & Denny, C. (2022). Alcohol consumption and binge drinking during pregnancy among adults aged 18–49 years—United States, 2018–2020. *Morbidity and Mortal Weekly Report, 71*, 10–13. https://doi.org/10.15585/mmwr.mm7101a2

Guille, C., & Aujla, R. (2019). Developmental consequences of prenatal substance use in children and adolescents. *Journal of Child and Adolescent Psychopharmacology, 29*(7), 479–486. https://doi.org/10.1089/cap.2018.0177

Hagan, J. F., Balachova, T., Bertrand, J., Chasnoff, I., Dang, E., Fernandez-Baca, D., . . . Zubler, J., on behalf of Neurobehavioral Disorder Associated with Prenatal Alcohol Exposure Workgroup; American Academy of Pediatrics. (2016). Neurobehavioral disorder associated with prenatal alcohol exposure. *Pediatrics, 138*(4), e20151553. https://doi.org/10.1542/peds.2015-1553

Landi, N., Avery, T., Crowley, M. J., Wu, J., & Mayes, L. (2017). Prenatal cocaine exposure impacts language and reading into late adolescence: Behavioral and ERP evidence. *Developmental Neuropsychology, 42*(6), 369–386. https://doi.org/10.1080/87565641.2017.1362698

Lester, B. M., Tronick, E. Z., LaGasse, L., Seifer, R., Bauer, C. R., Shankaran, S., . . . Lu, J. (2004). Summary statistics of neonatal intensive care unit network neurobehavioral scale scores from the maternal lifestyle study: A quasinormative sample. *Pediatrics, 113*(3 Pt. 2), 668–675.

Marcellus, L., & Badry, D. (2021). Infants, children, and youth in foster care with prenatal substance exposure: A synthesis of two scoping reviews. *International Journal of Developmental Disabilities, 69*(2), 265–290. https://doi.org/10.1080/20473869.2021.1945890

NIDA Notes. (2004). *Conference provides overview of consequences of prenatal drug exposure.* http://www.drugabuse.gov/NIDA_notes/Nnvol19N3/Conference.html

Paul, R., & Cascella, P. (2007). *Introduction to clinical methods in communication disorders* (2nd ed.). Paul H. Brookes Publishing.

Rivkin, M. J., Davis, P. E., Lemaster, J. L., Cabral, H. J., Warfield, S. K., Mulkern, R. V., . . . Frank, D. A. (2008). Volumetric MRI study of brain in children with intrauterine exposure to cocaine, alcohol, tobacco, and marijuana. *Pediatrics, 121*(4), 741–750. https://doi.org/10.1542/peds.2007-1399

Substance Abuse and Mental Health Services Administration. (2020). *2019 National Survey of Drug Use and Health.* https://www.samhsa.gov/data/release/2019-national-survey-drug-use-and-healthnsduh-releases

Wilhoit, L., Scott, D., & Simecka, B (2017). Fetal alcohol spectrum disorders: Characteristics, complications, and treatment. *Community Health Journal, 53,* 711–718. https://doi.org/10.1007/s10597-017-0104-0

Wymore, E. M., Palmer, C., Wang, G. S., Metz, T. D., Bourne, D. W. A., Sempio, C., & Bunik, M. (2021). Persistence of Δ-9-tetrahydrocannabinol in human breast milk. *JAMA Pediatrics, 175*(6), 632–634. https://doi.org/10.1001/jamapediatrics.2020.6098

SICKLE CELL DISEASE
CASE 7
Nicole: Auditory and Neurocognitive Impact of Sickle Cell Disease in Early Childhood
Diane M. Scott

Conceptual Knowledge Areas

Sickle cell disease (SCD) is a group of inherited red blood cell disorders. It is an inherited abnormality of the hemoglobin molecule, responsible for carrying oxygen in red blood cells (RBCs). Healthy red blood cells are round, soft, and flexible, and they move through small blood vessels to carry oxygen to all parts of the body. Inside normal RBCs, hemoglobin is dissolved in a watery solution and remains dissolved under all conditions. Inside the RBCs of a person with SCD, hemoglobin stays dissolved under some conditions and not under others. Instead of remaining liquid, hemoglobin forms crystals that twist the RBCs out of shape, making them sickle shaped. Crystallized hemoglobin has the following consequences:

1. RBCs clog small blood vessels and blood flow backs up. Oxygen is not delivered to organs that need it.
2. When an organ's oxygen supply is cut off, it is damaged and produces pain. Damage can be serious and pain severe (referred to as "painful episodes" or "crises").

3. When RBCs are damaged, the body destroys them. These RBCs cannot be reproduced as rapidly as normal RBCs. So many RBCs are damaged and destroyed in people with SCD that they suffer from chronic anemia.

4. SCD can cause pain and other serious problems such as infection, acute chest syndrome, and stroke (Centers for Disease Control and Prevention [CDC], 2021).

SCD is defined by the presence of the sickle cell gene (HbS). The most common types of SCD are (1) HbSS, where people inherit two sickle cell genes ("S"), one from each parent (this is commonly called *sickle cell anemia* and is usually the most severe form of the disease); (2) HbSC, where people inherit a sickle cell gene from one parent and from the other parent a gene for an abnormal hemoglobin called "C" (this is usually a milder form of SCD); and (3) HbS beta thalassemia, where people inherit one sickle cell gene from one parent and one gene for beta-thalassemia, another type of anemia, from the other parent. There are two types of beta-thalassemia: "0" and "+." Those with HbS beta 0-thalassemia usually have a severe form of SCD. People with HbS beta +-thalassemia tend to have a milder form of SCD. People who have sickle cell trait (SCT) inherit one sickle cell gene ("S") from one parent and one normal gene ("A") from the other parent (HbAS). People with SCT usually do not have any of the signs of the disease and live a normal life, but they can pass the trait on to their children.

SCD affects millions of people worldwide. It is estimated that SCD affects approximately 100,000 Americans, though the exact number is unknown. SCD occurs among about 1 out of every 365 African American births and among about 1 out of every 16,300 Hispanic American births. About 1 in 13 African American babies is born with sickle cell trait (CDC, 2021).

Universal newborn screening programs for SCD (and SCT) exist in all 50 states and the District of Columbia and in Puerto Rico and the Virgin Islands. Children with SCD start to have signs of the disease during the first year of life, usually around 5 months of age. At birth, 50% to 95% of hemoglobin is fetal hemoglobin (HbF). After birth, the percentage drops off at a rate of 3% to 4% each week, changing to HbA, HbS, or another hemoglobin. Thus, by 4 to 5 months of age, RBCs in children with SCD are capable of sickling. Children with SCD routinely are given prophylactic antibiotics and a pneumococcal vaccination to prevent infections. They are especially susceptible to *Streptococcus pneumoniae* (which can cause septicemia or meningitis) and *Hemophilus influenzae* (which can cause nose, throat, and ear infections). Penicillin is generally begun at 2 months of age, while the pneumococcal vaccine is given at 2 years of age.

During early infancy, the baby is usually without symptoms. Infections start after 2 to 3 months; many children remain symptom free for a year or more. In early childhood, hand-foot syndrome (blocked blood flow in the bones of the hands and feet causing local swelling accompanied by pain and fever) is often the first presenting problem. Infections begin at about the same time, though administration of prophylactic antibiotics can modify their incidence. In the absence of prophylactic antibiotics, children may die of infections between the ages of 1 and 3 years (CDC, 2021). Infections are often associated with painful episodes or crises. Symptoms and complications of SCD are different for each person and can range from mild to severe.

SCD is a disease that worsens over time. Treatments are available that can prevent complications and lengthen the lives of those who have this condition. These treatment options can be different for each person depending on the symptoms and severity (CDC, 2021).

Hydroxyurea is a medicine that can decrease several complications of SCD. This medicine increases the amount of fetal hemoglobin (hemoglobin F) in the blood. The Food and Drug Administration has approved a new medicine to reduce the number of sickle cell crises in adults and children older than age 5; it is called Endari (L-glutamine oral powder). A third treatment, which can actually cure SCD, is a stem cell (or bone marrow) transplant. This procedure infuses healthy cells, called stem cells, into the body to replace damaged or diseased bone marrow (bone marrow is the center of the bone where blood cells are made).

Transplants of bone marrow require a matched donor (CDC, 2021).

The presence of SCD may affect hearing, speech, and language skills. One clinical manifestation of SCD is that sickle-shaped cells tend to occlude smaller veins and capillaries, possibly including those supplying blood to the cochlea (Scott, 2000). Compared to adults with SCD, children with SCD appear to have a lower prevalence of sensorineural hearing loss. Recently, Stuart and Smith (2019) examined a large medical and research database to investigate the emergence and prevalence of hearing loss in children with HbSS. They identified 128 children with HbSS. When using the three-frequency average of the thresholds at 500, 1000, and 2000 Hz, the prevalence rate of hearing loss was 34%. This prevalence rate is higher than those usually reported for children in North America (Feder et al., 2017; Su & Chan, 2017). Strum et al. (2021) conducted the first systematic investigation of the relationship between SCD and sensorineural hearing loss (SNHL) in pediatric patients worldwide. There was a statistically significant increase in the prevalence of SNHL in children with SCD compared to the general population.

A stroke can happen if sickle cells get stuck in a blood vessel and clog blood flow to the brain. In addition, damaging strokes that do not cause obvious symptoms can be seen on magnetic resonance imaging (MRI) of the brain. Ischemic lesions of the brain that occur without clinical evidence of neurological deficits, or silent cerebral infarcts (SCIs), are among the most common forms of neurological disease in children with SCD (DeBaun et al., 2012). Pediatric hematologists screen children with SCD (HbSS and HbS beta 0-thalassemia) for risks of stroke. Children who have SCI are at increased risk of overt stroke (Miller et al., 2001; Pegelow et al., 2002) and progressive silent infarction (Pegelow et al., 2002).

Impairments in verbal abilities have been found among children with SCD (Sanchez et al., 2010; Schatz et al., 2009), primarily among children with the HbSS genotype (Schatz et al., 2009), and are associated with cerebrovascular disruptions and high cerebral blood flow velocities on transcranial Doppler (TCD) ultrasound (Sanchez et al., 2010). Some studies suggest the verbal abilities of children with SCD may be affected across language domains (syntax, semantics, and phonology), but their performance within these domains is not impaired to the same degree (Schatz et al., 2009).

Description of the Case

Background Information

Nicole J. was a 21-month-old African American female referred by her pediatrician to the University Speech, Language and Hearing Clinic because of concerns regarding her hearing abilities, given her history of middle ear infections. Nicole was accompanied to the clinic by her mother, Ms. J. She was scheduled for a complete audiologic assessment. Student clinicians conducted the assessment with supervision by the audiologist. Nicole was the youngest of three children who lived with both of her parents and her two brothers. Her 28-year-old mother was an elementary school teacher, and her 32-year-old father was a social worker. Nicole's brothers were 5 and 8 years of age. Nicole had HbSS of moderate severity. Both Nicole and an older brother had been identified with HbSS at birth. The oldest sibling had normal hemoglobin. The parents were not screened for the sickle cell gene until the birth of their second son. Nicole attended daycare but was absent from time to time when she was having a crisis. She had been hospitalized once during a crisis. Her first bout of otitis media was at 8 months of age with three more subsequently. Nicole's regular medications at that time included penicillin and folic acid. Although she was small for her age, her developmental milestones were within normal limits except for her speech and language skills. She was somewhat unintelligible and had not started communicating in two-word utterances. Ms. J. described Nicole as a "happy child," though she was becoming frustrated when unable to communicate her wants and needs. Ms. J. believed that Nicole did not hear normally when she had a middle ear infection. The audiologist noted that Ms. J.

seemed to be handling the chronic health problems of two of her children well. She had extended family to call for assistance. Ms. J. had educated herself about SCD. The audiologist noted that Nicole was an amiable child. She sounded congested on the day of testing.

Findings of the Evaluations

The otoscopic examination revealed clear ear canals, though it was difficult to visualize the tympanic membrane due to small ear size. Immittance testing revealed negative middle ear pressure with rounded peaks in both ears. Acoustic reflex testing revealed elevated contralateral thresholds for both ears. Given the constraints based on Nicole's age and attention span, audiological testing was abbreviated. Testing revealed that Nicole had air conduction thresholds of 15 to 20 dB HL across the speech frequencies bilaterally. The speech reception thresholds (SRTs) were obtained using a picture-pointing response with a limited set of choices; the SRTs agreed with the pure-tone averages. Bone conduction testing could not be completed.

The results of the evaluation indicated borderline normal to mild hearing impairment across the speech frequencies bilaterally. SRTs agreed with pure-tone thresholds. Negative middle ear pressure was found in both ears suggesting Eustachian tube dysfunction.

Case history information and observations clearly showed that Nicole was unintelligible at times and delayed in language development. Ms. J. stated that Nicole never had a transcranial Doppler ultrasound or MRI, and the pediatrician had not suggested one. Nicole's brother with SCD had shown no delays in his speech and language development, and no concerns were noted when he was tested with an established test of skills appropriate to kindergarten.

Representation of the Problem at the Time of Evaluation

Are Nicole's delays in speech and language skills due to her recurrent bouts of otitis media alone, or is the presence of sickle cell disease more directly affecting both the occurrence of the otitis media and her speech and language delays?

Nicole had a documented history of otitis media, a common disorder of childhood. Though otitis media is less prevalent in African Americans, that does not necessarily make Nicole less susceptible to otitis media; however, the presence of SCD may have made her more susceptible to ear infections. Nicole's speech and language skills were delayed. Was the history of otitis media the reason for the delays in Nicole's speech and language skills, or does the presence of SCD and the speech and language delays indicate the possibility of a silent infarct?

Treatment Options Considered

Recommendations were as follows:

- Nicole should be retested in 3 weeks to determine her middle ear status and her pure-tone thresholds. In the interim, Nicole's communication partners were encouraged to modify their communication with her. Recommendations included getting her attention before speaking, speaking with her at her height (level), and turning down or removing background noise or other distractions. These recommendations would be made regardless of the cause of the otitis media. The status of Nicole's auditory system should be monitored.
- Nicole should receive audiological reevaluations every 3 months, given her history of otitis media and the developmental level of her speech and language skills. This recommendation would be made regardless of the cause of the recurrent ear infections. The test battery should consist of pure-tone thresholds (air and bone conduction), speech reception thresholds, word recognition testing, immittance testing including (multifrequency)

tympanometry and acoustic reflex testing, and electrophysiologic tests including auditory brainstem response (ABR) and otoacoustic emissions (transient and distortion product). Tests should be added as she ages and her attention span lengthens. Some of these tests were chosen because Nicole has sickle cell anemia. For example, changes in Wave I of the ABR may reflect the modulation of cochlear blood flow. Otoacoustic emissions provide an objective measure of hair cell function independent of retrocochlear activity (confirming a cochlear origin of hearing impairment associated with SCD) (Burch-Sims & Matlock, 2005).

■ Another question relates to the long-term monitoring of Nicole's hearing once the bouts of otitis media disappeared. Given the presence of SCD, would Nicole develop a sensorineural or central auditory hearing impairment as she aged? A higher incidence of hearing impairment in children with SCD compared to children with normal hemoglobin has been observed (Scott, 2000). Possible long-term effects of SCD on the central nervous system were a concern. Steen et al. (2002) tested the hypothesis that young children with SCD and no history of stroke are at risk for cognitive impairment. The scores on a developmental skills checklist of kindergarten children in the Memphis schools with no history of stroke were examined. Children with SCD scored lower than controls in auditory discrimination; there was a trend toward lower scores in language.

■ Nicole should receive a speech and language assessment; thus, a referral was made to a speech-language pathologist. This recommendation would be made regardless of the cause of the speech and language delays. However, cerebrovascular disease is a common cause of morbidity in patients with sickle cell anemia. Nicole's speech and language skills may need to be monitored even if she is dismissed from therapy. Some researchers have suggested an association of some type between deficits in verbal abilities and lesions in frontal areas of the brain (Sanchez et al., 2010). Verbal deficits could be the consequence of neurological insult to frontal lobe areas directly related to language processing, such as Brodmann's areas 44 and 45 (Sanchez et al., 2010; Schatz et al., 2009), or they could be a side effect of other neurocognitive impairments caused by SCD, such as deficits in working memory or executive function (Brandling-Bennett et al., 2003).

■ Nicole's pediatrician should be contacted, with the permission of Ms. J. to discuss research recommending a transcranial Doppler ultrasound as a predictor of the possibility of stroke and/or MRI as a means to determine the presence of silent infarcts. One or both tests should be scheduled for Nicole.

Course of Treatment

Nicole returned for audiological retesting in 4 weeks and her pure-tone thresholds had improved to 5 to 10 dB HL across the speech frequencies. Tympanograms indicated normal middle ear pressure and compliance. Acoustic reflex thresholds were within normal limits. She had been seen by a speech-language pathologist for a speech and language diagnostic. Nicole had begun receiving therapy twice a week at daycare.

It took time to get Ms. J. to agree to allow the audiologist to discuss the issue of a transcranial Doppler ultrasound with Nicole's pediatrician. Ms. J. felt it was unnecessary given her son's normal development, even though he also had sickle cell anemia. The pediatrician recommended the transcranial Doppler ultrasound. The velocities of the large artery blood flow indicated low risk for stroke.

Analysis of the Client's Response to Intervention

Nicole's speech and language skills improved while in therapy. Ms. J., a teacher, worked with all her children on their language and mathematical skills. Nicole continued to have audiological reevaluations on a regular basis. No permanent peripheral or central hearing loss has been noted.

Author's Note

This case is not based on an actual patient.

References

Brandling-Bennett, E. M., White, D. A., Armstrong, M. M., Christ, S. E., & DeBaun, M. (2003). Patterns of verbal long-term and working memory performance reveal deficits in strategic processing in children with frontal infarcts related to sickle cell disease. *Developmental Neuropsychology, 24*(1), 423–434. https://doi.org/10.1207/S15326942DN2401_01

Burch-Sims, G. P., & Matlock, V. R. (2005). Hearing loss and auditory function in sickle cell disease. *Journal of Communication Disorders, 38*, 321–329.

Centers for Disease Control and Prevention. (2021, October 21). *Sickle cell disease (SCD).* https://www.cdc.gov/ncbddd/sicklecell/index.html

DeBaun, M. R., Sarnaik, S. A., Rodeghier, M. J., Minniti, C. P., Howard, T. H., Iyer, R. V., . . . Casella, J. F. (2012). Associated risk factors for silent cerebral infarcts in sickle cell anemia: Low baseline hemoglobin, sex, and relative high systolic blood pressure. *Blood, 119*(16), 3684–3690. https://doi.org/10.1182/blood-2011-05-349621

Feder, K. P., Michaud, M., McNamee, J., Fitzpatrick, E., Ramage-Morin, P., & Beauregard, Y. (2017). Prevalence of hearing loss among a representative sample of Canadian children and adolescents, 3 to 19 years of age. *Ear and Hearing, 38*(1), 7–20. https://doi.org/10.1097/AUD.0000000000000345

Miller, S. T., Macklin, E. A., Pegelow, C. H., Kinney, T. R., Sleeper, L. A., Bello, J. A., . . . DeBaun, M. R. (2001). Silent infarction as a risk factor for overt stroke in children with sickle cell anemia: A report from the Cooperative Study of Sickle Cell Disease. *Journal of Pediatrics, 139*(3), 385–390. https://doi.org/10.1067/mpd.2001.117580

Pegelow, C. H., Macklin, E. A., Moser, F. G., Wang, W. C., Bellow, J. A., & Miller, S. T., . . . Kinney, T. R. (2002). Longitudinal changes in brain magnetic resonance imaging findings in children with sickle cell disease. *Blood, 99*, 3014–3018. https://doi.org/10.1182/blood.v99.8.3014

Sanchez, C., Schatz, J., & Roberts, C. (2010). Cerebral blood flow velocity and language functioning in pediatric sickle cell disease. *Journal of the International Neuropsychological Society, 16*(2), 326–334. https://doi.org/10.1017/S1355617709991366

Schatz, J., Puffer, E. S., Sanchez, C., Stancil, M., & Roberts, C. W. (2009). Language processing deficits in sickle cell disease in young school-age children. *Developmental Neuropsychology, 34*, 122–136. https://doi.org/10.1080/87565640802499191

Scott, D. M. (2000). Managing hearing impairment in culturally diverse children. In T. J. Coleman (Ed.), *Clinical management of communication disorders in culturally diverse children* (pp. 271–294). Allyn & Bacon.

Steen, R. G., Hu, X. J., Elliott, V. E., Miles, M. A., Jones, S., & Wang, W. C. (2002). Kindergarten readiness skills in children with sickle cell disease: Evidence of early neurocognitive damage? *Journal of Child Neurology, 17*(2), 111–116. https://doi.org/10.1177/088307380201700204

Strum, D., Kapoor, E., Shim, T., Kim, S., Sabetrasekh, P., & Monfared, A. (2021). Prevalence of sensorineural hearing loss in pediatric patients with sickle cell disease: A meta-analysis. *Laryngoscope, 131*(5), 1147–1156. https://doi.org/10.1002/lary.29199

Stuart, A., & Smith, M. R. (2019). The emergence and prevalence of hearing loss in children with homozygous sickle cell disease. *International Journal of Pediatric Otorhinolaryngology, 123*, 69–74. https://doi.org/10.1016/j.ijporl.2019.04.032

Su, B. M., & Chan, D. K. (2017). Prevalence of hearing loss in US children and adolescents: Findings from NHANES 1988–2010. *JAMA Otolaryngology-Head & Neck Surgery, 143*, 920–927. https://doi.org/10.1001/jamaoto.2017.0953

SWALLOWING
CASE 8
Leona: Oromotor Entrainment Therapy to Develop Feeding Skills in the Preterm Infant
Steven M. Barlow, Meredith Harold, and Emily Zimmerman

Conceptual Knowledge Areas

Suck is a precocial ororhythmic motor behavior in humans and is integral to competent oral feeds. However, premature infants often demonstrate oromotor dyscoordination and are unable to suck and feed orally (Bu'Lock et al., 1990; Comrie & Helm, 1997). This represents a frequent and serious challenge both to the neonatal intensive care unit (NICU) survivors and the physician-provider-parent teams. The potential causes for delayed or impaired suck development are numerous and may result from neurologic insult to the developing brain, feeding intolerance or aversion, postsurgical recovery, diabetes, or as a result of ventilator interventions, which interfere with ororhythmic pattern formation. For example, lengthy oxygen supplementation procedures in the NICU cost the preterm infant precious sensory and motor experiences during a critical period of brain development while the central patterning of suck and prefeeding skills are being refined. Even the presence of a nasogastric (NG) feeding tube has negative effects on sucking and breathing outcomes (Shiao et al., 1995). Trussing the lower face with polytubes and tape also restricts the range and type of oral movements and limits cutaneous experiences with the hand and fingers. Interruption of these experiences may impair fragile syntheses of how the brain maps these functions (Bosma, 1970; Hensch, 2004). Moreover, failure to establish oral feeding skills in the NICU may result in the infant being discharged home on gavage or G-tube feedings and hinder the development of coordinated oromotor behavior.

For instance, for some preterm infants, poor suck and oromotor dyscoordination can persist well into early childhood and may lead to significant delays in feeding, babbling, and speech-language production (Adams-Chapman, 2006; Ballantyne et al., 2006). The difficulties associated with establishing oral feed competence along with the additional costs for extended hospitalization underscore the need for assessment and therapeutic tools to facilitate the development of normal oromotor skills (da Costa et al., 2008; Fucile et al., 2002, 2005; Lau & Hurst, 1999).

Feeding readiness is often evaluated by an infant's display of nonnutritive sucking (NNS) and oromotor patterning (Bingham et al., 2008; Lau, 2006). Suck appears in utero between 15 and 18 weeks' gestational age (GA) and is remarkably stable and well patterned by 34 weeks' postmenstrual age (PMA) (Hack et al., 1985). The NNS, defined as any repetitive mouthing activity on a blind nipple or pacifier that does not deliver a liquid stimulus (Goldson, 1987; Wolff, 1968), typically consists of a series of compression bursts of sucking and pause intervals for breathing. Each burst contains 6 to 12 suck cycles that manifest an initial deceleration phase of frequency modulation over the first 5 cycles to a steady state of approximately 2 Hz (Urish et al., 2007). The maturation and coordination of the NNS precedes the suck-swallow-breathe pattern associated with the slower 1 Hz pattern characteristic of the nutritive suck (Gewolb et al., 2001; Lau & Schanler, 1996; Medoff-Cooper, 2005).

Establishing a patterned NNS for the developing infant benefits growth, maturation, and gastric motility, while decreasing stress (Abbasi et al., 2008; DiPietro et al., 1994; Field, 1993; Lau & Hurst, 1999; Lau & Schanler, 1996; Pickler et al., 1996; Pickler et al., 1993), improving state control prefeed (DiPietro et al., 1994; Gill et al., 1992; Gill et al., 1988; McCain, 1992; Pickler et al., 1996) and postfeed (Pickler et al., 1993), and enhancing oral feeds (Barlow et al., 2008; McCain, 1995; Poore et al., 2008). Use of a pacifier for NNS appears to decrease the frequency of apnea and cyanosis and to improve breastfeeding scores (Volkmer & Fiori, 2008). The NNS accelerates the transition from tube to independent oral feeding and is presumed to enhance the maturation of neural systems responsible for ororhythmic activity (Bernbaum et al., 1983; Field et al., 1982; Measel & Anderson, 1979). The sensory consequences associated with the production of NNS appear to provide beneficial effects on oral feeding performance and the development of specific sucking skills (Fucile et al., 2002, 2005). Accurate assessment of oromotor dyscoordination in the preterm infant extends beyond the immediate issues surrounding the transition to oral feed competency and may serve as a potent clinical marker for brain development and neurodevelopmental outcomes (Mizuno & Ueda, 2005). Infants with perinatal distress and neurologic impairments demonstrate a significantly slower mean rate and greater variability of NNS (Dreier & Wolff, 1972). Children with severe neurodevelopmental problems at 18 months tend to have arrhythmic nutritive expression/suction patterns as premature infants (Mizuno & Ueda, 2005). This trend continues until age 5, where evidence links NNS patterns in infancy to motor skills, balance, overall IQ, verbal intelligence, performance intelligence, and language, with the better neonatal sucking positively correlated with higher test scores (Wolthuis-Stigter et al., 2017).

Suck Central Pattern Generator

The mammalian suck is the earliest-appearing somatic motor rhythm and is primarily controlled by a neural network known as the suck central pattern generator (sCPG). The sCPG consists of bilateral, linked internuncial circuits within the brainstem pontine and medullary reticular formation (Barlow & Estep, 2006; Barlow et al., 2010; Iriki et al., 1988; Tanaka et al., 1999). Based on animal models, the minimal circuitry for ororhythmic activity resides between the trigeminal motor nucleus and the facial nucleus in the brainstem (Tanaka et al., 1999), situated to function as premotor inputs to lower motor neurons. The sCPG is centrally modulated by multiple inputs, including descending pathways from the sensorimotor cortex and reciprocal connections with the cerebellum (Boughter et al., 2007; Bryant et al., 2007), which serve to modulate ororhythmic activity. Thus, it is important to assist infants to regulate their behavioral "state" through careful posturing and orientation during clinical testing as this will affect the nature of descending inputs to the sCPG. The sCPG can also be modified by sensory input arising from oral mechanoreceptors that encode the consequences of oral movements and external stimulation (i.e., breast, pacifier or bottle nipple, touch) along central pathways of the trigeminal system. Suck entrainment has been demonstrated in term infants through 6 months of age using a patterned orocutaneous stimulus delivered to perioral and intraoral tissues (Finan & Barlow, 1998). Entrainment is the phase locking of centrally generated suck motor patterns to an external stimulus and represents a powerful method of achieving neural synchrony among sensorimotor pathways. Therefore, it is not surprising that stimulation of the lips and tongue are methods used to evoke sucking behaviors (Fucile et al., 2002, 2005; Rocha et al., 2007).

Oromotor Entrainment: NTrainer

The neuroscientific principles underlying sensorimotor entrainment of ororhythmic motor activity have been translated to a new clinical application for preterm infants who exhibit poor suck and feeding difficulties. A new biomedical device known as the NTrainer system (approved by the Food and Drug Administration [FDA]) is coupled to a popular silicone pacifier common to many NICUs worldwide. The NTrainer transforms the Soothie pacifier into a pressurized orocutaneous stimulator suitable for use with premature infants. This motorized pacifier is presented to the infant for alternating 3-minute stimulus epochs during NG tube feeds in the NICU. The novel orosensory experience afforded by the NTrainer mimics the spatiotemporal dynamics of NNS and has been correlated to rapid organization of suck and shorter transition time to independent oral feeds in infants who exhibit poor feeding skills (Barlow et al., 2008; (Barlow, Lee, Wang, Oder, Knox, et al., 2014; Barlow, Lee, Wang, Oder, Oh, et al., 2014; Barlow et al., 2021a, 2021b; Barlow, 2022; Poore et al., 2008; Song et al., 2019).

The NTrainer system consists of a servo-controlled pneumatic actuator and microprocessor to dynamically modulate intraluminal pacifier pressure. This system includes (1) integrated real-time data acquisition and waveform analytics to sample and assess the infant's NNS and ororhythmic patterning at crib side in the NICU and (2) programmable somatosensory entrainment module to synthesize and deliver patterned pneumocutaneous stimulation via a pressurized silicone pacifier placed in the newborn's mouth during NG feeds or immediately before a scheduled PO feed (breast/bottle) (Barlow et al., 2017).

NNS Assessment

The NNS compression pressure waveforms, sampled from the infant, are digitized periodically (daily recommended) at the bedside 15 minutes prior to a scheduled feed (either oral or NG) using the mobile NTrainer system running the NeoSuck RT software. Infants remain connected to the pulse-oximetry monitors to ensure that respiration, heartbeat, and oxygen saturation levels are adequate to support oromotor activity. The portable, battery-powered NTrainer system is shown in Figure 8–1. A Soothie silicone pacifier serves as the interface to the NTrainer's handheld receiver (Figure 8–2), which is instrumented to sample intraluminal air pressure from within the pacifier (Honeywell sensor, DC-coupled, Butterworth low-pass filter @ 50 Hz, 3,000 samples/s @ 16-bit voltage resolution) during the suck sample. The NTrainer handpiece is the same one used when

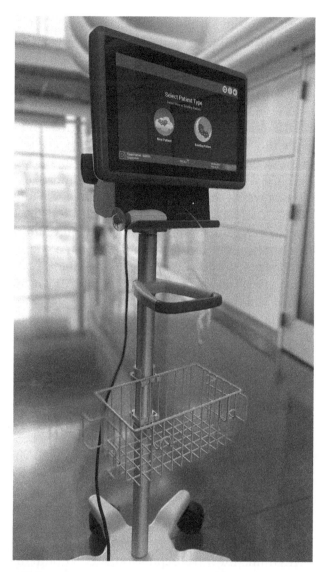

Figure 8–1. Mobile NTrainer System including battery-powered microprocessor, entrainment stimulator, and NT handpiece with pacifier receiver. Courtesy of Innara Health, Inc., Olathe, KS, USA.

the infant received the pneumotactile entrainment therapy.

Infants are held in a developmentally supportive semi-inclined posture. Background and overhead lighting are dimmed in the immediate area to promote eye contact with the developmental specialist (neonatal nurse, neonatologist, developmental speech-language pathologist, physical therapist, parent/guardian). (The personnel

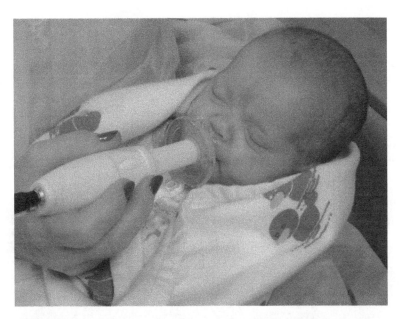

Figure 8–2. Preterm neonate receiving NTrainer somatosensory therapy to promote NNS patterning simultaneous with gavage (tube) feeding in the NICU. Source: Communication Neuroscience Laboratories, University of Nebraska.

who administer the NTrainer in the NICU vary by hospital site and may or may not be affiliated with the feeding team.) Sampling of NNS behavior is initiated when the infant achieves an optimal behavioral state, that is, drowsy to active alert (state 3, 4, or 5 as described by the Naturalistic Observation of Newborn Behavior, Newborn Individualized Developmental Care and Assessment Program; NIDCAP) (Als, 1995). Three minutes of NNS behavior is typically digitized for each infant per session, with the most productive 2-minute epoch automatically parsed using software recognition algorithms and subjected to formal quantitative and statistical analysis.

A sample output from the NeoSuck RT is shown for a healthy preterm infant at 35 weeks' PMA (Figure 8–3) and a tube-fed preterm infant at 35 weeks' PMA with RDS (Figure 8–4). The real-time display provides the clinician with the NNS compression waveforms and associated histogram updates for suck amplitude (cmH_2O), inter-NNS burst-pause periods (s), and intra-NNS burst-suck cycle periods (s). For the healthy preterm infant, well-organized NNS bursts with peak pressures averaging approximately 25 cmH_2O alternate with pause periods. The nipple compression cycle count for the 3.5-minute sample is 108. In contrast, the dissolution of the NNS burst structure for the tube-fed RDS infant corresponds to a disorganized nipple compression pattern and indistinguishable NNS bursts. The amplitude of oral compression output is likewise reduced to approximately 5 cmH_2O, with only 25 compression cycles identified in the 3.5-minute sample of digitized records.

During the NTrainer intervention, infants receive alternating 3-minute epochs of patterned orocutaneous stimulation, typically during gavage feeds. This helps the infant develop an association between oral stimulation and satiation from liquid nutrient entering the stomach. The NTrainer stimulus train currently used has been programmed to mimic the temporal features of NNS. Precise stimulus control is achieved with a custom-designed servo linear motor (H2W Technologies, Inc.) operating under position feedback and coupled in series with a pneumatic Airpel glass cylinder actuator and the pacifier receiver. A magnetostrictive displacement sensor is used for position feedback

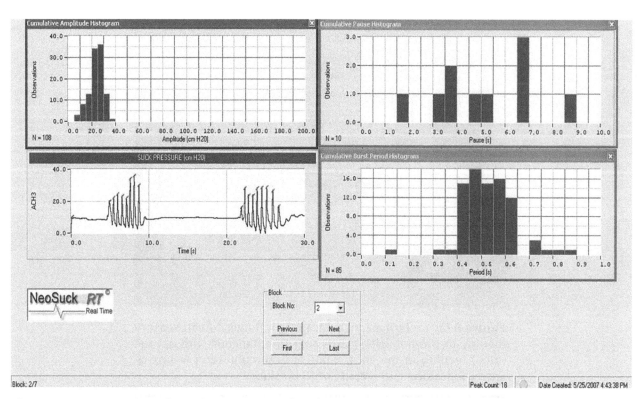

Figure 8–3. Screenshot of graphical user interface for sampling NNS from a healthy preterm infant.

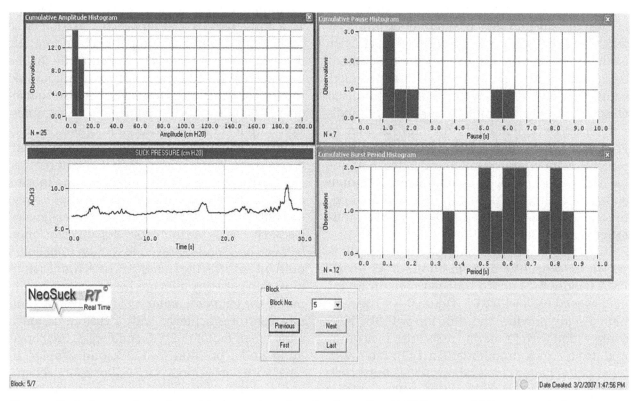

Figure 8–4. Screenshot of graphical user interface for Sampling NNS from an RDS preterm infant.

of the pneumatic linear motor in order to deliver a repeatable stimulus to the infant's mouth. A 16-bit digital-to-analog converter is used to synthesize an orocutaneous pneumatic pulse train, which consists of a series of six-cycle bursts and 2-second pause periods. Individual cycles within-burst are frequency modulated around a center frequency of 1.8 Hz. This synthetic pulse train is used to drive the servo motor to modulate the intraluminal pressure and shape of the infant's Soothie pacifier. The changes in intraluminal pressure yield a radial expansion of the pacifier nipple of approximately 135 microns (Barlow et al., 2008). This novel instrumentation transforms the infant's pacifier into a "pulsating nipple" that resembles the temporal pattern of a well-formed NNS burst. A total of 34 synthetic NNS burst-pause trains are presented to the infant during a single 3-minute entrainment session. Infants are typically treated with the NTrainer stimulus three to four times per day during tube feeding over a 10-day period, or until the infant attains 90% oral feeds for 2 consecutive days (Barlow, Lee, Wang, Oder, Knox, et al., 2014; Barlow, Lee, Wang, Oder, Oh, et al., 2014; Song et al., 2019). An ongoing National Institutes of Health (NIH) randomized controlled trial (RCT) (ClinicalTrials.gov NCT02696343) is examining the effects of a progressive dose NTrainer stimulation in extremely preterm infants that is initiated at 30 weeks' PMA (Barlow, 2022; Barlow et al., 2017).

Advanced NNS Digital Signal Processing

In studies of NNS fine structure (Estep et al., 2008; Poore et al., 2008; Stumm et al., 2008; Zimmerman & Barlow, 2008), 2-minute samples reflecting the most active period of NNS behavior generated by the preterm infant are selected from each raw data file for analysis. These are identified based on a waveform discrimination and pressure threshold detection algorithm in our NeoNNS software program (Liao et al., 2019), which indexes pressure peaks at a user-defined pressure threshold. Identification of the time-amplitude intercepts for individual pressure peaks is achieved by calculation of the first derivative of the pressure signal.

Zero-crossings in the pressure derivative function along with a pressure recruitment rate and hysteresis function are used to index nipple compression pressure peaks in the digitized waveforms. This algorithm permits objective identification of NNS burst activity as distinct from nonorganized mouthing compressions. Several objective measures can be extracted from indexed records of suck, including the following minute-rate variables: (1) *Total Compressions*, defined as the sum of all pressure events per minute; (2) *Non-NNS Events*, defined as nipple compression pressure events not associated with an NNS burst sequence; (3) *NNS Cycles*, defined as suck compression cycles with cycle periods less than 1,200 milliseconds and occurring within the NNS burst structure per minute; and (4) the number of *NNS Bursts* that consisted of two or more nipple compression cycles. The remaining NNS performance measures are (5) mean number *NNS Cycles/Burst*, and (6) a ratiometric calculation known as *NNS Cycles%Total*, defined as NNS Cycles expressed as a percentage of total nipple compressions ([Burst-related NNS cycles/Total Mouthing Events] × 100). Recently developed analytics (Liao et al., 2019) permit the user to explore the ontogeny of NNS burst pattern formation in the frequency domain, which is useful for repeated-measures analyses to map development of ororhythmic patterning beginning as early as 29 weeks' PMA.

NNS Spatiotemporal Index

The physiological approach to the assessment and habilitation of suck in the NICU includes a functional assessment of the integrity of the neural circuitry driving the suck central pattern generator through an analysis of suck pattern structure and stability (Liao et al., 2019; Poore et al., 2008). Coordinated NNS that is minimally variable from burst to burst indicates motor system integrity and is an important foundation for coordination with other emergent behaviors, such as swallow and respiration. A highly promising digital signal processing technique known as the Non-Nutritive Suck Spatiotemporal Index (NNS STI) has been developed to quantify the emergence of stable nonnutritive suck in preterm infants. The mathematical tenets underlying this computational technique have been used successfully to assess kinematic variability and pattern formation in limb (Atkeson & Hollerbach, 1985; Georgopoulos et al., 1981) and speech (Smith et al., 2000; Smith & Zelaznik, 2004) motor subsystems. The NNS STI provides the clinician with a single numerical value, calculated from the cumulative sum of the standard deviations of an amplitude and time-normalized set of suck pressure waveforms, and represents the stability of the infant's oromotor sequence. In essence, this measure provides a quantitative composite index of nonnutritive suck pattern stability. This metric eliminates the need to count suck pressure peaks or measure individual cycle periods. Instead, the Non-Nutritive Suck Spatiotemporal Index is designed to quantify the infant's suck over a selected burst pattern epoch, thereby providing NICU clinicians with a summative index or "gestalt" of oromotor pattern formation and stability. Obtaining a 2-minute sample of NNS behavior daily in the NICU with the NTrainer bedside system is sufficient to chart an infant's progress toward stable suck production (Poore et al., 2008). The NNS STI measure has also been used successfully to document the effects of the NTrainer patterned orocutaneous therapy on suck development among tube-fed premature infants with respiratory distress syndrome who have endured, on average, 40 days of oxygen supplementation therapy (Poore et al., 2008).

Description of the Case

Leona is a preterm infant, the first child of a 25-year-old mother who received prenatal care. Leona was born at 31 weeks' GA by cesarean section with a birth weight of 1,300 g, birth length of 39 cm, and head circumference of 28 cm. Soon after birth, she received a diagnosis of respiratory distress syndrome (RDS) and was prescribed 26 days of oxygen therapy. Like many preterm infants, she exhibited poor oromotor skills and a delayed suck pattern. This was evident in both her NeoSuck RT assessments and resultant NNS STI scores. At 36 weeks' PMA, Leona had an NNS STI of 89 (Figure 8–5). Thus, her poor suck output and delayed transition to oral feeds made her an ideal candidate for the NTrainer. The NTrainer was initiated at 36 weeks' PMA. One week after pairing the NTrainer stimulus with gavage feeds three to four times per day, she had her first PO feed at 37 weeks' PMA. During this feed, she took 62.5% of her bottle. Following this initial PO feed, she took 100% of all of her bottles and was discharged a week later. At 37 weeks' PMA, her NNS STI score had improved to 50, demonstrating the potent effect of the NTrainer therapy on improving NNS and feeding outcomes.

For comparison, a preterm control infant, Harrison, is included in this report. He was born the third of triplets by cesarean section at 31 weeks' GA, birth weight of 1540 g, birth length of 42 cm, and head circumference of 28 cm. His mother was 48 years old at the time of delivery and received prenatal care. Harrison received 11 days of oxygen therapy and also was diagnosed with RDS. He received weekly NeoSuck RT assessments. The nursing staff offered him a pacifier on a regular basis; however, the NTrainer patterned orocutaneous intervention was not provided. At 36 weeks' PMA, he had an STI of 71 (see Figure 8–5). Feeding by mouth was a significant challenge, requiring 44 days to attain a modest 36% oral feed level. His final STI score was completed at 38 weeks' PMA and increased slightly to 72, indicating that he regressed on his ability to suck. Due to the difficulty Harrison had with transitioning successfully to oral feeds, he was sent home on gavage feed. During his scheduled 6-month NICU follow-up clinic at Stormont-Vail Medical Center, Harrison was starting to eat cereal and fruit by spoon but still relied mostly on his tube feeds for all liquid nourishment.

Summary and Conclusions

Human brain development is a dynamic process that continues throughout gestation (Adams-Chapman, 2006; Barlow et al., 2021a, 2021b). A critical period of brain growth and development occurs in late gestation (Bosma, 1970; Hensch,

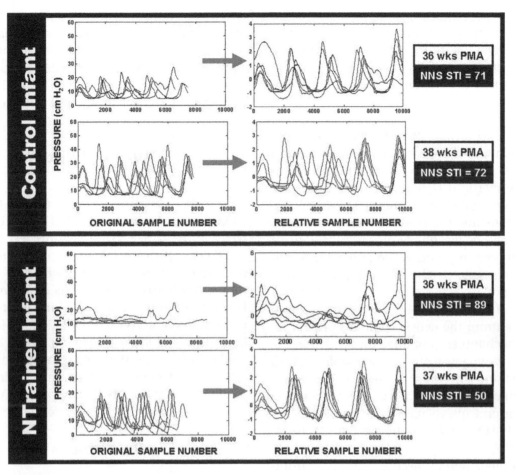

Figure 8–5. Upper panel block depicts the Non-Nutritive Suck Spatiotemporal Index (NNS STI) digital signal processing results for a control (No Intervention) tube-fed infant with RDS at 36 weeks' PMA and again at 38 weeks' PMA. Five superimposed raw NNS records (*left*) are transformed to normalized records (*right*) to demonstrate pattern formation resulting from suck CPG activity with the NNS STI scores. The bottom panels show the normalized NNS records and resultant STI values. The lower panel block depicts the NNS STI results for the present case report, a tube-fed RDS preterm infant at 36 weeks' PMA before intervention (36 weeks' PMA) and following NTrainer somatosensory intervention (37 weeks' PMA).

2004) that is vital for the development of various neural structures and pathways involved in oromotor control and coordination of suck, swallow, and breathe to support safe nutritional feeds. The premature infant is predisposed to multiple factors related to developmental immaturity, which mediates the risk for brain injury and subsequent abnormal neurologic sequelae, including the risk for development of intraventricular hemorrhage (IVH), periventricular leukomalacia (PVL),

hypoxic respiratory failure, hyperbilirubinemia, and infection. Importantly, the late preterm brain is only a fraction of the full-term brain weight. A significant proportion of brain growth, development, and networking (connectivity) occurs during the last 6 weeks of gestation and across the life span. These tissues are vulnerable to injury during this critical time period of development. Disruption of critical pathways needed for neuronal or glial development may result from sensory deprivation and/or motor restriction associated with respiratory distress syndrome and interventions that truss the infant's face with tubing and tape to support oxygen therapies.

Fortunately for the human infant, the brainstem sCPG responds to peripheral input (Barlow et al., 2008; Barlow, Lee, Wang, Oder, Knox, et al., 2014; Barlow, Lee, Wang, Oder, Oh, et al., 2014; Finan & Barlow, 1998; Rocha et al., 2007) and adapts to changes in the local oral environment (Zimmerman & Barlow, 2008). Collective results from studies in neonatal intensive care units demonstrate the potent effects of a motorized silicone pacifier nipple on the development of NNS in preterm infants. The patterned orocutaneous experience is physiologically salient and spectrally patterned to resemble the "burst-pause" structure of the NNS. This form of stimulation serves to entrain the activity patterns of populations of mechanoreceptor afferents located in the lips, tongue, and jaw of the neonate, which in turn influence firing patterns of the respective orofacial lower motor neurons. This is a central tenet of one of the basic principles of pathway formation, "neurons that fire together, will wire together" (Löwel & Singer, 1992).

The application of mechanosensory entrainment as a habilitation strategy has ecological validity in assisting the infant to produce appropriate oromotor output. This approach is consistent with contemporary ideas on the role of sensory-driven neural activity in pathway formation (Marder & Rehm, 2005; Penn & Shatz, 1999) and the notion that appropriate oral experiences may be critical in the final weeks of gestation for the formation of functional central neural circuits.

The richness of the patterned orocutaneous experience offered by the NTrainer presents a new neurotherapeutic application for the habilitation of suck in premature infants in the NICU (Barlow et al., 2008; Poore et al., 2008). The regimen includes repeated exposure to patterned orocutaneous events, distributed over three or four feeds totaling approximately 45 minutes per day in the NICU. Intervention is delivered concurrent with NG tube feeds over 7 to 10 days. It provides the preterm infant with a neural entrainment experience that facilitates the development of central neural pathways that regulate suck. Use of an orocutaneous entrainment stimulus has the advantage of being safe and pleasurable for the neonate and easily administered by the physician-provider-parent teams in the NICU, including developmental speech-language pathologists.

Authors' Note

This work was supported by grants NIH R01 DC003311 (S. M. Barlow, PI), NIH R01 HD086088, NIH P30 HD02528 (S. M. Barlow, PI), NIH P30 DC005803. Special thanks to the physicians, nurses, staff, and parents/guardians who care for these fragile newborns in the NICUs at Stormont-Vail HealthCare (Topeka, KS), Overland Park Regional Medical Center (Overland Park, KS), CHI St. Elizabeth's Regional Medical Center (Lincoln, NE), Tufts Medical Center (Boston, MA), Santa Clara Valley Medical Center (San Jose, CA), and Children's Hospital of Orange County (Los Angeles, CA).

References

Adams-Chapman, I. (2006). Neurodevelopmental outcome of the late preterm infant. *Clinical Perinatology, 33*, 947–964. https://doi.org/10.1016/j.clp.2006.09.004

Als, H. (1995). A manual for naturalistic observation of the newborn (preterm and full term infants). In E. Goldson (Ed.), *Nurturing the premature infant: Developmental interventions in the neonatal intensive care nursery* (pp. 77–85). Oxford University Press.

Atkeson, C. G., & Hollerbach, J. M. (1985). Kinematic features of unrestrained vertical arm movements. *The Journal of Neuroscience, 5*, 2318–2330. https://doi.org/10.1523/JNEUROSCI.05-09-02318.1985

Ballantyne, M., Frisk, V., & Green, P. (2006). Language impairment in extremely-low-birthweight infants. *Pediatric Academic Society*, Session 5532.178.

Barlow, S. M. (2022). Neonatal Feeding Club: Somatosensory-modulated ororythmic patterning and transition to oral feeds in EPIs: NIH RCT data. *Pediatric Academic Society*, Session 114367.

Barlow, S. M., & Estep, M. (2006). Central pattern generation and the motor infrastructure for suck, respiration, and speech. *Journal of Communication Disorders*, *39*, 366–380. https://doi.org/10.1016/j.jcomdis.2006 .06.011

Barlow, S. M., Finan, D. S., Chu, S., & Lee, J. (2008). Patterns for the premature brain: Synthetic orocutaneous stimulation entrains preterm infants with feeding difficulties to suck. *Journal of Perinatology, 28*, 541–548. https://doi.org/10.1038/jp.2008.57

Barlow, S. M., Lee, J., Wang, J., Oder, A., Knox, K., Hall, S., . . . Thompson, D. (2014). Frequency-modulated orocutaneous stimulation promotes non-nutritive suck development in preterm infants with respiratory distress syndrome or chronic lung disease. *Journal of Perinatology, 34*(2), 136–142. https://doi.org/10.1038/ jp.2013.149

Barlow, S. M., Lee, J., Wang, J., Oder, A., Oh, H., Hall, S., . . . Thompson, D. (2014). Effects of oral stimulus frequency spectra on the development of non-nutritive suck in preterm infants with respiratory distress syndrome or chronic lung disease, and preterm infants of diabetic mothers. *Journal of Neonatal Nursing, 20*, 178–188. https://doi.org/10.1016/j.jnn.2013.10.005

Barlow, S. M., Lund, J. P., Estep, M., & Kolta, A. (2010). Central pattern generators for speech and orofacial activity. In S. M. Brudzynski (Ed.), *Handbook of mammalian vocalization* (pp. 351–370). Elsevier.

Barlow, S. M., Maron, J. L., Alterovitz, G., Song, D., Wilson, B. J., Jegatheesan, P., . . . Rosner, A. O. (2017). Somatosensory modulation of salivary gene expression and oral feeding in preterm infants. *JMIR Research Protocols, 6*(6), e113. https://doi.org/10.2196/ resprot.7712

Barlow, S. M., Rosner, A., & Song, D. (2021a). Feeding and brain development in preterm infants: Central pattern generation and suck dynamics. In B. Govindaswami (Ed.), *Practical approaches to newborn care: A global perspective in the age of information* (pp. 255–263). Jaypee Brothers Medical Publishers.

Barlow, S. M., Rosner, A., & Song, D. (2021b). Feeding and brain development in preterm infants: Role of sensory stimulation. In B. Govindaswami (Ed.), *Practical approaches to newborn care: A global perspective in the age of information* (pp. 264–274). Jaypee Brothers Medical Publishers.

Bernbaum, J. C., Pereira, G. R., Watkins, J. B., & Peckham, G. J. (1983). Nonnutritive sucking during gavage feeding enhances growth and maturation in premature infants. *Pediatrics, 71*, 41–45.

Bingham, P. M., Thomas, C. S., Ashikaga, T., & Abbasi, S. (2008). Non-nutritive sucking measure predicts feeding skills in tube-fed premature infants. *Pediatric Academic Society, 3778*(1), 93.

Bosma, J. F. (1970). Summarizing and perspective comments: Part V. Form and function in the infant's mouth and pharynx. In J. F. Bosma (Ed.), *Second symposium on oral sensation and perception* (pp. 550–555). Charles C Thomas.

Boughter, J. D., Bajpai, T., St. John, S. J., Williams, R. W., Lu, L., & Heck, D. H. (2007). Genetic analysis of oromotor movements in inbred and BXD recombinant inbred mice. *Society for Neuroscience*, Session *407.12*.

Bryant, J. L., Roy, S., Boughter, J. D., Goldowitz, D., Swanson, D., Morgan, J. I., & Heck, D. H. (2007). A proposed new function of the mouse cerebellum: Temporal modulation of brain stem pattern generator activity. *Society for Neuroscience*, Session *78.17*.

Bu'Lock, F., Woolridge, M. W., & Baum, J. D. (1990). Development of coordination of sucking, swallowing and breathing: Ultrasound study of term and preterm infants. *Developmental Medicine and Child Neurology, 32*, 669–678. https://doi.org/10.1111/j.1469-8749.1990.tb08427.x

Comrie, J. D., & Helm, J. M. (1997). Common feeding problems in the intensive care nurseries, maturation, organization, evaluation, and management strategies. *Seminars in Speech and Language, 18*, 239–261. https://doi.org/10.1055/s-2008-1064075

da Costa, S. P., van den Engel-Hoek, L., & Bos, A. F. (2008). Sucking and swallowing in infants and diagnostic tools. *Journal of Perinatology, 28*, 247–257. https://doi.org/10.1038/sj.jp.7211924

DiPietro, J. A., Cusson, R. M., Caughy, M. O., & Fox, N. A. (1994). Behavioral and physiologic effects of nonnutritive sucking during gavage feeding in preterm infants. *Pediatric Research, 36*, 207–214. https://doi .org/10.1203/00006450-199408000-00012

Dreier, T., & Wolff, P. H. (1972). Sucking, state, and perinatal distress in newborns. *Biology of the Neonate, 21*, 16–24. https://doi.org/10.1159/000240491

Estep, M., Barlow, S. M., Vantipalli, R., Lee, J., & Finan, D. (2008). Non-nutritive suck burst parametrics in preterm infants with RDS and oral feeding complications. *Journal of Neonatal Nursing, 14*(1), 28–34. https://doi.org/10.1016/j.jnn.2007.12.005

Field, T. (1993). Sucking for stress reduction, growth and development during infancy. *Pediatric Basics, 64*, 13–16.

Field, T., Ignatoff, E., Stringer, S., Brennan, J., Greenberg, R., Widmayer, S., & Anderson, G. (1982). Nonnutritive sucking during tube feedings: Effects on preterm neonates in an intensive care unit. *Pediatrics, 70*, 381–384.

Finan, D. S., & Barlow, S. M. (1998). Mechanosensory modulation of non-nutritive sucking in human infants. *Early Human Development, 52,* 181–197. https://doi.org/10.1016/s0378-3782(98)00029-2

Fucile, S., Gisel, E., & Lau, C. (2002). Oral stimulation accelerates the transition from tube to oral feeding in preterm infants. *Journal of Pediatrics, 141,* 230–236. https://doi.org/10.1067/mpd.2002.125731

Fucile, S., Gisel, E., & Lau, C. (2005). Effect of an oral stimulation program on sucking skill maturation of preterm infants. *Developmental Medicine & Child Neurology, 47,* 158–162. https://doi.org/10.1017/s0012162205000290

Georgopoulos, A. P., Kalaska, J. F., & Massey, J. T. (1981). Spatial trajectories and reaction times of aimed movements: Effects of practice, uncertainty and change in target location. *Journal of Neurophysiology, 46,* 725–743. https://doi.org/10.1152/jn.1981.46.4.725

Gewolb, I. H., Vice, F. L., Schweitzer-Kenney, E. L., Taciak, V. L., & Bosma, J. F. (2001). Developmental patterns of rhythmic suckle and swallow in preterm infants. *Developmental Medicine and Child Neurology, 43,* 22–27. https://doi.org/10.1017/s0012162201000044

Gill, N. E., Behnke, M., Conlon, M., & Anderson, G. C. (1992). Nonnutritive sucking modulates behavioral state for preterm infants before feeding. *Scandinavian Journal of Caring Sciences, 6,* 3–7. https://doi.org/10.1111/j.1471-6712.1992.tb00115.x

Gill, N. E., Behnke, M., Conlon, M., McNeely, J. B., & Anderson, G. C. (1988). Effect of nonnutritive sucking on behavioral state in preterm infants before feeding. *Nursing Research, 37,* 347–350.

Goldson, E. (1987). Nonnutritive sucking in the sick infant. *Journal Perinatology, 7*(1), 30–34.

Hack, M., Estabrook, M. M., & Robertson, S. S. (1985). Development of sucking rhythm in preterm infants. *Early Human Development, 11,* 133–140. https://doi.org/10.1016/0378-3782(85)90100-8

Hensch, T. (2004). Critical period regulation. *Annual Review of Neuroscience, 27,* 549–579. https://doi.org/10.1146/annurev.neuro.27.070203.144327

Iriki, A., Nozaki, S., & Nakamura, Y. (1988). Feeding behavior in mammals: Corticobulbar projection is reorganized during conversion from sucking to chewing. *Developmental Brain Research, 44,* 189–196. https://doi.org/10.1016/0165-3806(88)90217-9

Lau, C. (2006). Oral feeding in the preterm infant. *Neoreviews, 7,* 19–27.

Lau, C., & Hurst, N. (1999). Oral feeding in infants. *Current Problems Pediatrics, 29,* 105–124. https://doi.org/10.1016/s0045-9380(99)80052-8

Lau, C., & Schanler, R. J. (1996). Oral motor function in the neonate. *Clinics in Perinatology, 23,* 161–178.

Liao, C., Rosner, A. O., Maron, J. L., Song, D., & Barlow, S. M. (2019). Automatic non-nutritive suck waveform discrimination and feature extraction in preterm infants. *Computational and Mathematical Methods in Medicine, 2019,* Article ID 7496591. https://doi.org/10.1155/2019/7496591

Löwel, S., & Singer, W. (1992). Selection of intrinsic horizontal connections in the visual cortex by correlated neuronal activity. *Science, 255,* 209–212. https://doi.org/10.1126/science.1372754

Marder, E., & Rehm, K. J. (2005). Development of central pattern generating circuits. *Current Opinion in Neurobiology, 5,* 86–93. https://doi.org/10.1016/j.conb.2005.01.011

McCain, G. C. (1992). Facilitating inactive awake states in preterm infants: A study of three interventions. *Nursing Research, 41,* 157–160.

McCain, G. C. (1995). Promotion of preterm infant nipple feeding with nonnutritive sucking. *Journal of Pediatric Nursing, 10,* 3–8. https://doi.org/10.1016/S0882-5963(05)80093-4

Measel, C. P., & Anderson, G. C. (1979). Nonnutritive sucking during tube feedings: Effect upon clinical course in preterm infants. *Journal of Obstetric, Gynecologic, and Neonatal Nursing, 8,* 265–271. https://doi.org/10.1111/j.1552-6909.1979.tb00960.x

Medoff-Cooper, B. (2005). Nutritive sucking research: From clinical questions to research answers. *The Journal of Perinatal and Neonatal Nursing, 19,* 265–272. https://doi.org/10.1097/00005237-200507000-00013

Mizuno, K., & Ueda, A. (2005). Neonatal feeding performance as a predictor of neurodevelopmental outcome at 18 months. *Developmental Medicine and Child Neurology, 47,* 299–304. https://doi.org/10.1017/s0012162205000587

Penn, A. A., & Shatz, C. J. (1999). Brain waves and brain wiring: The role of endogenous and sensory-driven neural activity in development. *Pediatric Research, 45,* 447–458. https://doi.org/10.1203/00006450-199904010-00001

Pickler, R. H., Frankel, H. B., Walsh, K. M., & Thompson, N. M. (1996). Effects of nonnutritive sucking on behavioral organization and feeding performance in preterm infants. *Nursing Research, 45,* 132–135. https://doi.org/10.1097/00006199-199605000-00002

Pickler, R. H., Higgins, K. E., & Crummette, B. D. (1993). The effect of nonnutritive sucking on bottle-feeding stress in preterm infants. *Journal of Obstetric, Gynecologic and Neonatal Nursing, 22,* 230–234. https://doi.org/10.1111/j.1552-6909.1993.tb01804.x

Poore, M., Barlow, S. M., Wang, J., Estep, M., & Lee, J. (2008). Respiratory treatment history predicts suck pattern stability in preterm infants. *Journal of Neonatal Nursing, 14*(6), 185–192. https://doi.org/10.1016/j.jnn.2008.07.006

Poore, M., Zimmerman, E., Barlow, S. M., Wang, J., & Gu, F. (2008). Patterned orocutaneous therapy improves sucking and oral feeding in preterm infants. *Acta Paediatrica, 97*, 920–927. https://doi.org/10.1111/j.1651-2227.2008.00825.x

Rocha, A., Moreira, M., Pimenta, H., Ramos, J., & Lucena, S. (2007). A randomized study of the efficacy of sensory-motor-oral stimulation and non-nutritive sucking in very low birth weight infants. *Early Human Development, 83*, 385–389. https://doi.org/10.1016/j.earlhumdev.2006.08.003

Shiao, S.-Y. P. K., Youngblut, J. M., Anderson, G. C., DiFiore, J. M., & Martin, R. J. (1995). Nasogastric tube placement: Effects on breathing and sucking in very-low-birth-weight infants. *Nursing Research, 44*, 82–88.

Smith, A., Johnson, M., McGillem, C., & Goffman, L. (2000). On the assessment of stability and patterning of speech movements. *Journal of Speech, Language, Hearing and Research, 43*, 277–286.

Smith, A., & Zelaznik, H. N. (2004). Development of functional synergies for speech motor coordination in childhood and adolescence. *Developmental Psychobiology, 45*, 22–33. https://doi.org/10.1044/jslhr.4301.277

Song, D., Jegatheesan, P., Nafday, S., Ahmad, K. A., Nedrelow, J., Wearden, M., . . . Govindaswami, B. (2019). Patterned frequency-modulated oral stimulation in preterm infants: A multicenter random-ized controlled trial. *PLoS One, 2019*(14), e0212675. https://doi.org/10.1371/journal.pone.0212675

Stumm, S., Barlow, S. M., Estep, M., Lee, J., Cannon, S., & Gagnon, K. (2008). The relation between respiratory distress syndrome and the fine structure of the non-nutritive suck in preterm infants. *Journal of Neonatal Nursing, 14*(1), 9–16. https://doi.org/10.1016/j.jnn.2007.11.001

Tanaka, S., Kogo, M., Chandler, S. H., & Matsuya, T. (1999). Localization of oral motor rhythmogenic circuits in the isolated rat brainstem preparation. *Brain Research, 821*, 190–199. https://doi.org/10.1016/s0006-8993(99)01117-8

Urish, M. M., Barlow, S. M., & Venkatesan, L. (2007). Frequency modulation of the sCPG in preterm infants with RDS. In *Abstracts for the American Speech-Language-Hearing Association, Boston, MA*. Session 1993.

Volkmer, A. S., & Fiori, H. H. (2008). Nonnutritive sucking with a pacifier in preterm infants. *Pediatric Academic Society, 3535*(1), 75.

Wolff, P. H. (1968). The serial organization of sucking in the young infant. *Pediatrics, 42*, 943–956.

Wolthuis-Stigter, M. I., Da Costa, S. P., Bos, A. F., Krijnen, W. P., Van Der Schans, C. P., & Luinge, M. R. (2017). Sucking behaviour in infants born preterm and developmental outcomes at primary school age. *Developmental Medicine & Child Neurology, 59*(8), 871–877. https://doi.org/10.1111/dmcn.13438

Zimmerman, E., & Barlow, S. M. (2008). Pacifier stiffness alters the dynamics of the suck central pattern generator. *Journal of Neonatal Nursing, 14*(3), 79–86. https://doi.org/10.1016/j.jnn.2007.12.013

Part II
PRESCHOOL CHILD CASES

ANKYLOGLOSSIA
CASE 9
Kyle: To Clip or Not to Clip . . . What Is the Answer?
Ann W. Kummer

Conceptual Knowledge Areas

What Is Ankyloglossia?

Ankyloglossia (commonly referred to as "tongue-tie") is a relatively common congenital condition that is usually detected soon after birth. It is characterized by partial fusion—or, in rare cases, total fusion—of the tongue to the floor of the mouth due to an abnormality of the lingual frenulum (also called "lingual frenum").

A *frenum* is a narrow fold of mucous membrane connecting a movable body part to a fixed part. Its purpose is to stabilize and check undue movement of that body part. A *frenulum* is a small frenum. The *lingual frenulum* is a fold of mucous membrane that arises from the floor of the mouth and typically attaches to the midportion of the tongue. Its function is to stabilize the tongue without interfering with tongue tip movement. Ankyloglossia is a condition in which the lingual frenulum is attached near the tip of the tongue (Figure 9–1) or is unusually short, thus restricting tongue tip movement.

How Common Is Ankyloglossia?

Reports of the prevalence of ankyloglossia vary significantly because the threshold between normal and abnormal is subjective. Regardless, most reports place the prevalence of ankyloglossia in newborns at about 4% to 10% (Segal et al., 2007).

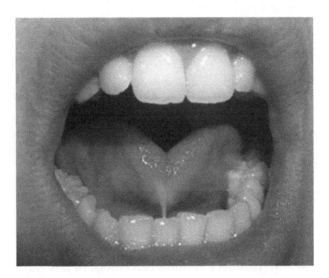

Figure 9–1. Ankyloglossia with the lingual frenulum attached to the tongue tip. Reproduced with permission from the Cleft and Craniofacial Center at Cincinnati Children's Hospital Medical Center.

How Is Ankyloglossia Diagnosed?

Diagnosing ankyloglossia is usually simple. With protrusion attempts, the tongue tip appears notched in midline due to the pull of the lingual frenulum. This results in a heart-shaped edge. An individual with ankyloglossia is unable to protrude the tongue past the edge of the mandibular incisors (or lower gingiva if there are no teeth). In addition, the individual is unable to touch the alveolar ridge with the tongue tip when the mouth is open and the jaw is lowered (Figure 9–2).

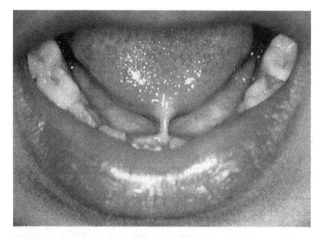

Figure 9–2. Ankyloglossia with a short lingual frenulum. Reproduced with permission from the Cleft and Craniofacial Center at Cincinnati Children's Hospital Medical Center.

What Are the Functional Effects of Ankyloglossia?

Most individuals with ankyloglossia experience little or no effect on function. In addition, the lingual restriction noted in infants tends to decrease over time due to changes in the oral cavity with growth. However, a small percentage of individuals with severe ankyloglossia do experience functional difficulties. Potential functional difficulties include the following:

■ **Feeding:** Approximately 25% of newborns with a diagnosis of ankyloglossia have trouble latching on to the nipple for feeding. Older individuals with ankyloglossia may have difficulty moving a bolus around in the oral cavity and clearing food from the sulci and molars with the tongue. This problem could result in chronic halitosis and contribute to dental decay.

■ **Dentition:** If the lingual frenulum is attached high on the gingival ridge behind the lower mandibular incisors, it can pull the gingiva away from the teeth and even cause a mandibular diastema (separation of the mandibular central incisors). This is usually not a problem until the child is 8 to 10 years old.

■ **Cosmetics:** There is no doubt that ankyloglossia may look abnormal when protruding the tongue. It has even been described as a forked or "serpent" tongue.

■ **Kissing:** Adults may complain of difficulty with French (i.e., with tongue) kissing.

■ **Speech:** Through the centuries, it has been commonly believed that tongue-tie causes speech disorders. However, there is no empirical evidence to support this belief. On the contrary, many authors over the past few decades have disputed the belief that there is a causal relationship between ankyloglossia and speech. A review of the literature results in very few articles that even mention ankyloglossia as a possible contributor to speech problems (Francis et al., 2015; Kummer, 2005; Messner et al., 2020).

What Sounds Could Be Affected by Ankyloglossia?

It makes sense that ankyloglossia does not affect the production of sounds that do not require tongue tip movement, such as bilabial, labiodental, or velar sounds. In contrast, it is often assumed that ankyloglossia affects lingual-alveolar (tongue tip) speech sounds. However, even tongue tip sounds are rarely affected by ankyloglossia. Lingual elevation to the alveolar ridge is usually only a problem when the jaw it dropped to open the mouth. This is because the tongue goes down with the jaw. It is rarely a problem when the jaw is in the normal position for speech, which positions the tongue tip directly under the alveolar ridge. The lingual-alveolar sounds (/t/, /d/, /n/, /s/, /z/, /ʃ/, /ʒ/, /tʃ/, /dʒ/) are produced with the top of the tongue tip so that very little tongue tip elevation or mobility is required. The initial and medial /r/ and the final /ɚ/ sounds are produced with the back of the tongue elevated on both sides. The tongue tip can be either up (retroflexed) or down (bunched) because the sound is actually produced with the back of the tongue—not the front.

The sound that requires the most lingual elevation is /l/. However, the /l/ sound can be produced with the tongue tip down so that the dorsum of the tongue articulates against the alveolar ridge. The sounds that require the most protrusion are the /θ/ and /ð/ sounds. However, these sounds can be produced with the tongue tip against the mandibular incisors. Given these facts, ankyloglossia is unlikely to affect the production of English speech sounds and, therefore, is not a common cause of speech sound disorders. Theoretically, ankyloglossia may affect the production of the lingual trill sound used in Spanish, as in the word "perro" meaning dog, although there is no evidence to support this.

How Can You Determine If Ankyloglossia Is Affecting Speech?

The examiner should determine if the child is able to produce the /l/ and /θ, ð/ sounds, which are the sounds that are most likely to be affected by ankyloglossia. If the child cannot achieve normal placement in isolation, yet there are multiple other articulation errors, the problem may be an articulation disorder rather than lingual restriction due to ankyloglossia. Ankyloglossia could be considered a contributing factor to a speech problem if the child cannot produce the /l/ and /θ, ð/ sounds. In this case, speech therapy is indicated to teach the child to produce these sounds with the tongue tip down, which elevates the dorsum of the tongue to produce these sounds. Surgery (e.g., frenotomy) is rarely, if ever, needed for speech purposes.

How Is Ankyloglossia Treated?

If ankyloglossia is noted at birth, but it is not causing problems with feeding, nothing needs to be done. It can always be treated in the future if problems arise. If the child demonstrates one or more of the problems noted, a *frenulotomy* (surgical release of the tongue) can be done. In the past, midwives used a sharpened fingernail to slit the frenulum immediately after birth. Currently, frenulotomies are performed by surgeons, pediatricians, otolaryngologists, or even dentists. Frenulotomies can be done with local anesthetic, although young children usually require general anesthesia. The procedure is simple and takes only a few minutes to perform. The frenulum is divided with scissors or with electrocautery. Sutures are usually not required.

The risks of frenulotomy are minimal, but they include pain, minor bleeding, or infection. In most cases, the mobility of the tongue after frenulotomy prevents scarring from occurring during the healing process. In rare cases, however, scarring occurs and can further limit the mobility of the tongue. If this happens, the scar tissue is excised and a series of flaps are created on the floor of the mouth to close the defect.

A major concern is that frenulotomy is often done in hopes of improving speech production, when ankyloglossia is not the true cause of the disorder. This results in an unnecessary surgery with unnecessary pain, inconvenience, and expense. Therefore, it is imperative that the speech-language pathologist make a correct diagnosis of cause before recommending frenulotomy!

Summary

Both ankyloglossia and speech problems commonly occur in children. Therefore, it is not surprising that these conditions are often seen together. A co-occurrence of these two findings does not mean that there is a causal relationship between the two. There is very little in the literature that even addresses ankyloglossia and speech—perhaps because a causal relationship is not commonly seen. Most experienced speech-language pathologists would suggest that ankyloglossia is unlikely to cause speech problems. Therefore, frenulotomy is rarely indicated for speech-related reasons, unless it is very severe or there are concomitant oral-motor problems. Although frenulotomy is a minor procedure with a low risk of morbidity, the true danger is the disappointment that can result when parents are led to believe that this will correct speech problems that are actually due to other causes. Frenulotomy may be warranted for problems with early feeding, bolus manipulation, dentition, or aesthetics.

Description of the Case

The following case report describes a child who was diagnosed with ankyloglossia and underwent a frenulotomy for treatment.

Background Information and Reason for Referral

Kyle, age 4 years, 10 months, was seen for a speech evaluation at the request of an attorney. Kyle had a history of ankyloglossia and speech problems. When he was about 4 years old, one of his speech-language pathologists told the parents that Kyle's "tongue-tie" was contributing to his speech problems. She therefore referred Kyle back to his otolaryngologist for a frenulotomy, which was done at the age of 4 years, 2 months. The frenulotomy had been done 8 months previously. The parents reported that there was no change in Kyle's speech following the surgery. The parents assumed this was because of habit strength. Therefore, they were suing the child's pediatrician for not recommending a frenulotomy earlier, preferably before Kyle started talking.

Pertinent History

Both parents accompanied Kyle to the evaluation and served as informants. They provided the following information:

Neonatal History. Kyle was the product of a full-term pregnancy and normal delivery. The only neonatal problem reported was difficulty with breastfeeding. Once the mother switched from breastfeeding to bottle feeding, the feeding difficulties resolved.

Medical History. Other than the frenulotomy, medical history was unremarkable.

Developmental History. According to his mother, Kyle's motor milestones were accomplished within normal limits. However, his speech development was somewhat delayed (due to the tongue-tie, in her opinion). Kyle seemed to understand speech as well as other children his age and started putting words together well before his second birthday, but his speech was always hard to understand.

Treatment History. Kyle began speech therapy just before the age of 3 years. He was still receiving speech therapy at a local hospital and at his preschool. His mother reported that although his articulation had improved as a result of therapy, progress had been very slow. She admitted that the frenulotomy did not seem to have the positive effect on Kyle's speech as they had expected.

Findings of the Evaluation

The following is a summary of the evaluation results:

Language

Kyle was communicating with sentence-length utterances, although there were frequent omissions of morphemes.

Speech Sound Production

Articulation was characterized by the following errors on the single word level: bilabials for labiodentals (p/f, b/v), fronting of velars (t/k, d/g), stopping of sibilants (t/s, d/z, t/ʃ, t/ʧ/, d/ʤ), substitution of /w/ or /y/ for /l/, f/θ, reduction of blends, and inconsistent voiced for voiceless substitutions. Kyle was able to produce most misarticulated phonemes in isolation, including /l/ and /θ, ð/. When asked to repeat words such as "money," "baby doll," "teddy bear," and "buddy," Kyle did reasonably well because these words contain mostly the bilabial and lingual-alveolar plosives—the phonemes that he could produce. However, when asked to produce one of these words repetitively, his articulation completely broke down. In connected speech, there were inconsistent errors and frequent phoneme omissions. Intelligibility of connected speech was fair to poor.

Resonance and Voice

Resonance was variable. During the production of single words, resonance was normal. In conversational speech, however, there was inconsistent hypernasality and sometimes even hyponasality on nasal consonants. Voice quality was normal.

Intraoral Examination

An intraoral examination revealed an intact velum, moderately enlarged tonsils, and normal occlusion. Kyle was able to protrude, lateralize, and elevate the tongue without difficulty.

Examiner Impressions

Kyle demonstrated a severe speech disorder characterized by the use of primarily early developmental sounds, such as nasals and plosives (bilabial and lingual-alveolar), inconsistent voiced/voiceless substitutions, inconsistent nasal for oral and oral for nasal substitutions, and an increase in errors and omissions with increased utterance length and/or phonemic complexity. These are characteristics of apraxia of speech. The irony is that Kyle had learned to produce lingual-alveolar sounds (tongue-tip sounds) as a substitution for other sounds, including velars (which involve the back of the tongue). Also, Kyle was able to produce the /l/ and /θ, ð/ sounds in isolation without difficulty. These speech characteristics strongly suggest a diagnosis of apraxia.

Parent Counseling

The parents were counseled regarding the results of the evaluation. They were told that apraxia is a motor speech disorder that has a neurological basis. There was no evidence that this history of ankyloglossia was a contributing factor in Kyle's case. In fact, there was evidence to the contrary.

Treatment Options Considered

Further speech therapy was recommended but with increased involvement of the family. It was explained to the parents that speech therapy involves instruction, trial and error, and then feedback, which are components of *motor learning*. They were then told that once the child can produce the sound in isolation, then frequent, short practice sessions every day would be required, which enhances *motor memory*. Therefore, the parents and other family members need to be involved. The parents were instructed on methods of incorporating speech practice into their daily routine. They were told that even 3 minutes of practice counts as a session but that they should try to do 3 minutes several times per day.

Follow-Up

The parents seemed to understand the explanations regarding Kyle's speech disorder. A few weeks after the evaluation, they chose to drop the lawsuit against the pediatrician and even sent him a letter of apology.

Further Recommendations

This case illustrates the critical importance of considering evidence and engaging in analytical thinking when making clinical decisions. Because there was the co-occurrence of ankyloglossia and a speech disorder, the speech-language pathologist assumed that there was a causal relationship. This was done without considering the evidence.

Due to this misdiagnosis, there were several negative consequences. The child underwent unnecessary (albeit minor) surgery. The parents expended time and money for the procedure and were given false hope that it would help to correct Kyle's speech. Finally, the parents and pediatrician went through months of unnecessary angst and expense related to the lawsuit.

A lesson in this case is that health care practitioners (including speech-language pathologists) need to be cautious of jumping to conclusions, particularly those that can have significant consequences. Instead, they should examine the evidence prior to making a referral for treatment, particularly one that involves surgery. In cases like this, the speech-language pathologist should study the literature and use appropriate evaluation procedures to come to the best conclusion regarding diagnosis, etiological factors, and appropriate treatment.

Author's Note

This information was taken from an actual case, but the name was changed.

References

Francis, D. O., Chinnadurai, S., Morad, A., Epstein, R. A., Kohanim, S., Krishnaswami, S., . . . McPheeters, M. L. (2015, May). Treatments for ankyloglossia and ankyloglossia with concomitant lip-tie [Internet]. *Agency for Healthcare Research and Quality* (Report No.: 15-EHC011-EF). https://pubmed.ncbi.nlm.nih .gov/26065053/

Kummer, A. (2005, December 27). Ankyloglossia: To clip or not to clip? That's the question. *The ASHA Leader, 10*(17), 6–7, 30.

Messner, A. H., Walsh, J., Rosenfeld, R. M., Schwartz, S. R., Ishman, S. L., Baldassari, C., . . . Satterfield, L. (2020). Clinical consensus statement: Ankyloglossia in children. *Otolaryngology-Head and Neck Surgery, 162*(5), 597–611. https://doi.org/10.1177/0194599820 915457

Segal, L. M., Stephenson, R., Dawes, M., & Feldman, P. (2007). Prevalence, diagnosis, and treatment of ankyloglossia: Methodologic review. *Canadian Family Physician, 53*(6), 1027–1033.

APRAXIA

CASE 10

Matthew: The Changing Picture of Childhood Apraxia of Speech: From Initial Symptoms to Diagnostic and Therapeutic Modifications

Diane Garcia

Conceptual Knowledge Areas

Conceptual knowledge relevant to this case study includes, first, a basic understanding of phonological development in preschool children. The time frame, from 3 to 6 years old, is vital for the acquisition of speech sounds and syllable shapes. It is therefore important that the clinician have a well-founded conceptual framework of normal acquisition patterns versus those that are considered deviant.

Second, the clinician should have a working knowledge of the symptom complex known as *childhood apraxia of speech* (CAS). Although the exact characteristics associated with this diagnostic label have changed over time, this case study draws on resources such as the American Speech-Language-Hearing Association (ASHA) position statement and technical report on childhood apraxia of speech (ASHA, 2007a, 2007b) and other current resources, which are found throughout the case study and in the references section.

Third, the clinician should be acquainted with three treatment approaches: the *cycles approach* (Hodson, 1997, 2007; Hodson & Paden, 1991), *integral stimulation techniques* (Strand & Skinder, 1999), and the *multiple oppositions approach* (Williams, 2000a, 2000b; Williams & Sugden, 2021). The cycles approach has been used to treat unintelligible children for decades regardless of the etiology. Although it was not specifically designed for children with motor-planning difficulties, this method has been successfully combined with integral stimulation to specifically address those motor-planning problems (Berman, 2001; Berman et al., 2007). The multiple oppositions approach directly addresses the collapse of multiple phonemes within a child's phonemic inventory. These three approaches were utilized during different phases of the treatment program. Integral stimulation and the multiple oppositions approach are explained in some detail in the following case study.

Description of the Case

Background Information

Matthew was originally seen at age 3 years, 1 month at a university clinic for a 2-hour diagnostic evaluation. He was accompanied by his mother. He was a rather serious child with a pleasant smile, sandy-colored hair, and freckles, who was intent on pleasing the clinicians. He cooperated throughout the entire diagnostic session; thus, the results that were obtained were considered to be representative of his skills at that time.

Reason for Referral

Matthew was referred to the clinic by his mother, who was concerned about his speech skills. She stated that he was hard to understand and that, although he enjoyed talking to people, his speech was often unintelligible. She had become proficient at interpreting his utterances and thought that she understood him approximately 50% to 70% of the time. Other people, however, typically could not understand Matthew and he occasionally became frustrated.

Family History

Matthew lived with his biological parents and one younger sister, who was 17 weeks old at the time of the initial evaluation. The family was considered upper middle class; the mother was a teacher who was staying home with the two children and the father was a lawyer. All family members were Caucasian, and English was the only language spoken at home. It was noted that Matthew's father, paternal aunt, and paternal uncle had experienced speech difficulties and that his father and aunt had received speech services as children.

Medical History

Matthew was born full-term with no complications during the pregnancy or labor and delivery. He had no current medical concerns, although he did have mild allergies and was considered to have occasional mild asthmatic symptoms. Both vision and hearing were evaluated and were within normal limits.

Developmental History

His mother described Matthew's development as "average" during the first 3 years. He sat alone at 4 to 5 months, walked alone at 11½ months, drank from a cup at 1 year, dressed himself at 2 years, said his first word at 9 to 10 months, and put two words together at 18 months. His verbalizations were considered very difficult to understand from the beginning of his speech attempts, and no dramatic changes had occurred in his speech development over the past 2 years.

Educational History

Matthew was not enrolled in school. He had attended speech therapy since the age of 2 years, 3 months. However, the family had moved several times, and therapy was of short duration and inconsistent.

Findings of the Evaluation

The results of the Goldman-Fristoe Test of Articulation-2 (GF-2) (Goldman & Fristoe, 2000) are summarized in Table 10–1. Matthew exhibited vowel errors and frequent substitutions of [b], [d], and [n] for other consonants. His speech was characterized by the diagnostic team as being "highly unintelligible." Results of the oral peripheral exam indicated possible oral apraxia. For example, Matthew had difficulty executing volitional oral-motor movements after a model; he could not pucker his lips or move his tongue from side to side when a model was provided. He also had difficulty moving his tongue without moving his head.

Although a language test was not given, Matthew's pragmatic skills and language comprehension were judged as being within normal limits. He was able to follow directions and answer questions in an age-appropriate manner. However, his speech was so unintelligible that a formal assessment of expressive semantics and morphosyntax was not attempted, and a language sample could not be completed.

It was hypothesized that Matthew demonstrated childhood apraxia of speech (CAS). Thus, the primary contributor to his speech production difficulties was thought to be impairment in planning or programming movement sequences (ASHA, 2007b). Matthew exhibited many characteristics of CAS identified in the literature (Caruso & Strand, 1999; Flahive et al., 2005; Smit, 2004; Strand, 2017). During the initial evaluation, Matthew exhibited signs of oral apraxia, as well as vowel distortions. Matthew had difficulty imitating speech sounds in the absence of any oral-motor weakness, and the frequency of his errors increased in longer words and utterances. He also demonstrated occasional initial consonant deletion (for example, "up" for "cup"), assimilation errors (e.g., "mum" for "gum"), and epenthesis, particularly insertion of the schwa vowel at the end of words. Although his mother remarked about the consistency of his productions, Matthew often produced the same word several different ways during the initial evaluation. This inconsistency contributed to the hypothesis of apraxia of speech.

Treatment Options Considered

Individual speech therapy was recommended for Matthew, twice weekly for 50-minute sessions. This case study spans the course of three semesters of treatment, each semester consisting of approximately 12 weeks. A different pair of student clinicians was assigned each semester to implement Matthew's remediation program under the close guidance of a university supervisor. Upon initiation of therapy, approximately 1 month after the diagnostic evaluation, further assessment of Matthew's expressive phonology and articulation was conducted using the GF-2 (Goldman & Fristoe, 2000), the Hodson Assessment of Phonological Patterns-3 (HAPP-3; Hodson, 2004), the Receptive One-Word Picture Vocabulary Test (ROWPVT; Brownell, 2000), and intelligibility measures. These results are summarized in Table 10–2.

Course of Treatment

The cycles approach (Hodson, 1997, 2007; Hodson & Paden, 1991) was selected as an appropriate therapy program for Matthew. It is specifically designed for young children with multiple error patterns and highly unintelligible speech. This

Table 10–1. Goldman-Fristoe Test of Articulation-2 Scores From Initial Evaluation

Test, Date, Age of Child	Error Score	Standard Score	95% Confidence Interval	Percentile Rank
Goldman-Fristoe 2, 12-05-07, Age 3;1	65	66	60–72	3

Table 10–2. Results of Testing at Beginning of Therapy

Test	Score	Standard Score	Percentile Rank/ Percentage
GF-2	Error score = 60	68	5
HAPP-3	Total occurrence of major phonological deviations = 131	Ability score = <55	<1 = Severe
ROWPVT	Raw score = 34	96	39
Speech Sample	6/25 completely intelligible responses		24% completely intelligible responses

method provides clear guidelines for target selection and implementation, as well as specific directions on how to structure remediation sessions—distinct advantages for student clinicians with little expertise in developing therapeutic protocols. In addition, the cycles approach includes a home program component that is easy and quick to administer, allowing Matthew's parents to be active participants in his treatment without placing unrealistic demands upon their time. Studies supporting the effectiveness of pattern-based approaches are primarily case studies (Kamhi, 2006). Despite the absence of large clinical trials, the cycles approach has been used to successfully treat highly unintelligible children for decades, regardless of etiology (Hodson, 1997, 2007; Hodson & Paden, 1991).

An initial cycle of targets was developed for Matthew following Hodson's recommendations (Hodson, 1997, 2007), with minor modifications. Error patterns that occurred with more than 40% frequency were targeted, including specific initial and final consonant deletions, anterior-posterior contrasts, s-clusters, and liquids. The initial consonants /m/ and /w/ were targeted to address class deficiencies in the categories of nasals and glides, as well as to decrease initial consonant deletion. Stimulability for each exemplar was probed the week prior to implementation. Initial /k/, /l/, /r/, and final s-clusters were deleted from the first cycle because Matthew was unable to produce these sounds (or, in the case of /r/, modify the production), despite maximum cueing.

Therapy sessions were structured according to guidelines developed by Hodson and Paden (1991) for the cycles approach and incorporated auditory bombardment, production practice, and a home program (as outlined in Figure 10–1). Each week, a small set of words was carefully selected containing the target sound (e.g., initial /w/). Remediation sessions were designed to maximize productions of the target words while keeping Matthew actively engaged and motivated. His favorite activities proved to be bowling and fishing—in fact, he wore his fishing hat to every session in hopes that a fishing rod might appear.

An initial cycle of targets was developed for Matthew following Hodson's (1997, 2007) guidelines. See Tables 10–3 and 10–4 for a summary of the target patterns.

Although the cycles approach was not specifically designed for children with motor planning difficulties, experts have suggested that it may be an appropriate program when combined with remediation techniques proven effective for childhood apraxia of speech (Berman, 2001; Flahive et al., 2005). Therefore, based upon the initial provisional diagnosis of CAS, aspects of integral stimulation therapy were incorporated into Matthew's therapy program. First, a continuum of temporal relationships between the clinician's presentation of stimulus and Matthew's response was utilized, including simultaneous production, immediate repetition, and delayed repetition. Second, during imitation tasks, a slow rate was initially employed and the rate was slowly increased until Matthew

1. Review	Child reviews previous session's word cards.
2. Auditory Bombardment	Amplified stimulation for 1 to 2 minutes of clinician reading approximately 12 words with target sound.
3. Target Word Cards	Three to five target word cards are prepared. Client repeats words modeled by the clinician.
4. Production Practice	Games are used as the clinician and child take turns naming the pictures. Clinician provides models and/or tactile cues so that the child achieves 100% success on target patterns.
5. Stimulability Probes	Child's stimulability is assessed for potential targets of next session. Child should be able to produce the next target sound with support.
6. Auditory Bombardment	Step 2 is repeated.
7. Metaphonological Awareness Activities	Clinician and parent implement activities such as reading short rhyming poems or engaging in syllable segmentation with the child.
8. Home Program	Parent participates in a 2-minute per day home program. Words are read from the week's auditory bombardment list (Step 2) and the child names word cards from Step 3.
Source: Hodson and Paden (1991).	

Figure 10–1. Overview of cycles therapy session.

could successfully imitate at a normal rate (Flahive et al., 2005; Gildersleeve-Neumann, 2007; Strand, 2017; Strand & Skinder, 1999). In addition, principles of motor learning were incorporated into the intervention program, including an initial emphasis on mass practice (many repetitions of a few targets), moving later to more distributed practice (fewer repetitions of a larger variety of targets). [Note to reader: Dynamic temporal and tactile cueing (DTTC) is a contemporary, modified version of integral stimulation that has been proven to be effective for children with severe CAS. Readers are referred to DTTC literature and training videos for details (e.g., Murray et al., 2014; Strand, 2017; Strand et al., 2006).]

Other therapeutic adaptations that have been recommended for children with motor planning difficulties were also utilized. Selection of target words involved careful attention to phonetic complexity (Bauman-Waengler, 2008; Hodson &

Paden, 1991). Words with simple syllable shapes were chosen initially. For example, when targeting initial /m/, words with a consonant-vowel (CV) syllable shape were used, such as "me," "my," and "mow." Coarticulatory effects were considered, including the movements necessary to achieve transitions between consonants and vowels. Thus, "mop" was chosen as a target to represent the CVC syllable shape because it included two bilabials and a final consonant (/p/) that was already present in Matthew's inventory, whereas "mug" was eliminated as a potential target word because it involved movement from the front to the back of the mouth and included a phoneme (/g/) not yet produced by Matthew.

Another adaptation of the cycles approach that was implemented was increasing the number of sessions devoted to each exemplar. Hodson recommends 1 hour of therapy for each target sound, yet Matthew received 3 hours of therapy

Table 10–3. Primary Target Patterns—Early Cycles

Error Pattern[a]	HAPP-3 Results	Potential Target?
Early developing patterns		
Syllableness	Could produce vowel nuclei of multisyllabic words	No
Initial early developing consonants—stops, nasals, glides (e.g., /p, b, m, w/)	Could produce /b, d, n/ Class deficiencies—difficulties with initial glides and nasals (including initial /w/ and /m/)	Yes, initial glides or nasals
Final consonants /p, t, k/ and/or /m, n/	Consistently deleted	Yes
Anterior-posterior contrasts		
Velars: initial /k/, final /k/, initial /g/, and/or glottal /h/	Consistently was unable to produce /h/, deleted or replaced /k/ and /g/	Yes
Alveolars /t, d/ (possibly /n/)	Could produce these sounds	No
/S/ clusters		
Word-initial /e.g., sp, st, sm/	Consistently deleted or replaced word-initial s-clusters	Yes
Word-final /e.g., ts, ps/	Consistently deleted or replaced word-final s-clusters	Yes
Liquids (Facilitation)		
Word-initial /l/	Consistently deleted or replaced word-initial /l/	Yes
Word-initial /r/	Consistently deleted or replaced word-initial /r/	Yes

[a]*Source:* Hodson (2007).

for each exemplar identified in his cycle. The extra time allowed Matthew more success. The initial session to learn a new sound was usually difficult and tiring for both Matthew and his clinicians as he required intensive cueing and instruction. The use of multimodality cueing, another recommended technique for children with CAS (ASHA, 2007b; Smit, 2004), was instrumental in achieving the correct manner and placement of new targets. The clinicians utilized visual, auditory, tactile, and kinesthetic cues. Although some cueing strategies were deemed ineffective (Matthew found the use of a mirror distracting), continued experimentation usually resulted in the identifi-

cation of effective prompts. Gestural cues, with tactile and kinesthetic elements, were the most facilitative. Matthew enjoyed throwing his arms up when producing a /w/ and sliding one hand down the other arm for /s/. As therapy progressed, he spontaneously used learned gestures to self-cue correct productions.

Progress

After Matthew had participated in speech therapy at the university clinic for approximately 1 year, his parents expressed concerns regarding their son's progress. Although they had noted some

Table 10–4. Targets for Cycle Approach With Matthew

Pattern	Exemplar
Initial glide deficiency	Initial /w/
Initial nasal deficiency	Initial /m/
Final consonant deletion	Final /p/
Final consonant deletion	Final /t/
Final consonant deletion and anterior-posterior contrasts	Final /k/
Anterior-posterior contrasts	Initial /k/
s-clusters	Initial /sn/
s-clusters	Initial /st/
Liquids	Initial /l/

improvement, Matthew's speech was still highly unintelligible to most people; they were hoping for a faster rate of progress and wanted to explore other therapy options. A careful review of Matthew's progress and current status was conducted in response to his parents' concerns. Results of the HAPP-3 indicated a pattern of slow but steady progress over the two semesters of treatment. Matthew's severity rating had improved from "severe" to "moderate" and the "Total Occurrences of Major Phonological Deviations" (the TOMPD score) had decreased from 131 to 95. His improved scores were attributable to an increase in production of /s/ blends in the initial and final positions of words, /k/ in the final position, and /w/ and /j/ in the initial position. However, the HAPP-3 results did not reflect the continued presence of voicing errors and a strong preference for alveolar sounds (particularly /d/) that resulted in frequent assimilation errors. Tables 10–5 and 10–6 summarize the Hodson Assessment of Phonological Patterns-3 and the Goldman-Fristoe Test of Articulation-2.

It was time to revisit the question of childhood apraxia of speech. Matthew had just turned 3 years old when he was originally evaluated. It is difficult to diagnose CAS in young children (ASHA, 2007a), and sometimes early indicators of apraxia may resolve into patterns that are more consistent

with a phonological disorder or other idiopathic developmental speech disorders (McCauley & Strand, 1999; Strand, 2017). Reviewing the initial list of characteristics demonstrated by Matthew, several changes were evident. He no longer demonstrated initial consonant deletion or epenthesis. The occurrence of vowel errors had significantly decreased and was now largely restricted to difficulties with rhotic vowels (i.e., "r" vowels). His ability to imitate both nonspeech motor movements and speech sounds had dramatically improved. In fact, his consonant inventory in imitative contexts had expanded to include most age-appropriate phonemes, although in spontaneous speech, he continued to demonstrate frequent sound substitutions.

Subsequent to the initiation of Matthew's therapy program, ASHA released a technical paper and position paper on childhood apraxia of speech identifying three characteristics of apraxia that had "gained some consensus among investigators" (ASHA, 2007b, p. 4). These segmental and suprasegmental features included (1) inconsistency of errors, (2) difficulty transitioning between sounds and syllables, and (3) prosodic difficulties. Matthew did not demonstrate these features at the end of his second semester of therapy. His inconsistent production of words during therapy sessions was attributed to attempts at self-correction. Error patterns were consistent at both the word and sentence level, so the frequency of his errors no longer increased with the length of utterances. Difficulties transitioning between sounds were occasionally noted when Matthew was learning a new sound but not during spontaneous productions. In addition, his prosody (including lexical and phrasal stress) was appropriate. Matthew was now telling elaborate stories to his clinicians, with his mother acting as interpreter. Her uncanny ability to interpret Matthew's speech was likely due, at least in part, to the consistency of his productions and his adult-like prosody. As Matthew's language developed and the length of his utterances increased, his sentences were riddled with homonyms. In the case of children with phonological-based errors, the substitution and omission of sounds may result in the production of the same combination of phonemes (e.g., /du/) for multiple lexical

Table 10–5. Test Results from Hodson Assessment of Phonological Patterns-3

Date of Testing, Age	Total Occurrences of Major Phonological Deviations	Severity Interval	Consonant Category Deficiencies Sum	Ability Score	Percentile
Initial Date: 1-07 CA: 3-2	131	Severe	87	<55	<1
End of first semester Date: 5-07 CA: 3-6	118	Severe	81	<55	<1
End of second semester Date: 12-07 CA: 4-0	95	Moderate	64	<55	<1

Table 10–6. Test Results From the Goldman-Fristoe Test of Articulation-2

Date, Age	Error Score	Standard Score	Percentile
Initial Date: 1-07 CA: 3-2	60	68	5
End of first semester Date: 5-07 CA: 3-6	58	58	4
End of second semester Date: 12-07 CA: 4-0	53	64	4

items (e.g., "two" /tu/, "stew" /stu/, "flu" /flu/). The term *homonymy*, as used here, thus refers to the substitution of a preferential consonant (e.g., /d/) for many potential phonemes (e.g., /t/, /st/, /fl/), resulting in one string of sounds produced for many lexical items.

Although his receptive vocabulary continued to grow (as evidenced by his performance on the Receptive One-Word Picture Vocabulary Test), Matthew's expressive vocabulary development was hindered by his restricted phonemic inventory. By frequently collapsing many different sounds to the /d/ phoneme, Matthew created homonyms that do not exist in the adult lexicon. For example, he pronounced the words "two," "shoe," "flu," and "stew" as "do." He intended to produce different words, yet they all sounded the same to an unfamiliar listener, resulting in low speech intelligibility and considerable frustration during therapy.

Treatment—Revised

The inability to utilize the contrastive features of sounds to create meaning (i.e., new words) is the hallmark of a phonological disorder. As the occurrence of homonyms in Matthew's speech increased and the characteristics of a motor planning disorder (CAS) diminished, a shift in both diagnostic and intervention strategies was needed. Therapy that emphasized the linguistic function of sounds, rather than their motor production, was now deemed appropriate. The multiple oppositions approach, as described by A. Lynn Williams (2000a, 2000b, 2005), seemed a perfect fit for Matthew. The purpose of this approach is to reduce homonymy in a child's system by increasing phonemic contrasts.

Multiple oppositions therapy involves larger treatment sets than traditional minimal pair therapy. Rather than targeting one contrast pair (e.g., "do" and "shoe"), a whole family of homonyms is targeted simultaneously (e.g., "do," "shoe," "two," "flu," "stew"). Each child's unique phonological system is analyzed to identify phonemic collapses, and targets are developed to systematically expand the sound inventory, increase contrast, and reduce homonymy. Analysis of Matthew's speech revealed that the following phonemes were substituted by /d/: /w/, /b/, /p/, /t/, /f/, /k/, /g/, /v/, /l/, /s/, "sh," "ch," "j" (as in "judge"), and "th" (voiced and unvoiced). In addition, almost all consonant blends were produced as a singleton /d/, including /bl/, /br/, /dr/, /fl/, /fr/, /gl/, /gr/, /kl/, /kr/, /kw/, /sk/, /sl/, /sm/, /sn/, /st/, /sw/, /skw/, and /tr/.

Williams (2005) recommends the selection of target phonemes that are maximally distinct from the preferred sound and represent maximal classification—that is, the target sounds represent different categories of place, manner, and voicing. Focusing on the collapses created by substitution of the /d/ phoneme, /p/, /k/, /st/, and "sh" were initially chosen. Each of the chosen sounds contrasted with the /d/ phoneme across two or more distinctive and/or descriptive features. For exam-

ple, "sh" differs from /d/ because it is voiceless as opposed to voiced, and it is a continuant strident, not a stop. The four phonemes also represented a variety of places and manners of production in addition to including both singleton phonemes and a cluster. The selection of targets that are very different from the error sound (i.e., represent maximal distinction) and are very different from each other (i.e., represent maximal classification) is designed to facilitate phonological reorganization and generalization to untreated phonemes (Bauman-Waengler & Garcia, 2018; Williams, 2000a, 2005).

The next step was to create families of words that were produced by Matthew as homonyms and contained these target sounds. The first attempts to identify groups of words that contained /p/, /k/, /st/, and "sh" yielded mixed results. Here are some examples:

- day pay K stay shay?
- die pie kie? sty shy
- doe poe? koe? stow show

As illustrated by the question marks above, some combinations produced words that did not exist in American English (e.g., "kie" and "koe"), and in other instances, the word did not occur in Matthew's lexicon (e.g., "sty" and "stow"). Williams (2010) promotes the use of real words whenever possible (although nonsense words are acceptable, if given meaning such as the name of a character). The decision was made to revise the list of target sounds beyond the initial four that were identified, in order to create word families that included functional, age-appropriate vocabulary. The singleton consonants "s," "l," and "w" were added to the list and /k/ was replaced by /g/, yielding homonym families such as these:

- day pay way say lay
- die pie why lie shy
- doe go low sew show

Initial consonant blends were also expanded beyond the initial selection of /st/ to include other /s/ blends as potential targets:

- day pay way say lay *stay*
- die pie why lie shy *sky*
- doe go low sew show *snow*

Attention was given to the function of syllable shapes in the creation of homonym families due to Matthew's restricted phonotactic inventory—his preferred syllable shape was CV (consonant-vowel). By deleting a consonant from a blend, Matthew changed the syllable shape of CCV words to CV. Thus, "stay" was produced as "day." In a similar fashion, by deleting the final consonant of words in connected speech, Matthew reduced CVC words to CV. Thus, CVC words such as "wait" and "late" were also produced as "day" as Matthew changed the initial phonemes to /d/ and deleted the final phonemes. Even CCVC words (e.g., "skate") became CV words (e.g., "day") as several processes occurred within a single word. Therefore, word families were expanded to include various syllable shapes, including CV, CCV, CVC, and CCVC, as illustrated:

- day (CV) pay (CV) way (CV) say (CV) lay (CV) stay (CCV)
- date (CVC) wait (CVC) late (CVC) gate (CVC) skate (CCVC)

The multiple oppositions approach is primarily a target selection approach. Unlike the cycles approach, it does not provide specific guidelines for the structuring of therapy sessions. In this regard, it requires more independent decision-making by clinicians. Matthew's clinicians chose to target one group of homonyms each week (for two 50-minute sessions), alternating between words with open syllables (CV and CCV) and words with closed syllables (CVC and CCVC). For example, one week, the target words included day, pay, way, say, lay, and stay; the following week, the target words included day, date, wait, late, gate, and skate. Each week, the previous week's targets were reviewed before proceeding to new words. Twice during the 4-month treatment period, a week was devoted to reviewing all the word families that had been introduced so far. [Note to reader: Please see literature on multiple oppositions for a recommended practice schedule model based on a child's progress data (e.g., Williams & Sugden, 2021).]

Target words for therapy were represented by pictures. Activities were similar to those utilized during implementation of the cycles approach, including matching and hunting games, as well as (of course!) fishing. This semester, though, the clinicians emphasized the meaning of words and the semantic consequences of misproductions—similar to recommendations for minimal pair therapy (Barlow & Gierut, 2002; Bauman-Waengler & Garcia, 2018). Opportunities were created for Matthew to produce the target words while directing the clinicians to carry out an activity. For example, Matthew might be required to tell the clinician which fish to catch. If he intended the clinician to catch the fish with a picture of "pay" on it, yet he said "day," he would experience the semantic consequence of his error as the clinician chose the wrong fish.

Matthew's mother successfully employed similar strategies when reviewing the pictures sent home each week. She reported that she would lay the pictures on a table and ask Matthew to tell her which picture to pick up, thus requiring accuracy on his part. If she displayed pictures of "pie," "shy," and "sky" on the table and Matthew said "die," she would emphasize the semantic differences between his actual production and his intended production. She noted that the word families helped her son understand that he was producing different words as the same word. Over the course of this final semester of treatment, she witnessed Matthew exerting more effort to produce words correctly and increased self-awareness of both errors and progress. "He feels like he's getting somewhere," his mother stated. "He is feeling success."

Progress—Final

Overall, Matthew's mother expressed greater satisfaction with the multiple oppositions approach than the cycles approach. Discussing the third semester of treatment, she reported that once Matthew learned a target word, he did not forget it; she often observed him using the new words at home in various speaking contexts. In addition, as Matthew's expressive lexicon expanded, his mother noticed that sounds that had been targeted within the homonym families (e.g., initial /w/, /p/, /s/) were spontaneously produced in new vocabulary words that had not been worked on in therapy. Her only concern was that the new sounds were not carrying over to words that had been in Matthew's vocabulary since a young age. For example, Matthew tended to produce the "sh" sound as /d/, so one of his families of homonyms included "show" as a target word. Matthew learned the word "show"—a new vocabulary word for him—and produced it correctly in various contexts. He also demonstrated accurate production of the "sh" sound in new words that he learned at home, such as "shave." However, the word "shoe," which was a word he had used for over a year and had not been included in any word families, continued to be produced as "do."

Matthew's parents, clinicians, and supervisor all reported great progress during the third semester, so results of the standardized assessments were surprising and a bit disappointing. Although test results indicated some improvement (a reduction of the TOMPD on the HAPP-3 from 95 to 84 and the error score on the GF-2 from 53 to 48—see Tables 10–7 and 10–8), they did not reflect the subjective perception of progress shared by the adults

in Matthew's environment. His mother stated that while watching the administration of the HAPP-3, she thought to herself, "Oh no, it [the improvement] is not showing up." Why? Perhaps the items on the tests included many "old" words that Matthew was continuing to produce as he always had and did not reflect his new phonological knowledge. Or perhaps the tests were not measuring the specific skills that Matthew had gained.

Item analysis of Matthew's responses indicated that many areas of improvement were not scored on the HAPP-3 and/or the GF-2, thus preventing significant numerical gains. For example, Matthew demonstrated remarkable improvement in his production of vowel sounds, and yet neither test includes vowel errors in the calculations for standardized scores. HAPP-3 scores also do not include voicing errors, and, therefore, Matthew's decreased use of prevocalic voicing was not noted. Although the GF-2 results did reflect the improvement in voicing, they did not numerically account for the significant increase in substitution errors with a corresponding decrease in omission errors. For example, "cup" was produced as "up" on the initial GF-2, whereas Matthew produced it as "tup" during the final administration of this test.

Both productions were scored as errors, yet the latter production demonstrates significant progress—in intelligibility, production of the CVC word

Table 10–7. Test Results After the Third Semester of Therapy

HAPP-3, Date, Age	Total Occurrences of Major Phonological Deviations	Severity Interval	Consonant Category Deficiencies Sum	Ability Score	Percentile
End of third semester Date: 4-08 CA: 4-5	84	Moderate	56	<55	<1
GF: 2, date, age	Error score	Standard score			Percentile
End of third semester Date: 5-08 CA: 4-6	48	65			5

Table 10–8. Intelligibility of Speech Samples Throughout Treatment

	Completely Intelligible	Partially Intelligible	Unintelligible	Completely or Partially Intelligible
Initial Date: 1-07 CA: 3-2	6/25 24%	6/25 24%	13/25 52%	12/25 48%
End of first semester Date: 5-07 CA: 3-6	12/25 48%	6/25 24%	7/25 28%	18/25 72%
End of second semester Date: 12-07 CA: 4-0	11/25 44%	9/25 36%	5/25 20%	20/25 80%
End of third semester Date: 5-08 CA: 4-6	16/25 64%	9/25 36%	0/25 0%	25/25 100%

shape, reduction of initial consonant deletion, and expansion of his phonemic inventory to include initial /t/. In addition, many of Matthew's other productions during the final assessment were much closer approximations of the target word or sound than they had been a year earlier. Consonant clusters now often contained at least one of the target sounds; "truck" was now produced as "tuck" rather than "dud," and "spoon" was produced as "poon" rather than "boon." Atypical substitution patterns were in many instances replaced by typical phonological patterns. For example, /r/ was now substituted by a /w/ and not a /d/, and an initial b/k substitution was replaced by a t/k substitution, representing the emergence of gliding and velar fronting—common error patterns exhibited by many young children.

These improvements in vowel production and voicing, along with decreases in omission errors and atypical patterns, likely explain the improvement in overall speech intelligibility reflected in the analysis of spontaneous speech samples (see Table 10–8). When Matthew started treatment, slightly over half of his utterances were completely unintelligible to an unfamiliar listener. By the end of the third semester of treatment, none of his utterances were completely unintelligible—all of them were either partially or completely understood. Thus, this method of assessing Matthew's speech production abilities provided a better representation of the progress described by his parents and clinicians than the formal articulation and phonological assessments that were administered.

Analysis of Client's Response to Intervention

It appears that Matthew experienced more progress than was reflected by the formal assessment results. Yet the question remains: Did Matthew achieve more progress during the final semester of treatment than during each of the preceding semesters? That is, was the multiple oppositions approach more effective than the combination of the cycles approach and integral stimulation? The data collected over the course of the three semesters indicate a steady expansion of Matthew's sound and syllable structure inventories. Acquisition of vowels, velars, glides, and stridents, as well as CVC and CCVC word shapes, occurred over the entire course of treatment. There was a steady decline in omission errors, accompanied by a corresponding increase in substitutions. However, a qualitative change occurred during the third semester in the nature of the substitutions. Previously, Matthew had substituted a /d/ phoneme, and occasionally a /b/ or /n/ phoneme, for almost all initial consonants. Upon completion of 4 months of multiple opposition therapy, he demonstrated a significant increase in the variety of initial consonants that he produced, thus reducing the occurrence of homonyms—the exact effect hoped for. The decrease of homonymy and increase in more typical substitution patterns contributed to larger gains in overall speech intelligibility during the last semester. Other advantages of the multiple oppositions approach reported by Matthew's mother were generalization to untreated targets, better retention of learned skills, and more self-awareness of errors and successful productions.

In conclusion, Matthew demonstrated significant progress over the course of his three semesters of treatment, thanks in large part to the dedication of his clinicians and the active participation of his parents. The catalyst for his accelerated growth during the final semester may have been multifaceted. A shift in diagnosis, the implementation of the multiple oppositions approach, greater client maturity, and attention to parental concerns—all may have played a role in Matthew's improved speech production abilities.

Author's Note

The author would like to acknowledge the significant contributions of the coauthor of this case study in its original form, Jacqueline Bauman-Waengler. Thank you also to all those who contributed to Matthew's therapy, including his parents, his clinicians (Nancy Alyssa McFall, Larissa Lapine, Gina Tashjian, Lisa Iland, and Nicole Clark), and his other clinical supervisor, Cynthia Wineinger. This project was reviewed and accepted by the IRB board at the University of Redlands, IRB # 21-06.

References

American Speech-Language-Hearing Association. (2007a). *Childhood apraxia of speech: Position statement.* http://www.asha.org/docs/html/PS2007-00277.html

American Speech-Language-Hearing Association. (2007b). *Childhood apraxia of speech: Technical report.* http://www.asha.org/docs/html/TR2007-00278.html

Barlow, J., & Gierut, J. (2002). Minimal pair approaches to phonological remediation. *Seminars in Speech and Language, 23*(1), 57–67.

Bauman-Waengler, J. (2008). *Articulatory and phonological impairments: A clinical focus* (3rd ed.). Allyn & Bacon.

Bauman-Waengler, J., & Garcia, D. (2018). *Phonological treatment of speech sound disorders in children: A practical guide.* Plural Publishing.

Berman, S. (2001). *Phonology targets: More patterns and themes for groups.* Pro-Ed.

Berman, S., Garcia, D., & Bauman-Waengler, J. (2007, November). *Cycles approach and integral stimulation: Outcome measures for unintelligible children.* Poster session presented at the American Speech-Language-Hearing Association, Boston, MA.

Brownell, R. (Ed.). (2000). *Receptive One-Word Picture Vocabulary Test.* Academic Therapy Publications.

Caruso, A., & Strand, E. (1999). Motor speech disorders in children: Definitions, background, and a theoretical framework. In A. Caruso & E. Strand (Eds.), *Clinical management of motor speech disorders in children* (pp. 1–28). Thieme.

Flahive, L., Velleman, S., & Hodson, B. (2005, November). *Apraxia and phonology.* Seminar presented at the American Speech-Language Hearing Association, San Diego, CA.

Gildersleeve-Neumann, C. (2007). Treatment for childhood apraxia of speech: A description of integral stimulation and motor learning. *The ASHA Leader, 12*(15), 10–13, 30.

Goldman, R., & Fristoe, M. (2000). *Goldman-Fristoe Test of Articulation* (2nd ed.). American Guidance Service.

Hodson, B. (1997). Disordered phonologies: What have we learned about assessment and treatment? In B. Hodson & M. Edwards (Eds.), *Perspectives in applied phonology* (pp. 197–224). Aspen.

Hodson, B. (2004). *Hodson Assessment of Phonological Patterns (HAPP-3).* Super Duper.

Hodson, B. (2007). *Evaluating and enhancing children's phonological systems: Research and theory to practice.* Thinking Publications University.

Hodson, B., & Paden, E. (1991). *Targeting intelligible speech: A phonological approach to remediation*. College-Hill Press.

Kamhi, A. (2006). Treatment decisions for children with speech-sound disorders. *Language, Speech, and Hearing Services in Schools, 37*, 271–279.

McCauley, R., & Strand, E. (1999). Treatment of children exhibiting phonological disorder with motor speech involvement. In A. Caruso & E. Strand (Eds.), *Clinical management of motor speech disorders in children* (pp. 187–208). Thieme.

Murray, E., McCabe, P., & Ballard, K. (2014). A systematic review of treatment outcomes for children with childhood apraxia of speech. *American Journal of Speech-Language Pathology, 23*, 486–504. https://doi.org/10.1044/2014_AJSLP-13-0035

Smit, A. (2004). *Articulation and phonology resource guide for school-age children and adults*. Thomson Delmar Learning.

Strand, E. (2017). *Diagnosis and treatment of CAS using DTTC [MOOC]*. Child Apraxia Treatment: Once Upon a Time Foundation. https://childapraxiatreatment.org/diagnosis-and-treatment-of-cas-online-course/

Strand, E., & Skinder, A. (1999). Treatment of developmental apraxia of speech: Integral stimulation methods. In A. Caruso & E. Strand (Eds.), *Clinical management of motor speech disorders in children* (pp. 109–147). Thieme.

Strand, E. A., Stoeckel, R., & Baas, B. (2006). Treatment of severe childhood apraxia of speech: A treatment efficacy study. *Journal of Medical Speech-Language Pathology, 14*(4), 297–307.

Williams, A. (2000a). Multiple oppositions: Case studies of variables in phonological intervention. *American Journal of Speech-Language Pathology, 9*, 289–299.

Williams, A. (2000b). Multiple oppositions: Theoretical foundations for an alternative contrastive intervention approach. *American Journal of Speech-Language Pathology, 9*, 282–288.

Williams, A. (2005). From developmental norms to distance metrics: Past, present, and future directions for target selection practices. In A. G. Kamhi & K. E. Pollock (Eds.), *Phonological disorders in children: Clinical decision making in assessment and intervention* (pp. 101–108). Paul H. Brookes Publishing.

Williams, A. L. (2010). Multiple oppositions intervention. In A. L. Williams, S. McLeod, & R. J. McCauley (Eds.), *Interventions for speech sound disorders in children* (pp. 73–93). Paul H. Brookes Publishing.

Williams, A. L., & Sugden, E. (2021). Multiple oppositions intervention. In A. L. Williams, S. McLeod, & R. J. McCauley (Eds.), *Intervention for speech sound disorders in children* (2nd ed., pp. 61–90). Paul H. Brookes Publishing.

AUGMENTATIVE COMMUNICATION AND ASSISTIVE TECHNOLOGY/CEREBRAL PALSY
CASE 11
Katie: An Augmentative and Alternative Communication Pathway to Desired Outcomes in Early Intervention
Carla Wood

Conceptual Knowledge Areas

Cerebral palsy (CP) is among the most common physical disabilities in childhood, affecting 2 to 3 children out of every 1,000 (Novak et al., 2012). CP is a nonprogressive disorder that affects the ability to move, coordinate muscles, and maintain balance and posture. It is the result of an injury to parts of the brain (Centers for Disease Control, 2019; National Institute of Neurological Disorders and Stroke, 2020). Individuals with CP present with a motor impairment characterized by ataxic CP due to cerebellar damage or spastic CP due to damage to the motor cortex causing increased tone and stiff movements. In addition, individuals may demonstrate athetoid CP characterized by slow, writhing, involuntary movements due to damage to the indirect motor pathways or mixed CP with symptoms of spastic, athetoid, and ataxic CP appearing simultaneously. Although children with CP often have normal cognition or a mild to moderate intellectual disability, difficulty with the precise muscle movements for speech often contributes to complex communication challenges (Pirila et al., 2007). They generally require support from a number of different professionals, including physical therapists, speech-language pathologists (SLPs), occupational therapists, special education teachers, and personal aides. Due to the physical constraints of the condition, children with cerebral palsy commonly benefit from augmentative and alternative communication (AAC), including speech-generating devices (SGDs).

AAC refers to all forms of tools and strategies (e.g., symbols, pictures, and speech-generating devices) that are used to compensate for speech and language disorders to express thoughts, needs, wants, and ideas (International Society Augmentative and Alternative Communication, 2018). An AAC system is an integrated group of components including the symbols, aids, strategies, and techniques used by individuals to enhance communication. AAC use with younger children has grown substantially over the past few decades, with a wide variety of AAC systems that can be used to develop language skills (National Joint Committee, 2016). Research suggests that children with complex communication needs show superior outcomes to speech-only approaches (Langarika-Rocafort et al., 2021). Hence, there is a pressing need for SLPs to be knowledgeable about providing AAC supports for young children with intellectual and developmental disabilities, autism, childhood apraxia of speech, and other disabilities (O'Neill et al., 2018).

An individual's AAC system may involve multiple components including unaided and aided forms. Unaided communication forms such as gestures, sign language, eye gaze, and facial expressions do not require external aids separate from the individual. Aided communication systems include those that are external to the person's body such as picture communication boards, speech-generating devices, and switches. Selecting appropriate AAC supports entails consideration of desired characteristics of the system tailored to the individual's strengths and needs. Considerations include selection technique (direct or scanning), display (lexical items, representations, organization), and presentation (e.g., array, size, spacing, location, and color).

There is growing evidence that early use of AAC facilitates or enhances communicative exchanges in young children with complex communication needs (Holyfield et al., 2019; Solomon-Rice & Soto, 2014). Assistive technology can also be effective in increasing the frequency of environmental control, switch interface, and supporting cause-effect understanding in young children with severe motor disabilities (Sullivan & Lewis, 2000). Additionally, research findings suggest increased communicative interaction following integration of speech-generating devices and other communication aids with communication partners across learning contexts in naturalistic routines in home and preschool classroom settings (Brady et al., 2016; Shire & Jones, 2014).

Description of the Case

Background Information

Katie is the youngest child in her family, a bright-eyed little girl diagnosed with severe cerebral palsy at 9 months old. Katie is nonambulatory, presenting with both hyper- and hypotonic muscle tone and limited range of motion. Katie initially communicated primarily through crying and body language, prompting her family and service providers to consider assistive technology to support her communication development. Throughout her early years, Katie's augmentative communication system evolved in response to changes in her interests and preferences, communication demands, skill development, environment, and communication partners. Aside from her challenges, Katie is a typical child. Her parents stated, "Katie enjoys all the things other kids do. We just have to assist her in the enjoyment of these activities."

Reason for Referral

Family and Child History

Katie was born to a middle-class family in the suburbs of a midwestern university community. She was referred to the Part C Infant-Toddler Coordinating Council (ICC) at 6 months of age due to delays in her acquisition of developmental milestones. Although she was drinking formula through a bottle, she was not adequately gaining weight. Her parents were concerned that she was not holding her head up or rolling over independently. They also noticed that she was not babbling or vocalizing as often as her older sister did at that age. A developmental pediatrician confirmed the diagnosis of severe cerebral palsy (CP).

Desired Outcomes

Katie's parents wanted her to vocalize more frequently to encourage the development of speech. They hoped she would acquire a means to communicate her wants and needs at home and in the childcare center. It was important to her parents that Katie play and engage in interactions with her sister and interact with peers and be accepted by them. Sitting upright so that she could interact with her environment was also a high priority. They wanted to improve her muscular strength, tone, and control for later walking. Katie's parents were concerned about her growth and nutrition, noting that she became fatigued easily during feedings and was not gaining weight.

Findings of the Evaluation

Interprofessional Teaming

Assessments were conducted using a team-based approach. Given the multifaceted aspects, service provision included diverse perspectives and expertise extended through collaboration with service providers from different disciplinary backgrounds (Sylvester et al., 2017). Because CP affects multiple systems, assessment is often dynamic across time in different situations and generally includes consideration of multiple areas: sensory needs, motor abilities and needs (positioning, strengths, range of motion), social communication, learning, nutrition, and feeding (Brady et al., 2016).

Katie's initial service team consisted of Katie's parents and her sibling, an SLP, a physical therapist, the lead teacher at Katie's childcare center, a family resource specialist, and the early childhood resource specialist who served a dual role as the family service coordinator. The therapists were employed by agencies in the community that contracted with the ICC. The family resource specialist was employed by the local ICC and consulted with the therapists and family to assist in providing access to desired resources and supports. For example, if the physical therapist recommended specific equipment for physical support and positioning, the family service coordinator and family resource specialist worked together with the team to secure access through lending agencies, funding sources, and/or the family's insurance.

The team members cotreated in pairs to maximize cross-training and provide consultation to caregivers. When reflecting on services, Katie's parents wrote, "We want the providers to communicate more with the paras (i.e., paraeducators), because they spend the most time with her. We often learn the paras are left out of the discussions with the providers." In response, therapists alternated between the family's home and the childcare setting for service delivery. During visits, therapists conversed with caregivers about progress, discussed and demonstrated strategies, and brainstormed opportunities to facilitate progress toward achieving desired outcomes. Her parents valued having service delivery at home, which allowed for identification of routine activities of daily living as opportunities for facilitating outcomes and coaching and problem solving within everyday contexts.

Treatment Options Considered

Intervention for Katie was informed by the family's priorities and desired outcomes, available evidence, clinical experiences, and Katie's preferences. Therapists worked together with the family to identify appropriate supports and implement evidence-based strategies to promote desired outcomes.

Course of Treatment

The SLP provided informational resources to the staff at the childcare center regarding encouraging vocalizations. The team determined that underlying cognitive milestones of object permanence and cause-and-effect understanding could be targeted during playtime routines. In initial steps, a switch-activated SGD was proposed as a low-tech support for requesting "more." A high-caloric flavored PediaSure formula was provided to encourage weight gain. Since the nipple on the bottle required great effort for Katie, a sippy cup was introduced as well as a special-order feeding cup with a preloadable straw. The physical therapist worked with the family resource specialist to support seating and positioning. Katie responded well to the use of thermoform in the center of a booster seat or donut-shaped pillow, which allowed her to play on the floor in an upright position with her sister. This seating made Katie more accessible for inclusion in play with dolls with her sister at home, as well as play with others at the childcare center. Other positioning supports for Katie varied by routine. At home she acquired a lap tray for a booster seat for mealtimes and an adapted bath seat to assist in the bathtub.

One of her parents' highest priorities was to ensure that Katie be integrated with peers, adapt socially, and have a way to communicate in those environments, as they believed this would facilitate her learning. This belief was consistent with research findings that highlight the importance of supporting successful interactions with communication partners across learning contexts (Shire & Jones, 2014). Service providers discussed communication opportunities and routines with Katie's family and teachers at the childcare center and preschool classroom. Teachers reported that mealtime was challenging because they wanted Katie to increase her caloric intake with the least amount of exertion, so choice making or requests were not seen as feasible. Floor play and bath time were determined to be the best times to regularly focus on Katie's communicative exchanges at home. Katie would be encouraged to request desired items and indicate a preference or choice through any means. At childcare, social exchanges with peers were identified as a priority during playtime and outdoor activities.

The team was also challenged to identify appropriate assistive technologies and AAC to meet Katie's communication needs. While the SGD was initially attempted, it was quickly apparent that Katie had an aversive reaction to the "click" of the switch. In response, a flat plate switch was used to activate a small speech-generating device with up to eight switch ports. Multiple plate switches of bright contrasting colors could be presented on her tray at one time with the SGD positioned under the tray. Utilizing direct selection appeared to be appropriate for Katie since scanning required her to have more precise timing and control of her selection timing.

Other considerations for assistive technologies for Katie included lexical items, representations, organization, and presentation. Katie's team brainstormed to ensure the items were concrete, appealing or motivating, and personalized to Katie's unique interests, opportunities, and communication partners. By considering AAC options with quick recording or programming options, adults could employ *just-in-time* programming approach, meaning that adults could program new vocabulary in the moment throughout the day to respond to choices or opportunities as they unfold (Holyfield et al., 2019). Designing Katie's system involved consideration of social play opportunities in her environment, Katie's visual access to items, and motor access or positioning. Free play activities with peers in the childcare setting provided frequent opportunities for making choices. During free play, the children had an opportunity to select specific toys or activities. This routine provided frequent opportunities for Katie to select preferred activities such as playing with peers using cheerleading pom-poms, having books read to her, and having the children play with toys on her lap tray. This use of assistive technology was expanded over time to support Katie to participate and communicate in repeti-

tive lines of stories, songs, and simple games in the preschool classroom.

Adaptations were necessary with evolving iterations of Katie's AAC system over time in individualizing AAC to her preferences using a trial-and-error process and initially tailoring support in consideration of her unique sensory needs. To illustrate, Katie demonstrated hypersensitivity to light as a toddler. Her vision was negatively affected by glare. In an effort to optimize her visual access, during initial presentations, the lexical items on the brightly colored plate switches were represented with both a picture and a miniature object (miniature book) or remnants (e.g., strings of the pom-pom). Due to Katie's motor constraints, the plate switches were placed at least 6 to 8 inches apart across Katie's tray two to three at a time. Katie was given time to explore and play with the items that were presented. Katie's selections were spontaneous and unsupported physically but generally involved stiff arm movements, and therefore her choices appeared most successful when items were presented with adequate space between them. When positioned with trunk support and her feet in contact with the floor or seating equipment, Katie reached across midline to activate a colorful plate switch without verbal prompting.

A visual scene display (VSD) organizational layout was also considered for Katie's AAC technology options. VSDs refer to the use of a digital photo or picture scene in which vocabulary items are embedded as "hot spots" (defined areas with speech output) within the picture (Wilkinson et al., 2012). For some children, VSDs offer the potential advantage of facilitating lexical access through the inclusion of a context-rich scene (Drager et al., 2004). It has been suggested that referents may be more comprehensible or recognizable in a visual scene that preserves the item's contextual relevance, coherence, and size integrity (Wilkinson et al., 2012). VSDs were not utilized during Katie's early years. Katie's access to pictures and photos was limited by visual and motor constraints in physically accessing items. Hot spots on the VSD needed to be large, preferably with three-dimensional remnants, and 6 to 8 inches apart. Visual scene displays could be considered in the future as Katie's physical access improves, particularly considering potential benefits of just-in-time programing with VSDs (Holyfield et al., 2019).

Analysis of Katie's Response to Intervention

As Katie advanced to preschool, her sensitivity to appropriate auditory selection feedback ("click") became less apparent and other section options could be incorporated. Service providers consulted with the preschool teacher and paraeducators to identify social communication opportunities within evolving daily routines. Assistive technology supports were identified to enhance communicative exchanges with peers. During recess, the paraeducator held the SGD while supporting Katie at the top of the slide. She activated the SGD, "Go down the slide! Wee!" when she was ready to launch. Caregivers also encouraged Katie to vocalize simultaneously using an open vowel such as /o/ for "go" or /i/ for "wee." Katie quickly began to anticipate this activity, and peers began to use the SGD as well. The interaction with peers provided natural reinforcement for her use of the speech-generating device while giving her increased control over her environment.

A dynamic display device was considered to facilitate Katie's access to a large number of pages with stored vocabulary, while only needing a few items on each display page at a time. Because Katie's choices had to be large and spaced apart, static displays or object choices limited the number of items she could select from at any time. A dynamic display allows multiple pages of vocabulary to be linked together electronically, so a single selection may result in a new array of choices. Findings of studies have shown that young children (2.5-year-olds) are able to learn to use dynamic display AAC technologies but may have initial difficulty learning to locate vocabulary on dynamic display systems. Given the potential advantages for Katie's access to linked pages of vocabulary, a dynamic display AAC device was explored with Katie when she was in preschool. At the time, Katie's physical access to the device was compromised by the glare and limited visual contrast of a dynamic display screen. Additionally, motor constraints prohibited Katie from using direct selection when choices were positioned within 6 to 8 inches of each other. Katie did not initially have precise or anticipatory control of the timing of motor movements needed to facilitate the use of a scanning selection technique.

Katie's parents reflected positively on their experiences during her early years. They expressed gratitude for positive outcomes and their support systems, including family, friends, and faith-based community. They stated, "Katie has taught us a lot about patience, compassion, and not to take anything for granted." When asked for their advice to other parents of children with complex communication challenges, her parents wrote,

> Take advantage of support services as soon as you can. Learn as much as you can from those services and resources. Learn to be patient. You must advocate for your child. It is indeed a balancing act to make sure your child receives proper services. Build positive relationships early on. Also, be vocal in the development of the IEP and make sure goals are met or adjusted accordingly.

When asked about advice they would share with service providers, Katie's parents advised, "They need to realize that every situation is different. There is no one-size-fits-all."

References

Brady, N. C., Bruce, S., Goldman, A., Erickson, K., Mineo, B., Ogletree, B. T., . . . Wilkinson, K. (2016). Communication services and supports for individuals with severe disabilities: Guidance for assessment and intervention. *American Journal on Intellectual and Developmental Disabilities, 121*(2), 121–138. https://doi.org/10.1352/1944-7558-121.2.121

Centers for Disease Control, National Center on Birth Defects and Developmental Disorders. (2019). *What is cerebral palsy?* https://www.cdc.gov/ncbddd/cp/facts.html

Drager, K., Light, J., Carlson, R., D'Silva, K., Larsson, B., Pitkin, L., & Stopper, G. (2004). Learning of dynamic display AAC technologies by typically developing

3-year-olds: Effect of different layouts and menu approaches. *Journal of Speech, Language, and Hearing Research, 47*, 1133–1148.

Holyfield, C., Caron, J., & Light, J. (2019). Programming AAC just-in-time for beginning communicators: The process. *Augmentative and Alternative Communication, 35*(4), 309–318. https://doi.org/10.1080/07434618.2019.1686538

International Society for Augmentative and Alternative Communication. (2018). *What is AAC?* https://www.isaac-online.org/english/what-is-aac/

Langarika-Rocafort, A., Idoiaga Mondragon, N., & Roman Etxebarrieta, G. (2021). A systematic review of research on augmentative and alternative communication interventions for children aged 6–10 in the last decade. *Language Speech and Hearing Services in Schools, 52*, 899–916. https://doi.org/10.1044/2021_LSHSS-20-00005

National Institute of Neurological Disorders and Stroke. (2020). *Cerebral palsy detailed: Signs, causes, risk factors, diagnosis, treatment, and research.* https://www.ninds.nih.gov/Disorders/Patient-Caregiver-Education/Hope-Through-Research/Cerebral-Palsy-Hope-Through-Research

National Joint Committee for the Communication Needs of Persons With Severe Disabilities (NJC) (2016). Publications, presentations, and learning module. *American Speech-Language Hearing Association.* https://www.asha.org/njc/articles-and-presentations

Novak, I., Hines, M., Goldsmith, S., & Barclay, R. (2012). Clinical prognostic messages from a systematic review on cerebral palsy. *Pediatrics, 130*(5), e1285–e1312.

O'Neil, T., Light, J., & Pope, L. (2018). Effects of interventions that include aided augmentative and alternative communication input on the communication of individuals with complex communication needs: A meta-analysis. *Journal of Speech Language Hearing Research, 61*, 1743–1765. https://doi.org/10.1044/2018_JSLHR-L-17-0132

Pirila, S., van der Meere, J., Pentikainen, T., Ruusu-Niemi, P., Korpela, R., Kilpinen, J., & Nieminen, P. (2007). Language and motor speech skills in children with cerebral palsy. *Journal of Communication Disorders, 40*(2), 116–128.

Shire, S. Y., & Jones, N. (2014). Communication partners supporting children with complex communication needs who use AAC: A systematic review. *Communication Disorders Quarterly, 37*(1), 3–15. https://doi.org/10.1177/1525740114558254

Solomon-Rice, P. L., & Soto, G. (2014). Facilitating vocabulary in toddlers using AAC: A preliminary study comparing focused stimulation and augmented input. *Communication Disorders Quarterly, 35*(4), 204–215. https://doi.org/10.1177/1525740114522856

Sullivan, M., & Lewis, M. (2000). Assistive technology for the very young. Creating responsive environments. *Infants and Young Children, 12*, 34–52.

Sylvester, L., Ogletree, B., & Lunnen, K. (2017). Cotreatment as a vehicle for interprofessional collaborative practice: Physical therapists and speech-language pathologists collaborating in the care of children with severe disabilities. *American Journal of Speech-Language Pathology, 26*, 206–216. https://doi.org/10.1044/2017_AJSLP-15-0179

Wilkinson, K. M., Light, J., & Drager, K. (2012). Considerations for the composition of visual scene displays: Potential contributions of information from visual and cognitive sciences. *Augmentative and Alternative Communication, 28*, 137–147. https://doi.org/10.3109/07434618.2012.704522

LATE LANGUAGE EMERGENCE/ DEVELOPMENTAL LANGUAGE DISORDER
CASE 12
Cameron: Targeted Treatment for a Preschool Child With Developmental Language Disorder
Erin E. G. Lundblom and Danielle Brimo

Conceptual Knowledge Areas

Late Language Emergence

Some children between the ages of 2 and 4 years present with late language emergence (LLE) (also referred to as "late talkers"), which is a delay in language acquisition with no other identified disabilities or developmental delays. Some children with LLE may have only expressive deficits marked by delayed vocabulary acquisition, sentence structure development, and articulation skills. Some children have a mixed presentation with delays in oral language production and language comprehension. Children with both receptive and expressive delays are at greater risk for language and literacy difficulties (Marchman & Fernald, 2013).

Early assessment and periodic monitoring are critical on a regular basis (e.g., every 6 months) to track language development and identify if any problems emerge. A comprehensive speech and language assessment should include a broad check of speech and language development using both standardized instruments and authentic measures. Assessment can include caregiver interviews, developmental observations, and communication sampling. The assessment process should consider the most common concerns for children with LLE—an expressive vocabulary of fewer than 50 words and a failure to combine 2 words together in the second year of life (Paul, 1991; Rescorla, 2002). Other areas to consider include grammar,

language comprehension, social communication skills, and play behaviors. Hearing and speech sound assessments should also be included. See the "Typical Components of the Speech and Language Assessment" in the ASHA Practice Portal: Late Language Emergence (American Speech-Language-Hearing Association, n.d.).

Intervention approaches for children with LLE can vary for each child and family. Children learn language in the context of interacting with persons close to them. The overarching goal of intervention is to support language development and teach language facilitation skills to promote communication. A key component is working closely with families. Collaborating with parents and caregivers helps to determine the communication goals for the child while identifying opportunities such as routines or activities that happen in the home, community, or school to embed intervention techniques.

Developmental Language Disorder

A developmental language disorder (DLD) is a neurodevelopmental language deficit that affects the acquisition, comprehension, and use of language (McGregor et al., 2020). Children with DLD have persistent language deficits and are unresponsive to universal educational instruction (McGregor et al., 2020). DLD varies across individuals, depending on the age of the child, language domain(s) impacted, and current level of language development. DLDs are heterogeneous, and the severity level can vary considerably. Each individual with language difficulties has a unique profile of strengths and needs.

Not all children with LLE will be diagnosed with DLD (Paul, 1996; Rescorla, 2002), which complicates the diagnosis of DLD. Many (approximately 50% to 70%) children with LLE demonstrate normal language development by late preschool and school age (Dale et al., 2003; Paul, 1996). One in five children with LLE have language impairment at the age of 7 years (Rice et al., 2008). It is important, then, that speech-language pathologists consider the variability in vocabulary growth and word combinations in young children by reviewing ongoing assessment and intervention data. Speech-language pathologists should use data collected to differentiate a language delay from a language disorder (Rescorla & Turner, 2015).

Description of the Case

The following description reports a hypothetical case based on experiences with a variety of pediatric cases.

Reason for Referral

Cameron, a 3-year, 7-month-old male, was referred by his court-appointed legal guardian for a clinical evaluation of his communication skills. Cameron's guardian is his great-aunt Sylvia, who became his guardian almost 2 years prior to this evaluation. When she received guardianship of Cameron at 2 years of age, she explained that he was "not talking." Sylvia indicated that a speech-language evaluation was completed when Cameron was around 2½ years old. Sylvia did not provide a copy of the evaluation. She explained the evaluation results indicated a speech delay with no recommendations for treatment. Sylvia requested another evaluation after discussing Cameron's communication skills with his pediatrician. Sylvia accompanied Cameron to the evaluation with his biological mother, Shauna.

Background Information

Sylvia and Shauna both provided information about Cameron's development jointly and separately. Both indicated that Cameron experienced a typical birth and delivery. Shauna reported that Cameron passed his newborn hearing screening. Shauna also explained that developmental milestones were typical except for his communication. For example, Shauna indicated that Cameron walked around 13 months of age. With specific questioning, Shauna explained that Cameron began gesturing prior to babbling. She thought he started babbling around 9 months old. He produced his first word, "momma," at 1 year 3 months. Shauna was unable to provide more information about Cameron's communication development past 15 months of age.

Sylvia was interviewed separately from Shauna to provide additional developmental information. Sylvia indicated that she cannot provide information from 15 to 24 months because she is unclear of Cameron's development. Sylvia explained that she became Cameron's court-appointed guardian when he was 24 months of age. She indicated she was contacted by the Department of Children and Family Services in a nearby state as the next of kin and closest living relative to Cameron. She explained that Cameron and his brother, Chase, had been living in an unsafe environment, and law enforcement found the children after serving a search warrant for suspected criminal activity at the residence. Law enforcement removed the children and contacted the Department of Children and Family Services. Sylvia agreed to take legal guardianship of Cameron and his older sibling, Chase.

Sylvia explained that when she received Cameron at 24 months of age that he did not combine words and his expressive vocabulary was fewer than 25 words. Cameron had difficulty communicating with her and he was difficult to understand, but over time she began to figure out what he was trying to say through his words and pointing. Cameron has had at least three ear infections since birth, which were treated with antibiotics and resolved. At the time of the evaluation, it was suspected Cameron had an ear infection.

Over the past 3 months, Shauna has moved to the area to be closer to her children. Sylvia agreed to let Shauna live in her home. Sylvia indicated that Shauna is adhering to a methadone maintenance program, and she attends a local chapter of Narcotics Anonymous.

At the time of the evaluation, Cameron lived with Sylvia (court-appointed guardian), Shauna (biological mother), his older 5-year-old brother (Chase), and three other individuals. Cameron attended daycare 5 days a week from 9 a.m. to 5 p.m. Sylvia reported that his "talking" had improved since starting daycare. His preschool teachers reported to Sylvia that Cameron is reserved but is beginning to engage with peers. He follows the classroom schedules and routines and enjoys attention from his teachers.

Evaluation Results

The evaluation team evaluated Cameron's speech and language using norm-referenced instruments, behavioral observations during play-based activities, and language sample analyses. The following is a summary of the evaluation results.

Hearing Screening

Upon consultation with an on-site audiologist, nonmedical otoscopy revealed cerumen blockage in both of Cameron's ears and an abnormal appearance of the eardrum. Tympanometry was attempted, but a seal could not be obtained. Pure-tone audiometry was not attempted. The audiologist recommended referral to an otolaryngologist.

Behavioral Observations

Cameron separated easily from Sylvia and Shauna. He appeared hesitant to interact initially but demonstrated comfort as the session continued. For example, he often wanted to sit in the clinician's lap throughout the evaluation session. Cameron used mostly two-word utterances and gestures to communicate demonstrating multiple functions of communication—requesting, protesting, commenting, and greeting, for example.

Cameron appeared eager to play with toys in the room. He engaged in symbolic play during social pretend play interactions. For example, he played with items in a kitchen using the items realistically and appropriately. At one point, he made coffee and poured it into cups. He refilled the cups, collected the cups, and washed the cups in the kitchen sink. Another play interaction involved doctor toys and a baby doll. Cameron engaged in a routine where he checked the doll's temperature, heartbeat, and administered a shot. During play, Cameron also followed simple one- and two-step commands using a barn toy and associated toys.

Cameron demonstrated an interest in books. He demonstrated several book-handling skills like being able to hold the book in the correct position. He also enjoyed turning the pages and identifying familiar pictures in books. When the clinician asked Cameron to tell the clinician a story about the pictures, Cameron had difficulty describing what was happening on each page. At the end of the session, Cameron drew a picture of his brother, mother, and Sylvia.

Language Sample Analysis

A language sample was gathered during play. Communication facilitation strategies, such as engaging Cameron in play-based activities (e.g., fixing the cars, washing the cars, driving the car to the store), commenting on actions within the play-based activities (e.g., "my car is going fast."), and providing wait time (i.e., pausing after making a comment to encourage Cameron to communicate) were used.

Cameron's mean length of utterance (MLU) and number of different words (NDW) were calculated to obtain an objective measure of his linguistic productivity and vocabulary diversity, respectively. Both were calculated from two play-based samples of 50 utterances. MLU and NDW can be indicative of atypical language development because typically developing children have predictable MLUs and NDWs. The expected MLU for a child Cameron's age is 3.2 to 4.3 (Paul et al., 2018). The expected NDW for a child Cameron's age is 76 (Paul et al., 2018). Cameron's MLU and NDW during the diagnostic session were measured to be:

MLU Sample 1 = 2.80   MLU Sample 2 = 2.88

NDW Sample 1 = 58   NDW Sample 2 = 65

Interpretations of Results

Table 12–1 presents a summary of the norm-referenced and criterion-referenced assessment results.

Cameron's semantic and syntactic comprehension (i.e., receptive language) were evaluated. Cameron understood commands with two modifying adjectives, more than one clause, and passive voice. For example, when presented a picture, Cameron identified the object and/or picture described (e.g. "Point to the white kitten that is sleeping," "Find the big brown dog," and "Point to Grandfather was kissed by the baby"). Cameron also understood qualitative concepts (e.g., tall, long, and short) and shapes (e.g., circle, square, and triangle). Lastly, Cameron responded correctly to "where" and "why" questions. Cameron's receptive vocabulary score on the Peabody Picture Vocabulary Test-4 (PPVT-4) and auditory comprehension subtest from the Preschool Language Scales-5 (PLS-5) was within the average range (i.e., 85–115) when compared to peers his age. Based on Cameron's performance on norm-referenced assessment and informal observation while interacting with him during play, Cameron's receptive language was judged to be age appropriate.

Cameron's semantic, morphosyntactic, and syntactic production (i.e., expressive language) were evaluated. Cameron used words when communicating with the clinician during the play interaction. He used the following words consistently: car, water, truck, boy, girl, soap, wash, push, give, down, go, no, yes, and bye. Cameron also named superordinate categories assessed on the PLS-5. For example, Cameron identified the following as *toys*: blocks, doll, ball, puzzle. Cameron marked the third-person singular and copula/auxiliary BE in statements and questions approximately 50% of the time. He produced copula/auxiliary BE more accurately in statements than questions. He had difficulty producing the DO verb (i.e., do and does) correctly in questions and the most difficulty marking past tense in statements. Cameron produced one- to two-word utterances (i.e., noun, noun + complement, and noun + verb). For example, when asked, "Where do you sleep?" Cameron replied, "Bed"; when asked, "Why do we wear jackets?" Cameron responded, "It cold"; and when asked to describe a bird, Cameron responded, "Bird fly." Based on Cameron's performance on the norm-referenced and criterion-referenced assessments and communication sample, Cameron's expressive language was judged to be below what is expected for children his age.

Cameron's articulation and use of phonological patterns were evaluated. When compared to developmental norms, Cameron produced one error that was considered beyond the age range of speech acquisition: production of medial /m/ (e.g., "swimming"). The age of acquisition is the age at which mastery of a sound is demonstrated (e.g., the age of acquisition for the sound /m/ is 3 years; this means that most children consistently produce the sound /m/ by age 3). The age of acquisition for medial /m/ is 3 years. Cameron's scores on the Khan-Lewis Phonological Analysis-3 (KPLA-3) are within the range of normal for children Cameron's age. Specific sound error patterns are expected during different ages of speech development but should disappear by specific ages, or ages of elimination. The error patterns listed below should no longer appear in speech of children Cameron's age.

Phonological Process	Percentage of Use	Age of Elimination
Deletion of final consonants *"ka" for "car"*	6/44 (14%)	3 years
Stopping of fricatives and affricates *"fedder" for "feather"*	6/31 (19%)	3 years

Table 12–1. Norm-Referenced and Criterion-Referenced Assessment Results

Measurement	Description	Score Description	Probe Score	%ile	Standard Score[b]
Peabody Picture Vocabulary Test-4	Measures listening comprehension of spoken words.			37%ile	95
Preschool Language Scale-5	Offers a comprehensive developmental language assessment with items that range from preverbal, interaction-based skills to emerging language and literacy skills.	**Total language** addresses receptive and expressive communication skills.		23%ile	89
		Auditory Comprehension testing examines the subject's ability to understand spoken language.		37%ile	95
		Expressive Communication tests the quality and quantity of spoken language.		14%ile	84
Test of Early Grammatical Impairment	Measures grammatical ability. Child percentages are compared to criterion scores.	**Phonological Probe**	15/15		
		Final /s/	5/5		
		Final /z/	5/5		
		Final /t/	5/5		
		Final /d/	5/5		
		Third-person singular probe	50% (80%)[a]		
		Past-tense probe	.05% (80%)[a]		
		Be/Do probe (Be score)	54% (>80%)[a]		
		Be/Do probe (Do score)	30% (~70%)[a]		
		Elicited Grammar Composite	33%		
Goldman-Fristoe Test of Articulation-3	Examines the production of speech sounds.	**Sounds in Words Subtest**		30%	92
Khan Lewis Phonological Analysis-2	Identifies patterns of speech sound errors.			23%	89
Primary Test of Non-Verbal Intelligence	Provides information about children's nonverbal reasoning skills by evaluating a series of pictures and identifying the picture that does not belong.			73%	109

[a]Represents the criterion score for each subtest on the TEGI.

[b]Norm-referenced standardized measures: mean: 100; standard deviation: 15; average range: 85–115.

Phonological Process	Percentage of Use	Age of Elimination
Syllable reduction	5/26 (19%)	3 years to 4 years
"nana" for "banana"		

Overall, Cameron's receptive language and articulation skills were judged to be appropriate for his age; however, his expressive language was judged to be an area of weakness. Cameron should have been communicating with multiple word utterances, producing a variety of verbs and adjectives, and using grammatical morphemes. Cameron's weaknesses in his expressive language skills were consistent with a diagnosis of developmental language disorder.

Treatment Options

There are a number of different treatment approaches and strategies for children with DLD. The goal of intervention is to facilitate language development to enhance everyday communication, and treatment goals are selected with consideration for developmental appropriateness and the potential for improving the effectiveness of communication (Fey et al., 2003).

One approach for treatment is to target Cameron's use of grammatical morphemes since he is not producing these targets at the same rate as other 3-year-old children with typical language. Facilitating a child's grammar is important because it supports their spoken and written language (Owen Van Horne, 2020). The use of enhanced conversational recasting (also referred as recasting, conversational recasting, and focused recasting) is a highly effective intervention approach to facilitate children's grammar (e.g., Cleave et al., 2015; Plante et al., 2014; Plante et al., 2019). A recast is defined as a clinician's production of a grammatical target following a child's correct or incorrect production of a grammatical target. The clinician's production does not add content (i.e., additional vocabulary words, phrases, or clauses). For example, if a child says, "It red," the clinician would present a recast by saying, "It is red."

An example goal to target for Cameron would be production of third-person singular. According to Fey et al. (2003), "Grammatical forms and operations that the child uses correctly on occasion but either omits or uses incorrectly on other occasions" are appropriate grammatical targets for intervention. The clinician could select motivating activities for Cameron, like book reading and playing with preferred toys. The clinician would then select 24 unique verbs to recast for each session. For example, Cameron prefers to play with cars. The clinician could select a car book to read. Verbs across both activities could include wash, take, ride, drive, hit, push, clean, drop, fix, dry, open, rinse, use, crash, hear, get, see, look, sit, turn, need, roll, help, and cover. The clinician could set up a play routine with other toys and wait for the child to produce the target verbs or to elicit the target verbs by saying, "What's happening here?" "Tell me about . . . ," and "What does the car do?" The clinician can provide a recast after Cameron's correct and incorrect production of the third-person singular targeting a minimum of 24 times within the session. For example, when Cameron says, "He wash it," the clinician should say, "He washes it." The clinician should also vary the noun that is used in the recast. For example, if Cameron also says, "He move the car," the clinician should say, "The man moves the car." See Hall and Plante (2020), Plante et al. (2014), and Plante et al. (2019) for detailed information.

Another approach for treatment is to target Cameron's use of new words, specifically his verb lexicon. Improving Cameron's semantic knowledge of verbs will support his syntactic growth (Hadley et al., 2016) and success in reading (e.g., Catts et al., 2002). Research evidence confirms that children with DLD have poor word-learning skills (e.g., Adlof et al., 2021), and they require more exposure to learn a word than peers with typical language (Rice et al., 1994). Interactive book reading is an activity that can facilitate children's learning of new words (Justice et al., 2005). Children with DLD require 36 exposures to a word to learn the word (Storkel et al., 2017).

An example goal to target for Cameron would be production of new Tier 2 words, words that a child will likely hear and read and that add new, mature ways to express concepts (Beck et al., 2002). The clinician could select a book and Tier 2 words that are used in the book (see Justice et al., 2005, and Storkel et al., 2017, for a list of books and list of words). The clinician should identify the word, provide a definition of the word, use the word in a sentence, and provide a synonym of the word. This can occur before reading the book, while reading the book, and after reading the book. The clinician should track the number of exposures of the word in a session and during repetitive readings of the book in subsequent sessions to achieve 36 exposures of each word. See Storkel et al. (2017) and Storkel et al. (2019) for detailed information and supplemental materials.

Treatment Outcomes

An example of Cameron's progress producing the third-person singular across an 8-week treatment period is presented in Table 12–2.

An example of Cameron's vocabulary progress is captured in Table 12–3. The book *Stellaluna* (Cannon, 1993) was used over 4 weeks to provide

multiple exposures as described above to the following Tier 2 vocabulary terms.

Language is developing at a rapid pace in preschoolers. For children like Cameron with language difficulties, this process may be delayed. Future areas of treatment for Cameron may focus on vocabulary expansion through targeting adjectives, conjunctions, and/or concept vocabulary while focusing on building semantic relationships. Additionally, a continued focus of treatment may be on the use of age-appropriate morphemes like auxiliary and copula BE verbs and the use of complex syntax. Other potential areas to consider for treatment include the development of narrative skills and building emergent literacy skills through understanding story structure. Continued support and education of Cameron's family is also a key component to a successful intervention program.

References

Adlof, S. M., Baron, L. S., Bell, B. A., & Scoggins, J. (2021). Spoken word learning in children with developmen-

Table 12–2. An Example of Cameron's Progress Producing the Third-Person Singular

Baseline	Week 4	Week 8
45% correct	62% correct	83%
Week 0 = 45% (11/24)	Week 1 = 50% (12/24) Week 2 = 58% (14/24) Week 3 = 54% (13/24) Week 4 = 62% (14/24)	Week 5 = 66% (16/24) Week 6 =79% (18/24) Week 7 = 91% (22/24) Week 8 = 83% (20/24)

Table 12–3. An Example of Cameron's Vocabulary Progress Over 4 Weeks

Week 1	Week 2	Week 3	Week 4
# exposures	# exposures	# exposures	# exposures
Grasp = 6	Grasp = 10	Grasp = 10	Grasp = 10
Gather = 6	Gather = 10	Gather = 10	Gather = 10
Swoop = 6	Swoop = 10	Swoop = 10	Swoop = 10
Dodge = 6	Dodge = 10	Dodge = 10	Dodge = 10

tal language disorder or dyslexia. *Journal of Speech, Language, and Hearing Research, 64*(7), 2734–2749. https://doi.org/10.1044/2021_JSLHR-20-00217

American Speech-Language-Hearing Association. (n.d.). *Late language emergence.* https://www.asha.org/prac tice-portal/clinical-topics/late-language-emergence/

Beck, I. L., McKeown, M. G., & Kucan, L. (2002). *Bringing words to life.* Guilford Press.

Cannon, J. (1993). *Stellaluna.* Houghton Mifflin Harcourt.

Catts, H. W., Fey, M. E., Tomblin, J. B., & Zhang, X. (2002). A longitudinal investigation of reading outcomes in children with language impairments. *Journal of Speech, Language, and Hearing Research, 45*(6), 1142–1157. https://doi.org/10.1044/1092-4388(2002/093)

Cleave, P. L., Becker, S. D., Curran, M. K., Owen Van Horne, A. J., & Fey, M. (2015). The efficacy of recasts in language intervention: A systematic review and meta-analysis. *American Journal of Speech-Language Pathology, 24*(2), 237–255. https://doi.org/10.1044/2015_AJSLP-14-0105

Dale, P. S., Price, T. S., Bishop, D. V., & Plomin, R. (2003). Outcomes of early language delay: Part I. Predicting persistent and transient language difficulties at 3 and 4 years. *Journal of Speech, Language, and Hearing Research, 46*(3), 544–560. https://doi.org/10.1044/1092-4388(2003/044)

Dunn, L. M., & Dunn, D. M. (2007). *Peabody Picture Vocabulary Test* (4th ed.). Pearson.

Ehrler, D. J., & McGhee, R. L. (2008). *Primary Test of Nonverbal Intelligence.* Pro-Ed.

Fey, M. E., Long, S. H., & Finestack, L. H. (2003). Ten principles of grammar facilitation for children with specific language impairment. *American Journal of Speech-Language Pathology, 12*(1), 3–15. https://doi.org/10.1044/1058-0360(2003/048)

Goldman, R., & Fristoe, M. (2015). *Goldman-Fristoe Test of Articulation* (3rd ed.). PsychCorp.

Hadley, P. A., Rispoli, M., & Hsu, N. (2016). Toddlers' verb lexicon diversity and grammatical outcomes. *Language, Speech, and Hearing Services in Schools, 47,* 44–58.

Hall, J., & Plante, E. (2020). Data-informed guideposts for decision making in enhanced conversational recast treatment. *American Journal of Speech-Language Pathology, 29*(4), 2068–2081. https://doi.org/10.1044/2020_AJSLP-20-00017

Justice, L. M., Meier, J., & Walpole, S. (2005). Learning new words from storybooks: An efficacy study with at-risk kindergartners. *Language, Speech, and Hearing Services in Schools, 36,* 17–32. https://doi.org/10.1044/0161-1461(2005/003)

Khan, L. M. L., & Lewis, N. (2015). *Khan-Lewis Phonological Analysis* (3rd ed.). PsychCorp.

Marchman, V. A., & Fernald, A. (2013). Variability in real-time spoken language processing in typically developing and late-talking toddlers. In L. A. Rescorla & P. S. Dale (Eds.), *Late talkers: Language development, interventions, and outcomes* (pp. 145–166). Brookes.

McGregor, K. K., Goffman, L., Owen Van Horne, A., Hogan, T., & Finestack, L. H. (2020). Developmental language disorder: Applications for advocacy, research, and clinical service. *Perspectives of the ASHA Special Interest Groups SIG 1 Language Learning and Education, 5*(1), 38–46. https://doi.org/10.1044/2019_PERSP-19-00083

Owen Van Horne, A. J. (2020). Forum on morphosyntax assessment and intervention for children. *Language, Speech, and Hearing Services in Schools, 51*(2), 179–183. https://doi.org/10.1044/2020_LSHSS-20-00018

Paul, R. (1991). Profiles of toddlers with slow expressive language development. *Topics in Language Disorders, 11*(4), 1–13.

Paul, R. (1996). Clinical implications of the natural history of slow expressive language development. *American Journal of Speech-Language Pathology, 5*(2), 5–21. https://doi.org/10.1044/1058-0360.0502.05

Paul, R., Norbury, C., & Gosse, C. (2018). *Language disorders from infancy through adolescence: Listening, speaking, reading, writing, and communicating* (5th ed.). Elsevier/Mosby.

Plante, E., Mettler, H. M., Tucci, A., & Vance, R. (2019). Maximizing treatment efficiency in developmental language disorder: Positive effects in half the time. *American Journal of Speech-Language Pathology, 28*(3), 1233–1247. https://doi.org/10.1044/2019_AJSLP-18-0285

Plante, E., Ogilvie, T., Vance, R., Aguilar, J. M., Dailey, N. S., Meyers, C., . . . Burton, R. (2014). Variability in the language input to children enhances learning in a treatment context. *American Journal of Speech-Language Pathology, 23*(4), 530–545. https://doi.org/10.1044/2014_AJSLP-13-0038

Rescorla, L. A. (2002). Language and reading outcomes to age 9 in late-talking toddlers. *Journal of Speech, Language, and Hearing Research, 45*(2), 360–371. https://doi.org/10.1044/1092-4388(2002/028)

Rescorla, L. A., & Turner, H. L. (2015). Morphology and syntax in late talkers at age 5. *Journal of Speech, Language, and Hearing Research, 58*(2), 434–444. https://doi.org/10.1044/2015_JSLHR-L-14-0042

Rice, M. L., Oetting, J. B., Marquis, J., Bode, J., & Pae, S. (1994). Frequency of input effects on word comprehension of children with specific language impairment. *Journal of Speech, Language, and Hearing Research, 37*(1), 106–121. https://doi.org/10.1044/jshr.3701.106

Rice, M. L., Taylor, C. L., & Zubrick, S. R. (2008). Language outcomes of 7-year-old children with or without a history of late language emergence at 24 months. *Journal of Speech, Language, and Hearing Research, 51*(2), 394–407. https://doi.org/10.1044/1092-4388(2008/029)

Rice, M. L., & Wexler, K. (2001). *Test of Early Grammatical Impairment.* The Psychological Corporation.

Storkel, H. L., Komesidou, R., Pezold, M. J., Pitt, A. R., Fleming, K. K., & Swinburne Romine, R. (2019). The impact of dose and dose frequency on word learning by kindergarten children with developmental language disorder during interactive book reading. *Language,*

Speech, Hearing Services in Schools, 50(4), 518–539. https://doi.org/10.1044/2019_LSHSS-VOIA-18-0131

Storkel, H. L., Voelmle, K., Fierro, V., Flake, K., Fleming, K. K., & Swinburne Romine, R. (2017). Interactive book reading to accelerate world learning by kindergarten children with specific language impairment: Identifying an adequate intensity and variation in treatment response. *Language, Speech, and Hearing Services in Schools, 48*(1), 16–30. https://doi.org/10.1044/2016_LSHSS-16-0014

Zimmerman, I. L., Steiner, V. G., & Pond, R. E. (2011). *PLS-5: Preschool language scales.* Pearson/PsychCorp.

BILINGUAL/LANGUAGE
CASE 13
Bartolomeo "Bart": A Bilingual Preschool Child

Mariateresa (Teri) H. Muñoz, Shelly S. Chabon, and Noma B. Anderson

Conceptual Knowledge Areas

Children in bilingual environments have different language learning tasks than children in monolingual environments. A child who is developing language in a monolingual environment has the task of acquiring, receptively and expressively, the content, forms, and functions of one language. Being bilingual means that an individual exists in settings where two or more languages operate (Kohnert et al., 2021). The extent to which the individual is exposed to and uses both languages can vary as a function of the people with whom and where the person interacts, and with the function of the linguistic task, that is, speaking, listening, reading, and writing. A child developing language in a bilingual environment must acquire, receptively and expressively, the content, forms, and functions of two (or more) languages. The nature of the child's linguistic input is a crucial factor.

Linguistic input refers to the language models to which the child is exposed (Flaherty et al., 2021). The linguistic goal for many bilingual children is to develop proficiency in both languages across modalities.

There are two processes of bilingual language acquisition. The first, simultaneous language acquisition, refers to acquiring both languages (L1 and L2) at the same time, which is referred to as dual-language learning (Fogle, 2019; Kohnert et al., 2021) and occurs with children 3 years old or younger. In the second process, successive or sequential language acquisition, a child 3 years old or older acquires a second language (L2) after having developed a first, or primary, language (L1). A typical occurrence of successive language acquisition is a young child who acquires L1 in the home and community settings, enters school as an English language learner (ELL), and subsequently acquires English as his or her L2 (Fogle, 2019). A child who is learning English as his or her

L2 follows the same sequence of language acquisition as does a monolingual child who is acquiring English (Höhle et al., 2020).

Irrespective of the child's age or whether the child is displaying simultaneous or successive language acquisition, all of the child's languages should be promoted. Optimum linguistic, cognitive, and academic development occurs when ongoing and continual development of L1 and L2 is facilitated by parents, caregivers, teachers, speech-language pathologists, siblings, peers, and the community. As the successive bilingual language learner progresses through L2 settings, care should be directed to ensure that language skills in L1 are maintained and that the child continues to advance in the acquisition of L1 while acquiring L2 (Fogle, 2019).

Competent assessment of the communication of a bilingual child through the use of standardized tests can be challenging. Appropriate selection and use of norm-referenced tests is dependent upon many factors, including (a) the standardization methodology employed, (b) the comprehensiveness of the assessment, and (c) the accuracy with which these measures diagnose the presence, patterns, and severity of a communication disorder. Speech-language pathologists (SLPs) utilizing a battery of diagnostic tests should make every effort to select language tests that represent the cultural and linguistic systems of the child being tested. SLPs also gather case history information by interviewing parents about their perceptions and knowledge of their child's physical, emotional, linguistic, medical, academic, and social development. Parents provide an overview of the child's development and medical history. Parents' perceptions are particularly important when assessing ELL children. They have a keen sense of the typical development of L1, as demonstrated by typically developing children of that culture.

An overarching professional responsibility of SLPs is to become culturally competent and to fully understand second language acquisition (American Speech-Language-Hearing Association [ASHA], n.d.-a). SLPs recognize that, as bilingual children acquire their language skills, they display language acquisition behaviors that monolingual English-speaking children do not.

Code-switching, which means that the child uses both languages within an utterance, is typical. An example is: "Mommy, where is *mi muñeca* (my doll)?" SLPs appreciate that this is not an example of a communication disorder but rather two languages learned in a typical, not atypical, manner. Another example is when an ELL child in the early stages of language acquisition responds in silence in L2 settings. This silence is often typical of bilingual language acquisition, although the length of the silent phase depends on the individual. A characteristic of simultaneous bilingual language acquisition is the child who develops dual-language systems. For example, the words "water" and "*agua*" initially are not equivalent forms because the child has learned "*agua*" in one context (e.g., bathtub) and "water" in a different context (e.g., water fountain). Accordingly, there may be a period of time when each word is produced with the initial referents. Gradually, the words become equivalent. This example demonstrates a typical feature of bilingual language acquisition and is not considered a communication disorder.

Competent assessment includes analyzing language across a variety of settings and interactions. This ecologically valid assessment procedure is essential because bilingual children's communication behaviors are connected to the setting and the people with whom they interact. Such a comprehensive process is most effectively conducted when the SLP is a member of a multidisciplinary assessment team.

Competent assessment requires that the SLP determines whether the child is (a) displaying second language learning behaviors (i.e., dialectical differences), (b) presenting a communication disorder, or (c) manifesting both dialectical differences related to second language acquisition and a communication disorder (Li'el et al., 2019). The assessment of bilingual ELL children is best performed by an SLP who is proficient in the languages spoken by the child and in the appropriate use of assessment instruments. Since the purpose of the assessment is to appraise the bilingual child's communication development, the child's capability in both languages should be considered. A monolingual speech-language pathologist may choose to work with a translator who is knowledgeable of the assessment process and assessment instruments to assist with this process.

ASHA (2000) takes the position that an essential responsibility of SLPs is to provide clinical services to those who present with communication disorders. It is inappropriate for SLPs to recommend speech-language pathology services for ELL children who do not present with communication disorders (ASHA, Committee on the Status of Racial Minorities, 1983; Li'el et al., 2019).

There are several approaches SLPs employ to facilitate the acquisition of English for ELL children who do not exhibit a communication disorder. One approach is to collaborate with parents to guide the linguistic input that children receive in the home setting (Li'el et al., 2019). SLPs may encourage parents to maintain L1 in the home during daily activities and family interactions, such as storytelling, reading, and communicating verbally (Marchman et al., 2020). The same recommendation may be offered regarding L2, if this is a comfortable language for family interaction in the home. If L2 is not used for family interaction, then L1 must be as rich as possible to ensure its continued development. SLPs may also collaborate with the child's teacher(s) to guide the linguistic input that the child receives in the classroom to foster the acquisition of L2, emphasizing language content, language forms, and language functions that promote academic success. ASHA (n.d.-a) acknowledges that parents of a bilingual child may seek the expertise of an SLP to teach the child the phonology, semantics, syntax, and pragmatics of English. Though this is elective therapy, it represents a common decision for many parents.

It is the responsibility of the SLP to treat the communication disorders that the bilingual child exhibits (ASHA, Committee on the Status of Racial Minorities, 1985). Analysis of the phonological, syntactic, and pragmatic errors is presented in L1 and L2. A treatment plan is designed that addresses the child's L1 and L2 communication errors.

When a bilingual child is assessed, the child's development in both languages should be captured to obtain an appropriate diagnosis. For instance, if speech and/or language skills in both languages are poor or atypical, this could be indicative of a language disorder. If the child's Spanish (L1) and English (L2) receptive language skills are commensurate with a child's developmental and/or chronological age level and the expressive language skills in both Spanish (L1) and English (L2) are significantly below the respective receptive language skills, developmental level, or chronological age, then the child more than likely presents with a language disorder. However, if the child's Spanish (L1) language skills are commensurate with the chronological age level and significantly higher than his or her English (L2) language skills, then the SLP may consider ruling out a language disorder and instead implement appropriate strategies to assist the child with the acquisition of English.

Description of the Case

Background Information

Bartolomeo (Bart) is a 4-year, 11-month-old boy who was born in the United States and lives with his mother, aunt, two older cousins (Kana and Rita), and maternal grandmother. Both his aunt and mother are second-generation immigrants from Cuba. Therefore, in his household, Spanish is the prominent language spoken. His maternal family owns a small neighborhood restaurant. Spanish is generally spoken in the restaurant, although there are some English-speaking patrons. His parents separated when he was 3 years of age. He visits his father, a monolingual Spanish speaker, every Wednesday night and stays overnight every other weekend from Saturday to Sunday. Therefore, he speaks only Spanish when he is with his father. However, he has opportunities to speak both Spanish and English in his home environment since his cousins, Kana and Rita, prefer to speak in English. Bart has other opportunities to listen to the English language when watching his favorite cartoons and at school. Bart is in prekindergarten in Florida. Since the school instruction and activities are conducted in English, Bart has frequent opportunities to use his L2 with his teacher and peers. Since his intellectual quotient (IQ) is 110, as measured by a psychoeducational test, his development and language skills should be commensurate with his chronological age. However, there were some concerns about his expressive language skills in both Spanish and English.

Reason for Referral

Initially, Bart was placed in the English Speakers of Other Languages (ESOL) program due to his limited English expressive language abilities during classroom activities and performance on the English Proficiency Test. The ESOL program aims to provide students whose first language is not English with the opportunity to improve their English language proficiency (Villegas & Pompa, 2020). An English Proficiency Test is initiated at a public school in Florida when the parent or guardian responds "yes" to at least one of the following questions: *Is another language other than English* (a) *spoken at home*, (b) *the primary language*, and/ or (b) *used at home* (Villegas & Pompa, 2020)? Based on the English Proficiency Test results, the students are classified into an ESOL level ranging from Levels 1 (lowest) to 5 (highest, indicating proficiency as a native speaker). The classification of an ELL with an ESOL Language Proficiency Level 3 (*Developing*) (Grapin & Lee, 2021) was selected since Bart (a) understood basic knowledge of the language content; (b) produced short sentences with a limited syntax model, such as *subject + verb + object*; (c) demonstrated the use of frequent syntax (grammatical) errors; and (d) maintained a conversation using simple related sentences. Once participating in the English proficiency class for 2 weeks, his ESOL teacher felt that the program was not an appropriate placement. Mrs. Villa, a Spanish-English bilingual speaker, noticed that, similar to his English expressive language skills, Bart's Spanish expressive language skills were not at age level compared to his typically developing peers. Mrs. Villa referred Bart to a bilingual SLP to evaluate his communication skills and determine whether there was a *language difference* (influence of L1 on second language learning) or a *language disorder*.

Findings of the Evaluation

Bart was evaluated by the school's bilingual SLP, Mrs. Hernández, in both Spanish and English. The following language and speech assessments and informal assessments were administered: (1) Preschool Language Scales 5th Edition, Spanish (PLS-5, Spanish); (2) Preschool Language Scales 5th Edition (PLS-5) (Zimmerman et al., 2011); (3) Informal Language Sample Analysis in Spanish and English; (4) Pragmatic Checklist; (5) Goldman-Fristoe Test of Articulation-3, Spanish; (6) Goldman-Fristoe Test of Articulation-3; (7) oral-motor peripheral examination; (8) voice screening; and (9) fluency screening.

Standardized Measurements of Receptive and Expressive Language Skills

Bart's receptive and expressive language skills were assessed using a standardized instrument available in Spanish and English, the PLS-5, Spanish and PLS-5, respectively. The initial and 6-month evaluations demonstrated that Bart's receptive language skills were within his chronological age level. However, his performance on the expressive subtests in both languages indicated that his expressive language skills, although commensurate with each other, were significantly below his receptive language skills, age level, and overall potential, as indicated by his IQ. This disparity between his receptive language and expressive language skills was indicative of an expressive language disorder in both languages.

Language Sample Analysis

A language sample analysis (LSA) was used to determine Bart's morphosyntactical level in Spanish and English by calculating his mean length of utterance (MLU). The calculation of the MLU is frequently used to identify language disorders in children (Finestack & Satterlund, 2018; Gallagher & Hoover, 2020). To determine Bart's MLU of morphemes in Spanish (MLU-m), Mrs. Hernández used the Linares-Orama and Sanders (1977) methodology. This methodology accounts for gender, number, diminutive, and augmentative inflections for nouns and adjectives; pronoun case; and the person, tense, and mood used in verbs (Gutiérrez-Clellen et al., 2000). To calculate Bart's MLU in English, Mrs. Hernández referred to Roger Brown's (1973) *Stages of Syntactic and Morphological Development* (1973), which identifies the age acquisition of common morphosyntactical features in typically developing children (Ezeizabarrena & Garcia Fernandez, 2018; Gallagher & Hoover, 2020). However, due to the syntactical variance among both languages, the MLUm in Spanish will account for a higher number of morphemes than a comparable level in English. For instance, in Spanish, "Ellos bañan perro" has a morpheme count of 8. This breakdown is as follows: (a) "Ellos" (stem "El" + third-person + gender + plural), $n = 4$; (b) + "bañan" (stem "baña-" + third person), $n = 2$; and (c) + "perro" (stem "perr-" + gender), $n = 2$, which is a total morphological count of $N = 8$. Whereas the morpheme count for "They *wash* dog" in English is "they" (pronoun), $n = 1$; + "wash" (verb), $n = 1$; + "dog" (noun), $n = 1$, which is a total morphological count of $N = 3$. When calculating Bart's MLUm in Spanish, 7.5 was derived. In English, his MLU was 2.5. Although the count differed in both languages, Bart's expressive language skills during conversational speech yielded a comparable level since his syntax skills were analyzed differently for each language, as indicated in the aforementioned example. However, both calculations indicated that Bart's expressive language skills were significantly delayed for a child his chronological age in both languages, which was consistent with the results on the PLS-5, Spanish and PLS-5.

Pragmatic Language Checklist

Bart's pragmatic skills were assessed to determine his ability to use language appropriately. During conversational speech and play activities, he was able to take turns during three to four exchanges. Bart was also able to follow two- to three-step commands. Additionally, he was able to initiate and maintain topics, make requests, and maintain eye contact with the speaker. His pragmatic language skills were deemed appropriate for a child his chronological age.

Standardized Assessment of Articulation Skills

The Goldman-Fristoe Test of Articulation-3 (GFTA-3) is a standardized norm-referenced test that assesses a child's articulation skills in words and sentences. This instrument has a Spanish and English version. The GFTA-3, Spanish was administered to assess Bart's production of Spanish consonant speech sounds in single words only. In Spanish, Bart was unable to produce /r/, /g/, /ɲ/ for ñ, /ʧ/, and /r/ for "rr." Bart's raw score on this instrument was $n = 5$. This score yielded a standard score of 111, with a confidence interval range at 90% of 104 to 116 and a percentile rank of 76.8. These scores indicated that Bart's articulation errors in Spanish were developmental in nature since it is frequently seen in children of his chronological age. On the GFTA-3, he also demonstrated several phonemic errors in English words. He had difficulties with earlier developing phonemes, such as /v/, /ʤ/, /s/, / ʧ/, /l/, /ʃ/, and /z/, which are typically acquired between 4:0 and 4:11 (Crowe & McLeod, 2020). The phonemes /ɹ/, /ð/, /ʒ/, and consonant clusters, acquired between 5:0 and 5:11 (Crowe & McLeod, 2020), were either omitted or substituted. He also substituted the /θ/ with the /s/, which is dialectal (accent related) in nature. Other sound errors consisted of dialectical variations, such as the substitution of /d/ for/ ð/ and /ʃ/ for /ʧ/. The dialectal errors related to the absence of these phonemes in the Spanish phonology system are commonly seen in children whose L1 is Spanish and L2 is English. Of the 11 phonemic errors, 7 were dialectal variations. Since some earlier and later developing errors, /v/, /ʤ/, /ʧ/, /z/, /ɹ/, /ð/, /θ/, demonstrated the influence of Spanish phonemes on the production of English phonemes, these errors were not included in Bart's raw score. Bart's true raw score on the GFTA-3 was $n = 4$, yielding a standard score of 109, with a confidence interval range at 90% of 102 to 115 and a percentile rank of 73%. These results in both languages suggested that the phonemic errors were all developmental in nature. Additionally, Bart's oral-motor, voice, and fluency skills were deemed within normal limits.

Summary

Based on the evaluation results, Bart's oral-motor development, articulation, voice, fluency, and pragmatic skills were within normal limits for his chronological age and gender.

Bart's Spanish and English receptive language skills also appeared to be within normal limits. A spontaneous English language sample included several instances of syntax models typically seen in Spanish. For example, he said, "Car blue" when asked to describe a car. In Spanish, the adjective is placed after the noun, "*Carro azul*." Although this syntax model was an influence of L1 on L2, Bart's expressive language skills were significantly below age level in both languages. Results on formal and informal measurements indicated an expressive language disorder.

Clinical Impressions

This 4-year, 11-month-old boy presented with a moderate to severe expressive language disorder. His expressive language skills in both languages led to this diagnosis and were the focus of the treatment plan. Bart's norm-referenced results yielded a standard deviation of –1.73 (moderate disorder) and –2.06 (severe disorder) in his Spanish and English expressive language skills, respectively. Therefore, language therapy was recommended to address his expressive language skills in both languages. Two bilingual SLPs implemented coordinated therapy; one addressed expressive language skills in Spanish (clinical setting), and the other focused on his use of English in the school setting. Bart received 60 minutes of language therapy twice weekly. Although his articulation errors were developmental and dialectical in nature, articulation errors were monitored to determine if future remediation is warranted.

Course of Treatment

Therapy Goals and Objectives

Long-Term Goal. Improve expressive language skills in Spanish and English

Short-Term Objectives. Bart will be able to:

1. improve MLU by combining four to five words in spontaneous conversational speech with 80% accuracy within three consecutive sessions in Spanish and English;
2. name pictures of objects at a 4- to 5-year-old level with 80% accuracy within three consecutive sessions in Spanish and English;
3. improve syntax by using adjectives using the model article + adjective + noun + verb in English utterances with 80% accuracy within three consecutive sessions; and
4. improve syntax by using adjectives using the model article + noun + adjective + verb in Spanish utterances with 80% accuracy within three consecutive sessions.

Therapy Approach

Therapy sessions included techniques, such as the use of the hierarchy of prompting (gestural cues, verbal cues, visual cues, model, partial physical assistance, full physical assistance), storytelling, and hands-on activities to elicit target objectives. This therapeutic approach aimed to improve expressive vocabulary and elicit age-appropriate utterances that demonstrated an increase in utterance length and complexity (MLU) and the use of morphosyntactical markers, such as auxiliary verbs, articles, and pronouns (ASHA, n.d.-b).

Age-appropriate materials, such as toys, familiar household and environmental objects, and pictures, were important for language elicitation.

Therapy Outcomes

After 6 months of therapy, improvement was noted in Bart's expressive language skills in Spanish and English. He combined four to five words in connected discourse in Spanish 40% of the time spontaneously and an additional 20% when provided with verbal cues. In English, he produced four- to five-word utterances spontaneously 30% of the time and an additional 10% when provided with verbal and gestural cues. He named pictures of household objects 40% of the time in Spanish and English spontaneously. After 6 months of therapy, Bart produced the following syntax models spontaneously: *article + noun + adjective + verb* (in Spanish) and *article + adjective + noun + verb* (in English), 40% of the time in Spanish and 25% of the time in English, respectively.

Analysis of Client's Response to Intervention

Bart received bilingual expressive language therapy services from two bilingual SLPs, one conducted therapy in Spanish one day and the other in English on another day. With intense and linguistically coordinated therapy services, in 6 months, Bart made favorable progress in both languages. Bart's therapy continued until his expressive language skills reached age appropriateness. It is very important for children who speak more than one language to have experiences that continuously foster their linguistic, cognitive, and social development in all of their languages across a wide variety of settings—home, school, clinical setting, and community.

Authors' Note

This case is fictionalized and was inspired by several children we have worked with.

References

American Speech-Language-Hearing Association. (n.d.-a). *Bilingual service delivery* [Practice portal]. https://www.asha.org/Practice-Portal/Professional-Issues/Bilingual-Service-Delivery/

American Speech-Language-Hearing Association. (n.d.-b). *Spoken language disorders*. https://www.asha.org/

American Speech-Language-Hearing Association. (2000). *Guidelines for the roles and responsibilities of the school-based speech-language pathologist* [Guidelines]. https://www.asha.org/policy/

American Speech-Language-Hearing Association, Committee on the Status of Racial Minorities. (1983).

Social dialects. *ASHA, 25,* 23–27. https://www.asha.org

American Speech-Language-Hearing Association, Committee on the Status of Racial Minorities. (1985). Clinical management of communicatively handicapped minority language populations [Position statement]. *ASHA, 27*(6), 29–32. https://www.asha.org

Brown, R. (1973). *A first language: The early stages.* Harvard University Press. https://doi.org/10.4159/harvard.9780674732469

Crowe, K., & McLeod, S. (2020). Children's English consonant acquisition in the United States: A review. *American Journal of Speech-Language Pathology, 29*(4), 2155–2169. https://doi.org/10.1044/2020_AJSLP-19-00168

Ezeizabarrena, M. J., & Garcia Fernandez, I. (2018). Length of utterance, in morphemes or in words? MLU3-w, a reliable measure of language development in early Basque. *Frontiers in Psychology, 8,* 2265, 1–17. https://www.frontiersin.org/articles/10.3389/fpsyg.2017.02265/full

Finestack, L. H., & Satterlund, K. E. (2018). Current practice of child grammar intervention: A survey of speech-language pathologists. *American Journal of Speech-Language Pathology, 27*(4), 1329–1351. https://doi.org/10.1044/2018_AJSLP-17-0168

Flaherty, M., Hunsicker, D., & Goldin-Meadow, S. (2021). Structural biases that children bring to language learning: A cross-cultural look at gestural input to homesign. *Cognition, 211,* 104608. https://doi.org/10.1016/j.cognition.2021.104608

Fogle, P. T. (2019). *Essentials of communication sciences & disorders.* Jones & Bartlett Learning.

Gallagher, J. F., & Hoover, J. R. (2020). Measure what you treat: Using language sample analysis for grammatical outcome measures in children with developmental language disorder. *Perspectives of the ASHA Special Interest Groups, 5*(2), 350–363. https://doi.org/10.1044/2019_PERSP-19-00100

Grapin, S. E., & Lee, O. (2021). WIDA English language development standards framework, 2020 edition: Key shifts and emerging tensions. *TESOL Quarterly, 56*(2), 827–839. https://doi.org/10.1002/tesq.3092

Gutiérrez-Clellen, V. F., Restrepo, M. A., Bedore, L., Peña, E., & Anderson, R. (2000). Language sample analysis in Spanish-speaking children: Methodological considerations. *Language, Speech, and Hearing Services in Schools, 31*(1), 88–98. https://doi.org/10.1044/0161-1461.3101.88

Höhle, B., Bijeljac-Babic, R., & Nazzi, T. (2020). Variability and stability in early language acquisition:

Comparing monolingual and bilingual infants' speech perception and word recognition. *Bilingualism: Language and Cognition, 23,* 56–71. https://doi.org/10.1017/ S1366728919000348

Kohnert, K., Ebert, K. D., & Pham, G. T. (2021). *Language disorders in bilingual children and adults.* Plural Publishing.

Li'el, N., Williams, C., & Kane, R. (2019). Identifying developmental language disorder in bilingual children from diverse linguistic backgrounds. *International Journal of Speech-Language Pathology, 21*(6), 613–622. https://doi.org/10.1080/17549507.2018.1513073

Linares-Orama, N., & Sanders, L. J. (1977). Evaluation of syntax in three-year-old Spanish-speaking Puerto Rican children. *Journal of Speech and Hearing Research, 20*(2), 350–357. https://doi.org/10.1044/ jshr.2002.350

Marchman, V. A., Bermúdez, V. N., Bang, J. Y., & Fernald, A. (2020). Off to a good start: Early Spanish-language processing efficiency supports Spanish-and English-language outcomes at 4½ years in sequential bilinguals. *Developmental Science, 23*(6), e12973. https://doi.org/10.1111/desc.12973

Villegas, L., & Pompa, D. (2020). *The patchy landscape of state English learner policies under ESSA.* Migration Policy Institute. https://www.migrationpolicy.org/ research/state-english-learner-policies-essa

Zimmerman, I. L., Steiner, V. G., & Pond, R. E. (2011). *Preschool Language Scale, Fifth edition (PLS-5)* (p. 52). Pearson.

LANGUAGE
CASE 14
Lilly: A Case Study of a Preschool Child Who Was Internationally Adopted
Jenny A. Roberts and Kathleen A. Scott

Conceptual Knowledge Areas

Many children who were internationally adopted (IA) are part of a high-risk group who frequently have communication delays upon arrival to their new homes. It is therefore important to understand what puts some IA children at risk for communication disorders. IA children adopted into the United States represent a diverse population. Their preadoption experiences can vary widely as a function of the settings in which they reside, their nutrition and health, quality and amount of caregiver interaction, and duration of time spent in institutional or foster care (Johnson et al., 1998). The social, economic, and political factors related to the country of origin influence the adoption process and the subsequent early development of

the IA child (Eckerle et al., 2021; Pollock, 2020). For example, children adopted into the United States between 1950 and 1980 came mainly from Korea, due to effects of the Korean War, whereas in the late 1980s and early 1990s, large numbers of international adoptees came from Romania and Russia (see Pollock, 2020). Poverty, illness, war, and social upheaval in their home countries have led to the adoption of many children from Ethiopia, Haiti, Columbia, and Guatemala.

A different set of social, economic, and political concerns impacts the preadoption experiences of children adopted from China, when children were abandoned largely due to China's one-child policy, beginning in the early 1990s and peaking in 2005. During the 1990s and 2000s, these children were mostly girls adopted as infants and young toddlers (Pollock, 2020). Special needs adoption from China became official in 2000 (Tan et al., 2007) and a dramatic increase in adoption of children of special needs adoption was seen between 2005 and 2009, increasing from 9% to 49% (Selman, 2015). Currently, almost all children adopted from China are adopted from the "Waiting Child" program; they are either older children with or without special needs or younger children with special needs, which include conditions such as congenital heart disease, cleft lip and/or palate disorders, limb differences, and other conditions (Miller et al., 2016; Pollock, 2020; waitingchildinfo.com). Overall, the average age at the time of adoption has increased; from 2018 to the present, 66% of children from China were adopted between the ages of 3 and 12 years (U.S. Department of State, 2022).

While international adoption has seen historic changes and the rates of adoption continue to shift, international adoption worldwide is declining (Eckerle et al., 2021; Selman, 2022). Furthermore, the preadoption care of IA children worldwide has improved, with better institutional living environments and an increased number of children living in foster care. Nevertheless, factors such as the number of caregivers, frequency of caregiver interactions in orphanages, and whether a child receives foster placement vary for individual children (Windsor et al., 2007); these variables can impact communication development. Although conditions have improved, institutional living environments negatively affect the development of children residing within them, and as a result, IA children are at risk due to their preadoption experiences.

In addition to challenging early life experiences, children who were internationally adopted into the United States are overwhelmingly adopted by monolingual English-speaking families, (e.g., Glennen, 2020) and must adjust to an abrupt loss of exposure to their native language. Because of the lack of maintenance of the native language, they are in effect "second first language" learners (Glennen, 2020; Pollock, 2020; Roberts, Pollock, Krakow, Price, et al., 2005), in that they are acquiring a second language prior to full acquisition of a first language and at a time when their first language is no longer available to them (see Glen-

nen, 2020, for further discussion). While some IA children will develop their second first language rapidly and without apparent difficulty, other children may struggle (e.g., Roberts, Pollock, & Krakow, 2005). An important question for parents and clinicians alike is whether the trajectory of growth and achievement of language milestones for any individual IA child is within the expected abilities of other IA children. The story of Lilly will help illustrate how to determine this.

Description of the Case

Lilly, a 3-year, 3-month-old child, was adopted from China when she was 2;1 years of age. She was adopted by Tim and Barbara M., who have one biological son, Toby, who is 11 years old. The family lives in a suburb of New York City. Tim, age 51, holds a PhD in electrical engineering and commutes to New York City daily. Barbara, age 46, has a master's degree in English literature and works part-time as a proofreader for a major economics magazine. She works at home 2 days a week and commutes to her office 1 day a month. Their son attends a nearby public elementary school and is active in sports most days after school. Tim and Barbara are typical of many parents that adopt internationally in that they are older than parents of preschool-aged children, well educated, and financially secure (Roberts, Pollock, Krakow, Price, et al., 2005). Tim and Barbara have close friends who adopted two girls from China as infants. Tim and Barbara wanted a second child and were interested in adopting from China. They discovered, however, that unlike for their friends, the children available from China came exclusively from the Waiting Child program, and they were provided by their adoption agency with a list of possible special needs to consider when applying for adoption. They indicated their preferences to their agency and were matched with a toddler, Lilly, who had a correctable heart condition for which she would need surgery. Tim and Barbara's adoption agency reported that currently Lilly was in fair medical health, underweight, and that she tired easily. Her language skills were reported to be adequate but her overall communication ability had not been formally evaluated.

Shortly after arrival to the United States, Lilly's heart was successfully repaired and her doctors indicated that her recovery and prognosis were excellent. Tim and Barbara were pleased with Lilly's progress since they recognized that many children with special needs may have substantial medical needs requiring significant and continuing medical intervention (Miller et al., 2016). Lilly soon settled into her new life and began to gain weight rapidly, though she remained small for her age. Because Tim and Barbara were familiar with the development of the children from China adopted by their friends, they were initially not concerned that Lilly seemed to be slow to produce new English words, especially since she seemed to understand most of what was said to her. When she did speak, her speech sounded "garbled" to them. They assumed that when she learned additional English words, she would soon be speaking clearly and regularly.

However, after 6 months of being home, Barbara and Tim began to be concerned that her language skills might not be developing as expected, especially since she had recovered very well from her surgery and in all other ways appeared to be thriving. A few months after her surgery, Lilly received a multidisciplinary evaluation at an early intervention clinic that included language assessment on a general assessment measure in English. Barbara also completed several questionnaire-based instruments, including the MacArthur Communicative Development Inventories: Words and Sentences (CDI; Fenson et al., 1993), a parent report instrument of expressive vocabulary and early sentence development. Lilly was producing 113 English words at 32 months on that instrument. On the general assessment measure, Lilly demonstrated limited use of expressive language, although receptive language abilities were emerging well, and she showed good pragmatic abilities. A Mandarin-Chinese interpreter who translated directions from English into Mandarin indicated that Lilly understood numerous words and sentences. However, Lilly provided only a few single-word responses in Mandarin when prompted. She also demonstrated slightly delayed fine motor skills.

Lilly was determined to be eligible for early intervention services in occupational therapy and speech/language. She began receiving language stimulation in her home from a developmental educator 3 hours per week for 5 months, until she turned 3 years of age. In addition, because she was approaching her third year, Barbara made an appointment for Lilly to be evaluated as part of the process to potentially transition Lilly to preschool special education services. Due to a planned month-long family vacation, as well as scheduling difficulties, Lilly was not evaluated until she was 3 years, 3 months of age. The following describes her assessment and subsequent treatment plan.

Assessment Procedure

To prepare for the evaluation, Janice Mohegan, the preschool speech-language pathologist (SLP) assigned to assess Lilly's communication skills, reviewed the literature on the language development of IA children. Janice learned that by 2 years postadoption, children adopted from China were performing within the average or above-average range on norm-referenced tests normed on monolingual English speakers (e.g., Roberts, Pollock, Krakow, Price, et al., 2005; Tan & Yang, 2005). Janice knew from her research that best current practice dictated the use of local norms, which would allow her to interpret Lilly's performance on norm-referenced tests in accordance with the norms of IA children established by these research studies, not only by the performance of the normative sample of the tests (Glennen, 2007; Roberts, Pollock, & Krakow, 2005). However, given that children with medical conditions like Lilly were not included in these studies, she realized she would need to exercise caution in her interpretation.

At the evaluation, Janice collected a careful case history and medical history from Barbara, and obtained copies of reports from Barbara of Lilly's prior assessment and treatment plan in Early Intervention. Janice obtained permission from Barbara to contact the developmental educator who had worked with Lilly in her home, who reported that Lilly was a "delightful child" with appropriate play and social interaction skills, and "slowly improving" language skills. Next, Janice chose a battery of tests that assessed a range of language abilities and whose local norms could be found in the IA literature for children fairly similar to Lilly in age and who had been adopted as toddlers. She administered the Peabody Picture Vocabulary Test–Fifth Edition (PPVT-5; Dunn, 2019); the Clinical Evaluation of Language Fundamentals Preschool, Third Edition (CELF-P 3; Wiig et al., 2020); and the Goldman-Fristoe Test of Articulation-3 (GFTA-3; Goldman & Fristoe, 2015).

In addition, Janice obtained a language sample, during which time Lilly and Barbara played with a toy dollhouse, farm, and accessories in her office, which Janice recorded and later transcribed using a computer program that automates transcription and analysis of language samples (Systematic Analysis of Language Transcription [SALT]; Miller & Iglesias, 2020). Because SALT provides limited information about syntactic structures, Janice scored an Index of Productive Syntax (IPSyn) to examine the breadth and types of syntactic structures Lilly produced during the language sample (Altenberg et al., 2018). She examined four subscales of noun phrase, verb phrase, question and negation structures, and other sentence structures, looking for evidence of up to two exemplars each for 59 syntactic structures.

Janice planned to score the IPSyn and then to determine if additional testing would provide more insight into Lilly's language acquisition. If additional testing was necessary, Janice planned to elicit more advanced structures on a subsequent visit, using a list of probes (Roberts et al., 2022) and a dynamic assessment method to judge whether Lilly required significant examiner effort (in the form of cues and repetition) in order to produce structures. Janice knew that dynamic assessment could be a powerful form of assessment for determining if a child who is learning English is demonstrating difficulties more consistent with a language disorder, as static, norm-referenced tests often overidentify language impairment in that population (Bedore & Peña, 2008). She recognized that Lilly was not experiencing a typical form of sequential bilingualism but was instead a second first language learner. Thus, she reasoned that

tapping into the language-learning process could provide insights into Lilly's language abilities.

Findings of the Evaluation

Table 14–1 shows the results of the norm-referenced tests. From this table, it can be seen that, in comparison to monolingual English-speaking norms, Lilly's receptive vocabulary on the PPVT-5 was in the average range of performance, and her receptive language composite on the CELF-P 3 was slightly above average. Inspection of individual subtests on the CELF-P 3 revealed that listening comprehension and understanding of basic concepts was well above average and that a measure of syntax comprehension (*Sentence Comprehension*) was in the low-average range. In comparison to monolingual English-speaking children, Lilly performed significantly more poorly on expressive language measures on the CELF-P 3, falling into the clinical range for monolingual English-speaking children on all three expressive language subtests. For example, when asked to repeat sentences said by the examiner in the context of a story (*Recalling Sentences*), Lilly frequently omitted whole words of the sentences. On a measure of single-word production, however, the GFTA-3, Lilly performed within the average range of ability.

From the language sample, Janice obtained scores of mean length of utterance (MLU), number of different root words (NDW), and total number of words used during the session (TNW), along with other basic measures of language that SALT provides. Lilly's MLU was 1.98, her NDW was 71, and her TNW was 181. In comparison to English monolingual peers derived from the SALT database, all three of these values fell more than 2 standard deviations below the mean of these children. Janice obtained a printout from SALT of the grammatical morphemes that Lilly used while playing with Barbara. Using Brown's developmental morphemes as a guide, as seen in the IPSyn scoresheet (Roberts et al., 2022), she determined that Lilly produced plural –s frequently and had one occurrence of the copula "is." No other free or bound morphemes from Brown's list of 14 grammatical morphemes were observed.

Table 14–1. Norm-Referenced Language Assessment Results

Area Assessed	Measure[a]	Standard Scores
Receptive vocabulary	PPVT-5	111
Single-word articulation	GFTA-3	92
Receptive Language Index	CELF-P 3	111
Following Directions		13
Basic Concepts		15
Sentence Comprehension		8
Expressive Language Index	CELF-P 3	69
Recalling Sentences		3
Formulating Labels		6
Words and Sentences		5

Note. CELF-P 3 = Clinical Evaluation of Language Fundamentals–Preschool 3; GFTA-3 = Goldman-Fristoe Test of Articulation-3; PPVT-3 = Peabody Picture Vocabulary Test-5.

[a]"Measure" is not meant to endorse a particular instrument or method of assessment.

Typical sentences that Lilly produced were "draw mommy," "this fork," and "I want blue." An examination of the IPSyn showed that Lilly had limited production of structures across all four subscales, verb phrase structures were particularly sparse, and she produced no complex sentences. Lilly produced many one-word labels of objects in the room and used these single-word utterances to draw her mother's attention to them. After Janice scored the IPSyn, when she saw the limited use of structures, she decided to attempt to elicit more advanced structures on a subsequent visit. In that visit, she used a list of probes for the IPSyn (Roberts et al., 2022) and a dynamic assessment procedure. She first provided two practice items for target probes, then a test item. For example, to elicit a third-person singular verb form, she presented pictures that could elicit a sentence such as "she likes to eat." If Lilly did not produce the form, Janice provided repetition, elicited imitation, and cueing. She was able to elicit a prepositional phrase and a copula with effort but was not successful in eliciting any additional structures.

Representation of the Problem at the Time of Evaluation

Janice first compared the assessment results with the published normative data. The normative data indicated that, in comparison to monolingual English-speaking children of the same age, Lilly was having primary difficulties with expressive language. Her receptive language appeared to be developing without difficulty. Though syntax comprehension was low average, her other receptive language scores were well within or above the average range on both the CELF-P 3 and the PPVT-5. In fact, vocabulary understanding was a particular strength. For expressive language, articulation at the single word level was in the average range according to the results of the GFTA-3, but the CELF-P 3 expressive language scores were low across all the subtests. The results of the language sample, in comparison to monolingual English-speaking children, also confirmed that in spontaneous use, expressive language appeared below age expectations.

However, Janice was not ready to conclude where Lilly was performing in the clinical range of ability. She first needed to consult the available literature of IA children of similar age, length of exposure to English, and preadoption circumstances to see how Lilly compared to them, as well as examine results from the language sample, IPSyn, and dynamic assessment.

First, she examined Lilly's performance on the CDI when she was 32 months old. Recall that Lilly was administered the CDI in her initial evaluation. Janice consulted several research reports of vocabulary growth of children adopted from China and determined that 113 words produced on the CDI was a significantly fewer number of words than those produced by other children adopted from China at a similar age and for a similar duration of English language exposure (Krakow & Roberts, 2003; Pollock, 2005; Price et al., 2006). For example, Janice learned that for children adopted after 24 months of age, Pollock (2005) reported that after 6 months of English language exposure, they were producing on average approximately 280 words on the CDI. Thus, not only was Lilly a late talker by monolingual English-speaking norms, but more importantly, she was a late talker in comparison to other IA children from China.

Second, Janice examined Lilly's performance on the norm-referenced measures with the available normative information on similar norm-referenced measures for children adopted from China. She also examined performance of individual low-scoring subjects when it was reported in these papers. She determined that on similar instruments for IA children of a comparable age and duration of English language exposure, Lilly was performing below her IA peers in expressive language. For example, Roberts and her colleagues (Roberts, Pollock, Krakow, Price, et al., 2005) reported norm-referenced test scores for 55 preschool children adopted from China between 8 and 25 months of age. They reported that the average standard score on the PPVT-III was 117.6, the CELF-P II Receptive language composite score was 120.8, the CELF-P II Expressive language composite score was 118.6, and the GFTA-II standard

score was 112.6. Test standard scores across all tests ranged considerably, from a low of 48 to a high of 142. However, only 3 of 55 children performed below 1.25 standard deviations of the mean on two or more composite or test measures. For those three children, Roberts, Pollock, Krakow, Price, et al. (2005) reported that their standard scores ranged from 76 to 113 on the PPVT-III, 66 to 96 on the CELF-P II Receptive language composite, 67 to 73 on the CELF-P II Expressive language composite, and 48 to 104 on the GFTA. Thus, Lilly's norm-referenced expressive language scores were much more comparable to the *low*-scoring children in the study than to the group averages.

Janice also consulted the literature with respect to language sample outcomes. Language sample analysis has been used historically by SLPs primarily as a supplement to data obtained from norm-referenced testing and to examine the language of children from culturally and linguistically diverse backgrounds (Gutiérrez-Clellen & Simon-Cereijido, 2009); Janice found limited data available on the spontaneous language abilities of IA children, making results particularly hard to evaluate in diagnostic terms. She could locate only one study of the spontaneous language of IA children adopted from China (Price et al., 2006), which provided language sample data on six girls adopted from China as infants. At age 3, the children's MLUs ranged from 1.9 to 4.0, NDWs ranged from 72 to 132, and TNWs ranged from 137 to 375. Of these six girls, the one with the lowest values on all of these measures also was performing in the below-average range on norm-referenced test measures similar to those used to examine Lilly. The researchers also found that parental concern was an important factor in determining the language abilities of the children. The authors of that study concluded that this child was in the delayed range in comparison to other children adopted from China.

On the IPSyn, Lilly's overall production of syntactic structures and total IPSyn score of 33 were similar to that of late-talking monolingual toddlers (Rescorla et al., 2000) and at the lower end of their range of scores. Lilly showed limited use of structures in all four subscales of the instrument.

Following guidelines from the American Speech-Language-Hearing Association's (ASHA, n.d.) practice portal on dynamic assessment, Janice judged that it had required high clinician effort to elicit only a few forms from Lilly and that no additional structures could be elicited. As indicated by ASHA, high examiner effort combined with low child responsiveness on a suitable dynamic assessment task typically indicates the presence of a language disorder rather than normal acquisition processes of children learning a new language.

Janice noted that Lilly's other language sample scores were similar to those of the delayed child in Price et al.'s (2006) study. In addition, Janice knew that Tim and Barbara were concerned about Lilly's language development. As such, Janice felt that the language sample analysis, coupled with parent report, provided crucial information regarding Lilly's overall language skills. Janice recognized that language samples are often used as criterion-referenced measures and are suitable as a source of goal formation (Roberts et al., 2022). Janice determined that many appropriate language goals for Lilly could be drawn from her initial sample, and with the collection of a second sample, she could use these as baseline and outcome measures in determining progress in therapy.

Janice also considered that although Lilly was a toddler upon arrival, and she was within the age range of studies of the language development of children adopted from China, she was different from the children in those studies in that she had a special need. However, Janice felt comfortable that her assessment and interpretation of the outcome of the assessment had been appropriate for Lilly. Based upon the careful examination of all of the available assessment evidence including norm-referenced test scores, language sample outcomes, IPSyn scores, and dynamic assessment, along with the established literature of IA children, Lilly's prior treatment history, Janice's clinical experience, and the concern of the family, Janice concluded that Lilly was performing outside of the average range for expressive language in comparison to other girls adopted from China and should receive services.

Treatment Options and Considerations

From her analysis, Janice formulated long-term treatment goals for Lilly, which were to increase sentence length, particularly in verb phrase structures including use of Brown's grammatical morphemes, and increase vocabulary diversity. Janice decided to simultaneously address these goals by targeting infrequently used or unused free and bound grammatical morphemes to lengthen sentences. Her specific goals for Lilly were to increase Lilly's use of three grammatical morphemes that occur early in development (present progressive –ing, irregular past tense, and articles a/the) that were not present or little used in Lilly's language sample. For example, sentences such as "This is fork" would be targeted to be produced with an article ("This is *a* fork").

Janice discussed her findings with Tim and Barbara and presented them with her treatment plan. Janice recommended that Lilly be provided with a hybrid method for increasing target structures; this method would include a combination of child-centered and clinician-directed approaches (Eisenberg, 2013). The therapist would provide explicit instruction with imitation drills and prompts, in addition to scaffolded practice, during which she would utilize conversational recasts to expand Lilly's phrases and sentences (McCauley et al., 2017). For example, sentences such as "I want blue" might be recast to Lilly as "You want *the* blue *ball.*" The therapy would occur in the context of play with familiar toys and during shared book reading activities. Lilly's parents were pleased with these therapy options and felt that therapy occurring in a play context was in keeping with their own beliefs of child interaction. They agreed to weekly treatment for 3 months, with a reevaluation at the end of that period.

Janice provided treatment to Lilly for 3 months as planned, compiling data of the number of grammatical morphemes offered in each weekly therapy session (which she kept record of with a silent handheld "clicker" that added a value each time she clicked it). Janice pooled the results of morphemes provided in the form of recasts as well as in other contexts. She entered on a simple record sheet the total stimulations offered during each session, which ranged from 32 to 71 occurrences during each session. She also made notes unobtrusively on a clipboard during the sessions when she heard Lilly spontaneously produce any of the target morphemes. Her records showed steady improvement in Lilly's production of the target morphemes.

To find out whether Lilly's use of the target morphemes in the therapy sessions had generalized to include the use of other communicative partners, at the end of 3 months, Janice obtained a sample of Lilly's language while Lilly interacted with her mother, which she transcribed in SALT. She also scored an IPSyn from the sample. Basic measures obtained from SALT revealed that Lilly's MLU was now 2.25, her NDW was 108, and her TNW was 231. Although all of these basic measures had increased since the language sample obtained 3 months earlier, Lilly's NDW and TNW had particularly improved, with her NDW falling within the range of monolingual English-speaking peers obtained from the SALT database. With respect to Brown's grammatical morphemes, Lilly continued to produce plural –s frequently, and several instances of the copula and past tense –ed were observed. For the morphemes targeted during therapy, Lilly produced two instances of present progressive –ing ("is going" and "he is running"), one instance of the irregular past tense (fell), and four instances of the article "the." The article "a" was not observed. Her IPSyn total score had increased from 33 to 38, and there were significant improvements in the verb phrase subscale.

Janice presented her results to Barbara, who agreed that Lilly appeared to be responding to the therapy. Janice demonstrated to Barbara how she might use recast techniques at home and provided her with some parent handouts about increasing language use in preschool-aged children. Because Lilly was responsive to the therapy, they agreed to continue the therapy for another 3 months and to reevaluate at that time whether additional therapy was needed.

In summary, Janice was able to determine that Lilly, a 3.3-year-old child with special needs adopted from China as a toddler, was performing below the range of what is expected for other similar children adopted from China. She was able to provide appropriate therapy for Lilly, targeted directly at those language structures that were slow to develop. It was important to Lilly's parents that Janet was well versed in the literature of the language development of IA children, was respectful of their wishes and childrearing beliefs, and consulted and included them in the therapeutic process. Janice kept careful data of Lilly's progress and was able to demonstrate good improvement in the target structures of language that she targeted.

References

Altenberg, E. P., Roberts, J. A., & Scarborough, H. S. (2018). Young children's structure production: A revision of the Index of Productive Syntax. *Language, Speech, and Hearing Services in Schools, 49*(4), 995–1008. https://doi.org/10.1044/2018_LSHSS-17-0092

American Speech-Language-Hearing Association. (n.d.). *Module 4: Clinical decision making with dynamic assessment.* https://www.asha.org/practice/multicultural/dynamic-assessment/module-4/

Bedore, L. M., & Peña, E. D. (2008). Assessment of bilingual children for identification of language impairment: Current findings and implications for practice. *International Journal of Bilingual Education and Bilingualism, 11*(1), 1–29. https://doi.org/10.2167/beb392.0

Dunn, D. M. (2019). *Peabody Picture Vocabulary Test* (5th ed.) [Measurement instrument]. NCS Pearson.

Eckerle, J. K., Bresnahan, M. M., Kroupina, M., Johnson, D. E., & Howard, C. R. (2021). International adoption: A review and update. *Pediatrics in Review, 42*(5), 245–257. https://doi.org/10.1542/pir.2019-0120

Eisenberg, S. L. (2013). Grammar intervention: Content and procedures for facilitating children's language development. *Topics in Language Disorders, 33*(2), 165–178. https://doi.org/10.1097/TLD.0b013e31828ef28e

Fenson, L., Dale, P. S., Reznick, J. S., Bates, E., Thal, D. J., Pethick, S. J., . . . Stiles, J. (1994). Variability in early communicative development. *Monographs of the Society for Research in Child Development, 59*(5), i–185. https://doi.org/10.2307/1166093

Glennen, S. (2007). Predicting language outcomes for internationally adopted children. *Journal of Speech*

Language & Hearing Research, 50, 529–548. https://doi.org/10.1044/1092-4388(2007/036)

Glennen, S. L. (2020). Speech and language development in adopted children. In G. M. Wrobel, E. Helder, & E. Marr (Eds.), *The Routledge handbook of adoption* (pp. 337–352). Routledge. https://doi.org/10.4324/9780429432040-24

Goldman, R., & Fristoe, M. (2015). *Goldman-Fristoe Test of Articulation (3rd ed., GFTA-3).* Pearson.

Gutiérrez-Clellen, V. F., & Simon-Cereijido, G. (2009). Using language sampling in clinical assessments with bilingual children: Challenges and future directions. *Seminars in Speech and Language, 30*(4), 234–245. https://doi.org/10.1055/s-0029-1241722

Johnson, K., Huang, B., & Wang, L. (1998). Infant abandonment and adoption in China. *Population and Development Review, 3,* 469–510. https://doi.org/10.2307/2808152

Krakow, R. A., & Roberts, J. (2003). Acquisition of English vocabulary by young Chinese adoptees. *Journal of Multilingual Communication Disorders, 1,* 169–176. https://doi.org/10.1080/14769670310001603862

McCauley, R. J., Fey, M. E., & Gillam, R. (2017). *Treatment of language disorders in children* (2nd ed.). Paul H. Brookes Publishing.

Miller, J., & Iglesias, A. (2020). *Systematic Analysis of Language Transcripts (SALT),* Version 20 [Computer software]. SALT Software, LLC.

Miller, L., Pérouse de Montclos, P., & Sorge, F. (2016). Special needs adoption in France and USA 2016: How can we best prepare and support families? *Neuropsychiatrie de l'Enfance et de l'Adolesence, 64,* 308–316. https://doi.org/10.1016/j.neurenf.2016.05.003

Pollock, K. (2005). Early language growth in children adopted from China: Preliminary normative data. *Seminars in Speech and Language, 26,* 22–32. https://doi.org/10.1055/s-2005-864213

Pollock, K. E. (2020). Second first language acquisition following international adoption. *Child Bilingualism and Second Language Learning: Multidisciplinary Perspectives, 10,* 189–220. https://doi.org/10.1075/bpa.10.10pol

Price, J. R., Pollock, K., & Oller, D. K. (2006). Speech and language development in six infants adopted from China. *Journal of Multilingual Communication Disorders, 4,* 108–127. https://doi.org/10.1080/14769670601092622

Rescorla, L., Dahlsgaard, K., & Roberts, J. (2000). Late-talking toddlers: MLU and IPSyn outcomes at 3;0 and 4;0. *Journal of Child Language, 27*(3), 643–664. https://doi.org/10.1017/s0305000900004232

Roberts, J., Altenberg, E. P., Ferrugio, H. S., & Rosenberg, J. E. (2022). How to use the Index of Productive Syntax to select goals and monitor progress in preschool children, *Language, Speech, and Hearing Services in Schools, 53*(3), 803–824. https://doi.org/10.1044/2021_LSHSS-21-00096

Roberts, J., Pollock, K., & Krakow, R. (2005). Continued catch-up and language delay in children adopted from China. *Seminars in Speech and Language, 26,* 76–85. https://doi.org/10.1055/s-2005-864218

Roberts, J., Pollock, K. E., Krakow, R., Price, J., Fulmer, K. C., & Wang, P. P. (2005). Language development in preschool-age children adopted from China. *Journal of Speech, Language and Hearing Research, 48,* 93–107. https://doi.org/10.1044/1092-4388(2005/008)

Selman, P. (2015, June). *Twenty years of the Hague Convention: A statistical review* [PowerPoint slides]. https://www.hcch.net/en/publications-and-studies/details4/?pid=6319

Selman, P. (2022). *Global statistics for intercountry adoption: Receiving states and states of origin 2004–2020.* https://assets.hcch.net/docs/a8fe9f19-23e6-40c2-855e-388e112bf1f5.pdf

Tan, T. X., Marfo, K., & Dedrick, R. F. (2007). Special needs adoption from China: Exploring child-level indicators, adoptive family characteristics, and correlates of behavioral adjustment. *Children and Youth Services Review, 29*(10), 1269–1285. https://doi.org/10.1016/j.childyouth.2007.05.001

Tan, T. X., & Yang, Y. (2005). Language development of Chinese adoptees 18–35 months old. *Early Childhood Research Quarterly, 20,* 57–68. https://doi.org/10.1016/j.ecresq.2005.01.004

U.S. Department of State. (2022). *Intercountry adoptions—adoption statistics.* https://travel.state.gov/content/travel/en/Intercountry-Adoption/adopt_ref/adoption-statistics-esri.html

Wiig, E. H., Secord, W. A., & Semel, E. (2020). *Clinical Evaluation of Language Fundamentals Preschool-3 (CELF-P3).* Pearson.

Windsor, J., Glaze, L. E., Koga, S. F., & The Bucharest Early Intervention Project Core Group (2007). Language acquisition with limited input: Romanian institution and foster care. *Journal of Speech, Language and Hearing Research, 50,* 1365–1381. https://doi.org/10.1044/1092-4388(2007/095)

SUBMUCOUS CLEFT PALATE
CASE 15
Sarah: Submucous Cleft Palate and 22Q11.2 Deletion Syndrome: A Typical Case of Late Diagnosis
Ann W. Kummer

Conceptual Knowledge Areas

Velopharyngeal Function

The velopharyngeal valve is responsible for closing off the nasal cavity from the oral cavity during speech. Normal velopharyngeal closure is accomplished by the coordinated action of the velum (soft palate) and the pharyngeal walls (the walls of the throat). Velopharyngeal closure is necessary for the production of all speech sounds, with the exception of nasal sounds (/m/, /n/, /ŋ/). Closure of the velopharyngeal valve is also important for singing, whistling, blowing, sucking, kissing, swallowing, gagging, and vomiting.

During nasal breathing and the production of nasal sounds, the velum rests against the base of the tongue so that the pharyngeal cavity is unobstructed. During the production of oral speech, however, the velum rises in a superior and posterior direction and then closes against the posterior pharyngeal wall. As it elevates, the velum has a type of "knee action," where it bends to provide maximum contact with the posterior pharyngeal wall over a large surface. The point where the velum bends is where the paired levator veli palatini muscles interdigitate and pull the velum up and back during contraction. This area can be seen on the oral surface during phonation and is called the *velar dimple*. Examination of the nasal surface of the velum through nasopharyngoscopy reveals a muscular bulge on the top of the "knee" during phonation, called the *velar eminence*. It is the result

of contraction of the paired musculus uvulae muscles. These muscles provide internal stiffness to the velum and better closure in the midline.

The lateral pharyngeal walls contribute to velopharyngeal closure by moving medially to close against the velum or, in rare cases, behind the velum. Both lateral pharyngeal walls move during closure, but there is great variation among normal speakers in the extent of movement. In addition, there is often asymmetry in movement so that one side may move significantly more than the other side.

During velar movement, anterior movement of the posterior pharyngeal wall is noted in some speakers, but its contribution to closure is much less than that of the velum and lateral pharyngeal walls. Some normal as well as abnormal speakers have a defined area on the posterior pharyngeal wall that bulges forward during speech, called the Passavant's ridge. This is a normal variation and is the result of contraction of the superior constrictor muscles.

Velopharyngeal Dysfunction

Velopharyngeal dysfunction (VPD) refers to a condition in which the velopharyngeal valve does not close consistently and completely during the production of oral sounds (Kummer 2020). *Velopharyngeal insufficiency (VPI)* is the term usually used to describe an anatomical or structural defect that prevents adequate velopharyngeal closure. Velopharyngeal insufficiency is the most common type of VPD because it includes a short velum, which is common in children with a history of cleft palate after the palate repair and also common in children with submucous cleft. *Velopharyngeal incompetence (also VPI)* refers to a neuromotor or physiological disorder that results in poor movement of the velopharyngeal structures. Finally, *velopharyngeal mislearning* refers to inadequate velopharyngeal closure secondary to faulty development of appropriate articulation patterns.

A velopharyngeal opening can cause hypernasality and/or nasal emission with speech (Kummer, 2011). If there is significant nasal emission, consonants will be weak in intensity and pressure, and utterance length will be short due to the need to take frequent breaths to replace the lost air through the nose (Kummer et al., 1992; Kummer et al., 2003). Compensatory articulation productions may also develop due to inadequate intraoral air pressure for consonant production. Because the air coming from the lungs is perpendicular to the velopharyngeal valve, even a very small velopharyngeal opening will cause a leak into the nasal cavity and will, therefore, be symptomatic for speech (Kummer, 2020).

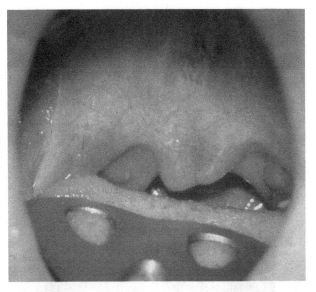

Figure 15–1. Note the zona pellucida (thin velum) and wide uvula with a line in midline. Reproduced with permission from the Cleft and Craniofacial Center at Cincinnati Children's Hospital Medical Center.

Submucous Cleft Palate (SMCP)

Submucous cleft palate (SMCP) is a congenital defect that affects the underlying structure of the palate, while the oral surface mucosa is intact. It often involves the muscles and nasal surface of the velum but can involve the bony structure of the hard palate. Depending on the severity of the SMCP, the defect can range from a slight bifid uvula to a complete submucosal cleft that extends from the uvula to the alveolar ridge.

The characteristics of an SMCP include a bifid or hypoplastic uvula, *zona pellucida* (thin, bluish appearing area) and *diastasis* (separation) of the levator veli palatini muscles, which normally elevate the velum during speech (Figure 15–1) (Kummer, 2020). The diastasis of the muscles can often be seen because instead of interdigitating in the middle of the velum, the muscles insert into the posterior border of the hard palate. When they contract during phonation, the velum appears to "tent up" in the shape of an inverted "V"

(Figure 15–2). If the submucous cleft extends through the velum all the way to the hard palate, there may also be a palpable notch in the posterior surface of the hard palate or a groove in the roof of the hard palate.

An *overt submucous cleft palate* is one that can be seen on the oral surface through a simple intraoral examination. An *occult submucous cleft* is a defect in the velum that is not apparent on the oral surface but can be clearly identified on the nasal surface through a nasopharyngoscopy exam. Because the word "occult" means "hidden" or "not revealed," this malformation is aptly named.

The incidence of SMCP is estimated to be 1 in 1,200 to 2,000 live births, with the true incidence unknown, as many individuals with this condition have few clinical manifestations and often go undiagnosed. SMCP can occur in isolation or as part of a genetic syndrome (such as 223q11.2 deletion syndrome or Stickler syndrome).

The biggest concern with SMCP is that it can cause velopharyngeal insufficiency (VPI); Jung et al., 2020). This is because the velum is either too short to reach the posterior pharyngeal wall during

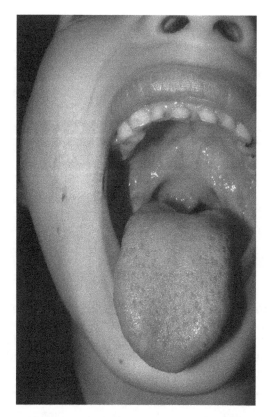

Figure 15–2. Note the inverted "V" shape that occurs during phonation. This is the result of abnormal muscle insertion. Reproduced with permission from the Cleft and Craniofacial Center at Cincinnati Children's Hospital Medical Center.

speech, or there is a midline defect that interferes with a complete seal of the velum against the pharyngeal wall. It has been estimated that one fourth to one half of individuals with submucous cleft have associated velopharyngeal insufficiency causing abnormal speech. On the other hand, it is important to recognize that most individuals with a submucous cleft have normal speech.

22q11.2 deletion syndrome (22q11.2 DS)

22q11.2 deletion syndrome (22q11.2 DS), also known as 22q, velocardiofacial syndrome (VCFS), and DiGeorge syndrome, is often identified in patients who demonstrate hypernasality with no known cause. In addition to the characteristic hypernasality, affected individuals often have language and learning problems, speech sound disorders, and hearing loss. Because communication disorders are common characteristics with 22q, it is often the speech-language pathologist (SLP) who first detects the problem and refers the individual for further medical assessment and intervention.

The characteristics of 22q have been described by many authors (Boyce, et al., 2019; Cable & Mair, 2003; Finkelstein et al., 1993; Ford et al., 2000; Gothelf, 2007; Hay, 2007; Kummer, 2020; Motzkin et al., 1993; Shprintzen, 2000; Stevens et al., 1990; Vo, McNeill, & Vogt, 2018). The basic characteristics are as follows:

- **Velo:** There is usually velopharyngeal dysfunction because of an overt or submucous cleft or pharyngeal hypotonia. Hypernasality and nasal emission are common findings.
- **Cardio:** Minor cardiac and vascular anomalies are common, including ventriculoseptal deviation (VSD), atrial septal defect (ASD), patent ductus arteriosus (PDA), pulmonary stenosis, tetralogy of Fallot, right-sided aortic arch, medially displaced internal carotid arteries, and tortuosity of the retinal arteries. The child may have had a heart murmur at birth.
- **Facial:** Facial characteristics include microcephaly, long face with vertical maxillary excess; micrognathia (small jaw) or retruded mandible often with a Class II malocclusion; nasal anomalies including a wide nasal bridge, narrow alar base, and bulbous nasal tip; narrow palpebral fissures (slit-like eyes); malar (cheek bone) flatness; thin upper lip; minor auricular anomalies; and others (Figure 15–3).
- **Learning and Cognitive Problems:** Learning disabilities and mild to moderate cognitive dysfunction are common. Affected individuals often have difficulty with abstract thinking.

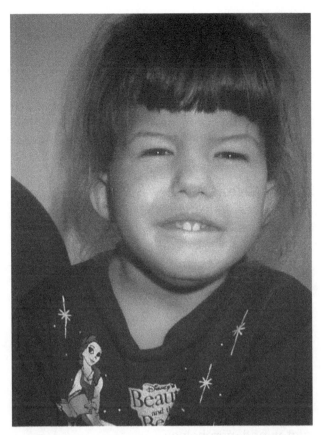

Figure 15–3. Typical facies of a child with 22q11.2 deletion syndrome. Note the narrow palpebral fissures (eye openings), wide nasal bridge, bulbous nasal tip, thin upper lip, long maxilla (which is why the teeth show), small mandible, and low-set ears. Reproduced with permission from the Cleft and Craniofacial Center at Cincinnati Children's Hospital Medical Center.

- **Communication Problems:** Hypernasality due to velopharyngeal insufficiency and pharyngeal hypotonia is the most common finding. In addition, affected individuals may demonstrate multiple misarticulations, often due to verbal apraxia (Kummer et al., 2007); a high-pitched voice; conductive and/or sensorineural hearing loss; or language disorders with learning problems (D'Antonio et al., 2001; Kok & Solman, 1995; Scherer et al., 1999; Scherer et al., 2001; Ysunza et al., 2003).

- **Other Common Physical and Medical Characteristics:** Other common findings include long slender digits; hyperextensibility of the joints; short stature, usually below the 10th percentile; Pierre Robin sequence (cleft palate, micrognathia, and glossoptosis with airway obstruction); umbilical and inguinal hernias; and laryngeal web.

- **Other Common Functional Problems:** There may be early feeding problems, gross and fine motor delays, social disinhibition, and risk of psychosis in adolescence.

Although there are many common characteristics with 22q, the expressivity is widely variable among individuals. Some have only a few characteristics, while others have many. In general, abnormal speech (usually due to velopharyngeal insufficiency and apraxia) is most common.

The cause of 22q is a genetic deletion on chromosome 22q11.2, which can occur sporadically in a family that has never had an individual with the syndrome. Once it occurs, it is an autosomal dominant condition so there is a 50% recurrence risk for the affected individual's offspring.

Description of the Case

Background Information

The following case report describes a child who was seen in the Velopharyngeal Insufficiency/Incompetence Clinic (VPI Clinic) at Cincinnati Children's Hospital Medical Center. The VPI Clinic is staffed by an interdisciplinary team of professionals, including an SLP, otolaryngologist, and geneticist.

Reason for Referral

Sarah, age 7 years, 4 months, was referred to the VPI Clinic by her pediatrician at the urging of the school SLP, who wanted an evaluation of velopharyngeal function due to Sarah's hypernasality.

Pertinent History

Both parents accompanied Sarah to the evaluation. The father was very quiet during the interview, although he occasionally nodded in agreement with the mother's comments. The mother, therefore, was the primary informant, and she provided the following information:

Neonatal History. Sarah was the product of a full-term pregnancy and normal delivery. She weighed 6 lbs. 10 oz and her Apgar scores were 7 and 9. The only neonatal problem was significant difficulty with breastfeeding. The mother reported that after a short period of time, she gave up trying to breastfeed and switched to bottle feeding. Even with the bottle, it took a long time for Sarah to feed. Once she switched to solid foods, Sarah seemed to do fine.

Medical History. Sarah had a heart murmur at birth that did not require surgery. She was hospitalized at the age of 4 years for an inguinal hernia repair. Sarah had chronic ear infections, requiring the insertion of pressure equalizing (PE) tubes on four occasions. When asked where Sarah was on the growth chart, the mother reported that she was at about the 10th percentile for height and close to that for weight. Sarah had been followed by an endocrinologist. She had never been seen by a geneticist or diagnosed with a syndrome.

Developmental History. The mother reported that Sarah's developmental milestones were a little delayed. She sat alone at 7 months and walked at 14 months. She used single words around 18 months and combined words into short utterances around the age 2 years. Her mother reported that Sarah's speech was initially hard to understand and has always sounded "nasally."

Treatment History. Sarah received early intervention services in the home from about 20 months of age until she was 3 years old. When she turned 3, she was enrolled in speech therapy through her school. Sarah continued to receive 2 half-hour sessions per week of individual therapy at her school.

The mother noted that although Sarah's articulation and language skills had improved, her speech remained very nasal.

Social History. Sarah was the youngest of three children. Her brother and sister had normal speech and no significant medical issues. Her father had received speech therapy as a child and had some learning issues.

School History. Sarah was in the second grade. Her mother said Sarah was generally doing well but had some difficulties with math.

Findings of the Evaluation

The following is a summary of the evaluation results:

Language

Sarah was communicating with complete sentences. An informal screening revealed normal syntax and morphology.

Speech Sound Production

Articulation placement was characterized by fronting of velars (t/k, d/g), inconsistent nasalization of pressure-sensitive sounds, substitution of ŋ/l, reduction of blends, and inconsistent voiced/voiceless substitutions. On the sentence level, however, there were many additional inconsistent errors and phoneme omissions, particularly with an increase in utterance length and phonemic complexity.

Airflow and Air Pressure

There was consistent nasal emission on all pressure sounds, but this was barely audible. However, consonants were very weak in intensity and pressure because of the nasal emission. Utterance length was short due to the loss of airflow through the nose, which resulted in the need to replenish the air supply by taking frequent breaths.

Resonance

Resonance was severely hypernasal.

Phonation

Voice quality was high in pitch and low in volume.

Nasometry

Using the Simplified Nasometric Assessment Procedures–Revised (SNAP-R) Test (Kummer, 2005), nasometry revealed a severely high degree of nasalance. The average nasalance score for the oral picture-cued passages was 64. A normal score for these oral passages is under about 21. These scores indicated that most acoustic energy during speech was being emitted from the nasal cavity rather than from the oral cavity.

Intraoral Examination

An intraoral examination revealed a submucous cleft. The uvula was hypoplastic with a line in the middle. During phonation, the velum formed an inverted "V" shape, which suggested diastasis of the levator veli palatini muscle. The tonsils were not enlarged. Dental occlusion was in a normal Class I relationship.

Nasopharyngoscopy

Nasopharyngoscopy showed evidence of a hypoplastic musculus uvulae muscle (on the top of the velum) during phonation. There was also a visible midline notch on the posterior border of the velum. These findings were consistent with a submucous cleft palate. During speech, there was a large velopharyngeal gap due to a short velum and poor lateral pharyngeal wall movement. Observation of the velopharyngeal port during normal nasal breathing showed pulsation of the left carotid artery on the posterior pharyngeal wall, which is often seen in patients with 22q. An assessment of the vocal folds revealed a small laryngeal web, which is also a common finding in this population.

Additional Physical Observations

Sarah exhibited several dysmorphic facial features, including a wide nasal bridge, bulbous nasal tip, and narrow palpebral fissures. She had a long, narrow face and micrognathia. As the mother reported, Sarah appeared to be very small for her age. Her fingers were long and tapered. On observation, the father had several of the same facial features and similarly tapered fingers.

Examiner Impressions

The results of the examination confirmed the presence of a submucous cleft (which caused a short velum) and pharyngeal hypotonia (which caused poor lateral pharyngeal wall movement). Both conditions caused severe velopharyngeal insufficiency due to a large velopharyngeal opening during speech. As a result, speech was characterized by hypernasality, nasal emission, nasalization of consonants, weak consonants, and short utterance length. There were also signs of verbal apraxia, which included voiced for voiceless phonemes, inconsistent articulation errors, and an increase in errors and omissions with increased sentence length and phonemic complexity.

The speech characteristics, physical findings, and history strongly supported a diagnosis of 22q as the primary cause. There was also a suspicion that the father might have had a mild form of 22q, given his facial features, tapered fingers, and history.

Parent Counseling

The parents were counseled regarding the results of the evaluation. Considerable time was spent providing them with information about submucous clefts, normal velopharyngeal function, and, finally, velopharyngeal insufficiency. The causes of Sarah's specific speech characteristics were explained. Then, treatment options were discussed. Informational handouts were given to them to reinforce the learning.

The parents were then told of the suspicion of 22q. This news initially came to them as a shock.

However, as the features were further described, they expressed a degree of relief in knowing that this could explain many of the problems that Sarah was experiencing and that her father had experienced in the past.

Treatment Options Considered

The team recommendations included the following:

Genetics Test

The geneticist told the parents that, although the diagnosis of 22q seemed very likely, this needed to be confirmed with a specific genetic test. He recommended that the father also have the test.

Surgery for the Velum and VPI

The team explained to the parents that Sarah would need a palate repair of the soft palate and VPI surgery before any progress could be expected with speech therapy. The team also explained that improving the structure, and thus function, of the velopharyngeal valve would give Sarah the oral airflow needed to improve her articulation skills. A Furlow Z-plasty was recommended for the palate repair. A pharyngeal flap was recommended for the VPI because it closes the pharyngeal port in midline, which is most affected by a submucous cleft. The parents were counseled that the surgery would improve oral airflow and oral resonance, as well as increase loudness. However, perfect speech may not be attainable because of the pharyngeal hypotonia and apraxia.

Surgery for the Laryngeal Web

Excision of the laryngeal web was recommended, not only to improve the voice but also to improve the airway.

Postoperative Speech Therapy

The parents were told that, although the pharyngeal flap would improve the physical ability to produce sounds, Sarah would require postoperative speech therapy to learn to produce sounds that she couldn't produce before the surgery. They were also informed about the importance of daily practice at home.

Course of Treatment

About 6 weeks following her clinic evaluation, Sarah had the palate repair, pharyngeal flap, and laryngeal web excision. The postoperative course was unremarkable. A postoperative VPI Clinic appointment was made for 3 months later.

Postoperative Evaluation History Update

The parents reported that since the surgery, Sarah's speech was louder and much easier to understand. Even her grandparents could understand her on the phone. Although speech improvement was noted, the mother reported that she still noticed a little "nasality."

When asked about the airway, the mother noted that Sarah was not snoring much at night and that she was sleeping well. She had no signs of sleep apnea.

By this appointment, the genetics test results were available. They revealed that both the father and Sarah had a deletion on chromosome 22q11.2, thus confirming the diagnosis. Again, the parents indicated that they were relieved to know what caused these problems, what to expect, and what to do about it.

Postoperative Evaluation Findings

The following is a summary of the changes noted as a result of the surgery:

Speech Sound Production. Articulation placement was the same as with the preoperative evaluation. However, oral consonants were no longer nasalized, and pressure-sensitive sounds (plosives, fricatives, and affricates) were clearer with better intraoral air pressure. Utterance length was significantly improved.

Airflow and Air Pressure. There was still nasal emission, but it was more audible than before. In addition, there was an inconsistent nasal rustle (a loud, friction/bubbling sound). (The increase in audibility occurred because the velopharyngeal opening went from large to small.)

Resonance. Resonance was normal, and with the increased oral resonance, the volume seemed to be louder.

Voice. Voice quality was normal, as opposed to the high pitch, which was noted before the release of the laryngeal web.

Nasometry. Nasometry showed significant improvement in nasalance. The average nasalance score for the oral picture-cued passages was 28, which was significantly lower than the preop score of 64. Because normal is under about 21, these scores were just a little high, suggesting a small remaining gap.

Intraoral Examination. An oral examination showed evidence of the flap donor site. However, the flap could not be seen, which suggested that it was in a good position behind the velum.

Nasopharyngoscopy. Nasopharyngoscopy showed the flap to be in good vertical position and in midline. The width of the flap appeared appropriate. Both ports were open wide for normal nasal breathing. During speech, the right port closed completely, but a small opening remained in the left port. The vocal folds appeared healthy and moved normally.

Analysis of Client's Response to Intervention

Examiner Impressions

The evaluation results revealed significant improvement in velopharyngeal function and thus speech as a result of the pharyngeal flap. However, there was still audible nasal emission due to incomplete closure of the left port. The nasal emission was actually more noticeable than before due to the effect of airflow going through a smaller opening.

Further Recommendations

Because the problem was with the left port, a left unilateral sphincter procedure was discussed by the team. However, this is the side of the medially displaced carotid artery, making surgery in that area somewhat more difficult. After much discussion, it was decided that the procedure could be done safely, and it was recommended to the family.

The family thought about the recommendations for additional surgery, but they were not anxious to put Sarah through another procedure right away. Therefore, they decided to postpone a decision about a touch-up procedure for another year. This seemed reasonable given that the remaining nasal emission was merely "cosmetic." The pharyngeal flap had given Sarah the intraoral airflow and oral resonance to improve speech production skills through speech therapy.

Author's Note

This was based on an actual case. The patient's name was changed to protect her identity. It should be noted that at the time that this child was treated, a pharyngeal flap was the most common and most effective surgical procedure for the treatment of velopharyngeal insufficiency. In recent years, this has changed. Another procedure using buccal flaps (tissue from the cheeks) is now more commonly used at our Center. In this procedure, the velum is surgically separated from the hard palate. The surgeon then rotates a flap from the inside of each cheek and sutures these flaps in the opening between the hard palate and velum. This pushes the velum posteriorly so that during speech, the velum is more likely to reach the pharyngeal wall for complete closure. In our experience, this improves outcomes and reduces the need for surgical revisions.

References

Boyce, J. O., Sanchez, K., Amor, D., Reilly, S. Da Costa, A., Kilpatrick, N., & Morgan, A. T. (2019). Exploring the speech and language of individuals with non-syndromic submucous cleft palate: A preliminary report. *International Journal of Language & Communication Disorders, 54*(5), 767–778. https://doi.org/10.1111/1460-6984.12474

Cable, B. B., & Mair, E. A. (2003). Avoiding perils and pitfalls in velocardiofacial syndrome: An otolaryngologist's perspective. *Ear, Nose, & Throat Journal, 82*(1), 56–60.

D'Antonio, L. L., Scherer, N. J., Miller, L. L., Kalbfleisch, J. H., & Bartley, J. A. (2001). Analysis of speech characteristics in children with velocardiofacial syndrome (VCFS) and children with phenotypic overlap without VCFS. *Cleft Palate-Craniofacial Journal, 38*(5), 455–467. https://doi.org/10.1597/1545-1569_2001_038_0455_aoscic_2.0.co_2

Finkelstein, Y., Zohar, Y., Nachmani, A., Talmi, Y. P., Lerner, M. A., Hauben, D. J., & Frydman M. (1993). The otolaryngologist and the patient with velocardiofacial syndrome. *Archives of Otolaryngology-Head & Neck Surgery, 119*(5), 563–569. https://doi.org/10.1001/archotol.1993.01880170089019

Ford, L. C., Sulprizio, S. L., & Rasgon, B. M. (2000). Otolaryngological manifestations of velocardiofacial syndrome: A retrospective review of 35 patients. *Laryngoscope, 110*(3 Pt 1), 362–367. https://doi.org/10.1097/00005537-200003000-00006

Gothelf, D. (2007). Velocardiofacial syndrome. *Child and Adolescent Psychiatric Clinics of North America, 16*(3), 677–693. https://doi.org/10.1016/j.chc.2007.03.005

Hay, B. N. (2007). Deletion 22q11: Spectrum of associated disorders. *Seminars Pediatric Neurology, 14*(3), 136–139. https://doi.org/10.1016/j.spen.2007.07.005

Jung, S. E., Ha, S., Koh, K. S., & Oh, T. S. (2020). Clinical interventions and speech outcomes for individuals with submucous cleft palate. *Archives of Plastic Surgery, 47*(6), 542–550. https://doi.org/10.5999/aps.2020.00612

Kok, L. L., & Solman, R. T. (1995). Velocardiofacial syndrome: Learning difficulties and intervention. *Journal of Medical Genetics, 32*(8), 612–618. https://doi.org/10.1136/jmg.32.8.612

Kummer, A. W. (2005). *Simplified Nasometric Assessment Procedures-Revised* (SNAP-R): *Nasometer Test and Manual.* KayPENTAX.

Kummer, A. W. (2011). Disorders of resonance and airflow secondary to cleft palate and/or velopharyngeal dysfunction. *Seminars in Speech and Language, 32*(2), 141–149. https://doi.org/10.1055/s-0031-1277716

Kummer, A. W. (2020). *Cleft palate and craniofacial conditions: A comprehensive guide to clinical management* (4th ed.). Jones & Bartlett Learning.

Kummer, A. W., Briggs, M., & Lee, L. (2003). The relationship between the characteristics of speech and velopharyngeal gap size. *Cleft Palate–Craniofacial Journal, 40*(6), 590–596. https://doi.org/10.1597/1545-1569_2003_040_0590_trbtco_2.0.co_2

Kummer, A. W., Curtis, C., Wiggs, M., Lee, L., & Strife, J. L. (1992). Comparison of velopharyngeal gap size in patients with hypernasality, hypernasality and nasal emission, or nasal turbulence (rustle) as the primary speech characteristic. *Cleft Palate–Craniofacial Journal, 29*(2), 152–156. https://doi.org/10.1597/1545-1569_1992_029_0152_covgsi_2.3.co_2

Kummer, A. W., Lee, L., Stutz, L. S., Maroney, A., & Brandt, J. W. (2007). The prevalence of apraxia characteristics in patients with velocardiofacial syndrome as compared with other cleft populations. *Cleft Palate-Craniofacial Journal, 44*(2), 175–181. https://doi.org/10.1597/05-170.1

Motzkin, B., Marion, R., Goldberg, R., Shprintzen, R., & Saenger, P. (1993). Variable phenotypes in velocardiofacial syndrome with chromosomal deletion. *Journal of Pediatrics, 123*(3), 406–410. https://doi.org/10.1016/s0022-3476(05)81740-8

Scherer, N. J., D'Antonio, L. L., & Kalbfleisch, J. H. (1999). Early speech and language development in children with velocardiofacial syndrome. *American Journal of Medical Genetics, 88*(6), 714–723.

Scherer, N. J., D'Antonio, L. L., & Rodgers, J. R. (2001). Profiles of communication disorder in children with velocardiofacial syndrome: Comparison to children with Down syndrome. *Genetics in Medicine, 3*(1), 72–78. https://doi.org/10.1097/00125817-200101000-00016

Shprintzen, R. J. (2000). Velocardiofacial syndrome. *Otolaryngologic Clinics of North America, 33*(6), 1217–1240. https://doi.org/10.1016/s0030-6665(05)70278-4

Stevens, C. A., Carey, J. C., & Shigeoka, A. O. (1990). DiGeorge anomaly and velocardiofacial syndrome. *Pediatrics, 85*(4), 526–530.

Vo, O. K., McNeill, A., Vogt, K. S. (2018). The psychosocial impact of 22q11 deletion syndrome on patients and families: A systematic review. *American Journal of Medical Genetics Part A. 176*(10), 2215–2225. https://doi.org/10.1002/ajmg.a.38673

Ysunza, A., Pamplona, M. C., Ramirez, E., Canun, S., Sierra, M. C., & Silva-Rojas, A. (2003). Videonasopharyngoscopy in patients with 22q11.2 deletion syndrome (Shprintzen syndrome). *International Journal of Pediatric Otorhinolaryngology, 67*(8), 911–915. https://doi.org/10.1016/s0165-5876(03)00157-5

FLUENCY

CASE 16

Mateo: A Preschool Child Who Stutters

Kristin M. Pelczarski and J. Scott Yaruss

Conceptual Knowledge Areas

Stuttering is a communication disorder that is typically characterized by the production of certain types of disruptions, or *disfluencies*, in the forward flow of speech (Bloodstein et al., 2021). These disfluencies often take the form of part-word repetitions ("li-li-like this"), prolongations ("lllllike this"), and blocks ("l—ike this"). Other types of disfluencies, including phrase repetitions ("like this—like this"), interjections ("um," "uh"), and revisions ("I want—I need that"), are also seen, though these are typically judged to reflect typical speech and language development (Conture, 2001).

Notably, disfluent speech is not the only important characteristic of the stuttering that must be considered. Fluent and disfluent speech may be accompanied by tension or struggle behaviors as the speaker tries to compensate for the feeling of "loss of control" that accompanies the moment of stuttering (e.g., Tichenor & Yaruss, 2019a). Stuttering can result in significant negative consequences for the speaker, including negative affective and cognitive reactions, limitations in the ability to perform daily activities involving communication, and restricted participation in social and vocational endeavors (e.g., Craig et al., 2009; Klein & Hood, 2004; Tichenor & Yaruss, 2019b; Yaruss & Quesal, 2004). For children, stuttering can result in an adverse educational impact that limits the child's ability to succeed in academic and social settings (Daniels et al., 2012). These negative consequences may be less common in very young children who stutter, though preschoolers (even preschoolers who do not stutter) may experience negative reactions associated with speech disfluencies (e.g., Boey et al., 2009; Clark et al., 2012; Ezrati-Vinacour et al., 2001; Glover et al., 2019; Vanryckeghem et al., 2005).

Stuttering typically begins in the preschool years, when a child is between 2½ and 4 years old (Yairi & Ambrose, 2005, 2013). It may begin gradually and increase in frequency and severity over time, though rapid or sudden onset is also reported (Bloodstein et al., 2021). Most young children stop stuttering within the first 1 to 2 years post onset (Månsson, 2000; Yairi & Ambrose, 1999, 2005, 2013). Later recovery is also reported, though recovery after approximately age 5 years appears to be significantly less likely (Walsh et al., 2018; Yairi & Ambrose, 2013).

Research has demonstrated a strong genetic link for stuttering (e.g., Dranya & Kang, 2011; Frigerio-Domingues & Drayna, 2017; Han et al., 2014; Polikowsky et al., 2022). Boys are more likely to stutter than girls, with an adult male-to-female ratio of approximately 4 or 5 to 1 (Bloodstein et al., 2021). Interestingly, the male-to-female ratio in young children is only approximately 2 to 1, suggesting that young girls may be more likely to stop stuttering than young boys (Yairi & Ambrose, 2013). Numerous other factors appear to contribute to the likelihood that young children who stutter will recover from stuttering, including children's language development, motor abilities, and temperament (e.g., Ambrose et al., 2015; Singer et al., 2020; Singer et al., 2022; Smith & Weber, 2017; Walsh et al., 2021; Walsh et al., 2018). At present, however, there is no way to determine with certainty which specific children will stop stuttering and which children will continue to stutter.

Because of this uncertainty about who is likely to continue stuttering, combined with the high percentage of children who ultimately stop stuttering, caregivers may be advised to delay the start of therapy to see if "natural recovery" will occur. Such advice is of concern because children who do continue to stutter face an increased likelihood of developing negative speech and communication attitudes. Thus, the majority of stuttering specialists recommend early intervention, particularly when the child exhibits several of the risk factors indicated above (Conture, 2001; Singer et al., 2020; Singer et al., 2022; Walsh et al., 2021; Yairi & Ambrose, 2005; Yaruss & Reardon-Reeves, 2017). Studies have shown that the majority of young children who stutter can be helped through treatment (Bernstein Ratner, 2018; de Sonneville-Koedoot et al., 2015; Harris et al., 2002; Millard et al., 2008; Onslow et al., 1996; Yaruss et al., 2006). Therefore, we believe that speech-language pathologists can and should recommend intervention for a young child who stutters if they judge that the child is at risk for continuing to stutter.

This case presentation highlights some of the issues clinicians should consider in the diagnosis and treatment of preschool children who stutter. We describe the experiences of Mateo, his caregivers, and his speech-language pathologist (SLP), beginning with the onset of stuttering and continuing through the successful conclusion of treatment. Although some aspects of the scenario are idealized, all facts reflect the real-life experiences of many of the families that we and our colleagues have evaluated and treated over many years.

Description of the Case

Background Information

Mateo was a young boy of Hispanic descent, aged 3 years, 6 months, who lived at home in an urban setting in the Southwest United States with his caregivers, maternal grandparents, and younger sister. He was the product of an unremarkable pregnancy, with no known medical, neurological, behavioral, or social concerns. The family described themselves as being from a middle-class background; both English and Spanish were spoken in the home. Mateo exhibited typical hearing abilities and had achieved all early speech, language, and motor milestones within typical age expectations. His maternal grandfather had reportedly been a person who stuttered, though there was no other known or reported family history of communication disorders. Mateo was described by his caregivers, family members, and others as an outgoing child who was "very talkative" and "bright." They added that he "liked to get things right" and sometimes became upset when he made mistakes.

Reason for the Referral

According to caregiver reports, Mateo started exhibiting disruptions in his speech when he was approximately 2 years, 10 months old. The caregivers described these disruptions as including repetitions of parts of words with increasing pitch, stretching of sounds at the beginning of words, and tense pauses when Mateo would move his mouth, but no sounds would come out. The caregivers stated that these disruptions started "overnight" and that Mateo's speech had previously been "really smooth." They indicated that prior to the onset of stuttering, Mateo had been developing language and speaking skills at an accelerated rate. They added that he routinely used long and complicated utterances compared to other children his age and that he liked to "tell stories" every night about what he did with his friends during the day.

Mateo's stuttering behavior fluctuated in severity for a period of several months, including some periods when he did not seem to stutter at all and other times when he "could hardly get a word out," according to the caregivers. They stated their belief that he was largely unaware of his speaking difficulties, though he occasionally expressed frustration when he was unable to say what he wanted to say. He continued to talk freely most of the time, though he would occasionally say "never mind" and stop talking when he was having particular difficulty with a word. This behavior caused the caregivers significant concern; they indicated that they were worried that Mateo might ultimately start talking less because of his stuttering.

After Mateo had stuttered for approximately 3 months, his caregivers contacted a pediatrician for advice. The pediatrician responded that "most kids outgrow stuttering" and advised them to just "wait and see" whether Mateo would stop stuttering. The pediatrician also advised them not to mention or draw attention to Mateo's speech or to do anything else that might cause him to become aware of his speaking difficulties. Unfortunately, these recommendations served to increase the caregivers' fears about the stuttering, for they did not want to do anything that might cause harm to their child. They did their best to comply but often found it difficult to "stand by and watch" when Mateo's stuttering was at its most severe and he was struggling to say even short phrases. On occasion, when Mateo was exhibiting great difficulty speaking, they would tell him, "slow down," and "think about what you are saying." Although this appeared to help him speak more fluently in the moment, the caregivers felt increasingly guilty for talking about Mateo's speaking difficulties in front of him when the pediatrician had told them not to do so.

As the next 3 months passed, the caregivers' concerns increased dramatically. They began to feel that Mateo was not talking as much as he had when he was younger. They noticed that he was telling fewer stories and giving shorter answers to questions. Episodes of frustration and moments of physical struggle were also more frequent. By this time, Mateo had been stuttering for approximately 6 months, and the caregivers were becoming very worried that the stuttering might not go away as easily as the pediatrician had suggested. They were still fearful of drawing attention to stuttering, but they also felt that they had to do something to help their son.

The Search for a Clinician

As a result of their growing fears about Mateo's speech, the caregivers began to search for information about stuttering. They contacted their pediatrician again, but the pediatrician still expressed reservations about whether action was necessary.

This contributed to the caregivers' apprehension about whether they were "doing the right thing for their child." Still, to be certain about whether Mateo might need help, they searched online to find additional information. They found websites for organizations such as the Stuttering Foundation (http://www.StutteringHelp.org), the National Stuttering Association (http://www.WeStutter.org), Friends: the National Association of Young People Who Stutter (http://www.FriendsWhoStutter.org), and other sites with suggestions for what they should do (e.g., the Stuttering Home Page, http://www.StutteringHomePage.com; Stuttering Therapy Resources, Inc.; http://www.StutteringTherapyResources.com), and many more. At first, they found the volume of material overwhelming. Upon closer reading, they realized that the some of the sites provided valuable information about the nature of stuttering in children, while others seemed to offer more dubious claims. One consistent pattern they noticed was that the credible sources recommended that caregivers consult a licensed and certified SLP about their child's speech, preferably one who specializes in stuttering. Through booklets, pamphlets, and streaming videos, the caregivers learned that although many children do recover indeed stop stuttering, it is impossible to tell in advance who would do so without treatment. They also learned that Mateo's family history of stuttering placed him at a greater risk for continuing to stutter. This knowledge helped them overcome their reluctance to contact an SLP directly.

The caregivers sought to locate a Board-Certified Specialist in Fluency via the website of the American Board of Fluency and Fluency Disorders (http://www.StutteringSpecialists.org), but they were unable to find one in their area. They contacted several specialists by e-mail and found them to be helpful in providing general information about how to help their child. In particular, the specialists confirmed the importance of finding a clinician with expertise in childhood stuttering. Through various sources, the caregivers obtained the names of several local SLPs whom they interviewed about their experience with children who stutter. They discovered that not all clinicians felt comfortable with fluency disorders (Beita-Ell &

Boyle, 2020; Byrd et al., 2020; Tellis et al., 2008; Yaruss & Quesal, 2002), and some even echoed the pediatrician's advice to wait to see what would happen. The caregivers persisted until they found a clinician they trusted who was knowledgeable about stuttering. That clinician agreed that, based on the length of time since Mateo started stuttering (now more than 8 months), combined with the confirmed family history and the caregivers' strong concerns, it was appropriate to conduct an evaluation of Mateo's fluency. The goal of the initial evaluation would be to determine whether treatment for Mateo's stuttering would be indicated.

Findings of the Evaluation

Prior to the date of the scheduled evaluation, the caregivers completed a detailed case history form, in which they provided background information about Mateo's speech and language development, his achievement of developmental milestones, and his early experiences with stuttering and communication. This allowed the clinician to tailor the evaluation to Mateo's individual needs and focus on the specific concerns expressed by Mateo's caregivers. In particular, the clinician focused the evaluation on trying to determine whether Mateo was at risk for continued stuttering and, as a result, whether he would need treatment to increase the likelihood that stuttering would ultimately stop while simultaneously ensuring the development of healthy and appropriate attitudes toward his communication abilities.

The evaluation itself consisted of three primary components, each of which was designed to contribute to the clinician's assessment of Mateo's risk for continued stuttering. These components are summarized in the following paragraphs in roughly the same order in which they occurred in the evaluation (Brundage et al., 2021; Yaruss, 1998; Yaruss & Reardon-Reeves, 2017).

Parent Interview

While Mateo played with some toys in the therapy room, the clinician conducted a detailed interview with the caregivers. The interview focused on (a) the onset and development of Mateo's stuttering, (b) the family history of stuttering, (c) Mateo's reactions to his communication difficulties, and (d) the caregivers' concerns about stuttering. The clinician learned that Mateo had been stuttering for approximately 8 months (2 months having elapsed between the caregivers' decision to seek an evaluation and the scheduling of the evaluation) and that his stuttering had fluctuated somewhat after starting relatively suddenly. The clinician learned about Mateo's sensitivity and occasional negative reactions to stuttering (e.g., the apparent reduction in his willingness to speak freely), as well as his positive family history of stuttering through his maternal grandfather. The clinician also learned about the caregivers' concerns about "putting too much pressure" on Mateo while he was young, as well as their fear (based, in part, on what they were told by the pediatrician) about increasing his sensitivity to stuttering. The results of the interview suggested to the clinician that Mateo was at some risk for continuing to stutter and that treatment would be prudent (e.g., Singer et al., 2020; Singer et al., 2022; Walsh et al., 2021). At the same time, the clinician would need to gather additional information without increasing the caregivers' fears about exacerbating Mateo's stuttering.

Observation of Speech Fluency

Next, the clinician observed while Mateo and his caregivers engaged in a free play dialogue. That is, Mateo continued playing with the toys while his caregivers joined him. The clinician watched from the corner of the room and collected data on the frequency, duration, and type of disfluencies that Mateo exhibited (Yaruss, 1997a, 1998).

Although Mateo was relatively talkative during the evaluation, he exhibited very few speech disfluencies during a 300-word parent-child dialogue. His overall frequency of disfluencies was approximately 9%, and the majority of these disfluencies were phrase repetitions and interjections. Only 6 words out of 100 (6%) were characterized as so-called "stuttered" or "stutter-like" disfluencies (i.e., part-word repetitions, prolongations, and blocks; see Ambrose & Yairi, 1999). The majority of Mateo's disfluencies were brief (less than 1 second) and free of observable physical tension. The clinician observed occasional struggle behaviors during some of Mateo's disfluencies, but the overall surface severity of Mateo's stuttering in the parent-child dialogue was judged by the clinician to be "mild."

The caregivers immediately expressed their concern that Mateo stuttered so little during the evaluation. They explained that he typically stuttered far more than the clinician had observed. In fact, when asked how the speech sample compared to Mateo's speech in other situations, they indicated that it was a "1 or 2" on a 10-point scale, in which a "5" represented Mateo's typical level of stuttering. The caregivers added that they observed far more physical tension and struggle in Mateo's speech than he exhibited during the evaluation. The clinician sought to ease the caregivers' concerns by explaining that it is not uncommon for children to stutter less in clinical settings (Johnson et al., 2009) and that this would be accounted for in the recommendations following the evaluation.

The clinician observed Mateo in other speaking situations to learn more about the variability of Mateo's stuttering (e.g., Yaruss, 1997b). These included two in-clinic speaking situations: a free play dialogue with the clinician in which Mateo described a favorite television show, followed by a picture description task. Again, Mateo exhibited relatively few stuttered speech disfluencies—far fewer than the caregivers reported seeing in other situations. The caregivers then provided video recordings of Mateo interacting with his brother and with his grandparents to show his speech in the home environment. The clinician observed more visible tension and struggle in these less-formal situations. Even without the home videos, however, the clinician judged that Mateo's stuttering behaviors were sufficient to cause concern about his speech.

In collecting these data about Mateo's observable speech disfluencies, the clinician was mindful of research showing that children who speak more than one language are *not* more likely to stutter than other children (Bedore et al., 2006; Byrd, 2018; Byrd et al., 2015; Choo et al., 2020), even

though they may exhibit more of the so-called "stutter-like disfluencies." Sharing this information with the caregivers helped to set their minds at ease, because they had seen (incorrect) suggestions on the Internet that teaching children a second language could lead to problems with fluency.

Finally, the clinician considered other aspects of Mateo's speech and overall communication, including his speaking rate, his reactions to stuttering, and other characteristics. Mateo was judged by the clinician to use a relatively rapid speaking rate, ranging from approximately four to five syllables per second. (A typical rate of speech for a preschool child is approximately three syllables per second, e.g., Ahn et al., 2002.) The clinician also observed that Mateo displayed some perfectionistic tendencies. He became easily frustrated when playing with a set of building blocks, and he eventually said that he did not want to play anymore because he could not get his tower to stand up. These behaviors suggested to the clinician that Mateo may have increased difficulty tolerating disruptions in his speech (such as stuttering), and this could result in a stronger negative reaction to his speaking difficulties. The caregivers confirmed that such reactions were typical for Mateo.

Communication Attitudes

The clinician understood the importance of evaluating not only Mateo's observable speech fluency but also his thoughts and feelings about stuttering and his ability to communicate, for even preschool children can develop negative communication attitudes in response to stuttering (e.g., Guttormsen et al., 2015). The clinician therefore spoke openly with Mateo about his speaking experiences to give him the opportunity to talk about any concerns that he had. The clinician was aware that the caregivers were worried about "drawing attention to stuttering" based on the advice provided by the pediatrician; however, the clinician helped to calm their fears by pointing out that it can actually be helpful to give children the opportunity to explore their thoughts and feelings about stuttering in a safe and supportive environment (Logan & Yaruss, 1999; Yaruss & Reardon-Reeves, 2017). The clinician started the process by simply asking Mateo if he knew why he was visiting the clinician's office that day. To the caregivers' surprise (but not the clinician's), Mateo immediately responded, "because I don't talk right." The clinician then invited Mateo to share what he meant by that and learned that Mateo was aware that words sometimes did not come out easily. He also stated that he worried about what was happening sometimes. This not only helped the clinician to better understand Mateo's experiences; it also provided an opportunity to reassure Mateo that it is okay that this happens, saying, "Sometimes, when children are learning to talk, they can have trouble getting their words out. That's okay; it's just part of learning, but I'm here to help" (Yaruss & Reardon-Reeves, 2017). The caregivers reported that even though they were nervous about this conversation at first, they were pleased to see how easily Mateo was able to discuss his speaking difficulty—and how much better he appeared to feel after hearing that he was okay. The clinician assured them that they would continue to work on this important aspect of coping with stuttering throughout the therapy process.

Speech, Language, and Hearing Testing

The clinician then evaluated Mateo's speech, language, and hearing abilities. Because Mateo had not previously received a hearing screening, the clinician judged that it was appropriate to conduct a screening and did so using a portable audiometer. Mateo passed the screening bilaterally at 20 dB SPL.

Although the caregivers had not expressed any concerns about Mateo's speech sound production, receptive and expressive language, or overall communication, the clinician wanted to ensure that latent speech or language difficulties were not contributing to his communication difficulties. Mateo's scores on the screening portion of the Clinical Evaluation of Language Fundamentals–Preschool 3 (CELF-P 3; Wiig et al., 2020) revealed speech and language abilities within typical limits. In fact, Mateo's language skills were judged to be relatively advanced for his age. (Mateo's standard score was 114, indicating the 82nd percentile.) These results were supported by the clinician's observation that Mateo tended to use long, complex utterances during the free play interaction.

Screening and informal observation suggested that Mateo's speech sound production abilities were at the lower ends of typical limits. Mateo exhibited a number of consistent speech error patterns, and his intelligibility was occasionally reduced when the context of communication was unknown to the listener. Thus, the clinician conducted a more specific evaluation of Mateo's speech sound production using the Clinical Assessment of Articulation and Phonology-2 (CAAP-2; Secord & Donohue, 2013). Results indicated that Mateo's speech-sound abilities were at the 21st percentile (standard score = 88), with consistent error patterns affecting the liquids /l, r/ (which were consistently replaced by the glide /w/ or by a vowel at the ends of words), initial voiceless stops (which were sometimes voiced), and final consonants (which were occasionally deleted). The clinician was careful to differentiate any apparent speech sound errors from differences that might be associated with dialect or language/social background. Because most of Mateo's error patterns were inconsistent, they did not cause particular concern. The overall pattern indicated that Mateo's speech sound abilities were still developing. That said, speech sound abilities do factor into the consideration of "risk factors" for determining whether a child may continue stuttering (Singer et al., 2020; Singer et al., 2022; Walsh et al., 2021), so the clinician considered these results when formulating recommendations about therapy.

Clinical Decision-Making

Following the completion of formal testing, the clinician needed to make a decision about whether to recommend speech therapy for Mateo's stuttering. Aware that there was no way to determine for certain whether Mateo needed therapy, the clinician knew that various risk factors revealed in the assessment could make ongoing stuttering more likely (e.g., Singer et al., 2020; Singer et al., 2022; Walsh et al., 2021). Based on the full results of diagnostic testing (including not just the assessment of observable speech behavior but also the evaluation of Mateo's communication attitudes, speech and language skills, and the caregivers' reports), the clinician judged that treatment was indicated. Specifically, the need for treatment was justified by the positive family history of stuttering, the persistence of stuttering for more than 6 months, the fact that Mateo's speech sound abilities were still developing in the presence of seemingly advanced expressive language abilities, and the negative reactions and concern that he exhibited in response to his stuttering.

Treatment Options Considered

The clinician shared the results of the evaluation with the caregivers, emphasizing that it was still quite possible that Mateo would recover from stuttering without intervention (e.g., Yairi & Ambrose, 1999). Still, the clinician explained that the overall profile indicated that treatment would probably be beneficial to support Mateo's development of easier and more fluent communication.

The clinician then explained that a number of treatment options were available for children who stutter, including less-direct approaches to therapy (Gottwald & Starkweather, 1995; Hill, 2003; Starkweather et al., 1990), more-direct approaches to therapy (Walton & Wallace, 1998), combined approaches (de Sonneville-Koedoot et al., 2015; Kelman & Nicholas, 2008; Millard et al., 2008; Rustin et al., 1996; Yaruss et al., 2006; Yaruss & Reardon-Reaves, 2017), and operant conditioning therapy (Harris et al., 2002; Onslow et al., 1994; Onslow et al., 1996; Onslow et al., 2003). Based on a careful reading of the literature, the clinician reported both benefits and drawbacks for each of these approaches. Moreover, although certain fundamental aspects of the approaches do differ from one another, there are still significant areas of overlap and commonality across treatments (Eggers et al., 2022). The clinician expressed an intention to build upon these commonalities to construct an individualized treatment that was specifically tailored to meet Mateo's and his caregivers' needs.

For example, although all treatment for preschool children involves caregivers, the less-direct approaches do so without requiring specific corrections of the young child's stuttering as is seen in the operant approach (Onslow et al., 2003). This seemed appropriate for Mateo, a child who might become sensitive to comments about his speech. Still, the clinician explained that the empirical research supporting less-direct approaches is not fully developed and preferred to select a treatment approach that was supported by empirical evidence. On the other hand, although operant therapies are supported by a robust literature, the clinician's own experience suggested to her that these approaches may be better suited for somewhat older children (but not children in the school-age years). The clinician expressed the belief that using a purely research-driven approach to selecting a treatment for preschool children who stutter was not as straightforward as it might seem, because there are no studies that examine children who are *exactly* like Mateo in terms of their characteristics and experience. The clinician highlighted that this was another reason that it would be necessary to combine strategies from different data-based approaches to develop an appropriate individualized treatment to address Mateo's stuttering (Bernstein Ratner, 2018).

Based on the uncertainty about whether Mateo's stuttering might diminish on its own, the clinician recommended a *staged* treatment approach beginning with methods that were less directly focused on Mateo's speech and then moving toward more-direct methods as needed (e.g., Yaruss et al., 2006). This recommendation allowed the clinician to accommodate the caregivers' concerns about focusing too specifically on Mateo's stuttering, while still engaging in treatment that would help Mateo to communicate more easily. It would also provide the opportunity to directly address the caregivers' worries and fears at the same time. Importantly, the clinician assured the caregivers that talking openly about stuttering would not cause Mateo to become inappropriately concerned about speech; however, they continued to express fears about talking about stuttering. The recommendation of a staged treatment approach also allowed the clinician to continue monitoring Mateo's speech development to see whether more direct intervention would be required. The caregivers expressed their agreement with the treatment recommendation, as well as their relief that they would be able to engage in focused activities to help their child without causing him to become self-conscious about his speech.

The caregivers ended the evaluation by asking many questions about what they could do to help Mateo's speech at home. The clinician explained that learning such strategies would be a central focus of the early stages of therapy. The first recommendation was that they try to focus their attention *not* on Mateo's production of speech disfluencies but rather on his overall ability and willingness to communicate. The clinician emphasized that the most important thing for a young child like Mateo was to encourage and support his ability and desire to say what he wanted to say, regardless of whether or not he could always produce words fluently. By taking a broader view of the purpose of speaking, the caregivers would be able to support Mateo's overall *communication* development. This would promote his ability to say what he wants to say successfully regardless of whether he stuttered on a given word or phrase. The clinician explained that therapy would address Mateo's stuttering and that improvements in fluency and the ease of speaking would be sought *in the context of* good communication skills and healthy communication attitudes.

Course of Treatment

The clinician did not explain all the details to the caregivers at the time of the initial evaluation. Nevertheless, as a highly educated SLP, the clinician had a plan in mind for the path that treatment would likely follow, along with strategies for how to adapt the initial plan to meet Mateo's and his caregivers' needs.

The initial treatment plan that the clinician adopted was based on a comprehensive view of early childhood stuttering therapy that included both family-focused and child-focused components (e.g., de Sonneville-Koedoot et al., 2015; Kelman & Nicholas, 2018; Millard et al., 2008; Rustin et al., 1996; Yaruss et al., 2006; Yaruss &

Reardon-Reeves, 2017). Such treatment seeks to achieve improvements in a young child's fluency simultaneously working to ensure that both caregivers and child develop healthy, positive attitudes toward speaking and communication.

Less-Direct Aspects of Treatment

The caregiver-focused components of treatment used in this approach are similar to those described in so-called "indirect" (e.g., Conture, 2001; Gottwald & Starkweather, 1995; Hill, 2003; Kelman & Nicholas, 2008; Millard et al., 2008; Rustin et al., 1996; Starkweather et al., 1990) or "less-direct" (e.g., Yaruss & Reardon-Reeves, 2017) interventions. In general, these aspects of therapy involve helping *caregivers* learn to modify aspects of the child's communication environment to enhance the likelihood that the child will be able to speak more easily and, ultimately, more fluently. Common parental communication factors that are generally associated with reduced stuttering include (a) slower parental speaking rates (Guitar & Marchinkoski, 2001; Guitar et al., 1992; Kelly & Conture, 1992; Sawyer et al., 2017; Stephenson-Opsal & Bernstein Ratner, 1988; Zebrowski et al., 1996), (b) longer pause time following children's utterances (Bernstein Ratner, 1992; Kelly & Conture, 1992; Newman & Smit, 1989; Winslow & Guitar, 1994), and (c) reduced demands on the child's communication (e.g., minimizing the requirement that the child answer questions or speak in a particular manner) (Conture, 2001; Starkweather et al., 1990). Notably, the majority of these changes in the child's communication environment involve reductions in the *time pressure* that the child may experience when trying to speak (Yaruss & Reardon-Reeves, 2017). Thus, therapy does not focus on the specific speaking rate that the caregivers use; instead, the focus is the overall sensation of time pressure that the child may perceive. By reducing apparent time pressure, caregivers can help their child feel less rushed to initiate or complete utterances, and this, in turn, can have a positive influence on the child's ability to speak more easily (Yaruss et al., 2006).

Changes in the caregivers' communication patterns can be taught during a brief course of therapy, in which they (a) learn about stuttering and the factors that may contribute to the child's stuttering and then (b) learn strategies for reducing demands or stressors that make it harder for the child to speak easily. Analogies can be introduced to help them understand that children are more likely to have difficulty speaking when they experience increased time pressure, communication pressure, or general life stress. If these "stressors" or "demands" can be minimized in a particular situation, then the child is less likely to stutter in that situation. (Note that this does not mean that the child will *definitely* not stutter in that situation; it simply decreases the *likelihood* of stuttering.) The goal of the early stages of therapy, then, is to try to minimize those pressures as much as is feasible and thereby increase the likelihood that the child will be able to speak easily and, ultimately, more fluently across speaking situations. Inherent in this process is ample opportunity for the clinician to model, and the caregivers to practice, specific changes in their communication style that may help to reduce stressors. For example, the clinician may teach the caregivers to use *slightly* reduced speaking rates to reduce the child's perception of time pressure when speaking. (It is important that the changes in rate be minimal—the goal is not to "talk as slowly as you can" but rather to maintain a *natural* speaking rate and rhythm while reducing the feeling that one needs to rush while speaking.) In the context of therapy, the clinician first models the slight reduction in speaking rate while interacting with the child. The caregivers then try the modification themselves while receiving feedback from the clinician. This gives them the opportunity to directly observe how changes in their own communication style can support the child's production of easier speech. These modeling sessions continue until the caregivers have learned a number of strategies that support the child's communication (e.g., slightly slowing their speaking rates, increasing their use of pausing, and reducing other demands on the child's communication). Ultimately, this stage of therapy ends with a discussion about which strategies have been helpful for the child. The clinician then assesses whether additional treatment focused more directly on the child's speech and communication attitudes is warranted.

More-Direct Aspects of Treatment

More-direct aspects of treatment are addressed through an open-ended period of treatment in which children observe and then practice making changes in their speaking rate and physical tension in an attempt to reduce stuttering (e.g., Walton & Wallace, 1998; Yaruss & Reardon-Reeves, 2017). Specific communication factors that may be associated with reduced stuttering include (a) changes in the *timing* of the child's speech production and (b) changes in the physical *tension* the child exhibits during both stuttered and nonstuttered speech (Meyers & Woodford, 1992; Yaruss & Reardon-Reeves, 2017). Thus, children may be taught to use a *slightly* slower rate of speech in certain situations in an attempt to enhance their fluency. (As with the speaking rate changes recommended for caregivers, these changes must be minimal so that the naturalness of speech can be maintained.) Or they may be taught to reduce the tightness of their muscles during a moment of stuttering, so they are able to move through it more easily and more smoothly.

Many of these techniques have traditionally been reserved for older children (e.g., Healey & Scott, 1995; Ramig & Bennett, 1995, 1997; Ramig & Dodge, 2005; Reardon-Reeves & Yaruss, 2013; Runyan & Runyan, 1993); however, these approaches can also be used effectively with younger children (Yaruss et al., 2006; Yaruss & Reardon-Reeves, 2017). The primary challenge in using more-direct treatment strategies with the preschool population is that abstract discussions of concepts such as speaking rate, pausing, or physical tension are initially too advanced for very young children. These concepts can be made more accessible through analogies that help the child understand the distinction between "too much" (e.g., too much physical tension or too fast speaking rate), "too little" (e.g., too little physical or too slow speaking rate), and "just right" or "somewhere in the middle" (Yaruss & Reardon-Reeves, 2017). For example, when children are riding their bicycles, they know that there are some situations when they can ride as fast as they please, but there are other situations when they need to slow down (e.g., when coming to a curve or when the road is bumpy) or else they will be more likely to fall. When learning to ride a bike, children rapidly learn that that they will need to *change* their riding rate depending upon the situation: Sometimes they will ride more quickly (but not so quickly that they fall down) and other times they will ride more slowly (but not so slowly that they fall down). They seek a rate that is somewhere in the middle ("just right"), and the specific rate that is judged to be "just right" will necessarily change from situation to situation. (Note that similar analogies can be constructed for both timing and tension changes using behaviors such as running, shooting baskets, coloring, reading, playing computer games, and, ultimately, talking.)

Of course, treatment cannot rely entirely on analogies. Even when children understand the importance of using a "just right" rate when riding a bicycle, this does not mean that they will be able to transfer that understanding to using a "just right" rate when speaking. The clinician must explicitly tie the analogy to speech production by pointing out the similarities between riding too fast and talking too fast. For example, the clinician might say, "If we try to go too fast on our bicycle, we might fall down and have trouble going where we want to go. The same is true for talking—if we try to go too fast when talking, we might get stuck and have trouble saying what we want to say." Ultimately, the goal is for children to understand that they may have more difficulty saying what they want to say if they try to go too fast (or use too much tension). At the same time, they may have difficulty saying what they want to say if they try to go too slowly (or use too little physical tension). Thus, they must seek a combination of timing and tension that is "in the middle" so they can say what they want to say while increasing their speech fluency.

Just as it is important for children to understand changes in speech timing or tension, it is also important for children to have ample opportunity to *practice* making such changes in their speech production. This can be done through play-based drill work, in which children learn to intentionally modify their speech rate or tension, just as they do when riding their bicycle. A considerable amount of practice may be needed because changes to timing and tension are not easy to make. If the clinician starts by building a strong foundation for success (e.g., Yaruss & Reardon-Reeves, 2017), then this will increase the likelihood that children will learn when, why, and how to use these modifications so that they can speak as easily as possible across different situations.

Treatment Focused on Communication Attitudes

One critical way in which modern comprehensive treatment approaches differ from traditional indirect therapy approaches is that a significant amount of attention is paid throughout the therapy process to helping both the caregivers and the children to develop and maintain healthy, appropriate *attitudes* toward communication and stuttering (Kelman & Nicholas, 2008; Logan & Yaruss, 1999; Yaruss & Reardon-Reeves, 2017). The idea that clinicians can talk with preschool children about speaking and stuttering stands in contrast to the advice that has traditionally been given about the treatment of young children who stutter (Johnson, 1949; Johnson & Associates, 1959). Still, ample research has shown that talking to children about their speech does not increase stuttering (Harris et al., 2002; Kelman & Nicholas, 2008; Onslow et al., 1994; Onslow et al., 1996; Onslow et al., 2003; Yaruss et al., 2006). In fact, talking with young children about talking can actually help to *reduce* children's concerns about stuttering (Logan & Yaruss, 1999; Williams, 1985; Zebrowski & Schum, 1993). This even includes using the word "stuttering" when talking to children about their speech—a factor that is particularly important to consider given clinicians' traditional hesitation about using this word when talking about stuttering (Byrd et al., 2020).

Several strategies can be employed to help caregivers and children develop healthy attitudes about communication. Most important among these is simply addressing stuttering in an open, honest, and matter-of-fact manner. Thus, rather than avoiding talking about stuttering (Johnson, 1949), caregivers and children can learn to talk about stuttering openly, labeling it, and acknowledging that "stuttering is just something that happens sometimes when children are learning to talk" (e.g., Yaruss & Reardon-Reeves, 2017). Caregivers and other caregivers can learn to treat stuttering just like any other difficulty the child may experience when learning to perform a difficult task. For example, when learning to color, a child is likely to color outside the lines. Caregivers do not avoid talking about this for fear that the child will develop concerns about their coloring abilities! Instead, they simply acknowledge that the child has colored outside the lines and then refocus the child's attention on the purpose of coloring, that is, creating a picture. Caregivers respond in a similar fashion when a child trips while learning to walk, falls down while riding a bicycle, reverses letters and numbers, and more (see Yaruss & Reardon-Reeves, 2017, for more examples).

By acknowledging stuttering and the sensation of feeling stuck when talking, caregivers can help children understand that there is nothing to fear and that what they say is important, regardless of whether it is produced fluently or with stuttering. The matter-of-fact responses of parents and other caregivers (including extended family and even teachers) help to maintain a focus on the child's *communication* rather than on observable speech fluency. Of course, improved ease of speaking may still be an important part of an individual child's overall treatment program. That is why these strategies are used as just *part* of a comprehensive treatment approach that includes both less-direct and more-direct components. Before caregivers can discuss stuttering in an open, matter-of-fact manner, they must first come to terms with their own fears about the child's speech. For this reason, treatment is structured in a staged fashion, with early stages focusing on the caregivers and later stages addressing the child, as needed.

Structure of Treatment

In an evidence-based approach to treatment, it is important for clinicians to adapt their treatment to the individual needs and values of their clients. In the treatment of young children who stutter, this can be seen through the flexible application of various components of the treatment process. In general, however, the less-direct caregiver-focused components of treatment are typically provided prior to the more-direct child-focused components of treatment. The reason for this is that many children appear to require *only* the less-direct aspects of treatment to achieve a reduction in stuttering and an improvement in fluency (Kelman & Nicholas, 2008; Yaruss et al., 2006). Still, all aspects of therapy can be provided simultaneously if the clinician judges that the child is at high risk of continuing to stutter and the clinician is eager to begin work with the child. Combining the less-direct and more-direct components of treatment allows the clinician to address environmental factors that may contribute to stuttering while still working to help the child speak more easily. Finally, the more-direct child-focused components of treatment can be administered on their own in situations where the caregivers are unable or unwilling to participate in therapy. Regardless of how the clinician chooses to start therapy, it is always important to incorporate aspects of treatment aimed at helping both the caregivers and the child develop healthy, appropriate attitudes toward communication in an attempt to prevent the negative reactions that often affect older children and adults who stutter.

Analysis of Client's Response to Treatment

In the present case, the clinician judged that the caregivers would be active and willing participants in the less-direct caregiver-focused components of treatment. Thus, a plan was developed that started with treatment activities aimed at educating caregivers about stuttering and reducing their fears, while simultaneously seeking to improve the caregivers' and child's attitudes toward speaking and stuttering. More-direct child-focused components of treatment were planned for use, as needed, following the initial caregiver-child training program.

Less-Direct Aspects of Treatment

Both caregivers attended a "parent-child training program" (Yaruss et al., 2006) of six sessions, which were scheduled every other week to better accommodate their work schedules. During the first two sessions, they worked with the clinician to identify possible stressors on Mateo's communication, and then they explored ways of minimizing those stressors where possible. For example, they recognized that one factor that probably contributed to Mateo's stuttering was his use of long, complicated sentences, combined with his relatively rapid speaking rate. The caregivers asked if they should try to get Mateo to use shorter sentences (indicating that they had read this somewhere on the Internet). The clinician responded that it was not advised to discourage Mateo from speaking because of a fear of stuttering, adding that they might view Mateo's advanced language skills as a *positive* aspect of his communication abilities. The clinician underscored this point by reiterating the importance of seeking improvements in fluency and reductions in stuttering *in the context of good communication skills.*

Thus, rather than trying to restrict Mateo's speech output to perceptibly fluent utterances only, the caregivers and the clinician sought other ways of minimizing the impact that Mateo's long sentences had on his speech. The clinician highlighted Mateo's rapid speaking rate and suggested to the caregivers that he might be more able to speak more easily if he reduced his speaking rate slightly during those times when he was experiencing difficulty. The clinician added that, although many clinicians discourage caregivers from telling children to slow down, this advice is largely based on the fear that talking about speech might make the child's stuttering worse. Fortunately, there are other ways to help Mateo reduce his speaking rate than simply reminding him to slow down, including modeling and increasing pausing in their own speech. The clinician emphasized that the real issue was not the specific speaking rate that Mateo used but rather the *time pressure* that he might perceive when speaking. The caregivers stated that they had noticed that it was easier for Mateo to speak when they themselves spoke with

him in an unhurried manner, so they agreed that this strategy might be helpful. The clinician then showed the caregivers that they could help Mateo minimize his sense of time pressure by reducing their own speaking rates slightly to show Mateo that he could take the time that he needed in order to speak. Again, the caregivers were reminded that their rate of speech was *not* the cause of Mateo's stuttering—it was Mateo's own rate of speech that likely contributed to his stuttering. Still, the caregivers could help Mateo feel that he had more time to say what he wanted to say through changes to their own communication patterns.

During the next three sessions, the caregivers observed the clinician making specific changes in communication patterns while interacting with Mateo. The caregivers were given opportunities to try the modifications themselves while the clinician provided feedback. At first, the caregivers found it challenging to reduce their speaking rates and increase their pausing, particularly when engaged in free play. As previously mentioned, however, they had noticed that Mateo tended to speak more easily when he had more time to say what he wanted to say. As a result, they were encouraged to continue practicing until their ability to adjust their speaking rates improved. Throughout the process, the clinician emphasized that they were not speaking "too fast" and that they were not to blame for Mateo's stuttering.

Treatment Focused on Communication Attitudes

Throughout the six sessions of the caregiver-child treatment program, as well as the additional sessions of child-focused treatment described below, the clinician discussed other types of stressors that might affect Mateo's speech. One such stressor that the caregivers identified during the first two sessions was that Mateo became easily frustrated when he experienced difficulty performing any task, not just speaking. As a result, the clinician and caregivers together decided that it would be appropriate to model more appropriate, accepting attitudes toward mistakes of all sorts. For example, the caregivers learned to react in a matter-of-fact, calm manner when they themselves made minor mistakes, like missing the basket when throwing clothes in the laundry, putting a dish in the wrong cupboard, picking the wrong snack at the grocery store, and so on. Further, they learned how to treat stuttering in Mateo's speech just like other difficulties he might experience when performing complicated tasks. They worked to overcome their concerns about talking about stuttering. They also learned to pay attention to the *content* of Mateo's messages, not just the apparent fluency with which he produced them. This helped Mateo learn that it was okay to stutter. In time, this made it easier for him to say what he wanted to say without worrying about whether he was saying it correctly.

Data Collection and Clinical Decision-Making

During the last session of the initial caregiver-child training program, the clinician collected data about Mateo's speech fluency and stuttering in the clinical setting, as well as caregiver reports about other situations. Results indicated that Mateo's stuttering had decreased significantly and that he was talking more easily. The caregivers noted that this was particularly true during situations in which they were utilizing the strategies they had learned in treatment. Specifically, during a caregiver-child interaction in the therapy room, Mateo exhibited an average of only two observable stuttered disfluencies per 100 words of conversational speech (2% disfluent), a notable decrease from his stuttering frequency during the evaluation. More importantly, the caregivers also reported that Mateo's ease of speaking had improved in other situations. They indicated that they rarely saw him struggle with his speech during moments of stuttering, and they reported that physical tension in Mateo's speech was practically nonexistent. They stated that he still used a relatively rapid rate of speech most of the time, though they noted that he seemed less concerned when he stuttered. They also reported that he was speaking more and telling stories "like he had before." The caregivers were pleased with his progress, particularly because Mateo was speaking more freely again. Still, they agreed with the clinician that Mateo's continued stuttering indicated the need for ongo-

ing therapy. Thus, more-direct child-focused components of treatment were introduced.

More-Direct Aspects of Treatment

The goal of the more-direct components of treatment was primarily to help Mateo to slightly reduce his speaking rate when necessary. Treatment did not specifically address physical tension because of the clinician's observations and the caregivers' confirmation that his tension had already diminished. The clinician started by introducing the concept of speech disfluencies and explained that some children get stuck in their speech sometimes when they are learning to talk. The clinician further explained that Mateo could learn to change those disruptions by changing certain aspects of how he produced speech.

Various analogies about rate were introduced as described above (in particular, bicycle riding, shooting baskets, and coloring), and Mateo quickly saw that he had more difficulty performing these activities when he tried to do them more quickly. For example, he learned that he was more likely to miss when he tried to shoot a basket too quickly. The clinician then tied this to speech production by explaining that missing a basket when he tried to shoot too quickly was similar to getting stuck or stuttering when he tried to speak too quickly. The clinician showed Mateo that shooting slightly more slowly (not *too* slowly) would increase the chance that he could make the basket—and, similarly, talking slightly more slowly (but not *too* slowly), especially using some pauses in his speech, would increase the chance that he could say what he wanted to say more easily.

Treatment continued for nine additional sessions, during which the clinician reinforced lessons about rate modification through additional analogies and focused practice. Mateo's response to this aspect of therapy was rapid and positive. He quickly grasped the analogies and demonstrated and reinforced his understanding by explaining them to his caregivers. He showed them that he could change his speech in different ways and repeated that slowing down "makes it easier" to say what he wanted to say.

During this time, the clinician took additional data on Mateo's stuttering and observable fluency in the clinical setting and continued to probe Mateo's caregivers about his fluency at home and in other settings. After three sessions of this more-direct treatment, the caregivers reported that instances of stuttering had diminished further. They stated that they had directly observed Mateo slowing his speaking rate when he was having difficulty speaking. Following four more sessions, the caregivers indicated that they had not seen any stuttering in Mateo's speech, and they asked whether Mateo needed to continue in therapy. Being reluctant to dismiss Mateo too quickly, the clinician asked the caregivers to monitor Mateo's speech while he attended two additional sessions to ensure that the reductions in stuttering were not simply the result of natural fluctuations in speech fluency (Yaruss, 1997a). The caregivers reported that they had not seen Mateo speak this easily for this long a period of time since he first started stuttering. Still, they agreed that attending additional sessions would be worthwhile for ongoing monitoring. After these sessions, they confirmed that Mateo had continued to speak easily and fluently at home and in other situations, and they expressed their desire to discontinue therapy. The clinician recommended that they maintain contact through weekly phone conferences until it was clear that Mateo was no longer stuttering for 3 full months following the end of therapy. They maintained this contact for 6 weeks of phone calls, after which they explained that they no longer had any concerns about Mateo's stuttering and did not see the need for further follow-up. The clinician assured them that they could reach out at any time if they had any other concerns about Mateo's stuttering or overall speech and language development.

Authors' Note

This case summarized the evaluation and treatment of a preschool child who stuttered. Although certain aspects of the summary were generalized, the examples represent the types of experiences that clinicians have seen with numerous preschool children who stutter. As the case summary indicates, early intervention for stuttering can be successful in helping children improve their fluency while simultaneously helping them develop appropriate attitudes toward communication.

References

Ahn, J. B., Shin, M. S., & Kwon, D. H. (2002). The study of speech rate in normal-speaking adults and children. *Speech Sciences, 9*(4), 93–103.

Ambrose, N. G., & Yairi, E. (1999). Normative disfluency data for early childhood stuttering. *Journal of Speech, Language, and Hearing Research, 42,* 895–909. https://doi.org/10.1044/jslhr.4204.895

Ambrose, N. G., Yairi, E., Loucks, T. M., Seery, C. H., & Throneburg, R. (2015). Relation of motor, linguistic and temperament factors in epidemiologic subtypes of persistent and recovered stuttering: Initial findings. *Journal of Fluency Disorders, 45,* 12–26. https://doi.org/10.1016/j.jfludis.2015.05.004

Bedore, L. M., Fiestas, C. E., Pena, E. D., & Nagy, V. J. (2006). Cross-language comparisons of maze use in Spanish and English in functionally monolingual and bilingual children. *Bilingualism: Language and Cognition, 9*(3), 233–247. https://doi.org/10.1017/S1366728906002604

Beita-Ell, C., & Boyle, M. P. (2020). School-based speech-language pathologists' perceived self-efficacy in conducting multidimensional treatment with children who stutter. *Language, Speech, and Hearing Services in Schools, 51*(4), 1172–1186. https://doi.org/10.1044/2020_LSHSS-20-00044

Bernstein Ratner, N. (1992). Measurable outcomes of instructions to change maternal speech style to children. *Journal of Speech and Hearing Research, 35,* 14–20. https://doi.org/10.1044/jshr.3501.14

Bernstein Ratner, N. (2018). Selecting treatments and monitoring outcomes: The circle of evidence-based practice and client-centered care in treating a preschool child who stutters. *Language, Speech, and Hearing Services in Schools, 49*(1), 13–22. https://doi.org/10.1044/2017_LSHSS-17-0015

Bloodstein, O., Bernstein Ratner, N. B., & Brundage, S. B. (2021). *A handbook on stuttering* (7th ed.). Thomson/Delmar.

Boey, R., Van de Heyning, P., Wuyts, F., Heylen, L., Stoop, R., & De Bodt, M. (2009). Awareness and reactions of young stuttering children aged 2–7 years old towards their speech disfluency. *Journal of Communication Disorders, 42*(5), 334–346. https://doi.org/10.1016/j.jcomdis.2009.03.002

Brundage, S. B., Ratner, N. B., Boyle, M. P., Eggers, K., Everard, R., Franken, M.-C. C., . . . Yaruss, J. S. (2021). Consensus guidelines for the assessments of individuals who stutter across the lifespan. *American Journal of Speech-Language Pathology, 30*(6), 2379–2393. https://doi.org/10.1044/2021_ajslp-21-00107

Byrd, C. T. (2018). Assessing bilingual children: Are their disfluencies indicative of stuttering or the by-product of navigating two languages? *Seminars in Speech and Language, 39*(4), 324–332. https://doi.org/10.1055/s-0038-1667161

Byrd, C. T., Bedore, L. M., & Ramos, D. (2015). The disfluent speech of bilingual Spanish–English children: Considerations for differential diagnosis of stuttering. *Language, Speech, and Hearing Services in Schools, 46*(1), 30–43. https://doi.org/10.1044/2014_LSHSS-14-0010

Byrd, C. T., Werle, D., & St. Louis, K. O. (2020). Speech-language pathologists' comfort level with use of term "stuttering" during evaluations. *American Journal of Speech-Language Pathology, 29*(2), 841–850. https://doi.org/10.1044/2020_AJSLP-19-00081

Choo, A. L. & Smith, S. (2020). Bilingual children who stutter: Convergence, gaps, and directions for research. *Journal of Fluency Disorders, 63*, 1–22. https://doi.org/10.1016/j.jfludis.2019.105741

Clark, C. E., Conture, E. G., Frankel, C. B., & Walden, T. A. (2012). Communicative and psychological dimensions of the KiddyCAT. *Journal of Communication Disorders, 45*(3), 223–234. http://dx.doi.org/10.1016/j.jcomdis.2012.01.002

Conture, E. G. (2001). *Stuttering: Its nature, diagnosis and treatment.* Allyn & Bacon.

Craig, A., Blumgart, E., & Tran, Y. (2009). The impact of stuttering on the quality of life in adults who stutter. *Journal of Fluency Disorders, 34*(2), 61–71. https://doi.org/10.1016/j.jfludis.2009.05.002

Daniels, D. E., Gable, R. M., & Hughes, S. (2012). Recounting the K-12 school experiences of adults who stutter: A qualitative analysis. *Journal of Fluency Disorders, 37*, 71–82. https://doi.org/10.1016/j.jfludis.2011.12.001

de Sonneville-Koedoot, C., Stolk, E., Rietveld, T., & Franken, M. C. (2015). Direct versus indirect treatment for preschool children who stutter: The RESTART randomized trial. *PLoS One, 10*(7), e0133758. https://doi.org/10.1371/journal.pone.0133758

Drayna, D., & Kang, C. (2011). Genetic approaches to understanding the causes of stuttering. *Journal of Neurodevelopmental Disorders, 3*(4), 374–380. https://doi.org/10.1007/s11689-011-9090-7

Eggers, K., Millard, S., & Yaruss, J. S. (2022). Considering commonalities in stuttering treatment. In M. Leahy & K. Eggers (Eds.), *Case studies in fluency disorders* (pp. 142–185). Taylor and Francis.

Ezrati-Vinacour, R., Platzky, R., & Yairi, E. (2001). The young child's awareness of stuttering-like disfluency. *Journal of Speech, Language, and Hearing Research, 44*, 368–380. https://doi.org/10.1044/1092-4388(2001/030)

Frigerio-Domingues, C., & Drayna, D. (2017). Genetic contributions to stuttering: The current evidence. *Molecular Genetics & Genomic Medicine, 5*(2), 95–102. https://doi.org/10.1002/mgg3.276

Glover, H., St. Louis, K., & Weidner (2019). Comparing stuttering attitudes of preschool through 5th grade children and their parents in a predominantly rural Appalachian sample. *Journal of Fluency Disorders, 59*, 64–79. https://doi.org/10.1016/j.jfludis.2018.11.001

Gottwald, S., & Starkweather, C. W. (1995). Fluency intervention for preschoolers and their families in the public schools. *Language, Speech, and Hearing Services in Schools, 26*, 117–126. https://doi.org/10.1044/0161-1461.2602.117

Guitar, B., & Marchinkoski, L. (2001). Influence of mothers' slower speech on their children's speech rate. *Journal of Speech, Language, and Hearing Research, 44*, 853–861. https://doi.org/10.1044/1092-4388(2001/067)

Guitar, B., Schaefer, H. K., Donahue-Kilburg, G., & Bond, L. (1992). Parent verbal interactions and speech rate. *Journal of Speech, Language, and Hearing Research, 35*, 742–754. https://doi.org/10.1044/jshr.3504.742

Guttormsen, L. S., Kefalianos, E., & Næss, K. A. B. (2015). Communication attitudes in children who stutter: A meta-analytic review. *Journal of Fluency Disorders, 46*, 1–14. https://doi.org/10.1016/j.jfludis.2015.08.001

Han, T. U., Park, J., Domingues, C. F., Moretti-Ferreira, D., Paris, E., Sainz, E., . . . Drayna, D. (2014). A study of the role of the FOXP2 and CNTNAP2 genes in persistent developmental stuttering. *Neurobiology of Disease, 69*, 23–31. https://doi.org/10.1016/j.nbd.2014.04.019

Harris, V., Onslow, M., Packman, A., Harrison, E., & Menzies, R. (2002). An experimental investigation of the impact of the Lidcombe Program on early stuttering. *Journal of Fluency Disorders, 27*(3), 203–214. https://doi.org/10.1016/S0094-730X(02)00127-4

Healey, E. C., & Scott, L. A. (1995). Strategies for treating elementary school-age children who stutter: An integrative approach. *Language, Speech, and Hearing Services in Schools, 26*, 151–161. https://doi.org/10.1044/0161-1461.2602.151

Hill, D. (2003). Differential treatment of stuttering in the early stages of development. In H. Gregory (Ed.), *Stuttering therapy: Rationale and procedures* (pp. 142–185). Allyn & Bacon.

Johnson, K. N., Karrass, J., Conture, E. G., & Walden, T. (2009). Influence of stuttering variation on talker group classification in preschool children: Preliminary findings. *Journal of Communication Disorders, 42*(3), 195–210. https://doi.org/10.1016/j.jcomdis.2008.12.001

Johnson, W. (1949). An open letter to a mother of a stuttering child. *Journal of Speech and Hearing Disorders, 14*, 3–8. https://doi.org/10.1044/jshd.1401.03

Johnson & Associates. (1959). *The onset of stuttering.* University of Minnesota Press.

Kelly, E. M., & Conture, E. G. (1992). Speaking rates, response time latencies, and interrupting behaviors of young stutterers, nonstutterers, and their mothers. *Journal of Speech, Language, and Hearing Research, 35*(6), 1256–1267. https://doi.org/10.1044/jshr.3506.1256

Kelman, E., & Nicholas, A. (2008). *Practical intervention for early childhood stammering: Palin PCI.* Speechmark.

Klein, J. F., & Hood, S. B. (2004). The impact of stuttering on employment opportunities and job performance. *Journal of Fluency Disorders, 29*(4), 255–273. https://doi.org/10.1016/j.jfludis.2004.08.001

Logan, K. J., & Yaruss, J. S. (1999). Helping parents address attitudinal and emotional factors with young children who stutter. *Contemporary Issues in Communication Science and Disorders, 26*, 69–81. https://doi.org/10.1044/cicsd_26_S_69

Månsson, H. (2000). Childhood stuttering: Incidence and development. *Journal of Fluency Disorders, 25*(1), 47–57. https://doi.org/10.1016/S0094-730X(99)00023-6

Meyers, S. C., & Woodford, L. L. (1992). *The fluency development system for young children.* United Educational Services.

Millard, S., Nicholas, A., & Cook, F. (2008). Is parent-child interaction therapy effective in reducing stuttering? *Journal of Speech, Language, and Hearing Research, 51*(3), 636–650. https://doi.org/10.1044/1092-4388(2008/046)

Newman, L. L., & Smit, A. B. (1989). Some effects of variations in response time latency on speech rate, interruptions, and fluency in children's speech. *Journal of Speech, Language, and Hearing Research, 32*, 635–644. https://doi.org/10.1044/jshr.3203.635

Onslow, M., Andrews, C., & Lincoln, M. (1994). A control/experimental trial of an operant treatment for early stuttering. *Journal of Speech, Language, and Hearing Research, 37*, 1244–1259. https://doi.org/10.1044/jshr.3802.386

Onslow, M., Costa, L., Andrews, C., Harrison, E., & Packman, A. (1996). Speech outcomes of a prolonged-speech treatment for stuttering. *Journal of Speech, Language, and Hearing Research, 39*(4), 734–749. https://doi.org/10.1044/jshr.3904.734

Onslow, M., Packman, A., & Harrison, E. (2003). *The Lidcombe Program of early stuttering intervention.* Pro-Ed.

Polikowsky, H. G., Shaw, D. M., Petty, L. E., Chen, H., Pruett, D. G., Linklater, J. P., . . . Kraft, S. J. (2022). Population-based genetic effects for developmental stuttering. *Human Genetics and Genomics Advances, 3*(1), 100073. https://doi.org/10.1016/j.xhgg.2021.100073

Ramig, P. R., & Bennett, E. M. (1995). Working with 7-12 year old children who stutter: Ideas for intervention in the public schools. *Language, Speech, and Hearing Services in Schools, 26*, 138–150. https://doi.org/10.1044/0161-1461.2602.138

Ramig, P. R., & Bennett, E. M. (1997). Clinical management of children: Direct management strategies. In R. F. Curlee & G. M. Siegel (Eds.), *Nature and treatment of stuttering: New directions* (2nd ed., pp. 292–312). Allyn & Bacon.

Ramig, P. R., & Dodge, D. M. (2005). *The child and adolescent stuttering treatment and activity resource guide.* Thomson Delmar Learning.

Reardon-Reeves, N., & Yaruss, J. S. (2013). *School-age stuttering therapy: A practical guide.* Stuttering Therapy Resources.

Runyan, C. M., & Runyan, S. E. (1993). A Fluency Rules therapy program for school age stutterers: An update on the Fluency Rules program. In R. Curlee (Ed.), *Stuttering and related disorders of fluency* (pp. 101–114). Thieme Medical Publishers.

Rustin, L., Botterill, W., & Kelman, E. (1996). *Assessment and therapy for young disfluent children: Family interaction.* Whurr.

Sawyer, J., Matteson, C., Ou, H., & Nagase, T. (2017). The effects of parent-focused slow relaxed speech intervention on articulation rate, response time latency, and fluency in preschool children who stutter. *Journal of Speech, Language, and Hearing Research, 60*(4), 794–809. https://doi.org/10.1044/2016_JSLHR-S-16-0002

Secord, W., & Donohue, J. (2013). *Clinical Assessment of Articulation and Phonology-2.* Super Duper Publications.

Singer, C. M., Hessling, A., Kelly, E. M., Singer, L., & Jones, R. M. (2020). Clinical characteristics associated with stuttering persistence: A meta-analysis. *Journal of Speech, Language, and Hearing Research, 63*(9), 2995–3018. https://doi.org/10.1044/2020_JSLHR-20-00096

Singer, C. M., Otieno, S., Chang, S., & Jones, R. (2022). Predicting persistent developmental stuttering using a cumulative risk approach. *Journal of Speech, Language, and Hearing Research, 65*(1), 70–95. https://doi.org/10.1044/2021_JSLHR-21-00162

Smith, A., & Weber, C. (2017). How stuttering develops: The multifactorial dynamic pathways theory. *Journal of Speech, Language, and Hearing Research, 60*(9), 2483–2505. https://doi.org/10.1044/2017_JSLHR-S-16-0343

Starkweather, C. W., Gottwald, C., & Halfond, M. (1990). *Stuttering prevention: A clinical method.* Prentice-Hall.

Stephenson-Opsal, D., & Bernstein Ratner, N. (1988). Maternal speech rate modification and childhood stuttering. *Journal of Fluency Disorders, 13*(1), 49–56. https://doi.org/10.1016/0094-730X(88)90027-7

Tellis, G. M., Bressler, L., & Emerick, K. (2008). An exploration of clinicians' views about assessment and treatment of stuttering. *Perspectives on Fluency and Fluency Disorders, 18*(1), 16–23. https://doi.org/10.1044/ffd18.1.16

Tichenor, S. E., & Yaruss, J. S. (2019a). Stuttering as defined by adults who stutter. *Journal of Speech, Language, and Hearing Research, 62*(12), 4356–4369. https://doi.org/10.1044/2019_jslhr-19-00137

Tichenor, S. E., & Yaruss, J. S. (2019b). Group experiences and individual differences in stuttering. *Journal of Speech, Language, and Hearing Research, 62*, 4335–4350. https://doi.org/10.1044/2019_JSLHR-19-00138

Vanryckeghem, M., Brutten, G., & Hernandez, L. M. (2005). A comparative investigation of the speech-associated attitude of preschool and kindergarten children who do and do not stutter. *Journal of Fluency Disorders, 30*, 307–318. https://doi.org/10.1016/j.jfludis.2005.09.003

Walsh, B., Christ, S., & Weber, C. (2021). Exploring relationships among risk factors for persistence in early childhood stuttering. *Journal of Speech, Language, and Hearing Research, 64*(8), 2909–2927. https://doi.org/10.1044/2021_JSLHR-21-00034

Walsh, B., Usler, E., Bostian, A., Mohan, R., Gerwin, K. L., Brown, B., . . . Smith, A. (2018). What are predictors for persistence in childhood stuttering? *Seminars in Speech and Language, 39*(4), 299–312. https://doi.org/10.1055/s-0038-1667159

Walton, P., & Wallace, M. (1998). *Fun with fluency: Direct therapy with the young child.* Imaginart.

Wiig, E., Secord, W., & Semel, E. (2020). *Clinical Evaluation of Language Fundamentals–Preschool* (3rd ed.). The Psychological Corporation.

Williams, D. (1985). Talking with children who stutter. In J. Fraser (Ed.), *Counseling stutterers* (pp. 35–45). Stuttering Foundation of America.

Winslow, M., & Guitar, B. (1994). The effects of structured turn-taking on disfluencies: A case study. *Language, Speech, and Hearing Services in Schools, 25*, 251–257. https://doi.org/10.1044/0161-1461.2504.251

Yairi, E., & Ambrose, N. (1999). Early childhood stuttering I: Persistency and recovery rates. *Journal of Speech, Language, and Hearing Research, 42*, 1097–1112. https://doi.org/10.1044/jslhr.4205.1097

Yairi, E., & Ambrose, N. (2005). *Early childhood stuttering: For clinicians by clinicians.* Pro-Ed.

Yairi, E., & Ambrose, N. (2013). Epidemiology of stuttering: 21st century advances. *Journal of Fluency Disorders, 38*(2), 66–87. https://doi.org/10.1016/j.jfludis.2012.11.002

Yaruss, J. S. (1997a). Clinical implications of situational variability in preschool children who stutter. *Journal of Fluency Disorders, 22*, 187–203. https://doi.org/10.1016/S0094-730X(97)00009-0

Yaruss, J. S. (1997b). Clinical measurement of stuttering behaviors. *Contemporary Issues in Communication Science and Disorders, 24*, 33–44. https://doi.org/10.1044/cicsd_24_S_27

Yaruss, J. S. (1998). Real-time analysis of speech fluency: Procedures and reliability training. *American Journal of Speech-Language Pathology, 7*(2), 25–37. https://doi.org/10.1044/1058-0360.0702.25

Yaruss, J. S., Coleman, C., & Hammer, D. (2006). Treating preschool children who stutter: Description and preliminary evaluation of family-focused treatment approach. *Language, Speech, and Hearing Services in the Schools, 37*, 118–136. https://doi.org/10.1044/0161-1461(2006/014)

Yaruss, J. S., & Quesal, R. W. (2002). Academic and clinical education in fluency disorders: An update. *Journal of Fluency Disorders, 27*(1), 43–63. https://doi.org/10.1016/S0094-730X(01)00112-7

Yaruss, J. S., & Quesal, R. W. (2004). Stuttering and the International Classification of Functioning, Disability, and Health (ICF): An update. *Journal of Communication Disorders, 37*, 35–52. https://doi.org/10.1016/S0021-9924(03)00052-2

Yaruss, J. S., & Reardon-Reeves, N. (2017). *Early childhood stuttering therapy: A practical guide.* Stuttering Therapy Resources.

Zebrowski, P. M., & Schum, R. L. (1993). Counseling parents of children who stutter. *American Journal of*

Speech-Language Pathology, 2, 65–73. https://doi.org/10.1044/1058-0360.0202.65

Zebrowski, P. M., Weiss, A. L., Savelkoul, E. M., & Hammer, C. S. (1996). The effect of maternal rate reduction on the stuttering, speech rates and linguistic productions of children who stutter: Evidence from individual dyads. *Clinical Linguistics & Phonetics, 10*(3), 189–206. https://doi.org/10.3109/02699209608985171

HEARING

CASE 17

Amy: Late Identification of Hearing Loss in an Underresourced Community

Paul M. Brueggeman

Conceptual Knowledge Areas

Forbes magazine (DePietro, 2022) reported that according to the U.S. Census Bureau's 2019 American Community Survey, 7 of the 10 counties in the United States with the highest poverty rates were in South Dakota. While the U.S. poverty rate nationally was estimated at 13.4%, poverty rates in these South Dakota counties ranged between 44.8% and 55.5%.

The subject of this case study resides in one such county, on a Native American reservation. Over 80% of its population is Native American, with over a third of the population living below the poverty level. The population density is quite sparse, with only 6.5 people per square mile. The average population density for South Dakota in general is 11.3 people per square mile (States101.com, 2022). This county comprises an area that is over 1,000 square miles, so travel to any health care facility can be challenging. Teen pregnancy rates and high school dropout rates are above the national average on this reservation. There is also a well-documented gang problem among teenagers. This is a challenging environment in which to raise children and to find access to appropriate specialty health care in a timely fashion.

Audiologists are working to lower the age at which permanent hearing loss is identified. Via appropriate universal newborn hearing screening (UNHS) programs, professionals can identify most congenital hearing loss early and intervene before hearing loss causes a speech and language delay. Close adherence to recommendations of the Joint Committee on Infant Hearing (JCIH, 2019) by all physicians would better ensure that children with hearing loss were not lost in the system. Rural populations are particularly isolated from specialty care related to hearing disorders. Professions other than audiology often have the responsibility for conducting informal "hearing screenings." Unfortunately, these screenings often miss milder forms of hearing loss, and children with hearing loss become lost in the very system of screenings and assessments that is designed to help identify developmentally significant permanent hearing loss.

Description of the Case

Background Information

Content that appears in this case study in quotations are direct quotes taken from a recorded interview with the mother, when Amy was 6 years, 4 months old.

Amy was born full-term at a local hospital weighing 7 lbs., 4 oz. Amy's mother had an uncomplicated pregnancy and received normal prenatal care. At 3 days of age, Amy was rechecked for jaundice due to concern noted when she was born. The results of this recheck were normal. The initial newborn hearing screening performed at the hospital resulted in a "fail" on the screening otoacoustic emission test. Amy's mother was told by the nurse who performed the test that this was because her ear canals were too small. There was no evidence that Amy's ear canals were ever smaller than normal, with no record of a stenosis of the ear canal. Amy was rescheduled for a follow-up newborn hearing screening and failed two subsequent follow-up hearing screenings in her first 2 months of life using transient otoacoustic emissions (TEOAEs). Her mother recalled being told by the physician to "bring her back in a few years and we'll test her again." The JCIH (2019) guidelines for the identification of newborn hearing loss indicate that an immediate referral for an auditory brainstem response (ABR) test to rule out sensorineural hearing loss was in order.

This audiologist first met Amy and her mother at a developmental clinic on a Native American reservation in South Dakota when Amy was 5 years, 3 months old. This is a grant-funded clinic that provides assessments to children age birth through 5 years on reservation lands. Assessments offered are speech and language, audiology, psychology, nutrition, and others, including quarterly 2-day audiology clinics. The audiologist provided approximately 65 hearing evaluations for children at this one clinic each year. Due to the geography of South Dakota, access to specialty health care can be an issue, especially on reservation lands in western South Dakota. It is not uncommon for families to travel over 40 miles (one way) to have access to pediatric health care.

Accompanying the audiologist to this clinic were two doctoral students. One student was in her first year of study for their AuD degree, and the other was in their second year of doctoral study. The University of South Dakota (USD) department has a unique junior/senior clinician model, in which second-year students act as mentors who work alongside faculty in providing supervision and guidance to first-year clinical students. The reservation developmental clinic is housed in a double-wide trailer house converted into clinical space. There are several permanent staff who assist families, provide transportation for families who need specialty care outside of the tribal land area, provide in-home consultations, and perform initial screenings for developmental and other related problems. A wonderful benefit of this clinic is the homelike environment, which includes a cook who is busy throughout the day preparing meals for visiting families.

Services are provided to families who are concerned about their child's development (including hearing concerns) in a relaxed atmosphere where they feel safe and free to share their concerns. It is not uncommon for the staff to wait until the children finish some yogurt or oatmeal before testing begins. Flexibility is the key at these clinics, and that is a learning process in itself for students. Caregivers are asked about the whole family, which is appreciated by most families in this culture. This assists the staff in understanding each family's unique needs and helps to keep in perspective that scheduling an appointment to get cerumen (ear wax) out of a grandson's ear may not be a family's first priority.

Often, the caregiver accompanying a Native American child is an aunt, uncle, mother, great-uncle, grandmother, father, or grandfather. It is customary to ask about the relationship between caregiver and child because of how common it is for the network of care to be far-reaching and multigenerational. Before the AuD students travel to these clinics, they receive information regarding Native American culture. This is quite important as the students may not have the knowledge to appreciate Native American culture.

History Information

Amy's mother discussed the instance she first suspected that her daughter had a hearing loss:

> She was probably about 4 days old when she had already failed two screening tests, and, well

. . . by 6 months, I knew definitely. My mom even pulled me out of the room when we were trying to get her to respond to our clapping and she was, like . . . "she can't hear, but she can at least see you cry and you don't want her to see that you are scared. . . . " But, yeah . . . I knew early on before all the doctors did.

Amy had the normal colds, diaper rashes, runny noses, and coughs and received appropriate medical care when these occurred. She did not have any major medical problems and was generally a healthy baby.

Amy had her first bilateral ear infection when she was 5 months old and continued to have chronic bilateral middle ear infections (otitis media) for the next 7 months, which were continuously treated with antibiotics six more times during her first year. A medical examination when Amy was 1 year old included the diagnosis of bilateral otitis media, though the physician noted that "Amy's hearing is grossly intact." During this time, Amy's mother was becoming increasingly worried about Amy's hearing sensitivity, as she noticed that "I would clap my hands and she would just look straight ahead and I would clap over here and she was not getting it. It was scaring me."

By her report, the mother pleaded with her physician on multiple occasions to give her a referral for an ENT or audiologic consult but was not provided with a "purple card." "Purple cards" are referral approval cards for specialty services covered by Medicaid. When asked why she believed she did not get a referral, Amy's mother responded, "I don't think they [physicians] are educated enough about hearing loss to know what to pick up on. They don't have the equipment or the knowledge."

Amy's mother went on to say,

Yeah, I mean, it was like I was on a deserted island and the place I needed to go . . . I could see it and knew that it was there, but I just didn't have the bridge to get there. I would ask people and they never knew who I should go to.

Amy's mother finally sought specialty care on her own. She had not heard of an "audiologist" before

she had her daughter tested as outlined in the following section.

Previous Audiologic and Related Testing Related to Amy's Case

Amy first had an audiology evaluation when she was 15 months old at the closest audiology clinic to her home, located 100 miles away. On that date, Amy had been pulling on her right ear and was not responding to sounds coming from the right side. Tympanometric results were normal, but acoustic reflex testing and otoacoustic emission screening was not completed due to Amy's activity level. The audiologist recommended follow-up with a sedated auditory brainstem response test, with sound field visual reinforcement audiometry (VRA) testing noted secondarily. Certainly, as pointed out by Thompson and Wilson (1984), VRA testing could have been attempted on this date of testing.

Amy's second audiologic evaluation was completed at the same clinic when she was 16 months old. It was noted in the case history on test day that Amy was saying "mama, dad, tada, shut up, later, tic-tic, hot." Otoscopy revealed slightly vascular (red) tympanic membranes (eardrums) bilaterally. Tympanometry revealed negative middle ear pressure at −200 daPa in both ears with normal compliance of the eardrums. Acoustic reflex testing revealed absent reflexes from 500 to 4000 Hz bilaterally and a "fail" result on the otoacoustic emission (OAE) screening in both ears. No behavioral hearing assessment was attempted. The audiologist did complete a sedated auditory brainstem response (ABR) test, which included the use of 29.3 and 19.3 click rates as well as 500 Hz tone burst stimuli. The evaluation revealed identifiable wave V latencies down to 40 dBnHL for click stimuli and 35 dBnHL for 500 Hz tone-burst stimuli. Sound-field behavioral testing was not attempted because Amy was too groggy after the sedated ABR to respond in the sound-treated audiologic booth. Amy's mother was told that the test results were consistent with a very mild hearing loss suggestive of an upward (more in the low frequencies) sloping hearing loss. The report from this date notes the following:

While the ABR results would suggest a possible sensorineural component, the bilateral negative middle ear pressure causes me to pause before declaring today's results sensorineural in nature. Certainly, we have absent acoustic reflexes and failed OAEs. However, we can have these with this amount of negative middle ear pressure. It is also possible to have hearing sensitivity affected more in one region than the other due to changes in middle ear pressure.

The two recommendations noted on this date included a consultation with an ENT physician regarding Amy's middle ear status and a reevaluation of hearing in 3 months to include repeat tympanometry, OAEs, and sound-field behavioral testing.

A panel of clinical and academic audiologists completed a retrospective review of this case. An overwhelming majority found some major discrepancies in how they would interpret the original sedated ABR (and subsequent) sedated ABR test findings. There was considerable artifact error in the low-level stimuli ABR recordings, but the wave V latency found, even at lower intensity levels, is consistent with a sensorineural pathology, not conductive pathology, which was suggested by the audiologist on this date. Conductive pathologies tend to have much longer wave V latencies versus what is considered to be in the normative range for sensorineural pathologies. The consensus of the review panel was that the test results at the lowest level in which click-ABR results were present was 50 dBnHL in the left ear and 45 dBnHL in the right ear, an indication of the hearing sensitivity in the higher frequency region. Additionally, the lowest 500 Hz tone-burst stimuli level where responses were reliably seen (in retrospect) was at 45 dBnHL in the right ear and 40 dBnHL in the left ear with absent OAEs and absent acoustic reflexes. The interwave latencies, interaural latency differences, morphology, and absolute latencies of the waveforms were interpreted to be consistent with the recommendations published by Hall (2006).

At the ENT consultation, held 100 miles from the family's home, the decision was made to place pressure equalization (PE) tubes in both of Amy's ears when she was 18 months old. After Amy received PE tubes, her mother reported that

she got the tubes and . . . I wouldn't have to speak so loudly or look so directly at her so much . . . but I still had to be in close range. So it didn't, like, open them up like I thought it would have, but it did it enough to where the ear infections were coming down to a minimum.

Over a year went by before Amy returned to the same audiology clinic for follow-up testing. Amy's mother again had difficulty obtaining a referral for specialty (audiologic) evaluation. There also were problems with missed appointments and rescheduling during this period.

Amy was finally reevaluated at the same audiology clinic at 27 months of age. Between 16 and 27 months of age, no speech, language, or hearing evaluations were administered. The decision was made to repeat the sedated ABR. Otoscopy revealed purulent (pus-like) discharge from the right PE tube and an open PE tube in the left eardrum. Tympanometry was performed and results were consistent with an "occluded PE tube with material behind the eardrum" in the right ear and "an open tube that is functioning" in the left ear. There were some issues getting Amy sedated with chlorohydrate on this day, as it was noted it took over 45 minutes for it to "take effect." The results of the sedated ABR for the right ear were described as "no response was obtained at 60 dBnHL suggesting that we have at least a moderate conductive loss in the high frequencies." Amy woke up before 500 Hz tone-burst testing could be performed; however, according to the audiologist, "The last testing revealed responses that would suggest normal hearing in the low frequencies." The results of the sedated ABR for Amy's left ear were described as "able to follow wave V down to 30 dBnHL, which indicated hearing in about the 20 to 25 dBHL range for mid and high frequencies in the left ear." The audiologist noted that bone conduction testing was not performed because "Amy woke up from the sedation." In the discussion section, the audiologist stated that "we continue to have an incomplete picture of Amy's hearing sensitivity, and because she does not pass on OAE screenings, we feel compelled to arrive at a better picture of her hearing status." No specific recommendations were made for follow-up, except that "we will discuss our experiences with chlorohydrate today with Amy's physician." There was no attempt made to obtain behavioral hearing test information. It is important to test a child's hearing behaviorally at this age. Amy was over 2 years old and should have been able to respond behaviorally via visual reinforcement audiometry (VRA) or play audiometry.

Amy was reevaluated at the same audiology clinic when she was 30 months of age to repeat the sedated ABR. Amy's mother stated on this date that Amy was saying more words than during the previous assessment. She also reported that Amy was forming short sentences, such as "I said no!" However, Amy's mother and others indicated that many of Amy's words were not understood by others. It was reported that Amy had many articulation errors. Otoscopy revealed that the PE tubes were in place but appeared occluded. Tympanometric results confirmed that the PE tubes were occluded and that they obtained "normal" middle ear mobility on this measure, evidence that the PE tubes were plugged. The sedated ABR done reportedly showed normal wave V responses to 19.3/s and 29.3/s condensation and rarefaction click stimuli down to 20 dBnHL bilaterally. It was noted that the results of the 500 Hz tone-burst ABR test would be consistent with normal hearing sensitivity in the low frequencies. Amy's mother was told that the results suggested or correlated with normal hearing sensitivity. The audiologist noted, "We do know that Amy has struggled with middle ear problems for quite some time. This may have contributed to her speech and language delays. It would be advisable to have her screened for her speech/language development."

These final ABR results were reviewed retrospectively by a panel of academic and clinical audiologists. The results of this retrospective review were quite different from that of the original interpretation from the clinical audiologist who performed the ABR. This panel believed that there were no ABR responses to click stimuli below 40 dBnHL and to tone-burst stimuli below 45 dBnHL in either ear. The panel found that Amy's hearing loss was misdiagnosed as "normal hearing," which seriously delayed the initiation of intervention and treatment. This was the last hearing test performed before this audiologist first saw Amy and her mother 33 months later, when Amy was 5 years, 3 months. It should be noted that no behavioral testing of any kind was attempted up to this point and there had never been a record of present OAEs or acoustic reflexes.

At 42 months of age, Amy's speech and language development was evaluated by a speech-language pathologist in the local school district due to concerns by Amy's mother that "people don't understand Amy at times." The Goldman-Fristoe Test of Articulation-2 was administered and results showed an age-equivalent for single words at 3 years, 2 months (SS ~96, RS ~25). During conversation, it was noted that Amy used younger speech patterns; however, only single words were evaluated on this date. Some of the noted errors included /d/ for /g/, /t/ for /k/, /h/ for /t/, /s/ for /th/, final /s/ deletions, and /tl/ for /sl/. Lakota was the primary language spoken in the home, which could have influenced these findings. It was recommended that her progress be monitored.

Reason for Referral

The audiologist attended a 2-day developmental clinic at the Native American reservation center described earlier. The presenting complaint from Amy's mother was that "Amy says 'huh' a lot, and . . . turns up the TV and headphones way too loud."

Findings of the Evaluation

The audiologist interviewed Amy's mother about her daughter's hearing, academic, and medical history. Amy spoke loudly and without the suprasegmentals (rate, stress, pitch, etc.) expected of a girl her age. She had many articulation errors (particularly high-frequency phonemes) and appeared to be quite hypernasal. These behaviors, combined with her mother's concerns, raised serious "red flags." The audiologist did not yet know anything about the previous testing conducted at other clinics.

A test battery approach, such as that advocated by Diefendorf (1998), was implemented combining both objective and subjective test measures to ensure an accurate measurement of hearing. Results of the audiology testing were as follows.

Otoscopy

Normal-appearing eardrum landmarks and clear ear canals bilaterally.

Tympanometry

Testing revealed normal ear canal volumes, middle ear compliance, and tympanometric width bilaterally. Middle ear pressure was recorded at −250 to −265 daPa in both ears.

Pure-Tone Audiometry

Air conduction testing performed using ER-3A insert earphones revealed a gently sloping (nearly flat) mild to moderate hearing loss bilaterally. Masked bone conduction testing revealed slight (5–15 dB) air-bone gaps at 500 and 1000 Hz bilaterally. Because of this, the hearing loss was referred to as a mixed type. Amy was able to raise her hand very consistently throughout testing, and as such, test reliability was deemed to be very good. Speech reception thresholds, which were within 5 dB of agreement with Amy's three-frequency pure-tone average (PTA), were recorded at 40 dBHL in the right ear and at 45 dBHL in the left ear.

Representation of the Problem at the Time of the Evaluation

Following the audiologic evaluation, the results were discussed with Amy and her mother. The audiologist began, "I am sorry, but I have some potentially bad news for you. The results of today's testing are consistent with a hearing loss that has mostly a permanent component." At this point, Amy's mother cried and said, "I knew it, I always knew it. I should have just trusted myself." She was visibly upset about the way her daughter's case had been handled in the past. She said that she had told doctors for years that her daughter could not hear and that whenever she was tested, there always seemed to be something that "clouded" the accuracy of the results. A year after this visit, Amy's mother recollected,

I was thinking that day you told me about Amy's hearing, like . . . Did I not take care of myself well enough when I was pregnant? Did I do something while I was pregnant? Like, I ate a lot of hot sauce . . . does that matter? . . . I know it sounds crazy, but you blame yourself for ruining your child, you know. . . . I exercised. . . . I didn't drink or smoke . . . but you feel so guilty for what happened, you try to find a way to blame yourself. I see other moms drinking while they are pregnant and all this other stuff. You know, what made me so mad is that I did it by the book. Where the **** do other moms get off screwing up their kid's life? You know, it is like I felt I was being punished, like I did something so bad that my kid is being punished too for it. You think of your child of being nothing but perfect . . . then this happens and it's like getting punched in the stomach so hard. I love my kids, so much. . . . I just felt like I'd killed my kid. I was really down . . . I didn't have any help; I didn't know where to go after that day. . . . When they [the field of audiology] says it flips your world upside down, oh it does! There is no way to prepare. But I am glad now that she is taken care of and she is all good now . . . I remember that day because it was real hard on me and when we sat down at home, Amy asked if hearing aids are going to help and I said "I hope so. . . ." Amy said "Okay," then rubbed my back, gave me a kiss, and said she loved me. . . . I cried for a really long time.

Treatment Options Considered

Client Preferences

Four primary recommendations were made after the audiologic evaluation was completed. First, given Amy's articulation errors, an updated speech and language evaluation was requested through her local school district. Second, Amy should be evaluated by an ENT physician due to the small conductive component in her hearing loss and the unknown cause of the permanent sensorineural hearing loss. Third, Amy should have a follow-up hearing evaluation at a regional audiology clinic. Based upon the results of the hearing evaluation and ENT consult, the determination to continue with a hearing aid evaluation at that clinic would be decided. It was felt that Amy would be an appropriate candidate for bilateral BTE hearing aids, but follow-up medical clearance and testing were warranted to better define the nature of her hearing loss (i.e., whether a portion of her loss was medically treatable or whether her hearing loss was stable or going to progress). The fourth recommendation was for Amy to return to this clinic for at least annual evaluations after the hearing aids were ordered and fit to her hearing loss at the other regional audiology clinic.

Course of Treatment

Nineteen days after this audiologist tested Amy's hearing, she was seen at a local audiology clinic for a follow-up hearing test. The test results were consistent with the behavioral findings. Amy's mother was motivated to start the process of acquiring hearing aids for her daughter, so hearing aid options were discussed on this date at this same clinic. It was decided that bilateral mini-BTE hearing aids (pink in color) would be ordered as well as custom earmolds with pink sparkles. The hearing aids have direct-audio inputs (DAIs) that can work to link outside inputs (such as a personal FM system) to them. The next month, Amy was fit with her new hearing aids. As a standard of care, real-ear verification of the frequency response, gain, and output was performed at the regional audiology clinic. After the optimum gain setting was obtained for soft, moderate, and loud inputs, the volume control was disabled so that it would be held at a constant level.

Analysis of Client's Response to Intervention

Amy's mother's recollection of the day of the hearing aid fitting, as well as the months that followed, is filled with many successes and a few disappointments. When the audiologist first turned the programmed hearing aids on, Amy said, "Wow, mom, they're kind of loud!" She stood in front of the mirror just looking at them. Amy's mother recalled,

> Every day when she first had them we would tell her how pretty she was with them because some days when she first got them she would say, "I don't want to wear them." . . . I would be like, Amy, you are so pretty with them on, everybody is just jealous of you; they want your hearing aids. Then, she would slap them in!

Following the initial hearing aid fitting, they went to Walmart to get her a gift. There was an elderly woman at the checkout, and Amy said to her, "Look at my new hearing aids, I can hear you now!" Amy's mother reported that their joke on the trip back home was a game of "Can you hear me now?" When asked to recall when she noticed Amy's speech and language changing, she stated,

> Oh, it was like a matter of a week, not even a week, and her vocabulary changed. I mean, I am not kidding, just like that! Also, the day she got the hearing aids in, I was talking to her the same I had been for the past 5 years and Amy was like, "Whoa! Mom, I can hear you!" Then, I was like, "Oh, my, I am so sorry!" And then, within like a week we were still seeing more and more "words" from her.

Amy had to teach her dad and grandpa how to care for the hearing aids, because at first they did not know what it meant when they squealed.

When asked what her family thinks of the hearing aids, Amy's mother reported,

> We all think it is the greatest thing in the world, except a few of the distant relatives that were initially shocked and were like "oh my gosh,"

like they had never seen a hearing aid. They just had never seen a child with hearing aids. They have always seen a child with glasses but never a child with hearing aids. Well, now my family is totally on board in helping Amy with her hearing aids.

Amy's mother was asked about her impression of how hearing loss is viewed in the Native American culture. She reported,

Well, I know how a few people are. One of my really good friends used to act like she loved my kids and thought my kids were great. The day she saw Amy with her hearing aids she said, "Oh, I am so sorry that this happened to you guys and I am so sorry that you had to put those on her head." I was like, "Excuse me? I don't know who the h#@! you think you are, but my kid is beautiful. My kid has hearing aids. There isn't a damn thing wrong with her, she just can't hear well." I said this to Amy later, and she said, "Yep, mom, I know!"

Amy's mother recalled,

The first day when Amy got her hearing aids, it was like the big talk in grade school because the other kids did not know what Amy was going to get. The teacher told the other children that Amy had something really big that she had to do. So, everybody in her class was all curious. She walked in and showed the teachers and said . . . "Look at my hearing aid," and the teacher said "Wow!" and all the little girls came up to her in the classroom and said, "I want them too!" These girls went home and told their mom and dad they wanted hearing aids just like Amy. So, she never had a problem there [at school], but then, you know, as kids get older they tend to get mean. There are a few kids that bother her about it, but we taught her to tell them, "I am just the same as you are . . . I just can't hear well," and that shuts them up, I guess [laughing]. She has never had a problem. . . . Amy told her teacher how she likes things done with her hearing aids, where she

sits and about where the teacher is. So, then . . . after that, Amy got the freedom to sit wherever.

Amy is the only Native American student in her grade, and "even before she got the hearing aids, that was a big step for her to deal with because everybody would look at her [because of her color] everywhere she would go. All the kids now think she is just fine and it's not an issue."

Amy's mother reported,

After a while, the hearing aids just became routine. I didn't let her mess with them at first because it is an expensive piece of equipment . . . but then as she got used to them more and whenever I would clean them or take out the battery she would ask, "Well, mom, what's that, how come you are doing that?" Then, the batteries (size 13) come with cool little sticker things she loved and always wanted to do something with. So, she puts her own batteries in her aids and then she'll turn them on and say "I can hear you, mom!" Now, she gets up in the morning and puts on her robe. This is just so we can have coffee together. Or, she'll be like, "Oh wait, mom, I have to put in my hearing aids" and then she'll give me a hug! I love her.

Almost immediately after Amy was fit with hearing aids, a PLS-4 (Preschool Language Scale) and Battelle Developmental Inventory was administered, which revealed that her receptive and expressive language fell 1.5 standard deviations below the mean. That qualified her for speech and language therapy services within the school district. Amy was also qualified for services under South Dakota law as a child with hearing impairment. She began language therapy for her receptive and expressive delays, and her teacher performed daily amplification checks. Her speech and language skills continued to develop. Even though her parents separated, they provided a very supportive environment for her. She continued to excel in school and enjoyed playing with her peers.

When asked what she would like to say to future audiology and speech pathology students, Amy's mother reported that audiologists should

> never force anything really scary on a kid and get to know the kid for what they are. Always listen to the parent. A parent spends way more time with that kid than anybody else. If I would have had somebody that would have listened to me early on, we probably could have gotten this [intervention] done sooner. If they would have taken an extra 5 minutes and listened to me, they would have gotten to the source of Amy's problem a lot quicker. I mean, it was like Amy was the first Native American kid to ever get hearing aids. Nobody seemed to know I knew anything.

Author's Note

This material was based on a real case that occurred in South Dakota, 2007–2008. The content is the real words of an interview of a mother of a child with hearing loss. With permission, the interview was digitally recorded. Permission was received from the parent as well as the tribal committee where Amy's mother resides. All of the events listed are real, as are the people, test results, and emotions. It is hoped that the depth of feeling associated with this case is communicated to the reader.

References

Diefendorf, A. O. (1998). The test battery approach in pediatric audiology. In F. H. Bess (Ed.), *Children with hearing impairment* (pp. 71–81). Vanderbilt Bill Wilkerson Center Press.

DePietro, A. (2022, February 28). Counties with the highest and lowest poverty rates in the U.S. *Forbes Magazine.* https://www.forbes.com/sites/andrewdepietro/2022/02/28/counties-with-the-highest-and-lowest-poverty-rates-in-the-us/?sh=4b5f580965ec

Hall, J. W. (2006). *New handbook of auditory evoked responses.* Allyn & Bacon.

Joint Committee on Infant Hearing. (2019). *Year 2019 position statement: Principles and guidelines for early hearing detection and intervention programs.* https://digitalcommons.usu.edu/cgi/viewcontent.cgi?article=1104&context=jehdi

States101.com. (2022). *South Dakota, population, area, density.* https://www.states101.com/populations/south-dakota

Thompson, G., & Wilson, W. (1984). Clinical application of visual reinforcement audiometry. *Seminars in Hearing, 5,* 85.

LANGUAGE/DEVELOPMENT LANGUAGE DISORDER
CASE 18
Tessa T.: Preschool Child With Developmental Language Disorder
Kelley Nelson-Strouts, Tiffany P. Hogan, and Mindy S. Bridges

Conceptual Knowledge Areas

Everyone loves a good mystery. Children with developmental language disorder (DLD) represent an intriguing mystery in the field of speech-language pathology. Children with DLD are characterized by difficulty understanding and using spoken language despite normal cognitive development and adequate language stimulation. Herein lies the mystery: Why do these children have difficulty learning language when all of the key components to language development appear to be present? Moreover, these children are not rare: approximately 7% to 10% of children in kindergarten have DLD (e.g., Norbury et al., 2016; Tomblin et al., 1997), making it five times more prevalent than autism. Additionally, DLD seems to affect children of all races and socioeconomic classes (Tomblin, 1996).

Children with DLD are diagnosed using inclusionary and exclusionary criteria. The inclusionary criterion is a lasting impairment in language learning that is relatively nonresponsive to general education interventions (McGregor et al., 2020). The persistent nature of the language impairment differentiates children with DLD from very young children with language delays (i.e., "late talkers"). A diagnosis of DLD should also emphasize the impact of the language deficits on the child's academic and social emotional functioning. The exclusionary criteria comprise possible explanations for the observed language impairment: cognitive deficits, hearing impairments, autism, neuromuscular disabilities, or severe emotional disorders. However, it is crucial to note that noncausal, co-occurring conditions are permissible and even expected. Many conditions such as dyslexia (Catts et al., 2005), reading comprehension disorders (Nation et al., 2004), and anxiety and depression (St Clair et al., 2011) seem to frequently co-occur with DLD. Operationally, children are diagnosed with DLD if they have *impaired* language and *unimpaired* nonverbal intelligence—that is, intelligence above the level of intellectual disability (i.e., an IQ > 70).[1]

Clinical Note

School-based speech language pathologists "have never embraced" (Kamhi, 2007, p. 366) the use of nonverbal IQ assessments. As such, diagnoses of DLD according to language and nonverbal intelligence scores are common in research but rarely used in clinical settings. Instead, the diagnosis of "language impaired" is applied to describe a broad range of expressive and receptive language impairments in children. If DLD is to be diagnosed, SLPs often obtain a child's nonverbal intelligence scores as part of a multidisciplinary team assessment, such as from a psychologist.

Although the cause of the language impairment has not been pinpointed, numerous studies have been conducted to characterize children with DLD.

Family History

DLD tends to run in families. Rice et al. (1998) reported that the incidence of language disorders among immediate family members is approximately 22%; incidence of language disorders among family members of a child without DLD is approximately 7%. Further support for a genetic basis of DLD comes from twin studies, in which the risk for DLD is higher for monozygotic twins than dizygotic twins (Bishop et al., 1995).[2]

Language Impairment

Children with DLD have language learning deficits, likely present at birth. As such, these children typically produce their first words later than children without DLD (Rudolph & Leonard, 2016; Trauner et al., 1995). Vocabulary learning continues to be a struggle into early childhood (Gray, 2004). In addition, children with DLD have difficulty recalling words from memory (McGregor et al., 2002): They often use nonspecific words such as "stuff" and "thing." When first combining words to make phrases and sentences, children with DLD often omit finite verb markings (Rice et al., 1995). Common errors made by children with DLD include omitting past-tense inflections (e.g., "He kick the ball" instead of "He kicked the ball"), omitting present-tense inflection (e.g., "She read the book" instead of "She reads the book"), and asking questions without including the verbs "do" or "be" (e.g., "He going?" instead of "Is he going?"). As language skills develop, children with DLD tell stories with fewer specific character references (Finestack et al., 2006) and fewer story components (McFadden & Gillam, 1996). Moreover, many with DLD develop deficits in pragmatic language skills (i.e., the social use of language) as they become increasingly aware of their language shortcomings as related to their peers.[3]

It is important to note, however, that children with DLD comprise a heterogeneous group, both in severity of their language difficulties and in the individual language profiles exhibited. Some show more difficulty expressing themselves, while others have more trouble understanding language. Most often, though, these children have deficits in both expressive and receptive language (Alt et al., 2004; Leonard, 2020).

Comorbidity

Although a DLD diagnosis indicates that a child has a persistent *language* deficit, as noted above, these children are more likely than their typically developing peers to have certain other difficulties. In the preschool years, several children with DLD have speech sound disorders in which they have difficulty producing sounds in words (for review, see Leonard, 2020, but see Shriberg et al., 1999, for school-age data). Moreover, children with DLD have difficulty acquiring prereading skills such as letter naming and phonological awareness (i.e., the explicit awareness of sound structure of language; Boudreau & Hedberg, 1999). During the school years, approximately half of children with DLD have dyslexia (Catts et al., 2005), and many have difficulties understanding what they read (Nation et al., 2004). In addition, children with DLD are more likely to have attention-deficit disorders (Kovac et al., 2001) and social emotional difficulties (Norbury et al., 2016) as compared to peers without language impairments, which often manifest as poorer quality peer relationships and behavioral difficulties in classroom settings (St Clair et al., 2011).

Summary of Impairments in Children With DLD

- Acquire first words later than peers
- Use less complex sentences with filler words, such as "thing" and "stuff"
- Demonstrate decreased production and comprehension of grammatical markers, most notably verb tense
- Produce narratives that contain more syntactic errors and fewer essential story grammar components
- May demonstrate deficient preliteracy skills as preschoolers, including decreased phonological awareness abilities
- Often exhibit difficulties with word reading and reading comprehension

Description of the Case

Tessa T., a preschool-aged girl (4 years, 6 months), had difficulty communicating with her playmates and family members. As her mother watched her play side-by-side with cousins and friends, she noticed that Tessa T. frequently imitated their words and play but had trouble contributing in novel ways to the play or conversation. At home, she was good-natured, playful, and cooperative, but she had difficulty following her parent's instructions and struggled to express her ideas. Tessa T.'s mother described her conversational skills as choppy and noted that she often spoke using "immature" speech with short sentences lacking verb tense markings.

Tessa T.'s preschool teacher also noticed that Tessa T. had difficulty responding to questions about stories and struggled to stay on topic when describing pictures from books. Based on the above concerns, Tessa T.'s mother contacted the university clinic to learn the nature of Tessa T.'s difficulties and what could be done to help her daughter improve her communication.

Background Information

Tessa T. had not received a prior speech/language evaluation. An evaluation of her language and nonverbal skills was conducted in the spring of 2022. Over two evaluation sessions, Tessa T.'s language and cognitive abilities were evaluated using formal speech and language assessments, cognitive assessment, language sampling, parent interview, and informal observation.

In the spring of 2022, Tessa T. was seen twice a week for 50-minute sessions at the university pediatric clinic by a student clinician, Rebecca. Sessions were supervised by a clinical faculty member, with consultation from another faculty member.

Tessa T. was typically accompanied to therapy by her mother and less frequently by both her mother and father. Initially, Tessa T.'s attendance was intermittent because of her mother's inability to transport her to the clinic due to increased

work hours. However, over time, Tessa T. reliably attended 80% of her scheduled sessions as her mother adjusted her work schedule.

History Information

Per parent report, Tessa T.'s birth history was unremarkable following a lengthy 48-hour labor. Her neonatal reports were normal and she was discharged from the hospital to the care of her parents. She has remained healthy and only recently received hospital care to treat an idiopathic skin disorder. Gross motor developmental milestones reportedly occurred within normal limits: She sat alone at 6 months and began walking at 12 months of age. Language milestones were delayed: Tessa T. first babbled at 9 months, produced her first word at 24 months (i.e., "mama"), and began to combine words at 2½ years of age. Per parent report, Tessa T. has not had an ear infection. Tessa T. attends a local preschool. She will be attending kindergarten at the public school in her neighborhood in the fall.

An only child, Tessa T. resides with her parents in a single-family home. Tessa T.'s mother reported that she attended remedial reading and writing classes while in high school and that Tessa T.'s father repeated the fourth grade. Tessa T.'s mother works as a card dealer in a local casino. She reported that she did not finish high school and does not like to read. Tessa T.'s mother required a full hour to complete the history and background information documents. Completing the forms and attending to the task appeared to be effortful and fatiguing for her, and she required frequent breaks. Tessa T.'s father works in a local tire factory. He earned his high school diploma and completed a few years of technical training. English is the primary language in their home; however, Tessa T.'s mother speaks both English and Navajo. Per parent report, Tessa T. hears Navajo spoken infrequently at home and has never attempted to speak it. Tessa T.'s maternal grandparents live and work in the Navajo Nation, where they are both employed in the public school system. No information was provided on the paternal grandparents.

Reasons for Referral

Tessa T. was referred by her mother for a speech-language evaluation because of her concerns with Tessa T.'s language skills. Although Tessa T.'s mother had been concerned for some time, it was Tessa T.'s preschool teacher who encouraged her to contact the university clinic. Tessa T.'s teacher was concerned that Tessa T. had difficulty responding to questions about stories and struggled to stay on topic when describing pictures from books.

At our initial meeting, Tessa T.'s mother expressed concerns about frequent communication breakdowns at home. These included her not understanding Tessa T.'s attempts to express herself and her daughter's inability to pay attention and follow directions to complete tasks around the house. She described Tessa T.'s frustration with communication, indicating that Tessa T. often "checked out" of conversations with her parents and frequently felt left out by her playmates. Tessa T.'s mother expressed a desire to help Tessa T. before beginning kindergarten. She noted that Tessa T. has many talents that she feels are overlooked by her preschool teacher, such as drawing very detailed pictures and inventing stories that go with the pictures.

Findings of the Evaluation

Tessa T.'s evaluation consisted of informal observations and interactions, parent interviews, and standardized measures. The following data were obtained. Typical performance is characterized by scores above 85 standard score/16th percentile.

Hearing

A hearing screening (American Speech-Language-Hearing Association [ASHA], n.d.) was adminis-tered to rule out an undiagnosed hearing impair-ment. Tessa T. passed the screening at 20 dB for 1000, 2000, and 4000 Hz in both ears.

Speech Skills

The Goldman-Fristoe Test of Articulation-3 (GFTA-3; Goldman & Fristoe, 2015) was administered to assess Tessa T.'s speech sound system. As seen in Table 18–1, Tessa's scores for the GFTA-3 were 0 errors, 119 standard score, and >92 percentile rank. Based on these scores and conversational analyses of speech, Tessa T.'s speech sound system is considered within normal limits for her chrono-logical age.

Basic Pragmatic Skills

Tessa T.'s pragmatic skills were assessed to be within normal limits based on observations of her interactions with others. Tessa T.'s mother did not report any concerns regarding social function at Tessa T.'s preschool or home. During interactions with the clinician, Tessa T. engaged in appropriate turn-taking, eye contact, joint attention, and intonation and prosody for a child of her age and cultural background. Because there were no concerns in this area, no standardized tests were administered.

Expressive and Receptive Language Skills

The Preschool Language Scale–Fourth Edition (PLS-4; Zimmerman et al., 2002) was adminis-tered as a standardized measure to assess Tessa T.'s expressive and receptive language skills. The PLS-4 was chosen because it displays acceptable sensitivity (.80) and specificity (.88) for diagnos-ing developmental language disorder using a cut-point of z score >–1.5 (Spaulding et al., 2006).[4]

Table 18–1. Goldman-Fristoe Test of Articulation-3 Summary

Raw Score	Standard Score[a]	95% Confidence Interval	Percentile Rank	Concern?
0	119	113–125	>92	No

[a]The standard scores are based on a mean of 100 and a standard deviation of 15.

That is, based on the psychometric properties of the PLS-4, a clinician has confidence that a child scoring below −1.5 *z* score (77.5 standard score) is truly language impaired. Tessa T.'s scores on the PLS-4 are listed in Table 18–2 and followed by an interpretative summary.

Auditory Comprehension Summary

The auditory comprehension subscale of the PLS-4 assesses comprehension of basic vocabulary, concepts, and grammatical markers. Tessa T. was able to identify colors, understand negatives in sentences, and demonstrate appropriate use of objects in play. For example, Tessa T. was correctly able to identify a picture when given the prompt, "Look at all the babies. Show me the baby who is *not* crying" from a field of four pictures. However, Tessa T. had difficulty with inferences, identifying categories, following directions with cues, and qualitative concepts (e.g., long, tall, short, and shapes). Tessa T. had particular difficulty following verbal instructions such as, "Get the cup and give the bear a drink." Tessa T.'s performance on this subtest indicated that her receptive language abilities are markedly impaired, as she scored more than 2 standard deviations below the mean for her chronological age.

Expressive Communication Summary

The expressive communication subscale of the PLS-4 examines verbal development and social communication. Tasks include naming common objects, describing objects, and expressing quantity. Tessa T. was able to use basic word combinations (e.g., noun + verb, noun + verb + adjective) and quality concepts (e.g., "how many chicks are here"), as well as answer logical questions (e.g., "She is sleepy. What would you do if you were sleepy?"). She had difficulty using possessives, naming objects, completing analogies, and describing how objects are used. Tessa T.'s performance on this subtest indicated markedly impaired expressive language abilities as she scored more than 2 standard deviations below the mean for her chronological age.

Total Language Score Summary

Tessa T.'s overall performance on the PLS-4 indicates that her core language abilities are more than 2 standard deviations below the mean. To this end, Tessa T.'s overall language score is below the first percentile, indicating a significant impairment in both receptive and expressive language abilities.

Language Sample Analysis. A conversational sample of 50 utterances was collected during the evaluation. Tessa T. was friendly and talkative; therefore, the sample was obtained easily. An analysis of the language sample showed that Tessa T. had difficulty formulating grammatically and semantically correct sentences. She had particular difficulty with pronouns and often interchanged

Table 18–2. Preschool Language Score–Fourth Edition Summary

	Raw Score	Standard Score (SS)[a]	SS Confidence Band (95% Level)	Percentile Rank (PR)	PRs for SS Confidence Band Values	Concern?
Auditory Comprehension	35	65	56–74	1	1–4	Yes
Expressive Communication	38	65	58–72	1	1–3	Yes
Total Language Score	130	61	53–69	1	1–2	Yes

[a]The standard scores are based on a mean of 100 and a standard deviation of 15.

he/she within sentences. In addition, Tessa T. had some word-finding problems evident by many pauses and false starts. Moreover, she often used a circumlocutory sentence pattern including vacuous words such as "thing" and "stuff."

Emerging Literacy Skills

Tessa T.'s emergent literacy skills were assessed because children with language impairments are at significant risk for literacy impairments. The Test of Preschool Early Literacy (TOPEL; Lonigan et al., 2007) was administered to assess Tessa T.'s emerging literacy skills. A summary of Tessa T.'s results is presented in Table 18–3 and described below.

Print Knowledge Summary. The Print Knowledge subtest of the TOPEL measures a child's familiarity with print materials, such as holding books appropriately, turning pages, and pointing to pictures. Tessa T.'s score on this subtest indicated that she is developing print knowledge skills in line with her chronologically age-matched peers.

Definitional Vocabulary Summary. The Definitional Vocabulary subtest of the TOPEL measures a child's use of spoken vocabulary. Tessa T. was able to identify simple objects and their uses (e.g., "What do you put on pancakes?"). Tessa T.'s scores on this portion were within the normal range for her chronological age.

Phonological Awareness Summary. The Phonological Awareness subtest of the TOPEL measures a child's ability to manipulate sounds in words. Tessa T. was able to delete initial syllables and sounds from words and blend sounds to form words. Tessa T.'s scores on this portion were within the normal range for her chronological age.

Early Literacy Index Summary. The Early Literacy Index is an average score based on Tessa T.'s Print Knowledge, Definitional Vocabulary, and Phonological Awareness subtest scores. Based on Tessa T.'s Index, her prereading skills were age appropriate at this time.

Nonverbal Intelligence

The Kaufman Assessment Battery for Children–Second Edition (KABC-II; Kaufman & Kaufman, 2004) was administered to measure Tessa T.'s nonverbal intelligence. Tessa T. was able to accurately recognize faces, create matching patterns, and imitate hand movements. The results of the KABC-II, presented in Table 18–4, indicate that Tessa T.'s nonverbal intelligence scores were within normal limits compared to her age-matched peers.

Overall Summary

Tessa T. presented with impaired expressive and receptive language abilities. She struggled to express her thoughts and ideas, as characterized

Table 18–3. Test of Preschool Early Literacy Summary

	Raw Score	Standard Score[a]	Percentile	Concern?
Print Knowledge	12	92	30	No
Definitional Vocabulary	40	90	25	No
Phonological Awareness	14	93	32	No
Early Literacy Index	275	90	25	No

[a]The standard scores are based on a mean of 100 and a standard deviation of 15.

Table 18–4. Kaufman Assessment Battery for Children–Second Edition Summary

	Raw Score	Standard Score (SS)[a]	SS Confidence Band (95% Level)	Percentile Rank	Concern?
Nonverbal Index	33	89	82–98	23	No

[a]The standard scores are based on a mean of 100 and standard deviation of 15.

by word-finding problems, vacuous circumlocutions, and immature morphology and syntactic structure (e.g., omitted verb tense and agreement and gender reversal). In addition, Tessa T.'s discourse patterns were marked with broad and empty speech and cognitive inflexibility. She had problems following verbal instructions. Tessa T.'s pragmatic skills were normal and age appropriate. Her speech sound system was age appropriate. Her nonverbal intelligence was within normal limits. These observations were confirmed by Tessa T.'s mother. In sum, Tessa T. presented with developmental language disorder (DLD).

Treatment Options Considered

Treatment decisions were made using an evidence-based practice, three-pronged approach (ASHA, 2005; Sackett et al., 2000) in which client preferences, clinical experience, and scientific evidence were considered.

Parent Preferences

The ultimate goal of language treatment is to improve the client's language functioning in daily living. To better understand Tessa T.'s functional language needs, the clinicians had a discussion with Tessa T.'s parents. Both parents indicated that they wanted Tessa T. to communicate her ideas more clearly with precise words and age-appropriate grammar. Additionally, they expressed their desire for Tessa T. to be able to tell stories about her day and also to share stories, both real and make-believe, with her friends. They wanted Tessa T. to "develop friendships." Finally, they noted

that they were concerned that Tessa T. will struggle with the kindergarten curriculum that she will encounter next year. They want Tessa T. to "feel good" about her artistic strengths and to overcome her language weaknesses. Logistically speaking, they also said that transporting Tessa T. to therapy at the university clinic may be a struggle because of Tessa T.'s mother's variable work schedule.

Clinical Experience

The clinical team met to determine Tessa T.'s language goals in light of their discussions with Tessa T.'s parents. Based on parent concerns and observed language weaknesses, the clinicians decided treatment goals should focus on strengthening vocabulary, morphosyntax, and narrative skills. It was noted that Tessa T.'s parents would be informed of the Individuals With Disabilities Education Act (IDEA, 2004) and then be provided with contact information for Tessa T.'s public school special education services office. According to IDEA, children are eligible for free school-based services from birth to 21 years if they meet school-based criteria for treatment.

Before consulting the research literature, clinical experiences surrounding the treatment of language were discussed. The team considered the implementation of a therapy program that trains parents to stimulate language skills in the home environment (Girolametto & Weitzman, 2006). It was noted that this approach would accommodate Tessa T.'s parents' concern that they may have difficulty transporting Tessa T. to the university clinic due to work- and preschool-based scheduling conflicts. A treatment approach that targets grammar and vocabulary using focused stimulation revolving around play activities (Bruinsma et al., 2020; Ellis Weismer & Robertson, 2006) was also considered. Finally, it was noted that treatment research focused on improving expressive grammatical targets and vocabulary as well as narrative structure (Finestack et al., 2006). The team felt that a narrative-based treatment approach would meet Tessa T.'s parents' desire to see Tessa T.'s story-telling abilities improve. Moreover, they thought that Tessa T.'s pictures could be incorporated into treatment, and, as such, the treatment would provide a nice format for utilizing (and showcasing) Tessa T.'s artistic abilities. However, it was noted that many narrative interventions were geared toward older children with DLD (e.g., Hessling & Schuele, 2020; Swanson et al., 2005) and, as such, modifications would likely need to be in place for Tessa T., a preschool child. With these three treatment approaches in mind for Tessa T., the clinicians evaluated the external scientific evidence.

Scientific Evidence

To focus the search for scientific evidence, a foreground question was developed that included four components: (P) patient/problem, (I) intervention, (C) comparison/contrast, and (O) outcome. These questions have been termed PICO questions, an acronym for the four components (Dollaghan, 2007; Sackett et al., 2000). Our foreground question was:

> For a preschool child with DLD (**P**), does a focused stimulation treatment program (**I**) increase vocabulary and morphosyntax skills in narrative language (**O**) better than a parent training program aimed at stimulating language in the home environment (**C**)?

First, to learn about each technique and its supporting evidence, the clinicians read book chapters and journal articles outlining each treatment approach. The focused stimulation method is outlined in a chapter by Ellis Weismer and Robertson (2006). An article by Bruinsma et al. (2020)

addressing focused stimulation alongside additional language facilitation techniques supplemented the chapter reading. The parent-focused model for stimulating language in the home environment is outlined in a chapter by Girolametto and Weitzman (2006). Both chapters are located in a book edited by McCauley and Fey (2006). In addition, the narrative-based language intervention approach was reviewed by the clinicians. This approach is overviewed in a research article by Swanson et al. (2005) and a book chapter by Finestack et al. (2006). The literature confirmed that the narrative-based program was created for older children with DLD, while the focused stimulation and parent training approaches were geared toward younger children. Additional research groups have also begun to provide evidence of successful narrative-based language interventions for younger students with language impairment (e.g., Spencer et al., 2013). The book chapters and external evidence allowed the clinicians to determine that focused stimulation and parent training yielded similar vocabulary and morphosyntax improvements in children with language impairments (Girolametto et al., 1996).

Treatment Decision and Language Goals

After reading and reviewing the external evidence, the clinicians decided on a treatment approach for Tessa T., pending approval by Tessa T.'s parents. The intervention would include focused stimulation within a modified narrative-based language intervention approach administered by Rebecca during biweekly university clinic therapy sessions. Moreover, Tessa T.'s drawings would be used to generate stories for treatment. To supplement the clinic intervention plan, Tessa T.'s parents would watch and discuss the therapy sessions with the clinicians to learn language stimulation techniques for use in the home environment. The proposed intervention was presented to Tessa T.'s parents, who agreed that the approach targeted Tessa T.'s language needs and was a reasonable plan for both home- and clinic-based instruction. They especially liked the idea of using Tessa T.'s drawings in each session to promote her strength as an artist. They were hopeful that including narratives in the therapy sessions would directly improve Tessa T.'s ability to tell stories at home and at school. Tessa T.'s mother did not like the idea of including only a home-based program, as she did not feel comfortable being the sole stimulation for Tessa T.'s language. Instead, she wanted intervention to be provided at the clinic, where she could watch the sessions and learn techniques to supplement therapy at home. Thus, she was comfortable with learning from the clinicians and completing home-based assignments. In sum, the intervention for Tessa T. was chosen based on scientific evidence, clinical experience, and client preferences. It was determined that Tessa T.'s prognosis for success was good because she was motivated to produce language through narrative productions, Tessa T.'s parents were supportive of the intervention plan, and Tessa T.'s language sample indicated the presence of grammatical structures indicative of potential to learn more complex structures (Pawlowska et al., 2008).

Basic, intermediate, and specific treatment goals (Fey et al., 2003) were set for Tessa T. Overall, these goals address vocabulary, morphosyntax, and oral narratives.

Tessa T.'s Basic Goal

To improve Tessa T.'s ability to orally produce complete, sequential, meaningful narratives to increase her ability to communicate in her everyday environments such as home and preschool.

Tessa T.'s Intermediate Goals

Vocabulary. Tessa T. will show expressive knowledge of previously unknown words encountered in narratives.

Grammatical Forms. Tessa T. will spontaneously produce finite verb markings in oral narratives.

Tessa T. will spontaneously produce correct subject-verb agreement in oral narratives.

Narratives. Tessa T. will produce sequential, meaningful oral narratives that include key story elements.

Tessa T.'s Specific Goals

Vocabulary. Tessa T. will correctly label four pictures representing previously unknown words (two nouns and two verbs) encountered in narratives at 90% accuracy each week.

Tessa T. will use at least three of the four newly learned words when retelling one narrative in the therapy room each week.

Grammatical Forms. Tessa T. will correctly produce regular past-tense verbs at 90% accuracy while generating and retelling oral narratives in the therapy room.

Tessa T. will use a personal pronoun (i.e., he, she) when referencing characters at 90% accuracy while generating and retelling oral narratives in the therapy room.

Narratives. Tessa T. will include all essential story elements (i.e., characters, setting, problem/goal, actions, and resolution/ending) while generating and retelling oral narratives in the therapy room using her rainbow paper supports.

Course of Treatment

The language intervention chosen for Tessa T. was a hybrid approach that included focused stimulation on specific vocabulary and grammatical forms (Bruinsma et al., 2020; Ellis Weismer & Robertson, 2006) in the context of narrative-based language instruction (Finestack et al., 2006; Spencer et al., 2013). A horizontal goal attack strategy was implemented in which all specific treatment goals were targeted each session. In addition to the clinician-directed intervention, Tessa T.'s parents observed therapy sessions and were explicitly instructed on ways to mimic Rebecca's language stimulation techniques in the home. These included recasting Tessa T.'s productions and expanding them to include verb tense marking and targeted vocabulary.

Treatment Sessions

Each treatment session followed a similar sequence. One clinician-driven narrative was used per week (i.e., two sessions). Tessa T. generated two narratives each week (i.e., one each session). Each of the five specific language goals was targeted each session.

Vocabulary and Grammatical Forms Probes.

At the beginning of each session, Tessa T. was presented with pictures of two nouns and two verbs from the clinician-generated oral narrative previously presented in the treatment session. To elicit spontaneous productions of these newly learned words, the student clinician used the following prompts: For the nouns, she said, "These are new words you heard in the story you heard last session. What did we call this?" For the verbs, she said, "In our story, one of your characters did this—he/she _____." Then, Tessa T. was prompted to name the verb, including a past-tense verb marking. Finally, the clinician probed for pronouns by showing Tessa T. a picture of two characters, one male and one female, from previous narratives. Tessa T. was then prompted to say a sentence about the character after a clinician model. For example, "He likes to play. Who likes to play?" at which time Tessa T. would be required to say, "He likes to play." Each probe, verb and personal pronoun, included 10 test words. Corrective feedback was provided after each probe.

Clinician-Generated Narrative.

Each week, Rebecca generated a narrative in consultation with Tessa T.'s mother to include events from Tessa T.'s home and school. The narratives included two main characters, one male and one female. Noun and verb targets were chosen based on frequency counts (Dale & Fenson, 1996). Each story contained two high-frequency verbs that were not targeted for treatment (i.e., known verbs) and two mid- to low-frequency verbs that were targeted for treatment (i.e., unknown verbs). The same procedure was followed for the selection of nouns for each story. To visually represent the essential story elements, color-coded elements were presented to Tessa T. This procedure was adapted from the narrative-based language intervention discussed in Finestack et al. (2006). This is similar to other narrative interventions that have been shown to successfully utilize visual icons to represent story elements with young children (Spencer et al., 2013). First, Tessa T. was presented with the two story characters pasted on purple construction paper. Next, she was shown the story setting on blue construction paper. Third, Rebecca presented the picture of the story's problem pasted on green construction paper. Fourth, Tessa T. was shown the story's action (i.e., resolution to the problem) on red construction paper. Finally, a picture of the story's ending/resolution was shown pasted on an orange piece of construction paper. Rebecca explained to Tessa T. that stories have to include these colors of the rainbow. Each story element was explained as it was shown to Tessa T. For example, Rebecca told Tessa T. that characters are people in a story. Tessa T. was given a rainbow to represent the colors of the elements in the story. As Rebecca told the prescripted story, she picked up each color-coded element and placed it on a storyboard, a large whiteboard, which was on the therapy table. The title of the story was written on the board and read to Tessa T. When introducing each story element, Rebecca emphasized the target vocabulary words and grammatical forms (i.e., personal pronouns and regular past tense). Tessa T. was given a colored sticker to place on the rainbow for each story element. The sticker was a smiley face that was the same color as the story element. Tessa T. was prompted to repeat each sentence of the story as it was given. If errors were present in the sentence repetition, Rebecca modeled the sentence again for Tessa T. without requiring another repetition. An example story is below with target words and forms underlined for emphasis.

Example: Clinician-Generated Story

Title: The Fall

- Bob and Sue are friends (characters on purple paper).
- They go to school every day (setting on blue paper).
- One day Bob was playing outside. <u>He</u> <u>tripped</u> over a rock on the <u>sidewalk</u>. <u>He</u>

scraped his knee! (problem on green paper).

- Sue helped him. She pulled his hand. Bob stood up again. (action on red paper).
- Bob was happy that Sue helped him. He started to play on the merry-go-round. She played on the merry-go-round too. (resolution/ending on orange paper).

The vocabulary words targeted in this story were *sidewalk, merry-go-round, tripped,* and *scraped.* The familiar verbs were *helped, pulled, started,* and *played.* Rebecca emphasized personal pronouns and past-tense verb markings through increased loudness, raised pitch, and word elongation.

Client-Generated Narrative. After Tessa T. repeated each sentence of the clinician-generated story, she was asked to retell the story. During the retelling, Rebecca tallied Tessa T.'s use of the newly learned vocabulary words, personal pronouns, and past-tense verbs. Rebecca then told the story to Tessa T. one last time while highlighting the story elements using the rainbow visual prompts. Tessa T. was then presented with more color-coded character, setting, problem, action, and resolutions/ending pictures. She was instructed to create another story using "the rainbow" as a cue for including all story elements. Sequencing was not a focus; thus, she could choose story elements at random. Once Tessa T. had chosen all essential elements, she was then instructed to tell her story using all the colors of the rainbow. Rebecca tallied Tessa T.'s use of story elements, specific vocabulary words, and grammatical forms. If an error was present, she recast Tessa T.'s sentence including all relevant information with correct productions and, at times, expanded content.

Homework. At the end of the session, Tessa T.'s mother was given the clinician-derived story. She was asked to read it to Tessa T. as Tessa T. drew a picture of the story. Tessa T.'s mother was also provided the vocabulary that she was to emphasize while reading the story and while interacting with Tessa T. throughout the week. A rainbow and stickers were provided to Tessa T.'s mother; these were provided to assist Tessa T., as she used her drawing to retell the story while including all of the story elements. Tessa T.'s mother was encouraged to remind Tessa T. to "use the rainbow" when she told stories.

Narrative Probe. For each session, Tessa T. brought in a picture she had drawn representing the clinician-driven story that was presented in the previous therapy session. She was given a rainbow to represent story elements and asked to tell the story using the same words that Rebecca and her mother used as they told the story. Tessa T. was given a smiley face sticker color-matched to each of the story elements she successfully included in her narrative. Rebecca tallied Tessa T.'s use of targeted vocabulary and grammatical forms (i.e., personal pronouns and past tense) as Tessa T. retold the story. This probe was administered each session after the vocabulary and grammatical forms probe. Note the amount of opportunities to determine correct use of grammatical structures and new vocabulary learning varied across probes depending on richness of Tessa T.'s story retell. Thus, the narrative probe served two purposes: (a) to assess the use of story elements in narrative retell and (b) to determine the generalization of vocabulary and grammatical targets to functional language use (i.e., narrative production).

Analysis of the Client's Response to Intervention

Tessa T. has attended biweekly therapy sessions for 8 weeks. She has made the most progress learning new vocabulary words and using personal pronouns, while her production of past-tense verb markings has shown less improvement. Figure 18–1 displays data for each target across the twice-weekly sessions. Likewise, her narratives often continue to lack focus, and she struggles to learn the concepts associated with the story elements (e.g., characters). Nonetheless, her enthusiasm for learning showed each session, and she expressed how much she liked including her drawing in the story retell. Tessa T.'s mother reported that Tessa T. was more confident when telling stories at home, and Tessa T. asked her often, "Did

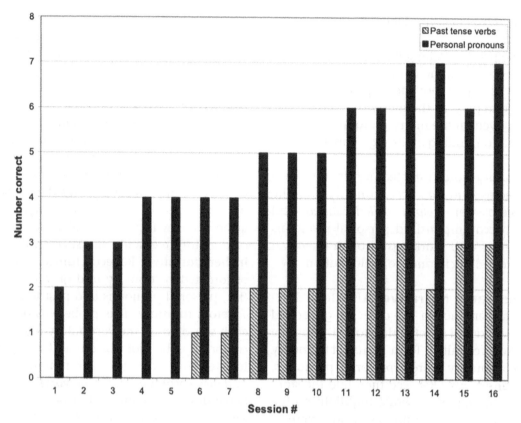

Figure 18–1. Treatment probe data across 8 weeks for grammatical forms: past-tense verbs and personal pronouns (10 total points possible per probe).

I use the rainbow?" Tessa T.'s parents reported that they feel better able to stimulate Tessa T.'s language at home by explicitly pointing out new vocabulary words, by expanding upon Tessa T.'s sentences emphasizing correct grammatical forms, and by "telling stories" each evening, a ritual they expressly enjoyed. Tessa T.'s preschool teacher noticed an increase in Tessa T.'s confidence but noted she continued to struggle when communicating in the classroom compared to peers.

The student clinician, in consultation with her supervisors, has implemented several adaptations to Tessa T.'s language intervention to respond to Tessa T.'s difficulty producing past-tense verb markings and narrative story elements. First, she has strived to use more concrete, direct language when explaining the story elements. It was hypothesized that Tessa T.'s receptive language problems impeded her ability to understand complex concepts. This adaptation seemed to be working, as Tessa T. has begun to show increased use of narrative elements. Of course, this improvement could have been due to time in therapy as well. Swanson et al. (2005) showed limited success using a narrative-based language intervention after 6 weeks. They predicted that a longer treatment likely would have led to more gains. This may be especially relevant when working with a pre-school-age child with more immature language. Another adaptation made in treatment has been the use of forced choice when probing past-tense verb acquisition. Tessa T. is asked to determine if a sentence with or without past-tense verb marking is grammatically correct. As such, receptive language goals have been added to supplement the original expressive language targets. She has shown progress in this area and, in turn, her production of past-tense verb markings has increased.

When Tessa T. generates her own narratives, she often loses sight of the narrative story elements and begins to stray from the story. The student clinician has begun to touch Tessa T.'s rainbow to cue her to include the story elements and stay on topic. This adaptation seems to be working; Tessa T.'s attention is often redirected to the rainbow, and she starts to include more story elements.

To date, Tessa T. is making progress in treatment; however, she has much to learn. Additionally, generalization to the attainment of goals outside of the therapy room will need to be explicitly addressed to ensure functional improvement in Tessa T.'s language abilities. For example, parent and teacher rating forms (cf. Newman & McGregor, 2006) may be included to determine generalization of treatment targets.

Other Considerations

- Tessa T.'s parents were directly instructed on ways to improve Tessa T.'s language skills in the home environment. Per parent request, goals were not set to quantify Tessa T.'s parents' learning of language stimulation techniques. Goals directly targeting parent training have been used by the clinical team in other cases.
- Narrative story elements were taught to Tessa T. to explicitly increase her narrative abilities. However, because Tessa T. is a preschool child, expectations for learning these elements were lower than they would have been if she were older and in grade school. Research shows that narrative development is a protracted process that spans from early childhood through the school years (Gillam & Pearson, 2017).
- Tessa T.'s narrative abilities were not formally assessed. A formal assessment (e.g., Gillam & Pearson, 2017; Hughes et al., 1997) would have more thoroughly quantified Tessa T.'s narrative skills to gain a better overall picture of her abilities and to determine the effect of treatment on targeted structures as well as untargeted structures.
- Repeated storybook readings have been shown to help younger children with DLD learn new words (Storkel et al., 2017; Storkel et al., 2019). This is another intervention strategy that could have been considered by the clinical team to address Tessa T.'s vocabulary deficits.

Endnotes

1. Normal nonverbal abilities in children with DLD are defined as the attainment of a standard score greater than 70 on a nonverbal intelligence test (see Plante, 1998). It should be noted that even though children with DLD exhibit *normal* nonverbal skills, on average, they score in the lower end of the normal range on nonverbal intelligence tests (e.g., 87–95 mean standard score).
2. See Leonard (2014, Chap. 6) for a detailed look into the genetic components of DLD (noted as in the book as specific language impairment, or SLI).
3. See Leonard (2014, pp. 103–134) for a comprehensive summary of crosslinguistic studies related to language use in children with DLD, including social language skills. See St Clair et al. (2011) for an additional resource on the social communication profiles of those with DLD (formerly SLI).
4. The PLS-4 was preferred to the more recent edition, the Preschool Language Scale–Fifth Edition (PLS-5; Zimmerman et al., 2011), due to psychometric concerns with the PLS-5 that could potentially impact Tessa T.'s scores. See Leaders Project (2013) for a complete review of the validity and reliability of the PLS-5.

Authors' Note

The authors thank their clients and their parents for serving as inspiration for our hypothetical case study. We also thank Mary Alt, Lizbeth Finestack,

Jill Hoover, and Cameron Kliner for helpful comments on drafts of the first edition of this chapter. Hogan's Fall 2008 Preschool Language Disorders course members provided value feedback from the "student" perspective.

References

Alt, M., Plante, E., & Creusere, M. (2004). Semantic features in fast-mapping: Performance of preschoolers with developmental language disorder versus preschoolers with normal language. *Journal of Speech, Language, and Hearing Research, 47,* 407–420. https://doi.org/10.1044/1092-4388(2004/033)

American Speech-Language-Hearing Association (n.d.). *Childhood hearing screening* [Practice portal]. http://www.asha.org/Practice-Portal/Professional-Issues/Childhood-Hearing-Screening

American Speech-Language-Hearing Association. (2005). *Evidence-based practice in communication disorders: Position statement and technical report.* https://www.asha.org/policy/ps2005-00221/

Bishop, D. V. M., North, T., & Donlan, C. (1995). Nonword repetition as a behaviour marker for inherited language impairment: Evidence from a twin study. *Journal of Child Psychology and Psychiatry, 37,* 391–403. https://doi.org/10.1111/j.1469-7610.1996.tb01420.x

Boudreau, D. M., & Hedberg, N. L. (1999). A comparison of early literacy skills in children with developmental language disorder and their typically developing peers. *American Journal of Speech-Language Pathology, 8,* 249–260.

Bruinsma, G., Wijnen, F., & Gerrits, E. (2020). Focused stimulation intervention in 4- and 5-year-old children with developmental language disorder: Exploring implementation in clinical practice. *Language, Speech, and Hearing Services in Schools, 51*(2), 247–269. https://doi.org/10.1044/2020_lshss-19-00069

Catts, H. W., Adlof, S. M., Hogan, T. P., & Ellis Weismer, S. (2005). Are specific language impairment and dyslexia disorders? *Journal of Speech, Language, and Hearing Research, 48,* 1378–1396. https://doi.org/10.1044/1092-4388(2005/096)

Dale, P. S., & Fenson, L. (1996). Lexical development norms for young children. *Behavior Research Methods, Instruments, & Computers, 28,* 125–127.

Dollaghan, C. A. (2007). *The handbook for evidence-based practice in communication disorders.* Brookes Publishing.

Ellis Weismer, S., & Robertson, S. (2006). Focused stimulation approach to language intervention. In R. J. McCauley & M. E. Fey (Eds.), *Treatment of language disorders in children* (pp. 77–103). Paul H. Brooks Publishing.

Fey, M. E., Long, S. H., & Finestack, L. H. (2003). Ten principles of grammar facilitation for children with specific language impairments. *American Journal of Speech-Language Pathology, 12*(1), 3–15. https://doi.org/10.1044/1058-0360(2003/048)

Finestack, L. H., Fey, M. E., & Catts, H. W. (2006). Pronominal reference skills of second and fourth grade children with language impairment. *Journal of Communication Disorders, 39,* 232–248. https://doi.org/10.1016/j.jcomdis.2005.12.003

Finestack, L. H., Fey, M. E., Sokol, S. B., Ambrose, S., & Swanson, L. A. (2006). Fostering narrative and grammatical skills with "syntax stories." In A. van Kleeck (Ed.), *Sharing books and stories to promote language literacy* (pp. 319–346). Plural Publishing.

Gillam, R. B., & Pearson, N. A. (2017). *Test of narrative language* (2nd ed.). LinguiSystems.

Girolametto, L., Pearce, P. S., & Weitzman, E. (1996). Interactive focused stimulation for toddlers with expressive vocabulary delays. *Journal of Speech and Hearing Research, 39,* 1274–1283. https://doi.org/10.1044/jshr.3906.1274

Girolametto, L., & Weitzman, E. (2006). It takes two to talk—The Hanen program for parents: Early language intervention through caregiver training. In R. J. McCauley & M. E. Fey (Eds.), *Treatment of language disorders in children* (pp. 77–103). Paul H. Brooks Publishing.

Goldman, R. & Fristoe, M. (2015). *Goldman-Fristoe Test of Articulation* (3rd ed.). Pearson Assessments.

Gray, S. (2004). Word learning by preschoolers with developmental language disorder: Predictors and poor learners. *Journal of Speech, Language, and Hearing Research, 47,* 1117–1132. https://doi.org/10.1044/1092-4388(2004/083)

Hessling, A., & Schuele, M. (2020) Individualized narrative intervention for school-age children with specific language impairment. *Language, Speech, and Hearing Services in the Schools, 51*(3), 687–705. https://doi.org/10.1044/2019_LSHSS-19-00082

Hughes, D. L., McGillivray, L., & Schmidek, M. (1997). *Guide to narrative language: Procedures for assessment.* Super Duper Publications.

Individuals With Disabilities Education Improvement Act. 20 U.S.C. § 126-16 *et seq.* (2004).

Kamhi, A. G. (2007). Thoughts and reflections on developmental language disorders. In A. G. Kamhi, J. J.

Masterson, & K. Apel (Eds.), *Clinical decision making in developmental language disorders*. Brookes Publishing.

Kaufman, A. S., & Kaufman, N. L. (2004). *KABC-II: Kaufman Assessment Battery for Children* (2nd ed.). Pearson Assessments.

Kovac, I., Garabedian, B., & Du Souich, C. (2001). Attention deficit/hyperactivity in DLD children increases risk of speech/language disorders in first-degree relatives: A preliminary report. *Journal of Communication Disorders, 34*, 339–354. https://doi.org/10.1016/s0021-9924(01)00054-5

Leaders Project. (2013, November 25). *Test review: PLS-5 English*. https://www.leadersproject.org/2013/11/25/test-review-pls-5-english

Leonard, L. B. (2020). A 200-year history of the study of childhood language disorders of unknown origin: Changes in terminology. *Perspectives of the ASHA Special Interest Groups, 5*(1), 6–11. https://doi.org/10.1044/2019_PERS-SIG1-2019-0007

Lonigan, C. J., Wagner, R. K., & Torgesen, J. K. (2007). *Test of Preschool Early Literacy*. Pro-Ed.

McFadden, T. U., & Gillam, R. B. (1996). An examination of the quality of narratives produced by children with language disorders. *Language, Speech, and Hearing Services in Schools, 27*, 48–56.

McGregor, K. K., Goffman, L., Owen Van Horne, A., Hogan, T. P., & Finestack, L. H. (2020). Developmental language disorder: Applications for advocacy, research and clinical service. *Perspectives of the ASHA Special Interest Groups, 5*(1), 38–46. https://doi.org/10.1044/2019_PERSP-19-00083

McGregor, K. K., Newman, R. M., Reilly, R. M., & Capone, N. C. (2002). Semantic representations and naming in children with developmental language disorder. *Journal of Speech, Language, and Hearing Research, 45*, 998–1014. https://doi.org/10.1044/1092-4388(2002/081)

Nation K., Clarke P., Marshall C. M., & Durand M. (2004). Hidden language impairments in children: Parallels between poor reading comprehension and specific language impairment? *Journal of Speech, Language, and Hearing Research, 47*(1), 199–211. https://doi.org/10.1044/1092-4388(2004/017)

Newman, R. M., & McGregor, K. K. (2006). Teachers and laypersons discern quality differences between narratives produced by children with and without DLD. *Journal of Speech, Language, and Hearing Research, 49*, 1022–1036. https://doi.org/10.1044/1092-4388(2006/073)

Norbury, C. F., Gooch, D., Wray, C., Baird, G., Charman, T., Simonoff, E., . . . Pickles, A. (2016). The impact of nonverbal ability on prevalence and clinical presentation of language disorder: Evidence from a population study. *Journal of Child Psychology and Psychiatry, 57*(11), 1247–1257. https://doi.org/10.1111/jcpp.12573

Pawlowska, M., Leonard, L. B., Camarata, S. M., Brown, B., & Camarata, M. N. (2008). Factors accounting for the ability of children with DLD to learn agreement morphemes in intervention. *Journal of Child Language, 35*, 25–53. https://doi.org/10.1017/s0305000907008227

Plante E. (1998). Criteria for SLI: The Stark and Tallal legacy and beyond. *Journal of Speech, Language, and Hearing Research, 41*(4), 951–957. https://doi.org/10.1044/jslhr.4104.951

Rice, M. L., Haney, K. R., & Wexler, K. (1998). Family histories of children with DLD who show extended optional infinitives. *Journal of Speech, Language, and Hearing Research, 41*(2), 419–432. https://doi.org/10.1044/jslhr.4102.419

Rice, M., Wexler, K., & Cleave, P. (1995). Developmental language disorder as a period of extended optional infinitive. *Journal of Speech and Hearing Research, 38*, 850–863. https://doi.org/10.1044/jshr.3804.850

Rudolph, J. M., & Leonard, L. B. (2016). Early language milestones and specific language impairment. *Journal of Early Intervention, 38*(1), 41–58. https://doi.org/10.1177/1053815116633861

Sackett, D. L., Strus, S. E., Richardson, W. S., Rosenberg, W., & Haynes, R. B. (2000). *Evidence-based medicine: How to practice and teach EBM*. Churchill Livingston.

Shriberg, L. D., Tomblin, J. B., & McSweeny, J. L. (1999). Prevalence of speech delay in 6-year-old children and comorbidity with language impairment. *Journal of Speech, Language, and Hearing Research, 46*, 1461–1481. https://doi.org/10.1044/jslhr.4206.1461

Spaulding, T. J., Plante, E., & Farinella, K. (2006). Eligibility criteria for language impairment: Is the low end of normal always appropriate? *Language, Speech, and Hearing Services in the Schools, 37*, 61–72. https://doi.org/10.1044/0161-1461(2006/007)

Spencer, T. D., Kajian, M., Petersen, D. B., & Bilyk, N. (2013). Effects of an individualized narrative intervention on children's storytelling and comprehension skills. *Journal of Early Intervention*. https://doi.org/10.1177/1053815114540002

St Clair, M. C., Pickles, A., Durkin, K., & Conti-Ramsden, G. (2011). A longitudinal study of behavioral, emotional, and social difficulties in individuals with a history of specific language impairment (SLI). *Journal of Communication Disorders, 44*(2), 186–199. https://doi.org/10.1016/j.jcomdis.2010.09.004

Storkel, H. L., Komesidou, R., Pezold, M. J., Pitt, A. R., Fleming, K. K., & Romine, R. S. (2019). The impact of dose and dose frequency on word learning by kindergarten children with developmental language disorder during interactive book reading. *Language, Speech, and Hearing Services in Schools, 50*(4), 518–539. https://doi.org/10.1044/2019_LSHSS-VOIA-18-0131

Storkel, H. L., Voelmle, K., Fierro, V., Flake, K., Fleming, K. K., & Romine, R. S. (2017). Interactive book reading to accelerate word learning by kindergarten children with specific language impairment: Identifying an adequate intensity and variation in treatment response. *Language, Speech, and Hearing Services in Schools, 48*(1), 16–30. https://doi.org/10.1044/2016_LSHSS-16-0014

Swanson, L. A., Fey, M. E., Mills, C. E., & Hood, L. S. (2005). Use of narrative-based language intervention with children who have developmental language disorder. *American Journal of Speech-Language Pathology, 14*, 131–143. https://doi.org/10.1044/1058-0360 (2005/014)

Tomblin, J. B. (1996). Genetic and environmental contributions to the risk of specific language impairment. In M. L. Rice (Ed.), *Toward a genetics of language* (pp. 191–210). Lawrence Erlbaum.

Tomblin, J. B., Records, N., Buckwalter, P., Zhang, X., Smith, E., & O'Brien, M. (1997). Prevalence of developmental language disorder in kindergarten children. *Journal of Speech, Language, and Hearing Research, 40*, 1245–1260. https://doi.org/10.1044/jslhr .4006.1245

Trauner, D., Wulfeck, B., Tallal, P., & Hesselink, J. (1995). *Neurologic and MRI profiles of impaired children* [Technical report CND-9513]. Center for Research in Language, University of California at San Diego.

Zimmerman, I. L., Steiner, V. G., & Pond, R. E. (2002). *Preschool Language Scales* (4th ed.). The Psychological Corporation.

Zimmerman, I. L., Steiner, V. G., & Pond, R. E. (2011). *Preschool Language Scales* (5th ed.). The Psychological Corporation.

PHONOLOGY/ARTICULATION
CASE 19
Sam: Complex Disorder Traits in a 3-Year-Old Boy With a Severe Speech Sound Disorder
Beate Peter

Conceptual Knowledge Areas

Typical and Disordered Speech Sound Development

Children typically acquire the speech sounds of their ambient language in a certain sequence. General patterns regarding manner of articulation are that nasals, glides, and stops are acquired at a young age, whereas fricatives, affricates, and liquids emerge later. Regarding place of articulation, anterior consonants are acquired before alveolar, palatal, and velar consonants. By age 6 years, most children in the world can correctly produce all sounds of their ambient language (McLeod & Crowe, 2018). In a unique case of a girl who did not speak until age 10 years, we showed that these acquisition patterns are not driven by age but rather by consecutive acquisition of motor skills (Peter et al., 2019).

Many children have difficulty with speech production, a condition commonly called speech sound disorder (SSD). They have more trouble being understood than their peers.

In a basic sense, disordered speech can be analyzed by what happens to the speech segments. Error types include omissions, substitutions, distortions, insertions, and sequential rearrangement. Probing beyond a basic description of segmental speech errors raises the question of how children with SSD can be grouped into distinct disorder subtypes. Bauman-Waengler (2020) summarizes commonly cited categories based on error typology, child age, and error consistency proposed by Dodd (2005). These categories are:

- **Articulation disorders**, characterized by speech sound errors that are phonetic in nature and usually represent errors of placement. An example of a phonetic error would be a laterally distorted /s/ sound ([sˡ]) in all attempts at the sound.
- **Phonological errors**, also referred to as phonological processes, are systematic in nature and can affect entire phoneme classes or word positions. Examples include reducing consonant clusters to singletons or omitting final obstruents, even though the omitted sounds are produced correctly in other phonological environments. Final devoicing and initial voicing are also commonly occurring systematic phonological processes.
- **Phonological delays**, diagnosed in children who produce phonological errors common in typically developing children at younger ages.

Phonological disorders (consistent or inconsistent) are diagnosed in children whose errors are unusual, for instance, omitting initial consonants but not final ones, devoicing initial consonants, or voicing final consonants. Whereas articulation disorders are thought to be based in habitually faulty articulator placement, phonological disorders are thought to originate from faulty knowledge of sound units in the context of words.

An alternate SSD taxonomy to the error type taxonomy based on Dodd (2005) is the **Speech Disorders Classification System (SDCS)** (Shriberg et al., 2019), an alternative model based on an etiological model. The distal causes are genomic and environmental, and proximal causes are allocated to processes of representation, planning/programming, and execution. Subtypes of SSD are speech delay, speech errors that affect /s, r/, and motor speech disorder.

Prompts for Restructuring Oral Muscular Phonetic Targets (PROMPT) (Grigos et al., 2010; Rogers et al., 2006) is a therapy approach designed for children with any type of SSD. It is based on shaping "motor-phoneme links" (i.e., gestures that connect higher-level phonological units to lower-level articulatory movements). The therapy uses tactile, kinesthetic, and proprioceptive inputs to refine the motor-phoneme links.

Phonological Processes

During the early years of clinical practice, speech sound errors were viewed as failure to acquire certain speech sounds, and therapy addressed each inaccurately produced speech sound individually. In contrast, a phonological view of speech sound errors is based on the idea that sounds can be grouped into classes, for instance, by place of articulation such as alveolar or velar; by manner of articulation such as stops, fricatives, or glides; or by voicing. Speech sound errors can affect several sounds within the same class. For instance, a child who has trouble with the /s/ sound, replacing it with [t], may also have difficulty with /f, θ/, substituting [p] or [t], a pattern called "stopping" because stops are produced instead of fricatives. In therapy, these processes are addressed by sound class rather than as individual sounds. Phonological processes can be observed in different linguistic structures, including segments, syllables, and words. Table 19–1 lists selected phonological processes and some actual examples from clinical practice. Because many children with severe SSD show several error patterns at once, some examples contain multiple errors.

Multiple processes can affect the same word production. For instance, [wiː]/tree shows evidence of both gliding and cluster reduction. Three phonological processes are evident in [daʊn]/clown: cluster reduction, velar fronting, and prevocalic voicing. In some cases, it may not be clear at first which phonological process is at play. For instance, [ɡɔɡ]/dog could be an example of assimilation or backing. A close look at other word productions

Table 19–1. Examples of Selected Phonological Processes, by Linguistic Level and Underlying Mechanism

Affected Structure	Mechanism	Phonological Process	Example
Segment	Place of articulation	Fronting	[ti]/key [so]/show
		Backing	[sʌm]/thumb
	Manner of articulation	Stopping	[ti]/see
		Gliding	[wɛd]/red
		Affrication	[haʊts]/house
	Voicing	Prevocalic voicing	[bədæmaz]/pajamas
		Final devoicing	[slaɪt]/slide
Syllable	Quantity of syllable constituents	Cluster reduction	[bu]/blue
		Final consonant deletion	[haʊ]/house
	Quality of syllable constituents	Assimilation	[lɛlo]/yellow
Word	Quantity of word constituents	Syllable deletion	[bun]/balloon
		Syllable insertion	[səlaɪd]/slide

will resolve the ambiguity based on additional evidence for these possibilities.

Care must be taken to distinguish between phonological processes and expressive language deficits. Final consonant deletion and unmarked plurals or missing third-person singular verb endings may result in the same word production. Probing for other syntactic markers will shed light on the underlying disorder mechanism.

Finally, note that errors in speech production can be explained through multiple models. For instance, a clinician working from a phonological process perspective might classify [bu]/blue as the phonological process of cluster reduction, while a clinician more comfortable in a motor planning framework may view this error type as a planning error triggered by a complex phonetic environment. The former perspective is a more linguistic-based one, while the latter emphasizes motoric elements of speech production.

Childhood Apraxia of Speech (CAS)

One form of SSD that is characterized neither by articulatory nor phonological loci of impairment but, rather, by difficulties with motor planning and programming is childhood apraxia of speech (CAS). The American Speech-Language-Hearing Association (ASHA, 2007) described CAS as "a neurological childhood (pediatric) speech sound disorder in which the precision and consistency of movements underlying speech are impaired in the absence of neuromuscular deficits." As thoughts are converted into speech sounds, motor planning and motor programming are conceptualized as steps preceding the actual muscle activity in the articulators. A recent review (van der Merwe & Steyn, 2018) conceptualized motor planning as the intent to speak, coupled with general motor programs stored in long-term memory, whereas motor programming refers to muscle-specific movement instructions and feedback loops that inform the execution of movement.

Many children with CAS have such severe speech difficulties that their speech is difficult to understand. Their speech can be characterized by small consonant inventories, vowel errors, inconsistent word productions, low intelligibility, and difficulty with multisyllabic words. Prosody is characterized by lack of differentiation between stressed and unstressed syllables, and mis-stressing syllables. Further, children with CAS have difficulty with rapid syllable repetition (diadochokinetic, DDK, tasks such as "papapa . . . ," "patapata . . . ") (Shriberg et al., 2011), and flow of speech is disrupted by characteristic pauses (Shriberg et al., 2017).

In recent years, some major advances in understanding CAS have emerged. First, in terms of phenotypic presentation, we and others have shown that motor planning and programming deficits are not limited to the motor speech system but can also affect fine motor and gross motor functions. These motor disruptions mainly affect complex and sequential movements (Peter et al., 2013), consistent with cerebellar dysfunction (Peter et al., 2020).

Second, in many cases, CAS is influenced by genetic variants. No single gene explains all cases of CAS; rather, many different genes play a role in different children with CAS. The first genetic cause that was identified for CAS was a variant in the *FOXP2* gene (Fisher et al., 1998) and other many genes are implicated in CAS (Peter et al., 2014).

Third, there is emerging evidence that knowledge of genotype-phenotype association can be leveraged toward proactive and personalized interventions. Typically, speech disorders cannot be assessed and treated until children are old enough to show that they have trouble learning to talk, not before age 2 or 3 years. If the risk for these disorders were known at birth, preventive interventions could be tried. Babble Boot Camp© is a bundle of activities and routines implemented via parent training. Parents learn to elicit, foster, and boost their children's speech and language productions starting with earliest signals of communication as early as infant age 2 months and ending with words, sentences, and pragmatics at age 2 years. The first attempt to evaluate the effectiveness of the Babble Boot Camp© was conducted in groups of infants and children with classic galactosemia, an inborn error of metabolism caused by recessively inherited variants in the *GALT* gene. Children with classic galactosemia are at risk for several health impairments but especially for severe speech and language disorders. CAS is much more common among children with classic galactosemia than other child populations. Children with classic galactosemia were selected as the ideal population for the clinical trial of Babble Boot Camp© because their risk for communication disorders is known soon after birth. Initial reports show evidence that targeting precursor and early speech and language skills may have beneficial effects on speech and language development (Peter et al., 2021; Peter et al., 2022). The intervention is implemented using a telehealth interface.

Description of the Case

Background Information

Sam had just celebrated his third birthday when he was referred for a clinical evaluation of his speech skills. Sam's father, Mike, is a pediatrician and his mother, Andrea, is a health insurance professional with expertise in early childhood education. They had been concerned about Sam's communication skills for some time, and as soon as Sam became eligible for an evaluation through the public school system, the local school district referred him to the nearest local speech-language pathologist (SLP), who was the author of this report.

During the phone interview prior to the evaluation, Andrea stated that Sam was generally in excellent health and that he was outgoing and curious, adding that he did not show interest in joint book reading, preferring other, more gross motor–based activities. Sam's speech development was his parents' main concern. Andrea reported that she and Mike could only understand approximately 50% of his utterances; that he produced sentences of three to four words in length, such as "help me, please" and "put it on, Mom"; and that they had no concerns regarding other aspects of his communication skills (e.g., voice, fluency, receptive and expressive language). She declined the school district's offer to conduct a full evaluation, including language and cognitive functioning, suggesting that Sam could be evaluated in these areas at a later point in time if concerns arose.

Sam was born at the conclusion of a normally progressing pregnancy with no birth complications. He appeared to be in perfect health during his early weeks and months. He reached all typical developmental milestones, with the exception that he did not start walking until age 15 months. Between the ages of 4 and 16 months, he spent time in a daycare setting, then was home full-time as his mother chose to stay at home. His main social contacts were his immediate family, including an older brother and his cousins.

Sam's parents began to notice that he was not starting to talk as expected. "He wasn't speaking," his mother said. "He showed no signs of verbal communication." They had experienced disordered speech in their extended families. One of Mike's nephews, a boy 5 years older than Sam, had received speech therapy because of severe speech delays, and Andrea's sister had been in speech therapy also as a young child. Mike's brother had undergone therapy as a child to remediate stuttering. Mike and Andrea were keenly aware of the difference between Sam's speech development and that of his older brother.

When Sam was 2 years old, his vocabulary consisted of five words that could be understood and an untold number of words he attempted to say unsuccessfully. To determine what Sam was trying to say, Andrea and Mike used various strategies. Often, they told him to "slow down and try again." When they thought he was requesting something, they guessed at what it might be and asked him to verify. Although they never questioned his ability to understand them, they requested a formal hearing evaluation at a local children's hospital when Sam was 2;7 (years; months). Findings were consistent with normal hearing in at least one ear, and hearing loss was ruled out as contributing to his speech delays.

By now, Sam was showing signs of frustration as his parents and older brother could not understand much of what he said. He expressed his frus-

tration by growling, crying, or lashing out, which seemed particularly out of character. Perhaps worst of all, sometimes he gave up trying to talk when he was asked to repeat what he just said.

In all other areas, Sam appeared to be developing within or above age expectations. His giftedness in spatial reasoning became apparent as he worked complicated puzzles, completed crafts projects, and drew pictures with a level of sophistication typical of much older children. Near his third birthday, Sam's parents decided to seek professional intervention. "It seemed to us that he was not nearly as independent as he should be for his age," his mother concluded. "He was not able to advocate for himself sufficiently."

Evaluation Findings

Sam arrived for his evaluation accompanied by his mother. The evaluation consisted of a conversational speech sample, an oral structural/functional examination, and standardized articulation testing.

Sam's conversational speech was highly unintelligible, with approximately 20% of his utterances judged as intelligible by an unfamiliar listener. He was unwilling to interact with the clinician directly, clinging to his mother. When the clinician tried to engage him in a conversation, he responded with single words or simply shouted, "No!" He seemed restless, jumping up from his chair frequently to explore materials in the room.

The oral structural/functional and articulation examinations were influenced by Sam's young age, his substantial frustration levels related to communication tasks, and the fact that he was not used to interacting with adults he didn't know. Although the oral/functional examination could not be completed fully, it revealed extremely large tonsils, a fairly large tongue, and a forward tongue carriage. A medical follow-up was suggested to rule out sleep apnea due to the size of the tonsils. Andrea was receptive to this advice and reported that Sam snored but never had any difficulty with chewing and swallowing food.

Articulation testing began with the Goldman-Fristoe Test of Articulation-2 (Goldman & Fristoe,

2000). When Sam became uncooperative, the Structured Photographic Articulation Test (SPAT) (Dawson & Tattersall, 2001) was used. Both tests sample all consonants of English in initial, medial, and final positions where phonotactically appropriate. Sam complied with the first few test items and then became unwilling to continue, shouting, "No!" and leaving his chair despite many efforts to redirect him. Andrea was able to elicit several more test words by asking him to imitate her model. She prompted additional speech samples by asking questions like "What is your favorite breakfast food?" Table 19–2 lists Sam's single-word productions from the two attempts to administer standardized testing, as well as single-word responses to questions posed by his mother.

An estimate of Sam's relational phoneme inventory was constructed from his single-word productions while naming pictures, imitating his mother's models, answering questions, and his conversational productions. Using the SPAT protocol, at least 30 errors were noted, which translated

Table 19–2. Word Productions During the Initial Evaluation

Items From Articulation Testing		Words Elicited in Conversation	
Word Transcription	**Gloss**	**Word Transcription**	**Gloss**
[haθ]	house	[to]	toy
[ðíðu]	scissors	[bókeno]	volcano
[kɛ́gi]	carrot	[piθ]	please
[naf]	knife	[dáma], [gáma]	grandma
[dʒɛ́wo]	jello	[nópaʊ]	snowplough
[ʃawáf]	shovel	[ʃʃɔtʃ]	sausage
[wun]	spoon	[pébʌkəʔ]	play bucket
[vɔtʃ]	watch	[bɔθ]	blocks
[túba]	toothbrush	[ða]	yeah
[bǽʔtʌb]	bathtub	[ðɛθ]	yes
[dʒǽmað]	pajamas		
[θek]	snake		
[vímɪŋ]	swimming		
[bun]	balloon		
[kɛθ]	skates		
[θíbɪŋ]	sleeping		
[pɛ́ðɛn], [pɛ́nɛ]	present		
[fi]	three		
[gáwað]	glasses		
[kɔʔ]	clock		
[ápen]	airplane		

to a percentile ranking of 5. If all phonemes in all tested word positions had been elicited, the error score would most likely have increased. Based on this estimate, Sam easily qualified for 30 minutes of weekly therapy services, using a cutoff rule of seventh percentile ranking or lower, compared to same-age children.

It was concluded that Sam had a severe SSD with components of multiple disorder subtypes. For instance, he had a frontal lisp, as evidenced by consistently placing his tongue too far forward during /s, z/, and he consistently substituted [ð] for /j/, even in high-frequency words like yeah and yes. This aspect of his speech would be classified as a phonetic error in taxonomies such as Dodd's (2005), and the clinician wondered whether the tongue size and carriage could be a physical contributor to these sound errors. Sam also showed evidence of several phonological processes. For instance, he exhibited cluster reduction as in [nópau]/snowplough, syllable deletion as in [bun]/balloon, and assimilation errors such as [kégi]/carrot and [ʃɔ́ʃotʃ]/sausage. Sam's speech sound inventory was additionally characterized by a kind of "musical chair" game for /θ, f, s / and their voiced cognates. Sam was perfectly capable of producing interdental fricatives, because he substituted them for /s, z, j/. In words requiring /θ/, however, Sam produced [f] instead. This aspect of his speech was clearly not a phonetic error; rather, it represented a phonologic system shift. Finally, several aspects of his speech were consistent with CAS, for instance, vowel errors as in [to]/toy and [naf]/knife, sequencing errors such as those in [ʃawáf]/shovel and [gáwað]/glasses, a lexical stress error as in [bókeno]/volcano, and variable productions of several words, for instance, [dáma, gáma]/grandma and [péðɛn, pénɛ]/present. The observation that Sam started to walk relatively late, at age 15 months, is consistent with a more general motor delay commonly seen in children with CAS.

The information gathered during the intake activities led to the clinical impression that Sam was a young child with a severe SSD of mixed type (phonetic, phonemic, and apraxic). The barriers he experienced in trying to express his thoughts had begun to cause him a significant level of frustration. His frequent use of the word "no" was seen as a desperate strategy to have at least some level of control using speech. Because of his lack of interest in joint book reading, he did not receive systematic exposure to hearing objects labeled with speech sounds.

Treatment Options Considered

The following therapy options were considered:

Traditional therapy, which includes auditory activities ("ear training") and structured speech production tasks. The target speech sounds are produced in increasingly complex contexts, beginning with the individual sound and progressing to syllables, words, phrases, and so on, until they have generalized to conversational speech. Targets are usually, but not always, selected starting with the most developmentally appropriate and most stimulable ones. This approach has been widely used and would be most appropriate for Sam's /s, z, j/ errors. See a recent summary for efficacy data on specific aspects of traditional articulation therapy (Preston & Leece, 2021).

Pattern-based therapy to address Sam's phonological processes, for instance, minimal opposition therapy, where target word pairs differ only in one aspect of articulation (manner, place, or voicing), or multiple opposition therapy, where target word pairs differ in multiple aspects, including manner and place of articulation, voicing, and linguistic unit. Efficacy data for various pattern-based therapy approaches are described in recent summaries, for instance, minimal pairs (Baker, 2021) and multiple opposition (Williams & Sugden, 2021).

Cycles (Hodson & Paden, 1991) is a programmed approach tailored to children with multiple phonological processes. Each session begins and ends with auditory exposure, preferably using amplified speech. Therapy focuses on one phonological process at a time, switching to another one after a short course of therapy, for instance, 6 to 18 therapy hours, regardless of whether the child mastered the pattern or not. Once all processes have been addressed in therapy, the next therapy cycle begins. Efficacy evidence has recently been summarized (Prezas et al., 2021).

Phonotactic therapy, which works on syllable and word shapes first and focuses on segment accuracy later. This approach facilitates the phonetic accuracy of segments (Velleman, 2002).

Course of Treatment

A therapy program was designed for Sam that took into consideration the different elements of his SSD, his need to focus attention on auditory representations of words, his young age, and his worrisome frustration with communication activities. A modified course of Hodson and Paden's *Cycles* approach (Hodson & Paden, 1991) was adopted because it provided focused listening activities and a systematic way to work on Sam's phonological processes. Goals related to phonetic, phonotactic, and apraxic errors were also incorporated into the overall framework. Therapy targets for the first cycle were switched every other month and included the following:

- Consonant clusters, regardless of accuracy of cluster constituents such as /s, l/ to build Sam's syllable shapes first, then refine the accuracy of the segments
- CVCV words with different consonants to address the apraxic-like sequencing errors and work on Sam's ability to sequence consonants across a bisyllabic word
- Vowels and diphthongs
- /θ, f/ contrasts, which were an area of confusion in Sam's phoneme inventory

The second cycle expanded on the scope of the first, to additionally include /j/. The [ð] substitution for /j/ was treated from an articulatory perspective. Articulatory work on /s, z/ was interspersed to reinforce the work on /θ, f/ contrasts, using an orthodontic model, a toy rubber tongue, and a mirror as visual aids. Because /s, z/ frequently do not emerge until later, they were not treated with the same intensity as the other sound errors.

Therapy was greatly enhanced by daily homework. Sam's parents were extremely supportive and made sure that Sam completed his assignments. They took turns reading word lists to him every night before bedtime, which became a soothing ritual for him. Home games and crafts activities were used to reinforce the relevant sound contrasts.

An additional goal of therapy was to address Sam's frustration with verbal communication. Therapy was designed to give him many opportunities to control his environment and to empower him as a stakeholder in his own therapy. One way to accomplish this was to create a speech folder for him and to give him responsibility for it. He was expected to carry his speech folder into the therapy room and to show his homework. Another strategy was to give him choices about his weekly therapy schedule. In a plastic pocket holder, pictures of all the activities for the therapy sessions were waiting for Sam. His job was to decide on the order ("What should we do first today, Sam?") and to check them off when completed. Because he was reluctant initially to participate in the listening activities using a tape recorder, Sam got to choose who would push the "Start" button, he or the clinician, and which stuffed animal was going to join him while listening.

Progress in Therapy

When Sam started therapy, he had never been in a structured school setting, and separating from his mother was too difficult. Having Andrea present during the first few sessions was actually helpful because she observed the activities and was able to continue them at home. Summer break came after the first 2 months of therapy, and during that time, Sam started preschool. When he returned for therapy the following September, he had acquired a whole new set of interaction skills and independence. He was now able to participate in therapy without his mother present, and his outbursts of frustration completely ceased.

The combined elements of therapy and the consistent home practice soon paid off. At the end of the first year of therapy, vowel accuracy was 100% in conversational speech, cluster reductions had been eliminated in words with prompts, CVCV words were 100% accurate in words with prompts, and /r/ had fully emerged without therapy. The Individual Education Plan (IEP) for Year 2 was modified accordingly. The residual consonant sequence errors and cluster reduction errors were combined into one goal ("produce all consonants in multisyllabic words in the correct sequence"). Sam's speech was still characterized by a consistent frontal lisp, a consistent /ð/ substitution for /j/, and [f] substitutions for /θ/. According to parent report, Sam's overall communication behaviors had improved dramatically. In preschool, he interacted with his teachers and peers, and his speech was understood by others most of the time.

During Year 2, Sam was served by a different SLP. Sam focused mainly on correct production of /s, z, j/ and progressed to the word level. At the end of Year 2, he began working on the [f] for /θ/ substitution again. All of his phonologic errors were fully resolved in conversational speech.

During the initial evaluation, the clinician had noted large tonsils and advised Sam's parents to rule out any medical sequelae such as inadequate oxygenation during sleep. Almost exactly 2 years later, Sam underwent tonsillectomy because of medical concerns. Andrea reported that the surgery had immediate and dramatic benefits, in that his breathing during the day had become much quieter, and he slept now without "snoring like a train."

Overall, Sam responded well to therapy. He is scheduled to start kindergarten soon. He will continue to receive speech therapy to address the residual issues related to his more phonetic-based errors and the [f] for /θ/ substitution. His SLP reports that he appears to have an extensive vocabulary and a good command of expressive syntax. With his new set of interaction skills, he has a great prognosis for a successful school experience socially and academically.

Author's Note

This case study is based on an actual client. The names of the child and his family members were changed to protect their identity. Sam is now an adult. He, his parents, and the school district provided consent to publish this case study. Sam was discharged from speech services when he was 6 years old. He reports no difficulty learning to read. Writing has been a persistent struggle, for two reasons: Sam found it challenging to organize his ideas into sentences into a cohesive flow, and he also struggled greatly with handwriting. Interestingly, organizing information into a well-flowing sequence involves the cerebellum in that this part of the brain influences processing sequential information, and handwriting, a complex fine motor activity, is also under cerebellar influence (Koziol et al., 2014). Thus, these difficulties with writing may be residual correlates of the childhood CAS.

References

American Speech-Language-Hearing Association. (2007). *Childhood apraxia of speech* [Position statement]. http://www.asha.org/policy

Bauman-Waengler, J. (2020). *Articulation and phonology in speech sound disorders*. Pearson.

Dawson, J., & Tattersall, P. (2001). *Structured Photographic Articulation Test II*. Janelle Publications.

Dodd, B. (2005). *Differential diagnosis and treatment of children with speech disorder* (2nd ed.). Wurr, Open Library.

Fisher, S. E., Vargha-Khadem, F., Watkins, K. E., Monaco, A. P., & Pembrey, M. E. (1998). Localisation of a gene implicated in a severe speech and language disorder. *Nature Genetics, 18*(2), 168–170. https://doi.org/10.1038/ng0298-168

Goldman, R., & Fristoe, M. (2000). *Goldman-Fristoe Test of Articulation 2*. American Guidance Service.

Grigos, M. I., Hayden, D., & Eigen, J. (2010). Perceptual and articulatory changes in speech production following PROMPT treatment. *Journal of Medical Speech-Language Pathology, 18*(4), 46–53. https://www.ncbi.nlm.nih.gov/pubmed/22984339

Hodson, B. W., & Paden, E. P. (1991). *Targeting intelligible speech: A phonological approach to remediation* (2nd ed.). Pro-Ed.

Koziol, L. F., Budding, D., Andreasen, N., D'Arrigo, S., Bulgheroni, S., Imamizu, H., . . . Yamazaki, T. (2014). Consensus paper: The cerebellum's role in movement and cognition. *Cerebellum, 13*(1), 151–177. https://doi.org/10.1007/s12311-013-0511-x

McLeod, S., & Crowe, K. (2018). Children's consonant acquisition in 27 languages: A cross-linguistic review. *American Journal of Speech-Language Pathology, 27*(4), 1546–1571. https://doi.org/10.1044/2018_AJSLP-17-0100

Peter, B., Bruce, L., Raaz, C., Williams, E., Pfeiffer, A., & Rogalsky, C. (2020). Comparing global motor characteristics in children and adults with childhood apraxia of speech to a cerebellar stroke patient: Evidence for the cerebellar hypothesis in a developmental motor speech disorder. *Clinical Linguistics and Phonetics 35*(4), 368–392. https://doi.org/10.1080/02699206.2020.1861103

Peter, B., Davis, J., Cotter, S., Belter, A., Williams, E., Stumpf, M., . . . & Potter, N. (2021). Toward preventing speech and language disorders of known genetic origin: First post-intervention results of Babble Boot Camp in children with classic galactosemia. *American Journal of Speech-Language Pathology, 30*(6), 2616–2634. https://doi.org/10.1044/2021_AJSLP-21-00098

Peter, B., Davis, J., Finestack, L., Stoel-Gammon, C., VanDam, M., Bruce, L., . . . Potter, N. (2022). Translating principles of precision medicine into speech-language pathology: Clinical trial of a proactive speech and language intervention for infants with classic galactosemia. *Human Genetics and Genomics Advances, 3*(3), 100119. https://doi.org/10.1016/j.xhgg.2022.100119

Peter, B., Matsushita, M., Oda, K., & Raskind, W. (2014). De novo microdeletion of BCL11A is associated with severe speech sound disorder. *American Journal of Medical Genetics Part A, 164A*(8), 2091–2096. https://doi.org/10.1002/ajmg.a.36599

Peter, B., Vose, C., Bruce, L., & Ingram, D. (2019). Starting to talk at age 10 years: Lessons about the acquisition of English speech sounds in a rare case of severe congenital but remediated motor disease of genetic origin. *American Journal of Speech-Language Pathology, 28*(3), 1029–1038. https://doi.org/10.1044/2019_AJSLP-18-0156

Preston, J. L., & Leece, M. C. (2021). Articulation interventions. In A. L. Williams, S. McLeod, & R. J. McCauley (Eds.), *Interventions for speech sound disorders in children* (2nd ed., pp. 419–445). Brookes.

Prezas, R. F., Magnus, L. C., & Hodson, B. (2021). The Cycles approach. In A. L. Williams, S. McLeod, & R. J. McCauley (Eds.), *Interventions for speech sound disorders in children* (2nd ed., pp. 251–278). Brookes.

Rogers, S. J., Hayden, D., Hepburn, S., Charlifue-Smith, R., Hall, T., & Hayes, A. (2006). Teaching young nonverbal children with autism useful speech: A pilot study of the Denver Model and PROMPT interventions. *Journal of Autism and Developmental Disorders, 36*(8), 1007–1024. https://doi.org/10.1007/s10803-006-0142-x

Shriberg, L. D., Kwiatkowski, J., & Mabie, H. L. (2019). Estimates of the prevalence of motor speech disorders in children with idiopathic speech delay. *Clinical Linguistics and Phonetics, 33*(8), 679–706. https://doi.org/10.1080/02699206.2019.1595731

Shriberg, L. D., Potter, N. L., & Strand, E. A. (2011). Prevalence and phenotype of childhood apraxia of speech in youth with galactosemia [Research Support, N.I.H., Extramural]. *Journal of Speech, Language, and Hearing Research, 54*(2), 487–519. https://doi.org/10.1044/1092-4388(2010/10-0068)

Shriberg, L. D., Strand, E. A., Fourakis, M., Jakielski, K. J., Hall, S. D., Karlsson, H. B., . . . Wilson, D. L. (2017). A diagnostic marker to discriminate childhood apraxia of speech from speech delay: I. Development and description of the pause marker. *Journal of Speech, Language, and Hearing Research, 60*(4), S1096–S1117. https://doi.org/10.1044/2016_JSLHR-S-15-0296

Thoonen, G., Maassen, B., Gabreels, F., & Schreuder, R. (1999). Validity of maximum performance tasks to diagnose motor speech disorders in children. *Clinical Linguistics and Phonetics, 13*(1), 1–12.

van der Merwe, A., & Steyn, M. (2018). Model-driven treatment of childhood apraxia of speech: Positive effects of the speech motor learning approach. *American Journal of Speech-Language Pathology, 27*(1), 37–51. https://doi.org/10.1044/2017_AJSLP-15-0193

Velleman, S. L. (2002). Phonotactic therapy. *Seminars in Speech and Language, 23*(1), 43–56. https://doi.org/10.1055/s-2002-23510

Williams, A. L., & Sugden, E. (2021). Multiple oppositions intervention. In A. L. Williams, S. McLeod, & R. J. McCauley (Eds.), *Interventions for speech sound disorders in children* (2nd ed., pp. 61–89). Brookes.

LANGUAGE/DEVELOPMENT LANGUAGE DISORDER
CASE 20
Noah: A Child With Developmental Language Delay Transitioning From Preschool to Kindergarten
Sue Grogan-Johnson

Conceptual Knowledge Areas

Language impairment in children can be loosely categorized into two categories, including language impairment as the primary diagnosis and language impairment that accompanies a secondary diagnosis (e.g., hearing impairment, Down syndrome) (Schuele & Hadley, 1999). When language impairment exists as the primary diagnosis, it is commonly described as children having difficulty acquiring spoken language in the absence of sensory, motor, intellectual, or other medical or neurological conditions (Gillam et al., 2018; Tomblin et al., 1997). This language impairment in children has been identified by multiple terms such as specific language impairment (SLI), language disorder, language learning disorder, and language delay. Bishop (2014) identified 32 different terms used for the disorder in published research and highlighted an ongoing debate on the most accurate term to use. Clinically, confusion can exist as children with language concerns may receive different labels for their disorder depending on their age or school performance. For example, a child may be identified as "language delayed" at preschool, which becomes SLI at school age and changed again to specific learning disability as school curriculum advances in later grades. Adding to this confusion, some published literature does not clearly differentiate between language as a primary diagnosis and language impairment that accompanies other disorders,

and the labels such as language impairment can refer to both disorders.

More recently, the term "developmental language disorder" (DLD) has been posited as the preferred term for children with a primary language impairment (McGregor et al., 2020). Proponents of the DLD term acknowledge that no single term can capture the heterogenous nature of language impairment but prefer DLD as its definition while, similar to SLI, highlights the nature and impact of the language difficulties. DLD is "a neurodevelopmental condition that emerges in early childhood and frequently persists into adulthood" (McGregor, 2020, p. 981) and "a language problem that endures into middle childhood and beyond and that has a significant impact on social or educational function" (McGregor et al., 2020, p. 38). The DLD definition emphasizes that language impairment interferes with the child's ability to communicate in relationships and will likely impact progress in school. In fact, published data indicate that children with DLD are six times more likely to have reading and spelling difficulties and four times more likely to struggle with math compared to their typically developing peers (McGregor, 2020; Young et al., 2002). Furthermore, language problems do not resolve spontaneously and are likely to persist into adulthood, resulting in a higher incidence of anxiety, depression, underemployment, and social-relational difficulties for adults with language impairment as compared with adults without a history of language impairment (Conti-Ramsden & Durkin, 2008; McGregor, 2020; RADLD, 2017). Proponents of the DLD label add that a child with a language disorder can have a co-occurring deficit in areas such as attention and memory but with an unknown causal relationship to the language dysfunction. Allowing for the inclusion of these components within the DLD label permits a more comprehensive description of the language disorder (McGregor et al., 2020).

Using the term DLD describes the nature of the language impairment, identifies the social and academic impact of the disorder, and importantly calls attention to the enduring nature of the deficit (McGregor, 2020; McGregor et al., 2020; RADLD, 2017). Given the risks associated with DLD, early identification and service provision is essential. It is widely held that DLD is a common disorder, with estimates of the prevalence ranging from 7.4% (Tomblin et al., 1997) to 7.58% (Norbury et al., 2016). However, available published data demonstrate that while this is a common disorder, children with DLD are less likely to be identified and to receive needed intervention. The Tomblin et al. (1997) study identified specific language impairment in 216 kindergarten children from a sample of 7, 218 students. Of the 216 students identified, "a large proportion of those children identified as language impaired had not been identified via systems with their schools and community" (Tomblin et al., 1997, p. 1257). In 2016, Norbury et al. found that among a sample of first-grade students in England, only 3.5% of children meeting the criteria for DLD were receiving therapy services in the schools and only 39% were receiving intervention outside of the school system. Rice (2016) conducted a broad comparison review including students with SLI, students with attention-deficit/hyperactivity disorder (ADHD) and SLI, children with autism spectrum disorder (ASD) and SLI, children who receive cochlear implants and have SLI, bilingual children with SLI, and children with nonstandard dialects and SLI. Among the findings, Rice reported that children with SLI were likely to be overlooked for intervention services unless they also had speech sound errors or an accompanying ADHD. Children with SLI were more likely to be bullied and suffer negative social consequences than children with ADHD without SLI.

"Children with DLD are not receiving the attention they deserve" (McGregor, 2020, p. 990). Children with this disorder are going underidentified, and the consequences for these students to become successful readers and writers are at risk. Recognizing DLD, advocating for expanded early intervention, and collaborating with general educators to improve speaking, listening, reading, and writing will be critical for children with DLD and their families.

Description of the Case

Background Information

Noah, a 5-year, 1-month-old boy had just completed 1 year in a public school preschool. Prior to the start of preschool, Noah participated in a multifactored evaluation (MFE). During the play-based assessment, Noah was observed and completed formal and informal assessments with a speech-language pathologist (SLP), preschool teacher, school psychologist, and school nurse. Case history information gathered from Noah's mother revealed an unremarkable medical and social history. Noah was the product of a normal pregnancy with no complications. He lived with his biological parents and siblings. Results of the MFE and parent report revealed that Noah had met all social/emotional, cognitive, and motor milestones for his chronological age and passed a vision and hearing screening. However, he did not meet developmental milestones for communication. Speech sound production was age appropriate, as was prosody and voice quality, but language functioning was delayed. Specifically, he scored greater than −1.5 SD from the mean on a standardized test of receptive and expressive language, with difficulty following directions, understanding relational terms (e.g., prepositions), using words to describe, and retelling a simple story or steps to complete a task. Analysis of a language sample identified a reduced mean length of utterance (MLU) of 3.0 words with errors in use of prepositions, verb tense and agreement, and pronouns. As a result, Noah was identified as a child with a speech or language impairment under the Individuals With Disabilities Act (2004). Noah received an Individualized Education Plan (IEP), which included goals to improve receptive and expressive language skills through participation in an integrated preschool curriculum as well as classroom-based and pull-out language therapy services twice weekly.

Reason for Referral

Noah's transition from preschool to kindergarten sparked a referral to an SLP in private practice. Noah's parents wanted continued language intervention over the summer months prior to kindergarten in the hopes of further improvement in Noah's language functioning. The private practice SLP was provided with copies of Noah's evaluation report, IEP, and progress reports along with the request from the parents to provide direct intervention services and a home practice program to be used between therapy sessions.

Findings of the Evaluation

After reviewing the supplied evaluation and intervention reports, it was determined that an informal language evaluation would be completed to establish goals for the summer intervention period. Components of the evaluation included a spontaneous language sample to collect data on Noah's use of targeted grammar goals (from preschool language intervention), telling of a personal narrative and retelling, and generating a fictional story. These assessment tasks were selected to identify Noah's areas of language difficulty related to kindergarten curriculum standards and aspects of school and social participation. The purpose of the informal assessment was to identify gaps between Noah's language abilities and the expectations of kindergarten (Hellmann et al., 2020). Beyond identifying discreet language skills, it is important to determine a child's communicative abilities in real-life contexts so that appropriate interventions are selected (Heilmann et al., 2020). A review of the kindergarten English language arts curriculum revealed that kindergarten students should

be able, with prompting and support, to retell familiar stories, including key details, and identify characters, settings, and main story events (Ohio Department of Education, 2017, p. 14). Kindergarteners are also expected to create and expand complete sentences in shared language activities when speaking or writing (Ohio Department of Education, 2017, p. 51) and describe familiar people, places, things, and events (Ohio Department of Education, 2017, p. 45).

Included in the informal assessment were the narrative tasks of telling a personal narrative and retelling and generating a fictional story. Narrative language skills, the ability of an individual to tell or retell a real or imagined event (Gilliam & Ukrainetz, 2006), are important for academic and social achievement. We now understand that narrative ability is predictive of later academic achievement (Spencer & Peterson, 2020). A child's ability to produce narratives in preschool predicts reading comprehension performance in the 4th, 7th, and 10th grades (Snow et al., 2007; Suggate et al., 2018). Published research highlights the interdependence of oral narration and literacy, indicating that oral narrative focused intervention can improve both reading comprehension and written expression in children (Language and Reading Research Consortium, 2019; Spencer & Petersen, 2018). Narrative skills are also important for adult and peer relationships. Parent and teachers need information about what happened at school or on the playground, and the ability to tell personal stories is important to making and keeping friends. Taken together, the results of the language sample and narrative assessment tasks were expected to provide direction for Noah's language intervention as he transitioned from preschool to kindergarten. The results of the informal evaluation are described in the following paragraphs.

Spontaneous Language Sample

A language sample was obtained during a free play session at the start of the assessment period. Noah was invited to select among toys and games and interacted with the SLP by playing with the toys and discussing related topics (e.g., favorite superhero). Traditionally, SLPs obtain a language sample by recording a 100-utterance sample, followed by transcription and analysis. The analysis includes multiple measures of language performance such as the number of different words used, mean length of utterance, and syntactic complexity. Language sample analysis conducted in this manner yields important information about a child's language system, but it is time-consuming and not always an efficient clinical practice (Schuele, 2010). A creative alternative is to establish beforehand the specific questions to be answered with language sample analysis and then collect the data from the sample to answer those questions (Schuele, 2010). I wanted to use language sample analysis to monitor Noah's use of the grammatical structures targeted during his preschool language intervention. I recorded the free-play session described above and then listened back to the recording several times, tallying the verbs that were and were not marked for tense; the correct and incorrect use of subjective, objective, and possessive pronouns; the presence and absence of auxiliary verbs; and the correct and incorrect use of prepositions. Results indicated that Noah was marking verb tense consistently. He was using subjective, objective, and possessive pronouns with increased accuracy but was still showing some confusion (e.g., Him was my friend.). Auxiliary verbs were present, but there were very few utterances that required an auxiliary verb. Most utterances were simple declarative present- or past-tense sentences. Prepositions were consistently used correctly in the sample.

Personal Narrative Retelling

Personal narratives are descriptions of real past experiences of the speaker or someone the speaker knows (Bliss & McCabe, 2012). They are an important component of the spontaneous language among children and contribute to connecting with family and friends (Preece, 1987). Noah's mother was especially concerned about Noah's personal narrative skills, indicating that one of her goals was for Noah to be able to tell her about his day at school.

Two personal narratives were obtained and transcribed orthographically using the procedure described by Bliss and McCabe (2012). The SLP told a brief personal experience and then asked Noah to respond, which resulted in two attempts that were analyzed for these features: topic maintenance, informativeness or completeness of the narrative, event sequencing, correct referencing, use of conjunctions to connect utterances and events, and fluency or the way the story is told (Bliss & McCabe, 2012). Noah's personal narratives were on topic but incomplete. He would omit specifics about people and actions that the listener had to try to fill in to understand the story. He did not always sequence events in chronological order or he would omit a past event that was essential to understanding the story. Noah talked about other people in his stories, but at times he would use pronouns without providing the referent. During his storytelling, Noah used very few conjunctions (e.g., and, but), and his manner of storytelling included disruptions such as false starts (e.g., "I . . . I . . . We), repetitions of words, and long pauses, which may have indicated word-finding difficulty or reduced planning or monitoring of his story.

Fictional Story Retelling and Generation

The ability to retell a familiar or new story and to create a novel story is important for school-age children as narrative ability is linked to better outcomes academically and socially (Davidson et al., 2017). Children with DLD typically have difficulty with many aspects of narration as it requires a high demand on linguistic-cognitive resources (Duinmeijer et al., 2012). Noah's narrative skills were assessed by asking him to retell a simple story and to create an original story. In order to assess story retell, a simple wordless picture book was provided. Noah followed along with the pictures in the story while the SLP read the story script. Then Noah was asked to retell the story using the pictures in the wordless book. Story generation was assessed by asking Noah to create a story in response to the story prompt, "Tell me an adventure story about outer space." Both the macrostructure (general logical-temporal structure or story grammar) and microstructure (sentence level or specific linguistic elements) of the stories were analyzed using an adaptation of Apel and Masterson's (2005) narrative analysis. Results of the macrostructure analysis revealed that Noah was not able to retell or generate a story with an age-equivalent macrostructure. According to Lahey's (1988) developmental stages of narrative macrostructure, a 5-year-old child should be able to tell a story that contains a series of statements with a causal connection or a complete episode. A complete episode consists of an initiating event or problem, an action by characters in the story in response to the initiating event, and a consequence for that action. Noah's stories contained a series of related utterances that had a temporal connection, which is a macrostructure expected of younger children. Another way of looking at the macrostructure of a story is to examine story grammar elements included by the child (Pico et al., 2021). Typically, story grammar elements include the characters, setting, initiating events, actions, consequences, and optionally the characters' internal responses, plans, and/or reactions (Pico et al., 2021). Noah's stories included characters and actions and took the form of picture description rather than a narrative. Noah's use of coherence devices and linguistic items that help the listener understand the story, such as providing a setting and an opening and closing to the story, were analyzed as part of the macrostructure. Noah did not include story openings or settings, but he did consistently close each story saying, "the end." Assessment of cohesive devices, such as the correct use of pronouns, articles, and conjunctions to help the sentences in the story relate to each other or "hold together," revealed that Noah utilized subjective and objective pronouns, but he did not always provide a clear referent for them. In addition, Noah infrequently utilized coordinating conjunctions (e.g., and, but) and did not utilize any subordinating conjunctions (e.g., so, because, when, who). Microstructure analysis of Noah's narratives revealed that Noah did not use compound or complex sentences in his stories. The use of coordinating and subordinating conjunctions to create compound and complex sentences is an important skill in expressing the complex and interrelated ideas in a story. In addition, he was infrequently using elaborated noun and verb phrases, and inconsistently omitted auxiliary verbs. He did mark present- and past-tense verbs, include prepositional phrases, and include simple declarative and interrogative sentences.

Summary and Recommendations

Analysis of a spontaneous language sample revealed that Noah was correctly using prepositions and marking present- and past-tense verbs in connected speech. He was using subjective, objective, and possessive pronouns with increasing accuracy, and the use of auxiliary verbs was emerging. These were all skills targeted in his preschool IEP. Assessment of narrative skills showed that Noah was not producing complete personal narratives, and he was not retelling and generating narratives with an adequate macro- and microstructure. Based on these results, it was recommended that Noah participate in narrative intervention, which included direct therapy as well as the provision of a home practice program.

Treatment Options Considered

Noah was already identified as a child with DLD when he was referred for summer language therapy services. His preschool IEP had goals for the comprehension and use of grammatical structures. A characteristic of DLD is delay in the acquisition of grammatical skills and, once started, slower progress than typically developing peers (Swanson et al., 2005). As a result, many children with DLD require intervention targeting grammatical comprehension and production (Fey et al., 2003). This was true for Noah as he had just completed a year of language therapy focused on grammatical comprehension and production in public school preschool.

Considering the curriculum expectations for kindergarten students, as well as the important foundation that narrative skills provide for becoming literate, the decision was made to focus on narrative intervention.

One of the many advantages of narrative intervention is that SLPs can utilize it to target story grammar, grammatical structures, complex language (use of coordinating and subordinating conjunctions), vocabulary, inferencing, and social language skills. Storytelling promotes the comprehension and production of complex language (Spencer & Petersen, 2020).

Course of Treatment

Individual 1-hour therapy sessions were conducted weekly in Noah's home. Following each session, the SLP discussed progress with Noah's mother and provided activities to complete during the week between sessions. Goals for therapy included the following.

Goal 1

Noah will tell personal narratives that contain an introduction, main point, or highlight and a conclusion with 90% accuracy over three sessions.

Intervention. The focus of Noah's personal narrative intervention was to provide an organizational structure for telling a personal narrative (Bliss & McCabe, 2012). That was accomplished by creating three interlocking puzzle pieces for the three main components of the narrative: the introduction (a way to alert the listener that you have a story to tell and provide introductory information), the highlight or the most important part (talk about one specific event that could be happy, funny, scary, or sad), and the ending (finish your story and ask your listener a question). The SLP modeled a personal narrative placing a puzzle piece on the table as she told that portion of her narrative. Then Noah practiced telling a personal story. If he omitted a component or put a component of the story in the wrong order, the puzzle pieces were a visual cue to correct the narrative. After initial instruction, Noah had a weekly

assignment to come prepared to tell the SLP a personal story at the start of the next therapy session. As a carryover activity, Noah's mother took advantage of spontaneous opportunities to highlight events that Noah could talk about. In addition, using a strategy recommended by Westby and Culatta (2016), she reminisced with Noah to recall past events and make connections between past and current events.

Goal 2

Noah will retell and generate stories that contain an opening, characters, setting, initiating event, action, consequence, and ending given a story prompt with 90% accuracy over three sessions.

Intervention. "There is no one right way to implement narrative intervention" (Spencer & Petersen, 2020, p. 1084). The method utilized with Noah was based on the work of Gilliam and Ukrainetz (2006) and involved explicitly teaching story grammar structure using visual representations of the story grammar elements with familiar, age-appropriate stories. Therapy sessions involved a prestory knowledge activation step in which the SLP reviewed the story and asked guiding questions to facilitate the child's knowledge of concepts related to the story. The story was then read aloud, followed by the SLP and Noah reviewing the story using story grammar visual supports. After the story was read, the SLP incorporated grammatical skill practice from Goal 3 utilizing the characters, vocabulary, and related events from the story, in addition to direct instruction on the story's grammar elements and retelling portions of the story. These activities were completed across two therapy sessions, and the narrative unit was finished with Noah retelling the story with the use of the story grammar visual supports and prompting from the SLP as needed. As Noah became successful in retelling stories, we transitioned to generating novel stories. For example, after reading the story *Dogzilla* by Dav Pilkey, we used a story grammar graphic organizer to create a parallel story about a favorite superhero. The SLP scribed Noah's ideas to complete the graphic organizer and then provided a blank "book" of stapled copy paper that Noah and his mother used to create and illustrate the story.

Goal 3

Noah will correctly use coordinating and subordinating conjunctions; mark verb tense; use subjective, objective, and possessive pronouns; and include auxiliary verbs during story retell and generation with 80% accuracy.

Intervention. Rather than providing drill-based instruction, the intervention approach for Goal 3 was indirect and incorporated into the activities of Goal 2. The SLP found that as Noah became engaged in retelling and creating stories, she only needed to bring a grammatical concept to Noah's attention, and he would typically incorporate it into the story he was creating. As an example, the SLP would put index cards with subordinating and coordinating conjunctions on the therapy table. As Noah retold or created his stories, the SLP would point to the conjunctions suggesting how they could be added to join thoughts. Noah's mother was aware of the grammatical targets and was instructed by the SLP on how to incidentally incorporate instruction as Noah was completing carry over activities for Goal 2.

Analysis of Client's Response

At the end of the summer intervention sessions, Noah was independently telling personal narratives, and they were no longer targeted in therapy. He was successfully generating novel stories that contained an opening, characters, setting, more than one episode, and a closing. Most notably, Noah was consistently using a variety of coordinating and subordinating conjunctions to create compound and complex sentences in his stories. He did not consistently carry over these sentence constructions into his conversational speech. He continued to exhibit inconsistent errors in marking verb tense, using auxiliary verbs, and correctly using subjective, objective, and possessive pronouns.

Conclusion

Narrative intervention can effectively and efficiently teach a variety of academically and socially meaningful skills when implemented following published evidence-based principles. Spencer and Petersen (2020) assert that narrative intervention is one of the most powerful approaches to SLP language intervention. This approach provided a successful transition for Noah from preschool to kindergarten.

Author's Note

DLD persists, and as Noah entered school-based language, therapy shifted to include goals for reading comprehension, written expression, understanding, and using expository text structures to improve learning in content areas (e.g., social studies, science) and meta language skills such as inferencing. Collaboration among the SLP, classroom teachers, intervention specialists, Noah, and his parents was essential to Noah's continued progress and academic success.

References

Apel, K., & Masterson, J. (2005). *Assessment and treatment of narrative skills: What's the story*. ASHA.

Bishop, D. V. M. (2014). Ten questions about terminology for children with unexplained language problems. *International Journal of Language & Communication Disorders, 49*(4), 381–415. https://doi.org/10.1111/1460-6984.12101

Conti-Ramsden, G., & Durkin, K. (2008). Language and independence in adolescents with and without a history of specific language impairment (SLI). *Journal of Speech, Language and Hearing Research, 51*, 70–83. https://doi.org/10.1044/1092-4388(2008/005)

Davidson, A. J., Walton, M. D., Kansal, B., & Cohen, R. (2017). Narrative skill predicts peer adjustment across elementary school years. *Social Development, 26*, 891–906.

Duinmeijer, I., de Jong, J., & Scheper, A. (2012). Narrative abilities, memory and attention in children with a specific language impairment. *International Journal of Language & Communication Disorders, 47*, 542–555. https://doi.org/10.1111/j.1460-6984.2012.00164.x

Fey, M. E., Long, S. H., & Finestack, L. H. (2003). Ten principles of grammar facilitation for children with specific language impairments. *American Journal of Speech-Language Pathology, 12*, 3–15. https://doi.org/10.1044/1058-0360(2003/048)

Gillam, S. L., Olszewski, A., Squires, K., Wolfe, K., Slocum, T., & Gillam, R. B. (2018). Improving narrative production in children with language disorders: An early-stage efficacy study of a narrative intervention program. *Language, Speech, and Hearing Services in Schools, 49*, 197–212. https://doi.org/10.1044/2017_LSHSS-17-0047

Gilliam, R. B., & Ukrainetz, T. A. (2006). Language intervention through literature-based unites. In T. A. Ukrainetz (Ed.), *Contextualized language intervention* (pp. 59–84). Thinking Publications.

Heilmann, J., Tucci, A., Plante, E., & Miller, J. (2020). Assessing functional language in school-aged children using language sample analysis. *Perspectives of the ASHA Special Interest Groups, 5*, 622–636.

Individuals With Disabilities Education Act, 20 U.S.C. § 1400. (2004).

Lahey, M. (1988). *Language disorders and language development.* Allyn & Bacon.

Language and Reading Research Consortium, Jiang, H., & Logan, J. (2019). Improving reading comprehension in the primary grades: Mediated effects of a language-focused classroom intervention. *Journal of Speech, Language, and Hearing Research, 62*(8), 1–17. https://doi.org/10.1044/2019_JSLHR-L-19-0015

McGregor, K. K. (2020). How we fail children with developmental language disorder. *Language, Speech, and Hearing Services in Schools, 51*, 981–992. https://doi.org/10.1044/2020_LSHSS-20-00003

McGregor, K. K., Goffman, L., Owen Van Horne, A., Hogan, T. P., & Finestack, L. H. (2020). Developmental language disorder; Applications for advocacy, research, and clinical service. *Perspectives of the ASHA Special Interest Groups, 5*, 38–46.

Norbury, D. F., Gooch, D., Wray, D., Baird, G., Charman, T., Simonoff, E., Vamvakas, G., & Pickles, A. (2016). The impact of nonverbal ability on prevalence and clinical presentation of language disorder: Evidence from a population study. *The Journal of Child Psychology and Psychiatry, 57*(11), 1247–1257. https://doi.org/10.1111/jcpp.12573

Ohio Department of Education. (2017). *Ohio's learning standards: English language arts.* https://education.ohio.gov/Topics/Learning-in-Ohio/English-Language-Art/English-Language-Arts-Standards

Pico, D. L., Hessling Prahl, A., Haring Biel, C., Peterson, A. K., Biel, E. J., Woods, C., & Contesse, V. A. (2021). Interventions designed to improve narrative language in school-age children: A systematic review with meta-analyses. *Language, Speech, and Hearing Services in Schools, 52*, 1100–1126. https://doi.org/10.1044/2021_LSHSS-20-00160

Preece, A. (1987). The range of narrative forms conversationally produced by young children. *Journal of Child Language, 14*, 353–373. https://doi.org/10.1017/s0305000900012976

RADLD. (2017, August 28). *Developmental language disorder (DLD): The consensus explained* [Video]. https://www.youtube.com/watch?v=OZ1dHS1X8jg&t=17s

Rice, M. (2016). Specific language impairment, nonverbal IQ, attention-deficit/hyperactivity disorder, autism spectrum disorder, cochlear implants, bilingualism and dialectal variants: Defining the boundaries, clarifying clinical conditions, and sorting out causes. *Journal of Speech, Language, and Hearing Research, 59*, 122–132. https://doi.org/10.1044/2015_JSLHR-L-15-0255

Schuele, C. M. (2010). The many things language sample analysis has taught me. *Perspectives on Language Learning and Education, 17*(1), 32–37.

Schuele, C. M., & Hadley, P. A. (1999). Potential advantages of introducing specific language impairment to families. *American Journal of Speech-Language Pathology, 8*, 11–22.

Snow, C. E., Porche, M. B., Tabors, P. O., & Harris, S. R. (2007). *Is literacy enough? Pathways to academic success for adolescents.* Brookes.

Spencer, T. D., & Petersen, D. B. (2018). Bridging oral and written language: An oral narrative language intervention study with writing outcomes. *Language, Speech, and Hearing Services in Schools, 49*(3), 569–581. https://doi.org/10.1044/2018_LSHSS-17-0030

Spencer, T. D., & Petersen, D. B. (2020). Narrative intervention: Principles to practice. *Language, Speech, and Hearing Services in Schools, 51*, 1081–1096. https://doi.org/10.1044/2020_LSHSS-20-00015

Suggate, S., Schaughency, E., McAnally, H., & Reese, E. (2018). From infancy to adolescence: The longitudinal links between vocabulary, early literacy skills, oral narrative, and reading comprehension. *Cognitive Development, 47*, 82–95.

Swanson, L. A., Fey, M. E., Mills, C. E., & Hood, L. S. (2005). Use of narrative-based language intervention with children who have specific language impairment. *American Journal of Speech-Language Pathology, 14*, 131–143. https://doi.org/10.1044/1058-0360(2005/014)

Tomblin, J. B., Records, N. L., Buckwalter, P., Shang, X., Smith, E., & O'Brien, M. (1997). Prevalence of specific language impairment in kindergarten children. *Journal of Speech, Language and Hearing Research, 40*(6), 1245–1260. https://doi.org/10.1044/jslhr.4006.1245

Westby, C., & Culatta, B. (2016). Telling tales: Personal event narratives and life stories. *Language, Speech, and Hearing Services in Schools, 47,* 260–282. https://doi.org/10.1044/2016_LSHSS-15-0073

Young, A. R., Beitchman, J. H., Johnson, C., Douglas, L., Atkinson, L., Escobar, M., & Wilson, B. (2002). Young adult academic outcomes in a longitudinal sample of early identified language impaired and control children. *The Journal of Child Psychology and Psychiatry, 43*(5), 635–645. https://doi.org/10.1111/1469-7610.00052

Part III
SCHOOL-AGE CHILD CASES

APRAXIA
CASE 21
Sarah: Childhood Apraxia of Speech: Differential Diagnosis and Evidence-Based Intervention

Kathy J. Jakielski

Conceptual Knowledge Areas

An understanding of this case requires the reader to have a strong knowledge base in phonetics and phonology. The reader will also benefit from having knowledge of the acquisition of speech in typically developing children, from canonical babbling through mastery, including an understanding of both segmental and suprasegmental speech components. Several textbooks contain overviews of these skills (e.g., Bauman-Waengler, 2020; Bernthal et al., 2022; Bleile, 2004; Vihman, 1996).

Childhood apraxia of speech (CAS) is a pediatric motor speech disorder that shares some common characteristics with non-CAS speech impairment; however, CAS is a distinct disorder that is differentially diagnosed using a complex of symptoms. It is important to discern if a child with disordered speech exhibits CAS or nonapraxic speech impairment based on the child's specific symptoms. The best single source currently available to increase the reader's broad understanding of the history of CAS is the Technical Report published by the American Speech-Language-Hearing Association (ASHA, 2007). It is important for the reader to be familiar with the principles of cognitive motor learning, as well as with how specific principles relate to speech production. It is also important for the reader to be familiar with recent research on the nature of CAS (e.g., Fiori et al., 2016; Iuzzini-Seigel, 2021; Murray et al., 2020),

as well as its diagnosis (e.g., de Oliveira et al., 2021; Murray et al., 2015) and intervention (e.g., Bahar et al., 2021; Murray & Iuzzini-Seigel, 2017; Murray et al., 2014). Many resources are listed in the references and additional suggested readings sections.

Description of the Case

Background Information

At age 6 years, 3 months, Sarah was brought to the College Center for Speech, Language, and Hearing (College Center) by her mother for a speech evaluation with concerns regarding the nature of Sarah's disorder. Sarah was first diagnosed with speech delay at age 2 years, 5 months and she had received ongoing speech intervention since that time. Sarah and her mother had recently moved to the area from another state, and the speech-language pathologist (SLP) at Sarah's new public grade school had referred Sarah to the local craniofacial clinic with concerns regarding Sarah's fluctuating hypernasal speech quality. Findings from the craniofacial team were negative for structural abnormalities; however, members of the team raised concerns regarding apraxic-like speech symptoms. The team then referred the family to the College Center for a differential assessment of Sarah's speech impairment.

Client History

The following information was secured from a parent questionnaire, a review of medical records, and parent conferencing that specifically explained and probed early and later vocal and verbal behaviors.

Sarah was the only child in a family that consisted of her biological mother and herself. Sarah's parents separated when she was 2½ years old; they divorced when she was 4 years old, so that Sarah's mother could secure employment. Sarah and her mother moved from another state to a neighborhood close to the College Center when Sarah turned 6 years old, just prior to her entering first grade. Sarah's mother had a high school diploma and worked in sales for a furniture company. Sarah's home life was reported to be stable, with an attentive mother and an environment in which Sarah's needs were met.

Sarah's birth followed a full-term, unremarkable pregnancy. She weighed 7 pounds, 11 ounces and was 20 inches long at birth. Her Apgar score 1 minute after birth was 7 and 5 minutes after birth was 9. She produced a healthy birth cry. Sarah was breastfed until she was approximately 6 months old; she demonstrated no difficulty sucking or swallowing. Early weight and height gains were normal for her age and sex. Throughout infancy, Sarah exhibited normal sleeping patterns, and her overall health was excellent. Hearing was normal, with no history of middle ear infections.

Sarah was described as a quiet infant, producing only a limited number of sounds and engaging in minimal sound play. Canonical babbling emerged at approximately 14 months of age; babbling volubility was low. Early vocalizations were characterized by reduplicated strings of stops and nasals combined with a limited number of vowels. Sarah's mother did not remember hearing Sarah produce jargon or long, variegated strings of babble. Sarah's early communication consisted of gestures, home signs, and vocalizations. Her first intelligible word, /du/ for juice, was produced at 20 months of age; first words consisted of juice, me, no, mama, dada, doggie, and more. The mother reported that Sarah always appeared to comprehend what was said to her, including single words, short sentences, and multistep commands. At age

2½ years, Sarah began to demonstrate behavior problems, such as throwing her toys, squealing in anger, and hitting others. Sarah's mother reported that those behaviors appeared to be linked to Sarah's frustration at not being able to communicate well enough to express her needs. Once Sarah began to receive early intervention services, her expressive language increased, and the negative behavior problems decreased.

Sarah's motor development was unremarkable except for delays in some fine motor hand skills, including stacking small blocks, placing pieces into shape sorters, and manipulating small toys; later Sarah exhibited difficulty correctly holding crayons/pencils and buttoning and zippering. No excessive drooling, eating problems, or food sensitivities were reported.

Shortly after Sarah's second birthday, her pediatrician referred her to the local early intervention program for motor and communication assessments. The physical therapist's assessment revealed normal gross motor development. The occupational therapist (OT) assessed Sarah's visual, sensory, and physical capabilities; results revealed mild delays in fine motor development, specifically in eye-hand coordination and in-hand manipulation. The SLP's assessment revealed normal play skills, normal receptive language development, moderate delays in expressive language, and mild delays in speech production. At age 2 years, 6 months, Sarah began receiving 60-minute sessions of combined, in-home OT and SLP services once every other week. Early speech goals targeted building a communication system comprising gestures and signs paired with verbalizations. CAS initially was suspected; however, it was ruled out based on Sarah's "age-appropriate oral-motor skills, including adequate tongue and jaw strength and movement, absence of excessive drooling, and good ability to chew and swallow food."

Sarah was enrolled in her public school's preschool speech and language program at age 3 years. She remained in the preschool program until she entered kindergarten at age 5 years. While in the preschool program, Sarah received direct speech and language services throughout the 9-month school year; however, OT services were decreased to monthly consultations for the first year that she was in the program, after which OT services were discontinued based on goal attainment. Speech and language goals consisted of increasing Sarah's expressive language and eliminating the phonological process of final consonant deletion using stops /p, b, t, d, k, g/ and nasals /m, n/ in single words. Sarah continued to make progress on the goals throughout her enrollment in the preschool program, although her progress remained slower than was predicted. These same goals were continued once Sarah reached kindergarten, with the addition of the goal of eliminating the phonological process of stopping of fricatives in words.

At the beginning of first grade, in her new school, Sarah had comprehensive language and cognitive testing. She also underwent an articulation screening; articulation testing was deferred pending the findings of the craniofacial clinic. Language testing was conducted by administering the Clinical Evaluation of Language Fundamentals, Fifth Edition (CELF-5; Semel et al., 2013) and by analyzing a 30-utterance spontaneous language sample. Testing revealed receptive language skills consistently in the average range of performance; expressive language performance in the areas of word structure, recalling sentences, formulated sentences, and morphosyntax was below average. Cognitive testing was conducted using the Wechsler Preschool and Primary Scale of Intelligence-III (WPPSI-IV; Wechsler, 2012). Findings revealed a low-average Verbal IQ score of 86 and an average Performance IQ score of 102—a 16-point difference between quotients. Results from the informal speech screening indicated a severe speech impairment characterized by highly unintelligible speech.

Sarah's mother described Sarah as easygoing, happy, shy, and socially immature and as a child who preferred to play alone. She stated that Sarah would willingly repeat herself in attempts to be understood.

Reasons for Referral

The family came to the College Center seeking a better understanding of the nature of Sarah's speech disorder. Sarah's school-based SLP also expressed the need for a differential diagnosis of Sarah's speech disorder. Sarah recently had language and cognitive testing upon transferring to her new school; therefore, the family and the SLP sought a speech-only evaluation.

Findings of the Evaluation

Sarah separated easily from her mother at the start of testing. Sarah interacted appropriately with the examiner and completed all tasks cooperatively and with good effort. She remained compliant throughout the 50-minute assessment session.

Sarah was tested using a variety of articulation measures, which included the Goldman-Fristoe Test of Articulation-3 (GFTA-3; Goldman & Fristoe, 2015), the Kaufman Speech Praxis Test for Children (KSPT; Kaufman, 1995), and the Fletcher Time-by-Count Test of Diadochokinetic Syllable Rate (DSR; Fletcher, 1973; see also Fletcher, 1972). During testing, informal attempts were made in conversation to elicit multiple tokens of words, as well as to elicit a variety of multisyllabic words. Informal observations focused on the suprasegmental aspects of Sarah's speech. A record review was completed to obtain information regarding Sarah's hearing ability and oral structures and functioning.

Following the completion of testing, standardized and informal analyses of the speech data were completed. Test scores were derived when possible; informal analyses yielded phonetic and error inventories for consonants, vowels, and word shapes, and observations were noted regarding suprasegmental production.

GFTA-3

The Sounds-in-Words subtest of the GFTA-3 was administered to assess Sarah's production of speech sounds in spontaneous single words. She exhibited a total of 40 errors on this subtest, resulting in a raw score of 40. This raw score equated to a standard score of 47 and placed her below the first percentile for her age and sex.

KSPT

The KSPT was designed to provide information regarding a child's motor speech proficiency. The KSPT consists of four levels—Oral Movement, Simple Phonemic and Syllabic, Complex Phonemic and Syllabic, and Spontaneous Length and Complexity levels—and contains a variety of tasks that increase in motor speech complexity within and across levels. The KSPT was normed on children up to 72 months of age (i.e., 6 years); therefore, Sarah's age of 6 years, 3 months exceeded the test's normative data, necessitating descriptive-only reporting of findings. On the first, most basic level, the Oral Movement level, Sarah exhibited one error on the 11 tasks, demonstrating difficulty rounding her lips to produce a lip pucker. All other oral-motor movements were completed easily, smoothly, and without difficulty. Sarah exhibited two errors on the 63 tasks on the Simple Phonemic and Syllabic Level. She exhibited no difficulty producing isolated vowel (monophthong and diphthong) imitations, singleton consonant productions, CV productions, reduplicative CVCV productions, and CVC homorganic productions (i.e., same place of articulation, as in the word /tod/, which has two alveolar consonants). She did exhibit one error out of four possible errors on tasks requiring V_1CV_1 or V_1CV_2 imitations and one error out of six possible errors on tasks requiring CV_1CV_2 imitations; in both instances, Sarah misarticulated a target vowel (as in, omə/umə, babo/bəbo). She also exhibited 2 out of 13 possible errors on simple consonant synthesis tasks requiring word-final /b/ and /d/ productions.

Tasks on the third level, the Complex Phonemic and Syllabic level, can be used to evaluate speech movements in six different contexts. Some tasks can be used to test complex consonant production (designated as C̲) in C̲, C̲VC, and CVC̲ productions. Other complex tasks include CCVC, C̲$_{front}$VC$_{back}$ and C$_{back}$VC$_{front}$, CVCVC, CVCVCV, and C̲VC to C̲VCV(C) to C̲VCV(C̲)CVC productions. Of the 91 productions elicited, Sarah misarticulated 39. Errors included difficulty producing affricates and some of the fricatives in isolation and in words. Sarah misarticulated 6 of the 15 clusters tested. She also exhibited difficulty imitating five of the

seven multisyllabic stimuli (i.e., cantaloupe, television, invitation, Cinderella, and puh-tuh-kuh); she assimilated sounds and omitted syllables. Sarah also demonstrated difficulty producing the medial syllable in the polysyllabic words tested; all her productions were reduced from three syllables to two (e.g., window/windowsill).

Sarah's performance on the Spontaneous Length and Complexity level was based on her spontaneous speech sample that was collected in play. Analysis revealed an increase in consonant, vowel, and word shape errors in conversational speech. Suprasegmental errors also were noted in rhythm (irregular syllable timing noted) and lexical stress (overstressing all syllables in multisyllabic words). There were numerous vowel errors exhibited in multisyllabic words and in spontaneous speech, and speech variability was noted on multiple productions of the same words. Overall, Sarah's conversational speech was given a score of 3 to 4 ("decodable"), which is described as partially intelligible.

DSR

The DSR was administered to assess Sarah's ability to rapidly and accurately sequence the reduplicated nonsense strings pə, tə, kə, fə, lə, pətə, pəkə, təkə, and pətəkə. Sarah's performance on all the diadochokinetic (DDK) tasks indicated production rates that ranged from two to four times slower than the normative data provided for other 6-year-old children. Sarah especially exhibited significant difficulty on the multisyllabic repetition tasks. In addition to the slower rates, Sarah's results revealed numerous misarticulations that were characterized by consonant substitutions and omissions, frequent vowel substitutions (i.e., a/ə substitutions), and poor rhythmicity.

Record Review

A review of recent findings from the craniofacial team assessment and past early intervention and kindergarten records revealed that Sarah's bilateral hearing was normal. She had no history of middle ear infections. Oral structures and functions were normal for speech production.

Phonetic Inventory

The phonetic inventory is a list of all the consonants, vowels, and word shapes a child produces, regardless of target accuracy. For example, the word "truck" consists of four speech sounds, /t/, /ɹ/, /ə/, and /k/, and the word shape is consonant-consonant-vowel-consonant (CCVC). If a child articulates "truck" correctly, then the child's phonetic inventory contains word-initial cluster /tɹ/, word-final singleton /k/, vowel /ə/, and word shape CCVC. On the other hand, for example, if a child produces the word as "tut," then the child's phonetic inventory would contain word-initial /t/, word-final /t/, vowel /ə/, and word shape CVC. The phonetic inventory provides important informa-

tion regarding what sounds and sound combinations a child can produce.

Sarah's consonant, vowel, and word shape phonetic inventories derived from the words she produced during testing are shown in Table 21–1. It is important to note that every singleton consonant and vowel had the opportunity to be produced at least three times. Almost all the consonants had the opportunity to occur in every permissible word position at least one time.

Error Inventory

The error inventory is a description of errors and error patterns exhibited by a child. Sarah's

Table 21–1. Sarah's Phonetic Inventory at the Time of Testing

Consonants		Vowels	Word Shapes
Initial position		**Monophthongs**	
Stops	p b t d k g	i ɪ e ɛ æ	CV
Nasals	m n	ə	CVCV(CV)
Glides	w j		CVC
Fricatives	f v s h	u ʊ o ɔ ɑ	CCVC
Affricates		**Diphthongs**	CVCCV
Liquids	l ɹ	a͡ɪ a͡ʊ ͡ɔɪ	VCVC
Clusters	pl bl kw gɹ fɹ	**Rhotics**	
Medial position		ɚ ͡ɪɚ ͡ɛɚ ͡ʊɚ	
Stops	p b t d k g	͡ɔɚ ͡aɪɚ ͡aʊɚ	
Nasals	n		
Glides			
Fricatives	s		
Affricates			
Liquids	l ɹ		
Clusters	mp nd		
Final position			
Stops	p t g		
Nasals	m n		
Glides			
Fricatives	s		
Affricates			
Liquids	l		
Clusters			

consonant, vowel, and word shape error inventories derived from the words she produced during testing are displayed in Table 21–2.

Suprasegmental Observations

The suprasegmental aspects of Sarah's speech that were evaluated included rate of speech, vocal pitch, vocal quality, loudness, and lexical stress.

Sarah's rate of speech was judged to be normal for her age. Her pitch was normal for her sex and age; however, she exhibited difficulty lowering her pitch to "sound like a monster" during play. The quality of her voice was good, except for intermittent hyponasal and hypernasal resonance that primarily was noted on words comprising nasal phonemes. Sarah produced speech with appropriate loudness and demonstrated the

Table 21–2. Sarah's Error Inventory at the Time of Testing

Consonants	Vowels	Word Shapes
Initial position	**Monophthongs**	
71% accuracy	85% accuracy	45% accuracy
Two most frequent types of errors:	Majority of errors were random substitutions of one monophthong for another monophthong	95% accuracy matching number of syllables in words
• Substitution of /d/ for consonants not in repertoire		
• Consistent substitution of /d/ for /s/	**Diphthongs**	Word shape errors were result of:
Medial position	85% accuracy	• Omissions of cluster segments
45% accuracy	Consistent error pattern of reducing a diphthong to a monophthong (for example, ɑ/aɪ)	• Omissions of final consonants
Two error patterns:		
• Substitution of /d/ for medial consonants 64% of the time	**Rhotics**	
• Reduplication of initial-position consonant 36% of the time	90% accuracy	
	Consistent error pattern of reducing a rhotic to a monophthong (for example, ə/ɑɚ)	
Final position		
42% accuracy		
Three observations:		
• Omitted final consonant in 58% of monosyllabic and multisyllabic words ending in a consonant		
• Omitted final consonant in 39% of words ending in a stop or fricative		
• Substitution of random consonant in 42% of words ending in a consonant		
Consonant clusters		
31% accuracy		
Two error patterns:		
• Reduced clusters to a single cluster segment in 65% of misarticulated clusters		
• Substitution of /d/ or another singleton consonant in 35% of misarticulated clusters		

ability to switch from whispered speech to normal speech to loud speech. She exhibited lexical stress errors on approximately 15% of the multisyllabic words she produced spontaneously; when in error, she tended to produce equal-excessive stress on all syllables.

Assessment Summary

Speech testing at the College Center when Sarah was age 6 years, 3 months revealed a severe speech impairment. The characteristics exhibited are as follows:

- An incomplete phonetic inventory for consonants /ŋ, θ, ð, z, ʃ, ʒ, t͡ʃ, d͡ʒ /
- An incomplete phonetic inventory for word shapes containing consonant clusters and final consonants
- Many more consonants and vowels in her phonetic inventory than produced correctly in words
- Atypical consonant and vowel substitutions
- A high percentage of consonant omission errors
- A nondevelopmental nature to her sound development (e.g., mastery of /l/ and /ɹ/ but omission of word-final stop consonants)
- Poor vowel accuracy in words
- An increased number of errors as stimuli increased in length and/or phonetic complexity
- An inaccurate production of lexical stress in 15% of multisyllabic words
- A reduced number of syllable productions on DDK tasks
- Arrhythmicity in syllable productions on DDK tasks
- Fluctuating nasal resonance in the absence of structural abnormalities or muscle weakness

A review of speech and language, medical, and parent reports revealed that Sarah also had a posi-

tive history of speech concerns that included the following:

- Delayed emergence of canonical babbling
- Decreased volubility of canonical babble
- A limited number of speech sounds in babble
- Decreased volubility of vocal play
- An absence of jargon
- Gestures substituted for words
- Delayed onset of first words
- An early diagnosis of speech and expressive language impairment
- Good language comprehension
- Behavior problems prior to increased expressive language output
- Highly unintelligible speech
- Slow progress in speech intervention
- Fine motor delays and history of occupational therapy
- Verbal IQ lower than performance IQ

Differential Diagnosis

There is no single marker that can be used to diagnose CAS; rather, a complex of characteristics must be considered. Speech characteristics that were considered when differentially diagnosing the nature of Sarah's speech impairment included the observed and reported symptoms in Table 21–3.

For additional evidence of motor speech impairment, a qualitative analysis of Sarah's specific speech errors was completed. Several findings revealed motor-based errors. Sarah's preference for a single-stop phoneme (/d/), numerous assimilation errors, numerous sound and syllable omissions, and reduction of clusters to singleton consonants all can be considered simplification of the motor speech plan. There was no evidence that Sarah omitted final consonants because she did not understand the concept of word-final consonants. In fact, she produced a limited but diverse variety of word-final consonants. Sarah's preference for open syllables was like the pattern found in infant canonical babbling in which open-syllable

Table 21–3. CAS Differential Symptoms

Characteristic	Observed/Reported Characteristic	Indicators[a]
Vocal development	Delayed onset; limited output	Characteristic of CAS
Oral structures	No structural abnormalities	Speech impairment cannot be attributed to a structural deficit
Nonspeech oral-motor functioning	Normal nonspeech oral-motor functioning	Speech impairment cannot be attributed to an oral-motor deficit
Hearing status	Normal hearing	Speech impairment cannot be attributed to an auditory deficit
Sensory-motor status	History of fine motor disorder	Characteristic of CAS
Diadochokinesis	Reduced number of productions Arrhythmic productions	Characteristic of CAS
Linguistic status	Average receptive language Below-average expressive language	Commonly reported finding in children with CAS
Cognitive status	Low-average verbal IQ Average-performance IQ	Speech impairment cannot be attributed to a cognitive deficit
Speech intelligibility	Highly unintelligible for age	Characteristic of CAS
Speech assessment findings	Numerous consonant errors Vowel errors Unusual consonant and vowel errors Nondevelopmental errors Increased complexity = increased number of errors Lexical stress errors	When all of these symptoms are combined, highly characteristic of CAS
Speech intervention	History of slow progress over 3½ years of speech intervention	Characteristic of CAS
Environmental factors	Attentive mother Enriched preschool/school environments History of medical care	Speech impairment cannot be attributed to an environmental deficit

[a]CAS is considered a symptom complex; a single marker for CAS does not exist.

productions predominate. It has been argued that syllables ending in vowels are motorically less complex than syllables ending in closants (i.e., consonant-like sounds; for an overview, see Davis & MacNeilage, 1995). Based on the complex of symptoms discussed and a preponderance of evidence suggesting a motor speech planning deficit, a diagnosis of CAS was confirmed.

Treatment Options Considered

Numerous approaches to remediating speech impairment are available; these approaches historically have been described as either articulatory or phonological in nature. Articulatory approaches also are referred to as phonetic- or motor-based approaches. Examples of articulatory approaches include traditional sound production training (Van Riper & Erickson, 1996), postural restructuring of motor planning therapy (PROMPT; Chumpelik, 1984; Namasivayam et al., 2021), rapid syllable transition treatment (ReST; McCabe et al., 2017), sensory-motor–based intervention (McDonald, 1964), and integral stimulation (Rosenbek et al., 1974; Strand & Skinder, 1999). Phonological approaches also are referred to as linguistic or language based. Examples of phonological approaches include the cycles approach (Hodson & Paden, 1991), Metaphon therapy (Howell & Dean, 1991), and minimal pair contrast therapy (Weiner, 1981).

CAS is a disorder that disrupts motor planning and/or programming for speech, and thus a motor-based intervention approach would be congruent with the inherent motor-planning difficulty experienced by children with CAS. Integral stimulation was selected for working with Sarah because it is a cognitive motor-based approach for remediating speech impairment (for an overview, see Maas et al., 2008). Several studies have been published on integral stimulation that provide evidence of its effectiveness in treating children with CAS (e.g., Rosenbek et al., 1974; Strand & Debertine, 2000; Strand et al., 2006). In addition, the College Center SLP had approximately 10 years of experience successfully employing this approach with several children with CAS, and Sarah's school SLP was willing to learn the techniques.

All the motor-based approaches, including integral stimulation, contain three similar components: an establishment phase (when a new movement pattern is learned), a stabilization phase (when a new movement pattern is produced automatically in practiced contexts), and a generalization phase (when a new movement pattern is produced automatically in novel contexts). Integral stimulation is a drill-intensive, cognitive-motor approach to speech intervention that is used to focus on decreasing the frequency and types of feedback cues provided to the child. Maximal cueing is the initial technique used to establish a new sound movement pattern, followed by (in decreasing order of support) simultaneous production, mimed production, immediate repetition, successive repetition, delayed repeti-

tion, question response, reading, and so on. Simultaneous production is when the SLP and child say the target utterance at the same time. Mimed production is when the SLP mouths the target while the child watches the SLP and says the target aloud. Immediate repetition is when the SLP models the target and the child repeats the target directly following the model. Successive repetition is when the child imitates the SLP's initial model several times successively without being provided an additional model. Delayed repetition is when the child imitates the SLP's model after waiting for several seconds after the model is provided. Question response is when the child spontaneously produces the target utterance after being asked a question by the SLP. Cueing begins with the SLP providing maximal multisensory input and a slowed speech rate. The SLP then slowly fades temporal and tactile cues as the child demonstrates the ability to take increasing responsibility for the assembly, retrieval, and execution of the motor speech plan at a normal speech rate.

Course of Treatment

Following the assessment, Sarah's mother enrolled her in twice-weekly 30-minute individual speech intervention sessions at the College Center. The College Center's schedule consisted of fall and spring 14-week semesters, separated by a 6-week winter vacation. Sarah's school SLP agreed to follow the speech goals developed at the College Center. Sarah's school speech intervention schedule consisted of two 30-minute individual sessions weekly; school speech intervention was scheduled on alternate days when Sarah was not seen at the College Center. Between both sites, Sarah received 30 minutes of speech intervention 4 days a week. The school SLP also saw Sarah for two 20-minute group language intervention sessions per week.

The integral stimulation cueing hierarchy used with Sarah consisted of six levels, including (from most to least support) simultaneous production, mimed production, immediate repetition, successive repetition, delayed repetition, and question response. Productions were scored using Strand and Debertine's (2000) 0- to 2-point scale. A score of 2 indicated that the utterance was produced with no articulation errors. A score of 1 indicated that the utterance was intelligible and contained only one to two articulation errors. A score of 0 indicated that the utterance did not meet the criteria for a score of 1 or 2. Sarah's school SLP learned integral stimulation methods and used the same cues and cueing hierarchy that were used at the College Center. Sarah's articulation goals for the dual-site, 9-month intervention period follow.

Goal 1

In response to cognitive-motor learning principles incorporated into integral stimulation intervention, Sarah will increase her phonetic inventory to include the fricatives /θ, ð, z, ʃ/.

Related Subgoal 1. To decrease Sarah's preference for open word shapes.

Related Subgoal 2. To increase Sarah's vowel accuracy in monosyllabic words.

- *Objective 1:* Sarah will correctly produce /θ/ and /ʃ/ in word-final position in functional monosyllabic words and short sentences.
- *Objective 2:* Sarah will correctly produce /ð/ and /z/ in word-initial position in functional monosyllabic words and short sentences.
- *Objective 3:* Once Sarah demonstrates approximately 50% accuracy on Objectives 1 and 2 at the level of successive repetition, vowel production accuracy will also be targeted.

Rationale. Increasing Sarah's phonetic repertoire to include the four target fricatives would increase her overall speech intelligibility. Learning how to produce these sounds in words would add an increased level of complexity to her motor speech skill repertoire. In typically developing children, voiceless fricatives emerge first in word-final position, so teaching word-final production

of /θ/ and /ʃ/ was selected to simulate the developmental context. In addition, teaching /θ/ and /ʃ/ in word-final position would help to eliminate Sarah's preference for open word shapes. Working on /ð/ and /z/ in word-initial position would increase intelligibility of Sarah's speech by eliminating her preference for /d/ in word-initial position. Last, addressing vowel accuracy once the consonant targets were emerging would lead to increased speech intelligibility. Stimuli initially consisted of monosyllabic words to minimize the articulatory demands on Sarah as she learned how to produce the four later-mastered fricatives.

Goal 2

In response to cognitive-motor learning principles incorporated into integral stimulation intervention, Sarah will increase correct production of a variety of speech sounds in functional multisyllabic words that comprise sounds already in her phonetic repertoire.

- *Objective 1:* Sarah correctly will produce all phonemes in 10 functional multisyllabic words selected by Sarah and her mother.
- *Objective 2:* Sarah correctly will produce all phonemes in up to 20 multisyllabic words selected from the Grade 1 National Reading Vocabulary List (TampaREADS, n.d.).

Rationale. Multisyllabic word production is similar to connected speech production, so Sarah's ability to correctly produce multisyllabic words would lead to increased overall articulatory proficiency and intelligibility. Sarah's ability to produce multisyllabic words should help her communicate more independently and help her to express her needs and wants more effectively at home and school and in other social situations. Using words that Sarah selects should help to increase her interest in intervention and should increase her practice time, as those words should have a high frequency of occurrence for Sarah. Using words from the Grade 1 National Reading Vocabulary List (e.g., before, after, today, tomorrow, cannot, etc.) should increase Sarah's speech intelligibility, as well as help to avert potential reading problems. Once one set of target words is mastered, another word set will be introduced.

Goal 3

In response to cognitive-motor learning principles incorporated into integral stimulation intervention, Sarah will correctly produce all the speech sounds in six functional sentences.

Rationale. Sarah's ability to correctly produce the sounds in the target sentences would increase her overall speech intelligibility and help her to communicate more independently. Sentences targeted contained personal information that was important for Sarah to be able to convey to unfamiliar listeners. Examples of target sentences included: "My name is Sarah xxx," "My phone number is 794-xxxx," "I live in Rock Island, Illinois," and "My address is xx Pine Road."

Analysis of Client's Response to Intervention

Sarah's overall response to speech intervention was slow but steady throughout the academic year. She remained positive and enthusiastic about attending therapy and worked hard during sessions at the College Center and at school. Sarah attended a total of 110 thirty-minute speech sessions over the 9-month period, totaling approximately 55 hours of speech intervention between both sites. Typically, all three goals were addressed in each session. The number of target utterances practiced varied, depending on her success on a goal within and across sessions. Smaller target sets tended to be used as Sarah established new sounds and word shapes, with stimuli increasing in number as she became more successful.

Goal 1 Progress

Sarah initially exhibited the slowest overall progress on this goal. Sarah began intervention able to produce the target phonemes only when provided

a very slow speech model and tactile cues. Sarah initially made the most rapid progress on /θ/ and /ʃ/ in word-final position; after approximately 16 sessions, she could produce these sounds in target words in immediate repetition with scores of 1 and 2. She made slower progress on /ð/ and /z/ in word-initial position; after approximately 16 sessions, Sarah could produce these sounds in words in mimed productions with scores of 1. After the first 50 sessions, she was able to produce all four fricatives in target words and contexts with scores of 1 on successive repetition tasks. Sarah demonstrated the most regression on this goal after she returned to the Center from winter break, even though she had received school-based intervention for 3 of the 6 weeks. By the end of the school year, Sarah was able to correctly produce the target fricatives in target utterances with scores of 1 and 2 on delayed repetition tasks.

Goal 2 Progress

Sarah demonstrated the most rapid progress on and interest in this goal. She began intervention producing target multisyllabic words with scores of 0 and 1 in simultaneous production with moderate cues (e.g., slowed model, exaggerated movements, etc.). Her most frequent error was omitting syllables. To initiate work on this goal, therapy began by having Sarah produce strings of three to five CV words containing sounds in her phonetic repertoire. For example, Sarah simultaneously produced baa-baa-baa-baa with the SLP, and once able to do this in successive repetition, the string would be changed (for example, to baa-bee-bee-baa). Toward the latter part of the first month of intervention, Sarah had learned to produce repetitive word strings containing sounds from her phonetic inventory intelligibly and with decreased cues; a list of 10 multisyllabic words then was developed by Sarah, her mother, and both SLPs. After approximately 40 sessions, Sarah consistently produced the 10 target words with scores of 2 in response to questions. Multisyllabic word targets then were selected from the Grade 1 National Reading Vocabulary List.

By the end of another 40 intervention sessions, Sarah was consistently producing those words with scores of 2 in response to questions. In addition, Sarah demonstrated the ability to read over half of the target words by sight.

Goal 3 Progress

Sarah exhibited good progress on this goal, demonstrating functional mastery after receiving the equivalent of 5 months of intervention (i.e., ~80 thirty-minute sessions). Sarah began intervention on this goal needing maximal cues (e.g., slowed model, exaggerated movements, simultaneous production, etc.) to achieve scores of 0 and 1. After approximately 2 months of intervention, she consistently produced target utterances with scores of 1 and 2 in immediate repetition of a model. After 5 months of intervention, she consistently produced all the target utterances with scores of 2 in delayed repetition and with scores of 1 and 2 in question response. This goal was discontinued in the middle of the spring semester (i.e., after the equivalent of approximately 5 months of intervention); however, Sarah's teacher periodically asked Sarah questions to elicit the target utterances. Her teacher reported that Sarah maintained intelligibility and largely correct articulation of all six sentences until the end of the school year.

In summary, Sarah demonstrated success on all three speech goals. Based on her progress in response to integral stimulation intervention at the end of first grade, the College Center SLP predicted that Sarah's speech disorder would likely resolve if she continued to receive frequent speech intervention over the next several years. Sarah's speech gains were also apparent to Sarah herself. She clearly expressed her excitement over "learning to talk better," and by the spring of first grade, Sarah more frequently initiated conversation with her peers, volunteered to answer in class, and talked on the telephone.

Author's Note

The case described is not based on an actual client.

References

American Speech-Language-Hearing Association. (2007). *Childhood apraxia of speech* [Technical report]. https://www.asha.org/policy/TR2007-00278/

Bahar, N., Namasivayam, A. K., & van Lieshout, P. (2021). Telehealth intervention and childhood apraxia of speech: A scoping review. *Speech, Language and Hearing.* Advance online publication. https://doi.org/10.1080/2050571X.2021.1947649

Bauman-Waengler, J. (2020). *Articulation and phonology in speech sound disorders: A clinical focus* (6th ed.). Pearson.

Bernthal, J. E., Bankson, N. W., & Flipsen, P. (2022). *Speech sound disorders in children: Articulation and phonological disorders* (9th ed.). Brookes Publishing.

Bleile, K. (2004). *The manual of articulation and phonological disorders: Infancy through adulthood* (2nd ed.). Thomson Delmar Learning.

Chumpelik, D. (1984). The PROMPT system of therapy: Theoretical framework and applications for developmental apraxia of speech. *Seminars in Speech and Language, 5,* 139–156.

Davis, B. L., & MacNeilage, P. F. (1995). The articulatory basis of babbling. *Journal of Speech and Hearing Research, 38,* 1199–1211. https://doi.org/10.1044/jshr.3806.1199

de Oliveira, A. M., Nunes, I., da Cruz, G. S., & Gurgel, L. G. (2021). Methods of assessing of childhood apraxia of speech: Systematic review. *Audiology Communication Research, 26,* 1–12. https://doi.org/10.1590/2317-6431-2021-2524

Fiori, S., Guzzetta, A., Mitra, J., Pannek, K., Pasquariello, R., Cipriani, P., . . . Chilosi, A. (2016). Neuroanatomical correlates of childhood apraxia of speech: A connectomic approach. *NeuroImage: Clinical, 12,* 894–901. https://doi.org/10.1016/j.nicl.2016.11.003

Fletcher, S. G. (1972). Time-by-count measurement of diadochokinetic syllable rate. *Journal of Speech and Hearing Research, 15,* 763–770.

Fletcher, S. G. (1973). *Fletcher time-by-count test of diadochokinetic syllable rate.* C.C. Publications.

Goldman, R., & Fristoe, M. (2015). *Goldman-Fristoe test of articulation* (3rd ed.). Pearson.

Hodson, B. W., & Paden, E. P. (1991). *Targeting intelligible speech: A phonological approach to remediation* (2nd ed.). Pro-Ed.

Howell, J., & Dean, E. (1991). *Treating phonological disorders in children: Metaphon—theory to practice.* Singular Publishing Group.

Iuzzini-Seigel, J. (2021). Procedural learning, grammar, and motor skills in children with childhood apraxia of speech, speech sound disorder, and typically developing speech. *Journal of Speech, Language, and Hearing Research, 64*, 1081–1103. https://doi.org/10.1044/2020_JSLHR-20-00581

Kaufman, N. R. (1995). *Kaufman speech praxis test for children*. Wayne State University Press.

Maas, E., Robin, D. A., Austermann Hula, S. N., Freedman, S. E., Wulf, G., Ballard, K. J., & Schmidt, R. (2008). Principles of motor learning in treatment of motor speech disorders. *American Journal of Speech-Language Pathology, 17*, 277–298. https://doi.org/10.1044/1058-0360(2008/025)

McCabe, P., Murray, E., Thomas, D., & Evans, P. (2017). *Clinician manual for Rapid Syllable Transition treatment*. The University of Sydney, Camperdown, Australia. https://rest.sydney.edu.au/wp-content/uploads/2019/07/rest-clinician-manual.pdf

McDonald, E. T. (1964). *Articulation testing and treatment: A sensory motor approach*. Stanwix House.

Murray, E., & Iuzzini-Seigel, J. (2017). Efficacious treatment of children with childhood apraxia of speech according to the International Classification of Functioning, Disability, and Health. *Perspectives of the ASHA Special Interest Groups, 2*, 61–76. https://pubs.asha.org/doi/10.1044/persp2.SIG2.61

Murray, E., Iuzzini-Seigel, J., Maas, E., Terband, H., & Ballard, K. (2020). Differential diagnosis of childhood apraxia of speech compared to other speech sound disorders: A systematic review. *American Journal of Speech-Language Pathology, 30*, 279–300. https://doi.org/https://doi.org/10.1044/2020_AJSLP-20-00063

Murray, E., McCabe, P., & Ballard, K. J. (2014). A systematic review of treatment outcomes for children with childhood apraxia of speech. *American Journal of Speech-Language Pathology, 23*, 486–504. https://doi.org/10.1044/2014_ajslp-13-0035

Murray, E., McCabe, P., Heard, R., & Ballard, K. J. (2015). Differential diagnosis of children with suspected childhood apraxia of speech. *Journal of Speech,* *Language, and Hearing Research, 58*, 43–60. https://doi.org/10.1044/2014_JSLHR-S-12-0358

Namasivayam, A. K., Huynh, A., Granata, F., Law, V., & van Lieshout, P. (2021). PROMPT intervention for children with severe speech motor delay: A randomized control trial. *Pediatric Research, 89*, 613–621. https://doi.org/10.1038/s41390-020-0924-4

Rosenbek, J. C., Hansen, R., Baughman, C. H., & Lemme, M. (1974). Treatment of developmental apraxia of speech: A case study. *Language, Speech, and Hearing Services in Schools, 1*, 13–22. https://doi.org/10.1044/0161-1461.0501.13

Semel, E., Wiig, E. H., & Secord, W. A. (2013). *Clinical evaluation of language fundamentals* (5th ed.). Pearson.

Strand, E. A., & Debertine, P. (2000). The efficacy of integral stimulation intervention with developmental apraxia of speech. *Journal of Medical Speech-Language Pathology, 8*, 295–300.

Strand, E. A., & Skinder, A. (1999). Treatment of developmental apraxia of speech: Integral stimulation methods. In A. Caruso & E. A. Strand (Eds.), *Clinical management of motor speech disorders in children* (pp. 109–148). Thieme.

Strand, E. A., Stoeckel, R., & Baas, B. (2006). Treatment of severe childhood apraxia of speech: A treatment efficacy study. *Journal of Medical Speech-Language Pathology, 14*, 297–307.

TampaREADS. (n.d.). *Reading key*. https://anyflip.com/rqqd/bnux

Van Riper, C., & Erickson, R. (1996). *Speech correction: An introduction to speech pathology and audiology* (9th ed.). Prentice-Hall.

Vihman, M. M. (1996). *Phonological development: The origins of language in the child*. Blackwell.

Wechsler, D. (2012). *Wechsler preschool and primary scale of intelligence* (4th ed.). Pearson.

Weiner, F. (1981). Treatment of phonological disability using the method of meaningful minimal contrast: Two case studies. *Journal of Speech and Hearing Disorders, 46*, 29–34. https://doi.org/10.1044/jshd.4601.97

ARTICULATION/PHONOLOGY
CASE 22
David: Of Mouth and Mind: An Articulation and Phonological Disorder in a Young School-Age Child
Sue T. Hale and Lea Helen Evans

Conceptual Knowledge Areas

Referral Questions and Assessment Decisions

When parents or school personnel report that a child has speech that is "delayed" or "difficult to understand" or even "unintelligible," the speech-language pathologist must make some important initial decisions about whether and how to assess the child. A referring statement, whether oral or written, brings immediate questions to mind.

- Is the child experiencing speech differences that are within the range of normal performance expected for children of the same age?
- Are the speech sound differences misarticulations or phonological error patterns, or is there evidence of both?
- Is it possible that there are other concomitant problems such as receptive or expressive language delays/disorders, hearing loss, oral-motor or structural differences, developmental delays, or behavioral issues?
- How consistent are the errors across speech contexts, and can the child improve the errored productions with instruction?
- What is the likelihood that the speech pattern will have an effect on academic achievement in the areas of reading, spelling, or writing?

Initial impressions about the possible answers to these questions will come from a thorough case history. However, each question must also be answered through direct observation and interaction with the child. An accurate assessment of a disorder of articulation/phonology rests not only on the information obtained from the case history and the direct observations but also on the clinician's sound conceptual and experiential framework for addressing articulation and phonological disorders. Specifically, the clinician must have the following knowledge and skills:

- Theoretical knowledge of normal aspects of development for articulation and phonology, which may affect both assessment and remediation decisions
- Clinical knowledge and skill using appropriate articulation/phonology assessment protocols
- Clinical knowledge and skill using evidence-based remediation approaches for articulation/phonological disorders

Developmental Articulation/ Phonology Models

To appropriately evaluate and remediate a phonological disorder, the clinician must have a working knowledge of the theories of developmental phonology. Many strategies have been suggested as possible models of phonological development. Vihman (2004) cites original authors and includes reasonably comprehensive descriptions of the following models: the behaviorist model, the natural phonology model, the generative phonology model, the prosodic model, the cognitive model, the biological model, the self-organizing model, and the nonlinear model.

Whereas the behavioral and structural models, based more on deductive rather than empirical thinking, have largely fallen out of favor, the remaining models address more currently accepted ideas regarding the presence or absence of universals, systematization, and the accuracy or inaccuracy of the child's speech perception from the beginning (Vihman, 2004). Maturation and practice clearly influence phonological development. Models that suggest the child engages in problem solving and also brings nonlinear learning related to prosody and segmental knowledge to the task complement most commonly used approaches for remediation (Vihman, 2004). As with any aspect of communication development, the model or models that the clinician accepts affect the clinical decision-making process. However, Vihman (2004) cites Macken and Ferguson, who stated that one point on which "virtually all theoretical persuasions can agree is the *systematic* nature of the child's simplifications and restructuring of adult words."

Assessment Rationale

In order to evaluate the presence or absence of a disorder of articulation or phonology, the well-prepared clinician should have a reasonably standardized protocol for assessment. Certain aspects of the child's history, physical makeup, and sensory and oral-motor abilities must be assessed. Physical causes (hearing loss, problems with oral structures or their functioning) for the disorder must be ruled out with accepted measurement protocols.

Objective, reliable, and valid assessment of the child's current speech and language status is essential. Receptive and expressive language must be evaluated to ensure that the problems in articulation are not compounded by problems in the language system. Additionally, the objective measures of speech sound production, which often occur in word-only contexts, must be supplemented with subjective observations in naturalistic and interactive environments.

Although the discussion of the current case focuses on thorough assessment illustrative of a clinical "ideal," Tyler et al. (2002) remind us that there is a need for balance between the ideals of thoroughness and efficiency. Evaluation appointments typically must progress from history to the final step of informing and counseling parents within a time span that is reasonable in the clinical setting and within the attention span of the child being evaluated. The current case is presented with the assumption that those measures not completed in the initial assessment were conducted during the first clinical session. Specific measures and their results are provided.

Intervention Models

In addition to a basic understanding of the theories of developmental phonology, the clinician must also have a working knowledge of the theoretical approaches to clinical remediation. Kamhi (2006) explored the fundamental similarities and differences in current clinical approaches. Accordingly, he delineates the following five models: (1) normative, (2) bottom-up, discrete skill, (3) language based, (4) broad based, and (5) complexity based. Williams et al. (2021) further described theoretical approaches and include minimal pairs intervention, multiple oppositions intervention, recasting, and examples of more narrowly defined or targeted language-based approaches. Similar ideological threads run through the theoretical approaches summarized by Kamhi (2006) and by Williams et al. (2021).

According to the normative view identified by Kamhi (2006), decisions regarding the presence or absence of a speech sound disorder, as well as decisions regarding the nature or severity of the disorder, are based on comparison of the client's speech to that of other children who are developing speech sounds typically. With this clinical approach, the clinician would begin treatment with targets no smaller than the syllable but would focus primarily on treatment beginning at the word level. Kamhi (2006) cautions that comparing the phonological learning of a child with a disorder to the normative sequence may lead to erroneous conclusions. Additionally, Kamhi (2006) suggests that most effective interventions for phonological disorders rely, at some point, on teaching the production of the target sound in isolation, a phenomenon that does not occur in normal development.

A bottom-up, discrete skill approach is the basis for two different treatment models. The traditional motor approach (Van Riper & Emerick, 1984) rests on the initial teaching of auditory discrimination for errored phonemes and moves to a stepwise progression of production in isolation, words, phrases, sentences, and, finally, conversation. The second branch of the bottom-up, discrete skill approach assumes that physical practice of the oral musculature outside the context of communication increases the accuracy of speech sound production in communication. Therefore, clinicians adhering to this approach incorporate oral-motor exercises into a treatment protocol. Both models are widely used. Kamhi (2006) reports a lack of evidence that the oral-motor approach improves speech production. He further indicates that while the traditional motor approach is supported by efficacy data, it has notable limitations (Kamhi, 2006).

Language-based approaches consider speech to be inexorably entwined with language. Taking into account the synergistic nature of phonology and language, clinicians who adhere to this approach focus therapy within the context of naturally occurring interactions and do not decontextualize the communication with direct instruction or practice. This protocol indirectly addresses speech sound errors. Kamhi (2006) cites prevailing findings that indicate that direct treatment is necessary for children with significant speech delays.

A broad-based approach to therapy combines parts from many different treatment approaches, including the normative approach and the bottom-up discrete skill approach. The broad-based

paradigm is probably most widely applied in the form of Hodson's cycles approach (Hodson & Paden, 1991). This model considers movement in a stepwise progression as well as in teaching speech sound motor movements. Like the normative approach, this broad-based approach bases target selection on typical speech sound development. Finally, this model gives the clinician the flexibility to use any form of evidence-based treatment that is effective for a particular child. Kamhi (2006) cites limited studies supporting a cycles approach as being more efficacious than other approaches.

Finally, the complexity approach addresses more complex targets first, which, when corrected, create the greatest positive change in overall speech sound production with a resulting generalization to nontargeted (less complex) sounds. Kamhi (2006) notes that despite numerous studies supporting the efficacy of this model of treatment, clinicians do not typically select goals in regard to complexity principles.

Regardless of the approach chosen, current research has indicated that all of the models detailed above are effective (Kamhi, 2006). Gierut (2005) indicated that the treatment target chosen for therapy was more important than the way in which it was taught. Kamhi (2006) summarizes this viewpoint by stating that "one treatment approach has not proved to be better than another."

Description of the Case

Background Information

David, a 6-year, 4-month-old male, was seen for a speech-language evaluation in the Pediatric Speech-Language Clinic of the Vanderbilt Bill Wilkerson Center (the Center), Nashville, Tennessee. A certified and state-licensed speech-language pathologist saw David for his evaluation. David was accompanied to the evaluation by his mother, his two younger sisters, and his maternal grandmother. The clinician briefly observed David interacting with his sisters. Then, his sisters left the examination room with the grandmother to play on the playground. David's mother provided case history information and then observed the testing session from the observation room. She returned to the examining room at the conclusion of the session to receive the results of the assessment. David separated from his sisters and mother easily and was readily engaged with the toys in the testing room. He then transitioned smoothly to the activities of the evaluation. He was cooperative and communicative throughout the session. When the clinician had difficulty understanding him, he repeated his messages up to three times before showing signs of frustration. When asked why he thought he was at the Center, David responded, "Because my friends don't understand me sometimes."

History

David was from an upper-middle-class family who had just moved to the area. His father was an attorney, and his mother did not work outside the home. She indicated that "my children are my focus" at this particular stage in life. She held a degree in elementary education. David was the oldest of three siblings. He had two younger sisters, one age 3 years and one who was 15 months old. The parent reported that the two younger children had speech and language development commensurate with other children their ages. Other familial communication disorders were not reported.

Pregnancy and birth history for David were unremarkable. Medical history was significant for recurrent otitis media (three to four episodes per year) treated with antibiotics. After placement of pressure equalization (PE) tubes when David was 3 years old, further ear infections were not noted. David achieved all developmental milestones at the expected ages.

At the time of the evaluation, David had just completed kindergarten. He had not attended a daycare, preschool, or prekindergarten program in his previous hometown. Teacher checklists indicated that while he was very reticent in groups of his peers and in volunteering to answer questions aloud in class, David excelled in kindergarten and surpassed all of the state-determined benchmarks, including phonetic awareness and iden-

tification and conceptual knowledge of numbers and colors. He had a sight-word vocabulary of 50 words. Additional teacher report revealed that David exhibited some aggressive interactions on the playground that typically occurred when he attempted to verbally engage his peers.

David's mother brought him to the Center due to his poor intelligibility. She expressed concern about the discrepancy between his level of intelligence and his speech intelligibility and his growing frustration level. Additionally, his mother reported that David's sisters were more intelligible even though they were younger than he and that unfamiliar adults in unfamiliar contexts were not able to understand David much of the time. On the day of the speech-language evaluation, the clinician, as an unfamiliar listener, noted that David's intelligibility in connected speech was less than 50%. Intelligibility improved when the clinician could relate David's word production to a limited and known context or when he was producing single words. David's sisters did not seem to be concerned about his speech. They did not respond verbally when David said something that they did not understand; however, they were attentive to his words and actions and seemed to gain an understanding of his intended messages through the gestalt of the situation. David had no prior history of evaluation or therapy for speech or language issues.

Reasons for Referral

The concern of the parents, which was supported by observations from David's kindergarten teacher, caused the mother to seek a speech-language consultation. She was most anxious to proactively address any barriers to academic achievement that his speech and language might present and to reduce the presence of social frustration.

Findings of the Evaluation

Oral Mechanism Examination

An examination of the oral mechanism revealed normal and intact oral structures. General symmetry of the face at rest and while making specific movements was observed to be within normal limits. Off-target groping, uncoordinated movements, or signs of weakness were not noted. Structural and functional integrity of the lips and tongue were intact. Structural and functional integrity of the hard and soft palates appeared to be intact. Velopharyngeal incompetence or insufficiency was not noted; however, there was a slight inflammation of the faucial tonsils (located between the anterior and posterior faucial pillars). When asked about it, the mother indicated that David was just getting over a sore throat. The integrity of the teeth and dental arches was intact with normal occlusal relationships. However, the upper right central incisor was noted to be loose, which was judged to be normal at David's age for a deciduous tooth. Repetitive tongue and lip movements and palatal elevation for the sustained /ah/ vowel were judged to be within normal limits.

Standardized Assessment Measures

Goldman-Fristoe Test of Articulation-3 (GFTA-3; Goldman & Fristoe, 2015). This assessment instrument, initially published in 1969, is appropriate for clients 2 years of age through 21 years, 11 months of age. It measures speech sound production in the word initial, medial, and final positions as well as in consonant blends. Using 47 pictures and 60 words, this evaluation of sound production uses indications of substitutions, distortions, and omissions to describe speech sounds at the word level. In addition to assessing speech sound production in individual words, the assessment also evaluates connected speech in a somewhat restricted manner by eliciting sentences/conversational speech from the client through story retelling. A third component of the GFTA-3 is a stimulability assessment of individual phonemes at the syllable, word, and sentence levels. David's raw score on the GFTA-3 was 24. This raw score converted to a standard score of 70, a percentile rank of 7, and an approximate age equivalent of less than 2 years. Errors included the data in Table 22–1.

Khan-Lewis Phonological Analysis-2 (KLPA-3; Khan & Lewis, 2015). Originally published in 1986, this assessment instrument uses the information obtained by the GFTA-3 to identify phonological processes that could be active in the child's speech sound system. This assessment evaluates the GFTA-3 information for 12 developmental and 3 nondevelopmental processes. David's raw score on the KLPA-3 was 31. This raw score converted to a standard score of 62, a percentile rank of 1, and an approximate age equivalent of 3 years to 3 years, 1 month. Developmental processes and percentage of occurrence noted included deletion of final consonants (2% occurrence), stopping of fricatives and affricates (42% occurrence), cluster simplification (11%), and liquid simplification (45%).

Preschool Language Scale-5 (PLS-5; Zimmerman et al., 2011). Originally published in 1969, this assessment instrument for children birth to age 6 years, 11 months evaluates the child's ability to understand language directed toward him or her (auditory comprehension subtest) as well as

Table 22–1. The Goldman-Fristoe Test of Articulation-3—Errors

Initial Position	Medial Position	Final Position
w/r, t/ th (voiceless), b/v, t/s, d/z, d/th (voiced), bw/br, dw/dr, fw/fr, gw/gr, kw/kr, t/sl. t/st, tw/tr	t/sh, w/r, -/th (voiceless), b/v, t/w, and d/th (voiced)	w/r, t/ th (voiceless), b/v, and t/s

Note: In the notations, errors are listed by position with slash marks; that is, if a child produced "dog" as "gog," the substitution would be indicated as being in the initial position as g/d. If the consonant was omitted, the omission would be indicated as a "-." For example, if the child produced "dog" as "do," the error would be indicated in the final position as -/g/. Results of stimulability testing indicated that David was stimulable for all phonemes in at least one context with the exception of /r/, which was not stimulable at any level.

to use language to communicate with others and to effect change in the environment (expressive communication subtest). David's raw score on the auditory comprehension subtest of the PLS-5 was 61. This raw score converted to a standard score of 103, a percentile rank of 58, and an approximate age equivalent of 6 years, 6 months. David's raw score on the expressive communication subtest of the PLS-5 was 65. This raw score converted to a standard score of 115, a percentile rank of 84, and an approximate age equivalent of 7 years, 11 months. Combined, these raw scores were 126. The combined standard scores converted to a total language percentile rank of 75 and an approximate age equivalent of 7 years, 1 month.

Informal Descriptive Measures

An analysis of a connected speech sample was used to augment the information obtained from the standardized assessment measures, since the standardized measures focused primarily on production of speech sounds at the single word level. Assessment of the speech sample was accomplished with both an independent analysis (assessment of speech sound productions without reference to the adult targets of the word) and a relational analysis (assessment of the child's speech sound production as those productions relate to the adult targets). Results of independent and relational analyses performed on a connected speech sample taken while David engaged in free play with his sisters and later his mother yielded speech sound inventories as well as phonological process usage similar in nature to those found with the standardized assessments.

Audiological Screening and Screening Tympanometry

Normal results were obtained from a hearing screening at 20 dB SPL for the frequencies 500 to 8000 Hz. Otoscopic evaluation of the external ear and middle ear was unremarkable. It was noted that the PE tubes were no longer in place. Screening tympanometry revealed Type A tympanograms bilaterally, suggesting normal mobility of the mid-

dle ear structures. Results suggested the presence of normal hearing for speech purposes as well as middle ear functioning within normal limits.

Speech Sound Discrimination Testing

Informal testing indicated that David was able to appropriately discriminate between speech sounds in a variety of contexts.

Voice

Voice quality and pitch were normal for David's age and gender.

Fluency

David had normal speech fluency in connected speech.

Representation of the Problem at the Time of Evaluation

David exhibited age-appropriate receptive and expressive language skills, normal fluency, and normal voice production. However, his production of the sounds of language did not appear to be age appropriate at the time of the evaluation. Standardized and informal assessments indicated that he exhibited both an articulation disorder (inability to produce /r/) and immature phonological processes (stopping of fricatives and affricates and cluster reduction). Although analysis indicated the presence of the process of gliding of liquids, it was judged that this finding was due to David's inability to produce /r/ rather than to a phonological process affecting all of the liquids. This observation was supported by David's ability to produce /l/ in a variety of contexts.

In summary, David exhibited delayed articulatory/phonological development. He substituted w/r in word initial and medial positions and in all consonant blends containing /r/, and this pattern was judged to be a motor error for the production of /r/. In addition, he exhibited the phonological processes of stopping of fricatives and affricates, as well as cluster reduction. The process of cluster reduction did not occur at a level of consistency to warrant remediation. However, the process of stopping of fricatives and affricates was strongly present and had a significant impact on David's intelligibility. Individual therapy was recommended at a frequency of two times per week for 1-hour sessions to address /r/ errors and the phonological process of stopping of fricatives/affricates.

Treatment Options Considered

In accordance with the preceding hypothesis, David had both phonological process usage as well as motoric articulation errors. The two types of errors warranted different remediation approaches. In view of the treatment models presented and the conclusions regarding efficacy by Kamhi (2006), a hybrid approach to speech sound remediation was chosen. This approach included elements of the traditional model (to address his articulation error in the production of /r/) and the broad-based approach (to address those speech sound errors that occurred due to inappropriate phonological process usage, notably, stopping of fricatives and affricates).

Course of Treatment

Therapy was designed to work briefly on the traditional, motoric production of /r/ before moving to a more cycles-based approach for remediation of the phonological process of stopping of fricatives and affricates. After a short traditional production activity designed to teach the placement of the /r/ phoneme, each therapy session was divided into the following sequence: (1) review of previous session's production targets, (2) listening activity for the identified phonological process, (3) target word review to incorporate new exemplars for the process being addressed, (4) production practice in play-based activities, (5) stimulability probing, (6) return to listening activity for the day's exemplars, and (7) discussion of home programming.

A vertically structured articulation treatment approach was employed. At the initiation of therapy, activities were planned to coincide with David's current level of functioning. Comprised of drill play, these activities consisted of turn-taking games in which turns focused on the imitation and then spontaneous production of the /r/ phoneme initially in isolation, syllables, monosyllabic CVC words, and sentences. David had to reach a criterion of mastery at each level before moving to the next.

Although a more broad-based phonological approach was chosen, only one phonological process was deemed to be severely affecting David's intelligibility—the stopping of fricatives and affricates. The percentage of occurrence of the phonological process of gliding of liquids was directly attributed to the absence of the /r/ phoneme. The percentage of occurrence of the phonological process of cluster reduction was fairly small and was not felt to affect intelligibility to a great extent. Since the clinician and client were only focused on one phonological process, the treatment approach was more vertical in nature, though the sequence of therapy activities from a cycles-based approach was incorporated. For each session, the first activity incorporated review of the previous week's practice words with the client. The client was not required to make any judgments of the words or to produce any of the previous week's targets.

The second activity consisted of a listening activity in which the child did not actively participate but rather listened to the clinician's production of the week's target words. For the listening activity, there were typically between 10 and 12 words that contained the target sound. (Although it was not used with David, this activity may be done with the use of an amplification device. Additionally, during this activity, the clinician may contrast the correct production of the target with the misarticulation.)

The third activity consisted of creation of target word cards. Within the context of this activity, the clinician and the client chose between three and five of the target words, which were represented by created pictures. These representations took different forms, including line drawings, photocopied pictures, stickers, and appropriate representations from magazines. The name of the picture represented was written on each of the cards.

The fourth activity comprised the majority of each therapy session and consisted of production practice, which is similar to production practice in many other therapy approaches. The client and the clinician engaged in experiential play that focused on the target words and required production of the target in order to continue with or take a turn in the activity. By incorporating experiential play, all aspects of environmental stimuli can be utilized to aid in production.

The fifth activity, stimulability probing, is used to plan for the target words for the following week. During this activity, the clinician attempted to discover what words the client possessed the ability to imitate. After the stimulability probing, the listening activity implemented earlier in the therapy session was repeated using the same word list.

The final activity, the home program, was discussed with the client's parent at the end of the therapy session. With this activity, the parent was given a word list of 10 to 12 target words similar in nature but different from the target words used in therapy. The parent was instructed to read the list to the child at least once a day in a manner similar to the listening activities used in therapy. Additionally, the picture cards that were created by the clinician and child at the beginning of the therapy session were sent home for daily practice.

Analysis of the Client's Response to Intervention

Following 1 month of therapy, David was able to produce /r/ imitatively following direct clinician model and was suppressing the phonological process of stopping of fricatives to 37% in words. Following 3 months of therapy, David was still mispronouncing the /r/ in words when he produced them spontaneously; however, he was beginning to self-correct at the word level. Additionally, he was suppressing the phonological process of stopping of fricatives to 20% or less in words. Following 6 months of the previously described therapy, David was able to spontaneously produce /r/ in words and had decreased the use of the phonological process of stopping of fricatives to 20% occurrence in connected speech.

Further Recommendations

The treatment regimen recommended after the evaluation was effective in improving David's speech. After 6 months of intervention, he was observed to be 90% intelligible in connected speech. His production of /r/ was correct in all contexts with the exception of highly complex consonant blends; that is, he still produced a w/r in the words *mushroom* and *shrub* in single-word contexts. Additionally, his production of /r/ in conversational contexts continued to be inconsistent, but it was accurate in at least 80% of the conversational contexts. Also after 6 months of remediation, he no longer used a stop for fricatives, but stops were observed occasionally for the affricates in phrases and in conversation. Following the reevaluation at the 6-month juncture, it was recommended that David continue with the current course of therapy until spontaneous production of /r/ was noted consistently in conversational speech and until the use of the phonological process of stopping of affricates was extinguished.

David's mother was pleased with his progress after 6 months of treatment. A conference with David's first-grade teacher resulted in the report that David was eager to participate in class discussions and to answer questions or read words from the board. She also stated that the other children understood David readily and that there were few instances when he was requested to repeat what he had said in conversation. David's mother wanted him to continue in therapy until his speech was error free and asked frequently if it was reasonable to expect that he would no longer need therapy once this school year was completed.

Authors' Note

David is a fictional school-age client who was used to represent common articulation and phonological error patterns as well as an expected course of treatment and recovery.

References

Gierut, J. (2005). Phonological intervention: The how or the what? In A. Kamhi & K. Pollock (Eds.), *Phonological disorders in children: Clinical decision making in assessment and intervention* (pp. 201–210). Brookes.

Goldman, R., & Fristoe, M. (2015). *Goldman-Fristoe Test of Articulation-3*. Pearson Assessments.

Hodson, B., & Paden, E. (1991). *Targeting intelligible speech: A phonological approach to remediation* (2nd ed.). Pro-Ed.

Kamhi, A. G. (2006). Treatment decisions for children with speech-sound disorders. *Language, Speech, and Hearing Services in Schools, 37*, 271–279. https://doi.org/10.1044/0161-1461(2006/031)

Khan, L., & Lewis, N. (2015). *Khan-Lewis Phonological Analysis-3*. American Guidance Service.

Tyler, A. A., Tolbert, L. C., Miccio, A. W., Hoffman, P. R., Norris, J. A., Hodson, B., . . . Bleile, K. (2002). Five views of the elephant: Perspectives on the assessment of articulation and phonology in preschoolers. *American Journal of Speech-Language Pathology, 11*, 213–214.

Van Riper, C., & Emerick, L. (1984). *Speech correction: An introduction to speech pathology and audiology* (7th ed.). Prentice-Hall.

Vihman, M. M. (2004). Early phonological development. In J. E. Bernthal & N. W. Bankson (Eds.), *Articulation and phonological disorders* (5th ed., pp. 63–104). Allyn & Bacon.

Williams, A. L., McLeod, S., & McCauley, R. J. (2021). *Interventions for speech sound disorders in children* (2nd ed.). Paul H. Brookes.

Zimmerman, I. L., Steiner, V. G., & Pond, R. E. (2011). *Preschool Language Scale* (5th ed.). Pearson Assessments.

AUDITORY PROCESSING
CASE 23
Allie and Connor: School-Age Children With Auditory Processing Disorder (APD)
Deborah Moncrieff

Conceptual Knowledge Areas

Children are suspected of having auditory processing disorder (APD) when they demonstrate difficulties with sound localization, following auditory directions, discriminating between sounds, maintaining attention, and needing repetition of auditory information for understanding despite normal hearing acuity (Task Force on Central Auditory Processing, 1996). Children with APD struggle to understand speech or environmental sounds, especially in the presence of background noise, and often present with histories of delayed receptive and expressive language, learning difficulties, and problems developing reading skills.

Auditory processing is typically assessed by presenting challenging auditory information to one or both ears to determine whether the child can achieve an age-appropriate level of performance. Poor performance on auditory processing tasks when there is no evidence of hearing acuity loss is likely to stem from dysfunction within the central auditory nervous system (CANS).

Description of Case 1

The first case illustrates standard assessment procedures that have been historically used to diagnose an APD and the recommendations that are routinely made following results from a comprehensive battery of tests.

Reason for Referral

Allie was brought to the clinic by her mother to be evaluated for APD. At the time of the appointment, Allie was 8 years, 11 months old and in the third grade at a local elementary school. She was receiving special education services under a 504 Plan that had been initiated when she was 6 years old, shortly after she had been diagnosed with an APD. Under the 504 Plan, Allie was given a remote microphone hearing device (FM listener) to use in school, but her mother reported that Allie was still having difficulty learning and that she had failed to develop age-appropriate reading skills.

History

Allie was born following a protracted labor of 44 hours. During her toddler years, she experienced multiple chronic ear infections and was once hospitalized for an ear infection and allergic reaction to medication but was otherwise in good health and developing normally. She wore glasses for reading. She lived with her parents and a younger sister and was generally cheerful, enthusiastic, and cooperative both at home and school.

The earlier diagnosis of APD at age 6 years was based upon an overall performance level of 81% on half of the Staggered Spondaic Words Test (SSW) (Katz, 1986), 26% in the right ear and 20% in the left ear on the Binaural Separation of Competing Sentences (Willeford, 1977), 20% in the right ear and 28% in the left ear on Filtered Speech (Willeford, 1977), and 90% in both ears on Rapid Alternating Sentences Perception (Willeford & Bilger, 1978). The SSW result was interpreted as a moderate deficit, and the results from the Filtered Speech and Binaural Separation Competing Sentences subtests were reported to be 3 and 2 standard deviations below normal, respectively. It was recommended that in addition to the use of an FM listener, Allie would benefit from simplified instructions, preferential seating, additional visual cues for teaching, and verbal rehearsal.

Over the next 2 years, Allie continued to have significant academic difficulties in school and was assessed for intelligence, attention, and psychosocial, emotional, and speech and language abilities. Results from those evaluations are detailed in Table 23–1. Of particular note was the discrepancy between a high-average nonverbal intelligence score of 135 on the Test of Non-verbal Intelligence (TONI) (Brown et al., 1997) and a low average verbal score of 85 on the Test of Oral Language Development–Preschool (TOLD-P) (Hammill & Newcomer, 1996). Further testing also revealed low-average performance on several language and

Table 23–1. Evaluation Results

Test	Age	Test/Subtest	Score	Interpretation
TOLD-P	6–9		SS = 85	Low average verbal
TONI	6–9		SS = 135	High average nonverbal
WJ Cog	8–2	Short Term Memory	SS = 85	Low-average
		Memory for Sentences	SS = 88	Low-average
		Memory for Words	SS = 86	Low-average
		Comprehension Knowledge	SS = 94	Average
		Picture Vocabulary	SS = 92	Low-average
		Oral Vocabulary	SS = 96	Average
		Auditory Processing	SS = 92	Low-average

continues

Table 23–1. *continued*

Test	Age	Test/Subtest	Score	Interpretation
WISC-III	8–2	Verbal	97	Average
		Performance	100	Average
		Full Scale	98	Average
CELF-3 (After FastForWord)	8–2 8–6	Receptive Language	88	
		Expressive Language	84	
		Total Language	85	Age equivalent 7–3
		Receptive Language	114	
		Expressive Language	98	
		Total Language	106	Age equivalent 8–7
GORT	8–2	**Form A:** Reading Rate	GE = 2.5	
		Reading Accuracy	GE = <1.9	
		Reading Passage	GE = <1.9	
		Reading Comprehension	GE = 3.7	
		Oral Reading Quotient	97, rank 42%	Average
		Form B: Reading Rate	GE = 2.2	
		Reading Accuracy	GE = <1.9	
		Passage Score	GE = <1.9	
		Comprehension Oral Reading	GE = 1.9	
		Oral Reading Quotient	85, rank 16%	Low-average, below cognitive
WIAT	8–2	Reading	SS = 94, 34%	Low-average
		Basic Reading	SS = 93, 32%	Low-average
		Reading Comp	SS = 98, 45%	Average
		Mathematics	SS = 112, 79%	High-average
		Numerical Operations	SS = 107, 68%	Upper-average
		Spelling	SS = 101, 53%	Average
Child Behavior Checklist	8–2	Behavior Problems	WNL	
Copeland Symptom Checklist for ADD	8–2	Inattention/Distractability	WNL	
		Impulsivity	WNL	
		Overactivity/Hyperactivity	WNL	
		Underactivity	WNL	
		Noncompliance	WNL	
		Attention-Getting Behavior	WNL	
		Immaturity	WNL	
		Emotional Difficulties	WNL	
		Poor Peer Relations	WNL	
		Family Interaction Problems	WNL	
		Poor Achievement	Mild to moderate	
		Cognitive & Visual-Motor Problems	Mild to moderate	

reading measures. At the age of 8 years, 3 months, Allie completed the FastForWord™ (Scientific Learning Corporation, 1997) training program and achieved excellent performance scores across all of the program subtests. A posttraining speech and language evaluation with the Clinical Evaluation of Language Fundamentals-3 (CELF-3) (Semel et al., 1995) reflected language gains of 1 year, 4 months within a period of 5 months.

Despite these successes, Allie continued to have difficulty attending to and understanding auditory information. She was getting As and Bs in school but struggling with reading. Knowing the importance of good reading skills, Allie's mother wondered whether auditory processing weaknesses might be interfering with Allie's ability to learn to read.

Findings From the APD Evaluation

At the current APD evaluation, Allie's pure-tone air conduction thresholds and speech recognition thresholds were within normal limits for both ears (PTA < 20 dB HL; SRT = 5–10 dB HL). There was no evidence of middle ear disorder, and ipsilateral acoustic reflexes were present in both ears. Word recognition scores were 100% in both ears, suggesting an excellent ability to repeat words one ear at a time in quiet.

Two auditory processing tests were used to evaluate Allie's performance, the Test for Auditory Processing Disorders in Children (SCAN-C) (Keith, 2000) and the Staggered Spondaic Words Test (SSW) (Katz, 1986). The results from those tests are detailed in Table 23–2. Based on standard scores alone, the results obtained by Allie on the SCAN-C indicated normal performance, but her right ear significantly outperformed her left ear on the two subtests in which her ears were placed in competition. A comparison of the individual results obtained for each ear demonstrated that for both dichotic listening subtests of the SCAN-C (Competing Words and Competing Sentences) and for the SSW (also a dichotic listening test), Allie had significant difficulties identifying words presented to her left ear at the same time that words were being presented to her right ear.

Interpretation

Allie has reduced ability to successfully integrate competing information arriving simultaneously at the two ears. Binaural integration of competing information during dichotic listening tests depends upon structural integrity within the ascending auditory nervous system as well as appropriate allocation of attentional resources during challenging listening experiences (Blauert, 1997). There is strong evidence of binaural integration deficits among children with learning and reading disorders who have been assessed with dichotic listening tests (Lamm & Epstein, 1994; Moncrieff & Black, 2008; Morton & Siegel, 1991).

Table 23–2. Results From the SCAN-C and SSW Tests

Test	Age	Test/Subtest	Score	Interpretation
SCAN-C	8–11	Filtered Words	SS = 14	WNL
		Auditory Figure Ground	SS = 10	WNL
		Competing Words	SS = 10	WNL
			R 83%, L 47%	Significant interaural asymmetry
		Competing Sentences	SS = 8	WNL
			R 100%, L 10%	Significant interaural asymmetry
SSW	8–11	Right Non-Competing	100%	WNL
		Right Competing	95%	WNL
		Left Competing	73%	Abnormal
		Left Non-Competing	93%	WNL

The structural model of dichotic listening states that (1) information ascends via contralateral auditory pathways to the opposite side of the brain, and (2) ipsilateral auditory pathways are suppressed when both ears are simultaneously activated by differing input (Kimura, 1967). As a result, information presented to the right ear ascends directly to the language-dominant left hemisphere of the brain (typical in 80% of right-handed and 50% of left-handed individuals). Information presented to the left ear ascends indirectly, arriving first in the right hemisphere and then transferring via the corpus callosum to the language-dominant left hemisphere. This indirect routing of the auditory signal from the left ear can account for some loss of information, but in most individuals, the loss leads to only a small decrement in performance for material presented toward the left ear. A significant decrement has been attributed to poor interhemispheric transfer via the corpus callosum, but it is also possible that auditory neural pathways ascending from the left ear may be disordered. Structures within the auditory brainstem, specifically in the superior olivary complex, provide neural patterns to characterize interaural timing and intensity differences that are important for localization, lateralization, and spatial stream segregation (Middlebrooks & Green, 1991).

The attention model of dichotic listening states that once linguistic material is presented, there is a priming of the language-dominant left hemisphere, which then leads to an advantageous allocation of attention to material being presented toward the right ear (Kinsbourne, 1970). Under this hypothesis, a listener who performs normally in the right ear and poorly in the left ear may be experiencing difficulties with appropriate allocation of attentional resources. This would result in a decreased ability to overcome the natural bias toward the right ear and to attend more to the information being presented toward the left ear. Attention is thought to be dependent upon and integrated with a listener's verbal working memory, which develops throughout childhood. An early model of working memory that defined it as a limited-capacity system to temporarily retain auditory sensory information while processing it (Baddeley & Hitch, 1974) was expanded to include central executive processes of attention, updating, and inhibition of irrelevant information (Baddeley, 1986), processes that are involved in repeating multiple elements in a dichotic listening (DL) task. Working memory depends on maturation (Cowan, 2016) and is significantly impaired in children (Arjona Valladares et al., 2020) and adults (Kim et al., 2014) with diagnosed attention-deficit disorders.

Because there had been no evidence that Allie had an attention-deficit disorder (see results in Table 23–1), it seemed unlikely that her difficulty with processing the words presented toward her left ear was the result of poor attentional resources during the dichotic listening tests. Her strong performance for information presented toward the right ear is consistent with the most recent language results that also indicated no significant disorder of language for Allie. It seemed plausible that Allie's difficulty with binaural integration may stem from poor transmission of auditory information arriving at the left ear. Whether this was due to poor interhemispheric transfer via the corpus callosum or was the result of poor transmission through ascending auditory pathways from the left ear was not known from these results.

Recommendations

Allie's mother had considered the Earobics™ program (Cognitive Concepts, 2000), and it was recommended that Allie complete Earobics™ and that she continue in ongoing language exercises (Wiig, 1992) as recommended by her speech-language pathologist. In order to explore potential physiologic weaknesses that may be underlying her binaural integration deficit, it was recommended that Allie be evaluated with a middle latency response (MLR).

Findings From the MLR Evaluation

An MLR was recorded in response to biphasic click stimuli presented at the rate of 12 per second to the right and left ears. The early components of the MLR, the Na response and the Pa response, were present for input to both ears at latencies of approximately 19 ms and 35 ms, respectively. As shown in Figure 23–1, the peak-to-peak amplitude of the MLR (from maximum negativity of the Na response to maximum positivity of the Pa) was delayed in overall latency and larger for input to the left ear (0.514 µV) than for input to the right ear (0.378 µV). This pattern of greater amplitude for the response from the left ear had been observed in other children with binaural integration deficits (Moncrieff et al., 2002). A recent study reported stronger β and γ neural oscillations for input to the right ear (Momtaz et al., 2021) and an insensitivity to stimulus rate changes in children with similar dichotic listening deficits (Momtaz et al., 2022). These oscillations that synchronize activity throughout the brainstem to cortex neuronal circuits are important for analysis of auditory temporal information and may contribute to abnormal excitatory and inhibitory interactions in patients with known dichotic listening deficits (Bahmer & Gupta, 2018).

Follow-Up Evaluation

Despite As in conduct, Allie had even greater difficulty in the fourth grade. Her average grades at the end of the school year were an A in Science/Health; Bs in Language, Spelling, Social Studies, and Mathematics; and a C in Reading. Her performance had been inconsistent throughout the school year, with Ds recorded for Social Studies and Mathematics and a C– in Language during individual grading periods. Her mother was concerned that despite the language exercises and participation in Earobics™ training, Allie's difficulties were not diminishing. Allie was reevaluated by the student services department of her public school district near the end of her fourth-grade year. Results from this reevaluation are detailed in Table 23–3.

Findings From the Follow-Up Evaluation

Allie's mother asked the school district to provide an independent educational evaluation for Allie, including a language evaluation. Her request was denied and the matter referred for a due process hearing. In the meantime, Allie returned to the clinic for a follow-up evaluation for APD to see if any of the binaural integration difficulties had resolved. The goal was to use different dichotic listening tests to see if the same pattern of a left ear weakness would emerge with new stimuli. Allie was now 10 years, 2 months of age. She was

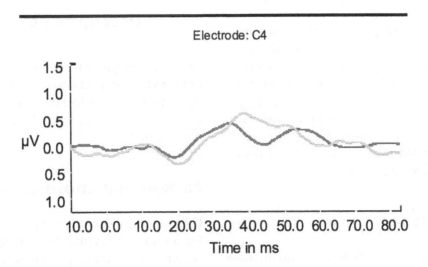

Figure 23–1. Findings from the MLR evaluation.

Table 23–3. Evaluation Results Near the End of the Fourth-Grade Year

Test	Age	Test/Subtest	Score	Interpretation
WISC-III	9–8	Verbal	95	Average
		Performance	99	Average
		Full Scale	97	Average
WJ-R	9–8	Letter-Word Identification	103	Average
		Passage Comprehension	97	Average
		Calculation	118	Average
		Applied Problems	105	Average
		Dictation	98	Average
		Broad Reading	99	Average
		Broad Math	112	Average
		Skills (E Dev)	101	Average
		Proofing	122	Average
		Basic Writing Skills	111	Average

assessed with three dichotic listening tests, Competing NU-6 Words (Moncrieff, 2004), Dichotic CVs Test (Hugdahl & Andersson, 1987), and the Randomized Dichotic Digits Test (Moncrieff & Wilson, 2009). She was also assessed with the Pitch Pattern Sequence Test (Pinheiro & Musiek, 1985). The results of those tests are detailed in Table 23–4.

Interpretation

The significant interaural asymmetry observed in the initial APD evaluation a little more than a year previously was still present in this evaluation. Across all three tests, Allie performed significantly better with information presented toward her right ear than with information presented toward her left ear. Despite efforts to remediate her auditory processing difficulties with Earobics™ and language intervention programs, Allie still demonstrated a significant binaural integration deficit during dichotic listening tasks.

Recommendation

A novel therapy approach that would involve training the weaker ear to perform at more nor-

mal levels during dichotic listening tasks was proposed. The therapy involves presentation of dichotic material during four weekly 1-hour sessions. Allie was encouraged to enroll in the therapy, but her parents requested additional computer-based strategies that she could complete at home because her parents worked and the driving time between her home and the training site was 1.5 hours each way.

Description of Case 2

This case highlights the benefits that may be obtained when a child with similar dichotic listening deficits is identified at the first evaluation and then provided auditory training targeted specifically at that deficit.

Background Information

Following enrollment in Auditory Rehabilitation for Interaural Asymmetry (ARIA), children have shown significant improvements during dichotic listening tests (Moncrieff et al., 2017). In an early

Table 23–4. Results From the Competing NU-6 Test, Randomized Dichotic Digits Test, and Pitch Pattern Sequence Test

Test	Age	Test/Subtest	Score	Interpretation
Competing NU-6 Words Test	10–2	Right Ear	66%	Significant interaural asymmetry
		Left Ear	40%	
Dichotic CV Test	10–2	Nonforced Condition		
		Right Ear	53%	Large right ear advantage
		Left Ear	20%	
		Forced Right Condition		
		Right Ear	50%	
		Left Ear	23%	
		Forced Left Condition		
		Right Ear	33%	Demonstrates ability to attend preferentially toward left ear
		Left Ear	33%	
Randomized Dichotic Digits Test	10–2	Single Digits		
		Right Ear	100%	
		Left Ear	89%	
		Double Digits		
		Right Ear	94%	WNL
		Left Ear	59%	Abnormal
		Triple Digits		
		Right Ear	93%	
		Left Ear	57%	
Pitch Pattern Sequence	10–2	Right Ear	67%	Below normal
		Left Ear	77%	Borderline

study with ARIA training, children also demonstrated significant improvements in untrained listening skills (Moncrieff & Wertz, 2008). In this case, a binaural integration deficit identified through dichotic listening tests was remediated following enrollment in ARIA shortly after initial diagnosis. A highlight of this case is that the child continued to demonstrate difficulties with short-term memory for some complex stimuli following the training, which led to a recommendation for additional training beyond ARIA. The primary justification for the triage approach to diagnose a dichotic listening deficit first and provide remediation for it is that ARIA training can improve access to auditory information, which should facilitate

other training approaches to improve auditory skills important for learning, language, and reading development.

Reason for Appointment

Connor was brought to the clinic by his father for an evaluation for APD when he was 7 years, 11 months of age. Connor was in the second grade at a local elementary school where he was receiving special education resources through an Individualized Education Program (IEP). He was referred to the laboratory by his speech-language pathologist who had been working with him on difficulties with articulation, syntax, and pragmatic language skills.

History

Connor was born prematurely and was diagnosed immediately after birth with jaundice. In the newborn nursery, he was given oxygen treatment. He began to speak at 1 year of age, but he was slow to put words together. He had eight ear infections by age 3 in the left ear (five) or in both ears (three). At age 6, Connor's parents had his hearing evaluated because of concerns that he frequently misunderstood words. At that time, his hearing results were normal, but the audiologist recommended that he use a remote microphone hearing device (FM system) at school. Connor used the device for several months, but his parents asked that it be discontinued when he was beginning the next school year. At that time, Connor was 7 years old and was using Earobics™ at home and working on language skills at a university speech and language clinic. The clinician noted concerns that Connor may have an auditory processing disorder and recommended an evaluation.

Findings From the APD Evaluation

Connor's father provided responses to the Children's Auditory Processing Performance Scale (CHAPS) (Smoski et al., 1998). Connor had the greatest difficulty when listening in background noise. He also had mild difficulties when listening with multiple inputs, with skills involving memory, and with skills involving attention. His score on the CHAPS placed him in the at-risk category. On an Auditory Processing Difficulties Checklist, Connor's father noted the greatest difficulties in the types of skills related to the integration type of APD with some mild difficulties in the types of skills related to the auditory decoding type of APD (Bellis & Ferre, 1999).

Connor's pure-tone air conduction thresholds and speech recognition thresholds were within normal limits for both ears (PTA < 20 dB HL; SRT = 0–5 dB HL). There was no evidence of middle

ear disorder, and ipsilateral acoustic reflexes were present in both ears. Word recognition scores were 100% in both ears, suggesting an excellent ability to repeat words one ear at a time in quiet.

Connor was evaluated with the Test for Auditory Processing Disorders in Children (SCAN-C) (Keith, 2000), Digits in Multi-talker Babble (Wilson et al., 2005), Words in Noise (Wilson et al., 2003), the Randomized Dichotic Digits Test (RDDT) (Moncrieff & Wilson, 2009), and the Dichotic Words Test (DWT) (Moncrieff, 2004). The results from all tests are detailed in Table 23–5. Based on standard scoring, Connor had difficulties listening in background noise and identifying dichotic material in the competing words and sentences tests.

In Connor's case, performance on the Competing Words subtest was below normal for both ears (43% in the right ear and 7% in the left ear), but there was also a significant interaural asymmetry of 36%. This same pattern was observed on the other two dichotic listening tests, the DWT and the two-digit condition of the RDDT. This pattern of performance is characterized as amblyaudia by the significant difference between the listener's dominant and nondominant ears and dichotic dysaudia by the significantly poor performance in the listener's dominant ear (Moncrieff, 2011; Moncrieff et al., 2016). The characterization of normal performance on the SCAN-C Competing Sentences test is based on the combined scores for the right and left ears. Connor was able to ignore the stimuli in his left ear and correctly identify all of the sentences presented to his right ear but was not able to direct his attention to the sentences in his left ear while ignoring the sentences arriving at his right ear. The 90% difference between the two ears is a significant sign of dichotic listening weakness that is not apparent when the scores for the two ears are combined to derive a standard score for this subtest.

The two speech-in-noise tests were included to establish a baseline for Connor's ability to handle speech presented in background noise, and he showed weaknesses in all of the tests, Auditory Figure Ground from the SCAN-C, Digits in Babble, and Words in Noise. These results confirm that Connor struggles to identify vocabulary words presented in background noise as suggested by

Table 23–5. Results for the Test for Auditory Processing Disorders in Children, Digits in Multitalker Babble, Words in Multitalker Babble, and the Dichotic Words Tests

Test	Age	Test/Subtest	Score	Interpretation
SCAN-C	7–11	Filtered Words	SS = 10	WNL
		Auditory Figure Ground	SS = 5	Borderline
		Competing Words	SS = 4	Disordered
			R 43%, L 7%	Significant interaural asymmetry
		Competing Sentences	SS = 9	WNL
			R 100%, L 0%	Significant interaural asymmetry
Digits in Babble	7–11	Right Ear	−3.33 dB SBR	Borderline
		Left Ear	0.67 dB SBR	Abnormal
				Normal for age 7 is approximately −6 to −9 dB SBR
Words in Noise	7–11	Binaural	14.4 dB SBR	Abnormal
				Normal for age 7 is approximately 7–10 dB SBR
Dichotic Words Test	7–11	Right Ear	58%	Abnormal
		Left Ear	14%	Abnormal
		Asymmetry	44%	Poorer than normal in both ears with a significant interaural asymmetry
Randomized Dichotic Digits Test–2 pairs	7–11	Right Ear	67%	Abnormal
		Left Ear	22%	Abnormal
		Asymmetry	45%	Poorer than normal in both ears with a significant interaural asymmetry
Frequency Pattern Test-V	7–11	Binaural	40%	Abnormal
Frequency Pattern Test-H			80%	WNL

his father in response to the two initial questionnaires. Connor's significantly poor results from the Frequency Pattern Test when he was asked to verbally label the tonal patterns are not uncommon in children with dichotic listening difficulties. When asked to hum the patterns, Connor was able to identify them at an age-appropriate level.

Interpretation

Results from the APD evaluation supported a diagnosis of amblyaudia plus (i.e., a combination of amblyaudia and dichotic dysaudia). Results were consistent with scores from the two listening questionnaires filled out by Connor's father.

Recommendation

ARIA training was recommended for Connor. Dichotic listening was reevaluated to determine the stability of the results obtained at this first appointment. A directed response condition was added to further assess his performance on the DWT. In the meantime, the speech-language pathologist at Connor's school tested him with the Test of Auditory Processing Skills (TAPS-3) (Martin & Brownell, 2005).

Follow-Up Evaluation

Results from the TAPS-3 at school and the two additional dichotic listening tests at the clinic reevaluation supported the initial diagnosis of amblyaudia plus. As shown in Table 23–6, Connor continued to demonstrate significant weaknesses for input primarily to his left ear with a significantly large asymmetry between the ears.

Interpretation

The improved performance in his right ear to more normal levels across the dichotic tests suggests that Connor may have been more comfortable with the testing situation at this second appointment. The weaknesses attributed to dichotic dysaudia because of poor performance in his right ear at the first appointment may have been due to discomfort and anxiety. Connor was a very conscientious child and may have been concerned that he might displease someone by his behavior. He often asked how he was doing throughout the

testing session and needed lots of encouragement, so it is plausible that as he became more relaxed by the second appointment, performance in his right ear improved.

Recommendation

It was recommended that Connor enroll in ARIA training. The training would take place at the same time each week for 60 minutes per session. ARIA involves listening to a variety of dichotic material presented while the intensity of information delivered to the listener's dominant ear is reduced adaptively to prevent overdominance of either ear. Generally, this means that the intensity of presentations to the listener's dominant ear begins at a significantly reduced level to overstimulate the listener's nondominant ear. When the listener repeats more stimuli from each list presented to the nondominant ear (greater than a 10% difference between the ears), intensity in the dominant ear is raised in increments of 1 or 5 dB through a standardized protocol. Conversely, if the score in the nondominant ear falls 10% or more below the score in the dominant ear, the intensity of presentations to the dominant ear is reduced. As such, ARIA is an individualized, adaptive training pro-

Table 23–6. Results From the TAPS-3 and Two Additional Dichotic Listening Tests at the Clinic Reevaluation

Test	Age	Test/Subtest	Score	Interpretation
Test of Auditory Processing Skills	8–1	Word Memory	SS = 5	Abnormal
		Sentence Memory	SS = 4	Abnormal
		Auditory Comprehension	SS = 6	Abnormal
Dichotic Words Test	8–2	Free Recall Conditions		
		Right Ear	76%	WNL
		Left Ear	28%	Abnormal
		Asymmetry	46%	Significant interaural asymmetry
		Directed Response Conditions		
		Right Ear	80%	WNL
		Left Ear	28%	Abnormal
		Asymmetry	52%	Significant interaural asymmetry
Randomized Dichotic Digits Test	8–2	Right Ear	83%	Abnormal
		Left Ear	31%	Abnormal
		Asymmetry	52%	Significant interaural asymmetry

tocol that utilizes perceptual learning techniques often used in constraint-induced therapies to train the once nondominant ear to perform at levels more equivalent to performance in the listener's dominant ear. Children with amblyaudia like Connor have demonstrated significant improvements in their nondominant ears, often attaining normal levels of performance in both ears during dichotic listening tests (Moncrieff et al., 2017). Some demonstrate significant improvements in their nondominant ears, but performance in one or both ears may continue to be below the age-appropriate normal level. With the adaptive procedures that depend on each individual participant's performance, children with more severe deficits tend to demonstrate greater dichotic listening gains from ARIA therapy.

Results From the ARIA Training

Connor participated in ARIA for the standard 4-week period. As shown in Figures 23–2 and 23–3, his dominant right ear showed steady improvement for both words and digits across the ARIA training. Performance in his nondominant ear increased immediately with the constraint placed

on his dominant right ear in the first ARIA session and then adaptively changed across the four sessions.

At the end of ARIA, the average performance level in Connor's nondominant ear was normal for words (left ear = 72%) and digits (left ear = 68%). The average performance level in his dominant ear was at the 10th percentile for digits (right ear = 72%) and borderline normal at the 25th percentile cutoff for words (right ear = 76%). These results support significant improvement in Connor's nondominant left ear and little change in his dominant right ear for the dichotic test with words but with some reduction in performance on his dichotic performance with digits. Connor was instructed to wait 3 months and then to return for a post-ARIA assessment after rest and consolidation of effects from the auditory training experience.

Posttraining Evaluation

Connor was tested 3.8 months later with the same dichotic listening tests that were used before training. Connor was also reassessed with the TAPS-3 by his speech-language pathologist. Results of the posttraining evaluation are detailed in Table 23–7.

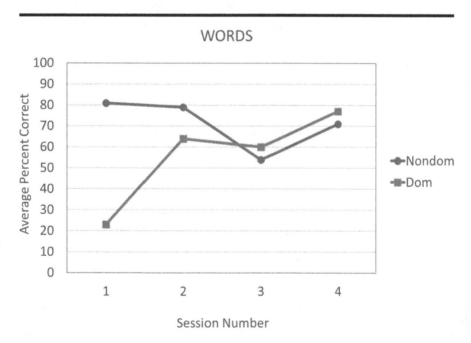

Figure 23–2. Results after training sessions.

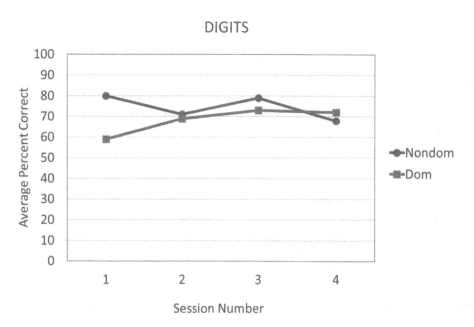

Figure 23–3. Average scores for digits and words throughout training.

Table 23–7. Results of the Posttraining Evaluation

Test	Age	Test/Subtest	Score	Interpretation
Test of Auditory Processing Skills	8–8	Word Memory	SS = 8	WNL
		Sentence Memory	SS = 7	WNL
		Auditory Comprehension	SS = 8	WNL
SCAN-C Competing Words Subtest	8–8	Overall	SS = 10	WNL
		Right Ear	67%	WNL
		Left Ear	60%	WNL
Dichotic Words Test	8–8	Right Ear	80%	WNL
		Left Ear	72%	WNL
Randomized Dichotic Digits Test–2 pairs	8–8	Right Ear	89%	WNL
		Left Ear	78%	WNL
Words in Noise	8–8	Binaural	8.2 dB SBR	WNL
Digits in Babble	8–8	Right Ear	−6.8 dB SBR	WNL
		Left Ear	−7.3 dB SBR	WNL
Frequency Pattern Test-V	8–8	Binaural	47%	Abnormal

Interpretation

Left ear performance with all dichotic materials improved following ARIA training. At this evaluation, results were normal for both ears and for interaural asymmetry across all the tests. In addition, Connor's scores from the three subtests of the TAPS were all within the normal range.

Recommendations

Dichotic deficits are no longer evident in Connor's test results following ARIA training, but this alone does not resolve all possible auditory processing weaknesses. Results from the TAPS suggest that there are no remaining weaknesses in memory for words or sentences or for general auditory comprehension. Other auditory processing assessments should be performed to determine whether there are any remaining weaknesses in Connor's ability to process auditory information as evidenced in his original evaluation. Tests that revealed initial weaknesses include Words in Noise, Digits in Babble, and Frequency Pattern Test, and Connor performed normally on all of these tests except the Frequency Pattern Test. Children who participated in ARIA have demonstrated improvements in untrained auditory processing skills such as speech-in-noise (Moncrieff, 2019) and on the oral reading, listening comprehension, and word recognition subtests from the Brigance battery (Moncrieff & Wertz, 2008).

Connor's parents reported that he was engaging more actively in peer-related conversations at home and at school and that he appeared to be significantly better able to follow auditory instructions. They noted that it was much easier for Connor to stay focused on auditory messages in general, especially when there were no other distractions. They wondered if Connor's auditory abilities would be stressed by multiple inputs and more challenging schoolwork. They also expressed concern that Connor continued to show some weakness in reading skills. It was suggested that Connor might benefit from additional therapies with a speech-language pathologist who specializes in literacy issues and that he return for another follow-up auditory processing evaluation in 1 year.

References

Arjona Valladares, A., Gómez, C. M., Rodríguez-Martínez, E. I., Barriga-Paulino, C. I., Gómez-González, J., & Díaz-Sánchez, J. A. (2020). Attention-deficit/hyperactivity disorder in children and adolescents: An event-related potential study of working memory. *European Journal of Neuroscience, 52*(10), 4356–4369. https://doi.org/10.1111/ejn.14767

Baddeley, A. D. (1986). *Working memory.* Oxford University Press.

Baddeley, A. D., & Hitch, G. J. (1974). Working memory. In G. H. Bower (Ed.), *The psychology of learning and motivation* (Vol. 8, pp. 47–89). Academic Press.

Bahmer, A., & Gupta, D. S. (2018). Role of oscillations in auditory temporal processing: A general model for temporal processing of sensory information in the brain? *Frontiers in Neuroscience, 12*, 793. https://doi.org/10.3389/fnins.2018.00793

Bellis, T. J., & Ferre, J. M. (1999). Multidimensional approach to the differential diagnosis of central auditory processing disorders in children. *Journal of the American Academy of Audiology, 10*, 319–328.

Blauert, J. (1997). *Spatial hearing: The psychophysics of human sound localization.* MIT Press.

Brown, L., Sherbinou, R. J., & Johnsen, S. K. (1997). *Test of Nonverbal Intelligence* (3rd ed.). Pearson Education.

Cognitive Concepts. (2000). Earobics [Computer software]. Houghton Mifflin Harcourt.

Cowan, N. (2016). Working memory maturation: Can we get at the essence of cognitive growth? *Perspectives on Psychological Science, 11*(2), 239–264. https://doi.org/10.1177/1745691615621279

Hammil, D. D., & Newcomer, P. L. (1996) *Test of Language Development–Primary* (3rd ed.). Pearson Education.

Hugdahl, K., & Andersson B. (1987). Dichotic listening and reading acquisition in children: A one-year follow-up. *Journal of Clinical and Experimental Neuropsychology, 9*, 631–649.

Katz, J. (1986). *SSW test user's manual.* Precision Acoustics.

Keith, R. (2000). Development and standardization of SCAN-C Test for Auditory Processing Disorders in Children. *Journal of the American Academy of Audiology, 11*, 438–445.

Kim, S., Liu, Z., Glizer, D., Tannock, R., & Woltering, S. (2014). Adult ADHD and working memory: Neural evidence of impaired encoding. *Clinical Neurophysiology*, *125*(8), 1596–1603. https://doi.org/10.1016/j.clinph.2013.12.094

Kimura, D. (1967). Functional asymmetry of the brain in dichotic listening. *Cortex*, 3, 163–168.

Kinsbourne, M. (1970). The cerebral basis of lateral asymmetries in attention. *Acta Psychologica Amsterdam*, *33*, 193–201. https://doi.org/10.1016/0001-6918(70)90132-0

Lamm, O., & Epstein, R. (1994). Dichotic listening performance under high and low lexical work load in subtypes of developmental dyslexia. *Neuropsychologia*, *32*, 757–785. https://doi.org/10.1016/0028-3932(94)90016-7

Martin, N. A., & Brownell, R. (2005). *Test of Auditory Processing Skills* (3rd ed.). Super Duper Publications.

Middlebrooks, J. C., & Green, D. M. (1991). Sound localization by human listeners. *Annual Review of Psychology*, *42*(1), 135–159.

Momtaz, S., Moncrieff, D., & Bidelman, G. M. (2021). Dichotic listening deficits in amblyaudia are characterized by aberrant neural oscillations in auditory cortex. *Clinical Neurophysiology*, *132*(9), 2152–2162. https://doi.org/10.1016/j.clinph.2021.04.022. Erratum in: *Clinical Neurophysiology* (2022, August), *140*, 256–257.

Momtaz, S., Moncrieff, D., Ray, M. A., & Bidelman, G. M. (2022). Children with amblyaudia show less flexibility in auditory cortical entrainment to periodic non-speech sounds. *International Journal of Audiology*. Advance online publication. https://doi.org/10.1080/14992027.2022.2094289

Moncrieff, D. (2004, November). *New tests of auditory processing*. Paper presented at the Annual Convention of the American Speech-Language-Hearing Association, Philadelphia, PA.

Moncrieff, D. (2011). Dichotic listening in children: Age-related changes in direction and magnitude of ear advantage. *Brain and Cognition*, *76*(2), 316–322. https://doi.org/10.1016/j.bandc.2011.03.013

Moncrieff, D. (2015). Age-and gender-specific normative information from children assessed with a dichotic words test. *Journal of the American Academy of Audiology*, *26*(7), 632–644.

Moncrieff, D. (2019, November). *It's time to take amblyaudia seriously*. Paper presented at the Tennessee Association of Audiology and Speech-Language Pathology Annual Convention, Chattanooga, TN.

Moncrieff, D., Keith, W., Abramson, M., & Swann, A. (2016). Clinical evidence on the diagnosis of amblyaudia, a binaural integration type of auditory processing disorder. *International Journal of Audiology*, *55*(6), 333–345. https://doi.org/10.3109/14992027.2015.1128003

Moncrieff, D., Keith, W., Abramson, M., & Swann, A. (2017). Evidence of binaural integration benefits following ARIA training in children and adolescents diagnosed with amblyaudia. *International Journal of Audiology*, *56*(8), 580–588. https://doi.org/10.1080/14992027.2017.1303199

Moncrieff, D. W., & Black, J. R. (2008). Dichotic listening deficits in children with dyslexia. *Dyslexia*, *41*, 54–75. https://doi.org/10.3766/jaaa.14096

Moncrieff, D. W., Byrd, D. L., & Bedenbaugh, P. H. (2002, March). *MLR in children with a dichotic left-ear deficit*. Paper presented at the American Auditory Society Annual Meeting, Scottsdale, AZ.

Moncrieff, D. W., & Wertz, D. (2008). Auditory rehabilitation for interaural asymmetry: Preliminary evidence of improved dichotic listening performance following intensive training. *International Journal of Audiology*, *47*, 84–97. https://doi.org/10.1080/14992020701770835

Moncrieff, D. W., & Wilson, R. H. (2009). Recognition of randomly presented one-, two-, and three-pair dichotic digits by children and young adults. *Journal of the American Academy of Audiology*, *20*(1), 58–70. https://doi.org/10.3766/jaaa.20.1.6

Morton, L. L., & Siegel, L. S. (1991). Left ear dichotic listening performance on consonant-vowel combinations and digits in subtypes of reading-disabled children. *Brain and Language*, *40*, 162–180. https://doi.org/10.1016/0093-934x(91)90123-i

Pinheiro, M. L., & Musiek, F. E. (1985). Sequencing and temporal ordering in the auditory system. In M. L. Pinheiro & F. E. Musiek (Eds.), *Assessment of central auditory dysfunction: Foundations and clinical correlates* (pp. 219–238). Williams & Wilkins.

Scientific Learning Corporation. (1997). Fast ForWord Language [Computer software].

Semel, E., Wiig, E. H., & Secord, W. A. (1995). *Clinical evaluation of language fundamentals* (3rd ed.). Psychological Corporation.

Smoski, W. J., Brunt, M. A., & Tannahill, J. C. (1992). Listening characteristics of children with central auditory processing disorders. *Language, Speech, and Hearing in Schools*, *23*, 145–149.

Task Force on Central Auditory Processing Consensus Development. (1996). Central auditory processing: Current status of research and implications for clinical practice. *American Journal of Audiology*, *5*(2), 41–52. https://doi.org/10.1044/1059-0889.0502.41

Wiig, E. H. (1992). *Language intervention for school-age children: Models and procedures that work.* EDUCOM Associates.

Willeford, J. (1977). Assessing central auditory behavior in children: A test battery approach. In R. W. Keith (Ed.), *Central auditory dysfunction* (pp. 43–72). Grune & Stratton.

Willeford, J. A., & Bilger, J. M. (1978). Auditory perception in children with learning disabilities. In J. Katz (Ed.), *Handbook of clinical audiology* (2nd ed., pp. 410–425). Williams & Wilkins.

Wilson, R. H., Abrams, H. B., & Pillion, A. L. (2003). A word-recognition task in multitalker babble using a descending presentation mode from 24 dB to 0 dB signal to babble. *Journal of Rehabilitation Research and Development, 40,* 321–327. https://doi.org/10.1682/jrrd.2003.07.0321

Wilson, R. H., Burks, C. A., & Weakley, D. G. (2005). A comparison of word-recognition abilities assessed with digit pairs and digit triplets in multitalker babble. *Journal of Rehabilitation Research and Development, 42,* 499–510. https://doi.org/10.1682/jrrd.2004.10.0134

AUGMENTATIVE AND ALTERNATIVE COMMUNICATION
CASE 24
Rocky: AAC for a School-Age Child With Complex Communication Needs
Pamela Hart and Shatonda S. Jones

Conceptual Knowledge Areas

Augmentative and alternative communication (AAC) is a type of assistive technology (AT) used to support effective communication for individuals with severe speech and/or language impairments who are unable to meet their communication needs through verbal and/or written modalities (American Speech-Language-Hearing Association, 2005). AAC includes all the tools, strategies, theories, and methods used to evaluate and/or compensate for deficits in verbal and/or written communication (Loncke, 2022). At the core of AAC is the belief that everybody deserves a voice, and the lack of verbal speech does not indicate the absence of thoughts, ideas, beliefs, or desire for social closeness.

In the current case, Rocky exhibits developmental disabilities across physical, sensory, linguistic, and cognitive areas of development. To achieve effective AAC outcomes for clients such as Rocky, researchers have consistently identified the need for highly skilled, multidisciplinary teams working toward the shared goal of communicative competence (Hart & Scherz, 2017; McNaughton et al., 2019). Professionals from a variety of backgrounds, including speech-language pathology, occupational therapy, special education, regular education, psychology, and assistive technology, collaborated to support Rocky's successful use of AAC.

The case of Rocky provides an opportunity to explore assessment and intervention with AAC for a school-age child with complex communication needs and physical impairments. Foundational knowledge related to general AAC strategies, alternative access for those with physical impairments, and school-based AAC services is provided to support discussion of this case.

Overview of AAC Foundations and Terminology

AAC tools and methods are broadly divided into aided and unaided strategies. Aided AAC strategies require a device or tool for message transmission such as a communication book, mobile device (e.g., tablet or phone), voice output communication aid (VOCA), or dedicated speech-generating device (SGD). Unaided AAC strategies use the individual's body to communicate and include gestures, eye movements, facial expressions, and vocalizations coded to communicate specific messages. Many individuals with complex communication needs will use a variety of aided and unaided AAC strategies depending on communication needs and context. For example, unaided strategies may be useful when interacting with those most familiar who understand the individual's vocalizations and gestures, while unaided strategies may support message clarity when communicating with less familiar partners (Blackstone & Hunt-Berg, 2003; Coburn et al., 2021). There is no single "best" AAC device or strategy. The best AAC strategy is the one that supports the current needs of the individual while also allowing for future growth and development. As the name implies, AAC encompasses both augmentative communication strategies and alternative communication strategies. This distinction is characterized by the level of support provided by the AAC system. Individuals with some verbal speech may only require intermittent AAC support. In these cases, AAC is considered "augmentative." In contrast, when AAC is used as a replacement for verbal and/or written language, it is considered "alternative" (Beukelman & Light, 2020). Additionally, the use of AAC may be temporary, as in a case of acute vocal injury in which recovery is expected, or permanent when required across the life span, such as the case of Rocky. While previously viewed as a strategy of last resort, this is no longer the case. There are no prerequisite skills, cognitive requirements, or age requirements to use AAC. Young children with communication impairments should have access to AAC early in development to facilitate the emergence of intentional communication (Drager et al., 2010).

In Rocky's case, his unmet needs should be considered across communication, language, and speech. Briefly reviewed, communication is the general exchange of ideas between a sender and receiver and includes verbal and nonverbal

strategies. Communication is not solely limited to humans as other animals communicate through body language and vocalizations. Language, in contrast, is considered a uniquely human achievement and characterized as a code in which arbitrary symbols stand for real things and ideas. Languages may be verbal or nonverbal and are generative with capacity to generate an infinite number of messages from a finite number of symbols. Speech, also limited to humans, is the sensorimotor process of producing the language code (Owens, 2020). Applied to AAC, some individuals with complex communication needs will only exhibit difficulty with speech production, while others will also exhibit difficulty with expressive language formulation and/or receptive language understanding. Still others may not yet demonstrate intentional communication. AAC should be viewed as an integrated component of overall intervention planning. The myth that AAC inhibits development of verbal speech has been consistently refuted by researchers. In fact, modest gains in verbal speech have been reported with use of AAC (Millar, Light, & Schlosser, 2006).

Access Strategies for Augmentative and Alternative Communication Devices

Direct selection access is a familiar strategy most of us have used when typing on a keyboard. Applied to AAC, the individual who uses direct selection will choose the desired item by directly touching or otherwise directly accessing the item with a pointer or eye gaze. The use of keyguards and high-tech device setting controls are sometimes used to increase direct selection accuracy. If motor or sensory impairments prevent the use of direct selection, indirect selection methods such as switch scanning may be required. While there are many different scanning methods, most require the individual to activate some type of switch using a reliable motor movement that does not adversely affect muscle tone, posture, or positioning or cause overfatigue of the muscles. Current switch activation technologies allow multiple ways to activate a switch, including direct physical contact, muscle contraction, eye blink, approximation of physical contact, and vocalization/sound activation, to name a few (Loncke, 2022).

In addition to selection of an appropriate switch activation strategy, the scanning mode and pattern must also be considered. Scanning patterns include options such as linear, in which items are highlighted from left to right, one at a time, and pattern-based scanning that highlights larger sections such as quadrants of the screen. Pattern-based scanning allows quicker access to desired messages but requires higher levels of cognitive skills to understand the concept. Scanning modes include options such as automatic scanning or step scanning. When automatic scanning is used, the switch is activated to begin the scanning process and activated again when the desired item is highlighted. This requires the ability to plan and complete the activation movement while the item is highlighted: a difficult task for those with motor planning, muscle tone, or muscle strength impairments. While it is possible to decrease the scanning speed to allow additional time for activation of the switch, this increases the wait time for message activation. Another option is step scanning. There are different versions of step scanning, but the basic premise is the individual activates the switch to advance the scanning sequence (Beukelman & Light, 2020). Two-switch step scanning uses one switch to advance the scanning sequence and a second switch to choose the desired item. The individual then has control over the speed of the scanning, but this method requires increased activation movement and two reliable motor movements to select the desired message. Regardless of the scanning method, successful switch use requires a volitional movement that can be initiated, consistently released, and repeated without negatively influencing muscle tone or fatigue and while allowing for adequate time to process the scanned items.

Eye gaze access technologies have existed for several decades, and while early systems produced inconsistent results, recent advancements display arrangement and technology that have increased the viability of this access method (Liang & Wilkinson, 2018; Wilkinson & Madel, 2019). While these improvements are exciting, a word of caution regarding the understandable tendency to consider eye gaze as an easier access method than switch input. The physical effort and time demand of learning eye gaze technology are sometimes underestimated, resulting in client and caregiver disappointment. It is important to develop realistic expectations regarding time, effort, and efficacy of the various alternative access strategies (Hsieh et al., 2021).

An emerging access method known as Brain Computer Interface (BCI) may provide future hope for those who struggle to produce volitional movement (e.g., locked-in syndrome). BCI uses implanted or surface sensors that detect electrical signals produced by the brain and then translates these signals to commands that control electronic devices such as an AAC device. Researchers have reported positive outcomes but have also noted a great deal of variability in current methodologies, which increases the difficulty of generalizing these findings to broader populations (Peters et al., 2022). BCI is not yet available in commercially developed AAC devices.

Description of the Case

Rocky is a 7-year-old male with bilateral cerebellar hypoplasia (BCH) who attends his neighborhood elementary school, where he receives a variety of regular education, special education, and therapy services. Rocky lives with his biological mother and father, two older siblings (both developing typically), and his paternal grandmother, who recently moved in with the family following declining health. Mainstream American English is the only language spoken in the home. Both of Rocky's parents work full-time outside the home and reported the grandmother to be settling in nicely after a period of adjustment for the family. Rocky enjoys interacting with all his family members but demonstrates particular attachment and interest in his grandmother.

Rocky was born moderately prematurely at 32 weeks' gestation following an uneventful pregnancy until that point. Magnetic resonance imaging (MRI) indicated BCH. Additional testing determined the absence of other genetic and/

or metabolic abnormalities (e.g., Walker-Walker syndrome and Williams syndrome). A moderate sensorineural hearing loss and intermittent visual nystagmus with suspected vertigo were also reported. Maternal health was unremarkable during pregnancy with expected progression until Rocky's premature birth. Paternal health was noted to include type 2 diabetes (A1C of 10%), hypertension (average blood pressure 190/100), and angina.

Rocky has experienced steady progress in all areas of development but continues to exhibit moderate impairments in motor, cognitive, self-help, and communication domains. Motor impairments include hypotonia, reduced strength, and difficulties with coordination. Due to the nature and severity of Rocky's impairments, it is anticipated he will require long-term support for mobility, communication, and self-care. At school, Rocky uses a manual wheelchair and requires total assistance to move from place to place. At home, Rocky moves around on his own by using a combination of crawling and scooting on his tummy. Rocky is an incredibly determined child and recently surprised his family by attempting to climb the stairs on his own, which he had not previously attempted. The family has now installed safety gates in appropriate areas.

Rocky received speech-language pathology, occupational therapy, and physical therapy intervention services in the home from birth through age 3. At 3, Rocky transitioned to the school district's special needs preschool, where he received the same therapies and special education classroom-based services two mornings each week. Goals included (a) increased strength and coordination for mobility, self-care, and feeding; (b) sustained attention to developmentally appropriate activities; (c) increased engagement with toys/peers in the environment; and (d) development of communicative intent for highly desired items. Rocky demonstrated good progress in all areas and, at the age of 5, was reevaluated to determine appropriate kindergarten placement for the following year. The evaluation team included a neuropsychologist, speech-language pathologist, occupational therapist, special education teacher, vision specialist, and audiologist. The team deter-

mined that Rocky would benefit from a general education setting with instructional aids and support services to maximize participation. Since that time, Rocky's speech-language pathologist has explored the use of low-tech, symbol-based communication strategies with positive results and has now requested a comprehensive AAC evaluation by the school-based team. The goal of the AAC evaluation is to determine strategies to support Rocky's unmet communication needs in the general education environment and maximize his communicative competence.

Initial Team Considerations

Person-centered planning by knowledgeable professionals is critical to achieving effective outcomes in AAC assessment and intervention. The team will consider all of Rocky's current and emerging communication skills and seek solutions to support unmet needs. Additional considerations include (a) evaluation of Rocky's motor, sensory, linguistic, and cognitive strengths and needs as related to use of AAC; (b) determination of an effective access method; and (c) determination of additional required device features. Initial intervention considerations will include use of the selected AAC device(s) in meaningful contexts and environments across Rocky's unmet needs. With expanding technology in dedicated and mobile device platforms, it is likely that several AAC strategies could meet Rocky's current and future needs. As such, the following description focuses on broad features of devices rather than specific brands or applications.

AAC Evaluation Results

Expressive Language

Rocky's communication environments include home, school, and community settings. Rocky's physical impairments limit his ability to produce verbal speech, and he currently uses gestures and vocalizations to indicate basic wants, needs, and yes/no responses. For example, Rocky turns his head to the right to indicate "yes" and points his head down to his chest to indicate "no." At home, Rocky produces several vocalizations to indicate basic needs such as discomfort, boredom, tiredness, hunger, and a desire to be snuggled. Rocky is beginning to initiate hand movements to approximate "hi" and "bye" in social communication settings. Rocky needs an AAC system that will support expressive language development by allowing Rocky to initiate, respond, question, socialize, comment, and offer ideas and opinions.

Receptive Language

Rocky's receptive language skills are an area of strength. He responds to yes/no questions via head movements with 75% accuracy, follows one-step directions with 80% accuracy, and demonstrates age-appropriate understanding of speech at a conversation level as indicated by appropriate facial expressions and gestures. For example, during shared book reading activities Rocky smiles, and if the story pauses, Rocky claps to indicate he wants to hear more. When Rocky was asked to identify pictures of 50 common objects from a field of four, he did so with 80% accuracy.

Motor Speech Skills

Rocky exhibits speech characteristics associated with ataxic dysarthria. His respiratory support is adequate for speech production, but hypotonia and coordination impairments result in breathy/strained phonation, imprecise phoneme production, decreased coordination of respiration and phonation, and significant difficulties with sequenced speech movements. Specific phonemes Rocky produces include /p/, /b/, /m/, /h/, /w/, and /n/, but he is not yet able to approximate verbal word productions.

Physical/Motor Skills

Rocky uses a wheelchair at school and is dependent for all activities of daily living. Evaluation with SGDs was conducted with the device placed on his wheelchair tray and mounted at eye level. Rocky experienced the most interest and success when the device was placed on his wheelchair tray. This device position requires a downward head position to visualize the screen, and fatigue/strain of Rocky's neck and upper body should be carefully monitored.

AAC Device Access

Direct selection was attempted, but Rocky was not able to accurately use this strategy due to movement accuracy and intention tremor difficulties. Use of various pointers and keyguards did not improve this accuracy. Use of switch scanning was first introduced with switch-activated toys. He demonstrated clear understanding of the switch activation process. Rocky's most consistent volitional motor movement was a sideways movement of his right arm when resting on his wheelchair tray. A small jellybean switch was placed on the right side of the wheelchair tray, approximately 2 inches from his wrist. Rocky was able to consistently activate the switch with his wrist and did not experience abnormal muscle tone or excessive fatigue. Automatic switch scanning with an eight-item SGD was then introduced with 40% accuracy from a field of eight icons. Rocky appeared to understand the task but struggled to time the movement/switch activation when the requested item was highlighted on the SGD screen. Step scanning was introduced, and Rocky was able to repeatedly activate the switch to advance the scan sequence to the desired item and pause for message activation. Regarding device placement, Rocky experienced the greatest attention and success when the device was placed on his wheelchair tray.

Hearing and Vision

As previously reported, Rocky exhibits a moderate sensorineural hearing loss and wears bilateral hearing aids that function effectively. Rocky receives regular follow-up from his audiologist, and no additional concerns related to hearing are reported. Rocky exhibits intermittent visual nystagmus but is otherwise reported to have 20/20 acuity (per parent report). The district vision specialist completed an evaluation and expressed concerns related to Rocky's visual attention, convergence, and tracking abilities. The use of high contrast on the SGD screen improved Rocky's visual attention, and he was able to visually attend to eight icons/scanning patterns on the SGD. Additional follow-up with the district vision specialist and occupational therapist will occur to explore Rocky's visual tracking and convergence with appropriate supports provided. Overall, Rocky exhibited vision skills to effectively operate the SGDs.

Summary

Rocky's comprehension skills far exceed his language production abilities. He currently uses unaided AAC strategies to meet basic needs, but these are not adequate to support Rocky's current and future communication needs. Based on the preceding results, an SGD that allows for switch input is recommended. The device should be positioned on the wheelchair tray with switch placement to the right side of his right arm. Step scanning should be further explored to determine the possibility of adding a second switch for increased message activation control.

Intervention Planning

In Rocky's case, it is important to consider the balance between immediate communication needs while allowing for future vocabulary development and overall language growth. To support his current and future needs, a core vocabulary approach will be used. With this approach, high-frequency single words that apply across multiple contexts and situations comprise the majority of Rocky's AAC system. Rather than storing multiple word messages within the device, the use of core vocabulary allows single words to be used flexibly and reduces cognitive and time demands. As Rocky gains competence with the core vocabulary, word combinations will be facilitated to support communication of more complex, nuanced messages. The core words remain in their original positions within the device to support memory and motor planning. The system will also allow for fringe vocabulary specific to Rocky's environment and interests not covered by the core vocabulary. The

fringe vocabulary will likely shift and change as Rocky's interests change. As these messages evolve, the core vocabulary words remain in their original locations unless adaptations are needed.

To demonstrate effective use of the device, the team will also use a strategy known as aided language stimulation (ALS). With this strategy, the communication partner models use of the device during interactions while also verbalizing their message. This type of scaffolding provides Rocky with a model of more competent AAC use. Since Rocky is the only child in his regular classroom who uses AAC, it is important that he interact with more competent AAC users, which will be modeled by his educational team (Beukelman & Mirenda, 2005; Oommen & McCarthy, 2014). The team will also coach Rocky to use his unaided vocalization strategies to gain the attention of caregivers and peers when he has a message to share.

Analysis of Client Response to Intervention

By the end of the second month of intervention with the SGD, Rocky has met the following goals:

- Rocky will use one-switch step scanning to choose a desired activity or item in 8 of 10 opportunities.
- Rocky will respond to questions during shared reading activities with 80% accuracy.
- Rocky will initiate interaction with peers by vocalizing to first gain their attention at least five times each school day.

Future Considerations

Rocky's initial progress is encouraging. The usability of the SGD should remain central to the school-based team's intervention considerations. This person-centered approach emphasizes a human factors model and is based on Baker's ergonomic equation, as adapted by King (1999) for assistive technology. In this adapted model of Baker's ergonomic equation, Rocky's unmet communication needs must exceed the sum of his physical effort (the actual physical exertion required to complete the task), cognitive effort (the overall level of cognition necessary to operate the system), linguistic effort (the level of linguistic knowledge required to understand the language representation of the system), and time load (the amount of time it takes Rocky to communicate a message) to result in a successful outcome. If, for example, a particular access strategy requires too much physical effort, it is likely the team will notice decreased communication initiations as a result. Additional future areas of focus should include expansion of opportunities to use the SGD across school and home environments. The use of varied functions and intentions of language should be modeled to include asking questions, making comments, expressing ideas/opinions, and developing narrative skills. It is also critical for Rocky's team to begin incorporating interventions to support literacy development. Individuals who use AAC often struggle to attain literacy skills, which limits expressive language development and vocational opportunities.

Authors' Note

The presented case was fictional.

References

American Speech-Language-Hearing Association. (2005). *Roles and responsibilities of speech-language pathologists with respect to augmentative and alternative communication: Position statement* [Position statement]. http://www.asha.org/policy

Beukelman, D. R., & Light, J. C. (2020). *Augmentative & alternative communication: Supporting children and adults with complex communication needs* (5th ed.). Brookes Publishing.

Beukelman, D., & Mirenda, P. (2005). *Augmentative and alternative communication, supporting children and adults with complex communication needs*. Brookes Publishing.

Blackstone, S., & Hunt-Berg, M. (2003). *Social networks: A communication inventory for individuals with complex communication needs and their communication partners.* Augmentative Communication.

Coburn, K., Jung, S., Ousley, C., Sowers, D., Wendelken, M., & Wilkinson, K. (2021). Centering the family in their system: A framework to promote family-centered AAC services. *Augmentative and Alternative Communication, 37*(4), 229–240. https://doi.org/10.1080/0743 4618.2021.1991471

Drager, K., Light, J., & McNaughton, D. (2010). Effects of AAC interventions on communication and language for young children with complex communication needs. *Journal of Pediatric Rehabilitation Medicine, 3*(4), 303–310. https://doi.org/10.3233/PRM-2010-0141

Hart, P., & Scherz, J. (2017). Perceptions of teamwork in AAC. *Online Journal of the Missouri Speech-Language-Hearing Association, 3*, 8–21.

Hsieh, Y. H., Borgestig, M., Gopalarao, D., McGowan, J., Granlund, M., Hwang, A. W., & Hemmingsson, H. (2021). Communicative interaction with and without eye-gaze technology between children and youths with complex needs and their communication partners. *International Journal of Environmental Research and Public Health, 18*(10), 5134. https://doi .org/10.3390/ijerph18105134

King, T. W. (1999). *Assistive technology: Essential human factors.* Allyn & Bacon.

Liang J., & Wilkinson, K. M. (2018). Gaze toward naturalistic social scenes by individuals with intellectual and developmental disabilities: Implications for augmentative and alternative communication designs. *Journal of Speech, Language, and Hearing Research, 61*, 1157–1170.

Loncke, F. (2022). *Augmentative and alternative communication, models and applications* (2nd ed.). Plural Publishing.

McNaughton, D., Light, J., Beukelman, D., Klein, C., Nieder, D., & Nazareth, G. (2019). Building capacity in AAC: A person-centred approach to supporting participation by people with complex communication needs, *Augmentative and Alternative Communication, 35*(1), 56–68. https://doi.org/10.1080/07434618 .2018.1556731

Millar, D., Light, J., & Schlosser, R. (2006). The impact of augmentative and alternative communication intervention on the speech production of individuals with developmental disabilities: A research review. *Journal of Speech, Language, and Hearing Research, 49*(2), 248–264. https://doi.org/10.1044/1092-4388(2006/021)

Oommen, E. R., & McCarthy, J. W. (2014). Natural speech and AAC intervention in childhood motor speech disorders: Not an either/or situation. *Perspectives* on *Augmentative and Alternative Communication, 23,* 117–123.

Owens, R. (2020). *Language development: An introduction.* Pearson.

Peters, B., Eddy, B., Galvin-McLaughlin, D., Betz, G., Oken, B., & Fried-Oken, M. (2022). A systematic review of research on augmentative and alternative communication brain-computer interface systems for individuals with disabilities. *Frontiers in Human Neuroscience, 16,* 952380. https://doi.org/10.3389/fnhum.2022.952380

Wilkinson, K., & Madel, M. (2019). Eye tracking measures reveal how changes in the design of displays for augmentative and alternative communication influence visual search in individuals with Down syndrome or autism spectrum disorder. *American Journal of Speech-Language Pathology, 28*(4), 1649–1658. https://doi.org/10.1044/2019_AJSLP-19-0006

AUTISM
CASE 25
Benny: A School-Age Child With an Autism Spectrum Disorder

Nerissa Hall and Christina Rizzo Tatreau

Conceptual Knowledge Areas

Autism spectrum disorder (ASD) affects 1 in every 44 (2.3%) 8-year-old children, is 4.2 times more prevalent among boys, and occurs in all racial and ethnic groups (National Institute of Mental Health [NIH], 2022). ASD is a neurological disorder. Although one can be diagnosed at any age, the onset of symptoms typically occurs in the first 2 years of life, and ASD is therefore considered a developmental disorder. ASD affects communication, behavior, and learning, and a diagnosis is based on continuing challenges in the areas of social communication and interaction, with co-occurring restricted, repetitive behaviors.

Autism, or "autism disorder," used to be a distinct diagnosis under the umbrella term "pervasive developmental disorders" (PDDs), along with childhood disintegrative disorder, Rett syndrome, Asperger's disorder, and pervasive developmental disorder–not otherwise specified (PDD-NOS). In May 2013, the American Psychiatric Association's *Diagnostic and Statistical Manual, Fifth Edition* (DSM-5) was released with a new definition of autism, grouping the five previously listed conditions together under the term ASD. The DSM-5 provides standardized diagnostic criteria and severity measures to help diagnose ASD. This resource stipulates "persistent deficits in social communication and social interaction across multiple contexts . . . [as well as] restricted, repetitive patterns of behavioral, interests, or activities" (Centers for Disease Control and Prevention [CDC], 2022, paras. 2–3). Severity is categorized into three severity levels (detailed in Table 2 of U.S. Department of Health & Human Services, n.d.): Level 3, "Requiring very substantial support"; Level 2, "Requiring substantial support"; and Level 1, "Requiring support."

Some examples of social communication and interaction challenges include difficulties with initiation, reciprocal communicative exchanges, sharing of interests, and misaligned affect and/or limited facial expressions, along with deficits in developing and maintaining social relationships. Restricted, repetitive patterns of behavior apply to motor movements, speech, and/or use of objects and can also include inflexibility and adherence to specific routines, intense and fixated interests, and responses to sensory input that are either hypo- or hyperactive. The *DSM-5* further specifies that these symptoms need to occur in early development and result in a clinically significant impairment that adversely affects everyday functioning and that cannot otherwise be better explained by an alternative diagnosis or etiology. It is important to note that "intellectual disability and autism spectrum disorder frequently co-occur; [but] to make comorbid diagnoses of autism spectrum disorder and intellectual disability, social communication should be below that expected for general developmental level" (CDC, 2022, para. 4).

There is an element of flexibility inherent to a diagnosis of ASD. "Spectrum" suggests enormous variability in how autism manifests in an individual, and although the *DSM-5* details specific diagnostic criteria, a diagnosis is based on several symptoms that collectively have a clinically significant impact on an individual's functioning across contexts. No two people with ASD will present in the same way with respect to their communication, behavior, interaction, and learning. It is therefore beneficial to recognize the symptomology as "neurodivergent," honoring brain differences that lead to variances in how one learns, behaves, and engages.

For most, ASD is a lifelong condition, and "timely psycho-educational intervention can significantly improve the level of autonomy reached by the individual" (Posar & Visconti, 2019, p. 210). With core symptoms in the areas of social communication and repetitive interests, speech-language pathologists (SLPs) are well equipped with the knowledge and skills to provide meaningful assessment, intervention, and consultation. Depending on the presentation of symptoms, intervention focused on speech, language, literacy, and/or pragmatics will likely be essential for the individual. Additionally, given the impact on interaction and behavior, oftentimes board-certified behavior analysts (BCBAs) are just as critical a team member as the SLP and can help affect socially significant changes in behavior.

It is estimated that 40% of individuals with ASD are functionally nonspeaking (Autism Speaks, n.d.), and greater proportions present with complex language and communication needs. Challenges with expressive and receptive language, as well as different learning trajectories and profiles, make individually tailored evidence-based practice essential for individuals with ASD. Additionally, by its very nature, the social element integral to the diagnosis of ASD involves communication partners. "The social communication issues experienced by individuals with ASD also affect their communication partners. Family members, friends, teachers, and coworkers face the challenge of learning to recognize and respond to subtle bids for communication and to interpret the communication functions of challenging behaviors." (American Speech-Language-Hearing Association [ASHA], n.d., para. 11) Depending on the nature and severity of the communication and/or pragmatic impairment, augmentative and alternative communication (AAC) may be warranted.

Description of the Case

Benny is 5. He recently received a diagnosis of ASD from his developmental pediatrician, to whom he had been referred by his local pediatrician. He is an engaging boy with a complex medical history and complex communication needs. He has a primary diagnosis of a rare gene mutation associated with ASD. This diagnosis, combined with the outcomes of the Autism Behavior Checklist (ABC; Krug et al., 1993) and other measures, led to a formal diagnosis of ASD.

Background Information

Developmental, Medical, Family, and Educational History

Benny presents with a complex medical history. He was born 2 weeks premature, and immediate physical abnormalities were noted, such as torticollis and microtia of the right ear. He spent approximately 2 weeks in the neonatal intensive care unit (NICU), and when medically stable, he transitioned home with his mother, Emily, and father, Dan.

Benny failed to meet developmental milestones in a timely manner. By 1 year of age, Benny made very few sounds and wasn't yet approximating words or even many gestures (such as waving or gesturing for someone to "come"). He wasn't attempting to pick up items in a refined manner and was only just starting to pull himself up to stand. His parents described him as "unflappable" and noted that he rarely reacted to what they thought should be painful and didn't often seek their comfort. By age 2, Benny's limited interest in others was evident and made more notable with the birth of his baby brother, Jake. Benny made very few sounds but was smiling more frequently and using physical manipulation to guide his parents to a desired item. Benny was walking but was wobbly and fell frequently (with little to no pain response). Additionally, he appeared to be developing slightly coarse facial features (like a broadened nasal bridge and full lips). Benny's pediatrician referred him to a developmental pediatrician, and Benny was subsequently diagnosed with a genetic mutation, global developmental delay, microtia, and torticollis. His family was prescribed regular visits with the specialist and audiologist, and Benny was referred to Early Intervention (EI) given his delayed fine and gross motor skills, as well as speech and language deficits.

Benny's family immediately followed up on the referrals, and Benny was placed on a waiting list for EI. He got an appointment with an audiologist, but it was hard to complete the exam as Benny was scared and not easily soothed by his parents. The audiologist did feel that the microtia resulted in a maximal conductive hearing loss and that there was possibly mild hearing loss in the other ear based on Benny's limited response levels obtained in the sound field.

EI services were established shortly before Benny turned 3. He was seen briefly by an occupational therapist (OT) and SLP, who called for services three to four times a week given the severity of his presentation, particularly with respect to Benny's speech and language. At this age, Benny was able to point and physically manipulate items the size of a matchbox car or bigger and was continuing to physically guide his parents to a desired item or area (i.e., to where the TV remote or iPad

were located). Benny was smiling and laughing, usually in response to motivating items (cars, songs, TV shows) but not really human interaction or engagement. He made only an "ah" sound and showed limited articulatory movement for the purposes of speech production, struggling to bring his lips together to make bilabial sounds (like /p/ and /b/) or even alveolars (like /t/ and /d/). This articulatory imprecision also resulted in difficulty managing his saliva.

Benny's EI team noticed a discrepancy between what he understood (his receptive language abilities) and how he could express himself, and it appeared that he understood far more than he could communicate. They started to introduce photos and icons and placed an array of 10 color-copied 2-in. × 2-in. laminated images on the side of the fridge with magnets (which are easier to remove from the fridge than Velcro) and encouraged Benny to travel to the fridge and point to or hand over an image that helped communicate his message. Benny showed a quick and clear understanding that the images of movies (i.e., *Sing, Cars,* and *Toy Story*) represented his preferred shows, but he didn't yet seem to recognize that an abstract symbol of a stick figure drinking meant "drink" or the yawning face meant "tired."

In March 2020, EI services were no longer able to be provided in person in Benny's home due to COVID-19. Both the EI OT and SLP worked to provide remote consultation to the family via telepractice. Although Benny's parents said they appreciated being offered ideas about how they could support Benny's fine and gross motor skills, they were longing for the direct services provided previously by the specialists and found it hard to parent Benny and his younger brother while also trying to support skill advancement. From about age 3 to 4, Benny was unable to receive in-home, outpatient, or at-school services due to the pandemic.

Right around when Benny turned 4, COVID-19 restrictions were lifted enough to enroll Benny in preschool through his local school district. Given his learning profile and medical needs, Benny was offered an Individualized Education Plan (IEP) with SLP and OT services to be provided in (push-in) and outside (pull-out) of the district's half-day integrated preschool program. Around other peers, Benny's challenges with social engagement and communication quickly became apparent, and Benny spent most of his time playing independently. When he did engage with a same-aged peer, he often offered physical aggression to communicate (pulling toys from peers, throwing items toward them, and sometimes hitting him). When he was asked to do age-appropriate schoolwork, he would clear the items from the table, throwing them to the ground, or cry. The school's BCBA was asked to observe Benny in class to offer some input about behavioral interventions. She suggested involving visuals for communication as well as to support task completion and scheduling. She also referred the family back to their specialist given the presentation of new symptoms in the school environment.

Benny's developmental history, particularly his genetic diagnosis and behavior at home and at school, combined with the outcomes of the ABC (Krug et al., 1993) and Autism Diagnostic Observation Schedule (ADOS-2; Lord et al., 2000), led to a formal diagnosis of ASD. Additionally, given his age and the nature and severity of his communication needs, increased speech therapy was advised, along with an updated audiological exam.

Benny's parents met with the school, and increased SLP and BCBA services were added to the service delivery grid of Benny's IEP. He also went to the audiologist, who was better able to assess Benny's current hearing and compare it to previous findings. She noted fluctuations in hearing due to changes in middle ear status, placing him at a listening disadvantage and at significant risk for accessing communication and education. Tubes were placed and listening accommodations were provided to the family and school, primarily regarding Benny's positioning and orientation toward those speaking as well as pairing auditory information with visual information whenever possible.

Reason for Referral

Benny was referred for an outpatient speech and language evaluation given the question of poten-

tial augmentative and alternative communication (AAC). When this had been raised at the IEP meeting with the school, Benny's parents expressed concern about assessing for AAC, explaining they felt worried about "giving up" on Benny's speech without intensive intervention. However, they agreed to complete a thorough assessment and wait to review the findings with the specialists completing them.

The Evaluation Process

Benny was seen at an outpatient clinic specializing in speech, language, and literacy for individuals with complex communication needs. He was accompanied to the clinic by his mother and father and worked with the SLP team. Benny was given an opportunity to explore the environment and the toys within. All toys were available to him, and he chose ones with which he was motivated to engage. He was provided time to just play, and the clinicians "paired" themselves (and the learning environment) with the reinforcing activity: a technique used to help form and maintain rapport with a learner. Once it was clear that Benny was comfortable, the clinical team used various AAC tools and strategies, modeling AAC use for Benny to see, without requiring him to use the tools in the same way, with the purpose being to establish a culture of multimodal communication for all present in the room with Benny.

Behavioral Observations

Benny appeared content and relaxed for the entirety of the diagnostic session. He showed a distinct interest in puzzles and letters, and he really enjoyed silly, pretend play, where the clinician would pretend to have the container "eat" the letters as Benny placed them within. While engaging in play, Benny was always encouraged to communicate verbally and through gestures. He was also simultaneously encouraged to interact with AAC tools designed to explore different AAC features. Additionally, Benny's responsiveness to different AAC support strategies was assessed. Given the nature and severity of Benny's communication needs, more dynamic, criterion-referenced assessment measures were used, rather than standardized assessment measures. This allowed the clinicians to better determine Benny's areas of strength and needs, as well as offer specific guidance around intervention and implementation plans to provide the necessary degree of intensity for Benny's current and future needs.

As previously noted, Benny enjoyed playing with puzzles and letters. When presented with letters, he consistently oriented them right-side up before placing them in the puzzle, handing them to the clinician, or putting them in a container. He had some difficulty positioning shapes to fit in a shape sorter but accepted help from the clinician to complete the task. Benny smiled frequently, and on a few occasions, he kicked his feet in what appeared to be excitement. When he was done playing with toys and puzzles, he indicated this by putting them back into containers and subsequently back onto the shelves. His mother reports that this is an established part of his routine. Toward the end of the session, Benny was motivated to listen to music on YouTube, and he explored the iPads and phones available in the room. He independently put down iPads that didn't have YouTube and also tolerated switching from the clinician's phone to his mother's. When an unknown peer entered the room (on multiple occasions), Benny remained focused on what he was doing and on one occasion turned his body away from the visitor, as if to indicate that he wanted to play on his own at that time. He was accepting of the clinicians' involvement in playing with him, as well as the systematic increase and decrease of demands, prompting, and scaffolding throughout the session.

Physical Engagement (Gross and Fine Motor)

Benny moved around the space with ease. He sat with his legs straight in front of him, as well as in a "W" position. He got up from standing on his own and on a few occasions kneeled to scan the cubbies of toys. He used the furniture to stabilize himself when bending to look for items lower than eye level. He was able to hold an iPad and phone with both hands. With the smaller phone size, he held the iPhone in one hand and used the other to scroll and select. When working with the iPad and AAC apps, he generally attempted to make a selection with a few fingers extended. He didn't form a distinctive point but rather adjusted his positioning to angle his fingers differently to help him select the intended target. He worked well with the capacitive screen of the iPad, which reacted quickly to the slightest touch (rather than requiring pressure).

Sensory Engagement (Vision and Hearing)

Benny worked in a quiet and controlled environment. In this setting, he responded to the auditory and visual input and output features of the tools trialed. More specifically, he scanned the ~10-in. screen of the trialed iPad, responded well to the high-contrast visual display and backlighting, tracked clinician visual point prompts, and reacted to the auditory output offered by the tool (i.e., smiling to express affirmation when hearing the voice output or reattempting a selection if the device didn't say anything or said a message other than the one he intended). Benny tolerated a range of prompting techniques, including physical prompting (like hand-under-hand), and didn't demonstrate an aversive response to gentle touch to support his learning and success.

Communication

While Benny presented as nonspeaking, he said a lot with his body and other intrinsic, unaided modes of communication. During the assessment, he consistently communicated by orienting and positioning his body toward or away people/items, physically manipulating items and handing them to his communication partner, kicking his legs (which reportedly can occur when excited, happy, and frustrated), using facial expressions, and eye contact (although oftentimes fleeting).

With respect to aided communication strategies, Benny worked with Proloquo2Go, TouchChat, and LAMP Words for Life on the clinicians' iPads during the assessment, and it was reported that at home, he uses a modified picture communication exchange system adhered to his fridge. Prior consultation with the school-based team confirmed that additionally, Benny is working with a mid-tech AAC multimessage switch with his SLP to support participation in group activities at school. Lastly, Benny's parents confirmed that he has been exposed to some signed English, and during his work in the clinic, Benny demonstrated his understanding of signs for "more," "all done," "help," "drink," "mom," and "dad."

Benny was presented with a diagnostic app on the clinician's iPad designed to better assess Benny's speech, language, and AAC-related skills. Benny showed limited interest in working with semistructured diagnostic tasks and demonstrated work avoidance and work refusal behaviors (pushing the iPad away and turning away from the iPad and clinician). When the SLP reverted to the "pairing" technique described earlier, Benny was able to engage in some clinician-led tasks designed to elicit specific skills for diagnostic purposes. He was most successful in play-based tasks and struggled when asked to receptively identify specific targets or to offer an expressive label using multimodal communication.

Benny was interested in the high-tech AAC tools available. He worked with three different overlays designed to explore his responsiveness to various AAC features and strategies. When working with the 15-button grid size in Proloquo2Go, Benny showed that he was responsive to clinician modeling and could also access icons that size (approximately 1 × 1.5 in. in size). When he worked with LAMP Words for Life, Benny consistently attempted to make selections in the 84-button grid but struggled to access the smaller-sized icon. However, what he did show when working with LAMP was his success leveraging principles of motor learning. More specifically, LAMP places icons in consistent locations, ensuring that AAC access and word retrieval are extremely predictable. This helps individuals build a motor automaticity (just like touch-typing) and reduces the burden related to visual scanning.

Given Benny's success with this way of programming and organizing vocabulary, he was presented a modified Proloquo2Go overlay with only the core words *I, more, eat,* and *sleep* showing. Visual point prompting was used to help Benny use the tool in the context of the game being played and was systematically faded to encourage Benny to independently and autonomously use the AAC device.

With this overlay, Benny was able to differentiate "eat" from "sleep" without prompting toward the device. For example, if he selected "sleep," the clinicians pretended to fall asleep while snoring loudly. Benny quickly learned that he didn't intend for them to sleep, but rather to "eat" the magnetic letters, and learned to differentiate between the two and self-correct his AAC selection if he had made a mistake. Additionally, Benny responded to clinician modeling to build two-word combinations and was able to make the phrases "more eat," "I eat," and "eat more" with minimal to no prompting.

Assessment Findings

Benny worked hard during the assessment session. Although he did not engage with more traditional standardized assessment materials, the play-based activities completed helped the SLP team determine the discrepancy between what Benny understands and what he can express. The clinical tasks completed yielded the following information:

- Comprehension of nouns from a variety of categories (food, toys, places, vehicles, colors)
- Ability to combine words and icons to be more expressive ("more eat," "I eat," and "eat more" as detailed above)
- Ability to access icons in a field of at least 25 icons with hide-and-show keys enabled (where superfluous vocabulary is hidden from view to help support Benny's attention and focus on a specific subset of vocabulary)
- Understanding of concepts big/small, hot/cold, fast/slow, in/out, up/down on/off
- Understanding of "no" (even though he didn't like to be denied access or told "no")
- Success using a capacitive screen

- Responsiveness to the auditory and visual feedback offered by the tool (i.e., he adjusted his selections if what he heard was not what he intended to select)
- Motor learning strengths (as he became faster and more effective when icons were placed in consistent locations)

Given Benny's performance, his age, and the nature and severity of his medical profile, further work with high-tech AAC was recommended. As discussed with the family, AAC for Benny is likely to be a process and an approach, rather than a single tool, and team members across settings were advised to work in concert to build Benny's skills as a total communicator using multiple means of expression. Emily and Dan's fears about "giving up on speech" were calmed by detailing the difference between speech and language and how access to the vocabulary of the device empowered Benny to expand upon his language abilities irrespective of his speech progress, as well as offering Benny the autonomy to communicate on his own terms more effectively. Additionally, continued work with lite-tech and mid-tech AAC tools, as well as unaided methods of communication, was highlighted as important for Benny. Based on Benny's performance, it was suggested that he has access to high-tech AAC with:

- Voice output
- A robust language system
- The ability to hide and show keys
- Options to accommodate motor learning
- Visual and auditory accommodations
- A sturdy case and carrying strap/handle

Lastly, it was advised that the AAC tool should be distinct from his iPad(s) used for recreation and leisure activities. The SLPs that completed the assessment met with the family and school team, and it was agreed that Benny would use Proloquo2Go on the family's iPad. The school did offer to purchase Benny an iPad to ensure access to his curriculum as prescribed by educational law, but given how new this was for Benny and the family, they opted to start with their personal iPad to explore it.

Treatment Plan

Given Benny's responsiveness to play-based activities and modeling from the clinicians throughout the assessment, the team's approach to treatment planning was to structure a learning environment with all of Benny's preferred items. A 1-hour parent/caregiver interview was completed to determine any preferences that may not have been evident to the clinicians during the initial assessment and observation. The parents were encouraged to share Benny's preferences for things that may be causing some difficulty in the home setting. Instead of limiting or restricting these items from Benny, the team provided Benny with all things he likes. The clinician made note of any items that Benny might need to be taught to pause, stop, or transition away from. Ecological setup in this scenario prioritized a highly enriched environment over one that can be tightly controlled.

Movies and music and, at times, cars were identified as Benny's primary preferred items. Observations of his engagement with movies on the iPad, in particular, showed very little tolerance for giving up the iPad once he had it or having his access to it restricted in any way. Not having the iPad would lead to crying, kicking, and throwing, and Benny needed to physically leave the room in which the iPad was to be able to be redirected (which could often take up to 15 minutes). At the start of treatment, Benny showed little understanding of "first ___, then ___" language and did not have an established visual schedule/reinforcement system in place (illustrating for Benny that if he completed x number of tasks, he could earn time with a preferred movie or song). Empowering Benny to ask for the iPad using AAC also didn't help, as he did not respond to "not available" or being told he couldn't have the iPad.

Benny's outside speech sessions were conducted in collaboration with a BCBA trained to implement programming that emphasizes client assent/consent and prioritizes establishing a trusting relationship between client and clinician. All of Benny's favorite things were available to him in this enriched setting. Because the clinical team knew that Benny would choose to engage with the iPad and would struggle if asked to give it up given his history of this behavior when adults would take it away, indicate that they were planning to take it away, or when given warnings like "one more minute," they agreed that they would teach Benny to incrementally tolerate having to transition away from this preferred item.

At first the clinicians would give Benny some time to relax with the iPad and would say "my turn!" If Benny showed he didn't want to move on from the iPad, they would honor this and wait a few more minutes and try again. After doing this a number of times, they prompted Benny to ask for "my turn" using AAC if they asked him to transition away from the iPad. It took a few prompted opportunities, but Benny quickly responded to this prompting strategy. Sometimes Benny wanted to watch the iPad and scoot a car on the table at the same time, and he was able to gain access to these activities using the omnibus request of "my turn." Eventually, Benny showed some interest in moving on from the iPad at the clinician's direction. After just a minute or so, the clinician welcomed him back to the iPad, to show that it was readily available to him.

At first, the clinicians prioritized this back and forth. Over the course of the first week of sessions, Benny used AAC to access the things he felt most comfortable with and the clinicians always honored his request. Benny quickly developed a positive relationship with the session area and with the clinicians. It was only after developing this strong rapport, honoring his requests consistently, and prioritizing his assent with instruction that the clinicians began to attempt to deny Benny access to more iPad. Through careful observation of Benny's interaction with the iPad, his behavioral responses, and his use of "my turn" and "iPad" on his AAC device, the clinical team and family were able to empower Benny to better tolerate any denied access to the iPad and his response to hearing "not right now," "one more minute," and "not available."

Benny's overall needs were well managed across his team. At school, Benny's SLP worked on lip closure and early sound development. She also used preprogrammed phrases and some individual words programmed into Proloquo2Go, as well as universally understood gestures, to sup-

port Benny's participation in classroom activities and social routines. The goal was to help Benny communicate quickly and meaningfully with little effort, and therefore she focused on helping Benny turn his head toward the speaker and smiling, waving "hi," pressing a mid-tech switch to state "my turn" during bubble play, and another multimessage switch to randomly tell a joke for the "joke of the day" opportunity. She also programmed biographical information and weather vocabulary into the device to ensure Benny had the vocabulary needed to engage in classroom routines. Once a week, she and the district occupational therapist (OT) treated Benny together to continue to refine his physical use of Proloquo2Go and to work with a stylus.

Benny also received outpatient speech support one time a week in his home, as well as one time a week in the clinic. Because access to peers was not available in these settings, the goal of his time in outside speech was to work on maintaining his appropriate engagement with the iPad and addressing his language through access to high-tech AAC. With the improved instructional control and highly controlled, enriched environment established early on in Benny's treatment plan, these sessions focused on increasing his length of utterance through combining words (like "more go," "I want car," "different car," etc.), being empowered to say "no" and "not," and exploring vocabulary and building on his item-to-icon correspondence. These goals were addressed while engaging with puzzles, reading books together, and playing with cars (especially ones that go fast and do flips). Critical elements of literacy (like book handling, labeling pictures within, pointing out letters) were embedded, and it helped that Benny was so interested in letters.

Outside speech services represented a very fluid, play-based way of targeting skills. However, careful data were collected on what was modeled on the device for Benny to see (i.e., how did the clinician use the device when engaging with him) and what he outputted using the device. The team kept a data sheet formatted for quick data taking and ease of use to mark whether the AAC use was following a model or independent and what the utterances were.

Next Steps

Even though Benny is young, he still requires access to AAC and support using total communication to express himself and build upon his language skills. To be empowered to "use his voice" (irrespective of whether it is a point, a gesture, a smile, verbal approximation, a picture, or AAC) in lieu of an unwanted behavior remains a primary focus of Benny's programming. The well-coordinated consultation between the SLPs and BCBAs on Benny's team has been integral to his success and needs to be maintained as a major tenet of his treatment plan and academic programming, alongside parent involvement. Programming should continue to prioritize assent with instruction and a careful recalibration of the learning space and items available so that Benny's programming occurs in an enriched learning environment that supports dynamic and sustained progress.

References

American Psychiatric Association. (2013). *Diagnostic and statistical manual of mental disorders* (5th ed.). https://doi.org/10.1176/appi.books.9780890425596

American Speech-Language-Hearing Association (n.d.). *Autism* [Practice portal]. https://www.asha.org/Practice-Portal/Clinical-Topics/Autism/

Autism Speaks. (n.d.). *Autism statistics and facts.* https://www.autismspeaks.org/autism-statistics-asd#:~:text=An%20estimated%2040%20percent%20of,wander%20or%20bolt%20from%20safety

Centers for Disease Control and Prevention. (2022). *Autism spectrum disorder (ASD).* https://www.cdc.gov/ncbddd/autism/hcp-dsm.html

Krug, D. A., Arick, J. R., & Almond, P. J. (1993). Autism Behavior Checklist (ABC). In *Autism Screening Instrument for Educational Planning (ASIEP-2).* Pro-Ed.

Lord, C., Risi, S., Lambrecht, L., Cook, E. H., Leventhal, B. L., DiLavore, P. C., & Rutter, M. (2000). The Autism Diagnostic Observation Schedule-Generic: A standard measure of social and communication deficits associated with the spectrum of autism. *Journal of Autism and Developmental Disorders, 30,* 205–223. https://doi.org/10.1023/A:1005592401947

National Institute of Mental Health. (2022). *Autism spectrum disorder (ASD).* https://www.nimh.nih.gov/health/statistics/autism-spectrum-disorder-asd

Posar, A., & Visconti, P. (2019). Long-term outcome of autism spectrum disorder. *Turkish Archive of Pediatrics, 54*(4), 207–212. https://doi.org/10.14744/TurkPediatriArs.2019.16768

U.S. Department of Health & Human Services. (n.d.). *Autism spectrum disorder.* https://iacc.hhs.gov/about-iacc/subcommittees/resources/dsm5-diagnostic-criteria.shtml

BILINGUAL/LANGUAGE
CASE 26
Manuela: Cultural and Linguistic Diversity: A Bilingual Child With a Phonological and Language Disorder
Brian A. Goldstein

Conceptual Knowledge Areas

Providing clinical services to bilingual children is not the same as providing them to monolingual children. Having input in and using more than one language complicates the process of assessment and subsequent treatment. Thus, speech-language pathologists (SLPs) must be prepared to alter their "standard of care" with bilingual children. The purpose of this case is to show how assessment and treatment differ for bilingual children in comparison to monolingual peers. To that end, three aspects of the clinical process will be the focus of this case: (1) assess speech and language skills in both languages, (2) take into account sociolinguistic variables, and (3) provide treatment in both languages (Goldstein, 2006).

Assess in Both Languages

Research on the speech and language development (and disorders) of bilingual children indicates that it is similar, although *not* identical, to monolingual development (e.g., Marchman et al., 2000). This finding holds for bilingual children with language disorders as well. For example, Paradis et al. (2003) found that the morphological skills of bilingual children with specific language impairment (SLI) were commensurate with those of age-matched monolingual English and monolingual French speakers with SLI. Thus, as bilin-gual children gain more linguistic experience over time, their speech and language skills become more like those of monolinguals. However, it is also likely that the language skills of bilinguals will be asymmetrically distributed across the two languages such that knowledge in one language is not necessarily replicated in the other. For example, Peña et al. (2003) found that bilingual children showed better performance in English than in Spanish on some tasks (e.g., receptive similarities and differences) but also better performance in Spanish on other tasks (e.g., expressive functions). Findings from these types of studies show the necessity of completing an assessment in both of the bilingual child's languages.

Consider Sociolinguistic Variables

Although the speech and language skills of bilingual children are similar to monolingual peers, those skills might be tempered differentially by the sociolinguistic environment (Escobar et al., 2022). Historically, sociolinguistic variables have been related to language dominance (i.e., which is the "stronger" language?) and type of bilingual (e.g., simultaneous or sequential). However, these descriptors do not allow the clinician to delve deeply into the child's bilingual background. Thus, in assessing bilingual children, SLPs should obtain information on language history (age at which the child hears and uses each language), language environment (environments in which the child hears and uses each language), language input/output (frequency with which the child hears and uses each language), and language proficiency (how well the child uses each language). Consideration of how the bilingual child develops and uses both languages will result in a more reliable and valid assessment and subsequently will link more directly to treatment.

Provide Treatment in Both Languages

Because bilingual children show distributed skills in each of their two languages and bilingual speech and language development is not equivalent to that of monolingual speakers, it is almost certain that treatment will need to occur in both languages at some point during the treatment process. Kohnert and Derr (2012) and Kohnert et al. (2005) proposed two approaches to treating speech and language disorders in bilingual children. First, the bilingual approach maintains that SLPs should improve language skills common to both languages. Along those same lines, Yavas and Goldstein (1998) recommended initially treating errors/error patterns exhibited with relatively equal frequency, in both languages. Second, the cross-linguistic approach maintains that the linguistic skills unique to each language should be targeted. Kohnert and colleagues emphasize that SLPs likely will utilize both approaches during treatment with bilingual children.

Analyzing the speech and language skills of bilingual children is a complicated task. Analysis is aided by assessing in both languages, considering the sociolinguistic variables, and providing intervention in both languages. These three parameters set the backdrop for the following learning objectives and case study.

Description of the Case

Manuela Torres is a 5-year, 8-month-old bilingual (Spanish-English) female who attends first grade at the Marín School. She was referred to the speech-language pathologist (SLP) by her classroom teacher as she tends to be "quiet" in class and is not making expected academic progress. Her mother, Sra. Ana Torres, was interviewed by phone in Spanish, her language of preference. During the evaluation, which occurred in both Spanish and English, case history information was obtained, formal testing was performed, and a language sample was recorded. The results of the evaluation are summarized in the following paragraphs.

Background Information

Manuela's birth history was normal. Her mother reported that she reached all developmental motor milestones at the appropriate times, but she had difficulty with toilet training; Manuela was completely trained at age 3 years, 6 months. Regarding Manuela's medical history, her mother stated that Maneula has had multiple cases of whooping cough, which have not recurred for over 2 years. Sra. Torres reported that results from an in-school hearing screening were normal, and she has no concerns about Manuela's hearing. According to school records, Manuela's hearing (pure tone and impedance) was screened at school approximately 3 months prior to the assessment and found to be within normal limits.

Manuela lived at home with her mother, father, and two brothers (age 4 years and age 8 months). Sra. Torres did not work outside the home, and Sr. Torres worked for the school district. Manuela also spent time with her grandmother. Manuela attended preschool for 1 year at a community preschool 5 days a week and was instructed in both Spanish and English. Manuela's 4-year-old brother attended the same preschool program.

Reason for Referral

Manuela's language environment has consisted of both English and Spanish since birth. However, until the time she entered preschool, she heard and used more Spanish than English. Sra. Torres estimated the frequency with which Manuela heard and used each language was 75% Spanish and 25% English. Manuela spent the majority of her day hearing and using English (approximately 80% of the time) in school. The rest of the day (about 20% of the time), she heard and used the Puerto Rican dialect of Spanish. At the Marín School, Manuela heard English almost exclusively in her classroom from the classroom teacher, although the aide in the classroom used Spanish to reinforce instructions and information from the classroom teacher. In school, nearly 100% of Manuela's productions were in English, according to Manuela's teacher. Manuela's teacher reported her English proficiency as a 3 (speaks the language with some errors) on a 0- to 4-point scale (Restrepo, 1998). Sra. Torres rated Manuela's Spanish proficiency (how well she uses the language) as a 2 (speaks the language with a relatively large number of errors) on the same 0- to 4-point scale.

Sra. Torres reported that at age 2 years, Manuela spoke her first words, which were in Spanish (e.g., *iej* [give me] and *mío* [mine]), and that at age 3 years, she began combining two and three words in Spanish and English (e.g., *mi perro* [my dog]; *iej manzana* [give me apple]; *uh-oh mommy*). Sra. Torres started showing concern about Manuela's speech and language skills 1 year prior to this evaluation as she noticed Manuela was not "speaking as well as the other children" in her preschool class. She did not express her concern to the school as she thought they would let her know "if something was wrong." Her main concern was Manuela's articulation, especially in Spanish, as she understood less than half of Manuela's utterances in Spanish. At the time of this study, intelligibility had increased to about 75%. Manuela's teacher was concerned not only about her articulation in English but also about her expressive language skills, especially her grammar in English.

Findings of the Evaluation

Manuela's speech and language skills were assessed in both Spanish and English. To assess those skills, the phonology subtest of the Bilingual English-Spanish Assessment (BESA) (Peña et al., 2018) and the Wiig Assessment of Basic Concepts–

English (Wiig, 2004) and Spanish (WABC) (Wiig & Langdon, 2006) were administered. An oral-peripheral mechanism screening was conducted, and language samples in both Spanish and English were collected.

Behavior

Manuela behaved well and appeared to have an attention span typical for her age. She interacted well with the clinician during play and was engaged in the testing activities but was initially reluctant to talk.

Oral-Peripheral Examination

An informal oral-peripheral assessment was completed during the evaluation. Her facial symmetry and oral musculature appeared to be within normal limits. Her mouth appeared to be symmetrical during speech and at rest. Diadochokinetic rate was within normal limits (Shipley & McAfee, 2020).

Phonology

Manuela's phonology was assessed in Spanish and English using the BESA phonology subtest. Scoring was completed taking dialect features into account such that those features were not scored as errors (Goldstein & Iglesias, 2001). Manuela exhibited a severe phonological disorder based on consonant accuracy (<50%) in both languages (Gruber, 1999). Scores for the Spanish and English phonology subtests are displayed in Figure 26–1.

Phoneme accuracy is listed in Table 26–1. These results provide further evidence of a phonological disorder given the expectation of near 100% accuracy on the majority of phonemes at this age in English (Smit et al., 1990) and in Spanish (Jimenez, 1987).

Manuela demonstrated a high frequency of occurrence (>10%) for phonological patterns in Spanish and English (Table 26–2): cluster reduction, initial cluster reduction, final consonant deletion, stopping, and backing.

These patterns are ones that are typically suppressed by the time a child reaches Manuela's

Consonant Accuracy: Spanish	48.78%
Vowel Accuracy: Spanish	87.14%
Consonant Accuracy: English	48.5%
Vowel Accuracy: English	84.91%

Figure 26–1. Scores for BESA Phonology Subtest—Spanish and English.

Table 26–1. BESA Phonology Subtest—Phoneme Accuracy

Phoneme	Percent Correct: Spanish	Percent Correct: English
p	100%	89%
b	86%	100%
t	85%	80%
d	70%	65%
k	67%	89%
g	75%	75%
m	100%	100%
n	80%	55%
ɲ	90%	n/a
ŋ	n/a	100%
f	67%	50%
v	n/a	50%
θ	n/a	15%
ð	50%	22%
s	14%	17%
z	n/a	50%
ʃ	n/a	12%
ʒ	n/a	n/a
tʃ	66%	50%
dʒ	n/a	42%
l	33%	20%
ɹ (as in _red_)	n/a	9%
r (flap)	11%	n/a
r (trill)	6%	n/a
w	n/a	95%
j	85%	90%

Table 26–2. Phonological Patterns Displayed

Phonological Pattern	Percentage of Occurrence		Example	
	Spanish	English	Spanish	English
Cluster reduction	71%	69%	"nego" for "negro"	"toe" for "toast"
Initial cluster reduction	87%	83%	"tabo" for "clavo"	"dop" for "stop"
Final consonant deletion	15%	33%	"ku" for "cruz"	"bri" for "bridge"
Initial consonant deletion	20%	0%	"ama" for "cama"	n/a
Stopping	30%	24%	"keño" for "señor"	"tum" for "thumb"
Consonant backing	15%	13%	"ke" for "tren"	"come" for "thumb"
Gliding	0%	22%	n/a	"wing" for "ring"

age. It also should be noted that the frequencies of occurrence were largely similar in both languages, although there were two exceptions: initial consonant deletion occurred in Spanish but not in English, and gliding occurred in English but not in Spanish.

Language

Receptive and expressive language skills were assessed in both English and Spanish using the WABC–Level 2 (English and Spanish).

Receptive Language. Results from the receptive portion of the WABC indicated receptive skills that were within normal limits. Manuela achieved a standard score of 88 on the WABC-English and a standard score of 90 on the WABC-Spanish, which placed her scores slightly below the mean but still within normal limits. She could follow one- and two-step commands. In both Spanish and English, she accurately identified many objects, parts of objects, and objects within a category (body parts, food items, animals, and clothing). She pointed to the correct use of objects, recognized actions in pictures and in play, and made inferences. Manuela demonstrated comprehension of quantitative concepts, part/whole relationships, and descriptive concepts such as *heaviest*, *slowest*, and *dark* in English and *débil* (weak), *menos* (less),

and *tarde* (late). She also appeared to understand pronouns and accurately identified the colors of objects (in English only). Although Manuela had difficulty with spatial concepts in both languages during testing (e.g., *inside*), she was able to demonstrate this skill during play. Concepts that were not answered correctly on the test tended to be condition concepts in Spanish (e.g., *oscuro* [dark]) and quantity concepts in English (e.g., *half*). During play, Manuela appeared to understand all wh-questions with the exception of *when*.

Expressive Language. Results from the expressive portion of the WABC (English and Spanish) found Manuela's skills to be moderately delayed. She achieved the following scores:

	English	Spanish
Standard score	80	73
Confidence interval (90%)	72–89	64–82
Percentile rank	9th	1st

Manuela showed similarities and differences on the WABC by language. In both languages, she knew concepts of weight/volume (e.g., *thin*, *heavy* in English and *bajo* [under], *delgada* [thin] in Spanish) and distance/speed/time (e.g., *slow*, *late* in English and *lejos* [far], *iejo* [old] in Spanish). She exhibited differences across languages as well. In English, she showed difficulty with concepts of condition/quality (e.g., *neat*, *quiet*, *straight*). In Spanish, she showed difficulty with concepts of location/direction (e.g., *izquierdo* [left], *tercera* [third], *al frente* [in front]).

A conversational language sample of 75 utterances in English and 62 utterances in Spanish was collected. In the sample, Manuela mainly used three- and four-word utterances in both languages, although she did show that she is capable of producing longer utterances (e.g., *My mom come in the car over here*). By this age, children typically should be able to produce complex utterances of at least five to six words. Mean length of utterance words (MLUw) was calculated in both languages as a measure of grammatical complexity. MLUw was calculated rather than MLUm (morphemes) to provide comparable measures across languages (Anderson, 1999). Manuela's MLUw from the conversational sample was 3.74 in Spanish and 3.85 in English. An MLUw under 4 places her language complexity at the level of a child age 3 years, 6 months to 4 years.

In the sample, Manuela used more nouns than verbs in both languages. To answer questions, she also produced a relatively large number of unconjugated verbs (infinitives such as *comer* [to eat] in Spanish and "to sleep" in English). When producing verbs, she used many general all-purpose verbs such as *tengo* [I have] and *quiero* [I want] in Spanish and *like*, *got*, *put*, *want* in English, as well as action verbs in Spanish (*ven* [come], *salta* [jump]) and in English (kick, crash, jump), and modal auxiliaries and concatenatives in English (wanna, gonna). She used possessive (*mío* [mine], *tuyo* [yours], his, my) and personal pronouns in Spanish (*yo* [I], *tú* [you]) and in English (he, you, I, it, me). Manuela inconsistently used the following constructions (*denotes omission of required element):

- **Articles:** *put **the** car* vs. *my mom crashed in front of * police*
- **Irregular past tense** (in English only): *My mom **bought** it* vs. *I can **broke** it*
- **Plurals:** *uvas* (grapes) vs. *two ball**
- **Possessive nouns:** *my, his* vs. *you see my ma* car right there?*

- **Auxiliaries and copulas:** *I * tired, what * this?, then he * leaving, I wish my mother * buy me that*

To measure lexical diversity, number of different words (NDW) was calculated. NDW was .31 (23 different words) in English and a slightly higher .42 (26 different words) in Spanish. In both languages, NDW was less than expected for her age (Miller, 1987). By age 7 years, English-speaking children produced, on average, 173 different words in a 100-utterance sample (Leadholm & Miller, 1992). In Spanish, children of approximately the same age as Manuela produced 70 different words (Muñoz et al., 2003).

Manuela did not always demonstrate the ability to communicate her wants and needs in an age-appropriate fashion. At times, she relied on action verbs to make requests. For example, when a toy did not function, she brought it to a clinician and said, "Do this." When asked, "Do what?" she replied, "Jumping," to refer to the balls that moved up and down inside the toy. When asked what she was doing while playing with the hula hoop, she responded, "*Trata* (try)." There were instances, however, when she demonstrated the ability to construct appropriate requests but did not do so. For example, to ask the clinician to tie her shoe, she said, "My tie it" and "Make it." Afterward, however, she said, "My dad can tie it" and "I can tie my shoes."

By 5 to 6 years old, a child typically uses adult-like grammar most of the time. Manuela's inconsistent omission of articles, verbal morphology, auxiliaries, and copulas is not typical for a child her age. By this age, she should put five- to six-word sentences together consistently. Although the sample shows that she is capable of producing longer utterances (e.g., *I gonna throw hard over there* and *Tengo un gato en mi casa* [I have a cat at my house]), she typically used short utterances that did not adequately communicate her thoughts or requests.

Pragmatics. Manuela's pragmatic skills were demonstrated in informal (play) testing situations. She engaged in play with the clinician and warmed up quickly. She showed appropriate levels of eye contact, turn-taking, and joint attention. She demonstrated an excellent ability to request information and actions from the clinician (e.g., *¿qué es esto?* [what is this?]). With puppets, Manuela created characters and told the clinician which one was the daddy, the mommy, and the baby (based on sizes of the dolls). Manuela was outgoing and playful with any task asked of her.

Voice and Fluency. Voice and fluency were examined informally and found to be within normal limits.

Treatment Options Considered

Manuela was evaluated using standardized and nonstandardized approaches in both English and Spanish. Based on the results of testing, she exhibited a moderate expressive language disorder and a severe phonological disorder in both languages that was impacting her ability to be understood. Both areas of weakness should be addressed in therapy twice per week.

Course of Treatment

Results of Manuela's comprehensive assessment revealed that she exhibited a moderate expressive language disorder and a severe phonological disorder in both languages. Manuela received two 1-hour treatment sessions per week, and this phase of treatment lasted 8 weeks.

Three initial treatment goals were implemented. For Goals 1 and 2, a bilingual treatment approach was utilized initially, given that both languages were affected, although not identi-

cally. The selection of this approach was based on the work of Kohnert and colleagues (Kohnert & Derr, 2012; Kohnert et al., 2005) and Yavas and Goldstein (1998), who suggested initially treating errors/error patterns exhibited with relatively equal frequency in both languages. For Goal 3, a cross-linguistic approach was utilized as all errors were in only one language. The following description states the goal, rationale, implementation procedure, and results of treatment.

Goal 1

Manuela will suppress the use of the phonological patterns: stopping and cluster reduction.

- **Rationale:** Both patterns were frequently occurring in both languages. By Manuela's age, both patterns should be suppressed entirely or infrequently occur in English (Bernthal et al., 2022) and Spanish (Goldstein, et al., 2005). Moreover, these goals represented two types of patterns: syllabic (cluster reduction) and substitution (stopping).
- **Implementation:** Treatment occurred in both languages, with equal time in English and Spanish. One session per week was conducted in English, and one session per week was conducted in Spanish. Both types of patterns (syllabic and substitution) were addressed in each session.
- **Results of Treatment:** As noted in Table 26–3, percentages of occurrence decreased for both patterns. However, the frequency of occurrence decreased more for cluster reduction in Spanish

Table 26–3. Results of Treatment for Phonological Patterns

Pattern	Spanish		English	
	Pretreatment	Posttreatment	Pretreatment	Posttreatment
Cluster reduction	71%	33%	69%	50%
Stopping	30%	18%	24%	15%

than in English. This result was most likely due to differences in clusters in the two languages. Spanish has only two-member clusters in onset position (e.g., *plato* [plate]) versus two (e.g., *plate*) and three for English (e.g., *string*) (Hammond, 2001).

Goal 2

Manuela will increase her mean length of utterance to 4.5 words in conversation in both Spanish and English.

- **Rationale:** MLUw was below age expectations in both languages (Bedore et al., 2022, for Spanish and Shipley & McAfee, 2020, for English). In conversation, Manuela produced mainly utterances of three and four words.
- **Implementation:** Treatment occurred equally in both languages. One session per week was conducted in English, and one session per week was conducted in Spanish.
- **Results of Treatment:** After 8 weeks of treatment, MLU increased in both languages, although slightly more so in English. The slight English advantage is likely the result of two factors. First, Manuela was exposed to more English during the day than to Spanish. In the classroom setting, instruction was almost exclusively in English. Second, Spanish is a pro-drop language, meaning that subject nouns and pronouns are largely optional (Bedore et al., 2022). Thus, utterance length may be less than that of English, which is not a pro-drop language. Results are displayed in Table 26–4.

Goal 3

To produce irregular past-tense verbs in English in 80% of obligatory contexts.

- **Rationale:** Manuela produced irregular past-tense verbs only in English. Accuracy for these verbs was approximately 30%. At her age, she should be producing these verbs accurately (Shipley & McAfee, 2020).
- **Implementation:** Treatment occurred in English only. However, cross-linguistic generalization was monitored in Spanish through the use of a probe list of sentences containing irregular past-tense verbs and via elicitation in conversation.
- **Results of Treatment:** After a course of treatment, accuracy on irregular past-tense verbs in English increased from 30% to almost 50%. In Spanish, Manuela accurately produced 1 of 10 irregular verbs in the elicited sentences. In conversational speech, six irregular verbs were attempted and one was produced correctly. Thus, even though irregular verbs in Spanish were not targeted, some cross-linguistic generalization might have been occurring.

Further Recommendations

Assessing and treating bilingual children with speech and language disorders is a complicated task given the increasing but general lack of developmental research studies, paucity of valid and reliable assessment tools, and few treatment studies with this group of children. Evidence-based practice, however, also dictates considering clini-

Table 26–4. Results of Treatment for MLU

	Spanish		English	
	Pretreatment	Posttreatment	Pretreatment	Posttreatment
MLUw	3.74	4.10	3.85	4.25

cal judgment and the client's goals in the provision of clinical services (Dollaghan, 2007). The interaction of these three components suggests that SLPs need to assess in both languages, consider sociolinguistic variables, and treat in both languages as a means to provide reliable and valid services to bilingual children.

Author's Note

The case study presented is hypothetical.

References

Anderson, R. (1999). Loss of gender agreement in L1 attrition: Preliminary results. *Bilingual Research Journal, 23*, 319–338.

Bedore, L., & Cooperson, S. (2022). Morpho-syntactic development. In B. Goldstein (Ed.), *Bilingual language development and disorders in Spanish-English speakers* (3rd ed., pp. 171–191). Brookes.

Bernthal, J., Bankson, N., & Flipsen, P. (Eds.). (2022). *Articulation and phonological disorders* (9th ed.). Brookes.

Dollaghan, C. (2007). *The handbook for evidence-based practice in communication disorders*. Brookes.

Escobar, K., Smith, J, Hammer, C. S., & Rodriguez, B. L. (2012). Bilingual language acquisition and the child socialization process. In B. Goldstein (Ed.), *Bilingual language development and disorders in Spanish-English speakers* (3rd ed., pp. 45–65). Brookes.

Goldstein, B. (2006). Clinical implications of research on language development and disorders in bilingual children. *Topics in Language Disorders, 26*, 318–334.

Goldstein, B., Fabiano, L., & Washington, P. (2005). Phonological skills in predominantly English, predominantly Spanish, and Spanish-English bilingual children. *Language, Speech, and Hearing Services in Schools, 36*, 201–218. https://doi.org/10.1044/0161-1461(2005/021)

Goldstein, B., & Iglesias, A. (2001). The effect of dialect on phonological analysis: Evidence from Spanish-speaking children. *American Journal of Speech-Language Pathology, 10*, 394–406.

Gruber, F. (1999). Probability estimates and paths to consonant normalization in children with speech delay. *Journal of Speech, Language, and Hearing Research, 42*, 448–459. https://doi.org/10.1044/jslhr.4202.448

Hammond, R. (2001). *The sounds of Spanish: Analysis and application (with special reference to American English)*. Cascadilla Press.

Jimenez, B. C. (1987). Acquisition of Spanish consonants in children aged 3–5 years, 7 months. *Language Speech and Hearing Services in the Schools, 18*(4), 357–363.

Kohnert, K., & Derr, A. (2012). Language intervention with bilingual children. In B. Goldstein (Ed.), *Bilingual language development and disorders in Spanish-English speakers* (2nd ed., pp. 337–363). Brookes.

Kohnert, K., Yim, D., Nett, K., Fong Kan, P., & Duran, L. (2005). Intervention with linguistically diverse preschool children: A focus on developing home language(s). *Language, Speech, & Hearing Services in Schools, 32*, 153–164. https://doi.org/10.1044/0161-1461(2005/025)

Leadholm, B., & Miller, J. (1992). *Language sample analysis: The Wisconsin guide*. Wisconsin Department of Public Instruction.

Marchman, V., Martínez-Sussman, C. & Price, P. (2000, June). *Individual differences in early learning contexts for Spanish and English speaking children*. Paper presented at Head Start's 5th National Research Conference, Washington, DC.

Miller, J. F. (1987). A grammatical characterization of a language disorder. In J. A. M. Martin, P. Fletcher, P. Grunwell, & D. Hall (Eds.), *Proceedings of the First International Symposium on Specific Speech and Language Disorders in Children* (pp. 100–113). London: AFASIC.

Muñoz, M., Gillam, R., Peña, E., & Gulley Faehnle, A. (2003). Measures of language development in fictional narratives of Latino children. *Language, Speech & Hearing Services in Schools, 34*, 332–342. https://doi.org/10.1044/0161-1461(2003/027)

Paradis, J., Crago, M., Genesee, F., and Rice, M. (2003). French-English bilingual children with SLI: How do they compare with their monolingual peers? *Journal of Speech, Language, and Hearing Research, 46*, 113–127. https://doi.org/10.1044/1092-4388(2003/009)

Peña, E., Bedore, L. M., & Rappazzo, C. (2003). Comparison of Spanish, English, and bilingual children's performance across semantic tasks. *Language, Speech & Hearing Services in Schools, 34*, 5–16. https://doi.org/10.1044/0161-1461(2003/001)

Peña, E. D., Gutiérrez-Clellen, V. F., Iglesias, A., Goldstein, B. A., & Bedore, L. M. (2018). *BESA: Bilingual English-Spanish Assessment*. Brookes.

Restrepo, M. A. (1998). Identifiers of predominantly Spanish-speaking children with language impairment. *Journal of Speech, Language, and Hearing Research, 41*, 1398–1411. https://doi.org/10.1044/jslhr.4106.1398

Shipley, K., & McAfee, J. (2020). *Assessment in speech-language pathology: A resource manual* (6th ed.). Plural Publishing.

Smit, A., Hand, L., Freilinger, J., Bernthal, J., & Bird, A. (1990). The Iowa Articulation Norms Project and its Nebraska replication. *Journal of Speech and Hearing Disorders, 55*, 779–798. https://doi.org/10.1044/jshd.5504.779

Wiig, E. (2004). *Wiig Assessment of Basic Concepts–English*. Super Duper Publications.

Wiig, E., & Langdon, H. (2006). *Wiig Assessment of Basic Concepts–Spanish*. Super Duper Publications.

Yavas, M., & Goldstein, B. (1998). Phonological assessment and treatment of bilingual speakers. *American Journal of Speech-Language Pathology, 7*, 49–60.

RESONANCE/HYPERTROPHIC TONSILS
CASE 27
Alice: Diagnosing the Cause of Her Resonance Disorder

Robert J. Shprintzen, Karen J. Golding-Kushner, and Ellen R. Cohn

Conceptual Knowledge Areas

This case debunks some widely held misconceptions. First, therapies such as palatal massage, chewing plastic rods, blowing exercises, sucking thickened liquid through a straw, gagging with a tongue blade, and external neck massage cannot eliminate hypernasality. (Nor can speech therapy improve a structurally faulty velopharyngeal valve.) Second, removing hypertrophic tonsils will not increase hypernasality. And third, the presence of a submucous cleft palate does not necessarily require surgery. The case describes the examinations implemented by imaging experts who are able to interpret the anatomy and function of the entire upper airway to assess the roles of hypertrophied tonsils, adenoids, and the velopharyngeal valve in causing abnormal resonance (nasality) and/or articulation errors.

Description of the Case

Reason for Referral

This case describes Alice, first seen by the authors as a 9-year-old female in the third grade. When Alice was age 3 years, an otolaryngologist who had been following her for chronic middle ear disease and middle ear effusion noted a bifid uvula and a presumed submucous cleft palate (Figure 27–1).

The otolaryngologist thought Alice had velopharyngeal insufficiency (VPI) and had referred her to a community private speech-language pathologist (SLP) for speech therapy. The SLP scheduled the child for once-weekly 1-hour therapy sessions. During the therapy sessions, they did palatal massage, chewing plastic rods, blowing exercises, sucking thickened liquid through a

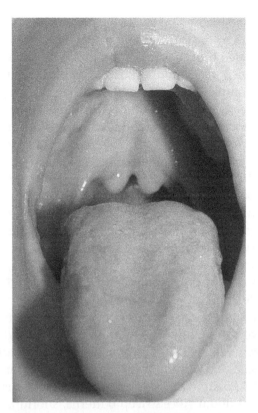

Figure 27–1. Submucous cleft showing a bifid uvula and zona pellucida in the midline of the hard palate.

straw, gagging with a tongue blade, and external neck massage. Because not one of these strategies intended to address resonance-based disorders (i.e., caused by velopharyngeal insufficiency) are supported by evidence-based research, we highly discourage readers from employing any of them. Doing so will delay referral and appropriate treatment.

The report of the evaluation from this therapist noted "nasality" without mentioning how severe it was and without mentioning the presence or observation of nasal air emission or the consistency of the "nasality." According to the mother, after beginning speech therapy at age 3 years, Alice was talking more, but very predictably given the treatment strategies, "nasality" was still present.

In addition to Alice's chronic otitis media, she was noted to have large tonsils described as "kissing tonsils," but the otolaryngologist was concerned about removing them because he thought it might result in more severe VPI. Alice was noted to have loud but intermittent snoring and restless sleep, which included wakening frequently, and substantial movement during sleep, including leg kicking, tossing and turning, and several instances of falling out of bed during the night.

The family lived in an area where the nearest large academic medical center was more than 120 miles away, and they relied on community physicians, dentists, and other health care professionals to provide care for Alice. There was no local specialty program for cleft palate or craniofacial disorders. The best option for speech- and language-based disorders was the public school district. The SLP newly assigned to Alice's elementary school had completed her MA degree in speech-language pathology at a highly regarded graduate program that was ASHA approved. Her degree had required her to take an introductory-level anatomy course that included a description of cleft palate disorders, mention of cleft-related resonance as part of a single-day lecture in a voice disorders class, and a course in sound production disorders that covered articulation impairment, dyspraxia, dysarthria, and developmental disorders. There was unfortunately no requirement for a separate course in cleft or craniofacial anomalies and none was even offered in the curriculum.

During first grade, Alice was absent from school on multiple occasions due to bilateral acute otitis media requiring treatment that was initially with amoxicillin; after the third infection, the prescription was changed to Augmentin, and on the fourth infection to a cephalosporin, Ceclor. For the fifth infection, erythromycin was prescribed. Although each infection responded to immediate treatment, all were followed by recurrences within a month. Therefore, the otolaryngologist suggested a myringotomy with insertion of pressure-equalizing tubes in both ears along with an adenoidectomy, but not a tonsillectomy, because of (misplaced) concern about VPI as a consequence. During the visit to the otolaryngologist, flat tympanograms and a conductive hearing loss of 40 to 50 dB were present in both ears.

The intraoperative report noted effusion in both ears, and permanent tubes were placed. Adenoidectomy was performed. The report did not state if adenoidectomy was complete or partial. A postoperative audiogram done some weeks later showed that hearing was within the normal range, and the tubes were seen to be patent and functioning properly in terms of aerating the middle ear.

Speech remained unchanged. A number of articulation errors were noted by the school SLP, including substitution of /k/ for /t/ and /g/ for /d/, that were also resistant to treatment. The family was concerned that the "nasality" was not responding to speech therapy and asked both the private and public school SLPs why no progress had been made. The school SLP replied that Alice was not motivated. The private therapist suspected often difficult to treat dyspraxia.

The parents decided that solutions were not being offered, and the lack of progress over more than 5 years of treatment was unacceptable, so they went to the Internet for alternative options. They searched the terms "submucous cleft palate," "hypernasal speech," and "speech therapy for nasality." Their search yielded many literature citations, multiple book titles, and a large number of definitions of the disorders on the websites of hundreds of institutions. The search on submucous cleft palate alone yielded hundreds of thousands of hits. After several days of reading material from the Internet, they concluded that they would try to connect with a person or institution that was closest to them or most convenient for an overnight trip. They found one such place in a metropolitan area that was a 140-mile drive but within their state, so that there was a high probability their medical insurance would be accepted, and they could return home without having to spend a night at an expensive hotel. They called and were directed to the institution's craniofacial center. Within a few minutes, they were connected to the director of the craniofacial center who asked them the outcomes so far. The director first suggested that they make an appointment at the craniofacial center for an initial intake to be followed, if appropriate, by two imaging procedures: flexible fiberoptic nasopharyngoscopy and multiview videofluoroscopy. The director took a detailed history and focused on the present treatments implemented by the local community professionals and suggested that the current therapies be discontinued until the evaluation by the craniofacial team was completed. The family was then turned over to a secretary, who arranged an appointment for the procedures recommended by the director, followed by a meeting with the director and the SLP to go over the findings.

The family left their home early in the morning on the Thursday of the first visit and arrived on time for their appointment. They met the center's director and an SLP who participated in the interview and initial examination. A detailed speech and language history was taken first, and then Alice was examined by the director and SLP. The SLP did an oral examination and listened to Alice while reading a passage from a book, during conversation, and when imitating a standardized speech sample. The director did a more detailed physical examination and asked Alice's parents about possible eating and choking problems, as well as about Alice's sleep patterns, snoring, and nighttime awakenings. The parents noticed that when the SLP first looked in Alice's mouth, she said, "oh my" and called over the director, who nodded silently. The director then asked the parents if tonsillectomy had ever been considered, and the parents said that everyone who had seen Alice previously warned that removing the tonsils could cause a worse speech disorder than was already present. The parents were also asked about food preferences and related that Alice tended to prefer things that did not require a lot of chewing, that she occasionally choked on foods that were more difficult to chew such as meats, and that eating usually took a long time compared to the rest of her family. They also discussed her snoring and sleep disturbance. They related that when she had her adenoidectomy and myringotomy and tube procedure, there was no change in her eating or sleeping, and her speech was unaffected.

At this point, the director asked the SLP if a brief articulation test could be done prior to the nasopharyngoscopy. It was, and about 30 minutes later, the family was told that the nasopharyngoscopy would be done at that point and the family could have lunch afterward before the videofluoroscopy. The director and the SLP brought Alice over to a chair that looked like a dental chair and asked her to sit there. They described what the nasopharyngoscopy was going to be like. The director told Alice that they would start by putting a piece of cotton in her nose using a pair of "tweezers." The tweezers were actually very slender forceps, but the examiners liked to explain things to children using words with which they would be familiar. The director told Alice that she might feel a little tickle in her nose like she had a "booger" there but that the cotton had a medicine on it that would make it so that her nose would not feel anything. The director then showed Alice the flexible endoscope and told her that if she did not feel the cotton, she would not feel the endoscope. Alice noticed she was facing a TV and that there was another TV behind her. The director told her that the TV in front of her was for Alice to watch the inside of her nose and throat, and the one behind her was for everyone else to see. The director and the SLP put on latex gloves again and started the video system and a video recorder. They asked Alice to hold a microphone so her speech would also be recorded on the video. The director then brought over the forceps and a thin strip of cotton about 3 inches long and showed it to Alice. The director dipped the cotton in a blue solution (pontocaine) and twisted the cotton so it was even thinner and brought it over to Alice's nose and asked her to smell it so she could see it had no odor. The director then told her that the cotton, which looked like blue spaghetti, would be slid into her nose using the forceps and left there for a few minutes until her nose was numb. This was done, and Alice cooperated perfectly, at first being a bit tense, but when she realized that she did not feel anything, she cooperated and relaxed. About 5 minutes later, the director pulled the end of the cotton that was hanging out of Alice's nose to remove it and told her she should watch the TV as the endoscope was slid into her nose. The director guided the endoscope through the turbinates and into the nasopharynx, describing all that was being seen on the TV. The SLP then had Alice repeat some sounds, words, and phrases. As Alice saw the structures of her palate and pharynx move, she giggled. "Is that me?"

The director then advanced the instrument into the oropharynx and hypopharynx, saying, "There they are." The SLP said, "They [the tonsils] are blocking most of the airway and touching the arytenoids on the left!" The director then visualized the vocal cords and asked Alice to say a high-pitched "eeeeeee." The endoscope was withdrawn and the director placed his hand in front of Alice and said, "Give me five," which Alice did immediately.

The parents were told to go to lunch and then return in an hour, at which time the director would take them to the Department of Radiology for videofluoroscopy. After the family left for lunch, the director and the SLP reviewed the video recording of the endoscopy with the resident present. Alice and her parents returned and were escorted to the Department of Radiology, where they were brought to a fluoroscopy room for the multiview assessment of the velopharyngeal mechanism. The SLP brought Alice into the fluoroscopy suite and explained the procedure. With the fluoroscopy table positioned horizontally, Alice was given a lead apron to wear and then placed on the table in a supine position. Strawberry-flavored barium was mixed to the consistency of heavy cream and, using a pipette, several milliliters of barium were squirted into each side of the nose. Then, with the patient still supine, the image intensifier was passed over Alice's face, about 2 feet over her head, and a quick look under fluoroscopy was done to be sure the pharynx was well coated with barium. The SLP stood close to Alice for moral support and to explain everything that was being done. Alice held the SLP's hand and a microphone on her chest with the other hand. The SLP told Alice to look straight up in order to obtain the frontal (P-A) view and then asked Alice to repeat the same series of sounds, words, and phrases that were used during nasopharyngoscopy. The radiology technician outside of the fluoroscopy suite operated the video recorder. Once the first set of phrases was completed, Alice was asked to turn over in a sphinx-like position with her chin elevated, the SLP stood at the end of the table in front of Alice, and the speech sample was repeated for the base view. Alice was then told to lie on her back and the table was rotated to an upright vertical position and Alice was turned 90°, and the SLP stood in front of Alice and asked her to hold the microphone and repeat the speech sample for a third time. This final fluoroscopic position, the lateral (midsagittal) view, was completed and reviewed quickly to make sure all the necessary information was obtained. Alice was taken back to her parents, and the director asked them to return to his office to go over everything.

Results of Imaging Assessment

Nasopharyngoscopy

The nasal surface of the soft palate had a deep midline groove indicative of a separation of the muscle fibers on the nasal surface of the soft palate, confirming the presence of a submucous cleft (Croft et al., 1978; Shprintzen et al., 1985). There was a remnant of adenoid tissue on the posterior pharyngeal wall that was just slightly above the soft palate (Figure 27–2).

It was unclear if there was regrowth of the adenoid or if a prior surgical procedure had been a partial adenoidectomy to remove the tissue in close proximity to the eustachian tube orifice. During the repetition of words and phrase with nonnasal sounds (sounds other than m, n, ŋ), a small leak of air was seen in the midline of the soft palate as it approximated the base of the adenoid mass remaining in the nasopharynx. However, during the production of words and phrases with an /s/ or /z/ sound, the gap through which the air leak occurred was larger and the airflow became audible, which was not true for other pressure consonants. As the endoscope was advanced into the oropharynx, the upper pole of both tonsils immediately became visible, and during speech production, the lateral edges of the velum could be seen compressing the tonsils against the posterior pharyngeal wall, thereby partially inhibiting the velum from making a broad contact against the posterior pharynx. Lateral pharyngeal wall motion could not be visualized because the tonsils blocked the view bilaterally (Figure 27–3). The

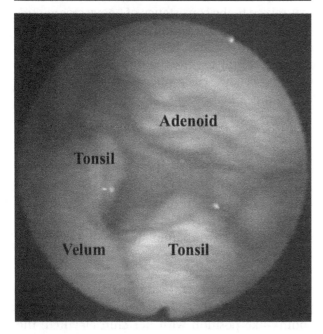

Figure 27–2. Tonsils and adenoid with the tonsils extending into the nasopharynx behind the velum (soft palate).

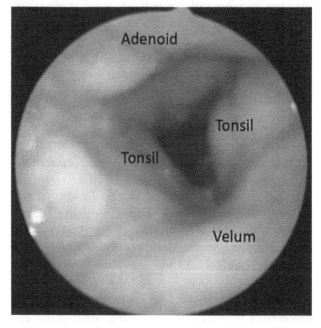

Figure 27–3. Tonsils blocking the lateral pharyngeal walls bilaterally.

tonsils were also seen to extend inferiorly to the level of the arytenoid cartilages, and on the left side, the tonsil completely obstructed the pyriform sinus. Vocal cord function was normal.

Multiview Videofluoroscopy

The fluoroscopic procedure provided a three-dimensional view of the entire pharynx from three different angles so that the entire speech mechanism relative to velopharyngeal constriction could be seen. The first thing the examiners noted was variability of movement during the different sounds in the speech samples and abnormal tongue positions for front and back pressure consonants. The tonsils were well coated with barium, and they could be seen extending posteriorly behind the soft palate, interfering with its contact to the posterior pharyngeal wall. The adenoids were not obstructing the nasopharyngeal airway. The tonsils could be seen intruding posteriorly behind the velum, preventing the velum from contacting the posterior pharynx (Figure 27–4).

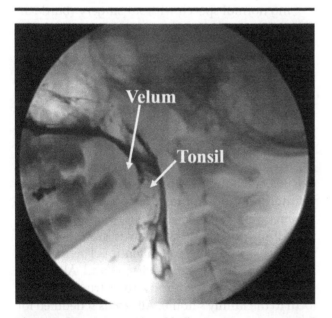

Figure 27–4. Lateral videofluoroscopic image of tonsils posterior to the velum during speech preventing the velum from approximating to the posterior pharynx or adenoid.

The lateral pharyngeal wall motion also seemed to be inhibited by the tonsillar location. Airflow into the nasopharynx could be seen but was variable depending on the sound being produced. The lateral video videofluoroscopic image during speech showed the tonsils sat posterior to the velum and were physically preventing the velum from approximating to the posterior pharynx or adenoid.

Results of Speech Evaluation

An articulation screening prior to the imaging studies revealed variable hypernasal and hyponasal resonance relative to speech sound production, as well as an odd pattern of articulatory substitutions, including tongue backing for front placement pressure sounds /p/, /b/, /t/, and /d/. Increased nasal air escape was seen on /s/ and /f/. Resonance was "muffled," often described as "potato in the mouth" resonance. (The therapists who had been previously providing treatment erroneously labeled this muffled quality as hypernasality.) Nasal occlusion during an imitated speech sample of nonnasal sounds did not alter the resonance of speech, but it did eliminate the short bursts of audible nasal air emission on anterior pressure phonemes. Nasal occlusion also did not alter resonance during normally nasal phoneme production for /m/, /n/, and /ŋ/, although it should have, consistent with the hyponasal resonance that was observed.

Conclusions and Recommendations

In reviewing the data obtained in the evaluation, the clinicians' conclusions were as follows:

1. The nasal air escape was being caused by the hypertrophic tonsils interfering with the movements of the velum and the lateral pharyngeal walls. The resonance pattern was caused by the tonsils obstructing the majority of the hypopharyngeal and oropharyngeal airway, thereby preventing both normal oral

resonance and even normal nasal resonance for nasalized phonemes.

2. The abnormal articulatory pattern was caused by a learning error induced by the partial airway obstruction caused primarily by the tonsils. The backing pattern on anterior sounds was caused by the easy path to retract the tongue slightly to cause a pressure consonant, whereas moving the tongue anteriorly was likely causing some anterior displacement of the tonsils decreasing oral airflow for anterior pressure consonant production.

3. The recommendation of the otolaryngologist to do an adenoidectomy but to leave the tonsils in place was rejected as an appropriate course of action. The tonsils were clearly severely hypertrophic. Tonsillar size was being reported based only on oral examination and, because most of the tonsillar tissue had grown behind the tonsillar pillars, both up into the nasopharynx and also down into the hypopharynx, they could not be fully visualized by looking in the mouth. The conclusion is that rating tonsillar size based on growth toward the midline is not adequate for determining a pathological state; the endoscopic and/or radiographic views of their size and position in the airway are also needed. They can grow posteriorly into the pharyngeal airway even though their attachment is in the oral cavity between the faucial pillars. This can be assessed endoscopically by an experienced endoscopist who knows how to maneuver a fiber-optic instrument from side to side in addition to looking at the midline of the pharynx. This tonsillar phenomenon is quite common, especially in people with muffled oral resonance and also in individuals who prefer soft foods over foods that are more difficult to chew and spend more time in the mouth before swallowing, thereby reducing breathing space. Reports of resonance disorders related to tonsillar hypertrophy have been available for more than 35 years (Shprintzen et al., 1987; MacKenzie-Stepner et al., 1987). Also, because this case had a submucous cleft as confirmed by the endoscopy, adenoid removal could have certainly prompted VPI, while ton-

sillectomy is not known to unmask VPI and would only cause a problem if there were surgical complications that would extend to the velum or the faucial pillars. This was exactly the opposite of what the ENT had said.

4. The recommendation after complete evaluation was for tonsillectomy without further adenoidectomy, speech reevaluation 1 month after surgery, and follow-up endoscopy 3 months after surgery. The rationale was to eliminate the physical obstruction of the tonsils while leaving the adenoids in place as the primary contact point for the velum as seen in lateral view videofluoroscopy. Because the lateral walls were also moving based on fluoroscopic assessment, although also partially obstructed by the tonsils, the thought was that the tonsillectomy was necessary regardless of the speech outcome. Data have demonstrated that performing tonsillectomy prior to pharyngeal reconstruction for VPI reduces the risk of postoperative obstructive sleep apnea (OSA) dramatically (Chegar et al., 2007). Furthermore, the decision was also based on most people with submucous cleft palate having normal speech without surgery (Bardach, 1995, p. 280; Shprintzen et al., 1985).

Posttonsillectomy Outcomes

One month following tonsillectomy, Alice returned for follow-up speech assessment. The muffled oral resonance that had been a prominent feature of Alice's speech was no longer present, and there was no clinical evidence of nasal air escape for normally nonnasal pressure consonants. Alice's parents were very pleased. Snoring during sleep had diminished, and Alice was sleeping better with fewer episodes of awakening. The articulation errors, of course, persisted, and Alice was referred for speech therapy to a trusted source local to the family's home. Alice was scheduled for therapy three times each week for 30 minutes per session with specific assignments for the parents to reinforce the normal sound productions being taught in therapy. Alice was scheduled for follow-up nasopharyngoscopy 2 months after this visit.

At the next follow-up visit, nasopharyngoscopy was performed in the same manner as the first study. Entering the nasopharynx, once again the midline groove of the velum was evident and the adenoid was seen posteriorly in the pharynx occupying approximately 50% of the postnasal space. On repetition of the standardized speech sample, the velum made broad contact against the posterior pharyngeal wall, and the lateral pharyngeal walls were seen to move medially almost to the midline, resulting in a circular closure pattern (Shprintzen & Golding-Kushner, 1989; Siegel-Sadewitz & Shprintzen, 1982; Skolnick et al., 1973). Alice had made excellent progress with her articulation therapy with almost complete elimination of the abnormal substitution pattern shown on first evaluation.

Alice was seen twice more, 6 months and 2 years later, at the age of 13 years, after the onset of puberty and significant adult-like facial growth changes. Her history of middle ear disease had resolved, and it was more than 18 months since her last ear infection. She had normal articulation and resonance, and speech therapy had been discontinued shortly after her last visit. The family was advised against any additional recommendation for adenoidectomy and that if there was any additional evidence of otitis media, it should be treated symptomatically or with myringotomy and tubes, if recurrent, but not to have adenoid removal.

Clinical Implications

This case points out a number of important issues. The first is that the submucous cleft palate became the obvious focus of attention related to the possibility that the patient's speech was hypernasal. While this is something that obviously requires investigation, it must be understood that the majority of people with submucous cleft palate have normal speech without need for surgical repair. The second is that the presence of hypertrophic tonsils can frequently cause resonance disorders, both oral and nasal. That some people believe that tonsillectomy is contraindicated in people with clefts is an error. Tonsils do not con-

tribute positively to velopharyngeal closure, and removal of tonsils will not impair nasal resonance and may in some cases eliminate VPI (MacKenzie-Stepner et al., 1987; Shprintzen et al., 1987).

It is also important that the presence of submucous cleft palate not be an indication for early palate repair before the onset of speech because most people with submucous clefts develop normal speech rendering surgery unnecessary.

We strongly recommend both nasopharyngoscopy and multiview videofluoroscopy as essential to fully understand the complete picture of VPI in essentially all cases (Golding-Kushner et al., 1990). Neither procedure alone provides all of the information required to determine specificity of the surgical approach to VPI.

Finally, when the parents had asked both SLPs why Alice was not making progress after 5 years of therapy, they both "blamed" Alice (she was "not motivated" or she must have "dyspraxia"), rather than asking themselves if the presumed diagnosis was accurate and if the treatment and therapy procedures were correct. The first assumption should never be that the client is the problem.

Authors' Note

Alice is a hypothetical client who illustrates actual clinical findings seen in a large sampling of cases drawn from the authors' clinical experiences.

References

Bardach, J. (1995). Secondary surgery for velopharyngeal insufficiency. In R. J. Shprintzen & J. Bardach (Eds.), *Cleft palate speech management: A multidisciplinary approach* (p. 280). Mosby.

Chegar, B. E., Shprintzen, R. J., Curtis, M. S., & Tatum, S. A. (2007). Pharyngeal flap and obstructive apnea: Maximizing speech outcome while limiting complications. *Archives of Facial Plastic Surgery, 9,* 252–259. https://doi.org/10.1001/archfaci.9.4.252

Croft, C. B., Shprintzen, R. J., Daniller, A. I., & Lewin, M. L. (1978). The occult submucous cleft palate and the musculus uvuli. *Cleft Palate Journal, 15,* 150–154.

Golding-Kushner, K. J., Argamaso, R. V., Cotton, R. T., Grames, L. M., Henningsson, G., Jones, D. L., . . . Skolnick, M. L. (1990). Standardization for the reporting of nasopharyngoscopy and multi-view videofluoroscopy: A report from an international working group. *Cleft Palate Journal, 27*, 337–347. https://doi.org/10.1597/1545-1569(1990)027<0337:sftron>2.3.co;2

MacKenzie-Stepner, K., Witzel, M. A., Stringer, D. A., & Laskin, R. I. (1987). Velopharyngeal insufficiency due to hypertrophic tonsils: A report of two cases. *International Journal of Pediatric Otorhinolaryngology, 14*, 57–63. https://doi.org/10.1016/0165-5876(87)90050-4

Shprintzen, R. J., & Golding-Kushner, K. J. (1989). Evaluation of velopharyngeal insufficiency. *Otolaryngologic Clinics of North America, 22*(3), 519–536.

Shprintzen, R. J., Schwartz, R., Daniller, A., & Hoch, L. (1985). Morphologic significance of bifid uvula. *Pediatrics, 75*, 553–561. https://doi.org/10.1542/peds.75.3.553

Shprintzen, R. J., Sher, A. E., & Croft, C. B. (1987). Hypernasal speech caused by hypertrophic tonsils. *International Journal of Pediatric Otorhinolaryngology, 14*, 45–56. https://doi.org/10.1016/0165-5876(87)90049-8

Siegel-Sadewitz, V., & Shprintzen, R. J. (1982). The relationship of communication disorders to syndrome identification. *Journal of Speech and Hearing Disorders, 47*(4), 338–354. https://doi: 10.1044/jshd.4704.338

Skolnick, M. L., McCall, G. N., & Barnes, M. (1973). *The Cleft Palate Journal, 10*, 296–305.

HEARING LOSS
CASE 28
Jon: Assessing and Supporting the Speech, Language, and Literacy Skills of a School-Age Child With Late Identified Hearing Loss

Wilder M. Roberts and Victoria S. Henbest

Conceptual Knowledge Areas

It is estimated that approximately two to three children per 1,000 are born deaf or hard of hearing (DHH) each year in the United States and of those, 90% are born to hearing parents (U.S. National Institutes of Health [NIH], 2021). Children who are DHH are at risk for delayed and disordered speech, spoken language, and literacy development, even if the degree of hearing loss is minimal (Bess et al., 1998). For parents who have chosen spoken language as the communication mode for their children who are DHH, a number of factors such as age at identification, age of intervention, severity of loss, parent involvement, and classroom acoustics may impact the child's success with learning spoken and written language (American Speech-Language-Hearing Association, 1997–2022; Tomblin et al., 2015; U.S. NIH, 2005; Wolfe et al., 2013). Children who are DHH may have particular difficulty with marking grammatical morphemes (e.g., -ing, plural "s," past tense -ed) and vocabulary development in spoken language (Trussell & Easterbrooks, 2017). They also may not easily develop phonological awareness skills, including the ability to think about and manipulate individual speech sounds (i.e., phonemic awareness), critical to successful reading and spelling (Lund et al., 2015; Runnion & Gray, 2019). While the severity of hearing loss in children can range from minimal to profound, all levels will impact communication and academic success (ASHA, 1997–2022).

The timing of identification of hearing loss is critical. Children who are identified by 6 months and receive intervention have better outcomes than those identified later (Yoshinaga-Itano et al., 1998). According to Holstrum et al. (2008), even children who experience minimal to mild hearing loss require early identification and intervention to support their communication needs; these children are the least likely to be identified early. Children who are DHH and wear hearing aids full-time (i.e., 10+ hours/day) may have grammar and vocabulary skills similar to children with normal hearing, whereas children who do not wear hearing aids consistently, regardless of degree of hearing loss, are at risk for poorer language skills (Walker et al., 2015).

Ideally, management of hearing loss should include the coordination of a number of individuals, including but not limited to clinical and school audiologists, otolaryngologists, speech-language pathologists (SLPs), teachers of the deaf (TODs), parents and other family members, classroom teachers, principals, and special education teams (Garber & Nevins, 2012). While there is scant research on the impact of audiologist, teacher, and SLP-based collaborations, such interaction is within their scopes of practice (Ukstins & Welling, 2017). Research has shown collaboration to be effective in improving the language outcomes of children in the school setting (e.g., Henbest et al., 2019; Mitchell et al., 2022). Unfortunately, collaboration is often not the case. School-based SLPs and audiologists may have limited professional relationships with care providers outside of the school setting, leading to gaps in the coordination of services needed for successful management of children's hearing loss. Geographical access to health care service also may limit coordination.

Description of the Case

Jon was identified late, at the age of 6 years, with a mild hearing loss. Currently, at the age of 9, he continues to have difficulty with speech sound production and is falling behind in school. Jon has deficits in speech, language, and literacy develop-ment. We provide a detailed overview of the child's history of clinical services as well as the impact of a lack of coordination of services between Jon's family and clinical providers. Included is a description of audiological and speech and language assessments at the age of 9 years and the subsequent implementation of a coordinated intervention plan developed between the school-based SLP, family, and external clinical audiologist.

Background Information

Jon, a 9-year-old boy, had been living in a rural town with his parents and younger sister. He was attending the local school prior to his diagnosis of bilateral hearing loss. Jon had a history of recurrent otitis media with pressure equalization (PE) tube placement, failed hearing screenings, and speech-language difficulties. He was enrolled in early intervention prior to attending school and received speech services for articulation at his school. By first grade, he was not meeting grade-level reading standards, so his mother brought him to his ENT physician complaining that he was not hearing well. Testing at that time indicated bilateral mild hearing loss (see the audiogram shown in Figure 28–1), and he was referred to the speech and hearing center at the local university for a comprehensive audiologic evaluation.

That evaluation confirmed a bilateral mild hearing loss and that Jon was a candidate for bilateral hearing aids. Medical clearance for hearing aids was obtained from the ENT physician. He was fit with hearing aids in both ears, and his mother extensively counseled that Jon should wear his hearing aids during all waking hours and not only in the school setting.

An ear-level FM System was recommended, and his audiologist, who had previous experience working in the public school setting, told Jon's mother that the FM System should be provided by the school under the Individuals with Disabilities Education Act (IDEA, 2006) as assistive technology. An FM System (formerly known as frequency modulated) is actually now a digital signal (RF) that uses a microphone (transmitter) worn by the teacher that wirelessly delivers a signal captured

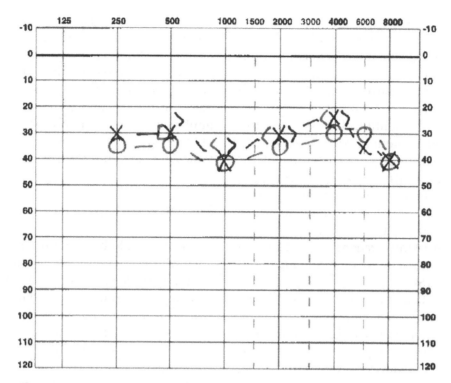

Figure 28–1. Pure-tone audiogram 1 (mild loss). Threshold in decibels (dB) on *y*-axis; frequency (Hz) on *x*-axis. O = right ear. X = left ear.

by the microphone to the receivers in the child's hearing aids. Because Jon's hearing aids have an integrated FM receiver, they are compatible with an educational-grade FM microphone system to be worn by the teacher. At his follow-up appointment, Jon's mother reported benefit from the hearing aids, noting his teachers have seen increased classroom participation. Datalogging, however, indicated only 2.5 hours of use daily. Consistent daily use of hearing aids was emphasized to Jon's mother and to Jon.

Jon returned to the speech and hearing center for routine monitoring approximately 6 months later. His mother reported that he was repeating first grade. An FM System had not yet been provided by the school. Jon's mother was concerned that his hearing had gotten worse. His hearing was retested and had indeed worsened to a mild-to-moderate hearing loss (Figure 28–2).

Jon's hearing aids were reprogrammed to accommodate this change in hearing. Comprehensive speech and language services and the use of an FM System in the classroom were again recommended. Given the number of speech sound errors impacting Jon's intelligibility, clinic-based speech services were also recommended. A letter detailing the need for an FM System and school-based speech services was sent to his school.

Datalogging showed hearing aid use now averaged 3.5 hours per day. His mother stated that she often allowed Jon to decide if he needed to wear his hearing aids. She and Jon were counseled on the importance of full-time use of hearing aids and the concept of "eyes open, ears on." Over several monitoring appointments, datalogging of hearing aid wear time was 6 hours of daily use. Jon's wear time of his hearing aids had improved, but he had not achieved full-time use, which is considered 90% of hours awake. Jon and his mother were praised for the improvement and encouraged to continue to the goal of full-time use.

At his last appointment, Jon's lack of academic progress was discussed, including retention in the first grade and his current academic performance.

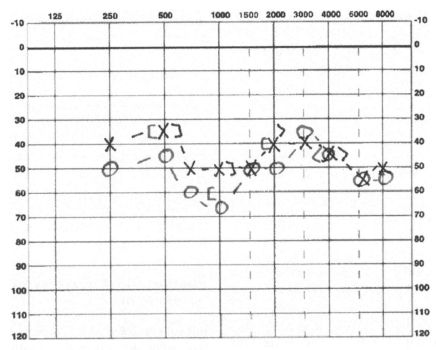

Figure 28–2. Pure-tone audiogram 2 (mild-to-moderate loss). Threshold in decibels (dB) on *y*-axis; frequency (Hz) on *x*-axis. O = right ear. X = left ear.

The audiologist discussed the correlation between hearing loss and language impairment, including late identified hearing loss. Because Jon's previous and current speech services focused on his speech intelligibility, the audiologist administered the Clinical Evaluation of Language Fundamentals–5th Edition Screening Test (CELF-5ST; Wiig et al., 2013). At the time, Jon was 8 years old, and a criterion-referenced passing score was considered 17. Jon scored a 6, indicating the need for comprehensive language testing. Jon had difficulty on all subtests. The results were discussed with Jon's mother.

Referral for Spoken Language and Literacy Evaluation

At 9 years of age, Jon's family moved to a different home within the same rural school district at the beginning of his second grade year, which meant he would attend a different school. His new teacher observed academic difficulties, particularly in language arts and reading. This was her first experience having a child with hearing loss in her class, so Jon's mother contacted her for a conference to familiarize her with Jon's hearing loss and past difficulties. At this time, Jon also was due for his 3-year special education reevaluation. He had been receiving school-based speech services since early childhood, although his hearing loss was unknown at that time. The speech-language pathologist (SLP) at his new school was a recent graduate and in her clinical fellowship year (i.e., first year of practice). Upon reading Jon's audiologic evaluation records and Individualized Education Program (IEP), she became concerned with his current services. The SLP was aware that children who are DHH may be at significant risk for literacy impairment, and she noted that Jon had been receiving speech articulation services for *only* 30 minutes per week and on the CELF-5ST screener (Wiig et al., 2013), he scored well below the cutoff. She thought it was odd that his eligibility for receiving special education services was under "speech and language impairment" and not under "deaf or hard of hearing." She brought her concerns regarding his eligibility classification to the lead special education resource teacher.

Evaluation

Case History: School Records

According to school records, Jon had received special education services for a brief time in preschool. There was no record of a full psychoeducational testing battery. His initial eligibility report stated he had passed his hearing screening. Since kindergarten, Jon had received 30 minutes of articulation therapy per week in a school-based group. Though he had repeated first grade, his file did not contain information about his reading level. The SLP therefore reached out to his former teacher, who reported that Jon had consistently struggled with foundational literacy skills. He had difficulty learning alphabet letters, reading basic words, and his spelling skills were below those of his classmates. His current second-grade teacher also reported poor spelling skills.

Case History: The Audiologist

In preparation for Jon's reevaluation, with his mother's consent, his new SLP contacted his clinical audiologist to obtain information related to his hearing. The audiologist reported that Jon did not receive hearing aids until the spring of his first-grade year. There was a substantial lag between determining candidacy and when he was fit with hearing aids. She explained that Jon's late diagnosis of hearing loss, combined with limited wear of his hearing aids (according to datalogging), were likely the largest contributors to his limited academic progress. The audiologist and school SLP met via videoconferencing so that the audiologist could discuss the audiological documentation, as well as research on the importance of wearing hearing aids during all waking hours. The audiologist posited that Jon's specific hearing loss was negatively impacting his speech perception and language comprehension.

Spoken Language Evaluation

As recommended by the audiologist, prior to evaluating Jon's spoken and written language skills, the SLP conducted a hearing aid check and low-middle-high (LMH) frequency sound check (Madell, 2021) to determine whether Jon could perceive and/or produce the following phonemes: /u/, /a/, /i/(ee), /m/, /ʃ/, /s/, /dʒ/, /h/, /n/. Jon detected all sounds, although he produced /ʃ/ and /s/ incorrectly, as expected.

Standardized Norm-Referenced Assessment

Jon's receptive and expressive spoken language skills were formally assessed with the CELF-5 (Wiig et al., 2013). Jon's scaled and standard scores are provided in Table 28–1. Scaled scores between 7 and 13 and standard scores between 85 and 115 represent the average range. The percentile rank indicates the percentage of students who would be expected to perform similarly or below Jon (e.g., a percentile rank of 50 indicates performance that is the same as or better than 50% of children who complete this assessment).

Jon's performance on the CELF-5 was consistent with what the audiologist shared about his performance on the CELF-5ST. His receptive and expressive language indices as well as his Core Language Score were more than 2 standard deviations below the mean, indicating spoken language skills significantly below his same-age peers.

As recommended by the audiologist, the SLP readministered some of the receptive items from the CELF-5 employing "acoustic highlighting" when prompting a response. Acoustic highlighting, a technique used in auditory verbal therapy, is when a specific sound or word is emphasized in speech in various ways to render it more audible (Estabrooks et al., 2020). The SLP used the following strategies: She sat in close proximity next to Jon, used acoustic highlighting via a slowed rate of speech, and emphasized key words/sounds

Table 28–1. Jon's CELF-5 Scores

CELF-5 Subtest	Item Example	Scaled or Standard Score	Percentile Rank	Compared to Same-Aged Peers
Word Classes (WC)	"Tell me the two words that go together: milk, apple, banana" (Wiig et al., 2013, p. 47).	4	2	Well below
Following Directions (FD)	"Point to the pictures in the order I tell you. Point to the circle and a square" (Wiig et al., 2013, p. 52).	4	2	Well below
Formulated Sentences (FS)	"Make a sentence about this picture using the word ___" (Wiig et al., 2013, p. 56).	4	2	Well below
Recalling Sentences (RS)	The child is asked to repeat sentences spoken by the examiner: "listen carefully and say exactly what I say" (Wiig et al., 2013, p. 75).	3	1	Well below
Sentence Assembly (SA)	"Make two sentences using the words I show you: saw, the girl, the boy . . . now make a different sentence with those words" (Wiig et al., 2013, p. 94).	3	1	Well below
Semantic Relationships (SR)	"Listen to this question and the possible answers . . . tell me the two answers that are correct . . . Jan saw Pedro. Dwayne saw Francis. Who was seen?" (Wiig et al., 2013, p. 98).	5	5	Well below
Receptive Language Index	Sum of Scaled Scores for WC, FD, and SR	69	2	Well below
Expressive Language Index	Sum of Scaled Scores for FS, RS, and SA	61	0.5	Well below
Core Language Score	Sum of Scaled Scores for WC, FS, RS, SR	66	1	Well below

when readministering a sample of items from the CELF-5 (e.g., "Point to the houseES" with care not to increase the volume of her voice, but rather to lean in closer to Jon and lowlight the vowels). Speaking more softly increases the volume of the voiceless consonants in a word. She also highlighted the voiceless consonant by prolonging the production of that consonant. Jon's receptive performance inconsistently improved with acoustic highlighting. For example, on the Following Directions subtest, Jon initially selected

the incorrect item for "Point to the last circle. Go" (Wiig et al., 2013, p. 53), but when prompted with "Point to the *last* circle," he selected the correct corresponding picture. In this example, *last* is used with a pause before and after the word. The word is given with a slight change in pitch, similar to parentese (Saint-Georges et al., 2013), to add emphasis to the key word. However, for some other items on this same subtest, when the clinician used appropriate highlighting, his performance did not change.

Speech and Language Sample

Jon's speech and spoken language skills within a communicative context were observed in two settings, with peers in the lunchroom and while explaining to the SLP how to play his favorite game. Consistent with Jon's type and severity of hearing loss as well as the errors documented on his initial evaluation and current IEP, he was observed to delete or distort fricative sounds when explaining how to play the game. Cluster reduction was observed for consonant blends that contained a voiced and voiceless consonant; he almost always deleted the voiceless consonant (e.g., /-mɛl/for /smɛl/; /-le/ for /ple/). Both consonants were deleted when attempting to produce words with clusters containing two voiceless consonants, and final voiceless singleton consonants were often deleted (e.g., /--a-/ for /stap/). To assess intelligibility, Jon was audio-recorded naming 10 picture cards. A nonfamiliar listener wrote down the 10 words they heard; they understood 3 of the 10 words.

Jon was observed to produce lengthy utterances so there was no concern regarding his mean length of utterance (MLU). However, the parts of his utterances that were intelligible appeared to be run-ons with an overuse of the coordinating conjunction "and" to describe the procedure for playing his favorite game (e.g., "You have to roll the dice and count and take your turn and play the game." [Jon's speech errors are not represented in this example]). He did not use any subordinating conjunctions or temporal terms when describing the procedure. Jon exhibited difficulty answering questions, particularly questions that required him to infer information. Instead, he would change the topic as an avoidance strategy. Nonspecific vocabulary use (e.g., it, this, there) was noted.

When Jon was observed during lunch, his peers turned away from him to talk to one another, leaving Jon out of the conversation. Jon did not seem to notice his friends' rejection and kept talking, which appeared to frustrate them. On more than one occasion, his peers rolled their eyes and said "never mind" when attempting to converse with Jon.

Written Language Evaluation

Phonological Awareness. The Elision and Blending Words subtests from the Comprehensive Test of Phonological Processing–2nd Edition (CTOPP-2; Wagner et al., 2013) were administered to assess Jon's phonological awareness, an important oral metalinguistic skill foundational to word-level reading and spelling success. The Elision task required Jon to say a word and then say what is left of the word after dropping out designated syllables or sounds (e.g., "Say bold. Now say bold without saying /b/"). The Blending Words task required that Jon listen to sounds in isolation and then blend them together to make a word (e.g., /m/-/ æ/-/d/ > mad). On these measures, standard scores between 7 and 13 are considered the average range.

Word-Level Literacy. Word-level reading was measured using two subtests from the Woodcock Reading Mastery Tests–Third Edition (WRMT-3; Woodcock, 2011). The Word Identification subtest measured Jon's ability to read single real words in isolation, and the Word Attack subtest measured his ability to decode single nonwords. Standard scores between 85 and 115 are considered the average range.

The Test of Written Spelling–Fifth Edition (TWS-5; Larsen et al., 2013) was administered to assess Jon's word-level spelling skills. This task required that he spell to dictation. The examiner said a word in isolation, used it in a sentence, and then said the word again in isolation. Standard scores between 85 and 115 are considered the average range.

Reading Comprehension. Jon's silent reading comprehension was measured using the Passage Comprehension subtest of the WRMT-3 (Woodcock, 2011). This subtest required that he read increasingly complex sentences/passages silently and then state the correct word that fit in the blank space of each sentence or passage. Standard scores between 85 and 115 are considered the average range.

Jon's performance on the measures of phonological awareness and written language are presented in Table 28–2. As with the CELF-5, Jon's performance on the measures of phonological awareness and written language were in the significantly low range.

Oral Reading of Connected Text. Jon's teacher provided a second-grade-level text and a text one grade level below. The SLP had a copy of the books' transcripts to conduct a miscue analysis while he was reading. Even with encouragement and ensuring that he was not being assessed for a grade, Jon was reluctant to read aloud. While reading, he was noted to use a "guess and go" strategy in that he would guess the word based on the first letter or couple of letters in the word. He also appeared to be using the pictures to guess the words. When applying this strategy, the word guessed was never the correct one. Jon was not observed to apply decoding strategies when he came to a word he did not know. His performance was minimally better reading the first-grade passage.

Classroom Spelling/Writing Samples. The SLP reviewed Jon's classroom folder that included his morning journal entries and spelling tests. She noticed that Jon's journal entries were brief (i.e., five sentences or fewer) and contained no complex sentences with more than one verb, which would be expected at his age. Consistent with observations of his spoken language, Jon used nonspecific vocabulary words (e.g., it, this, there) in his writing where specific referents would have been needed to express the meaning of the sentence clearly (e.g., "it got their ball" [spelling errors are not represented in this example]). Jon did not use punctuation, and he spelled very few words correctly. He was observed to use the same word to describe an action or an object throughout the sample, which made the SLP wonder if Jon may have avoided words he could not spell or if his hearing loss impacted his vocabulary.

Spelling Error Analysis. Jon was asked to spell several words to dictation that contained a variety of spelling patterns he would be expected to know at his age and grade, including the spelling of multimorphemic words. To determine the linguistic nature of his spelling errors, the SLP analyzed his spelling attempts and found that for several words, Jon often did not represent every sound in the word with a letter (e.g., "go" for "got"), a finding that indicates potential phonemic awareness difficulty (Henbest & Apel, 2021; Masterson & Apel, 2010). This corroborated Jon's low performance on the CTOPP-2. He represented some consonant phonemes with the correct letter and had little difficulty representing short vowels and consonant sounds when only one vowel or consonant letter was required. Jon did not spell any multimorphemic words correctly and rarely represented long vowels with two vowel letters or adhered to consonant doubling rules when

Table 28–2. Jon's Performance on Measures of Phonological Awareness and Written Language

Skill/Measure	Standard/ Scaled Score	Percentile Rank	Compared to Same-Aged Peers
Phonological Awareness-Elision/CTOPP-2	2	<1	Well below
Phonological Awareness-Blending/CTOPP-2	2	<1	Well below
Word Identification/WRMT-3	64	1	Well below
Word Attack/WRMT-3	60	1	Well below
Spelling/TWS-5	62	1	Well below
Passage (reading) Comprehension/WRMT-3	55	0.1	Well below

required (e.g., "buk" for "books"; "bez" for "bees"; "meld" for "smelled"; "jum" for "jumped"; "runi" for "running"; "bak" for "bake"), suggesting limited morphological awareness skills and knowledge of orthographic patterns.

Recommendations Based on Evaluation

Along with the school-based psychometrist who completed a full psychoeducational battery, the SLP reported the findings of her evaluation to the school-based team. The team determined that Jon's primary eligibility would be categorized under a label of Deaf or Hard of Hearing. He also was determined to meet criteria for Speech and Language Impairment and Specific Learning Disability in Reading.

Treatment Options Considered

The school-based team met with Jon's family to review the results of the evaluation and collaboratively propose a treatment plan. The first option considered was continuing with speech articulation–only intervention 30 minutes per week. That option was quickly dismissed because the significant spoken and written language needs identified during the evaluation could not be adequately addressed in that limited amount of time. Jon was not considered to receive the majority of his instruction in a special education classroom, as that would not be considered his least restrictive environment for interaction with normal-hearing peers in the general education setting. The school professionals proposed that Jon work with the literacy coach in a small group outside of the classroom each day for 30 minutes. Initially, the SLP wanted to support Jon's goals inside the classroom setting twice weekly for 30 minutes to reduce the amount of time he was pulled out, but the university-based clinical audiologist who attended the meeting suggested all speech and/or resource intervention occur in a quiet setting to optimize Jon's speech perception to improve speech production. She also encouraged the team

to consider an increase in Jon's intervention minutes, but Jon's mother was apprehensive about Jon being pulled away from his peers for that much of the school day, as he was on the local baseball team and several of his teammates were in his class. Jon's mother was worried that removing him would alienate him. The team decided that Jon would receive 30 minutes of instruction with the SLP three times each week individually or in a pair. Additionally, the SLP would consult with his teacher and literacy specialist 30 minutes each month to review Jon's progress to ensure alignment of goals and approaches.

Aware of her own minimal training and experience addressing the speech, language, and literacy needs of children who are DHH, the SLP requested school district support to acquire professional development to work with these children. She provided the district with online learning opportunities available to her (e.g., hearingfirst.org). The university-based clinical audiologist offered an in-service training to the IEP team for hearing aid checks, FM System troubleshooting, and understanding an audiogram. Given that the TOD was itinerant, the SLP agreed to be the building-based point person for Jon's immediate daily hearing aid or FM needs. Under assistive technology needs, an FM system would be provided by the school district, to be worn by any teacher interacting with Jon, including teachers in the general education classroom, resource room, speech room, library, PE gym, art room, music room, and so on. Services from a TOD to provide additional support and guidance would be provided under "related services."

Course of Treatment-Direct SLP Services

Priorities for direct service provision included focusing on Jon's speech intelligibility, his morphosyntactic spoken language development, and his word-level reading and spelling. As with the evaluation, prior to the start of each session, the SLP made sure to complete a hearing aid check and an LMH sound check (Madell, 2021) to ensure that Jon had access to speech sounds. She made note of any consistent changes in Jon's responses to the LMH sounds and communicated this with Jon's mother, teacher, and audiologist.

Speech Sound Production

The SLP continued to consult with the clinical audiologist when planning for Jon's speech sound production intervention. Jon had made little progress with traditional speech articulation/phonological intervention, and she suspected that the audiologist might provide some insight. The audiologist explained that traditional articulation and phonological approaches alone were likely to be unsuccessful because Jon's speech sound production was the result of a lengthy history of impoverished auditory input due to his late identified hearing loss and the limited wear of his hearing aids. That is, the basis for his speech production errors may have been due to difficulty perceiving the speech sounds rather than motorically not being able to produce them. As was used in the evaluation, the audiologist encouraged the SLP to use acoustic highlighting and lowlighting as well as the FM System during her sessions with Jon to ensure that his perception of the sounds was not impacting his production. For example, when addressing Jon's deletion of final consonants, the SLP offered a prompt for the missing sound; when Jon stated his team "bee" the Expos at the ballpark, the SLP looked confused and asked, "Your team bee or beaT" the Expos?" She then paused and gave an expectant look to offer Jon another opportunity to produce the correct word. She encouraged additional speech production trials with increased expression by having Jon tell another student in the session about the triumphant win using the word "beat."

Spoken Language and Literacy

The SLP referred to a school-age language and literacy textbook (Ukrainetz, 2015a) as an initial decision-making guide for Jon's spoken language and literacy intervention. She recalled that school-age intervention needed to be explicit, and she wanted to acquire more specifics. Because Jon demonstrated phonemic-based spelling errors and performed poorly on the measures of phonemic awareness, she studied the chapter covering the phonological basis of reading (Ukrainetz, 2015b) as well as the scientific literature, which confirmed that phonemic awareness instruction was a priority, including for children with hearing loss (Runnion & Gray, 2019).

Jon's morphological weaknesses in spoken language production and written spelling were also were determined to be a priority. The SLP remembered talking extensively about morphology in her graduate courses. In particular, one of her instructors emphasized the importance of morphological awareness, the ability to "think about" morphemes (Apel, 2014). She recalled learning that children who are morphologically aware are more likely to be successful readers and spellers and that morphological awareness intervention results in improved literacy skills (Apel et al., 2013; Wolter & Dilworth, 2014). She thought this was important given Jon's difficulties marking grammatical morphemes in spoken language and the morphologically based spelling errors. Targeting morphology also would support Jon's production of final consonants given that grammatical morphemes occur at the ends of words and often in consonant clusters (e.g., books). A focus on morphology would also inherently support Jon's vocabulary development and was consistent with Common Core Standards for second grade (e.g., Council of Chief State School Officers, n.d.). Prioritizing morphology for children with hearing loss was corroborated from her review of the scientific literature (e.g., Trussell & Easterbrooks, 2017). She decided to use a speech-to-print (Wasowicz, 2021) multilinguistic word study approach to target phonemic awareness and morphological awareness simultaneously (Masterson & Apel, 2007; Wolter, 2015).

Explicit Instruction

Given Jon's significant difficulty with phonological awareness, the SLP made sure early in the treatment to address the "basics," including definitions of vowels and consonants, with repeated practice identifying these sounds and their associated letters. As soon as Jon had a good foundation with these skills, the SLP moved on to targeting linguistic features specific to Jon's needs. The example activity below describes the use of the "I Do, We Do, You Do" framework (Keesey et al., 2015) to address plural "s" by bringing to Jon's attention the sounds, spelling, and meaning of words when plural "s" is added. This type of instruction is considered explicit because the teaching is direct with explanations and substantial modeling.

- **I DO:** For each new target morpheme/skill, the SLP first introduced the activity explaining the reason it was important: "Remember we are working on thinking about plural 's' which, when added to a word, means more than one. Our next word is 'books' (using acoustic highlighting). I'm going to say each of the sounds in the word 'books'—/b/-/ʊ/-/k/-/s/. 'Books' has 4 sounds." As each sound was spoken in isolation, the SLP pushed small blocks forward to represent each sound. Next, she placed the blocks on a piece of paper and wrote the letter(s) to represent each phoneme while saying the sound-letter associations aloud, "The /b/ sound is represented by the letter 'b' and the /ʊ/ sound by the letters 'oo.'" To emphasize that the "s" represents a separate unit of meaning in the word, the SLP restated the meaning of the base word alone, the affix, and what they mean together (e.g., "That 's'-/s/- on the end. It means there is more than one book. Two books . . . three books . . . four books . . . tons of books!"). During this portion, the SLP also underlined the letter(s) that represent the plural "s," stating, "I'm underlining the letter 's' in this word because it stands for the /s/ sound—the plural 's,' which means more than one book." Note that also included in the plural "s" lessons were instructions on the various pronunciations of the plural "s" and rules for spelling "s" versus "-es" (Wasowicz, et al., 2012).

- **WE DO:** After several models, Jon was encouraged to segment the words by their sounds and write the corresponding letters with the SLP's support as needed, "I think there may be more than two sounds in that word. Let's say each sound together." After writing the letters, he was encouraged to state the meaning of the base word and how the addition of the plural "s" changed the quantity of the base word, "When plural 's' is added to the word 'book,' it means there is more than one book." During the initial treatment sessions, Jon indicated that he likes to draw, so the SLP had him draw pictures to represent the plural "s." For example, on a notepad, the target base word was written on the left-hand side of the paper along with its corresponding drawing (e.g., word "book" with a picture of one book). Then an arrow was drawn to the word "books" with an underline to indicate that the "s" represents a meaningful part along with a drawing of two books.

- **YOU DO—Analysis of Client's Response to Treatment:** After substantial practice with the SLP's support, Jon's progress was assessed by asking him to complete the intervention activities or parts of them independently. For example, after working on segmenting words into their sounds for over the course of 2 weeks, the SLP administered a probe assessing Jon's phonemic segmenting using 10 words that varied in syllable structure (e.g., CVC, CCVC, CCVC, etc.), including words with and without plural "s," some of which were included during the intervention sessions and some of which were novel. The purpose was to determine (a) if Jon could independently segment words taught directly, (b) whether his phonemic segmentation skills had generalized to untaught words with and without plural "s," and (c) whether it was appropriate to proceed or if simpler syllable structures needed to be targeted. Similarly, mini spelling tests were administered monthly to assess whether Jon's skills were transferred to independent spelling tasks.

- **Additional Sample Activities for Explicit Instruction:** Using the scaffolding approach as previously described, the SLP engaged with Jon in a variety of activities designed to increase his awareness of the phonemes, spellings, affixes, and meaning of words.
  - The SLP strategically targeted orthographic patterns and suffixes that were developmentally appropriate goal areas for Jon.
  - An activity used often was "word sorts" (e.g., sorting words that end with the /t/ sound dependent on whether the word did or did not contain past-tense -ed (e.g., adapt vs. walked) (Wasowicz, et al., 2012).
  - Jon's skills were supported in authentic contextualized activities as soon as he was ready. In the classroom, Jon's teacher incorporated his goals into writing assignments and lessons. This worked out well given that Jon's target skills were already well aligned with the lesson plans.
  - The SLP used extension activities to give Jon opportunities to practice target skills within the context of connected text. He enjoyed looking for words with target affixes in written passages, highlighting and defining them, and then creating sentences using those words. Jon's SLP leveraged his interests by incorporating passages on topics such as baseball and other team sports.

Implicit Instruction

In addition to supporting Jon's morphosyntactic development through instruction in written language, the SLP wanted to support Jon's spoken language in a naturalistic context. The SLP engi-neered activities and projects that she and Jon could complete together to provide opportunities to model the target linguistic structure (e.g., plural "s," past-tense -ed). When targeting plural "s," they built objects together that required multiples of the same item (e.g., LEGO spaceship—three rectangle LEGOs; two wheels; four red ones; two spaceships). To leverage Jon's interests, they built a baseball field diorama (e.g., four bases; two dugouts; six infielders). At the beginning of each session, they spent 5 minutes in shared book reading; the SLP intentionally selected books that had several instances of the linguistic structure being targeted, and she used acoustic highlighting when reading the words with the target structure. Priming in this way, when combined with explicit instruction, has been shown to support the language skills of children with language disorders (e.g., Wada et al., 2020). To assess Jon's progress with spoken morphosyntactic production, the SLP obtained a language sample at each quarter to assess Jon's use of grammatical morphemes.

Further Recommendations

It was recommended that Jon's teacher, reading specialist, TOD, and school-based SLP continue to prioritize their alignment of goals, terminology, procedures, and approach to literacy instruction so that Jon receives consistent and repeated instructional support. It is important that the isolated skills learned by Jon in therapy are reinforced in the classroom. Additionally, perhaps the SLP and teacher could initiate a coteaching collaboration to support the language and literacy skills of all children in Jon's classroom. The SLP recognizes that the severity of Jon's spoken and written language disorder will require long-term intervention with goals that change over time and that his hearing and hearing aid use must be consistently monitored.

Take-Aways

Understanding a student's diagnosis and communicating with outside providers will enhance school-based services. Failing to do so for a child such as Jon with late identified hearing loss may result in an inappropriate service eligibility designation for an IEP and negatively impact access to appropriate services and assistive technology. Practitioners are encouraged to seek additional knowledge when unfamiliar with a diagnosis or population. Collaboration among all those serving the student is imperative for IEP planning and implementation.

Authors' Note

This case is based on a hypothetical client and the clinical experiences of the authors.

References

American Speech-Language-Hearing Association. (1997–2022). *Effects of hearing loss on development*. https://www.asha.org/public/hearing/effects-of-hearing-loss-on-development/

Apel, K. (2014). A comprehensive definition of morphological awareness: Implications for assessment. *Topics in Language Disorders, 34*(3), 197–209.

Apel, K., Brimo, D., Diehm, E., & Apel, L. (2013). Morphological awareness intervention with kindergartners and first-and second-grade students from low socioeconomic status homes: A feasibility study. *Language, Speech, and Hearing Services in Schools, 44*, 161–173.

Bess, F. H., Dodd-Murphy, J., & Parker, R. A. (1998). Children with minimal sensorineural hearing loss: Prevalence, educational performance, and functional status. *Ear and Hearing, 19*(5), 339–354.

Council of Chief State School Officers. (n.d.). *Common Core State Standards Initiative: Preparing America's Students for College and Career*. https://learning.ccsso.org/common-core-state-standards-initiative

Estabrooks, W., Morrison, H. M., & MacIver-Lux, K. (Eds.). (2020). *Auditory-verbal therapy: Science, research, and practice*. Plural Publishing.

Garber, A. S., & Nevins, M. E. (2012). Child-centered collaborative conversations that maximize listening and spoken language development for children with hearing loss. *Seminars in Speech and Language, 33*(4), 264–272.

Henbest, V. S., & Apel, K. (2021). The relation between a systematic analysis of spelling and orthographic and phonological awareness skills in first-grade children. *Language, Speech, and Hearing Services in Schools, 52*(3), 827–839.

Henbest, V. S., Apel, K., & Mitchell, A. (2019). Speech-language pathologist–guided morphological awareness instruction in the general education classroom. *Perspectives of the ASHA Special Interest Groups, 4*(5), 771–780.

Holstrum, W. J., Gaffney, M., Gravel, J. S., Oyler, R. F., & Ross, D. S. (2008). Early intervention for children with unilateral and mild bilateral degrees of hearing loss. *Trends in Amplification, 12*(1), 35–41.

Individuals with Disabilities Education Act, 34 CFR § 300.105. (2006)

Keesey, S., Konrad, M., & Joseph, L. M. (2015). Word boxes improve phonemic awareness, letter–sound correspondences, and spelling skills of at-risk kindergartners. *Remedial and Special Education, 36*(3), 167–180.

Larsen, S., Hammill, D., & Moats, L. (2013). *Test of written spelling* (5th ed.). Pro-Ed.

Lund, E., Werfel, K. L., & Schuele, C. M. (2015). Phonological awareness and vocabulary performance of monolingual and bilingual preschool children with hearing loss. *Child Language Teaching and Therapy, 31*(1), 85–100.

Madell, J. (2021, August). Hearing health and technology matters. *The LMH Test for Monitoring Listening-Jane Madell and Joan Hewitt*. https://hearinghealthmatters.org/hearingandkids/2021/3245/

Masterson, J., & Apel, K. (2007). *Spelling and word-level reading: A multilinguistic approach*. In A. Kamhi, J. Masterson, & K. Apel (Eds.), *Clinical decision making in developmental language disorders* (pp. 249–266). Paul H. Brookes Publishing.

Masterson, J. J., & Apel, K. (2010). The spelling sensitivity score: Noting developmental changes in spelling knowledge. *Assessment for Effective Intervention, 36*(1), 35–45.

Mitchell, M. P., Ehren, B. J., & Towson, J. A. (2022). Vocabulary outcomes with third graders in a teacher and speech-language pathologist collaboration. *Perspectives of the ASHA Special Interest Groups, 7*(6), 2067–2087. https://doi.org/10.1044/2022_PERSP-22-00008

Runnion, E., & Gray, S. (2019). What clinicians need to know about early literacy development in children with hearing loss. *Language, Speech, and Hearing Services in Schools, 50*(1), 16–33. https://doi.org/10.1044/2018_LSHSS-18-0015

Saint-Georges, C., Chetouani, M., Cassel, R., Apicella, F., Mahdhaoui, A., Muratori, F., . . . Cohen, D. (2013).

Motherese in interaction: at the cross-road of emotion and cognition? (A systematic review). *PLoS One*, *8*(10), e78103. https://doi.org/10.1371/journal.pone.0078103

Tomblin, J. B., Harrison, M., Ambrose, S. E., Walker, E. A., Oleson, J. J., & Moeller, M. P. (2015). Language outcomes in young children with mild to severe hearing loss. *Ear and Hearing, 36*(1), 76S. https://doi.org/10.1097/AUD.0000000000000219

Trussell, J. W., & Easterbrooks, S. R. (2017). Morphological knowledge and students who are deaf or hard-of-hearing: A review of the literature. *Communication Disorders Quarterly, 38*(2), 67–77.

Ukrainetz, T. (Ed.). (2015a). *School age language intervention: Evidence based practices*. Pro-Ed.

Ukrainetz, T. (2015b). Awareness, memory, and retrieval: Intervention for the phonological foundations of reading. In Ukrainetz (Ed.), *School-age language intervention: Evidence-based practices*. Pro-Ed.

Ukstins, C. A., & Welling, D. R. (2017). The speech-language pathologist in audiology services: An interprofessional collaboration. In D. R. Welling & C. A. Ukstins (Eds.) *Fundamentals of audiology for the speech-language pathologist* (2nd ed., pp. 2–14). Jones & Bartlett Learning.

U.S. National Institutes of Health. (2005). *Hearing loss: Determining eligibility for Social Security benefits*. National Academy of Sciences, National Library of Medicine. https://www.ncbi.nlm.nih.gov/books/NBK207837/

U.S. National Institutes of Health (NIH), National Institute on Deafness and Other Communication Disorders. (2021, March). *Quick statistics about hearing*. https://www.nidcd.nih.gov/health/statistics/quick-statistics-hearing#:~:text=About%202%20to%203%20out,in%20one%20or%20both%20ears.&text=More%20than%2090%20percent%20of%20deaf%20children%20are%20born%20to%20hearing%20parents

Wada, R., Gillam, S. L., & Gillam, R. B. (2020). The use of structural priming and focused recasts to facilitate the production of subject- and object-focused relative clauses by school-age children with and without developmental language disorder. *American Journal of Speech-Language Pathology, 29*(4), 1883–1895. https://doi.org/10.1044/2020_AJSLP-19-00090

Wagner, R. K., Torgesen, J. K., Rashotte, C. A., & Pearson, N. A. (2013). *Comprehensive Test of Phonological Processing–Second Edition (CTOPP-2)*. Pro-Ed.

Walker, E. A., Holte, L., McCreery, R. W., Spratford, M., Page, T., & Moeller, M. P. (2015). The influence of hearing aid use on outcomes of children with mild hearing loss. *Journal of Speech, Language, and Hearing Research, 58*(5), 1611–1625.

Wasowicz, J. (2021). A speech-to-print approach to teaching reading. *Learning Difficulties Australia, 53*(2), 10–18.

Wasowicz, J., Apel, K., Masterson, J. J., & Whitney, A. (2012). *SPELL-links to reading and writing* (2nd ed.). Learning By Design.

Wiig, E. H., Semel, E., & Secord, W. A. (2013). *Clinical Evaluation of Language Fundamentals–Fifth Edition (CELF-5)*. NCS Pearson.

Wolfe, J., Morais, M., Neumann, S., Schafer, E., Mülder, H. E., Wells, N., . . . Hudson, M. (2013). Evaluation of speech recognition with personal FM and classroom audio distribution systems. *Journal of Educational Audiology, 19*, 65–79.

Wolter, J. A. (2015). Spelling and word study: A guide for language-based assessment and intervention. In Ukrainetz (Ed.), *School-age language intervention: Evidence-based practices* (pp. 527–563). Pro-Ed.

Wolter, J. A., & Dilworth, V. (2014). The effects of a multilinguistic morphological awareness approach for improving language and literacy. *Journal of Learning Disabilities, 47*(1), 76–85. https://doi.org/10.1177/0022219413509972

Woodcock, R. W. (2011). *Woodcock reading mastery tests–Third Edition (WRMT-3)*. Pearson.

Yoshinaga-Itano, C., Sedey, A. L., Coulter, D. K., & Mehl, A. L. (1998). Language of early- and later-identified children with hearing loss. *Pediatrics, 102*(5), 1161–1171. https://doi.org/10.1542/peds.102.5.1161

FLUENCY

CASE 29

Emily: Lidcombe Program to Treat Stuttering in a School-Age Child

Rosalee C. Shenker, Verity MacMillan, Stacey Sheedy, and Sally Hewat

Conceptual Knowledge Areas

Stuttering is a speech disorder that involves disruptions to normal verbal behavior, including (1) repeated movements of whole or part-words, (2) fixed postures with or without audible airflow, and (3) superfluous behaviors such as grimacing (Teesson et al., 2003). The onset of stuttering typically occurs in the early years of life. A prospective, community-ascertained cohort study found the cumulative incidence of stuttering to be 8.5% of children by the age of 3 years (Reilly et al., 2009) and 11% by 4 years (Reilly et al., 2013). If left untreated, the disorder may be associated with adverse consequences because of negative peer and social reactions to stuttering (Smith et al., 2014).

Early intervention for stuttering is crucial as it is generally agreed that stuttering is most tractable during the preschool years. Tractability decreases with age, presumably as neural networks for speech become established (Wohlert & Smith, 2002). The school-age period, between the ages of 7 and 12 years, is considered a transitional time prior to the point where stuttering becomes intractable. While treatment during the school years is one of the final opportunities to manage stuttering in childhood, clinical management can be more difficult (Conture & Guitar, 1993). The impact of negative consequences of stuttering that may begin in the preschool years (Langevin et al., 2009) becomes more intense as a child progresses through school. A school-age child is faced with increasing demands on social interactions, which may lead to teasing, bullying, social isolation, and rejection (Blood et al., 2011), as well as impact their ability to generalize and maintain stutter-free speech. Additionally, the presence of other factors, including language and phonological skills, attention deficit, temperament, and executive functioning, may play a role in the profile of stuttering and could affect progress in treatment (Choo et al., 2020; Unicomb et al., 2020). When a child who stutters reaches the school-age years, it is likely that they have experienced unsuccessful attempts at treatment or relapses after successful treatment, which will likely decrease motivation to comply with any further attempts at treatment.

Description of the Case

Background Information

Emily presented to the clinic as a 9-year-old. She lives with her parents, who sought further intervention for her stuttering. During the assessment, Emily spoke with interest about books she enjoyed reading, animals, and watching movies and shows. Emily attends her local public school. She began stuttering consistently at 4 years of age and had intervention at that time with a positive treatment outcome. Her speech remained mostly fluent for several months, but she did not complete the maintenance stage of the treatment. Her stuttering has been variable in severity since then, increasing in severity in recent months.

Reason for Referral

This was Emily's second presentation at the clinic. Emily had attended several years previously and at the time presented with moderate stuttering consisting of repeated movements, including sound and syllable repetitions and fixed postures without audible airflow (i.e., short-duration blocks). She was treated with the Lidcombe Program of Early Stuttering Intervention (Jones et al., 2005; Onslow, 2003). After 18 clinic visits, Emily reached the criteria for entry into Stage 2 (maintenance), which was mostly stutter-free speech or very occasional mild stuttering for 3 consecutive Stage 1 appointments. Emily continued to meet this criterion for the first four appointments of the criterion-based Stage 2 of the Lidcombe Program over the following 3 months. However, against the advice of the speech-language pathologist (SLP), the maintenance stage of the treatment was discontinued because Emily's parents were satisfied with the outcome. Emily maintained stutter-free speech for several months posttreatment; however, she gradually relapsed. Treatment was not sought immediately because her stuttering was mild and infrequent. Hence, her parents did not re-refer her for intervention until now, when the severity had increased more significantly.

Findings of the Evaluation

Emily's parents reported a normal birth and developmental history, with no other speech or language problems. Emily's pretreatment stuttering measure was 5% syllables stuttered (%SS), consisting of repeated movements and frequent fixed postures with audible airflow. Very infrequent, short-duration fixed postures without audible airflow were noted (i.e., blocks). The Lidcombe Program severity rating scale was used as a perceptual severity rating (SR) of her speech.[1] On the scale where 0 = no stuttering, 1 = extremely mild stuttering, and 9 = extremely severe stuttering, her severity in the clinic was assigned SR 6. Emily's parents reported that this speech sample was quite representative of her usual speech, with severity ranging from SR 4 to SR 7 in various speaking situations. A video-recorded sample from home confirmed this.

During the assessment, Emily expressed specific concerns about participating in class discussions. She explained that other children were imitating her stutter in the playground, and as a result, she was becoming self-conscious about talking. The Overall Assessment of the Speaker's Experience of Stuttering (OASES; Yaruss & Quesal, 2016) was used as a pretreatment measure of Emily's reaction to her stutter and its impact on her daily life. Emily's overall impact rating was moderate. Results from these measures suggested that addressing Emily's level of concern was an essential component of the treatment plan.

Before treatment began, the SLP provided information to Emily about stuttering and ensured that Emily understood that her stutter was not a result of an emotional disorder. The SLP explained that her stuttering was associated with how the brain processes speech (Packman & Attanasio, 2004). The SLP also incorporated discussions related to Emily's concerns throughout the treatment. This included explaining to her that as stuttering persists, negative feedback from listeners can affect a child who stutters, and this experience sometimes leads to "worries" about stuttering and avoidance of some speaking situations. Confronting these feelings and learning coping skills can lead to an openness about stuttering and an ability to self-advocate for personal needs, strengthening resilience in the face of teasing and other negative feedback.

Treatment Options Considered

Emily's previous experience of therapy was the Lidcombe Program (Onslow et al., 2021), a behavioral

---

[1]As of December 2022, the Severity rating scale was amended to a 0- to 11-point scale where 0 = no stuttering, 1 = extremely mild stuttering, and 10 = extremely severe stuttering. Stated in Onslow, M. (2022, December). *Stuttering and its treatment: Twelve lectures.* Retrieved January 09, 2023, from https://www.uts.edu.au/asrc/resources. ISBN-13:978-0-646-92717-6, ISBN:0-646-69816-0 .

treatment developed for preschool children who stutter and administered by parents. The child attends the clinic weekly with the parent, and the SLP trains the parent to present verbal contingencies for the child's stutter-free speech and occasionally for unambiguous stuttering. Initially, the parent presents these verbal contingencies in short, structured daily practice sessions, designed to increase stutter-free speech. The parent then administers the contingencies in the natural conversations of daily life to generalize stutter-free speech to these situations. The SLP uses the 10-point perceptual rating scale to measure the child's stuttering severity in the clinic, while the parent records a daily speech measure at home using the same scale. These measures are used to guide clinical process decisions. In the case of a preschool child, when the child's fluency has been reduced to no stuttering or almost no stuttering for three consecutive clinic visits, Stage 2 (maintenance) commences.

The Lidcombe Program has been shown to be an effective treatment for reducing stuttering in preschool-age children (Jones et al., 2005). However, as a child who stutters enters the school years, the demands on daily life increase in terms of schoolwork and social activities, limiting time available to dedicate to treatment. Other factors that may impact treatment are the likely persistence and decreased tractability of stuttering, previous treatment failure, and the possible suffering of teasing and bullying. These factors increase the importance of efficient and efficacious treatment for this group of children.

Stuttering in school-age children has also been shown to respond to the Lidcombe Program, which is a simple and replicable treatment. While evidence is limited (e.g., Harrison et al., 2010; Hewat et al., 2021), stuttering severity was reduced within the same time frame as reported for preschool children, although all studies reported more variability in Stage 2 speech measures compared to preschool children. Some advantages of using the Lidcombe Program over other treatments with school-age children include (1) no need for a novel speech pattern and (2) a more mature cognitive ability may increase self-monitoring/self-correction. Most children require no modification from the manualized treatment format; however, some adjustments may be appropriate. These include changing the language used to provide praise with more age-appropriate vocabulary, incorporating reading as a practice activity, having the child involved in taking daily severity ratings, adjusting the activities during natural conversation to be more representative of the child's age, and altering the criteria and schedule of Stage 2, particularly during the first few months (Harrison et al., 2010).

Alternatively, speech-restructuring/fluency shaping provides the highest level of evidence for school-age children (Hancock et al., 1998). However, this style of treatment is based on intensive formats requiring 100 or more treatment hours (Koushik et al., 2009), children are required to use a novel speaking pattern to increase stutter-free speech, and there is a high rate of relapse reported (Boberg & Kully, 1994).

Another possible treatment option is using syllable-timed speech to treat stuttering for school-age children. While the results of a nonrandomized clinical trial may not be as promising as for the Lidcombe Program with this age group, the treatment is the most procedurally simple of school-age treatments (Andrews et al., 2016).

On review of the evidence, the SLP was convinced of the value of commencing treatment using the Lidcombe Program for Emily. Her stuttering severity having successfully reduced during her previous treatment experience and since during a brief trial to apply verbal contingencies, the SLP was able to elicit a conversation with reduced stuttering severity.

Course of Treatment

Emily's treatment was guided by the Lidcombe Program treatment guide (Onslow et al., 2021). The SLP reviewed the key components of the Lidcombe Program with Emily and her parents, including measurement, verbal contingencies across practice sessions and natural conversations, and the two stages of the program. Since Emily and her father indicated that they spend a lot of time together at home, he agreed to take the primary responsibility for completing the daily practice sessions with Emily. The SLP demonstrated a practice session using a picture description as stimulus for the conversation and discussed the type and number of verbal contingencies that Emily would be amenable to. As a result of this discussion, acknowledgment of stutter-free speech was established as an important verbal contingency as it matched Emily's quiet, relaxed interaction with her father. Some gentle praise for stutter-free speech (for example, "nice," "smooth, good job," "good one") was also introduced. Following this demonstration, Emily's father participated in a practice session conversation with Emily and was able to maintain the reduced stuttering established in the interaction with the SLP. He also delivered appropriate acknowledgment and praise contingent on stutter-free speech during the conversation. Emily and her father commenced daily measurement and daily practice sessions, supported by weekly clinic appointments.

Over the first 4 weeks of the treatment, the SLP added requests for self-evaluation and self-correction to the practice sessions, and it was noted that Emily was able to spontaneously self-monitor stutter-free speech and began to spontaneously self-correct her unambiguous stutters. Acknowledgment of stuttering was attempted with Emily in the clinic, but Emily's father reported that at home, Emily had told him "Don't say that" and so it was discontinued. Since Emily was able to spontaneously self-monitor her fluent speech accurately and was beginning to spontaneously self-correct moments of stuttering, her parents agreed to focus on praise or acknowledgment of spontaneous self-correction rather than acknowledgment of stuttering. However, Emily also suggested that occasional requests for self-correction of stuttered speech could be helpful from her parents, and a maximum of two per day was agreed upon. Emily preferred a "nonverbal" reinforcement to be used sometimes when she was talking without stuttering, especially when others were present (e.g., a thumbs-up).

Praise and acknowledgment contingent on stutter-free speech were also incorporated into naturally occurring conversations at home. Emily continued to accurately monitor her stuttering during school days, using the severity rating scale. Emily was able to identify some short time periods during the school day in which she was able to increase her stutter-free speech. According to her father's daily ratings, Emily's stuttering reduced from a weekly average of SR 6 to a weekly average of SR 4. Emily agreed that her stutters had decreased and, when asked, reported that she felt better about her talking.

As her familiarity with the SLP increased, Emily became more open about her experiences at school. She revealed that she often spent her lunch break in the school library and that she didn't usually volunteer to say things in class. With consent from the family, the SLP contacted Emily's teacher, who indicated that Emily was a quiet, intelligent child who made friends with likeminded, often less assertive children. Her teacher had noticed the stutter and reported that she had responded to it by trying not to actively nominate Emily to answer questions in class. The teacher acknowledged that this had resulted in Emily not contributing to class discussions. The SLP and teacher reviewed options for encouraging Emily to contribute to class discussions and agreed that it would be appropriate to talk to Emily about the value of sharing her thoughts with the class. The teacher theorized that as an initial step, Emily might like to be regularly invited to contribute to the weekly class discussion about books students had read since Emily was known to be a voracious reader.

Emily's father reported that when he opened further conversation with Emily about her talking experiences at school, she had revealed that last year, a school child had imitated one of her repetitions in the school playground. Together, Emily, her SLP, and her parents addressed the issue of teasing and implemented treatment goals to increase her resilience and openness to these concerns. The SLP reminded Emily of her strengths by starting a journal that listed "things that I am good at" to help her refocus on strengths rather than weaknesses. Together with her parents and the SLP, Emily began to discuss imperfections, acknowledging "that it is ok to make mistakes," taking risks and trying new things that help people to learn and grow, as well as encouraging a "can-do" attitude toward daily activities. This discussion transitioned to creating hierarchies of difficult/easier speaking situations, openness about stuttering, self-advocacy, and shifts in focus of attention to deal with the response of others to stuttering. Each session started with a discussion of "what is going well" to focus on positive change. She started to talk about how much more confident she was feeling overall, specifically describing an increased willingness to contribute to class discussions.

After 8 weeks of treatment, Emily's father rated her daily stuttering severity consistently SR 3 or SR 4. Daily practice sessions were ongoing, and 15 to 20 acknowledgments or praises for stutter-free speech in naturally occurring conversations were being delivered daily, along with an agreed maximum of two requests for self-correction. Emily's father demonstrated significant skill during clinic appointments in maximizing opportunities to deliver verbal contingencies for stutter-free speech in practice sessions and at identifying very subtle stutters. The SLP opened discussion with Emily and her father about how to encourage further progress, resulting in a decision to try to make verbal contingencies more powerful through use of a supplemental visual reinforcement system. Emily was enthusiastic, and she developed a personalized tally system, whereby her father would pair some of his verbal contingencies with a tally mark on a chart. Following the implementation of this system driven by Emily, her daily stuttering severity ratings indicated that her severity had decreased further. After 4 weeks of using Emily's visual tally system, her father reported that she did not seem to be motivated by the chart any longer, and Emily agreed that she was ready to discontinue the system.

On completion of 14 weeks of treatment, Emily's father rated her typical daily severity as SR 2. In the clinic, the SLP observed predominantly syllable repetitions with occasional small, fixed postures without audible airflow. At this stage of the program, daily practice sessions did not rely on external stimuli such as pictures to prompt conversation; rather, the sessions were conducted during conversations that mirrored typical interactions between Emily and her father at home. Emily reported that her speech did not really bother her

anymore and that she would rate her own severity as usually SR 1 with SR 0 sometimes. While this was not in strict agreement with her father's SR 2 evaluation, it was a positive reflection of Emily's personal experience of talking.

Feedback from Emily's teacher confirmed that Emily was stuttering less noticeably in school and was more willing to engage in conversations, answer questions, and take a turn reading in front of the class. Emily had indicated that if she was to read aloud in class, she preferred to be called on as one of the first to read, which the teacher respected. Emily and her teacher agreed that on those days when Emily preferred not to contribute before the whole class, she could indicate that to the teacher.

Emily, her father, and the SLP discussed Stage 2, focusing on the importance of completing this phase of treatment to maintain low levels of stuttering and manage relapse. Stage 1 of the Lidcombe Program continued for another 3 weeks with Emily maintaining a typical SR 2 and a weekly average parental SR less than 2.5. Considering this stability, the criteria for entering Stage 2 were adjusted to allow for a bit more stuttering than is typical for children under 6 years of age. A beyond clinic typical SR 2 or lower with a maximum SR 3 occurring not more than once per week was determined to be appropriate ratings in the week preceding a clinic appointment. Because of the variability noted in Stage 2 with older children, the schedule of meetings was altered to decrease in frequency more slowly. The schedule for Emily's Stage 2 appointments was that she attends the clinic twice monthly for 2 months, then twice 3 weeks apart, then another appointment after 1 month followed by two appointments 2 months apart, concluding with two appointments each separated by 4 months. Emily was to progress through this schedule if she continued to meet the accepted criteria.

Analysis of Client's Response to Intervention

The SLP trained Emily and her parents to record average stuttering severity each day in everyday speaking situations, using a 10-point SR scale where 0 = no stuttering, 1 = extremely mild stuttering, and 9 = extremely severe stuttering. Emily's measure represented her speaking during the school day, while her parents rated their time spent with her at home. At each subsequent clinic visit, the SLP also assigned Emily a SR during a conversational interaction and asked Emily and her parents to do the same. In this way, ratings were compared and discussed until reasonable agreement was achieved, with SR scores being no more than 1 scale value different. Figure 29–1 presents the mean weekly SR scores collected by Emily's parents. Emily and her parents compared their severity ratings, and at one point, the ratings differed by more than 1 point. Emily then disclosed that her stuttering was often more severe in the classroom, particularly when asked to answer a question or read out loud in front of the class. This disclosure led to a discussion on how to support Emily better in these concerns.

Emily progressed to a criterion-based maintenance program after she achieved three consecutive appointments of within the clinic and beyond the clinic SR scores averaging 2.5 or below, with no more than one occasion of a score of 3 beyond the clinic. Emily maintained this low level of stuttering for the duration of her 17-month maintenance schedule, except on one occasion during which she had an increase in her stuttering measures to a few scores of SR 3 in a row for several days. At that time, Emily and her father increased the practice, and Emily's speech fluency improved. Hence, this was considered a mild regression. Toward the final stages of maintenance, Emily's perception of her own speech improved.

In addition to daily severity ratings, the SLP measured percentage of syllables stuttered (%SS) in the clinic at assessment, at transition to Stage 2, and at the end of Stage 2. These %SS measures, supplemental to the daily SRs, were based on a conversational speech sample that was a minimum

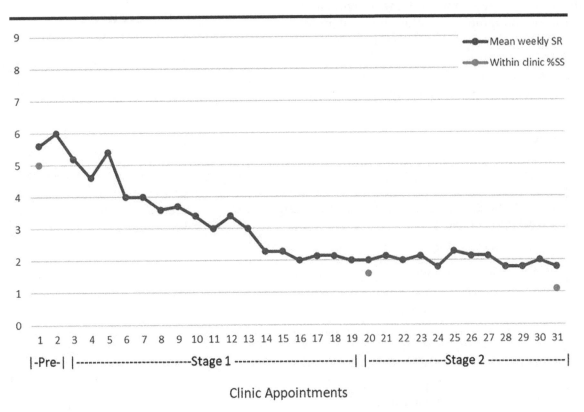

Figure 29–1. Mean weekly beyond-clinic severity rating (SR) scores—collected by Emily's parents the week before clinic appointments.

of 300 syllables or 10 minutes in duration. Emily completed the Overall Assessment of the Speaker's Experience of Stuttering (OASES; Yaruss & Quesal, 2016) pretreatment, on entry to Stage 2, and at the end of Stage 2. An additional quick and useful measure is the Subjective Units of Distress Scale (SUDS). This measure involved asking the parent to score their concern, the child's concern, and the impact of the stutter on a scale, with 0 = no concern/impact and 10 = extremely concerned/severe impact. Emily completed this outcome measure at those same points in time, as well as at completion of Stage 2. The %SS and SR scores recorded by the SLP during the clinic sessions, OASES scores pretreatment and at end Stage 2, and SUDS scores recorded by Emily and her parents are presented in Table 29–1.

Emily's case illustrates some advantages of using the Lidcombe Program to treat school-age children who stutter. First, the treatment was simple and did not require that the child adapt a novel speaking pattern to be fluent. This allowed Emily to concentrate on what she was saying in a natural-sounding manner, rather than talking in an unnatural manner to be more fluent. Second, the treatment plan required the involvement of Emily's parents, which added to their understanding of stuttering. As such, the compliance issues that are known to relate to this age group may be overcome. Third, the treatment was efficient. Following the assessment, only 18 clinic visits were required to reach the criteria set for maintenance. Emily's everyday speech was judged to sound quite natural by her SLP and parents, adding to her confidence in speaking.

It is not possible to generalize from Emily's case to the population of school-age children who require treatment for their stuttering, as further systematic clinical trials will be needed with a cohort of school-age children. Nonetheless, the results of this single case are encouraging.

Authors' Note

The name of the client and some details of her case have been changed for confidentiality.

References

Andrews, C., O'Brian, S., Onslow, M., Packman, A., Menzies, R., & Lowe, R. (2016). Phase II trial development of a syllable-timed-speech treatment for school

Table 29–1. Within-Clinic Measures (Percent Syllables Stuttered [%SS], OASES, and SUDS) Collected by the Treating Clinician

Measure	Pretreatment	Entry to Stage 2	Completion of Stage 2
% syllables stuttered	5%	1.6%	1.1%
In-clinic severity rating	6	2	1
OASES overall impact rating	Moderate		Mild
SUDS—parent concern (0–10, 1 = no concern, 10 = extremely concerned)	8	1	1
SUDS—Emily's concern (0–10, 1 = no concern, 10 = extremely concerned)	6	2	2
SUDS—impact on communication (0–10, 1 = no impact, 10 = severe impact)	7	1	1

age children who stutter. *Journal of Fluency Disorders, 48*, 44–55.

Blood, G. M., Blood, I.., Tranamontana, M., Sylvia, A. J., Boyle, M. P., & Motzko, G. R. (2011). Self-reported experience of bullying of students who stutter: Relations with life satisfaction, life orientation, & self-esteem. *Perceptual Motor Skills, 113*(2), 253–264.

Boberg, E., & Kully, D. (1994). Long-term results of an intensive treatment program for adults and adolescents who stutter. *Journal of Speech & Hearing Research, 37*(5), 1050–1059. https://doi.org/10.1044/jshr.3705.1050

Choo, A., Smith, S. A., & Li, H. (2020). Associations between stuttering, comorbid conditions and executive function in children: A population-based study. *BMC Psychology, 8*(1), 113. https://doi.org/10.1186/s40359-020-00481-7

Conture, E., & Guitar, B. (1993). Evaluating efficacy of treatment of stuttering: School-age children. *Journal of Fluency Disorders, 18*, 253–287.

Hancock, K., Craig, A., McCready, C., McCaul, A., Costello, D., & Gilmore, G. (1998). Two-to-six-year controlled trial stuttering outcomes for children and adolescents. *Journal of Speech, Language and Hearing Research, 41*, 1242–1252. https://doi.org/10.1044/jslhr.4106.1242

Harrison, E., Bruce, M., Shenker, R., & Koushik, S. (2010). The Lidcombe Program with school-age children who stutter. In B. Guitar & R. McCauley (Eds.), *Treatment of stuttering: established and emerging approaches* (pp. 150–166). Lippincott Williams & Wilkins.

Hewat, S., Unicomb, R., Dean, I., & Cui, G. (2021). Treatment of childhood stuttering using the Lidcombe Program in mainland China: Case studies. *Speech, Language and Hearing, 23*, 55–65.

Jones, M., Onslow, M., Packman, A., Williams, S., Ormond, T., & Schwarz, I. (2005). Randomised controlled trial of the Lidcombe programme of early stuttering intervention. *British Medical Journal, 331*(7518), 659–661. https://doi.org/10.1136/bmj.38520.451840.E0

Koushik, S., Shenker, R., & Onslow, M. (2009). Follow-up of 6-10-year-old stuttering children after Lidcombe Program treatment: A phase I trial. *Journal of Fluency Disorders, 34*(4), 279–290. https://doi.org/10.1016/j.jfludis.2009.11.001

Langevin, M., Packman, A., & Onslow, M. (2009). Peer responses to stuttering in the preschool setting. *American Journal of Speech-Language Pathology, 18*(3), 264–276. https://doi.org/10.1044/1058-0360(2009/07-0087)

Onslow, M. (2003). Evidence-based treatment of stuttering: IV. Empowerment through evidence-based treatment practices. *Journal of Fluency Disorders, 28*(3), 237–244. https://doi.org/10.1016/s0094-730x(03)00041-x

Onslow, M., Webber, M., Harrison, E., Arnott, S., Bridgman, K., Carey, B., . . . Hearne, A. (2021). *The Lidcombe Program Treatment Guide* (Ver. 1.3). https://www.uts.edu.au/asrc/resources/lidcombe-program

Packman, A., & Attanasio, J. S. (2004). *Theoretical issues in stuttering*. Taylor & Francis.

Reilly, S., Onslow, M., Packman, A., Cini, E., Conway, L., Ukomunne, O., . . . Wake, M. (2013). Natural history of stuttering to 4 years of age: A prospective community-based study. *Pediatrics, 132*(3), 460–467. https://doi.org/10.1542/peds.2012-3067

Reilly, S., Onslow, M., Packman, A., Wake, M., Bavin, E., Prior, M., . . . Ukoumunne, O. C. (2009). Predicting stuttering onset by age 3 years: A prospective, community cohort study. *Pediatrics, 123*, 270–277. https://doi.org/10.1542/peds.2007-3219

Smith, K., Iverach, L., O'Brian, S., Kefalianos, E., Reilly, S. (2014). Anxiety of children and adolescents who stutter: A review. *Journal of Fluency Disorders, 40*, 22–34. https://doi.org/10.1016/j.jfludis.2014.01.003

Teesson, K., Packman, A., & Onslow, M. (2003). The Lidcombe Behavioral Data Language of stuttering. *Journal of Speech, Language, and Hearing Research, 46*(4), 1009–1015. https://doi.org/10.1044/1092-4388(2003/078)

Unicomb, R., Kefalianos, E., Reilly, S., Cook, F., & Morgan, A. (2020). Prevalence and features of comorbid stuttering and speech sound disorder at age 4 years. *Journal of Communication Disorders, 13*, 84. https://doi.org/10.1016/jcomdis.2020.105976

Wohlert, A., & Smith, A. (2002). Developmental change in variability of lip muscle activity during speech. *Journal of Speech, Language, and Hearing Research, 45*, 1077–1087.

Yaruss, J. S., & Quesal, R. W. (2016). *Overall Assessment of the Speaker's Experience of Stuttering (OASES)*. Stuttering Therapy Resources.

CLUTTERING
CASE 30
Paul: Treatment of Cluttering in a School-Age Child

Kathleen Scaler Scott and Kenneth O. St. Louis

Conceptual Knowledge Areas

Cluttering is a much misunderstood and under-researched disorder, a fact that stands in sharp contrast to the extensive literature that exists for its more famous relative, stuttering. In contrast to stuttering, cluttering lacks visibility to (a) the cluttering client, wherein lack of awareness is regarded as a clinical symptom among many who clutter, (b) the public, and (c) clinicians, many of whom report that they are uncertain how to identify, diagnose, and treat this disorder (Reichel & Bakker, 2009; Scaler Scott et al., 2010; Scaler Scott et al., 2022). There is no single known cause for cluttering, although many believe it reflects genetic and/or physiological differences resulting in difficulties with rate regulation at its core (see Bakker et al., 2011; St. Louis et al., 2007). There has been continuing evidence that cluttering has a strong relationship with stuttering, with which it commonly co-occurs.

Onset and Development

Like stuttering, cluttering is considered a developmental disorder, although there have been occasional reports of cluttering arising following neurological trauma (e.g., LeBrun, 1996; Thacker & De Nil, 1996). Cluttering typically is not diagnosed until 7 or 8 years of age (Diedrich, 1984; Ward, 2017). Reasons for late diagnoses include lack of awareness of the disorder and the fact that cluttering often becomes salient in more complex,

later developing language or motor achievements (Pitluk, 1982; St. Louis et al., 1985; Ward, 2017). It may also be that, because the difficulties with speech motor control, language, or fluency that a young clutterer might experience are usually at a high level, many children go either undiagnosed or unseen by speech-language pathologists. Ward (2017) noted that cluttering is often diagnosed after a referral for stuttering, with older children and adults often expressing surprise when they find that they not only stutter but have cluttering as well.

Two core reasons may account for the lack of understanding of cluttering: (a) differences of opinion as to which features may be regarded as essential to the disorder versus those that are merely incidental to it and (b) the reality that cluttering (particularly severe cluttering) rarely occurs in isolation and most commonly is seen in combination with stuttering or other disorders (Freund, 1952; Preus, 1996; St. Louis et al., 2007; Weiss, 1964). Although more data are needed to establish a firm prevalence of coexisting cluttering and stuttering, a review of the literature suggests that between one-third and two-thirds of those who stutter also clutter (Ward, 2017). Cluttering has also been found to co-occur with other language and nonlanguage disorders such as intellectual disability (Coppens-Hofman et al., 2013; Farmer & Brayton, 1979), Down syndrome (Van Borsel & Vandermeulen, 2009), fragile X syndrome (Bangert et al., 2022), autism spectrum disorders (Scaler Scott et al., 2014), learning disabilities (Van Zaalen et al., 2009), and attention-deficit/hyperactivity disorder (ADHD) and/or auditory processing disorder (Blood et al., 2000; Molt, 1996; Scaler Scott, 2018; St. Louis & Schulte, 2011). Some of the speech characteristics inherently seen in these disorders are somewhat similar to those identified in cluttering, thus lending ambiguity as to whether these may be attributed exclusively to cluttering.

Despite these difficulties, there are some features of cluttering that are apparently readily recognized by clinical practitioners. In a survey of the opinions of 60 expert clinicians, Daly and Cantrell (2006) observed high interrater agreement for the following features: fast and irregular speech rate, telescoped words, imprecise articulation, poor intelligibility, and word-finding difficulties. Other characteristics thought important included a lack of pausing, lack of awareness, lack of self-monitoring skills, and disorganized language. Using these areas of agreement as a foundation, St. Louis and Schulte (2011) developed the lowest common denominator (LCD) definition of cluttering. Under this definition, clients receive a diagnosis of cluttering based upon meeting the mandatory criteria of perceived rapid or irregular rate and at least one of the following consequent symptoms: (1) excessive nonstuttering disfluencies, (2) pauses in places not expected grammatically, and (3) excessive over-coarticulation.

Assessment

There is now an emerging consensus that cluttering is a multifaceted disorder and as such requires comprehensive assessment in order to arrive at an informed diagnostic decision (Scaler Scott et al., 2022; St. Louis et al., 2007; Ward, 2017). In addition to a thorough case history, a comprehensive assessment is needed to gain a secure diagnosis. Depending on the age of the client, the clinician may need to assess (formally or informally) overall speaking rate, fluency, language function, motor speech, articulation, and speech rhythm (smoothness vs. jerkiness) (Scaler Scott et al., 2022). When assessing a suspected clutter in a client, the clinician may also need to consider related disorders, such as stuttering, ADHD, developmental language disorder, childhood apraxia of speech,

and autism spectrum disorders. It is important to differentiate speech symptoms that may be due to cluttering versus those due to a separate diagnosis, as well as to determine the contribution of concomitant diagnoses to cluttering symptoms (Scaler Scott, 2018). A comprehensive assessment of the client's medical history is necessary in order to rule out neurological trauma or disease as a causal factor. See Scaler Scott (2018, 2022) and Scaler Scott et al. (2022) for comprehensive assessment protocols.

Description of the Case

Background Information

Paul was a 10-year-old, fifth-grade boy whose mother, Mrs. R, contacted the first author for a speech-language evaluation. She indicated that Paul tended to speak quickly and at a low volume, making it difficult for others to understand him. In her judgment, Paul's speech problem had worsened within the previous year.

Paul had been diagnosed with autism spectrum disorder, Level 1 (i.e., highest functioning, without intellectual disability, formerly regarded as Asperger's disorder) in the second grade. He was also diagnosed with anxiety, for which a selective serotonin reuptake inhibitor had been prescribed. At the time of the evaluation, he had been receiving individual counseling biweekly. Within the previous year, Paul's family had relocated from a suburban to a rural area after Paul's father, whose job required frequent travel, was transferred by his employer. The family was in temporary housing awaiting a final decision about staying in the area. Paul's mother was a nonemployed speech-language pathologist who cared for Paul and his first-grade younger brother at home.

Paul's birth and medical histories were unremarkable. There was a familial history of stuttering (maternal grandmother and great-uncle). Paul stuttered for approximately 6 months when he was 4 years old. The stuttering, consisting of repetitions and prolongations, reportedly resolved spontaneously.

Reason for Referral

Paul enjoyed school and participated in gifted and talented programs both within school and elsewhere. Paul's second-grade teacher reportedly could not read his handwriting because of improper letter spacing, but this later resolved in Grade 2 when he easily mastered cursive writing. Paul received occupational therapy to address such fine motor difficulties as handwriting and tying his shoes and physical therapy to increase speed and coordination for gross motor activities, for example, running and jumping rope. His mother had noticed improvement in both fine and gross motor skills but described Paul as "slower" and "slightly less coordinated" than normal in gross motor skills. At the time of the evaluation, Paul commented that he enjoyed his current participation in karate, swimming, and spinning classes but did not enjoy team sports.

Paul indicated that he had had a best friend in his neighborhood prior to the recent move but had no friends at his new school. Paul's mother noted that he spoke with a few girls in his current class, and sometimes a friend (who also has social difficulties) from his new school came to his home, which she regarded as positive for Paul.

Findings of the Evaluation

As children with ASD Level 1 are often found to exhibit at least average performance on formal speech and language measures (Shriberg et al., 2001; Tager-Flusberg, 1995) and to have greatest difficulty integrating language skills appropriately in context (Barnhill, 2001; Szatmari, 1991), language skills were assessed informally in conversational speech rather than through standardized testing. Accordingly, for the evaluation, samples of conversation and oral reading were video recorded and later analyzed for speaking rate, intelligibility, and disfluencies. Paul's mother, a speech-language pathologist, raised no concerns about his grammatical skills or vocabulary, nor were any such difficulties observed during the evaluation. Table 30–1 summarizes the evalua-

tion findings. Using Yairi's (1996) criteria, Paul exhibited 2% stuttering-like disfluencies (SLDs) (i.e., mostly blocks/tense pauses plus one prolongation and occasional part-word repetitions) and 11% nonstuttering-like disfluencies (NSLDs) (i.e., revisions, interjections, and phrase repetitions) during the 5-minute conversation speech sample. Paul's blocks/tense pauses and prolongations were brief, that is, up to 1 second in duration and less than 1 second, respectively. The Stuttering Severity Instrument for Children and Adults, Third Edition (SSI-3; Riley, 1994), administered for both conversation and reading, placed Paul in the mild range of stuttering. On the Communication Attitude Test–Revised (CAT-R; Brutten & Vanryckeghem, 2007), Paul scored more than 2 standard deviations below children his age who do not stutter and within the same range as children his age who do stutter, indicating considerable negative attitudes toward speaking.

Speech intelligibility was judged by the first author to be "fair to poor" in unknown contexts and "fair" in known contexts. Rate and articulation contributed to the difficulty in understanding Paul. His rate tended to increase as he went on with a sentence or topic. He intermittently failed to pronounce word endings and/or weak syllables fully, which gave the impression of words blending into one another. This was differentiated from the phonological process of weak syllable deletion as it was not a consistent pattern, but related to increased rate, and therefore determined to be the cluttering symptom of over-coarticulation. Additionally, Paul sometimes exhibited tense pauses between his words or phrases, producing an atypical rhythm (i.e., an irregular rate of speech). Finally, Paul's frequent low vocal intensity further compromised his intelligibility.

While formulating language, Paul did not always include the necessary background information for the listener. At times he appeared to become "lost" in the content of what he was saying, going into specific details before giving general information or realizing he was veering from the main topic. Such "lost" or empty speech is known as *mazes* (Loban, 1976; Ward, 2006). It was speculated that Paul's decreased awareness

Table 30–1. Summary of Pretherapy Evaluation Findings

Area	Measures Used	Data
Fluency	Conversation sample	SLDs: 2% NSLDs: 11%
Fluency	Reading sample	SLDs: 1% NSLDs: 0.5%
Fluency	Combined reading and conversation	SSI-3 score: 10 SSI-3 severity rating: mild
Articulation	Examiner judgment	Intermittent weak syllable deletion Decreased vocal intensity
Speech rate	Examiner judgment Overall speaking rate[a]: 4.7 syllables/s Articulation rate[b]: 5.1 syllables/s	Rapid, irregular
Language usage	Examiner judgment	Excessive use of fillers and mazing Decreased inclusion of background information
Attitudes	CAT-R	$z = -2.06$[c]
Parent ratings	Ward Cluttering Checklist	68[d]

[a]Number of syllables per second including disfluencies, pauses, and hesitations (i.e., rate of message transmission).

[b]Number of syllables per second excluding disfluencies, pauses, and hesitations (i.e., rate of motor movements of mouth).

[c]As compared to school-age children with no speech/language issues, where average $z = 0.00$.

[d]See Table 30–4 for comparison of pre- and postscores, with decrease in score indicating movement toward more normalized speech.

precluded him from "tuning in" to the listener's nonverbal feedback to assist him in regulating his speech. When the clinician directly asked him for clarification, he responded, "Never mind," even when told the clinician wanted to hear what he had to say.

On occasions when Paul had difficulty formulating his ideas, he tended to insert filler words (e.g., "like," "um," "uh"), use nonspecific language (e.g., "stuff"), or revise or restart his utterance, all making his message difficult to follow.

He also seemed to insert phrases as a means of getting himself started, such as "Okay, well," "Okay," or "You see." The following represents a sample of Paul's speech in which these patterns were noted:

"So like then we had to figure out this pro—, group project that we wanted to do. And then well, like, it was one of us, I don't know, it was me. I came up with like, you see we went to Bixby Village in like the fall it's like this historical place where there were like all, all it's like, back in li—, it's like, like, it was like, in New Ham—, yeah it's in New Hampshire like Sussex County. There's like this Buffalo Village. Of course that's not what it's all about. I don't remember what time period it was but it was long ago."

Diagnostic Hypotheses

Paul was diagnosed with coexisting disorders of cluttering, stuttering, and ASD. Knowing that individuals with ASD tend to have difficulties with executive functioning skills (Hill & Bird, 2006), the role they were suspected to play in Paul's speech and language could not be overlooked (Scaler Scott, 2018).

Normal executive functioning skills, such as self-regulation, planning, organizing, and problem solving, control and affect the outcome of performance in everyday tasks. They allow a child to plan an action, hold that plan in memory and sequence, and inhibit irrelevant responses (Denckla, 1996; Scaler Scott, 2018; Singer & Bashir, 1999). Although Paul presumably possessed the language *information* to formulate messages clearly and concisely, his difficulties with executive functioning skills likely resulted in verbal planning and organizing difficulties. Accordingly, although some of Paul's excessive nonstuttered disfluency may have been habitual (e.g., excessive use of the filler word "like"), such disfluencies significantly decreased during reading tasks when language formulation was not required. This suggested that most of these disfluencies were the result of language formulation issues. It was hypothesized that he first had difficulty formulating a message, followed by weaknesses in regulating and problem solving to compensate effectively for this language formulation difficulty. Although he appeared to be compensating for this difficulty by inserting excessive disfluencies or frequently revising his message to hold his conversational turn, he did not employ the most effective compensatory strategies that would make it easy for

listeners to follow his ideas. Therefore, the difficulty lay not in his language skills alone, but in integration of language and executive functioning skills that is necessary for efficient and effective communication to take place.

The combination of rapid and/or irregular rate with decreased intelligibility and excessive use of NSLDs confirmed a diagnosis of cluttered speech, following the LCD definition of cluttering (St. Louis & Schulte, 2011):

Cluttering is a fluency disorder wherein segments of conversation in the speaker's native language typically are perceived as too fast overall, too irregular, or both (although measured syllable rates may not exceed normal limits). The segments of rapid and/or irregular speech rate must further be accompanied by one or more of the following: (a) excessive ; "normal" disfluencies; (b) excessive collapsing or deletion of syllables; and/or (c) abnormal pauses, syllable stress, or speech rhythm. (pp. 241–242)

Although debate remains as to whether language formulation issues are obligatory or incidental features of cluttering, under the LCD definition, formulation issues were not used to diagnose Paul's cluttered speech. However, since language formulation difficulties had a negative impact upon communicating his message effectively, they would be addressed clinically as a concomitant symptom in the treatment of overall effective communication. Paul also exhibited mild stuttering. Because the stuttering was mild and Paul did not engage in such behaviors as communication avoidance, tension, or struggle in relation to these moments of stuttering, it was determined that addressing cluttering should be the first treatment priority. Treatment would determine whether once cluttering was addressed, stuttering might worsen. Scaler Scott et al. (2010) found increased stuttering in a young clutterer-stutterer taught to use pausing to decrease rate of speech. The investigators hypothesized that because stuttering often involves difficulty with initiation of voicing, reducing speaking rate in cluttering via pausing may increase the challenge of initiating voice after each pause, thereby increasing the frequency and/or severity of stuttering blocks. This area would need to be monitored during treatment with Paul and stuttering strategies introduced if and when appropriate.

Treatment Options Considered

Therapy Model

At present, there is a weak evidence base for the treatment of cluttering. Although large-scale, well-controlled empirical trials on treatment efficacy are lacking, some small studies have demonstrated improvement in cluttering symptoms through the use of pausing, emphasizing sounds and syllables (Healey et al., 2015), and an auditory-visual training approach (Van Zaalen & Reichel, 2019).

From a clinical perspective, cluttering can be thought of as a modular disorder, with separately identifiable components that nonetheless interrelate; for example, excessive coarticulation is likely to correlate with an overrapid speech rate. A synergistic model was adopted, that is, the idea that successful intervention within one area may have positive effects in another (Myers & Bradley, 1992; St. Louis et al., 2007). It can provide the maximal benefit with minimal clinical time if treatment goals are based on interrelated or hierarchically organized skill deficits. Therefore, in this model, individualized treatment plans must be individually tailored, using information gained from a careful evaluation. In addition to disfluency, therapy may well address such areas as awareness, speech rate, speech rhythm, articulation, and language formulation.

Course of Treatment

Because Paul had an active after-school schedule, he was seen for 10 two-hour therapy sessions over the course of a 2-week period. Most sessions occurred in the evenings after a full day of activities. Despite initial concerns that Paul might be too fatigued from his day to focus on an area of challenge such as his speech, he sustained sufficient attention for all sessions.

Goals, Principles, and Sequence of Treatment

Initial goals were:

1. To increase awareness of specific speech difficulties (i.e., fluency, articulation, rate, and language usage) and effective versus ineffective responses to these difficulties
2. To increase use of effective executive functioning strategies when communication breakdowns occur and to:
   a. Identify the potential source of communication breakdown (i.e., Paul would come up with a "hypothesis")
   b. Respond with a repair strategy related to this hypothesis
   c. Self-evaluate and debrief in structured conversations with the clinician and mother
   d. Use pausing and language organization strategies in functional contexts by progressing through a hierarchy from more- to less-structured language

Three specific principles of treatment were applied to ensure effective therapy. First, to build Paul's self-esteem regarding his speech, the approach needed to be supportive rather than confrontational. His score on the CAT-R indicated that he was not comfortable as a speaker and had negative feelings associated with speaking. Two hours of nightly focus upon something about which Paul had negative feelings could easily become demoralizing. Paul needed to know that, despite speech difficulties, he had many other assets. Second, to foster Paul's enthusiastic participation in therapy, the approach needed to be lighthearted and fun, building on his interests and strengths. Paul was a gifted child who, like many children with ASD Level 1, enjoyed intellectual activities. Therefore, he was frequently assigned the role of "teacher" and/or "researcher" when examining how changes in one's speech result in changes in listener reactions. Third, to help ensure carryover, goals needed to be incorporated as soon as possible into everyday contexts, and whenever possible, Paul's family needed to be involved. To accomplish this, Paul was given assignments such as explaining things he had learned to family members, designing and administering quizzes on strategies and information he had learned, and reporting the results back to the clinician. These activities enhanced Paul's sense of empowerment in therapy and allowed the clinician to address any misperceptions as they occurred.

Within the context of these three principles, the long-term goals were addressed in a sequence of specific therapy focus areas. Table 30–2 summarizes the sequence.

Awareness

Experience indicates that although many with cluttered speech are unaware of how they come across to others, they may be somewhat aware that something is not "right" about their speech, if only because of vague feedback they have received from listeners (Dewey, 2005). Paul's CAT-R score seemed to suggest that he was not completely unaware of his speech. Over the years, he had received feedback from professionals and

his family about his rapid rate of speech. Therefore, in introducing the concept of awareness, it was decided to take the conversation beyond Paul and apply it to everyone's speech in general. Children with social and/or severe communication issues such as Paul's are often ignored, teased, or reminded about their speech by others (Gertner et al., 1994). Because communication occurs throughout a child's day, reminders can be frequent. The feedback can become quite tiring and can lead to feelings of guilt and shame, especially when a child knows that he or she should change his or her speech (based upon what others are saying) but does not know how to do so effectively (Murphy, 1999). Often by school age, students have developed defense reactions in response to unwanted feedback about their speech. Many assert that there is "nothing wrong" (Weiss, 1964; Wilhelm, 2020). Paul responded exactly in this way during baseline measurement. This denial suggested that a "back door" approach might be more effective than even gentle confrontation about Paul's speech (Scaler Scott & Ward, 2013). As often happens, when brainstorming with Paul reasons that people might not understand a speaker in general—rather than himself specifically—he volunteered that several of the options presented were characteristic of him (e.g., "I do that one all the time").

Table 30–2. Summary of Therapy Session Structure

Focus Area	Activities
Awareness	Identify potential errors that impact intelligibility; negative practice; games to identify errors in self and others; flowcharts; practice "tuning in" to and responding to nonverbal communication
Pausing	Insertion of pauses in structured hierarchy
Language	Expediter and Pyramid strategies
Home carryover	Designing, administering, and reporting on family quizzes; email assignments with clinician for accountability

Desensitization

Next, therapy involved identifying and experiencing through negative practice different types of less-than-intelligible speech segments, for example, mumbling or deleting syllables. Much of this was done in a game context, with client and clinician competing for points for correctly identifying the types of each other's unintelligible speech. This fostered desensitization to the negative connotations that might surround drawing attention to Paul's speech. Rather than regarding his speech as a weakness or failure, it helped Paul become an "expert" at identifying and producing unintelligible speech (Murphy et al., 2007). Paul gradually became more aware of his compromised intelligibility and open to discussing it. For example, when commended for accurately identifying mumbling combined with rapid speech during a game, Paul commented, "That's easy for me to guess. I do it all the time!"

Pausing

Paul was taught to use pauses to improve the clarity of his speech. Visual markers, that is, slash marks, were inserted into oral reading passages. The clinician explained that pausing would help him both in slowing down and in having time to think about what he wanted to say (St. Louis & Myers, 1995). A science experiment (Scaler Scott & Ward, 2013) was designed whereby Paul read 10 sentences to his mother, 5 during which he used pausing and 5 during which he did not use pausing. He scored the number of words his mother could correctly repeat for each sentence and compared her overall combined accuracy for sentences with and without pausing. Paul repeated this task with his father. In the case of both parents, Paul was able to see how accuracy scores dropped dramatically when pauses were not used. This activity focused on his intellect and motivated him to use the pausing strategy in the future. Once he was "hooked," Paul practiced pausing in a speech hierarchy, progressing through sentences, paragraphs, book chapters, short structured conversations (i.e., one- to two-sentence answers), and spontaneous conversations.

Language Strategies

As Paul became proficient at pausing, he learned how to use the strategy in response to nonverbal feedback from others. Paul had developed a flowchart of "hypotheses" about the source of listener confusion and corresponding repair strategies. The strategies were applied to two broad categories of listener confusion: confusion because of "what I said" (e.g., omitted background information) or "how I said it" (e.g., too soft) (Scaler Scott & Ward, 2013). At this point, the "what" of Ward's (2004, 2006) "Pyramid Approach" and Scaler Scott's (Scaler Scott & Ward, 2013) "Expediter Rules" were introduced (Table 30–3). It is important to note that Paul, like many children with ASD, frequently was unaware of feedback from others because he

Table 30–3. Summary of Language Strategies

Principles adapted from the "Pyramid Approach" (Ward, 2006)[a]
Progress from the "big picture" to small details in descriptions.
Resist providing additional information or asides before the "big picture" is explained.
Resist using fillers.
Principles adapted from "Expediter Rules" (Scaler Scott, 2002)
Use short sentences.
Get right to the point.
Do not use too many examples.
Do not use nonspecific pronouns.
Give the listener background information.

[a]Highlights of the program used with Paul; for a full program description, see Ward (2006, pp. 371–372) and Scaler Scott and Ward (2013).

often found speaker-listener eye contact aversive. As a desensitizing activity, Paul and the clinician played games wherein each took turns identifying when the listener's face looked confused. Once desensitized, Paul was ready to use eye contact to apply what he had learned about identifying listener confusion and making the appropriate repair. During games, Paul and the clinician practiced guessing the source of listener confusion and making the necessary speech repairs. In this activity, Paul again was engaged in the game while not being focused upon his shortcomings, that is, how difficult eye contact could be for him. He began to regard feedback as valuable rather than aversive and as something over which he had control (Ward, 2006). If direct eye contact had remained aversive for Paul due to his ASD, a modified strategy of looking at the listener's forehead or other part of the face would have been presented.

Self-Monitoring and Carryover

As therapy progressed, Paul became more and more successful in self-monitoring his speech: (a) proactively, to speak intelligibly in the first place (through use of pausing, "Pyramid," and "Expediter" strategies), and (b) reactively, to respond either to his own knowledge that he was unclear, or to feedback from others (see Scaler Scott & Ward, 2013). He was praised for attempts at all of these levels.

By the seventh session, Paul was typically able to utilize all strategies effectively and independently in structured communication situations, including such structured daily situations as conversing with his mother in the car. In order to increase distraction and thereby make speech monitoring more challenging, the last three sessions focused solely on spontaneous speech involving Paul, his mother, and his younger brother. In Session 8, the trio and the clinician played several games ("Game Night"), and Paul was required to use clear speech, even when excited. Session 9 involved one of Paul's interests, a cooking activity. In Session 10, Paul ordered lunch at a restaurant and was asked to speak to his server in a loud and clear voice.

To foster carryover, the clinician helped Paul construct a hierarchy of 10 speaking situations, arranged from least to most challenging. Additionally, she asked Paul to email her nightly with his commitment for the following day's practice and then follow up the following night with an evaluation of how it went. In this way, treatment would continue beyond structured therapy.

Analysis of Client's Response to Treatment

Paul's speech was reevaluated 2 days following his last therapy session and again at 3 weeks posttherapy. At all follow-up sessions, Paul's mother indicated that she felt he was more aware of his lack of speech clarity and made more efforts to self-correct. She also indicated that Paul was much less defensive when she intermittently reminded him to repeat or use pauses to regulate his rate. Parent training was implemented for Mrs. R to avoid "overdoing" her reminders and to remember to praise Paul for independent attempts at either using clear speech proactively or repairing communication breakdowns reactively.

Table 30–4 shows that in a posttherapy repeat conversation sample, Paul's NSLDs decreased from 11% to 5%. Without any cueing from the clinician, he made concerted efforts to use pauses in his speech. He did the same during a repeat oral reading task, in which his NSLDs decreased from 0.5% to 0%. His SLDs remained at 2% in conversation and increased from 1% to 2% in oral reading. On the CAT-R, Paul's negative scores increased in comparison to children who do not stutter (i.e., 2.65 standard deviations below this group). This increase in score is likely related to increased speech awareness after therapy. In addition, Paul's comments on the CAT-R indicated that he moved closer toward more positive feelings, but given the opportunity on the test to select only "true" or "false," his score did not change for several items. For example, in response to "I don't talk like other children," Paul responded "true" in both pre- and posttesting, but on posttesting, he qualified this answer with "sometimes." At the 3-week follow-up, Paul's score on the CAT-R had decreased dramatically to –0.88, suggesting his positive feelings about his speech were continuing to increase over time. His mother's rating on Ward's (2006) "Checklist of Cluttering Behavior" showed that Paul's speech ratings changed in the direction of normal scores, that is, from 68 to 60, and increased only slightly at 3-week follow-up to 62.

Overall, Paul responded favorably to intensive intervention and showed increased clarity of speech in structured situations. He became more comfortable with his speech and with monitoring it. He was empowered in being able to modify his speech so that others could understand him. He demonstrated a desire to use these strategies to be more clear to his listener, evidenced by numerous examples of modifying and repeating his message when unclear rather than saying, "Never mind." Paul initiated modifications on his own speech or in response to the nonverbal feedback indicating listener confusion. Three weeks after therapy had ended, he had carried out the aforementioned email assignments approximately one to two times weekly, rather than every day as assigned. At 3-week follow-up, Paul indicated that he was having difficulty remembering to do the email

Table 30–4. Summary of Pre- and Postdata

Area	Pre	Post	3-Week Follow-Up
Disfluencies			
Conversation	SLDs: 2% NSLDs: 11%	SLDs: 2% NSLDs: 5%	SLDs: 3% NSLDs: 13%
Reading	SLDs: 1% NSLDs: 0.5%	SLDs: 2% NSLDs: 0%	SLDs: 1% NSLDs: 0.5%
Fluency	SSI-3 score: 10 SSI-3 severity rating: very mild	SSI-3 score: 12 SSI-3 severity rating: mild	SSI-3 score: 10 SSI-3 severity rating: very mild
Articulation Examiner judgment	Intermittent weak syllable deletion; frequent instance of decreased vocal intensity	Fewer instances of weak syllable deletion and decreased vocal intensity	Intermittent weak syllable deletion continues; increased regularity of vocal intensity maintained
Speech rate	Examiner judgment: rapid, irregular Overall speaking rate[a]: 4.7 syllables/s Articulation rate[b]: 5.1 syllables/s	Examiner judgment: Deliberate pauses used and increased regularity Overall speaking rate[a]: 3.1 syllables/s Articulation rate[b]: 3.0 syllables/s	Examiner judgment: pauses and regularity maintained Overall speaking rate[a]: 3.8 syllables/s Articulation rate[b]: 4.6 syllables/s
Language usage	Informal observations: Excessive use of fillers, mazing, and decreased inclusion of background information	Informal observations: Decreased use of fillers and mazing; increased inclusion of background information	Informal observations: Fillers increase; increased provision of background information; increased cohesion of message
Attitudes	$z = -2.06$[c]	$z = -2.65$[c]	$z = -0.88$[c]
Parent ratings	68	60	62
Executive functioning	Examiner judgment: Decreased self-monitoring of clarity persistence when not understood	Examiner judgment: Increased self-monitoring and persistence when not understood	Examiner judgment: Slightly decreased self-monitoring when excited but persistence when not understood maintained

[a]Number of syllables per second including disfluencies, pauses, and hesitations (i.e., rate of message transmission).
[b]Number of syllables per second excluding disfluencies, pauses, and hesitations (i.e., rate of motor movements of mouth).
[c]As compared to school-aged children with no speech/language issues, where average $z = 0.00$.

assignments. At his mother's suggestion, Paul agreed to make the email a part of his daily routine after dinner and before homework; however, even with this plan in place, Paul continued to complete assignments only once or twice weekly.

Further Recommendations

Initial evaluation results revealed stuttering and cluttering. As previously mentioned, it was possible that as Paul decreased his cluttered speech, stuttering might increase (Scaler Scott et al., 2010). His overall score on the SSI-3 did reflect a slight increase at posttesting, with a return to baseline Level 3 weeks later. Given the variability of stuttering behaviors, this slight fluctuation is not surprising. However, possibly because they were not directly addressed in this intervention plan, Paul's SLDs also did not *decrease* with therapy. As the treating clinician became increasingly familiar with Paul, his typical stuttering pattern became apparent. The majority of the SLDs were "tense pauses," that is, minor blocks of less than 1 second in duration with no impact upon his willingness to communicate. Throughout treatment, Paul repeatedly denied other symptoms of stuttering, such as feelings of words getting "stuck" in his mouth. Given his dramatic improvement in attitude toward himself as a speaker even though SLDs were not addressed, it seems valid to state that the SLDs had negligible impact upon Paul as a communicator. Therefore, it was felt that giving Paul another strategy to use in response to his SLDs would only result in an unnecessary additional self-monitoring load. As a next step, the clinician recommended that Paul receive continued assistance and coaching with current cluttering strategies through daily situations on his hierarchy. The clinician also recommended that Paul's SLDs continue to be monitored for signs that further intervention is warranted (such as increased tension, struggle, or word or communication avoidance).

Paul's NSLDs also increased to baseline Level at 3 weeks posttesting. Qualitatively, however, a difference was noted in the functional use of his NSLDs. That is, at 3-week follow-up, he did make frequent revisions in his speech (which are coded as NSLDs) but often did so as a means of revising an unclear message. This functional use of NSLDs was in contrast with his baseline use of NSLDs as time fillers to gather his thoughts. Nonetheless, although Paul had maintained many of his gains in self-monitoring by 3 weeks posttesting, he also was demonstrating some slips in self-monitoring when regular therapy sessions ceased. One such slip was decreased monitoring of speech when excited. Paul's data demonstrate that although

therapy can result in great improvement in the short term, consistent therapy in the long term is required for maintenance of gains. Finally, since Paul's clarity of speech improved after introduction of language strategies and pausing—notably *without* specific exercises to address motor speech—a synergistic approach to treatment (Myers & Bradley, 1992) was validated.

Authors' Note

The authors wish to acknowledge the participation of "Paul" (all names and identifying information changed to maintain confidentiality) and his family. This case study is based upon a real client and has met the requirements for institutional review board exemption.

References

Bakker, K., Raphael, L. J., Myers, F. L., & St. Louis, K. O. (2011). A preliminary comparison of speech rate, self evaluation, and disfluency of people who speak exceptionally fast, clutter, or speak normally. In D. Ward & K. Scaler Scott (Eds.) *Cluttering: Research, intervention and education.* (pp. 45–65). Psychology Press.

Bangert, K., Scaler Scott, K., Adams, C., Kisenwether, J. S., Giuffre, L., Reed, J., . . . Klusek, J. (2022). Cluttering in the speech of males with fragile X syndrome. *Journal of Speech, Language, and Hearing Research, 65,* 954–969. https://doi.org/10.1044/2021_JSLHR-21-00446

Barnhill, G. P. (2001). Social attributions and depression in adolescents with Asperger syndrome. *Focus on Autism and Other Developmental Disabilities, 16,* 46–53. https://doi.org/10.1177/108835760101600112

Blood, G. W., Blood, I. M., & Tellis, G. (2000). Auditory processing and cluttering in young children. *Perceptual Motor Skills, 90,* 631–639. https://doi.org/10.2466/pms.2000.90.2.631

Brutten, G., & Vanryckeghem, M. (2007). *Behavior Assessment Battery for Children Who Stutter.* Plural Publishing.

Coppens-Hofman, M. C., Terband, H. R., Maassen, B. A. M., van Schrojenstein Lantman-De Valk, H. M. J., Van Zaalen op't Hof, Y., & Snik, A. F. M. (2013). Dysfluencies in the speech of adults with intellectual disabilities and reported speech difficulties. *Journal of Communication Disorders, 46*(5–6), 484–494. https://doi.org/10.1016/j.jcomdis.2013.08.001

Daly, D. A., & Cantrell, R. P. (2006, July). *Cluttering: Characteristics identified as diagnostically significant by 60 fluency experts.* Paper presented at the Fifth World Congress of Fluency Disorders, Dublin, Ireland.

Denckla, M. B. (1996). A theory and model of executive function: A neuropsychological perspective. In G. R. Lyon & N. A. Krasnegor (Eds.), *Attention, memory, and executive function* (pp. 263–278). Paul Brookes.

Dewey, J. (2005, October). *My experiences with cluttering.* Paper presented at the Eighth Annual International Stuttering Awareness Day (ISAD) Online Conference.

Diedrich, W. M. (1984). Cluttering: Its diagnosis. In H. Winitz (Ed.), *Treating articulation disorders: For clinicians by clinicians* (pp. 307–323). University Park Press.

Farmer, A., & Brayton, E. R. (1979). Speech characteristics of fluent and dysfluent Down's syndrome adults. *Folia Phoniatrica, 31,* 284–290. https://doi.org/10.1159/000264175

Freund, H. (1952). Studies in the interrelationship between stuttering and cluttering. *Folia Phoniatrica, 4,* 146–168. https://doi.org/10.1159/000262621

Gertner, B. L., Rice, M. L., & Hadley, P. A. (1994). Influence of communicative competence on peer preferences in a preschool classroom. *Journal of Speech and Hearing Research, 37,* 913–923. https://psycnet.apa.org/doi/10.1044/jshr.3704.913

Healey, K., Nelson, S., & Scaler Scott, K. (2015). A case study of cluttering treatment outcomes in a teen. In S. K. Millard, D. T. Rowley, & K. Fenton (Eds.) *Proceedings of the 10th Oxford Dysfluency Conference, Oxford, United Kingdom* (pp. 141–146). Elsevier: Science Direct.

Hill, E. L., & Bird, C. M. (2006). Executive processes in Asperger syndrome: Patterns of performance in a multiple case series. *Neuropsychologia, 44,* 2822–2835. https://doi.org/10.1016/j.neuropsychologia.2006.06.007

LeBrun, Y. (1996). Cluttering after brain damage. *Journal of Fluency Disorders, 21,* 289–295. https://doi.org/10.1016/S0094-730X%2896%2900031-9

Loban, W. (1976). *The language of elementary school children.* National Council of Teachers of English.

Molt, L. F. (1996). An examination of various aspects of auditory processing in clutterers. *Journal of Fluency Disorders, 21,* 215–225. https://doi.org/10.2466/pms.2000.90.2.631

Murphy, W. P. (1999). A preliminary look at shame, guilt, and stuttering. In N. Bernstein Ratner & E. C. Healey (Eds.), *Stuttering research and practice: Bridging the gap* (pp. 131–143). Erlbaum.

Murphy, W. P., Yaruss, J. S., & Quesal, R. W. (2007). Enhancing treatment for school-age children who stutter. I. Reducing negative reactions through desensitization and cognitive restructuring. *Journal of Fluency Disorders, 32,* 121–139. https://doi.org/10.1016/j.jfludis.2007.02.002

Myers, F. L., & Bradley, C. L. (1992). Clinical management of cluttering from a synergistic framework. In F. L. Myers & K. O. St. Louis (Eds.), *Cluttering: A clinical perspective* (pp. 85–105). Far Communications. (Reissued in 1996 by Singular)

Pitluk, N. (1982). Aspects of the expressive language of cluttering and stuttering schoolchildren. *The South African Journal of Communication Disorders, 29,* 77–84.

Preus, A. (1996). Cluttering upgraded. *Journal of Fluency Disorders, 21,* 349–357. https://doi.org/10.1016/S0094-730X(96)00038-1

Reichel, I., & Bakker, K. (2009). Global landscape of cluttering. *Perspectives of Fluency and Fluency Disorders, 19*(2), 62–66.

Riley, G. D. (1994). *Stuttering severity instrument for children and adults* (3rd ed.). Pro-Ed.

Scaler Scott, K. (2018). *Fluency plus: Managing fluency disorders in individuals with multiple diagnoses.* SLACK, Inc.

Scaler Scott, K. (2022). Cluttering in a school-aged child: Tackling the challenges step by step. *Seminars in Speech and Language, 43*(2), 130–146. https://doi.org/10.1055/s-0042-1743537

Scaler Scott, K., Sonsterud, H., & Reichel, I. (2022). Cluttering: Etiology, symptomatology, education and treatment. In P. M. Zebrowski, J. D. Anderson, & E. G. Conture (Eds.), *Stuttering and related disorders of fluency* (4th ed., pp. 244–254). Thieme.

Scaler Scott, K., Tetnowski, J. A., Flaitz, J. R., & Yaruss, J. S. (2014). Preliminary study of disfluency in school-aged children with autism. *International Journal of Language & Communication Disorders, 49*(1), 75–89. https://doi.org/10.1111/1460-6984.12048

Scaler Scott, K., Tetnowski, J. A., Roussel, N. C., & Flaitz, J. R. (2010, April). Impact of a pausing treatment strategy upon the speech of a clutterer-stutterer. In K. Bakker, F. L. Myers, & L. J. Raphael (Eds.), *Proceedings of the First World Conference on Cluttering* (pp. 132–140). http://associations.missouristate.edu/ICA

Scaler Scott, K., & Ward, D. (2013). *Managing cluttering: A comprehensive guidebook of activities.* Pro-Ed.

Shriberg, L. D., Paul, R., McSweeny, J. L., Klin, A., Cohen, D. J., & Volkmar, F. R. (2001). Speech and prosody characteristics of adolescents and adults with high-functioning autism and Asperger syndrome. *Journal of Speech, Language, and Hearing Research, 44*, 1097–1115. https://doi.org/10.1044/1092-4388(2001/087)

Singer, B. D., & Bashir, T. S. (1999). What are executive functions and self-regulation and what do they have to do with language-learning disorders? *Language, Speech and Hearing Services in Schools, 30*, 265–273. https://doi.org/10.1044/0161-1461.3003.265

St. Louis, K. O., Hinzman, A. R., & Hull, F. M. (1985). Studies of cluttering: Disfluency and language measures in young possible clutterers and stutterers. *Journal of Fluency Disorders, 10*, 151–172. https://doi.org/10.1016/0094-730X(85)90008-7

St. Louis, K. O., & Myers, F. L. (1995). Clinical management of cluttering. *Language Speech and Hearing Services in Schools, 26*, 187–195. https://doi.org/10.1044/0161-1461.2602.187

St. Louis, K. O., Myers, F. L., Bakker, K., & Raphael, L. J. (2007). Understanding and treating cluttering. In E. Conture & R. Curlee (Eds.), *Stuttering and related disorders of fluency* (3rd ed., pp. 297–325). Thieme.

St. Louis, K. O., & Schulte, K. (2011). Defining cluttering: The lowest common denominator. In D. Ward & K. Scaler Scott (Eds.), *Cluttering: Research, intervention and education.* (pp. 233–253). Psychology Press.

Szatmari, P. (1991). Asperger's syndrome: Diagnosis, treatment and outcome. *Psychiatric Clinics of North America, 14*, 81–92.

Tager-Flusberg, H. (1995). Dissociation in form and function in the acquisition of language by autistic children. In H. Tager-Flusberg (Ed.), *Constraints on language acquisition: Studies of atypical children* (pp. 175–194). Erlbaum.

Thacker, R. C., & De Nil, L. F. (1996). Neurogenic cluttering. *Journal of Fluency Disorders, 21*, 227–238. https://doi.org/10.1016/S0094-730X(96)00025-3

Van Borsel, J., & Vandermeulen, A. (2009). Cluttering in Down syndrome. *Folia Phoniatrica et Logopaedica, 60*(6), 312–317. https://doi.org/10.1159/000170081

Van Zaalen, Y., & Reichel, I. (2019). Clinical success using the audio-visual training for cluttering. *Perspectives in Global Issues in Communication Science and Related Disorders, 4*(6), 1589–1594. https://doi.org/10.1044/2019_PERS-SIG17-2019-001

Van Zaalen, Y., Wijnen, F., & Dejonckere, P. (2009) Language planning disturbances in children who clutter or have learning disabilities. *International Journal of Speech-Language Pathology, 11*(6), 496–508. https://doi.org/10.3109/17549500903137249

Ward, D. (2004). Cluttering, speech rate and linguistic deficit: A case report. In A. Packman, Meltzer, & H. F. M. Peters (Eds.), *Theory, therapy and research in fluency disorders: Proceedings of the 4th World Congress on Fluency Disorders* (pp. 511–516). Nijmegan University Press.

Ward, D. (2006). *Stuttering and cluttering: Frameworks for understanding and treatment.* Psychology Press.

Ward, D. (2017). *Stuttering and cluttering: Frameworks for understanding and treatment* (2nd ed.). Psychology Press.

Weiss, D. A. (1964). *Cluttering.* Prentice-Hall.

Wilhelm, R. (2020). *Too fast for words: How discovering that I don't stutter but clutter changed my life.* Big Time Publishers.

Yairi, E. (1996). Applications of disfluencies in measurements of stuttering. *Journal of Speech and Hearing Research, 39*, 402–403. https://doi.org/10.1044/jshr.3902.402

CASE 31

Archie: Using the Multisensory Syllabic Unit Approach to Treat the Fricative Productions of a Child With Moderate-to-Severe Hearing Loss

Sheila R. Pratt

Conceptual Knowledge Areas

Hearing loss has a notable effect on the development of speech production when the loss is congenital or occurs in infancy and early childhood. The treatment of speech impairment secondary to hearing loss typically is viewed from a sensory modality perspective—whether speech production should be stimulated and treated via the impaired auditory system or through multiple modalities, including the auditory system. Unisensory approaches argue for strengthening the auditory system, whereas multisensory approaches argue for training flexibility in access and use of the best available set of speech cues across modalities.

Description of the Case

Background Information

Relevant Facts

This report describes a child with a moderate-to-severe sensory hearing loss who had difficulty with fricative production and was treated with the Multisensory Syllabic Unit Approach. The Multisensory Syllabic Unit Approach was first used at the Central Institute for the Deaf and described by Carhart (1947, 1963) and later by Silverman (1971). It was subsequently adapted and incorporated into other, more current treatment approaches for children with speech impairment secondary to hearing loss.

History

Archie was a 6-year-old boy with a genetic bilateral hearing loss that was identified at 1 year of age, so by current standards, he was late identified (Joint Committee on Infant Hearing, 2019; Yoshinaga-Itano et al., 2021). He was fitted bilaterally with behind-the-ear hearing aids at 3 years of age and enrolled into intervention through a local day-school program for deaf and hard-of-hearing children. This placement continued through elementary school. The school used an auditory-oral approach to education and treatment, although students were allowed to use sign language in casual conversations outside of the classroom. American Sign Language was the child's native language in the home, but he used oral English at school and when communicating with oral-aural communicators. During school, the child's speech production was promoted through auditory stimulation and training and not through direct speech production intervention.

Reason for Referral

The child was referred by his parents for treatment because he had difficulty producing fricatives and affricates and was not making substantive gains in speech intelligibility. There was concern that because of his age, further gains in speech production skills would be limited without direct intervention.

Initial Findings and Representation of the Problem

Archie presented with clear ear canals upon otoscopic inspection and normal tympanograms bilaterally (American Speech-Language-Hearing Association [ASHA], 1997). Pure-tone thresholds revealed a moderate-to-severe sensorineural hearing loss in both ears (Figure 31–1). The hearing loss configuration was symmetrical across ears and relatively flat. Word recognition was measured with the Northwestern University–Children's Perception of Speech (Elliott & Katz, 1980a) presented at 30 dB HL. Performance was 82% correct in the right ear and 74% correct in the left.

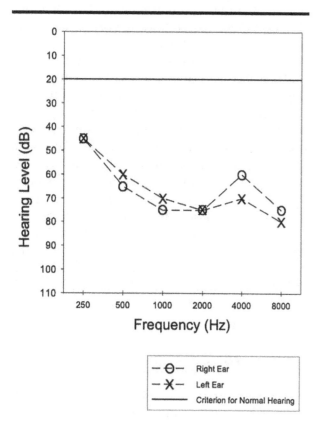

Figure 31–1. The child's unaided pure-tone thresholds obtained with insert earphones.

These results were consistent with age and hearing loss severity, yet over 2 *SD* below that expected by normal-hearing children of Archie's age (Elliott & Katz, 1980b).

Archie's oral-aural language skills were consistent with his age and hearing loss but delayed when compared to normal-hearing children. On the Peabody Picture Vocabulary Test–Revised (Dunn & Dunn, 1981), he produced a standard score of 59 and percentile rank of 1. On the Rhode Island Test of Language Structure (Engen & Engen, 1983), which was administered in oral English, his percentile rank was 49.2 when compared to children with hearing loss but <1 when compared to normal-hearing children his age. With sign language considered, his mother reported that he was at age level on the expressive and receptive language subtests of the Child Development Inventory (Ireton, 1992), as well as on the inventory overall. This suggested that although his ability to comprehend and produce language was intact, oral-aural language was constrained by the hearing loss.

Archie's auditory-verbal memory span was assessed with the Digit Span subtest of the Wechsler Intelligence Scale for Children–Third Edition (Wechsler, 1991). The results were borderline with a subtest scaled score of 5 (Kramer, 1993). This result was not unexpected because auditory working memory often is depressed in children with prelingual hearing loss and oral-aural language delay (Heinrichs-Graham et al., 2021). In contrast, the child's performance on the Motor-Free Visual Perception Test (Colarusso & Hammill, 1972) was at age level (standard score of 95). These results confirmed that the impact of this child's hearing loss was limited to auditory dependent skills.

Consistent with this argument, the child's speech production was impaired, but his oral-motor function appeared to be normal. An oral peripheral examination revealed intact oral structures and normal movement and coordination for speech (Robbins & Klee, 1987). The Goldman-Fristoe Test of Articulation (Goldman & Fristoe, 1986) was administered at the single-word level, and most of Archie's errors were on fricative and affricate sounds, /r/, and blends. Fricatives and affricates in the final word position were typically omitted, whereas those in the initial and medial position were substituted with plosives of comparable place and voicing. For example, /f/ was replaced by /p/ and /v/ was replaced by /b/, /s/ was substituted with /t/, and /z/ was substituted with /d/. The /r/ sound was usually replaced with /w/, and most blends were reduced. Other speech sounds were correctly produced at the single-word level. However, in conversational speech, his consonant inventory primarily consisted of stops, nasals, and early emerging liquids and glides. Fricatives were globally affected and either stopped or omitted. Affricates were omitted in conversation. Some inconsistent voicing distortions (shifts toward the perceptual boundary) were common and indicated issues with coarticulatory timing. Voice quality, resonance, and prosody were normal in ongoing speech, which was somewhat surprising given the severity of the child's hearing loss. Single-word intelligibility, as assessed with the CID Picture SPINE (Monsen et al., 1988), was 60%, but in conversation, the child was understood most of the time, especially when he reduced his speaking rate. He was quite social and talkative, and his speech production problems did not appear to substantively interfere with casual communication with his peers and teachers in the school setting.

Archie presented a speech production disorder secondary to prelingual hearing loss that was characterized by omission of fricatives in the final word position and the substitution of initial and medial fricatives with plosives. Affricates followed this pattern in single words but tended to be omitted in all word positions in conversational speech. Of note was the substitution of /f/ and /v/, highly visible continuants typically produced correctly by children with moderate-to-severe hearing loss. With the mix of substitutions, omissions, and inconsistent voicing, it was difficult to determine if the disorder was solely a phonological or a sensorimotor disorder. The consistent stopping of initial and medial fricatives was suggestive of a phonological disorder, but the omissions and inconsistent control of voicing were more characteristic of a sensorimotor disorder. It is likely that both levels were affected, although a primary motor impairment was not indicated.

Archie's hearing loss was associated with delayed auditory vocabulary and immature oral-aural language structure. Both likely adversely impacted speech intelligibility, but manual communication skills were age appropriate. As mentioned, auditory verbal memory span was borderline normal but visual processing skills were age typical.

Treatment Options Considered

Well-Established Knowledge and Scientific Evidence

The nature and severity of speech production delays and impairment secondary to prelingual hearing loss in pediatric populations vary across infants and children (Blamey, Barry, et al., 2001; Paatsch et al., 2006; Sininger et al., 2010). The impact of hearing loss on speech production can be pronounced in children with profound and severe hearing losses, although in most cases, severity is moderated by early and appropriate fitting of hearing aids and cochlear implants and behavioral interventions (Fulcher et al., 2014; Sininger et al., 2010). Profound and severe hearing losses in infancy and early childhood can affect the entire speech production mechanism from respiration to coarticulation and prosody. Without hearing aids and cochlear implants, most children with severe and profound hearing losses fail to produce intelligible speech. In contrast, children with mild-to-moderate hearing loss usually develop intelligible speech, but they remain at risk for resonance, vocal, and segmental speech differences and delays (Pratt & Tye-Murray, 2008; Tomblin et al., 2014).

However, not all studies have found early identification and intervention to account for the development of speech sound production in children with hearing loss (Kennedy et al., 2006). Quality of intervention, hearing technology wear time (dosage), and speech perception skills may be more critical to the long-term development of speech production in children with prelingual hearing loss (Farquharson et al., 2022; Paatsch et al., 2006).

Most children with hearing loss also require behavioral intervention to speak intelligibly and in a manner acceptable to the average listener. Intervention usually begins shortly after diagnosis and typically is a long-term process that continues through early childhood. Despite an acknowledged need, well-controlled studies documenting speech treatment effectiveness and efficacy are limited for this population. Published studies comparing behavioral treatment approaches for children with hearing loss are rare (Paatsch et al., 2001, 2006). Most recent studies of speech production outcomes assess them as a component of comprehensive therapeutic and educational approaches and do not detail specific procedures used in speech therapy (Farquharson et al., 2022; Paatsch et al., 2006).

Nearly all speech treatments used with children with hearing loss optimize the use of residual hearing and/or compensate for the hearing loss by using other sensory modalities for input and feedback (Pratt, 2005; Pratt & Tye-Murray, 2008). Concentrating on the auditory modality typically is preferred if the auditory system can be treated (i.e., hearing technologies and auditory training) and sufficient sensory input and feedback can be made accessible. However, if children with hearing loss are unable to develop and interface with a complete internal auditory representation of speech, production will be impaired. As a result, a substantive number of children with hearing loss fail to develop normal phonological and sensorimotor speech production skills despite proper and early fitting of hearing technologies and appropriate behavioral intervention (Blamey, Sarant, et al., 2001; Cupples et al., 2018; Serry & Blamey, 1999; Uchanski & Geers, 2003). For some children, augmenting or supplementing speech information through other sensory modalities is required for speech skill acquisition or correction to occur. The visual modality frequently is used to provide supplementary sensory input and feedback during speech treatment, although this is not without controversy.

Ling (2002) and others have argued that nonauditory input and feedback, especially if artificial, can interfere with the retention and generalization of speech sound acquisition. Ling acknowledged that visual and other forms of nonauditory sensory information can benefit some children when initially learning to produce certain sounds but that a dependency can develop. He warned that visual and other nonauditory cues and feedback should be withdrawn as quickly as possible once a child has acquired a sound. This argument has not been tested in children with hearing loss but is supported by the motor-learning literature (Lintern et al., 1990). During motor learning tasks, a dependency can result during practice as artificial cues and feedback become a part of motor memory and interfere with the weaker intrinsic cues of the target movement (Proteau & Cournoyer, 1990; Proteau et al., 1987). This dependence on nonintrinsic cues and feedback is particularly problematic if the task and feedback are simple and feedback is provided with every trial (Weinstein & Schmidt, 1990; Wulf et al., 1998). Yet, behaviors that are complex with multiple characteristics, such as speech, might be less affected by feedback frequency.

In contrast, Carhart (1947, 1963) advocated teaching speech production to children with hearing impairment through a multisensory approach. He suggested speech production should be improved by optimizing auditory performance through auditory training and appropriate amplification, especially with children who have substantial residual hearing. However, Carhart also argued that children should be taught to focus on the face of speakers, first for gestural information and then for speech articulation cues. Furthermore, kinesthetic and vibrotactile information should be integrated into speech production training to promote the development of self-monitoring. That is, children should be taught to monitor their speech production by how it sounds and by how it feels. Carhart's description of what has been referred to as the Multisensory Syllabic Unit Approach or the Traditional Approach was expanded by Silverman (1971). Silverman included the use of other visual and tactile systems such as orthography, graphic displays, visual displays of acoustic signals, fingerspelling, cued speech, and tactile aids.

The Multisensory Syllabic Unit Approach is largely analytic. As its name implies, the basic unit of treatment is the syllable. Phonemes are taught in a predetermined sequence, with most children beginning with bilabial consonants in combination with mid and back vowels (Davis & Hardick, 1981, p. 272). Treatment highlights the visual cues and feedback typically associated with the targeted sounds, as is other sensory information. More artificial information is added as needed. The targeted phonemes are taught first in isolation or consonant-vowel (CV) and vowel-consonant (VC) syllables. The training then advances to more complex syllable combinations such as CVC, CCVC, and CVCCC syllables. Although treatment starts at the syllable level, natural voice and prosody are promoted. However, prosody is directly treated in an analytic fashion once the children have acquired a sizable phoneme repertoire. Finally, the social act of speech, not the precise articulation of segments, is the goal of the approach, so children are encouraged to use newly acquired speech skills in context.

Clinical Experiences

Previous work has shown that visual information, such as visual feedback from computer-based feedback systems, improves the speech of children who have limited auditory function, although a large number of sessions are needed to reach criterion and for the behaviors to stabilize and generalize (Pratt, 2003, 2007; Pratt et al., 1993). Other investigators have observed similar findings (Dagenais et al., 1994; Ertmer & Maki, 2000).

Client Preferences

The child and his parents did not have a preferred treatment approach and were comfortable with the treatment implemented. The child was very willing to attend the sessions and was engaged in the treatment process.

Course of Treatment

The child was seen for individual treatment two times a week for approximately 30 minutes a session, with the sessions conducted at least 2 but no more than 5 days apart. The treatment was conducted at the child's school by an ASHA-certified speech-language pathologist who had experience treating speech and language disorders in children who have hearing loss. A single-subject multiple-baseline design was used with /f/ (and later /s/) as the targeted sound in CV syllables. The vowels were limited to /a/, /o/, /u/, and /i/. Probes of /f/ in CV syllables were used to monitor and document treatment effects. The criterion for acquisition was 80% correct production on the CV probes for four consecutive sessions. Also probed were /v/, /s/, and /z/ in CV syllables. These syllables were monitored to assess generalization to related sound and developmental effects. The production of /f/ and /v/ in words was probed to assess generalization to larger linguistic units. The words were probed by having the child label pictures. All probes were conducted at the beginning of the subsequent session to document learning and retention from the previous treatment session.

The treatment was an adaptation of the Multisensory Syllabic Unit Approach and consisted of a multisensory syllabic imitation task preceded by an auditory identification task. The auditory identification task consisted of the clinician presenting the targeted sound or its common substitution in a CV syllable (e.g., /fo/ vs. /po/) to the child live-voice but without visual lip cues. The child was then asked to indicate by pointing to one of two letters whether an /f/ or a /p/ sound was heard. This was followed by the clinician modeling the /f/ in the CV syllable combination for the child while pointing to her lips. The child was then required to produce the syllable. This sequence was completed 10 times for each of the CV combinations with the order of the combinations randomized for each session. Performance was judged online by the clinician as correct or incorrect, and feedback was provided for both the identification and imitation tasks on 80% of the treatment trials. The child did not receive any concurrent speech therapy while receiving this treatment.

Analysis of Response to Treatment

Treatment results were assessed visually by the clinician from graphic display of the data and with

Table 31–1. Tests of Treatment and Generalization Effects

Effects	C-statistic	z-score	p-value
Treatment			
/f/ Treatment 1	0.554	3.507	.001**
/f/ Treatment 2	0.655	4.095	.001**
/s/ Treatment 2	0.816	5.716	.001**
Generalization of /f/ Treatment 1			
/v/ CV	0.363	2.439	.007*
/s/ CV	0.166	1.053	.146
/z/ CV	−0.043	−0.287	.612
/f/ Words	0.769	0.045	.001**
/v/ Words	0.626	3.865	.001**
Generalization of /f/ Treatment 2			
/v/ CV	0.657	4.361	.001**
/s/ CV	0.110	0.692	.244
/z/ CV	0.029	0.194	.422
/f/ Words	0.802	2.821	.002*
/v/ Words	0.742	4.580	.001**
Generalization of /s/ Treatment 2			
/z/ CV	0.694	4.505	.001**

*$p \leq .01$. **$p \leq .001$.

the C-statistic. Jones (2003) previously demonstrated that the C-statistic is a reasonable statistical test for assessing clinical treatment data that are serially dependent, especially when associated with a flat pretreatment baseline. Treatment analysis and generalization results are displayed in Table 31–1. The clinician's judgments agreed with the statistical results and are thus not presented separately. The child's auditory identification was 80% to 100% correct after the first treatment session, so is not reported further.

The results of the treatment upon /f/ production in CV syllables are illustrated in Figure 31–2. The figure displays the child's production accuracy for the treatment session and the probes collected during the following session. However, determination of treatment effects, generalization, and maintenance were based only on probe data (open circles). With the treatment, the child appeared to acquire the /f/ sound but had difficulty stabilizing performance sufficiently to meet criterion. So, starting at Session 39, it was decided to remove the finger-pointing cue from the treatment. This was done because the child appeared to focus excessively on the finger point and because of cautions associated with using artificial visual cues (Ling, 2002). The removal of the finger point did facilitate stabilization of the /f/ production as well as generalization to the /v/ syllables (which met criterion without treatment) and /f/ and /v/ words. After reaching criterion, correct /f/ production maintained during the treatment of /s/ production. Although the treatment of /s/ was not completed due to the onset of the child's summer break from school, it too showed a positive response to the treatment and generalization to /z/.

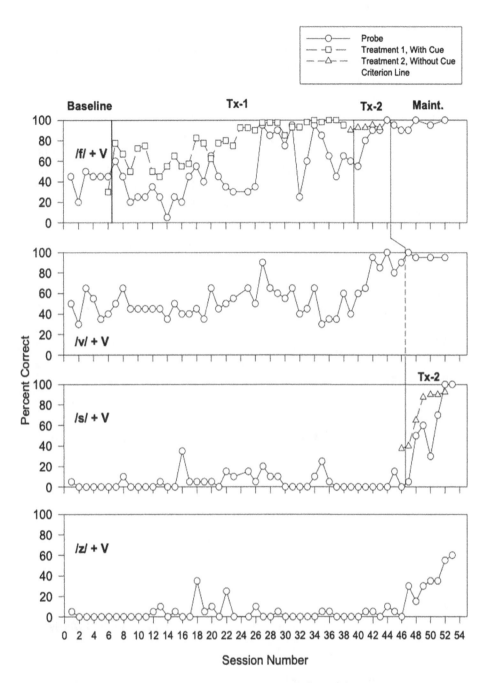

Figure 31–2. Treatment and generalization results at the CV level.

Despite the generalization of the treatment of /f/ to the production of /v/ in CV syllables (especially after removal of the finger cue), there was no generalization to /s/ and /z/ syllables, indicating that the effects of the treatment were not only limited to /f/ and /v/, but also that there was no general improvement in the child's speech production that could be attributed to development or educational activities. That is, the initial flat /s/ and /z/ baselines supported the notion that the significant changes in /f/ and /v/ production were caused by the treatment and not by some other uncontrolled influence.

In addition to generalization at the CV level, the treatment of /f/ was associated with generalization to /f/ and /v/ at the CVC and multisyllabic word level (Figures 31–3 and 31–4). Somewhat surprising was that generalization to the word level was a bit more pronounced for the /v/ than the /f/ words. The /f/ words might have been more difficult linguistically or phonetically than the /v/ words. It also is possible that for this child, producing a voiceless fricative at the word level was more difficult than producing a voiced frica-tive. It is not unusual for children with hearing loss to demonstrate difficulty turning the voice on and off in coordination with the upper airway articulators.

Single-word intelligibility on the CID Picture SPINE improved from 60% to 84% correct over the course of the treatment. The child was producing /f/ and /v/ correctly in conversation and in the classroom by the time treatment was terminated. The teachers and parents expressed approval of the child's progress.

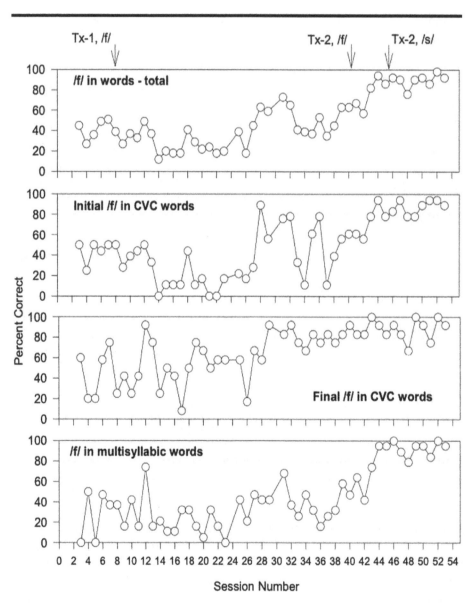

Figure 31–3. Generalization to /f/ in words.

Reformulated Hypothesis and Further Recommendations

Treatment produced a positive and significant response with substantive generalization to the voiced cognate and to more complex linguistic levels. It was concluded that for Archie, a structured multisensory treatment approach at the syl-labic level was effective, although the use of an artificial visual cue interfered with stabilization and generalization. The auditory task might have facilitated the treatment but because the child was near ceiling levels after one session, it was difficult to ascertain its role in the treatment. It was recommended that this child continue speech treatment when school resumed.

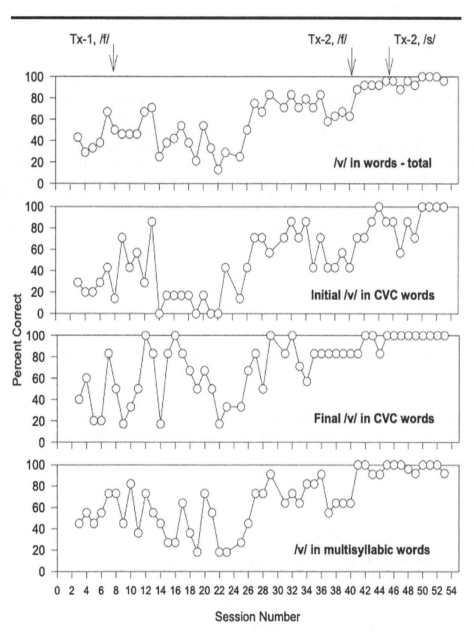

Figure 31–4. Generalization to /v/ in words.

Author's Note

This chapter describes a real case. The treatment was provided gratis by the author and permission was previously obtained to present this case for instructive purposes. Identifiable information was excluded.

References

American Speech-Language-Hearing Association. (1997). *Guidelines for audiologic screening.* http://www.asha.org/policy

Blamey, P. J., Barry, J. G., & Jacq, P. (2001). Phonetic inventory development in young cochlear implant users 6 years postoperation. *Journal of Speech, Language, and Hearing Research, 44,* 73–79. https://doi.org/10.1044/1092-4388(2001/007)

Blamey, P. J., Sarant, J. Z., Paatsch, L. E., Barry, J. G., Bow, C. P., Wales, R. J., . . . Tooher, R. (2001). Relationships among speech perception, production, language, hearing loss, and age in children with impaired hearing. *Journal of Speech Language and Hearing Research, 44,* 264–285. https://doi.org/10.1044/1092-4388(2001/022)

Carhart, R. (1947). Conservation of speech. In H. Davis (Ed.), *Hearing and deafness, a guide for laymen* (pp. 300–317). Murray Hill Books.

Carhart, R. (1963). Conservation of speech. In H. Davis & S. R. Silverman (Eds.), *Hearing and deafness* (Rev. ed., pp. 387–302). Holt, Rinehart and Winston.

Colarusso, R., & Hammill, D. (1972). *Motor-Free Visual Perception Test.* Academic Therapy Publications.

Cupples, L., Ching, T. Y., Button, L., Seeto, M., Zhang, V., Whitfield, J., . . . Marnane, V. (2018). Spoken language and everyday functioning in 5-year-old children using hearing aids or cochlear implants. *International Journal of Audiology, 57*(Suppl. 2), S55–S69. https://doi.org/10.1080/14992027.2017.1370140

Dagenais, P., Critz-Crosby, P., Fletcher, S., & McCutcheon, M. (1994). Comparing abilities of children with profound hearing impairments to learn consonants using electropalatography or traditional aural-oral techniques. *Journal of Speech and Hearing Research, 37,* 687–699. https://doi.org/10.1044/jshr.3703.687

Davis, J., & Hardick, E. (1981). *Rehabilitative audiology for children and adults.* John Wiley & Sons.

Dunn, L., & Dunn, L. (1981). *Peabody Picture Vocabulary Test-Revised.* American Guidance Service.

Elliott, L., & Katz, D. (1980a). *Northwestern University–Children's Perception of Speech.* Auditec of St. Louis.

Elliott, L., & Katz, D. (1980b). *Development of a new children's test of speech discrimination.* Auditec of St. Louis.

Engen, E., & Engen, T. (1983). *Rhode Island Test of Language Structure.* Pro-Ed.

Ertmer, D. J., & Maki, J. E. (2000). A comparison of speech training methods with deaf adolescents: Spectrographic versus noninstrumental instruction. *Journal of Speech, Language, and Hearing Research, 43,* 1509–1523. https://doi.org/10.1044/jslhr.4306.1509

Farquharson, K., Oleson, J., McCreery, R. W., & Walker, E. A. (2022). Auditory experience, speech sound production growth, and early literacy in children who are hard of hearing. *American Journal of Speech-Language Pathology, 31,* 2092–2107. https://doi.org/10.1044/2022_AJSLP-21-00400

Fulcher, E., Baker, E., Purcell, A., & Munro, N. (2014). Typical consonant cluster acquisition in auditory-verbal children with early-identified severe/profound hearing loss. *International Journal of Speech-Language Pathology, 16,* 69–81. https://doi.org/10.3109/17549507.2013.808698

Goldman, R., & Fristoe, M. (1986). *Goldman-Fristoe Test of Articulation.* American Guidance Service.

Heinrichs-Graham, E., Walker, E. A., Eastman, J. A., Frenzel, M. R., Joe, T. R., & McCreery, R. W. (2021). The impact of mild-to-severe hearing loss on the neural dynamics serving verbal working memory processing in children. *Neuroimage: Clinical, 30,* 102647. https://doi.org/10.1016/j.nicl.2021.102647

Ireton, H. (1992). *Child Development Inventory.* Behavior Science Systems, Inc.

Joint Committee on Infant Hearing. (2019). Year 2019 Position Statement: Principles and guidelines for early hearing detection and intervention programs. *Journal of Early Hearing Detection and Intervention, 9*(1), 9–29. https://doi.org/10.1044/1059-0889(2000/005)

Jones, W. P. (2003). Single-case time series with Bayesian analysis: A practitioner's guide. *Measurement and Evaluation in Counseling Development, 36,* 28–39.

Kennedy, C. R., McCann, D. C., Campbell, M. J., Law, C. M., Mullee, M., Petrou, S., . . . Stevenson, J. (2006). Language ability after early detection of permanent childhood hearing impairment. *New England Journal of Medicine, 354*(20), 2131–2141. https://doi.org/10.1056/NEJMoa054915

Kramer, J. H. (1993). Interpretation of individual subtest scores on the WISC-III. *Psychological Assessment, 5,* 193–196.

Ling, D. (2002). *Speech and the hearing-impaired child: Theory and practice* (2nd ed.). A. G. Bell Association for the Deaf.

Lintern, G., Roscoe, S. N., & Sivier, J. (1990). Display principles, control dynamics, and environmental factors in pilot training and transfer. *Human Factors, 32*, 299–317.

Monsen, R., Moog, J., & Geers, A. (1988). *CID Picture SPINE*. Central Institute for the Deaf.

Paatsch, L. E., Blamey, P. J., & Sarant, J. Z. (2001). Effects of articulation training on the production of trained and untrained phonemes in conversations and formal tests. *Journal of Deaf Studies and Deaf Education, 6*, 32–42. https://doi.org/10.1093/deafed/6.1.32

Paatsch, L. E., Blamey, P. J., Sarant, J. Z., & Bow, C. P. (2006) The effects of speech production and vocabulary training on different components of spoken language performance. *Journal of Deaf Studies and Deaf Education, 11*, 39–55. https://doi.org/10.1093/deafed/enj008

Pratt, S. (2003). Reducing voicing inconsistency in a child with severe hearing loss. *Journal of the Academy of Rehabilitative Audiology, 36*, 45–65.

Pratt, S. (2005). Aural habilitation update: The role of auditory feedback on speech production skills of infants and children with hearing loss. *ASHA Leader, 10*(4), 8–9, 32–33.

Pratt, S. (2007). Using electropalatographic feedback to treat the speech of a child with severe-to-profound hearing loss. *The Journal of Speech and Language Pathology—Applied Behavior Analysis, 2*, 213–237.

Pratt, S., Heintzelman, A., & Deming, S. (1993). The efficacy of using the IBM SpeechViewer Vowel Accuracy Module to treat young children with hearing impairment. *Journal of Speech and Hearing Research, 36*, 1063–1074.

Pratt, S. R., & Tye-Murray, N. (2008). Speech impairment secondary to hearing loss. In M. R. McNeil (Ed.), *Clinical management of sensorimotor speech disorders* (2nd ed., pp. 204–234). Thieme Medical Publishers.

Proteau, L., & Cournoyer, L. (1990). Vision of the stylus in a manual aiming task: The effects of practice. *Quarterly Journal of Experimental Psychology, 42B*, 811–828. https://doi.org/10.1080/14640749008401251

Proteau, L., Marteniuk, R. G., Girouard, Y., & Dugas, C. (1987). On the type of information used to control and learn an aiming movement after moderate and extensive training. *Human Movement Science, 6*, 181–199.

Robbins, J., & Klee, T. (1987). Clinical assessment of oropharyngeal motor development in young children. *Journal of Speech and Hearing Disorders, 52*, 271–277. https://doi.org/10.1044/jshd.5203.271

Serry, T. A., & Blamey, P. J. (1999). A 4-year investigation into phonetic inventory development in young cochlear implant users. *Journal of Speech, Language, and Hearing Research, 42*, 141–154. https://doi.org/10.1044/jslhr.4201.141

Silverman, S. (1971). The education of deaf children. In L. E. Travis (Ed.), *Handbook of speech and language pathology* (pp. 399–430). Prentice-Hall.

Sininger, Y. S., Grimes, A., & Christensen, E. (2010). Auditory development in early amplified children: Factors influencing auditory-based communication outcomes in children with hearing loss. *Ear and Hearing, 31*, 166–185.

Tomblin, J. B., Oleson, J. J., Ambrose, S. E., Walker, E., & Moeller, M. P. (2014). The influence of hearing aids on the speech and language development of children with hearing loss. *JAMA Otolaryngology-Head and Neck Surgery, 140*, 403–409. https://doi.org/10.1001/jamaoto.2014.267

Uchanski, R. M., & Geers, A. E. (2003). Acoustic characteristics of the speech of young cochlear implant users: A comparison with normal-hearing agemates. *Ear and Hearing, 24*(Suppl.), 90–105. https://doi.org/10.1097/01.AUD.0000051744.24290.C

Wechsler, D. (1991). *Wechsler Intelligence Scale for Children–Third edition*. Psychological Corporation.

Weinstein, C. J., & Schmidt, R. A. (1990). Reducing frequency of knowledge of results enhances motor skill learning. *Journal of Experimental Psychology: Learning, Memory and Cognition, 16*, 677–691.

Wulf, G., Shea, C. H., & Matschiner, S. (1998). Frequent feedback enhances complex skill learning. *Journal of Motor Behavior, 30*, 180–192. https://doi.org/10.1080/00222899809601335

Yoshinaga-Itano, C., Manchaiah, V., & Hunnicutt, C. (2021). Outcomes of universal newborn screening programs: Systematic review. *Journal of Clinical Medicine, 10*(13), 2784. https://doi.org/10.3390/jcm10132784

LANGUAGE
CASE 32
Jessica: A School-Age Child With Specific Language Impairment: A Case of Continuity
Amy L. Weiss and Michelle Flippin

Conceptual Knowledge Areas

To be prepared to understand this case, it is necessary to have a thorough knowledge of the definition and characteristic profiles of children diagnosed with specific language impairment (SLI). SLI is defined as "a communication disorder that interferes with the development of language skills in children who have no hearing loss or intellectual disabilities. SLI can affect a child's speaking, listening, reading, and writing" (National Institute on Deafness and Other Communication Disorders [NIDCD], 2019). Just as important as an understanding of what SLI is, is an appreciation of what it is not. That is, there are several etiological factors that disqualify children with language problems from being diagnosed with SLI (e.g., hearing impairment, intellectual disability, autism spectrum disorder). Most typical of individuals diagnosed with SLI is their difficulty in learning and consistently using the grammatical morphemes of their language, although disruptions in the learning and use of other language areas, both receptively and expressively, are frequently observed (Leonard, 1998, 2014). In addition, it is critical to understand that SLI is a disorder that may underlie both the learning of oral language comprehension and production and written language comprehension and production (i.e., reading and writing). Moreover, whereas some children with SLI demonstrate early difficulties in word reading, other children with SLI may have no struggles in early word reading, with deficits in reading only detected in later elementary grades, when decoding no longer determines reading comprehension skills (Catts et al., 2005). Given the bridging between oral and written language learning, the speech-language pathologist (SLP) must also be well versed in foundations of typical development in both of these communication modes, and a number of texts do a fine job of providing this information (Adlof, 2020; Catts et al., 2002; Stone et al., 2004). In particular, see Paul et al. (2018) for a very useful set of definitions delineating differences among learning disabilities, language-learning disabilities, reading disabilities, and dyslexia. In terms of course work, graduate students are advised to have completed courses in language development, language disorders in school-age children, assessment and diagnosis, and a course covering the principles of intervention prior to beginning practicum with a school-age client diagnosed with SLI. Further, because federal, state, and local jurisdictions mandate specific requirements for service delivery (e.g., eligibility, accountability), SLPs should frequently check appropriate websites for updated information (e.g., Department of Education, http://www.ed.gov; American Speech-Language-Hearing Association, http://www.asha.org; NIDCD, http://www.nidcd.nih.gov/health/specific-language-impairment).

Description of the Case

Background Information

Jessica was referred by her parents to a local university speech and hearing clinic that served as a training site for speech-language pathology graduate students. At this time, Jessica was 10 years, 3 months of age and enrolled in the fourth grade. The child's parents wanted to know why their daughter was struggling to keep up with her classmates in terms of academic achievement. More specifically, Jessica demonstrated impaired oral language skills characterized by immature grammar that immediately set her apart in conversations from her same-age peers. Specifically, she often omitted grammatical morphemes that were obligatory in the contexts used. For example, although Jessica's home and school dialect were Standard American English, she often omitted third-person singular verb forms as in "Lester **walk** to school but Henry **ride** the bus." In addition, her ability to follow multistep directions, necessary for successful completion of classroom tasks, was also well below grade-level expectations, perhaps indicating a concomitant comprehension problem. Jessica's parents reported that their daughter demonstrated problems with decoding, reading comprehension, and spelling and were concerned that she was not meeting the reading and writing expectations for her grade. Recent benchmark assessments at school reported that Jessica was reading at the second-grade level, and her parents noted that "reading for pleasure" was not an activity that Jessica willingly selected.

When asked about Jessica's history of speech and language development, her parents reported that Jessica began receiving speech and language therapy at 28 months of age. Although some early progress had been made, they were certain that their daughter remained behind her classmates in her language competencies when she entered kindergarten. Jessica's parents have served as good advocates for their daughter's special needs both within their local school district and by securing outside service providers (e.g., a home-based tutor for reading). They described that their concerns about Jessica's language had escalated over the last several years as literacy-learning expectations exponentially increased. Jessica's parents indicated that they had two goals for the present evaluation. First, they were seeking advice for ways to help their daughter catch up through working with her at home. In addition, they sought rec-ommendations for the appropriate services Jessica should be provided in school.

History Information

The following information was gleaned from a combination of direct interview and medical reports released to the clinic. Jessica was born at 36 weeks' gestation, weighing 5.5 lbs., the product of an otherwise unremarkable pregnancy. During her first 2 years of life, Jessica was reported to have had frequent upper respiratory infections, occasionally accompanied by bouts of otitis media with effusion (OME) and subsequent mild hearing loss. A diagnosis of allergies to spring grasses and tree pollen was also made. Jessica's bouts of OME were typically treated with antibiotics, and an antihistamine that caused drowsiness was administered as needed to manage seasonal allergies. Although Jessica's early motor milestones appeared within the typical age-expected range, her speech and language milestones—both receptive and expressive—were delayed. Jessica was enrolled in an Early Intervention (EI) home program when she was 2 years, 4 months of age. At that time, the most remarkable characteristic about Jessica's communication was the presence of multiple misarticulations that made the limited speech she did produce highly unintelligible. Once Jessica was no longer eligible for EI services, she was transitioned to speech-language therapy services through her local school district, where she received once-weekly therapy for 30-minute sessions during the 2 years of preschool. The focus of therapy was on increasing Jessica's intelligibility, although standardized testing indicated that along with multiple misarticulations, Jessica exhibited a more global deficit in both receptive and expressive language. During these 2 years, Jessica also attended an inclusive preschool program five mornings each week. When Jessica entered kindergarten, she continued to receive one weekly, 30-minute session of speech therapy and one 30-minute session of resource support per week to targeted phonological awareness skills. When she entered first grade, her individual pull-out therapy was terminated as Jessica's speech sound production was judged to be intelligible enough for classroom success. However, in second grade, Jessica began receiving some additional reading support in the classroom. For the next 2 years, Jessica failed to meet eligibility requirements for SLP services in school as results of annual screenings conducted by the school's SLP demonstrated oral language skills that were within normal limits. Jessica has remained in the lowest-achieving reading group in her class, and although the resource teacher works with this group twice weekly, Jessica's parents have not observed appreciable changes in their daughter's ability to understand what she has read. In third grade, a neighbor's daughter, who was completing a degree in special education at a local college, was hired by the family to help Jessica with her homework twice a week after school.

According to Jessica's mother, Jessica enjoys attending school despite struggling academically. Jessica excels in both art class and physical education activities and was described by her mother as someone who "enjoys interacting with her friends" and is a "bright, fun-loving, and social child." Jessica's mother did express concerns that Jessica's continued frustration with reading might result in her deciding not to continue her education beyond high school. It was clear that Jessica's parents were very concerned about the impact her current difficulties would have on her future endeavors.

Reason for the Referral

Jessica's parents' primary concern was that they did not understand why their daughter's problems with language and literacy learning had persisted for so long despite the many years of therapy and other supports received. Because Jessica's language problems had transcended oral language understanding and production to reading and writing, her mother expressed urgency in finding an effective therapy program. Her father also noted that Jessica appeared to be falling further behind in her schoolwork. Jessica's parents were concerned what was once a year lag in development had become a 2-year lag—their daughter was now almost 3 years behind in reading comprehension.

Children with SLI are underdiagnosed compared to their same-age peers (Rice, 2020a). Thus, for children like Jessica, accurate identification of SLI is critical, and measuring multiple language dimensions enhances understanding of strengths and challenges and informs selection of appropriate treatment approaches (Rice, 2020b). To better describe Jessica's speech and language understanding and performance as well as investigate some of the underlying competencies that supported that performance, several standardized tests and two nonstandardized assessment tools were employed. More specifically, the intent was to be sure to cover the areas of language learning that supported reading and writing development. The following standardized tests were administered over two 90-minute evaluation sessions:

- Peabody Picture Vocabulary Test–Fifth Edition (PPVT-5; Dunn, 2018) to evaluate the student's receptive vocabulary. Jessica's receptive vocabulary as measured by the PPVT-5 (Form A) yielded a standard score of 75, placing her between 1 and 2 standard deviations below the mean for her age.
- Comprehensive Test of Phonological Processing–Second Edition (CTOPP-2; Wagner et al., 2013) to determine the student's ability to manipulate the phonological system as it may relate to literacy learning. Only the seven core subtests were administered. Although Jessica's phonological awareness composite (i.e., elision and blending words subtests) placed her in the low-normal range, her phonological memory composite (i.e., memory for digits, nonword repetition subtests) and rapid naming composite (i.e., rapid digit naming and rapid letter naming subtests) both placed her performance in the lowest quartile when compared with other students her age.
- Test of Narrative Language–Second Edition (TNL-2; Gillam & Pearson, 2017) to determine both the student's

comprehension (i.e., inferencing) and production of narrative text. A comparison of Jessica's understanding and production of stories clearly showed that her performance in both modalities was significantly below age-expected levels. As the amount of support for storytelling diminished (i.e., retelling, to sequence pictures, to one stimulus picture), Jessica demonstrated increased difficulty including story grammar elements in a logical manner. Her ability to accurately respond to questions that evaluated her understanding of narratives consistently revealed problems with inferencing.

- Test for Auditory Comprehension of Language–Fourth Edition (TACL-4; Carrow-Woolfolk, 2014) to evaluate the student's comprehension of grammatical morphemes and elaborated sentence types. Scores for the vocabulary, grammatical morphemes, and elaborated phrases and sentences subtests consistently placed Jessica in the below-average range (standard scores ranged from 8 to 6).

- Comprehensive Assessment of Spoken Language for Ages 7 to 21–Second Edition (CASL-2; Carrow-Woolfolk, 2017) to evaluate more advanced pragmatic, lexical, and syntactic language understanding and use. The five core subtests appropriate for Jessica's chronological age were administered (i.e., antonyms, syntax construction, paragraph comprehension, nonliteral language, pragmatic judgment). Jessica had the least difficulty providing opposites for the words in the antonyms subtest and the most difficulty with the pragmatic judgment task, often remaining silent when given the task prompt. Except for the antonym subtest, the remaining subtests placed Jessica in the lowest quartile of performance.

- A 100-utterance spontaneous language sample was also collected and analyzed using Systematic Analysis of Language Transcripts (SALT; Miller & Iglesias, 2018). Jessica was not easy to engage in conversation. Thus, the language sample used for analysis was pieced together from incidental language output gathered across test sessions. Having noted this, the results of the language sample analysis should not be considered representative of her best language performance. However, the utterances that were collected substantiated the inconsistencies observed in Jessica's use of grammatical morphemes.

- To evaluate Jessica's written language competencies, she was asked to use the picture stimuli from Task 4 of the TNL-2 (Gillam & Pearson, 2017) to write a story. This nonstandardized probe was administered approximately 30 minutes after the TNL-2 was administered to prevent contamination of the results. It was difficult to motivate Jessica to attempt writing the story. Moreover, she wrote only one sentence for each picture, characterized by frequent misspellings, use of nonspecific words (e.g., that, it), and lack of cohesion. Throughout the assessment, it was not clear that Jessica was using the pictures to support a story with a beginning, a logical middle, and an end.

- Given Jessica's history of OME with documented episodes of hearing loss, information about her hearing status was sought before beginning an evaluation. A hearing evaluation was scheduled just prior to the speech and language evaluation. The results demonstrated that her hearing thresholds were within normal limits bilaterally, and tympanometry revealed normal middle ear pressure in both ears. There were no concerns about Jessica's peripheral hearing at the time of testing. Note that this evaluation did not include any tests specific to a central auditory processing evaluation.

Findings of the Evaluation

Observations

Jessica was compliant during both test sessions. Although testing covered concepts that were clearly difficult for her, Jessica appeared to try her best. However, it was noted during the testing sessions that she was reticent and reluctantly engaged in conversation with the examiner despite the use of various motivating and engaging materials. As had been stated by Jessica's mother, Jessica also appeared to be acutely aware of her difficulties communicating throughout the assessment process.

Interview Revelations

During the evaluation sessions, it was necessary to remind Jessica's mother several times that some of the material presented to her daughter would likely be too difficult for her to handle successfully, but it was important to determine Jessica's present level of performance without supports. Jessica's mother expressed concern that repeated frustrations with testing would result in her daughter not wanting to continue trying her best. The examiner did not share this opinion.

Representation of the Problem at the Time of Evaluation

Jessica's test results confirmed her parents' impressions that Jessica did indeed have a significant delay in both age-expected receptive and expressive language competencies in the absence of any obvious cognitive deficit, peripheral hearing loss, social-emotional difficulties, or oral-motor problems (i.e., there was no indication of either dysarthria or apraxia). Given the absence of any disqualifying etiological factor and the presence of multiple areas of language learning that were below age expectations, a working diagnosis of SLI was supported. In addition to the results gleaned from formal testing, Jessica's long history of impairments in speech and language learning

pointed to a diagnosis of SLI. Although speech sound errors were discerned through testing and observation, they did not negatively affect Jessica's intelligibility. However, longstanding problems with the speech sound system may be indicative of a problem with phonological memory that can impact new word learning and word retrieval, concerns that are not uncommon to many children with the diagnosis of SLI. In addition, impairments in the phonological processing component of language learning also would contribute to a diagnosis of dyslexia, a particular type of reading disability (Catts et al., 2005).

Taken together, it appeared that Jessica was at risk for falling further behind without a significant, team-based approach to working on her underlying language-learning issues. Although Jessica might not have initially qualified for speech and language services based on early oral language screening results, she did now qualify for services as indicated by her low performance on several standardized tests. In fact, given the student's poor reading performance and the longstanding nature of her difficulties, service delivery was felt to be a high priority. Her Individualized Education Plan (IEP) would specify the objectives, therapy approach, the intensity of the therapy received, and who would be providing the services. The plan was not only to recommend services but also to provide some guidance about the type of program thought best given what was known about Jessica's needs and available therapy approaches.

Treatment Considerations

Clinical Experiences

Clinical experiences led to the belief that any successful treatment program for Jessica would have to include the following features:

- Selection of specific goals for Jessica would be developmental, functional, and classroom curriculum based. The continuity between oral language understanding and production and successful literacy learning (i.e., learning to read and write) would have to be enhanced.

- Both the classroom teacher and the school SLP would play integral roles in the planning and implementation of the treatment program to enhance carryover of language-learning strategies.
- Multiple modalities would be utilized to maximize Jessica's learning.
- Evidence-based data supporting the success of the program for students with language-learning needs like Jessica's were available.

Intervention Approach

The intervention approach selected for Jessica was the Writing Lab Approach (WLA) as described by Nelson and Van Meter (2006b). The WLA involves the use of computer technology to target writing skills and can be easily integrated into the classroom curriculum. This language program focuses on the enhancement of writing competencies by providing frequent opportunities to produce and receive feedback on written assignments. Although the products are primarily written, the authors note that the underlying targeted features of language development include both the oral and written modalities from words and sounds at the most basic level of discourse (p. 384). There are three main portions of the WLA: (1) writing process instruction, (2) computer support, and (3) inclusive instructional practices. Students are presented with writing projects that are "authentic" (p. 384). That is, a specific genre is practiced (e.g., narrative, expository) related to the intended audience of the product. Fulfillment of the program requires collaboration between SLPs, general education teachers, and special education teachers as appropriate to ensure that the objectives are curriculum based. Nelson and Van Meter (2006a) claim that support for the WLA program can be traced to studies that have demonstrated the efficacy of "process-based approaches to writing" (p. 389) such as 4th-, 8th-, and 12th-grade stu-

dents' results on the National Assessment of Educational Process exams taken in 1992, when the students who were most successful on the exam described their teachers as providing them with frequent writing exercises accompanied by practice with strategies that encouraged organization of writing products. The authors also cited work by MacArthur and colleagues (Graham et al., 1995; MacArthur et al., 1993) demonstrating that computer-based and process instruction models of intervention were effective in improving the maturity of essays produced by the students in the experimental groups. Research aimed at evaluating the WLA has shown growth for students with language-learning disabilities at all three levels of writing assessed: the word, sentence, and discourse (Nelson et al., 2004; Nelson & Van Meter, 2006b). In addition, most participating students made appreciable gains in written word production fluency and in production of well-formed stories, although less far-reaching were positive changes in the production of more complex sentences.

Selection of Treatment Approach

It was decided that the WLA program was a good choice for Jessica for several reasons. First, the WLA program was founded on the principle of the continuity between oral and written language. It is a flexible program, and the specific written projects can easily be altered to fit within the boundaries of the student's curriculum (e.g., creating a diary as if written by an explorer to the "New World" would be appropriate for a social studies unit about explorers). Second, the WLA, by design, is implemented with collaboration between the SLP and the classroom teacher to maximize functionality and carryover. Third, the WLA includes a computer instructional portion but is not completely reliant upon this modality. Jessica most likely would benefit from inclusion of visual cuing (e.g., graphic organizers) in addition to activities based on computer instruction. Finally, the foundational skills on which the program is based (e.g., the continuity between oral and literate language learning) are accepted as viable instructional principles (Nelson & Van Meter, 2006a).

Course of Treatment

The clinician was asked to work with the school in determining the treatment program to be implemented. After careful consideration, a consensus was reached on the WLA. According to Nelson and Van Meter (2006b), implementation of the WLA requires that the SLP be involved in the daily, hourlong intervention sessions conducted in the classroom two to three times per week. Consistent with the district's Response to Intervention (RTI) plan, it was decided that the seven children in the fourth grade who were in similar need of language-learning instruction/writing instruction would be assigned to meet as a group for 1 hour daily. The resource room teacher was designated as the expert who would be trained in the WLA model and would meet with the children. For these group sessions, one of the three fourth-grade classroom teachers was always present, rotating through the program on a weekly basis. The school SLP also participated three times a week. The professionals on the team met weekly to discuss goals, lesson plans, and the students' progress. Because the WLA approach was as new to the school personnel as it was to the fourth-grade students, the team experienced a period of adjustment. Fortunately, the elementary school had a strong history of administrative support for both continuing education and preparation time for its faculty, and thus the personnel involved had ample time to prepare to implement this new service delivery model. The plan was to begin the program by November 1 and to informally assess the students' classroom performance 6 weeks prior to the beginning of the December break. Because the activities that were employed as part of the WLA could be very useful for enhancing the writing competencies for all fourth-grade students, the teachers decided that after December, they would expand the program with every fourth-grade student participating at least once weekly. The role of the SLP was to provide additional assistance with feedback to Jessica and her cohort and in analyzing the individual lessons to maximize the learning benefits for the children with IEPs. Jessica thrived in this environment.

Analysis of the Client's Response to Intervention

According to her mother and the classroom teachers, Jessica enjoyed the activities planned for her and her group. Because of the care taken by the school personnel to individualize the program for each of the students with IEPs, Jessica was provided with sufficient support to be successful most of the time. She appeared to gain confidence in her ability to complete the assigned writing tasks. Jessica also became more willing to offer information in class. When the typical language learners were included in the WLA approach, the teachers began to develop writing projects that fostered collaboration between Jessica and her classmates who were not having difficulty with language learning. The SLP facilitated these group endeavors to be certain that Jessica was not left out of the decision-making process. At the end of the school year, standardized testing revealed that Jessica had gained approximately 1.5 grade levels in her reading and writing performance. There was also a notable change in the maturity of the sentences she produced in conversation. It appeared that the use of frequent orthographic cuing had made the presence of obligatory morphemes more salient to Jessica. She was now consistently including regular plurals, past-tense verb forms, and third-person singular verb forms, among other grammatical morphemes. The WLA had also had a positive effect on Jessica's vocabulary. It was noted by her classroom teacher that her use of nonspecific words had also noticeably diminished.

Further Recommendations

As hoped, the WLA intervention made an appreciable difference in providing Jessica the support she needed to learn the foundational skills for achieving grade-level reading and writing competencies. Her progress in the WLA program substantiated the belief that Jessica's difficulty with the oral language modality was inextricably tied to her difficulties with reading and writing. At the next IEP meeting, the SLP suggested that Jessica receive an additional session per week of SLP services to specifically address some of her remaining problems with expressive grammar (Smith-Lock et al., 2013) and, specifically, the formulation of complex sentence structures (e.g., adverbial clauses, noun + post modification).

Authors' Note

Jessica's case study is not based on an actual client. Rather, her case represents a composite of several hundred school-age clients the authors have worked with in more than 30 years as SLPs.

References

Adlof, S. M. (2020). Promoting reading achievement in children with developmental language disorders: What can we learn from research on specific language impairment and dyslexia? *Journal of Speech, Language, and Hearing Research, 63*(10), 3277–3292. https://doi.org/10.1044/2020_JSLHR-20-00118

Carrow-Woolfolk, E. (2014). *Test for Auditory Comprehension of Language–Fourth Edition*. Pro-Ed.

Carrow-Woolfolk, E. (2017). *Comprehensive assessment of spoken language*. WPS.

Catts, H. W., Adlof, S. M., Hogan, T. P., & Ellis Weismer, S. (2005). Are specific language impairment and dyslexia distinct disorders? *Journal of Speech, Language, and Hearing Research, 48*(6), 1378–1396. https://doi.org/10.1044/1092-4388(2005/096)

Catts, H. W., Fey, M. E., Tomblin, J. B., & Zhang, X. (2002). A longitudinal investigation of reading outcomes in children with language impairments. *Journal of Speech, Language, and Hearing Research, 45*(6), 1142–1157. https://doi.org/10.1044/1092-4388(2002/093

Dunn, L. (2018). *Peabody Picture Vocabulary Test–Fifth Edition*. Pearson.

Gillam, R., & Pearson, N. (2017). *Test of Narrative Language–Second Edition*. Pro-Ed.

Graham, S., MacArthur, C., & Schwartz, S. (1995). Effects of goal setting and procedural facilitation on the revising behavior and writing performance of students with writing and learning problems. *Journal of Educational Psychology, 87*, 230–240. https://doi.org/10.1037/0022-0663.87.2.230

Leonard, L. (1998). *Children with specific language impairment*. MIT Press.

Leonard, L. B. (2014). Children with specific language impairment and their contribution to the study of language development. *Journal of Child Language, 41*(1, Suppl. 1), 38–47. https://doi.org/10.1017/S0305000914000130

MacArthur, C., Graham, S., & Schwartz, S. (1993). Integrating strategy instruction and word processing into a process approach to writing instruction. *School Psychology Review, 22*, 671–681. https://doi.org/10.1080/02796015.1993.12085681

Miller, J., & Iglesias, A. (2018). Systematic Analysis of Language Transcripts (SALT), Version 2018 [Computer software]. SALT Software, LLC.

National Institute on Deafness and Other Communication Disorders. (2019). *Fact sheet: Specific language impairment*. https://www.nidcd.nih.gov/health/specific-language-impairment

Nelson, N., Bahr, C., & Van Meter, A. (2004). *The writing lab approach to language instruction and intervention*. Paul H. Brookes Publishing.

Nelson, N., & Van Meter, A. (2006a). Partnerships for literacy in a writing lab approach. *Topics in Language Disorders, 26*(1), 55–69.

Nelson, N., & Van Meter, A. (2006b). The writing lab approach for building language, literacy, and communication abilities (pp. 383–422). In R. McCauley & M. Fey (Eds.), *Treatment of language disorders in children*. Paul H. Brookes Publishing.

Paul, R., Norbury, C., & Gosse, C. (2018). *Language disorders from infancy through adolescence: Listening, speaking, reading, writing, and communicating* (5th ed.). Elsevier.

Rice, M. L. (2020a). Advances in specific language impairment research and intervention: An overview of five research symposium papers. *Journal of Speech, Language, and Hearing Research, 63*(10), 3219–3223. https://doi.org/10.1044/2020

Rice, M. L. (2020b). Clinical lessons from studies of children with specific language impairment. *Perspectives of the ASHA Special Interest Groups, 5*(1), 12–29. https://doi.org/10.1044/2019_persp-19-00011

Smith-Lock, K. M., Leitao, S., Lambert, L., & Nickels, L. (2013). Effective intervention for expressive grammar in children with specific language impairment. *International Journal of Language & Communication Disorders, 48*(3), 265–282. https://doi.org/10.1111/1460-6984.12003

Stone, C., Silliman, E., Ehren, B., & Apel, K. (Eds.). (2004). *Handbook of language & literacy: Development and disorders*. The Guilford Press.

Wagner, R. K., Torgesen, J. K., Rashotte, C. A., & Pearson, N. A. (2013). *Comprehensive Test of Phonological Processing–2nd Edition. (CTOPP-2)*. Pro-Ed.

LANGUAGE/BEHAVIORAL DISORDERS
CASE 33
Kevin: A School-Age Child With Emotional Disturbance and Language-Learning Disabilities: Applying Written Language and Behavioral Support Interventions

Robyn A. Ziolkowski and Howard Goldstein

Conceptual Knowledge Areas

The co-occurrence of language disabilities and emotional disturbance has been well documented in the research literature (e.g., Beitchman et al., 1996; Benner et al., 2002; Chow & Wehby, 2018; Hollo et al., 2018; Hollo et al., 2014). Recent research indicates that 68% to 97% of students with emotional disturbance (ED) are likely to experience significant receptive, expressive, and/or pragmatic language impairments (LIs) (Chow & Wehby, 2018). Moreover, in children with ED, these language impairments are stable across age (Nelson et al., 2005).

In addition to the connection between LI and ED, Beitchman and colleagues (1996) expanded this relation to include evidence of a joint association among LI, ED, and learning disabilities. They found that children who demonstrated concomitant LI and psychiatric conditions, including ED, also had school learning problems. In fact, research indicates that most children with ED function below grade level when compared to peers without disabilities (Trout et al., 2003); have lower graduation rates, lower reading and math scores; are less likely to attend postsecondary school (Kauffman, 2001); and have difficulty maintaining employment (Walker et al., 2004). Many students with ED become involved in criminal activity and are involved in the justice system

at an early age (U.S. Department of Health and Human Services, 1999).

There is considerable consensus that language, reading, and behavioral deficits of students with ED become harder to remediate as they become older (J. R. Nelson et al., 2004). Thus, we need to address the underlying skills and processes required for a student to become a better, more independent learner as early as possible. We also need to identify effective intervention strategies, such as structured literacy (Moats, 2019) and explicit instruction (Archer & Hughes, 2011; Graham et al., 2012; Rogers & Graham, 2008), that can affect multiple deficit areas. Speech-language pathologists (SLPs) who work with school-age children should be familiar with the American Speech-Language-Hearing Association (2001) guidelines for providing literacy-focused language intervention, understanding that interventions should focus on improved spoken and written language proficiency. Further, intervention goals should be relevant to the expectations of the general education curriculum. This is facilitated through an alignment of literacy-focused language intervention goals with state and district achievement standards and benchmarks and to the district curriculum. Standards and benchmarks can be found on state Department of Education websites or by contacting the state department offices directly. District information is available by contacting the curriculum and instruction departments or on websites as well. One must keep in mind that standards and benchmarks are normative and are set for students with typically developing skills. They serve as guidelines for the skill sets that students should possess at a specific grade level.

Students with LI and ED are at high risk for developing academic deficits, particularly in the area of written language (Nelson et al., 2003). Some students appear to be fairly proficient in handwriting in earlier grades but begin to experience difficulties as demands increase as they progress in school. These difficulties have been attributed to the increased complexity of the classroom content (Westby, 2004).

The expectation to produce more complex written discourse necessitates self-regulation for students to more independently manage their own learning and behavior (Scott, 2002; Zimmerman & Schunk, 2001). But children with LI, reading disabilities (RDs), and ED typically exhibit delays in their ability to self-regulate (Westby, 2004). Zimmerman (2002) describes self-regulated learners as metacognitively, motivationally, and behaviorally active participants in their own learning process. Self-regulation contributes to systematic efforts to direct thoughts, feelings, and actions toward the attainment of one's goals. Upper elementary students with ED and LI often have difficulty organizing their time, completing assignments, and doing independent seat work. These students often hold negative opinions about themselves and their ability to gain control over their academic environment. It is difficult for these students to formulate, work toward, and attain goals. However, well-designed interventions can accommodate and support development of self-regulated learning (Harris & Graham, 1998). Studies of self-regulated strategy development (SRSD) have shown uniformly positive effects for school-age students with ED and LI (Sreckovic et al., 2014).

Students with ED and LI who struggle academically often have depressed vocabulary levels when compared to peers without disabilities (Ebbers & Denton, 2008). Numerous encounters with new words facilitate greater word knowledge (Nagy & Scott, 2000). However, students with literacy difficulties spend less time engaged in literacy activities, subsequently limiting encounters with new words and inhibiting their vocabulary growth (Baker et al., 1998). Intervention researchers have developed a number of strategies to facilitate word learning, including (1) teaching word study strategies that fuse root words and affixes (Reed, 2008), (2) using semantic maps (Kim et al., 2004), and (3) providing robust instruction with repeated exposures to new words in different contexts (Beck et al., 2002).

Children with LI and ED also have difficulty with written language (Lane et al., 2008). The writing of these students typically contains more mechanical errors and is less expansive, coherent, and effective (Moxley et al., 1995). These difficulties may exist secondary to students with disabilities engaging in writing tasks with little or no planning, limiting revisions to minor errors, and having problems with punctuation, spelling, or handwriting (Gersten & Baker, 2001). Students with LI and ED may increase their writing proficiency when taught in an explicit and direct manner using a basic framework of planning, writing, and revision, as the SRSD approach exemplifies (Graham et al., 2012).

The SRSD model (Graham & Harris, 1999) is an empirically validated instructional approach designed to improve students' strategic thought processes. It has been used to teach strategies for improving academic skills such as reading, writing, and math to students with attention-deficit/hyperactivity disorder (ADHD) or students with learning disabilities, and it appears to be a promising intervention for children with ED (Lane et al., 2008). To date, more than 84 studies have been conducted using SRSD to teach planning and drafting strategies for narrative and expository text with strong treatment effects and maintenance of skills over time (Graham et al., 2012). Students are taught self-regulatory strategies such as self-monitoring, goal setting, and self-instruction in conjunction with specific writing task strategies. These self-regulatory strategies help students manage undesirable behaviors that interrupt task performance. The use of self-monitoring is very motivating because it provides a visual account or record of performance over time (Goddard & Sendi, 2008).

The following case study is a descriptive account of how the SLP can play a significant role in establishing and implementing a contextualized language and self-regulated writing intervention for a student diagnosed with LI and ED.

Description of the Case

Background Information

Kevin was an 11.3-year-old Caucasian male student who had just completed the fourth grade. He presented with a history of oppositional defiant disorder (ODD), ADHD, receptive and expressive language impairment (specific language impairment, SLI), and a reading disability (RD) (American Psychiatric Association, 2013). He had just returned home after spending 2 weeks in a residential treatment center, where he was receiving psychiatric intervention after threatening bodily harm to his previous fourth-grade teacher and running away on the last day of school. He was taking Ritalin for ADHD management and was enrolled in individual psychotherapy to develop effective anger management and daily coping skills. He had a history of explosive temper tantrums, active defiance, and refusal to comply with adult requests and rules. To avoid academic tasks, he would make deliberate attempts to get into trouble and annoy others around him. He often talked about "seeking" revenge when he became angry. Kevin lived with his maternal grandparents, who had been his primary caregivers and custodial guardians since he was 5 years old, and his mother gave up her custodial rights due to ongoing substance abuse issues, resulting in social services intervention for neglect. Kevin's mother had minimal contact with him. Unfortunately, his grandparents were not able to provide much history on his development from birth to age 5 because of his mother's transient lifestyle. Kevin's father, an artist, died when he was an infant.

Kevin's psychiatrists referred him to the examiner in the summer between his fourth- and fifth-grade school years because of concerns that his language impairment and reading disability were contributing factors in the sudden exacerbation of his psychiatric condition. The report from the psychologist indicated that Kevin's nonverbal IQ was in the average range. History and background information were obtained from an in-depth interview with Kevin's grandparents and review of Kevin's medical records. Kevin was diagnosed with a receptive/expressive language disorder at 6 years of age and received ongoing language therapy through the school system provided by the SLP. Kevin was retained in kindergarten secondary to not meeting school benchmarks and at his grandparents' insistence. His reading disability was diagnosed at the end of his third-grade school year. Kevin also demonstrated difficulty with written language. At the end of the fourth grade, he received grades of C, D, and F and did not pass the state competency exam for reading or writing. Even though Kevin did not meet the entire fourth-grade requirements for promotion, Kevin's school decided that he would be passed on to fifth grade based on his special education status. No additional information related to Kevin's current level of language or reading level was available from the school at the time of his referral.

Kevin's grandparents stated that Kevin was an exceptional artist and loved to draw people and animals. They indicated that the only time Kevin would complete his homework without arguing was when the teacher assigned some type of art project. In fact, many times they resorted to hiding Kevin's sketch paper, paints, and special drawing pencils so he would complete his homework.

Language and Writing Assessments

The Clinical Evaluation of Language Fundamentals–4th Edition (Semel et al., 2003) was used to evaluate Kevin's receptive and expressive language. Kevin obtained a receptive language standard score of 72 and an expressive language standard score of 62. Overall, his total language standard score was 65, confirming a severe receptive/expressive language disorder. In addition, the Peabody Picture Vocabulary Test-V (PPVT-V; Dunn, 2019) was administered to assess receptive vocabulary. Kevin's yielded a standard score of 80, indicating his receptive vocabulary was in the below-average range.

After reviewing the results of the language assessments, it appeared that Kevin's difficulty with writing might have been due to underlying language impairment. However, records could not be obtained from the school district in a timely manner, and as per his grandparents' report, district placement testing was completed during the last semester of Kevin's third-grade year. This would make the evaluation results over 1 year old. Subsequently, an informal writing assessment was administered.

Prior to the writing assessment session, Kevin's grandparents were instructed to have Kevin complete two forms of writing, one story and one essay. Kevin refused to complete the written sample task and threatened to run away from home if they made him do it. After they provided a rationale for the assessment, Kevin complied with the request to complete a 3-minute Writing Curriculum-Based Measure (WCBM). A WCBM is a short, simple measure of writing skill that has been used successfully with students with and without disabilities (Watkinson & Lee, 1992). Students write for 3 minutes after they are given an instructional-level story starter. Several components of written communication can then be evaluated, including fluency, syntactic maturity, vocabulary, content, and conventions (e.g., spelling, punctuation, and capitalization) (Epsin et al., 1999). Norms are available for certain components such as Total Number of Words and Correct Writing Sequences (Powell-Smith & Shinn, 2004). In addition to the WCBM, Kevin completed a checklist of indicators assessing his ability to apply self-regulation strategies during the writing process (modified version of Harris and Graham's [1998] full checklist) and a Motivation to Write Survey tool developed by the clinician.

Kevin's timed WCBM samples were scored for (1) total number of words written (TWW), (2) total number of different words (NDW), and (3) total number of correct writing sequences (CWS; i.e., "two adjacent, correctly spelled words that are acceptable within the context of the phrase to a native speaker of the English language" [Videen

et al., 1982]). Samples were further analyzed for syntax and vocabulary. Kevin's writing sample included (1) short length for his age and grade level based on published norms from Deno and colleagues (1982), (2) minimal diversity in word use or inclusion of novel vocabulary, and (3) fragmented sentences and incorrect writing sequences. Punctuation and capitalization were judged as generally proficient, although errors in grammar use were observed. Kevin's writing scores were similar to the scores of a student in the middle of the third-grade school year. In addition, the checklist indicated that Kevin demonstrated poor self-regulation during the writing process, particularly in the areas of planning, organizing information, and revising. The motivational survey results were not surprising: Kevin had significantly depressed motivation to engage in and complete writing tasks.

Hypothesis

It was clear from the outcome of the standardized language assessments that Kevin's receptive and expressive language difficulties, specifically in the areas of grammatical understanding, language production, and semantic understanding, were likely affecting his ability to perform proficiently in the areas of expressive language and writing. Further, it was hypothesized that Kevin's ability to self-regulate and apply metacognitive strategies when engaging in reading and writing tasks was decreased, and this difficulty was negatively impacted by his decreased motivation. He would likely benefit from direct and explicit instruction aimed at increasing his ability to formulate and utilize more complex grammatical structures, improve his understanding of unknown vocabulary, and increase his written expression. It was hypothesized that Kevin's ability to self-regulate would improve if he could effectively implement self-regulating strategies while engaging in language formulation and written expression tasks, such as planning, organizing, and revising written material. Likewise, intrinsic motivation to engage in these tasks would likely increase if Kevin could monitor his own progress and visually determine that his efforts were successful.

Treatment Options

Three different treatment options were considered and discussed with Kevin's grandparents and with Kevin. All the options were based on empirically supported strategies found to be effective for children with ED, LI, and RD. Two of these options incorporated the same treatment goals (stated above); however, the instructional delivery and session time differed.

Option 1: Individualized Treatment

The first treatment option was to begin individualized treatment specific to Kevin's language impairment and difficulties with writing. Intervention would utilize direct and explicit instruction through the Writing Lab Approach (N. Nelson et al., 2004) to increase grammar and vocabulary combined with elements of SRSD to increase written language. Weekly data would be taken, and ongoing intervention goals would be determined by data outcomes. Kevin would be seen in 2 individual hourlong treatment sessions per week for 10 weeks, for a total of 20 hours of intervention. The advantages of this treatment option included individualized attention, ongoing assessment for treatment planning, and convenient session blocks for the grandparents. The greatest disadvantage of this treatment plan was that Kevin would not have multiple opportunities to engage in collaborative learning with fellow students with the expected outcome of improved social and emotional skills.

Option 2: Intensive Small Group

The second treatment option considered was an intensive small group (i.e., four students) program for school-age students, all of whom were diagnosed with ED. Programming would be designed to develop oral and written language skills using components of the Writing Lab Approach (N. Nelson et al., 2004). In addition to the self-regulation component, the group intervention would focus on developing appropriate peer relationships and social skills. Explicit/direct intervention, small group instruction, positive emotional support, and repeated practice have led to powerful student outcomes (Foorman & Torgesen, 2001). These strategies would be incorporated into the planning for this group and implemented in a manner that was responsive to Kevin's language level, reading level, and ED needs. Weekly data would monitor progress for ongoing intervention goals. The group would meet for 90 minutes three times a week for 10 weeks, for a total of 45 hours of intervention. The advantages of this option included the small group format, with embedded social and emotional learning opportunities. Further, Kevin would be engaged in practice with peers as opposed to just the clinician. The disadvantage was that Kevin's behavior problems might prevent his full participation.

Option 3: Consultation and Home-Based Intervention

The third treatment option considered was a combination of consultation and home-based intervention using the home computer. It was proposed that Kevin's grandparents would consult with the clinician once every week to review the previous week's outcomes, preview the coming week's instruction, and complete a weekly WCBM. Kevin would independently work on his writing, grammar, and vocabulary goals via the computer. The clinician would give the grandparents a series of assignments for Kevin to complete each week. Although this model has not been validated for teaching SRSD, utilizing word processing has been shown to have moderate effects on writing outcomes (see Bangert-Drowns, 1993) and is a recommended strategy for students with ADHD (Simonson et al., 2008). The recommended instructional time for this model was three times per week for half an hour via computer for 10 weeks, for a total of 15 hours of instruction. The advantages of this program were minimal: It was convenient for Kevin's grandparents. The disadvantages included potential poor home participation and follow-through with minimal scaffolding support and social encouragement during intervention.

Kevin's grandparents chose the second option (i.e., small group) based on the premise that he would be able to interact and learn with peers his own age. They felt that Kevin's challenging behaviors would be less likely to occur in the presence of a peer group and that this option would be the most motivating to Kevin in the long run. Kevin indicated that he "didn't care one way or the other because either way he would not do anything anyway."

Intervention Approach and Activities

Developing Treatment Goals

Kevin's school district website was reviewed and language, reading, and writing content standards and benchmarks and curriculum matrix were easily obtained for intervention goal planning. The following state standards were incorporated:

- Write personal or fictional narratives using a logical sequence of events and demonstrating an effective use of techniques such as descriptions and transitional words and phrases
- Correct sentence formation, grammar, punctuation, capitalization, and spelling are applied to make the meaning clear to the reader
- With guidance and support from peers and adults, develop and strengthen writing as needed by planning, revising, and editing

Third- and fourth-grade curriculum map goals were utilized secondary to Kevin's language and writing assessment results that indicated he demonstrated difficulty with many of the skill areas targeted. Intervention was planned to include the following treatment goals: (1) Increase production and application of more complex grammatical forms, focusing on those targets that would support growth in Kevin's writing; (2) increase understanding and use of novel vocabulary,

including recognizing meaning of select prefixes and suffixes; (3) improve written expression in TWW (baseline = 39 words), NDW (baseline = 17 words), and CWS (baseline = 23) when writing narratives; (4) independently incorporate self-regulating strategies during each stage of writing (criterion for each stage = 5 based on self-reported checklist); and (5) independently incorporate the main idea and supporting details using elements of story grammar.

Developing the Therapeutic Community

On the first day of intervention, students were introduced to each other, and intervention commenced. Kevin and the other three group members created a series of rules and group expectations that the small group would abide by and named the expectations the "Cooperation Code." The Cooperation Code was posted in the intervention area and systematically reviewed by the students at each session. Student and clinician roles and responsibilities were clearly defined, as were the cooperative learning procedures (i.e., interactive dialogue procedures such as turn-taking and asking for help) and the specific negotiating actions that were to be implemented when group members did not agree. This type of behavioral management strategy has been shown to decrease off-task behavior and increase academic engagement, leadership, and conflict resolution (see Simonson et al., 2008). Further, the clinician and group members agreed to use positive statements and praise during interactions, including when feeling discouraged or unsuccessful. Kevin did not demonstrate any challenging behavior and fully participated. The students appeared to enjoy setting up their own therapy "community."

The students also were expected to develop their own management hierarchy related to how the independent practice center would run. The students decided to create a leadership role and determined that "what the boss says goes." This role was to be rotated each week so each student had the opportunity to be "the boss." This strategy appeared to be a positive motivator for group participation as well as a facilitator of self-regulated behavior when in the boss role. The leadership rules became part of the Cooperation Code.

Self-Monitoring

Kevin and his group members had completed baseline assessments at their first evaluation appointment. To determine whether this baseline measure was stable, three more 3-minute samples were completed. On the first day of intervention, the self-monitoring strategy was introduced. Kevin and his fellow group members learned how to count and graph the TWW and the NDW. Procedures used were modeled after Goddard and Sendi (2008), who found significant increases in writing quantity and quality after students began self-monitoring. Students would then graph their own data from the WCBM on the TWW and NDW that were administered at the end of every week.

General Intervention Procedures

Students with ED appear to require increased structure, minimal distractions, decreased transition time, and active engagement with multiple opportunities to respond to promote academic and social behaviors (Simonson et al., 2008). Thus, the structure of the therapy sessions was consistent; although the content and intervention targets were data driven, the form of delivery did not change for the 10 weeks. Separate "centers" were developed to structure each intervention component. Centers ran as follows: (1) 2 minutes for reviewing rules and garnering materials, (2) 15 minutes of direct grammar and vocabulary instruction, (3) 13 minutes of partner pairs for reviewing vocabulary words and practicing newly learned grammatical forms, (4) 5 minutes for planning, (5) 10 minutes for organizing, (6) 15 minutes for writing (varied among direct clinician instructional time, collaborative peer work, independent work), (7) 15 minutes for revising (varied among direct clinician instructional time, collaborative peer work, independent work), (8) 10 minutes for drawing illustrations to complete the narrative, and (9) 5 minutes for wrap-up. The centers were timed with a 2-minute warning for transitions between the eight phases.

Based on recommendations from extant research, the following instructional components were implemented during the intervention sessions: (1) reviews of previously covered material, (2) clearly stated purpose of the new lesson, (3) explicit and direct strategy instruction, (4) active modeling, (5) scaffolding of student responses, (6) guided practice in collaborative groups or pairs, (7) motivating and culturally sensitive corrective feedback, and (8) practice to mastery (Swanson, 1999).

Strategies were first introduced via direct, explicit instruction and supported through clinician models. The students were required to attempt the strategies presented with clinician support. The self-monitoring data were used to determine when the students required less support. As the students demonstrated increased proficiency, the level of support was decreased.

Strategic Programming

The program was designed to address goals in a comprehensive manner. Intervention was delivered in units. The unit components were thoughtfully chosen so the grammar/vocabulary elements would be utilized and included in the writing product. Each unit comprised the following components:

1. A theme intended to target a social emotional area (e.g., making friends)
2. A starter that was tied to the theme and would guide the choice of grammar and vocabulary targets (e.g., One morning I woke up and saw a . . . ?)
3. Grammar targets (examples):
   a. Adjectives (bright, sunny, dark, gloomy)
   b. Adverbs (quickly, tearfully, happily)
   c. Auxiliary verbs (are, will, have, has, can, does)
   d. Homophones (their, there, they're)
   e. Cohesive units (and, but, also, even though)
   f. Prefix (re-)
   g. Simple versus compound sentences
4. Vocabulary: words that assist with providing rich, colorful, accurate, and precise language

and descriptions (e.g., pal [n], enemy [n], respect [v], entice [v], loyal [a], reluctant [a])

Task-Specific Strategy for Planning and Writing

The "3-5-3" model of story writing, a modified version of the Think, Plan, and Write—SPACE approach (Graham & Harris, 1999), also was introduced and utilized over the course of the 10 weeks. It is based on the SRSD model (Graham & Harris, 1993) and incorporates six stages of instruction that can be reordered, combined, revisited, or modified if required by the students' individualized needs. These stages are: *develop background knowledge, discuss it, model it, memorize it, support it,* and *perform it independently.* As illustrated below, the 3-5-3 model of writing is introduced in the *discuss it* stage and carries through the rest of the instructional sequence. This approach to writing story narratives also was adapted for teaching essay construction using approaches called PLAN—WRITE, as well as DARE—STOP (De La Paz, 1999; De La Paz & Graham, 1997).

Develop Background Knowledge. During the first session, the purpose of the small group intervention and potential outcomes were discussed with Kevin and the other group members. Each group member provided a reason for becoming a better writer (e.g., to pass tests, to get better grades, to earn my art supplies back, so I can go to the sixth grade). Each reason was written on construction paper and posted to serve as a reminder of their personal goals.

Discuss It. Next, the clinician discussed what mnemonics are and why it is important for Kevin to apply these strategies to his writing. The clinician introduced the 3-5-3 model as the steps needed to construct a well-written story. The first three strategies were introduced as follows:

1. *Prompt*—Pay attention to the prompt! Underline it. Is this story going to be funny? Happy? Scary?
2. *Plan*—Visualize! Brainstorm! Who is the main character? What are some of the attri-

butes you want to make sure the reader understands? What is the setting? What is the action or problem in the story? What are the consequences? How did the character feel?
3. *Put (in order)*—Visualize what happens first.

Then, the clinician introduced the five elements of story grammar. The students were taught to write about the story grammar elements using the SPACE acronym. The strategies were introduced as follows:

1. *Setting*—the character(s), place, and time
2. *Problem*—the problem or conflict faced by the main character
3. *Action*—the actions or events the main character completes in order to overcome the problem
4. *Consequence*—the resolution or consequences of the actions taken by the main character
5. *Emotions*—the feelings of the characters in the story

SPACE was described to Kevin as the time to write his ideas for the most common or basic parts of a story. After each part was defined, the clinician and the group went through numerous picture books and short stories to learn how to identify these elements in well-known stories (Graham & Harris, 1999). The students were taught how to visualize as well as to brainstorm when thinking about ideas that fit into the SPACE elements.

The final step in the 3-5-3 model of story writing was described to Kevin as the time to write and create the story. The clinician and Kevin discussed how to create the whole story in the mind as if it were a movie, to use a graphic organizer if needed, and then to write it down to ensure all the SPACE elements were included. Finally, the clinician discussed how Kevin needed to go back into the story to look for the elements of grammar and the vocabulary words previously taught to see if they were included. The strategies were introduced as follows:

1. *Create*—the story on paper
2. *Count*—the new vocabulary words and grammar that were learned and ask, "Are all of the elements of story grammar included?"

3. *Create again*—another version. Revise—Make sure elements of story grammar are clear; include more words; elaborate and expand on what is already written. Can you sequence the story in frames? What happened first, second, next, and then last?

Model It. The clinician used the 3-5-3 model for writing by implementing each strategy using a story from one of the picture books used. Kevin was shown how to begin writing the story on paper after he visualized the complete story sequence in his mind. The clinician then modeled the self-monitoring process and charted the TWW.

Memorize It. Kevin and the other students put on a presentation for their grandparents/parents, modeling the different components of the 3-5-3 model. The family members were informed that each student must memorize the strategies used in the model, including the mnemonics, and that this was very important to the group's success. Kevin's grandparents agreed to help Kevin memorize the strategies. During the presentation, Kevin appeared very proud after his grandfather stated that "he was learning a thing or two about writing too."

Support It. Kevin demonstrated full awareness of the 3-5-3 strategies after the first 2 weeks. Although he did not require support to verbally state the steps, he required ongoing support to write about all the SPACE elements during implementation. He wanted to skip this step and just write his story. The importance of clearly defining each story grammar piece before composing the full story was discussed. At the end of each intervention week, Kevin's progress was monitored using the 3-minute WCBM. He charted his own progress at the end of each week. After the first few times, Kevin became independent at charting and proudly showed his scores to his grandparents.

Perform It Independently. To help facilitate independent use of the new grammatical elements and vocabulary learned, a word wall was developed and served as a visual prompt during the first 4 weeks of intervention. This prompt was then faded in the fifth week and totally removed by the sixth week. When the word wall was taken down, Kevin developed a personal goal, which was to include at least five different, newly learned grammatical elements in his weekly WCBM. To facilitate this, he made up a rap that contained all the new words learned during the grammar/vocabulary center. This caught on quickly, and Kevin and the group members expanded on his approach and made up a rap that included the 3-5-3 strategies. Each week, during the independent learning center, Kevin and the other group members created a new rap that incorporated the 3-5-3 elements and the new grammar and vocabulary. It was clear that they were utilizing this strategy independently during their writing; each was observed quietly restating key elements (i.e., rapping) during the 3-minute weekly CBM.

Peer Revising Strategy

Prior to participation in the revising center, Kevin and the other students were taught how to participate as members of the writing group by sharing their writing and collaborating (Graham et al., 2012). They also received direct instruction on the appropriate way to provide feedback to peers. To aid in this process, they were given a checklist and a list of specific feedback messages. After 4 weeks, the list was faded out and the students provided peer feedback without the visual aid, with the clinician continuing to monitor. The revising strategy helped Kevin develop his ability to monitor others' written products, and eventually he became more proficient at revising his own work. In addition, Kevin learned appropriate ways to deliver constructive criticism and how to incorporate others' feedback into his work.

Intervention Outcomes

The activities and procedures implemented in this intensive intervention program appeared to advance Kevin's understanding and use of specific strategies when engaged in the writing process. Kevin was highly responsive to the intervention, as evidenced by postintervention scores. A series of three 3-minute WCBMs were used to describe postintervention progress. During baseline, Kevin's stories were incomplete and brief. After 10 weeks of intervention, the number of total words written increased from a baseline mean of 37 words to 48 words postintervention. This brought Kevin close to the fifth-grade mean of 54 (Deno et al., 1988). Kevin also increased the number of different words from a baseline mean of 17 to a postintervention mean of 25 words. The number of correct writing sequences increased from a baseline mean of 23 to a postintervention mean of 49, which indicated Kevin was beginning to close the gap to the fifth-grade norm of 58 (Powell-Smith & Shinn, 2004).

In addition, Kevin demonstrated a positive change in the number of story grammar elements from a mean of two in baseline (i.e., setting and problem) to including all five. His three WCBMs contained clearly delineated main ideas. He also demonstrated increased use of auxiliary verbs, adjectives, and adverbs and was utilizing cohesive units correctly in his final stories. Although growth was observed in the use of novel vocabulary, Kevin did not demonstrate increased recognition of select prefixes and suffixes.

The clinician was able to determine that Kevin was independently incorporating self-regulating strategies during writing by readministering the self-report checklist. An increase in Kevin's motivation to write was evident based on clinician observation of Kevin's active engagement in the writing process and independent implementation of the 3-5-3 rap. This observation also was supported through comments and statements made by Kevin's grandparents, including that Kevin had started "writing some books at home."

Kevin's progress highlights the positive effect of intervention that incorporates self-regulated learning strategies into contextualized intervention planning for a child diagnosed with language-learning disabilities and ED. Within a relatively brief amount of time, Kevin made significant growth in his writing abilities, as well as in his use of novel vocabulary and grammar in his writing. The behavioral and instructional principles applied to the intervention program

represented strategies known to aid in increasing on-task behavior and student learning (Swanson, 1999). Direct, explicit instruction was provided in a highly concentrated manner with many opportunities for the students to engage and respond. Learning was based on modeling and scaffolding of new strategies and active employment of the SRSD model, including self-monitoring.

Conclusion

The assessment and current intervention approach used in this case study was implemented in a manner that reflected current research in writing instruction. Clinicians who practice in schools and clinic settings can utilize this case study as a model for intervening effectively with students who have language-learning disabilities or, as in Kevin's case, both language-learning disabilities and emotional disturbance.

Kevin still needs to self-regulate his communication at times. In fact, he will be attending a new elementary school in the fall after threatening his previous fourth-grade teacher. However, the school district has inclusive classrooms in place, and Kevin will be served in a general education classroom with support from the school psychologist, counselor, special education teacher, and the SLP. The school SLP is excited to continue with Kevin's current programming.

Authors' Note

Although this case is based on past and recent experiences working in schools, Kevin is a fictional school-age client who was used to represent a student with a dual diagnosis of language impairment and emotional disturbance. This case is hypothetical but depicts a course of treatment and expected improvements in written language proficiency when students like Kevin are taught in an explicit and direct manner utilizing strategic language instruction combined with the self-regulated strategy development approach.

References

American Psychiatric Association. (2013). *Diagnostic and statistical manual of mental disorders* (5th ed.). https://doi.org/10.1176/appi.books.9780890425596

American Speech-Language-Hearing Association. (2001). *Roles and responsibilities of speech-language pathologists with respect to reading and writing in children and adolescents* [Position statement]. http://www.asha.org/docs/html/PS2001-00104.html

Archer, A., & Hughes, C. (2011). *Explicit instruction: Effective and efficient teaching*. Guilford Press.

Baker, S. K., Simmons, D. C., & Kame'enui, E. J. (1998). Vocabulary acquisition: Instruction and curricular basics and implications. In D. C. Simmons & E. J. Kame'enui (Eds.), *What reading research tells us about children with diverse learning needs: Bases and basics* (pp. 219–238). Erlbaum.

Bangert-Drowns, R. (1993). The word processor as an instructional tool: A meta-analysis of word processing in writing instruction. *Review of Educational Research, 63*, 69–93.

Beck, I. L., McKeown, M. G., & Kucan, L. (2002). *Bringing words to life: Robust vocabulary instruction*. Guilford.

Beitchman, J. H., Wilson, B., Brownlie, E. B., Inglis, A., & Lancee, W. (1996). Long-term consistency in speech/language profiles: II. Behavioral, emotional, and social outcomes. *Journal of American Academy of Child and Adolescent Psychiatry, 35*, 804–814.

Benner, G. J., Nelson, J. R., & Epstein, M. H. (2002). The language skills of children with emotional and behavioral disorders: A review of the literature. *Journal of Emotional and Behavioral Disorders, 10*, 43–59.

Chow, J. C., & Wehby, J. H. (2018). Associations between language and problem behavior: A systematic review and correlational meta-analysis. *Educational Psychology Review, 30*, 61–82.

De La Paz, S. (1999). Teaching writing strategies and self-regulation to middle school students with learning disabilities. *Focus on Exceptional Children, 31*, 3–16.

De La Paz, S., & Graham, S. (1997). Effects of dictation and advanced planning instruction on the composing of students with writing and learning problems. *Journal of Educational Psychology, 89*, 203–222.

Deno, S. L., Martson, D., & Mirkin, P. (1982). Valid measurement procedures for continuous evaluation of written expression. *Exceptional Children Special Education and Pediatrics: A New Relationship, 48*, 368–371.

Dunn, D. M. (2019). *Peabody Picture Vocabulary Test* (5th ed.) [Measurement instrument]. NCS Pearson.

Ebbers, S. M., & Denton, C. A. (2008). A root awakening: Vocabulary instruction for older students with reading difficulties. *Learning Disabilities Research and Practice, 23*, 90–102.

Epsin, C. A., Scierka, B. J., Skare, S., & Halvorson, N. (1999). Criterion-related validity of curriculum-based measures in writing for secondary school students. *Reading and Writing Quarterly: Overcoming Learning Difficulties, 15*, 5–27.

Foorman, B. R., & Torgesen, J. K. (2001). Critical elements of classroom and small group instruction promote reading success in all children. *Learning Disabilities: Research and Practice, 16*(4), 203–212.

Gersten, R., & Baker, S. (2001). Teaching expressive writing to students with learning disabilities: A meta-analysis. *Elementary School Journal, 101*, 251–272.

Goddard, Y. L., & Sendi, C. (2008). Effects of self-monitoring on the narrative and expository writing of four fourth-grade students with learning disabilities. *Reading and Writing Quarterly, 24*, 408–433.

Graham, S., Bollinger, A., Booth Olson, C., D'Aoust, C., MacArthur, C., McCutchen, D., & Olinghouse, N. (2012). *Teaching elementary school students to be effective writers: A practice guide* (NCEE 2012-4058). National Center for Education Evaluation and Regional Assistance, Institute of Education Sciences, U.S. Department of Education. http://ies.ed.gov/ncee/wwc/publications_reviews.aspx#pubsearch

Graham, S., & Harris, K. R. (1993). Self-regulated strategy development: Helping students with learning problems develop as writers. *Elementary School Journal, 94*, 169–181.

Graham, S., & Harris, K. R. (1999). Assessment and intervention in overcoming writing difficulties: An illustration from the self-regulated strategy development model. *Language, Speech, and Hearing Services in Schools, 30*, 255–264.

Graham, S., Kiuhara, S., McKeown, D., & Harris, K. R. (2012). A meta-analysis of writing instruction for students in the elementary grades. *Journal of Educational Psychology, 104*, 879–896.

Harris, K. R., & Graham, S. (1998). *Making the writing process work: Strategies for composition and self-regulation*. Brookline.

Hollo, A., Chow, J. C., & Wehby, J. H. (2018). Profiles of language and behavior in students with emotional disturbance. *Behavioral Disorders, 44*, 195–204. https://doi.org/10.1177/0198742918804803

Hollo, A., Wehby, J. H., & Oliver, R. M. (2014). Unidentified language deficits in children with emotional and behavioral disorders: A meta-analysis. *Exceptional*

Children, 80, 169–186. https://doi.org/10.1177/0014 40291408000203

Kauffman, J. M. (2001). *Characteristics of emotional and behavioral disorders in children and youth* (7th ed.). Merrill/Pearson.

Kim, A., Vaughn, S., Wanzek, J., & Wei, S. (2004). Graphic organizers and their effects on reading comprehension of students with learning disabilities: A synthesis of research. *Journal of Learning Disabilities, 37,* 105–118.

Lane, K. L., Harris, K. R., Graham, S., Weisenbach, J. L., Brindle, M., & Morphy, P. (2008). The effects of self-regulated strategy development of the writing performance of second-grade students with behavioral and writing difficulties. *The Journal of Special Education, 41,* 234–253.

Moats, L. (2019). Structured literacy: Effective instruction for students with dyslexia and related reading difficulties. *Perspectives on Language and Literacy, 45*(2), 9–11.

Moxley, R. A., Lutz, P. A., Ahlborn, R., Boley, N., & Armstrong, L. (1995). Self recorded word counts of free writing in Grades 1–4. *Education and Treatment of Children, 18,* 138–157.

Nagy, W. E., & Scott, J. A. (2000). Vocabulary processes. In M. L. Kamil, P. Mosenthal, P. D. Pearson, & R. Barr (Eds.), *Handbook of reading research* (Vol. 3, pp. 269–287). Erlbaum.

Nelson, J. R., Benner, G. J., & Cheney, G. (2005). An investigation of the language skills of students with emotional disturbance served in public school settings. *The Journal of Special Education, 39,* 97–105.

Nelson, J. R., Benner, G. J., Lane, K., & Smith, B. W. (2004). An investigation of the academic achievement of K-12 students with emotional and behavioral disorders in public school settings. *Exceptional Children, 71,* 59–74.

Nelson, J. R., Benner, G. J., & Rogers-Adkinson, D. L. (2003). An investigation of the characteristics of K-12 students with comorbid emotional disturbance and significant language deficits served in public school settings. *Behavioral Disorders, 29*(1), 25–33.

Nelson, N., Bahr, C., & Van Meter, A. (2004). *The writing lab approach to language instruction and intervention.* Paul H. Brooks Publishing.

Powell-Smith, K. A., & Shinn, M. R. (2004). *Administration and scoring of written expression curriculum-based measurement for use in general outcome measurement.* Edformation.

Reed, D. K. (2008). A synthesis of morphology interventions and effects on reading outcomes for students in grades K–12. *Learning Disabilities Research and Practice, 23,* 36–49.

Rogers, L. A., & Graham, S. (2008). A meta-analysis of single subject design writing intervention research. *Journal of Educational Psychology, 100,* 879–906.

Scott, C. M. (2002). A fork in the road less traveled: Writing intervention based on language profile. In K. G. Butler & E. R. Silliman (Eds.), *Speaking, reading and writing in children with language learning disabilities* (pp. 219–237). Erlbaum.

Semel, E., Wiig, E. H., & Secord, W. H. (2003). *Clinical Evaluation of Language Fundamentals–Fourth Edition.* Harcourt.

Simonson, B., Fairbanks, S., Briesch, A., Myers, D., & Sugai, G. (2008). Evidence-based practices in classroom management: Considerations for research to practice. *Education and Treatment of Children, 31,* 351–380.

Sreckovic, M. A., Common, E. A., Knowles, M. M., & Lane, K. L. (2014). A review of self-regulated strategy development for writing for students with EBD. *Behavioral Disorders, 39*(2), 56–77.

Swanson, H. L. (1999). Instructional components that predict treatment outcomes for students with learning disabilities: Support for a combined strategy and direct instruction model. *Learning Disabilities Research and Practice, 14,* 12–140.

Trout, A. L., Nordess, P. D., Pierce, C. D., & Epstein, M. H. (2003). Research on the academic status of students with emotional and behavioral disorders: A review of the literature from 1961–2000. *Journal of Emotional and Behavioral Disorders, 11,* 198–210.

U.S. Department of Health and Human Services. (1999). *Mental health: A report of the surgeon general.*

Videen, J., Deno, S., & Martson, D. B. (1982). *Correct word sequences: A valid indicator of written expression* (Rep. No. 84). Institute for Research on Learning Disabilities. (ERIC Document Reproduction Service No. ED 225112.)

Walker, H. M., Ramsey, E., & Gresham, F. M. (2004). *Antisocial behavior in school: Evidence-based practices* (2nd ed.). Wadsworth.

Watkinson, J. T., & Lee, S. W. (1992). Curriculum-based measures of written expression for learning-disabled and nondisabled students. *Psychology in the Schools, 29,* 184–191.

Westby, C. E. (2004). Executive functioning, metacognition, and self-regulation in reading. In A. Stone, E. Silliman, B. Ehren, & K. Apel (Eds.), *Handbook of language and literacy development and disorders* (pp. 398–428). Guilford.

Zimmerman, B. J. (2002). Becoming a self-regulated learner: An overview. *Theory Into Practice, 41*(2), 64–70. https://doi.org/10.1207/s15430421tip4102_2

Zimmerman, B. J., & Schunk, D. H. (Eds.). (2001). *Self-regulated learning and academic achievement: Theoretical perspectives.* Erlbaum.

LITERACY
CASE 34
Ana: Treating the Reading and Spelling Skills of a Bilingual Elementary-Age Student with Word-Level Literacy Deficits
Victoria S. Henbest, Lindsey Hiebert, and Shurita Thomas-Tate

Conceptual Knowledge Areas

This case is based on Masterson and Apel's (2007) multilinguistic model of five factors involved in word-level reading and spelling. The first component, *phonemic awareness*, involves the ability to attend to and manipulate individual sounds within words. The second component, *orthographic knowledge*, denotes how speech translates to print. Orthographic knowledge can be divided into two components: (1) orthographic pattern knowledge or understanding of the rules for how spoken words are written (i.e., spelling rules) and (2) the ability to store and use *mental graphemic representations* (MGRs; Apel et al., 2019). MGRs depend on adequate exposure to print, experience with phonemic analysis, and appreciation for sound-letter correspondences (Apel et al., 2019). The further component, *semantic knowledge*, is a child's understanding of the meaning of words and how meaning influences written spelling (e.g., choosing the appropriate homonym as in *bear* vs. *bare*). The final component, *morphological awareness*, broadly involves conscious attention to spoken and written morphemes and is needed to decode and spell multimorphemic words, both inflectional and derivational. According to Masterson and Apel (2000, 2010), failure to represent a sound in spelling suggests a problem with phonemic awareness (e.g., "spill" spelled as "sill"), whereas use of illegal spellings suggest problems in knowledge of orthographic rules (e.g., "boat" spelled as "'bot") or, in the case of multimorphemic words, morphological awareness (e.g., "magician" spelled as "magishun"). A legal but incorrect spelling suggests problems in adequate MGRs (e.g., "boat" spelled as "bote").

Description of the Case

Background Information

At the beginning of the spring semester, Ana D. was referred to the university clinic by her mother due to concerns about a lack of progress in reading. Graduate students supervised by clinical faculty conducted the evaluation and subsequent treatment. At the time of the initial evaluation, Ana was 9 years old, a Spanish-English bilingual, and in the third grade at a public school. Ana's parents were Spanish-English bilinguals. Although Spanish was their first language, they report speaking more English than Spanish at home. According to her mother, Ana's spoken language skills had always been adequate when compared to her siblings and cousins. However, Ana often used "odd" spellings that frequently changed into other "odd" spellings in subsequent written work, which were sometimes impacted by Spanish sounds (e.g., "wuaked" for "walked"; "rich" for "reach"; "goot" for "goat"). Ana was described as easy to understand, able to comprehend and remember what was said to her, and good at following instructions in both Spanish and English. Her Spanish expressive abilities were limited at the time of this evaluation; she easily expressed herself in English. Ana attended an English-dominant preschool. In kindergarten, she was reportedly observed to misread words in English with long vowel patterns (e.g., "seat" as /si/-/æt/) when reading. She had not received any reading instruction in Spanish, so this was not assessed. Sra. D. indicated that in preschool and kindergarten, Ana would often memorize familiar English books from the classroom and verbalize them aloud in both Spanish and English, without reading the words.

Math was a relative strength, while spelling performance was "low satisfactory," and reading was reported to be "below grade level." Although Ana did well on weekly spelling tests via memorization, she reportedly failed to retain knowledge of the correct spellings, often misspelling those words in written composition. She had a good attendance record. Ana had received tutoring to improve her reading skills, as she had previously struggled with reading fluency and comprehension skills. Sra. D. had Ana's older sister assist her with homework by reading instructions and some textbooks aloud. No special education services were being provided through the school at the time of the evaluation.

Reason for Referral

Ana's parents desired more information regarding her current reading level and information as to how to help Ana at home. Sra. D. stated that Ana had difficulty making sense of written words and consistently read below grade level. Ana's classroom teacher observed that she had difficulty getting started on writing assignments independently, did not like to read on her own and when asked to read aloud in class, and was slow and stilted.

Findings of the Evaluation

Speech and Spoken Language Skills

Ana's articulation, fluency, voice, and hearing were within normal limits. Expressive spoken English language skills in syntax, semantics, and morphology were observed during a conversation and also appeared to be typical. Conversational skills and pragmatics were excellent. Ana was able to retell and generate narratives in English with complete episodes, supporting details, listener-friendly devices, and accurate sequence without difficulty. She used predominantly English for producing narratives with occasional use of Spanish nouns (e.g., *niño, gato*).

Spelling

The Test of Written Spelling–5th Edition (TWS-5; Larsen et al., 2013), which measures single-word written spelling to dictation, was administered in English, and Ana's standard score was below typical limits (76). A written narrative sample was obtained in English that contained multiple spelling errors (21%). Ana's handwriting was neat and legible. Her writing (typewritten) sample appears in Figure 34–1.

Reading

Subtests from the Woodcock Reading Mastery Tests–3rd Edition (WRMT-3; Woodcock, 2011) were administered to assess Ana's word-level reading skills in English. The Word Identification subtest measured Ana's MGR knowledge; she scored low average (86). On the Word Attack subtest, a measure of nonsense word decoding, her standard score was 85, also indicating low-average performance. She scored an 86 on the Passage Comprehension subtest, which measures understanding of written sentences and passages, again indicating borderline performance.

> *Once upon a time there was a turtle named shelly. shelly Loved egvenchers Once shelly pretened she was a piret with a long black beard. and once she wasa spy. She never thot of a real egvencher and one day she was in the pond and sudinly!!!!! A huge net came uround her she was stond she trid to screem but nothing came out she fanted she was so scarde when she yockup she didn't know where she was it looked like one of those things that in a newspaper that was by the pond she looked over a bruck wall a and lion the lion said. HI! My is lary, what is your name I am selly and were am I. lary said your're at the zoo [reversed z]. The ZOO [reversed z] we've got to exap!!! Lary and shelly made a plan it worked out great. THE END PS. if you whant to find out what happends next get the next book.*

Figure 34–1. Ana's generated narrative with original spellings and punctuation.

Finally, the Gray Oral Reading Test–5th Edition (GORT-5; Weiderholt & Bryant, 2012) was administered in English to further evaluate comprehension and to examine reading fluency. Accuracy and Comprehension scores at that time were borderline average, with scaled scores of 7. Rate and fluency were below typical limits, with scaled scores of 6. The overall Oral Reading Index was 82, which is below the average range.

Evaluation Summary and Treatment Options Considered Within Evidence-Based Practice Framework

Ana demonstrates deficits in word-level literacy skills, as evidenced by a low performance on reading fluency, spelling, and difficulty decoding nonsense words. Her scores in real-word reading and comprehension were slightly better, although still compromised. Thus, treatment would focus heavily on word-level reading and spelling, with additional support to increase fluency and improve comprehension. Ana's English spoken language skills, including narrative skills, were determined to be strong.

According to the American Speech-Language-Hearing Association (ASHA, 2022), clinical decisions that are evidence based incorporate (1) the clinician's expertise, (2) external research evidence and clinician-collected data, and (3) client/caregivers' perspectives. Working within this framework, the clinicians interviewed Ana's parents, who initially desired that treatment focus on spelling in the short term with reading to be addressed as a more long-term or secondary goal. In considering Ana's needs, the clinicians were mindful of current theory and research in combination with past clinical experiences. Ana's school, like most classrooms across the country, used the "Friday Test" as a strategy to teach spelling. This usually involved rote memory activities throughout the week. Students were asked to look up the meaning of each word and write it five times every day. The word list selection was often centered on classroom "themes." Rarely was any systematic attention paid to the lessons learned as time progressed and new lists were provided. This style of instruction neglects to address spelling as a multilinguistic skill that requires coordination of phonemic awareness, morphological awareness, and semantic and orthographic knowledge.

Because Ana struggled to retain spelling knowledge after memorizing words for the Friday Test, the clinicians agreed that a multilinguistic approach was preferable (e.g., Apel et al., 2013; Collins et al., 2020; Wolter & Dilworth, 2014; Wolter & Green, 2013). Because spelling and reading have a reciprocal relationship (i.e., we read what we spell, and we spell what we read), the clinicians planned to use Ana's spelling to determine the orthographic targets in focused word study to be supplemented with authentic reading and writing activities. To determine the initial targets and type of instruction needed, the Spelling Evaluation for Language and Literacy-2 (SPELL-3; Masterson et al., 2023), a prescriptive and adaptive spelling assessment, was administered in English. Ana's performance on SPELL-3 indicated needs in orthographic knowledge. Specific recommendations are illustrated in Figure 34–2.

Course of Treatment

Treatment began immediately following the evaluation. Word study lessons came from SPELL-Links to Reading and Writing (SPELL-Links; Wasowicz et al., 2017), and the implementation procedures described in Masterson and Apel (2007) were used. All treatment was conducted in English. Each lesson in SPELL-Links focuses on a particular orthographic target and emphasizes phonemic awareness, orthographic knowledge, morphological awareness, and semantic knowledge. Ana's needs were primarily in orthographic knowledge, and difficulty was noted with understanding spelling rules as well as establishment of clear MGRs. SPELL-Links activities such as Sort It Out establish two or three categories based on an orthographic pattern. A list of words representing the pattern to be learned along with a contrasting pattern were presented to Ana, who was encouraged to sort the words into two columns, one column of words that seem to follow one pattern and the other column for the other words/pattern.

High-frequency words were preferred stimuli to illustrate spelling patterns. Once Ana sorted the words successfully, she was asked to explain the pattern/rule aloud (e.g., *when a vowel says its name, it's a long vowel so there are two vowel letters in the word*). The pattern description was added to a

---

Develop clear and complete mental orthographic images of words containing the following spelling patterns for:

- consonants 'r, l'
- consonant digraph 'wh'

Develop clear and complete mental orthographic images of words containing spelling patterns for spelling of:

- short vowel /u/
- long vowel a̲ spelled as: 'ey, ay, ai'
- long vowel e̲ spelled as: 'ee, ea, y, ey, i, ie'
- long o̲ spelled as: 'oa, ough, ow'

Develop clear and complete mental orthographic images and orthographic knowledge sound symbol correspondence of:

- digraphs 'ch,' tch'

Develop clear and complete mental orthographic images and orthographic knowledge of sound symbol correspondence as well as long and short vowel principles for words containing the spelling pattern of:

- 'ck'
- Long o spelled as 'oCe'

Develop orthographic knowledge of sound-symbol correspondences for:

- Long vowel i̲ spelled as: 'y, ie, igh'

Develop ability to map letters to sound in words containing:

- Long u spelled as: 'uCe'
- Long u spelled as: 'ue, oo, o, ui'

Figure 34–2. Recommendations generated from SPELL (Level 1).

growing list of patterns and rules she wrote in her spelling journals.

An example of a SPELL-Links activity to facilitate Ana's establishment of complete MGRs was Picture This. This activity has both empirical and theoretical support (Glenn & Hurley, 1993; Richards et al., 2006). In the Picture This activity, Ana was first asked to look at a word and pay close attention to the specific parts it contained (Masterson & Apel, 2007; Wasowicz et al., 2017). The word was written, and a variety of strategies were implemented to support Ana's accurate storage of it as MGR. For example, consonants were colored blue and vowels red, and when spelling the word aloud, Ana used a "low voice" for letters that drop below the line (e.g., "p") and a "high voice" for those that go up ("h"). She also spelled the words backward to encourage her to form a complete mental picture of the word and in turn lead to accurate and quick reading and spelling of the word. When addressing individual words/MGRs, Ana was always encouraged to attempt to access other types of knowledge (phonemic awareness, orthographic knowledge, morphological awareness) first as most words do not need to be memorized completely.

The transfer from word study to authentic (i.e., contextualized) reading and writing activities was addressed directly. Texts containing current word-study targets were used and the clinician called Ana's attention to those orthographic structures during guided reading (Savage et al., 2018). Later, she read passages in which the targeted patterns had been replaced by blanks in words. As she read, she determined the correct word and then spelled the word correctly in the passage. Additionally, authentic writing opportunities that involved targeted orthographic patterns were provided each session.

Treatment continued by targeting syllable division rules for words containing r-controlled syllables, l-controlled syllables, accented and unaccented syllables, silent "e," and prefixes and suffixes. Spelling rules for doubling letters when adding suffixes and changing "y" to "i" when adding suffixes were also included in the lessons. During treatment, Ana used a word journal and stories she selected to find age-appropriate words

and identify similar spelling patterns and create her own flashcards. Over time, academic textbook reading was added to support study skills, and care was given to provide opportunities to read high-interest material.

Reading Fluency

Reading fluency, the ability to read accurately at a normal rate with expression, is important for good comprehension. According to the *Report of the National Reading Panel: Teaching Children to Read* (National Institute for Child Health and Development, 2000) and more recent investigations (e.g., Hudson et al., 2020; Kuhn, 2005; Zimmermann et al., 2019; Zimmermann et al., 2021), guided and repeated oral reading procedures improved word recognition, fluency, and comprehension skills across several grade levels.

The guided oral reading and rereading activities used with Ana included clinician modeling of fluent reading, choral reading (reading in unison with the clinician), echo reading (in which the clinician read a portion of the material with Ana immediately rereading the same portion), and rereading (asking Ana to reread the passage after feedback had been provided). Children's acting monologues were used for repeated readings and to encourage expression (e.g., Rowen et al., 2015). The selected materials were either at or slightly below Ana's reading level.

Analysis of Client's Response to Intervention

Ana's response to intervention was monitored in two ways: The clinician documented her success with the therapy activities (e.g., percentage correct with sorting according to spelling rules/patterns), and each quarter, Ana spelled a number of different grade-appropriate words containing patterns addressed in therapy. Masterson and Apel's (2010) Spelling Sensitivity System (SSS) scoring procedure was used to assign a score based on how phonemes and morphemes (i.e., elements) were represented linguistically. As examples, a correct spelling earned a score of 3 (e.g., the /l/ in "spill" is spelled with "ll"). An incorrect but "legal" spelling (e.g., "bote" for "boat") earned a score of 2. A 1 was assigned when an element was represented but with an orthographically implausible spelling (e.g., "bot" for "boat"), and a score of 0 was earned when an element was not represented (e.g., "sill" for "spill"). The element scores within each word were averaged and then an average across words was obtained. Using this continuum-based scoring procedure allowed the clinician to measure Ana's progress in learning orthographic patterns even when a word was spelled incorrectly. Ana received treatment for four 16-week academic semesters and two 8-week summer semesters. A formal evaluation of Ana's written language skills was completed at the end of her enrollment. Readministration of the WRMT-3, the GORT-5, and the TWS-5 was conducted in English and a comparison of pre- and posttreatment scores is shown in Tables 34–1 and 34–2.

Ana's literacy skills improved following inter-

vention. Word-level reading and reading comprehension skills had improved from borderline to well within normal limits, as measured by the WRMT-3. Ana's performance on the TWS-5 improved substantially, as did her oral reading. It should be noted that Ana continued to exhibit a slower than average reading rate, but her comprehension score had dramatically increased, likely contributing to the improved Oral Reading Index score. Individual profile scores on the GORT-5 are represented in Table 34–2.

The Written Expression Scale subtest from the Oral and Written Language Scales–2nd Edition (OWLS-2; Carrow-Woolfolk, 2011) also was administered to formally measure Ana's written conventions such as letter formation, spelling, punctuation, capitalization, and other structures and use of linguistic forms such as modifiers, verb phrases, question forms, vocabulary choice, and coherence. She earned a standard score of 116, indicating performance above expected levels.

Table 34–1. Ana's Literacy Performance Pre- and Postintervention

Test or Subtest	SS Pretreatment	SS Posttreatment
WRMT-III Word Identification	86	95
WRMT-III Word Attack	85	94
WRMT-III Passage Comprehension	86	103
GORT-5 Oral Reading Index	82	97
TWS-5	76	100

Note: SS = Standard score or quotient (mean = 100, *SD* = 15).

Table 34–2. Ana's Performance on the Individual Subtests of the GORT-5

Profile	SS Pretreatment	SS Posttreatment
Rate	6	6
Accuracy	7	8
Fluency	6	7
Comprehension	7	12

Note: SS = Standard score (mean = 10, *SD* = 3).

Parent Report

It has been a year since Ana stopped coming for services. She is now in Grade 6. Her parents feel Ana is happier in school compared to the frustration she was experiencing as a third grader. Specifically, she is more accepting of the extra time that is required for language arts and is willing to put forth the needed effort. Ana's parents also are pleased to report that recently, for the first time, Ana began reading silently for her own enjoyment.

Conclusion

This case described an elementary student whose primary needs were in written language. Both her spoken language and narrative skills were within normal limits in her dominant language of English and, in fact, were areas of strength that facilitated increased development of reading and spelling skills. The services delivered were beneficial, as evidenced by both assessment data and parental report. The information provided supports the benefits of speech-language pathologists' involvement in literacy intervention.

Authors' Note

This case is hypothetical; however, it represents a composite of the characteristics, treatment, and outcomes that have been associated with actual clients.

Acknowledgments. The authors thank Deborah Cron and Julie J. Masterson for their work on the original version of this case and for extending the opportunity for us to update and revise it into the current version.

References

American Speech-Language-Hearing Association. (2022). *Evidence-based practice.* https://www.asha.org/research/ebp/

Apel, K., Brimo, D., Diehm, E., & Apel, L. (2013). Morphological awareness intervention with kindergartners and first- and second-grade students from low socioeconomic status homes: A feasibility study. *Language, Speech, and Hearing Services in Schools, 44,* 161–173. https://doi.org/10.1044/0161-1461(2012/12-0042)

Apel, K., Henbest, V. S., & Masterson, J. (2019). Orthographic knowledge: Clarifications, challenges, and future directions. *Reading and Writing, 32*(4), 873–889.

Carrow-Woolfolk, E. (2011). *Oral and written language scales.* American Guidance Service.

Collins, G., Wolter, J. A., Meaux, A. B., & Alonzo, C. N. (2020). Integrating morphological awareness in a multilinguistic structured literacy approach to improve literacy in adolescents with reading and/or language disorders. *Language, Speech, and Hearing Services in Schools, 51*(3), 531–543.

Glenn, P., & Hurley, S. (1993). Preventing spelling disabilities. *Child Language Teaching and Therapy, 9,* 1–12. https://doi.org/10.1177/026565909300900101

Hudson, A., Koh, P. W., Moore, K. A., & Binks-Cantrell, E. (2020). Fluency interventions for elementary students with reading difficulties: A synthesis of research from 2000–2019. *Education Sciences, 10*(3), 52.

Kuhn, M. R. (2005). A comparative study of small group fluency instruction. *Reading Psychology, 26*(2), 127–146. https://doi.org/10.1080/02702710590930492

Larsen, S., Hammill, D., & Moats, L. (2013). *Test of written spelling* (5th ed.). Pro-Ed.

Masterson, J., & Apel, K. (2000). Spelling assessment: Charting a path to optimal instruction. *Topics in Language Disorders, 20*(3), 50–65. https://doi.org/10.1097/00011363-200020030-00007

Masterson, J., & Apel, K. (2007). Spelling and word-level reading: A multilinguistic approach. In A. Kamhi, J. Masterson, & K. Apel (Eds.), *Clinical decision making in developmental language disorders* (pp. 249–266). Paul H. Brookes Publishing.

Masterson, J. J., & Apel, K. (2010). The spelling sensitivity score: Noting developmental changes in spelling knowledge. *Assessment for Effective Intervention, 36,* 35–45. https://doi.org/10.1177/153450841038003

Masterson, J., Apel, K., & Wasowicz, J. (2023). *SPELL-3.* Leanring By Design. https://shop.learningbydesign.com/product/spell-3/

National Institute for Child Health and Development (NICHD). (2000). *Report of the National Reading Panel: Teaching children to read.* https://www.nichd.nih.gov/sites/default/files/publications/pubs/nrp/Documents/report.pdf

Richards, T. L., Aylward, E. H., Berninger, V. W., Field, K. M., Grimme, A. C., Richards, A. L., & Nagy, W. (2006).

Individual fMRI activation in orthographic mapping and morpheme mapping after orthographic or morphological spelling treatment in child dyslexics. *Journal of Neurolinguistics, 19,* 5–36. https://doi.org/10.1016/j.jneuroling.2005.07.003

Rowen, D., Biggs, D., Watkins, N., & Rasinski, T. (2015). Choral reading theater: Bridging accuracy, automaticity, and prosody in reading fluency across an academic unit of study. *Journal of Teacher Action Research, 1,* 53–69.

Savage, R., Georgiou, G., Parrila, R., & Maiorino, K. (2018). Preventative reading interventions teaching direct mapping of graphemes in texts and set-for-variability aid at-risk learners. *Scientific Studies of Reading, 22*(3), 225–247.

Wasowicz, J., Apel, K., Masterson, J., & Whitney, A. (2017). *SPELL-Links to literacy.* Learning By Design.

Wiederholt, J. L., & Bryant, B. R. (2012). *Gray Oral Reading Test–Fifth Edition.* Pro-Ed.

Wolter, J. A., & Dilworth, V. (2014). The effects of a multilinguistic morphological awareness approach for improving language and literacy. *Journal of Learning Disabilities, 47*(1), 76–85. https://doi.org/10.1177/0022219413509972

Wolter, J. A., & Green, L. (2013). Morphological awareness intervention in school-age children with language and literacy deficits: A case study. *Topics in Language Disorders, 33*(1), 27–41. https://doi.org/10.1097/TLD.0b013e318280f5aa

Woodcock, R. W. (2011). *Woodcock reading mastery tests–Third Edition (WRMT-3).* Pearson Assessment.

Zimmermann, B. S., Rasinski, T. V., Was, C. A., Rawson, K. A., Dunlosky, J., Kruse, S. D., & Nikbakht, E. (2019). Enhancing outcomes for struggling readers: Empirical analysis of the fluency development lesson. *Reading Psychology, 40*(1), 70–94. https://doi.org/10.1080/02702711.2018.1555365

Zimmermann, L. M., Reed, D. K., & Aloe, A. M. (2021). A meta-analysis of non-repetitive reading fluency interventions for students with reading difficulties. *Remedial and Special Education, 42*(2), 78–93. https://doi.org/10.1177/0741932519855058

LITERACY/PHONOLOGY
CASE 35
Josh and Steve: Enhancing Phonological and Literacy Skills in Twins With Highly Unintelligible Speech

Kathy H. Strattman, Barbara W. Hodson, and Karissa J. Marble-Flint

Conceptual Knowledge Areas

By the time most children reach kindergarten, their understanding and productions in all domains of language typically have developed so that they are ready to learn. Speech and language deficiencies, including expressive phonological impairments that are unresolved by the time children begin to learn to read and write, have a negative impact on literacy development (Bishop & Adams, 1990; Overby et al., 2012). Mental phonological repre-sentations remain "fuzzy" or not clearly established and adversely affect phoneme retrieval in decoding (Stackhouse, 1997; Sutherland & Gillon, 2007). Once children begin to fall behind peers in reading, they are likely to continue a downward spiral that Stanovich (1986) termed "Matthew effects" (i.e., the rich get richer, the poor get poorer). Good readers read more, gaining vocabulary and understanding about reading structures; poor readers read less and lose out on language and knowledge gained through reading. Duff et al. (2015) revisited "Matthew effects" and added that early word reading and rate of vocabulary growth affect academic and social success. In addition, there is evidence (Bird et al., 1995; Boada et al., 2022; Clarke-Klein & Hodson, 1995; Preston et al., 2013; Webster & Plante, 1992) that children with a history of unintelligible speech have poor phonological awareness skills important for literacy development (see Farquharson et al., in press, for more information).

Research results have shown that twins are at a higher risk for language delays and deficiencies (Lewis & Thompson, 1992; Rice et al., 2014) and evidence phonological deficiencies more frequently than single births (Dodd & McEvoy, 1994). What if twins continue to have phonological deficits beyond the critical age?

Description of the Case

Background Information

Josh and Steve, identical twin boys, were referred to the university clinic during their second semester of kindergarten at age 5 years, 10 months. According to their speech-language pathologist (SLP), they had already participated in phoneme-oriented treatment for a couple of years, but gains had been minimal, and they were still extremely unintelligible. Typically fewer than 10% of their utterances in connected speech could be identified. The Hodson Assessment of Phonological Patterns-3 (HAPP-3; Hodson, 2004) was administered at this time (Tables 35–1 and 35–2). Their initial scores on the HAPP-3 calculated using Hodson Computerized Assessment of Phonological Patterns (HCAPP-4; Hodson, 2021) placed both boys in the profound severity interval. Table 35–3 provides some samples of their productions at age 5 years, 10 months.

Reasons for Referral

According to the critical age hypothesis (Bishop & Adams, 1990), children need to speak intelligibly by age 5 years, 6 months or literacy acquisition will surely be hindered. Josh and Steve were already past the critical age. The boys were to enter first grade in the fall (at age 6 years, 2 months). School personnel and parents were extremely concerned about their literacy abilities because of intelligibility difficulties.

Birth and Medical History

Although they were born 6 weeks premature, prenatal and birth histories were relatively unremarkable. Josh weighed 3 lbs. 9 oz., and Steve weighed 4 lbs. 9 oz. They remained in the hospital initially to maintain body temperature and then to monitor growth and weight gain. The boys were raised in a two-parent, middle-income home. Their mother reported typical developmental milestones, except they used "some twin talk" but no real words until after they were 2 years of age. The boys had both undergone numerous surgeries for middle ear pathologies, vision, and polydactylism, but otherwise they were regarded as being generally healthy.

Findings of the Evaluation

Phonological Intervention

Beginning in first grade, both boys participated in individual weekly sessions for three semesters (approximately 35 contact hours). The emphasis at this time was on enhancing their phonological and metaphonological skills via the cycles phonological approach (Hodson, 2007; Magnus & Hodson, in press; Rudolph & Wendt, 2014).

Their target patterns for the first semester/cycle included (a) final consonants, (b) /s/ clusters (initial and final), (c) velars (final and initial), and (d) initial liquids. As the semesters progressed, velars, /s/ clusters, and liquids were recycled. Consonant clusters (e.g., medial /s/ clusters, velar clusters, liquid clusters, and three-consonant clusters) were targeted. By the end of the third semester of phonological intervention, the boys were able to produce all consonants and consonant patterns

Table 35–1. Phonological Deviation Scores on the Hodson Assessment of Phonological Patterns-3 for Steve Prior to Phonological Treatment (Age 5 Years, 10 Months) and Following Each of Three Semesters

	Percentages of Occurrences by Age			
	5:10	6:5	6:10	7:5
Omissions				
Syllables	25	0	0	0
Consonant Sequences	123[a]	38	23	23
Prevocalic Singletons	21	0	0	0
Intervocalic Singletons	50	29	7	7
Postvocalic Singletons	100	6	6	0
Consonant Category Deficiencies[b]				
Liquids	100	10	100	100
Nasals	62	5	14	0
Glides	90	20	20	20
Stridents	100	45	36	29
Velars	100	68	45	41
Other Anterior Obstruents (Backing)	43	6	3	3
TOMPD[c]	215	79	62	53

[a]The formula for Consonant Sequences on the HAPP-3 represents dividing the number of total omissions of consonants in sequences by the number of possible "reductions" to one consonant.

[b]Consonant Category Deficiencies are scored if the target consonant is omitted or if a consonant from another category as specified is substituted for the target.

[c]TOMPD stands for total occurrences of major phonological deviations, which is obtained by adding occurrences of Omissions and occurrences of Consonant Category Deficiencies. Totals above 150 represent profound; between 100 and 149, severe; between 50 and 99, moderate; below 50, mild.

in their production practice words, and considerable carryover into spontaneous utterances had occurred. Moreover, their severity intervals had decreased from profound to moderate or mild.

School personnel were expressing increasing concerns about literacy. Their second-grade teacher told the parents that she might retain both boys at the end of the year. The first two authors visited the school to confer with the teachers. It was evident that the boys were falling behind their peers because of their difficulties in literacy. The focus for the fourth clinic semester changed to literacy. Some phonology goals were still incorpo-

rated (e.g., multisyllabic word productions), but these were now secondary.

Literacy Assessment and Intervention

Beginning in January of second grade, at age 7 years, 8 months, the boys were assessed for abilities affecting literacy. Reading and spelling abilities rely on phonological processing, which includes phonological awareness, speech sound production, and automatic components that facilitate comprehension (Kamhi & Catts, 2012). In a study of 75 typical second graders (Strattman

Table 35–2. Phonological Deviation Scores on the HAPP-3 for Josh Prior to Phonological Treatment (Age 5 Years, 10 Months) and Following Each of Three Semesters

	Percentages of Occurrences by Age			
	5:10	6:5	6:10	7:5
Omissions				
Syllables	6	0	0	0
Consonant Sequences	123	51	33	13
Prevocalic Singletons	18	0	0	0
Intervocalic Singletons	36	0	0	0
Postvocalic Singletons	100	22	3	0
Consonant Category Deficiencies				
Liquids	100	79	58	26
Nasals	62	14	0	0
Glides	90	20	20	20
Stridents	93	60	36	7
Velars	100	68	59	9
Other Anterior Obstruents (Backing)	43	7	7	0
TOMPD	206	89	57	17

Note: See Table 35–1 for explanations.

Table 35–3. Phonetic Transcriptions of Sample Word Productions From HAPP-3 at Age 5 Years, 10 Months

Target Word	Productions by Both	
clouds	[taʊ]	
square	[tɛ]	
candle	[næ o]	
string	[ni]	
rock	[ɑʔ]	
queen	[ni]	
	By Steve	**By Josh**
screwdriver	[tudai]	[dudaiʊ]
glasses	[dæʔɪ]	[dædɪ]

& Hodson, 2005), children with good phonemic awareness skills demonstrated by deletion and manipulation tasks were better at decoding nonwords and spelling real words. Vocabulary understanding contributed positively to decoding performance. Improved phonological production as measured by productions of multisyllabic words contributed to spelling scores. Results of speech sound productions, receptive vocabulary, and reading assessment indicated new problems that could potentially interfere with reading and writing for Josh and Steve.

Speech Sound Productions

Although both boys were intelligible after three cycles of phonological treatment, speech sound errors were still noticeable. Results of the HAPP-3 demonstrated progress in phonology with a score in the high mild range for Josh and the low-moderate range for Steve. The Assessment of Multisyllabic Words screening instrument (HAPP-3) revealed some consonant cluster reductions (e.g., *Seeping Beauty* for Sleeping Beauty), a few consonant single-ton omissions within these more complex words, and also several word-specific assimilations.

Receptive Vocabulary. Receptive vocabulary was 1½ to 2 years below expectation for chrono-logical age (age equivalency 6 years, 2 months for Josh and 5 years, 11 months for Steve), accord-ing to results of the Peabody Picture Vocabulary Test-5 (Dunn 2018). Some believe that vocabu-lary increases reciprocally with reading skills. At this time, neither boy read for pleasure, although they enjoyed it when someone read to them. Their vocabularies were relatively simple, with little variety in verbs and limited use of synonyms for nouns and adjectives.

Reading and Spelling. Sight word reading scores were within the typical range for second graders; however, decoding and reading compre-hension were below age expectations. Reading real words was at grade level (2:6), as assessed by the Word Identification subtest of the Woodcock Reading Mastery Test (Woodcock, 1998, 2011). Scores on the Word Attack subtest indicated that decoding of nonwords was more difficult for Steve (grade equivalency 1:6) than for Josh (2:2). Results of the Passage Comprehension subtest demon-strated a significant problem for both boys (grade equivalency 1:3 for Josh; 1:4 for Steve). Spelling scores were at or just below 1 standard deviation from the mean. Josh scored 59 and Steve scored 56 on the spelling subtest of the Wide Range Achieve-ment Test ($M = 69$, $SD =12$) (Jastak & Jastak, 1993; Wilkinson & Robertson, 2017).

Representation of the Problem at the Time of Referral

Reading comprehension was compromised by early phonological impairment that had not been fully resolved before learning to read and spell. Because reading was difficult, the boys did not want to read and did not develop strategies for learning from written text. More and more demand for independent reading and demonstra-tion of comprehension is expected by third grade. Retention in second grade was not a guarantee of reading comprehension strategy development.

Course of Treatment

Treatment focused on needs identified in assess-ment that contribute to reading and spelling suc-cess. To support decoding, some treatment was continued to facilitate the development of con-sonant sequences that contained liquids /r/ and /l/ and also included productions of multisyllabic words. In addition, phonemic manipulation tasks were utilized. The primary emphasis was on the development of reading comprehension strategies.

Speech Sound Productions

The cycles phonological approach was contin-ued. Target patterns for liquid clusters included more complex three-consonant clusters (e.g., /spr/ *spring*, /spl/ *splash*). Active games (e.g., basketball, scavenger hunts) and table activities were alter-nated for motivation. Multisyllabic words from the stories were segmented by syllables, using felt squares. Letter tiles or plastic letters were placed on the felt squares to facilitate spelling any syl-lable that was deleted (e.g., *algator* for *alligator*) or contained an error (*agarium* for *aquarium*). No let-ters were placed on squares that were correct. After identifying the problem, correct syllable produc-tion was practiced, and then the entire word was rehearsed correctly and added to a list of "Really Long Words I Can Say."

Reading Comprehension Strategies

Second graders often need help with strategies for understanding narrative stories and exposi-tory texts. Their reading textbook included both strategies. Explicit strategies facilitate comprehen-sion but also help students engage in the story beyond just decoding the words. Josh and Steve often answered, "I don't know," when asked either an open-ended question (e.g., *What was that story about?*) or specific questions (e.g., *Who was the main character?*).

Strategies for narrative stories included identification of story *grammar* elements (characters, setting, initiating event, problem, problem-solving attempts, and resolution) within the story and using story grammar structure for answering questions, comparing stories, and retelling. Initially, narrative stories with school themes at the second-grade reading and interest level (e.g., *Arthur's Lost and Found, Arthur's Valentine*) were chosen. Story grammar elements were labeled with Post-it® notes during reading. Graphic or visual organizers (e.g., story webs) were used to analyze the stories. Venn diagrams, two circles that overlap, were used to compare stories. Similarities between stories were listed in the overlapping part, and those that were unique to each story were listed in the part of the circles that did not overlap. (See Paul et al., 2018, for more information on graphic organizers.) Steve enjoyed narrative stories, but Josh preferred "real" stories.

Strategies for comprehension of expository texts were introduced as stories about real things included identification of elements: topic, main idea, and details. The same model used by the classroom teacher, a triangle with the topic at the top and the main idea in the middle, was adopted in the clinic. Details were listed on lines off the lower portion of the triangle. Later, one boy read a narrative (e.g., *Shark Tale*; Herman, 2004) and alternated with the other boy, who read an expository book (e.g., *Hungry, Hungry Sharks*; Cole, 1986). The books had a related theme, and they exchanged books the following week.

At school, they followed a program for monitoring reading comprehension of library books read on their own. Books were chosen from a specified list read at home and assessed via a computerized test. A variety of questions often followed story grammar or expository elements.

The hierarchical levels of language abstraction used in the Preschool Language Assessment Instrument-2 (Blank et al., 2003) were designed to assess preschoolers' abilities to answer ques-

tions that follow the language of instruction at school (e.g., *Which one is different? What do you think might happen next?*). This hierarchical structure of language is appropriate for school-age students because it is based on the premise of a perceptual-language continuum, which refers to the "distance" between what is immediately apparent (e.g., Level 1—*How many sharks do you see?*) and an answer that requires more reasoning (e.g., Level 4—*How could fish breathe under water?*). Level 4 is the most abstract and requires the highest degree of reasoning. In Level 1 questions, what the child perceives matches what is seen or was just heard (e.g., *What color is this shark? How many sharks are there on this page?*). Level 2 requires some recall or reorganization (e.g., *What work did Lenny do at the Whale Wash? What lie did Oscar tell?*). Level 3 questions require reordering of information or inhibition of an anticipated response (e.g., *What swims in the ocean but is not a fish?*). Josh and Steve worked initially at Levels 1 and 2, followed by Levels 3 and 4. These questions were written on sticky notes throughout the books. The boys answered the questions as they were reading the story. Accuracy of answers was tallied. After the story was finished, some of the questions were asked again. They could look back in the book if they needed help recalling the answer.

Higher-level narrative skill requires understanding the feelings and motivations of the characters (Paul et al., 2018). The boys' skills were compromised by their simple vocabulary (e.g., Arthur was *happy* when he got a Valentine. Lenny was *sad* not to be with his friends.). Other activities were designed to develop synonyms for feelings and emotions of the characters. The boys took turns with their clinicians drawing words from a bag and determining whether or not words meant the same thing (e.g., *happy, delighted, pleased*). Emotional thermometers were used to rank the degree of feeling (e.g., *pleased, happy, delighted, ecstatic*) (Westby, 2012).

Analysis of the Client's Response to Intervention

By the end of the spring semester, both boys demonstrated progress. They could identify basic story grammar elements with minimal cuing. They generated the topic, main idea, and four details in high-interest nonfiction books with no cuing. Level 1 and 2 questions were answered accurately without cues. Each attempted to answer questions, even if unsure. Both boys were promoted to third grade because of their substantial gains in reading comprehension.

Further Recommendations

Although the case was not closed, a solution was apparent—explicit treatment of deficit areas is necessary and has positive results. Although both boys were promoted to the next grade level, they continued to receive treatment and were learning additional strategies for reading comprehension and spelling. Steve was checking books out of the library, often choosing Arthur books (e.g., Brown, 1998, 2000). His mother reported that he read three books in 1 week. Children with histories of severe speech sound deficits are at risk for later literacy problems, and appropriate intervention makes a difference.

Authors' Note

Real clients provided the basis for this study. Permission was obtained to present this information for instructional purposes. Names were changed and identifiable information was excluded.

References

Bird, J., Bishop, D. V. M., & Freeman, M. H. (1995). Phonological awareness and literacy development in children with expressive phonological impairments. *Journal of Speech and Hearing Research, 38*, 446–462. https://doi.org/10.1080/13682820600806672

Bishop, D. V. M., & Adams, C. (1990). A prospective study of the relationship between specific language impairment, phonological disorders, and reading retardation. *Journal of Speech and Hearing Research, 38*, 1027–1050. https://doi.org/10.1111/j.1469-7610.1990.tb00844.x

Blank, M., Rose, S. A., & Berlin, L. J. (2003). *Preschool language assessment instrument* (2nd ed.). Pro-Ed.

Boada, K. L., Boada, R., Pennington, B. F., & Peterson, R. L. (2022). Sequencing deficits and phonological speech errors, but not articulation errors, predict later literacy skills. *Journal of Speech, Language, Hearing Research, 65*, 2081–2097. https://doi.org/10.1044/2022_JSLHR-21-00241

Brown, M. (1998). *Arthur lost and found*. Little, Brown.

Brown, M. (2000). *Arthur's valentine*. Little, Brown.

Clarke-Klein, S., & Hodson, B. W. (1995). A phonologically based analysis of misspellings by third graders with disordered-phonology histories. *Journal of Speech and Hearing Research, 38*(4), 839–849. https://doi.org/10.1044/jshr.3804.839

Cole, J. (1986). *Hungry, hungry sharks*. Random House for Young Readers.

Dodd, B., & McEvoy, S. (1994). Twin language or phonological disorder? *Journal of Child Language, 21*, 273–289. https://doi.org/10.1017/s0305000900009272

Duff, D., Tomblin, J. B., & Catts, H. (2015). The influence of reading on vocabulary growth: A case for a Matthew effect. *Journal of Speech, Language, Hearing Research, 58*(3), 853–864. https://doi.org/10.1044/2015_JSLHR-L-13-0310

Dunn, D. M. (2018). *Peabody Picture Vocabulary Test, 5th Edition*. Pearson.

Farquharson, K., Cabbage, K. L., & Gillon, T. (in press). Phonological awareness: Implications for children with expressive phonological impairment. In B. W. Hodson (Ed.), *Evaluating and enhancing children's phonological systems*. PhonoComp Publishing.

Herman, G. (2004). *Shark tale: Lenny's fishy fib*. Scholastic.

Hodson, B. (2004). *Hodson Assessment of Phonological Patterns* (3rd ed.). Pro-Ed.

Hodson, B. (2007). Enhancing children's phonological systems: The cycles remediation approach. In B. W. Hodson (Ed.), *Evaluating and enhancing children's phonological systems* (pp. 87–113). PhonoComp Publishing.

Hodson, B. (2021). Hodson Computerized Analysis of Phonological Patterns (4th ed.; HCAPP-4) [Computer software]. PhonoComp Software.

Jastak, J. F., & Jastak, S. R. (1993). *Wide Range Achievement Test-3*. Jastak & Associates.

Kamhi, A. G., & Catts, H. W. (2012). *Language and reading disabilities* (2nd ed.). Pearson.

Lewis, B. A., & Thompson, L. A. (1992). A study of developmental speech and language disorders in twins. *Journal of Speech and Hearing Research, 35*, 1086–1094. https://doi.org/10.1044/jshr.3505.1086

Magnus, L., & Hodson, B. W. (in press). Enhancing children's phonological systems: The cycles remediation approach. In B. W. Hodson (Ed.), *Evaluating and enhancing children's phonological systems*. Phono-Comp Publishing.

Overby, M. S., Trainin, G., Smit, A. B., Bernthal, J. E., & Nelson, R. (2012). Preliteracy speech sound production skill and later literacy outcomes: a study using the Templin Archive. *Language, Speech, and Hearing Services in Schools, 43*(1), 97–115. https://doi.org/10.1044/0161-1461(2011/10-0064)

Paul, R., Norbury, C., & Gosse, C. (2018). *Language disorders from infancy to adolescence: Listening, speaking, reading, writing, and communicating* (5th ed.). Elsevier.

Preston, J. L., Hull, M., & Edwards, M. L. (2013). Preschool speech error patterns predict articulation and phonological awareness outcomes in children with histories of speech sound disorders. *American Journal of Speech-Language Pathology, 22*(2), 173–184. https://doi.org/10.1044/1058-0360(2012/12-0022)

Rice, M. L., Zubrick, S. R., Taylor, C. L., Gayan, J., & Bontempo, D.E. (2014). Late language emergence in 24-month-old twins: Heritable and increased risk for late language emergence in twins. *Journal of Speech, Language, and Hearing Research, 57*(3), 917–928. https://doi.org/10.1044/1092-4388(2013/12-0350)

Rudolph, J. M., & Wendt, O. (2014). The efficacy of the cycles approach: A multiple baseline design. *Journal of Communication Disorders, 47*, 1–16. https://doi.org/10.1016/j.jcomdis.2013.12.003

Stackhouse, J. (1997). Phonological awareness: Connecting speech and literacy problems. In A. Hodson & M. Edwards (Eds.), *Perspectives in applied phonology* (pp. 157–196). Aspen.

Stanovich, K. E. (1986). Matthew effects in reading: Some consequences of individual differences in the acquisition of literacy. *Reading Research Quarterly, 21*, 360–406.

Strattman, K. H., & Hodson, B. W. (2005). Variables that influence decoding and spelling in beginning readers. *Child Language: Teaching and Therapy, 24*, 1–26. https://doi.org/10.1191/0265659005ct287oa

Sutherland, D., & Gillon, G. T. (2007). Development of phonological representations and phonological awareness in children with speech impairment. *International Journal of Language & Communication Disorders, 42*(2), 229–250. https://doi.org/10.1080/13682820600806672

Webster, P. E., & Plante, A. S. (1992). Effects of phonological impairment on words, syllables, and phoneme segmentation and reading. *Language, Speech, and Hearing Services in Schools, 23*, 176–182. https://doi.org/10.1044/0161-1461.2302.176

Westby, C. (2012). Assessing and remediating text comprehension. In A. G. Kamhi & H. W. Catts (Eds.), *Language and reading disabilities.* (3rd ed., pp. 163–225). Pearson.

Wilkinson, G. S., & Robertson, G. J. (2017). *Wide Range Achievement Test, 5th ed.* Pearson.

Woodcock, R. W. (1998). *Woodcock Reading Mastery Test.* Pearson.

Woodcock, R. W. (2011). *Woodcock Reading Mastery Test, 3rd Edition.* Pearson.

SWALLOWING
CASE 36
Hannah: Dysphagia in the Schools: A Case Study

Emily M. Homer and Dorothy Kelly

Conceptual Knowledge Areas

For children to learn at school, they must have safe and efficient mealtimes that provide adequate hydration and nutrition for them to benefit from their curriculum (Homer, 2016). This case study profiles a student who has a primary classification of developmental delay with diagnosed impairments that include the following: cerebral palsy, encephalopathy, cortical blindness, and severe global developmental delays in motor, cognitive, self-help, language, and oral-motor skills.

Federal and State Laws

When working within the school setting, it is essential to understand that federal and state laws dictate the services provided to students with disabilities. The Individuals With Disabilities Education Act (IDEA, 2004) provides students with disabilities rights to special education and the protection of these rights. States must comply with IDEA but are able to set up their own policies and procedures. IDEA is a funded law, which ensures that students with disabilities have access to a free and appropriate public education (FAPE). Children with disabilities are entitled to special education services, including related services. According to IDEA, related services include speech-language therapy, occupational therapy, physical therapy, and health services. Medical services are included in IDEA and are limited to "diagnostic and evaluative purposes only," performed by a physician.

Health services are a related service designed to enable a student with a disability to participate in school and as a result receive FAPE. A nurse or other qualified professional may provide health services.

Educational Relevance

The educational goal for students with special needs is to optimize each student's developmental potential while maintaining adequate nutrition, hydration, and health so that he or she may access and benefit fully from the educational program (Arvedson, 2000). Health services are essential for some students to be able to access the curriculum. For example, a student with a seizure disorder may need the services of a nurse to train service providers to administer medication when the student has a seizure. Without this, the student would be unable to attend school. IDEA protects the rights of students with disabilities and ensures a free appropriate public education. Feeding and swallowing disorders may be considered educationally relevant and part of the school system's responsibility to ensure:

- safety while eating in school, including having access to appropriate personnel, food, and procedures to minimize risks of choking and aspiration while eating;
- adequate nourishment and hydration so that students can attend to and fully access the school curriculum;
- student health and well-being (e.g., free from aspiration pneumonia and illnesses

related to malnutrition or dehydration) to maximize their attendance and academic ability/achievement at school; and

■ skill development for eating and drinking efficiently during meals and snack times so that students can complete these activities with their peers safely and in a timely manner (American Speech-Language-Hearing Association, n.d.).

Students with swallowing and feeding disorders may miss school more frequently than other students due to related health issues. These may include repeated upper respiratory infections or other pulmonary problems related to aspiration during oral feeding or gastroesophageal reflux. In addition, students who have difficulty managing their saliva or who resist toothbrushing due to sensory-based disorders or autism spectrum disorders may have poor oral hygiene.

For students to participate fully in the educational program, they need to be efficient during regular meal and snack times, so that their meal and snack times are completed with their peers. Optimally, they should complete their meal or snack within 30 minutes or less. Prolonged mealtime is a "red flag" for a swallowing and feeding disorder. Prolonged feeding times are indicative of excessive effort and energy that interfere with other activities important to a student's school day experiences. Prolonged mealtimes often are stressful for the student, and this stress can carry over into the remainder of the school day. Some students may require more frequent snacks or meals to maximize educational performance.

Developmental Delay

The student profiled in this case study was diagnosed with developmental delay according to Louisiana Bulletin 1508 (Pupil Appraisal Handbook, 2017), which outlines eligibility criteria for special education classification in Louisiana. Developmental delay is a disability in which children ages 3 through 8 years are identified as experiencing developmental delays in one or more of

the following areas: physical development, cognitive development, communication development, and social, emotional, or adaptive development. According to Bulletin 1508, a child qualifies for services under developmental disability when he or she has met the following criteria: between the ages of 3 through 8 years and functioning significantly below age expectancy (i.e., exhibiting a delay of 25% or more on criterion-based measures or achieving a standard score greater than or equal to 1.5 standard deviations below the mean on norm-based measures) in one or more of the following areas:

1. Physical development, which includes gross motor skills, fine motor skills, sensory (visual or hearing) abilities, sensory-motor integration
2. Social, adaptive, or emotional development, which includes play (solitary, parallel, cooperative), peer interaction, adult interaction, environmental interaction, expression of emotions
3. Cognitive or communication development, which includes language (receptive or expressive), concrete or abstract reasoning skills, perceptual discriminations, categorization and sequencing, task attention, memory, essential developmental or academic skills, as appropriate (Pupil Appraisal Handbook, 2017)

Cerebral Palsy

Cerebral palsy (CP) is a group of permanent disorders of the development of movement and posture, causing activity limitation, that are attributed to nonprogressive disturbances that occurred in the developing fetal or infant brain (Malandraki & Malandraki, 2019). There are four main types of CP: spastic, dyskinetic, ataxic, and mixed (Centers for Disease Control and Prevention, n.d.). CP is further described as mild, moderate, or severe, as well as the area of involvement (Prontnicki, 1995). There are many symptoms and effects of cerebral palsy. The student in this study exhibited symptoms such as spasticity and rigidity of muscles, delayed motor development, history of cortical blindness, perceptual and attentional problems, dysarthria, language delays, decreased breath control, oral-motor deficits, and dysphagia.

Pediatric Feeding Disorders

Pediatric feeding disorder (PFD) is defined by the World Health Organization's *International Classification of Functioning, Disability, and Health* (IFC) as impaired oral intake that is not age appropriate and is associated with medical, nutritional, feeding skill, and/or psychosocial dysfunction. Medical factors include impaired structure/function of the gastrointestinal (GI), cardiorespiratory, and neurological systems that give rise to dysfunction through several mechanisms, including dysphagia and cerebral palsy. Nutrition factors include the risk of malnutrition, overnutrition, micronutrient deficiency or toxicity, and dehydration. Many children with PFD have altered feeding skills, resulting from illness, injury, or developmental delay that have led to impairments such as oral sensory functioning, oral-motor functioning, delayed feeding skills, unsafe oral feeding, and inefficient oral feeding. Psychosocial factors in the child and/or caregiver can also contribute to feeding dysfunction and are characterized as developmental factors, mental and behavioral health problems, social factors, or environmental factors (Goday, 2019). The student in this case study had a PFD as evidenced by medical, nutritional, feeding skills, and psychosocial concerns.

Dysphagia

This case profiles a student who had a pediatric feeding disorder that included dysphagia, secondary to cerebral palsy. A basic knowledge of the phases of dysphagia is essential to understand the issues surrounding this student's disorder. The phases of dysphagia include oral preparatory and transit, pharyngeal, and esophageal phases. The oral preparatory and transit phases are under voluntary neural control. Students with oral preparatory and transit phase dysphagia have difficulty preparing food for a swallow and propelling it to the pharynx. They often exhibit weak lip closure, poor mastication, pocketing of food in the oral cavity, and the inability to efficiently propel the food in a cohesive bolus to the back of the oral cavity, thus initiating the pharyngeal phase of the swallow. The pharyngeal phase of swallowing begins voluntarily with the initiation of a swallow. As the bolus travels down the pharynx, the action becomes involuntary. Students with a pharyngeal phase dysphagia often have delays in the swallow, pooling in the vallecula and pyriform sinuses, and aspiration. The esophageal phase of dysphagia is the automatic movement, which carries the bolus through the esophagus and is completed when the food passes through the gastroesophageal junction into the stomach. Children with esophageal dysphagia may have gastroesophageal reflux disorder, which may result in a structural esophageal obstruction or a reflux-induced esophageal stricture. Esophageal dysphagia can lead to food aversion (Arvedson & Brodsky, 2002; Arvedson et al., 2020).

The reader may recall a choking experience or swallowing liquid that went "down the wrong way." These experiences relate to what the subject in this case goes through on a daily basis.

Description of the Case

Hannah was a 5-year, 6-month-old female student with a primary exceptionality of developmental delay according to the Louisiana State Pupil Appraisal evaluation on July 15, 2018. Diagnosed impairments at that time included the following: cerebral palsy, encephalopathy, cortical blindness (originally, though vision has reportedly improved), and severe global developmental delays in motor, cognitive, self-help, language, and oral-motor skills.

Background Information

Hannah was born prematurely at 26 weeks' gestation, weighing 3 pounds, 2 ounces. Ventilation was subsequently required for 1½ weeks due to underdeveloped lungs. She remained in the hospital for 2 months so that she could gain enough weight to be discharged. She went home weighing 5 pounds and was given an apnea monitor, though her biological parents apparently did not use it. At 5 months old, she contracted respiratory syncytial virus (RSV), which apparently went untreated until she became unconscious and her parents took her to the hospital. At that time, she sustained a severe anoxic brain injury associated with metabolic acidosis, and she remained in the hospital for 1 month. As a result of this neglect, her biological parents lost custody of Hannah. Other pertinent health history included ear infections for which pressure equalization (PE) tubes were inserted at 1 year old as well as surgery for exotropia (divergent strabismus resulting in abnormal turning outward of one or both eyes) at the age of 2 years, 4 months. In addition, Hannah had seasonal allergies and reactive airway disease, resulting in a compromised respiratory system. Medications included Xopenex regularly for respiratory difficulties, Zantac and Reglan for acid reflux, and Zyrtec for allergies.

Hannah wore glasses to correct her vision. Hearing was tested by her third birthday and found to be within normal limits. Hannah underwent 120 hyperbaric dives from 1 year, 2 months to 2 years of age as an adjunct therapy treatment to improve skills in multiple areas. Hyperbaric dives have been used to treat a variety of conditions such as autism, strokes, wounds, burns, and so on. Hannah's adoptive mother reported improvements in her vision and hearing following this treatment.

A long history of dysphagia was found with multiple modified barium swallow studies (MBSS) revealing silent aspiration. Her initial MBSS revealed that only honey-thick (moderately thick) liquids could be safely swallowed without aspiration or penetration. Hannah received early intervention services for dysphagia as well as physical, occupational, and speech therapies. Subsequent MBSS revealed improvements with swallowing, though dysphagia persisted. At the time that Hannah entered the school system, the most recent MBSS, conducted at 3 years, revealed aspiration with thin liquids, and as a result, liquids were thickened to a nectar (mildly thick) consistency.

Reason for Referral and Findings of the Evaluation

Hannah participated in the Early Steps program that provided her with speech-language therapy, occupational therapy, and physical therapy. Due to the history of dysphagia from Early Steps, a referral was made for the school district's dysphagia team prior to Hannah's first day of school. The interdisciplinary observation (clinical evaluation) was conducted with Hannah's speech-language pathologist and occupational therapist on the first day of school. Input was also gathered from the special education nurse who wrote the emergency plan for Hannah and Hannah's adoptive parents, who provided information on mealtimes at home. Oral-motor difficulties consisted of labial, mandibular, buccal, and lingual weakness; reduced range of motion and incoordination, more prominent on the left side; oral hyposensitivity; and suspected apraxia. Based on these findings, symptoms that were suspected were the following: anterior loss due to decreased lip closure; oral residue and pocketing due to weakness, decreased coordination, and range of motion; and decreased mastication and multiple swallows due to decreased bolus formation, oral hyposensitivity, and apraxia. The symptoms described were noted during the interdisciplinary swallowing and feeding observation. Based on these observations, Hannah's medical history, and previous MBSS, the following recommendations were made:

1. Positioning in a rifton chair (an adaptive chair designed to encourage normal sitting or standing posture for students with neuromuscular disorders) with cushion harness on the chest and shoulders to assist with sitting balance
2. Diet/food preparation:
   - Liquids should be thickened to mildly thick according to the International Dysphagia Diet Standardization Initiative (IDDSI).
   - Soft foods such as vegetables should have crumbled crackers to add texture. (Hannah had oral hyposensitivity and thus has reduced tactile sensitivity; bland, smooth foods were difficult for Hannah to detect in her mouth.)

- Dry foods such as cornbread should be slightly moistened to facilitate Hannah forming a more cohesive bolus.
3. Swallowing and feeding plan techniques/precautions:
   - Liquids taken one very small sip at a time and all liquids thickened to 1.5 TBS per 8 ounces
   - Chewable foods placed to her right side and on her molar table to encourage her to chew her food and give her visual cues to chew as needed
   - Pace slowed, allowing her to swallow two to three times per one bite of food or sip of liquid (she did this independently)
   - Mouth checked periodically for pocketing and a small sip of thickened liquid given if oral residue is noticed
   - Ensure she does not tilt her head back—give verbal and/or tactile cues to move head midline.

Treatment Options Considered

Several treatment options were considered based on the results of the evaluation, including Beckman's (1986) oral-motor interventions as they do not require the child to follow oral-motor directions and thus can be passively performed on the child. In addition, these interventions target all oral-motor areas of difficulty. Hannah's speech-language pathologist (SLP) had attended the Beckman training and witnessed the effectiveness of the treatment on numerous students of various ages. In addition, the SLP had used these interventions on several other children with good results. Hannah had good family support, and it was hypothesized that these interventions would be trained for carryover at home. However, the SLP was unsuccessful in bringing in the adoptive mother for training with Beckman exercises with multiple attempts. Thermal/tactile stimulation was considered initially due to the delayed swallow reflex, though after attempts to train with Beckman were unsuccessful, this was not implemented as thermal/tactile stimulation needs to be done a minimum of three times daily to be effec-

tive (Logemann, 1998). Active oral-motor exercises could not be implemented due to difficulty following oral-motor directions. Chewing exercises and training utilizing the chewy tube were used with good success. The recommendations and swallowing precautions previously mentioned have been documented to facilitate improvements with areas of deficit as well as practice in swallowing various types and textures of foods. Hannah was followed by the dysphagia case manager (SLP) on a weekly basis, which included working with her during one of her lunch meals as well as consulting with the teachers and paraeducators who assisted with feeding (Homer, 2016).

Course of Treatment

Parent Perspective

Hannah's adoptive mother reported that the most difficult time for the family was in the initial stages of her dysphagia. Hannah was congested all the time, and the mother was unable to keep her well. This fear was alleviated following the initial diagnosis of dysphagia and the cause of her frequent illnesses was determined. Initially, Hannah's dysphagia was severe, and all liquids were reportedly thickened to pudding (extremely thick) using an infa-feeder. It was 2 years before Hannah was able to eat baby food by spoon. Hannah's swallowing problems were among many that the family faced. Projectile vomiting and reflux were also significant problems for which Hannah reportedly was on two different medications. During this period of time, Hannah required breathing treatments every 3 to 4 hours. Hannah's adoptive father worked full-time, and her adoptive mother did not have other family support as their families were upset with them for adopting a child with special needs. Furthermore, Hannah's adoptive mother reported that she and her husband fought with the Office of Community Services (OCS) for 8 months before the hyperbaric dives that Hannah needed were approved. The family also reportedly had to deal with negative medical comments, including that Hannah would never see or hear. Hannah's adoptive mother indicated that the hyperbaric dives significantly improved her hearing, sight, motor development, and swallowing. Hannah made much progress; however, the family continued to deal with medical and social issues such as wheelchairs and starting a baclofen pump to help with some persistent motor issues. Her swallowing and feeding improved significantly and Hannah was scheduled for an updated swallow study to see if she could handle thin liquids. Hannah's adoptive mother stated that Hannah's well-being is worth far more than the difficulties that the family has endured.

Analysis of Client's Response to Intervention

Hannah made significant progress over the course of treatment. At the time of the study, Hannah fed herself and chewed her food, even soft chewable foods such as macaroni and cheese, with good success independently. Adding texture to foods was no longer required. The need for moistening foods was also minimized. Hannah placed the food to the side of her mouth independently by lateralizing her tongue. Pocketing and the use of a small sip of liquid were also significantly reduced. Only slight oral residue was noted to persist with certain chewable foods. Liquids continued to be thickened due to difficulty controlling thin liquids as well as to a delayed swallow reflex and reduced laryngeal sensation identified with the latest modified barium swallow.

Authors' Note

This case study was based entirely on an actual student. The procedures and information provided reflect the actual treatment of this student by the school district's Interdisciplinary Dysphagia Team. Parents were aware of the case study and provided unconditional permission.

References

American Speech-Language-Hearing Association. (n.d.). *Pediatric feeding and swallowing* [Practice portal]. http://www.asha.org/practice-portal/clinical-topics/pediatric-dysphagia/

Arvedson, J. C. (2000). Evaluation of children with feeding and swallowing problems. *Language, Speech, and Hearing Services in Schools, 31,* 28–41. https://doi.org/10.1044/0161-1461.3101.28

Arvedson, J. C., & Brodsky, L. (2002). *Pediatric swallowing and feeding: Assessment and management* (2nd ed.). Singular Thomson Delmar Learning.

Arvedson, J. C., Brodsky, L., & Lefton-Greif, M. A. (2020). *Pediatric swallowing and feeding: Assessment and management* (3rd ed.). Plural Publishing.

Beckman, D. A. (1986). *Oral motor assessment and treatment.* Beckman and Associates.

Centers for Disease Control and Prevention (n.d.). *What is cerebral palsy?* https://www.cdc.gov/ncbddd/cp/facts.html

Goday, P., Huh, S., Sliverman, A, Lukens, C., Dodrill, P., Cohen, S., . . . Phalen, J. A. (2019). Pediatric feeding disorder—consensus definition and conceptual framework. *Journal of Pediatric Gastroenterology and Nutrition, 68*(1), 124–129. https://doi.org/10.1097/MPG.0000000000002188

Homer, E. M. (2016). *Management of swallowing and feeding disorders in schools.* Plural Publishing.

Individuals With Disabilities Education Improvement Act of 2004. P.L. No. 108–446, 8 Stat. 2647 (2004).

Logemann, J. (1998). *Evaluation and treatment of swallowing disorders* (Rev. ed.). Pro-Ed.

Malandraki, G. A., & Malandraki, J. B. (2019). Oropharyngeal dysphagia in children with cerebral palsy. In M. Gosa & D. Suiter (Eds.), *Assessing and treating dysphagia: A lifespan perspective.* Thieme.

Prontnicki, J. (1995). Presentation: Symptomatology and etiology of dysphagia. In S. R. Rosenthal, J. J. Sheppard, & M. Lotze (Eds.), *Dysphagia and the child with developmental disability: Medical, clinical and family interventions* (pp. 1–14). Singular.

Pupil Appraisal Handbook, Bulletin 1508. Title 28, Education Part CI. 31–32, Louisiana State Department of Education (2017).

VOICE
CASE 37
Adam: Vocal Cord Dysfunction in a Teenage Athlete
Gail B. Kempster

Conceptual Knowledge Areas

Knowledge of Vocal Fold Physiology in Breathing and Speech

The primary purpose of the structures of the larynx is for protection of the airway and the lower respiratory system. The true vocal folds (TVFs), also known as the vocal cords, are folds of tissue arising from the sides of the airway, protected by the cartilages of the larynx. The movements of the TVFs are controlled primarily by the intrinsic muscles of the larynx through innervation by branches of the vagus nerve. The posterior cricoarytenoid muscles open the TVFs, the lateral cricoarytenoid and interarytenoid muscles close the TVFs, and the thyroarytenoid and cricothyroid muscles tense and stiffen or elongate the TVFs. During quiet breathing, the TVFs remain open so that air may move through the respiratory tract for the exchange of oxygen and carbon dioxide (although small movements of the arytenoid cartilages are seen during breathing, toward abduction on inhalation, and toward adduction on exhalation). The TVFs and other supraglottal structures close momentarily for a number of functions. These include protecting the airway from foreign substances such as during the act of swallowing; vomiting; coughing to expel material; allowing for the increase of intrathoracic pressure for lifting, defecation, birthing, and the like; and for producing voice (Hixon et al., 2008).

Knowledge of Typical Stresses of Adolescence, Especially Those of an Athlete

Stress is a significant problem for many teenagers. It is characterized by feelings of tension, frustration, worry, sadness, and withdrawal that may last anywhere from a few hours to days. While the majority of teenagers are not depressed, it is common for young people to experience life events involving friends or family that involve conflict or loss. Some of these events include the breakup with a boyfriend or girlfriend; increased arguments with parents, siblings, and friends; changes in a family's financial status; and parents experiencing relationship difficulties. The majority of teenagers face such negative life experiences with the resources to cope, but for others, such stressors are overwhelming. For most adolescents, however, coping with life events involves learning skills to find positive ways to achieve peace of mind and assuming responsibility for oneself. These skills require practice and rely to a great extent on communication with others (Walker, 2005).

Athletics are one outlet for teenagers to learn positive coping skills and reduce stress. However, sports can promote both positive and negative stress. Researchers have found that adolescents' participation in competitive sports is linked with competition anxiety and self-centeredness. Also, balancing school and sports is not an easy task and can be very stressful. Some high-achieving teenagers are focused more on winning, on obtaining public recognition, and on their performance relative to others. This orientation and personality disposition may lead to additional stress on the teenager, which outweighs the positive benefits of the sports activity (Lyons, G., n.d.).

Knowledge of Signs, Symptoms, and Treatment for Vocal Fold Dysfunction

Vocal cord dysfunction (VCD) is a disorder in which the vocal folds move to an adducted or partially adducted position during inhalation and/or exhalation. This disorder has also been labeled paradoxical vocal fold motion disorder (PVFMD) and, under certain circumstances, more recently is called exercise-induced laryngeal obstruction (EILO) (Johnston et al., 2017). This "dysfunctional" closure of the TVFs results in difficulty breathing, sometimes with stridor, with a resultant increase in anxiety. The etiology of VCD is unclear. It frequently co-occurs in individuals with asthma and has also been associated with allergies, reflux, and psychosocial stress. Some individuals with VCD have triggering symptoms such as exercise or exertion or being in an environment with a particular odor (e.g., perfume, gasoline, coffee). A patient experiencing VCD typically indicates that tightness is experienced in the throat area versus in the upper chest. The classic diagnostic finding related to VCD is a shortened inspiratory flow volume loop found on pulmonary function testing. Many individuals also present with a posterior, diamond-shaped glottal chink, even when not symptomatic (Mathers-Schmidt, 2001).

A patient with a diagnosis of VCD should be determined to have good control of asthma, allergies, and reflux symptoms. If these related disorders are being controlled, the treatment for VCD involves cognitive-behavioral therapy directed toward respiratory retraining to produce relaxed abdominal breathing, often with attention diverted away from the area of tension in the throat. Johnston et al. (2017) describe three useful variations of respiratory retraining strategies, while Gallena et al. (2019) report a successful clinical trial of intensive short-term treatment of teenage athletes with this disorder.

Knowledge of Characteristics of and Treatment for Tourette Syndrome

Tourette syndrome (TS) is a neurological condition characterized by repetitive, involuntary movements or vocalizations known as tics. The etiology of this disorder is unknown, but TS is thought to involve multiple brain areas with complex interactions. There is evidence to suggest that TS is inherited. TS is more common in males and is often diagnosed first in childhood. Although there is no known cure, the disorder appears at its worst during the early teen years and often improves in adulthood.

Individuals with Tourette syndrome frequently have a concomitant diagnosis of attention-deficit/hyperactivity disorder (ADHD) and may experience anxiety and depression. For those patients whose symptoms of TS interfere with daily functional activities, neuroleptic medications are commonly prescribed for tic suppression. These medications may have side effects, and long-term use can lead to other movement disorders such as dystonia or even tardive dyskinesia (National Institute of Neurological Disorders and Stroke, n.d.).

Description of the Case

Background Information

The patient, Adam, a 15-year-old high school freshman, was referred to the Speech and Hearing Clinic at a large teaching hospital for evaluation. At the time of referral, Adam was active in several sports in high school as well as in church activities and scouting. He had two younger siblings, a brother with epilepsy and a sister diagnosed with central auditory processing disorder and dyslexia. His mother was a single parent who worked full-time at a local diner.

The family came to the medical center from a middle-class suburb some distance away. Adam attended a large high school with over 2,000 students. Despite his many activities, his grades were well above average, and he was on the honor roll almost every term. Adam's medical history included diagnoses of allergies, asthma, chronic otitis media, and ADHD. His current medications included Singulair, Advair, and Maxair for his asthma.

Reason for Referral

About 4 years prior to this evaluation, Adam began exhibiting tics and other symptoms, including sniffing, head jerks, and ear popping. He was evaluated by a neurologist and found to have Tourette syndrome. Clonodine and Concerta, prescribed for his ADHD, also seemed to help his symptoms of Tourette syndrome. The tics and other signs tended to recur when he was extremely anxious or tired. Sylvia, his mother, tried several homeopathic strategies to see if these relieved some of the symptoms. Based on trial and error, she and Adam believed a gluten-free diet had a positive effect.

Adam was monitored closely by his primary care physician and routinely by a consulting neurologist. Despite all of her children's many activities and their health issues, Sylvia was organized, knowledgeable, and proactive in dealing with their medical and educational needs. This attention was illustrated by her rousing all three of her children at 4:00 a.m. to come to the medical center on time for Adam's clinic appointment. Sylvia brought with her detailed records relating to Adam's medical history and supplemented his answers to our questions with specific information. She encouraged Adam to speak for himself and take ownership of the reason for his consult at our clinic.

Findings of the Evaluation

Adam was previously evaluated by his primary care doctor and by a pulmonary specialist. The pulmonologist ordered pulmonary function testing and determined that Adam's asthma was under optimal control. His flow volume study, however, revealed a reduced inspiratory flow volume loop. This suggested an extrapulmonary source of constriction and is associated with a diagnosis of vocal cord dysfunction. Adam was referred to this medical center for confirmation of this diagnosis.

During the interview, Adam reported that he began experiencing difficulty breathing during exercise in fifth grade. He described these periods as having trouble getting air in or out and "feeling pain in the back of the throat." Unlike his asthma episodes when he typically experienced a feeling of tightness in his chest, which lasted an hour or two, the symptoms he experienced with exertion lasted only for a minute or two. Adam was active in multiple sports, including swimming and cross-country, and he noticed that episodes of breathing difficulty had been happening more and more frequently, sometimes during practice, but even more so during competitions. These episodes, which often occurred multiple times during a single workout session, had a significant effect on Adam's ability to perform and stay competitive. In fact, his coaches, his teammates, and even spectators became noticeably concerned and anxious whenever the situation occurred, and he was restricted from participation during competitions. Adam seemed matter-of-fact in discussing these episodes, but he had difficulty maintaining eye contact with the clinician and became somewhat agitated and less forthcoming when pressed for more details.

The evaluation protocol followed that recommended by Mathers-Schmidt (2001). After obtaining information related to the patient's medical and social history and his current symptoms, other elements—respiratory support and control, laryngeal valving efficiency and control, respiratory driving pressure control, laryngeal musculoskeletal tension, and structural/functional integrity of the speech structures—were assessed.

This assessment revealed that Adam had normal vocal pitch, loudness, and quality and had no difficulty with voiced and voiceless onsets and offsets in connected speech. His phonational range was 38 semitones, which is normal. He had no difficulty varying loudness as requested in specific tasks. Maximum phonation time on a prolonged vowel was normal at 15.3 seconds, although this value was judged to be below his maximum ability. Adam had no difficulty sustaining a steady respiratory driving pressure of 5 cm H_2O for 5 seconds. His oral mechanism exam was normal.

Palpation of the laryngeal area during quiet breathing and speech revealed musculoskeletal tension to be mildly elevated in the clinician's judgment. No episodes of difficulty breathing outside of the range of normal were elicited, despite having Adam run up five flights of stairs. Because Adam was asymptomatic during the evaluation, videoendoscopy was not completed.

Adam appeared mildly anxious during the assessment and intermittently exhibited signs of boredom, irritation, and embarrassment. These reactions were not, however, considered out of the ordinary for the patient's age and the evaluation environment. A few signs of Tourette syndrome were noted during the 90-minute session, including two facial tics on the patient's left side and two slight head jerks to the left.

The results of the evaluation supported the diagnosis of vocal cord dysfunction. In particular, the specific nature of the symptoms reported, their duration, and the context in which they occurred (in addition to the pulmonary function test results) clearly pointed to this diagnosis.

Treatment Options Considered

The etiology of vocal fold dysfunction is unclear, except in cases associated with neurologic origins. Movement disorders are one such neurologic etiology, and Tourette syndrome can be categorized in this way. However, Adam's shortness of breath symptoms did not seem correlated with episodes of tics. Rather, he reflected one common profile of patients with VCD, who typically are young, tend to be high achievers and have competitive natures, have a history of allergies and asthma, and experience specific triggering episodes such as exertion.

Clinical experience revealed that treatment of patients with VCD must first achieve maximal control of conditions threatening the airway: that of asthma, allergies with chronic postnasal drip, and laryngopharyngeal reflux. Once the patient and his physicians assert that these conditions are well controlled medically, the patient is taught

to recognize the initial, subtle signs of laryngeal tension during typical triggering activities. Some patients find that they need to cough, clear their throat, or swallow more in response to a kind of tickle, irritation, or tightness in the throat. It is shortly after experiencing such signs that tension in the throat builds and breathing becomes difficult on inspiration, expiration, or both. Treatment for patients with vocal cord dysfunction consists of patient education, supportive counseling, and instruction in tension identification and control, and in relaxed open throat breathing (see Mathers-Schmidt, 2001). Clinicians often focus on respiratory retraining strategies (Gallena et al., 2019; Johnston et al., 2017). Adam's clinician began by describing the anatomy of respiration, differences seen in quiet breathing versus speech breathing, and the function of the vocal folds.

Course of Treatment

Adam acknowledged being aware of the change in feeling in his throat, so the clinician immediately taught him a relaxed, open throat breathing exercise (Blager, 1995). Many patients with symptoms of VCD recognize that if they force themselves to relax and breathe easily, the tension in the throat dissipates quickly. The difficulty, however, is in preventing the episodes from occurring.

Adam was instructed in the relaxed, open throat breathing exercise. Sitting quietly with his arms at rest and shoulders relaxed, he was taught to focus on relaxing his jaw with his lips closed and tongue resting on the floor of his mouth. After taking a moderately quick inhalation (a "sniff") through his nose, Adam was instructed to exhale slowly while quietly producing /s/ and to continue this exhalation focusing on the constriction at the front of the mouth until he had exhaled below resting expiratory level before inhaling again. This technique allowed two things to occur. First, his attention was distracted away from the tightness in the throat and drawn to the constriction in the front of the oral cavity during the exhalation. Second, exhaling below resting expiratory level promoted the need for an inhalation with a wide-open airway.

The clinician asked Adam to practice this exercise several times a day for a few weeks and to log any episodes of VCD, noting specific features about each episode, including the triggering situation, initial symptoms, and duration. Once Adam had experience with the exercise, his mother agreed to contact Adam's cross-country coach and the school nurse to inform them about this disorder and to see how support could be provided at school. Because the family lived so far from the medical center, the clinician recommended only a minimal amount of follow-up at the clinic with telephone contacts as needed.

Adam returned for follow-up 1 month later. He said that he had been practicing the relaxed breathing exercise several times a day and demonstrated this. He continued to sit on the bench during athletic contests and reported no episodes of VCD in the last month. The mother had spoken with Adam's cross-country coach, and he was willing to monitor and support Adam. A packet of information about VCD, including the Mathers-Schmidt (2001) article and written instructions for the relaxed open throat breathing exercise, was prepared for the coach and the school nurse. It was agreed that the coach and nurse would contact the SLP with any questions. The plan was for Adam to begin jogging, slowing down as needed, and using the breathing exercise whenever he felt the incipient tension beginning in his throat.

Ten weeks later, Adam returned to the clinic. He had practiced several times with his coach running with him. Each time the same thing happened: He would run three laps, would then sprint 100 yards, and then the VCD started. Adam described it this way: "I'll stop and breathe out, but then I choke and can't breathe in. It feels like someone's holding my head under water, and I need to breathe in, but I can't. Sometimes I almost feel like I'm gagging and need to throw up." Adam felt that the breathing exercise was not helping him. He was discouraged and stressed by what was occurring. At this session, signs of Tourette syndrome were more noticeable than before.

The clinician explored the pattern of the episodes thoroughly. Adam seemed to go from no problems to full-blown "choking" with almost no time in between despite his and his coach's best efforts. The clinician was convinced Adam was following the recommendations and had support there to help him. Although Adam received encouragement, he was clearly frustrated and felt any modifications of the strategy would be worthless. In a radical move, the clinician decided to recommend that Adam turn the breathing exercise "upside down"—that is, rather than using a quick inhalation and slow, controlled exhalation, he would try the opposite and use a slow, relaxed inhalation through pursed lips with a quicker, open-mouthed exhalation. Adam practiced this in the therapy room and reluctantly agreed to give it a try. The clinician asked him to test it and telephone with an update.

Analysis of Client's Response to Intervention and Further Recommendations

The clinician did not hear from Adam, but the mother brought him back for a recheck visit 5 months later. Adam reported no episodes of VCD while at camp over the summer. He did, however, experience some episodes when starting cross-country practice again. However, by then, Adam realized what to do and how to control the episodes. He needed to keep reminding himself to breathe and to maintain an even breathing rhythm, *not* to hold his breath during running. He was happy to report that he had had no episodes in the past 6 weeks.

The clinician discussed how to approach possible VCD episodes when Adam began swimming practice again. Adam's self-determined strategy seemed like a good one to stay with, and he was encouraged to do this. Because of the humid and chlorinated environment of indoor pools, the clinician asked Adam to be especially vigilant in following his daily treatment plan for his asthma.

Adam was asked to call in 2 months to provide an update, but he did not follow through. Because the clinician believed that the mother would have continued to seek follow-up should Adam have problems, it was assumed that he was coping well and experiencing few, if any, episodes of VCD.

Clinical experience and evidence from the literature suggest that most student athletes with VCD typically do not continue to experience episodes long term. It is unclear why this disorder resolves in this population. In fact, evidence in support of the efficacy of behavioral treatment for VCD with breathing exercises is largely anecdotal in nature, with very few high-quality clinical studies in the literature (Patel et al., 2015). However, patient education with strategies involving respiratory retraining appear promising.

Author's Note

This case is based on the experiences of the clinician with patients with this disorder. All identifying characteristics have been altered to protect any individual patient's privacy. Content altered in this way was approved for publication by the Rush University Medical Center Privacy Office.

References

Blager, F. (1995, September). Treatment of paradoxical vocal cord dysfunction. *Division 3 Newsletter*. American Speech-Language-Hearing Association.

Gallena, S., Johnson, A., & Vossoughi, J. (2019). Short-term intensive therapy and outcomes for athletes with paradoxical vocal fold motion disorder. *American Journal of Speech-Language Pathology, 28*, 83–95. https://doi.org/10.1044/2018_AJSLP-17-0223

Hixon, T., Weismer, G., & Hoit, J. (2008). *Preclinical speech science: Anatomy physiology acoustics perception*. Plural Publishing.

Johnston, K., Bradford, H., Hodges, H., Moore, C., Nauman, E., & Olin, J. (2017). The Olin EILOBI breathing techniques: Description and initial case series of novel respiratory retraining strategies for athletes with exercise-induced laryngeal obstruction. *Journal of Voice, 32*(6), 698–704. https://doi.org/10.1016/j.jvoice.2017.08.020

Lyons, G. (n.d.). *Sports-related stress in adolescents*. https://www.readkong.com/page/sports-related-stress-in-adolescents-3042992

Mathers-Schmidt, B. (2001). Paradoxical vocal fold motion: A tutorial on a complex disorder and the speech-language pathologist's role. *American Journal of Speech-Language Pathology, 10*, 111–125. https://doi.org/10.1044/1058-0360(2001/012)

National Institute of Neurological Disorders and Stroke. (n.d.). *Tourette syndrome fact sheet*. http://www.ninds.nih.gov/disorders/tourette/detail_tourette.htm

Patel, R., Venediktov, R., Schooling, T., & Wang, B. (2015). Evidence-based systematic review: Effects of speech-language pathology treatment for individuals with paradoxical vocal fold motion. *American Journal of Speech Language Pathology, 24*, 566–584. https://doi.org/10.1044/2015_AJSLP-14-0120

Walker, J. (2005). *Adolescent stress and depression*. University of Minnesota Extension Center for Youth Development. https://hdl.handle.net/11299/195269

Part IV
ADULT CASES

APHASIA
CASE 38
Andrew: A Case of Primary Progressive Aphasia in the Later Stages of the Disease
Michael de Riesthal and Kiiya Shibata

Conceptual Knowledge Areas

This chapter describes the management of an individual with primary progressive aphasia (PPA). To understand this case, it is important to be familiar with the definition and presentation of PPA and how it differs from *nonprogressive* aphasia. This includes understanding the changes to language systems, speech motor systems, and cognitive systems that may occur in progressive diseases.

Aphasia is a disorder of language formulation and comprehension that results in deficits across input (auditory and reading comprehension) and output (speaking and writing) language modalities (Rosenbek et al., 1989). Typically, nonprogressive aphasia results from a focal lesion in the cortical language areas due to a stroke and is abrupt in onset. Deficits are often maximal at onset of the stroke, and improvement in language function occurs during the acute and chronic stages of the disorder through the influence of spontaneous recovery and the implementation of treatment (Robey, 1998; Wertz et al., 1986). Definitions of aphasia often include exclusionary criteria to distinguish aphasia from communication disorders related to nonlinguistic physiologic, cognitive, and sensory deficits that differ with regard to diagnosis, prognosis, and management.

In contrast, PPA is a neurodegenerative disease involving insidious onset language difficulties in the context of relatively spared cognitive function, where language is the initial and dominant factor impacting activities of daily living (Mesulam, 2001). Gorno-Tempini et al., (2011) produced the

seminal international consensus paper, which established behavioral, neuroimaging, and pathophysiological diagnostic profiles for three variants of PPA: semantic variant (svPPA), logopenic variant (lvPPA), and nonfluent/agrammatic variant (nfvPPA). The earliest established variant, svPPA is characterized by impairments in single-word comprehension, confrontation naming, and surface dyslexia and dysgraphia. The clinical hallmarks of lvPPA are word-finding difficulties in connected speech and naming, impairments in sentence and phrase repetition, and phonemic paraphasias. To be diagnosed with nfvPPA, one must present with either apraxia of speech (AOS) or agrammatic language production, and may also present with impaired comprehension of syntactically complex sentences.

Progression through the disease is typically characterized by increasing severity of speech and language symptoms; development of secondary movement, behavioral, and cognitive syndromes; and mortality within the first 10 years (Kertesz et al., 2007; Ulugut et al., 2021). Ulugut and colleagues (2021) followed a cohort of individuals with PPA for a period of up to 6 years. Individuals with lvPPA had notable cognitive and language impairments relative to the other cohorts, with language progressing to include symptoms beyond the defining characteristics of the variant. Those diagnosed with nfvPPA demonstrated increased incidence of movement disorders and mortality, as well as progression of speech and language symptoms to the point of mutism. Participants who carried a diagnosis of svPPA were more likely to develop behavioral symptoms consistent with those seen in behavioral variant frontotemporal dementia, and while their semantic deficits continued to worsen, the language profile remained consistent with the defining characteristics of svPPA. It should be noted that prior to the Gorno-Tempini et al. (2011) consensus paper, individuals were typically diagnosed with either an svPPA or a nonfluent PPA that encompassed features of both nfPPA and lvPPA. The case to follow is an example of an individual who was diagnosed with nonfluent PPA prior to the publication of the consensus paper.

Description of the Case

Background Information

The patient, Andrew, a right-handed, native English speaker, was retired from a management position. He had an undergraduate degree in physics and a black belt in several forms of martial arts. When he was 55 years old, he began having difficulty with word finding and mathematical calculations. Concerned that these changes could be related to Alzheimer's disease (AD), he scheduled an appointment with his primary care physician, who referred him for psychological testing. Testing results were not consistent with AD, and it was felt that the changes could be due to depression and stress. He was prescribed Paxil and observed some improvement in speech and mathematical skill with an increased dose, but deficits persisted. He was referred to a neurologist for further assessment. Following the behavioral assessment and magnetic resonance imaging (MRI), Andrew was diagnosed with AD. He and his wife, Sarah, were not satisfied with this diagnosis and continued their search for an accurate diagnosis. After Andrew and Sarah retired and moved to a new city, his new primary care physician felt that, although the MRI of the brain was negative, the symptoms were more consistent with a stroke. The physician referred Andrew for speech therapy. According to Sarah, Andrew became frustrated with speech therapy and was frequently emotional when he left a session. Eventually, Andrew

was evaluated at a clinic that specialized in the assessment and diagnosis of individuals with progressive language and cognitive deficits. Following a thorough neuropsychological assessment, Andrew was diagnosed with PPA.

Reasons for the Referral

Andrew was referred for speech and language assessment and training of "augmentative and alternative communication and aggressive speech and language therapy" by his primary care physician due to the diagnosis of PPA.

Findings of the Evaluation

Neuropsychological testing was completed at another institution 11 months prior to Andrew being seen at Pi Beta Phi Rehabilitation Institute (PBPRI). Testing revealed a progressive, nonfluent language impairment characterized by single-word utterances and echolalia in conversational speech, as well as severely impaired confrontation and generative naming. He demonstrated a moderate impairment in comprehension of narrative information and a moderate-to-severe impairment in comprehension of single- and multistep commands. He was able to repeat some single words and high-probability phrases (i.e., Mother cooks dinner), but performance was poor with low-probability phrases (i.e., The pastry cook was elated). Andrew presented with a moderate impairment in visual immediate attention, conceptual reasoning, and immediate recall of visuospatial material. Evidence of motor perseveration was observed on the Luria three-step motor sequence task. It was determined that Andrew's deficits were consistent with progressive nonfluent aphasia, with the primary symptom being the onset of word-retrieval difficulty with progression of language dysfunction over the first 3 years of the disease.

At PBPRI, the Western Aphasia Battery–Revised (Kertesz, 2006) (language quotient subtests) and the Pyramids and Palm Trees Test (Howard & Patterson, 1992) were administered. Andrew's wife, Sarah, completed the ASHA–Functional Assessment of Communication Skills for Adults (ASHA-FACS; Frattali et al., 1995). The results (Table 38–1), which were similar to those of previous neuropsychological testing, suggested a progressive, severe nonfluent aphasia. Andrew spoke in mostly single-word utterances and tended to be more perseverative and echolalic on structured language and conversational tasks. Confrontation naming was severely impaired and was characterized by both paraphasic and perseverative errors. Generative naming was severely impaired, and naming to sentence completion was moderately to severely impaired. Andrew was able to repeat single words and short phrases but was unable to repeat sentence-length material. His yes/no response was inconsistent. Auditory comprehension of sequential commands was moderately to severely impaired and variable across stimuli of increasing complexity. Reading comprehension was severely impaired.

Relative strengths were also observed. Andrew demonstrated better performance on picture-to-written word matching than written word-to-picture matching, which suggested visual-picture information might be more useful in accessing the semantic system for communication. On informal testing, Andrew's auditory word-to-picture matching (field of two pictures) improved when the picture and written word stimuli were presented together. His accuracy also improved on a sentence description-to-picture matching task. Finally, Andrew demonstrated the ability to write a few single words to dictation and to copy simple words. Data from the ASHA-FACS revealed deficits in the areas of social communication, reading, writing, number concepts, and daily planning. However, according to Sarah, communication of basic needs was a relative strength.

Sarah reported that, recently, Andrew had experienced a change in social behavior and increased confusion. He was referred to a neurologist, who confirmed the diagnosis of PPA and determined that the onset of behavioral symptoms was consistent with frontotemporal dementia (FTD).

During the initial interview, it was clear that the changes in Andrew's speech, language, and cognitive functioning due to PPA had had a significant impact on Andrew and Sarah. Their financial situation had become strained since the onset of the illness. He was not able to continue in his profession due to his speech and language issues, and Sarah was not able to work because she had to care for him. They were on a fixed income and had to make many lifestyle changes. They lived far from their respective families and did not have any routine social support. Both Andrew and Sarah were frustrated that many medical professionals, including speech-language pathologists, did not seem to have much experience with PPA. As Andrew's condition worsened, Sarah accepted more and more of the burden of communication and the completion of activities of daily living (ADLs). Andrew had always been a fiercely independent and capable person, and his loss of independence was demoralizing. At times, their situation left them feeling alone and, according to Sarah, as if "you are stranded on an island and the sun isn't shining."

Representation of the Problem at the Time of Testing

Andrew's language function had declined significantly over the 5 years prior to the assessment, and this decline was the primary symptom experienced during the first few years postonset. His moderately severe to severe oral-expressive language, writing, auditory, and reading comprehension deficits made it very difficult for him to communicate with others. In addition, the recent change in social behavior and increased confusion had resulted in difficulty performing ADLs. Andrew's history and the results of neuropsychological and speech and language testing were consistent with the diagnosis of PPA. Moreover, the neurological evaluation indicated the onset of FTD.

Treatment Options Considered

At the time Andrew's treatment plan was developed, the treatment literature for PPA was significantly limited, as compared to the literature for nonprogressive aphasia. Only a few studies had

Table 38–1. Test Data for Andrew During Assessment at PBRRI

Western Aphasia Battery	Score
Spontaneous Speech	
Information content	3/10
Fluency, grammatical competence, and paraphasia	2/10
Auditory Verbal Comprehension	
Yes/no questions	33/60
Auditory word recognition	27/60
Sequential commands	39/80
Repetition	42/100
Naming and Word Finding	
Object Naming	22/60
Word Fluency	0/20
Sentence Completion	5/10
Responsive Speech	0/10
Reading	
Comprehension of Sentences	4/40
Reading Commands	3/20
Written Word-Object Choice Matching	0/6
Written Word-Picture Choice Matching	1/6
Picture-Written Word Choice Matching	3/6
Spoken Word-Written Word Choice Matching	2/6
Letter Discrimination	4/6
Spelled Word Recognition	0/6
Spelling	0/6
Writing	
Writing Upon Request	2/6
Writing Output	0/34
Writing to Dictation	0/6
Writing Dictated Words	1/10
Alphabet and Numbers	4/22.5
Dictated Letters and Numbers	2/7.5
Copying a Sentence	2/10
Pyramids and Palm Trees Test	29/52
ASHA FACS	
Social Communication	3.6/7
Reading, Writing, and Number Concepts	2.4/7
Daily Planning	2.0/7
Communication of Basic Needs	5.6/7

reported the therapeutic effect of specific treatment techniques for improving language function in individuals with PPA. The available data suggested that some individuals with PPA may benefit from a lexical-semantic treatment for word-retrieval deficits (McNeil et al., 1995), an oral and gestural training of verb tense for sentence production deficits (Schneider et al., 1996), and a reading and constrained summarization treatment for discourse deficits (Rogalski & Edmonds, 2008). Several guidelines or recommendations for clinical practice had been promoted based on case studies and clinical expertise (e.g., Murray, 1998; Rogers & Alarcon, 1998). While expert opinions differed on the efficacy of restitutive and maintenance therapies, there was agreement on the importance of preparing for decline by implementing low-tech AAC and training primary communication partners on strategies to support communication. Today, the benefit of restitutive and maintenance interventions is better understood. Some general underpinnings of these interventions include implementing formal therapy and home programs to facilitate maintenance, beginning therapy early in the disease process when possible (as gains are typically congruent to severity), and capitalizing on errorless learning modes and spared semantic knowledge (where possible) to facilitate generalization (Cadório et al., 2017; Henry et al., 2018; Henry et al., 2019; Jokel, 2019).

After considering the available literature, it was determined that Andrew's treatment plan should include (1) educating patient and family, (2) training with an AAC system to improve communication, and, potentially, and (3) implementing a behavioral treatment targeting a specific language impairment. Moreover, the treatment should be dyad oriented to promote successful communication between Andrew and his wife. Given that Andrew was not diagnosed until he was in the middle to later stages of PPA and had no previous experience with an AAC system, it was unclear how he would respond to this type of treatment. Moreover, while there is evidence that individuals with PPA respond to impairment-based behavioral language treatment (e.g., Schneider et al., 1996), Andrew was in a later stage of the disease and had more severe language deficits than the participants included in published reports. Thus, the potential influence of such a treatment was unknown.

Lasker and colleagues (2006) recommended that the objectives of AAC in the later stages of PPA should be to help maintain personal connectedness and participation in communicative activities and to find alternative methods to achieve personal fulfillment. The goals for communication with Andrew's AAC system were based on this idea. Because he and Sarah were frustrated by the frequent communication breakdowns and the recent onset of difficulty performing certain ADLs, these concerns became the focus for designing the picture-based AAC system. In addition to this system, Andrew and Sarah were trained to use the techniques from the program Supported Conversation for Adults with Aphasia (SCA; Kagan, 1998) as another means of facilitating communication. Finally, given Andrew's limited ability to copy some words during the initial language assessment, the Copy and Recall Treatment (CART) program was implemented. The therapeutic effect of CART on written naming performance has been shown in individuals with severe nonprogressive aphasia (Beeson et al., 2003) but not in individuals with PPA.

Course of Treatment

Andrew was seen twice weekly for the first 2 months of treatment. However, due to the distance he and his wife traveled to treatment, session frequency was reduced to once each week. Sarah participated in all sessions.

One of the first goals addressed in treatment was to improve the couple's knowledge and understanding of PPA. Andrew and Sarah entered treatment with some awareness of his disease. Prior to the diagnosis being made 11 months earlier, Sarah had suspected the diagnosis of PPA based on her own research. The speech-language pathologist was able to share his knowledge of the results of the assessment, the anticipated decline in function, and the treatment options available. Sarah was able to share her knowledge of PPA, verify the information, and ask questions. Education and counseling were incorporated throughout treatment during individual sessions and on the telephone. The speech-language pathologist shared literature regarding the expected course of the disease and the management of its associated communication deficits. Similarly, Sarah shared articles she found on the Internet and information she gathered from books. As Andrew's communicative function declined during treatment, the couple and the speech-language pathologist discussed changes with respect to the anticipated course of the disease and modified the treatment plan accordingly.

The AAC system was developed and introduced at the beginning of treatment. As mentioned, Sarah was concerned about Andrew's recent difficulty performing certain ADLs and the added burden this placed on her. In particular, Andrew was having difficulty carrying out the steps involved in organizing his clothes to get dressed in the morning, preparing his breakfast, washing his hands, brushing his teeth, and organizing his gym bag. Moreover, Sarah and Andrew were frustrated about their frequent communication breakdowns. To target these issues, a picture-based system was designed to facilitate Andrew's ability to perform certain ADLs and to communicate simple messages to his wife and other communication partners. The pictures were paired with printed words to provide multimodality input, which was found to aid comprehension during informal assessment. For each ADL identified, a set of pictures illustrating the steps in the process or the items needed to complete the process were printed and laminated. The pictures for each task were included on individual "storyboards" (using Velcro) that could be placed in the location where the activity took place (e.g., the kitchen counter, bathroom, closet). To improve communication of simple messages, picture/printed word cards were developed for yes/no responses, stores and restaurants, feelings/health, and frequently misplaced items.

The picture sets for the performance of ADLs and the communication of simple messages were introduced to Andrew one at a time during the treatment sessions. For the ADL picture sets, each picture was presented and the correct order of placement was demonstrated. He was asked to point to each picture on command in a field of three or four. Errors were corrected, and cueing was provided. The pictures were then scrambled, and Andrew was asked to place the pictures in correct order. Again, errors were corrected and cueing was provided as needed. When possible, performance of the actual activity was practiced in the clinic. Training was similar for the use of the yes/no, store/restaurant, feelings/health, and frequently misplaced items picture sets. He and his wife were instructed on using the system at home and were asked to keep a log of his daily use of the system. Review of the picture sets during treatment sessions depended on Andrew's ability to perform the task at home.

Communication techniques from SCA (Kagan, 1998) were trained throughout treatment. In general, training focused on the three basic principles for revealing an individual's communicative competence during a conversation. These include (1) ensuring the individual with aphasia comprehends the conversation partner's message by having the partner use multiple input modalities and stimuli (e.g., gesture, written key words, drawings, and additional materials), (2) ensuring the individual with aphasia has a means for responding (e.g., yes/no or fixed-choice response, multiple response modalities), and (3) verifying that the conversation partner comprehends the aphasic individual's message by expanding upon that message and requesting additional information. Communication techniques based on these principles were modeled repeatedly by the clinician during treatment sessions. Andrew and Sarah practiced in the clinic and were encouraged to use the principles to communicate at home. Andrew understood information and responded best when provided with written words, pictures, and maps. Sarah organized a book of photos to use during conversations about parents, siblings, children, nieces and nephews, and close friends. Maps were used to aid communication about local trips, past travels, and details about Andrew's childhood. For example, Andrew was able to communicate how to get to the hardware store from his house using a local street map. Despite his significant communication deficits and the onset of cognitive deficits, Andrew maintained fairly well-preserved map- and route-finding skills and responded well to the use of maps in conversation.

Finally, Andrew was introduced to the CART program (Beeson et al., 2003). This program is a lexical-semantic treatment designed to improve single-word spelling through repeated copying of target words while pairing the printed stimuli with the picture of the object or concept (Beeson et al., 2003). Typically, words are treated in groups of five. The individual is provided with daily homework sheets that require him or her to copy each of the five words up to 20 times. Daily self-test sheets are provided to practice writing the word from recall. Five words were chosen for Andrew based on Sarah's input. He attempted to complete the homework task each week, but his attempts to copy the words were often unsuccessful. His initial attempt was the most accurate, but each successive attempt was further from the target, and some perseverative responses were observed. Andrew was not able to learn to write the words without copying them directly. The use of CART was discontinued after 2 weeks of treatment so that resources could be focused on more successful communication tasks.

Analysis of Client's Response to Intervention

Andrew's response to intervention varied over the course of his treatment program. He and Sarah benefited from education and counseling. They became more knowledgeable of the deficits he was experiencing and what was expected in the future. Moreover, Andrew and Sarah had an opportunity to share their feelings of frustration regarding the challenges to communication and participated in "troubleshooting" the problems. Often, Sarah would describe her creative attempts to improve communication at home, and she appreciated having these ideas validated in the clinic. Communication at home continued to decline as Andrew's deficits worsened. However, having an outlet for discussion of these changes and frustrations was beneficial.

Use of the AAC system as originally designed during the first 2 months of treatment proved

useful. Initially, Andrew required occasional cueing from his wife to perform the ADLs targeted in the system. The log sheet indicated near daily use of the system to perform such tasks as preparing breakfast, dressing himself, brushing his teeth, washing his hands, and preparing popcorn. Moreover, Andrew and Sarah were able to use the system together to communicate feelings, plans to go to certain restaurants or shops, and misplaced items Andrew was trying to find (e.g., wallet, keys, etc.). During this time, Sarah reported that Andrew was exhibiting some increased independence in performing the ADLs targeted in treatment. This permitted Sarah to relax during the day for at least a short period of time (e.g., drink a cup of tea, read the newspaper, etc.).

After the first 2 months of treatment, Andrew began having more difficulty performing the tasks targeted in the AAC system. Sarah reported that he needed more cueing to perform many of the tasks, even when using the pictures as a guide. During treatment sessions, the system was changed to include more input from Sarah but still promote Andrew's independence. For example, Andrew still used the pictures to prepare his breakfast (bagel with butter), but Sarah placed the required materials (plate, knife, etc.) on the counter instead of having Andrew find the items in the kitchen. In addition, Sarah periodically modeled the task for Andrew and provided prompts to facilitate improved performance. Even with this change, Andrew required increased cueing from Sarah to perform the tasks.

Over the course of treatment, Andrew and Sarah benefited from using the principles of SCA to facilitate communication at home. As Andrew's communication skills deteriorated, Sarah accepted more responsibility during conversational interactions. At that point, supported conversation was the best means of communication, because Andrew required active participation by the listener. Having practiced utilizing the principles in the treatment sessions, Sarah was able to make this transition. Sarah used the picture stimuli from the AAC system, other referential graphics (e.g., picture book of family members, maps), and written key words to ensure that Andrew comprehended the information presented and had a means of responding.

Further Recommendations

When treating patients with PPA, the clinical profile for the patient continues to change as his or her communication and (possibly) cognitive skills deteriorate. Hypotheses about the patient's deficits are continually revised, as are the format and goals of treatment. As previously discussed, clinicians, patients, and family members should prepare for these changes in advance so that there is a smooth transition to the next phase of language treatment and use of communication strategies. Andrew had already experienced a significant decline in his language skills and communicative function before he was first seen for treatment. During treatment, language and communicative function continued to decline, and he began to demonstrate increased confusion at home. Andrew's treatment continues, and he and Sarah are preparing for the next modification that will shift additional communication and activity burdens to her, while promoting his independence for as long as possible. Continued education and support has been a healthy coping mechanism for this client and his wife.

Authors' Note

The case presented is of an actual client with PPA and his wife. He and his wife granted permission to the author to use their case in this text, and they actively participated in the creation of this manuscript through interviews and discussion. Both were excited to know that their experiences might help in the training of future clinicians.

References

Beeson, P. M., Rising, K., & Volk, J. (2003). Writing treatment for severe aphasia: Who benefits? *Journal of Speech-Language Hearing Sciences, 46*, 1038–1060.

Cadório, I., Lousada, M., Martins, P., & Figueiredo, D. (2017). Generalization and maintenance of treatment gains in primary progressive aphasia (PPA): A systematic review. *International Journal of Language & Communication Disorders, 52*(5), 543–560. https://doi.org/10.1111/1460-6984.12310

Frattali, C. M., Thompson, C. K., Holland, A. L., Wohl, C. B., & Ferketic, M. M. (1995). *The American Speech-Language-Hearing Association Functional Assessment of Communication Skills for Adults.* American Speech-Language-Hearing Association.

Gorno-Tempini, M. L., Hillis, A. E., Weintraub, S., Kertesz, A., Mendez, M., Cappa, S. F., . . . Grossman, M. (2011). Classification of primary progressive aphasia and its variants. *Neurology, 76*(11), 1006–1014. https://doi.org/10.1212/wnl.0b013e31821103e6

Henry, M. L., Hubbard, H. I., Grasso, S. M., Dial, H. R., Beeson, P. M., Miller, B. L., & Gorno-Tempini, M. L. (2019). Treatment for word retrieval in semantic and logopenic variants of primary progressive aphasia: Immediate and long-term outcomes. *Journal of Speech, Language, and Hearing Research, 62*(8), 2723–2749. https://doi.org/10.1044/2018_jslhr-l-18-0144

Henry, M. L., Hubbard, H. I., Grasso, S. M., Mandelli, M. L., Wilson, S. M., Sathishkumar, M. T., . . . Gorno-Tempini, M. L. (2018). Retraining speech production and fluency in non-fluent/agrammatic primary progressive aphasia. *Brain, 141*(6), 1799–1814. https://doi.org/10.1093/brain/awy101

Howard, D., & Patterson, K. (1992). *Pyramids and palm trees: A test of semantic access from pictures and words.* Thames Valley Publishing.

Jokel, R. (2019). Generalization (but not maintenance) of treatment gains from semantic therapy may differ by primary progressive aphasia variant. *Evidence-Based Communication Assessment and Intervention, 13*(4), 187–190. https://doi.org/10.1080/17489539.2019.1666492

Kagan, A. (1998). Supported conversation for adults with aphasia: Methods and resources for training conversational partners. *Aphasiology, 12*, 816–830.

Kertesz, A. (2006). *Western Aphasia Battery–Revised.* Harcourt Assessment.

Kertesz, A., Blair, M., McMonagle, P., & Munoz, D. G. (2007). The diagnosis and course of frontotemporal dementia. *Alzheimer's Disease and Associated Disorders, 21*, 155–163.

Lasker J., King, J., Fox, L., Alarcon, N. B., & Garrett, K. (2006, November). *AAC decision-making in chronic and progressive aphasia.* Seminar presented at the American Speech-Language Hearing Association Convention, Miami, FL.

McNeil, M. R., Small, S. L., Masterson, R. J., & Fossett, T. R. D. (1995). Behavioural and pharmacological treatment of lexicalsemantic deficits in a single patient with primary progressive aphasia. *American Journal of Speech-Language Pathology, 4,* 76–87.

Mesulam, M. M. (2001). Primary progressive aphasia—a language-based dementia. *New England Journal of Medicine, 349*(16), 1535–1542. https://doi.org/10.1056/nejmra022435

Murray, L. L. (1998). Longitudinal treatment of primary progressive aphasia: A case study. *Aphasiology, 12,* 651–672.

Robey, R. R. (1998). A meta-analysis of clinical outcomes in the treatment of aphasia. *Journal of Speech, Language and Hearing Research, 41,* 172–187.

Rogalski, Y., & Edmonds, L. A. (2008). Attentive Reading and Constrained Summarisation (ARCS) treatment in primary progressive aphasia: A case study. *Aphasiology, 22,* 763–775.

Rogers, M. A., & Alarcon, N. B. (1998). Dissolution of spoken language in primary progressive aphasia. *Aphasiology, 12,* 329–339.

Rosenbek, J. C., LaPointe, L. L., & Wertz, R. T. (1989). *Aphasia: A clinical approach.* Pro-Ed.

Schneider, S. L., Thompson, C. K., & Luring, B. (1996). Effects of verbal plus gestural matrix training on sentence production in a patient with primary progressive aphasia. *Aphasiology, 10,* 297–317.

Ulugut, H., Stek, S., Wagemans, L. E. E., Jutten, R. J., Keulen, M. A., Bouwman, F. H., . . . Pijnenburg, Y. A. L. (2021). The natural history of primary progressive aphasia: Beyond aphasia. *Journal of Neurology, 269*(3), 1375–1385. https://doi.org/10.1007/s00415-021-10689-1

Wertz, R. T., Weiss, D. J., Aten, J. L., Brookshire, R. G., Garcia-Buñuel, L., Holland, A. L., . . . Goodman, R. H. (1986). Comparison of clinic, home, and deferred language treatment for aphasia. *Archives of Neurology, 43*(7), 653. https://doi.org/10.1001/archneur.1986.00520070011008

APHASIA
CASE 39

Betty: Cognitive-Communication Impairments in a Woman With Right Hemisphere Disorder

Scott R. Youmans

Conceptual Knowledge Areas

Right hemisphere disorder (RHD) arises from damage to the nondominant hemisphere of the brain. Until somewhat recently, the impact of lesions to the right hemisphere of the brain on communication was underestimated and, therefore, understudied. This was perhaps because communication impairments in persons with RHD are subtler than the communication impairments observed following language-dominant hemisphere lesions (aphasia and/or apraxia). The communication impairments with which persons with RHD present are usually byproducts of the cognitive problems that underlie them.

RHD is typically characterized by cognitive impairments of memory and attention and related difficulties, some of which also impair communication. Some of the more commonly reported impairments include the person's inability to recognize that he or she has a disorder (anosagnosia), an inattention to stimuli on the left side (left neglect), visuospatial and visuoperceptual impairments (which may also inhibit constructional abilities), an inability to recognize or convey emotions, impulsivity, difficulties with executive functions (problem solving, reasoning, judgment), problems with the social aspects of speech (pragmatics), and higher language use and comprehension (Brookshire & McNeil, 2014; Carota & Bogousslavsky, 2018; Hewetson et al., 2017).

Description of the Case

Background Information

In January 2020, Betty had a stroke in her right frontal lobe with mild residual left-sided weakness. When she was discharged from the hospital to her home, she was referred by her speech-language pathologist to our university clinic as an outpatient. Betty began coming to the clinic for an evaluation and subsequent treatment in March 2020.

History Information

At the time of her referral, Betty was a 57-year-old, right-handed, African American woman. Betty lived alone and identified herself as being in the low socioeconomic range. She was a Brooklyn native and English was her first and only language. Betty completed high school but never attended college. Prior to her hospitalization, she worked as an office manager for a local business due to her stroke-related difficulties, she was no longer employed. The loss of income reportedly made it difficult for Betty to make ends meet financially.

Betty was a widow; her husband had died 7 years prior to her referral. She had two unmarried adult sons, Ronnie and Peter, who lived locally. Ronnie visited his mother biweekly and called daily. Betty confided that Ronnie, the older of the two men, was supportive and tried to help her as much as he could, both financially and with household responsibilities. Peter was apparently frustrated by the limitations Betty exhibited following her stroke and expressed his impatience at her slow recovery. Peter visited her daily during her hospital stay following her stroke, but he visited and called less often following her discharge from the hospital.

Prior to Betty's stroke, she had never been hospitalized or had surgeries other than minor dental work. Her past medical history was significant for high cholesterol and hypertension. Betty had normal, corrected vision and stated that her hearing was within normal limits. Her premorbid reading and writing abilities were also reportedly average.

Reasons for the Referral

Betty was originally referred to the speech-language pathologist by her primary hospital physician due to problems with swallowing. Upon Betty's release from the hospital, the speech-language pathologist reported that swallowing had returned to normal and that no further diet modifications or compensations were necessary but expressed the need for a further evaluation of Betty's cognitive-communication abilities by an outpatient speech-language pathologist. Betty was referred to our clinic due to its "sliding-scale" cost reduction for persons with low incomes.

Interview

When asked, Betty initially downplayed any problems with her cognition or communicative abilities resulting from her stroke. Upon further probing, Betty reported becoming confused during conversations, being easily distracted, and having difficulty concentrating during reading. Prior to concluding the interview, the examiner asked Betty if there was anything in particular that bothered her since her stroke. Betty again changed her response. This time she reported that it bothered her that she had difficulty reading because that was her favorite hobby prior to her stroke; however, she also reiterated that she really did not have any other difficulties.

Betty's son, Ronnie, who attended the evaluation, reported that his mother's personality seemed different since her stroke. He said she seemed "weird" and "like a different person."

When asked what, specifically, he noticed about her that was different, he responded that she was much more "literal" than she had been before, she was easily confused, and she talked on and on without conveying much information or getting to a point. He also mentioned that Betty's once dry, sarcastic sense of humor was no longer expressed.

Observations

During the interview, the examiner noted that Betty exhibited a flat affect and showed little emotion. She did not initiate eye contact often and maintained it only briefly once it was established. Betty was distractible and frequently had difficulty maintaining and shifting topics. She answered questions with utterances that were excessive in length and somewhat empty of content. Receptively, Betty appeared to understand shorter, simpler utterances but seemed to have more difficulty when the utterances became longer and more complex. She did not exhibit word-finding difficulties or manifest any grammatical problems. A slight speech impairment was detected, which did not affect her intelligibility.

Findings of the Evaluation

Hearing

Although Betty reported that her hearing was normal, she was seen by the clinic audiologist to rule out a hearing loss that could explain some of her impairments. Hearing was within normal limits. Additionally, the audiologist reported that Betty could adequately perceive speech.

Speech

An oral mechanism examination was conducted. The salient results were as follows: The client had slight tongue weakness and lower facial weakness on her left side in the absence of other abnormal findings. An analysis of her speech showed that Betty produced slightly distorted lingual and labial phonemes. Additionally, Betty's prosody during connected speech was observed to be flat; in other words, her speech was monotonous and somewhat robotic.

Assessment of Abilities Associated With the Right Hemisphere

The Mini Inventory of Right Brain Injury–Second Edition (MIRBI-2; Pimental & Kingsbury, 2000) was administered to assess some of the cognitive and linguistic abilities that are commonly affected by damage to the right hemisphere.

Betty demonstrated difficulty visually scanning for letters (e.g., circling all of the As in a particular row of letters). She did not exhibit left neglect. She made several errors during oral reading and was unable to answer a comprehension question. Betty was able to write to dictation with additional time but made several errors when writing spontaneously. She had difficulty expressing emotion, exhibited a flat affect, demonstrated poor eye contact, and displayed distractibility. She also had mild difficulty with several higher language skills, such as understanding humor and comprehending oral narratives. Betty did not have difficulty comparing or contrasting items. She did have difficulty with oral expression at the narrative level that was described as disorganized, verbose, and tangential. Throughout the assessment, Betty frequently requested that items be repeated, and she appeared to require concentrated attention and effort to answer questions; however, she did not exhibit impulsivity in her responses.

Conversation

Consistent with the observations made during her interview and on the MIRBI-2, Betty displayed moderate difficulty with verbal expression of her ideas when she was engaged in an unsupported, naturally paced conversation. Her verbal expression was frequently disorganized, fragmented, repetitive, irrelevant, and/or tangential to the topic at hand. She frequently used empty, nonspecific speech during conversation that was sometimes incomplete or ambiguous.

When conversation was supported with visual cues for the topic and sequencing of ideas, Betty performed somewhat better; however, she continued to become confused and distracted. Betty's affect appeared flat throughout the exchange. She did not maintain eye contact and displayed some difficulty turn-taking. Also consistent with the results of the other assessments and observations, Betty appeared able to attend to and comprehend simple utterances but appeared to get "lost" as listening and cognitive demands increased. The use of figurative language, abstract concepts, and humor by the examiner often elicited confused or inappropriate replies.

Informal Writing Evaluation

Betty was able to write and sign her name and was able to write short sentences to dictation. She generated short, novel written sentences in response to pictorial stimuli but with obvious effort and significant delay. Spelling and letter formation were accurate during this brief screening.

Informal Reading Evaluation

Betty was able to read short (5 to 10 sentences), seventh- to eighth-grade-level paragraphs orally but with frequent errors. Her errors consisted of word omissions and word-ending omissions. She inconsistently recognized and self-corrected these errors. She spontaneously and inconsistently used the strategy of finger pointing, which seemed to aid her oral reading ability. In terms of comprehension, Betty interpreted meanings literally, failed to understand humor, and had difficulty assigning a central theme or moral to a story.

Interpretation of the Findings

Betty presented with a mild unilateral upper motor neuron (UUMN) dysarthria. This type of dysarthria is typically mild and transient, and it involves phonemic distortions due to tongue and lower facial weakness. UUMN dysarthria commonly occurs following a unilateral stroke in the cortex of the brain. Although Betty exhibited slightly abnormal speech due to these distortions, they were not significant enough to impair her intelligibility.

Additionally, based on the data obtained from the formal and informal evaluations of her cognition and communicative abilities, Betty exhibited a mild-moderate cognitive-communication impairment characteristic of right hemisphere disorder (RHD). Betty exhibited behavioral abnormalities, such as her flat affect and reduced prosody, which made her verbal output relatively free of emotion and animation. Betty also displayed some of the classic pragmatic impairments that often occur as a result of RHD, such as poor turn-taking, limited eye contact, and excessive verbal output with limited information content and no central point or theme. Betty also was concrete and had difficulty interpreting abstract meanings, including metaphors, and humor. Additional problems included reduced visuoperceptual abilities, comprehension of oral and written narratives, perseveration on a topic, and limited insight into her disorders.

Many of the problems individuals exhibit due to RHD are attributable to underlying problems with attention, including an individual's ability to sustain attention without becoming distracted, focus attention while other distractions are present, divide attention to multitask, and shift attention from one point of focus to another. These underlying problems with attention can obviously explain Betty's distractibility and difficulty maintaining or shifting topics during conversation. In addition, Betty's inability to attend to specific details can also be seen as the underlying cause of her lack of insight into her disorder, her visuoperceptual difficulties, disorganization of verbal and written expression, auditory and reading comprehension problems, and pragmatic impairments (e.g., inability to attend to the listener).

In conclusion, at the time of the initial evaluation, Betty appeared relatively linguistically intact; however, her underlying cognitive problems, primarily with attention, interfered with her ability to efficiently express herself orally or in writing or comprehend higher-level oral or written language. Betty's strengths included her evident intelligence despite her stroke-related cognitive impairments, her ability to read and write premorbidly, her attempts to compensate for her impairments (i.e., finger pointing during reading and asking for repetitions when she did not understand a statement), her stimulability to treatment (i.e., conversation improved when conversation was supported), and her familial support. On the other hand, a major barrier to her treatment was Betty's lack of insight into her difficulties.

Treatment Options Considered

The speech-language pathologist considered various goals and treatment options for this client. Upon reflection, he came to the conclusion that no matter what treatment avenue was pursued, it was imperative that Betty's lack of insight into her disorders be addressed either first or concomitantly while working on other goals. Without insight into her impairments, Betty would have difficulty understanding the purpose or necessity of treatment, and she might also have difficulty maintaining motivation to come to therapy and to complete home assignments or follow recommendations made by the speech-language pathologist.

The speech-language pathologist also considered whether to work directly on Betty's dysarthria. He concluded that directly treating Betty's dysarthria would probably not be a priority unless it was her primary concern. His reasoning was that UUMN dysarthria is often transient (i.e., resolves itself spontaneously as the acute effects of the stroke diminish); Betty's intelligibility was not affected, so communication would not be compromised by the dysarthria, and therapy involved extensive verbal output. By using the lip and facial muscles to speak, she would strengthen them and further improve her ability to speak.

Because attention underlies many of the cognitive abilities with which Betty was having difficulty, directly treating attention was considered. The therapist could generate specific treatments that targeted each of the types of attention (focused, sustained, divided, and alternating). By removing the underlying cause, the problem would be expected to diminish. Some researchers have suggested that this is the best approach to treatment (Tompkins, 1995); however, the speech-language pathologist was concerned that Betty might not understand how this treatment approach related to her other problems.

Therapy could also focus on Betty's conversational abilities, including her pragmatics, such as turn-taking, eye contact, and topic maintenance, and her inferential abilities, such as understanding humor, metaphors, incongruence, sarcasm, and implied meanings (Myers, 1998). Improving these abilities would help Betty to better express and comprehend language. Additionally, her son specifically mentioned that Betty's premorbid sense of humor was one of the characteristics that defined her personality. Many of these abilities can be worked on in a conversational context, which tends to be well received by clients due to its naturalness.

Finally, the speech-language pathologist considered direct work on Betty's reading ability because she had expressed a specific concern about this. To maintain motivation in therapy, it is wise to attempt to focus treatment on areas that would not only improve a client's communication abilities but would have the maximum effect on quality of life. Additionally, because Betty lacked some insight into her disorders, working on something she recognized as disordered and effectively remediating it could help her "buy into" therapy. As reading was a hobby of Betty's, she might find the home assignments and treatment activities enjoyable as long as they were ability-appropriate and not overly frustrating. Finally, focus on reading would facilitate work on visual scanning, reading comprehension, and underlying attention problems at the same time, while treating attention directly might seem to Betty to be unrelated to her concerns.

Course of Treatment

The speech-language pathologist recommended that Betty attend individual 1-hour speech therapy sessions at the university clinic twice a week. The clinician also suggested that Betty attend an adult communication group that met for 1 hour a week and primarily included individuals with aphasia, apraxia, and RHD. It was further recommended that therapy focus on reading, conversational support strategies, and inferential abilities and that strategy practice occur in structured and unstructured conversation and reading tasks.

The therapist discussed these recommendations with the client to obtain her input into the appropriateness and sufficiency of the goals. The client reported her understanding and approved of the goals without desire to modify or eliminate any of them or to add others. She reported that she was most interested in working on her reading, but she was willing to "try anything."

At first, Betty attended individual sessions sporadically and did not come to the communication group. She rarely completed home assignments and made limited progress. When asked how she liked speech therapy and the tasks on which we were working, she said that she really liked them, but she could not explain why she was doing them despite the speech-language pathologist's repeated attempts to explain this to her. Furthermore, she reported that the transportation van that she used to get to the clinic was always late and the driver was rude to her.

The speech-language pathologist telephoned Betty's son, Ronnie, and asked if he would encourage her to come to therapy more frequently. He agreed and offered to drive her to therapy personally when he was able. True to his word, Ronnie began to bring Betty to therapy.

As Betty began to attend therapy more consistently, she became more enthusiastic about it, and she particularly enjoyed the communication group. In the speech-language pathologist's experience, communication groups often have a powerful effect on clients, who often respond better to comments or redirection from other clients than they do to the speech-language pathologist. In addition, they appreciate hearing from other people who have overcome some of the communication problems that they are experiencing. Clients often share strategies that they have found successful in solving their communication problems, and they share their feelings about life after a neurological incident, such as a stroke or traumatic brain injury.

Betty also attended individual therapy sessions regularly. Therapy had two general focuses: reading and conversation. Betty read aloud paragraphs that increased in length and was encouraged to use her finger to point to every word and to read slowly in a distraction-free environment. She was also asked to recall details from the story and to explain the theme or point of the story to address her attention and reading comprehension abilities. As Betty's reading abilities improved, the speech-language pathologist planned to provide stories that included humor, incongruence, and figurative language to address those impairments as well.

Betty's conversation abilities were addressed by first showing videos of people having a con-

versation (generated by the speech-language pathologist and two graduate students) in which the conversational partners demonstrated both successful conversations and communication breakdowns due to pragmatic impairments. Betty was asked to first differentiate between the successful and unsuccessful conversations, and then to specifically identify what made the conversations successful or unsuccessful. The speech-language pathologist and Betty practiced conversing, and the speech-language pathologist provided feedback following each conversation. Betty was encouraged to practice her conversational goals during the group therapy sessions. Each group session was videotaped (written consent was obtained from all of the group members). During the subsequent individual therapy session, the speech-language pathologist and Betty watched the videotape together and analyzed her communication, discussing her strengths and the areas that still needed work. The goals included turn-taking, eye contact, topic maintenance, topic shifting, expressing her thoughts concisely and in an organized way, and comprehension of the listener's point. Again, as Betty's conversational abilities improved, the speech-language pathologist planned to provide stories that included humor, incongruence, and figurative language to address those areas as well.

Analysis of Client's Response to Intervention

Betty continued to attend sessions regularly and reported that she liked coming. With the help of her son, she usually remembered to do her home assignments. She also practiced her conversational strategies with her son, who attended several of her therapy sessions and was informed of her goals. After 6 months, Betty was able to name all of her goals and to explain why they were important to successful reading and communication. She had begun to show slight improvement in reading comprehension but continued to have difficulty with long passages. Betty's conversational skills had improved as well, including her ability to establish and maintain eye contact, and to maintain her topic; she still had difficulty with excessive and "empty" speech, but her comprehension had improved somewhat due to her improved attention to the listener. Betty carried a card to remind her of her goals throughout the day in case she needed to use it as a reference. She appeared to have "bought into" therapy, and the therapist was now considering adding goals to directly address the various components of attention.

Author's Note

The case described is not based on an actual client. All of the names, background, and diagnostic information are fictitious.

References

Brookshire, R. H., & McNeil, M. (2014). *Introduction to neurogenic communication disorders* (8th ed.). Mosby-Year Book.

Carota, A., & Bogousslavsky, J. (2018). Minor hemisphere: Major syndromes. *Frontiers of Neurology and Neuroscience, 41,* 1–13. https://doi.org/10.1159/000475690

Hewetson, R., Cornwell, P., & Shum, D. (2017). Cognitive-communication disorder following right hemisphere stroke: Exploring rehabilitation access and outcomes. *Topics in Stroke Rehabilitation, 24*(5), 330–336. https://doi.org/10.1080/10749357.2017.1289622

Myers, P. S. (1998). *Right hemisphere damage: Disorders of communication and cognition.* Delmar Cengage Learning.

Pimental, P. A., & Kingsbury, N. A. (2000). *The Mini Inventory of Right Brain Injury* (2nd ed.). Pro-Ed.

Tompkins, C. A. (1995). *Right hemisphere communication disorders: Theory and management.* Singular Publishing Group.

APHASIA
CASE 40
Joel: A Case of Expressive Aphasia: Teletherapy Assessment and Multimodal Treatment With Visual Barriers
Linia Starlet Willis

Conceptual Knowledge Areas

The term *aphasia* typically refers to a classification system credited to the Boston Aphasia Research group and the neurologist Dr. Norman Geschwind and his associates. This classification, upon which many testing and treatment methods are based, divides aphasia into two major categories: nonfluent/anterior aphasia and fluent/posterior aphasia. Nonfluent aphasia is characterized by lesions around Broca's area (third convolution of the frontal cortex), resulting in agrammatism or "telegraphic speech" in which syntax is impaired but information words (nouns and verbs) may be present. There is relatively good auditory comprehension. The most frequent classification is that of Broca's aphasia. In addition to Broca's aphasia, nonfluent aphasia also includes the relatively rare transcortical motor aphasia, which is like Broca's aphasia but with better ability to perform repetition tasks. Finally, global aphasia is generally viewed as an anterior aphasia with severe to complete impairment in all language modalities, affecting areas beyond the anterior cortex.

The second major classification is that of fluent/posterior aphasia. When this framework is used to look at fluent or "receptive" aphasia, it is not possible to have purely receptive difficulties without concomitant expressive difficulties. Therefore, syndromes are examined that have strong receptive components (auditory comprehension difficulties) as fluent aphasias, typically caused by posterior lesions in the left cerebral cortex, usually around the area of the second temporal convolution. These are often classified as Wernicke's aphasia, conduction aphasia, anomic aphasia, transcortical sensory aphasia, and mixed aphasia. Conduction aphasia is generally found when there is a lesion in the area between Wernicke's and Broca's aphasia, known as the arcuate fasciculus. Transcortical sensory aphasia, a relatively rare phenomenon, is like Wernicke's aphasia but with preserved repetition. A complete discussion of these subtypes may be found in Davis (2007, pp. 33–39). In general, the most frequently seen syndrome within the fluent aphasias is that of Wernicke's aphasia, which has as its major deficit poor auditory comprehension with speech that runs from jargon to real words interspersed with "paraphasic" utterances. Many of these clients have particular difficulties with verbal repetition tasks. Clients with these symptoms are generally among the most difficult to treat because of their frequent lack of awareness of their symptoms and difficulties with attention. Often, clients with Wernicke's aphasia may fail to comprehend even simple conversation or writing. Clients with somewhat better processing abilities may be able to get the main points of a conversation but not the details. An excellent description of this type of aphasia may be found in Brookshire's (2014) *Introduction to Neurogenic Communication Disorders.*

Description of the Case

Background Information and Reason for Referral

The client, Joel, is one with a medically complex presentation. First, although he exhibited symptoms of what was clearly a nonfluent aphasia, his language problems were characteristic of Broca's aphasia paired with multiple cognitive-linguistic deficits. Although his expression was impaired, higher-level tasks such as memory, sequencing, and computing were severely delayed, as reflected on auditory processing/receptive tasks. Both expressive and receptive language may be explained by the etiology of multiple strokes during his recovery (indicating more widespread insults to the brain) related to the medical precipitating factor of coronary artery disease and multiple myocardial infections. Of note, he was recovering from COVID-19 at the time of referral. Despite the complexity of symptoms, Joel's case is a functional example of how speech-language pathologists deal with multiple aspects of language where aphasia is the primary diagnosis.

Findings of the Evaluation

Joel was a 57-year-old right-handed male who was referred to the university clinic for evaluation and treatment due to discharge from home health care. The client had an extensive cardiovascular history of myocardial infarction, multiple transient ischemic attacks (TIA), a left hemispheric middle cerebral artery (MCA) stroke impacting the occipital lobe in 2021, status post COVID-19 at the onset of speech-language treatment, and three additional infarcts in February 2022 impacting the right hemisphere. Medications included Keppra, which affected his alertness during late morning sessions. Joel had a high school education, and his premorbid occupation was a mechanic. In summary, this client suffered multiple recurrent strokes over several months while receiving anticoagulant therapy. His recovery was considered nonlinear due to comorbidities and recurrent hospitalizations that diminished the gains that he had received after his initial infarct.

Testing was administered via teletherapy due to pandemic protocols. Of note, Joel's vision had decreased prior to his stroke per dependency on eyeglasses use. At the time of evaluation, his vision was considered significantly impaired due to left occipital lobe damage. A modified assessment considering physical and environmental barriers was completed utilizing the Western Aphasia Battery–Revised (WAB-R; Kertesz, 2007).

Language Evaluation

Prior to the evaluation, this patient had already received speech-language intervention for 4 months via home health. Therapy was terminated when health insurance benefits expired. This evaluation was performed by a student clinician approximately 1 month after discharge, through teletherapy.

Joel exhibited symptoms of a moderately severe nonfluent aphasia (Broca's type). His auditory comprehension was mildly impaired, especially in response to open-ended questions. In conversational context, he presented with appropriate responses such as greetings and saying "thank you." His overall pragmatic skills were deemed to be within functional limits per his ability to initiate jokes and describe feelings. Visual options, spelling, and writing tasks were unable to be completed per decreased vision. Frustration with repeating "I don't know" and "I'm frustrated" paired with facial grimaces and heavy breathing were noted.

Writing, reading, and math computations were all considered severely impaired. His labored speech often resulted in his wife interpreting or clarifying his wants and needs. She was also considered his e-helper as she set up and logged him in for his sessions.

Testing

A mix of formal and informal measures were utilized in the university clinic via teletherapy delivery. The WAB-R is an individually administered assessment for adults with acquired neurological disorders (as a result of stroke, head injury, dementia). "This assessment identifies the linguistic skills most frequently affected by aphasia and key nonlinguistic skills" (Kertesz, 2007). Subtests of part one of this assessment were administered, including spontaneous speech, auditory/verbal comprehension, repetition and naming, and word finding. During the evaluation, Joel exhibited a moderately severe fluent aphasia with deficits in all language modalities due to bilateral multi-infarcts.

Treatment Options Considered

Joel's wife was concerned that he had experienced "setbacks" within his progress due to adjusting to medication changes and recovering from COVID-19. He reportedly experienced fatigue, and some of his medications caused drowsiness.

Per student-clinician implementation and collaboration, it was recommended that aspects of semantic feature analysis (Coelho et al., 2000) be used. This approach is a word-retrieval treatment in which the person with aphasia identifies semantic features of a target word that is difficult to retrieve. For example, if the individual experiences difficulty retrieving the word "oven," then he or she might be prompted with questions to provide information related to "oven" (e.g., Where is it located? [Kitchen]; What is it used for? [Cooking]). Modification of the SFA approach was necessary due to low vision. The picture was still included on the shared screen via teletherapy, so that the e-helper, Joel's wife, could observe the session and understand the expectations and target words.

Course of Treatment

A speech-language treatment plan was developed postevaluation. Joel's primary presentation was decreased expression, and therapy was directed at the use of functional communication to express wants and needs. The main objective was to provide Joel with strategies for self-advocacy and decreased assistance from his spouse. He received individual therapy twice weekly for 1 hour via teletherapy. The treatment goals included the following components:

1. Demonstrate ability to state personal information clearly (name, birthday, address)
2. Increase verbal expression of everyday items needed in his home

3. Improve short-term recall to review treatment strategies

Speech and language therapy consisted of the following:

- Use of tactile stimuli (such as pillow, remote control, glasses) of home objects within reach. The use of tactile stimuli versus visual allowed the client to establish a routine of naming objects and their function in his environment.
- Emphasize expressive strengths through rote activities, such as counting and naming days/months.
- Role-play functional situations such as checking in at a doctor's appointment and answering questions related to pain.
- Engage in breathing exercises and encourage closing of eyes to diminish frustration. The client was offered this strategy or his preference of a 3-minute rest break when he felt overstimulated. Breaks could include silence or listening to music.

Analysis of Client's Response to Intervention

Language Reevaluation

Fifteen out of 21 sessions were attended. After 3 weeks of treatment, Joel suffered multiple bilateral strokes and was hospitalized. This adversely affected his vision and progression made during the remainder of the semester. Titration of medication and polypharmacy were attributed to his morning session drowsiness and decreased attention. There were three sessions in which treatment ended approximately 15 minutes early due to chronic headaches and drowsiness.

In addition to the WAB, criterion-referenced baseline testing was completed based upon his discharge report from home health to ensure a smooth transition of services. He initially achieved 70% accuracy with word-finding tasks utilizing semantic feature analysis. He scored 50% accuracy with immediate recall tasks and 30% accuracy with delayed recall task.

Criterion-referenced posttesting was completed by the student-clinician. Independent expression was limited. With verbal prompting and cueing, he answered the questions and related to semantic features with 65% accuracy. Joel answered questions independently with 60% accuracy. During the immediate and delayed recall portions, he achieved 70% accuracy, noting marked improvement in this area.

Informal/Functional Conversation

Joel was able to frequently use appropriate phrases and provide short answers, such as two three-word sentences. His overall production of stating "I don't know" evolved into requests for more time or repetition. He was able to elaborate on topics that interested him, such as his former occupation and musical preferences, with increased fluency. Rapport building over time between the client, student-clinician, supervisor, and e-helper could also be attributed to Joel's willingness to share in informal conversation.

Further Recommendations

Joel's objective scores decreased for word-finding semantic features but increased for recall. Subjectively, Joel and his wife stated that they felt overall improvement was noted per establishing a routine and his decreased frustration. When not confronted with complex questions, and when conversation was informal and initiated by him, Joel appeared to communicate more effectively. Although he continued to display characteristics of a moderately severe nonfluent aphasia, his ability to communicate functionally seemed to be more efficient than on previous occasions. These observations may be a result of therapeutic efforts despite the lack of measurable improvement per formal clinical testing, and his intermittent absences and fatigue may have contributed to his performance. Joel also indicated awareness that he communicated with more ease than at the onset of therapy, his frustration was diminished, and his motivation to attend and continue treatment had increased. As a result, the prognosis for further improvement was fair, and continued therapy utilizing this approach was recommended.

When working with clients who have significant nonfluent aphasia, it is important to adopt a holistic treatment approach. Teletherapy in a pandemic era paired with managing comorbidities can be a challenge for both experienced and student-clinicians. Occasional technology connectivity issues may have negatively impacted the quality and clarity of auditory stimuli. The repetition of prompts by the e-helper should also be considered as it resulted in a need to process additional stimuli. A possible pause in treatment could have been warranted to determine if Joel's presentation was medication related, characteristic of post-stroke fatigue, and/or requiring more time for the homeostasis and neuroplasticity processes post-stroke to occur per multiple infarcts. His overall progress was difficult to quantify based on multiple factors in this limited timeframe. Joel's focus and alertness varied with his sleep cycle and the timing of medication. The results of this case suggest consideration be given to establishing new baselines for medically complex clients and reestablishing routines for functional communication, to promote clear dialogue for autonomy and safety as part of a patient-centered approach.

Acknowledgments. The author thanks Elaine S. Sands for their work on the original version of this case.

References

Brookshire, R. H. (2014). *Introduction to neurogenic communication disorders* (8th ed.). Mosby Elsevier.

Coelho, C. A., McHugh, R., & Boyle, M. (2000). Semantic feature analysis as a treatment for aphasic dysnomia: A replication. *Aphasiology, 14,* 133–142. https://doi.org/10.1044/1058-0360.0404.94

Davis, G. A. (2007). Aphasiology, disorders and clinical practice (2nd ed.). Pearson Education.

Kertesz, A. (2007). *Western Aphasia Battery–Revised* (WAB-R). Pearson.

APHASIA
CASE 41
Deb: Increasing Participation for a Person With Severe, Chronic Aphasia Using Augmentative and Alternative Communication

Aimee Dietz, Miechelle McKelvey, Michele Schmerbauch, Kristy S. E. Weissling, and Karen Hux

Conceptual Knowledge Areas

Aphasia is an acquired disorder most commonly associated with left hemisphere cerebrovascular accidents (CVAs) that impairs comprehension and production of spoken, written, and gestural language. The clinical features of aphasia are not due to intellectual, sensory, or motor deficits; rather, aphasia disrupts the symbolic processing underlying language comprehension and production (Papathanasiou & Coppens, 2022).

With restorative speech-language intervention, some people with aphasia can reestablish functional communication using natural speech. However, roughly half of people with aphasia cannot participate fully in conversational and information-transfer interactions (Dietz et al., 2020). As such, augmentative and alternative communication (AAC) can support their language comprehension and production via multimodal approaches incorporating readily available strategies (e.g., gesturing, drawing) as well as low-technology (e.g., communication books) and/or high-technology (e.g., electronic, iPad-based) materials.

This case study illustrates how one person with severe, chronic aphasia used multiple AAC strategies to support her interactions with a variety of communication partners and across multiple communication settings and activities. A low-technology communication book and a high-technology AAC device employing Visual Scene Displays (VSDs)—via an iPad—incorporated contextually rich, personally relevant photographs, written words, and, when appropriate, synthesized voice output to support message formulation and system navigation (Beukelman et al., 2015; Brock et al., 2017; Dietz et al., 2006; Weissling & Beukelman, 2006). Figures 41–1 and 41–2 provide example pages of low- and high-technology VSDs, respectively.

Case Description

Background and History

Deb was a 56-year-old, married mother of two and grandmother of four when she was referred to the speech-language pathologist (SLP). She had a high school education, and her primary career focus was her family. Four years previously, Deb had sustained a left hemisphere CVA resulting in severe aphasia. Following her stroke, Deb and her husband moved in with their adult daughter, son-in-law, and two grandsons due to financial strain. The family's socioeconomic status was lower middle class, and they resided in an urban area of a Midwestern state.

Deb regularly attended women's meetings at her church, traveled with her husband, and attended family gatherings with her children and grandchildren prior to her stroke. As often hap-

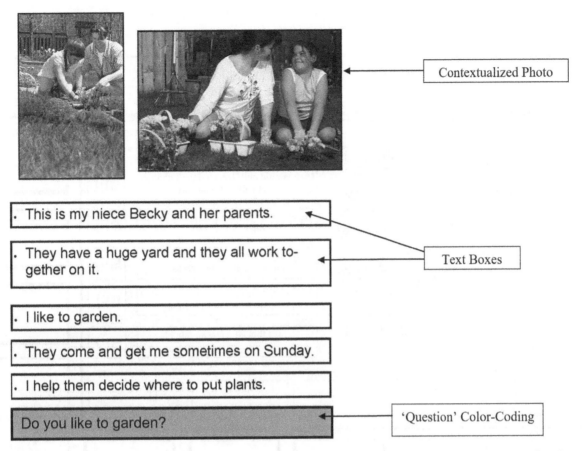

Figure 41–1. Example Visual Scene Display page from a low-technology communication book. Copyright © 2008 Kristy Weissling. Used with permission.

pens (Manning et al., 2019), Deb's participation in these activities ceased following her CVA. The family reported that Deb refused to attend functions due to embarrassment and communication challenges when interacting with people outside her immediate family. The family reported that she "refused to leave the house [even though] extended family members wanted to see her." Deb's adult daughter, son-in-law, and grandchildren expressed a strong desire for her to reestablish her social roles.

Reason for Referral

Deb had received restoration-based speech-language intervention immediately following her stroke that focused on facilitating speech produc-

tion and understanding what others were saying. After several months, Deb's recovery slowed, and she no longer was making significant gains in reducing her level of impairment. She was discharged from therapy without any exploration of participation-based solutions utilizing AAC strategies. After 3 years of increasing social isolation, Deb's family requested additional speech-language services, and they were referred to a speech and language clinic for development of an AAC system. Intervention over the next several months focused on implementing AAC strategies, including drawing, writing, using a low-technology communication book with contextually rich pictures and text, and using a high-technology AAC system with contextually rich pictures, written text, and synthesized speech. Due to hemiparesis and mobility challenges, an iPad served as

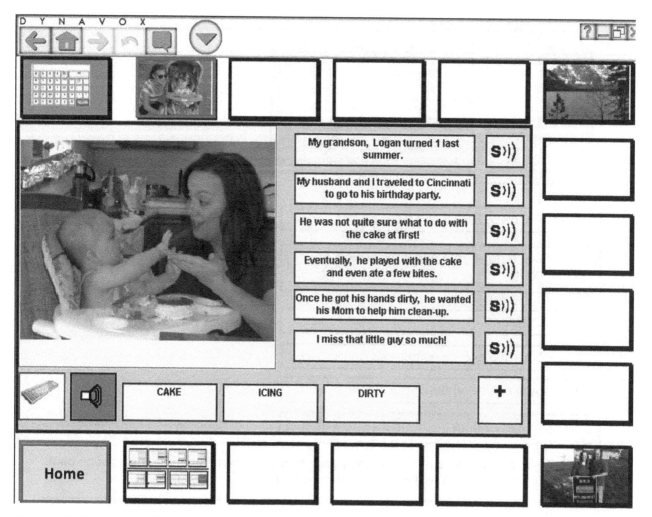

Figure 41–2. Example Visual Scene Display. Copyright © 2014 Aimee Dietz. Used with permission.

the platform for Deb's high-technology AAC system; assessment trials indicated she had sufficient dexterity and visuoperceptual skills to navigate the device. In addition to individual therapy sessions, Deb attended a weekly aphasia treatment group to increase her interactions with peers and to foster generalization.

Evaluation Findings

Administration of the Aphasia Quotient (AQ) portion of the Western Aphasia Battery–Revised (WAB-R) (Kertesz, 2007) established the type and severity of Deb's aphasia. AQ scores range from 0 to 100, and distinct performance patterns across subtests correspond with different aphasia types. Deb's AQ at the time of referral was 16.5 and corresponded with severe Broca's aphasia. Her communicative repertoire included vocalization of a single stereotypy (i.e., [apapa]), production of simple gestures such as pointing and tapping, fragmented writing of single letters and partial words, and pointing to items in a low-technology communication book containing mostly printed words. Deb exhibited moderate auditory comprehension deficits.

Hypothesis About the Problem

Deb was a partner-dependent contextual choice communicator (Garrett et al., 2020). She interacted with familiar people during structured situations but was largely reliant on communication partners to verbalize intended messages and repair communicative breakdowns. Deb's challenges generating meaningful speech and responding to others in novel contexts substantially limited her engagement in social interactions outside her home or speech-language intervention sessions. She needed communication strategies and techniques that supported her residual language processing skills and, at the same time, provided her with a nonlinguistic manner of expressing ideas and messages. Deb's SLP hypothesized that her communicative effectiveness and willingness to participate in social interactions would improve if she learned to implement a variety of AAC strategies. These techniques included the generation of simple drawings (Lyon, 1995), the writing of short words or partial words (Beeson, 1999), the use of a low-technology communication book that included VSDs (Beukelman et al., 2015; Weissling & Beukelman, 2006), and the use of the iPad that incorporated VSDs to support navigation and message formulation (Brock et al., 2017; Dietz et al., 2014; Wallace & Hux, 2014).

Intervention Options

A broad range of clinical practice methods can facilitate improved language recovery and communication for people with aphasia; hence, Deb's SLP had several options from which to choose when determining the best intervention approach. Language restoration approaches—such as lexical retrieval-focused interventions (e.g., Semantic Feature Analysis [Efstratiadou et al., 2018] and Verb Network Strengthening Treatment [Edmonds et al., 2014]), syntactic rebuilding treatments (e.g., Treatment of Underlying Forms; Thompson & Shapiro, 2005), constraint-induced aphasia therapy (e.g., Sickert et al., 2014), modality-specific training (e.g., reading comprehension; Purdy et al., 2018), and Melodic Intonation Therapy (e.g., Albert et al., 1973)—aim to reestablish natural speech and language processing.

In contrast, participation-based treatments aim to maximize communicative effectiveness by providing supports to residual language competencies and, simultaneously, teach multimodal strategies to supplement and serve as alternatives to natural speech (Beukelman & Light, 2020; LPAA Project Group, 2008). Participation approaches include instruction to people with aphasia and their communication partners in the creation of aphasia-friendly environments (Simmons-Mackie, 2018), the production of self-generated drawings (Lyon, 1995) and gestures (Raymer et al., 2006), and the use of low-technology (Beukelman et al., 2015; Weissling & Beukellman, 2006) and high-technology AAC techniques (Brock et al., 2017; Dietz et al., 2014; Dietz et al., 2018).

Clinicians implementing AAC with people with aphasia view it as integral to the therapeutic process rather than solely as a compensatory treatment. As such, using AAC is comparable to using a wheelchair or walker to traverse lengthy distances that would otherwise be too difficult due to weakness or fatigue (Dietz et al., 2020). AAC and restorative treatments are not mutually exclusive (Dietz et al., 2020; Weissling & Prentice, 2010). Instead, AAC can serve a dual purpose—to help compensate for inevitable communication breakdowns while simultaneously providing self-cueing to promote expressive skills (Dietz et al., 2018). Given that Deb had already received several restoration-based interventions that promoted minimal functional changes in speech and language production and comprehension, an alternate approach was warranted to support her interactions with multiple people, about multiple topics, and in multiple settings. A discussion of the presence and severity of concomitant disorders (e.g., apraxia of speech, cognitive impairments) evident in Deb's case is beyond the scope of this chapter; however, her frustration with minimal progress given restorative services made clear the need for a different treatment strategy. In keeping with the philosophy of multimodal support, Deb's SLP pursued a combination of AAC-based language compensation approaches, including (a) instruction in the production of self-generated drawings to clarify and expand her communicative intent, (b) reinforcement in the writing of simple words or partial words because this was a relative strength for her and a strategy she already had employed on occasion, (c) expansion of her low-technology communication book to include VSDs, and (d) exploration of high-technology AAC options.

The SLP's next decision concerned selection of an AAC interface design for Deb. Researchers have shown that people with aphasia can use high-technology AAC in specific situations such as answering the phone, ordering in restaurants or stores, and engaging in scripted conversations (e.g., Garrett et al., 2020). However, researchers have also found that people with aphasia may need months or even years to master such devices, and generalization to novel circumstances is often difficult and limited (Russo et al., 2017). Because a primary concern of Deb's family was her loss of social interactions both within and outside her family, attention to generalization was paramount; hence, Deb's SLP rejected AAC options that would only support specific situations.

Deb's SLP also had concerns about implementing AAC approaches requiring the substitution of a novel symbolic processing system for traditional written or spoken language. Such approaches not only require people with aphasia to learn symbols (i.e., icons or isolated pictures) substituting for written or spoken words, but they also force the sequential placement of those symbols to create sentence-like structures. The symbolic processing challenges of people with aphasia limit mastery of such systems, and given the severity and chronicity of Deb's aphasia, her SLP believed that introducing such a system was unlikely to be successful.

To reduce the symbolic processing demands of existing AAC technology and to facilitate interaction with multiple people on multiple topics and in multiple situations, the SLP decided to introduce a system that used VSDs to represent messages and support navigation (Beukelman et al., 2015). VSDs can serve as the foundation for low-technology or high-technology applications, so Deb's clinician decided to explore both options. Both would incorporate highly contextualized and personally relevant photographs and written words to represent situations, places, or experiences and to support message formulation. High-technology AAC devices incorporating VSDs have the additional benefits of providing synthesized voice output and a navigation structure based on contextually rich images.

Using highly contextualized photographs in an AAC system has distinct advantages for people with aphasia over other types of pictures or symbol sets. Most importantly, highly contextualized photographs depict elements in relation to the natural environment and provide support for referencing a variety of related information. As such, they convey the gist of an event or experience with little external explanation or interpretation needed. In contrast, portraits or isolated pictures of objects provide limited and decontextualized information that typically support only identification and labeling functions. With portraits or isolated pictures, viewers must generate any additional, supportive, or contextual information related to the circumstances prompting the image capture. This spontaneous generation of specific and detailed linguistic information is precisely the task with which people with aphasia struggle. The use of highly contextualized images in VSD formats helps communication partners infer information and, thus, decreases the demands placed on people with aphasia during communicative interactions (Beukelman et al., 2015).

An additional feature making VSDs appealing for constructing and organizing Deb's AAC system was the flexibility they allowed regarding content. By including multiple VSDs in her low- and high-technology systems, Deb would have access to numerous, diverse themes (see Figure 41–2) from which to choose communication topics. The low-technology communication book served as a backup system in the event of high-technology software or hardware failures or in situations not conducive to carrying or accessing the iPad. Access to multiple communication themes and maximal portability were crucial to supporting Deb's interactions with a variety of people and across diverse communication situations. Also, AAC systems constructed with VSDs are relatively transparent to people with aphasia regarding organization and navigation; hence, they master system use, theme expansion, and generalization to novel situations with relative ease (McKelvey et al., 2007). Because Deb's need for support was going to persist, her AAC system had to be flexible yet simple enough for use in virtually all communicative encounters.

Deb's Course of Intervention

Deb's SLP assisted in developing a low-technology communication book during individual intervention sessions and introduced the iPad during sessions when family members were present. Topics in the initial versions of both communication supports included themes to facilitate communication about immediate family members and their activities.

Deb's family expressed a strong desire for her to use the iPad, but Deb resisted. After 1 month of access to the system, Deb refused to use it for any interactions occurring outside intervention sessions. Deb's family expressed frustration with understanding her communication attempts and concern about her persisting lack of social interactions. To address these issues, the SLP arranged a joint meeting with Deb and her family. Each person present independently used 5-point Likert scales (5 = *strongly agree*; 1 = *strongly disagree*) to indicate their perceptions about the effectiveness of Deb's communication strategies and their preferences for strategies available to her. Deb's ratings as well as the averaged ratings of her family members appear in Table 41–1. Of note, Deb and her family members agreed that using the iPad provided the greatest communicative effectiveness; they differed in their preferences regarding

other strategies. Deb rationalized her preference for natural speech and writing by insisting she would eventually regain these functions and that her current strategies met her daily communicative needs. Only after the SLP shared with Deb her family members' effectiveness and preference ratings did she recognize the extent of their frustration with her current communicative strategies. She had assumed her family understood her natural speech and writing attempts and, therefore, did not see the purpose of using the iPad to supplement natural speech and writing attempts.

Deb's family suggested a compromise regarding the use of various communication strategies. They agreed that she would first try using speech or writing to communicate; however, if they did not understand her message, Deb would then use her low-technology communication book or iPad to resolve the breakdown. Deb also agreed to not persist with speech or writing attempts when breakdowns occurred. Everyone agreed this was an acceptable compromise because it allowed Deb to use her preferred communication modes yet simultaneously facilitated a gradual move toward increased multimodal approaches to communication. For the first time since her stroke, Deb seemed to accept that full recovery of natural speech was an unrealistic goal and that she needed to expand her use of AAC options.

Early VSD Content

Deb began using the low- and high-technology VSDs for a trial period. However, her family

Table 41–1. Likert-Scale Results From Deb and Her Family Members Regarding Communicative Effectiveness and Strategy Use Preferences

Strategy	Communicative Effectiveness		Preferences	
	Deb	Family	Deb	Family
iPad	5.0	4.25	3.0	4.25
Communication book	5.0	4.00	3.0	4.00
Writing	3.0	3.5	5.0	3.25
Natural speech	3.0	2.0	5.0	2.5

continued to report struggles concerning iPad use. The SLP promoted device use between Deb and a family member by demonstrating strategies or providing verbal cues when communication breakdowns occurred during naturally occurring conversations. The last 5 minutes of each session served as a time to summarize strategies and familiarize family members with newly added content. Additionally, Deb's family shared notebook entries reporting communication successes and challenges they had observed during the past week. This facilitated input from multiple family members, provided a means of idea exchange regarding new AAC content, and allowed the SLP to suggest alternative communication strategies and tips for use outside the clinical setting.

Family reports about continuing communication struggles prompted recognition of an immediate need to create VSD pages to support Deb's communication at home. Emerging themes addressed household activities such as doing laundry, cooking, washing dishes, going grocery shopping, watching television, and relaying messages about phone calls and visitors occurring when Deb was the only person home. The addition of these thematic pages alleviated considerable frustration for the family; specifically, they reported less need to guess when Deb communicated about these topics. This early success had the added benefit of encouraging Deb to consider participating in social activities beyond her immediate family.

Content Organization and Continuing Intervention

Deb's primary intervention goal shifted to a pragmatic issue as she gained confidence and skill using her low- and high-technology AAC strategies. Specifically, when using the iPad, Deb frequently selected speech output buttons in a sequential manner rather than a conversationally appropriate manner. For example, Deb often asked her communication partner a question, even if the person had just asked her a question. Thus, Deb required coaching on how and when to use the iPad to ask questions. To address this, the SLP implemented color-coding to facilitate Deb's

recall of the function of buttons on VSD screens. Text boxes containing questions and corresponding speak buttons were color-coded blue, and text boxes and speak buttons for statements had neutral backgrounds (see Figures 41–1 and 41–2). This strategy, combined with role-playing practice, reduced Deb's inappropriate asking of questions. Similarly, color-coding on Deb's social greetings VSD page helped her distinguish conversation starters and closers.

Another adjustment concerned the iPad's synthesized speech output. The quality and rate of synthesized speech output exacerbated Deb's auditory comprehension challenges. Degraded speech output also interfered with her communication partners' comprehension of synthesized messages, especially for members of her aphasia support group. Through trial and error, the SLP identified a more effective voice and speaking rate.

Expansion of VSD Content to Support Social Engagement

The next area of focus involved reintegrating Deb into some of her former social roles. With encouragement from her SLP and family, Deb agreed to develop VSD themes to facilitate social interactions outside her home. Deb experienced several positive interactions with people in the speech and language clinic where she received services. In particular, participation in an aphasia support group facilitated her recognition of benefits offered by expanding her communication repertoire. Several new VSD themes emerged. The first was a vacation theme about a trip she took with her husband several years before her stroke.

Deb's use of the vacation theme was pivotal regarding her acceptance of the iPad. She realized the potential this theme held for expanding her social network, and she became an active co-decision-maker regarding VSD content; previously, Deb had allowed family members to act as the primary decision-makers. Now, Deb began requesting new themes herself. First, she asked for a speech and language clinic theme to facilitate socialization before and after intervention sessions; Deb wanted to interact with other clients and clinic staff. Next, she requested a theme about her hobbies. Using the iPad, Deb asked others about their hobbies in hopes that they, in turn, would ask about hers. Then, she would use VSDs to show off her miniature cow collection and where she displayed the figurines in her home. Additional new themes addressed issues about her children and grandchildren, her extended family, her daughter's business, and her family's gatherings.

Deb's success led to a renewed interest in attending family gatherings. Six weeks after first introducing the iPad, Deb left her house to attend a social event—a family holiday gathering—for the first time since her stroke. Afterward, she rated her communication during the gathering as a 3 on a Likert scale ranging from 1 to 3 (i.e., 1 = *horrible*, 2 = *OK*, 3 = *great*). Her daughter and son-in-law confirmed that Deb interacted with several people at the gathering and that her communication partners were consistently successful in understanding her intent. Furthermore, Deb did not give up when confronted with challenges. For example, when a navigational link on one of her iPad VSD pages did not work, she independently navigated to the story using another route.

In time, Deb resumed participation in women's meetings at church, albeit on an intermittent basis. Initially, she appeared satisfied to interact with other women using small talk and sharing content from themes already available in her low-tech communication book and iPad. Over time, however, Deb expressed a strong desire to participate more actively in Bible study and prayer time. Her SLP identified a church member who could provide specific Bible passages for advance programming into Deb's iPad.

Analysis of the Client's Response to Intervention

Deb initially resisted using the iPad because she believed she could communicate successfully using natural speech. Once she realized the limitations associated with natural speech, Deb became receptive to incorporating AAC strategies and device use into her repertoire. The SLP was instrumental in helping Deb and her family identify themes and use personal photos to create VSDs to facilitate communication about daily activities and promote social closeness. As a result, Deb reestablished social roles within her family and began to explore communication opportunities outside her home.

Reformulated Hypothesis and Further Recommendations

Deb continued to live with severe, chronic Broca's aphasia; however, her communicative competence improved greatly after learning AAC strategies incorporating VSDs. Prior to development and implementation of a multimodal AAC system, Deb functioned as a partner-dependent contextual choice communicator; later, given multimodal communication strategies and AAC support, she functioned as a partner-independent generative communicator (Garrett et al., 2020). Incorporation of multiple AAC strategies, techniques, and materials prompted successful social interactions with familiar and unfamiliar communication partners across multiple settings and about multiple topics. Although communication breakdowns still occurred, Deb had a repertoire of approaches to resolve many of them. For example, she had learned to switch with relative ease among gesturing, drawing, and using either her iPad or low-technology materials rather than simply repeating [apapa] as she did prior to intervention. At last report, Deb had over 185 images and 377 written statements paired with voice output and corresponding to 21 unique themes programmed into her iPad. With continued practice, she is likely to refine further her communication techniques and materials to promote even greater success.

Deb's quick and steady progress with an AAC approach was impressive. Before her introduction to AAC supports, Deb had only received restorative interventions. This is a common scenario for people with aphasia; in fact, only about 2% receive AAC treatment prior to hospital discharge (Rogers et al., 2014), and only about half of caregivers receive AAC education during the early poststroke months (Elman et al., 2016). Neither Deb's poststroke treatment nor these data align with Best Practice Recommendations for Aphasia (Recommendation 4; Simmons-Mackie et al., 2017):

No one with aphasia should be discharged from services without some means of communicating his or her needs and wishes (e.g., using AAC, supports, trained partners) or a documented plan for how and when this will be achieved (Level: Good Practice Point). (p. 139)

Imagine how much Deb missed out on because AAC was not part of her original treatment plan. Aphasia rehabilitation must evolve to include AAC as an integral part of initial treatment plans rather than a last resort.

Authors' Note

Preparation of this chapter was supported in part by the Communication Enhancement Rehabilitation Engineering Research Center (AAC-RERC), which is funded by the National Institute on Disability and Rehabilitation Research of the U.S. Department of Education under grant number H133E980026. The opinions expressed in this chapter are those of the authors and do not necessarily reflect those of the Department of Education.

References

Albert, M., Sparks, R., & Helm, N. (1973). Melodic intonation therapy for aphasia. *Archives of Neurology, 29*, 130–131. https://doi.org/10.1001/archneur.1973.00490260074018

Beeson, P.M. (1999). Treating acquired writing impairment: Strengthening graphemic representations. *Aphasiology, 13*, 767–785.

Beukelman, D. R., Hux, K., Dietz, A., McKelvey, M., Weissling, K. (2015). Using visual scene displays as communication support options for people with chronic, severe aphasia: A summary of AAC research and future research directions. *Augmentative and Alternative Communication, 31*(3), 234–245. https://doi.org/10.3109/07434618.2015.1052152

Beukelman, D. R., & Light, J. C. (2020). *Augmentative & alternative communication: Supporting children and adults with complex communication needs.* Paul H. Brookes Publishing.

Brock, K., Koul, K., Corwin, M., & Schlosser, R. (2017). A comparison of visual scene and grid displays for people with chronic aphasia: A pilot study to improve communication using AAC. *Aphasiology, 31*(11), 1282–1306. https://doi.org/10.1080/02687038.2016.1274874

Dietz, A., McKelvey, M., & Beukelman, D. R. (2006). Visual scene display (VSD): New AAC interfaces for persons with aphasia. *Perspectives on Augmentative and Alternative Communication, 15*, 13–17. https://doi.org/10.1044/aac15.1.13

Dietz, A., Vannest, J., Maloney, T., Altaye, M., Holland, S. H., & Szaflarski, J. P. (2018). The feasibility of improving discourse in people with aphasia through AAC: Clinical and functional MRI correlates. *Aphasiology, 32*(6), 693–719. https://doi.org/10.1080/02687038.2018.1447641

Dietz, A., Wallace, S. E., & Weissling, K. (2020). Revisiting the role of augmentative and alternative communication in aphasia rehabilitation. *American Journal of Speech-Language Pathology, 29*, 909–913. https://doi.org/10.1044/2019_AJSLP-19-00041

Dietz, A., Weissling, K. Griffith, J., McKelvey, M., & Macke, D. (2014). The impact of design during an initial high-technology AAC: A collective case study of people with aphasia. *Augmentative and Alternative Communication, 30*(4), 314–328. https://doi.org/10.3109/07434618.2014.966207

Edmonds, L. A., Mammino, K., & Ojeda, J. (2014). Effect of a verb network strengthening treatment (VNeST) in persons with aphasia: Extension and replication of previous findings. *American Journal of Speech-Language Pathology, 23*, S312–S329. https://doi.org/10.1044/2014_AJSLP-13-0098

Efstratiadou, E. A., Papathanasiou, I., Holland, R., Archonti, A., & Hilari, K. (2018). A systematic review of semantic feature analysis therapy studies of aphasia. *Journal of Speech, Language, and Hearing Research, 61*(5), 1261–1278. https://doi.org/10.1044/2018_jslhr-l-16-0330

Elman, R. J., Cohen, A., & Silverman, A. (2016, May). *Perceptions of speech-language pathology services provided to persons with aphasia: A caregiver survey.* Paper presented at the Clinical Aphasiology Conference, Charlottesville, VA.

Garrett, K., Lasker, J., & Fischer, J. (2020). AAC supports for adults with severe aphasia and/or apraxia of speech. In D. Beukelman & J. C. Light (Eds.), *Augmentative and alternative communication: Supporting children and adult with complex communication needs* (5th ed., pp. 553–604). Paul H. Brooks.

Kertesz, A. (2007). *Western Aphasia Battery–Revised.* The Psychological Corporation.

LPAA Project Group. (2008). Life participation approach to aphasia: A statement of values for the future. In R. Chapey (Ed.), *Language intervention strategies in aphasia and related neurogenic communication disorders* (5th ed., pp. 279–289). Lippincott Williams & Wilkins.

Lyon, J. G. (1995). Drawing: Its value as a communication aid for adults with aphasia. *Aphasiology, 9,* 33–49. https://doi.org/10.1080/02687039508248687

Manning, M., MacFarlane, A., Hickey, A., & Franklin, S. (2019). Perspectives of people with aphasia post-stroke towards personal recovery and living successfully: A systematic review and thematic synthesis. *PLoS One, 14*(3), e0214200. https://doi.org/10.1371/journal.pone.0214200

McKelvey, M., Dietz, A., Hux, K., Weissling, K, & Beukelman, D. R. (2007). Performance of a person with chronic aphasia using a visual scene display prototype. *Journal of Medical Speech Language Pathology,* 15(3), 305–317. https://www.researchgate.net/publication/287007347_Performance_of_a_person_with_chronic_aphasia_using_personal_and_contextual_pictures_in_a_visual_scene_display_prototype

Papathanasiou, I. & Coppens, P. (2022). *Aphasia and related neurogenic communication disorders* (3rd ed.). Jones & Bartlett Learning.

Purdy, M., Coppens, P., Madden, E. B., Mozeiko, E., Patterson, J., Wallace, S. E., & Donald, D. (2018). Reading comprehension treatment in aphasia: A systematic review. *Aphasiology,* 33, 6, 629–651. https://doi.org/10.1080/02687038.2018.1482405

Raymer, A. M., Singletary, F., Rodriguez, A., Ciampitti, M., Heilman, K. M., Gonzalez-Rothi, L. J. (2006). Effects of gesture+verbal treatment for noun and verb retrieval in aphasia. *Journal of International Neuropsychology Society,* 12(6), 867–882. https://doi.org/10.1017/S1355617706061042

Rogers, M. A., Roye, F., & Mullen, R. (2014, May). *Measuring outcomes in aphasia and apraxia of speech in the context of a learning health care system.* Paper presented at the 44th Clinical Aphasiology Conference, St. Simons Island, GA.

Russo, M. J., Prodan, V., Meda, N. N., Carcavallo, L., Muracioli, A., Sabe, L., . . . Olmos, L. (2017). High-technology augmentative communication for adults with post-stroke aphasia: A systematic review. *Expert Review of Medical Devices, 14*(5), 355–370. https://doi.org/10.1080/17434440.2017.1324291

Sickert, A., Anders, L., Münte, L., & Sailer, M. (2014). Constraint-induced aphasia therapy following sub-acute stroke: A single-blind, randomized clinical trial of a modified therapy schedule. *Journal of Neurological Neurosurgery Psychiatry, 85*(1), 51–55. https://doi.org/10.1136/jnnp-2012-304297

Simmons-Mackie, N. (2018). Communication partner training in aphasia: Reflections on communication accommodation theory. *Aphasiology, 32*(10), 1215–1224. https://doi.org/10.1080/02687038.2018.1428282

Simmons-Mackie, N., Worrall, L., Murray, L. L., Enderby, P., Rose, M. L., Paek, E. J., & Klippion, A., on behalf of the Aphasia United Best Practices Working Group and Advisory Committee. (2017). The top ten: Best practice recommendations for aphasia. *Aphasiology, 31,* 131–151. https://doi.org/10.1080/02687038.2016.1180662

Thompson, C. K., & Shapiro, L. P. (2005). Treating agrammatic aphasia within a linguistic framework: Treatment of underlying forms. *Aphasiology, 19,* 1021–1036. https://doi.org/10.1080/02687030544000227

Wallace, S. E., & Hux, K. (2014) Effect of two layouts on high technology AAC navigation and content location by people with aphasia. *Disability and Rehabilitation: Assistive Technology, 9*(2), 173–182. https://doi.org/10.3109/17483107.2013.799237

Weissling, K., & Beukelman, D. (2006). Visual scene displays: Low tech options. *Perspectives on Augmentative and Alternative Communication,* 15(4), 15–17. https://doi.org/10.1044/aac15.4.15

Weissling, K., & Prentice, C. (2010). The timing of remediation and compensation rehabilitation programs for individuals with acquired brain injuries: Opening the conversation. *SIG 12 Perspectives on Augmentative and Alternative Communication,* 19(3), 87–96. https://doi.org/10.1044/aac19.3.87

APHASIA
CASE 42
Faye: Acute Aphasia in Multiple Sclerosis
Brooke Hatfield and Suzanne Coyle

Conceptual Knowledge Areas

Multiple sclerosis (MS) is described by the MS Society as an unpredictable disease of the central nervous system (the brain, optic nerves, and spinal cord) that alters the way information travels between the brain and the body (MS Society, n.d.). It is an immune-mediated disease that impacts myelin, or the surrounding insulation of nerve fibers. As myelin is damaged or destroyed, it can result in a variety of neurological changes such as blurred or limited vision, reduced balance and coordination, slurred speech, and numbness. These damaged areas may also develop scar tissue.

Speech-language pathologists (SLPs) are frequently involved in the management of cognitive communication, speech, and swallowing impairments in clients with a medical diagnosis of multiple sclerosis. These deficits are most commonly associated with white matter involvement, including decreased episodic memory, slowed information processing, and decreased executive functions (Hulst et al., 2013; Sofologi et al., 2020), as well as sensorimotor impairments of dysarthria and dysphagia (Ansari et al., 2020; Feenaughty et al., 2018). While the presentation of MS has wide clinical variation, until the past few decades, the traditional understanding of MS is that language and intellectual function remain intact, though the patient may be easily fatigued, which can impact performance.

The acute onset of aphasia is most commonly associated with gray matter involvement of the left hemisphere via cerebral vascular accident or focal trauma. Aphasia is not commonly a present-ing complaint in those with autoimmune disease, which is associated with white matter lesions. As neuroimaging and understanding of the complexity of MS have advanced, however, magnetic resonance imaging (MRI) is detecting cortical *gray matter* lesions even in the earliest stages of MS and may be its earliest clinical manifestation (Calabrese et al., 2013).

Nevertheless, aphasia continues to be rarely reported in the MS population outside of single case studies, occurring in only 0.7% to 3% of cases (Devere et al., 2000; Erdem et al., 2001; Lacour et al., 2004). Even when specific language modality impairments such as decreased word finding are described, researchers are reluctant to provide a diagnostic label of aphasia, preferring to describe performance on naming tasks as attributable to general cognitive slowing, reduced attention, and changes in visual processing (Renauld, 2016; Sofologi et al., 2020).

A large-scale study of acute aphasia in MS (Lacour et al., 2004) reviewed cases of French patients with a primary diagnosis of MS. Of the 2,700 cases reviewed, only 22 (0.81%) were diagnosed with acute onset of aphasia. Of those 22 patients, 100% presented with nonfluent or unclassified aphasia, and 91% presented with a relapsing, remitting form of MS at onset. Aphasia was the *first clinical manifestation* of MS in 36% of the patients. Information regarding the prevalence of aphasia is not reported in the two other forms of MS, secondary-progressive and primary-progressive. Studies of this size have not been repeated, likely due to the relative paucity of reporting.

The anticipated course of recovery following the acute onset of aphasia from a stroke is mitigated by such anagraphical and neurolinguistic prognostic factors as age and severity (Nakagawa, 2019). By comparison, recovery of communication impairments related to autoimmune disease is mitigated by periods of relapse and remission, as well as response to medication. Treatment strategies with MS frequently emphasize compensatory strategies and energy conservation, while treatment strategies for aphasia frequently address remediation of targeted, modality-specific language deficits and compensatory strategies to facilitate successful functional communication in the patient's environment. The same study by Lacour et al. in 2004 revealed that of the 22 patients with acute aphasia as a result of MS, 86% of them were treated with methylprednisolone, a medication to suppress inflammation. A "full recovery" was reported in 64% of the cases, while in the remaining 36%, residual sequelae were "not severe." Details of SLP treatment interventions or whether or not subjects actively used compensatory strategies were not described. Mean recovery time was reported to be 15.7 weeks.

Description of the Case

Background Information and Reason for Referral

Faye is a 35-year-old right-handed female who was diagnosed with MS after developing both upper extremity and lower extremity weakness approximately 3 months earlier. Four weeks after diagnosis, she presented to her local emergency room with speech difficulties and minimal unilateral right-sided weakness over a period of 2 days. An MRI revealed a 4-cm lesion in the left centrum semiovale and small lesions in the left frontal subcortical white matter consistent with demyelinating disease. Faye was admitted to acute care for 1 week with the diagnosis of an MS exacerbation. She was not thought to have had a stroke despite the acute onset of both a speech impairment and unilateral weakness. Her medical team included radiologists, neurologists, and MS specialists, with all disciplines agreeing that there had been no

cerebral vascular accident. Faye began a course of steroid treatment, which is a common management strategy for MS exacerbations. This steroid treatment resulted in significant improvement in motor function during her hospitalization, but speech difficulties persisted. She did not receive SLP services while in acute care; however, following 1 week of hospitalization, Faye was discharged with the recommendation to pursue outpatient SLP services.

Faye was employed as a government contractor and had a master's degree in literature. She lived with her husband and had a very supportive family and network of friends in the area. Prior to the recent MS diagnosis, her medical history had been unremarkable. Her husband described her as "very bright" and "a bookworm." She was active in her community and enjoyed many hobbies, including reading and participating in a book club, working out at her gym, and cooking.

Faye's job responsibilities included analysis and synthesis of information from multiple data sources and quickly consolidating and summarizing information. She needed to read, comprehend, and retain technical information and abstract theory. She also needed to verbally brief her staff and communicate effectively and efficiently via email. Faye was very concerned about the severity of her language impairment and was highly motivated to return to work.

Faye's husband was employed full-time and was able to continue as such throughout Faye's rehabilitation, thus reducing the urgency with which Faye needed to return to work for financial reasons. However, she was highly motivated to return to work as soon as possible because she loved her work and considered it a large part of her identity. Her manager was supportive of Faye's medical leave and rehabilitation, and was willing to provide any accommodations that would support Faye's successful return to work.

Both Faye and her husband had researched commonly linked changes in speech and cognitive-communication skills with MS and explored Internet resources about aphasia. Faye's husband returned to work a few days after Faye was discharged from the hospital, as she appeared to be safe while unattended at home during the day. In his research regarding aphasia, he read patient and family accounts reporting that daily practice on structured tasks resulted in improved language skills. He enlisted the help of friends who worked in education and gathered a variety of resources to serve as practice materials. When he left for work in the morning, Faye went to what they called "boot camp" at the kitchen table, with Faye working on language-based activities for 3 to 4 hours/day with telephone check-ins from her husband.

Following a few weeks of intensive home practice, Faye began outpatient SLP services at the recommendation of her physician to address residual communication difficulties. She was accompanied to the initial evaluation by her husband.

Findings of the Evaluation

No medical records were available at the time of the evaluation with the exception of the therapy order reading "speech and language therapy for MS exacerbation." Faye and her husband provided the medical history, relaying specific details and summarizing the results of neuroimaging and the impressions of her medical team. The information presented by the patient and her husband was judged to be accurate given their extensive notes and preparedness for the session.

A combination of objective and subjective measures was used to assess Faye's functional status, along with Faye's report and specific examples of difficulties/errors noted at home as Faye attempted to return to participation in her previous leisure activities.

In a cursory oral mechanism evaluation, Faye presented with facial symmetry at rest and in active movement. She denied changes in sensation. She was able to achieve and sustain all articulatory positions to command without groping or delay. Diadochokinesis was within normal limits.

In a spontaneous speech sample, Faye was fully intelligible in connected speech with no evidence of dysarthria. Vocal quality was within normal limits (WNL). She demonstrated occasional phonemic errors in her spontaneous speech, consistent with phonemic paraphasias versus apraxic errors (e.g., "skihorse" for "seahorse").

In conversation and structured diagnostic tasks, Faye was able to demonstrate comprehension of moderately complex auditory information when provided extended time and slightly reduced rate of presentation. She frequently requested repetition of auditory information to improve her comprehension; however, gestalt comprehension of both conversational and structured inferential paragraphs was intact. She followed multistep directions without difficulty. Faye reported that she felt that she "missed things" in conversations when there was more than one speaker.

Faye was able to demonstrate comprehension of factual written paragraphs such as brief newspaper articles with intact gestalt comprehension. Her oral reading of single paragraphs revealed rapid, efficient processing. However, Faye demonstrated difficulty as the abstract components and grammatical complexity of written material increased, and as a result, her efficiency decreased. Prior to onset of this MS exacerbation, Faye had been an avid reader. She reported significant frustration with reading at the time of the evaluation. Faye reported and demonstrated that she was able to retain details from previously read information following a delay.

Expressive language skills appeared to be Faye's greatest difficulty. She relayed moderately complex novel information to an unfamiliar listener in nonfluent language with assistance for clarification of her intended message. Her attempts at expressing thoughts were characterized by frequent hesitations and phonemic and semantic paraphasic errors. Faye demonstrated excellent awareness of her paraphasias yet was generally unable to correct her errors. Attempts at narrative discourse generally resulted in a deletion of functors. Her spontaneous verbal expression included a higher percentage of nouns than verbs. Confrontation and generative naming were significantly reduced, which proved to be Faye's greatest frustration. She benefited equally from semantic and phonemic cueing. She frequently supplemented her attempts at verbal expression with gesture. Repetition was intact at both the single word and sentence level. Faye's pragmatic language skills (e.g., maintaining eye contact, maintaining topic, transitioning between topics, proxemics) were well within normal limits. In a structured picture description task, Faye produced the following: "Um, uh, the um, um, dishwasher, um is running out the, you know. Teacups, no, not teacups, and uh, um, now. I don't know. Cookie jar, um, and um, the um, the boy is um, tipping over. And, um the girl wants cookies."

Faye's written expression in a simple picture description task was semantically and syntactically accurate at a single sentence level. She continued to have weakness in her dominant right hand, which reduced the legibility of her writing and slowed her written output. Attempts at expressing abstract thoughts in writing resulted in significant frustration and reduced ability to accurately formulate complex written sentence structures, which somewhat mirrored her verbal expression.

Faye and her family reported no significant change in cognitive skills. Faye was an excellent historian of recent events and medical history. She was able to sustain attention to conversation and diagnostic tasks without redirection. Functional problem solving was not an area of concern for Faye or her family, as she had been managing her own medication and staying at home during the day unattended without incident. She consistently initiated alternative modes of communication when one method failed and revised her performance based on her communication partner's feedback. She reported feeling generally tired but did not feel that her performance significantly deteriorated over the course of the day. Despite extensive probing, no cognitive deficits were indicated by Faye or observed by the clinician or her friends and family.

Treatment Options Considered

Several management questions presented themselves given the constellation of cognitive-linguistic impairments that are commonly associated with MS and the relapsing/remitting nature of the disease, including decreased sustained attention, organization, and short-term memory, in the face of the patient's presentation of impaired language in all modalities suggesting aphasia.

The first question was whether it was appropriate to provide treatment given the relapsing/remitting nature of MS and the client's anticipated response to medication. If the communication impairments present upon initial evaluation were likely to improve as the disease process remits or medication lessens its impact, it would be difficult to attribute change and progress to specific therapeutic interventions. There are little to no data to suggest or refute that when aphasia results from MS, it shares the relapse/remission pattern of motor-based sequelae or that it is directly impacted by medication. However, withholding treatment in favor of providing extensive education regarding management strategies would not adequately address Faye's current functional language status and the impact it had on her quality of life and ability to return to work. In this particular case, the client, her physicians, family, and the clinician all agreed that SLP intervention was warranted given the acute onset of the impairments, Faye's motivation, and stimulability.

Once the decision to treat was made, an understanding of the source of the impairment was needed to formulate a diagnosis that would later shape the treatment plan. Given the more commonly seen cognitive-linguistic impairments in patients with MS, it was possible that Faye's presentation was resulting from a grossly impaired organizational system impacted by significant fatigue rather than aphasia. To develop a working diagnosis for guiding treatment, standardized assessments including portions from the Western Aphasia Battery (Kertesz, 1982), Boston Diagnostic Aphasia Exam (Goodglass, Kaplan, & Barresi, 2001), and Boston Naming Test (Goodglass, Kaplan, & Weintraub, 2001) were administered to identify patterns of impairment and facilitating strategies. These measures provided a baseline of language abilities and described her status but did not provide specific information regarding other potentially mitigating factors or contributors.

To look at specific cognitive-linguistic areas both in isolation and as they interacted with each other, the Cognitive Linguistic Quick Test (Helm-Estabrooks, 2001) was used. This provided information regarding attention, memory, visuospatial skills, and executive functions in addition to language skills, with limited expressive language demands. Faye met and surpassed age criteria in all cognitive-linguistic areas with no single target area as an outlier. This was in direct contrast to the results of her aphasia battery, which indicated impairment across all modalities of varying degrees of severity. Given this profile, the clinicians felt comfortable developing a diagnosis of aphasia rather than cognitive-linguistic impairment. Following the initial evaluation, Faye's language impairment was described as moderate transcortical motor aphasia.

In this case, the process of developing a differential diagnosis of aphasia was not confounded by visual impairments, dysarthria, or limited attention and/or short-term memory. One should be cautioned that in clients with MS, these sequelae could certainly muddy the diagnostic waters, and subjective observation of performance on standardized measures may prove more beneficial than the objective results when any of these are present.

Another factor in treatment planning for this case was the appropriate dosing. As previously mentioned, Faye and her family were highly motivated to begin treatment and to complete daily home practice activities, both those provided by the therapist and those developed by Faye, her family, and friends. However, one of the obstacles for clients with MS is rapid fatigue and the need for energy conservation. In the "more is more" approach that Faye and her family had adopted, with the extensive time spent in structured activities, was this as likely to result in a positive change as it would with someone with aphasia resulting from stroke? Should both SLP sessions and home practice be limited in favor of energy conservation? Given the positive prognostic indicators for recovery, including Faye's age, time postonset, progress to date, and motivation, coupled with Faye's report that her performance did not deteriorate over time, a schedule of therapy consistent with a client with similar prognostic variables with acute aphasia was chosen. It was recommended that Faye attend two to three individual SLP sessions per week, with sessions lasting 50 minutes, for an anticipated time frame of approximately 8 weeks.

A final factor in treatment planning was how to prioritize time within each session. Again, given the relapsing and remitting nature of Faye's MS but little understanding of how this impacts aphasia, the clinicians needed to decide how best to use each treatment session—in activities that target remediation of a deficit area, compensate for a deficit area, or a combination of the two. Faye's preference was for a combination of the two, which she felt would provide her with the best opportunity for a timely, successful return to work by potentially strengthening her efficiency in using compensatory strategies. The clinicians developed long-term goals over an anticipated 8-week period to address circumlocution, naming in all forms, syntax at the discourse level, and reading comprehension for work-related information. Auditory comprehension and written expression were to be probed and monitored; however, at the onset of treatment, Faye felt these areas to be grossly functional for meeting her daily and vocational needs. Verbal expression and reading comprehension were the biggest areas of frustration and the biggest obstacle to returning to activities of daily living.

Course of Treatment

SLP Interventions

Therapy began with extensive training of word-retrieval strategies. Faye frequently demonstrated anomia in conversation but did not have an efficient system to facilitate word retrieval. Therapy focused on word-retrieval exercises, such as semantic feature analysis, convergent and divergent naming, and work with synonyms and antonyms. Faye quickly initiated the use of compensatory word-retrieval strategies such as circumlocution and substitution in conversation, which significantly reduced her frustration. The frequency of Faye's anomic episodes and paraphasias significantly declined, and she was able to correct these errors with greater efficiency. Faye was always anxious for homework and was provided with regular word-retrieval exercises to complete between sessions.

To address Faye's concerns of slowed reading efficiency, the Multiple Oral Re-reading (MOR) approach as described by Beeson and Hillis (2001) was utilized to improve her overall reading speed. The philosophy behind the MOR program is that repeated oral reading will improve the graphemic recognition of written words and improve overall reading speed and efficiency. In the MOR program, Faye was presented with a series of novel, 100-word written passages. Her initial oral reading rate was recorded, and then Faye practiced oral reading of these passages at home until she could achieve her criterion of 100 words per minute (wpm). Faye was highly successful with this program, beginning with an initial oral reading rate of novel passages of less than 50 wpm. Throughout the course of treatment, Faye's initial oral reading rate of novel information improved with each new passage presented. By the end of treatment, Faye was able to achieve an oral reading rate of greater than 90 wpm with novel information.

Throughout the course of therapy, counseling centered on methods for implementation of learned compensatory strategies into interactions in home, work, and community settings, as well as discussion of energy conservation strategies and resource allocation should Faye experience a change in status with future exacerbations.

Analysis of Client's Response to Intervention

Faye attended a total of 18 SLP sessions over 12 weeks. Additional scheduled sessions were missed due to an unrelated illness. Throughout the course of her treatment, Faye's family was very involved in her care. They frequently attended sessions with her, helped her complete homework assignments, and were supportive of her efforts to utilize compensatory word-retrieval strategies.

Faye also found ways to enhance her communication opportunities at home, such as returning to her book club. Although reading the lengthy novels and participating in complex discussions were more difficult than before the exacerbation, Faye was able to use her book club as an opportunity to challenge both her verbal expression and her reading skills.

Ultimately, Faye was discharged from SLP treatment having reached her long-term goals and feeling equipped to implement both verbal expression and reading comprehension strategies as needed. She planned to return to work on a part-time basis the following month. Faye and her family were very satisfied with the improvement that she made throughout the course of treatment. Although it is uncertain if formal SLP treatment was responsible for Faye's improvement, Faye felt that therapy gave her an opportunity to learn compensatory strategies to help her, by her own report, "be a better communicator with aphasia."

Conclusion and Further Recommendations

The course of therapy and the recovery pattern were consistent with those of a young, educated, motivated woman with acute onset of aphasia, despite having several prognostic indicators unique to the MS population, which are both positive and negative. The positive indicators include the age of the individual—those with MS are often younger than the cerebrovascular accident (CVA) population—and use of medications such as steroids to suppress inflammation. The negative prognostic indicators include recovery patterns related to medical stability—the CVA population often demonstrates a linear recovery pattern versus the relapsing, remitting pattern of MS, and rapid access to treatment of aphasia is much more commonly identified in the CVA population. While the mechanism of aphasia in the MS population is not definitively known, this case supports the notion that management of aphasia, when careful differential diagnosis between aphasia and other cognitive-linguistic impairments is established, is not altogether different from management in those with aphasia resulting from stroke or other focal gray matter lesions. However, a careful eye on energy conservation and education in preparation for future exacerbations may be warranted.

Authors' Note

The medical information, initial presentation, course of treatment, and outcomes described above are drawn from an actual case; however, the client's name, quotations, and psychosocial details have been changed, as have the specific diagnostic measures used in the initial evaluation.

References

Ansari, N., Tarameshlu, M., & Ghelichi, L. (2020). Dysphagia in multiple sclerosis patients: Diagnostic and evaluation strategies. *Degenerative Neurological and Neuromuscular Disease*, *10*, 15–28. https://doi.org/10.2147/DNND.S198659

Beeson, P. M., & Hillis, A. E. (2001). Comprehension and production of written words. In R. Chapey (Ed.), *Language intervention strategies in adult aphasia* (4th ed., pp. 572–595). Lippincott, Williams & Wilkins.

Calabrese, M., Favaretto, A., Martini, V., & Gallo, P. (2013). Grey matter lesions in MS. *Prion*, *7*(1), 20–27. https://doi.org/10.4161/pri.22580

Devere, T. R., Trotter, J. L., & Cross, A. H. (2000). Acute aphasia in multiple sclerosis. *Archives of Neurology*, *57*(8), 1207–1209. https://doi.org/10.1001/archneur.57.8.1207

Erdem, H., Stalberg, E., & Calgar, L. (2001). Aphasia in multiple sclerosis. *Upsala Journal of Medical Science*, *106*, 205–210.

Feenaughty, L., Tjaden, K., Weinstock-Guttman, B., & Benedict, R. (2018). Separate and combined influence of cognitive impairment and dysarthria on functional communication in multiple sclerosis. *American Journal of Speech-Language Pathology*, *27*(3), 1051–1065. https://doi.org/10.1044/2018_AJSLP-17-0174

Goodglass, H., Kaplan, E., & Barresi, B. (2001). *Boston Diagnostic Aphasia Exam* (3rd ed.). Lippincott, Williams & Wilkins.

Goodglass, H., Kaplan, E., & Weintraub, S. (2001). *Boston Naming Test* (2nd ed.). Lippincott, Williams & Wilkins.

Helm-Estabrooks, N. (2001). *Cognitive Linguistic Quick Test*. The Psychology Corporation. https://doi.org/10.1007/978-3-319-56782-2_9082-2

Hulst, H., Steenwijk, M., Versteeg, A., Pouwels, P., Vrenken, H., Uitdenhaag, B., . . . Barkhof, F. (2013). Cognitive impairment in MS: Impact of white matter integrity, gray matter volume, and lesions. *Neurology*, *80*(11), 1025–1032. https://doi.org/10.1212/WNL.0b013e31828726cc

Kertesz, A. (1982). *Western Aphasia Battery*. Grune & Stratton.

Lacour, A., de Seze, J., Revenco, E., Lebrun, C., Masmoudi, K., Vidry, E., . . . Vermersch, P. (2004). Acute aphasia in multiple sclerosis: A multicenter study of 22 patients. *Neurology*, *62*(6), 974–977. https://doi.org/10.1212/01.WNL.0000115169.23421.5D

Nakagawa, Y., Sano, Y., Funayama, M., & Kato, M. (2019). Prognostic factors for long-term improvement from stroke-related aphasia with adequate linguistic rehabilitation. *Neurological Sciences*, *40*(10), 2141–2146. https://doi.org/10.1007/s10072-019-03956-7

National Multiple Sclerosis Society [MS Society]. (n.d.). *Definition of multiple sclerosis*. https://www.nationalmssociety.org/What-is-MS/Definition-of-MS

Renauld, S., Mohamed-Said, L., & Macoir, J. (2016). Language disorders in multiple sclerosis: A systematic review. *Multiple Sclerosis and Related Disorders*, *10*, 103–111. https://doi.org/10.1016/j.msard.2016.09.005

Sofologi, M., Markou, E., Kougioumtzis, G., Kamari, A., Tsandiou, A., Porfyri, G., . . . Tachmatzidis, D. (2020). Linguistic deficiencies in primary progressive multiple sclerosis. *Dual Diagnosis Open Access*, *5*(1), 1–4. https://bgro.repository.guildhe.ac.uk/id/eprint/727

APRAXIA
CASE 43
Douglas: A Novel Combination Approach to Treating Apraxia of Speech

Julie A. G. Stierwalt and Joanne P. Lasker

Conceptual Knowledge Areas

In order to understand this case, readers should possess a basic understanding of apraxia of speech as an impairment in motor planning, an understanding of basic properties of augmentative and alternative communication (AAC) speech-generating devices (SGDs), and a basic understanding of treatment concepts related to drill/practice modeling, feedback, and stimuli selection.

Apraxia is an impairment of learned skilled movement not attributable to muscle weakness, movement disorders, comprehension deficits, sensory disturbance, or cognitive disorders (Geschwind, 1975). Derived from this definition and applied to the oral-motor system, apraxia of speech (AOS) is a motor speech disorder that results from a disruption of the *motor program* for speech production. For example, when you want to formulate an utterance, first you must select the ideas and the words you want to put together (e.g., "That was a great party last night!"). Once you have formulated what you want to say, the message must be relayed to the oral-motor system with all the sounds in their proper order so the listener can process the series of sounds as recognizable words and thus understand the communicative intent. That *message* relayed from the brain, which informs the speech mechanism how to move muscles in order to precisely execute the words, takes the form of a motor program. Thus, the disruption in apraxia of speech does not occur in formulating language, because individuals with apraxia know what they want to say. Instead, the disruption comes somewhere between formulating the language and coordinating the structures of the speech mechanism to produce speech.

Description of the Case

The case example provided in this chapter illustrates an approach to treating apraxia of speech with an individual (Douglas) who suffered from profound AOS. The features of this treatment combine principles of motor learning and accessing an AAC device for home practice. This approach allowed Douglas, who was initially without meaningful speech, to talk functionally with his family and friends using words, phrases, and sentences.

Background Information and Reason for Referral

At the time of our initial evaluation, Douglas was a 49-year-old right-handed retired sheriff who had experienced a series of three strokes 4 years earlier. As part of his rehabilitation plan, a voice-output AAC device using digitized speech recording to store messages was recommended and obtained; however, Douglas never used the device because he felt that it did not meet his needs. The first phase of Douglas's treatment ended 3 years prior to our evaluation. Immediately before our assessment, a diagnostic treatment trial was terminated when Douglas remained unable to speak. At the end of that treatment trial, the speech-language pathologist referred Douglas to our university clinic for an AAC evaluation.

Before his strokes, Douglas served 20 years in the military and worked as a corrections officer and a sheriff. His educational history included 2 years of college in addition to the training he obtained in the military. Douglas had limited functional use of his right arm and used a cane to walk. Despite his hemiparesis, he drove his own vehicle, used a cell phone, and managed all activities of daily living independently. Douglas was a highly strategic problem-solver. When driving to his first appointment, he went into the college bookstore, handed his cell phone and the clinician's card to the clerk, and indicated that he was lost and needed directions. The clerk called the clinician's number to explain the situation, and Douglas followed the directions to find his way to the appointment.

Prior to the series of strokes, Douglas enjoyed fishing, attending church, participating in the fraternal order of Freemasons, shopping, cleaning, and cooking. According to Douglas's sister, he spent the bulk of his time watching TV, shopping, cleaning, cooking, and attending church. His sister reported that Douglas had a desire to communicate with family members, friends, and his pastor. He also wished to be able to communicate on the telephone. When contacted before our evaluation, Douglas's sister reported that she hoped we "weren't going to give him one of those talking machines again because Douglas wanted to talk." That statement was not in line with the referral to our clinic for an AAC device by the former clinician but was an important consideration when selecting treatment options.

Findings of the Evaluation

Speech and Language

Douglas continued to demonstrate apraxia of speech consistent with prior evaluations. Our assessment using the Apraxia subtest of the Western Aphasia Battery (Kertesz, 2007) indicated that Douglas demonstrated a profound AOS without accompanying limb or oral apraxia. Unfortunately, Douglas's speech impairment did not allow for the completion of formal or standardized testing; thus, we were unable to obtain an Aphasia Quotient from the Western Aphasia Battery–Revised (Kertesz, 2007). Specifically, Douglas had a severely restricted repertoire of speech sounds and had difficulty producing even isolated vowel sounds either through imitation or in unison production with the clinician. Informal evaluation revealed that attempts at verbal output were limited to phonation on command and imitation of /ah/ and /oh/. Although verbal expression was limited, he was able to communicate successfully using a variety of partner-supported conversation techniques, such as the Written Choice Communication Strategy (Garrett & Beukelman, 1995), some handwriting, residual speech sounds, and gestures. When asked to sing along with familiar songs, he was able to imitate melodic line well but unable to sing the words. Throughout the evaluation, Douglas's receptive language skills appeared to be within functional limits for basic conversation.

Because the assessment results confirmed a profound AOS, Douglas was tested for stimulability using the Motor Learning Guided (MLG) approach (Hageman et al., 2002). He was presented with five index cards containing the words "so," "ah," "no," "mow," and "oh" (targeting vowel sounds "a" and "o"). The vowel "o" was used in four of the five words because it was the easiest vowel to elicit based on our testing. The clinician provided a model of the target and asked him to repeat it. Following the first repetition, Douglas was instructed to wait 4 seconds between repeating the stimulus an additional three times. He was instructed to use the intervening pause time to "listen" to his production and change it if necessary to make it sound more like the target. Douglas produced an approximation of the target for 5 of 15 trials. When the clinician did not provide him with a model (a much more difficult task), Douglas produced approximations on 3 of 15 trials. Many of his productions included delays, articulatory groping, and perseverative errors. However, given his extremely limited output, even an incorrect production was considered a relatively promising prognostic indicator. For example, when Douglas produced "no" instead of the targets "so" or "mow," this demonstrated at least some degree of speech control. Douglas required cueing and encouragement to "say anything" in order to produce a response for every stimulus card. It was clear that Douglas was, in fact, surprised when he was able to produce any speech at all. Based on the results of this limited trial, we believed that employing the MLG protocol had the potential to improve aspects of Douglas's speech production.

Augmentative and Alternative Communication

At the initial evaluation, the voice-output communication device that Douglas owned was a speech-generating device (SGD) funded by his insurance. The device was a portable digitized speech communication device, meaning it had no text-to-speech capability. A user could not type a letter, word, or phrase into the SGD to hear them produced by the machine. This device was not the optimal choice for Douglas, who had no usable speech and no follow-up support for programming relevant messages into the system. However, Douglas clearly possessed the ability to formulate and access messages using a variety of letters, words, and phrases. The SGD employed a dynamic display system, meaning that when Douglas pressed a button, the screen changed to reveal a new set of potential messages. This feature of the device made sense for a strategic user like Douglas, and he demonstrated adequate skills in navigating from page to page of the SGD. He also appreciated the portability of the system.

During the evaluation, the clinicians presented Douglas with a different voice-output communication device that was also highly portable. Salient features of this device included a dynamic display, which gives communicators the capability to move from page to page by pressing certain areas on the screen, and text-to-speech synthesis. When a user selected different "buttons" on the

screen, representing letters, words, and phrases, the speech synthesizer within the device produced a message using a computer-generated voice. Douglas easily navigated to various locations on the screen to access specific messages. For example, when asked which button he would press to find messages related to shopping, he immediately pressed the correct message square linking to the "shopping" page. He clearly understood the concept of navigation and of returning to the "home" page to find other categories of potential messages. When he and his sister heard the machine producing a message using synthesized speech for the first time, it was clear that they were both surprised and impressed by the fact that AAC devices had such capability.

Douglas was also shown the conversation overlay on the SGD, which consisted entirely of whole phrases on buttons arranged according to conversation function, such as greetings, comments, and conversation breakdown repair messages. Douglas was given two hypothetical situations and asked how he would respond. When the clinician presented him with a situation (i.e., "If someone told you that you couldn't drive, what would you say to them?"), he successfully navigated through the system choosing the representation for "it isn't fair." In another situation, when asked by the clinician what he would say if his niece or nephew drew a picture for him, he responded by choosing the phrase "I love it" from a page of comments.

When asked, through partner-supported conversation strategies, if he liked the speech-generating device that we trialed during the evaluation, Douglas clearly indicated he did. We suspected that part of his reluctance in using a speech-generating device prior to our evaluation was related to the fact that he owned an inappropriately prescribed device and received no support or follow-up to help him use it effectively. Given his limited natural speech output, relatively strong reading skills, and strategic communication behaviors, Douglas clearly could benefit from voice-output AAC approaches. We began the process of searching for and acquiring a different, more appropriate speech-generating device.

To summarize our evaluation findings, Douglas exhibited profound AOS characterized by his inability to imitate vowel sounds or produce any usable speech. We believed that it was likely that Douglas also had some degree of expressive aphasia, but we were unable to confirm the type or extent due to his motor speech impairment. Douglas demonstrated strengths in the areas of auditory comprehension (i.e., following verbal commands) and reading comprehension in context (selecting choices presented in Written Choice Conversation). Douglas possessed skills to use multiple communication strategies, including gesture, some writing of letters and words with his nondominant hand (when he was seated), and partner-supported conversation strategies. Douglas's pragmatic behaviors in conversation were good. He appeared to understand requests, and his responses were appropriate given his expressive speech constraints. Based on the changes in speech production he achieved using the MLG approach, it appeared that the potential to benefit from a motor learning–guided approach was positive. Finally, when provided with an appropriate AAC device, Douglas was able to operate it successfully and was pleased with the benefits that it provided.

Treatment Options Considered

In making decisions regarding treatment, there are important guidelines to follow, which include selecting a treatment that has the following aspects:

- Has established evidence or, when evidence is not available, is based on sound theory
- Has shown clinical efficacy through the clinician's experience or through case report
- Targets behaviors and/or objectives in line with a person-centered approach (McNaughton et al., 2019)

With these guidelines in mind, there are several treatments that were considered. Melodic Intonation Therapy (MIT) (Albert et al., 1973) is a treatment approach used with AOS that has some documented success in the literature. However, that evidence has been mixed and our attempts to probe the technique in our assessment (singing well-known songs such as "Happy Birthday") were not successful in eliciting expression; thus, MIT was not selected for treatment. Traditional approaches (such as the Eight-Step Continuum approach) had not provided therapeutic benefit in previous treatment with Douglas; therefore, they were not selected (Wambaugh et al., 2006). As another option, we considered additional training using AAC, since Douglas appeared more amenable to the concept when provided with an appropriate device. Finally, we decided on a combined approach. Because Douglas *was* able to demonstrate changes in his speech using the MLG approach within the assessment, trial therapy using the technique was warranted. Additionally, while the referral to our university clinic was specifically for an AAC device, Douglas and his sister expressed that they wanted to focus on "speech." Although somewhat new as a technique at the time, MLG is based on sound motor learning theory (Hageman et al., 2002; Mass et al., 2008; Schmidt & Wrisberg, 2000), and we have had tremendous success with its application for individuals with acquired and developmental AOS. The second piece of the combined approach was to utilize AAC as a supplemental practice tool. The combination approach was successful with a similar client we had treated in our clinic. Implementing this approach successfully addressed each of the treatment selection guidelines. There was existing evidence and sound theoretical support, as well as personal clinical experience with the technique, and this technique addressed the client's primary wish to target speech.

Course of Treatment

Treatment sessions were conducted in a university clinic once weekly as Douglas drove 100 miles both to and from the clinic. The initial portion of every session (retention probes) was videotaped and recorded with a lavalier microphone. As an expansion of clinic treatment sessions, Douglas practiced the treatment targets at home for 15 minutes a day with the aid of an AAC speech-generating device. These sessions were monitored using a log that was completed weekly. The trained stimuli were programmed into the speech-generating device, with a single target item stored under a single button. When a specific area on the device was selected, the target utterance was "spoken" aloud by the device. For Cycles 1 and 2, Douglas used a small digitized device to practice targets. For Cycles 3 and 4, he used a device with synthesized voice output. Douglas reported that he had no strong preference toward either digitized or synthesized voice output models for home practice.

Stimuli

During each treatment cycle, 20 stimuli were selected for direct treatment and 20 were designated as untrained items. These untrained items were probed approximately every three sessions to determine whether there was a generalization effect of the treatment. We attempted to create lists of trained and untrained stimuli that were similar in terms of length and phonetic structure; however, the primary emphasis was on functionality of the target items. We also took care to create stimuli that were consistent with Douglas's dialect and cultural experiences. The first cycle of stimuli consisted of "real- word" CV combinations, including items such as "no," "day," "hi," and "see." Cycle 2 stimulus items included two-syllable words and phrases such as "amen," "no way," "maybe," "how much," "sweet tea," and "Jesus." In Cycle 3, stimuli included three- to seven-syllable words and phrases, including biographical information such as the client's name, medical history, and phone number, and terms Douglas wanted to say in church. These items included: "I had three strokes," "paralyzed," "Jerusalem," "arrogance," and "Holy Ghost." Cycle 4 stimuli ranged from two to five syllables in length, focusing on phrases that Douglas needed in his daily activities in church, as a member of the Aphasia Group, and using his cell phone, including items such as "How was your weekend?" "seven years ago," "peace be with you," and "I'll call you back."

Session Procedure

Each MLG treatment session began with random elicitation of the treatment targets as a measure of motor retention. Eliciting treatment targets prior to the treatment is a critical element of this approach, as the utterances reveal true retention, without the added benefit of the practice that took place during each session (Hageman et al., 2002; Johnson et al., 2018). Following the retention task, treatment ensued. The MLG treatment hierarchy is described in Figure 43–1.

The unique features of MLG drawn from motor learning theory include the type and schedule of feedback provided and the variable nature of practice (Husak & Reeve, 1979; Johnson et al., 2018; Kim et al., 2012; Mass et al., 2008; Schmidt & Bjork, 1992). The feedback clinicians provided was of a "knowledge of results" type, at an approximately 30% schedule. Knowledge of results differs from traditional "knowledge of performance" feedback in which clinicians provide specific instruction on how to change productions (e.g., "Move your tongue between your teeth"). "Knowledge of results" is general information about production accuracy, namely, how close the attempt is to the target item. Feedback consisted of statements such as, "That second try was really good" or "I heard the last part of the target clearly." Knowledge of results encourages the client to self-evaluate his or her productions relying on the auditory, tactile, and kinesthetic feedback, rather than the clinician's interpretation of accuracy.

The schedule of feedback is another important consideration. Historically, clinicians have been trained to provide a high schedule of feedback, sometimes as high as 100%. However, delivering feedback at such a high schedule may actually interfere with the client's self-evaluation, which will reduce long-term accuracy (motor learning) (Hula et al., 2008; Kim et al., 2012; Lee et al., 1985).

Variable practice is another feature incorporated in MLG. It calls for randomizing targets/stimuli during practice. This is in direct contrast to "massed practice" in which a single target is practiced repeatedly for an extended time period. The theoretical difference between these forms of practice is simple. During massed practice, an

The Motor Learning Guided (MLG) Treatment Protocol
Environment/Stimuli
Treatment will take place in a quiet treatment atmosphere as free from distraction as possible. The participant will be instructed to refrain from asking questions during the practice and, more importantly, asked to refrain from talking during the delay interval in between production attempts. Approximately 20 stimulus items (presented in written form) will be selected for treatment. The stimuli will range from single words to full sentences selected on the basis of their high functionality by the participant or a family member who is well acquainted with the participant and their routines. An additional 20 items will be generated and used as untreated items (randomly mixed with trained items) to probe every 3rd–4th session.
Retention Measure
Each session will begin with random elicitation of the treated items. These items are scored according to an 11-point multidimensional rating scale (Figure 43–2). These ratings demonstrate the extent of motor learning retained from the previous session; thus, they serve as a true index of motor learning. They are uniformly elicited prior to the treatment phase of the session to eliminate potential practice effects.
Step 1: The clinician selects a block of 5 stimulus items at random from the group of 20 treated items to be used for Steps 1 and 2. The clinician produces an utterance, waits 4 seconds, and the utterance is elicited from the participant using a written stimulus card. Participant attempts utterance without assistance. (No feedback). Participant produces utterance 3 times with a 4-second pause between each attempt. After the 3 attempts, the clinician repeats the stimulus and provides knowledge of results feedback (general feedback regarding the accuracy of the client's productions). (Step 1 continues for a block of 5 stimulus items.)
Step 2: Using the same 5 stimulus items as in Step 1, the utterance is elicited from the participant using a written stimulus card in random order. Participant attempts utterance without assistance. (No feedback). Participant produces utterance 3 times with a 4-second pause between each attempt. After the 3 attempts, the clinician repeats the stimulus and provides knowledge of results feedback. (Step 2 continues for a block of 5 stimulus items.)
Step 3: Repeat steps 1–2 with another block of 5 stimulus items until all trained items are completed.
Step 4: Upon completion of the 20 treated items, the utterances are randomly elicited from written stimulus cards. Participant attempts utterance without assistance. (No feedback). Participant produces utterance 3 times with a 4-second pause between each attempt. After the 3 attempts, the clinician repeats the stimulus and provides knowledge of results feedback.

Figure 43–1. The Motor Learning Guided Treatment Protocol.

individual will retrieve and execute the motor program one time, then hold that program in working memory during massed repetitions. The variable practice in MLG requires that a client retrieve and execute the motor program for a few repetitions, then move on to another target. Each time these targets are revisited, the motor plan is retrieved. The multiple occurrences of retrieval provide a greater opportunity for motor learning to occur (Johnson et al., 2018; Kim et al., 2012; Newell & Shapiro, 1976).

To rate Douglas's performance on the target items at the beginning of the session, clinicians used an 11-point multidimensional scale. See Figure 43–2 for details of this rating scale. Items were judged to be some degree of "correct" or "intelligible" when ratings were above or equal to a 5 on this scoring system.

Treatment Fidelity

Douglas worked with different student clinicians for each of the four treatment cycles. The student clinicians transcribed his utterances elicited during the retention measure at the start of each session. They transcribed actual productions in real time and then viewed videotapes to correct any transcription or scoring errors. Discrepancies were resolved by viewing the session recording and consulting with supervisors. Reliability checks were conducted on a minimum of 30% of all transcripts for each treatment cycle. The overall mean interobserver agreement for correct productions for all sessions was 88%. Treatment fidelity for each clinician's adherence to the steps of the MLG protocol was determined for all of the treatment sessions in each cycle and found to be 100%.

Retention Measure Rating Scale

11   Accurate, immediate (may include distortion but maintains immediate intelligibility)

10   Delayed (greater than 2 seconds)

9   Delayed (includes silent or audible articulatory groping and/or posturing)

8   Immediate, acceptable approximation, though not immediately intelligible

7   Delayed (2+ seconds) acceptable approximation, though not immediately intelligible

6   Self-correction

5   Repeat, asks for repetition

4   Incomplete, similar characteristics but not the target

3   Error (clearly not the target)

2   Error plus a delay (2+ seconds)

1   Perseveration (produces previous response)

Figure 43–2. Multidimensional Retention Rating Scale.

Analysis of Client's Response to Intervention

Figures 43–3, 43–4, 43–5, and 43–6 illustrate the accuracy of production of trained and untrained stimulus items from retention probes conducted in Cycles 1, 2, 3, and 4. In Cycle 1, Douglas did not initially produce any of the treated or untreated stimuli successfully. By the end of the first cycle, accuracy had increased steadily until his produc-

tions of treatment targets stabilized at 13 out of 20. Within the first 3 weeks of Cycle 2, 8 out of 20 of the targets were being produced at an intelligible level. At the end of the second cycle, 16 of the 20 targets were produced at an intelligible level. Generalization to untrained items was also seen for 10 of the 20 untreated stimuli that were produced at an intelligible level. At the end of Cycle 3, 15 of the 20 items were produced accurately. Due to the complexity of items in the Cycle 3 treatment

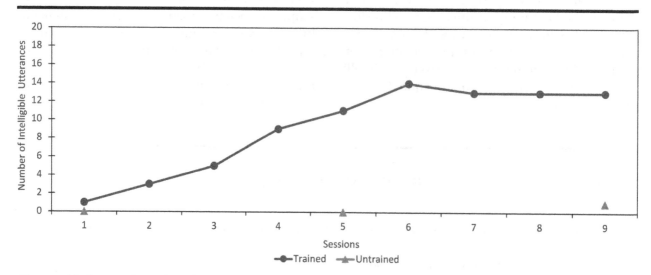

Figure 43–3. Number of intelligible utterances (scores of 5 or higher) of trained and untrained stimuli in Cycle 1.

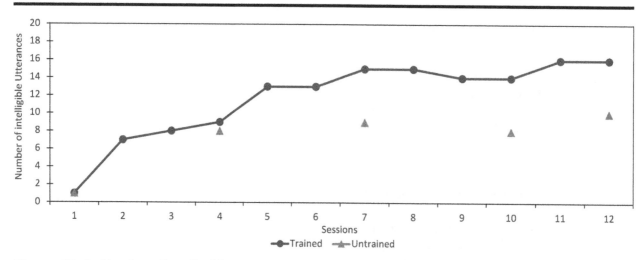

Figure 43–4. Number of intelligible utterances (scores of 5 or higher) of trained and untrained stimuli in Cycle 2.

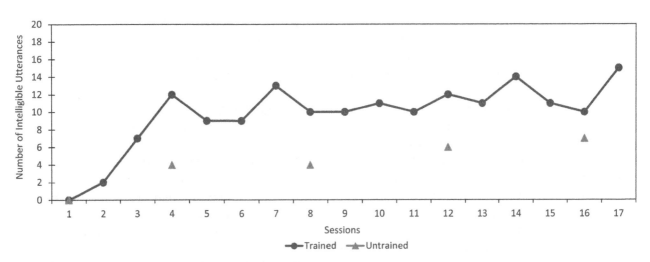

Figure 43–5. Number of intelligible utterances (scores of 5 or higher) of trained and untrained stimuli in Cycle 3.

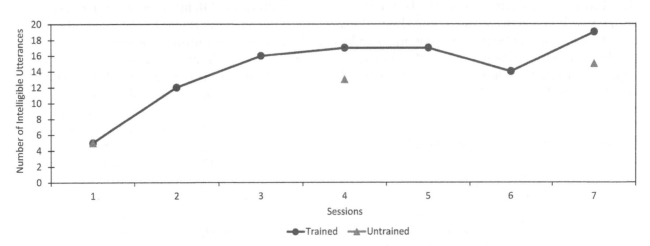

Figure 43–6. Number of intelligible utterances (scores of 5 or higher) of trained and untrained stimuli in Cycle 4.

set (e.g., "arrogance," "runs a daycare"), the cycle continued for two academic semesters. All treated and untreated stimuli from Cycles 1, 2, and 3 were probed at the end of Cycle 3, and Douglas retained correct production of 46 of 65 targets (71%). When Douglas returned after a summer break to begin Cycle 4, treated and untreated stimuli from Cycle 3 were probed, and Douglas retained correct production of 15 of the trained utterances and 10 of the untrained utterances for a total of 25 of 40 items (63%). Given the fact that Douglas reported

that he had not practiced Cycle 3 items over the summer break, it is interesting to note that he retained correct production of both trained and untrained items over a period of 4 months without targeted treatment. Cycle 4 began with both trained and untrained items at a score of 5 correct. By the seventh week of Cycle 4, Douglas produced 19 of 20 trained stimuli and 15 of 20 untrained items correctly.

In addition to changes noted on weekly retention probes, Douglas, his family, and other clinicians reported positive changes in Douglas's spoken productions in "real-life" activities. While participating in Cycle 2, Douglas attended a weekly Aphasia Group conducted at a university clinic and began to verbalize during group sessions. He attempted novel and trained words in contexts outside of treatment sessions, as observed by clinicians and through reports from his sister. Douglas continued his participation in Aphasia Group through Cycle 3 with ever-increasing numbers of verbal attempts noted each week. During a particularly engaging group session, Douglas attempted to produce novel one- to three-word utterances at least 40 times. Douglas now speaks during one-to-one conversations with clinicians on a regular basis, usually producing untrained responses. For example, when asked how tall he was, Douglas replied "6–2." He recited his phone number for a clinician when asked and commented on a supervisor's new hairstyle by saying, "your hair." In a recent conversation about Thanksgiving, he independently produced the utterances "fried turkey," "dinner," "fresh," "peanut oil," "throw it away," "nephew," and "Georgia."

Implications and Hypotheses

The combined treatment approach that employed both the MLG approach for apraxia of speech and AAC was effective for this client with longstanding, profound apraxia of speech. The gains Douglas made were particularly notable given his time poststroke (4 years at the start of treatment) and the severity of his impairment (essentially nonverbal). Based on these results, we have noted several interesting features related to this treatment approach:

- While clearly effective for Douglas, this approach was quite effortful, especially at the beginning; he expended both physical and mental effort to complete retention probes. For example, it took a full 60-minute session for Douglas to produce 40 items (all CVs) in Cycle 1 due to persistent groping and restarts.

- As cycles progressed, Douglas's facility in producing utterances improved and the time required to produce each utterance decreased. However, he continued to rely heavily on written input (e.g., concentrating carefully on the written cue card), particularly for untrained stimuli.

- As utterances increased in complexity, it took Douglas a greater number of weeks to acquire them. For example, he required 17 weeks to reach mastery of trained items in Cycle 3, compared with 9 weeks in Cycle 1.

- In Cycle 1, minimal change was noted in untrained stimuli as trained stimuli were acquired. In Cycles 2, 3, and 4, untrained items were acquired in conjunction with trained items; however, retention of trained items was always better than retention of untrained items.

- As Douglas's speech outside of clinic settings improved, agrammatism became more evident. For example, he left a message on one author's voicemail to report car trouble, stating his name and the words, "car—no." With more words in his spoken repertoire and greater facility to produce untrained words, we saw evidence of the nonfluent aphasia that coexisted with his apraxia of speech. When using handwriting or his AAC device to augment his natural speech, Douglas clearly demonstrated difficulty spelling words, retrieving words, and organizing words into sentences.

- At the end of 2 years of treatment, equivalent to four academic semesters, Douglas used primarily natural speech to communicate, which he augmented and supplemented with handwriting, gesture, scrolling through names on his cell phone, and accessing prepared messages on his speech-generating device. He best fit the category of a "generative communicator" as defined by the AAC-Aphasia Framework continuum (Garrett et al., 2020), in that he was highly strategic and used multiple approaches to formulate novel messages for communication partners with limited need for partner support.

- Based on our work with Douglas and other clients like him, we have noted characteristics of individuals who appear to benefit most from this combined treatment approach. Clients who benefit demonstrate a greater degree of motor speech impairment (AOS) compared with a language impairment (aphasia) have adequate auditory comprehension to discriminate accurate from inaccurate productions and are highly motivated to improve speech production.

Authors' Note

We would like to express our thanks to Douglas (pseudonym). We are grateful for his willingness to share his story and are sincerely impressed by the time, effort, and spirit he exhibits in pursuing his goals. We also thank the following graduate student clinicians, Stephanie Fountain, Min-Jung Kim, Dorian Chen, and Katie Ames, who worked with Douglas and were just as "bowled over" as we were by his dedication and tremendous progress.

References

Albert, M. L., Sparks, R. W., & Helm, N. A. (1973) Melodic intonation therapy for aphasia. *Archives of Neurology, 29*, 130–131. https://doi.org/10.1001/archneur.1973.00490260074018

Garrett, K. L., & Beukelman, D. R. (1995). Changes in the interaction patterns of an individual with severe aphasia given three types of partner support. *Clinical Aphasiology, 23*, 237–251.

Garrett, K. L., Lasker, J. P., & Fischer, J. K. (2020). AAC supports for adults with severe aphasia and apraxia of speech. In D. Beukelman & J. Light (Eds.), *Augmentative and alternative communication: Supporting children and adults with complex communication needs* (pp. 553–603). Paul H. Brookes.

Geschwind, N. (1975). The apraxias: Neural mechanisms of disorders of learned movement. *American Scientist, 63*(2), 188–195.

Hageman, C. F., Simon, P., Backer, B., & Burda, A. N. (2002, November). *Comparing MIT and motor learning therapy in a nonfluent aphasic speaker.* Symposium conducted at the annual meeting of the American Speech-Language-Hearing Association, Atlanta, GA.

Hula, S. N. A., Robin, D. A., Maas, E., Ballard, K. J., & Schmidt, R. A. (2008). Effects of feedback frequency and timing on acquisition, retention, and transfer of speech skills in acquired apraxia of speech. *Journal of Speech, Language, and Hearing Research, 51*, 1088–1113.

Husak, W. S., & Reeve, T. G. (1979). Novel response production as a function of variability and amount of practice. *Research Quarterly, 50*, 215–221.

Johnson, R. K., Lasker, J. P., Stierwalt, J. A. G., MacPherson, M. K., & LaPointe, L. L. (2018). Motor learning guided treatment for acquired apraxia of speech: A case study investigating factors that influence treatment outcomes. *Speech, Language and Hearing, 21*(4), 213–223. https://doi.org/10.1080/2050571X.2017.1388488

Kertesz, A. (2007). *Western Aphasia Battery–Revised.* The Psychological Corporation.

Kim, I., Lapointe, L. L., & Stierwalt, J. A. G. (2012). The effect of feedback and practice on the acquisition of novel speech behaviors. *American Journal of Speech-Language Pathology, 21*(2), 89–100. https://doi.org/10.1044/1058-0360(2011/09-0082

Lee, T. D., Magill, R. A., & Weeks, D. J. (1985). Influence of practice schedule on testing schema theory predictions in adults. *Journal of Motor Behavior, 17*(3), 283–299.

Mass, E., Robin, D. A., Austermann Hula, S. N., Freedman, S. E., Wulf, G., Ballard, K. J., & Schmidt, R. A. (2008). Principles of motor learning in treatment of motor speech disorders. *American Journal of Speech-Language Pathology, 17*(3), 277–298.

McNaughton, D., Light, J., Beukelman, D. R., Klein, C., Nieder, D., & Nazareth, G. (2019). Building capacity in AAC: A person-centred approach to supporting participation by people with complex communication needs. *Augmentative and Alternative Communication, 35*(1), 56–68. https://doi.org/10.1080/07434618.2018.1556731

Newell, K. M., & Shapiro, D. C. (1976). Variability of practice and transfer of training: Some evidence toward a schema view of motor learning. *Journal of Motor Behavior, 8*(3), 233–243.

Schmidt, R., & Bjork, R. (1992). New conceptualizations of practice: Common principles in three paradigms suggest new concepts for training. *Psychological Science, 3*(4), 207–217.

Schmidt, R. A., & Wrisberg, C. A. (2000). *Motor learning and performance* (2nd ed.). Human Kinetics.

Wambaugh, J. L., Duffy, J. R., McNeil, M. R., Robin, D. A., & Rogers, M. A. (2006). Treatment guidelines for acquired apraxia of speech: A synthesis and evaluation of the evidence. *Journal of Medical Speech-Language Pathology, 14*(2), xv–xxxiii.

AMYOTROPHIC LATERAL SCLEROSIS/ AUGMENTATIVE AND ALTERNATIVE COMMUNICATION
CASE 44
Thomas: An Adult With ALS Using AAC
Telina Caudill and Nerissa Hall

Conceptual Knowledge Areas

Amyotrophic lateral sclerosis (ALS) is a degenerative neurological disorder that leads to profound weakness, fatigue, and paralysis of the muscles necessary for walking, using our hands, as well as those for respiration, speech, and swallowing (Beukelman et al., 2007). ALS can be further classified as bulbar, spinal, or mixed, based on the location of onset.

Persons with ALS (pALS) experience communication impairments (such as dysarthria, anarthria, dysphonia, and aphonia). Given the nature of this progressive disease, communication abilities for pALS deteriorate over time, and more than 75% of pALS are unable to use natural speech or writing at some point during the disease progression (Beukelman et al., 2011) and therefore require access to augmentative alternative communication (AAC). Speech-language pathologists (SLPs) play a critical role in the care for pALS. Planning for scheduled SLP sessions to assess motor speech, voice, and cognitive functions over time facilitates timely and successful AAC assessment, acquisition, and intervention services

and a plan of care that evolves as the needs of pALS change.

Communication Symptoms

As the muscles related to speech, swallowing, and respiration weaken, pALS may exhibit different communication challenges. Most often, dysarthria, voice disorders, cognitive-linguistic changes, and dysphagia are communication symptoms prevalent for pALS.

Dysarthria

ALS results in mixed flaccid-spastic dysarthria given upper and lower motor neuron involvement. According to Ball et al. (2002), an accurate prediction of eventual intelligibility demise is a speaking rate of lower than 125 words per minute, irrespective of ALS type. Spasticity or flaccidity is most often seen with mild dysarthria; however, ALS can progress and lead to profound impairments and anarthria (Beukelman et al., 2011). Bulbar ALS is the most aggressive type of ALS and progresses rapidly, initially affecting speech and swallowing, and is commonly associated with pseudobulbar affect (Makkonen et al., 2018).

Voice Disorder

Poor breath support leads to decreased vocal intensity and short phrasing and can ultimately lead to dysphonia. Individuals who require noninvasive ventilation, such as bilevel positive airway pressure (BiPAP), typically those with spinal ALS, often present with relatively intact speech. However, verbal communication becomes laborious, and sometimes impossible, due to the physical barriers associated with ventilation masks that cover the whole face, partial face, or the nares. Coordinating speech muscle movement with breathing through the nose or mouth becomes difficult, and vocal intensity and resonance are disturbed. The pALS may need to remove their mask to speak (leading to fatigue and shortness of breath) or rely on others to adjust their mask for them (which affects spontaneity and autonomy). Invasive ventilation increases the life expectancy of pALS as well as the duration of AAC use (Beukelman et al., 2011). However, invasive ventilation for pALS can lead to aphonia. Strategies for the adult with aphonia can include methods such as exaggerated articulation to support lip reading, use of an electrolarynx, or an in-line speaking valve.

Cognitive Communication

Cognitive-linguistic changes do occur in ALS. Yunusova et al. (2016) report that these tend to be more distinct with bulbar involvement, with 10% exhibiting frontotemporal dementia (FTD) symptoms and up to 50% demonstrating more global cognitive decline on neuropsychological testing. There are four variants of FTD, one of which is primarily behavioral deviation with the remaining variants of primary progressive aphasia (PPA) mainly characterized by language impairment.

Dysphagia

Sialorrhea or excessive drooling is a result of muscle weakness and deterioration. This may disrupt the flow of verbal speech as the pALS need to swallow more frequently, wipe their mouths more often, or even maintain gauze or towels intra-orally to minimize secretion overflow. Any of these factors may result in social isolation and avoidance of communicative interactions.

Communication Needs

High-tech voice output AAC interventions (speech-generating devices [SGDs]), as well as low-tech, paper-based AAC tools, should focus on personally relevant messages within the four purposes of communicative interaction that include expression of needs and wants, information transfer, social closeness, and social etiquette (Light & McNaughton, 2015). Additionally, communicative environments and partners should be identified by the SLP and incorporated into the AAC treatment plan to maximize generalization and carryover.

Intervention for ALS

DeRuyter (2002) proposed five ALS intervention stages adapted from the Revised Amyotrophic Lateral Sclerosis Functional Rating Scale (ALSFRS-R) (Cedarbaum et al., 1999):

- Stage 1: Normal Speech Processes
- Stage 2: Detectable Speech Disturbances
- Stage 3: Reduction in Speech Intelligibility
- Stage 4: Use of AAC
- Stage 5: No Functional Speech

Beukelman et al. (2007) list three general phases of AAC service provision for pALS:

- Phase 1: Monitor, Prepare, and Support
- Phase 2: Assess, Recommend, and Implement
- Phase 3: Adapt and Accommodate

Intervention at each stage or phase may occur via inpatient, outpatient, home-health, and/or remote service delivery (i.e., tele-AAC) depending on the needs and abilities of the client. Additionally, intervention should involve the caregiver(s) and/or significant other within treatment to support generalization of learned skills within the natural environment(s).

Phase 1: Monitor, Prepare, and Support

Stage 1: Normal Speech Processes

Stage 2: Detectable Speech Disturbances

At this point in the disease process, the speech of the pALS is either intact or functional, with only perceived changes.

Monitor

First, the SLP should evaluate the speaking rate and intelligibility of the pALS during 15-minute multidisciplinary clinic visits once every 3 to 4 months.

Prepare

Second, systematic, consistent, individualized, and timely discussion of the known course of the disease; AAC supports available (no-tech to high-tech); and adjustments to new communication norms for AAC users are critical to help them prepare for the anticipated progression of the disease. The SLP should prepare caregivers by discussing role changes (from supporters to translators) and pragmatic changes resulting from energy conservation methods (telegraphic speech), which may appear blunt or rude (Judge et al., 2018).

Compensatory Speech Strategies and Communication Partner Tips. Support for pALS and their communication partners is critical. Strategy training for pALS may include:

- Use slow speaking rate
- Overarticulate
- Pause between words
- Use alphabet supplementation, gestures, writing, or communication boards

- Avoid talking on residual air
- Conserve energy (strategically engaging in anticipated conversations when least fatigued, using a voice amplifier, taking breaks)
- Discourage oral-motor exercises and articulation practice that increase fatigue (and educate that normal speaking is enough exercise)

Strategy training for the caregiver and/or significant other may include:

- Speak facing one another, maintain eye contact, and try to offer your full attention
- Optimize speaking environments by reducing/eliminating background noise
- Minimize the space between communication partners

Voice Banking. Voice banking helps to preserve a piece of the identity of pALS. It involves creating synthetic voices that are personalized and modeled after the client's natural speech patterns, which can then be programmed as the default voice on an SGD. Voice banking should be discussed when speech is intact, though often pALS defer in the absence of any signs or symptoms of dysarthria. It is the responsibility of the SLP to review disease progression and optimal recording situations prior to onset of dysarthria, respiratory impairment, or poor endurance.

Although participation in voice banking is optimal when the client's speech is intact, pALS may participate when experiencing early onset of speech changes. The SLP should explore various software options that meet the client's needs to ensure voice banking participation and completion. Some software options require as few as 50 phrase recordings to create a personalized synthetic voice.

Message Banking. Message banking is the term used for creating digitized recordings of vocal utterances of the individual's choosing. These are sometimes referred to as legacy messages. They are recordings of the person's natural voice that can be stored electronically until an SGD is required and then transferred and programmed within the software at that time. pALS can also message bank directly into an SGD should they already have one. Message banking can also be completed on a handheld voice recorder, a voice recording app, native sound recorders on computers, teddy bears, and children's recordable story books.

Hurtig and Downey (2009) underscore the value of the personalized voice for both acceptance and use of the AAC device with the pALS and their loved ones. Notably, Oosthuizen and colleagues (2018) found in their study that pALS who chose to message bank ranked messages related to social closeness as most important to them. Inclusion of idiosyncratic comments, curse words, expressions of anger and sarcasm, pet commands, and absolutely anything personally relevant to the pALS is highly recommended.

Support

Support pALS by providing access to community resources, reputable online content, and individualized handouts and materials that they can explore both with you and on their own, self-paced, when they have reached acceptance to learn about ALS. Consider educational materials that meet accessibility standards for those with disabilities.

Phase 2: Assess, Recommend, and Implement

Stages 3: Reduction in Speech Intelligibility

Stage 4: Use of AAC

At this stage, the pALS's speech intelligibility is reduced, requiring repetition and/or use of AAC. Functionally, the pALS is now likely compensating by texting or writing instead of calling or speaking. No-tech to low-tech systems such as gestural communication, alphabet and topic supplementation, written aids, communication boards, voice amplifiers, and palatal lifts should be considered while procurement of a high-tech AAC system, for those indicated, is initiated.

Assess

The SLP should provide or assist with the coordination of a comprehensive AAC evaluation with device trials to ensure the client has access to an AAC system that meets their communication needs aligned with those identified in feature-matching analysis. The SLP uses information gathered during the comprehensive evaluation to prepare for intervention following procurement. For example, the client and caregiver are assigned the task of listing favorite webpages, preferred browsers, email accounts, and favorite television channels. Additionally, the SLP provides a list of default categories and phrases from within the selected AAC software and guides the client and caregiver in customizing the list in advance. If upper extremity weakness is present, alternative access methods to direct selection such as partner-assisted scanning, eye-tracking, laser-pointing, switch-scanning, and optical tracking are indicated.

Recommend

Immediate, consistent, and frequent training for the pALS and the caregiver to maximize learning of high-tech systems while residual speech remains functional is imperative. A suggested schedule of SLP intervention to achieve competency with an AAC system is three times a week for 12 weeks. The SLP should evaluate the client's barriers to access AAC services and assess potential solutions to mitigate them. For example, transportation to an outpatient clinic may be physically challenging for the client. One solution could be to evaluate if the service is available closer to the client's home or if tele-AAC is a viable option for both the client and the therapist. This can occur during inpatient, outpatient, home health, tele-AAC, or a combination of the above service modalities as well as in conjunction with training from the device vendor.

Implement

The focus of intervention should be toward obtaining strategic and communicative competency for not only the client but also the caregiver. Initial training is typically performed by the device representative upon installation in the home. The SLP provides the device representative with individualized client input as stated above to maximize efficiency during setup. The SLP supplements vendor training in the appropriate treatment modality providing hands-on training, ongoing programming and customization, role-playing, and modeling. Training resources developed by the SLP (i.e., picture guides, video tutorials, written step-by-step instructions, and links to online learning content) are invaluable and empower caregivers and AAC facilitators to maintain their SGD.

The SLP should determine client preference for AAC facilitators and communication partners to "guess" or complete sentences on their behalf. Education on the benefits and challenges of communication partners engaging in anticipatory completion of an utterance is warranted with both the client and their communication partners. The client should be provided with a script to navigate requests for communication partners to use and/or to terminate use of anticipatory completion of an utterance. Findings from a study by Bloch (2011) reveal both advantages and disadvantages of anticipatory completion of an utterance. The strategy may save time and effort if accurately predicted but could increase time and effort if inaccurately predicted.

Phase 3: Adapt and Accommodate

Stage 5: No Functional Speech

At this stage, the pALS has no functional speech and is completely dependent on the AAC systems in place to engage with others.

Adapt

In this "maintenance" phase of intervention, the SLP monitors and modifies the communication methods and systems to meet the changing needs of the client associated with disease progression. This may include access methods, selection settings, language representations, and page layouts. The SLP should transition from weekly sessions to monthly follow-ups. Once the client demonstrates independence and has no ongoing current needs, follow-up service can now convert to an as-needed basis as indicated by the client. The SLP should ensure that the client has means to independently contact their provider if necessary.

Accommodate

Maintaining high-tech systems includes software upgrades, troubleshooting, sustaining contact with device representatives, and technical support and ability to connect with remote assistance. In this phase, the pALS must maintain competency with low-tech backup communication methods, as technological issues are inevitable. The SLP can support nonverbal means of communication by training others on partner-assisted scanning, developing a reliable nonverbal yes/no response mechanism, creating a gestural legend for unfamiliar partners, and developing a list of frequently used messages or topics to minimize demands on the pALS. Early intervention with recurring treatment sessions specific to the client's communication needs may improve participation in personally relevant activities and quality of life and reduce abandonment of AAC among adults with diseases that cause speech, language, and cognitive impairments.

Description of the Case

Background Information

Thomas, a 73-year-old married man, was a veteran and retired architect who started experiencing shortness of breath and changes in his speech (particularly articulation) in 2013. He was diagnosed with bulbar-onset ALS early in 2014. He was evaluated by a pulmonologist and prescribed a BiPAP and cough assist given his respiratory dysfunction. By June of that year, he was exhibiting mild dysarthria and was referred to an SLP. By 2015, the disease had progressed quickly, and Thomas suffered neuromuscular respiratory failure, requiring intubation and mechanical ventilation. He underwent a tracheostomy due to ventilator dependence. He was followed by his outpatient ALS interdisciplinary team before he was admitted to long-term care. In long-term care, he continued to receive interdisciplinary services, until his death in 2020.

Thomas was prescribed single vision lens glasses and bilateral hearing aids. He rarely used the equipment because he was able to perform functional activities without them. At initial assessment, Thomas ambulated without an assistive device and was independent for all activities of daily living (ADLs). However, respiratory impairment was a significant barrier for participation in activities and he was easily fatigued. His speech was mildly dysarthric, characterized by impaired articulation, reduced intensity, and slowed rate though significantly worsened with fatigue. His performance fell within the range of Stage 2, "Detectable Speech Disturbance" on the ALSFRS-R (Cedarbaum et al., 1999) and Group 1 "Adequate Speech & Adequate Hand Function," per the Classification of Functional Capabilities scale (Yorkston et al., 2013).

Thomas identified maintaining in-person communication, long-distance communication, environmental control, and Internet access as top communication goals. Message and voice banking were discussed with Thomas in the initial evaluation, but he politely declined using either. Thomas's language and cognition were within normal limits; however, he was unable to meet his communication needs using compensatory speech strategies, and therefore, an AAC evaluation was recommended. Thomas and his spouse had good basic technology skills, and Thomas was motivated to learn novel communication software and access methods in advance of needing them. Within 2 years of his initial assessment, Thomas's physical abilities had deteriorated, and he presented with complete quadriplegia.

AAC Considerations

A dedicated SGD was ruled out during Thomas's initial assessment because at that time, he presented with intact upper extremity function and

effective use of compensatory speech strategies to help meet his communication needs. However, given the rapid progression of Thomas's symptoms, access to AAC emerged as a necessity.

Thomas was an iPhone user and very familiar with the iOS operating system. Having this prior knowledge and familiarity reduced the cognitive burden of needing to use a novel tool. iOS has a multitude of SGD apps appropriate to meet his communicative needs while allowing access to the Internet and ease of portability, which were features important to Thomas. Additionally, procurement could be expedited with low-cost everyday mobile device apps.

The AAC System

Following app and device trials, Thomas was asked to rate each SGD app on a rating scale for ease of use for various features, such as using word prediction, adding new phrases, navigating among features, and correcting typos (Bardach, 2017). The ratings for each device across features were totaled and an average percentage was calculated. Other user feedback, such as overall satisfaction with the user interface and access to integrated features, were discussed subjectively (Bardach, 2017). The objective and subjective data indicated an appropriate match with Predictable for iPhone and the Tobii C12. Thomas utilized his iPhone SGD for 2 years before transitioning to the C12. When he required a power chair for mobility and alternative access to his SGD, mounting solutions and an infrared (IR) phone were integrated into his AAC system.

Thomas's long-term communication system until his death consisted of the high-tech Tobii C12, floor mount, wheelchair mount, and IR phone. The system was identified as an appropriate match following the feature-matching process and comprehensive assessment discussed previously. Thomas primarily utilized his iPhone SGD via direct selection when access was intact. Once the C12 was approved by VA Prosthetics, purchased, and received (3 to 4 months later), he was able to access the equipment directly and learn Communicator software at his own pace, without significant burden or fatigue.

Course of Treatment

Thomas customized his phrase bank by editing the default phrases and supplementing with his own personalized messages. He selected his preferred homepage, features to include and discard from the homepage, keyboard settings, and the addition of contacts. These programming adjustments were done on a trial/clinic device with Thomas's SLP and were transferred to his purchased device by the vendor when it arrived. Prior programing and customization increased the vendor's productivity and allowed for more time to provide direct client training. Through a combination of vendor in-home visits, clinical in-home visits, and SLP service provision during brief hospital admissions, Thomas participated in multiple scheduled follow-up sessions to ensure his operational and strategic competency of the Tobii C12.

After 2 years from his initial visit, direct select access became challenging and Thomas transitioned to using a modified tracker ball mouse and the RNET BT module from his power wheelchair for joystick control. Eventually, Thomas needed eye-tracking access technology to accommodate for the changes in his access needs. It was around this period when Thomas was admitted to long-term care at his nearest veterans hospital. However, given the physical distance from his home, he became more reliant on social media, phone calls, and email to maintain social connectedness.

Treatment goals upon admission to long-term care included the following at a frequency of three times a week for 12 weeks:

- Use AAC to repair communication breakdowns and to convey more complex communication needs given setup and moderate cues.
- Demonstrate mastery of basic maintenance and operation of SGD with 100% accuracy.
- Collaborate with the SLP to program his SGD in order to customize the device for his individualized communication needs 100% of the time.
- Use rate enhancement strategies (i.e., word prediction and abbreviation expansion) on SGD to expedite message production independently and with 100% accuracy.
- Compose and respond to electronic messages and social media on SGD given minimum assistance within 8 weeks.

Thomas experienced improved access to technology support directly and indirectly from the assistive technology (AT) providers with his long-term care admission due to the elimination of the travel burden.

As Thomas progressed toward his goals and as his status evolved, SLP intervention shifted from direct services to consultative/training services of the nursing staff. It was imperative that the nursing staff acknowledged the importance of setting up Thomas's SGD and eye-tracking device everyday just as one would provide daily respiratory and tracheostomy care. Multiple interactive in-services across nursing shifts to target all staff was vital to Thomas's communication success. The implementation of a hands-on experience that simulated life without use of extremities, natural voice for self-expression, total dependence on assistive technology to interact with the world, and reliance on others to position the device was invaluable to carryover training objectives to Thomas's daily care.

The AT and SLP team provided ongoing assistance with SGD customization through equipment programming, assisting with integration of environmental controls, maintaining the software, supporting Wi-Fi connectivity issues, and managing general technology glitches or accidental setting changes (by patient or staff). Training of new staff was required intermittently, as was patient education (specifically around managing fatigue). Practice using backup systems (like no-tech and low-tech options) was incorporated into both client and partner training. Thomas's backup options included:

- Partner-assisted scanning for either spelling or identifying preset messages using low-tech communication boards
- Low-tech eye-tracking system offering spelled communication for spontaneous utterances as well as prearranged phrases or general topics

■ Posted signage at bedside alerting staff and visitors of Thomas's nonverbal yes/no system (e.g., eyebrow raise for yes and squeeze eyes shut tight for no)

Communication with ALS providers, such as hospice, palliative care, and psychology, would not have been possible without AAC as Thomas began to discuss end-of-life desires. It was his wish to be removed from the ventilator when communication was no longer feasible for him, when his eye movements deteriorated, and it became labor intensive. He utilized his AAC system to say goodbye to his family surrounding his bed as he died.

References

Ball, L. J., Beukelman, D. R., & Pattee, G. L. (2002). Timing of speech deterioration in people with amyotrophic lateral sclerosis. *Journal of Medical Speech-Language Pathology, 10*(4), 231–235.

Bardach, L .G. (2017). CommNeedsQuestionnaire.pdf. https://cehs.unl.edu/documents/secd/aac/CommNeedsQuestionnaire.pdf

Beukelman, D., Fager, S., & Nordness, A. (2011). Communication support for people with ALS. *Neurology Research International, 2011,* 1–6. https://doi.org/10.1155/2011/714693

Beukelman, D. R., Garrett, K. L., & Yorkston, K. M. (Eds.). (2007). *Augmentative communication strategies for adults with acute or chronic medical conditions.* Paul H. Brookes Publishing.

Bloch, S. (2011). Anticipatory other-completion of augmentative and alternative communication talk: a conversation analysis study, *Disability and Rehabilitation, 33*(3), 261–269. https://doi.org/10.3109/09638288.2010.491574

Cedarbaum, J. M., Stambler, N., Malta, E., Fuller, C., Hilt, D., Thurmond, B., & Nakanishi, A. (1999). The ALSFRS-R: A revised ALS functional rating scale that incorporates assessments of respiratory function. *Journal of the Neurological Sciences, 169,* 13–21.

DeRuyter, F. (2004). Speech pathologist's clinical pathway for communication changes with ALS. *ALS Clinical Pathways.* http://aac-rerc.psu.edu/index.php/files/list/type/1

Hurtig, R. R., & Downey, D. A. (2009). *Augmentative and alternative communication in acute and critical care settings.* Plural Publishing.

Judge, S., Bloch, S., & McDermott, C. J. (2018). Communication change in ALS: Engaging people living with ALS and their partners in future research. *Disability and Rehabilitation: Assistive Technology, 14*(7), 675–681. https://doi.org/10.1080/17483107.2018.1498924

Light, J., & McNaughton, D. (2015). Designing AAC research and intervention to improve outcomes for individuals with complex communication needs. *Augmentative and Alternative Communication, 31*(2), 85–96. https://doi.org/10.3109/07434618.2015.1036458

Makkonen, T, Ruottinen, H., Puhto, R., Helminen, M., & Palmio, J. (2018). Speech deterioration in amyotrophic lateral sclerosis (ALS) after manifestation of bulbar symptoms. *International Journal of Language and Communication Disorders, 53*(2), 385–392. https://doi.org/10.1111/1460-6984.12357

Oosthuizen, I., Dada, S., Bornman, J., & Koul, R. (2018). Message banking: Perceptions of persons with motor neuron disease, significant others and clinicians. *International Journal of Speech-Language Pathology, 20,* 756–765. https://doi.org/10.1080.17549507.2017.1356377

Yorkston, K. M., Miller, R. M., Strand, E. A., & Britton, D. (2013). *Management of speech and swallowing disorders in degenerative diseases* (3rd ed.). Pro-Ed.

Yunusova, Y., Graham, N. L., Shellikeri, S., Phuong, K., Kulkarni, M., Rochon, E., . . . Green, J. R. (2016). Profiling speech and pausing in amyotrophic lateral sclerosis (ALS) and frontotemporal dementia (FTD). *PLoS ONE, 11*(1), Article e01475373. https://doi.org/10.1371/journal.pone.01475373

AUTISM
CASE 45
George: An Autistic Adult Without Intellectual Disability: Language and Communication Challenges at Work
Diane L. Williams

Conceptual Knowledge Areas

DSM-5 Diagnostic Criteria for Autism Spectrum Disorders

According to the *Diagnostic and Statistical Manual of Mental Disorders* of the American Psychiatric Association (APA, 2013), to meet the requirements for a diagnosis of autism, an individual must have a deficit in social communication and interaction and demonstrate restricted, repetitive behaviors that interfere with daily functioning. Individuals who meet the diagnostic criteria for autism are then characterized by the level of support needed to meet the demands of daily living. The three levels of support are (1) Level 1: Requiring Support, (2) Level 2: Requiring Substantial Support, and (3) Level 3: Requiring Very Substantial Support.

Complex Information Processing Model of Autism

The complex information processing model of autism is based on the results from a neuropsychological study of adults on the autism spectrum (Minshew et al., 1997) and supported by additional studies with children on the autism spectrum (Williams et al., 2006) and a second sample of adults on the autism spectrum (Williams et al., 2015). This conceptualization of autism is derived from models of information processing. According to this model, individuals on the autism spectrum perform simple information processing tasks across the cognitive domains at or above the level of age-matched comparison groups but have more difficulty with tasks as the processing demands increase. "Complex" refers to the processing demands of the task. Large amounts of information, unorganized information, information that requires integration across domains, information that must be processed quickly, information that must be processed parallel to other information, and information that must be processed when the individual is stressed or anxious are all examples of complex processing. Decreasing performance with increasing complexity is not unique to individuals on the autism spectrum; however, these individuals show challenges at lower levels of complexity than expected relative to age and general ability level. The selective challenges in higher-order cognitive functions mean that individuals on the autism spectrum must accomplish tasks using lower-order abilities, resulting in inefficiencies of learning and the oddities of performance associated with the autism spectrum.

Pragmatic Language (Formation of Gist, Conversational Turn-Taking, Topic Maintenance, Topic Shifting)

Pragmatic language refers to the functional use of language, especially for conversation and discourse. This is an area of language that is particularly affected in individuals on the autism spectrum even if they are very verbal. For example, an individual who is not on the autism spectrum who wants to tell someone else about a personal experience or a movie may form a gist of the event or the story, telling only the information needed for the other person to understand what happened. Individuals on the autism spectrum may fail to do this. Instead, they tell all the details of the event or story. Individuals on the autism spectrum may monopolize the conversation and not take turns during conversation, may stay on one topic too long, or jump from topic to topic, making it difficult for listeners to interact with them.

Generalization

Generalization is the cognitive process by which information learned in response to stimuli in one context is transferred and used in a new context. Individuals on the autism spectrum may have a great deal of difficulty with generalization. This seems to occur because during the learning process, the information is strongly connected to both the stimuli that elicit the responses and to the context in which the information is learned.

Emotion Regulation

Emotion regulation is the ability to control emotional responses so that they (1) are appropriate to the situation and (2) do not interfere with performance or learning. The ability to regulate emotions is a developmental skill. Older children and adults continue to experience strong emotions but use their information processing skills so that their responses are measured in consideration of the social situation. Individuals on the autism spectrum may have pronounced difficulty with emotion regulation even when they have cognitive intelligence that is average or above. They may have age-inappropriate "meltdowns" that interfere with their performance in academic and employment settings.

Supported Employment

Some individuals on the autism spectrum require assistance to learn job tasks and/or to learn the behaviors that are required in a work setting. Supported employment is employment in an actual work setting but with the assistance of a job coach or counselor who helps the individual learn to perform the tasks essential to successful job performance. The job coach or counselor may break down the steps of the job tasks to make them more explicit and easier for the individual to learn. The job coach or counselor may also work with the individual on the social skills required to keep the job such as how to interact appropriately with supervisors and fellow employees.

Vocational Rehabilitation Services

Vocational Rehabilitation Services, commonly known as OVR or the Office of Vocational Rehabilitation Services, is a state-run agency that provides assessment, funding for job training, and assistance with employment for individuals who need additional support but have the potential to work independently. OVR was created by a mandate from the federal government but receives a combination of state and federal funding and is administered at the state level. Individuals who are 18 years old or older who have documented needs for support are potentially eligible for services. Eligibility is usually determined following a comprehensive evaluation that includes psychological testing to ascertain general functioning level. OVR works with community educational programs (such as colleges and vocational training programs) and job assistance programs (such as the Work for Life program described in the case of George) to provide for the needs of their clients.

Description of the Case

George W. was a 26-year-old male diagnosed on the autism spectrum. His Full-Scale IQ was above 70 so he does not have an intellectual disability.

George lived with his parents, Ed and Marjorie W. He had been employed at several part-time jobs in the past. His most recent job was as a stock clerk at a large discount department store. George was laid off from that job about 3 months prior to the evaluation.

Background Information

Early Development/Diagnosis

George's parents had been concerned about his development since before he was 3 years of age. He did not talk until he was almost 2.5 years old. When he began to talk, George spoke in full sentences. However, these sentences were primarily imitations of the speech of his mother and father or phrases from television. As a young child, George had some behaviors that his parents had difficulty managing. He had frequent tantrums. Mrs. W. reported that she was never sure what triggered the tantrums. George also spent time turning light switches on and off or opening and closing doors. Mrs. W. said that George would spend hours lining up blocks and toy vehicles. Mr. and Mrs. W. did not have any other children and neither had been around young children very much, so, at the time, they did not think these behaviors were unusual.

From an early age, George had remarkable memory abilities. He could recite children's books word for word after only one hearing. In fact, he would become extremely upset if his mother changed even one word of a book when reading it to him. At first, Mr. and Mrs. W. thought George was precocious because he was reading before the age of 4. However, something about his reading struck them as odd. George seemed to get more pleasure from saying the words in the books over and over to himself than from reading to or with someone.

When George entered preschool at age 4 years, his teacher became concerned that he did not join in with the other children, preferring to play by himself. George spent large amounts of time picking up sand from the sandbox and watching it as it fell slowly from his hand. At other times, he would start squealing and run wildly around the playground. George was attracted to anything with a string and would flick the string back and forth while intently examining it. The teacher noticed that, although George seemed to know a lot, he had difficulty answering her questions and she could not engage him in conversation. George would focus on a subject of his own interest; for example, he would talk at length about different types of rocks. He continued to have frequent tantrums.

The teacher suggested that George's parents have him evaluated. George was seen at age 4 years, 8 months at the Child Development Unit of Children's Hospital by a developmental pediatrician, who completed the Childhood Autism Rating Scale (CARS; Schopler et al., 1980). Based on the responses of his mother and father, George received a score of 34 (scores less than 30 are not consistent with autism and scores of 36 or greater indicate severe autism). The doctor diagnosed George with autism and referred him for a neuropsychological evaluation. The neuropsychological evaluation indicated that George's overall cognitive functioning was in the low-average range. He was advanced in his ability to decode written words. George had the first of many speech-language evaluations. He received a standard score of 77 in Auditory Comprehension and a standard score of 83 in Verbal Ability on the Preschool Language Scale-3 (PLS; Zimmerman et al., 1992). He received a standard score of 103 on the Peabody Picture Vocabulary Test–Revised (PPVT-III; Dunn & Dunn, 1997), which measured his understanding of the meanings of single words. George was referred to his local school district for special education services.

Elementary School

At the age of 5 years, George was enrolled in a kindergarten program for children who required additional support. He received speech therapy once weekly for 50 minutes in a small group with three other children. The therapy focused mainly on following directions and answering questions. As he progressed in school, George continued to be enrolled in a special education classroom and to receive speech therapy once weekly. Beginning in fourth grade, he continued to be taught his academic subjects in the special education classroom but attended general classes for music, art, and physical education. George continued to demonstrate behaviors that his teachers had difficulty managing. He would rock his body back and forth and flick papers with his right hand while flapping his left hand. If George had difficulty with a task, he would begin to scream and would sometimes throw himself onto the floor.

Middle School and High School

By seventh grade, George's parents became concerned that he was not being challenged enough academically. Therefore, at that year's Individualized Education Plan (IEP) meeting, they pressed for George to be placed in general math, science, and social studies classes. George would continue to receive reading and English in a resource room with other students with learning differences. George's interfering behaviors were reduced, but he continued to have occasional angry outbursts when he became frustrated. Because George's behaviors could be disruptive, a teaching assistant was assigned to the regular education classes that George attended. This general plan continued through high school. As George matured, he managed more of his behaviors in public. He kept a wad of string in his pocket, playing with it to help manage his anxiety. George's rocking and hand flapping decreased significantly. Emotional outbursts or "meltdowns" were much less frequent.

George had a comprehensive speech-language evaluation at age 15. The results of the Clinical Evaluation of Language Fundamentals-4 (CELF-4; Semel et al., 2003) indicated that George had slight weaknesses in following directions, explaining the relationships between associated words, and formulating sentences when given three targeted words. He had relative strengths in vocabulary and syntax. A conversational speech sample revealed that he could hold a conversation on a topic that he initiated for at least 2 minutes. However, George's turns took up significantly more time than those of his conversational partner, and he had difficulty with shifting topic. George did not change what he was saying in response to information provided by his communication partner.

Prior to the beginning of his senior year in high school, George was seen for a comprehensive assessment by a psychologist from the local Office of Vocational Rehabilitation Services. The results of that assessment indicated that George had a Verbal IQ of 85, a Performance IQ of 106, and a Full-Scale IQ of 95. George was described as being a visual learner, and it was suggested that he go to the local community college to study a visually based field such as computer programming.

George continued to receive speech therapy during high school in a small group once weekly. He practiced social communication skills, including conversational turn-taking and social forms such as ordering food in a restaurant and placing phone calls. George graduated from high school at 18 years of age. He finished with a 2.2 (out of 4.0) grade point average. His reading and writing skills were at an eighth-grade level.

Postsecondary Education

After high school, George enrolled in classes at the community college. He struggled with the coursework. Tutoring was available at a center on campus, but George did not go. He failed to pass his English and history classes and received a grade of D in his math and computer classes. When it was time for the next semester to begin, George refused to attend class and became upset any time his parents mentioned college.

Work History

Through a friend of the family, his parents helped George get a job at a local pizza restaurant. George worked there 10 hours a week, helping with setup for the dinner shift. He rolled silverware sets into napkins and put paper placemats on the tables. One afternoon, a first-grade class on a field trip was eating at the restaurant. They were in the room that George used to roll the silverware sets. George became increasingly agitated at the noises the children were making. He knocked over the silverware tray and, when he tried to leave the room, he used such force that he pulled the knob off the door. This greatly upset the children, and the manager fired George.

George was unemployed for several months. Then his former resource room teacher called. She had a friend, Mr. D., who was the manager at a local discount department store. Mr. D. was interested in hiring employees who might need additional support. George began working at the store 15 to 20 hours a week. He stocked the shelves, did daily cleaning (sweeping the aisles, cleaning up spills), and gathered the shopping carts from the parking lot. Mr. D. worked patiently with George until he could perform these tasks proficiently. George worked at the store for 3 years. Then Mr. D. was promoted and moved to a new location. After the new manager came, George began to exhibit more agitation and had occasional outbursts. One day, he could not get a shopping cart to fit in the long line of carts he was gathering from the parking lot. George became upset and pushed the cart really hard, hitting a parked car and causing considerable damage. George was let go from his job.

George sat at home for 3 months while his parents tried to figure out what to do. Mrs. W. finally called the local autism support group, and they referred her to the Work for Life program.

Reasons for the Referral

George is currently a client at Work for Life, an agency that provides evaluations and supported employment services to adults with developmental disabilities. George has had difficulty in his past jobs related to his problems with social communication and emotional regulation. The case manager requested an evaluation of George's language skills to provide suggestions to the support team that would be working with him.

Proposed Vocational Placement

Following occupational and interest evaluations performed by the support team at Work for Life, and with input from George and his parents, a vocational training plan was developed. It was decided that George needed a work environment that (1) limited his contact with the public to struc-

tured interactions, (2) provided supervision by a caring and supportive manager, (3) included tasks in which he had a high degree of interest and knowledge, and (4) allowed him to use skills that he had been successful in using in previous jobs.

Since childhood, George has had a persistent interest in rocks and other areas of geology. He knows the names of all the rocks that are native to the area where he lives and is expert at identifying them and relating relevant facts about the rocks. George reported that one task he enjoyed from his previous job was cleaning and putting stock in order.

George's support team arranged for him to get a part-time job at a state park not far from his home. George's duties would include cleaning up and removing trash and clearing overgrown walking trails. He would also help to clean and maintain the displays of geological items and wildlife at the park's education center. The director of the education center planned to work with George on giving short presentations about the rocks and other geological formations that could be found at the state park.

The questions for the speech-language pathologist were: (1) Does George currently have the language/communication skills to be successful in the proposed job placement? (2) If not, what skills would George need to develop? (3) What form of intervention would be most appropriate for the development of these skills?

Planning the Evaluation

The first decision to be made in planning the evaluation was what form it should take. George had had a number of evaluations throughout his life. He had already been diagnosed with autism without intellectual disability and had the characteristic language problems associated with that disorder. Therefore, the questions to be answered by an evaluation of George's language skills were more specific. The primary need was to determine whether George had the language and communication skills to be successful in the proposed job placement. In addition, George had significant problems in the *social* use of language and communication or *pragmatic language*, an area that a formal assessment measure might not detect. Therefore, a *functional or ecologically based assessment* appeared to be most appropriate. However, a second consideration was for the evaluation to fulfill the agency requirements of documenting the need for speech and language therapy services. The agency required that all individuals have a formal test measure as the basis for this determination. Therefore, the evaluation needed to include at least one formal measure of language. George's evaluation would be a combination of (1) an ecologically based assessment related to the proposed job placement and (2) a formal test measure to fulfill the agency requirements of documentation of the need for services.

Findings of the Evaluation

Ecologically Based Assessment

An ecologically based assessment is focused on the environments in which the individual needs to communicate to determine the specific demands of those environments. An inventory of the individual's communication skills is also made. The communication demands and the communication skills are then compared to determine what skills need to be developed. The intervention plan targets those skills. Ecological assessments typically include the elements of (1) interviewing parents and other key individuals who can provide information about the demands of the environments and the individual's current skills and (2) observing the individual in the relevant environments (Elksnin & Elksnin, 2001).

Interview With the Parents

The parents knew not only George's history but were also George's primary communication partners. They reported that George did well in interacting with others when he had a clear understanding of what was expected of him. They had successfully taught him a few basic social scripts such as asking people how their days were going. They thought that George would have difficulty telling visitors to the Education Center about the items in the display cases. They were afraid that he would talk about what he was interested in rather than what the visitor was interested in. They were concerned that George would talk on and on about an item and that his listeners would become impatient with him.

Interview With Past Employer

After securing permission from George, Mr. D., the manager at the department store where George previously worked, was interviewed. He provided information about the challenges George encountered with language and social communication in a work setting. Also, because he had trained George, Mr. D had insight into what learning strategies worked with George. Mr. D. said that whenever George learned a new task, the task needed to be broken down into small, explicit steps. George seemed to remember the steps better if each was given a short verbal description and that verbal description was used repeatedly (First you look at the barcode on the package. Then you find the barcode on the shelf. Then you put the package on the shelf by that barcode.). Mr. D. said that George did better when he worked in an area by himself and did especially well at remembering the order of the tasks to be done during a shift if he was given some choice of how to arrange his schedule.

Interview With George

George was shown several rock samples and asked to explain the names of the rocks, how they were formed, and what they could be used for. George picked up a piece of granite and talked for 2 minutes without stopping. He did not use the provided organizational structure. When he was asked a question, George answered but then returned to his list of facts about the rock.

Observations

The speech-language pathologist accompanied George and his job coach on an initial visit to the state park where he was scheduled to work. While George shadowed one of the park maintenance workers, the speech-language pathologist made observations to determine the communication demands of the environment and what skills George had. These observations indicated that George needed to develop language and communication skills to (1) interact with supervisors and coworkers regarding work assignments and to ask for assistance with unfamiliar tasks, (2) use language to talk himself through unfamiliar tasks, and (3) answer basic informational questions from park visitors.

Formal Assessments

A challenge in planning a speech-language evaluation for adults on the autism spectrum is the lack of standardized test instruments to use with this population. Many of the test instruments created for developmental language disorders only provide norms to the age of 21 years. Most of the language tests that are available for older adults were constructed for adults with acquired language disorders such as those resulting from a traumatic brain injury (TBI) or a cerebral vascular accident (CVA). Therefore, if the use of a standardized test is important, a speech-language pathologist has to decide whether to use an instrument that is slightly out of age range (using the norms for the oldest age group) or whether to restrict choices to the limited number of language areas, such as expressive and receptive vocabulary, for

which age-appropriate normed tests are available. In George's case, the Test of Adolescent and Adult Language (TOAL-4; Hammill et al., 2007) was administered. The TOAL-4 has norms to age 24 years, 11 months. George was age 26 years at the time the test was administered. When the scores were reported, it was noted that the norms for the oldest age groups were used. George's performance on this test is shown in Table 45–1.

Based on a mean of 100 and a standard deviation of 15, George's score of 75 for Written Language and his score of 85 for Spoken Language indicate that he had weaknesses with reading and writing, with more strength in spoken language.

Treatment Options Considered

Individual Speech-Language Therapy

In individual sessions, George could be explicitly taught about communication interactions with his supervisors, coworkers, and park visitors. He could also be taught scripts to use when teaching park visitors about items displayed in the Education Center.

- ■ *Advantages:* George's attention could be focused on the skills that the speech-language pathologist wanted to address

Table 45–1. Results of the TOAL-4

Subtest	Standard Score[a]	Percentile	Interpretation
Spoken Language	85	16	Average
Word Opposites	7	16	Average
Word Derivations	11	63	Average
Spoken Analogies	6	9	Below average
Written Language	75	5	Below average
Word Similarities	6	9	Below average
Sentence Combining	5	5	Below average
Orthographic Usage	5	5	Below average
General Language	80	9	Below average

[a]Scores are based on a mean of 10 and a standard deviation of 3.

without the distractions present in an actual work environment. The cognitive processing load could be more carefully managed in a one-to-one session than during teaching that is embedded in the actual work environment. George might be more willing to try skills that he had not mastered if he did not have other people watching him.

- *Disadvantages:* Like other individuals on the autism spectrum without intellectual disability, George had difficulty with *generalizing* knowledge learned in one setting to a different one. Even if he performed the desired language/social skill during the one-to-one session, George might not generalize this skill to the actual work environment. Social communication cannot be adequately addressed in a session in which the only communication partner is the therapist. Other models of service delivery are more effective for addressing functional outcomes and training of communication partners. Because of these limitations, if used, individual, one-to-one sessions should be directly related to functional outcomes and used on a limited basis for the development of skills that are then quickly translated and established in an actual work environment (American Speech-Language-Hearing Association [ASHA], 2016).

Social Communication Group

Another option considered for George was group therapy in the form of a social skills group or social "club" (Ke et al., 2018). In this approach, the speech-language pathologist plans each session around preset topics related to social communication challenges. Topics may include general social problems such as meeting new people, being different, or dealing with stress. The speech-language pathologist may also design the program around topics that relate to the specific needs of the participants. Sessions usually include modeling of appropriate behavior and feedback

to the participants about the effectiveness of their communication.

- *Advantages:* Interactive behaviors can be targeted because multiple communication partners are available. Under the guidance of the speech-language pathologist, group members can serve as models for one another.
- *Disadvantages:* George may spend time on topics that are not directly relevant to him if the needs and skill levels of other participants are different from his own. Other individuals with social communication problems may be inadequate models. George may not generalize what he learns in the social communication group to his work setting.

Ecological Treatment

Ecological treatment, or treatment within the context where the skills will be used, has been demonstrated to be beneficial for the development of the social communication skills of individuals on the autism spectrum (National Research Council, 2001).

- *Advantages:* Treatment can focus directly on the skills needed for particular language and social communication tasks. George will not need to generalize the skills learned in one setting to another setting. The skills and strategies will be made explicit to him during the treatment process.
- *Disadvantages:* Treatment within the work setting is time-consuming for the professionals involved. The speech-language pathologist would need to travel to the work setting and spend time with George and his communication partners. Different types of tasks require different language and communication demands. Intervention would need to address the skills required for each of these tasks rather than on social

communication skills in general. Development of the scripts for George's educational talks might be more difficult within the work setting than during a one-on-one session.

Peer Modeling

Peer modeling is a strategy that may be used as part of an ecological treatment approach. Peer modeling or mediation has been used successfully with children on the autism spectrum to develop social communication skills (Bellini et al., 2014). George's peers were fellow employees in the work setting. Peers would receive instruction so that they knew what was expected of them and what they were trying to help George do. An example of a strategy that a peer might model is to say aloud what he is thinking while doing the task. George would then use this language to talk himself through the task. This language would help George to structure the task and provide cues so that he could perform the task independently. Peers could also serve as models for social communication with each other and with park visitors.

- *Advantages:* The peers are available to provide guidance on an ongoing basis until the skills become well established. The peers may have an insight into the language needed to do a task that is not obvious to others.
- *Disadvantages:* The availability of an appropriate peer model depends on who else is employed at the work setting. These peers may also have limitations in language and social communication, making them inadequate models for George.

Course of Treatment

Training of the Supported Employment Trainer

As he began his new job placement at the state park, George would be assisted by a job coach from Work for Life. This individual would work with him for at least the first 3 months of his placement. Although this individual had a degree in rehabilitation, he might not have experience in working with an individual on the autism spectrum in general and in working with George specifically. George's speech-language pathologist would provide preservice and continuing education to this person (ASHA, 2016). This training would include background information about autism, the language and social communication challenges encountered by individuals on the autism spectrum, and specific information about George's abilities and the skills needed to support George so that he is successful in his job. The speech-language pathologist would work with the job coach to develop the teaching strategies to be used with George as he learned about the environment and duties of his new job.

Training of the Job Supervisor

The job supervisor was given background information about autism and specific information about George's abilities. The supervisor received advice on an ongoing basis as particular situations arose. The job coach, the speech-language pathologist, and job supervisor also developed a plan to help George use his language to manage when he experienced emotional dysregulation.

Environmental Adaptations

Visual schedules have been shown to be effective for individuals on the autism spectrum of a variety of skill levels (Bryan & Gast, 2000). Because George had literacy skills, his weekly and daily schedule could be provided in written form rather than with pictures. The weekly schedule let him know what days and times he was to report for work. The daily schedule informed him of the specific tasks to do during each work day. When possible, the daily schedule was arranged by time of day so that George knew which tasks to do in a particular time period. George was given the tasks that needed to be completed that day and could choose the order in which they would be addressed (Watanabe & Sturmey, 2003).

Training of the Client

Skills to be developed with George were language and social communication for work-related interactions with his supervisors, social chit-chat with coworkers, and interactions with park visitors. He needed to learn scripts to structure his work and complete tasks. Peer modeling was used as previously described for language and communication that was needed when completing tasks and interacting with supervisors and coworkers.

George worked with the speech-language pathologist to develop written scripts for use when explaining the displays in the Education Center. Written scripts have been shown to be an effective teaching strategy to use with individuals on the autism spectrum (Charlop-Christy & Kelso, 2003). During the development of these scripts, George needed to be guided so that he (1) focused on what was the important or salient information that his listeners needed to know, and (2) expressed the information using appropriate pragmatic skills.

To reduce inappropriate behaviors, George was taught socially appropriate ways to communicate frustration. Social stories were developed for this purpose. This technique is effective in reducing inappropriate behaviors such as tantrums in individuals on the autism spectrum (Samuels & Stansfield, 2012).

Although this technique was not used with George, video modeling has been used successfully with adults and children on the autism spectrum to teach a variety of different skills (Bellini et al., 2014). For this technique, a 1- to 3-minute video is made of a peer or the individual on the autism spectrum demonstrating the target behavior. The video is then used to teach the skill through repeated guided viewing and then practicing the behavior.

Analysis of the Client's Response to Treatment

George's response to treatment will not be measured by formal assessment instruments. Rather, his response to treatment will be measured by how successful he is in his job placement. If George per-

forms well and not only is able to retain his job but also becomes a valuable employee, this will indicate that he has the language and social communication skills necessary for that job. However, if George experiences difficulty with completion of his tasks or interactions with his supervisor, coworkers, and/or park visitors, this will suggest that the impact of his difficulties with language and social communication on his job performance need to be further assessed and additional supports will need to be planned and implemented.

Further Recommendations

If the job supervisor changes, the new supervisor will need to be trained. The job supervisor needs a consistent person to contact if changes occur in either the demands of the job or in George's needs. George's parents need to remain vigilant for any signs that George is having difficulty at work. These signs might include changes in George's behavior such as increased anxiety as the time to go to work approaches, increases in verbalizations that are not directed to anyone, increase in pacing, sudden outbursts of anger, and other difficulty with emotional regulation.

Author's Note

George W. is a fictional person who represents a compilation of several adults on the autism spectrum and the persons in their support networks that the author has provided services to during her clinical career.

References

American Psychiatric Association. (2013). *Diagnostic and statistical manual of mental disorders* (5th ed.). https://doi.org/10.1176/appi.books.9780890425596
American Speech-Language-Hearing Association. (2016). *Scope of practice in speech-language pathology* [Scope of practice]. https://www.asha.org/policy/

Bellini, S., Gardner, L., & Markoff, K. (2014). Social skills interventions. In F. R. Volkmar, S. J. Rogers, R. Paul, & K. A. Pelphrey (Eds.), *Handbook of autism and pervasive developmental disorders: Vol. 2. Assessment, interventions, and policy* (4th ed., pp. 887–906). John Wiley & Sons.

Bryan, L. C., & Gast, D. L. (2000). Teaching on-task and on-schedule behaviors to higher functioning children with autism via picture activity schedules. *Journal of Autism and Developmental Disorders, 30*, 553–567.

Charlop-Christy, M. H., & Kelso, S. E. (2003). Teaching children with autism conversational speech using a cue card/written script program. *Education and Treatment of Children, 26*, 103–127.

Dunn, L. M., & Dunn, L. M. (1997). *Peabody Picture Vocabulary Test–III.* American Guidance Service.

Elksnin, N., & Elksnin, L. (2001). Adolescents with disabilities: The need for occupational social skills training. *Exceptionality, 9*, 91–105. https://doi.org/10.1080/09362835.2001.9666993

Hammill, D. D., Brown, V. L., Larsen, S. C., & Wiederholt, J. L. (2007). *Test of Adolescent and Adult Language* (4th ed.). Pro-Ed.

Ke, F., Whalon, K., & Yun, J. (2018). Social skill interventions for youth and adults with autism spectrum disorder: A systematic review. *Review of Educational Research, 88*(1), 3–42. https://doi.org/10.3102/0034654317740334

Minshew, N. J., Goldstein, G., & Siegel, D. J. (1997). Neuropsychologic functioning in autism: Profile of a complex information processing disorder. *Journal of the International Neuropsychological Society, 3*, 303–316. https://doi.org/10.1017/S1355617797003032

National Research Council. (2001). *Educating children with autism.* National Academy Press, Committee on Educational Interventions for Children with Autism, Division of Behavioral and Social Sciences and Education.

Samuels, R., & Stansfield, J. (2012). The effectiveness of Social Stories™ to develop social interactions with adults with characteristics of autism spectrum disorder. *British Journal of Learning Disabilities, 40*(4), 272–285. https://doi.org/10.1111/j.1468-3156.2011.00706.x

Schopler, E., Reichler, R. J., DeVellis, R. F., & Daly, K. (1980). Toward objective classification of childhood autism: Childhood Autism Rating Scale (CARS). *Journal of Autism and Developmental Disorders, 10*, 91–103. https://doi.org/10.1007/BF02408436

Semel, E. M., Wiig, E. H., & Secord W. (2003). *Clinical Evaluation of Language Fundamentals-4 (CELF-4).* Psychological Corporation.

Watanabe, M., & Sturmey, P. (2003). The effect of choice-making opportunities during activity schedules on task engagement of adults with autism. *Journal of Autism and Developmental Disorders, 33*, 535–538.

Williams, D. L., Goldstein G., & Minshew, N. J. (2006). Neuropsychologic functioning in children with autism: Further evidence of disordered complex information processing. *Child Neuropsychology, 12*, 279–298. https://doi.org/10.1080/09297040600681190

Williams, D. L., Minshew, N. J., & Goldstein, G. (2015). Further understanding of complex information processing in verbal adolescents and adults with autism spectrum disorders. *Autism, 19*(7), 859–867. https://doi.org/10.1177/1362361315586171

Zimmerman, I., Steiner, V., & Pond, R. (1992). *Preschool Language Scale-3* (3rd ed.). The Psychological Corporation.

BILINGUAL/ACCENT

CASE 46

Dr. JN: An Adult Nonnative Speaker of English: High Proficiency

Amee P. Shah

Conceptual Knowledge Areas

Census 2021 indicates that the immigration number is now 84.8 million in the United States, almost three times the growth in 15 years since the first publication of this book. With such a large proportion of nonnative speakers of English in the total population, speech-language pathologists (SLPs) are often consulted for intelligibility and accent issues due to foreign (and regional) accents. Recognizing this need, ASHA's 1983 and 1985 position papers have included communication problems related to dialects and accents in the scope of SLP practice. Thus, a majority of graduate programs in the country now address accent modification in the clinical services and academic training of graduate students. Surveys of accredited programs (Schmidt & Sullivan, 2003; Shah, 2005) have revealed several areas of need, including inadequate preparation in accent modification of students, limited coursework focusing on cross-language issues, and a dearth of efficacy-based accent modification clinical practices. Shah (2005) concluded that the absence of normative assessment tools and clinical programs forced clinicians to combine subtests from diverse tests, find and use less-known or obscure tools, and devise their own training procedures. From as early as 2005, this author has been advocating for evidence-based accent services that would help address the gaps and provide consistency in serving clients with their accent needs (Shah, 2005, 2010a, 2010b, 2011). Accent modification needs to be grounded in theory and research, thus fostering an efficacy-

based effort (also called *evidence based*). Further, in light of increased awareness in being culturally responsive and socially just, Shah (2016, 2019) has advocated for a departure from traditional notions of accent modification to a more comprehensive approach that involves accent management that goes beyond the speaker and works on transforming the environment, including listeners. A recent systematic review of accent trainings (Gu & Shah, 2019) showed the gaps and inconsistencies that are present in published accounts of accent modification, intervention, or management. The case studies in this chapter and the next one are offered as a means to help fill some of those gaps.

This case presents a high-proficiency client as a successful model of systematic, evidence-based practice from interview to intervention. Specifically, the ideas and evidence obtained from research conducted in fields such as psychology, sociolinguistics, and speech perception were adapted and applied to various aspects of accent management practice. Specific areas of clinical practice described include initial case history and interview, assessment as guided by quantitative analyses, and therapy as planned using structured, systematic principles.

Background Information

The Communicating for Impact program (Shah, 2010a) was designed to cater to the highly specialized communication needs of international physicians and scientists at the Cleveland Clinic. Based on experience with a large cohort of such physicians and scientists who had been referred for therapy over the course of the last year, this author was able to design and successfully implement such a program. Specifically, as high-proficiency (or advanced) speakers of English, this particular client group's communication needs are subtle and advanced.[1] Thus, this program consisted of specialized goals and methods to specifically meet the language needs and cognitive styles of such physicians and scientists. In particular, the *goals* addressed advanced skills such as professional vocabulary, language rhythm (suprasegmental features), advanced grammar, and subtle pragmatic differences that may have impeded socialization and acculturation and thus, indirectly, affected perceived spoken intelligibility. This program helped address these goals in *methods* that would appeal to the cognitive and learning styles of an analytic, knowledgeable, learned, technologically savvy group of professionals. The program used acoustic software that provided audio and visual cues of the clients' speech on computers. The clinician guided the clients to edit and change speech patterns with such audio and visual feedback. Extensive use of clients' recorded samples was used in training, as well as in pre- and posttraining comparisons. The structure of the program was established as more of an equal partnership with the clients, wherein they were consulted and informed at every juncture of the process. Thus, after the initial interview and assessment, they were given a detailed summary of their communication deficits and, together with the clinician, planned therapy priorities. They maintained the diagnostic profile report and referred to it at periodic junctures to monitor their own progress and work on goals at home.

Description of the Case

Background Information

Dr. JN, a 38-year-old Asian (Japanese) female anesthesiologist working at the Cleveland Clinic, was referred by her supervisor to the Communicating for Impact program offered by the Office of Diversity at the clinic. The area of primary concern for the referring superior was that Dr. JN was very difficult to understand as she had a strong foreign accent that interfered with her communication with her patients as well as the hospital personnel.

Reasons for Referral

Based on the Language Background Questionnaire that is part of the Comprehensive Assessment of Accentedness and Intelligibility (CAAI; Shah, 2007), *language history* is as follows: Dr. JN was born and raised in Tokyo, Japan, and spoke Japanese as her primary and native language. In addition, she spoke English and had partial knowledge of French. Her self-rated proficiency in Japanese was "strong" in all language areas, including reading, writing, and speaking. She rated her English proficiency as "average" for speaking and "good" for reading and writing, respectively. Her self-rated proficiency for French was "low" in all areas of speaking, reading, and writing. She reported using English and Japanese with nearly equal frequency in the course of her week: English at work and Japanese at home, in her local neighborhood, and among friends. She considered Japanese to be her strongest language and continued to prefer using it over English or French. Dr. JN's age of language learning (AOL) for English was 13 years, when she was formally taught English in her middle school in Japan exclusively by Japanese teachers who spoke English with a distinct Japanese accent. Dr. JN's age of arrival (AOA) in the United States was 24 years, and her length of residence (LOR) in the United States was 14 years. Dr. JN came to the United States to pursue her medical degree and completed 8 years of her medical education, leading to her present job as an anesthesiologist. Upon arrival, she had been enrolled in an English as Second Language (ESL) class through her university; she participated for one semester and received English instruction once a week for 2 hours for 16 weeks. Dr. JN's educational history included an MD and a postgraduate fellowship in anesthesiology. Her language needs at her work involved spending about 70% of her time conversing in English during active patient care (conversing with patients, their family, the hospital personnel, and colleagues) and about 30% of her time in activities such as giving presentations in conferences or in meetings with colleagues, collaborating on research, reading professional journals, writing journal articles in medical journals, and training residents. Thus, her English language skills were called upon in all areas of communication, including speaking, listening, reading, and writing. Her self-reported areas of concern with her communication abilities included primarily needing help with her strong foreign accent to be better understood. She expressed difficulty listening and attempting to understand other speakers of English. Her listening skills were reportedly good in casual conversation and watching television but markedly reduced with unfamiliar work and people. She needed help in acquiring and using more advanced vocabulary skills, especially professional terminology, idiomatic expressions, and slang. Goals involved being able to communicate more intelligibly with patients and colleagues, as well as during her presentations and meetings. She considered her grammar skills to be fairly good in English and did not seek any further direct intervention in speaking and writing.

Her self-perceived communication difficulties included her awareness that, while people appeared to be able to understand the gist of her message and a large number of her sentences, they had frequent trouble understanding single words in her sentences and often asked her to repeat individual words. As part of her awareness and attempts to circumvent her communication challenges, she tried to implement strategies, such as speaking slower, segmenting syllables, and planning the sentence grammar ahead of time as she spoke English. She commented that her communication difficulties had markedly improved after she increasingly attempted to "think in English." No other medical, social, or family history was reported as relevant to the nature of her communication difficulties.

Note: Factors such as AOL, AOA, and LOR were part of the interview questions, in keeping with the extensive research conducted by James Flege and colleagues (e.g., Flege, 1984) that describes how these variables can affect and shape second language learning and, ultimately, predict success in learning that second language.

Findings of the Evaluation

After the interview, the CAAI (Shah, 2007) was administered to determine Dr. JN's performance in various aspects of speech, language, and overall communicative abilities in English. The CAAI is *comprehensive* in that it targets a multitude of typical errors that pose communication difficulties for dialect and accented clients. Foreign accentedness and intelligibility issues span speech production, speech perception, and other language areas such as grammar, vocabulary, and nonverbal behavior. It is important to assess the range of area(s) that are implicated and determine which of those specifically interfere with the individual client's communication and integration into mainstream society. Consequently, this test addresses various levels of speech and nonspeech extralinguistic areas. This test distinguishes *articulatory* from *phonological errors* and *segmental errors* of consonants and vowels from *prosodic errors* that span varied lengths of spoken material from syllables and words to sentences and narratives. Auditory and perceptual discrimination abilities are tested in order to make judgments about the underlying causes of accented speakers' production errors, thereby helping to predict goals and target areas for intervention. The test also addresses *language performance* as measured by *grammatical, semantic,* and *pragmatic* differences.

Dr. JN completed 22 sections of the CAAI, which required activities such as reading aloud words, sentences, and/or paragraphs, answering questions, and role-playing dialogues. The 22 sections yield numeric data through the scores from each section, which can then be used to make pre- and posttherapy comparisons. In particular, the Diagnostic Profile (Table 46–1) provided with the Individual Scoring Form helps categorize the scores and enables the examiner to get a quick snapshot of areas of relative difficulty and thus arrive at the priority order of targeting them in later therapy/training.

Table 46-1. Diagnostic Profile for Dr. JN (From the CAAI)

Comprehensive Assessment of Accentedness & Intelligibility: Complete Diagnostic Report					
Amee P. Shah, Ph.D. Date: Client Name: Dr. J.N.					
SECTION TITLE	**Total Possible Score**	**90% Performance**	**70% Performance**	**50% Performance**	**Client's Score**
Degree of difficulty ⟶		Mild difficulty	Moderate	Strong difficulty	
SECTION 1: INTELLIGIBILITY RELATIVE TO ACCENTEDNESS e.g., "The committee was composed of ten members . . ."	1 to 5	2	3	4 or more	2.5
SECTION 2: INTELLIGIBILITY SCORE & RATE OF SPEECH ON NARRATIVE PASSAGE Stimulus: Rainbow Passage	100%	90%	70%	50%	89%, normal rate
SECTION 3: SENTENCE LEVEL INTONATION "I got promoted!"	10	9	7	5	7
SECTION 4: WORD LEVEL INTONATION e.g., ("Tuesday comes after Monday.") "Good!"	4	3.6	2.8	2	3
SECTION 5: LEXICAL STRESS IN SINGLE, MULTISYLLABIC WORDS e.g., "Repellent."	12	10.8	8.4	6	7
SECTION 6: DERIVATIVE STRESS IN MULTISYLLABIC WORDS e.g., "democracy/democratic"	24	21.6	16.8	12	15
SECTION 7: CONTRASTIVE LEXICAL STRESS e.g., "I have a birthday present for you."/present	28	25.2	19.6	14	17
SECTION 8: EMPHASIS e.g., ("Which one was it?") "I made the pumpkin pie."	12	10.8	8.4	6	10
SECTION 9: SENTENCE PHRASING e.g., "I need milk, eggs, and bread from the market."	7	6.3	4.9	3.5	7
SECTION 10: CONTRASTING SENTECE PAIRS e.g., "Ben would never leave Woody/would he?"	10	9	7	5	10
SECTION 11: CONSONANTS WORD LIST e.g., Initial position /p/ in "pan."	65	58.5	45.5	32.5	56
SECTION 12: CONSONANT CLUSTERS WORD LIST e.g., /r/ blend in "brush."	59	53.1	41.3	29.5	38
SECTION 13a: VOWEL WORD LIST e.g., /i/ in "meat."	18	16.2	12.6	9	12
SECTION 13b: VOWEL WORD LIST e.g., /æ/ in "packed."	22	19.8	15.4	11	13
SECTION 14: PHONOLOGICAL PROCESSES	13	11.7	9.1	6.5	4

continues

Table 46–1. *continued*

SECTION TITLE	Total Possible Score	90% Performance	70% Performance	50% Performance	Client's Score
SECTION 15: AUDITORY DISCRIMINATION	75	67.5	52.5	37.5	53
SECTION 16: PREPOSITIONS e.g., "I live _____ Ohio." (in)	20	18	14	10	13
SECTION 17: COLLOQUIAL/IDIOMATIC USE OF PREPOSITIONS e.g., Are we still on _____ tonight? (for)	8	7.2	5.6	4	6
SECTION 18: CONTRASTING IDIOMATIC PHRASES e.g., "hold on" vs. "hold out."	17	15.3	11.9	8.5	15
Secondary Cues: sentence fill-in (comprehension of phrases)	Secondary score: 8	7.2	5.6	4	n/a
SECTION 19: COMPREHENSION OF IDIOMATIC PHRASES "Don't be upset, he's only pulling your leg." (teasing)	12	10.8	8.4	6	10
SECTION 20: ADVANCED VOCABULARY Defining a word given four choices.	20	18	14	10	13
SECTION 21: CONVERSATIONAL GRAMMAR					
SECTION 22: PRAGMATIC PROBLEMS					

The interview and assessment session of the CAAI was audio-recorded and later analyzed and scored by two speech-language pathology students to ensure reliability in test scoring and analysis. Results of the analysis are as presented in Table 46–1, which consists of the diagnostic profile for Dr. JN. The table provides a quantitative estimate of the client's accent severity in each of the 22 sections, as well as an overall estimate of the baseline intelligibility and speaking rate.

Summary of Assessment Results

Based on the assessment findings, the client was found to typically exhibit a mild to moderate degree of difficulty in most areas. As Section 2 in the CAAI indicated, the client's rate of speech was normal and baseline intelligibility was only mildly affected (89%). The client had a distinct moderate accent that did not appear to affect conversational intelligibility (2.5 on a scale of 1–5) and was labeled as a "Mild-Moderate Foreign Accent."

Areas that were judged to be only mildly impaired and relatively low priority for further intervention included suprasegmental aspects such as sentence-level intonation, word emphasis, sentence phrasing, and contrasting sentence phrasing. Areas with moderate degree of impairment and high priority for intervention included word-level stress features (word-level intonation, lexical stress in multisyllabic words, derivative stress, and contrastive lexical stress). In addition, segmental properties were moderately affected and included errors on many consonants (/r/, /ɾ/, /l/, /pʰ/, /tʰ/, /kʰ/, /v/, /θ/, and /ð/), a marked number of clusters (predominantly /r/ blends and /l/ blends), and a variety of vowels (/ɪ/, /æ/, /ʊ/, /a/, /ɚ/, and /ʌ/). Four phonological processes were noted, including final /s/ or /z/ deletion, addition of intrusion schwa, vowel reduction, and de-aspiration of initial voiceless consonants.

Auditory discrimination abilities were found to be moderately implicated as well and included confusion between sounds such as (/r/-/l/, /v/-/b/,

/θ/-/ð/, /ð/-/d/, /θ/-/t/, /f/-/p/, /f/-/v/, /m/-/n/, /v/-/w/, /ɪ/-/ɛ/, /ɪ/-/e/, /ɔ/-/ʌ/). Other nonspeech aspects of language were affected to a moderate degree and consisted of errors with the colloquial use of prepositions, knowledge of idiomatic expressions, and technical/advanced vocabulary.

Therapy[2] Options Considered

Therapy goals were identified and an order of priority determined in the overall therapy hierarchy. This goal-setting was done on the basis of the baseline numeric scores and the strength of their deviation from the norm (mild, moderate, or strong), as seen on the diagnostic profile for the client (see Table 46–1). Areas that were either moderately or strongly impaired were considered to have the highest priority in treatment.

The following areas were selected, in the order in which they were addressed in therapy:

1. Production and discrimination of consonants
2. Production and discrimination of vowels
3. Phonological processes
4. Word-level stress, including contrastive stress
5. Understanding and appropriate use of prepositions
6. Understanding and appropriate use of everyday idiomatic expressions
7. Everyday conversational skills relevant to client's professional and social settings: addressing all of the preceding goals, with emphasis on overall prosody
8. Presentation skills focusing on technical vocabulary, overall language prosody (intonation, juncture, and pacing), and pragmatics

In determining the selection of these goals, their priority status, and their respective methods of intervention, several factors were considered along with the immediate results and scores of the assessment battery, including *client preference*, *experience*, and *need*. Moreover, in keeping with the client's professional needs, the area of improvement in presentation skills was addressed. The selected goals were incorporated in activities involving conversational role-play and making professional presentations (lectures).

The examiner also reviewed well-established knowledge/scientific evidence. For example, Strange and Dittmann (1984) have shown how Japanese speakers benefit from training on discrimination and production of /r/-/l/ sound contrasts. Learning accomplished through such training appears to be transferred outside the laboratory situation and maintained for longer periods even after the training is discontinued. As a result of such documented information, /r/-/l/ contrasts were selected for the client. Similarly, Derwing and Rossiter (2003) have shown the importance of suprasegmental aspects in the perceived improvement of nonnative speakers' intelligibility. Thus, therapy focused on language prosody skills, including various aspects of lexical stress, and overall sentence intonation through conversational role-plays. Segmentals were addressed before the prosodic goals as the former were relatively few, were easier to target, and provided good initial encouragement and reinforcement. After some preliminary practice and improvement with segmentals, prosody aspects were soon introduced in Dr. JN's therapy. Prosody aspects were targeted in a variety of ways, including conversations and presentation skills, and were continued long after segmental goals were discontinued.

The issue of accentedness has been treated here as a category distinct from intelligibility. Munro and Derwing (1995) have shown that the phenomena of perceived accentedness and intelligibility are related, yet distinct. Intelligibility refers to the actual process of decoding the message and is estimated by transcribing each utterance heard by listeners to arrive at the number of words understood. Perceived accentedness, on the other hand, is determined by conducting an accent rating task on a scale from "no foreign accent" to "strong foreign accent." Although clinical accent modification and ESL programs are typically geared toward addressing only those speech characteristics that affect intelligibility, these programs should instead test and address perceived accentedness as separate from intelligibility. Indeed, accented speech, even when free of intelligibility concerns, may be stigmatized and pose difficulties to speakers in their personal and professional communication. The CAAI was used to address and separate the methods for arriving at measures of perceived accentedness as distinct from and independent of performance on intelligibility. Sections 1 and 2 in the test help separate these two measures and, consequently, help separate therapy priorities for different clients. Thus, for some clients, the goal may be to improve intelligibility, whereas with others, therapy may need to address subtle aspects of speech to minimize the "foreignness."

A third factor considered in therapy was the clinician's *clinical experiences*. Clinical experience revealed intervention on segmentals to be a good starting point in therapy as it gives the client practice with listening to various sounds and identifying subtle differences. Targeting segmentals also allows clients opportunities to vary articulatory maneuvers on individual sounds (as opposed to the length of an entire sentence). Finally, segmentals allow clients to visually *see* the difference in their productions (e.g., on programs where sound waveforms are shown, clients can see the improvement in changing duration, intensity, stress on specific syllables, aspiration for voiceless stops, pause and juncture across syllable and word boundaries, and overall word or sentence contour). A multimodality approach was followed because it was found to yield maximum and relatively fast improvements in therapy. Such an approach involves listening to sounds, producing them and noticing the tactile and kinesthetic differences across articulatory movements, and observing the acoustic properties on a spectrograph or waveform.

The CAAI's individual scoring forms allow recording and comparing baseline and follow-up testing scores side-by-side to track progress as well as show clients their achievements. It is recommended that portions of CAAI be readministered at periodic junctures after a goal in therapy has been addressed for a few sessions. These follow-up scores will ensure a more quantified comparison with baseline scores than their clinician-generated "impressions."

Course of Treatment

Session Structure

Therapy consisted of eight sessions, once a week, for 60 minutes each. The number of sessions was determined by clients' availability in the Communication for Impact program (these physicians were able to devote only 8 hours of time to their communication needs, hence this program had to provide maximum results in the least possible time).

Of the eight sessions, one was devoted to the initial interview and the comprehensive assessment using CAAI. Two sessions were reserved for consonant intervention (including auditory discrimination and production), and two more were reserved for vowels. The sessions focusing on segmentals (consonants and vowels) also included 15 minutes of reading paragraphs and producing free-form conversation, wherein prosody goals were introduced and addressed in tandem with the segmentals. One session was dedicated entirely to introducing and practicing details of suprasegmentals. Two more sessions were used for *real-life* speaking opportunities, wherein all previously addressed segmental and prosodic goals were addressed together as relevant.

Specific Procedures

Segmentals: Consonants and Vowels. Consonants were targeted before intervention with vowels. Each session dealing with segmentals involved auditory discrimination exercises first, to allow the client to hear and perceive the differences between the target phoneme in contrast with other phonemes. These minimal pairs were selected from the examples found in the two auditory discrimination subtests in the CAAI. If necessary, additional examples were selected for practice from other accent modification books (see, for example, Celce-Murcia et al., 1996). The clinician would say aloud minimal pairs to provide the client with listening experiences in differentiating various phonemes in these minimal pairs. She was asked to identify these phonemes as "same or different" and write the exact word pairs heard. The clinician provided verbal feedback to point out differences between the sounds if the client failed to identify the difference on her own. Repetitions were provided as necessary until the client began to perceive the difference with at least 80% accuracy.

After this perception experience, the second half of the session dealt with practice on production of these phonemes. For each target phoneme (consonant or vowel), the production exercises began by showing the client a picture of the typical articulatory position to produce the sound. Concurrently, the clinician demonstrated that movement, asked the client to mimic it, and provided direct instructions to modify the movement, as necessary. For phonemes whose productions were relatively difficult to visualize via pictures and/or clinician's model (e.g., velar and palatal consonants and back vowels), a visual animation software program was used to demonstrate the movement of the articulators on a computer screen. The client was asked to imitate the articulatory movements for each phoneme until the clinician was satisfied that the client realized these gestures correctly on individual sounds. Once the client understood the correct articulatory placement, that target phoneme was introduced in all three positions in words of varying syllable length (one-, two-, and three- or four-syllable words). These words were selected from Blockcolsky et al. (1979). The client read individual word lists varying in syllable length and monitored the correct production of the articulatory position on the target phoneme. Each list of words was followed by practice with a list of short sentences containing these phonemes. Finally, the client read a paragraph with all target sounds underlined. The client attended to the related articulatory positions, especially as she read the underlined parts. Simultaneously, as the client read these sentences and paragraphs, the prosody goals were introduced and addressed in tandem with the segmentals. The prosody goals involved aspects such as lexical stress, contrastive syllable stress, word emphasis, overall sentence intonation, and pausing at phrase boundaries. Where necessary, the client was instructed and provided appropriate prosodic models for imitation at various junctures.

Suprasegmental/Prosody. A session was exclusively dedicated for the prosodic goals. The client's goals involved *word-level stress features* (word-level intonation, lexical stress in multi-syllabic words, derivative stress, and contrastive lexical stress). Activities involved reading word lists with appropriate syllable stress patterns and, where incorrect, repeating after the corrected models provided by the clinician. These word lists were compiled from the corresponding sections of the CAAI as well as from other practice books (such as Celce-Murcia et al., 1996; Sikorski, 1988). These words varied in syllable length and ranged from two to five syllables. A wide range of examples was included in these word lists to allow the client to intuit English stress patterns and remap existing stress patterns carried over from the mora-timed Japanese stress patterns. Once the client achieved 80% success rate in her word-level stress productions, she was presented with sentence lists and paragraphs containing the previously used words from the word lists. The client read these sentences and paragraphs as naturally as possible and focused on the appropriate syllable stress patterns. Where necessary, reinstruction and clinician's models were provided.

Real-Life Conversational Speaking Opportunities. The final two sessions of the program were dedicated to bringing together the learning accomplished on the segmental and prosodic goals in the previous sessions and to transferring and generalizing these goals to the client's routine conversational situations. Thus, a secondary goal was to provide specific skills and strategies to enable the client to communicate effectively in her meetings and professional presentations/lectures.

Analysis of Client's Response to Intervention

At the end of the 8-week program, a determination was made to assess whether the client had made adequate progress and functional improvement to be discharged from therapy or whether a continuation of therapy was warranted. Three criteria were used to arrive at this decision: (1) pre- and posttherapy scores on the CAAI, (2) intelligibility judgments by neutral listeners, and (3) client's personal response to intervention.

Pre- and Posttherapy Scores on the CAAI

Selected sections of the CAAI were readministered. The client showed marked improvement in most of the targeted areas/sections. Overall intelligibility scores improved from the previous 2.5 to the present 1.5, and baseline passage intelligibility increased from 89% to 97%; these scores indicated a nearly normal range of functioning. Perfect scores were obtained on word-level intonation and contrastive lexical stress, and mild difficulty was noted on lexical stress on multisyllabic words and derivative stress. Consonant production scores improved from 56 to 62, and consonant clusters' scores improved from 38 to 55, indicating normal functioning. Vowel production scores showed mild difficulty, especially with the back vowels. The client demonstrated good use of compensatory strategies and self-cueing in the section of phonological processes, and as a result, scores showed a marked improvement from 4 to 10.5 on a scale of 1 to 13. The nonspeech language areas revealed marked improvement as well. Scores on the two sections of prepositions improved to a normal range, as did use and understanding of idiomatic expressions. Marked progress was seen with vocabulary, and the client's score improved from 13 to 17. Pragmatic issues were noted to improve as the client now made direct eye contact with the speaker and used better sitting posture and vocal loudness to allow projection of voice and its audibility. The client demonstrated better awareness of communication breakdown and immediately responded to listeners' cues. Based on CAAI scores, it was determined that the client had made marked gains in all areas, and problems that persisted were of a mild degree. More importantly, she knew and used compensatory strategies and independently self-cued to address communication breakdowns. Thus, based on CAAI scores alone, it appeared that the client did not need further intervention and could be discharged from therapy. However, it was still important to determine whether this improvement was apparent to neutral listeners and also whether the client was satisfied with her current communication status.

Intelligibility Judgments by Neutral Listeners

Audio recordings made of the client reading Sections 1 and 2 (sentences and the Rainbow Passage; Fairbanks, 1998) were presented individually to three neutral listeners for judgment. They were undergraduate students at Cleveland State University and received partial credit in their class for participating in this task. These listeners had no prior listening training or familiarity with the client's speech or voice. Individual scores were computed from each listener, and interrater reliability of their scores yielded a high 96% correlation. An average of their scores was 2 in Section 1 and 92% in Section 1, thus matching the CAAI scores reported above very closely (1.5 and 97%, respectively). It appeared that neutral, untrained listeners' judgments corresponded well with the trained speech-language pathologist's estimation of the client's functional improvement.

Further Recommendations

It was important to ascertain whether the client felt there were any areas that were not addressed and to determine whether she had any additional concerns that would prevent her from demonstrating gains and/or independently using speech strategies in real-life situations. Thus, in the course of debriefing and discussing the follow-up scores on the CAAI, the clinician probed for her opinion about her performance. Pre- and posttherapy audio recordings were also played to the client for an objective comparison. This discussion revealed that the client was very pleased with the outcome of therapy. She reported that the scores confirmed her own intuitions and self-assessment of progress. She noted feeling more comfortable and confident in her communication with patients and during professional presentations. Her concerns were about how to ensure that she would retain what she had accomplished. To address this concern, some long-term maintenance skills and strategies were provided. She was given samples of the audio recording files from her baseline and final sessions. Specific issues in her baseline recording were identified and strategies to articulate those consonants, vowels, or prosodic patterns were reviewed. The client recorded these detailed instructions and where necessary included examples and drawings of articulators showing the incorrect and correct postures of sound production. Additional examples of sentences and paragraphs were provided for take-home practice and review. She was asked to continue practicing the sounds and their pronunciation daily on her own as well as in conversations with others. Finally, a 6-month follow-up visit was scheduled to monitor and review her status and maintenance of the progress achieved at present.

Author's Note

This report is based on a real case; some of the background details of the case, including the client's name, have been altered in order to preserve anonymity. The research and therapy treatment were conducted with the appropriate permissions from Cleveland State University's Institutional Review Board and the Cleveland Clinic Foundation's Office of Diversity. All necessary permissions to present the data and the case findings have been sought and obtained from the client and the collaborating colleagues and institutions.

Acknowledgments. This research was supported in part by the Faculty Research Development Grant awarded to the author from Cleveland State University. Assistance of the personnel and students in the Speech Acoustics and Perception Laboratory is greatly appreciated. The author appreciates the support and resources provided by the director, Dr. Deborah Plummer, and various staff members of the Office of Diversity at Cleveland Clinic Foundation.

Endnotes

1. In contrast, skills, goals, and methods that apply to low-English-proficiency clients are addressed in the following case.

2. In recent work (Shah, 2010b, 2016, 2019), the author has offered a more culturally appropriate terminology for accent management that uses the word "Implementation" rather than the traditional "Therapy," "Treatment," or "Intervention." However, these chapters are using the latter terms in keeping with what was standard practice when these case studies took place. That said, readers are encouraged to depart from the medical model philosophy to more culturally sensitive terminology by using neutral terms for clients rather than the medically informed terms used with patients with communication disorders.

References

Blockcolsky, V. D., Frazer, D. H., & Frazer, J. M. (1979). *40,000 selected words*. Communication Skill Builders.

Celce-Murcia, M., Brinton, D., & Goodwin, J. (1996). *Teaching pronunciation: A reference for teachers of English to speakers of other languages*. Cambridge University Press.

Derwing, T. M., & Rossiter, M. J. (2003). The effects of pronunciation instruction on the accuracy, fluency, and complexity of L2 accented speech. *Applied Language Learning, 13*, 1–17.

Fairbanks, G. (1998). *Voice and articulation drill-book*. Addison Wesley Educational.

Flege, J. E. (1984). The detection of French accent by American listeners. *Journal of the Acoustical Society of America, 76*, 692–707. https://doi.org/10.1121/1.391256

Gu, Y., & Shah, A. (2019). A systematic review of interventions to address accent-related communication problems in healthcare. *Ochsner Journal, 19*(4), 378–396. https://doi.org/10.31486/toj.19.0028

Munro, M. J., & Derwing, T. M. (1995). Foreign accent, comprehensibility and intelligibility in the speech of second language learners. *Language Learning, 45*(1), 73–97. https://doi.org/10.1111/j.1467-1770.1995.tb00963.x

Schmidt, A. M., & Sullivan, S. (2003). Clinical training in foreign accent modification: A national survey. *Contemporary Issues in Communication Science and Disorders, 30*, 127–135. https://doi.org/10.1044/cicsd_30_F_127

Shah, A. (2005, November). *Accent modification: Is it efficacy-based? Results from a nationwide survey.* Paper presented at the Annual Conference of the American Speech and Hearing Association (ASHA), San Diego, CA. Abstract in *ASHA Leader, 10*(11), 86, 513.

Shah, A. P. (2007). *Comprehensive Assessment of Accentedness and Intelligibility (CAAI)*. EBAM Institute. https://www.caaiassessment.com

Shah, A. P. (2010a, November). *CAAI: An evidence-based assessment model for foreign-accented speech*. One-hour seminar presented at the ASHA annual meeting, Philadelphia PA.

Shah, A. P. (2010b). *Comprehensive assessment of foreign-accented speech*. An online CEU peer-reviewed web seminar prepared in collaboration with the American Speech-Language-Hearing Association (ASHA), Rockville, MD.

Shah, A. P. (2011). *Evidence-based assessment of accented speech leading to structured therapy: Diagnostic tools, assessment model, & case studies*. Cross-Country Education Seminar Series. Peer-reviewed, Continuing

education, full-day workshops offered nationwide. June 2011: Spokane, WA; Portland, OR; Seattle, WA (Northwest tour), July 2011: El Paso, TX, Phoenix, AZ, Albuquerque, NM (Southwest tour).

Shah, A. P. (2016, November). *Evidence-based accent management: Where are we?* Poster presented at the Annual Convention of the American Speech-Language-Hearing Association (ASHA), Philadelphia, PA.

Shah, A. P. (2019). Why are certain accents judged the way they are? Decoding qualitative patterns of accent bias. *Advances in Language and Literary Studies, 10*(3), 128–139. https://www.journals.aiac.org.au/index.php/alls/article/view/5548/4015

Sikorski, L. (1988). *Mastering the intonation patterns of American English*. LDS and Associates.

Strange, W., & Dittmann, S. (1984). Effects of discrimination training on the perception of /r-l/ by Japanese adults learning English. *Perception & Psychophysics, 36*, 131–145. https://doi.org/10.3758/BF03202673

BILINGUAL/ACCENT
CASE 47
Ms. PW: An Adult Nonnative Speaker of English: Low Proficiency
Amee P. Shah

Conceptual Knowledge Areas

This case offers a profile of a low-English-proficiency client to contrast and supplement the information in the previous case on a high-English-proficiency client. Together, these cases provide speech-language pathology students and professionals with evidence-based models to attempt systematic assessment and treatment for clients with regional and foreign accents. Accent modification is a relatively recent area of practice in the discipline of speech-language pathology and thus lacks a sufficiently robust research base to inform its clinical practice. A systematic review of

accent interventions (Gu & Shah, 2019) showed all of the gaps that are still present in published accounts of accent modification, intervention, or management. These cases are intended to introduce clinicians to a relevant literature base, available assessment tools and methods, and variables to consider in treatment as related to accent modification therapy in contrasting scenarios (low- and high-proficiency speakers of English). It is suggested that the previous case be read first for additional details that are relevant to this case as well, but not repeated here to prevent redundancy.

The present case was undertaken in the course of an ongoing research project in the Speech Acoustics and Perception Laboratory at Cleveland

State University (CSU). International students on the CSU campus were recruited to participate in a pilot program to help them with speech and language difficulties related to their foreign accents. This training study was geared toward relatively low-proficiency speakers of English, newly arrived in the United States, who were struggling to navigate the classroom and to acculturate and adapt to their new country.

As low-proficiency (or introductory) speakers of English, this specific client group's communication needs are in contrast to the subtle and advanced skills reported in the previous case. Communication issues in a low-proficiency subgroup would typically involve markedly low intelligibility; wide-ranging differences in the production of consonants, vowels, and consonant clusters; marked carryover of phonological patterns from the native language; and limited experience perceiving the second-language sound contrasts. An overall difficulty with the second language is also predicted, including issues such as limited vocabulary, limited fluency, and presence of a large number of grammatical errors. Furthermore, due to limited acculturation, knowledge of idiomatic expressions, colloquialisms, and pragmatic awareness of the mainstream culture tends to be rather restricted.

Description of the Case

Background Information and Reason for Referral

Ms. PW, a 21-year-old female, presented with a moderate-strong foreign accent characterized by difficulties in the production of Standard American English phonemes common to native Russian speakers. A graduate student in engineering at Cleveland State University, she was concerned that her dialect would interfere with her ability to obtain gainful employment. She was referred to the Speech Acoustics and Perception Laboratory by her psychology class instructor, who noticed PW's marked difficulty in understanding what other people were saying to her and her inabil-

ity to make herself understood. The initial interview revealed that PW had moved to the United States at the age of 19 years (AOA = 19 years) and had lived in the United States for 2 years (LOR = 2 years). She began learning English at age 10 years (AOL = 10 years) in her home country.[1] She never received any English as Second Language (ESL) or accent modification training. She was a bilingual speaker, with Russian as her first and dominant language and English as the second language. She rated her English as medium proficiency in speaking and writing modalities but strong in reading. She had brief experiences as a cashier in a Subway sandwich franchise and was a parking attendant on campus. She reported severe difficulty with pronunciation relative to her listening skills, vocabulary issues, and writing skills. The latter were reported to be mildly affected and grammar issues were reported to be moderately affected.

Findings of the Evaluation

The Comprehensive Assessment of Accentedness and Intelligibility (CAAI; Shah, 2007) was administered to determine performance in various aspects of speech, language, and overall communicative abilities in English. Please refer to the previous case for details and an overview of CAAI, including the test design rationale, purpose, and structure. To briefly review, the CAAI consists of 22 sections including intelligibility, consonant and vowel production, phonological processes, auditory discrimination, prosody and contrastive stress, emphasis, prepositions, idiomatic phrases, grammar, vocabulary, and pragmatics. The 22 sections yield numeric data in the form of individual section scores, which can be used to make pre- and posttherapy performance comparisons. The resulting diagnostic profile for PW summarizing the scores, patterns, and severity of disruption to communication is provided in Table 47–1.

Summary of Assessment Results

Based on the assessment findings (see Table 47–1), the client exhibited a moderate to strong degree of difficulty in most areas. As Section 2 in the CAAI

Table 47–1. Diagnostic Profile for Ms. PW (From the CAAI)

Comprehensive Assessment of Accentedness & Intelligibility: Complete Diagnostic Report					
Amee P. Shah, Ph.D. Date: Client Name: Ms. PW.					
SECTION TITLE	Total Possible Score	90% Performance	70% Performance	50% Performance	Client's Score
Degree of difficulty ⟶		Mild difficulty	Moderate	Strong difficulty	
SECTION 1: INTELLIGIBILITY RELATIVE TO ACCENTEDNESS e.g., "The committee was composed of ten members . . ."	1 to 5	2	3	4 or more	4.08
SECTION 2: INTELLIGIBILITY SCORE & RATE OF SPEECH ON NARRATIVE PASSAGE Stimulus: Rainbow Passage	100%	90%	70%	50%	44%, normal rate
SECTION 3: SENTENCE LEVEL INTONATION "I got promoted!"	10	9	7	5	9
SECTION 4: WORD LEVEL INTONATION e.g., ("Tuesday comes after Monday.") "Good!"	4	3.6	2.8	2	4
SECTION 5: LEXICAL STRESS IN SINGLE, MULTISYLLABIC WORDS e.g., "Repellent."	12	10.8	8.4	6	8
SECTION 6: DERIVATIVE STRESS IN MULTISYLLABIC WORDS e.g., "democracy/democratic"	24	21.6	16.8	12	19
SECTION 7: CONTRASTIVE LEXICAL STRESS e.g., "I have a birthday present for you."/present	28	25.2	19.6	14	19
SECTION 8: EMPHASIS e.g., ("Which one was it?") "I made the pumpkin pie."	12	10.8	8.4	6	10
SECTION 9: SENTENCE PHRASING e.g., "I need milk, eggs, and bread from the market."	7	6.3	4.9	3.5	7
SECTION 10: CONTRASTING SENTECE PAIRS e.g., "Ben would never leave Woody/would he?"	10	9	7	5	9
SECTION 11: CONSONANTS WORD LIST e.g., Initial position /p/ in "pan."	65	58.5	45.5	32.5	35
SECTION 12: CONSONANT CLUSTERS WORD LIST e.g., /r/ blend in "brush."	59	53.1	41.3	29.5	32
SECTION 13a: VOWEL WORD LIST e.g., /i/ in "meat."	18	16.2	12.6	9	13
SECTION 13b: VOWEL WORD LIST e.g., /æ/ in "packed."	22	19.8	15.4	11	16
SECTION 14: PHONOLOGICAL PROCESSES	13	11.7	9.1	6.5	8

continues

Table 47–1. *continued*

SECTION TITLE	Total Possible Score	90% Performance	70% Performance	50% Performance	Client's Score
SECTION 15: AUDITORY DISCRIMINATION	75	67.5	52.5	37.5	42
SECTION 16: PREPOSITIONS e.g., "I live _____ Ohio." (in)	20	18	14	10	15
SECTION 17: COLLOQUIAL/IDIOMATIC USE OF PREPOSITIONS e.g., Are we still on _____ tonight? (for)	8	7.2	5.6	4	1
SECTION 18: CONTRASTING IDIOMATIC PHRASES e.g., "hold on" vs. "hold out."	17	15.3	11.9	8.5	8
Secondary Cues: sentence fill-in (comprehension of phrases)	Secondary score: 8	7.2	5.6	4	n/a
SECTION 19: COMPREHENSION OF IDIOMATIC PHRASES "Don't be upset, he's only pulling your leg." (teasing)	12	10.8	8.4	6	3
SECTION 20: ADVANCED VOCABULARY Defining a word given four choices.	20	18	14	10	2
SECTION 21: CONVERSATIONAL GRAMMAR					
SECTION 22: PRAGMATIC PROBLEMS					

indicated, the client's rate of speech was normal, but her baseline intelligibility was strongly reduced (44%). The client was found to have a "Strong Foreign Accent" as her accent markedly affected conversational intelligibility.

Areas with moderate-strong degree of impairment and, in turn, those considered high priority for intervention included segmental errors, namely, errors with the following consonants (/r/, /ɾ/, /w/, /v/, /s/, /z/, /θ/, /ð/, /ŋ/, /pʰ/, /tʰ/, /kʰ/), and a variety of vowels (/ɪ/, /i/, /æ/, /o/, /ɔ/, /ʊ/, /a/, /ɚ/, /ə/, and /ʌ/). The phonological processes noted included de-aspiration of initial voiceless stops, devoicing of final fricative (/s/ for /z/), and tense-lax vowel confusion. Auditory discrimination abilities were found to be markedly implicated as well and included confusion between sounds such as a/ɛ, i/e, v/w, e/ɛ, s/θ, z/g, ʃ/s, ɔ/ʌ, æ/ɛ, d/t, ŋ/n, ɪ/e, aʊ/æ, a/o, a/ʌ, and o/ɔ.

Among suprasegmental features that appeared to be moderately impaired were lexical stress in multisyllabic words, derivative stress,

and contrastive stress; these were targeted next in the hierarchy. Suprasegmental features that were relatively spared and did not require further intervention at this point included word emphasis, sentence phrasing, and contrasting sentence pairs. Other nonspeech aspects of language were markedly affected and needed to be addressed as well, although they played less of a role on perceived intelligibility and accentedness and were thought not as high a priority. These included prepositions, advanced vocabulary, understanding and use of idiomatic phrases and colloquialisms, and certain pragmatic features of conversation.

Therapy Options Considered

The following areas were selected and are included in the order in which they were addressed:

1. Production/auditory discrimination of consonants

2. Production/auditory discrimination of vowels
3. Phonological processes
4. Word-level stress properties (lexical stress, contrastive stress, and derivative stress)
5. Everyday conversational skills

As mentioned in the previous case, important factors in selecting the goals and their importance were the *client's preference, experience*, and *need*. In contrast to the high-proficiency client in Case 46, the present client was relatively new to the country and not very proficient in English. Limited English skills precluded working on any of the advanced language skills targeted with the previous client. Instead, the emphasis was on speech pronunciation abilities and, in particular, those that would directly influence intelligibility and the strength of accent. Thus, the majority of the treatment sessions focused on segmentals, including consonant and vowel discrimination practice, articulation drills, and coarticulation of these sounds in narratives and conversations.

Course of Therapy[2]

Session Structure

Therapy consisted of 12 once-weekly sessions of 1.5 hours each. The number of sessions was determined by the client's availability (once a week), and session duration was determined by the severity of the client's communication needs (moderate-severe).

Goals and Specific Procedures[3]

Long-Term Goal. PW will use Standard American English (SAE) patterns and speech sounds with 80% accuracy in two 10-minute conversational speech samples as measured by analysis of the speech samples.

Short-Term Goal 1. PW will discriminate sound pairs (consonants or vowels) with 80% accuracy while listening to the clinician read from a list of minimal pairs of words.

■ Client will discriminate contrasting vowels /i/, /ɪ/, /ɛ/ at the word level with 80% accuracy while listening to the clinician read from a list.

■ Client will discriminate contrasting consonants /r/ and /l/ at the word level with 80% accuracy while listening to the clinician read from a list.

■ Client will discriminate contrasting consonants /v/ and /w/ at the word level with 80% accuracy while listening to the clinician read from a list.

Short-Term Goal 2. PW will use SAE to produce the following consonant sounds in all positions of words with 80% accuracy:

■ Client will correctly produce aspiration on word-initial voiceless consonants /pʰ/, /tʰ/, and /kʰ/.

■ Client will correctly produce /r/ in all positions of words using SAE with 80% accuracy.

■ Client will correctly produce contrasting consonants /r/ and /l/ at the word level while reading from word lists with 80% accuracy.

■ Client will correctly produce /s/ in all positions of words using SAE with 80% accuracy.

■ Client will produce /z/ in all positions of words using SAE with 80% accuracy.

■ Client will produce /v/ and /w/ contrasts at the word level while reading from word lists with 80% accuracy.

Short-Term Goal 3. PW will use SAE to produce vowel sounds in all positions of words with 80% accuracy.

■ Client will correctly produce /ʌ/ in all positions of words using SAE with 80% accuracy.

■ Client will correctly produce /a/ in all positions of words using SAE with 80% accuracy.

- Client will correctly produce /o/ in all positions of words using SAE with 80% accuracy.
- Client will produce contrasting vowels /i/ and /ɪ/ at the word level while reading from word lists with 80% accuracy.

Short-Term Goal 4. PW will correctly use SAE stress and intonation patterns in conversational speech with 80% accuracy.

- Client will produce correct syllable stress in multisyllable words at both word and sentence levels while reading from word lists and passages with 80% accuracy.
- Client will use SAE stress patterns when asking a question with 80% accuracy.
- Client will use SAE stress patterns when answering a question with 80% accuracy.
- Client will use SAE intonational patterns in scripted conversation with 80% accuracy following the clinician's model.

Specific Procedures

Segmentals: Consonants and Vowels. Intervention began with work on consonants, including /r/, /w/, /v/, /s/, /z/, /pʰ/, /tʰ/, and /kʰ/. Vowels including /ɪ/, /i/, /o/, /a/, and /ʌ/ were then addressed. Initially, auditory discrimination exercises were conducted using examples from the CAAI and other word samples from accent modification books. The clinician read minimal pairs of words with target sound contrasts, and the client had to indicate which of the two words represented a given target sound. The exercise was varied on other days to require the client to say "same" or "different" in response to hearing these minimal pairs with either the same sounds (e.g., "rate-rate") or different sounds (e.g., "rate-late"). Word identification exercises required the client to write the string of words that the clinician read aloud.

These listening exercises were conducted before addressing production errors. Consonants were targeted before vowels in production exercises. For each target sound goal, the activity

started by showing the client a picture of the articulatory position for that sound. Next, the clinician demonstrated and asked the client to mimic the correct posture and movement for that sound and provided direct instructions to modify the movement, as necessary. Once the client had learned the correct posture and movement for a sound in isolation, words containing that sound were presented to the client to be read aloud. These lists of words were taken from the book of 40,000 words by Blockcolsky et al. (1979). Words were selected so that each target sound occurred in word-initial, medial, and final positions, as well as in words increasing in syllable length, that is, two-, three-, and four- or five-syllable words. The client practiced producing these various word positions and word lengths. In tandem, the client practiced to contrast the target sound with others in minimal pairs. For example, while working on /p/, words with /f/ and /b/ were also presented for practice. Once 80% of mastery was accomplished with these word-level sound productions, the client was led through practice with sentences containing these sounds. All sounds were practiced in the two consonant-dedicated sessions. Finally, the client was asked to read a paragraph wherein all the sounds targeted thus far were underlined and to pay attention to the related articulatory positions while reading the underlined parts.

Suprasegmental/Prosody. The client's prosody goals involved *word-level stress features* (lexical stress in multisyllabic words, derivative stress, and contrastive lexical stress). Activities involved reading word lists with contrastive lexical stress (e.g., OBject vs. obJECT) and varying degrees of lexical stress over words with increasing syllable length (one to five syllables). Once the client achieved 80% success rate in word-level stress productions, she was presented with sentence lists and paragraphs containing previously used words. The client read these sentences and paragraphs as naturally as possible and focused on the appropriate syllable stress patterns. In addition to reading word lists and sentences, the client engaged in roleplays with scripted conversations to produce stress and sentence intonation patterns that matched appropriate contexts such as asking questions, answering factual questions, exclaiming, conveying sadness, and so on. The sentences represented a variety of pitch contours reflecting a wide range of pragmatic contexts. Where necessary, reinstruction and clinicians' models were provided.

Analysis of Client's Response to Intervention

At the end of the semester, a follow-up evaluation was conducted to determine the client's progress and gauge whether to continue therapy. Progress was noted as follows. The client discriminated contrasting vowels /i/, /ɪ/, and /ɛ/ at the word level with 60% accuracy while listening to the clinician read from a list. She discriminated contrasting sounds /r/ and /l/ with 90% accuracy at the word level. She produced voiceless consonants with marked improvement, /pʰ/ and /tʰ/ with 90% accuracy, and /kʰ/ with 85% accuracy in all positions. She produced /r/ with 65% accuracy in all positions of words using SAE, /s/ in all positions with 70% accuracy, and /z/ in all positions with 60% accuracy. In the vowel category, she produced /ʌ/ in all positions of words with 75% accuracy, /a/ in all positions of words with 80% accuracy, and /o/ in all positions of words with 80% accuracy. She used SAE stress patterns when asking a question with 80% accuracy, SAE stress patterns when answering a question with 80% accuracy, and SAE intonation patterns in scripted conversation with 80% accuracy.

A debriefing discussion was conducted with the client to elicit her response to intervention, check her evaluation of her progress, and understand her expectations. She reported noticing marked improvement in her ability to perceive the differences in the sound patterns in English as they differ from her native language, Russian. Moreover, she reported being better able to self-correct her production errors when they occurred in conversations by reminding herself of their correct articulatory position and specific oral movements. She learned when to slow down and repeat, when to paraphrase, when to enunciate carefully, and when to speed up her utterances in order to sound more natural. She reported maximum success with producing and monitoring the produc-

tion of the voiceless consonants, /pʰ/, /tʰ/, and /kʰ/. She expressed continued difficulties in producing vowels and a few consonant clusters.

Further Recommendations

In light of these evaluation findings and the client's self-report, it was concluded that the client had benefited from speech therapy and shown marked progress and that therapy needed to be continued further in the course of the next semester. The client had fewer errors and communication issues but needed increased practice with gains made and future ones expected. Thus, it was determined that the client would be seen three times a week (instead of once weekly as before) for 30-minute (instead of 1.5-hour) sessions. The client was provided with strategies and assignments for the winter break to maintain the progress and learning achieved thus far. These assignments included copies of materials involving words, sentences, and paragraphs with highlighted sounds, all of them targeting the specific consonant and vowel targets addressed. In addition, the client was given conversational assignments wherein she was supposed to role-play situations with her sister at home to mimic interactions with various people in her everyday situations and audio-record these situations (e.g., discussing a product in a store with a sales clerk, discussing a simple banking transaction with a bank teller, placing an order over the telephone). She analyzed these recordings and identified features in which she had incorporated the new strategies learned in therapy, as well as those features in which she failed to do so. Finally, she was asked to practice pronouncing the individual words that she identified as errors from this analysis and to bring recordings to the therapy sessions.

Author's Note

This report is based on a real case; some of the background details of the case, including the client's name, have been altered to preserve anonymity. The research and therapy treatment were conducted with the appropriate permissions from Cleveland State University's Institutional Review Board and from the Speech and Hearing Clinic at Cleveland State University. All necessary permissions to present the data and the case findings have been sought and obtained from the client and the collaborating colleagues and institutions.

Acknowledgments. This research was supported in part by a Faculty Research Development Grant awarded to the author from Cleveland State University. Assistance of the personnel and students in the Speech Acoustics and Perception class and the Speech and Hearing Clinic is greatly appreciated.

Endnotes

1. For information regarding the terms *AOA*, *AOL*, and *LOR*, please refer to the case history information in the previous case.

2. In recent work (Shah, 2010, 2016, 2019), the author has offered a more culturally appropriate terminology for accent management that uses the word "Implementation" rather than the traditional "Therapy," "Treatment," or "Intervention." However, these chapters are using the latter terms in keeping with what was standard practice when these case studies took place. That said, readers are encouraged to depart from the medical model philosophy to more culturally sensitive terminology by using neutral terms for clients rather than the medically informed terms used with patients with communication disorders.

3. Please note that the format of this section is different from that of the previous case. The clients seen in the Speech Acoustics and Perception lab are treated in keeping with the structure of the speech and hearing clinic. Thus, long- and short-term goals, procedures, and report writing reflect those followed in the clinic. This structure is different from that specially designed for the high-proficiency clients seen in the Communication for Impact program described in the previous case.

References

Blockcolsky, V. D., Frazer, D. H., & Frazer, J. M. (1979). *40,000 selected words.* Communication Skill Builders.

Gu, Y., & Shah, A. (2019). A systematic review of interventions to address accent-related communication problems in healthcare. *Ochsner Journal, 19*(4), 378–396. https://doi.org/10.31486/toj.19.0028

Shah, A. P. (2007). *Comprehensive Assessment of Accentedness and Intelligibility (CAAI).* EBAM Institute. https://www.caaiassessment.com

Shah, A. P. (2010). *Comprehensive Assessment of Foreign-Accented Speech.* An online CEU peer-reviewed web seminar prepared in collaboration with the American Speech, Language, and Hearing Association (ASHA), Rockville, MD.

Shah, A. P. (2016, November). *Evidence-based accent management: Where are we?* Poster presented at the Annual Convention of the American Speech-Language-Hearing Association (ASHA), Philadelphia, PA.

Shah, A. P. (2019). Why are certain accents judged the way they are? Decoding qualitative patterns of accent bias. *Advances in Language and Literary Studies, 10*(3), 128–139. https://www.journals.aiac.org.au/index.php/alls/article/view/5548/4015

DEMENTIA
CASE 48
Mrs. P: Screening, Assessment, and Cognitive-Linguistic Interventions for a Bilingual Adult With Dementia Secondary to Alzheimer's Disease
Manaswita Dutta and Arpita Bose

Conceptual Knowledge Areas

Dementia Overview

Dementia is an acquired neurological syndrome characterized by "a decline from previous levels of cognitive functioning with impairments in two or more cognitive domains . . . not entirely attributable to normal aging which significantly interferes with independence in the person's performance of activities of daily living" (International Classification of Diseases-11; World Health Organization [WHO], 2018). Cognitive deterioration in dementia is typically observed in the absence of delirium or psychiatric condition, initially marked by a pervasive decline in memory followed by related impairments in language, attention, executive functioning, and visuospatial skills (McKhann et al., 2011).

The clinical syndrome of dementia can be caused by a wide range of underlying diseases. Alzheimer's disease (AD) remains the most common cause of dementia, accounting for 60% to 80% of the dementia cases (Alzheimer's Association [AA], 2022). Other causes of dementia that cause irreversible progressive neurological changes and cognitive decline include cerebrovascular disease, Lewy bodies, and frontotemporal degeneration. The cognitive profiles associated with each dementia type vary based on the underlying pathology and syndromes. This chapter focuses on dementia related to AD.

Alzheimer's Disease (AD)

AD most commonly affects individuals who are 65 years of age or older; it can also impact younger adults (early-onset AD; AA, 2022). Currently, AD affects over 55 million individuals worldwide. With rapid increases in the aging population globally, an exponential growth is expected, with 78 million in 2030 and 139 million by 2050, with the greatest increase in low- to middle-income Asian countries (Guerchet et al., 2020). Furthermore, with over half of the world's population speaking more than one language, the incidence of older bilingual speakers with AD is rising. Within the United States, an estimated 6.5 million older adults (i.e., ≥ 65 years of age) live with AD. Women are twice as likely to develop AD than men. Older Hispanic and African Americans are 1.5 to 2 times more likely to be diagnosed with AD compared to older Whites (AA, 2022).

Neuropathology of AD

AD is identified by core neuropathological biomarkers, including increased amyloid deposition (neuritic plaques), accumulation of pathologic neurofibrillary tau (tangles), and cortical pyramidal cells' neurodegeneration (Jack et al., 2019). The initial changes in AD are marked by generalized atrophic brain changes beginning in medial temporal structures, including the hippocampus, as well as parietal and association cortices with later involvement of the prefrontal, primary visual, and sensorimotor regions.

Stages of AD

The clinical diagnosis of AD is typically preceded by three stages: the *preclinical phase* (precedes the onset of clinical AD by 10–20 years); the prodromal phase, characterized by *mild cognitive impairment* (MCI; transitional stage characterized by mild impairments in one or more cognitive domains and signs of AD pathology); and the *clinical stage of dementia* (marked by a global cognitive decline and a significant deterioration of everyday functional abilities). Although the presence of biomarkers associated with the preclinical and MCI stages (i.e., neuronal atrophy, beta-amyloid proteins) is indicative of a higher risk of conversion to AD, some individuals who show such pathophysiological biomarkers may never manifest clinical symptoms or progress to the clinical stage of dementia (Vermunt et al., 2019).

Cognitive-Communication Impairments Associated With AD

Cognitive Impairments in AD. With the early neuropathological changes occurring in the medial temporal structures, including the hippocampal, entorhinal, and perirhinal cortices, cognitive deterioration is first noted in memory, typically affecting episodic memory. Episodic memory is one's capacity of recalling individual-specific and personal experiences and events such as remembering what one had for dinner or their wedding day. During the initial stages, procedural memory (i.e., supports the learning and execution of motor and cognitive skills) and sensory and motor skills remain relatively spared (Almkvist, 1996; Baddeley, 2001). Individuals with AD may also present with deficits in verbal and visuospatial working memory, and semantic memory or the ability to retrieve information related to meaning, world knowledge, and universal facts (Hodges et al., 1992; Huntley & Howard, 2010).

Whereas episodic memory impairments are ubiquitously seen in AD, deficits in other cognitive domains such as attention, executive functioning, visuospatial functions, and language emerge early on as well as during the later stages of the condition (Mandal et al., 2012). Individuals with AD commonly encounter attentional impairments during daily life tasks (e.g., difficulty participating in large group conversations, being easily distracted). Different aspects of attention frequently impacted in AD include sustained attention, selective attention, attentional shifting, and divided attention (Malhotra, 2019; Perry & Hodges, 1999). Executive functioning deficits affecting inhibitory control, cognitive flexibility, idea generation, strategic planning, organization, and problem solving are also common in AD (Guarino et al., 2019).

Language and Communication Impairments in AD. Language and communication changes are commonly seen with the progression of the condition. During the initial stages of AD, a gradual degradation of the underlying semantic system results in failure to successfully access the semantic representations (Balthazar et al., 2008). With disease progression, changes in other linguistic domains including phonology, morphology, syntax, fluency, and pragmatics become more apparent (Bayles et al., 1987). While impaired lexical retrieval is the most prominent characteristic of AD, individuals also demonstrate deficits in auditory and written comprehension and oral reading (Ahmed et al., 2013; Martínez-Sánchez et al., 2013).

Single word-level tasks (e.g., confrontational naming, word repetition, object recognition, verbal fluency [i.e., semantic, phonemic, and verb] tasks) are commonly used to examine language comprehension and production revealing lexical-semantic impairments in AD (e.g., Paek & Murray, 2021; Weiner et al., 2008). Among bilinguals, naming tasks have revealed differential patterns of language deterioration. Costa et al. (2012) found similar patterns of impairments in balanced Catalan-Spanish bilinguals with mild-to-moderate AD, and Gollan et al. (2010) and Ivanova et al. (2014) found differing results in non-balanced Spanish-English bilinguals: Gollan et al. reported the dominant language to be more affected; in contrast, Ivanova et al. noted a decline in the nondominant language. While single-word tasks are sensitive to semantic system breakdowns in AD, performance on such isolated tasks does not fully capture the breadth of linguistic impairments or communication in everyday situations, providing an incomplete picture of an individual's language skills (Mueller et al., 2016). Therefore, use of naturalistic discourse is more representative of language breakdowns in AD.

Persons with AD frequently demonstrate impairments in naturalistic language use or spoken discourse (Carlomagno et al., 2005; Mueller et al., 2018; Slegers et al. 2018). These impairments can affect both the structural (i.e., microlinguistic) and global (i.e., macrolinguistic) levels of discourse. At the microlinguistic level, the language output in AD can be characterized by slower speech rate, increased pausing, frequent disruptions (i.e., hesitations, reformulations), less complex morphosyntax, and frequent lexical retrieval deficits (Bose et al., 2021; Cuetos et al., 2007; Sajjadi et al., 2012). At the macrolinguistic level, individuals with AD may demonstrate reduced informativeness and accuracy of semantic content, impaired coherence, and empty speech characterized by lack of referencing, inappropriate conversational topic shifts, and tangential utterances (Ehrlich et al., 1997; Pistono et al., 2019).

Although the presentation of certain core AD-related language markers in spoken discourse may be universally seen across monolinguals and bilinguals (e.g., slowed speech rate, fluency disruptions, and reduced information content), the presentation of language deficits varies based on several factors, including the structure of the language examined, tasks used, and participants' bilingualism profiles (Bose et al., 2021; Bose et al., 2022). For instance, in contrast to English speakers with AD who tend to overproduce pronouns and have noun and verb inflection impairments, speakers with AD using structurally distinct language from English show differential patterns (e.g., production of a lower proportion of pronouns among Bengali speakers; no inflectional morphology impairments in Hebrew and Bengali speakers; Bose et al., 2021; Kavé & Levy, 2003).

Overall, very little is known regarding the language changes associated with AD in bilingual/multilingual adults. Much of the empirical evidence regarding language changes in AD is derived from monolinguals or English speakers. To obtain a more holistic profile of the individuals' language abilities, a combination of impairment-focused testing batteries and naturalistic language tasks must be incorporated routinely during clinical assessment. This is especially important for individuals with AD from different linguistic and cultural backgrounds for whom formal language assessment options are limited.

Role of Speech-Language Pathologists in AD Care Pathway

Speech-language pathologists (SLPs) are key members in the interdisciplinary rehabilitation process and serve an important clinical role in identifying, monitoring, and managing cognitive-communicative changes associated with different types of dementia and in differential diagnosis of dementia with other neurogenerative disorders such as primary progressive aphasia (Bourgeois, 2019). SLPs are involved in providing nonpharmacological behavior-based interventions that focus on cognitive-linguistic remediation, compensation approaches, increased social interactions and multimodal communication, and long-term care planning to maintain independence, engagement, and safety with daily living and recreational activities (Rodakowski et al., 2015). SLPs also engage in research related to dementia-related communication disorders and support clients, their families, and care partners via education, counseling, and advocacy throughout the continuum of care (ASHA, 2016). Given the continuous rise in individuals living with AD, the SLP's role is expected to become even more critical.

Description of the Case

Background Information

Mrs. P is a 66-year-old right-handed Bengali[1]-English bilingual speaker who presented to the neurologist at the memory clinic with a chief complaint of progressive forgetfulness and verbal communication difficulties starting 4 years prior to her first clinic visit. Mrs. P's husband reported that she seemed to have difficulties with finding words or using incorrect words during conversations. When questioned, Mrs. P expressed no major concerns with her language but did admit to experiencing difficulties with remembering the content of recent conversations or recently completed daily activities. She noticed that she would often repeat information during conversations and had limited interest in her ability to complete activities/tasks that she previously enjoyed (e.g., driving, cooking, reading).

Mrs. P was born in India and immigrated to the United States in 2004 at the age of 48 years. Mrs. P completed 17 years of education (master's degree in Mathematics) in India. She was a mathematics teacher in a public school in Portland, Oregon. She retired early from teaching as she was no longer able to cope with ongoing work demands. She lives with her husband. Apart from being a sincere, dedicated, and popular teacher, she also managed household responsibilities. She

was involved in raising her two children and fulfilling her responsibilities as a mother.

Neurological Examination and Screening of Global Cognitive Functioning

Mrs. P's clinical diagnosis was made following collation of the multidisciplinary team's report on several assessments. She underwent a detailed medical history, physical and mental status examinations, neuroimaging (single photon emission computed tomography [SPECT], magnetic resonance imaging [MRI]), and laboratory tests (see Figure 48–1 for results).

Neuropsychological Examination Findings

Mrs. P's neurology team administered the Clinical Dementia Rating Scale (Morris, 1993), the adapted Bengali versions of the Mini-Mental State Examination (Folstein et al., 1975), and

---

Mrs. P's medical history and neurological exam findings

Medical History	Neurological Exam Findings	Neuroimaging Findings

- Hypertension
- Hypercholesterolemia
- Nondiabetic and euthyroid
- No family history of AD or any other neurodegenerative disease
- Vitamin B12 - not done
- Lipid profile - not done
	- Normal cranial nerves, motor coordination, gait, and reflexes
	- Mild peripheral neuropathy
	- Comprehension difficulty
	- Reading and writing problems
	- Loss of empathy
	- Visuospatial difficulties
	- No evidence of:
	  o Recognition difficulty for objects and faces
	  o Disinhibition, aggression, repetitive and stereotypic behaviors, environmental dependency behaviors
	  o Delusion, hallucinations
	  o Stroke, loss of consciousness, falls, rigidity, dystonia, gait disturbance, urinary incontinence, myoclonic jerks, swallowing difficulty
		- Brain MRI revealed focal atrophy and minimal white matter hyperintensity
		
		- SPECT showed mild left temporal and parietal hypometabolism

Figure 48–1. Mrs. P's medical history and neurological examination findings.

Addenbrooke's Cognitive Examination (Hsieh et al., 2013) to determine Mrs. P's dementia severity and overall cognitive functioning. The memory clinic at which Mrs. P was tested had access to normative data on these tests from Bengali-English bilinguals (Table 48–1). The neuropsychological evaluation revealed significant impairments in multiple cognitive domains including attention, memory, executive functions, and visuoconstructional skills. Verbal fluency tasks revealed lower scores for Mrs. P compared to the normative scores (i.e., below fifth percentile) in both languages.

Clinical Diagnosis

Mrs. P was diagnosed with mild to moderate probable AD as per the criteria developed by the National Institute of Neurological and Communicative Disorders and Stroke (NINCDS) and the Alzheimer's Disease and Related Disorders Association (ADRDA; McKhann et al., 2011).

Reasons for SLP Referral

Mrs. P was referred to the SLP with concerns related to her declining cognitive status and difficulty with communication. Mrs. P's neurologist noted that she had fluent speech but demonstrated word-finding difficulties. She had difficulty paying attention or concentrating. Mrs. P found it increasingly challenging to organize her thoughts and communicate them through speech. Her husband also reported that she struggled finding words during complex conversations.

Table 48–1. Neuropsychological Test Scores for Mrs. P

Assessment	Total Score Obtained	Normative Scores (Mean [SD])
MMSE	16/30	30 (0)
CDR	1	0 (0)
ACE-III	31/100	92.7 (2.3)
Attention	8/18	17.7 (0.7)
Memory	3/26	25.3 (0.7)
Fluency	1/14	8 (1)
Language	14/26	25.9 (0.3)
Visuoconstructional	3/16	15.8 (0.4)
Semantic fluency[a]		
Bengali	3	14.4 (3.6)
English	2	12.3 (4.2)
Phonemic fluency[a] **(average)**		
Bengali	7	12.7 (3.2)
English	5	11.3 (4.5)

Note. MMSE = Mini-Mental Status Examination; ACE = Addenbrooke's Cognitive Examination; CDR = Clinical Dementia Rating Scale.

[a]Verbal fluency was assessed using phonemic (i.e., words starting with the letters F, A, and S [English]; letters K, P, and M [Bengali]) and semantic (i.e., naming animals) tasks, and the total number of correctly produced exemplars was calculated from each category.

SLP Evaluation

Consistent with the International Classification of Functions framework proposed by the WHO (2016), Mrs. P's rehabilitation plans entailed profiling her AD-related cognitive-linguistic deficits at the impairment level and evaluating her activity and participation in everyday communication activities. Additionally, personal and environmental facilitators and barriers impacting Mrs. P's functioning were addressed.

Case History and Interview

An important starting point of a comprehensive speech and language evaluation is a detailed case history, which involves interviewing the client and family members and reviewing the medical record. According to her husband, Mrs. P's symptoms began 4 years prior to receiving her AD diagnosis. She would frequently forget to complete work and household-related tasks. For example, she forgot to submit her course exam grades at the school before leaving for a holiday, which was unusual for her. On a few occasions, Mrs. P's elder son observed that she was very anxious, did not enjoy her work, and had a poor appetite. She would also repeat questions. Although the quality of her work was not affected, she eventually stopped participating in weekly chores such as grocery shopping.

One year after the onset of symptoms, behavioral changes were more evident. She became withdrawn and did not converse much with her friends. Memory problems also worsened. During group conversations, she would often confabulate (i.e., create false or erroneous memories without the intent of deceit). Considering that these changes were caused by the increased stress related to her job, Mrs. P's husband suggested that she discontinue work. Initially, she did not agree, but 2 years after her first symptoms, her husband persuaded the school authorities to allow her to retire early. Mrs. P ultimately accepted this decision as she agreed that her personal life and health were affected by stress at work.

Further memory problems gradually emerged. For example, she would forget recent conversations, to convey messages, what she had for her meals, and her friends' birthdays. She also had difficulty recognizing familiar routes. She became increasingly dependent on her husband for any decision-making regarding household matters. Three years since her initial symptoms, while on a trip with her husband, she could not remember her hotel room or floor and was also unable to recognize the car she was traveling in.

Five months prior to her neurological evaluation, she experienced increasing difficulty with comprehension and recalling names of places. For instance, when her husband asked her to sign a document, she appeared confused and had difficulty determining whether she had to sign below or above the signature line. She was only able to sustain attention for a few minutes during reading. Although Mrs. P had been a good painter, she became unable to do pencil sketching.

Over time, changes were also observed in Mrs. P's emotional expression. She did not express happiness when her son gave her a surprise visit. Her husband also noted that she had become submissive. At the time of her assessment, she continued to do daily routine activities and took proper personal care. Her husband spent time with her every day. He took her out for walks, dinners in restaurants, and to meet her friends in social settings.

Background Assessments

Hearing and Vision Screening. Sensory impairments are prevalent among older adults and can confound cognitive-linguistic assessment (Dupuis et al., 2015), and thus any changes in hearing and vision must be documented. Mrs. P complained of some difficulty hearing mostly in noisy situations. She passed a pure-tone audiometric screening at or above 35 dB HL at 500, 1000, 2000, and 4000 Hz in her right ear but demonstrated hearing loss at 4000 Hz in her left ear. Mrs. P achieved >90% accuracy on a picture-matching task, indicating that her vision was within functional limits.

Depression Screening. Concomitant issues such as depression can emerge with the progression of AD (Rapp et al., 2008). Therefore, Mrs. P was screened using the Patient Health Questionnaire (PHQ-9; Spitzer et al., 1999), a brief depression screener, which revealed mild depression (score = 9 out of 27).

Activities of Daily Living. The Instrumental Activities of Daily Living Scale for Elderly (Mathuranath et al., 2005) was administered to evaluate Mrs. P's ability to complete everyday activities including cognitive, social or recreational, community, household, and self-care activities (e.g., taking medication, pursuing hobbies, shopping, meal preparation, and personal care). Mrs. P exhibited a score of 36 (a score of >16 is in the impaired range).

Bilingualism Measures. The clinic where Mrs. P was assessed used an adapted questionnaire developed by Muñoz et al. (1999) to assess Mrs. P's language acquisition history, language instruction during education, self-rated language proficiency across different modalities (i.e., in speaking, understanding, reading, and writing), and her current language usage pattern.

The *language acquisition questionnaire* indicated that Mrs. P was born and raised in a Bengali-speaking household. She reported an early onset of exposure to English (at around 4 years of age), both formally and informally; thus, she was considered a sequential bilingual. She had greater immersion initially in Bengali compared to English. Since moving to the United States, she has used English more frequently at work and in social settings while Bengali remained her preferred language for family interaction at home. Mrs. P demonstrated similar proficiency and usage in English and Bengali and is considered a more "balanced" bilingual. Per Mr. P, her proficiency in English was very good, almost native like, especially after living in the United States for several years. Much of her higher education was in English. Since her dementia onset, Mrs. P reported losing fluency (spoken) in English. Mrs. P's current preferred language is Bengali, although she remains proficient in English.

Evaluation of Cognitive-Communication Abilities

Although neuropsychological testing revealed significant cognitive impairments, a detailed evaluation was warranted to assess the extent of cognitive-communication difficulties and determine the significant areas of impairments to be addressed in therapy. The goal of this assessment was to obtain a comprehensive picture of the pattern of impairments observed across both spoken languages. All assessments were completed by a certified bilingual SLP with assistance from a health care colleague proficient in Bengali. Mrs. P's spouse also assisted as an interpreter with the portion of testing that was conducted in Bengali. The SLP administered the assessments listed below to evaluate language. Normative data for these assessments were collected from Bengali-English bilinguals (see Table 48–2 for Mrs. P's language assessment scores).

a. **Western Aphasia Battery–Revised (WAB-R):** The English and Bengali (Kertesz, 2007; Keshree et al., 2013) versions of this test were used to assess Mrs. P's language performance on the spontaneous speech, auditory verbal comprehension, and naming subtests.

b. **Spoken discourse:** Language performance at the discourse level was assessed using a picture description task (i.e., the picnic scene from the WAB-R). Measures related to speech rate, mean length of utterance, and correct information units (CIU); (Nicholas & Brookshire, 1993) were derived from the analysis.

c. **Behavioral observations:** Observations of Mrs. P's functional interactions with her family members were obtained by the SLP throughout the session. During the evaluation, Mrs. P exhibited frequent difficulties understanding and remembering task instructions and was slow in responding. She displayed frustration when she struggled with tasks. She experienced cognitive fatigue and demonstrated difficulties with memory (e.g., she asked the same questions multiple times) and orientation (e.g., she incorrectly stated the city she lived in and was unaware of the day of the week). Her conversations mostly revolved around past personal events. She was observed to converse with familiar communication partners in Bengali but could switch to using English upon request.

Table 48–2. Language Testing Results for Mrs. P

Assessment	Total Score Obtained (English)	Total Score Obtained (Bengali)	Normative Scores (Mean [SD]), English	Normative Scores (Mean [SD]), Bengali
WAB-R				
Spontaneous Speech	6/20	10/20	19.40 [0.15]	19.65 [0.11]
Auditory Comprehension	120/200	130/200	198.56 [0.87]	197.43 [0.93]
Naming	24/100	38/100	99.04 [0.64]	99.12 [0.35]
Discourse Analysis				
Speech rate (words/min)	42.17	69.76	78.67 [5.43]	76.93 [4.61]
Total number of CIUs	118	70	95.7 [20.4]	74.86 [29.96]
CIU%	49.48	70	78.86 [8.45]	84.85 [8.55]
CIUs/min	33.78	48.84	73.14 [5.04]	65.17 [6.51]
MLU	3.34	5.46	9.18 [1.00]	5.11 [0.68]

Note. WAB-R = Western Aphasia Battery–Revised; CIU = Correct Information Units; MLU = mean length of utterances.

Mrs. P demonstrated difficulties with both language comprehension and production, but language expression was more significantly affected than comprehension abilities in both languages. She had trouble following multistep commands and accurately understanding task directions. Additionally, she exhibited deficits with numerical processing on the auditory verbal subtest of the WAB-R, albeit only in English. Mrs. P had pronounced noun-retrieval difficulty during the confrontational naming and picture description tasks in English. She only demonstrated occasional lexical retrieval issues when completing tasks in Bengali. To compensate, she often used circumlocutions to explain the target item (e.g., producing "I use this every day to get into my house, it is in my purse" for "key" during object naming in the WAB-R). During the naming task, she had greater difficulty with low-frequency and multisyllabic words (e.g., safety pin, screwdriver) compared to single syllabic highly frequent words (e.g., ball, book) in English.

When Mrs. P's spoken discourse performances in both languages were compared, she demonstrated a slower speech rate, shorter utterances, and reduced semantic content and efficiency in English compared to Bengali (Table 48–3). Addi-

tionally, she produced semantic errors (e.g., "goat" to describe the "dog" in the picnic scene) and used nonspecific language (e.g., "something") while describing the WAB-R picnic scene elements. She also demonstrated frequent repetition of previously mentioned picture elements, which compromised her fluency.

Treatment Options Considered

A combination of direct training of communication and memory strategies and indirect intervention approaches (i.e., caregiver training and education) was considered with the goal of maximizing her overall communication, social participation, and quality of life outcomes while supporting her family members along the course of disease progression.

Mrs. P and her family were consulted during the treatment planning process to ensure the co-construction of functionally relevant goals. Based on Mrs. P's assessment findings and upon discussion with Mrs. P and her family, the main goals of intervention were to work on her word-retrieval and episodic memory abilities. A secondary goal was to educate Mrs. P's family members and care

Table 48–3. Excerpt of Mrs. P's Picnic Scene Picture Description (WAB-R Picnic Scene) Compared to a Neurotypical Bengali-English Speaker

Mrs. P
There is a um (inaudible)
It's a picnic
So a couple with their children uh have gone to uh this picnic
And they were **trying to** *in th- in uh* **they're trying to** *uh* **trying to** *uh* trying to *uh g-* get a lot of fun *and all they want to*
So they have the father and mother
They are *uh* sitting *there* on the grass
*And uh ch-***children** *uh there* children were there *in the* at the back
And the uh-the **the um** the man was you *uh* reading a book
And **the man** *was uh an- and* the lady was *you know* taking out *the uh things every* everything *from the* for the picnic
Taking out everything from there *and then they from uh* the children *the uh* started *uh fl-* a kite
Then they were busy
There was *a ba-sorry* a goat there *and*
At the corner there we can find uh a person who is *perhaps th-* trying to *uh* pick up some *f- uh* fish *or something*
The child was there to find our something for its
And then the child is *uh* also very happy *seeing uh* for **kiting**
Then and-and the whole it's a there's a very nice couple
And children are also nice
And they are also *having* enjoying their trip
Neurotypical Bengali-English Speaker
This is a beautiful picture
There is a house beside a river
It's a holiday
So the family has come out to spend time with each other
They have placed the picnic basket under the tree
The man is reading a book
And the woman is drinking juice
The boy is flying a kite
His dog is looking at him and waiting for him to play with him
There is a flag hoisted in the front in front of the house
The flag *there s-* there is a boat sailing on the river
A man is probably *doing so-* doing something by the riverside

Note. Words marked in italics indicate words that were not counted as correct information units; bolded text indicates fluency disruptions (i.e., repetitions, revisions, and reformulations of thoughts).

partners about the progression of her cognitive-linguistic skills over the course of AD and provide strategies to support Mrs. P in challenging communication settings (see Figure 48–2 for a description of the treatment options considered). Given that Mrs. P relied on both Bengali and English, a decision was made to provide intervention in both languages.

Treatment Procedures and Responsiveness

Treatment sessions occurred twice weekly. Mrs. P was seen for a total of eighteen 50-minute sessions. Her cognitive-linguistic performance was reassessed immediately after the completion of therapy and during a follow-up visit 3 months after treatment.

a. **Spaced Retrieval Training (SRT; Bourgeois et al., 2003):** As Mrs. P's attention and ability to follow one- to two-step commands remained relatively preserved at the time of testing, SRT was considered a viable approach for therapy

(Mahendra et al., 2011). SRT was used to train Mrs. P in remembering names and personal information (e.g., family birthdays [semantic memory]) and future appointments/activities (prospective memory) using a memory aid (i.e., Mrs. P's phone calendar). Mrs. P was given a set of information for immediate recall. If she succeeded, she would be asked to recall repeatedly over increasing time intervals (5, 10, 15, and 20 minutes). In case of a recall failure, the time interval was reduced to the previous trial or half the time.

Mrs. P responded well to the SRT approach. After 9 weeks of therapy, her ability to independently recall personally relevant information (e.g., SLP's name, husband's birthday, upcoming dental appointment) increased over three sessions consecutively to 90% accuracy. At follow-up, Mrs. P demonstrated 70% accuracy with independently recalling the trained prompts and new information that she practiced at home with her husband. She required reminders to use her memory aid in recalling details.

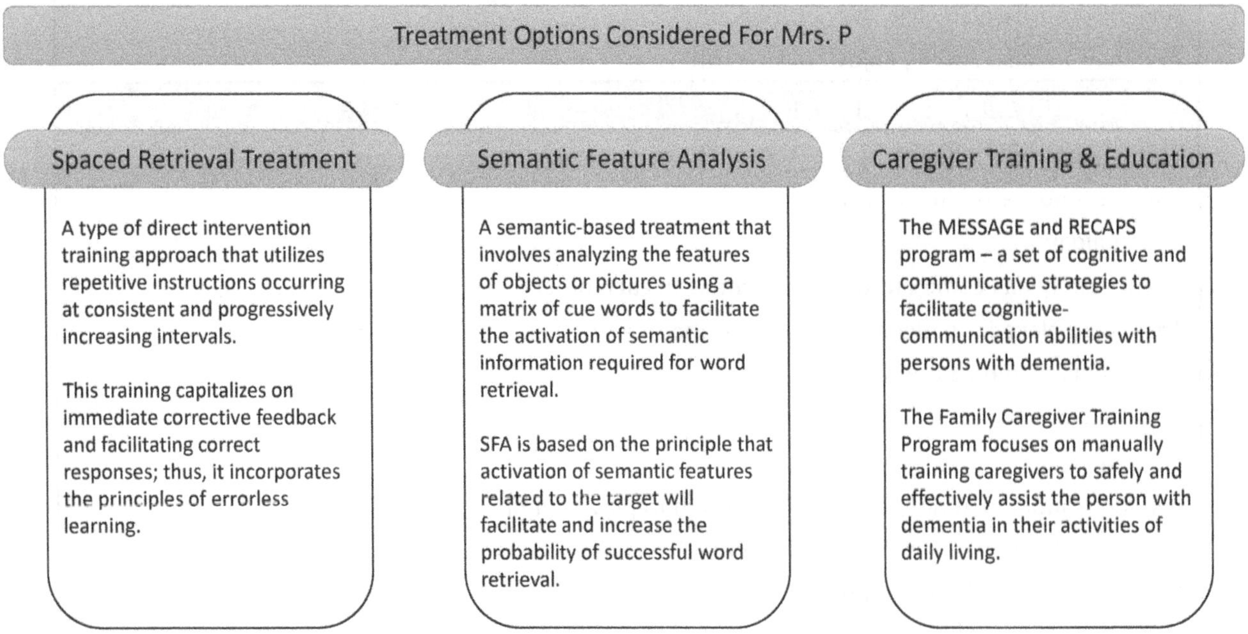

Treatment Options Considered For Mrs. P

Spaced Retrieval Treatment	Semantic Feature Analysis	Caregiver Training & Education
A type of direct intervention training approach that utilizes repetitive instructions occurring at consistent and progressively increasing intervals.

This training capitalizes on immediate corrective feedback and facilitating correct responses; thus, it incorporates the principles of errorless learning. | A semantic-based treatment that involves analyzing the features of objects or pictures using a matrix of cue words to facilitate the activation of semantic information required for word retrieval.

SFA is based on the principle that activation of semantic features related to the target will facilitate and increase the probability of successful word retrieval. | The MESSAGE and RECAPS program – a set of cognitive and communicative strategies to facilitate cognitive-communication abilities with persons with dementia.

The Family Caregiver Training Program focuses on manually training caregivers to safely and effectively assist the person with dementia in their activities of daily living. |

Figure 48–2. Treatment options considered for Mrs. P.

b. **Semantic Feature Analysis (SFA; Boyle & Coelho, 1995):** Thirty photographs that were functional and personally relevant for Mrs. P were selected as training items for word retrieval. Regardless of her success with naming the target items, she was trained to produce associated features of each item based on the following cues: group, use, action, properties, location, and association. Relatedly, SRT was incorporated to help Mrs. P in remembering to describe the items and use this as a strategy when she could not think of their names.

Immediately posttreatment, Mrs. P named 24 out of the 30 pictures spontaneously. For the remaining six items, she retrieved the item names once she went through the semantic features associated with them. Three months later, she maintained 80% accuracy on the trained items, but she inconsistently remembered to use the circumlocutory word-retrieval strategy. Discourse efficiency (i.e., CIU%) also improved after SFA treatment (from 70% to 85%), but only in Bengali.

c. **Caregiver education and training:** The SLP spent considerable time educating Mrs. P's family members about the signs of dementia progression and introducing various strategies and caregiver training programs such as MESSAGE and RECAPS (Smith et al., 2011; Figure 48–3) and the Family Caregiver Training Program (DiZazzo-Miller et al., 2014), which consisted of different modules involving presentations, discussions, real-life demonstrations, and role-playing. Mrs. P's SLP also worked with her caregivers on an ongoing basis and scheduled biweekly phone calls to check in. Mrs. P's husband found this support helpful and utilized the trained communication strategies consistently. However, he became frequently frustrated by increased caregiver burden and stress. He was given information about local support groups and community resources.

With progressive cognitive deterioration, Mrs. P began experiencing more significant challenges in communicating and making choices, resulting in undesirable behaviors (e.g., increased frustration, aggression). Given Mrs. P's cognitive-linguistic limitations, the SLP recommended environmental modifications to support her communication and reduce challenging behaviors. Mrs. P's family was educated to use concrete referencing (e.g., referencing visible objects that are present in her environment), asking simple yes/

M - Maximize attention

E - Expressions and body language

S - Keep it simple

S - Support their conversation

A - Assist with visual aids

G - Get their message

E - Encourage and engage in conversation

R – Reminders

E – Environment

C - Consistent routines

A – Attention

P – Practice

S - Simple steps

Figure 48–3. The MESSAGE and RECAPS program designed for care partners of individuals living with dementia (Smith et al., 2011).

no and choice questions to reduce cognitive load while still encouraging Mrs. P to make decisions. With these modifications, her caregivers reported that care routines took less time and she visibly appeared less frustrated.

Further Recommendations

SLPs play a unique role in the AD care pathway and are involved in providing person-centered care through a range of services, including the identification of initial cognitive-linguistic symptoms, differential diagnosis, and monitoring and managing changes over the course of the disease progression.

With the growing population of bilingual/multilinguals and those with different linguistic and cultural backgrounds globally, the quality of our AD-related services for culturally and linguistically diverse clients is increasingly important. When working with bilinguals or non-English speakers with AD, care should be individualized, considering cultural-linguistic differences as well as perceptions regarding dementia-related disability. Clinicians should not assume that a person's dominant language is always their first language, and all languages may not show similar patterns of linguistic decline in AD (Stilwell et al., 2016).

At present, the assessment options for bilingual/multilingual non-English speakers with AD remain limited. Aphasia tests (e.g., the Bilingual Aphasia Test; Paradis & Libben, 1987) are heavily relied on while evaluating language in dementia with no dementia-specific language assessment options available for non-English and/or multilingual speakers. Most of the newly adapted versions of cognitive-linguistic assessments have primarily focused on select languages such as Spanish (e.g., the Cognitive Linguistic Quick Test–Spanish; Helm-Estabrooks, 2017). Apart from Spanish-language speakers, South Asians are among the largest and fastest growing minority groups within the United States (Faroqi-Shah, 2012; Mahendra, 2012). Thus, it is critical that we expand our understanding of how AD impacts other languages (e.g., Bengali, Hindi, Urdu, Punjabi) and determine the rehabilitation needs of such speakers. Clinicians

may consult the literature for information about normative data for standardized tests in other languages. Although it may not be possible for SLPs to learn multiple languages, they must be aware of the influence of cultural and linguistic factors on cognitive-linguistic assessment performances so as to suit their clients' needs. Clinicians should involve the family members, care partners, interpreters, and professionals who share the individual's language and culture (Volkmer et al., 2020). Educating and advocating for patients when working with individuals with AD and especially those from diverse cultural, linguistic, and ethnic backgrounds is critical.

Authors' Note

The present client's description is based on a real bilingual client with Alzheimer's disease who had participated in our research study. The client's name, personal, demographic details, and assessment and treatment data have been altered to provide anonymity. We are also grateful to Dr. Nidhi Mahendra and her chapter on dementia in the first edition of this book for providing us with a structure for our current chapter.

Endnote

1. Bengali (also known as Bangla) is a pro-drop South Asian language with very rich morphology allowing extensive inflections of verbs, nouns, and other lexical categories. It belongs to the Aryan branch of the Indo-Iranian of the Indo-European group of languages and is spoken by natives of Bangladesh; the states of West Bengal, Assam, and Tripura in India; and a significant diaspora in the United States, United Kingdom, Middle East, and several Western countries. It is the seventh most spoken language in the world, with over 265 million speaking Bengali as their first or second language.

References

Ahmed, S., Haigh, A. M. F., de Jager, C. A., & Garrard, P. (2013). Connected speech as a marker of disease progression in autopsy-proven Alzheimer's disease. *Brain, 136*(12), 3727–3737. https://doi.org/10.1093/brain/awt269

Almkvist, O. (1996). Neuropsychological features of early Alzheimer's disease: Preclinical and clinical stages. *Acta Neurologica Scandinavica, 94*(S165), 63–71. https://doi.org/10.1111/j.1600-0404.1996.tb05874.x

Alzheimer's Association. (2022). 2022 Alzheimer's disease facts and figures. *Alzheimer's Dementia, 18*(4), 700–789.

American Speech-Language-Hearing Association. (2016). *Scope of practice in speech-language pathology.*

Baddeley, A. (2001). The concept of episodic memory. *Philosophical Transactions of the Royal Society of London. Series B: Biological Sciences, 356*(1413), 1345–1350. https://doi.org/10.1098/rstb.2001.0957

Balthazar, M. L. F., Cendes, F., & Damasceno, B. P. (2008). Semantic error patterns on the Boston Naming Test in normal aging, amnestic mild cognitive impairment, and mild Alzheimer's disease: Is there semantic disruption? *Neuropsychology, 22*(6), 703–709. https://doi.org/10.1037/a0012919

Bayles, K. A., Kaszniak, A. W., & Tomoeda, C. K. (1987). *Communication and cognition in normal aging and dementia.* College-Hill Press/Little, Brown & Co.

Bose, A., Dash, N. S., Ahmed, S., Dutta, M., Dutt, A., Nandi, R., . . . D. Mello, T. M. (2021). Connected speech characteristics of Bengali speakers with Alzheimer's disease: Evidence for language-specific diagnostic markers. *Frontiers in Aging Neuroscience, 13*, 707628. https://doi.org/10.3389/fnagi.2021.707628

Bose, A., Dutta, M., Dash, N. S., Nandi, R., Dutt, A., & Ahmed, S. (2022). Importance of task selection for connected speech analysis in patients with Alzheimer's disease from an ethnically diverse sample. *Journal of Alzheimer's Disease, 87*(4), 1475–1481. https://doi.org/10.3233/JAD-220166

Bourgeois, M. S. (2019). Caregiving for persons with dementia: Evidence-based resources for SLPs. *Topics in Language Disorders, 39*(1), 89–103. https://doi.org/10.1097/TLD.0000000000000166

Bourgeois, M. S., Camp, C., Rose, M., White, B., Malone, M., Carr, J., & Rovine, M. (2003). A comparison of training strategies to enhance use of external aids by persons with dementia. *Journal of Communication Disorders, 36*(5), 361–378. https://doi.org/10.1016/s0021-9924(03)00051-0

Boyle, M., & Coelho, C. A. (1995). Application of semantic feature analysis as a treatment for aphasic dysnomia. *American Journal of Speech-Language Pathology, 4*(4), 94–98. https://doi.org/10.1044/1058-0360.0404.94

Carlomagno, S., Santoro, A., Menditti, A., Pandolfi, M., & Marini, A. (2005). Referential communication in Alzheimer's type dementia. *Cortex, 41*, 520–534. https://doi.org/10.1016/s0010-9452(08)70192-8

Costa, A., Calabria, M., Marne, P., Hernández, M., Juncadella, M., Gascón-Bayarri, J., & Lleó, A. (2012). On the parallel deterioration of lexico-semantic processes in the bilinguals' two languages: Evidence from Alzheimer's disease. *Neuropsychologia, 50*(5), 740–753. https://doi.org/10.1016/j.neuropsychologia.2012.01.008

Cuetos, F., Arango-Lasprilla, J. C., Uribe, C., Valencia, C., & Lopera, F. (2007). Linguistic changes in verbal expression: A preclinical marker of Alzheimer's disease. *Journal of the International Neuropsychological Society, 13*(3), 433–439. https://doi.org/10.1017/S1355617707070609

DiZazzo-Miller, R., Samuel, P. S., Barnas, J. M., & Welker, K. M. (2014). Addressing everyday challenges: Feasibility of a family caregiver training program for people with dementia. *The American Journal of Occupational Therapy, 68*(2), 212–220. https://doi.org/10.5014/ajot.2014.009829

Dupuis, K., Pichora-Fuller, M. K., Chasteen, A. L., Marchuk, V., Singh, G., & Smith, S. L. (2015). Effects of hearing and vision impairments on the Montreal Cognitive Assessment. *Aging, Neuropsychology, and Cognition, 22*(4), 413–437. https://doi.org/10.1080/13825585.2014.968084

Ehrlich, J. S., Obler, L. K., & Clark, L. (1997). Ideational and semantic contributions to narrative production in adults with dementia of the Alzheimer's type. *Journal of Communication Disorders, 30*(2), 79–99.

Faroqi-Shah, Y. (2012). Linguistic and sociocultural diversity among south Asians. *Perspectives on Communication Disorders and Sciences in Culturally and Linguistically Diverse (CLD) Populations, 19*(1), 6–11. https://doi.org/10.1044/cds19.1.6

Folstein, M. F., Folstein, S. E., & McHugh, P. R. (1975). "Mini-mental state": A practical method for grading the cognitive state of patients for the clinician. *Journal of Psychiatric Research, 12*(3), 189–198. https://doi.org/10.1016/0022-3956(75)90026-6

Gollan, T. H., Salmon, D. P., Montoya, R. I., & Da Pena, E. (2010). Accessibility of the nondominant language in picture naming: A counterintuitive effect of dementia on bilingual language production. *Neuropsychologia, 48*, 1356–1366. https://doi.org/10.1016/j.neuropsychologia.2009.12.038

Guarino, A., Favieri, F., Boncompagni, I., Agostini, F., Cantone, M., & Casagrande, M. (2019). Executive functions in Alzheimer disease: A systematic review. *Frontiers in Aging Neuroscience, 10*, 437. https://doi.org/10.3389/fnagi.2018.00437

Guerchet, M., Prince, M., & Prina, M. (2020). Alzheimer's Disease International. *Numbers of people with dementia around the world.* https://www.alzint.org/resource/numbers-of-people-with-dementia-worldwide/

Helm-Estabrooks, N. (2017). *Cognitive linguistic quick test-plus.* The Psychological Corporation.

Hodges, J. R., Salmon, D. P., & Butters, N. (1992). Semantic memory impairment in Alzheimer's disease: Failure of access or degraded knowledge? *Neuropsychologia, 30*(4), 301–314. https://doi.org/10.1016/0028-3932(92)90104-t

Hsieh, S., Schubert, S., Hoon, C., Mioshi, E., & Hodges, J. R. (2013). Validation of the Addenbrooke's Cognitive Examination III in frontotemporal dementia and Alzheimer's disease. *Dementia and Geriatric Cognitive Disorders, 36*(3–4), 242–250. https://doi.org/10.1159/000351671

Huntley, J. D., & Howard, R. J. (2010). Working memory in early Alzheimer's disease: A neuropsychological review. *International Journal of Geriatric Psychiatry, 25*(2), 121–132. https://doi.org/10.1002/gps.2314

Ivanova, I., Salmon, D. P., & Gollan, T. H. (2014). Which language declines more? Longitudinal versus cross-sectional decline of picture naming in bilinguals with Alzheimer's disease. *Journal of the International Neuropsychological Society, 20*(5), 534–546. https://doi.org/10.1017/S1355617714000228

Jack, C. R., Jr., Bennett, D. A., Blennow, K., Carrillo, M. C., Dunn, B., Haeberlein, S. B., . . . Silverberg, N. (2019). NIA-AA research framework: Toward a biological definition of Alzheimer's disease. *Alzheimer's & Dementia, 14*(4), 535–562. https://doi.org/10.1016/j.jalz.2018.02.018

Kavé, G., & Levy, Y. (2003). Morphology in picture descriptions provided by persons with Alzheimer's disease. *Journal of Speech Language Hearing Research, 46*, 341–352. https://doi.org/10.1044/1092-4388(2003/027)

Kertesz, A. (2007). *Western Aphasia Battery–Revised.* Grune & Stratton.

Keshree, N. K., Kumar, S., Basu, S., Chakrabarty, M., & Kishore, T. (2013). Adaptation of the Western Aphasia Battery in Bangla. *Psychology of Language and Communication, 17*(2), 189–201. https://doi.org/10.2478/plc-2013-0012

Mahendra, N. (2012). South Asian stories: Firsthand client perspectives on barriers to accessing speech-language pathology services. *SIG 14 Perspectives on Communication Disorders and Sciences in Culturally and Linguistically Diverse (CLD) Populations, 19*, 29–36. https://doi.org/10.1044/cds19.1.29

Mahendra, N., Scullion, A., & Hamerschlag, C. (2011). Cognitive-linguistic interventions for persons with dementia: A practitioner's guide to 3 evidence-based techniques. *Topics in Geriatric Rehabilitation, 27*(4), 278–288. https://doi.org/10.1097/TGR.0b013e31821e5945

Malhotra, P. A. (2019). Impairments of attention in Alzheimer's disease. *Current Opinion in Psychology, 29*, 41–48. https://doi.org/10.1016/j.copsyc.2018.11.002

Mandal, P. K., Joshi, J., & Saharan, S. (2012). Visuospatial perception: An emerging biomarker for Alzheimer's disease. *Journal of Alzheimer's Disease, 31*(Suppl. 3), S117–S135. https://doi.org/10.3233/JAD-2012-120901

Martínez-Sánchez, F., Meilán, J. J. G., García-Sevilla, J., Carro, J., & Arana, J. M. (2013). Oral reading fluency analysis in patients with Alzheimer disease and asymptomatic control subjects. *Neurología, 28*(6), 325–331. https://doi.org/10.1016/j.nrl.2012.07.012

Mathuranath, P. S., George, A., Cherian, P. J., Mathew, R., & Sarma, P. S. (2005). Instrumental activities of daily living scale for dementia screening in elderly people. *International Psychogeriatrics, 17*(3), 461–474. https://doi.org/10.1017/s1041610205001547

McKhann, G. M., Knopman, D. S., Chertkow, H., Hyman, B. T., Jack, C. R., Jr., Kawas, C. H., . . . Phelps, C. H. (2011). The diagnosis of dementia due to Alzheimer's disease: Recommendations from the National Institute on Aging-Alzheimer's Association workgroups on diagnostic guidelines for Alzheimer's disease. *Alzheimer's & Dementia, 7*(3), 263–269. https://doi.org/10.1016/j.jalz.2011.03.005

Morris, J. C. (1993). The Clinical Dementia Rating (CDR): Current version and scoring rules. *Neurology, 43*, 2412–2414. https://doi.org/10.1212/wnl.43.11.2412-a

Mueller, K. D., Hermann, B., Mecollari, J., & Turkstra, L. S. (2018). Connected speech and language in mild cognitive impairment and Alzheimer's disease: A review of picture description tasks. *Journal of Clinical and Experimental Neuropsychology, 40*(9), 917–939. https://doi.org/10.1080/13803395.2018.1446513

Mueller, K. D., Koscik, R. L., Turkstra, L. S., Riedeman, S. K., LaRue, A., Clark, L. R., . . . Johnson, S. C. (2016).

Connected language in late middle-aged adults at risk for Alzheimer's disease. *Journal of Alzheimer's Disease, 54*(4), 1539–1550. https://doi.org/10.3233/JAD-160252

Muñoz, M. L., Marquardt, T. P., & Copeland, G. A. (1999). Comparison of the codeswitching patterns of aphasic and neurologically normal bilingual speakers of English and Spanish. *Brain and Language, 66*, 249–274. https://doi.org/10.1006/brln.1998.2021

Nicholas, L. E., & Brookshire, R. H. (1993). A system for quantifying the informativeness and efficiency of the connected speech of adults with aphasia. *Journal of Speech, Language, and Hearing Research, 36*(2), 338–350. https://doi.org/10.1044/jshr.3602.338

Paek, E. J., & Murray, L. L. (2021). Quantitative and qualitative analysis of verb fluency performance in individuals with probable Alzheimer's disease and healthy older adults. *American Journal of Speech-Language Pathology, 30*(1, Suppl.), 481–490. https://doi.org/10.1044/2019_AJSLP-19-00052

Paradis, M., & Libben, G. (1987). *The assessment of bilingual aphasia.* Lawrence Erlbaum Associates.

Perry, R. J., & Hodges, J. R. (1999). Attention and executive deficits in Alzheimer's disease: A critical review. *Brain, 122*(3), 383–404. https://doi.org/10.1093/brain/122.3.383

Pistono, A., Jucla, M., Bézy, C., Lemesle, B., Le Men, J., & Pariente, J. (2019). Discourse macrolinguistic impairment as a marker of linguistic and extra-linguistic functions decline in early Alzheimer's disease. *International Journal of Language & Communication Disorders, 54*(3), 390–400. https://doi.org/10.1111/1460-6984.12444

Rapp, M. A., Schnaider-Beeri, M., Purohit, D. P., Perl, D. P., Haroutunian, V., & Sano, M. (2008). Increased neurofibrillary tangles in patients with Alzheimer disease with comorbid depression. *The American Journal of Geriatric Psychiatry, 16*(2), 168–174. https://doi.org/10.1097/JGP.0b013e31816029ec

Rodakowski, J., Saghafi, E., Butters, M. A., & Skidmore, E. R. (2015). Non-pharmacological interventions for adults with mild cognitive impairment and early-stage dementia: An updated scoping review. *Molecular Aspects of Medicine, 43*, 38–53. https://doi.org/10.1016/j.mam.2015.06.003

Sajjadi, S. A., Patterson, K., Tomek, M., & Nestor, P. J. (2012). Abnormalities of connected speech in semantic dementia vs Alzheimer's disease. *Aphasiology, 26*(6), 847–866. https://doi.org/10.1080/02687038.2012.654933

Slegers, A., Filiou, R. P., Montembeault, M., & Brambati, S. M. (2018). Connected speech features from picture description in Alzheimer's disease: A systematic review. *Journal of Alzheimer's Disease, 65*(2), 519–542. https://doi.org/10.3233/JAD-170881

Smith, E. R., Broughton, M., Baker, R., Pachana, N. A., Angwin, A. J., Humphreys, M. S., . . . Chenery, H. J. (2011). Memory and communication support in dementia: Research-based strategies for caregivers. *International Psychogeriatrics, 23*(2), 256–263. https://doi.org/10.1017/S1041610210001845

Spitzer, R. L., Kroenke, K., Williams, J. B., & the Patient Health Questionnaire Primary Care Study Group. (1999). Validation and utility of a self-report version of PRIME-MD: The PHQ primary care study. *JAMA, 282*(18), 1737–1744. https://doi.org/10.1001/jama.282.18.1737

Stilwell, B. L., Dow, R. M., Lamers, C., & Woods, R. T. (2016). Language changes in bilingual individuals with Alzheimer's disease. *International Journal of Language & Communication Disorders, 51*(2), 113–127. https://doi.org/10.1111/1460-6984.12190

Vermunt, L., Sikkes, S. A., Van Den Hout, A., Handels, R., Bos, I., Van Der Flier, W. M., . . . Coley, N. (2019). Duration of preclinical, prodromal, and dementia stages of Alzheimer's disease in relation to age, sex, and APOE genotype. *Alzheimer's & Dementia, 15*(7), 888–898. https://doi.org/10.1016/j.jalz.2019.04.001

Volkmer, A., Spector, A., Warren, J. D., & Beeke, S. (2020). Speech and language therapy for primary progressive aphasia: Referral patterns and barriers to service provision across the UK. *Dementia, 19*(5), 1349–1363. https://doi.org/10.1177/1471301218797240

Weiner, M. F., Neubecker, K. E., Bret, M. E., & Hynan, L. S. (2008). Language in Alzheimer's disease. *Journal of Clinical Psychiatry, 69*(8), 1223–1227. https://doi.org/10.4088/jcp.v69n0804

World Health Organization. (2018). *ICD-11 for mortality and morbidity statistics.*

World Health Organization. (2016). *International classification of functioning, disability, and health.*

FLUENCY
CASE 49
Jessica: Treatment of Stuttering for an Adult
Sue O'Brian, Mark Onslow, Ross G. Menzies, and Tamsen St Clare

Conceptual Knowledge Areas

Stuttering is a genetically influenced disorder of neural speech processing. Typically, it begins in early childhood. In adulthood, the incidence is around 1% to 2%, with a male to female ratio of 4:1. Adults who stutter may find normal communication extremely difficult, and in severe cases, their rate of transfer of information can be reduced by up to half that of nonstuttering speakers. They may also avoid speaking for much of their day-to-day lives. Anxiety is a common clinical symptom associated with stuttering, with up to 60% of those seeking clinical help warranting a comorbid psychiatric diagnosis of social phobia (Blumgart et al., 2010; Iverach et al., 2009; Stein et al., 1996). Not surprisingly, then, those who stutter may have poor quality of life and failure to attain educational and occupational potential.

Social phobia, or social anxiety disorder, is one of the commonly diagnosed anxiety disorders. It involves a morbid and debilitating expectation of negative evaluation by others in social situations, with the expectation of being humiliated and embarrassed. The response of those affected is disproportionate to the reality of the threat and, in severe cases, involves high levels of avoidance and social isolation.

Cognitive behavior therapy (CBT) is widely considered the most efficacious treatment for anxiety. Several meta-analytic reviews (for example, Fedoroff & Taylor, 2001; Gould et al., 1997; Taylor, 1996) have summarized studies evaluating cognitive and behavioral therapies for social anxiety. All have reached a similar conclusion: that

behavior therapy and CBT are consistently more efficacious than wait-list conditions. Taylor (1996) concluded that CBT is superior to placebo and various control conditions. CBT has been found to be significantly more efficacious in reducing social anxiety than both pharmacologic interventions (Clark et al., 2003) and alternate forms of psychotherapy (for example, Heimberg et al., 1993).

Cognitive behavior therapy has been associated with excellent maintenance of gains following treatment. Heimberg and colleagues (1993) found that patients receiving CBT maintained their gains at 5-year follow-up and remained significantly less symptomatic than those who had received the control intervention of education and supportive counseling.

Description of the Case

Background Information

Jessica presented at the Australian Stuttering Research Centre as a pleasant, somewhat reserved, articulate young woman of 29 years at the time of assessment. She was single and lived alone, having recently moved from South Africa to Sydney. She had no immediate family support and a very small circle of friends. She had initially trained as a librarian, but soon after beginning treatment, she began work with a publisher of educational texts.

Jessica said she had had difficulty with her speech for as long as she could remember. Although it had been a consistent problem for her throughout her primary school years, it was only during adolescence that she identified her problem as stuttering. Her family never discussed the issue with her, and she had always been too embarrassed to bring it up with them. Jessica was unaware of any other family members who stuttered but had never felt able to ask about its existence in her extended family.

Jessica's stuttering had remained mild but persistent throughout her years at school and university. She had never sought treatment, although she had tried many techniques herself to overcome the problem. She had practiced reading out loud when nobody was listening. She had tried to slow down her speech rate when experiencing difficulty, and she reported scanning ahead when talking and substituting other words for those on which she anticipated stuttering. However, she reported that none of these techniques had any impact on her stuttering.

Findings of the Evaluation

A speech sample in conversation with the clinician at the first clinic visit revealed 3.4% syllables stuttered (%SS) and a clinician severity rating (SR) of 3 on a 9-point scale (0 = *no stuttering*, 8 = *extremely severe stuttering*; O'Brian et al., 2004). Repeated movements, usually several incomplete syllable repetitions, characterized Jessica's stuttering and very occasional, short, fixed postures. Jessica's self-reported stuttering SRs in five situations representative of her daily life confirmed typical severity ratings of between 2 and 3.

Jessica's speech history also revealed several cognitive and behavioral indicators of speech anxiety. First, she had never sought advice about or discussed her stuttering with anyone, including family members and friends, despite experiencing considerable long-term concern about her speech. She reported being tormented by embarrassment and feelings of inadequacy all her life because she sounded different from her peers. She felt that her stuttering had significantly affected her social relationships as well as her occupational potential because she avoided many speech-related situations. She felt continually frustrated by using word avoidance strategies because this meant that she

was unable to express herself precisely. Her presentation to the clinic at 29 years of age was significant because it was the first time she had ever acknowledged her stuttering to another person.

During the assessment, Jessica showed symptoms of speech-related anxiety, which were considered to be in excess of those expected in the context of a quite mild stuttering problem. It was acknowledged that Jessica might have difficulty applying speech techniques in everyday social settings and that consequently her speech outcomes might be compromised by her anxiety.

During her treatment (see "Description of Course of Treatment"), Jessica was assessed by a clinical psychologist (the third author). The clinical psychologist conducted a comprehensive clinical interview to determine the specific nature of Jessica's anxiety and to assess for comorbid psychiatric disorders. Jessica reported the following specific anxiety symptoms in the three domains of anxiety.

Cognitive symptoms included acute embarrassment when she stuttered and high levels of anticipatory anxiety when thinking about speaking situations. Reported beliefs about stuttering included: "People will notice that I stutter," "I won't be able to say what I want to say," "People will think I'm incompetent because I stutter," and "People will evaluate me negatively because I stutter." She also expressed concern that other people would discover not only that she stuttered but also that she became anxious about speaking. *Behavioral* symptoms reported were marked avoidance of the following speaking situations: the telephone, formal work meetings, and telephone answering machines. She also reported using word avoidance. Physiological symptoms reported were blushing, dry throat, sweaty hands, nausea, and stomach distress.

Jessica met the modified diagnostic criteria for social phobia (Stein et al., 1996). She also reported having been diagnosed with irritable bowel syndrome (IBS). This is common in anxious people, and stress is thought to exacerbate the symptoms. Her IBS symptoms included intermittent stomach bloating, decreased appetite, and abdominal pain. Jessica did not meet criteria for any other psychiatric diagnoses.

In addition to the clinical interview, Jessica completed a battery of psychometric measures to assess social anxiety. The measures chosen were the Fear of Negative Evaluation (FNE) Scale, the Social Avoidance and Distress (SAD) Scale, and the Social Phobia and Anxiety Inventory (SPAI). Results from these measures show that Jessica scored significantly above the mean on the three measures. This confirmed that she was suffering from high levels of social anxiety despite having mild stuttering.

Reason for Referral

In summary, Jessica presented as an intelligent 29-year-old woman with mild stuttering, which was complicated by significant speech-related anxiety. Her stated aim in seeking therapy at the time of assessment was to eliminate or at least reduce her stuttering.

Treatment Options Considered

Onslow et al. (2008) argue that, based on consensus within the field, a reasonably liberal definition of a clinical trial is a prospective study involving speech measures beyond the clinic with at least 3 months of follow-up. By far the best evidence for control of stuttering in this age group is for speech restructuring techniques, with more than 30 trials published that meet the Onslow et al. criteria (for an overview, see Onslow, 2022). These treatments control stuttering by changing aspects of speech production, such as reduced rate, prolonged vowels, "soft" articulatory contacts, and "gentle" vowel onsets. However, despite short-term benefits from these treatments, posttreatment relapse is common. In addition, posttreatment speech with these treatments often feels unnatural to the speaker, takes effort to maintain, and may sound unnatural to the listener.

An alternative treatment technique, for which there are three clinical trials according to the definition of Onslow et al. (2008), is time-out (Hewat et al., 2001; Hewat et al., 2006). Time-out is a verbal response-contingent procedure that involves a person pausing for a short period contingent on stuttering. It may be imposed by the clinician or by the client, or some combination of the two. Clinical trials of this procedure have demonstrated up to 80% reduction in stuttering in some clients in as few as 6 to 8 treatment hours. Another advantage of this procedure is that clients do not have to learn to use a new speech pattern. There has been one clinical trial showing positive results when time-out is combined with speech restructuring (James et al., 1989). According to the Onslow et al. criteria, there has been one clinical trial of the regulated breathing method (Saint-Laurent & Ladouceur, 1987). Additionally, there are many reports of drug treatments for stuttering, particularly using haloperidol, risperidone, and olanzapine. However, these interventions were not considered because of the limitations of their evidence base (Boyd et al., 2011).

A CBT treatment designed specifically for the speech-related anxiety of those who stutter has been developed and trialed successfully in a clinic format (Menzies et al., 2008) and in a standalone online format (Menzies et al., 2016). Subsequent randomized trials showed that the online format was noninferior to the clinic format (Menzies, Packman, et al., 2019) and that adding the online version to speech restructuring treatment improved speech outcomes in terms of stuttering severity and quality of life (Menzies, O'Brian, et al., 2019).

Course of Treatment

Referral to a clinical psychologist for treatment (the third author) was considered at the start of treatment. However, since stuttered speech was Jessica's primary complaint, a trial of speech treatment was offered first. Referral to a clinical psychologist could follow later if required.

The clinician tried self-imposed time-out (SITO) as a first treatment option for Jessica for the following reasons:

1. She had no previous successful or unsuccessful stuttering treatment to take into consideration.

2. Her stuttering was quite mild and therefore might not need the continued effort and focus involved in using a speech restructuring technique.
3. She had a fear of "sounding different" that may have made her feel uncomfortable using any speech restructuring technique.
4. SITO involves a shorter period of clinical time than speech restructuring techniques.
5. Speech restructuring could be introduced if a trial of SITO was unsuccessful.

A stable baseline was first established for Jessica's stuttering in the clinic, and then several 2-minute monologues using clinician-imposed time-out were trialed. Jessica's stuttering did not decrease at all in response to this technique. A further period of 2-minute monologues, this time using SITO, showed Jessica's stuttering to be unresponsive to the SITO technique, although she was able to use it very well. She identified accurately all instances of stuttering and timed herself out for several seconds; however, her stuttering rate did not reduce sufficiently during preliminary trials for the technique to be considered viable. Therefore, the clinician decided to introduce speech restructuring treatment. The Camperdown Program (Carey et al., 2010; O'Brian et al., 2003) was the treatment model chosen because the evidence at the time suggested that it was the simplest and least time-consuming delivery model for speech restructuring. Materials for this program, including the exemplar video, can be downloaded from the website of the Australian Stuttering Research Centre (O'Brian et al., 2018).

Description of Course of Treatment

The Camperdown Program consists of four stages: (1) teaching of the treatment components, (2) within-clinic control of stuttering, (3) generalization of stutter-free speech into everyday speaking situations, and (4) maintenance. It can be implemented in group or individual sessions and in weekly or intensive format. A telehealth version of this treatment is known to be efficacious in two clinical trials available (Carey et al., 2010;

O'Brian et al., 2008); however, the face-to-face version (O'Brian et al., 2003) was chosen.

Jessica attended weekly 1-hour sessions for Stage 1 of the program. She easily learned to use the fluency technique as demonstrated by the models shown on the ASRC website (https://www.uts.edu.au/asrc/resources/camperdown-program), although she commented that she did not like the sound or the feel of the technique and was initially somewhat uncomfortable and embarrassed using it even in the clinic. She had no difficulty learning to use the 9-point severity and fluency technique scales. These can also be found on the ASRC website (https://www.uts.edu.au/asrc/resources/camperdown-program).

She attended a group day with two other people for Stage 2 of the program as it was thought that she might benefit from exposure to and support from other adults who stuttered. At the completion of this day, she was able to use natural-sounding, stutter-free speech consistently within the clinic.

Stage 3 of the program was again implemented in weekly individual sessions. The initial focus of these problem-solving sessions was to establish appropriate speech practice routines with familiar and supportive partners, and general consolidation of the speech restructuring technique in everyday situations. Practice routines were difficult for Jessica because she had not told anyone that she was attending treatment, had never spoken to her friends or family about her stuttering, and still was uncomfortable to do so. Therefore, she had no one with whom she could overtly practice her speech. Arrangements were therefore made for her to practice over the telephone with another client who had attended the group day with her and with a clinic reception staff member. She was also encouraged to begin to use her speech technique in various everyday situations and to collect severity and fluency technique ratings of her speech in these situations. These ratings assisted her in learning to problem-solve around daily fluctuations in stuttering severity.

After a few sessions, Jessica returned to South Africa for a month to attend a family wedding. During this time, she did no speech practice and did not attempt to use speech restructuring to control her stuttering in any situation. When her mother decided to return to Australia with her for a holiday, Jessica felt compelled to tell her about the stuttering treatment program. Her mother was critical and unsupportive of her decision to attend therapy and, in particular, her use of a speech technique.

After a few clinic sessions, Jessica's self-reports of stuttering severity beyond the clinic differed little from those reported before treatment. She could be consistently stutter-free and natural-sounding, with fluency technique scores of 1 to 2, while talking to the clinician, the clinic reception staff member, the other members of her initial group, and her mother. However, Jessica was reluctant to attempt to use her speech technique to control her stuttering in everyday situations. She was only comfortable using the fluency technique to control her stuttering with people with whom she had discussed her problem, which involved a limited group, particularly as her mother had now returned home.

In summary, despite being able to use speech restructuring to control her stuttering at a fluency technique level of 1 to 2, and listening to recordings of this speech and agreeing that it sounded quite normal, Jessica was unwilling to use it in everyday situations. She remained concerned about other people's reactions to both her stuttering and her use of the speech technique. Jessica's speech-related anxiety had not decreased as a result of her speech treatment, and it was prohibiting her from making further progress with her speech treatment.

Consequently, a referral was made for Jessica to be assessed by a clinical psychologist. At the time of referral to the clinical psychologist (see "Findings of the Evaluation," above), Jessica had attended approximately 16 hours of speech therapy: 3 initial teaching hours, 7 group hours, and 6 problem-solving hours.

Given that Jessica met diagnostic criteria for social anxiety disorder, was motivated to overcome her anxiety, and did not exhibit any comorbid diagnoses thought to interfere with response to treatment, she was considered an ideal candidate for CBT. Her CBT program was based on the package developed by McColl and colleagues (2001),

with modifications to reflect current best practice in the treatment of social anxiety. The individual CBT components are outlined in the following paragraphs.

Education. Jessica was provided with information on the following topics: (1) the relationship between anxiety and speech performance, (2) the nature of anxiety, (3) the cognitive-behavioral model of anxiety acquisition and maintenance, and (4) cognitive-behavioral interventions for anxiety. Detailed information was presented and Jessica's own experiences were discussed.

Cognitive Restructuring. Jessica was taught to identify and change her dysfunctional beliefs about stuttering using the following steps.

1. Jessica was taught that there are many possible ways to interpret a specific situation. This was achieved with a series of "thinking exercises" in which she was required to generate several alternative interpretations for an ambiguous hypothetical situation.
2. Jessica learned to identify the thoughts that led her to feel anxious in speaking situations. She was asked to analyze the various components of her anxiety response by writing the following information in a diary each time she became aware of anxiety symptoms: date and time, situation, feelings, perceived threat, and behavior.
3. Jessica learned to challenge her thoughts by analyzing how realistic and helpful they were. She was asked to explore the evidence for and against her unhelpful thoughts. She was then asked to consider other ways in which that same situation could have been interpreted and to generate more adaptive thoughts and beliefs about the social situations she entered.
4. As is typical of social anxiety, Jessica's primary fear was of negative evaluation by others. She tended to overestimate both the likelihood and "badness," or cost, of negative evaluation. Cognitive therapy was aimed at helping Jessica learn to analyze the real probability and cost of such evaluation by others, and repeatedly to challenge her automatic

interpretations by generating more realistic and helpful alternatives.

Behavioral Experiments. Behavioral experiments are another method of producing cognitive change. They involve testing beliefs and interpretations with direct experiments. Initially, Jessica was convinced that her stuttering was obvious to others and that the likelihood that others would notice it increased as she became more anxious. She was also convinced that as she became anxious, she would show other signs of physiological arousal, such as blushing and sweating, and that others would notice them. She was convinced that once others knew of her stuttering, or once they noticed her blushing and sweating, they would judge her as being incompetent.

Jessica was encouraged to test these beliefs rather than accepting them as true without supporting evidence. One task involved her speaking to a large group and videotaping her presentation. She then analyzed the video and compared her predicted speech and appearance with her actual speech and appearance. She discovered that she did not stutter as much as expected and that there were no obvious signs of physiological arousal. A second task involved her telling several close friends that she had a stutter and comparing their reactions to her predictions. Interestingly, her best friend had not realized that Jessica stuttered, despite having known her for more than 20 years. Once Jessica collected evidence from these behavioral experiments, she was encouraged to use it in her cognitive restructuring exercises to further facilitate cognitive change.

Attentional Training. Many socially anxious people have difficulty focusing on the task in which they are engaged, such as the speech they are giving or the content of the conversation they are having. This is because their attention is focused on how they are being perceived by others. Jessica described having a mental image of herself stuttering, blushing, and sweating when talking to others and that this preoccupied her to such an extent that she could not focus on the content of conversations. In order to overcome this, Jessica was taught an attentional training exercise, which she was asked to practice twice each day.

The attentional training component involved two tasks. First, Jessica was encouraged to strengthen her attentional ability with meditation exercises. In this task, she learned to focus on alternative cognitive targets by counting her breaths rather than focusing on intrusive thoughts. The second task involved intentionally changing the focus of her attention when in anxiety-provoking speaking situations.

The above components were delivered across 10 weekly 1-hour sessions. Jessica was then reassessed to determine treatment response. Jessica made significant improvements in her social anxiety. She described being less anxious when speaking in formal work meetings and said that she no longer avoided participating in them. She was no longer concerned that others might see her blush or sweat and was markedly less concerned about other people noticing her stutter. She had reduced her use of email and was making many more telephone calls to customers. She was actively confronting difficult words rather than avoiding them. Posttreatment scores on psychometric measures reflected this reported reduction in anxiety. Posttreatment questionnaire scores are presented in Table 49–1. This shows that Jessica had significantly reduced her scores on all three measures following CBT.

Analysis of Client's Response to Intervention and Further Recommendations

After completing the CBT program, Jessica attended several further sessions with the speech-language pathologist before moving into a performance-contingent maintenance program. During these sessions, strategies were discussed for using her speech technique when needed to control her stuttering in everyday speaking situations. Her maintenance sessions, some of which occurred by telephone, were spaced as she took control of her stuttering management. Clinical measures collected before and after treatment are presented in Table 49–2.

Table 49–1. Jessica's Pretreatment and Posttreatment Scores and Population Means for Social Anxiety Measures

Measure	Jessica Pretreatment	Jessica Posttreatment	Nonanxious Control Subjects
FNE	27	16*	13.97[a]
SADS	18	10*	11.2[a]
SPAI difference score	98	62*	32.7[b]

[a] Watson and Friend (1969).
[b] Turner et al. (1986).
*$p < .05$.

Table 49–2. Pretreatment and Posttreatment Percent Syllables Stuttered (%SS) and Severity Ratings (SR) for Jessica

	Pretreatment	Posttreatment
Within clinic (%SS)	3.4	0
Within clinic (SR)	3	0
Talking to family (SR)	2	0
Social—friends (SR)	3	1
Telephone (SR)	3	1
Work—talking to clients (SR)	3	1
Work—seminar presentations (SR)	3	1

Note: SRs are measured on a 9-point scale where 0 = *no stuttering* and 8 = *extremely severe stuttering*.

Authors' Note

This case was based on a real client. Names, places, and some details of treatment were changed to preserve anonymity.

References

Blumgart, E., Tran, Y., & Craig, A. (2010). Social anxiety disorder in adults who stutter. *Depression and Anxiety, 27,* 687–692. https://doi.org/10.1002/da.20657

Boyd, A., & Howell, P. (2011). Pharmacological agents for developmental stuttering in children and adults. *Journal of Clinical Psychopharmacology, 31,* 740–744.

Carey, B., O'Brian, S., Onslow, M., Block, S., Jones, M., & Packman, A. (2010). Randomized controlled non-inferiority trial of a telehealth treatment for chronic stuttering: The Camperdown Program. *International Journal of Language and Communication Disorders, 45,* 108–120. https://doi.org/10.3109/13682820902763944

Clark, D. M., Ehlers, A., McManus, F., Hackmann, A., Fennell, M., Campbell, H., . . . Louis, B. (2003). Cognitive therapy versus Fluoxetine in generalized social phobia: A randomized placebo-controlled trial. *Journal of Consulting and Clinical Psychology, 71,* 1058–1067. https://doi.org/10.1037/0022-006X.71.6.1058

Federoff, I. C., & Taylor, S. (2001). Psychological and pharmacological treatments of social phobia: A meta-analysis. *Journal of Clinical Psychopharmacology, 21,* 311–324. https://doi.org/10.1097/00004714-200106000-00011

Gould, R. A., Buckminster, S., Pollack, M. H., Otto, M. W., & Yap, L. (1997). Cognitive-behavioral and pharmacological treatment for social phobia: A meta-analysis. *Clinical Psychological Science Practice, 4*, 291–306. https://doi.org/10.1111/j.1468-2850.1997.tb00123.x

Heimberg, R. G., Salzman, D. G., Holt, C. S., & Blendell, K. A. (1993). Cognitive-behavioral group treatment for social phobia: Effectiveness at 5-year follow-up. *Cognitive Therapy and Research, 14*, 1–23. https://doi.org/10.1007/BF01177658

Hewat, S., O'Brian, S., Onslow, M., & Packman, A. (2001). Control of chronic stuttering with self-imposed time-out: Preliminary outcome data. *Asia Pacific Journal of Speech, Language, and Hearing, 6*, 97–102. https://doi.org/10.1179/136132801805576716

Hewat, S., Onslow, M., O'Brian, S., & Packman, A. (2006). A phase II clinical trial of self-imposed time-out treatment for stuttering in adults and adolescents. *Disability and Rehabilitation, 28*, 33–42. https://doi.org/10.1080/09638280500165245

Iverach, L., O'Brian, S., Jones, M., Block, S., Lincoln, M., Harrison, E., . . . Onslow, M. (2009). Prevalence of anxiety disorders among adults seeking speech therapy for stuttering. *Journal of Anxiety Disorders, 2*, 928–934. https://doi.org/10.1016/j.janxdis.2009.06.003

James, J. E., Ricciardelli, L. A., Rogers, P., & Hunter, C. E. (1989). A preliminary analysis of the ameliorative effects of time-out from speaking on stuttering. *Journal of Speech and Hearing Research, 32*, 604–610. https://doi.org/10.1044/jshr.3203.604

McColl, T., Onslow, M., Packman, A., & Menzies, R. G. (2001). A cognitive behavioural intervention for social anxiety in adults who stutter. In L. Wilson & S. Hewat (Eds), *Proceedings of the 2001 Speech Pathology Australia National Conference* (pp. 93–98), Speech Pathology Australia.

Menzies, R., O'Brian, S., Lowe, R., Packman, A., & Onslow, M. (2016). International Phase II clinical trial of CBTPsych: A standalone Internet social anxiety treatment for adults who stutter. *Journal of Fluency Disorders, 48*, 35–43. https://doi.org/10.1016/j.jfludis.2016.06.002

Menzies, R., O'Brian, S., Onslow, M., Packman, A., St Clare, T., & Block, S. (2008). An experimental clinical trial of a cognitive behavior therapy package for chronic stuttering. *Journal of Speech, Language, and Hearing Research, 51*, 1451–1464. https://doi.org/10.1044/1092-4388(2008/07-0070)

Menzies, R., O'Brian, S., Packman, A., Jones, M., Helgadóttir, F. D., & Onslow, M. (2019). Supplementing stuttering treatment with online cognitive behavior therapy: An experimental trial. *Journal of Communication Disorders, 80*, 81–91. https://doi.org/10.1016/j.jcomdis.2019.04.003

Menzies, R., Packman, A., Onslow, M., O'Brian, S., Jones, M. & Helgadóttir, F. J. (2019). In-clinic and standalone Internet CBT treatment for social anxiety in stuttering: A randomized trial of iGlebe. *Journal of Speech, Language and Hearing Research, 62*, 1614–1624. https://doi.org/10.1044/2019_JSLHR-S-18-0340

O'Brian, S., Carey, B. Lowe, R. Onslow, M., Packman, A., & Cream, A. (2018). *The Camperdown Program stuttering treatment guide.* https://www.uts.edu.au/asrc/resources/camperdown-program

O'Brian, S., Cream, A., Onslow, M., & Packman, A. (2000). Prolonged speech: An experimental attempt to solve some nagging problems. In C. Lind (Ed.), *Proceedings of the 2000 Speech Pathology Australia National Conference, Sydney, Australia.* Speech Pathology Australia.

O'Brian, S., Cream, A., Onslow, M., & Packman, A. (2001). A replicable, nonprogrammed, instrument-free method for the control of stuttering with prolonged-speech. *Asia Pacific Journal of Speech, Language, and Hearing, 6*, 91–96. https://doi.org/10.1179/136132801805576680

O'Brian, S., Onslow, M., Cream, A., & Packman, A. (2003). The Camperdown Program: Outcomes of a new prolonged-speech treatment model. *Journal of Speech, Language, and Hearing Research, 46*, 933–946. https://doi.org/10.1044/1092-4388(2003/073)

O'Brian, S., Packman, A., & Onslow, M. (2004). Self-rating of stuttering severity as a clinical tool. *American Journal of Speech-Language Pathology, 13*, 219–226. https://doi.org/10.1044/1058-0360(2004/023)

O'Brian, S., Packman, A., & Onslow, M. (2008). Telehealth delivery of the Camperdown Program for adults who stutter. *Journal of Speech, Language, and Hearing Research, 51*, 184–195. https://doi.org/10.1044/1092-4388(2008/014)

Onslow, M. (2022, December). *Stuttering and its treatment: Twelve lectures.* https://www.uts.edu.au/asrc/resources

Onslow, M., Costa, L., Andrews, C., Harrison, E., & Packman, A. (1996). Speech outcomes of a prolonged-speech treatment for stuttering. *Journal of Speech and Hearing Research, 39*, 734–749. https://doi.org/10.1044/jshr.3904.734

Onslow, M., Jones, M., O'Brian, S., Menzies, R., & Packman, A. (2008). Biostatistics for clinicians: Defining, evaluating, and identifying clinical trials of stuttering treatments. *American Journal of*

Speech-Language Pathology, 17, 401–415. https://doi.org/10.1044/1058-0360(2008/07-0047)

Onslow, M., O'Brian, S., Packman, A., & Rousseau I. (2004). Long-term follow-up of speech outcomes for a prolonged-speech treatment for stuttering: The effects of paradox on stuttering treatment research. In A. K. Bothe (Ed.), *Evidence-based treatment of stuttering: Empirical issues and clinical implications.* (pp. 231–244). Lawrence Erlbaum Associates. https://doi.org/10.4324/9781410610522

Saint Laurent, L., & Ladouceur, R. (1987). Massed versus distributed application of the regulated-breathing method for stutterers and its long-term effect. *Behaviour Therapy, 18*, 38–50. https://doi.org/10.1016/S0005-7894(87)80050-3

Stein, M. B., Baird, A., & Walker, J. R. (1996). Social phobia in adults with stuttering. *American Journal of Psychiatry, 153*, 278–280.

Taylor, S. (1996). Meta-analysis of cognitive-behavioral treatments for social phobia. *Journal of Behavior Therapy and Experimental Psychiatry, 27*, 1–9. https://doi.org/10.1016/0005-7916(95)00058-5

Turner, S. M., Beidel, D. C., & Dancu, C. V. (1986). *SPAI: Social Phobia and Anxiety Inventory.* Multi-Health Systems.

Watson, D., & Friend, R. (1969). Measurement of social-evaluative anxiety. *Journal of Consulting and Clinical Psychology, 33*, 448–457. https://doi.org/10.1037/h0027806

HEAD AND NECK CANCER/SWALLOWING
CASE 50
Joel: Management of a Patient With Advanced Head and Neck Cancer
Roxann Diez Gross

Conceptual Knowledge Areas

To work successfully with patients that are being treated for head and neck cancer, the speech-language pathologist (SLP) must have an understanding of normal oral, laryngeal, and pharyngeal anatomy and function. Competency in evaluating and treating adult speech intelligibility disorders and dysphagia is required. The clinician must also be familiar with a variety of swallowing exercises, postural strategies, and swallowing maneuvers. Examples of swallowing exercises and maneuvers that are often used for this patient population are the effortful swallow, Mendelsohn maneuver, Shaker exercise, super-supraglottic swallow, and tongue hold maneuver. The effortful swallow increases the strength of all swallowing muscles by requiring patients to repeatedly swallow as hard and long as they can. The Mendelsohn maneuver improves the strength of the muscles that elevate the larynx by teaching the patient to maintain laryngeal elevation for several seconds when swallowing. The Shaker exercise increases the opening of the upper esophageal sphincter and is completed by lying on the back and raising the head to the chest while keeping the shoulders down. The super-supraglottic swallow increases airway protection and ensures correct breathing-swallowing coordination by teaching the patient to breathe in and close the vocal folds, bear down to close the laryngeal vestibule, and then swallow. The tongue hold maneuver improves the anterior motion of the posterior pharyngeal wall. It is completed by protruding the tongue and holding it between the teeth while swallowing. Positional strategies alter bolus (food or drink) flow from the mouth and into the esophagus. For example, turning the head to a weak side diverts the bolus to the stronger side. Tucking the chin to the chest can have a variety of effects on the swallow, from preventing premature spillage from the back of the mouth to narrowing the laryngeal vestibule.

Clinicians should also have basic knowledge of the different surgical procedures that are used to excise tumors and the potential effects on speech and swallowing. Additionally, familiarity with the imaging techniques and fundamental terminology that physicians use in relation to the medical management of these patients is beneficial. Strong counseling skills are necessary because these patients are often upset about their diagnoses and have little knowledge about speech and swallowing function. Furthermore, many patients are now aware of the painful side effects involved in cancer treatment and are understandably anxious about the effects of any pending surgical procedures or chemotherapy drugs.

Small tumors of the oral tongue and true vocal folds can be treated with surgical procedures that do not often impair speech or swallowing function; however, large tumors require wide excisions and can profoundly impair communication and swallowing.

Treatment that preserves organs is rapidly becoming the primary method to destroy tumors in the larynx and oropharynx; however, the function of these organs can decline as a result of this form of management. Currently, the main organ preservation treatment for oropharyngeal and laryngeal tumors is the combination of chemotherapy and radiation therapy. The main purpose for the chemotherapy is to increase the effects of the radiation. Chemotherapy drugs are continually being evaluated, and clinicians should be familiar with the names of the drugs and aware of the potential side effects. New methods that limit radiation exposure to surrounding tissues are also continually in development. The SLP should recognize the terminology used to describe the different modalities that deliver radiation as well as the effects of radiation on the surrounding tissues. Basic understanding of diagnostic imaging and tumor staging is also beneficial and can assist in determining the size and location of the tumor when postulating the potential effects on speech

and swallowing in light of the various treatments. Observational and interview experience in providing emotional support is crucial, because patients are often very fearful and seek assurance from the medical community. Speech-language pathologists should be sensitive to the patient's fears and anxiety in relation to a diagnosis as grave as cancer and should provide emotional support without exceeding the scope of practice (such as by implying that a cure is certain or uncertain).

Description of the Case

Background Information and Reasons for Referral

Joel was a 48-year-old male, nonsmoker, nondrinker, with no significant past medical history. He had a college education and was employed full-time as an accountant. His family history included a father who died of heart disease and a mother who died of colon cancer. His sister had diabetes and a remote history of stroke. He initially presented to his primary care physician with a persistent "sore throat" of 4 weeks' duration. Two courses of antibiotics were not effective in relieving his symptoms. A dental exam found the need for a root canal, which was performed in hopes of providing relief, yet the pain did not subside. In fact, Joel began to develop increased pain upon swallowing (rated by the patient as 6 on a scale of 10), and he began to experience a new onset of intermittent ear pain.

Joel was then referred by his primary care physician to an otolaryngologist, who, based upon the recent medical history, completed a thorough head and neck assessment. During the examination, the physician palpated a firm base of tongue mass. A transnasal endoscopic examination was then performed by the doctor. The mucosal surface of the nasopharynx and soft palate were normal in appearance. When the flexible scope was advanced into the oropharynx, a large, irregular base of tongue mass was clearly visible. Upon continued visual inspection, the tumor did not appear to involve laryngeal structures or the pyriform sinuses. A small portion of the mass was excised and sent to pathology. A more in-depth imaging procedure called positron emission tomography (PET) and computerized tomography (CT) or a PET CT scan was ordered.

Findings of the Evaluation

Joel's case was discussed by the head and neck cancer team at the weekly multidisciplinary conference. The team discussed treatment options and weighed the effects of surgery alone versus surgery with radiation versus organ preservation treatment to determine which treatment would provide the maximum potential to cure the disease while limiting the impact on Joel's posttreatment quality of life. The biopsy results confirmed the presence of squamous cell carcinoma. PET CT scan images showed strong uptake of the radiopharmaceutical and increased metabolic activity in the tongue base and bilaterally in the neck. Measurements of the size of the tumor and nodes were made so that the tumor could be staged. The 2.5 × 2.4-cm mass in the base of the tongue extended up to the right palatine tonsil and down to the pediole of the epiglottis. Several lymph nodes within the neck also showed increased activity. None of the nodes were greater than 6 cm. The biopsy was also positive for human papillomavirus (HPV). The possibility that the tumor was a result of HPV was discussed (Venkatesh et al., 2021). The tumor was staged as T2, N2C, M0, indicating stage IV head and neck cancer (Takes et al., 2010).

Treatment Options Considered

The risks and benefits of surgical, radiation, and combined treatment modalities were discussed by the medical team. Treatment options included a wide surgical excision of the base of the tongue and selected neck dissection to remove the cancerous nodes and surrounding nodes. The removal of a tumor that large with so much lingual tissue would most likely result in permanent and severe pharyngeal dysphagia as well as articulatory impairment from reduced range of motion of the tongue. In addition, Joel would still require radiation and could develop other unwanted effects. For these reasons, team members agreed that a combination of chemotherapy and radiation (CRT) was the best option for successful treatment and functional outcome. Chemotherapy treatment options were (1) neoadjuvant or induction chemotherapy, which is chemotherapy given prior to radiation therapy, and (2) adjuvant chemotherapy, where the chemotherapy drug(s) are given concomitantly with radiation therapy (chemoradiotherapy).

The radiation was to be given in a "fractionated fashion," meaning that a total dose would be given in fractions over a period of time. Additional options for radiation therapy were (1) conventional external beam radiation and (2) intensity-modulated radiation therapy (IMRT), a more advanced form of radiotherapy that uses a computer-controlled method to deliver a more precise radiation dose to tumors that invade deeply into tissue.

The effects of the CRT on swallowing can vary, but the probability is that patients are at risk to develop some degree of speech and/or swallowing impairment during and after treatment (Ihara et al., 2018). Consequently, referral to speech-language pathology was made. The team decided that Joel should be followed and periodically assessed by the dietitian throughout the course of treatment to assist with nutritional counseling as necessary.

The primary reason for the initial referral was to enable the SLP to instruct Joel in the appropriate swallowing exercises prior to the start of his cancer treatment (Paleri et al., 2014), to take a baseline quality of life (QOL) measurement and a baseline evaluation of swallowing function, and to provide counseling in relation to preservation of speech precision and swallowing function during CRT. Joel and his wife came to the outpatient speech-language pathology clinic 3 days after he received his final diagnosis from the otolaryngologist and following a meeting with the radiation oncologist and medical oncologist. He stated that he was to receive one dose of chemotherapy prior to the initiation of radiation therapy (induction chemotherapy), followed by adjuvant chemotherapy and radiation therapy over the course of

7 weeks. Because of the tumor characteristics, he would receive IMRT, which can deliver high doses of radiation with reduced exposure to surrounding and uninvolved tissues such as the parotid gland, mandible, and spinal cord. Joel stated that he was eager to begin CRT so that the cancer would not progress, but he was also anxious about both the short- and long-term side effects of the treatment.

Course of Treatment

Joel had a large tumor that appeared to have a negative effect on swallowing function primarily by causing pain; however, there was a very real possibility that the tumor could alter or partially obstruct bolus flow. Perceptually, his speech intelligibility was within normal limits at this time. When questioned further, he revealed that he had lost 10 pounds in the past 4 weeks. His taste sensation was unchanged (normal) at the time of the initial visit. Although he was evaluated endoscopically by a physician, a swallowing assessment had not been completed.

The large tumor would likely obstruct the view should a fiber-optic endoscopic evaluation of swallowing take place (FEES); therefore, a videofluoroscopic evaluation of swallowing or modified barium swallow study was planned. Because pre-CRT treatment swallowing exercises have been shown to improve swallowing outcomes (Carroll et al., 2008; Peng et al., 2015), Joel would be instructed in a series of exercises during the first visit. Also, counseling was necessary in relation to the need to continue to swallow despite the onset of odynophagia (painful swallowing), dysgeusia (altered taste sensation), and hypogeusia (low taste sensation).

During the first visit, Joel was instructed in prophylactic range-of-motion exercises (ROM) for tongue and mandible to prevent loss of motion from scarring and synechia (adhesions) that can result from high doses of radiation that are intensified further by the chemotherapy. Both he and his wife were counseled on the importance of continuing to swallow throughout the course of CRT even if he could only swallow water. They stated that they had received the same suggestion from

the radiation oncologist. It was also recommended that, should he develop the side effect of painful mucositis (inflammation and ulceration of the oral and pharyngeal mucosa), he should take the prescribed pain medicine rather than stop eating and/or drinking. Because CRT would alter taste sensation and cause eating to be unpleasant, he was given guidance to change his expectation of food and drink from "pleasure" to "medicine," or to think of himself as an athlete in training in which food is consumed for a purpose (i.e., build muscle). Joel, his wife, and the SLP were hopeful that he could continue to obtain adequate nutrition and hydration by mouth and avoid the necessity of having a feeding tube placed into his stomach.

Joel was then instructed in a series of strengthening exercises such as effortful swallow, Mendelsohn, and tongue-hold maneuver. He was unable to perform them with sufficient effort at the time because of pain and tumor size. He was able to perform the Shaker exercise and agreed to do at least three repetitions every other day. He was instructed to make the lingual and mandibular ROM exercises part of his morning and evening grooming routine, such as face washing and teeth brushing, and to use the mirror for visual feedback. It was explained that the purpose of the ROM exercises was not to increase motion but to maintain the current function, particularly lingual motion for speech and swallowing. These twice-daily exercises were to continue for the rest of his life (adding that, hopefully, he will be doing the ROM exercises for many years). It was explained that the effects of the radiation would continue long after the radiation therapy had ended and that some of the tissue changes would be permanent. The MD Anderson Dysphagia Inventory (MDADI) was also administered for the purpose of obtaining a baseline quality of life measurement (Chen et al., 2001). This scale has been shown to be valid and reliable for use in patients with head and neck cancer. The scale runs from 0 (*extremely low functioning*) to 100 (*high functioning*). The results showed that, overall, Joel felt that his quality of life (QOL) was high with a global score of 100/100, emotional score of 96/100, and functional score of 92/100. He gave the lowest rating to his physical status with a score of 87.5/100.

A baseline videofluoroscopic swallowing study or modified barium swallow was completed while Joel sat in lateral view and swallowed a variety of standardized viscosities from thin liquid to pudding and a solid. The evaluation showed that the oral phase was within normal limits as indicated by complete and controlled mastication, anterior to posterior movement of each entire bolus, no posterior oral cavity loss, and no oral residue. There was good velar seal and a prompt pharyngeal response. The large base of tongue tumor was easily visible in the lateral view and altered but did not obstruct bolus flow. Pharyngeal transit was within functional limits with hyoid elevation to the level of the mandible, laryngeal elevation was within normal limits for both height and duration of elevation, the posterior pharyngeal wall moved well, and the upper esophageal sphincter opening was adequate for bolus passage. There was no pharyngeal residue or aspiration observed during the evaluation. It was recommended that he continue with his current diet and food selections, including thin liquids.

As stated previously, CRT side effects can include mucositis (painful inflammation and ulceration of the tongue and mucous membranes), making it too painful to eat by mouth, and/or hypogeusia (reduced taste ability) and/or dysgeusia (distortion of taste), which make it difficult and undesirable to eat. Joel began CRT the next week with chemotherapy to be given at the beginning, middle, and end of 7 weeks of radiation. He was scheduled to return to the clinic in 3 weeks or sooner if he noticed a decline in swallowing function indicated by symptoms such as coughing during meals and/or a sensation of food sticking.

After approximately 3 weeks into his cancer treatment, Joel developed painful oropharyngeal mucositis and voluntarily switched to very soft and then smooth puree as tolerated. He continued to drink thin liquids. He lost his sense of taste and had a very poor appetite. He was reminded to try to change his expectation of food and to consider only the nutritional aspects as well as the importance of trying to continue to swallow, even if it was only water. He was not able to overcome the barriers to oral intake that had developed and lost greater than 10% of his body weight. At that point, the dietitian recommended the placement of a percutaneous endoscopic gastrostomy (PEG) tube so that nonoral nutrition and hydration could be given. Joel's preference was to be relieved of the burden of eating by mouth, and he had the PEG placed. During the next session, he and his wife were again advised as to the importance of continuing to swallow even if only small sips of water were taken. He was encouraged to continue to complete the daily ROM activities and Shaker exercise.

Two weeks after the CRT was completed, Joel's pain had resolved; however, he refused to eat because he felt that it was unsafe to do so. He continued drinking water because his salivary glands were affected by the CRT, and he developed severe mouth dryness, called xerostomia. He stated that all other liquids tasted bitter and, although he did attempt to take small amounts of food on occasion, he was unable to consume anything because he "couldn't swallow" and "everything tasted like paper." Because CRT patients' perceptions of their swallowing ability is not always consistent with their function, and having nothing by mouth for as little as 2 weeks is associated with a poorer outcome (Hutcheson et al., 2013), a second videofluoroscopic swallowing evaluation was scheduled. Additionally, it was felt that a fluoroscopic examination of swallowing would make it possible to identify the pathophysiology that might have resulted from the CRT so that a treatment plan specific to the patient could be designed. Also, compensatory and positional strategies could be explored, if indicated.

At this point, Joel's swallowing ability was likely functional, but anxiety and perhaps altered sensation were, in part, preventing him from eating by mouth. In addition, dysgeusia, or significantly altered taste sensation, had a significant negative impact on his desire for food. Radiation-induced xerostomia was another major complaint that often causes patients to perceive greater swallowing difficulty than may actually be present (Logemann et al., 2003).

The videofluoroscopic evaluation was completed in lateral and anterior-posterior views using the same standardized amounts and viscosities as the baseline exam. It was found that the oral phase had remained unchanged from the baseline examination. The large base of tongue tumor was no longer visible. Reduced base of tongue retraction was identified by the lack of normal posterior motion and failure to contact the posterior pharyngeal wall. Laryngeal elevation was also reduced as indicated by reduced superior motion from approximately 1½ vertebral bodies on the first exam to less than 1 cervical body. The anterior motion of the posterior pharyngeal wall was mildly diminished when compared to the baseline evaluation. Epiglottic inversion was not observed on any swallow, a finding that further supported the reduced range of motion of the base of tongue and laryngeal elevation. These changes combined to result in moderate residue in the valleculae (cavity approximately 50% full) with puree and soft solid (cookie), plus mild bilateral residue in the pyriform sinuses (bases only contained residue) with puree and solid. No material given was observed to enter the laryngeal vestibule or subglottis. A liquid wash was found to be an effective method to clear all residue. A deep chin tuck narrowed the pharyngeal space and altered biomechanics sufficiently to improve pharyngeal transit and prevent residue in the pharyngeal spaces. A soft diet with thin liquids was recommended. Based upon this assessment and Joel's concerns for swallowing safety, the video of the swallowing study was reviewed with him and his wife so that it could serve as a teaching tool. After a brief orientation to the swallowing structures and review of basic swallowing function, both stated that they were assured that the material he consumed had not entered his airway. They were also able to determine the effectiveness of the compensatory strategies, since this was observed directly. The patient stated that he was motivated to work toward having the feeding tube removed.

In a therapy session that followed, Joel was instructed to resume oral intake gradually using chin tuck and/or a liquid wash to manage pharyngeal residue. To assist with anxiety related to swallowing safety, the clinician gave him smooth purees and liquids during the treatment session and allowed him to practice the chin tuck and liquid wash. Because his pain had resolved, Joel and the clinician both felt that he was able to

begin an exercise program. Therefore, based upon the pathophysiology observed fluoroscopically, the following therapeutic exercise program was established: To increase base of tongue retraction, the effortful swallow and super-supraglottic swallow were to be the primary exercises. To improve laryngeal elevation, the Mendelsohn maneuver was instructed using submental EMG biofeedback for instruction. In addition, he was to continue to perform the Shaker head lift exercise. To increase anterior motion of the posterior pharyngeal wall, the tongue hold maneuver was instructed. The exercises were to be completed independently at home in sets of 20, every other day. He was asked to return in 1 week, so that it could be assured that he was performing the exercises correctly. The results of the fluoroscopic swallowing study and the recommendation to gradually resume oral intake were sent to the dietician, so that she could manage the gradual transition from nonoral to oral feedings without compromising nutritional status.

Upon his return, Joel demonstrated that he could perform each exercise accurately. He had not been able to reach 20 repetitions but was gradually increasing the intensity of his home program. Because he demonstrated independence with his exercises, he was not scheduled to be seen again for 1 month. Clinician contact information was provided along with written instructions. During this time period, it was expected that he would have begun to transition off the PEG feedings and resume oral intake to meet at least 50% of his nutritional and hydration needs. A fiberoptic endoscopic examination of swallowing function (FEES) was to be performed upon his return. FEES was selected for the reevaluation because the absence of residue in the valleculae and pyriform sinuses would indicate improved functioning and benefit from therapy without additional exposure to radiation. FEES was also indicated because there had been no oral phase swallowing impairment, and an endoscopic swallowing examination could easily be performed in the office.

After 1 month, Joel returned to the clinic. He stated that he had maintained his weight and possibly gained a pound or two. A quick weight check confirmed a 2-pound weight gain. He stated (and his wife confirmed) that he had been completing his swallowing exercises on a consistent basis with improved motivation since subsidence of his pain and reduced anxiety. In addition, he stated that he felt more confident about his ability to swallow safely since viewing his swallowing function under fluoroscopy. Despite the expected trepidation in relation to having a nasoendoscope passed, he was eager for the examination because he expected to see significant improvement. Although it is out of the scope of practice of the SLP to evaluate or comment on tumors and masses, and Joel was informed of this, he and his wife were anxious to visually inspect the base of his tongue.

The FEES was completed using a range of viscosities that had contrast color added to assist with visualization. Joel's head was in neutral position. Preswallowing observations showed slight swelling of the arytenoid cartilages and a smoothed appearance of the pharyngeal mucosa, both of which are indicative of dryness and radiation changes. The presence of obvious tumor was not appreciated and the tongue base appeared to be normal in size. There was no pooling of secretions. The true vocal folds adducted well. Premature spillage was not observed with any consistency. Postswallowing observations showed minimal, diffuse residue throughout the pharynx with pudding consistency only. An effortful swallow eliminated the residue. No contrast color of any of the materials given was observed within the laryngeal vestibule or subglottis. The impressions were that Joel no longer required a chin tuck or liquid wash because pharyngeal transit was much improved. The recommendations were to continue with a soft diet and thin liquids. It was also recommended that he continue to work with the dietitian until he was able to obtain all nutrition and hydration by mouth. The physician and dietitian were then to decide when to remove the PEG tube.

Analysis of Client's Response to Intervention

At this time, Joel was asked to take the MDADI once again so that his quality of life in relation to eating and drinking could be reassessed. His post-CRT global score was 60 (down from 100), the emotional subscale was 80 (down from 96), the physical component score was 70.5 (down from 87.5), and the functional score was 96 (increased from 92). The lower scores likely reflected his lack of taste, dryness, and other postradiation changes. The importance of continuing to complete twice-daily lingual and mandibular range-of-motion exercises to prevent scar tissue formation that can negatively affect speech and swallowing was reinforced, and Joel was discharged.

Author's Note

The case is highly typical of patients who undergo organ preservation treatment of head and neck cancer; however, many personal details are fictional.

References

Carroll, W. R., Locher, J. L., Canon, C. L., Bohannon, I. A., McColloch, N. L., & Magnuson, J. S. (2008). Pretreatment swallowing exercises improve swallow function after chemoradiation. *Laryngoscope*, *118*(1), 39–43. https://doi.org/10.1097/MLG.0b013e31815659b0

Chen, A. Y., Frankowski, R., Bishop-Leone, J., Hebert, T., Leyk, S., Lewin, J., & Goepfert, H. (2001). The development and validation of a dysphagia-specific quality-of-life questionnaire for patients with head and neck cancer: The M. D. Anderson dysphagia inventory. *Archives of Otolaryngology-Head and Neck Surgery*, *127*(7), 870–876.

Hutcheson, K. A., Bhayani, M. K., Beadle, B. M., Gold, K. A., Shinn, E. H., Lai, S. Y., & Lewin, J. (2013). Eat and exercise during radiotherapy or chemoradiotherapy for pharyngeal cancers: Use it or lose it. *JAMA Otolaryngology-Head and Neck Surgery*, *139*(11), 1127–1134. https://doi.org/10.1001/jamaoto.2013.4715

Ihara, Y., Crary, M. A., Madhavan, A., Gregorio, D. C., Im, I., Ross, S. E., & Carnaby, G. D. (2018). Dysphagia and oral morbidities in chemoradiation-treated head and neck cancer patients. *Dysphagia*, *33*(6), 739–748. https://doi.org/10.1007/s00455-018-9895-6

Logemann, J. A., Pauloski, B. R., Rademaker, A. W., Lazarus, C. L., Mittal, B., Gaziano, J., . . . Newman, L. A. (2003). Xerostomia: 12-month changes in saliva production and its relationship to perception and performance of swallow function, oral intake, and diet after chemoradiation. *Head and Neck, 25*(6), 432–437. https://doi.org/10.1002/hed.10255

Paleri, V., Roe, J. W., Strojan, P., Corry, J., Grégoire, V., Hamoir, M., . . . Ferlito, A. (2014). Strategies to reduce long-term postchemoradiation dysphagia in patients with head and neck cancer: An evidence-based review. *Head and Neck, 36*(3), 431–443. https://doi.org/10.1002/hed.23251

Peng, K. A., Kuan, E. C., Unger, L., Lorentz, W. C., Wang, M. B., & Long, J. L. (2015). A swallow preservation protocol improves function for veterans receiving chemoradiation for head and neck cancer. *Otolar-yngology-Head and Neck Surgery, 152*(5), 863–867. https://doi.org/10.1177/0194599815575508

Takes, R. P., Rinaldo, A., Silver, C. E., Piccirillo, J. F., Haigentz, M., Suárez, C., . . . Ferlito, A. (2010). Future of the TNM classification and staging system in head and neck cancer. *Head and Neck, 32*(12), 1693–1711. https://doi.org/10.1002/hed.21361

Venkatesh, A., Elengkumaran, S., Ravindran, C., & Malathi, N. (2021). Association of human papilloma virus in oral squamous cell carcinoma: An alarming need for human papillomavirus 16 screening in cancer patients. *Journey of Pharmacy and Bioallied Sciences, 13*(Suppl. 2), S1224–S1227. https://doi.org/10.4103/jpbs.jpbs_370_21

HEARING
CASE 51
Denise: Adult Auditory Rehabilitation: The Case of the Difficult Patient

Jessica R. Sullivan, Shamine Alves, and Darchayla Lewis

Conceptual Knowledge Areas

We present the case of a patient referred to as Denise and explore the concept of the "difficult patient." Some of the clinicians who have worked with Denise found her to be demanding and "difficult to treat." Denise exhausted multiple auditory rehabilitation tools (i.e., hearing aids, group auditory rehabilitation classes, and counseling sessions). Her case provides a unique perspective on the effectiveness of auditory rehabilitation and the importance of cultural competency.

Denise first came to a private pay audiology practice in 2015. She presented with a moderate precipitously sloping to profound sensorineural hearing loss (Figure 51–1). Her subjective experience related to this hearing loss was reflected in a questionnaire completed prior to her appoint-ment. Denise's responses on the questionnaire indicated that she heard poorly in group settings and noisy environments (i.e., restaurants, her children's school events, and church services). Denise was new to wearing hearing aids and had some reluctance about paying for technology.

During the 6 months that Denise was in the care of the practice, the audiologists became frustrated with her indecisiveness and failure to commit to a device; see Table 51–1 for a listing of all visits during this period. She was fitted with hearing aids once and seen for programming adjustments to her initial amplification twice. When her first trial period was complete, she returned to the office to request a different hearing aid brand, reporting inconsistent loudness and "how things just didn't sound right." The audiologist then fitted her for a new pair of behind-the-ear hearing aids, but after her 30-day trial, she complained

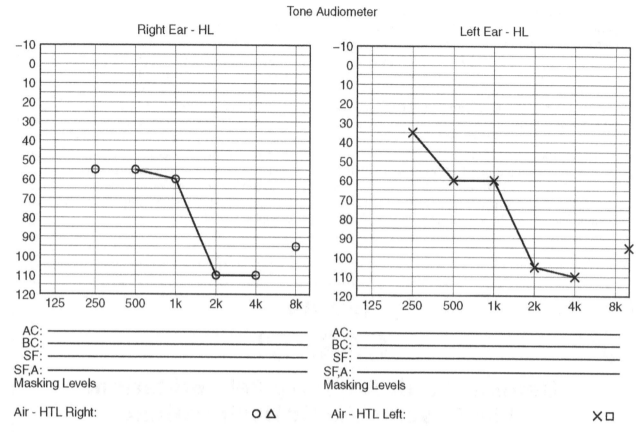

Figure 51–1. Denise's audiometric results. She presents with a bilateral moderate precipitously sloping to profound sensorineural hearing loss. HAE = hearing aid evaluation; HAF = hearing aid fitting; PROG = patient request for hearing aid reprogramming; CHECK = hearing aid check/cleaning; ADP = assistive device purchase; ADR = assistive device return; IN = hearing aid in office repair; OUT = out of office repair.

about its softness and bulkiness and requested to go back to her initial selection. Denise's audiologists were troubled by her indecisiveness and asked her to make a decision after 6 months of fittings and readjustments.

During clinical rotations, students likely hear stories about "difficult" patients. Practicing clinicians may describe a difficult patient as an individual who makes unreasonable demands, or one whose outcomes are poorer than would be expected based on their physical condition. It is not clear that this was the case with Denise. However, before addressing the question of whether Denise was a difficult patient, we will describe the auditory rehabilitation process and how it related to Denise's treatment. First, we review the process of auditory rehabilitation; then we examine reha-

bilitation principles through the lens of Denise's case, describing her experiences with hearing aid use and group auditory rehabilitation. Finally, we explore the concept of "the difficult patient" and whether Denise fits that concept.

What Is Auditory Rehabilitation?

There is confusion among students and professionals about the definition of *auditory rehabilitation*. Some professionals view auditory rehabilitation quite narrowly and consider it to be services ancillary to the provision of hearing aids, cochlear implants, and/or assistive listening devices. These ancillary services might include speechreading training, auditory training, and group auditory

Table 51–1. Denise's Visits

Date	Services Requested
September 1, 2015	Initial fitting
September 11, 2015	Requested reprogramming
September 21, 2015	Requested reprogramming
October 1, 2015	Requested new hearing aid
October 14, 2015	Requested reprogramming
October 29, 2015	Requested reprogramming
November 3, 2015	Return to initial selection of hearing aids
November 19, 2015	Requested reprogramming
December 2, 2015	Requested reprogramming
December 23, 2015	Requested new hearing aid
January 5, 2015	Requested reprogramming
January 21, 2015	Requested reprogramming
February 2, 2015	Requested reprogramming
March 3, 2015	Purchased hearing aids

rehabilitation. However, we prefer to take a broader view. According to Boothroyd (2007), auditory rehabilitation should be a holistic intervention that aims to reduce the negative effects of hearing loss on the quality of life of an individual. With this broad definition, it becomes clear that auditory rehabilitation includes many services. To determine which auditory rehabilitation services are most appropriate for a particular patient, the audiologist should consider both the communication difficulties imposed by hearing loss as well as the psychosocial ramifications of the hearing loss. The psychosocial aspects of hearing loss are multidimensional and have been well described in the literature (Hetu, 1996; Hogan, 2001; Trychin, 2002). Trychin (2002) has classified reactions to hearing loss in terms of emotional, cognitive, interpersonal, behavioral, and physical responses.

Research has consistently demonstrated that hearing aids can alleviate the psychological, social, and emotional effects of hearing loss (Chisolm et al., 2007). However, in many cases, resid-

ual hearing loss–related participation restrictions and activity limitations remain. These limitations can occur in an individual with a particularly severe hearing loss or in an individual who is having difficulty adjusting to and/or accepting hearing loss. Although in these cases, it can be difficult for the audiologist to determine the appropriate course of treatment, self-assessment scales may be useful in identifying a particular patient's needs.

Self-Assessment Scales

Hearing loss–specific quality of life scales measure the degree to which patients' hearing loss or hearing aids affect their self-perception of daily functioning and well-being and provide a systematic measure of the success of treatment and/ or the need for further treatment (Chisolm et al., 2007). Appropriate scales can also be useful in determining the most beneficial type of auditory rehabilitation treatment. For example, a hearing aid benefit scale such as the Abbreviated Profile of Hearing Aid Benefit (Cox & Alexander, 1995) can determine whether a hearing aid fitting is successful. If it is not, results on the scale might suggest whether assistive listening technologies should be added. A scale such as the Communication Strategies Scale for Older Adults (Kaplan et al., 1997) measures whether a patient uses communication strategies successfully. Those who do not may benefit from an individual or group auditory rehabilitation program that focuses on communication strategy training. A hearing loss–related quality of life scale such as the Hearing Handicap Inventory (for the Elderly or for Adults; Newman et al., 1990; Ventry & Weinstein, 1982) is useful in determining whether an individual has effectively dealt with the emotional reactions and interpersonal reactions to hearing loss. Those who have not effectively dealt with these reactions could benefit from participation in a group auditory rehabilitation program that focuses on the psychosocial aspects of hearing loss.

The preceding discussion of auditory rehabilitation and self-assessment scales demonstrates how treatment might occur under ideal conditions. In a busy clinic, there is a risk that a professional may find it challenging to adhere to best practices. Important data may go uncollected and useful treatment options ignored.

Description of the Case

Background Information and Reason for Referral

Hearing Aid Use

Denise was treated by the audiology private practice for 6 months. During that time, she had two primary problems with her hearing aids: commitment problems and unresolved hearing loss–related participation restrictions and activity limitations. When Denise became a patient in the practice, the audiologists switched her from in-the-ear-style hearing aids to behind-the-ear-style (BTE) hearing aids to provide her with increased gain. The clinician did not consider potential problems with this approach. Since her initial fitting, as Denise was a devoted wife and mother, she reported little time to care for her physical appearance. As a result of her busy schedule and hereditary hair loss, she decided to cut her hair into a short, curly pixie style. This came with an entirely new set of hair products and an increased frequency of Denise leaving home with her hair wet. Merely 1 month after she was fitted with her new hearing aids, the right hearing aid casing cracked. Over the course of 3 years, her hearing aid casing cracked nine different times. The clinicians eventually discovered (through conversations with a representative from the hearing aid manufacturer) that the cracking was likely caused by contact with Denise's new hair products. Despite the use of hearing aid coatings and care while styling her hair, this problem never resolved satisfactorily.

Findings of the Evaluation

If Denise's problems were restricted to the cracked casing of her hearing aids, the clinicians would have been glad to repair them every few months.

However, despite wearing two hearing aids, Denise continued to experience significant communicative difficulties. This is evident by her frequent visits for hearing aid adjustments (nine times shown in Table 51–1). These adjustments are referred to as "tweaking" by some audiologists. Denise's requests for tweaking were sometimes contradictory (she asked for increased gain at one visit and requested reduced gain at the next visit). It is not clear if tweaking actually improves speech understanding or just "appeases" the patient. Cunningham et al. (2001) and Saunders et al. (2009) found that there was little evidence to support patient benefit from tweaking despite it being a routine part of the fitting process. Cunningham and colleagues found that there were no differences in level of benefit, measured subjectively and objectively, between the groups, while Saunders and colleagues found that there is a slight benefit of prefitting counseling and positive expectations going into the hearing aid fitting process.

Treatment Options Considered

Rather than "tweak" Denise's hearing aids, the clinicians might have attempted to determine why Denise was so dissatisfied with her hearing aids and whether additional assessment and/or treatment was warranted. The reasons for Denise's limited hearing aid benefit can begin to be understood by examining the left and right ear following Denise's first hearing aid fitting in 2015. These graphs are basically an audiogram flipped upside down. The y-axis of the graphs shows the sound pressure level (the intensity of the sound), and the x-axis of the graphs shows the frequencies of the sounds. The Xs and Os connected by straight lines represent Denise's left ear and right ear hearing thresholds. The shaded region above the thresholds is the target area for the audiologist to place speech sounds presented through Denise's hearing aids. If the audiologist adjusts the hearing aids to amplify sounds of different frequencies to reach the target (shaded) area, all the speech signals will be audible. Finally, the squiggly lines represent the speech sounds that were presented to Denise. Due to Denise's profound hearing loss above 1500 Hz, the audiologist could not provide functional amplification in those frequencies. (The squiggly lines fell below the shaded area above 1500 Hz in each ear.) Denise was unaidable in the mid to high frequencies.

Another way to look at the success of the hearing aid fitting is to consider the articulation index (AI). The articulation index is a method to calculate the audibility of speech for a particular individual (American National Standards Institute, 1969; Pavlovic, 1989). Without hearing aids, Denise has an AI of approximately .02 for each ear. That is, if someone were to speak to her at a normal level, only 2% of the speech signal would be audible. When Denise wore her hearing aids, her AI improved to 23%. While this may seem to represent poor hearing aid performance, with an articulation index of .23, it is expected that she would be able to understand about 50% of sentences presented to her in quiet listening situations (American National Standards Institute, 1969). That is not surprising considering Denise's significant hearing loss but not good enough considering her communication demands. Despite their best efforts, the clinicians were not able to improve Denise's audibility to 100%. Unfortunately, Denise never understood this, as will be discussed later.

Notwithstanding careful hearing aid fitting and multiple reprogramming, Denise had unmet needs. The staff knew this because she kept coming back to the practice, but they were unable to determine the exact nature of her concerns because a standardized hearing loss–related quality of life scale was never used. Thus, the genesis of her unmet needs was unclear. Despite this lack of information, Denise's audiologists tried several additional auditory rehabilitation strategies.

Remote Microphone and Apps

The use of commercially available remote microphones has increased in popularity. Adult hearing aid users can use their cellular phone as a remote microphone in group settings without purchasing additional accessories. The new lines of hearing aid accessories are sleek in design and better in technology. Because of the improvement in remote microphone and hearing aid accessories, modern hearing aids come with apps that can aid in overcoming noise, distance, and reverberation in a variety of listening situations.

It was believed that, in Denise's case, the ability to take control of difficult listening situations might reduce her frustration and become empowering. Being able to use apps on her phone at work or group dinners could also help aid communication with family and friends.

Group Auditory Rehabilitation Classes

During Denise's sixth year of treatment in the practice, a research study was initiated at the university evaluating the efficacy of auditory rehabilitation (AR) programs. Denise was invited to participate and attended a 6-hour, 6-week program. Each week, a group of seven experienced hearing aid users discussed the problems and feelings associated with their hearing loss. In addition, they were given informational lectures about hearing loss, hearing aids, assistive devices, and communication strategies. Prior to beginning the study, Denise completed the Hearing Handicap Inventory (HHI; Ventry & Weinstein, 1982). This is a 25-item hearing loss–related quality of life scale that measures social and emotional responses to hearing loss. A score near 0 indicates no hearing loss–related difficulties, while a score near 100 suggests severe hearing loss–related participation restrictions and activity limitations.

Before participating in the group program, Denise scored 86, which indicates a significant impairment due to hearing loss. Despite her hearing aid use, Denise reported significant social and emotional reactions to her hearing loss. Hetu (1996) developed a framework for understanding the psychosocial effects of hearing loss. According to this author, most individuals consider their hearing loss to be a "stigma," defined as a discredited or discreditable attribute, or perceived disgrace associated with something that is regarded as socially unacceptable. As a result, individuals may isolate themselves, avoid social interactions, and/or bluff their way through communication breakdowns. These behaviors and feelings can result in a change in one's social identity and an enduring sense of social uncertainty (Barker et al., 2017; Hetu, 1996; Hogan, 2001). Participation in group auditory rehabilitation programs is one way to deal with feelings related to the loss of social identity associated with hearing loss (Hetu, 1996). An outcome of group participation is that hearing loss is seen as typical rather than deviant and leads to feelings of belonging (Hetu, 1996).

Auditory rehabilitation groups may focus exclusively on the needs of individuals with hearing loss or provide information and training for individuals with hearing loss as well as their significant others (Getty & Hetu, 1991; Preminger, 2003, Rolfe & Gardner, 2016). Groups that include significant others may provide training specifically designed for them, such as suggestions on how and when to communicate: "only speak to the person with hearing loss when you are in the same room and when he or she can see your face" (Krause & Panagiotopoulos, 2019; Schum, 1996).

After participating in the 6-week group program for people with hearing loss, Denise's HHI score dropped from 86 to 58, a significant improvement (Weinstein et al., 1986). Denise also reported to the group leader that for the first time, she understood why she was having so much difficulty understanding, even with her hearing aids. She told the group leader, "I have come to realize I have no miracle coming that will improve my hearing. I feel I have the best type of hearing aid for me. I have always felt like my audiologists did not understand how wearing hearing aids would affect my lifestyle. I didn't want to be perceived as 'less than' while at work and other social settings. I already am perceived differently because of my background and didn't want to give them another reason to view me as less than. I am thankful because now I have found the hearing aid style that suits my needs."

In 2015, Denise told the audiologist who led her group class that for the first time, she understood the benefits of her hearing aids. Yet in 2010 and 2012, previous audiologists had discussed the same information with Denise at her hearing aid evaluation and at her subsequent hearing aid counseling sessions. Unfortunately, this is a common occurrence. Research indicates that patients remember only about 50% of what is told to them during their office visits (Margolis, 2004). Patient retention of information could improve with teletherapy, counseling sessions, and auditory training applications. Patient retention of information could improve with teletherapy, counseling sessions, and auditory training applications.

Family-Centered Care

Denise and her husband were referred to counseling to help them work through their communication difficulties. Denise had not been as involved in her family's church and in her daughter's parent teacher association (PTA) meetings since switching to BTE hearing aids. Her husband noticed that she also seemed more introverted and shyer. Through therapy, Denise expressed that she felt embarrassed to wear BTE hearing aids because she didn't want people to know about her hearing loss. Unfortunately, due to her recent haircut, she was no longer able to hide her hearing aids.

When prompted by her husband to explain why she felt embarrassed for her friends and colleagues to know that she wore hearing aids, Denise explained that she never sees people in her community wearing hearing aids. She felt that she was not socially acceptable and worried that she would be treated differently.

Diverse cultures may have their own unique views on hearing loss, and thus, it is important to ensure that the client is comfortable with the services provided. Cultural awareness is crucial for the successful acceptance of hearing services (Lin et al., 2017).

Cochlear Implant Use

While Denise benefited from the group auditory rehabilitation program, that benefit was brief. Six months after completing the program, her HHI score increased to 82, a significant hearing handicap. Denise's audiologists recommended that she consider a cochlear implant. Denise's puretone audiogram and lack of perceived benefit from hearing aids made her a potential cochlear implant candidate when she first began treatment in the practice in 2001. Denise could have been recommended for a cochlear implant evaluation in 2001 when she purchased a new set of hearing aids or in 2004 when she purchased another set of hearing aids. However, the audiologist might not have recognized that Denise was a cochlear implant candidate at those times. When the U.S. Food and Drug Administration first approved cochlear implants for adults in 1985, only adults with hearing losses greater than 100 dB HL and with no discernible communication benefit from hearing aids were considered candidates (Zwolan, 2007). According to these old guidelines, Denise would not have been a candidate for a cochlear implant. Candidacy has changed over time as cochlear implants have improved and benefits from cochlear implantation have increased. Between 1998 and 2001, candidacy for the three major cochlear implant companies changed to moderate to profound hearing loss in the low frequencies and profound hearing loss in the middle to high speech frequencies (pure-tone average at 0.5, 1, and 2 kHz of 70 dB HL or greater) with limited benefit from amplification, as defined by open set sentence recognition scores of 50% correct or less in the ear to be implanted and 60% or less in the best aided condition (Food and Drug Administration, 2018). Denise's audiologist was either not aware of the change in candidacy or simply did not think about Denise as a cochlear implant candidate since she was already viewed as a hearing aid user. In addition, Denise had quite a bit of "aid-able" hearing in the lower frequencies, which might have prevented her audiologists from viewing her as a cochlear implant candidate. Denise received a cochlear implant in 2007. Two and a half months after the implant's activation, she scored 60 on the HHI, a significant decrease of 22 points compared to her preimplantation score. It was anticipated that her benefit from the cochlear implant would continue to improve, as adult cochlear implant patients typically see some slow improvements in performance over time (Valimaa et al., 2002a, 2002b). There was a growing body of evidence that adult cochlear implant users benefit from auditory training, which can speed the rehabilitation process and improve peak performance (Fu & Galvin, 2007). Although many facilities do not offer auditory training for adult cochlear implant users today, the use of mobile apps with intervention programs has increased (Ferguson et al., 2019).

Analysis of Client's Response to Intervention

Is Denise a Difficult Patient?

Hahn and colleagues have described three characteristics of "difficult" patients: (1) patient psychopathology, (2) abrasive interpersonal style, and (3) multiple physical symptoms (Hahn, 2001; Hahn et al., 1994; Hahn et al., 1996). These characteristics combine in a variety of ways that may foster negative feelings in the clinician, including frustration and dislike (Wasan et al., 2005). Based on informal reports from audiologists who participated in this patient's care, Denise was considered a "difficult" patient. There have been no reports of psychopathology in Denise's case; however, all the audiologists indicated that Denise had an abrasive interpersonal style and presented with significant communicative impairment and self-perceived participation restrictions.

According to Hahn, the term *difficult patient* is really a misnomer as the "difficulty" is experienced by the clinician; therefore, the clinician's characteristics also influence the level of difficulty attributed to the patients (Hahn, 2001; Hahn et al., 1996). Part of the frustration involved in treating a difficult patient is generated by the clinician's perceived inability to successfully diagnose and/or treat the patient. Denise's abrasive personality, significant activity limitations, and participation restrictions, as well as the frustration her case had generated for the clinicians involved in her care, led to her classification as a difficult patient. However, three clinician-related variables may have also contributed to the difficulties experienced by the clinicians in Denise's case. First, the clinicians never measured Denise's perception of her activity limitations or participation restrictions. Second, the clinicians never documented Denise's expectations for rehabilitation. Therefore, Denise's expectations and prognosis were never clarified. A patient's expectations can be assessed through administration of questionnaires, such as the Hearing Demand, Ability, and Need Profile (Palmer & Mormer, 1997). The questionnaire allows the patient to establish goals for treatment and then document expectations in meeting those goals. The audiologist can suggest modifications to the patient's goals based on the evidence and professional expertise. Unrealistic patient goals for rehabilitation can dramatically confound rehabilitation outcomes. Many patients expect hearing aids to "fix" their hearing, just as glasses "fix" vision. These patients may not understand the complexity of hearing loss, including outer versus inner hair cell damage, loss of compressive qualities within the cochlea, and changes to the central auditory nervous system (Hardie & Shepherd, 1999; Moore, 2007; Oxenham & Bacon, 2003). Denise's expectations may have contributed to the multiple requests for "tweaking" made throughout her time in the practice and her lack of satisfaction with amplification. Retrospectively, the clinicians treating Denise might not have provided her with the optimum treatment tools. Indeed, Denise's pure-tone audiogram, lack of perceived benefit from hearing aids, challenging auditory environment, and motivation to achieve better communication made her a potential cochlear implant candidate when she first arrived for rehabilitation in 2015.

Further Recommendations

Although Denise's clinician continued to report that she had an abrasive personality, her communicative needs are being met more appropriately by her current treatment plan (i.e., bimodal cochlear implant and hearing aid use). It is possible that the perception of Denise's "abrasive" personality could be a mismatch in cultural differences or misperception. The new treatment plan's efficacy is evidenced by the reduction in her hearing loss participation restrictions and activity limitations, as noted on the Hearing Handicap Inventory. It may be argued that a significant portion of the "difficulty" associated with Denise could be attributed to inadequate verification of treatment efficacy, delay in provision of best treatment options, and her poor communicative abili-

ties coupled with high communicative demands. If Denise's rehabilitative progress continues to be monitored through validated self-assessment measures, and as cochlear implant technology advances, she might benefit from further bilateral implantation in the future. In the meantime, an auditory training program may help Denise adjust to and benefit from her cochlear implant, and both Denise and her spouse may find value in attending an auditory rehabilitation program designed for significant others of people with hearing loss.

Acknowledgements. The authors thank Jill E. Preminger and Jonathon P. Whitton for their work on the original version of this case and for extending the opportunity for us to update and revise it into the current version.

References

American National Standards Institute. (1969). *American National Standard methods for the calculation of the articulation index* (ANSI S3.5–1969).

Barker, A. B., Leighton, P., & Ferguson, M. A. (2017). Coping together with hearing loss: A qualitative meta-synthesis of the psychosocial experiences of people with hearing loss and their communication partners. *International Journal of Audiology*, 56(5), 297–305. https://doi.org/10.1080/14992027.2017.1286695

Boothroyd, A. (2007). Adult aural rehabilitation: What is it and does it work? *Trends in Amplification*, 11(2), 63–71. https://doi.org/10.1177/1084713807301073

Chisolm, T. H., Johnson, C. E., Danhauer, J. L., Portz, L. J. P., Abrams, H. B., Lesner, S., . . . Newman C.W. (2007). A systematic review of health-related quality of life and hearing aids: Final report of the American Academy of Audiology task force on the health-related quality of life benefits of amplification in adults. *Journal of the American Academy of Audiology*, 18, 151–183. https://doi.org/10.3766/jaaa.18.2.7

Cox, R. M., & Alexander, G. C. (1995). The Abbreviated Profile of Hearing Aid Benefit (APHAB). *Ear and Hearing*, 16, 176–186. https://doi.org/10.1097/00003446-199504000-00005

Cunningham, D. R., Williams, K. J., & Goldsmith, L. J. (2001). Effects of providing and withholding post fitting fine-tuning adjustments on outcome measures in novice hearing aid users: A pilot study. *American Journal of Audiology, 10*, 13–23. https://doi.org/10.1044/1059-0889(2001/001)

Ferguson, M., Maidment, D., Henshaw, H., & Heffernan, E. (2019). Evidence-based interventions for adult aural rehabilitation: That was then, this is now. *Seminars in Hearing, 40*(1), 68–84. https://doi.org/10.1055/s-0038-1676784

Food and Drug Administration. (2008). Devices @ FDA. http://www.fda.gov/medical-devices/cochlear-implants/fda-approved-cochlear-implants

Fu, Q. J., & Galvin, J. J., III. (2007). Perceptual learning and auditory training in cochlear implant recipients. *Trends in Amplification, 11*, 193–205. https://doi.org/10.1177/1084713807301379

Getty, L., & Hetu, R. (1991). Development of a rehabilitation program for people affected with occupational hearing loss: 2. Results from group intervention with 48 workers and their spouses. *Audiology, 30*, 317–329. https://doi.org/10.3109/00206099109072894

Hahn, S. R. (2001). Physical symptoms and physician-experienced difficulty in the physician-patient relationship. *Annals of Internal Medicine, 134*, 904. https://doi.org/10.7326/0003-4819-134-9_Part_2-200105011-00014

Hahn, S. R., Kroenke, K., Spitzer, R. L., Brody, D., Williams, J. B., Linzer, M., & deGruy, F. V. (1996). The difficult patient: Prevalence, psychopathology, and functional impairment. *Journal of General Internal Medicine, 11*(1), 1–8. https://doi.org/10.1007/BF02603477

Hahn, S. R., Thompson, K. S., Will, T. A., Stern, V., & Budner, N. S. (1994). The difficult doctor-patient relationship: Somatization, personality and psychopathology. *Journal of Clinical Epidemiology, 47*, 647–657. https://doi.org/10.1016/0895-4356(94)90212-7

Hardie, N. A., & Shepherd, R. K. (1999). Sensorineural hearing loss during development: Morphological and physiological response of the cochlea and auditory brainstem. *Hearing Research, 128*, 147–165. https://doi.org/10.1016/S0378-5955(98)00209-3

Hetu, R. (1996). The stigma attached to hearing impairment. *Scandinavian Audiology, 25*, 12–24.

Hogan, A. (2001). *Hearing rehabilitation for deafened adults: A psychosocial approach.* Whurr.

Kaplan, H., Bally, S., Brandt, F., Busacco, D., & Pray, J. (1997). Communication Scale for Older Adults (CSOA). *Journal of the American Academy of Audiology, 8*(3), 203–217.

Krause, J. C., & Panagiotopoulos, A. P. (2019). Speaking clearly for older adults with normal hearing: The role of speaking rate. *Journal of Speech, Language, and Hearing Research, 62*(10), 3851–3859. https://doi.org/10.1044/2019_JSLHR-H-19-0094

Lin, C. J., Lee, C. K., & Huang, M. C. (2017). Cultural competence of healthcare providers: A systematic review of assessment instruments. *Journal of Nursing Research, 25*(3), 174–186. https://doi.org/10.1097/JNR.0000000000000153

Margolis, R. H. (2004). Page ten: What do your patients remember? *The Hearing Journal, 57*, 10–17. https://doi.org/10.1097/01.HJ.0000292451.91879.a8

Moore, B. C. J. (2007). *Cochlear hearing loss* (2nd ed.). John Wiley & Sons.

Newman, C. W., Weinstein, B. E., Jacobson, G. P., & Hug, G. A. (1990). The Hearing Handicap Inventory for Adults: Psychometric adequacy and audiometric correlates. *Ear and Hearing, 11*, 430–433. https://doi.org/10.1097/00003446-199012000-00004

Oxenham, A. J., & Bacon, S. P. (2003). Cochlear compression: Perceptual measures and implications for normal and impaired hearing. *Ear and Hearing, 24*, 352–366. https://doi.org/10.1097/01.AUD.0000090470.73934.78

Palmer, C. V., & Mormer, E. (1997). A systematic program for hearing aid orientation and adjustment. *Hearing Review, 1*, 45.

Pavlovic, C. V. (1989). Speech spectrum considerations and speech intelligibility predictions in hearing aid evaluations. *Journal of Speech and Hearing Disorders, 54*, 3–8. https://doi.org/10.1044/jshd.5401.03

Preminger, J. E. (2003). Should significant others be encouraged to join adult group audiologic rehabilitation classes? *Journal of the American Academy of Audiology, 14*, 545–555. https://doi.org/10.3766/jaaa.14.10.3

Rolfe, C., & Gardner, B. (2016). Experiences of hearing loss and views towards interventions to promote uptake of rehabilitation support among UK adults. *International Journal of Audiology, 55*(11), 666–673. https://doi.org/10.1080/14992027.2016.1200146

Saunders, G. H., M. S. Lewis, & Forsline, A. (2009). Expectations, pre-fitting counseling, and hearing aid outcome. *Journal of the American Academy of Audiology, 20*(5), 320–334. https://doi.org/10.3766/jaaa.20.5.6

Schum, D. J. (1996). Intelligibility of clear and conversational speech of young and elderly talkers. *Journal of the American Academy of Audiology, 7*, 212–218.

Trychin, S. (2002). *Guidelines for providing mental health services to people who are hard of hearing* (Rep. No. ED466082). University of California, San Diego.

Valimaa, T., Maatta, T., Lopponen, H., & Sorri, M. (2002a). Phoneme recognition and confusions with multichannel cochlear implants: Consonants. *Journal of Speech, Language, and Hearing Research, 45,* 1055–1069. https://doi.org/10.1044/1092-4388(2002/085)

Valimaa, T., Maatta, T., Lopponen, H., & Sorri, M. (2002b). Phoneme recognition and confusions with multichannel cochlear implants: Vowels. *Journal of Speech, Language, and Hearing Research, 45,* 1039–1054. https://doi.org/10.1044/1092-4388(2002/084)

Ventry, I. M., & Weinstein, B. E. (1982). The hearing handicap inventory for the elderly: A new tool. *Ear and Hearing, 3,* 128–134. https://doi.org/10.1097/000 03446-198205000-00006

Wasan, A. D., Wooton, J., & Jamison, R. N. (2005). Dealing with difficult patients in your pain practice. *Regulatory Anesthesia and Pain Medicine, 30,* 184–192. https://doi.org/10.1016/j.rapm.2004.11.005

Weinstein, B. E., Spitzer, J. B., & Ventry, I. M. (1986). Test-retest reliability of the Hearing Handicap Inventory for the Elderly. *Ear and Hearing, 7,* 295–299. https://doi.org/10.1097/00003446-198610000-00002

Zwolan, T. (2007). Selection of cochlear implant candidates. In S. Waltzman & J. T. Roland (Eds.), *Cochlear implants* (2nd ed., pp. 57–68). Thieme Medical Publishers.

HEARING
CASE 52
Claude: Evaluation and Management of Vestibular Problems and Tinnitus Following Head Trauma
Richard A. Roberts

Conceptual Knowledge Areas

Benign Paroxysmal Positional Vertigo

This vestibular disorder is the number one peripheral cause of spinning dizziness (vertigo; Bhattacharyya et al., 2017). It is common in most age groups and becomes more prevalent as we get older. Benign paroxysmal positional vertigo (BPPV) occurs with displacement of the crystalline otoliths from the utricle of the vestibular labyrinth into the semicircular canals, which do not have such structures in a normal state. Common causes of BPPV include the normal aging process, head trauma, ear surgery, ear infection, and so on. Movement of the otoliths within the semicircular canal causes an inappropriate response to changes in head position, leading to intense vertigo and nystagmus (eye movement) in the plane of the affected canal. BPPV also has a negative influence on balance and can contribute to falls, particularly in older patients. Approximately 90% of the time, the posterior semicircular canal becomes affected by the displaced otoliths given its inferior location relative to the utricle. The Dix-Hallpike maneuver is used to identify BPPV. To complete this test, the patient is seated on an examination table with the clinician positioned behind. The patient is then gradually lowered until lying flat on the exam table with the clinician seated behind in a position to observe the eyes of the patient. The clinician is supporting the head and neck of the patient during this maneuver. A positive response includes a subjective report of vertigo along with a transient rotary-type nystagmus. This disorder does not respond to medication, although there are surgical interventions that are successful. Most agree that canalith repositioning maneuvers (CRMs), which consist of moving the head and body of the patient through a set protocol, are able to deposit the otoliths back to the utricle with complete resolution of symptoms in one to two repositioning treatments 80% to 96% of the time (Roberts, 2016).

Uncompensated Peripheral Vestibulopathy

This terminology describes the status of the balance system following insult to one or both of the vestibular structures. This insult may be secondary to disorders, such as labyrinthitis, vestibular neuritis, Meniere's disease, and so forth, and can follow head trauma, which may lead to labyrinthine concussion. When one or both of the vestibular structures become damaged, there is often a functional alteration in the two primary reflex pathways, which rely on vestibular information to a great extent: the vestibulo-ocular reflex (VOR) and the vestibulospinal reflex (VSR). The VOR pathway is in large part responsible for stabilization of gaze on a visual target during head movement. Correspondingly, damage to the vestibular structure(s) may lead to blurred vision with head movement (Roberts & Gans, 2007). Reportedly, visual acuity may degrade from 20/20 with no head movement to 20/200 with head movement, which can be debilitating for the patient. The VSR pathway connects the vestibular structures to antigravity muscles and is key to maintenance of postural stability. Patients with disruption of VSR may notice difficulty maintaining balance during ambulation, particularly in poorly lit environments with an uneven walking surface.

Patients with uncompensated peripheral vestibulopathy often experience significant reduction of symptoms through vestibular rehabilitation therapy (VRT; Hall et al., 2016). The goal of VRT is not to "fix" the peripheral vestibulopathy but to get the VOR and VSR pathways to utilize information from unaffected vestibular structures, as well as other resources such as visual and somatosensory input (Whitney & Rossi, 2000). In this way, the balance system recalibrates to the altered set of inputs. This is accomplished through an individualized VRT program incorporating specific exercises to target *adaptation* to the altered vestibular information, *habituation* to head and body movements that lead to unpleasant symptoms (i.e., nausea, fatigue), and *substitution* of other resources to supplement vestibular information. Following successful VRT, a patient may be said to have compensated to the peripheral vestibulopathy when there is no longer any negative functional impact.

Tinnitus

Perception of sound(s) in the ears or head without an acoustic/vibratory source is tinnitus. Types of tinnitus include ringing, roaring, whistling, buzzing, humming, crickets, pulsing, and so on. There are many causes of tinnitus, such as buildup of ear wax (cerumen), temporomandibular joint problems, head and neck trauma, certain medications (including aspirin), and thyroid problems (Henry et al., 2005; Tunkel et al., 2014). By far, hearing loss is the most common cause of tinnitus. It is estimated that 90% of patients with cochlear-based sensorineural hearing loss report the presence of tinnitus. Damage to the hair cell structures in the cochlea by excessive noise, ototoxic medications, and the normal aging process are often implicated as causes of tinnitus. For many patients with tinnitus, there is little effect on quality of life. Other patients with tinnitus find it extremely troubling and potentially debilitating with difficulty concentrating, relaxing, and sleeping (Henry, Schechter, et al., 2005).

Given the relationship between hearing loss and tinnitus, it is fortunate that many patients report a decrease in their tinnitus when fitted with hearing aid amplification (Henry, Dennis, et al., 2005). The hearing aids reduce stress from communication difficulties related to the hearing loss and also increase the perception of other sounds in the environment of the patient. The patient is less likely to focus on the tinnitus in this situation. Likewise, many patients with tinnitus report a decrease in perception of their tinnitus when they maintain an acoustically rich environment. Other forms of tinnitus intervention include masking devices, tinnitus retraining therapy, and biofeedback (Tunkel et al., 2014). Often, appropriate counseling about the causes of tinnitus by a trained audiologist or physician will reduce the impact of tinnitus on the patient's quality of life.

Description of the Case

Background Information

Claude was a 71-year-old male with onset of symptoms following a motor vehicle accident (MVA) during which a head trauma occurred. Immediately postimpact, the patient developed constant vertigo with nausea and emesis that gradually improved over 3 days. There was no change in hearing status or tinnitus reported at the time of hospital admission. He was placed on medication to suppress his symptoms. A computed axial tomography scan was unremarkable. His symptoms improved to brief episodes of vertigo with slight nausea. The patient was tapered off the suppressant medication and discharged after 5 days.

Reasons for the Referral and Findings of the Evaluation

Claude reported two types of dizziness. One was described as "a strange sensation of dizziness that was not quite spinning" and that was provoked by head movement. He felt best when he was lying still in bed. Claude reported experiencing very intense but brief vertigo when lying down or turning over in bed. In between the episodes of vertigo, he reported imbalance worse with ambulation in the dark and outside his home. He noted having to touch the walls inside his home and other objects such as furniture to steady himself during ambulation. Claude also reported that his "eyes do not keep up with his head." He noticed difficulty reading the newspaper, which was always an activity he enjoyed prior to onset of the current symptoms. He noticed that his constant ringing tinnitus, which was present prior to the MVA, was more troubling since his discharge from the hospital and was causing him some difficulty falling asleep at night.

Claude was referred for comprehensive vestibular evaluation to rule out a peripheral vestibular involvement contributing to his symptoms. Audiometric evaluation revealed a bilateral, symmetric mild to moderately severe sensorineural hearing loss. Otoacoustic emissions and immittance results were in agreement with audiometric data. Tinnitus was matched to a 3 kHz tone with 20 dB sensation level. Claude reported that the tinnitus seemed momentarily softer following a presentation of 60 seconds of 3 kHz narrow-band noise. He stated that his tinnitus immediately became more noticeable when he entered the sound-treated suite. Subjective assessment with the Tinnitus Handicap Inventory (THI) was 73 (Newman et al., 1996).

The vertebrobasilar artery screening test (VAST; Roberts, 2016) revealed a slight transient dizziness with hyperextension of the neck and rotation of the head to the right. Results to the left were unremarkable. Postural stability testing revealed a vestibular pattern with a right turn on the Fukuda stepping test and a fall on dynamic surface with eyes closed. This was consistent with functional impairment of the VSR as the patient could not remain standing without visual information, though vestibular information should have been available.

During the Fukuda stepping test, Claude was asked to march in place for about 30 steps with eyes closed. The fact that he turned instead of staying in one place is remarkable. Dynamic visual acuity testing revealed a degradation from 82% correct with no head movement to 42% with horizontal volitional head movement and 60% with vertical volitional head movement. These results are consistent with functional impairment of the VOR (Roberts & Gans, 2007). Greater difficulty with horizontal compared to vertical is also a common finding with VOR dysfunction.

Vestibular evoked myogenic potentials (VEMPs; ocular and cervical) revealed normal waveforms with stimulation to both ears. Utricle and superior vestibular nerve function is required for normal ocular VEMP responses. Saccule and inferior vestibular nerve function is required for normal cervical VEMP responses. Random saccade, smooth pursuit, and optokinetic results were unremarkable, which is consistent with intact oculomotor function. Gaze testing was unremarkable, but high-frequency headshake elicited a transient left-beating nystagmus. Claude also reported a subjective increase in his dizziness, though not to the point of vertigo. Dix-Hallpike positioning to the right provoked an intense sensation of vertigo and upbeating torsional nystagmus consistent with right posterior semicircular canal BPPV (Roberts, 2016). Results to the left were negative. Static positional testing was unremarkable. Caloric testing produced a 50% right unilateral weakness. Directional preponderance and fixation suppression index were within normal limits. Subjective assessment with the Dizziness Handicap Inventory (DHI) was 85 (Jacobson & Newman, 1990).

Key Findings

- Right posterior semicircular canal BPPV (from head trauma)
  - Supported by positive modified Hallpike
- Partial peripheral vestibulopathy affecting the right labyrinth (labyrinthine concussion due to head trauma)
  - Supported by provokable left-beating nystagmus, right unilateral weakness in presence of normal VEMP responses
- Functional VOR and VSR deficits related to vestibulopathy and possibly contributed to by BPPV
- Bilateral sensorineural hearing loss
- DHI = 85 points, classified as severe with activity limitation and participation restriction
- THI = 73 points, also consistent with a severe perception of handicap (McCombe et al., 2001)

Treatment Options Considered

Benign Paroxysmal Positional Vertigo

Medications are not typically successful in treating BPPV. There are surgical options (singular neurectomy and semicircular canal occlusion), but these are quite involved and are usually reserved for patients who do not respond to repositioning maneuvers. Clearly, the literature indicates that repositioning the displaced otoliths into the utricle is the most efficient intervention that provides immediate relief of symptoms in 80% to 96% of patients (Roberts, 2016). Brandt-Daroff exercises have been reported to be successful but usually require 9 to 14 days of patients working on their own to disperse the otoconia. This is not a good choice for treatment given that most of the other repositioning techniques provide an immediate positive response. The canalith repositioning maneuver initially described by Epley is a good choice for many patients. In the current case, Claude had a positive VAST. Although that response may be related to the presence of BPPV on the right, the clinician cannot be certain. The CRM requires the patient to be in a state of hyperextension for an extended time and would certainly be contraindicated in the current case in view of the positive VAST (Roberts, 2016). The Semont Liberatory Maneuver (SLM) and Gans Repositioning Maneuver (GRM; Roberts et al., 2006) are both excellent alternatives to the CRM as both methods avoid the neck hyperextension associated with the CRM but have the same efficacy. For this case, a GRM was chosen, but the SLM could have been used quite easily.

Uncompensated Peripheral Vestibulopathy

Overall, the results of the current case indicated a unilateral right peripheral vestibulopathy for which the patient is uncompensated. Although some patients will compensate to the peripheral vestibulopathy over time, the literature indicates that an individualized program of VRT allows the patient to realize a faster functional recovery (Hall et al., 2016). Patients who are highly motivated with predominantly a disruption of VOR are often candidates for a self-directed program of VRT. The audiologist or physical therapist would work with the patient in a single session to teach the appropriate form for the various exercises. Ideally, the clinician then follows the patient by phone until an appointment to determine the outcomes.

In other cases, and especially with VOR and VSR deficits, a clinician-directed program is more appropriate with either an audiologist or a physical therapist. As the level of VSR dysfunction increases and if there are additional comorbid factors such as peripheral neuropathy, artificial knee or hip, and so on, a physical therapist (PT) would be the appropriate choice. Since there was an obvious functional impact on VSR (supported by postural stability findings and patient symptoms), it was decided that the patient should be referred for a clinician-directed program with a PT.

Tinnitus

In view of the complexity of this case in terms of the dizziness and imbalance along with tinnitus, it was not felt that more time-intensive tinnitus interventions such as tinnitus retraining therapy (TRT), biofeedback, and so forth were appropriate. Claude was a candidate for hearing aid amplification based on the bilateral sensorineural hearing loss. It was decided to fit the hearing loss of the patient as an initial plan and keep other tinnitus intervention options open if there was not an appropriate level of improvement following successful use of hearing aid amplification. The hearing aid amplification was expected to reduce communication stress by allowing him to hear sounds important for speech intelligibility (Henry, Schechter, et al., 2005). It was anticipated that VRT would diminish any stress associated with Claude's dizziness and imbalance. Decreasing the overall stress in his life, it was hoped, would produce a concomitant decrease in perception of the tinnitus.

Course of Treatment

Claude was immediately treated for the BPPV using a GRM, which was well tolerated. After two successive treatment maneuvers, he no longer exhibited symptoms of BPPV when placed in the provoking position, which is suggestive of a successful treatment maneuver. He was scheduled to return in 1 week for follow-up to treatment of the BPPV to ensure treatment efficacy.

Vestibular retraining therapy (VRT) was initiated with a local physical therapist 1 week after treatment for BPPV. The therapy was scheduled for twice weekly 45-minute sessions. Claude was provided with supplemental VRT exercises to complete at home. Therapy incorporated adaptation and habituation techniques for home and clinic use. Substitution strategies were used mainly with the clinician in a controlled situation and focused more on the patient's balance. Claude became frustrated during the first week of VRT because the therapeutic exercises provoked his symptoms quite a bit. This is expected with VRT, and all patients should be warned that this may occur, but they should be encouraged to continue with the program (Hall et al., 2016). Encouragement by the audiologist and physical therapist helped the patient continue with VRT for the remaining 3 weeks, during which he noted significant subjective improvement. Claude admitted that he was not diligent about his home VRT exercises initially but performed them faithfully after he started noticing improvement during the second week.

Claude was fitted with appropriate hearing aid amplification at the start of his VRT. He became frustrated and felt that "nothing was working." It was decided to wait until he noted improvement in the symptoms of dizziness and imbalance and then refit the hearing aid amplification. In the third week of VRT, Claude noted that his tinnitus was less troubling. At that point, the hearing aid amplification was refitted. He felt that he was receiving excellent benefit from the amplification and decided to keep the instruments at the end of his trial period. The tinnitus was only noticeable intermittently by the end of the trial period.

Analysis of Client's Response to Intervention

On his follow-up to treatment of the BPPV, Claude indicated that he was no longer experiencing any vertigo. He did note that the dizziness with head movement was still present, but he was quite pleased with the immediate resolution of the vertigo. He was checked with side-lying and there was no BPPV response. Rechecking of his VAST was initially positive and then was also negative, suggesting that the initial responses were likely related to the BPPV in the right ear. Claude was then checked using a Dix-Hallpike position since there was no issue with vertebrobasilar insufficiency. This was also negative. He was placed in left and right lateral positions to ensure that no otoconial debris migrated into the adjacent right horizontal canal, and this was negative. Deep head-hanging was also negative for anterior canal BPPV. Claude was considered clear of the BPPV.

As mentioned above, Claude reported some initial frustration with VRT. This was due, in part, to the immediate success he experienced with the treatment for BPPV. It was explained that VRT takes longer and requires more effort on the part of the patient. He continually used a rating scale from 0 (no dizziness) to 5 (extreme dizziness) to report his subjective impressions of each exercise. During the first week, most of the VRT exercises elicited reports of "4" and "5." This gradually declined until the fourth week, when the reports were mainly of "0" and "1." Claude reported little to no dizziness with head movement and also noted significantly improved balance. Posttherapy DHI was assessed by the patient and was a 4 compared to his initial DHI of 85, suggesting no activity limitation or restriction of participation.

Claude returned to the audiologist for follow-up assessment. His static postural stability was normal with no fall on dynamic surface with eyes closed. This result indicated functional recovery of the VSR. His DVA scores were 76% and 72% for horizontal and vertical volitional head movement, respectively. This result indicated functional recovery of the VOR. In addition, no provocable nystagmus was recorded during headshake testing using video-oculography. This is also consistent with improved VOR function. All results suggested that Claude was compensated to the peripheral vestibulopathy.

Tinnitus intervention via hearing aid amplification was initially postponed to allow the patient time to see the positive effects of BPPV treatment and get over the initial symptoms provoked during VRT. Claude noticed a decrease in his tinnitus symptoms after the BPPV was resolved and after

he began to experience some positive outcomes in VRT. This continued with successful fitting of hearing aid amplification, and a postfitting THI was 24. This was consistent with a mild impact with tinnitus easily masked by environmental sounds and easily forgotten during activity (McCombe et al., 2001). This was a significant improvement over the initial THI score.

Further Recommendations

Over 5 months, this patient was able to achieve (1) complete resolution of BPPV, (2) significant functional and subjective improvement in dizziness and imbalance symptoms associated with uncompensated peripheral vestibulopathy, and (3) significant improvement in subjective perception of tinnitus through appropriate fitting of hearing aid amplification.

Upon release from treatment, Claude was advised that recurrence rates for BPPV range from 5% to 30%, barring a precipitating event such as head trauma or inner ear infection. He was to contact the audiologist immediately with any recurrence of positional vertigo.

Outcome studies indicated the patient compensated to the peripheral vestibulopathy. It was explained that some patients experience a "relapse" of symptoms occasionally with extreme fatigue or acute illness. He was to begin his home program of VRT immediately after onset of these symptoms. If the symptoms persisted, he was to contact the audiologist for further evaluation.

It is quite possible that reducing the stress associated with the dizziness and imbalance as well as any hearing loss–related communication stress helped to decrease this patient's perception of his tinnitus. Claude will continue to wear his hearing aid amplification and was instructed to maintain an acoustically rich environment. It was emphasized that this is especially important when he is in quieter situations, such as trying to go to sleep at night. The use of environmental noise machines was discussed, and Claude will consider these if needed. At this time, there is no reason to pursue ear-level tinnitus maskers and/or tinnitus retraining therapy.

Author's Note

The patient described in this case is fictional but based on a composite of real cases evaluated and managed by the author.

References

Bhattacharyya, N., Gubbels, S., Schwartz, S., Edlow, J., El-Kashlan, H., Fife, T., . . . Corrigan, M. D. (2017). Clinical practice guideline: Benign paroxysmal positional vertigo. *Otolaryngology Head & Neck Surgery, 156*(3, Suppl.), S1–S47. https://doi.org/10.1177/0194599816689667

Hall, C. D., Herdman, S. J., Whitney, S. L., Cass, S. P., Clendaniel, R. A., Fife, T. D., . . . Woodhouse, S. N. (2016). Vestibular rehabilitation for peripheral vestibular hypofunction: An evidence-based clinical practice guideline: From the American Physical Therapy Association Neurology Section. *Journal of Neurologic Physical Therapy, 40*(2), 124–155. https://doi.org/10.1097/NPT.0000000000000120

Henry, J. A., Dennis, K. C., & Schechter, M. A. (2005). General review of tinnitus: Prevalence, mechanisms, effects, and management. *Journal of Speech, Language, and Hearing Research, 48*, 1–32. https://doi.org/10.1044/1092-4388(2005/084)

Henry, J. A., Schechter, M. A., Loovis, C., Zaugg, T. L., Kaelin, C., & Montero, M. (2005). Clinical management of tinnitus using a "progressive intervention" approach. *Journal of Rehabilitation Research and Development, 42*(4, Suppl. 2), 95–116. https://doi.org/10.1682/jrrd.2005.01.0005

Jacobson, G., & Newman, C. (1990). The development of the Dizziness Handicap Inventory. *Archives of Otolaryngology-Head and Neck Surgery, 116*, 424–427. https://doi.org/10.1001/archotol.1990.01870040046011

McCombe, A., Bagueley, D., Coles, R., McKenna, L., McKinney, C., & Windle-Taylor, P. (2001). Guidelines for the grading of tinnitus severity: The results of a working group commissioned by the British Association of Otolaryngologists, Head and Neck Surgeons, 1999. *Clinical Otolaryngology, 26*, 388–393. https://doi.org/10.1046/j.1365-2273.2001.00490.x

Newman, C., Jacobson, G., & Spitzer, J. (1996). Development of the Tinnitus Handicap Inventory. *Archives of Otolaryngology-Head and Neck Surgery, 122*, 143–148. https://doi.org/10.1001/archotol.1996.01890140029007

Roberts, R. (2016). Technique and interpretation of positional testing. In G. Jacobson & N. Shephard (Eds.), *Balance function assessment and management* (2nd ed., pp. 251–282). Plural Publishing.

Roberts, R., & Gans, R. (2007). Comparison of horizontal and vertical dynamic visual acuity in patients with vestibular dysfunction and non-vestibular dizziness. *Journal of the American Academy of Audiology, 18*, 236–244. https://doi.org/10.3766/jaaa.18.3.5

Roberts, R., Gans, R., & Montaudo, R. (2006). Efficacy of a new treatment for posterior canal benign paroxysmal positional vertigo. *Journal of the American Academy of Audiology, 17*, 598–604. https://doi.org/10.3766/jaaa.17.8.6

Tunkel, D. E., Bauer, C. A., Sun, G. H., Rosenfeld, R. M., Chandrasekhar, S. S., Cunningham, E. R., . . . Whamond, E. J. (2014). Clinical practice guideline: Tinnitus. *Otolaryngology-Head and Neck Surgery, 151*(2, Suppl.), S1–S40. https://doi.org/10.1177/0194599814545325

Whitney, S., & Rossi, M. (2000). Efficacy of vestibular rehabilitation. *Otolaryngology Clinics of North America, 33*, 659–672. https://doi.org/10.1016/s0030-6665(05)70232-2

HEARING
CASE 53
Ella: Sudden Idiopathic SNHL: Autoimmune Inner Ear Disease
Lauraine L. Wells

Conceptual Knowledge Areas

Sudden Sensorineural Hearing Loss (SSHL)

Sudden sensorineural hearing loss (SSHL) presents complex emotional and physical challenges for the patient as well as unique diagnostic and treatment challenges for audiologists and other medical professionals. As the name implies, the onset of the hearing loss occurs over a short period of time, typically within 3 days or less. The degree of change is generally defined as a 30 dB or greater decrease in hearing thresholds at three adjacent audiometric frequencies and is sensorineural in nature. SSHL accounts for 1% of all cases of sensorineural hearing loss (Das et al., 2019; Hughes et al., 1996). Of the approximately 15,000 cases of sudden hearing loss reported around the world each year, about 4,000 occur in the United States (Hughes et al., 1996). The reported incidence of SSHL is approximately 5 to 20 cases in every 100,000 people (Byl, 1984).

Idiopathic Sudden Sensorineural Hearing Loss (ISSHL)

Only about 10% of SSHL cases ever receive a formal diagnosis. Those without a known etiology are termed *idiopathic* SSHL. It is estimated that 60% to 65% of idiopathic sudden sensorineural hearing loss (ISSHL) cases recover spontaneously, without medical intervention, within the first 14 days after onset (Mattox & Simmons, 1977).

This characteristic further complicates the ability of researchers to judge treatment effectiveness. Most SSHL prevalence studies do not distinguish between idiopathic or known etiology.

SSHL appears to affect women and men in equal numbers, and there is no right or left ear preference. It occurs at nearly any age, with few reported pediatric cases (Argup, 2008), and is most common in those who are middle aged, 50 to 60 years (Bly, 1984). SSHL is often accompanied by tinnitus and vestibular symptoms (Wynne et al., 2001). It is estimated that vertigo accompanies hearing loss in 40% of SSHL cases (Mattox & Simmons, 1977). Possible causes of SSHL can be broadly classified into six categories: (1) viral infections, (2) compromised immune system, (3) vascular disease/disorder limiting the blood supply to the inner ear, (4) neurologic disorders, (5) neoplastic lesions, and (6) inner ear trauma such as disruptions of the membranous system within the cochlea. Diagnosis of hearing loss requires physical examination, detailed medical history, comprehensive audiological assessment, and laboratory studies including hematologic, urinalysis, serologic, and immunologic studies (Muller et al., 2001). Timing of intervention is critical in terms of hearing recovery. The opportunity for reversal of the hearing loss improves if treatment is received within the first 1 to 2 weeks of onset (Sing, 2006).

Immune System in the Inner Ear

It was long thought that the inner ear was not capable of housing immune activity because the blood-labyrinth barrier, which separates the labyrinth from circulation, was presumed to separate the inner ear from cellular and humoral activity. However, in 1958, Dr. E. Lenhardt speculated that the inner ear could be affected by anticochlear antibodies in a group of patients with bilateral sudden sensorineural hearing loss (Bovo et al., 2006). Many studies followed in an attempt to define the role of the immune system in the inner ear. Since the early 1980s, studies have shown immune activity within the cochlea. It appears that the enolymphatic sac plays a key role. Damage to the delicate inner ear structures can occur secondary to the inflammatory process of immune activity but also from the autoimmune reactions of the immune system response (Stroudt & Vrabec, 2000).

Autoimmune Inner Ear Disease (AIED)

In 1979, Dr. Brian McCabe introduced the term *autoimmune hearing loss* and described the first cohort of 18 patients exhibiting similar clinical characteristics, whose symptoms did not fit into an existing disease classification. McCabe described a disease manifested as sensorineural hearing loss, which is bilateral, asymmetrical, and advances over a period of weeks or months, rather than in hours, days, or years, and which responds favorably to treatments traditionally used for autoimmune disease. The argument for a separate designation as autoimmune inner ear disease (AIED) was largely due to the potential for treatment, unlike the other causes of sensorineural hearing losses (McCabe, 1979). Many studies have been conducted to determine the exact relationship of the immune system to the audiovestibular system, and although much has been discovered, there is still no known cause for the disorder. Because the pathophysiology of the immune system in the inner ear has not been directly linked, another term for the disease process has been introduced: *immune-mediated ear disease.*

Although incidence figures are inexact, AIED is considered a rare disease, making up less than 1% of all cases of hearing loss or dizziness (Bovo et al., 2006). AIED appears to affect more women (65%) than men (35%) and is most apt to occur in middle age (Hughes et al., 1996). There may be a genetic component to acquiring AIED. AIED can be a localized event, but in 15% to 30% of patients, there is an underlying systemic autoimmune disorder (systemic lupus, Cogan's syndrome, rheumatoid arthritis, etc.; Bovo et al., 2006).

The hallmark indicator for AIED is the progressive sensorineural hearing loss, which advances too quickly to be age-related hearing loss and too slowly to be classified as SSHL. It is often fluctuating and may originate in one ear first, followed several months later by symptoms in the other ear (79% of patients have bilateral hearing loss). Nearly 50% of patients also experience vestibular symptoms, which range in severity from general imbalance to violent, episodic vertigo. Tinnitus and fullness of the ears occurs in nearly 25% to 50% of cases (Bovo et al., 2006). Typically, the otologic physical examination of the patient is normal with no visible sign of disease to the outer or middle ear. Because they share similar symptoms, it is difficult to differentiate between AIED, autoinflammatory disease, and Meniere's disease (MD). Autoinflammatory disease is a rare family of immune-mediated diseases, some of which manifest in sensorineural hearing loss. Accurate diagnosis is needed to allow treatment and prevent conditions that could lead to organ failure (Vambutas & Pathak, 2016). There is some evidence that MD may have an underlying autoimmune etiology, and one proposed subcategory of AIED is immune-mediated Meniere's disease (Harris & Keithley, 2003).

Laboratory Testing for AIED

There is no specific diagnostic test available to definitively identify AIED. Diagnosis is achieved with a combination of clinical manifestation of hearing loss and vestibular symptoms, a detailed medical history, the response to immunosuppressant drugs, and evidence of immune activity in the blood. In a detailed comparison of patients with progressive hearing loss, Hirose et al. (1999) recommended using either erythrocyte sedimentation rate (ESR) or C-reactive protein (CRP) and

Western blot hsp-70 to investigate immune activity in the blood.

Sedimentation Rate (Erythrocyte Sedimentation Rate or ESR).

ESR or "sed-rate" is a measure of inflammatory or immune activity in the body. When erythrocytes, or red blood cells, are placed in a test tube, they settle to the bottom, creating sediment, while leaving the clear blood serum above it. The sed-rate is the distance in millimeters from the top that the layer of red blood cells falls within a given time, typically 1 hour. An elevated sed-rate indicates the presence of particular proteins generated during the inflammation process. The proteins cause the red blood cells to clump together and fall more quickly. Thus, the higher the sed-rate, the greater the degree of inflammation. Using a Westegren method, normal sed-rate is 0 to 15 millimeters per hour for males and 0 to 20 millimeters per hour for females.

C-Reactive Protein (CRP).

CRP is a specific protein that, with increased presence in the blood, indicates immune activity. It is a marker of inflammation but also is theorized to have a protective mechanism against autoimmune disease (Szalai, 2004).

Western Blot Analysis.

Western blot analysis is a technique used to identify the presence of a specific antibody in the serum. Specifically, a positive test for an antibody to an antigen of the molecular weight 68 kDA was considered evidence of AIED. Later studies suggest this antigen was actually heat shock protein 70 (hsp 70); however, this conclusion has since been disproved (Bovo et al., 2006). Presence of the antibody was also thought to predict a favorable response to steroids (Moscicki et al., 1994); however, the value of the Western blot analysis is now in question, since as many as 50% to 60% of patients who do respond favorably to steroid treatments are Western blot negative (Bovo et al., 2006).

Treatment for AIED

Successful treatment of AIED involves both medical and audiological management. It is impor-

tant for both to be coordinated to maximize outcomes.

Medical Treatment.

There is little consensus regarding the treatment regimens for AIED due to limited research, the relatively few cases seen, and the high number of hearing losses that spontaneously recover. Many cases of sudden hearing loss may be either ignored or discovered only as a secondary finding when investigating a different complaint. Unfortunate delays in identifying SSHL and/or AIED diminish the chances for treatment and potential recovery. Sudden hearing loss should be considered a medical emergency and warrants immediate attention. Steroid therapy is the typical treatment for SSHL and AIED, although the exact mechanism of steroid interaction with cochlear function is not well understood. The type of steroid, the length of treatment, and the delivery mechanism are all variables. A classic regimen is the administration of oral prednisone of up to 1 mg/kg for up to 1 month, with a tapered dosage to diminish use over the next 2-week period. Alternatives to steroids are methotrexate and cyclophosphamide (Cytoxan), but these medications have serious side effects and must be monitored closely (Sargent, 2002).

Aural Rehabilitation.

Contralateral routing of signal (CROS) and bilateral CROS (BiCROS) hearing aids are designed for people with unilateral hearing loss, to the extent that the poorer ear cannot benefit from traditional amplification (Hayes, 2006). Patients with relatively normal hearing in the "good" ear and no aidable hearing in the "poor" ear can benefit from the technology of CROS. A CROS aid is used to direct sound received on the patient's poor-hearing side and transmit it to the better-hearing side. This is done by placing a microphone on the poor ear, which receives the signal and transmits it to a receiver worn on the good ear. The patient hears the sound from the poor ear through the receiver on the good ear, while hearing sound from the good side naturally through the open ear canal. This can be accomplished either by hardwiring the transmitter and receiver together with a wire worn behind the head or wirelessly by frequency-modulated transmission.

The BiCROS aid was developed for patients who also need amplification on the good ear due to reduced hearing acuity. The BiCROS differs from the CROS in that the good ear is fitted with a hearing aid, which receives the transmitted sound from the poor ear but also functions as a stand-alone device for the better-hearing ear.

CROS and BiCROS hearing aids allow users to hear sound they might otherwise miss from the poor ear. This gives awareness of sound and also some idea about location of the sound source. However, not all unilateral hearing loss patients will accept the aided configuration, because the sound crossed over to the good ear may interfere with processing natural sound in the better-hearing ear and may prove confusing as to directionality of sound.

Description of the Case

"Suddenly, I realized I couldn't hear anything from my right ear," she recalled. This dramatic discovery triggered a long journey: medical intervention, audiological rehabilitation, and an emotional struggle that continues today, nearly 35 years later. This case illustrates a classic sudden hearing loss of unknown etiology including the evolution of the disease, the number of specialists involved, and the emotional struggle of the patient and her family as they all learn to cope with the hearing and balance disorder. Information for this case presentation has been compiled from medical record review and personal interview with the patient.

Background Information

Rev. Ella Star is an 85-year-old woman. An only child, she learned to entertain herself by reading, writing, and imaginative play. Her father was a high school principal and her mother a piano teacher in rural Kansas. Rev. Star grew up in a small town and loved summertime, when she lived with her grandparents on their farm. Perhaps it was these early experiences that allowed her to better cope with her eventual audiovestibular disability.

Reason for the Referral

Onset of the Hearing and Balance Disorder

Rev. Star graduated from college with a bachelor's degree in music education. After marriage, she and her husband settled in Iowa, where they raised their son and daughter. She supplemented the family income by teaching piano lessons, substitute teaching in the elementary schools, freelance writing, and apprenticing in the local string instrument repair shop. She is Caucasian, is a nonsmoker, and does not drink alcohol. Rev. Star was always physically active: walked, exercised regularly, and coached her daughter's church basketball team. After the youngest child left home for college, Rev. Star pursued her own dream: She enrolled in seminary at the age of 50 years and became an ordained United Methodist minister. Her new career allowed her to study, write, teach, and counsel people of all ages.

Rev. Star underwent a hysterectomy due to a fibroid tumor, and as she recalls, sometime during her 5-day hospitalization, she developed "chirping sounds, like crickets" in the right ear. Approximately 6 weeks later, she consulted a local ear, nose, and throat physician to investigate the tinnitus complaint. An audiology evaluation was conducted and Rev. Star was surprised to learn that she had a "50% hearing loss" in the right ear. Until then, she had no awareness of a hearing problem. Neither medical intervention nor rehabilitation was prescribed by the ear, nose, and throat physician (Dr. 1), who told her she might have Meniere's disease, for which no treatment was recommended. She coped with the tinnitus by learning to "tune out" the sound much as she did as a child when she learned to ignore the sounds of her mother's piano students.

Approximately 1 year later, Rev. Star and her husband were vacationing. During the outbound flight, Rev. Star conversed with her fellow passenger seated to her right. Oddly, after the plane landed, she could no longer hear what the gentleman was saying to her. As they deplaned, Mr. Star noted that Rev. Star was also having difficulty negotiating the ramp. He had to hold her hand to steady her as he guided her through the airport. When they greeted their friends outside the airport, Rev. Star remembered apologizing because she couldn't hear anything from the right ear. No one paid much attention, and she eventually returned to her hotel room to be alone. Assuming that her hearing would return, she didn't consider it to be an emergency and vacation plans were unaltered.

Ironically, one of Rev. Star's parishioners had a daughter who had recently graduated with a master's degree in audiology. When learning of Rev. Star's condition, the parishioner volunteered to call her daughter for advice. The young audiologist contacted a colleague, who quickly arranged an appointment with an otologist at a national medical facility. Three weeks later, Mr. and Rev. Star drove out of state for the consultation.

Findings of the Evaluation

The otologist (Dr. 2) found nothing remarkable on the physical examination. However, a detailed medical history evoked some additional information, including a previous vertiginous attack approximately 2 years prior. His handwritten chart notes follow:

> 51 y.o. w.f. Pastor United Methodist Church who first noted a fullness and rushing sound like fluid in R ear 3 years ago. This eventually resolved. She developed sudden onset of vertigo and nausea ~ 2 years ago lasting 6 24 h but followed by ~ 8 weeks of unsteadiness. This was followed by mild positional vertigo which to some extent persists. More tinnitus and decreased hearing became apparent in January 1984—this fluctuated some in the past year and a half—most recent outside audiogram 2/11/1985 shows 50+dB loss & 36% discrimination. No vertiginous episodes. Audio today—ō R. Now had fluctuation in L ear after flying ~ 1 month ago. No pain.

A diagnostic audiology evaluation on August 22, 1985, revealed a mild-degree, sloping sensorineural hearing loss in the left ear with excellent word recognition at 40 dB SL. There was no response to air or bone conduction stimuli in the right ear. Stenger was negative. Immittance findings showed Type A tympanograms in both ears. Contralateral and ipsilateral acoustic reflex thresholds were absent when stimulating the right ear and present at expected levels when stimulating the left ear. Acoustic reflex decay was negative at 500 and 2000 in the left ear.

Electronystagmography, also conducted on August 22, revealed no spontaneous nystagmus observed in any of the positions tested. Cold and warm water caloric stimulation revealed a unilateral weakness on the right: 0% response in the right ear and 100% in the left ear (nystagmus was suppressed with eyes open). Ice water caloric stimulation to right ear revealed 3.7 degrees/second left-beating nystagmus. Findings were consistent with right peripheral deficit.

Dr. 2 noted that the condition "may be hydrops but unusual scenario." He ordered a computed tomography (CT) scan, which was negative with no evidence of lesion. He suggested a repeat audiological evaluation in 1 year and a hearing aid evaluation for a CROS aid. It was speculated that the right ear hearing loss was the result of a viral infection, which would be unlikely to affect the hearing in the left ear.

In December that same year, Rev. Star experienced increased difficulty communicating on the telephone. Terrified that she was losing hearing in her left ear, she immediately made an appointment with her local ear, nose, and throat physician, Dr. 1. After reviewing the results of a new audiogram, Dr. 1 told her that he "didn't see much difference since the last visit." Astonished and angered, Rev. Star responded, "I've lost all of the hearing and balance in my right ear. Now I'm starting to lose the hearing in my left ear, and you don't see the difference?" Dr. 1 left the room and called Dr. 2., the otologist who had seen her in August. After discussing her case, it was agreed to refer her to another otologist, Dr. 3, who had expertise in autoimmune inner ear disease (AIED). An appointment was scheduled within 2 weeks.

Diagnosis: AIED

When she asked Dr. 3 how one arrives at a diagnosis of autoimmune inner ear disease, he replied, "By ruling out every other known disease." The process of elimination was well under way, and a pattern was beginning to emerge. By looking at Rev. Star's total health history, rather than at the audiovestibular mechanism as an isolated system, seemingly unrelated symptoms became connected. A review of salient points follows:

- In college, Rev. Star had episodes of canker sores in her mouth, throat, and bronchial tubes. Later episodes included lesions in the throat and mouth that responded to prednisone treatments.
- Rev. Star's mother had a long history of Meniere's disease and wore hearing aids in both ears.
- During a routine physical done in her early 40s, a blood test revealed an extremely high erythrocyte sedimentation rate (ESR). Her internal medicine physician told her at the time that she could expect to develop rheumatoid arthritis in the future.
- In approximately 1982, she experienced aural fullness and a rushing sound in the right ear, which spontaneously resolved.
- In 1983, she experienced vertigo so severe that she was hospitalized overnight. She was treated with medication for 3 months and had lingering unsteadiness.
- In 1984, she experienced tinnitus in the right ear while hospitalized for a hysterectomy. That summer, she noticed that she couldn't keep her balance when riding her bicycle and was unable to make turns when riding. When ascending and descending the steps in her home, she found herself reaching for the banister to make the turn at the bottom of the stairwell.
- In May 1984, she was diagnosed with sensorineural hearing loss in the right ear.

- Later that year, she developed severe episcleritis in both eyes. She was treated by her internal medicine physician with monthly steroid injections, which alleviated the symptoms.
- She frequently experienced shortness of breath, which she attributed to being out of shape, although she was physically active. She described "huffing and puffing" when walking a short distance uphill. She was easily fatigued despite being weight appropriate.
- In July 1985, she lost all hearing and balance function in the right ear and had mild hearing loss in the left ear. In December 1985, hearing in the left ear decreased.
- In December 1985, her ESR was 93 mm/h (abnormal).

For Rev. Star, the AIED diagnosis was based on her medical history, which included other autoimmune conditions: canker sores, episcleritis (inflammation of the connective tissue between the conjunctiva and the sclera), and unspecified lung condition causing shortness of breath. The acquisition of the hearing loss fit the time course of AIED, namely, sensorineural hearing loss in one ear, occurring over weeks or months, followed by fluctuating hearing loss in the opposite ear. The hearing loss was preceded by aural fullness, tinnitus, and vertigo. She had at least a 10-year history of high ESRs. In the subsequent years after the initial diagnosis, her CRP has been abnormally high. In 1999, during an episode of reduced hearing, Rev. Star tested negative for the Western blot 69 kDA, even though she did respond favorably to the steroid treatment.

Course of Treatments

In 1985, Dr. 3 prescribed aggressive treatment to stop the progression of hearing loss in the left ear. Rev. Star underwent 2 weeks of chemotherapy with intravenous injection of cyclophosphamide (Cytoxan): 30 minutes/day, followed by 3 months of oral prednisone and immunosuppresants. Cytoxan has been used for treating rheumatoid arthritis, multiple sclerosis, and leukemias. After the conclusion of the treatment, Rev. Star had a mild, sloping to moderate-degree sensorineural hearing loss in the left ear. Word recognition scores were excellent when tested in quiet environments. She became extremely ill from the side effects of the powerful drug; however, Rev. Star credited this treatment with preserving the hearing in the left ear.

Rev. Star's subsequent health care involved a team of subspecialty physicians under the supervision of a rheumatologist for her continued physical ailments. She continued to exhibit ulcerations in the throat, soft palate, and mouth; dyspnea upon exertion; and episcleritis, scleral thinning, and arthritis. In November 1986, she was diagnosed as possibly having Wegener's granulomatosis. This and also Behcet's disease were subsequently ruled out after a nasal septum biopsy. Pulmonary function testing and an open lung biopsy led to diagnoses of pulmonary hypertension with possible thromboembolic component. Her symptoms are managed by medication: anticoagulant, immunosuppressants, and tapered doses of both oral and topical prednisone for the recurring bouts of episcleritis. Because of past Cytoxan treatment, she was monitored for hematuria (blood in urine). Due to long-term steroid treatment, a medication was given to counteract the effect of calcium malabsorption.

From the time of the initial AIED diagnosis (December 1985) until December 2008, Rev. Star has experienced multiple recurrences of left ear hearing fluctuations. There were approximately four episodes/year between 1986 and 1988, which reduced in frequency to two episodes/year until 2006. There was one recurrence in 2007 and one in 2008. Each episode was treated with high doses of oral prednisone in tapered regimen. The most recent course prescribed was 60 mg/day for 2 weeks, followed by 1 day each at 40 mg/day, 30 mg/day, 20 mg/day, and 10 mg/day. Additional diagnostic tests were conducted over the years, including in 1998 "ENG Tullio and neurocom pressure" tests, which were negative in both ears.

Audiology evaluations are conducted throughout the treatment to monitor hearing change. Typically, there is a 10- to 25-dB drop in the low- to mid-frequency thresholds. Usually, 1 to 2 days after beginning the prednisone treatment, Rev. Star noticed a marked subjective improvement in hearing. Objectively, her hearing thresholds showed a return to her baseline levels at the end of the steroid therapy; however, over the course of 23 years, there was some permanent decrease of about 15 to 20 dB across all test frequencies. Interestingly, word recognition remained excellent at a comfortable listening level in a quiet environment. Refer to Figure 53–1 for audiogram results from 1985 to 2008.

Living With Hearing and Balance Loss

Because communication is so integral to human interaction, the effects of hearing loss extend to all relationships. Adjusting to a loss of hearing and balance function has implications for both career and family life.

At Work

According to Rev. Star, being a good pastor was "more about listening than it is about preaching." Several listening situations are encountered, from one-on-one counseling sessions to large social gatherings, with all types of meetings in between. She needed to hear children when teaching Sunday school, elderly people in nursing homes, and sick patients in hospitals. There were weddings, funerals, and multiple worship services to officiate weekly. She was integrally involved in composing, rehearsing, and performing music in her ministry. The repercussions of not responding appropriately in conversation or, worse, failing to respond at all could be severe. Parishioners tend to take it personally when the pastor doesn't acknowledge them. While there were humorous situations caused by misunderstanding words, there were more serious instances of parishioners with hurt feelings from being "ignored" and accusations of purposeful neglect. She desperately needed to hear well and decided she must be open and honest about her hearing loss with her congregation. To maximize sound reception, Rev. Star was fitted with a wireless behind-the-ear BiCROS hearing aid. Having a transmitter on the right side allowed her to know when someone on her right side was speaking;

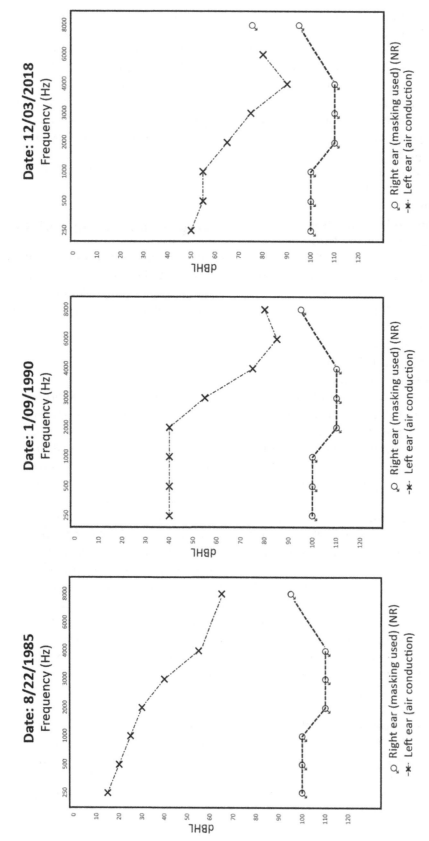

Figure 53–1. Air conduction thresholds for three audiograms: 1985, after initial onset of total right hearing loss; 1990; and most current, 2018.

however, she still struggled with sound localization and with understanding speech in a noisy environment, such as the fellowship hour after a church service. As her hearing and other health conditions worsened, she eventually applied for and received medical disability many years before she would have voluntarily retired.

At Home

Mr. Star, a loving and devoted husband, had to face the reality of his wife's disabilities. He battled his own impatience with having to repeat himself and the frustration of watching his normally astute wife misunderstand conversations, and he grieved lost intimacy and easy laughter. To be effective, communication had to be purposeful and calculated, rather than spontaneous and unconscious. Simple accommodations included rearranging the furniture in the living room so that Mr. Star's chair was on Rev. Star's left side. More difficult accommodations included controlling anger and exasperation in his voice when saying things the second or third time. There were countless medical appointments and the constant worry that someday, the left ear will suddenly drop permanently, making natural communication all but impossible.

The Stars' son and daughter were both grown and away from home when the symptoms of the disease began. At first, there was denial regarding the severity and permanency of the disorder. Like most people, they were unfamiliar with the complications hearing loss adds to conversations and family activities. As the hearing loss fluctuations occurred, their daughter noticed that the quality of Rev. Star's voice changed when her hearing loss increased. This became an important indicator to identify the need for intervention. Both children have become very supportive of their parents through the years. Their daughter researched options for amplified telephones and encouraged Rev. Star to request assistive listening devices at the theater.

Hearing loss changed many of Rev. Star's daily activities. Although she was able to continue playing piano, she eventually withdrew from singing in the choir and from participating in other

musical groups. Listening to recorded music at home became less pleasurable, and she stopped listening to music as a pastime. She still enjoyed attending live music events, and she and Mr. Star held season tickets to the symphony.

Coping Strategies

Accepting Rev. Star's new identity as "disabled" came with many changes. The Stars got a puppy and trained her to bark when the phone and doorbell rang. Rev. Star learned that she had to see where she was walking to compensate for the lack of balance. She began to carry a flashlight with her to illuminate the pathway whenever it was dark. Her physical activity changed since something as simple as ducking to avoid a Frisbee could result in a fall. Often, she steadied herself by holding on to another person as she walked, making her feel older than her true age. She stopped swimming and boating to avoid the danger of disorientation while under water. The side effects of large doses of prednisone caused extreme weight gains and mood swings. She constantly apologized for getting things wrong and sensed the negative reactions of others when she did not hear accurately. As painful as it was to give up her ministry, she could no longer trust her hearing ability. She was unable to answer questions with certainty or assume that what she heard was correct. When asked recently what it was like to have a hearing loss, Rev. Star said, "The most insulting part for me is that I am an educated, intelligent woman. Yet when I make a mistake in a conversation, people look at me as if I am *stupid*."

The combination of the general health disorders and the effort involved to listen made it easier to retreat into her hobbies. Being on immunosuppressant medication makes one more susceptible to any infection, and the patient is advised to avoid crowds of people and germ-rich environments. While the autoimmune disease kept her away from many social gatherings, she enjoyed being alone to write, sew, and create jewelry. When she stopped working, she discontinued using the BiCROS-style hearing aid. Over the years, she used in-the-ear aids and now used a monaural digital behind-the-ear–style hearing aid with FM compatibility on her left ear. Her positive attitude toward overcoming her limitations contributed to an eagerness to teach others about hearing loss, balance disorders, and autoimmune disease. Rev. Star intended to donate her temporal bones to research and registered with the National Temporal Bone, Hearing, and Balance Pathology Resource Registry.

Analysis of Client's Response to Intervention

Key to understanding this case is the difficulty with regard to diagnosing AIED. Rev. Star experienced the importance of consulting physicians and audiologists who were current with the latest research and connected with their professional peers. The diagnosis of AIED occurred in 1985, just 6 years after the hallmark study proposing the definition of AIED was published. It took three different physicians, three different audiologists, and over 1 year of elapsed time to arrive at a diagnosis. There are several relevant observations in reviewing the facts of this case study:

- Technological and scientific advancements have yielded new understandings of autoimmune and autoinflammatory disease, and new diagnostic tools and therapeutics have been developed. Still, the primary diagnostic information for AIED are the clinical manifestations, supplemented by medical history and laboratory studies. Today, a multidisciplinary team approach including the audiologist, otolaryngologist, and rheumatologist can benefit the patient and support early identification and appropriate treatment (Ciorba et al., 2018).
- Current audiology test batteries might include:
  - Pure-tone air and bone conduction audiometry
  - Stenger
  - Speech audiometry
  - Multifrequency tympanometry
  - Contra and ipsilaterally stimulated acoustic reflexes
  - Acoustic reflex decay
  - Otoacoustic emissions
  - Electrophysiological tests including early, middle, late evoked potentials
  - Electrocochleography
  - Electronystagmography/ videonystamography
  - Posturography
  - Rotary chair testing
  - Hearing aid evaluation and appropriate aural rehabilitation
  - Cochlear implantation
  - Tinnitus assessment and treatment
  - Vestibular rehabilitation
- The disease process began several years before the diagnosis was made. A culmination of episodes and comprehensive medical history intake were needed to identify the pattern of the audiovestibular disorder and connect the seemingly unrelated symptoms. According to Rev. Star's report, Dr. 1 did not advise any further investigation or rehabilitation for her symptoms in 1984. There is still risk today that a diagnosis of AIED will be overlooked because there is not one definitive diagnostic test (Bovo et al., 2006).
- The diagnostic process involved ruling out several known disease patterns, including vestibular schwannoma, Meniere's disease, viral infection, and vascular disorder.
- The effectiveness and necessity of Cytoxan chemotherapy is questionable. Though the patient attributes this treatment with stopping the progression of the left ear hearing loss, there is no way of knowing how the outcome would differ with a different treatment approach. The side effects of Cytoxan are unpleasant to the patient and have potential long-term serious effects. For Rev. Star, there was no recovery of hearing thresholds after the Cytoxan

treatment. Subsequent record review by another physician indicated the treatment was "to no avail."

- Although early in the disease process, Rev. Star experienced vertigo severe enough to be hospitalized, she apparently did not see an ear, nose, and throat specialist or an audiologist at the time. The primary care physician, emergency room physician, otologist, and audiologist should be consulted when patients exhibit audiovestibular dysfunction.

- Unilateral hearing loss has unique behavioral effects: difficulty localizing sound, increased difficulty hearing in background noise, and lack of awareness of activity on the impaired side. CROS or BiCROS hearing aids offer some benefit for some but not all patients.

- Fluctuation of the hearing thresholds in the left ear pose challenges for treatment and rehabilitation management.

- The patient must be quick to recognize a subtle change in hearing to obtain medical/pharmacological treatment as quickly as possible.

- The hearing aid must be adaptable to compensate for swings in hearing acuity.

- The spouse and family must learn to accept variations in the patient's ability to communicate and respond to sound.

- Professionals often focus on the effects of hearing loss, yet overlook the complications caused by loss of balance function.

- After the initial diagnosis and treatment, a multidisciplinary approach to medical management is important. Rev. Star had numerous subspecialty physicians all under the supervision of her rheumatologist. She relied heavily on her audiologist to communicate test results with the otologist and manage her hearing aid status. An audiologist has the opportunity to become an advocate for the hearing-impaired patient and may also be a resource for the patient when filing a disability claim for hearing loss.

The process of acquiring and adjusting to AIED challenged Rev. Star physically, emotionally, and spiritually. Her family strived to be supportive and understanding. They became keenly aware of the value of good hearing and the fragility of health. Regardless of the hardship, Rev. Star was determined to hear and to be heard no matter how much effort it took. She knew that although the disease changed her, she was still the vital, intelligent, and strong woman she was before the disease.

Author's Note

Many of the facts in this case were drawn from medical records and personal patient interview, used with permission from the patient. However, some descriptive and identifying information, as well as location references, has been fabricated to preserve anonymity. Any resemblance to actual people or places should be assumed to be accidental. Note that all instances of sudden sensorineural hearing loss and autoimmune disease are different and should be treated on a case-by-case basis. This case study is not to be used as a treatment protocol.

References

Argup, C. (2008). Immune-mediated audiovestibular disorders in the paediatric population: A review. *International Journal of Audiology, 47*(9), 560–565. https://doi.org/10.1080/14992020802282268

Bovo, R., Aimoni, C., & Martini, A. (2006). Immune-mediated inner ear disease. *Acta Oto-Laryngologica, 126*, 1012–1021. https://doi.org/10.1080/00016480600606723

Byl, F. M., Jr. (1984). Sudden hearing loss: Eight years' experience and suggested prognostic table. *Laryngoscope, 94*(5, Pt. 1), 647–661.

Ciorba, A., Corazzi, V., Bianchini, C., Aimoni, C., Pelucchi, S., Skarzynski, P., & Hatzopoulos, S. (2018). Autoimmune inner ear disease (AIED): A diagnostic challenge. *International Journal of Immunopathology and Pharmacology, 32*, 1–5. https://doi.org/10.1177/2058738418808680

Das, S., Bakshi, S. S., & Seepana, R. (2019). Demystifying autoimmune inner ear disease. *European Archives of Oto-Rhino-Laryngology, 276*, 3267–3274. https://doi.org/10.1007/s00405-019-05681-5

Harris, J., & Keithley, E. (2003). Autoimmune inner ear disease. In J. Snow Jr. & J. Ballenger (Eds.), *Ballenger's otorhinolaryngology head and neck surgery* (16th ed., pp. 396–407). BC Decker.

Hayes, D. (2006). *A practical guide to CROS/BiCROS fittings*. Audiology Online. http://www.audiologyonline.com/articles/article_detail.asp?wc=1&article_id=1632

Hirose, K., Wener, M. H., & Duckert, L. G. (1999). Utility of laboratory testing in autoimmune inner ear disease. *Laryngoscope, 109*, 1749–1754. https://doi.org/10.1097/00005537-199911000-00005

Hughes, G., Freedman, M., Haberkamp, T., & Guay, M. (1996). Sudden sensorineural hearing loss. *Otolaryngologic Clinics of North America, 29*(3), 393–405.

Mattox, D., & Simmons, F. (1977). Natural history of sudden sensorineural hearing loss. *Annals of Otology, Rhinology & Laryngology, 86*, 463–480. https://doi.org/10.1177/000348947708600406

McCabe, B. (1979). Autoimmune sensorineural hearing loss. *Annals of Otology, Rhinology, and Laryngology, 88*(5), 585–589. https://doi.org/10.1177/000348947908800501

Moscicki, R. A., San Martin, J. E., Quintero, C. H., Rauch, S.D., Nadol, J. B., Jr., & Bloch, K. J. (1994). Serum antibody to inner ear proteins in patients with progressive hearing loss. Correlation with disease activity and response to corticosteroid treatment. *Journal of the American Medical Association, 272*(8), 611–616.

Muller, C., Vrabec, J., & Quinn, F. (2001). *Sudden sensorineural hearing loss*. Grand Rounds Presentation, UTMB, Dept. of Otolaryngology. http://www.utmb.edu/otoref/Grnds/SuddenHearingLoss-010613/SSNHL.htm

Sargent, E. W. (2002). *Autoimmune inner ear diseases: Autoimmune disease with audiovestibular involvement*. Audiology Online. http://www.audiologyonline.com/articles/article_detail.asp?article_id=364

Sing, T. (2005). Prognostic indicators in idiopathic sudden sensorineural hearing loss in a Malaysian hospital. *The Internet Journal of Otorhinolaryngology, 5*(2). https://ispub.com/IJORL/5/2/3445

Stroudt, R., & Vrabec, J. (2000). *Autoimmune inner ear disease*. Grand Rounds Presentation, UTMB, Dept. of Otolaryngology. http://www.utmb.edu/otoref/grnds/Autoimmune-Ear-200001/AutoimmuneInner-Ear.doc

Szalai, A. (2004). C-reactive protein and autoimmune disease: Facts and conjectures. *Clinical & Developmental Immunology, 11*(3/4), 221–226. https://doi.org/10.1080/17402520400001751

Vambutas, A., & Pathak, S. (2016). AAO: Autoimmune and autoinflammatory (disease) in otology: What is new in immune-mediated hearing loss. *Laryngoscope Investigative Otolaryngology, 1*(5), 110–115. https://doi.org/10.1002/lio2.28

Wynne, M., Diefendorf, A., & Fritsch, M. (2001, December 26). Sudden hearing loss. *The ASHA Leader*. https://doi.org/10.1044/leader.FTR2.06232001.6

HEARING
CASE 54
Jack: Noise-Induced Hearing Loss: A Work-Related Investigation
Deanna K. Meinke

Conceptual Knowledge Areas

Noise-Induced Hearing Loss

The relationship between exposure to high levels of sound on the job and hearing loss has been known for over 300 years. Occupational noise-induced hearing loss (NIHL) was first described by Bernardo Ramazzini in a medical text entitled *De Morbis Artificum Diatriba* (translation *Diseases of Workers*), first published in 1700 and revised in 1713 (Ramazzini, 1964). Ramazzini observed that hearing loss was common in coppersmiths and corn millers who were exposed to loud sounds. He also suggested that a remedy might be to "stuff their ears with cotton so that the inner parts [of the ear] receive less shock from the loud noise." Today we know that noise-induced damage to the auditory system is a risk for workers in many industries and is prevalent among workers in the military, construction, manufacturing, mining, and agriculture (Humes et al., 2005; Masterson et al., 2016), and efforts to prevent occupational noise-induced hearing loss are ongoing (Themann & Masterson, 2019).

Evidence of a Noise Notch

Hazardous sound exposure has the potential to damage delicate hair cells and other structures in the auditory system (Bielefeld, 2022; Henderson et al., 2006; Henderson et al., 2007). This results in hearing loss most evident at the frequencies of 3000, 4000, or 6000 Hz, with recovery at 8000 Hz, at least in the early stages (Kirchner et al., 2012; Mirza et al., 2018; Rabinowitz et al., 2022). When plotted on an audiogram, this characteristic dip in the hearing threshold data is commonly referred to as a "noise notch" and is first evident during the decade 10 to 19 years old (Figure 54–1). Gradual-onset NIHL may not be subjectively apparent to an individual until it worsens to a greater degree of loss and spreads to adjacent audiometric test frequencies due to continued unprotected exposures. The presence of a sensorineural hearing loss with a "noise notch" configuration in combination with a history of unprotected noise exposure usually distinguishes early-onset NIHL from other causes of hearing loss. The diagnosis of NIHL is confounded by the presence of age-related hearing loss in later decades, as the "notch" configuration erodes into a sloping configuration in Figure 54–1 for those 70+ years. Consequently, ongoing periodic monitoring records that include 500, 1000, 2000, 3000, 4000, 6000, and 8000 Hz are critical for occupational regulatory compliance and the determination of temporary or permanent work-related NIHL.

Temporary Versus Permanent Threshold Shift

Hazardous noise exposure can cause both temporary and/or permanent damage to the auditory system depending on the sound level and duration of sound exposure(s). Audiometric monitoring is used to detect changes in hearing, which

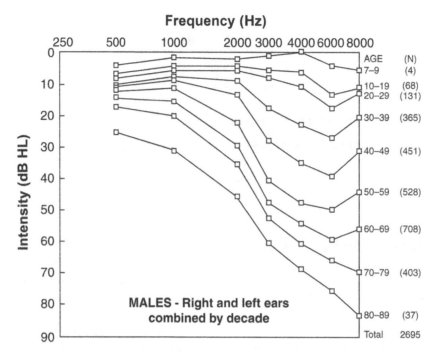

Figure 54–1. Averaged audiometric threshold values plotted by age decade for U.S. males engaged in farming. Reprinted with permission from ADVANCE Newsmagazines; Lankford, Zurales, Garrett, and Delorier. 10-Year Study of Agricultural Workers. *Advance for Audiologists*, 4(5), 34, 36–37, 2002.

may be either short-term noise-induced temporary threshold shift (NITTS) or long-term noise-induced permanent threshold shift (NIPTS). Both ongoing exposures over time and instantaneous hazardous sound exposures have the potential to cause NIPTS. In the case of acoustic trauma, hearing loss occurs instantaneously after noise exposure and is immediately evident to the affected individual. Specifically, unprotected exposure to a firearm shot (Humes et al., 2005), a vehicle airbag deployment (Yaremchuk & Dobie, 2001), or an explosion (Van Campen et al., 1999) is reported to cause sudden-onset NIPTS. In the occupational setting, long-term unprotected exposure to hazardous levels of noise leads to gradual-onset NIPTS. Repeat measurement of hearing thresholds before and after noise exposure can be used to differentiate NITTS (which recovers over a period of hours, days, or weeks depending on the extent of the noise exposure) from NIPTS (Meinke, 2022; Themann & Masterson, 2019).

Occupational Noise-Induced Hearing Loss and Tinnitus

Worldwide, an estimated 16% of disabling hearing loss in adults is attributed to hazardous noise exposure at work (Nelson et al., 2005). In the United States, 17% to 25% of nonmilitary U.S. workers (22–25 million) are exposed to hazardous noise at work (Kerns et al., 2018; Tak et al., 2009). Approximately 10 million persons in the United States (Jackson & Duffy, 1998) and 25 to 30 million in Europe (Quaranta et al., 2001) have permanent hearing loss from long-term continuous noise exposure or acoustic trauma. A more recent analysis of hearing threshold data from the 2011 to 2012 cycle of the U.S. National Health and Examination Survey (NHANES) reported audiometric notching suggestive of NIHL in 32.6% among working-age adults (20–69 years) with a history of workplace noise exposure (Carroll et al., 2017). Estimates of the prevalence of tinnitus in noise-exposed workers range from 10% to 58% (Axelsson, 1995; Coles et al., 1990; Cooper, 1994). Workers' compensation is given for tinnitus as well as hearing loss in some jurisdictions (Dobie & Cooper, 2022). Tinnitus is also implicated as an early warning indicator of NIHL (Griest & Bishop, 1998). The most commonly recognized "at-risk" occupations include agriculture (farming, forestry, commercial fishing), mining, construction, manufacturing, utilities, transportation (aircraft, railroad, and marine), service personnel (firefighters, emergency medical technicians, surgeons), musicians, and military.

Hearing Conservation Programs

Implementation of a workplace hearing conservation program is mandated in some of these industries in the United States by the Occupational Safety and Health Administration (OSHA, 1983), the Mine Safety and Health Administration (MSHA, 1999), the Federal Railroad Administration (FRA, 2006), and the U.S. Department of Defense (DoD, 2010). The National Institutes of Occupational Safety and Health (NIOSH, 1998) provide recommendations for hearing loss prevention based upon scientific evidence to support best practice. These programs all include the need to implement audiometric monitoring programs to track the hearing of workers and ideally identify early decreases (shifts) in hearing that would trigger intervention to prevent permanent NIHL.

Significant Threshold Shift

The audiometric monitoring component of the OSHA (1983) mandated hearing conservation program defines a significant threshold shift (STS) as an average change in hearing of 10 dB or more for the test frequencies of 2000, 3000, and 4000 Hz in either ear. Baseline testing is required to be performed on individuals who have not been exposed to noise within the previous 14 hours to avoid the effects of NITTS on baseline testing references. If an STS occurs and is confirmed on subsequent tests without pretest noise exposure, then the baseline reference is revised to a new reference for determining future significant changes in hear-

ing (McDaniel et al., 2013; Meinke, 2022). OSHA requires that individuals with an STS be notified and be refit/retrained in the use of hearing protection devices. Individuals not required to wear hearing protection on the job (exposed between 85 and 90 dBA time-weighted average [TWA] are now required to wear hearing protection for exposures above 85 dBA TWA. There is an option for employers to retest the worker's hearing within 30 days to confirm the presence of an STS.

Work-Related Hearing Loss

Employers are required to report the specifics of any work-related hearing loss on the OSHA 300 log per the requirements of 29 CFR 1904.10 (OSHA, 2002). An OSHA recordable hearing loss is triggered when there is an average hearing threshold change of 10 dB or more at 2000, 3000, and 4000 Hz (e.g., a standard threshold shift occurred), and such shifts result in an absolute threshold average of 25 dB hearing level (HL) or more. Hager (2006) summarized the U.S. Bureau of Labor Statistics data relative to the OSHA injury and illness recordable hearing loss statistics for 2004 and reported that 11% of all OSHA recordable occupational injuries were due to hearing loss. Themann and Masterson (2019) note that there are serious limitations to the OSHA reporting requirements and recordability criteria that likely result in an underestimation of the true incidence of work-related hearing loss.

Role of the Audiologist

Audiologists are routinely involved in the evaluation, diagnosis, and treatment of patients with NIHL and tinnitus. Patients with hearing loss and/or tinnitus resulting from noise exposure are pervasive in the otological clinical population. Dobie (1993) estimates that approximately 20% of patients may attribute at least a part of their hearing loss to noise exposure.

Beyond the clinic, audiologists have specific roles and responsibilities within regulatory mandated hearing conservation programs. The audiologist may perform the noise exposure measurements and hearing testing services; review audiograms to identify threshold shifts; make referrals for workers needing follow-up care; select, fit, and measure the attenuation of hearing protectors; and provide training to workers and management. Additionally, the audiologist may determine if a hearing loss is work related and evaluate individuals for workers' compensation claims. The following case study illustrates the role of the audiologist in the context of a complex occupational noise-induced hearing loss.

Description of the Case

Adults are known to be at risk for progressive sensorineural hearing loss if unprotected from hazardous sound exposures over a lifetime. Early detection and intervention are critical for the prevention of noise-induced hearing loss whether due to occupational or avocational sources. In the absence of preventive action, hearing loss may occur and accrue to a disabling degree. Employees with hearing impairment are likely to seek workers' compensation for this condition if they believe the employer is responsible for the noise levels that may have damaged their hearing. This case illustrates that a professional team-based approach, combined with critical investigation and diagnostics, facilitates individual considerations for workers' compensation claim determinations and settlements. More importantly, it demonstrates that when opportunities for early intervention are missed, additional hearing loss ensues and may be costly to the employer and/or insurer as well as to the employee.

Background Information

This case of Jack, a worker with NIHL, describes the history, audiometric data, noise exposure profile, and interventions provided by a team of health and safety professionals. There were missed opportunities for the prevention of NIHL in Jack, and the reader is encouraged to identify these stages and implement a more proactive, preventive medicine approach in his or her own practice. Note that this case occurred in Colorado, so allowances should

be made for variations in workers' compensation laws in different states. It is imperative that clinicians be familiar with the workers' compensation statutes and requirements in their geographical region(s). Additionally, this case was uncontested and ultimately was processed through the state workers' compensation insurer for settlement. The employer was obligated under OSHA CFR 29 1910.95 (1983) for hearing loss prevention and OSHA 29 CFR 1904.10 (2002) for occupational injury and illness reporting requirements. Although the dates are decades old, this scenario might occur today since the same regulations and workplace requirements are still in effect and best practices in hearing loss prevention are yet to be implemented in many workplace hearing conservation programs. It is estimated that compliance with OSHA 29 CFR 1910.95 will still result in 25% of 60-year-old workers being at excess risk of material hearing impairment (defined as an average hearing loss at 1000, 2000, 3000, and 4000 Hz that exceeds 25 dBHL) after a 40-year working lifetime exposure to occupational noise (NIOSH, 1998, Table 3-4). Additionally, allowances are not made for off-the-job noise exposures, which further increase the risk of NIHL.

Relevant Facts

Jack, a 58-year-old male, was first evaluated for a workers' compensation claim in January 2003, and the claim was settled in November 2003. There was no evidence of functional hearing loss, and he did not require special testing to rule out malingering. The involved health and safety professionals and their affiliations included the following:

- Industrial hygienist (IH); employer affiliated
- Occupational health nurse (OHN); employer affiliated
- Occupational physician (OPhys); consultant to employer
- Occupational audiologist (OAud); consultant to employer and occupational physician
- Otolaryngologist (ENT); private practice provider

■ Clinical audiologist (CAud); private practice provider, affiliated with ENT
■ Patient (WRK); employed as a maintenance worker by the employer

The employee was never formally enrolled in a hearing conservation program at work, and hearing- and noise-related information is intermittent throughout his years of employment.

Patient-Reported History Information

The initial case history may be the most important adjunct to the audiologist's test battery, and it often requires more than one effort to complete since information has to be gathered not only from the patient and referring physician but also from the worksite. A comprehensive history provides direction and confidence for future clinical decisions and reporting. It also serves as a check for consistency between histories given to the occupational health nurse, the physicians, and the audiologists at different points in time. An example of the complete case history taken for WRK (Jack) via a patient interview (March 2003) is summarized in the following paragraphs. All relevant topics are included for reference.

General Medical History

Jack was negative for diabetes, kidney disease, thyroid disease, autoimmune disease, neurological disorders/disease, seizure disorders, high blood pressure, circulatory system disorders, stroke, cancer/tumors, metabolic disorders, head injury/unconsciousness, meningitis, and scarlet fever. There was a positive history of childhood mumps and measles. He had a long history of tobacco smoking.

Otologic Medical History

Jack had negative otologic history for ear pain, drainage, fullness, and discomfort. There were no reports of facial numbness/paralysis, head injuries, ear surgeries, cerumen impactions, or dizziness/vertigo. There were no reports of allergies or sinus/cold symptoms affecting his hearing in the past. He denied taking any ototoxic medications (quinines, -myacins, or long-term high-level aspirin regimens) or knowingly being exposed to chemicals/solvents. There was a negative history for familial hearing loss. Jack reported gradual onset of bilateral hearing loss and noted that he had problems communicating for the past several years. The loss was not subjectively asymmetrical and did not seem to fluctuate. He also reported bilateral mild tinnitus and described it as primarily "annoying in quiet." He had not been previously evaluated by an ENT or audiologist as part of his personal health care and had never worn hearing aids. He stated that his hearing was checked intermittently at work in the past and that the results were "abnormal, but nothing was done about it."

Communication History

Jack reported minimal problems understanding speech in quiet or communicating in the course of performing his job duties. He indicated difficulty understanding speech in noisy listening environments, in meetings, on the telephone, and while transcribing voice messages. Warning signals and safety hazard communications were audible and supplemented by a pager. His family complained about his ability to hear at home and during social activities.

Work-Related Environmental Noise Exposure and Hearing Protector Use History

Jack reported no school/vocational training, voluntary work, or second job noise exposure. His work-related history is as follows:

■ 1967–1969: Served in the United States Air Force with intermittent noise exposure from jet engine props; occasional earmuff use when exposed.
■ 1969–1971: Assembled vehicles with some noise exposure reported; no hearing protection was used.
■ 1971–1972:[1] Worked a variety of different jobs (building construction and

maintenance) in a large manufacturing plant with variable noise exposures; no hearing protection was used.

- 1973: Drove a truck for manufacturer; no hearing protection was used.
- 1973–1993: Worked in mechanical equipment rooms and provided maintenance services to the plant. No hearing protection was used in the early employment years. Earmuffs were required for specific tasks in the later employment years, with hearing protector use "some of the time."
- 1994–2003: Worked in a different mechanical division. Hearing protection was required in the work area, especially while grinding, welding, and using jackhammers. Jack reported faithful use of a foam moldable earplug on a cord over the past few years.

Jack was asked, "What do you think caused your hearing loss?" He answered that between 1989 and 1996, he was required to use a jackhammer and a hammer chisel to remove brittle tile epoxy and cut cement from the plant flooring. He stated that this was very difficult and time-consuming work. He reportedly worked on his hands and knees chiseling the floor for extended periods. He noted that earmuffs were the only style of hearing protection offered to employees at that time. Jack had to wear a face shield to keep tile pieces from flying into his face. The earmuffs were not compatible with the face shield, and consequently hearing protection was not worn. He stated, "I had to make a choice, my ears or my eyes, and I chose my eyes." Reportedly, earplug-style hearing protectors were not available to the workers until 1995. (Note: Jack reportedly had been advised by health and safety personnel that "earmuffs are better than earplugs"; the employer did not offer both styles to the workforce.)

Nonoccupational Noise Exposure and Hearing Protector Use History

- Firearms: Lifelong exposures as a hunter and target shooter. Jack reported that he is right-handed and shoots right-handed. Frequency of firearm use was reported as once a year while hunting big game. Hearing protection was not used when hunting. Earmuffs had been used for target shooting since the 1990s.
- Power tools: Operated household power tools including lawnmowers, weed eaters, and construction power tools (saws, sanders, etc.) with occasional use of earmuffs at home reported for "loud tasks."
- Chainsaw: Occasional use of chainsaw for firewood cutting. Earmuffs were used.
- Farm equipment: Grew up on a farm and returned to the family farm to help during planting and harvesting seasons. No hearing protection was used.

Supplemental Occupational Physician History and Exam Information (March 2003)

- Jack reported routine use of ibuprofen for headaches.
- Jack smoked one package of cigarettes per day for about 30 years; he was tobacco free for the past 4 years, but he began smoking again this year.
- Jack did not do woodworking or sheet metal work or have other noisy hobbies besides hunting.
- Jack enjoyed calf roping and arrowhead hunting as hobbies.
- On physical exams, ear canals were clear of wax impactions and otoscopy was normal bilaterally. No cervical adenopathy was evident and his throat was clear.

Employer-Reported History Information

The industrial hygienist (IH) and occupational health nurse (OHN) provided information in March 2003 after review and summary of noise surveillance and employer medical records.

Occupational Noise Exposure

Personal noise dosimetry measurements were not obtained on Jack during the course of employment. Area sound-level measurements were not completely available for most of Jack's employment period. Only a few potentially hazardous exposures were reported:

- 1994–1996: Mechanical room area sound-level measurement reported as 83 to 92 dBA. Hearing protection was required for these work areas.
- 1996–1998: Area sound-level measurements for various shops and mechanical rooms ranged between 74 and 100 dBA. Hearing protection was required when operating certain pieces of equipment such as metal hammers, handheld air motor grinders, welding grinders, band saws, metal spinner, metal shearer, metal saw, and metal hole-punch.
- 1998–2003: No noise exposure records were available. Employee frequented and maintained mechanical rooms with boilers, chillers, and large industrial building fans.

Hearing Protection Device (HPD) Records

Hearing protection became available at the plant in the mid-1980s. At the time the history was provided, the IH reported that Jack was utilizing a foam expandable earplug with a noise reduction rating (NRR) of 33 dBC. There were no records pertaining to compliance with hearing protection policies available from the employer. The 1995 IH report indicated that the worker should have been enrolled in the OSHA-mandated hearing loss prevention program and should have received annual audiometric exams and hearing conservation training. (Note: For unknown reasons, Jack was never formally enrolled in the hearing loss prevention program and annual audiometric monitoring exams and training were not provided.)

Audiometric Records

Jack's hearing had been monitored sporadically while employed. The initial baseline exam was obtained 2 days prior to the hire date. The baseline exam was essentially normal for both ears with the exception of a slight loss at 4000 Hz in the left ear. Subsequent audiograms were obtained in September 1979 and March 1984. No other onsite hearing testing was completed until his workers' compensation claim was filed in February 2003. Threshold comparisons indicated a progressive high-frequency hearing loss for both ears on all exams subsequent to the first (baseline) exam. The absolute hearing thresholds and standard threshold shift (STS) status are summarized in Table 54–1. Note that the employer used existing audiograms as the baseline test for OSHA 29 CFR 1910.95 compliance purposes after 1983. Under OSHA CFR 1910.95, the employer had the option to perform 30-day STS retests; however, none were completed for Jack.

STS Status

Retrospective analysis of the audiometric test data revealed age-corrected STSs were present in both of Jack's ears in 1979 (preregulation), 1984, and again in 2003. Note that the STSs would have met the OSHA criteria for recording on the injury and illness log in 1984 and again in 2003 if they had been detected at the time of the testing and if a work-related component to the hearing loss had been identified. There was no evidence of any audiometric follow-up, medical evaluation, or intervention at any time despite these progressive decreases in hearing. Seemingly, the audiometric technician filed the test results in Jack's medical file at the conclusion of the test without professional review or guidance.

Age corrections were applied to the calculation of STS in Jack's case as it was the standard procedure utilized by the employer for OSHA 29 CFR 1910.95 compliance. STSs were evident with or without the application of age correction. The NIOSH does not advocate correction for presbycusis for STS purposes (NIOSH, 1998, pp. 59–60):

Table 54–1. Hearing Threshold (dB HL) Summary and Age-Corrected STS Status

Ear	Date	500 Hz	1000 Hz	2000 Hz	3000 Hz	4000 Hz	6000 Hz	8000 Hz	STS Status
Left	January 1971	10	10	15	15	35	20	NT	Original baseline exam
	September 1979	15	10	20	40	55	40	30	Initial STS-A
	March 1984	10	05	30	60	65	65	45	Second STS-A
	February 2003	20	30	55	80	75	70	50	Third STS-A
	March 2003 diagnostic evaluation	10	20	55	65	75	75	55	Improved from 2003
Right	January 1971	10	00	00	10	00	25	NT	Baseline exam
	September 1979	10	05	15	25	35	15	00	Initial STS-A evident
	March 1984	05	15	35	35	40	35	20	Second STS-A evident
	February 2003	15	45	60	70	65	65	45	Third STS-A evident
	March 2003 diagnostic evaluation	15	40	55	65	65	65	45	Third STS-A confirm

Note: NT = not tested; STS-A = standard threshold shift, a ≥10 dB average change from baseline at 2000, 3000, and 4000 Hz after application of age corrections permitted by OSHA 29 CFR 1910.95.

"NIOSH does not recommend that age correction be applied to an individual's audiogram for significant threshold shift calculations. Although many people experience some decrease in hearing sensitivity with age, some do not. It is not possible to know who will and who will not have an age-related hearing loss. Thus, applying age corrections to a person's hearing thresholds for calculation of significant threshold shift will overestimate the expected hearing loss for some and underestimate it for others, because the median hearing loss attributable to presbycusis for a given age group will not be generalizable to that experienced by an individual in that age group."

(Note: The OSHA age correction procedure is available at https://www.osha.gov/laws-regs/regulations/standardnumber/1910/1910.95A ppF, and the current OSHA occupational hearing loss recording criteria reference is available at https://www.osha.gov/laws-regs/regulations/standardnumber/1904/1904.10.)

Audiological Evaluation

Jack was referred to the occupational audiologist by the occupational physician for a complete diagnostic exam for workers' compensation purposes in March 2003. The evaluation was scheduled when he had been away from noise for 48 hours. The absolute thresholds are included in Table 54–1. The audiologist report stated:

Left Ear: Normal hearing progressing to a severe high-frequency sensorineural hearing loss with partial recovery at 8000 Hz. Speech reception threshold was 20 dBHL and word recognition score was 80% when stimuli were presented at 50 dBHL. Type A tympanogram and normal compensated static acoustic admittance. Contralateral and ipsilateral acoustic reflexes were present at expected sensation levels for 500, 1000, and 2000 Hz and absent at 4000 Hz. The presence of an STS is confirmed as compared to the original 1971 baseline after age correction. The total age-corrected average shift is 29.33 dB. The hearing loss meets current OSHA 300 log requirements (the presence of an STS and average hearing thresholds at 2000, 3000, and 4000 Hz greater than or equal to 25 dBHL). Distortion product otoacoustic emissions presented at 65/55 dB SPL were marginally present at 1000 Hz (4 dB SNR) and absent for 2000 to 6000 Hz.

Right Ear: Normal hearing progressing to a severe high-frequency sensorineural hearing loss with partial recovery at 8000 Hz. Speech reception threshold was 30 dBHL and word recognition score was 80% when stimuli were presented at 60 dBHL. Type A tympanogram and normal compensated static acoustic admittance. Contralateral and ipsilateral acoustic

reflexes were present at expected sensation levels for 500, 1000, and 2000 Hz and absent at 4000 Hz. The presence of an STS is confirmed as compared to the original 1971 baseline after age correction. The total age-corrected average shift is 39.33 dB. The hearing loss meets current OSHA 300 log injury and illness reporting requirements (the presence of STS and average hearing thresholds at 2000, 3000, and 4000 Hz greater than or equal to 25 dBHL). Distortion product otoacoustic emissions presented at 65/55 dB SPL were absent for 1000 to 6000 Hz.

A graphic representation of the progressive hearing loss over the 32 years is provided in Figure 54–2.

Impairment Rating

Colorado uses the American Academy of Otolaryngology (AAO, 1979) impairment rating formula for workers' compensation determinations. The formula is:

- Monaural: [(Average threshold at 500, 1000, 2000, and 3000 Hz) – 25 dB] 1.5%
- Binaural: 5:1 better ear weighting

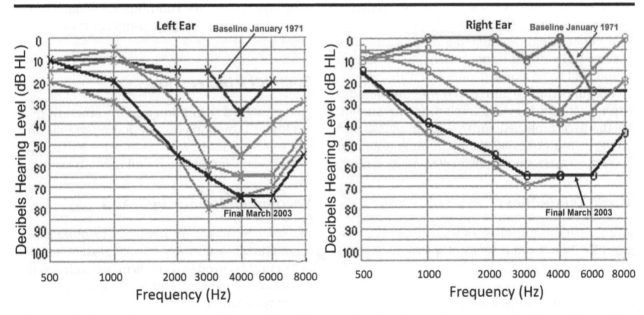

Figure 54–2. Serial audiograms from baseline in 1971 (*gray*) progressing to final audiogram in March 2003 (*black*). *NT is "not tested at 8000 Hz on baseline audiogram."

The subtraction of 25 dB is to account for "normal hearing" and is considered the "low fence." An online impairment calculator is available at http://www.occupationalhearingloss.com/master_calculator.htm.

Jack's AAO-1979 impairment rating at the time of the diagnostic evaluation in March 2003 was 28.1% for the right ear and 18.8% for the left ear. Binaural impairment was 20.3%. A disparity exists between the degree of hearing loss and the impairment rating values for NIHL due to the high-frequency nature of the disorder. This disparity is not as great in other jurisdictions in which high frequencies are included in the impairment formula, such as in Oregon, which includes threshold values for 500, 1000, 2000, 3000, 4000, and 6000 Hz (Dobie & Cooper, 2022).

Hearing Protection Assessment

Jack was asked to bring his current hearing protection to the evaluation. He used foam expandable earplugs with an NRR of 33. He was asked to insert his earplugs, and the relative fit was assessed both visually and by gently tugging on the earplug cord to check for resistance. Jack subjectively reported an occlusion effect especially when vocalizing. Upon removal, the earplugs were visually inspected and observed to be evenly compressed and reflected the contours of the canal. No creases or twisting that might impair the attenuation provided were observed. Hearing thresholds were measured in a sound field using warbled tones first with open ear canals (unoccluded) and second with the binaural earplugs inserted by Jack (occluded). Attenuation for the least protected ear was 15 dB at 250 and 500 Hz, 25 dB at 1000 Hz, 30 dB attenuation at 2000 to 3000 Hz, and 40 dB for 4000 to 8000 Hz.

Work Relatedness

The determination of work-relatedness is facilitated by addressing a series of questions relative to this employee:

1. Is there a hearing loss? Yes.
2. Is the hearing loss consistent with NIHL? Yes.
3. Was Jack exposed to noise at work? Yes.
4. Did he consistently wear HPDs at work? No.
5. Was he exposed to noise away from work? Yes.
6. Did he consistently wear HPDs for off-the-job noise exposures? No.
7. Did the HPDs have sufficient attenuation for workplace noise exposure? Probably.
8. Was the hearing protector fit adequate and did it provide effective attenuation? Yes.

Related to Question 8, individual ear hearing protector fit-testing equipment is available, and audiologists are encouraged to incorporate these ear-specific attenuation measures into their clinical assessment of NIHL (Tufts et al., 2012). It is widely recognized that the laboratory-measured noise NRR overestimates the actual attenuation achieved during field use (Berger & Voix, 2022). Individual attenuation measures will serve to quantify the actual field benefit and afford opportunities to improve hearing protector fit and use compliance.

Upon review of these questions, it is evident that Jack had unprotected hazardous noise exposure at work and also during nonoccupational activities. The Colorado workers' compensation system relies upon medical opinion for the determination of workers' compensation and does not require apportionment of the impairment between occupational and nonoccupational noise-induced hearing loss or for the contributions of aging. Also, there is no separate compensation for tinnitus in Colorado at this time.

Summary Impression

Jack presented with bilateral sensorineural hearing loss. His audiometric configuration and timeline were consistent with progressive NIHL. There was no suspicion of functional hearing loss.

Recommendations by OAud

1. Refer to an otolaryngologist or otologist for medical evaluation of progressive sensorineural hearing loss, medical determination of work relatedness, and medical clearance for amplification.
2. Refer to an audiologist for a hearing aid consultation.

3. Continue use of hearing protection for all noise exposures at or above 85 dBA at work and home.
4. Use electronic hearing protection for firearm noise exposures.
5. Monitor hearing loss via annual audiometry.
6. Obtain personal noise dosimetry for current job and HPD requirements.
7. Verify OSHA 29 CFR 1910.95 requirements for hearing loss prevention program after noise dosimetry completed. Recommend an STS follow-up including retraining and refitting of hearing protection.
8. Enroll in workplace hearing conservation program if noise exposed at or above 85 dBA time-weighted average work.
9. Consider submitting a request for employer accommodations for assistive listening device(s) for meetings and difficult on-the job communication settings.

ENT Evaluation

An ENT evaluation was conducted in April 2003. The ENT completed a comprehensive physical exam and diagnostic workup. No additional otologic history was provided; however, Jack's general health history indicated surgeries on his hand, shoulder, and stomach. Laboratory testing consisting of complete blood count (CBC), sedrate, thyroid stimulating hormone (TSH), Thyroxin (T4), and fluorescent treponemal antibody absorption (FTA-ABS) was conducted to rule out other systemic causes of sensorineural hearing loss. No radiographic studies were conducted. The tympanic membranes and ear canals were normal. The remainder of the head and neck exam was normal, except for smoker's pharyngitis. A repeat audiogram was conducted by the ENT-affiliated clinical audiologist and was consistent with the previously reported audiometric evaluation.

ENT Diagnostic Impression

Jack's diagnosis was a bilateral sensorineural hearing loss secondary to noise exposure. The greatest losses seemed to coincide with the period of unpro-

tected noise injury during Jack's jackhammer work activities. It was felt that the contribution of non-occupational noise exposure was minimal and, if any, might account for 5% of the total injury. Ninety-five percent of the loss was attributed to workplace noise exposure. (Note: Colorado does not require apportionment for workers' compensation purposes but does require a medical opinion that the hearing loss is work related. Hence, the ENT provided an indication that the majority of the hearing loss was felt to be attributed to work-related noise exposure.)

ENT and Clinical Audiologist Recommendations

1. Bilateral programmable hearing aids
2. Periodic audiological monitoring
3. Continued use of hearing protection for all noise exposures
4. Lifetime replacement of hearing aids on an approximately 4- to 6-year cycle

Final Disposition

Amplification

Binaural programmable hearing aids were dispensed 4 months after the workers' compensation claim was filed. Jack reported excellent subjective benefit and acceptance. He reported using the hearing aids full-time and especially noted the improved ability to hear his granddaughter better. The employee reportedly removed his hearing aids at work and continued to use foam earplugs. He declined the need for assistive listening devices at work and felt his hearing aids sufficed during meetings and other group situations. Electronic hearing protectors were encouraged to facilitate situational awareness while working in noise-hazardous environments and for recreational exposures (especially firearms).

Medical Treatment

No specific medical treatment was advised. The occupational physician (OPhys) completed the final impairment rating and concurred with the ENT's diagnosis. Medical follow-up was advised on an as-needed basis in the future.

Audiological Monitoring

This will be pursued on an annual basis either through the employer or the worker's personal audiologist even after retirement.

Workers' Compensation Claim

Confirmed work-related noise-induced hearing loss, bilaterally. Jack's final impairment rating was consistent with the previously reported impairment percentages. He received a $12,000 financial settlement and negotiated a lifetime provision for bilateral hearing aids, batteries, repairs, and audiological/medical care related to his hearing loss. It is worth noting that financial settlements vary greatly from state to state. Colorado is among the states providing the lowest monetary compensation for hearing loss (Dobie & Cooper, 2022). Compensation is based on a percentage of a lump-sum payment set by the workers' state compensation board. In addition, settlements can be negotiated to include the lifetime amplification needs of the worker, an important consideration given the limitations of monetary settlements, which may not be adequate for long-term hearing health care provision.

Summary

Jack's case illustrates the unique situations and multiple missed opportunities for intervention and prevention of permanent hearing loss. Each individual deserves the dedicated attention and efforts of a team of professionals to prevent NIHL.

Author's Note

The case presented is adapted from a real case with identifying features, absolute timelines, and noncritical components altered to provide ano-nymity. This is a unique case presentation and as such cannot be interpreted as applicable to all individuals presenting with NIHL. Work-related determinations are to be made on a case-by-case basis. The conceptional knowledge section has been updated to reflect advances since the first edition.

Endnote

1. Work history from 1971 to 2003 was for the same employer.

References

American Academy of Otolaryngology. (1979). Committee on Hearing and Equilibrium and the American Council of Otolaryngology Committee on the medical aspects of noise: Guide for the evaluation of hearing handicap. *Journal of the American Medical Association, 241*(19), 2055–2059.

Axelsson, A. (1995). Tinnitus epidemiology. In G. Reich & J. Vernon (Eds.), *Proceedings of the fifth international tinnitus seminar* (pp. 249–254). The American Tinnitus Association.

Berger, E. H., & Voix, J. (2022). Hearing protection devices. In D. K. Meinke, E. H. Berger, D. P. Driscoll, R. L. Neitzel, & K. Bright (Eds.), *The noise manual* (6th ed., pp. 67–78). American Industrial Hygiene Association.

Bielefeld, E. C. (2022). Anatomy and physiology of the ear: Normal function and the damage underlying hearing loss. In D. K. Meinke, E. H. Berger, D. P. Driscoll, R. L. Neitzel, & K. Bright (Eds.), *The noise manual* (6th ed., pp. 67–78). American Industrial Hygiene Association.

Carroll, Y. I., Eichwald, J., Scinicariello, F., Hoffman, H. J., Deitchman, S., Radke, M. S., . . . Breysse, P. (2017). Vital signs: Noise-induced hearing loss among adults—United States 2011–2012. *Morbidity and Mortality Weekly Report, 66*(5), 139–144. https://doi.org/10.15585/mmwr.mm6605e3

Coles, R., Smith, P., & Davis, A. (1990). The relationship between noise-induced hearing loss and tinnitus and its management. In B. Berglund, & T. Lindval (Eds.) *New advances in noise research* (Part I, pp. 87–112). Swedish Council for Building Research.

Cooper, J. C. J. (1994). Tinnitus, subjective hearing loss and well-being. Health and Nutrition Examination Survey of 1971–75: Part II. *Journal of the American Academy of Audiology, 5,* 37–43.

Dobie, R. A. (1993). *Medical-legal evaluation of hearing loss.* Van Nostrand Reinhold. https://doi.org/10.1121/1.412021

Dobie, R. A., & Cooper, S. (2022). Workers' compensation. In D. K. Meinke, E. H. Berger, D. P. Driscoll, R. L. Neitzel, & K. Bright (Eds.), *The noise manual* (6th ed., pp. 67–78). American Industrial Hygiene Association.

Federal Railroad Administration. (2006). *Occupational noise exposure* (49CFR Chapter 11, Part 227). Federal Railroad Administration, U.S. Department of Transportation.

Godlee, F. (1992). Noise: Breaking the silence. *British Medical Journal, 304*(6819), 110–113.

Griest, S. E., & Bishop, P. M. (1998). Tinnitus as an early indicator of permanent hearing loss: A 15 year longitudinal study of noise exposed workers. *American Association Occupational Health Nurses Journal, 46,* 325–329. https://doi.org/10.1177/216507999804600704

Hager, L. (2006). *Recordable hearing loss in the United States 2004.* Paper presented at the 31st Annual Conference of the National Hearing Conservation Association, Tampa, FL.

Henderson, D., Bielefeld, E. C., Harris, K. C., & Hu, B. H. (2006). The role of oxidative stress in noise-induced hearing loss. *Ear and Hearing, 27*(1), 1–19. https://doi.org/10.1097/01.aud.0000191942.36672.f3

Henderson, D., Bielefeld, E. C., Hu, B. H., & Nicotera, T. (2007). Cellular mechanisms of noise-induced hearing loss. In K. C. M Campbell (Ed.), *Pharmacology and ototoxicity for audiologists* (pp. 216–229). Thomson Delmar Learning.

Humes, L. E., Joellenbeck, L. M., & Durch, J. S. (2005). *Noise and military service: Implications for hearing loss and tinnitus.* National Academies Press. https://doi.org/10.17226/11443

Jackson, L. D., & Duffy, B. K. (1998). *Health communication research: A guide to developments and directions.* Greenwood Publishing Group.

Kerns, E., Masterson, E. A., Themann, C. L., & Calvert, G. M. (2018). Cardiovascular conditions, hearing difficulty, and occupational noise exposure within U.S. industries and occupations. *American Journal of Industrial Medicine, 61,* 477–491. https://doi.org/10.1002/ajim.22833

Kirchner, D. B., Evenson, E., Dobie, R. A., Rabinowitz, P., Crawford, J., Kopke, R., & Hudson, T. W. (2012). Occupational noise-induced hearing loss: ACOEM task force on occupational hearing loss. *Journal of Occupational and Environmental Medicine, 54*(1), 106–108. https://doi.org/10.1097/JOM.0b013e318242677d

Masterson, E. A., Themann, C. L., Luckhaupt, S. E., Li, J., & Calvert, G. M. (2016). Hearing difficulty and tinnitus among U.S. workers and non-workers in 2007. *American Journal of Industrial Medicine, 59*(4), 290–300. https://doi.org/10.1002/ajim.22565

McDaniel, M. Chinn, G., McCall, K., & Stewart, A. (2013). NHCA guidelines for audiometric baseline revision. *Spectrum, 30*(1), 16–17.

Meinke, D. K. (2022). Audiometric monitoring: Implementation and quality assurance. In D. K. Meinke, E. H. Berger, D. P. Driscoll, R. L. Neitzel, & K. Bright (Eds.), *The noise manual* (6th ed., pp. 67–78). American Industrial Hygiene Association.

Mine Safety and Health Administration. (1999). *Health standards for occupational noise exposure; final rule* (30 CFR Part 62, Fed. Regist. 64, 49548-49634, 49636-49637). Mine Safety and Health Administration.

Mirza, R., Kirchner, D. B., Dobie, R. A., Crawford, J., & ACOEM Task Force on Occupational Hearing Loss. (2018). Occupational noise-induced hearing loss. *Journal of Occupational and Environmental Medicine, 60*(9), e498–e501.

Nelson, D. I., Nelson, R. Y., Concha-Barrientos, M., & Fingerhut, M. (2005). The global burden of occupational noise-induced hearing loss. *American Journal of Industrial Medicine, 48*(6), 446–458. https://doi.org/10.1002/ajim.20223

NIOSH. (1998). *Revised criteria for a recommended standard: Occupational noise exposure* (NIOSH Publication No. 98–126).

OSHA. (1983). 29 CFR 1910.95, Occupational noise exposure. U.S. Department of Labor, Occupational Safety and Health Administration. *Federal Register, 48,* 9738–9744.

OSHA. (2002). 29 CFR 1904.10, Occupational injury and illness recording and reporting requirements. U.S. Department of Labor, Occupational Safety and Health Administration. *Federal Register, 67*(242), 77165–77170.

Quaranta, A., Sallustio, V., & Quaranta, N. (2001). Noise induced hearing loss: Summary and perspectives. In D. Henderson, D. Prasher, R. Kopke, R. J. Salvi, & R. P. Hamernik (Eds.), *Noise induced hearing loss: Basic mechanisms, prevention and control* (pp. 539–557). Noise Research Network Publications.

Rabinowitz, P. M., Davies, H. W., & Meinke, D. K. (2022). Auditory and non-auditory health effects of noise. In D. K. Meinke, E. H. Berger, D. P. Driscoll, R. L. Neitzel, & K. Bright (Eds.), *The noise manual* (6th ed., pp. 67–78). American Industrial Hygiene Association.

Ramazzini, B. (1964). *Diseases of workers, translated from the Latin text de morbis artificum of 1713 by Wilmer Cave Wright* (W. C. Wright, Trans.). Hafner Publishing.

Tak, S., Davis, R. R., & Calvert, G. M. (2009). Exposure to hazardous workplace noise and use of hearing protection devices among US workers—NHANES, 1999–2004. *American Journal of Industrial Medicine, 52*(5), 358–371. https://doi.org/10.1002/ajim.20690

Themann, C. L., & Masterson, E. A. (2019). Occupational noise exposure: A review of its effects, epidemiology, and impact with recommendations for reducing its burden. *The Journal of the Acoustical Society of America, 146*(5), 3879–3905. https://doi.org/10.1121/1.5134465

Tufts, J. B., Palmer, J. V., & Marshall, L. (2012). Measurements of earplug attenuation under supra-aural and circumaural headphones. *International Journal of Audiology, 51*(10), 730–738. https://doi.org/10.3109/14992027.2012.696217

U.S. Department of Defense. (2010). *Hearing Conservation Program.* U.S. Department of Defense Instruction, No. 6055.12. https://www.esd.whs.mil/Portals/54/Documents/DD/issuances/dodi/605512p.pdf%3Fver=2019-08-14-073309-537

Van Campen, L. E., Dennis, J. M., Hanlin, R. C., King, S. B., & Velderman, A. M. (1999). One-year audiologic monitoring of individuals exposed to the 1995 Oklahoma City bombing. *Journal of the American Academy of Audiology, 10*(5), 231–247. https://doi.org/10.1055/s-0042-1748495

Yaremchuk, K., & Dobie, R. A. (2001). Otologic injuries from airbag deployment. *Otolaryngology-Head and Neck Surgery, 125*(3), 130–134. https://doi.org/10.1067/mhn.2001.117872

LARYNGECTOMY
CASE 55
Mr. J: The Role of the SLP in Helping the Patient Through the Decision-Making Processes From Partial Laryngectomy to Total Laryngectomy With TEP
Tammy Wigginton and Jodelle F. Deem

Conceptual Knowledge Areas

For a basic understanding of the concepts in this case study, the reader should have had a course in anatomy and physiology of the speech and hearing mechanism with a specific focus on respiration, phonation, and swallowing. In-depth understanding of the case will be facilitated if the reader has had at least an introductory course in disorders of voice and/or an introductory course in alaryngeal speech. Some background in basic medical and surgical terminology would be beneficial as well.

Description of the Case

Background Information and Reason for Referral

Mr. J was a seemingly healthy and active 42-year-old man. He was evaluated by a general otolaryngologist (ENT) for throat pain, hoarseness, and progressive difficulty swallowing. During a mirror examination, the physician observed a large, suspicious-appearing, supraglottic mass and referred Mr. J for a more in-depth assessment and treatment planning with an ENT specializing in head and neck surgery and cancer oncology.

Mr. J was evaluated by the head and neck surgery specialist and a speech-language pathologist (SLP). He reported a 2-year history of increasing difficulty swallowing accompanied by a sensation of a "ping pong ball in his throat." Approximately 6 months prior at another facility, he had been seen for an esophagogastroduodenoscopy (EGD) and a barium swallow to determine the etiology of his swallowing difficulties. An EGD is an endoscopic procedure that allows a physician to examine the esophagus, stomach, and a portion of the small intestines. A barium swallow is a diagnostic test that involves ingesting barium while undergoing imaging to evaluate the integrity of the pharynx and esophagus when swallowing. A barium swallow is different from a modified barium swallow (MBS) or videofluoroscopic swallow study (VFSS), which is a collaborative procedure completed between a radiologist and an SLP to evaluate the safety and efficiency of the oropharyngeal phase of the swallow.

Mr. J reported there were no unusual findings, but those results were unavailable for review because the procedures were completed at another facility. Mr. J reported a sensation that solid-consistency foods were getting stuck in his throat and that he frequently "coughed up" pieces of food during and after meals. Despite difficulty swallowing, Mr. J continued to consume a general-consistency diet and his weight remained stable. Mr. J also reported a constant dull pain in his throat, which he rated an 8/10 with 10 representing intolerable pain. Over several weeks, his throat pain reportedly had begun to radiate to his left ear. In addition to the difficulty swallowing and throat pain, he also noticed a change in his overall vocal quality characterized by increased effort to speak and voice fatigue with use. Mr. J's wife, who accompanied him to the evaluation, reported that his voice sounded "muffled," and she also noticed he was snoring more frequently and much louder than he had in the past. Mr. J further complained of shortness of breath with activity.

Mr. J was not being treated for any chronic medical conditions. He denied all tobacco use.

He consumed two to four alcoholic beverages per week. He worked in sales and reported high voice demands associated with his sales job. He and his wife had two young children at home. In his free time, he helped coach and referee his children's softball and basketball games. Mr. J expressed a concern for throat cancer as there was a high incidence of cancer in his family.

Examination Findings

Laryngoscopy and Videostroboscopy

A flexible laryngoscopy was performed by the SLP. Under halogen light, a large endophytic lesion of the left aryepiglottic fold was observed. Endophytic lesions tend to grow underneath the mucosa inside the organ or other structures versus exophytic lesions, which tend to grow on the exterior surface of the mucosa of the organ or other structures. The right arytenoid and right posterior vocal fold could not be visualized due to the size and location of the mass. The mass did not appear to involve the right pyriform sinus or ventricular fold. The left arytenoid had a normal appearance and full mobility. When the scope was advanced below the mass to the level of the true vocal folds, the true vocal folds appeared to be free of obvious lesions, and the airway was fully patent. Under stroboscopic light, glottic closure appeared to be complete and the amplitude, mucosal wave, and vibratory parameters of the vocal folds were grossly symmetrical and intact bilaterally.

Perceptual Voice Evaluation

The GRBAS (Grade of hoarseness, Roughness Breathiness, Asthenia, and Strain) Scale (Hirano, 1981; Isshiki et al., 1969) was utilized to perceptually evaluate vocal quality (0 equals no deficit, 1 equals mild deficit, 2 equals moderate deficit, 3 equals severe deficit). Mr. J's GRBAS grade was as follows:

Hoarseness = 1; Roughness = 1; Breathiness = 0; Asthenia = 0; Strain = 1.

Impressions and Recommendations

The examination revealed a large, suspicious-appearing endophytic, supraglottic lesion resulting in dysphagia, dyspnea, and mild dysphonia. Endoscopic/stroboscopic images were reviewed with the ENT and with Mr. and Mrs. J. Mr. J was referred for a computed tomography (CT) scan, a positron emission tomography (PET) scan, and a diagnostic laryngoscopy and biopsy.

Additional Testing

CT Scan

A CT scan is a diagnostic tool used for detecting disease and injury. It uses a series of X-rays with computer enhancement to produce a three-dimensional image of soft tissue and bones. The images allow the radiologist to view thin "slices" of bones, muscles, organs, and blood vessels. In the context of cancer treatment, a CT scan helps locate tumors and determine the size of tumors and other structures, if any, that are being infiltrated by cancer. After treatment, a CT scan can help evaluate the effectiveness of treatment.

Mr. J's CT of the neck revealed a 24 × 22-mm infiltrating mass in the right aryepiglottic fold, the posterior wall of the hypopharynx, and immediate superior supraglottic larynx. Partial encasement of the arytenoids and superior cricoid cartilage was noted. No evidence of metastatic disease was observed.

PET Scan

A PET scan is a diagnostic tool that involves the injection of a radioactive glucose tracer into a vein. Cancer cells uptake more glucose than normal cells because they reproduce more quickly. Uptake of the glucose is imaged and allows detection of the location of cancer cells within the body.

Mr. J's PET scan revealed a mass of the larynx and hypopharynx that had the potential to be metastatic. However, no metastatic sites were noted outside of the larynx and hypopharynx.

Diagnostic Laryngoscopy and Biopsy

A diagnostic laryngoscopy is a procedure that is typically done under general anesthesia as an outpatient procedure. This procedure allows the surgeon to examine the larynx and adjacent structures more thoroughly. In the context of a cancer evaluation, this procedure allows the surgeon to directly view the size, location, and extent of the cancer and to obtain biopsies of the tumor. A biopsy involves removal of tissue from the tumor. The biopsied tissue samples are sent to a pathologist to determine the type of cancer as well as the presence of perineural invasion (through nerves and nerve sheaths) and/or lymphovascular (small lymphatic or blood vessels adjacent to the tumor) invasion. The presence of perineural and/or lymphovascular invasion negatively impacts the prognosis for long-term survival and makes it more likely radiation and/or chemotherapy will be required to treat the cancer.

Mr. J's laryngoscopy revealed a submucosal mass of the right aryepiglottic fold with extension to the arytenoid. The epiglottis, valleculae, tonsils, and true vocal folds all had a normal appearance. Biopsy results were consistent with adenoid cystic carcinoma. Adenoid cystic cancers are exceptionally rare and account for less than 1% of all malignant tumors of the larynx. This type of malignancy is characterized by slow progression and late distant metastasis. There are no distinct risk factors that predispose patients to this type of malignancy. Squamous cell carcinomas account for approximately 99% of laryngeal malignancies and are associated with tobacco and alcohol use, especially when combined (Zyrko & Golubović, 2009).

Review of Treatment Strategies

Multidisciplinary Tumor Board

Mr. J's case was presented at the Multidisciplinary Tumor Board, which is a team composed of professionals from different clinical specialties who meet to discuss the features of a patient's cancer and then work together to make customized recommendations about how a patient's cancer should ideally be managed based on the best evidence available at that time. In Mr. J's circumstances, the Tumor Board recommended primary surgery, followed by adjuvant therapy (e.g., radiation therapy).

Many cancers require multiple treatment modalities to be ideally cured or, at a minimum, to control the cancer. Adjuvant treatment is given *after* surgery with the goal of killing remaining microscopic cancer cells to reduce the risk of the cancer coming back or recurring. *Concurrent* therapy may also be used involving *simultaneous* delivery of two treatment approaches or modalities at one time. Concurrent chemoradiation (chemotherapy + radiation) therapy is commonly used to treat head and neck cancers. Neoadjuvant treatment such as chemotherapy may be provided *before* surgery with the goal of shrinking a tumor or stopping the spread of cancer to make surgery less invasive and more effective.

Partial Laryngectomy

Given the fact that the cancer did not involve the vocal folds, the possibility of performing a partial laryngectomy versus a total laryngectomy was discussed. A patient may be considered to be a candidate for a partial laryngectomy if the tumor is small, it does not involve structures that help maintain a functional airway or impact swallowing function to a significant degree, and adjuvant treatment (radiation therapy ± chemotherapy) is not anticipated to be required as an essential component of the treatment regime (T. Wigginton, personal communication, January 30, 2022). A successful partial laryngectomy would entail removal of the cancerous portion of the larynx and hypopharynx while ideally preserving a functional airway without the need for a tracheostomy. Overall vocal quality, while impaired to a certain extent, would likely be functional, and although Mr. J might have required dysphagia therapy, he would ideally be able to return to an oral diet.

Total Laryngectomy

In contrast, a total laryngectomy involves removal of the entire larynx (including all cartilages, mus-

cles, and membranes), the hyoid bone, and the upper two or three rings of the trachea. The trachea is pulled anteriorly and sutured to the external neck region just above the suprasternal notch. This permanent external opening, through which the patient breathes, is referred to as a tracheostoma or simply a stoma. For patients in whom the cancer has spread to the neck and cervical lymph nodes, a surgical procedure called a *neck dissection* may be performed on the right, left, or both sides of the neck (Deem & Miller, 2000). The majority of patients with a total laryngectomy return to an oral diet (Jung & Adams, 1980), and many patients develop functional communication using either an artificial larynx (Kaye et al., 2017) or via a secondary surgery called a tracheoesophageal puncture (TEP) (McAuliffe et al., 2000).

Tumor Board Recommendation

In exploring the possibility of a limited or a partial laryngectomy surgery, it was determined that Mr. J's lesion appeared to invade the arytenoids as well as the posterior paraglottic space. The surgeon voiced concern regarding the ability to obtain negative surgical margins with a partial laryngectomy. That is, the surgeon did not believe an edge or a border of tissue around the site where the cancer would be removed could be pathologically determined to be completely free of cancer cells. Moreover, if a negative margin could not be obtained, Mr. J would require radiation therapy after surgery, further increasing the likelihood of him having a nonfunctioning larynx after treatment. Chemotherapy, especially when combined with radiation therapy (chemoradiation therapy), is an effective method for preventing tumor recurrence but has also been highly correlated with impaired swallowing outcomes (Nguyen et al., 2004). The surgeon also noted if the arytenoids had to be removed to obtain negative margins, Mr. J would require a permanent tracheostomy or a surgical opening in the neck created to allow a patient with a larynx to breathe, and he would also lose his natural speaking voice.

From an oncologic and functional standpoint, the optimal surgical treatment was determined to be a total laryngectomy. With a total laryngectomy, Mr. J would likely be able to be treated with surgery alone and be spared chemoradiation treatment. Alternatively, primary chemoradiation could be attempted. However, given the extent of disease within his larynx, he would likely be unable to functionally produce a voice and would be tracheostomy and gastrostomy tube dependent afterward. It was determined Mr. J would likely have a better quality of life with a total laryngectomy than a partial laryngectomy. Although the total laryngectomy would result in the creation of a permanent tracheostoma (i.e., an opening created in the neck of a laryngectomized patient to allow them to breathe), he would be able to swallow without aspirating, and functional communication could be restored.

The Tumor Board recommendations were discussed with Mr. J and his wife. Anticipated advantages and potential disadvantages of the various treatment options were reviewed. At that time, Mr. and Mrs. J disclosed that they were in the process of seeking a second opinion regarding the best course of treatment at another facility. However, they were amenable to prelaryngectomy counseling and to tentatively scheduling a total laryngectomy.

Prelaryngectomy Counseling

Mr. J and his wife were seen for prelaryngectomy counseling. Comprehensive preoperative counseling that includes patients and their caregivers is an important aspect of preparation for surgery (Cady, 2002). Both Mr. J and his wife were noticeably distraught. They expressed concern not only about his survival but also how losing his natural voice might impact his quality of life and his ability to support their family. Pre- and postoperative anatomy and physiology were reviewed. Illustrations were used to enhance understanding. The full extent of a total laryngectomy surgery was explained. Mr. J and his wife became quite emotional and indicated they were unable to process the information provided as they were feeling overwhelmed. At that point, the counseling session was ended. They were given the clinician's

contact information and a variety of resources regarding living with a laryngectomy. Peer support was offered. The patient declined, but Mrs. J expressed an interest in speaking with a laryngectomee peer and his wife. She was provided with their contact information.

Treatment Course

Patient Decision—Partial Laryngectomy

Mr. J decided to seek a second opinion from another surgeon at a different institution. At that institution, he was offered the option of attempting a partial laryngectomy with the understanding that if he was unhappy with his quality of life after the partial laryngectomy, he could still have a complete laryngectomy at a later date. Unfortunately, during the partial laryngectomy procedure, Mr. J's arytenoids had to be resected to clear the tumor from his larynx. Resection of the arytenoids resulted in the need for a tracheostomy tube to maintain an open airway and also left Mr. J without a functional way to verbally communicate. In addition to the need for a tracheostomy and loss of his voice, a modified barium swallow revealed a nonfunctional swallow with aspiration of all presented consistencies. Given the nature and severity of his deficits, the prognosis for return to total oral intake was extremely guarded, so he was taken back to the operating room for placement of a percutaneous endoscopic gastrostomy (PEG) tube. A PEG tube is a flexible feeding tube inserted through the abdominal wall into the stomach. Surgical pathology revealed positive deep margins indicating the presence of cancer cells as well as perineural invasion, resulting in the recommendation that he receive adjuvant chemoradiation therapy.

Patient Decision—Total Laryngectomy

Mr. J and his wife were deeply disappointed in the results following the partial laryngectomy and subsequently opted to return to his original ENT surgeon and treatment team. Given the likelihood he would be tracheostomy and PEG tube dependent and would be unable to speak, Mr. and Mrs. J were ready to consider a total laryngectomy with the hope that some aspects of his function could be improved. Mr. J consented and was scheduled for a complete total laryngectomy.

Mr. J was taken to the operating room for a total laryngectomy with a modified radical neck dissection. A neck dissection is a surgical procedure to remove lymph nodes from the neck to determine if cancer has metastasized or spread from the lymphatic system to the lymph nodes of the neck. While in surgery, the previous arytenoidectomy was noted. An irregular lesion involving the right aryepiglottic fold was observed. A bilateral selective neck dissection was completed. A selective neck dissection involves removal of a limited number of lymph nodes and is a less invasive procedure with fewer postoperative complications than a modified radical neck dissection. A modified radical neck dissection involves removal of all the lymph nodes. An even more invasive procedure is a radical neck dissection, which involves removal of all the lymph nodes, muscles, nerves, salivary glands, and major blood vessels from the jaw to the collar bone.

Postoperatively, Mr. J's pathology report confirmed adenocystic carcinoma of the larynx. No residual tumor was noted in the laryngeal specimen or the lymph nodes. Two weeks after surgery, Mr. J was seen for a videofluoroscopic swallow study with results indicating safe swallowing of all presented consistencies. At that point, a liquid diet was initiated, and he was upgraded to a general consistency diet as his tolerance for oral intake improved.

Adjuvant Radiation Therapy

Twelve weeks after surgery, Mr. J underwent external beam radiation therapy. He received 30 treatments over a 39-day period to a total of 60 Gy (pronounced gray), which is a unit of measure for the amount or dosage of radiation administered. Mr. J tolerated radiation treatment with minimal side effects, but he did experience a sore throat, irritation, and inflammation of the stoma and anterior neck.

Communication Training

Artificial Larynx

Mr. J declined artificial larynx training during his acute care stay. He opted to write and/or mouth words, and he gestured to communicate. He was seen for artificial larynx training as an outpatient and developed intelligible speech. However, he was generally unhappy with the electronic sound of the device and was only willing to use his artificial larynx to communicate with familiar listeners. He had no interest in long-term use of an artificial larynx as his primary method of communication.

Tracheoesophageal Puncture and Voice Restoration

Since it first became available in the 1980s, tracheoesophageal (TE) voice restoration has been an excellent alternative for voice restoration (Blom & Singer, 1979). The TEP surgery is an endoscopic procedure that can be performed at the time of *primary laryngectomy*, or it can be performed later under general anesthesia as a secondary outpatient procedure.

With this approach, a small silicone voice prosthesis is inserted into a surgically created, midline, tracheoesophageal opening or fistula, and the patient uses pulmonary or lung air shunted from the trachea to the esophagus for voice production. The primary advantage of TE voice restoration is that patients use pulmonary air as their power source for speech production, rather than the limited air supply available when using esophageal speech. A second important advantage of the TEP voice restoration procedure is the surgical procedure can be performed on most patients, including those who have been irradiated. A third advantage of TEP is that the procedure and the design of the various voice prostheses have effectively eliminated the problems of aspiration and difficulties in swallowing (Deem & Miller, 2000).

Assessment of Candidacy for a TEP

Six weeks after completion of radiation therapy, Mr. J was seen for TEP candidacy assessment and counseling. He was found to be cancer free at that time and judged by his surgeon to be a good surgical candidate for TEP. He had resumed an oral diet of general-consistency foods and denied any difficulty swallowing. However, he was in the process of being treated for depression and anxiety and felt strongly that being able to functionally speak in a "more normal" voice would improve his sense of well-being.

TEP Education and Counseling

The anticipated benefits of TEP (i.e., a more natural-sounding voice) were reviewed with Mr. J. Typical postoperative care was explained, as well as the need for routine follow-up with his SLP team and ENT. The potential complications of TEP were explained, including leakage through or around the prosthesis, which could result in aspiration; accidental prosthesis dislodgement, which could result in aspiration of the prosthesis; and partial prosthesis dislodgment, which could result in spontaneous partial or complete closure of the puncture tract and TE voice loss. The patient was advised that the overall quality of his TE voice could not be guaranteed as quality varies from person to person. He was also told that if he is unhappy and wants the TEP removed, the puncture site may not close spontaneously and additional surgery might be required. The patient was advised there are various accessories such as baseplates, intraluminal devices, and handsfree valves that can be utilized to enhance functional voice outcomes (InHealth Technologies). The ability to utilize accessories varies from person to person, and individual insurance companies may or may not assist with the costs associated with TEP accessories.

Initial TEP Fitting Process

From a medical and clinical perspective, Mr. J met the criteria for TEP placement. He was seen on postoperative day 7 for TEP placement. Every procedure begins with the use of surgical gloves and universal precautions. Mr. J had a red rubber catheter sutured to his neck that was placed there to keep his tracheoesophageal tract open. The red rubber catheter was removed and discarded. The puncture tract appeared healthy. An 18 French dilator was gradually inserted into the puncture tract. After approximately 10 minutes, the dilator was removed, and a 16 French measuring tool was inserted into the tract. The tract measured 10 mm. The measuring tool was removed, and the dilator, replaced as a 17 French/10-mm Provox Vega (Atos Medical) voice prosthesis, was loaded into the inserter tool. The dilator was removed, and the prosthesis was placed without difficulty. Prosthesis placement was confirmed by rotating the prosthesis 360 degrees within the tract and pulling forward on the prosthesis to assess functional seating. No leakage was observed as Mr. J sipped water. Occlusion of the stoma revealed functional airflow, as evidenced by production of a "voice or neophonation." The insertion tab of the prosthesis was detached, and the prosthesis was functionally oriented within the tract per the manufacturer's instructions.

At this point, attention turned to helping Mr. J acquire functional use of the prosthesis. Mr. J was trained to coordinate respiration, stomal occlusion, and "voice" production. Initially, trials consisted of vowel sounds, but he quickly progressed to words, short phrases, and conversational speech activities. Accuracy of stoma occlusion was improved with use of an adhesive baseplate coupled with a heat moisture exchanger (HME). An adhesive baseplate is a device that adheres to the peristomal (area around the stoma) with medical-grade adhesive. An HME is a medical device that acts as an artificial nose. It filters particles from the air, much like the hairs in the nose, and heats or cools the ambient air to an appropriate temperature for the lungs much like the nose does. The HME snaps into the baseplate and can be pressed to occlude the stoma. This is particularly helpful if the stoma has an irregular shape and the patient is otherwise unable to successfully occlude the stoma. Moreover, using an HME coupled with a baseplate is more sanitary as the patients thumb or fingers are not coming into direct contact with stomal secretions (InHealth Technologies).

By the end of the session, Mr. J was able to coordinate respiration, stoma occlusion, and "voicing" to greater than 80% accuracy with minimal cueing. Overall, Mr. J's vocal quality was very good. He was counseled and educated regarding strategies for enhancing communication, basic TEP problem-solving techniques, and when to return for follow-up.

Conclusion

Mr. J was a patient in obvious need of successful voice restoration. Although Mr. J initially appeared to be a candidate for a partial laryngectomy procedure, the partial laryngectomy resulted in significant negative consequences. Ideally, cancer treatment should not only cure the disease but also leave the patient with what they would consider to be an acceptable quality of life. In some candidates, a partial laryngectomy may represent a better quality of life than a total laryngectomy because the patient is typically able to live without a tracheostomy, produce a more natural-sounding voice, and resume an oral diet.

In Mr. J's situation, the typical essential functions of the larynx (respiration, phonation, and airway protection for swallowing) could not be spared in the partial laryngectomy procedure. This was anticipated by the patient's original voice care team, and the potential risks and benefits of a partial versus a total laryngectomy were carefully reviewed with Mr. J and his wife. Ultimately, they chose a partial laryngectomy, desperately hoping that he could preserve his "normal" voice. Following the partial laryngectomy, both Mr. J and his wife realized the outcome was less than functionally acceptable to them, and they returned to the original voice care team to undergo a complete total laryngectomy.

Our patients often make choices that are not in keeping with recommendations of their care team. While these choices may seem unconventional or perhaps not in their best interest, ultimately the patient and/or caregivers have the right to make choices that they consider representative of their personal idea of what constitutes a functional quality of life. In this circumstance, the reality of living with the result of a partial laryngectomy helped the patient understand the need for a total laryngectomy. Because the lines of communication were kept open throughout the entire process, Mr. J and his wife were able to comfortably return to our primary voice care team for management and ultimately realize the functional postcancer outcome they were hoping for. Mr. J did not return to his sales job but was able to find other employment that allowed him to financially support his family. He remains cancer free and lives a very active life, including cheering for his daughters at sporting events and offering support to other patients with laryngeal cancer.

References

Blom, E. D., & Singer, M. I. (1979). Surgical-prosthetic approaches for postlaryngectomy voice restoration. In R. L. Keith & F. L. Darley (Eds.), *Laryngectomee rehabilitation* (pp. 251–276). College-Hill Press.

Cady, J. (2002). Laryngectomy: Beyond loss of voice—caring for the patient as a whole. *Clinical Journal of Oncology Nursing, 6*(6), 347–351. https://doi.org/10.1188/02.cjon.347-351

Deem, J., & Miller, L. (2000). *Manual of voice therapy* (2nd ed., pp. 261–294). PRO-ED.

Hirano, M. (1981). *Clinical examination of voice.* Springer Verlag.

Isshiki, N., Okamura, H., Tanabe, M., & Morimoto, M. (1969). Differential diagnosis of hoarseness. *Folia Phoniatrica Et Logopaedica, 21*(1), 9–19. https://doi.org/10.1159/000263230

Jung, T. T. K., & Adams, G. L. (1980). Dysphagia in laryngectomized patients. *Otolaryngology-Head and Neck Surgery, 88*(1), 25–33. https://doi.org/10.1177/019459988008800109

Kaye, R., Tang, C. G., & Sinclair, C. F. (2017). The electrolarynx: Voice restoration after total laryngectomy. *Medical Devices: Evidence and Research, 10,* 133–140. https://doi.org/10.2147/mder.s133225

McAuliffe, M. J., Ward, E. C., Bassett, L., & Perkins, K. (2000). Functional speech outcomes after laryngectomy and pharyngolaryngectomy. *Archives of Otolaryngology-Head & Neck Surgery, 126*(6), 705. https://doi.org/10.1001/archotol.126.6.705

Nguyen, N. P., Moltz, C. C., Frank, C., Vos, P., Smith, H. J., Karlsson, U., . . . Sallah, S. (2004). Dysphagia following chemoradiation for locally advanced head and neck cancer. *Annals of Oncology, 15*(3), 383–388. https://doi.org/10.1093/annonc/mdh101

Zvrko, E., & Golubović, M. (2009). Laryngeal adenoid cystic carcinoma. *ACTA Otorhinolaryngolica Italica, 29*(5), 279–282.

SWALLOWING
CASE 56
Janelle: Diagnosis and Management of Adult Dysphagia
Christina A. Baumgartner

Conceptual Knowledge Areas

Assessment of Dysphagia

Dysphagia, or impaired swallowing, can be defined as difficulty transferring a bolus from the mouth to the stomach. The swallowing impairment may occur in any or all of the three stages of swallowing: oral, pharyngeal, and esophageal. Both oropharyngeal dysphagia and esophageal dysphagia impact a person's overall health and nutrition. Dysphagia resulting in aspiration may lead to an aspiration pneumonia. Another common consequence of dysphagia is the inability to meet nutritional needs orally. The speech-language pathologist (SLP) is the professional who determines whether a patient has dysphagia.

Differential Diagnosis of Dysphagia

To manage dysphagia appropriately, it is necessary to determine the location (oral, pharyngeal, and/or esophageal) and cause(s) of the dysphagia. Some dysphagias can be managed therapeutically through changes in diet and liquids, through the use of swallowing compensatory techniques, or through therapy. Other dysphagias require medical management such as surgery or medications.

Ethical Considerations in Management of Dysphagia

For patients who have a poor prognosis or who are at the end of life, managing dysphagia requires the consideration of medical status, patient preferences, quality of life, and contextual features such as family preferences, social and cultural influences, and legal and financial issues (Sharp & Genesen, 1996). Recommendations change based on each patient's situation, prognosis, and personal wishes. A recommendation of nothing by mouth and nonoral nutrition might be appropriate for someone who is 55 years old, was relatively healthy, suffered an acute stroke, and is now significantly aspirating food and drink due to an oropharyngeal dysphagia. Based on what is known about general recovery patterns from stroke (Shin et al., 2022), this person is likely to improve. Therefore, an aggressive recommendation to provide the patient with nonoral nutrition only to reduce the risk of aspiration pneumonia and provide adequate nourishment and hydration may be made. The focus of dysphagia management in this case is on rehabilitating this patient's swallow function. However, if the patient is an 89-year-old nursing home resident with end-stage Alzheimer's disease, whose only pleasure in life was eating but aspirated everything he ate and drank, the recommendation might not be as aggressive. Instead, more conservative management focusing on quality of life might be more appropriate. In this case, after discussing evaluation findings with the patient's family and medical team, it may be decided that the patient should continue to eat and drink despite the high risk of developing an aspiration pneumonia, and dysphagia management would focus on facilitation. The goal would be to provide the patient with the safest feeding techniques and compensatory strategies that lead to the least amount of aspiration.

Description of the Case

Background Information and Reason for Referral

On April 17, Janelle, a 69-year-old female, was admitted to the hospital with complaints of a 1-week history of lethargy, shortness of breath, and poor appetite without significant weight loss. Relevant medical background revealed recent diagnosis of acute myelogenous leukemia (AML), esophageal cancer, and reflux. Janelle began chemoradiation therapy 21 days before she was admitted to the hospital. Janelle was a retired elementary school teacher who had been living independently with her husband of 40 years. She had two adult daughters who live in the area.

Physical examination by the internal medicine physician revealed reduced breath sounds bilaterally with poor inspiratory effort. Cranial nerve examination was normal. Chest x-ray showed progressive right upper lobe and right lower lobe infiltrates. Janelle was diagnosed with pneumonia and was to continue chemotherapy in the hospital and be treated for pneumonia.

Two hours after dinner that first evening in the hospital, Janelle's nurse entered her room and observed that she was minimally responsive. Janelle did not respond to her name and exhibited difficulty breathing. An emergency call was placed to the physicians. Janelle was intubated and transferred to the intensive care unit (ICU). The pulmonology service physician, a specialist in the diagnosis and management of lung disease, was consulted and determined that Janelle was in acute respiratory failure (ARF).

Janelle remained in the ICU for 9 days. She was intubated and sedated for 7 of those days and received medications and hydration through an IV. Janelle was extubated on day 8. She was diagnosed with mucositis at that time. Mucositis, a common side effect of chemotherapy, results in painful inflammation and ulceration of digestive tract mucous membranes (Rosenthal et al., 2006). Oral mucositis can result in difficulty talking, eating, and swallowing due to pain from oral sores or ulcers. Some medications used to treat muco-sitis, such as Lidocaine, are anesthetics that can produce reduced oral and pharyngeal sensation.

Findings of the Evaluation

On the eighth day of Janelle's ICU stay, the speech-language pathologist was consulted to determine whether Janelle could safely initiate oral intake after extubation. A clinical, bedside swallow evaluation was completed that morning. An oral mechanism examination revealed many atypical findings. Her oral cavity appeared red and inflamed. Overall mild, bilateral labial weakness and reduced range of motion (ROM) was exhibited during protrusion and retraction. Lingual ROM was mildly reduced upon protrusion, retraction, elevation, and lateralization. Lingual strength was also mildly reduced. Buccal tension was grossly within functional limits (WFL) and Janelle was able to impound air. Velopharyngeal function was WFL. Phonation was mildly breathy and hypophonic postextubation. Janelle exhibited difficulty initiating visceral swallows due to oral sores and dryness. The overall, mild generalized weakness and reduced ROM exhibited during the oral mechanism examination could be explained by a combination of any or all of the following factors: general debilitation from the cancer diagnosis, xerostomia, fibrosis, and neuromuscular damage due to chemoradiation (Kulbersh et al., 2006); oral pain caused by the mucositis (Rosenthal et al., 2006); and recent prolonged intubation (Colice et al., 1989).

Oral swallow stage at bedside appeared to be mildly impaired. Anterior loss of thin liquids by cup occurred, possibly due to labial weakness and/or reduced sensation. Bolus formation and control of nectar-thick liquids and pureed solids were grossly WFL. Janelle requested to defer soft solid trials due to oral cavity soreness. Bolus transit times were adequate. Swallow responses were timely with adequate laryngeal elevation. However, delayed throat clearing and wet vocal quality were exhibited following swallows of thin liquids indicating possible penetration and/or aspiration of the boluses. Pharyngeal stage dysphagia was suspected. A videofluoroscopic swallow study was recommended to further assess pharyngeal swallow function and to rule out aspiration. Janelle continued to receive nutrition intravenously through total parenteral nutrition (TPN) and remained NPO (nothing by mouth).

A videofluoroscopic swallow study was completed the following day. The patient sat at 90 degrees and lateral and anterior-to-posterior (A-P) views were taken. Swallow function was assessed with thin liquids by teaspoon and cup sip trials, nectar-thick liquid consistency by teaspoon and cup sip trials, pureed consistency, and solids (cracker). Oral swallow stage was moderately impaired, characterized by early spillover of thin liquids into the pyriform sinuses before the swallows. It was suspected that reduced lingual ROM due to oral pain from mucositis, as well as iatrogenic reduction of oral and pharyngeal sensitivity from the medication used to treat the mucositis, may have led to reduced bolus control. Improved bolus control with decreased premature spillage over base of tongue occurred with nectar-thick liquids and pureed consistency. The more viscous consistencies likely resulted in increased sensation. Janelle was unable to masticate a cracker due to oral pain from the mucositis and expectorated that trial.

Pharyngeal swallow stage was moderately impaired and characterized by reduced posterior lingual retraction and absent epiglottic inversion, resulting in consistent, trace penetration during swallows of thin liquids and after swallows from vallecular residue. Reflexive coughing did not clear the penetrated residue, and it was subsequently aspirated. The Rosenbek 8-point Penetration-Aspiration Scale score was 7 (Rosenbek et al., 1996). Chin-down posture was attempted to assess if widening the vallecular space would reduce the amount of residue and, hence, the potential of penetration and aspiration after the swallows. A chin tuck reduced the amount of vallecular residue but was inconsistently successful in eliminating the penetration events. Marked amounts of bilateral vallecular, pyriform sinus, and pharyngeal wall residue from pureed consistency remained after swallows due to reduced posterior tongue elevation, reduced hyolaryngeal elevation, and decreased pharyngeal wall contrac-

tions. Chin-down posture and alternating thinner consistencies with thicker consistencies helped to reduce but not eliminate this residue. The A-P view revealed reduced bilateral vocal fold adduction, which could also contribute to the penetration observed during the swallows.

Representation of Problem at the Time of Evaluation

Both prolonged intubation and chemoradiation can result in impaired swallowing. Laryngeal and tracheal injuries are commonly seen following prolonged intubation. Colice et al. (1989) assessed laryngeal damage in 82 patients who were intubated for more than 4 days. Laryngeal edema and mucosal ulcerations of the vocal folds were found in 94% ($n = 77$) of the patients. Adequate laryngeal adduction is required to protect the airway from food and liquid during swallows. Prolonged intubation commonly causes vocal fold mobility impairments (Colton House et al., 2011), which may result in impaired airway protection during swallowing. And, as mentioned previously, the videofluoroscopic swallow study documented reduced vocal fold adduction in the A-P view. In addition to prolonged intubation, Janelle had been undergoing chemoradiation, which was found to produce reduced range of motion of oral, laryngeal, and pharyngeal structures and could explain reduced posterior tongue elevation, reduced hyolaryngeal elevation, and reduced pharyngeal wall contractions (Kulbersh et al., 2006; Rosenthal et al., 2006).

Treatment Options Considered

Recommendations for a pureed diet, nectar-thick liquids, and swallow precautions were made. Swallow precautions of small bites, liquids by cup sip, chin-down posture, and alternating liquids and solids were posted at the head of Janelle's bed and reviewed with the patient, her family, nursing, and Janelle's physicians. The dietician was also contacted because a calorie count, which measures daily caloric intake, was recommended. Because of Janelle's fatigue and reduced endurance from generalized weakness, it was believed that she would not be able to meet nutritional needs orally at the time. Therefore, Janelle would continue to require nonoral supplementation of nutrition.

Maintaining ROM and strength through swallowing exercises during chemoradiation to prevent dysphagia and aspiration has been documented in the literature (Kulbersh et al., 2006; Rosenthal et al., 2006). However, Janelle had not seen a speech-language pathologist prior to beginning her course of treatment. A dysphagia exercise program was developed to help Janelle improve and maintain adequate range of motion and strength of oral, laryngeal, and pharyngeal structures during and after her course of chemoradiation.

The Masako, or tongue-holding maneuver (Fujiu & Logemann, 1996; Fujiu et al., 1995), was introduced for improved posterior tongue elevation and retraction. The super-supraglottic swallow (Logemann et al., 1997), combined with an effortful swallow (Kahrilas et al., 1993), were reviewed and demonstrated. The goals of these maneuvers are to improve hyolaryngeal elevation, tongue base retraction, and pharyngeal contraction. Due to Janelle's reduced endurance and oropharyngeal pain associated with mucositis, she was only able to perform these exercises minimally over the next few days.

Course of Treatment

Janelle remained hospitalized for 10 more days. During this period, she was followed daily by speech-language pathology services. Sessions included ongoing assessment of diet and liquid toleration, ongoing reassessment of swallow function, and swallowing exercises. Janelle was tolerating the pureed diet and nectar-thick liquids without clinical signs or symptoms of aspiration. She was able to state what her swallow precautions were and followed them independently with 100% carryover. During this time, the pain from the mucositis had almost resolved. Her endurance improved, and her phonatory quality was no longer hoarse and breathy. She was able to perform the prescribed swallowing exercises independently and accurately. Based on clinical examination

findings, Janelle exhibited overall improvement in swallow function during her hospital stay. After 7 days on a pureed diet and nectar-thick liquids, she tolerated trials of thin liquids and soft solids without clinical signs or symptoms of aspiration or complaints of pain. Janelle's diet was subsequently upgraded to mechanical soft with thin liquids, and it was recommended that she continue her swallowing precautions. TPN was discontinued as Janelle's endurance had improved and she was able to meet nutritional needs orally.

Janelle was discharged from the hospital on May 4. Her pneumonia had resolved and she was tolerating a mechanical soft diet and thin liquids. Discharge recommendations included continuing with the swallow precautions and exercises and returning for a follow-up videofluoroscopic swallow evaluation in 4 weeks, at the completion of her chemoradiation series.

On May 20, she was readmitted to the hospital with a new diagnosis of pneumonia. On May 21, the speech-language pathology service was consulted to assess swallowing and to rule out aspiration. A clinical swallow evaluation was completed that morning. Janelle reported that she had been on a mechanical soft diet with thin liquids at home and that she had been compliant with following her swallow precautions and completing her swallowing exercise program. She complained of increased coughing over the past 4 days with eating and drinking.

The results of the oral-motor-speech examination were WNL, including labial, lingual, buccal, velopharyngeal, and jaw ROM, strength, and coordination. Phonation was also WFL. Oral cavity inflammation secondary to mucositis, which was noted on prior admission, had resolved. Janelle was able to produce timely visceral swallows with adequate laryngeal elevation. Swallow function was assessed at bedside with teaspoon trials of water. No clinical signs or symptoms of aspiration were exhibited with the initial trial. A second teaspoon of water was given. Immediate coughing occurred after the swallow. Immediate coughing also occurred after a third teaspoon of water. Janelle was then given a teaspoon of nectar-thick liquid. Again, immediate coughing occurred after the swallow. Janelle's clinical swallowing presentation was concerning for penetration and/or aspiration. The speech-language pathologist spoke to the physician and nurse and recommended that Janelle be made NPO. An order for a videofluoroscopic swallow evaluation was obtained and completed that afternoon.

The patient was seated at 90 degrees and lateral views were taken. Swallow function was assessed with thin liquids by teaspoon and cup sip trials. Oral swallow stage was WFL and characterized by normal bolus formation and control, normal A-P transport, and timely oral bolus transit. Pharyngeal swallow stage also appeared to be WFL. Swallow responses were timely with adequate hyolaryngeal elevation, base of tongue retraction, epiglottic inversion, pharyngeal contractions, and upper esophageal sphincter (UES) opening. After 2 teaspoons and 2 small cup sips of thin liquids, there was no evidence of penetration or aspiration. Janelle was then instructed to take consecutive cup sips of the thin barium. After the last swallow, she began coughing markedly and barium was expelled from the trachea. However, the barium was not observed either entering the laryngeal vestibule or being retropropelled from the esophagus. Upon closer examination, it was suspected that the barium was entering the trachea through a fistula in the tracheoesophageal wall. The videofluoroscopic swallow study was stopped and the physician was immediately called. A STAT barium swallow study, or esophagram, and a computed tomography (CT) scan of the chest were ordered to rule out a tracheoesophageal fistula (TEF).

A tracheoesophageal fistula was confirmed that afternoon. Within the mediastinum, there was an air tract connecting the right aspect of the midesophagus to the posterior aspect of the trachea. Aspiration of barium into the right lung and the left lower lobe confirmed aspiration pneumonitis. Unfortunately, the CT scan of the chest also identified blastic osseous lesions of the thoracic spine. As the time in radiology progressed, Janelle's respirations became more labored and her oxygen requirements increased as a result of the aspiration through the TEF. Janelle was transferred to the intensive care unit, where she had to be intubated for 3 days.

The speech-language pathologist and primary physician met with Janelle and her family and explained the results of the videofluoroscopic swallow study, barium swallow, and CT scan of the chest. It was speculated that Janelle had developed three chloromas, or tumors in the trachea, which are often associated with AML. One of the tumors responded to the chemoradiation, which resulted in the TEF. As noted on the chest CT scan, it was confirmed that Janelle's cancer had metastasized, or spread, to her bones.

Analysis of Client's Response to Intervention

Further management by the speech-language pathologist was not indicated at this time as the oropharyngeal swallow was WFL, and the reason for the aspiration was a fistula. Medical management was required. It was determined that Janelle was not medically fit for surgery. Instead, a covered, self-expanding metal stent (SEMS) was placed on May 24 in an attempt to palliatively seal the fistula (Fan et al., 2002). The SEMS successfully closed the fistula, as confirmed by repeat esophagram. However, there was concern that the two remaining chloromas would respond in a similar fashion to the chemotherapy and result in TEFs.

A consult to the palliative care team was made. The palliative care team usually consists of a physician, frequently a nurse, and a social worker. In some settings, a pharmacist and spiritual advisor may be included. Palliative care specializes in medical management and decision-making at end of life. A decision needed to be made regarding the aggressiveness of Janelle's medical care, including whether to consider nonoral nutrition. Several new, and extremely unfortunate, pieces of information regarding Janelle's medical condition had been discovered in the past few days. The presence of two more tumors in the trachea put Janelle at risk for developing more TEFs, which could lead to other episodes of aspiration pneumonia.

Janelle was not expected to live beyond 6 months. She wished to continue with chemotherapy in an attempt to slow down the rate of the spreading cancer. Her endurance was poor due to her illness, and it was expected that she would not meet nutritional needs orally. In consideration of quality of life, she wanted to begin eating and drinking again. Janelle's physicians supported the initiation of oral intake. They explained that at end of life, the feeling of hunger subsides and that people are often satisfied with a few bites or sips of something they really enjoy (Slomka, 2003).

Janelle's husband and daughters were concerned that Janelle would develop another TEF and develop aspiration pneumonia. They convinced Janelle that she should remain NPO and receive a feeding tube. The palliative care team and speech-language pathologist conferenced again with Janelle and her family to review Janelle's prognosis and the importance of quality of life in her final days. The team suggested that if Janelle did receive a percutaneous endoscopic gastrostomy (PEG) tube, or feeding tube, oral pleasure feedings should accompany the nonoral nutrition. The speech-language pathologist explained that having a PEG tube did not guarantee that Janelle would not get aspiration pneumonia. With Janelle's history of reflux, it was very possible that she could aspirate refluxed tube feedings. The SLP also reviewed clinical signs and symptoms of aspiration. She suggested that since Janelle had exhibited clinical signs and symptoms of aspiration during her first two bouts with aspiration pneumonia, she would likely exhibit coughing and choking if aspiration due to a new TEF occurred. In this case, the family could immediately contact the physician and Janelle could return to NPO status.

The family was insistent that Janelle receive nothing by mouth to prevent aspiration pneumonia. Against her own wishes, Janelle agreed to receive a PEG tube. The tube was placed on May 25 and Janelle was discharged to home on hospice the following day.

Janelle passed away 1 week later. The feeding tube did not prolong Janelle's life. And, unfortunately, she did not enjoy any foods or liquids that could have contributed to her quality of life. The family, afraid to lose Janelle after a relatively short illness, influenced her to choose aggressive management in light of a very poor prognosis and focused on quantity of life versus quality of life. Although the medical team can provide information, recommendations, and support, ultimately, end-of-life decisions lie with our patients and their families. Providing the patient and family with education and resources to make these decisions is an important role of the medical team, which includes the speech-language pathologist.

Author's Note

This case study was not based on a single patient. Instead, it was developed from a compilation of patients with similar diagnoses, medical courses, and outcomes. Institutional review board approval was not required.

References

Colice, G. L., Stukel, T. A., & Dain, B. (1989). Laryngeal complications of prolonged intubation. *Chest, 96*, 877–884. https://doi.org/10.1378/chest.96.4.877

Colton House, J., Noordzij, J. P., Murgia, B., & Langmore, S. (2011). Laryngeal injury from prolonged intubation: A prospective analysis of contributing factors. *Laryngoscope, 121*(3), 596–600. https://doi.org/10.1002/lary.21403

Fan, A. C., Baron, T. H., & Utz, J. P. (2002). Combined tracheal and esophageal stenting for palliation of tracheoesophageal symptoms from mediastinal lymphoma. *Mayo Clinic Proceedings, 77*, 1347–1350. https://doi.org/10.4065/77.12.1347

Fujiu, M., & Logemann, J. A. (1996). Effect of a tongue-holding maneuver on posterior pharyngeal wall movement during deglutition. *American Journal of Speech-Language Pathology, 5*, 23–30. https://doi.org/10.1044/1058-0360.0501.23

Fujiu, M., Logemann, J. A., & Pauloski, B. R. (1995). Increased postoperative posterior pharyngeal wall movement in patients with anterior oral cancer: Preliminary findings and possible implications for treatment. *American Journal of Speech-Language Pathology, 4*, 24–30. https://doi.org/10.1044/1058-0360.0402.24

Kahrilas, P. J., Lin, S., Logemann, J. A., Ergen, G. A., & Facchini, F. (1993). Deglutitive tongue action: Volume accommodation and bolus propulsion. *Gastro-enterology*, *104*, 152–162. https://doi.org/10.1016/0016-5085(93)90847-6

Kulbersh, B. D., Rosenthal, E. L., McGrew, B. M., Duncan, R. D., McColloch, N. C., Carroll, W. R., & Magnuson, J. S. (2006). Pretreatment, preoperative swallowing exercises may improve dysphagia quality of life. *Laryngoscope*, *116*, 883–886. https://doi.org/10.1097/01.mlg.0000217278.96901.fc

Logemann, J. A., Pauloski, B. R., Rademaker, A. W., & Coangelo, A. (1997). Super-supraglottic swallow in irradiated head and neck cancer patients. *Head and Neck*, *19*, 535–540. https://doi.org/10.1002/(sici)1097-0347(199709)19:6<535::aid-hed11>3.0.co;2-4

Rosenbek, J. C., Robbins, J. A., Roecker, E. B., Coyle, J. L., & Wood, J. L. (1996). A penetration-aspiration scale. *Dysphagia*, *11*, 93–98. https://doi.org/10.1007/BF00417897

Rosenthal, D. I., Lewin, J. S., & Eisbruch, A. (2006). Prevention and treatment of dysphagia and aspiration after chemoradiation for head and neck cancer. *Journal of Clinical Oncology*, *24*, 2636–2643. https://doi.org/10.1200/JCO.2006.06.0079

Sharp, H. M., & Genesen, L. B. (1996). Ethical decision-making in dysphagia management. *American Journal of Speech-Language Pathology*, *5*(1), 15–22. https://doi.org/10.1044/1058-0360.0501.15

Shin, S., Lee, Y., Chang, W.H., Sohn, M. K., Lee, J., Kim, D. Y., . . . Kim, Y.-H. (2022). Multifaceted assessment of functional outcomes in survivors of first-time stroke. *JAMA Network Open*, *5*(9), e2233094. https://doi.org/10.1001/jamanetworkopen.2022.33094

Slomka, J. (2003). Withholding nutrition at the end of life: Clinical and ethical issues. *Cleveland Clinic Journal of Medicine*, *70*, 548–552. https://doi.org/10.3949/ccjm.70.6.548

TRAUMATIC BRAIN INJURY
CASE 57
Neil: A Holistic Rehabilitation Approach for an Adult With Traumatic Brain Injury
Patricia Kearns, Janelle Johnson Ward, Karen Hux, and Jeff Snell

---

Conceptual Knowledge Areas

Traumatic brain injury (TBI) results from the application of strong, external, physical forces to the skull and underlying brain. Common causes include violent shaking, whiplash injuries, and blows to the head from falls, assaults, sporting accidents, and motor vehicle accidents. The consequent damage to the brain results from a combination of initial or primary mechanisms occurring at the actual time of injury as well as secondary injury mechanisms occurring as aftereffects of the initial insult. Primary mechanisms of injury include cavitation effects and shearing strain and result in diffuse axonal injury; secondary mechanisms take the form of hematomas, acute cerebral swelling, cerebral edema, and increased intracranial pressure.

Blast injury represents a special class of TBI in that it results from one or more of four primary injury mechanisms:

1. an overpressure wave (i.e., a blast or percussion wave) striking the body surface,
2. projectiles (e.g., flying debris, bomb fragments) striking the body,
3. displacement of the victim (e.g., being thrown into other objects) and/or structural collapse (e.g., crush injuries) secondary to the blast, and
4. a direct consequence of the blast, such as burns, asphyxia, and exposure to toxins.

Secondary mechanisms of injury then follow, with the result being diffuse damage throughout the brain.

Treatment for TBI initially focuses on stabilizing the person from a medical standpoint, attending to any life-threatening injuries, and preventing or minimizing to the greatest extent possible the occurrence of secondary mechanisms of injury. Physical, cognitive, social, and emotional changes associated with the sustained damage only become evident as the person progresses through the recovery process. Long-term outcome and quality of life following TBI largely depend on the extent to which a person has spared abilities, is successful in reestablishing lost or impaired skills, or can learn to compensate for persistent deficits.

Cognitive rehabilitation is the process through which professionals assist people in achieving the best outcome possible. Over time, the focus of a person's cognitive rehabilitation program shifts from regaining lost abilities to mastering strategies that minimize the effects of persistent deficits. The cognitive rehabilitation process often extends over a period of several years and involves the efforts of professionals from multiple disciplines as well as friends and family members.

Description of the Case

Background Information

Neil grew up in an upper-middle-class home in a large Midwestern town. Neil's family described him as a "very bright" student throughout high school, in the gifted program, with plans to attend college. He entered college while also working part-time and then reportedly quit school in his first year because it was "too much like high school." Shortly thereafter, Neil joined the military. His medical history included a childhood diagnosis of Tourette's syndrome with tics that were treated and largely controlled with medication. He also had a history of occasional, although not excessive, alcohol use.

Neil sustained a severe TBI at 21 years of age while he was serving as an active-duty Operation Iraqi Freedom combat soldier. His injury occurred when a suicide bomber in a vehicle packed with explosives hit the vehicle Neil was driving and detonated the explosives. Neil was the only survivor. His injuries included a depressed skull fracture, bilateral subdural hematomas, right lung contusion, open fractures of the mandible, right facial fractures, right humeral fracture, C6 vertebral fracture, sternum fracture, clavicle fractures, extensive embedded shrapnel fragments in the right face and neck, and second- and third-degree burns on his right hand, thighs, and knees. Shortly following his initial trauma, he sustained a left frontoparietal stroke.

Neil was initially hospitalized and medically stabilized in Germany and then transported to the intensive care unit of an Army Medical Center in the United States. One month later, he began rehabilitation at the same facility. He had several other inpatient rehabilitation placements over the next year, eventually returning home to live with his mother approximately 1 year following his injury. Neil continued to require 24-hour care and supervision at that time. He received various home health support and outpatient services while living at home.

Reasons for Referral and Evaluation Findings

Neil entered a postacute residential rehabilitation facility approximately 3½ years after his injury to undergo assessment and intervention for persistent cognitive deficits. His initial assessment included speech-language and neuropsychological evaluations. Neil's hearing appeared adequate for conversational speech. Although he had some nearsightedness, he compensated for this by placing material close within his visual field. Neil was independent with walking over level surfaces, although he displayed significant ataxia affecting upper extremity use and gait steadiness over uneven surfaces. He demonstrated no bizarre or specifically psychotic thought processes, and his thinking appeared goal directed and concrete.

The initial speech-language evaluation revealed slowed processing speed and memory impairments affecting performance of lengthy and complex tasks. Neil answered concrete and abstract yes/no questions and followed two- and three-step commands, but he had difficulty with four-step commands. When read a paragraph, Neil immediately answered simple yes/no questions about the story with 80% accuracy. However, when asked to retell the story immediately after hearing it, Neil could not generate either the main idea or details. Further testing revealed that he had stored a portion of the concrete story information in memory but had difficulty accessing that stored information to generate the story retell. His expressive language abilities were largely intact, and he spoke in complete, grammatically accurate sentences. Neil performed sentence completion, object naming, and picture description tasks adequately, and his abstract language comprehension was functional. Given extended time, he generated multiple solutions and solved common as well as novel problems. Neil's speech was slightly imprecise, slurred, and hypernasal. He used several strategies, such as slowing down and taking frequent breaths, to increase speech intelligibility. At times, Neil expressed frustration about the way his voice sounded.

Neil's performance on neuropsychological assessments revealed significant deficits in memory, with scores on immediate recall, delayed recall, and recognition tasks falling within the borderline to impaired range. He evidenced substantial decay of information over a relatively brief time (e.g., 20 minutes) and could not retrieve information spontaneously or even recognize target information after that delay. Neil also demonstrated a general slowing of cognitive processing speed, impairments in divided attention, and significant ataxia. Consistent with the speech-language evaluation findings, Neil demonstrated relatively intact language functioning, with average performance on confrontation naming and abstract language reasoning tasks and superior performance on a vocabulary task. The only areas of language functioning with suppressed perfor-

mance were ones requiring rapid responses and verbal fluency. These challenges appeared to stem from slowed processing speed. From a behavioral perspective, Neil demonstrated substantial executive dysfunction, frequently erupting in angry outbursts when frustrated by his inability to perform tasks that were formerly not problematic for him. He was quick to anger and tended to exhibit behaviors disproportionate to the circumstances, such as yelling, cursing, and fleeing the location. Further complicating Neil's cognitive deficits and difficulty applying compensatory strategies was a general lack of awareness and insight. Neil did not demonstrate accurate insight and awareness "in the moment" when struggling with cognitive tasks or when experiencing an emotional/behavioral escalation and, therefore, did not spontaneously compensate for or initiate strategies to deal with the situation.

The most substantial and interfering deficits Neil displayed were those associated with memory functioning. These challenges limited Neil's independence and hampered his acquisition, mastery, and use of compensatory strategies to minimize the impact of his deficits. As a result, Neil required 24-hour support for initiating and completing all daily activities except dressing himself. Emotional issues, specifically anger, stemmed from Neil's perceived lack of independence and control over his environment. His anger resulted in outbursts and behaviors that compromised his safety.

Neil's family supported him for all functional deficits in an attempt to minimize his frustration and outbursts of anger, but after months of providing this level of care, his family reported substantial fatigue and discouragement. They described a deteriorating family unit focused only on meeting Neil's needs. Furthermore, constant family support to initiate and complete daily activities prompted Neil to become excessively dependent on others.

Neil expressed a goal of regaining his premorbid level of independent living and purposeful activity, including having his own apartment, engaging in relationships, driving, and working. Neil's family expressed a desire for him to increase independence with daily living skills and, more importantly, to be happy with his life again.

These were the goals forming the basis for his enrollment in the year-long, postacute treatment program.

Treatment Options Considered

A broad range of clinical practice methods exist in the area of cognitive rehabilitation; hence, several treatment options were available to serve as a basis for Neil's program (Gopi et al., 2021; Sander & van Veldhoven, 2014). Options included (a) *systems of total external support* (i.e., support from family or caregivers) to eliminate decision-making and the potential for failure; (b) impairment-specific *cognitive retraining tasks* (i.e., "mental muscle building") using activities such as computer memory games; (c) *academic-type training* using didactic material and homework focused on noncontextual learning and explicit memory; (d) *internal compensatory strategies* such as rehearsal, visual imagery, and organizational techniques to refine self-monitoring skills and teach methods of deficit compensation that could potentially generalize across multiple settings and activities; (e) *external compensatory devices* such as memory books, planners, and alarms to compensate for specific deficits; and (f) *skill-specific training* focused on contextual learning and use of implicit memory for development of routines.

Neil's treatment team was strategic in selecting a treatment option. They systematically considered the match between Neil's residual strengths and challenges and the skills needed for successful implementation of each cognitive rehabilitation technique. The team rejected the first option, systems of external control, because this was the strategy Neil's family had been implementing and with which they were currently struggling. Next, given the severity of Neil's memory and executive function deficits, the team felt that treatment options dependent on explicit memory and noncontextual learning would not be effective; hence, they also rejected cognitive retraining tasks and academic-type training as the basis for program development. Regarding the provision of compensatory strategy instruction, many practitioners consider this a "practice standard" for people with mild memory deficits who are actively involved in identifying and treating their challenges (Cicerone et al., 2011, 2019; Mahan et al., 2017; Velikonja et al., 2014). However, given the severity of Neil's memory deficits and his limited deficit awareness, the treatment team believed compensatory strategy training requiring self-regulation alone was unlikely to be successful. For people with more severe memory impairments, evidence suggests that externally directed compensatory devices such as alarms may be beneficial if training incorporates functional activities and ongoing staff support is provided (Cicerone et al., 2011, 2019). This was a possibility for Neil, but needing constant support was unlikely to lessen his excessive reliance on his family. Finally, the team considered the option of engaging Neil in skill-specific training. Evidence of success for this method exists for people with moderate to severe memory deficits when the treatment focuses on real-life functional activities, is completed in the context of real-world settings, and involves the use of implicit memory and learning (Cicerone et al., 2011; Gopi et al., 2021; Wilson & Fish, 2013, 2018). Based on their deliberations, the team believed this option would be the most effective in serving as a basis for increasing Neil's independence.

Neil's team focused on specific skill sets that would be functional within the real-world environment of the residential facility and the community. Successful mastery of skill sets relies primarily on implicit memory and the learning of routines through consistent repetitions (Wilson & Fish, 2013, 2018). To provide motivation, each routine centered on Neil's interests and goals, and the treatment program included psychology services to address awareness and acceptance issues as well as to deal with emotional issues as they arose. External memory compensation devices were integrated into specific skill sets to the degree they could be included in implicitly learned routines (Gopi et al., 2021).

The team hypothesized that helping Neil master a series of implicitly learned routines that included external compensatory devices would allow him to increase his independence when managing daily living skills and engaging in purposeful activity. They also hypothesized that Neil's emotional well-being would improve as he developed a sense of hope and optimism for his future through increased independence and control over his day.

Course of Treatment

Neil began his treatment in an on-site residential facility that provided 24-hour staff support. The setting was a single-story house with eight private bedrooms and community living, dining, kitchen, laundry, and shower areas. Neil's treatment team included a nurse, nutritionist, occupational therapist, physical therapist, speech-language pathologist, life skills specialist, recreational therapist, psychologist, family counselor, case manager, and five residential staff. His treatment program included three components. The first component addressed medical needs as they arose, although these were minimal. The second and primary component was education based and focused on developing skill sets. The third component was psychological in nature and targeted helping Neil regain hope and optimism for the future and an anticipation of pleasure. Neil's team speculated that addressing the psychological component in conjunction with the medical and education components would lead to optimal participation and maximize outcomes.

Based on the three treatment components, Neil's team identified functional skill sets necessary to meet his goals. In addition to discipline-specific formal evaluations of performance, the treatment team observed Neil closely for all waking hours over 3 consecutive days to assess the functional impact of his impairments on daily living skills. They also gathered specific information regarding his preferences and natural tendencies. Using this information, the team developed routines for each skill set. As appropriate, they considered various external compensatory strategies and devices for implementation with the routines. Initially, Neil refused to consider any external compensatory devices that he perceived as differentiating him from a "normal" person. Over time and as he became more aware of his deficits through regular counseling and staff encouragement, he began to participate in choosing and developing strategies and devices that allowed him to increase his independence when performing moderately complex and complex routines.

Implementation of routines focused on providing sufficient support to ensure Neil's success while, at the same time, avoiding excess support that would foster dependence on staff. The goal was for each routine to occur successfully (i.e., following principles of errorless learning) and without task failure (Clare & Jones, 2008; Gopi et al., 2021; Haslam, 2018). Therefore, the treatment team continuously and carefully monitored Neil's performance, and as Neil proved he was implicitly learning a routine by demonstrating initiation of parts or all of it, staff adjusted their support to allow for his increased independence. Each routine was implemented in Neil's real-life environment (i.e., residential and community settings) and with natural support from staff. Because overlap existed in the skill sets on which various team members focused, communication was imperative to ensuring consistency across disciplines. Communication with family members and their direct involvement in the treatment program was also critical.

Analysis of Client's Response to Intervention

Neil's team began his course of treatment by developing routines for basic functional skill sets. These basic routines included morning/evening grooming, basic orientation strategies, intake of adequate nutrition, and taking medications. To illustrate the sequence of a basic routine, consider Neil's morning grooming routine. The team first identified a specific location to keep all items Neil needed for morning grooming along with a written list of specific, sequential tasks to perform during showering, grooming, and dressing. The listed tasks included (a) shower, (b) put on clothes from basket, (c) brush teeth, and (d) put dirty clothes in hamper. Neil initially required verbal cues to retrieve needed items and then to attend to each task on the list. Without the cues and list, Neil completed some items multiple times and failed to complete others. The team taught all staff members working with Neil the exact type of support, interaction style, and support timing likely to be most effective. Specifically, a staff member was immediately present when Neil woke each day at 6:15 a.m. This was to ensure that Neil started the routine correctly every day and prevented him from making errors such as starting in the middle of the list. After 5 days, Neil had learned to initiate using the list, thereby allowing staff to eliminate that cue. With ongoing successful repetitions, staff gradually faded support, and Neil showered, dressed, and groomed independently. The team introduced all other basic routines in the same manner; that is, they used a variety of verbal cues and written lists, and the amount of staff support decreased as Neil demonstrated consistent success.

The team introduced skill sets of increasing complexity once a foundation of basic routines was in place. These included management of external memory compensation devices, simple meal planning and preparation, basic home management, and community access focusing on safety, emotional adjustment, and decision-making. Although implementing external memory compensation devices was a routine in and of itself, it also became an important step within other routines. To determine the best compensatory memory device, Neil first experimented with several possibilities ranging in complexity from a simple day planner to a smartphone. Based on his preferences, premorbid strategies, and physical challenges because of ataxia, he settled on using a personal computer with Microsoft Outlook® calendar.

The purpose for encouraging Neil to use a memory compensation device was twofold. First, it provided Neil with a consistent way of preparing for each day; second, it served as a way of reminding him to attend to daily activities. The memory compensation device routine started with staff providing verbal cues to assist Neil with locating the Outlook® icon on his computer desktop, opening the program and calendar, and printing the schedule for the next day. Neil performed this part of the routine in the evening, so he could use the printed schedule to make decisions for the next day (e.g., deciding what clothing to wear and for what time to set the alarm). After completing his next-day planning, Neil placed his printed schedule in a designated spot every evening (i.e., on a shelf near the door along with his watch, wallet, phone, and keys). In the morning, Neil gathered his schedule, watch, wallet, phone, and keys before walking out the door.

After 10 days of successful repetitions, Neil required a cue to initiate the memory compensation routine but independently accessed the program and printed his daily schedule. He also required a cue to put his schedule in the designated spot, but he located the schedule, along with his other items, independently in the morning. Neil continued to require cues throughout the day to look at his schedule. After 2 additional weeks, Neil became independent with placing his schedule on the shelf each evening, but he did not make further progress with using his schedule. To further decrease staff support needed to implement schedule use and complete activities, the team considered adding a second external memory compensation device—specifically, a watch with an audible alarm that Neil approved as an acceptable accommodation. After reviewing several options, use of a Timex® Data Link® watch that provided numerous alarm options as well as scrolling written text was implemented. The team's initial intent was to use the watch instead of the paper schedule; however, Neil's tendency to turn off the alarm and then quickly forget what the text cued him to do prevented successful implementation of this substitution. Therefore, the team opted to maintain use of the printed schedule and simplify the watch cues; they only served as reminders about medication times and the need to "check the schedule." With these strategies in place, the number of cues Neil needed throughout the day to use his schedule decreased.

Although Neil became more independent with his memory compensation device routine, he continued to need occasional reminders to check his schedule even after 8 months of treatment. The team investigated other strategies during this time period, but wearing a "normal" watch and discreetly carrying a paper schedule were the only options Neil considered acceptable. Because Neil implicitly learned through repetition of routines occurring on a daily basis (i.e., meals, ADLs), the team considered making his entire schedule exactly the same each day. As with most young adults, however, Neil preferred a variety of leisure activities and the option of changing or adding activities spontaneously to his schedule. Hence, this idea was not put into operation. The team introduced implementation and mastery of all remaining routines included in Neil's rehabilitation program in the same manner with modifications made as appropriate.

As Neil gained independence with activities meeting his basic health and safety needs, the team developed additional routines to address his emotional needs and allow him to have a sense of control over his day. Memory compensation devices that Neil could learn to use independently were again an important component of these complex routines. Proposed routines included money management, meal planning and shopping, leisure planning, community access, and medication management. Leisure planning was the most motivating routine for Neil and reinforced previously mastered skill sets. However, Neil required full support for generating ideas for leisure options and filling open time during his day. He frequently refused options offered by others, yet he demonstrated anger when time slots on his schedule were left empty. To manage this, staff encouraged Neil to develop lists of options based on prior interests and supported his investigation and participation in similar activities available in the surrounding community.

Leisure activities of particular interest to Neil included dining out, watching movies, and listening to music. To help him master routines associated with these options, team members developed separate written lists for interests Neil could access in his residence (e.g., downloading music, searching the Internet, or playing games online) versus in the community (e.g., going to restaurants, movie theaters, or concert venues). Then, staff assisted Neil with identifying free time in his schedule and choosing activities from his lists appropriate for the time of day and amount of time available. Specifically, each Sunday evening, Neil met with a staff member to identify short periods of free time throughout the upcoming week and then made selections from his list of residential leisure activi-

ties to fill those times. Two times per week, staff assisted Neil with identifying time slots of sufficient length to allow him to access the community. By again using his written list of choices, Neil selected an activity (e.g., dining out) and then a venue for that activity (e.g., Applebee's®). He then utilized the Internet to find the location, print the menu, and budget for the activity.

Neil initially needed maximum support to complete the multiple steps associated with implementing leisure option routines. In particular, Neil required significant encouragement to participate in making choices and following through with selected activities. His reluctance appeared to result from memory deficits (i.e., he would forget that he chose the activity) and poor acceptance of his deficits (i.e., he appeared embarrassed about his ataxia and the way his memory deficits affected his abilities). However, after several successful experiences with community-based activities, Neil became more cooperative with performing leisure option routines and began to demonstrate increased independence with parts of the planning and execution process. Over a period of approximately 6 months, Neil went from maximum staff dependence to requiring only one cue to access and make choices from his list. As Neil gained computer proficiency, the team transferred his written lists to a series of folders that he could access from his computer desktop. The folders were layered, representing the sequence from his areas of interests to category or venue options and specific venue information. For example, if he wanted to go out to eat for dinner, he would choose the "Dining Out" folder, then select a food category folder—such as the "American Food" folder—and, finally, choose a specific restaurant. This would link him to the restaurant website for further planning. Due to the complexity of the overall routine, Neil persisted in usually needing support to initiate planning for an upcoming evening or weekend activity, adding it to his schedule, and sequencing through the planning steps. However, on occasion, Neil independently found community activities to attend.

The team observed an overall improvement in Neil's mood as he gained independence and control over his day. That, in turn, appeared to increase his participation in the treatment program. His achievement of complex routines had the greatest impact on his mood, as they allowed for the anticipation of pleasure, a greater sense of control over his life, and increased confidence in his abilities. However, performing complex routines also caused Neil the most frustration because he could not complete the necessary steps with the same ease he did prior to injury. Overall, the team believed the benefits associated with Neil's improved mood and program participation outweighed the periods of frustration and anger. Over time, he responded to redirection with greater ease and acceptance.

With routines in place, Neil was ready to move from the structured rehabilitation setting to a community-based apartment that had 24-hour supervision available as needed. This move provided a means of simulating fully independent living while still ensuring Neil's access to staff support and supervision. Despite replication of all of Neil's previously mastered routines and compensatory devices in the apartment setting, the change of environment resulted in a need for increased staff support. Initially, Neil required maximum support for all routines and 24-hour supervision for safety. With structured repetitions, however, this need for support was gradually decreased to match his previously acquired levels. The team also came to realize that any interruption in Neil's routines necessitated a temporary increase in staff support. For example, after visiting his family for a 10-day vacation during which other activities interrupted his established routines, Neil again required maximum staff support to reestablish his routines in his apartment setting. This support was gradually decreased over a 2- to 4-week period to again match his previously acquired levels.

Further Recommendations

After a year of combined residential treatment and independent living simulation, Neil was independent with all basic routines as long as his environment remained consistent. He was also independent with mid-level routines within his familiar environment if his compensatory strategies were consistently available. Based on this increased level of independence, the support Neil needed decreased from 24 hours to 6 to 8 hours per day. Neil continued to require evening and weekend support to facilitate implementation of complex routines. In conjunction with his family and his funding source, the treatment team decided to discharge Neil from the postacute rehabilitation program and to arrange for him to live in a community apartment close to his family's home. Neil would transition and carry out his daily schedule and all functional skill sets and routines in this permanent environment. Because Neil was not receiving any traditional formal therapies at the time of discharge, the team did not recommend resumption of any such services. Rather, the treatment team recommended (a) continued provision of 6 to 8 hours per week of assistance from a companion to help manage complex routines and (b) provision of vocational rehabilitation to assist Neil in obtaining a job.

Neil had an extensive support system throughout his treatment, including immediate and extended family, childhood friends, and military friends and advocates. Neil's family and friends participated in extensive brain injury education and instruction about how to facilitate his routines successfully. Just prior to discharge, Neil's mother and father participated in a simulated companion role over a 1-week period. This gave them confidence that they could instruct others in using verbal cues, external devices, and interaction styles to maximize Neil's success.

The accuracy of the team's initial hypotheses about the type of rehabilitation program best suited to Neil's situation allowed for the selection of an effective treatment approach. However, the team did not anticipate that the success or failure of the program would be so dependent on the consistency of Neil's staff interactions, verbal supports, and environments. In particular, the team did not expect that a simple change of environment or interruption in Neil's daily schedule would lead to a notable decline in his independence with basic routines. Despite these types of setbacks, the team made accurate predictions about the amount of time Neil would need support to regain his independence with basic routines after returning to a familiar environment and predictable schedule. Neil's periods of regression when first introduced to a simulated independent living situation and when returning to that environment after a 10-day vacation provided important information for developing his discharge transition plan. In particular, the team realized that Neil's successful transition to a permanent independent living setting would require an initial period of increased support as well as exact or nearly exact replication of established routines and devices. They were confident, however, that given consistency and repetition, Neil could master both simple and complex routines that allowed for only minimal reliance on outside supervision and support.

Neil's case provides an example of the type of improved independent living possible for a person with severe and persistent cognitive and behavioral challenges following TBI. Often times, financial support is not available to fund the extended and intensive postacute rehabilitation services Neil received. However, when considered over an adult's typical life span, paying for services resulting in substantial improvement in independence and quality of life is more cost-effective than the alternative. Over multiple years, the financial saving associated solely with decreasing Neil's need for support services from 24 hours to 6 to 8 hours daily meant he could live in a community-based setting rather than a more restrictive and expensive facility.

Authors' Note

This chapter is based on a real case, although names and other identifying information were changed to protect individuals' privacy. Both the Institutional Review Board of the University of Nebraska–Lincoln and the facility's Research Committee and Human Rights Review Committee approved performance of this work. The client and his legal guardian provided assent and consent for participation.

References

Cicerone, K. D., Goldin, Y., Ganci, K., Rosenbaum, A., Wethe, J. V., Langenbahn, D. M., . . . Harley, J. P. (2019). Evidence-based cognitive rehabilitation: Systematic review of the literature from 2009 through 2014. *Archives of Physical Medicine and Rehabilitation, 100*(8), 1515–1533. https://doi.org/10.1016/j.apmr.2019.02.011

Cicerone, K. D., Langenbahn, D. M., Braden, C., Malec, J. F., Kalmar, K., Fraas, M., . . . Ashman, T. (2011). Evidence-based cognitive rehabilitation: Updated review of the literature from 2003 through 2008. *Archives of Physical Medicine and Rehabilitation, 92*(4), 519–530. https://doi.org/10.1016/j.apmr.2010.11.015

Clare, L., & Jones, R. S. P. (2008). Errorless learning in the rehabilitation of memory impairment: A critical review. *Neuropsychological Review, 18*(1), 1–23. https://doi.org/10.1007/s11065-008-9051-4

Gopi, Y., Wilding, E., & Madan, C. (2021, January 15). *Memory rehabilitation: Restorative, specific knowledge acquisition, compensatory, and holistic approaches.* PsyArXiv. https://doi.org/10.31234/osf.io/zjdn4

Haslam, C. (2018). The tyranny of choice: Deciding between principles of errorless learning, spaced retrieval and vanishing cues. In C. Haslam & R. P. C. Kessels (Eds.), *Errorless learning in neuropsychological rehabilitation: Mechanisms, efficacy, and application* (pp. 180–192). Routledge.

Mahan, S., Rous, R., & Adlam, A. (2017). Systematic review of neuropsychological rehabilitation for prospective memory deficits as a consequence of acquired brain injury. *Journal of the International Neuropsychological Society, 23*(3), 254–265. https://doi.org/10.1017/S1355617716001065

Sander, A. M., & van Veldhoven, L. M. (2014). Rehabilitation of memory problems associated with traumatic brain injury. In M. Sherer & A. M. Sander (Eds.), *Handbook on the neuropsychology of traumatic brain injury* (pp. 173–190). Springer. https://doi.org/10.1007/978-1-4939-0784-7_9

Velikonja, D., Tate, R., Ponsford, J., McIntyre, A., Janzen, S., & Bayley, M. (2014). INCOG recommendations for management of cognition following traumatic brain injury, part V: Memory. *The Journal of Head Trauma Rehabilitation, 29*(4), 369–386. https://doi.org/10.1097/HTR.0000000000000069

Wilson, B. A., & Fish, J. (2013). Memory disorders. In K. Ochsner & S. M. Kosslyn (Eds.), *The Oxford handbook of cognitive neuroscience: Vol. 2. The cutting edges* (pp. 473–487). Oxford University Press.

Wilson, B. A., & Fish, J. E. (2018). The past, present, and future of errorless learning in memory rehabilitation.

In C. Haslam & R. P. C. Kessels (Eds.), *Errorless learning in neuropsychological rehabilitation: Mechanisms, efficacy, and application* (pp. 11–25). Routledge.

VELOPHARYNGEAL DYSFUNCTION
CASE 58
Emily: Velopharyngeal Dysfunction in an Adolescent Girl: Neurological, Behavioral, or Anatomical in Origin?
Jeff Searl

Conceptual Knowledge Areas

1. Normal oral, pharyngeal, and velopharyngeal (VP) anatomy
2. Normal VP physiology
3. Impact of VP dysfunction on speech (impacts on resonance, articulation, phonation, breath units, etc.)
4. Experiences: completion of oral mechanism examination (particular focus on VP structure and function), articulation inventory, instrumental evaluation of VP function via endoscopy and aerodynamic measures

Description of the Case

Background Information

Setting and Time of Client Contact

Emily was seen for diagnostic and therapeutic speech services at a university-based hearing and speech clinic on the campus of a teaching hospital. Prior to initiating speech services, she was an outpatient in the Otolaryngology Depart-ment at this same hospital for reasons related to her speech. The clinical services described below took place within a 4-month time frame during Emily's eighth-grade school year. There were five individuals involved in Emily's case. The first was Emily herself. She contributed information regarding her social and educational history, social and psychological consequences of her speech, description of her speech, and judgments about the impact therapy had on her speech. Emily's mother prompted the initial consultation with the ENT doctor that resulted in referral to the hearing and speech clinic. The mother provided most of the history information; gave observations about the social, psychological, and educational impacts on Emily; motivated Emily to complete her speech "homework"; and served as another judge of therapy progress. The ENT physician saw Emily for one visit, providing an important review of her medical history and assessment of current health, physical appearance, and movement of VP structures. The ENT has exclusively seen pediatric patients for more than 20 years, including those with velopharyngeal (VP) function issues.

A speech-language pathologist (SLP) working in the university hearing and speech clinic provided services to Emily in the form of diagnostic testing and therapy. The SLP also supervised a graduate student who was in her first year of a 2-year master's degree program in Speech-Language Pathology. The SLP had 15 years of experience, including frequent clinical contact with individuals having VP problems. The graduate student provided most of the therapy over 2 months and participated in the initial diagnostic session. The graduate student had not had any substantial experience with clients with VP issues prior to this case but had completed related coursework.

History Information

Emily was 14 years old and in eighth grade at the time of the ENT evaluation that precipitated the speech pathology contact. She lived in an urban neighborhood with her mother, father, and a 2-year-old brother. Both parents had high school educations and worked full-time in the manufacturing industry. They had been married 16 years, and by the mother's account, the living situation was harmonious and stable. The household was lower to middle socioeconomic level based on household income, parental education, and other measures.

The mother smoked intermittently through the first trimester of the pregnancy; the pregnancy was normal in all other respects. Emily's birth was unremarkable. She was diagnosed with moderate pulmonary stenosis within the first week of life and underwent balloon dilation followed by several years of subacute bacterial endocarditis prophylaxis. She continues to be followed by a pediatric cardiologist up to the present. Persistent symptoms of general fatigue, shortness of breath, and a rapid heart rate are attributed to heart issues. Emily had bilateral myringotomy tubes placed at 1 year of age because of frequent middle ear infections that were not responsive to antibiotic regimens. Her hearing now is within normal limits per the ENT with tubes in place.

According to Emily's mother, Emily sat unsupported at 7 months of age, crawled at 9 months, and was walking unsupported by 13 months. She described Emily as being "clumsy" at a young age when running or throwing balls. Emily stated that she is less coordinated and athletic than most of her peers. Mom did not think Emily was a particularly messy eater as a young child. She described Emily as a "late talker" with first real words produced at approximately 2 years of age.

From a preschool screening when Emily was 3½ years old, physical and occupational therapy (PT and OT) were recommended to address motor development. A specific diagnosis was not offered other than general "developmental delay." The mother indicated that Emily continued to be seen by both PT and OT through third grade, but reports of the treatment were not available. She started speech therapy (ST) near the end of kindergarten, because the teacher was having trouble understanding Emily. Speech therapy continued through sixth grade. Mom reported that the reason for the ST during elementary school was because Emily did not "pronounce" many of her sounds correctly, had reduced speech intelligibility, and used short phrases and sentences. The mother also stated that Emily's speech has always sounded "nasally." At the end of sixth grade, the therapy ended because, according to the mother, the speech therapist felt that progress had stopped. Emily had an Individualized Education Plan (IEP) throughout her elementary and junior high school career, which included PT, OT, ST, and educational specialists for reading, writing, and mathematics.

Emily was reluctant to talk during the interview. Her responses to questions were brief and spoken quietly. She nodded affirmatively when asked if her speech bothered her. Mom felt strongly that Emily's shyness was directly related to her speech. Her school performance was negatively impacted by her speech as evidenced by her mom's observations that Emily does not raise her hand or speak up in class because of embarrassment about her speech. Emily is reticent to talk much with close friends.

Reason for Referral

The speech evaluation referral was an outcome of Emily's visit to an ENT. The reason for the ENT visit was "because of her adenoids" and the possibility that removing them might improve her speech, a suggestion from the school SLP. The following medical information was included in the ENT report: frequent nasal congestion, no known allergies, and family history of chronic fatigue, depression, and seizures. The ENT exam revealed the following: cranial nerves II though XII intact on cursory examination, no ear issues, mild nasal congestion from a cold, tonsils without erythema or exudates, and "some nasal emissions with plosives." Flexible fiber-optic nasopharyngoscopy was performed. This entailed passing a flexible scope down one side of the nose with the tip positioned superior to the VP port so that soft palate and pharyngeal wall motion during speech could be visualized (see Karnell, 2011) with the following observations: small adenoid pad, inconsistent but extensive palatal elevation during sustained vowels, intermittent closure of the VP port during productions of plosives and fricatives in syllables and short phrases, and a "very small indentation" in the soft palate near the point of attachment of the hard and soft palate. When VP closure was incomplete (~50% of trials), there was a central gap rather than a lateral air leak. The ENT's assessment was: "Hypernasality with mild velopharyngeal insufficiency, and history of developmental delays." The ENT recommended a speech evaluation and trial therapy to determine whether Emily could correct the VP insufficiency behaviorally; if not, the ENT was prepared to consider surgery to address the VP problem.

Findings of the Evaluation

Emily's evaluation was completed in one 75-minute meeting with her mother present. The evaluation consisted of the following: history interview, articulation inventory, perceptual ratings of voice and resonance, oral mechanism examination, aerodynamic assessment of VP function, and stimulability testing.

Interview

Relevant history from the interview was included in the Background section above. Direct observation of Emily during this interview was helpful in gauging the extent of her communication deficit in nonstructured speech tasks and gaining an impression of the impact that her speech has on her. The most striking observations were related to her communication style. Emily was very reticent to speak. Even with open-ended questions directed to her, she never gave more than a short-phrase response. She avoided eye contact completely, sat low in her chair with shoulders slumped and arms folded across her chest, and had her body turned slightly away from the table around which everyone sat. This did not come across as defiance but rather shyness, embarrassment, or perhaps reduced self-confidence. Almost without thinking about it, her mother answered most questions, even those intended for Emily. In contrast to Emily, her mother was very talkative. Her comments suggested a high level of concern about Emily's speech and the impact on school performance. When Emily did respond, her voice was quiet and mouth movements were minimal. The graduate clinician had to request several repetitions from Emily because of inaudibility and unintelligibility.

Articulation Inventory

A single-word repetition task was completed that sampled all consonants in initial and final position of syllables in Standard American English. This inventory is not standardized but rather used within the Cleft Palate Clinic at the facility to allow rapid and complete detailing of a speaker's articulation of all consonants.

Observations from the articulation inventory included substitution of /w/ for /r/ (when /r/ was a singleton and in a consonant cluster) and /s/ for /sh/. She produced /r/ correctly when asked to repeat words that were initially in error. Likewise, she could correctly produce /sh/ stimuli when asked to do so. All stop consonants were produced with perceptually weak bursts, regardless of the position of the consonant within a syllable. These weak bursts were sometimes accompanied by nasal airflow (nasal emission) but not always (the phenomenon co-occurred ~60% of the time). During a brief speech sample elicited with open-ended questions, Emily produced similar errors on /r/ and intermittently on /sh/; bursts and frication on stops and fricatives during more spontaneous speech were weak. Speech intelligibility was at or near 100% during the speech sample, although careful listening was required due to Emily's soft voice.

Perceptual Ratings of Voice and Resonance

During sustained vowel production, the articulation inventory, and spontaneous responses, Emily's laryngeal voice quality and her habitual pitch were judged to be normal for her age and gender. Pitch range on sustained vowels was approximately 1.5 octaves. As noted previously, she typically spoke with decreased loudness. Emily could increase loudness under instruction but did so reluctantly.

Hypernasality was judged on a 5-point scale where 0 = *no hypernasality* and 4 = *severe hypernasality*. Hypernasality is a resonance phenomenon defined as excess nasal resonance on oral sound production. Hypernasality occurs on phonemes that are principally defined by their resonance, namely, vowels and vowel-like consonants such as liquids and glides and (to a lesser extent) voiced consonants (Bzoch, 2004; Kummer, 2011a). Emily repeated sentences heavily loaded with the vowels /i/, /u/, and /a/ and voiced oral consonants. The sentences were, "He will read to Lee," "You were rude to Lou," and "Bob had our dollar," each repeated three times. Emily said each sentence on one breath at a comfortable loudness level while the graduate clinician intermittently closed the nares with her fingers (nasal flutter task, or the cul-de-sac test). If air escapes through the VP port during production of these fully oral sentences, obstructing the nares results in a perceptible shift in the vowel quality that can be noted by the clinician. Before completing this task, Emily blew her nose; if nasal congestion is present, it confounds this perceptual test. During the nasal flutter task, Emily's speech was rated as mildly hypernasal (rating of 2). She had some trials produced without any perceptible hypernasality.

Nasal emission ratings were made during production of sentences loaded with voiceless stop consonants and fricatives (e.g., "Paula paid Perry," "Terry told Teddy," etc.) using the same 5-point scale with 0 = *none* and 4 = *severe*. Each sentence was repeated three times, each on one breath. Nasal emission is a pressure-based phenomenon that is defined as a burst of air out the nose while an individual produces an oral burst or frication (Oren et al., 2020). This air burst is generally audible, but silent nasal emission can also occur. The nasal emission protocol included assessment of the pressure consonants /p, t, k, f, s, sh, ch/. Voiceless consonants are used because the oral pressure generated on voiceless stops and fricatives is greater than the voiced counterparts, increasing the likelihood of eliciting nasal emission if a VP gap is present (Trost-Cardamone, 2004). Emily had none-to-mild nasal emission that varied across consonants and across trials of the same consonant. She most consistently had mild nasal emission on /p/ and /s/; she never had nasal emission on /t/ or /k/. All other consonants had at least one trial with nasal emission.

Hyponasality is also a resonance phenomenon characterized by a reduction in nasal resonance during nasal consonant production. Hyponasality was rated on a 5-point scale (0 = *none*, 4 = *severe*) as Emily repeated sentences loaded with nasal consonants. The nose was intermittently obstructed. In this case, a change in resonance should occur if the nasal sounds are being produced with nasal airflow and acoustic energy. Obstructing the nares during nasal sound production causes cul-de-sac resonance, facilitating the clinician's ability to detect whether there is sufficient nasal resonance on nasal phonemes. Emily's speech was rated as having no nasal emission on any trial.

During the limited spontaneous speech productions from Emily, hypernasality was more consistently present than what was noted during the structured speech sampling. Nasal emission was also more prominent in the spontaneous productions (greater in magnitude and frequency of occurrence). Others have pointed out the need for clinicians to make observations about hypernasality, nasal emission, and hyponasality during connected speech in addition to the more structured tasks that are designed specifically to facilitate perceptual ratings of each phenomenon.

Oral Mechanism Examination

An oral mechanism examination is a vital part of the assessment protocol when there are VP concerns because the information derived is needed to rule in or out various structural or movement-related factors (Peterson-Falzone et al., 2009). There were no structural abnormalities noted during the oral mechanism examination. There were no scars on the lip or palate. There was not a bifid uvula, notching of the hard-soft palate juncture, or coloration change in the soft palate that might suggest a submucous cleft (Boyce et al., 2018). Emily allowed the SLP to place a gloved finger inside the oral cavity to palpate the hard and soft palate. There were no obvious bony or muscular defects (indentations) in the soft or hard palate that could be felt with the fingertip.

With the mouth open and the tongue resting low in the mouth, Emily sustained the vowel /a/ for 5 seconds on one breath; she repeated this several times as the SLP observed palatal and pharyngeal wall movement. Superior and posterior movement of the soft palate serves as the primary but often not the sole movement that results in VP closure (Raol & Hartnick, 2015). Females in particular may demonstrate more of a circular closure pattern than males who more frequently demonstrate a coronal closure pattern (Jordan et al., 2017). The posterior and lateral pharyngeal walls need to constrict around the elevated palate to fully occlude the VP port. Palatal elevation was consistently rated 2 on a 3-point scale where 0 = *no movement*, 1 = *minimal/slight movement*, and 2 = *moderate/marked movement*. Lateral pharyngeal wall movement during /a/ was consistently rated 1. There were no indications of discoordination of VP movements during the vowel productions.

Lip, tongue and jaw strength, range of motion, speed of movement, and coordination during rapid alternating movements were judged to be within normal limits based on observations of nonspeech movements. There were no indications of laryngeal or respiratory abnormalities based on informal observations of Emily at rest and when talking.

Aerodynamic Assessment

Simultaneous measurement of oral air pressure and nasal airflow was obtained using a Microtronics PERCI-SARS hardware-software arrangement as Emily produced various speech stimuli. By selecting stimuli appropriately, one can gather information from the aerodynamics recordings that reflect on VP closing. Oral pressure is measured with a small tube between the lips with the tip resting above the tongue just behind the upper central incisors. The tube is connected to a differential pressure transducer. Nasal airflow was measured by placing a mask over the nose; the mask was coupled to a pneumotachometer and differential pressure transducer (see Warren, 1979).

Emily produced /p/ in syllable series, words, and sentences. Syllable series and words with /p/ in a nasal context also were produced (e.g., /pam-pampam/, "hamper"). The /mp/ context can be particularly challenging for the VP mechanism because it must transition rapidly from an open position on /m/ to a closed position for /p/. Emily's oral pressure on /p/ was typically 2 to 3 cmH$_2$O and occasionally ranged up to 5 cmH$_2$O. Her oral pressures were at or below the low end of normal for teenagers and adults for whom pressures should be between 3 and 8 cmH$_2$O. For some samples, the nasal airflow tube and nasal air pressure tube were removed so that the nostrils could be manually occluded by the clinician as Emily produced some of the /p/ stimuli a second time. With the nose occluded, oral air pressure increased to an average of 5.2 cmH$_2$O, indicating that she has the respiratory drive and oral articulatory ability to produce adequate oral pressure if the air leakage through the nose is eliminated.

Nasal airflow on /p/ averaged ~150 cc/second (range: 65–230 cc/s). During /p/ production, nasal airflow should be essentially zero (less than ~20 cc/s is suggested by Zajac, 2000). There was significant variation in the magnitude of nasal airflow within and across stimuli. For example, during one trial saying a series of /pa/, Emily had nasal airflow on the first, second, and fifth /p/s of approximately 120 cc/s; however, flow on the third and fourth /p/s was ~30 cc/s. On /pi/ stimuli, she always had nasal airflows greater than 110 cc/s.

Nasal airflow was also measured on syllable series and sentences constructed with the consonants /t, k, f, s, ʃ, tʃ/; the oral tube is removed to allow normal oral articulation, so only nasal flow is recorded. Flow values ranged from ~60 to 270 cc/s. Again, these are oral consonants where nasal flow should be absent (or at least less than 20 cc/s).

Stimulability Testing

Emily was asked to manipulate her resonance and oral pressure. Most of the stimulability testing was with the pressure-flow equipment in place for two reasons: (1) Changes in nasal airflow and oral air pressure could be quantified, and (2) the visual display of airflow and pressure could be used as biofeedback to facilitate Emily's ability to change the requested parameters. The target behaviors tracked during stimulability testing were (1) oral pressure on /p/ with a target of at least 4 to 5 cmH$_2$O and (2) nasal airflow on all oral stimuli with a target <40 cc/s.

Initially, the stimulability testing was done with the aerodynamic equipment in place but with the computer display turned away from Emily. Later, the display was turned so she could watch the screen. The intent was to see whether she could manipulate the targets with just auditory models and instructions, and to see the impact of visual feedback on changing the behaviors. Without visual feedback, there were no reductions in nasal airflow with any of the following instructions: increase loudness, decrease loudness, increase articulatory precision, make bursts stronger ("really pop that /p/"), and a general command to "get rid of the nasal sound." These types of instruction have been suggested based on clinical experience as possible means of altering VP activity and/or minimizing perceptions of hypernasality, nasal emission, or weak oral pressures, although none have any significant empirical support (Tomes et al., 2004, provide a review of issues related to behavioral intervention approaches for VP impairment). For Emily, oral pressure increased to ~3 to 4 cmH$_2$O with increased loudness, but she appeared reluctant to increase loudness even with significant modeling. By happenstance, we observed Emily whispering with the equipment in place. During

the whisper (sentences loaded with /p/), oral air pressure was consistently greater than 6 cmH$_2$O, and nasal flow was less than 10 cc/s. When the computer display was turned for her viewing, the same set of manipulations was attempted. In this condition, she was able to increase oral pressure ~30% of the time with the general instruction to "make this peak go higher" and "make the /p/ more strongly." When doing so, she appeared to be engaging in exaggerated articulatory activity with slightly prolonged lip closure; there was a perceptibly louder burst under this instruction. When oral pressure increased, nasal flow decreased to ~0 to 10 cc/s, although occasional spikes up to 75 cc/s still occurred. During whispering, while watching the screen, Emily was able to engage in "negative practice" involving alternating between allowing nasal airflow through the nose on one production and then eliminating nasal airflow on the next. Sustained /s/ was also elicited. Without instruction, the sustained /s/ had consistent nasal flow of 80 to 125 cc/s when watching the screen. With the instruction, "make it all come out of your mouth," she could reduce nasal flow below 30 cc/s for 75% of the duration of a given trial.

Definition of the Problem Based on Assessment Information

Emily presented with two primary speech issues. The first was persistent articulatory substitutions on /r/ and /sh/, which were inconsistently present. She demonstrated the ability to accurately produce these phonemes with limited prompting. While these errors were not judged to have a large negative impact on intelligibility, they did draw attention to her speech and gave an impression of immaturity.

The second issue was mild hypernasality and none-to-mild nasal emission. A related factor was a general reduction in the strength of bursts and frication that appeared to be linked to nasal air leak when building air pressure for oral consonants. The aerodynamic recordings of oral pressure were consistent with the clinicians' perceptions of weak pressure consonants; the magnitude of the nasal airflow recordings was greater than expected compared to the rating of mild hypernasality from the clinicians. Additionally, Emily's spontaneous speech gave the impression of fairly constant hypernasality and nasal emission compared to the aerodynamic recording.

In addition to describing Emily's VP symptoms, a primary outcome of the assessment was to define the reason for the VP symptoms and to develop an appropriate treatment plan. It was clear to the clinicians, the mother, Emily, and the ENT that Emily's speech was not normal and that the VP symptoms were a primary feature that drew a listener's attention. The problem was of sufficient magnitude that the clinicians had some difficulty both hearing and, at times, understanding Emily. They also felt they had to "work harder" as a listener to determine when Emily was talking. These observations are consistent with the mom's report that teachers complained about Emily's speech. While Emily did not volunteer much about the impacts, she did say that she was reluctant to talk in class or with others whom she does not know well. All agreed that the problem was of sufficient magnitude to warrant treatment.

Determining etiology for VP symptoms is critical for treatment planning. Behavioral interventions with an SLP are usually only effective when the cause of symptoms is functional (rather than physical) or when symptom severity is limited. Emily presented with evidence that could support more than one etiology. The diagnostic thinking is presented below with the categories of etiology considered and specific pieces of evidence from the evaluation that seemed to favor one cause over another.

Determining the type of velopharyngeal dysfunction a person has involves distinguishing among three conditions (Table 58–1; Hopper et al., 2014; Naran et al., 2017). The first is velopharyngeal insufficiency, which involves insufficient tissue or some type of mechanical restriction in the ability to close the VP port (e.g., cleft palate, unusual proportions to VP structures, etc.). The second is velopharyngeal incompetency, which implies neuromotor impairment such as might occur from a stroke or various neurological conditions. The third is velopharyngeal mislearning, or a functional issue (Kummer et al., 2015).

Functional origins of VP symptoms imply that a speaker has the physical capability of achieving appropriate VP closure on oral phonemes (and also, opening on nasals) but does not do so. One might think of this as a phonological process in some speakers who early on in speech sound development incorporated use of nasalization on oral phonemes as part of their speech. In others, there may be specific sounds on which nasal air escape occurs; this is phoneme-specific nasal emission and is often conceptualized as a specific articulatory error similar to a speaker who substitutes or distorts other speech sounds.

Based on a weighing of the evidence, a functional or neurological etiology seemed most likely. A submucous cleft was a possibility as well, based on the report from the ENT's nasopharyngoscopy. An indentation on the nasal surface of the soft palate could indicate a defect in the muscle alignment in the soft palate. However, other indicators of submucous cleft were not present (i.e., a triad of symptoms is often described as bifid uvula, a notch in the posterior hard palate, and a zona pellucida or whitish blue tissue color in the soft palate; see Rourke et al., 2017). It was not possible based on the diagnostic information to exclusively rule in or out the functional over the neurological etiologies. A combination of causes might be at play. Perhaps there was some mild neurological involvement of the VP musculature (or even a structural defect such as a submucous cleft) that makes closure of the port more demanding and less consistent. At the same time, it might be possible that Emily has not fully maximized the use of a VP mechanism that appears to be structurally sound.

In addition to determining the etiology, the diagnostic process also revealed the following important pieces of information:

1. Emily appears able to exert more control over the VP mechanism in structured speech tasks and with some guidance (auditory, visual feedback) compared to what she exhibits in spontaneous speech. This was considered a positive prognostic variable for behavioral intervention, although such variation in performance is no guarantee of therapy success.

Table 58–1. Evidence From Emily Related to the Etiological Considerations

Etiology		Evidence Supporting	Evidence Against
Velopharyngeal insufficiency	A. Cleft of the palate	None.	No reported history or overt clefting.
	B. Submucous cleft	ENT noted a "very small "indentation" on the nasal surface of the soft palate during nasopharyngoscopy.	No obvious tactile perception of a defect in the bulk of the soft palate when digitally palpated by the clinician.
			None of the usual stigmata of submucous cleft were appreciated on the oral mechanism examination. The triad of usual features, namely, bifid uvula, posterior hard palate bony notch, and a zona pelucida (whitish blue tissue color) were not present.
	C. Congenital insufficiency in size or position of VP structures	None.	Length of soft palate was judged to be appropriate relative to the depth of the pharynx during the oral mechanism examination; no other structural insufficiencies noted during this exam.
			Nasopharyngoscopy showed evidence that the VP port could close at least a portion of the time (50% of trials per ENT).
	D. Surgical	None.	No history of surgery on tonsils or adenoids or any other structures in the mouth, nose, or throat.
Velopharyngeal incompetency	A. Acquired condition or disease	She did (and still does) have pulmonary stenosis, which can cause general fatigue and other symptoms. The general fatigue and low energy level might conceivably involve the motor activity of speech.	No report from the family of any acquired neurological conditions or diseases.
		Variability in the VP speech symptoms, as Emily demonstrated, is also often considered a potential marker for a neurological cause (developmental or acquired).	ENT reported cranial nerves 2–12 were intact based on cursory examination.
		Although not part of Emily's specific history, there is family history of neurological issues (seizure disorders, depression, etc.).	

continues

Table 58–1. *continued*

Etiology		Evidence Supporting	Evidence Against
Velopharyngeal incompetency *continued*	B. Developmental	Early development was worrisome enough ("clumsy," "late talker") that PT, OT, and speech therapy were all initiated in preschool or early elementary school.	No specific information against.
		Variability in the VP speech symptoms, as Emily demonstrated, is also often considered a potential marker for a neurological cause (developmental or acquired).	
Velopharyngeal mislearning (functional)		Nasopharyngoscopy suggests the VP port is capable of closing, at least some of the time.	No specific information against.
		Perceptually, Emily presented with some trials with no hypernasality or nasal emission. She also never had perceptible nasal emission on /t/ or /k/ productions.	
		Aerodynamically, nasal air flow on /p/ was intermittently absent or at least approached the expected range (<20 cc/s).	
		Stimulability testing indicated that Emily could reduce or eliminate nasal air flow (and increase oral pressure) under certain situations, at least some of the time.	

2. Emily's speech may be contributing to both her less than ideal academic and social functioning.

3. Emily did not show or verbalize much motivation to work on her speech, although her mother wanted to address the issue.

Treatment Options Considered

Treatment for VP speech problems is largely dictated by the underlying cause. Physical problems generally require a physical treatment such as surgery or a prosthetic device, while functional problems usually fall to the SLP for behavioral intervention (Kummer, 2011b). Magnitude of the VP symptoms should also be considered. Even if a VP problem is known to have a physical basis, a decision may be made to avoid physical interventions if the symptoms are limited in severity or if there are extenuating factors that make a speaker a poor candidate for a physical approach (e.g., poor surgical candidate). Conversely, there are situations of a functional VP problem addressed with a physical intervention; usually this occurs when an individual is unable to consistently maintain control over VP activity or if the learned pattern of VP dysfunction is resistant to change in behavioral therapy.

Treatment options considered for Emily included the following:

1. *Surgical or prosthetic management.* Several surgical approaches and prostheses have been utilized to minimize or eliminate VP symptoms, including pharyngeal flaps (e.g., Peterson-Falzone et al., 2009, for a review), augmentation of the posterior and lateral pharyngeal wall (e.g., Boneti et al., 2015), palatal lengthening procedures (e.g., Furlow, 1994), and pharyngeal obturators and palatal lifts (e.g., Reisberg, 2015). Many studies document success of surgical and prosthetic management of VP symptoms, the majority of which have focused on individuals with clefts of the palate. In Emily's case, the unknown etiology, variable presence of symptoms, and fairly limited magnitude of symptoms steered the clinicians away from immediately pursuing surgery or prosthetic interventions. The surgical risks, costs, and potential side effects (nasal airway obstruction, for example) and the costs and time commitment for making a prosthesis and refining it were all weighed against the possibility of improving her speech behaviorally. There are potential risks and complications to these surgical approaches, and so a recommendation for the physical intervention must be justified by the situation. In Emily's case, she demonstrated enough evidence of occasional VP closure during speech that we were intrigued to find out if she could do even more. In such cases, a period of trial speech therapy is appropriate (Kummer, 2011b).

2. *Behavioral therapy to eliminate her articulation errors with no attempt to directly address the VP symptoms.* The /r/ and /sh/ substitutions occur intermittently in Emily's spontaneous speech, and they give an impression of immature speech. These errors were not considered to be directly related to her VP function. For children with clefts exhibiting VP symptoms and compensatory articulation (usually moving the place of production more posteriorly in the vocal tract), some have advocated remediation of the articulation issue as a means of also reducing VP symptoms (Hoch et al., 1986; Ysunza et al., 1992). However, Emily did not have a cleft and her articulation errors are not considered the typical compensatory articulation errors associated with VP dysfunction. For these reasons, and because the family was most concerned about addressing the resonance issue, therapy to address the residual articulation errors was put on hold until behavioral attempts were made at remediating the hypernasality.

3. *Trial behavioral intervention to address hypernasality and nasal emission.* What was intriguing about trial behavioral intervention was Emily's demonstration (perceptually, aerodynamically, and endoscopically) of adequate VP closure at times, both under instruction with feedback about aerodynamic events, but also spontaneously in some instances. Others have suggested that individuals presenting with inconsistent "competency" may have the potential to profit from behavioral intervention (e.g., Golding-Kushner, 2001; Kummer, 2011b). During the stimulability testing, several possible therapeutic strategies were identified that facilitated VP closure (visual feedback of oral pressure; "stronger /p/"; whispering as a means of increasing oral pressure without evidencing nasal flow; sustained /s/) and could serve as a starting point for behavioral intervention. We considered this trial in nature because neurological causes could not be excluded, raising the possibility that Emily would not be able to exert any more control over VP function than she already was. She also had gone through several years of speech therapy and had apparently plateaued in her progress. While we did not know the specific focus of that therapy, it was possible that she had maximized her abilities to control VP activity for speech.

The plan for trial therapy, focusing on determining Emily's ability to reduce hypernasality and nasal emission and to increase oral air pressure, was discussed with Emily and her mom. The other possibilities of physical intervention and addressing the articulation errors were also discussed with the clinicians offering a rationale for starting with trial behavioral therapy. The mom did ask questions about surgeries in particular and how we would decide if Emily ultimately would need one (the ENT offered surgery as one possible recommendation). We discussed the issues of severity of the speech deficits, glimpses of Emily's ability to alter the symptoms, and the risks of surgery (these were only discussed in general; the mom was directed to the ENT for specific risks). After the discussion, the mom was eager to initiate therapy. She inquired about how long therapy would take. We indicated that within 4 to 6 weeks, we would expect to have a much better indication of whether Emily can control the symptoms but that an additional 4 to 8 weeks beyond that might be needed to maximize any abilities identified early on. This was based on the clinician's experience rather than any specific guidance from the literature. Emily had no questions and no visible reaction to the discussion about trial therapy. When directly asked if she understood the plan, she nodded "yes"; when asked if she was interested in starting the program, she simply shrugged; when asked if she was willing to come back the following week to work on her speech with the graduate clinician, she said "yes."

Description of the Course of Treatment

The goal of the trial therapy was to identify instructions, strategies, or behaviors that decreased hypernasality and/or nasal emission (ratings of 0–1 in structured stimuli >90% of the time over two sessions) and to identify instructions, strategies, or behaviors that resulted in stronger bursts and frication on stops and fricatives. In addition to the perceptual data that were kept, a parallel set of aerodynamic measures (nasal airflow and oral air pressure) were also logged regularly to help gauge changes.

The therapeutic approaches that were attempted included the following:

1. Visual biofeedback of nasal airflow on oral consonant productions with associated instructions to manipulate speech. Various types of biofeedback have been attempted over the years and have been shown to have positive results in many instances, particularly when paired with traditional speech therapy approaches (e.g., Gabriel et al., 2017; Neumann & Romonath, 2012). The goal for Emily was to generate oral sounds in sentences with nasal airflow less than 40 cc/s more than 90% of the time. Instruction that were paired with the visual feedback included:
   a. Nondirective instructions to simply "get rid of the air in the nose"
   b. Whispering (based on the observation of essentially no nasal airflow when doing so during the evaluation)
   c. Increasing the oral pressure for bursts or frication. We were essentially asking Emily to increase oral air pressure while watching the nasal flow signal.
2. Visual biofeedback of oral air pressure with instructions to elicit increased oral air pressure. The goal for Emily was to produce /p/ in sentences with oral air pressure peaks greater than 4 cmH$_2$O more than 90% of the time. The instructions utilized were:
   a. Nondirective instruction to "make this peak (pressure) go above this level"
   b. Whispering
   c. Increase overall loudness level
   d. Exaggerate the articulation of the consonant

All of the strategies were also attempted without the aerodynamic feedback. The graduate clinician provided verbal feedback regarding her perception of the strength of the burst/frication or the perception of hypernasality or nasal emission. For the latter, Emily was informed of the 5-point scale described above for perceptual judgments of hypernasality and nasal emission. She was given positive feedback when the clinician rated a production as a 0 to 1. For strength of the burst, a 3-point scale was devised with 0 = *no perceived increase from Emily's usual speech*, 1 = *minimal increase in the strength of the consonant*, and 2 = *a definite improvement in the strength of the consonant*.

Client's Response to Intervention

Emily returned 1 week after the evaluation for her first therapy session. She was fully engaged in the tasks at hand but remained reticent to talk and did not smile. Mom watched from an observation room. The first session was structured to sample Emily's performance in each of the conditions noted above. Within each condition, care was taken to record her performance across a variety of speech stimuli allowed by the recording equipment (the oral tube for pressure measurements poses limitations when it is in place) that was constructed to vary in terms of vowel environment, position of target consonants (syllable initiating vs. terminating position), length and complexity of the stimulus (sustained phoneme in some cases, CV and VC syllable series, short real words in isolation, phrases and longer sentences), and the target consonant itself. The first session was lengthy (nearly 90 minutes with frequent breaks), but Emily did not appear to fatigue or disengage.

The data at the end of the first session revealed the following:

1. Visual feedback for nasal airflow and oral pressure facilitated meeting the target behaviors. Reductions in nasal airflow were more consistent using the visual feedback than were reductions in hypernasality or nasal emission ratings when auditory-verbal feedback alone was presented. This was the case across all instructions.
2. Instruction designed to increase oral air pressure resulted in the greatest change in nasal airflow and oral air pressure during aerodynamic recordings and nasal emission and burst/frication strength rated perceptually. Several instructions were attempted to increase pressure, but simply asking for a "stronger" consonant, word, or phrase produced the most consistent results. In the first session using the

nasal flow and oral pressure feedback and instruction for "stronger" speech, Emily produced /p/ in the syllable initiating position at or above the 4 cmH_2O level 82% of the time in syllables series, 70% in real words, and 68% in short phrases compared to baseline measures of 30%, 32%, and 10% for the three stimulus constructions. In the instructed condition, nasal airflow remained below 40 cc/s 100% of the time when the pressure target was met (i.e., she could increase the pressure without increasing nasal escape—in fact, nasal flow decreased). When /p/ was placed in the syllable terminating position, the percentage of success on the pressure measure was even higher by roughly 10% across the three stimulus types.

3. Emily had greater trouble limiting nasal airflow and maintaining the target oral pressure when using the /i/ as opposed to the /a/ or /u/ contexts. Success rates generally dropped by ~5% to 10% for /i/.
4. Emily had greater success on increasing oral pressures (measured aerodynamically or judged perceptually as burst/frication strength) on stop consonants as opposed to fricatives. We simplified the stimuli further by having her sustain fricatives while watching the nasal airflow channel. After a short period of instruction involving negative practice ("put it all in your nose"; "make this line [nasal flow] higher—now lower") and derivation of /s/ from the alveolar stop /t/ (recall /t/ never had nasal airflow in the evaluation), she was able to produce a sustained /s/ with less than 10 cc/s nasal airflow 70% of the time.

Emily was seen 2 days later, and work focused on those strategies that seemed most effective from the first session. Visual feedback was used 100% of the time, and this second 45-minute session focused on "stronger" consonants/speech using mainly /p/ (both syllable initiating and terminating position) in the /a/ and /u/ contexts. She quickly met target oral pressure and nasal airflow goals at nearly 100% criterion within this session on these syllable and short-word stimuli; performance dropped to ~90% when using /i/ contexts or when shifting to sentence stimuli, but even this represented a gain from the prior session. She still required derivation techniques to generate a sustained /s/ without airflow ("start saying a /t/, but when you let the /t/ go, stretch out the sound"), and she was able to produce this derived /s/ in a CV syllable series only 25% of the time with nasal flow <40 cc/s. However, we discovered that when the derived /s/ was placed in a VC context, she was 100% accurate in meeting the nasal airflow goal.

Emily was seen three times a week for the first 3 weeks and then twice a week for 2 weeks. She was given homework to do two to three times a day (7 days a week) that reinforced behaviors targeted in therapy. The mom reported that Emily did the homework as prescribed (5–10 minutes' practice, two to three times a day), usually with the mom serving as a helper/judge of performance. Emily made very rapid progress within that first week. By the second week, we began fading the visual feedback (still recorded it for the clinician's benefit) with a goal of having Emily begin to serve as her own judge. This caused a slight regression in her performance that was made up within two to three sessions.

By the end of the second week, we updated Emily and the mom on the progress to date. At that point, Emily produced /p/ with adequate oral pressure (at or above 4 cmH$_2$O) nearly 100% of the time in structured phrases and sentences. Nasal flow was maintained below 40 cc/s 85% of the time when she was focused on "stronger" speech/consonants. She also produced /s/ and other voiceless fricatives in syllable series and words with perceptually acceptable strength of frication and essentially no measurable nasal airflow, but performance dropped to ~80% when speaking longer sentences. At the end of the second week, it had become clear that Emily could manipulate her speech and hit the aerodynamic and perceptual targets with limited input from the clinician or the visual display. At this point, we conferred with Emily and the mom, to tell them that therapy was shifting from trial to corrective. The trial therapy was completed because specific strategies and behaviors that consistently resulted in positive changes in Emily's speech had been identified. Additionally, she had shown the ability to begin

implementing these behaviors in increasingly complex stimuli, although still structured by the therapeutic tasks.

The third week of intervention represented the beginning of corrective therapy. The new goal was that Emily would produce spontaneous speech with perceptually acceptable bursts and frication and none-to-minimal hypernasality or nasal emission. The outcome measures shifted exclusively to perceptual events (i.e., clinician ratings). For bursts/frication, the goal was a rating of 2 on the 3-point scale described previously; for hypernasality and nasal emission, the goal was a rating of 0 to 1 on the 5-point scale. We considered this corrective in nature because of the extent of control that Emily demonstrated over the symptoms within the first 2 weeks.

Over the next several weeks, Emily made rapid progress in all areas. A rather traditional hierarchy of stimuli difficulty was constructed that varied target phoneme, phoneme position within the syllable, stimulus length, and level of distracters (environmental, cognitive load). By the end of the fifth week, she was able to offer short monologues (20–60 seconds) on clinician-selected topics with perceptually acceptable pressures >95% of the time and hypernasality and nasal emission ratings of 0 to 1 throughout. Most encouraging was the report from the mother that the classroom teacher had recently commented on how much better Emily sounded when called on in class. While Emily still was reluctant to talk freely in the therapy setting, there were noticeable changes in her communication. The student clinician noted greater eye contact and a more relaxed posture during communication exchanges. The school SLP was engaged at that point to continue the therapy plan. Emily returned to the clinic a few weeks later for a repeat of the aerodynamic measures. She was maintaining the progress as evidenced by oral pressure >4 cmH$_2$O on 100% of samples recorded on /p/ and associated nasal flow <20 cc/s. She also was maintaining nasal flow on other pressure consonants in syllable series and phrases well below the original target level of <40 cc/s. At that point, Emily was scheduled for a follow-up visit that coincided with the end of the school semester so that a final check on progress/maintenance could be made. However, when the time arrived, her mother politely refused the follow-up, stating that she (and presumably Emily) was happy with the outcome.

References

Boneti, C., Ray, P. D., Macklen, E. B., Kohanzadeh, S., de la Torre, J., & Grant, J. H. (2015). Effectiveness and safety of autologous fat grafting to the soft palate alone. *Annals of Plastic Surgery, 74*, S190–S192. https://doi.org/10.1097/SAP.0000000000000442

Boyce, J., Kilpatrick, N., & Morgan, A. (2018). Speech and language characteristics in individuals with nonsyndromic submucous cleft palate—A systematic review. *Child: Care, Health and Development, 44*, 818–831. https://doi.org/10.1111/cch.12613

Bzoch, K. R. (2004). A battery of clinical perceptual tests, techniques, and observations for the reliable clinical assessment, evaluation, and management of 11 categorical aspects of cleft palate speech disorders. In K. R. Bzoch (Ed.), *Communicative disorders related to cleft lip and palate* (pp. 375–462). Pro-Ed.

Furlow, F. T. (1994). Correction of secondary velopharyngeal insufficiency in cleft palate patients with the Furlow palatoplasty. *Plastic and Reconstructive Surgery, 94*, 942–943.

Gabriel, J. C., Mittelman, T., Braden, M. N., Woodnoerth, G. H., & Stepp, C. E. (2017). Video game rehabilitation of velopharyngeal dysfunction: A case series. *Journal of Speech, Language, and Hearing Research, 60*, 1800–1809. https://doi.org/10.1044/2017_JSLHR-S-16-0231

Golding-Kushner, K. J. (2001). *Therapy techniques for cleft palate speech and related disorders*. Singular Publishing.

Hoch, L., Golding-Kushner, K., Siegel-Sadewitz, V.L., & Shprintzen, R. J. (1986). Speech therapy. *Seminars in Speech and Language, 7*, 313–325.

Hopper, R., Tse, R., Smarrt, J., Swanson, J., & Kitner, S. (2014). Cleft palate repair and velopharyngeal dysfunction. *Plastic and Reconstructive Surgery, 133*, 852e–864e. https://doi.org/10.1097/PRS.0000000000000184

Jordan, H. N., Schenck, G. C., Ellis, C., Rangarathnam, B., Fang, X., & Perry, J. L. (2017). Examining velopharyngeal closure patterns based on anatomic variables. *The Journal of Craniofacial Surgery, 28*, 270–274. https://doi.org/10.1097/SCS.0000000000003284

Karnell, M. P. (2011). Instrumental assessment of velopharyngeal closure for speech. *Seminars in Speech and Language, 32*, 168–178. https://doi.org/10.1055/s-0031-1277719

Kummer, A. W. (2011a). Perceptual assessment of resonance and velopharyngeal function. *Seminars in Speech and Language, 32*, 159–167. https://doi.org/10.1055/s-0031-1277718

Kummer, A. W. (2011b). Speech therapy for errors secondary to cleft palate and velopharyngeal dysfunction. *Seminars in Speech and Language, 32*, 191–198. https://doi.org/10.1055/s-0031-1277721

Kummer, A. W., Marshall, J., & Wilson, M. (2015). Non-cleft causes of velopharyngeal dysfunction: Implications for treatment. *International Journal of Pediatric Otorhinolaryngology, 79*, 286–295. https://doi.org/10.1016/j.ijporl.2014.12.036

Naran, S., Ford, M., & Losee, J. (2017). What's new in cleft palate and velopharyngeal dysfunction management? *Plastic and Reconstructive Surgery, 139*, 1343e–1355e. https://doi.org/10.1097/PRS.0000000000003335

Neumann, S., & Romonath, R. (2012). Effectiveness of nasopharyngoscopic biofeedback in clients with cleft palate speech—a systematic review. *Lopedics Phoniatrics et Vocology, 37*, 95–106. https://doi.org/10.3109/14015439.2011.638669

Oren, L., Kummer, A., & Boyce, C. (2020). Understanding nasal emission during speech production: A review of types, terminology, and causality. *Cleft Palate-Craniofacial Journal, 57*, 123–126. https://doi.org/10.1177/1055665619858873

Peterson-Falzone, S. J., Hardin-Jones, M. A., & Karnell, M. P. (2009). *Cleft palate speech* (4th ed.). Elsevier.

Raol, N., & Hartnick, C. (2015). Anatomy and physiology of velopharyngeal closure and insufficiency. *Advances in Oto-Rhino-Laryngology, 76*, 1–6. https://doi.org/10.1159/000368003

Reisberg, D. J. (2015). Prosthetic management of velopharyngeal dysfunction. In J. E. Losee & R. E. Kirschner (Eds.), *Comprehensive cleft care* (2nd ed., pp. 1309–1320). CRC Press.

Rourke, R., Weinberg, S. M., Marazita, M. L., & Jabbour, N. J. (2017). Diagnosing subtle palatal anomalies: Validation of video-analysis and assessment protocol for diagnosing occult submucous cleft palate. *International Journal of Pediatric Otorhinolaryngology, 100*, 242–246. https://doi.org/10.1016/j.ijporl.2017.06.009

Tomes, L. A., Kuehn, D. P., & Peterson-Falzone, S. J. (2004). Research consideration for behavioral treatments of velopharyngeal impairment. In K. R. Bzoch (Ed.), *Communicative disorders related to cleft lip and palate* (pp. 797–846). Pro-Ed.

Trost-Cardamone, J. E. (2004). Diagnosis of specific cleft palate speech error patterns for planning therapy or physical management. In K. R. Bzoch (Ed.), *Communicative disorders related to cleft lip and palate* (pp. 463–491). Pro-Ed.

Warren, D. W. (1979). PERCI: A method for rating palatal efficiency. *Cleft Palate Journal, 16*, 279–285.

Ysunza, A., Pamplona, C., & Toledo, E. (1992). Change in velopharyngeal valving after speech therapy in cleft palate patients: A videonasopharyngoscopic and multi-view videofluoroscopic study. *International Journal of Pediatric Otorhinolaryngology, 24*, 45–54. https://doi.org/10.1016/0165-5876(92)90065-w

Zajac, D. (2000). Pressure-flow characteristics of /m/ and /p/ production in speakers without cleft palate: Developmental findings. *Cleft Palate-Craniofacial Journal, 37*(5), 468–477. https://doi.org/10.1597/1545-1569_2000_037_0468_pfcoma_2.0.co_2

VOICE
CASE 59
Catherine: Finding Catherine's Voice
Leo Dunham

Conceptual Knowledge Areas

Because this case concerns an individual with a disorder of the basal ganglia who demonstrates symptoms similar to those of people with Parkinson's disease, it will be helpful to have some understanding of motor speech problems associated with Parkinson's disease as well as practices appropriate for addressing those problems.

Darley et al. (1975) provide the classic description of the moderately severe hypokinetic dysarthria prevalent in individuals with Parkinson's:

Significantly reduced variability in pitch and loudness, reduced loudness level overall, and decreased use of all vocal parameters for achieving stress and emphasis. Markedly imprecise articulation is generated at variable rates in short bursts of speech punctuated by illogical pauses and by inappropriate silences. Voice quality is sometimes harsh, sometimes breathy. (p. 195)

The perceptual features of dysarthria in people with Parkinson's reflect the underlying pathophysiology. Yorkston et al. (1995) describe the relationship between the pathophysiology and these features in this way:

Reduced ranges of motion may be reflected in the features of monopitch, monoloudness, reduced stress, and short phrases. Variable rate, short rushes of speech, and imprecise consonants may also be reflective of the reduced range of speech movements. Inappropriate silences may be related to bradykinesia, with its feature of difficulty of initiating movements. The deviant voice dimensions . . . may be the result of rigidity of the laryngeal musculature. Dysarthria in those with Parkinson's affects all components of speech and voice: respiration, phonation, resonance (in a minor way), articulation and prosody. The feature of reduced loudness may indicate that the respiratory system is involved. (p. 112)

Voice disorders in Parkinson's are marked by many of the perceptual features noted by Darley et al. (1975), primarily those involving pitch, loudness, or changes in vocal quality. Although the vocal folds may appear normal and the movements of adductor and abductor muscles symmetrical, breathiness may be the result of incomplete vocal fold closure (Aronson, 1985).

Selection of intervention methods for people with Parkinson's has typically been based on physiologic features or on the presence of certain speech characteristics (Spencer et al., 2002). The respiratory and phonatory subsystems are critical to speech, the former because it provides the energy source for speaking and the latter because it provides the sound source (Spencer et al., 2002). It is these two areas that were the basis for this treatment.

Impairments in respiration and phonation can have a major impact on the production of speech. If functioning is reduced at this level, the impairment likely comes from one of three causes: decreased respiratory support, decreased respiratory/phonatory coordination, or decreased phonatory function (Spencer et al., 2002). All three of these areas were incorporated into the treatment plan in the present case: Increasing vital capacity and improving endurance for breathing were addressed by postural changes as simple as sitting upright, phonatory/respiratory coordination was improved by means of cued conversational scripts, and improvement in phonatory function was made by increasing loudness and improving self-monitoring of vocal loudness by means of instrumental feedback.

Description of the Case

Background Information

Catherine was admitted to a skilled nursing facility in the Kansas City metropolitan area. She was transferred to the facility from a hospital to which she had been admitted after falling at home. The admission diagnosis was status postfall, with her daughter reporting her admission to skilled nursing was primarily because she could no longer provide the care Catherine needed in her home with numerous other family obligations. Her medical history included the following:

- Progressive supranuclear palsy, a degenerative neurological disease with symptoms similar to Parkinson's disease, including problems with gait and balance, and rigidity. Additional symptoms are mild dementia and problems with voluntary movement of the eyes.
- Congestive heart failure, an inability of the heart to pump blood efficiently, caused by failure of one or both heart ventricles. Symptoms include shortness of breath and circulatory difficulties leading to stasis or edema and enlargement of the heart itself.
- Chronic bronchitis, or inflammation or swelling of the lining of the airways in the lungs, causing obstruction of the airways.
- Chronic obstructive pulmonary disease (COPD), which is any disorder that obstructs bronchial airflow in a persistent way.
- Atrial-fibrillation, an irregular heartbeat.
- Hypothyroidism, or reduced production of thyroid hormone. Symptoms include depression, edema, increased cholesterol levels, sleepiness, fatigue, weight gain, and decreased concentration.
- Hypertension, or high blood pressure.
- Gastroesophageal reflux disorder, or acid reflux, a chronic condition in which the liquid contents of the stomach are regurgitated into the esophagus, leading to inflammation of the esophageal lining.
- Pacemaker implantation, the installation of an electronic device to control an irregular or slow heart rate.

The original request for orders to evaluate and treat came from the nursing staff, because of difficulty understanding the patient's speech due to reduced loudness and strained voice. The family also found it difficult to understand her speech, making communication a frustrating experience.

History

Catherine was a 63-year-old female, widowed, with three children. She lived with one of her daughters for the 2 years prior to admission to the skilled nursing facility, at which time the daughter felt she could no longer adequately care for her mother.

Catherine was a high school graduate and grew up in what she described as a lower-middle-class household in the Kansas City area. Catherine worked for several years as a switchboard operator for local hospitals.

Visual examination of the throat by an ear, nose, and throat specialist indicated dystonia due to hyperfunction of false and true vocal folds, as well as notable dryness of the vocal folds.

Catherine was being treated with Lasix and Albuterol, among other drugs, for the edema caused by her congestive heart failure and for the pulmonary obstructive problems, respectively.

The patient reported that difficulties with speech interfered with relationships with family and fellow residents at the nursing home. Her relationships with other residents in the facility were of most concern to Catherine, as she particularly enjoyed conversations at her table during meals. Her communication problems caused her to withdraw from social situations and made her feel somewhat isolated from her tablemates at meals because she could not participate adequately in conversations.

Family involvement with Catherine was limited to occasional visits by one daughter. Following an initial visit at the skilled nursing facility between the therapist and that daughter, she communicated little to the therapist regarding any interest in treatment or outcomes. The therapist would communicate progress by way of telephone messages or through nursing if necessary.

Reasons for the Referral

The staff at the skilled nursing facility could not understand Catherine's speech secondary to reduced volume and moderately impaired articulation. Catherine herself reported difficulty with clarity and volume of speech, reporting that at times she "couldn't hear [herself] talking" and felt as though she were "shouting to be heard."

Findings of the Evaluation

The oral-mechanism examination revealed that Catherine's oral structures were within functional limits but that lingual and labial functions were impaired slightly. Catherine's face was symmetrical at rest and in movement. Facial sensation was intact. Tone appeared to be increased, with facial expressions slightly exaggerated and eyes protruded moderately. Both left and right nares were patent. Catherine was primarily a mouth breather, day and night. Her lips were symmetrical at rest and in movement, and sensation appeared intact. Lips were open slightly at rest, but Catherine could close them on request. Lip seal was adequate. The mandible was symmetrical at rest and in movement, and appeared to have an appropriate relationship to the maxilla. Catherine reported no discomfort in her temporomandibular joints. She was able to open her mouth adequately voluntarily and in speech movement. Dental occlusion appeared normal and dentition was complete, with teeth appearing in adequate condition. The tongue seemed relatively small in relation to the size of oral cavity and was symmetrical at rest and in protrusion. Range of movement for lingual protrusion, retraction, elevation, lateralization, and circular movements was slightly reduced. Width and height of the hard palate appeared to be within typical limits. The soft palate was symmetrical and appeared to move appropriately. The oral cavity appeared typical, including the oral mucosa and saliva. Catherine was able to produce an adequate cough voluntarily and could clear her throat.

Perceptual evaluation results confirmed generally reduced vocal intensity with occasional bursts of increased volume, inconsistent speech rate, poor and inconsistent breath support, intermittent pitch breaks, and poor ability to monitor voice production in terms of rate, volume, and clarity. Findings included sustained phonation of /a/ sound averaged 3.4 seconds over three trials, s/z ratio of 1.16 over three trials, and strained voice with reduced loudness.

Poor breath support was demonstrated by labored breathing and short bursts of speech. Breath support was sufficient only for very short phrasing. Respiration was labored, and breathing was shallow with her shoulders in a forward position when sitting. Catherine demonstrated reduced loudness, measuring at or slightly below the 60 dB range as measured with a sound level meter. Loudness increased rapidly at times, notably when she tried to complete a vocal phrase as she ran out of breath. Rate in running speech was generally consistent, with rate also increasing as breath supply ran low.

Pitch varied, rising especially at the end of vocalization as breath supply began running out. Pitch range was perceptually adequate. Catherine reported she felt that she could maintain phonation longer when using a higher pitch. Repeated measurement of sustained phonation showed this not to be the case. Oronasal resonance sounded balanced.

Catherine reported she consumed approximately five to six glasses of fluids per day (estimated to be about 30–36 ounces). As noted previously, her medications included Albuterol and Lasix. A former smoker, she was diagnosed with gastroesophageal reflux, drank one cup of coffee a day, and did not consume any alcohol. She reported no vocal abuse.

Catherine demonstrated few cognitive deficits. Long-term memory appeared intact, but she had a mild impairment of short-term memory. Auditory comprehension was appropriate. She followed all directions, including multistep directions, was able to read and write, and showed no problems with expressive or receptive language skills and had no impulsiveness. Insight and judgment regarding her communication problems were mostly appropriate, but her perception of her respiratory and phonatory deficits was at least moderately impaired, and she asked on more than one occasion during the evaluation, and at various times during treatment, whether she was doing something that caused her to lose her voice.

Catherine responded affirmatively to the question of whether the amount or degree of tension in the production of voice varied from day to day.

Representation of the Problem at the Time of Evaluation

Catherine's progressive supranuclear palsy caused symptoms including reduced volume and bursts of rapid speech. The chronic obstructive pulmonary disease compromised breath support for speech, causing her to speak with reduced volume and at times to increase pitch as breath support declined during speech. This rapid burst of speech and reduced loudness combined to impair the articulation of speech sounds as well. If the tension or rigidity in the laryngeal area was contributing to the effort required to vocalize, in combination with variable but generally poor breath support, then a treatment approach designed to address both issues was expected to allow for improved loudness, clarity, and rate of speech.

Progressive supranuclear palsy is often considered to be a form of "Parkinson's plus," a collection of neurodegenerative disorders that share symptoms with Parkinson's disease, such as bradykinesia, rigidity, and tremor. Since the respiratory and phonatory impairments Catherine demonstrated are found in people with Parkinson's disease, treatment options reflected the similarities.

Treatment Options Considered

Selection of intervention methods for people with Parkinson's disease has typically been based on physiologic features or on the presence of certain speech characteristics (Spencer et al., 2002). The respiratory and phonatory systems are critical to speech, the former because it provides the energy source for speaking and the latter because it provides the sound source (Spencer et al., 2002). Characteristics of Catherine's speech that would be commonly used as a rationale for intervention included reduced voice production and vocal loudness, and poor coordination of breath support and speech. The choice of intervention strategies was also based on prognostic factors, such as improved phonation when a person is instructed to speak more loudly. A final consideration was to choose treatment options that show some capacity for generalization, a particular problem for those with Parkinson's (Spencer et al., 2002).

Impairments in respiration and phonation can have a major impact on the production of speech. If functioning is reduced at this level, the impairment likely comes from one of three causes: decreased respiratory support, decreased respiratory/phonatory coordination, or decreased phonatory function (Spencer et al., 2002). Catherine's communication deficits could arguably have been caused by any of these conditions. Hyperfunction of her vocal cords could have caused decreased phonatory function, and chronic bronchitis and COPD could have diminished breath support for speech. Poor coordination of respiration and phonation was apparent.

Treatment options included increasing vocal intensity for its own sake and to aid in slowing speech rate and improving articulation and coordination of breath support for speech. Training in improved vocal hygiene and use of neck and shoulder relaxation exercises was also included. Exercises similar to those used in treatment have been effective in reducing tension (Dworkin & Meleca, 1997). As Catherine typically reclined in her bed at a 45-degree angle and demonstrated a shoulder-forward posture when sitting, she was encouraged to sit upright with shoulders back when speaking. This is helpful for those with inspiratory impairments in that it allows gravity to aid movement of the diaphragm in breathing (Duffy, 1995). The final component of the treatment plan was improvement of Catherine's ability to perceive variations in breath support and loudness so that she could adjust the length of vocal phrasing to minimize the effects of her respiratory and phonatory deficits on a daily basis.

The treatment plan included both speech and nonspeech tasks, with a preference for using speech tasks to improve respiratory support of speech and to improve phonatory production, in accordance with Duffy (1995), who argued that the use of nonspeech tasks for improvement of respiratory support is not merely unnecessary but also inappropriate.

Catherine wanted to improve communication skills, particularly with respect to loudness and coordination of breath with speech. Family and caregiver goals were to improve generally the quality of speech communication.

Course of Treatment

Initially, treatment would be primarily compensatory. The highest priority was to improve Catherine's ability to communicate with staff so she could express her wants and needs more effectively.

The treatment plan included improvement of coordination between speech and breathing, increased loudness of speech, and improved self-monitoring of loudness and clarity. Speech tasks began with Catherine reading out loud, then transitioned stepwise to spontaneous speaking.

Nonspeech treatment tasks in the form of shoulder and neck relaxation exercises were also used, with a gradual increase in endurance and intensity, as rated by the clinician. Treatment began with the goal of improving Catherine's vocal hygiene and providing her with strategies to make communication more effective immediately.

The treatment was provided five times per week for 11 weeks. The initial treatment goals were to establish good vocal hygiene, begin relaxation exercises to aid in improved phonation, and begin coordination of breathing and speaking. As Catherine became independent in vocal hygiene and performing relaxation exercises, these activities would be withdrawn from daily treatment sessions to continue progress on coordination of breath support and speech and to begin working toward goals of increased loudness and increased self-monitoring of speech in terms of loudness and breath support.

Catherine needed 2 weeks of training and monitoring with respect to vocal hygiene before withdrawing from sessions. Goals were written to ensure compliance with appropriate hydration, minimize vocal abuse by use of natural voice, and improve the effectiveness of her communication by reducing background noise when speaking with others. Daily conversation about these goals led to increased awareness and compliance. Once Catherine gained independence in this area, only occasional discussion about it occurred during the remainder of treatment.

Shoulder and neck relaxation exercises were a part of treatment sessions for 5 weeks. Catherine demonstrated adequate recall of the exercises after nearly 2 weeks, allowing the clinicians to modify short-term goals to increase endurance and quality of the exercises. The number of repetitions and number of sets of each exercise were slowly increased to the point that Catherine performed them consistently and reported that she could pursue the exercises on her own during the day. Acoustic measures such as pre- and postexercise duration of sustained phonation of the /a/ sound with multiple trials resulted in an increase in duration of approximately 15% during this period, indicating that the exercises reduced stress and tension.

It is noteworthy that the average duration of sustained phonation varied from as little as just over 3 seconds to over 15 seconds across treatment sessions, suggesting significant variability in breath support available to Catherine on a given day. The measure of sustained phonation became for Catherine a reliable daily indicator of breath support and of the relative length of phonation; she might be able to coordinate with respiration.

Treatment to improve coordination of phonation and respiration began with the initial session and continued throughout the course of treatment. Reading tasks were utilized at first, with Catherine progressing eventually to spontaneous speaking tasks. Reading tasks began with single words, which grew quickly in syllable length until she was able to read short phrases. At that point, reading materials were marked with phrase lengths appropriate for her breath support in sustained phonation for a given session. These cued conversational scripts allowed Catherine to anticipate the length of phrase to be spoken, making an effective transition to more independent anticipation of phrase length. She demonstrated a growing ability to coordinate phonation and respiration with use of breath pauses and phrase lengths suitable for the day. At this time, increasing loudness became a component of her speech goals.

Loudness of speech was measured instrumentally with a sound level meter set initially at the 60 dB range, with an analog indication of loudness. The goal was modified after a week to set a target level at 70 dB. As Catherine was still using reading tasks at this stage of treatment, she was given verbal cues to increase loudness when the analog indication fell below the target range. The transition to spoken tasks to coordinate phonatory and respiratory function allowed Catherine to view the analog indication of voice loudness herself. This transition was made quickly, in part for the practical improvement of eliminating interruption of her reading with verbal cues to speak more loudly.

As loudness became more consistent, use of the sound level meter was altered to verify Catherine's accuracy of gauging perceptually the loudness of her voice in various speaking tasks. This phase of treatment, to improve Catherine's reliability in monitoring her own vocal production, began 8 weeks into treatment. To improve her self-perception regarding loudness, Catherine began rating her coordination of speech and breath support. After speaking for a short time, usually no more than 30 seconds, Catherine and the clinician would each give a yes/no rating for loudness (at target level or not) and a scaled rating of phonatory/respiratory coordination between 1 and 10. Catherine's initial tendency was to rate her performance well below the clinician's rating. As the final weeks of treatment passed, her appraisal of her own performance became more consistent with the clinician's for breath support and coordination and that of the sound level meter in terms of loudness.

Analysis of the Client's Response to Intervention

Catherine was motivated to improve communication skills, and with consistent effort, she made steady progress in meeting treatment goals. Her improved awareness of her ability to coordinate speech and breathing affected the overall quality of her oral communication, to which she responded very positively.

A year after treatment, Catherine reported that she still "had her voice," though she had intermittent episodes in which she demonstrated strained vocalization and reduced volume for a day or so, usually once every 6 to 8 weeks. She continued to participate in group activities and socialized with several other residents. Nursing and therapy staff reported that Catherine's speech communication became more effective and remained clearer and louder.

Further Recommendations

There are many treatment options available for intervention involving phonatory and respiratory impairments. Some were considered and not chosen, and some were beyond the clinical experience of the therapist or not supported in the facility in terms of equipment needed.

Several treatment options exist for improving respiratory support, including maximum inhalation and exhalation tasks (Ramig & Dromey, 1996), and pushing and pulling techniques (Workinger & Netsell, 1992). Given the severity of Catherine's respiratory impairment and the variability from one day to another, it was felt to be more practical for her to reliably anticipate respiratory support and coordinate phonation to suit.

Various techniques for treatment of vocal fold hyperfunction exist but were outside the training or experience of the therapist. These include Lee Silverman Voice Therapy, which has been used effectively to treat a patient with progressive supranuclear palsy (Countryman et al., 1994).

Author's Note

This case is based on the treatment of a real patient. Catherine (not her real name) contin-ues to reside in the nursing facility, and she often calls out exercises and counts repetitions for the restorative therapy group. Catherine has benefited since the original treatment course with a refresher course approximately 1 year later. The facility granted approval for use of the information as it appears here.

References

Aronson, A. E. (1985). *Clinical voice disorder: An interdisciplinary approach* (2nd ed.). Thieme.

Countryman, S., Ramig, L. O., & Pawlas, A. A. (1994). Speech and voice deficits in parkinsonism plus syndromes: Can they be treated? *Journal of Medical Speech-Language Pathology, 2*(3), 211–226.

Darley, F. L., Aronson, A. E., & Brown, J. R. (1975). *Motor speech disorders*. W. B. Saunders.

Duffy, J. R. (1995). *Motor speech disorders: Substrates, differential diagnosis, and management*. Mosby.

Dworkin, J., & Meleca, R. (1997). *Vocal pathologies: Diagnosis, treatment and case studies*. Cengage.

Ramig, L. O., & Dromey, C. (1996). Aerodynamic mechanisms underlying treatment-related changes in vocal intensity in patients with Parkinson's disease. *Journal of Speech and Hearing Research, 39*(4), 798–807. https://doi.org/10.1044/jshr.3904.798

Spencer, K. A., Yorkston, K. M., Beukelman, D. R., Duffy, J., Golper, L. A., Miller, R. M., . . . Sullivan, M. (2002). *Practice guidelines for dysarthria: Evidence for the behavioral management of the respiratory/phonatory system* (Technical Report 3). Academy of Neurologic Communication Disorders and Sciences.

Workinger, M. S., & Netsell, R. (1992). Restoration of intelligible speech 13 years post head injury. *Brain Injury, 2*(6), 183–187. https://doi.org/10.3109/0269905 9209029657

Yorkston, K. M., Miller, R. M., & Strand, E. A. (1995). *Management of speech and swallowing in degenerative diseases*. Communication Skill Builders.

VOICE
CASE 60

Beth: Becoming Who You Are: A Voice and Communication Group Program for a Trans Woman Client

Sena Crutchley and Vicki McCready

Conceptual Knowledge Areas

Although in recent years more literature about speech-language pathologists (SLPs) serving persons who are transgender/nonbinary (TGNB) has appeared in journals, at conferences, in podcasts, and in textbooks written specifically for SLPs, more information is needed about this population and about service delivery models. The eighth version of the World Professional Association for Transgender Health's (WPATH) Standards of Care for the Health of Transgender and Gender Diverse People (Coleman et al., 2022) reports population estimates of TGNB persons within the general population. According to those survey-based studies reviewed for the latest Standards of Care document, TGNB adults make up 0.3% to 4.5% of the general population, and TGNB children and adolescents make up 2.5% to 8.4% of the general population. Despite carefully defined research inclusion criteria to determine population estimates, it is acknowledged that limitations in terms of geographic location could diminish accuracy as most data were reported from North America and Western Europe. In addition, varied definitions of who is considered TGNB and the age groups included are potential barriers to accuracy.

As individuals assigned male at birth (AMAB) socially transition as trans women, the services of a qualified SLP can help them develop a more readily perceived feminine vocal pitch, pitch range, and resonance pattern, as well as a more desirable

and authentic communication style. If their goal is to be perceived as women, one of their main concerns is that their resonance and typically low-pitched voices may instantly lead to a male gender attribution. Some of these individuals try to change their vocal pitch, resonance, and communication style by themselves or by watching online content and using various materials developed by individuals without specific training in voice. The problem with this approach is that the person might strain and misuse the voice, increasing the risk for vocal pathology. The same outcome might occur with a trans man attempting to independently lower his vocal pitch or a nonbinary individual who attempts to modify their pitch. A trained SLP can help the person develop their desired voice characteristics without vocal abuse (Adler & Antoni, 2019; Davies & Goldberg, 2006).

In addition to voice and resonance as gender indicators, communication characteristics can lead observers and listeners to a misperception of gender. It is important not only for TGNB clients but also for speech-language pathology students and practicing clinicians to know that no intervention program for this population is complete without considering these communication components (Hirsch & Boonin, 2019; Hooper, 2012). It is also important for the clinician and TGNB client to determine an authentic fit between the client and their desired characteristics instead of automatically conforming to society's gender-based stereotypes (Davies & Goldberg, 2006). As Hirsch and Boonin (2019) point out,

We are living in a time when gender stereotypes are being critically questioned socially, politically, and in the workplace; and rightly so. The work we do with gender diverse clients needs to be viewed through a number of lenses, not least of all the following: the client is the expert about their own sense of gender, and we must lead all teaching with context. (p. 277)

The overarching goal of this work will always be client authenticity and satisfaction. With an ever-increasing understanding and acceptance of gender on a continuum, it is critical for skilled clinicians to acknowledge that their TGNB clients may or may not desire a binary gender expression. In addition, clients may wish for a more variable gender expression depending on their communication partners and activities. It is important for clinicians to view their clients holistically and consider creative treatment approaches that may more efficiently lead to authentic gender expression (G. Robinson, personal communication, May 1, 2022).

The purpose of this chapter is to present a case based on an actual trans woman client who participated in one of our voice and communication groups. The group, which served as part of the clinical education program at the University of North Carolina Greensboro (UNCG), involved eight clients and a clinical team of four graduate students and four faculty members (two of whom are also the authors of this chapter) of the Department of Communication Sciences and Disorders. Since this case study was first presented (McCready et al., 2011), clinical work with transgender clients has become increasingly more client-centered and more reflective of the diversity of the TGNB community.

Basic Information About Transgenderism

Knowledge about the population to be served is crucial before any assessments or treatment programs are begun. The following definitions of selected concepts from various professional sources are a first step in this process. See https://lgbtqia

.ucdavis.edu/educated/glossary (University of California, Davis, 2020) for additional definitions.

- **Gender identity:** "Gender identity refers to your internal knowledge of your own gender—for example, your knowledge that you're a man, a woman, or another gender" (National Center for Transgender Equality, 2016).
- **Sex:** "Sex is typically assigned at birth (or before or during ultrasound) based on the appearance of external genitalia. . . . For most people, gender identity is congruent with sex assigned at birth (see cisgender); for TGNB individuals, gender identity differs in varying degrees from sex assigned at birth." (American Psychological Association [APA], 2015)
- **Transgender (TG):** "Transgender people are people whose gender identity is different from the gender they were thought to be at birth" (National Center for Transgender Equality, 2016).
- **Cisgender:** "An adjective used to describe a person whose gender identity and gender expression align with sex assigned at birth; a person who is not TGNB" (APA, 2015).
- **Nonbinary (NB):** "Identity label that may be used by individuals whose gender identity and/or role does not conform to a binary understanding of gender as limited to the categories of man or woman, male or female" (Bockting, 2008).
- **Transfeminine:** "A 'transfeminine' person is typically someone who was assigned male at birth (AMAB) but identifies more closely with femininity than masculinity. Transfeminine people are oftentimes non-binary, genderfluid, or intersex people who do not identify completely with the binary genders of man or woman but feel a close affinity to femininity." (LGBTQ Nation, 2022)
- **Gender dysphoria:** "Distress that is caused by a discrepancy between a person's gender identity and that person's sex assigned at birth (and the associated

gender role and/or primary and secondary sex characteristics)" (Knudson et al., 2010).

- *Intersex:* "Umbrella term to describe a wide range of natural body variations that do not fit neatly into conventional definitions of male or female. Intersex variations may include, but are not limited to, variations in chromosome compositions, hormone concentrations, and external and internal characteristics." (University of California, Davis, 2020)

Voice and Speech Differences Typically Attributed as Male or Female

Societal trends between cisgender males and females have been reported for speaking pitch, vocal quality, vocal intonation, resonance characteristics, and articulation patterns. Speaking fundamental frequency (SFF) refers to an individual's habitual speaking frequency. A higher SFF is generally associated with the perception of a feminine voice (Wolfe et al., 1990); however, a higher SFF alone is often insufficient for a person to be perceived as a female (Carew et al., 2007). In a systematic review and meta-analysis of 38 articles, Leung et al. (2018) found that SFF contributed "to 41.6% of the variance in gender perception" (p. 266). They reported that listener perception of gender is influenced by acoustic and auditory-perceptual measures of pitch and resonance, intonation, loudness, and articulation. Perception is not significantly impacted by rate or stress.

According to Hancock and Siegfriedt (2020), research into gender-based intonation patterns remains inconclusive. They suggest that gender-based notions of intonation may be based more on stereotypes rather than actual differences. Although findings have not been statistically significant, some studies have found a more rising intonation pattern in cisgender women and a downward pattern in cisgender men (Hancock et al., 2014; Wolfe et al., 1990). In addition, findings of the SFF range in women have varied from

being narrower to being larger than in men. Thus, Hancock and Siegfriedt conclude that intonation may be worth consideration in voice training but not for the sole purpose of gender attribution.

Currently, breathiness is the only vocal quality that may be associated with gender. Although a breathy voice quality often identifies a speaker as being feminine (Andrews & Schmidt, 1997; Van Borsel et al., 2009), the influence is variable (Leung et al., 2018).

Resonance refers to the quality of a sound that is generated at the level of the vocal folds and then passes through the vocal tract. There is a range of vocal resonance patterns associated with the masculine and feminine perceived voices. High front vowels and their formant frequencies can be associated with the perception of a female voice (Carew et al., 2007). Differences in vowel formant frequency values between men and women are too great to be due to structural differences alone (Günzburger, 1995). Functional differences, such as forward tongue carriage and lip spreading, increase vowel formant frequency by reducing the size of the vocal tract, thereby resulting in a voice that is perceived as more feminine (Carew et al., 2007).

In addition to pitch and resonance, rate of speech and articulation may affect the listener's perception of gender. Hancock and Siegfriedt (2020) report that studies of speech rate according to gender have been inconclusive and may be more representative of stereotypes than actual differences. In terms of articulation, Hirsch et al. (2019) report that cisgender women generally pronounce words with greater clarity and elongate their vowels more than men. Conversely, cisgender men have been found to distort or omit sounds. Gender perception can also be attributed to vocal tract physiology and dimension variations that impact articulation (Simpson, 2001).

Nonverbal and Verbal Communication

Although anywhere from 60% to 90% of a message is transmitted through nonverbal communication, human beings in general are far less aware of their nonverbal behaviors than they are of their verbal behaviors (Hirsch & Boonin, 2019). According to Hirsch and Boonin (2019), many transgender clients "initially have no idea of the communicative power of their biological gender habits" (p. 285).

Nonverbal communication (NVC) refers to "any nonverbal behavior that may be interpreted as having meaning for a receiver, even if not intended as such by the sender" (Hirsch & Boonin, 2019, p. 252). Extensive research in this area, though with cisgender individuals (Davies et al., 2015), has demonstrated that there are some gender-linked differences in how people engage in NVC. These differences are influenced by factors such as ethnicity, age, class, nationality, and the situation (e.g., gender and familiarity of communication partners, group size, activity) (Davies et al., 2015; Hancock & Siegfriedt, 2020). As Hancock and Siegfriedt (2020) have more recently pointed out, there is an indirect link between body language and gender and that link is "mediated by sociocultural power dynamics" (p. 165). These authors add that "anyone of any gender can be perceived as more powerful if they have open posture and use more space when communicating" (p. 165). Finally, a client's report matters. According to testimonials from transfeminine clients, "Anecdotally, nonverbal communication training appears to make a difference" (Hirsch & Boonin, 2019, p. 276). However, based on this first author's recent 5-year experience of routinely offering training in stereotypically feminine nonverbal behaviors to trans women, none of the clients chose to target nonverbal communication.

Verbal communication, according to Hooper et al. (2012), involves "a rule-based, brain-based, socially shared code or system for representing thoughts" (p. 298). It is in part through this language system that individuals express gendered identities from culture to culture (Wood, 2009). People assigned male or female at birth are typically socialized in different, subtle ways (as cited in Wood, 2009; see also Coates, 1997). One outcome of this socialization is a small though statistically significant impact of gender on language use known as Gender-Linked Language Use (GLLE) (Hancock & Siegfriedt, 2020; Leaper & Ayers, 2007); for example, men tend to be more talkative and directive and to use a more assertive communication style than women while women show more support and agreement and tend to use a more affiliative communication style than men. See Table 60–1 for further detail about communication styles. These differences are affected by such factors as speaker age, relationship, and familiarity as well as group size and gender composition, and communicative context and topic of conversation (Leaper & Ayers, 2007).

Leaper and Ayers (2007) also noted that their meta-analysis of 39 to 47 published studies involved primarily participants from middle-class, European American backgrounds. The exclusion of Black, Indigenous, and People of Color (BIPOC) and TGNB subjects from much of the research into gender expression highlights the need not only to use caution when applying the findings from this research but also the need for the inclusion of a more diverse subject base, especially in terms of race and gender (G. Robinson, personal communication, May 1, 2022). Experiencing gender and how it evolves for the individual varies by cultural group (Robinson & Toliver-Smith, 2021).

In addition, because of contextual influences on communication style, there may be instances in which men use an affiliative style (Ladegaard, 2011) and women use an assertive style (Hancock & Siegfriedt, 2020). There may even be times in which one uses both styles within a conversation or even within a single utterance (Hancock & Siegfriedt, 2020). Therefore, TGNB clients may benefit from viewing communication in these terms of affiliation and assertiveness in order to facilitate a language style that is more effective and authentic than a checklist of stereotypically male and female communication patterns (Hancock & Siegfriedt, 2020).

It is also important to consider the effects of gender stereotyping on perceptions and judgments (Deutschmann & Steinvall, 2020; Ladegaard, 2011). For example, in the research by Deutschmann and Steinvall (2020), subjects in two randomized groups evaluated the conversational

Table 60-1. Characteristics of Communication Styles

Dimensions	
Affiliative ("rapport talk"[a])	**Assertive ("report talk"[a])**
Interpersonal warmth and support	Powerful
Expression of agreement	Competitive
Sympathetic	Direct
Cooperative	Task oriented
Collaborative	Argumentative
Reflective comments	Contradictory
Probing questions	Giving information
Affectionate	Disagreeing with or criticizing
Expressions of connection to listener	Problem solving
Acknowledgment of the other's contributions	Combative
Engaging	Interrupting
Indirect and relationship oriented	Arguing forcefully
Appeasing	Giving opinions and suggestions
Not taking too much conversational space	Taking up conversational space
Active understanding	

Sources: Cheshire and Trudgill (1998); Deutschmann and Steinvall (2020); Ladegaard (2011); Leaper and Ayres (2007).
[a]Tannen (1990).

behaviors from a single recording that was modified only in terms of vocal parameters to sound female or male. After listening to their version (i.e., male versus female) of the recording, they rated the speaker's affiliative and assertive behaviors. Subjects who listened to the male version gave higher scores on conversational features associated with assertive styles while those who listened to the female version gave higher scores on affiliative features. These responses clearly demonstrated stereotyping tendencies.

While acknowledging existing gender-linked differences in nonverbal and verbal communication, it is important to emphasize those "social and behavioral contexts" that influence how individuals communicate (Adler et al., 2019, p. 74). A client's situation, desires, and needs must be considered relative to those contexts (Adler et al., 2019). According to Davies et al. (2015), modification of language and discourse should "be based on the client's own observations of gender markers in the specific environmental context of concern to the client (e.g., work, home, cultural community, social setting)" (p. 135). The client's real-world situations and communication partners must be explored as part of the treatment process in order to facilitate authenticity and satisfaction (Adler et al., 2019).

The Role of a Speech-Language Pathologist

The Scope of Practice and Code of Ethics

According to the Scope of Practice in Speech-Language Pathology from the American Speech-Language-Hearing Association (ASHA, 2016), clinical services delivered by SLPs include "Transgender (TG) and transsexual (TS) voice and communication: Educate and treat individuals about appropriate verbal, nonverbal, and voice characteristics (feminization or masculinization) that are congruent with their targeted gender identity."

ASHA (2016) states that "professionals are ethically and legally obligated to determine whether they have the knowledge and skills necessary to perform such services." It is necessary to possess clinical and cultural humility, responsiveness, and competency. In addition, ASHA's (2023) Code of Ethics states that "individuals shall not discriminate in the delivery of professional services or in the conduct of research and scholarly activities on the basis of age; citizenship; disability; ethnicity; gender; gender expression; gender identity; genetic information; national origin, including culture, language, dialect, and accent; race; religion; sex; sexual orientation; or veteran status."

Necessary Clinical Skills

SLPs need a strong understanding of voice and speech science, including theory, therapy techniques, and speech and voice disorders (Davies & Goldberg, 2006; Goldberg, 2006). They should also possess up-to-date knowledge of culturally based gender differences and cisgender-based norms in both verbal and nonverbal communication (Davies & Goldberg, 2006). In addition to training from programs in communication sciences and disorders, training in the theater, including such aspects as movement, makeup, and clothing style, can be invaluable to teach nonverbal feminine characteristics (Hirsch & Boonin, 2019). The clinician has the responsibility to determine his or her competency to serve the TGNB population.

Cultural Competency, Responsiveness, and Humility

SLPs must be sensitive to the needs and challenges of TGNB persons and must be cognizant of the client's gender pronouns, superlatives, and the name by which the client wishes to be identified and in what contexts (e.g., in the treatment room or only in the lobby) (Davies & Goldberg, 2006). This information can be gathered through case history forms and the interview process. It will go a long way in establishing trust if SLPs state their own pronouns first upon meeting the client and include their pronouns in written communication, as that helps to normalize the concept of individualized pronouns. If one accidentally misgenders the client by using the incorrect pronoun or the person's "deadname" (no longer desired name assigned at birth) (Robinson & Toliver-Smith, 2021), saying a simple "I'm sorry" and then trying not to make the same mistake again is the best course of action. Then the session can move forward and the client doesn't have to put energy into trying to assuage the clinician's regret. In addition, it is critical that SLPs approach their clients with care and respect that involves securing consent for aspects of care that might invoke feelings of hurt or discomfort (e.g., portions of an oral mechanism exam with a person who has had facial feminization surgery) (Goldberg, 2021).

The path that TGNB persons take if they choose to transition socially and/or medically from living as the gender they were assigned at birth to their gender identity is complex and varied. Not all TGNB persons choose to transition, nor do all TGNB persons experience gender dysphoria; however, clients who come specifically for gender-affirming care are in the transition process. That overall process may involve a vocal, social, legal, hormonal, and/or surgical transition as well as unique psychosocial issues (as cited in Davies & Goldberg, 2006; Goldberg & Lindenberg, 2001). The transition may or may not involve sex reassignment surgery and/or hormone therapy. TGNB clients, like cisgender clients, vary in their sexual orientation. TGNB persons may begin this journey at a point in their lives when they are married and have children. Some may stay married, while others may divorce. Others may begin this journey at a much younger age. Clearly, the TGNB population is heterogeneous. As mentioned earlier, the role of SLPs is to support client satisfaction and authenticity.

The Voice and Communication Group at the Speech and Hearing Center of UNC Greensboro

Description of the Group Program

The group met weekly for 2 hours over 14 weeks and included primarily small group work in the areas of vocal health, voice, communication styles, and nonverbal behaviors (if requested by a specific client). Four clinical faculty with expertise and background in theater, voice, and language supervised four CSD graduate students assigned to this group as part of their clinical practicum experience. Two of the clinical faculty had previous experience with transgender clients. The students, faculty members, and seven of the eight clients self-identified as white. The remaining client self-identified as Latina.

Description of the Case

Background Information

Beth (pseudonym) was a 55-year-old, white, trans woman practicing medicine in a small town in North Carolina. She was assigned male at birth (AMAB). Beth realized in her early years that she was different from boys; she played with girls and was attracted to activities that were considered stereotypically female ("I was the only boy taking tap, ballet, and jazz."). She eventually married a good friend from high school, and they went on to have two children. She went to medical school and became a family physician in her hometown. (As Beth pointed out: "We transsexuals become overachievers; we are the doctors, the lawyers, the black belts, the Navy SEALS. We do whatever we can to take the thoughts out.")

Reasons for Referral

Although Beth had wanted to transition in her 20s, she postponed the decision until her two children had graduated from high school. And so, 30 years later, at the time of her 25th wedding anniversary, after much anguish and depression, she "came out" to her wife and children and began the transition process. Although her wife was initially devastated, her children were supportive and told her, "You will always be my dad." She ultimately remained married.

Beth began the transition process with hormone treatment, psychotherapy, and her first facial feminization surgery. Her sex reassignment surgery (SRS) took place in 2016, after which Beth described herself as "extremely happy."

As a result of her transition, Beth was forced to resign from her group medical practice, was asked to leave a financial board on which she served with old friends from high school, and was "kicked out of the church" where she had been a member for 35 years. Eventually after being asked by the town manager as well as former patients and friends to stay in town and not relocate, Beth borrowed money and opened her own private practice in which she sees many TGNB patients. She shared further that serving the TGNB community was especially necessary given the widely reported healthcare disparities experienced by TGNB individuals.

Chief Complaint at Time of Referral

An email from client Beth in 2020: "I am a post-op trans woman physician in Smallwood [pseudonym], NC. I am currently practicing family medicine in Smallwood which is also my hometown. All is well except for my voice. I am constantly outed when calling in prescriptions or conversing with out-of-town physicians. Can you help me?"

Wanting her gender attribution to be female in all contexts, Beth was highly motivated to begin the group. When asked to share three situations in which she would like to sound more feminine, she reported the following: interacting with female patients, talking on the phone with colleagues or with pharmacies, and interacting with male colleagues at professional conferences and consultations.

Findings of the Evaluation

Evaluation Results

The evaluation included an assessment of voice, resonance, and hearing and observations of overall interpersonal communication style, including both verbal and nonverbal communicative behaviors. The voice evaluation involved an acoustic assessment, an assessment of laryngeal coordination, and an auditory-perceptual assessment. Measures of fundamental frequency (F_0) and the formant frequencies F_1 and F_2 were recorded with the KayPENTAX Visi-Pitch IV, Model 3950, and vocal intensity was measured using a Radio Shack Digital Sound Level Meter. The Consensus-Auditory Perceptual Evaluation of Voice (CAPE-V) (ASHA, 2009) was used for the auditory-perceptual assessment. Timed tasks, such as maximum phonation time (MPT), were measured using a digital stopwatch.

Voice and Resonance

Beth's mean F_0 on vowels (/a/ 161.50 Hz, /i/ 170.96 Hz) was in the range of 150 to 185 Hz, which is often perceived as gender-neutral in the absence of other features. Her mean F_0 (113.27 Hz), also referred to as speaking fundamental frequency (SFF), in connected speech was consistent with cisgender male norms (Baken & Orlikoff, 2000). Beth's formant frequencies, F_1 and F_2, were measured for /a/ (840 Hz for F_1 and 1195 Hz for F_2), /i/ (292 Hz for F_1 and 2301 Hz for F_2), and /u/ (306 Hz for F_1 and 1178 Hz for F_2) to obtain a baseline for later comparison. Measures of shimmer (/a/ 25.8%, /i/ 19.0%) and relative average perturbation (RAP) (/a/ 5.1%, /i/ 2.4%) were both high. Beth's MPT (12 seconds) was reduced.

Beth also completed the Trans Woman Voice Questionnaire (TWVQ) (Dacakis & Davies, 2012). She reported that her voice was "very male" and that her ideal voice would sound "somewhat female." The TWVQ is comprised of 30 questions that are answered on a 4-point Likert scale (1 = *never or rarely* and 4 = *usually or always*). Beth rated 23 of the 30 items with a 3 or 4, indicating some level of impairment or dissatisfaction with her voice.

Based on completion of the CAPE-V (ASHA, 2009), Beth's pitch was perceived to sound more masculine than feminine. Her voice quality was excessively breathy, and her resonance sounded hypernasal.

Hearing

Because Beth failed the initial hearing screening, she was referred for an audiological evaluation. Findings indicated a "notch-shaped" mild hearing loss at 3000 and 4000 Hz in the left ear and a moderate loss at 4000 Hz in the right ear. Overall, her hearing was adequate for participation in the group.

Interpersonal Communication— Verbal and Nonverbal

Beth's verbal and nonverbal behaviors were observed within a framework of style, with a "focus on effective interpersonal communication" (Hancock & Siegfriedt, 2020, p. 166) during a two-part 15-minute videotaped interview between Beth and a cisgender male clinician (Part 1) and then between Beth and one of the cisgender female clinical educators (Part 2). Interview topics included her personal history, background information about her transition, her more recent experiences as a trans woman physician, and her goals for this therapy experience. Conversation with both partners about her transition and experiences in Smallwood enabled the clinicians to observe the possible impact of an emotional topic on her communication style.

Observations

During both parts of the interview, Beth appeared friendly, talkative, and motivated to begin the therapy process. Considering the styles of assertive and affiliative behaviors, both clinicians noted that Beth displayed several characteristics of each. For example, when answering questions, she was cooperative and engaging, —both indicative of an affiliative style. In addition, in terms of an assertive style, she was direct and task oriented when sharing what her goals were. Finally, it was noted that with the male interviewer, she talked more extensively, gave more detailed information, and shared her opinions more frequently than she did with the female interviewer. With the female interviewer, she shared more of her emotions about the way she was treated by some in her hometown when she first transitioned. Other contextual factors besides gender that might explain Beth's responses with the female clinician versus the male student clinician include the similar age of the two women and the possibility of the more experienced female clinician asking more leading questions.

In terms of nonverbal communication behaviors (e.g., facial expression and gait), Beth displayed numerous examples of stereotypically masculine and feminine traits. When asked about her interest in targeting any of these, she denied any concerns and reported that she wanted her sessions to focus on voice, resonance, and style.

The Hypothesis

The clinical team hypothesized that by the end of the first 14-week group program, Beth would demonstrate a gender-neutral pitch range or higher with minimal cueing and increased use of her desired communication style in the clinical setting and two other outside settings as chosen by Beth. The team expected that it would take at least another 14-week program in order for Beth to generalize these new behaviors across all her desired settings, contexts, and conversational partners.

Intervention Options Considered

Knowledge/Scientific Evidence

Evidence-based practice (EBP) is recognized as integrating the best available research evidence with clinician experience and expertise and client/caregiver values. Although there are numerous published studies on communication therapy with the TGNB population (Davies et al., 2015; Hancock & Siegfriedt, 2020), the strength of evidence garnered from those studies is greatly limited (Oates, 2019). According to Oates (2019), based on an extensive review of the literature published from 1977 to 2005, there were "no published RCTs [randomized controlled trials] or large experimental studies in the field of voice therapy" (p. 31) for TGNB clients. Most studies involve few subjects or are case studies (Hooper, 2000). Ultimately, it is incumbent upon the clinician to critically analyze available research and glean from those studies what is most appropriate for the client(s) and what correlates best with clinical experience and expertise.

Although the evidence from the most recently published studies is not strong, one may identify potentially useful information about clinical practice with TGNB clients. For example, oral resonance modifications can successfully feminize the resonance characteristics of trans women (Davies et al., 2015; Hancock & Siegfriedt, 2020). A common target pitch range for trans women appears to be between 150 and 185 Hz (Pausewang Gelfer et al., 2019); however, depending on the goals of the individual, a transfeminine client might be satisfied with a lower target pitch in conjunction with other voice and resonance modifications. In a literature review, McNeill (2006) reported that subjective measures may be more appropriate in determining success in speech therapy than objective measures for the TGNB population. Davies et al. (2015) provide a thorough review of the literature and expert opinion related to clinical practice with communication in TGNB individuals. Group instruction has been found to be an effective approach to communication feminization for trans women, particularly when followed by individual services (Kayajian et al., 2019).

Other resources can be invaluable to the clinician working with TGNB clients. Textbooks by Adler et al. (2019) and Hancock and Siegfriedt (2020) provide thorough reviews of the literature combined with recommendations for clinical practice. Podcasts, websites, and other training resources, sometimes by SLPs or other representation from within the TGNB community, are often rich with useful clinical and cultural information.

In terms of the evidence base related to verbal and nonverbal communication (NVC) in the TGNB population, according to Byrne et al. (2003), "Despite the implication that components of speech and language other than voice should be considered when treating male-to-female transsexuals, research in this area is scant" (p. 16). Although gender differences in verbal and NVC have been described in the literature, these are often based on social stereotypes of cisgender persons that are inextricably related to cultural norms, generational differences, and social class (Davies & Goldberg, 2006). TGNB clients must be involved in the process of selecting which communication skills fit their individual lives.

Because Beth expressed concerns specifically related to her profession, the clinical team searched the literature for research into gender-based communication differences in physicians. Findings from a systematic review and meta-analysis by Jefferson et al. (2013) included increased partner building in female physicians. They also found that female physicians engaged in longer consultation times with patients and used more rapport-building behaviors such as offering encouragement and reassurance, attentively and silently listening, exhibiting concern and empathy, lowering dominance, and nodding and smiling more. Please refer to Table 60–1 for a more complete list of these affiliative behaviors.

Client Preferences

Beth reported early in the process her desire to improve her satisfaction with her pitch, intonation, resonance, and communication styles in different contexts with different communication partners. She had the freedom to select which communicative styles she felt comfortable integrating into her daily communication. In addition, with an emphasis on assertiveness and empowerment within a real-world context for her, Beth wanted to be able to communicate effectively with other physicians and medical professionals without dropping below her targeted vocal pitch range. From an individualized perspective addressing communicative effectiveness, Beth wanted to increase her use of a more affiliative style with her patients. The clinical team regularly sought Beth's feedback about the process and about her progress toward her communication goals.

Course of Intervention

Beth was one of eight trans women clients who began the UNCG Voice and Communication Group in the spring of 2020. Based on the overarching goal of client satisfaction and authenticity, her long-term goal was as follows: On a 5-point Likert scale of satisfaction with one's gender expression (1 = *not satisfied*, 3 = *neutral*, 5 = *completely satisfied*), Beth will rate herself at a 4, indicating "somewhat satisfied" while having the knowledge to continue making progress independently. Note that her baseline rating was a 1.5 (between unsatisfied and somewhat unsatisfied). Four short-term goals for the first semester targeted the following specific outcomes:

- Maintaining a gender-neutral pitch range or higher, without evidence of strain, with fewer than three visual or verbal cues during a 5-minute conversation over two consecutive sessions (topic, setting, and conversational partners to be determined by Beth)
- Maintaining a gender-neutral pitch range or higher and using at least three to four assertive behaviors during mock phone and in-person conversations of at least 2 minutes with a pharmacist and another with a physician, with no more than two visual cues over two consecutive sessions
- Using lip spreading to facilitate a "brighter"-sounding voice and resonance quality, with fewer than three visual or verbal cues during a 5-minute conversation over two consecutive sessions (topic, setting, and conversational partners to be determined by Beth)

- Using at least three to four affiliative behaviors during a mock 5-minute female patient/physician interaction with no more than two verbal or visual cues over at least two consecutive sessions for each conversation

The group met weekly for 2 hours over 14 weeks. After completion of initial evaluations, the weekly format of the group included an opening circle for the session's agenda and an exercise in a selected area, for example, vocal health; rotation through three small groups focusing on observation and use of voice and preferred communication styles in different contexts; and finally, a closing circle with the entire group sharing any feedback or reflections on the completed activities. Eventually, the small group work integrated voice and communicative style. Clients were encouraged to keep a weekly journal of observations of communication styles or characteristics not only of unfamiliar cisgender males and females in different settings and contexts but also of personal friends, family members, and co-workers in different settings.

Voice work focused on modifying pitch and resonance while minimizing the likelihood of damaging the vocal mechanism (Verdolini, 1998). In addition to the training in vocal health, the work supporting a foundation of a healthy vocal mechanism included components of resonant voice therapy (RVT) (Stemple et al., 2000) and Vocal Function Exercises (VFE) (Stemple et al., 1994). Semi-occluded vocal tract (SOVT) techniques, including the use of straws and lip/tongue trills with pitch glides, a messa di voce exercise, nasals, voiced fricatives, and the closed vowels /i, u/, were used to facilitate safely and efficiently a higher vocal register (Davies & Goldberg, 2006; Davies et al., 2015; Titze & Verdolini Abbott, 2012). Based on the work of Titze and Verdolini Abbott (2012), perceptual-motor learning principles were incorporated to facilitate acquisition and generalization of new vocal skills. Lastly, resonance was further addressed beyond forward focused resonance by training in a slight lip spread; a high, forward tongue placement; and limited jaw movement during speech (Carew et al., 2007; Gorham-Rowan & Morris, 2005).

Analysis of Client's Response to Intervention

Beth made excellent progress over the 14-week program, achieving each of her short-term goals. She often exceeded expectations in role-plays for use of specific communicative styles in different settings with different conversational partners. Beth effortlessly incorporated the use of some affiliative communication elements in mock physician/patient interactions as well as the use of some assertive elements with male colleagues. She reported satisfaction in beginning to carry over those techniques into her medical practice.

In addition, she safely maintained her target pitch range during conversation with the clinicians and phone conversations with colleagues; with visual cues, she was able to maintain a speaking fundamental frequency (SFF) just into the range that is consistent with normative data for cisgender women, and she incorporated trained resonance techniques. The RVT and SOVT approaches helped Beth to safely maintain target pitch levels. Breathing and stretching exercises completed during a 3-week period created an awareness of appropriate airflow and abdominal muscle support. By the end of the program, Beth no longer exhibited an excessively breathy vocal quality or hypernasal resonance. She completed weekly homework to begin generalization of her newly learned skills.

In addition to performance on short-term goals, a comparison of pre- and post-voice data indicated Beth's progress. As noted during initial assessment, her mean fundamental frequency of 113.27 Hz in conversation was in a range often perceived as male. During final assessment, Beth maintained a mean fundamental frequency of 159.74 Hz. As a result of the use of lip spreading in addition to her increased F_0, she also increased her F_1 and F_2 on /u/ from 306 and 1178 Hz to 329 and 1260 Hz, respectively. Beth increased her F_1 and F_2 on the vowel /a/ from 840 and 1195 Hz to 1255 and 2829 Hz, respectively. There was no notable change to her formants with /i/, and that is likely due to /i/ naturally being produced with lip spreading and a high, anterior tongue carriage, no matter the gender. Beth's increase in speaking fundamental frequency in combination with her changes in resonance resulted in a voice that was more satisfying to the client and more readily perceived as feminine.

Initially, Beth's RAP and shimmer percentages were higher than normal limits. During the final assessment, these values were within normal limits with the exception of perturbation during phonation of /i/, which was elevated at 1.23% (normal is below 1%). Beth's maximum phonation time doubled from 12 seconds to 24 seconds, well within normal limits.

Beth completed a written evaluation of her progress on two different measures: the TWVQ and a 5-point Likert scale assessing her satisfaction with her gender expression. Her responses on the TWVQ were quite different from those she gave initially. She rated her voice overall as "somewhat female," while on the first administration, she rated it as "very male." On all 30 items, she indicated that her voice was more female, reliable, natural, and less tense than she reported 3 months earlier.

Beth's response to the Likert scale assessing her satisfaction with her gender expression indicated a significant improvement as compared to her baseline rating of 1.5 (between unsatisfied and somewhat unsatisfied). Her final rating was a 4 (somewhat satisfied). Although Beth met her long-term goal, she reported wanting to continue receiving gender-affirming services in order to improve her communication effectiveness in personal situations that became more salient since the start of the program.

In addition to Beth's self-assessment of her progress, she completed a 12-item questionnaire asking her to rate on a 5-point scale (5 = *strongly agree*; 1 = *strongly disagree*) the overall group experience as well as the components of the program, Beth indicated that she strongly agreed with all parameters. For example, she strongly agreed that she learned about vocal health, her appropriate

pitch range, and different communication styles. She found the interactions with other group members extremely helpful ("I think this is key."). She gave an overall rating of "outstanding" to the group, and she strongly agreed that she would recommend the program to other TGNB individuals. Beth's responses to the open-ended interview questions were very positive and helpful to the authors, who will use clients' feedback in planning the next group. One of Beth's comments was as follows: "Other than my sex reassignment surgery and facial feminization, this group has been the most important aspect of my transition."

Further Recommendations

As expected, Beth achieved the goals for the 14-week program. In addition, she reported that she was beginning to apply what she had learned about voice production and her choices in terms of communicative styles in her daily life. In order to help her continue the generalization process, it was recommended that she continue in the Advanced Voice and Communication Group in the fall of 2020.

Not only did this group have an impact on Beth and the seven other trans women, but it also affected the four young graduate clinicians assigned to them. At the beginning of the semester, the students were nervous, apprehensive, and uncomfortable about working with the transgender population. At the end of this experience, when asked to compare their reactions to this group at the beginning and end, all four students expressed the personal and professional impact of this clinical assignment.

It seems fitting to end this chapter with one student's comments:

Being assigned to this group has been a blessing in disguise to me. It has made me step back and realize that the thoughts that I had prior to meeting this population were stereotypical and quite shallow. The transgender population is just as human as the rest of us; they just are struggling with different issues than most people.

It's a speech-language pathologist's responsibility to serve clients in a nonjudgmental way, regardless of the circumstances.

Authors' Note

Although the case presented in this chapter is based on a real client, it has been updated to reflect current practices in gender-affirming care. IRB approval (IRB #078326) was received for the original publication on April 4, 2008, from the Office of Research Compliance at UNC Greensboro (UNCG). The study did not need to be reopened for this chapter update. The authors would like to thank Beth (pseudonym) for her willingness to share her story in this chapter and the entire transgender group for their motivation, hard work, and support. The authors acknowledge the sensitive and competent work of the four UNCG graduate student clinicians assigned to this group: Jillian Bauman, Elizabeth Davis, Elizabeth Frye, and Kara Tietsort. In addition, the authors would like to thank the other two authors, Colette Edwards and Michael Campbell, who contributed to the original chapter but were unable to participate in this update.

A significant note of gratitude is also extended to Dr. Gregory C. Robinson for their skilled, meticulous review of the chapter and associated recommendations. The authors are also grateful for the awards from the Guilford Green Foundation in Greensboro, NC, and The Adam Foundation in Winston-Salem, NC, that reduced the cost of the group program. Finally, gratitude is extended to Dr. Celia Hooper, Dr. Robert Mayo, and Mr. David Arneke at UNCG for their support and encouragement.

References

Adler, R. K., & Antoni, C. (2019). Vocal health and phonotrauma. In R. K. Adler, S. Hirsch, & J. Pickering (Eds.), *Voice and communication therapy for the transgender/gender diverse client: A comprehensive clinical guide* (pp. 127–140). Plural Publishing.

Adler, R. K., Hirsch, S., & Pickering, J. (2019). *Voice and communication therapy for the transgender/gender diverse client: A comprehensive clinical guide* (3rd ed.). Plural Publishing.

American Psychological Association. (2015). Guidelines for psychological practice with transgender and gender nonconforming people. *American Psychologist, 70*(9), 832–864. https://doi.org/10.1037/a0039906

American Speech-Language-Hearing Association. (2016). *Scope of practice in speech-language pathology* [Scope of practice]. http://www.asha.org/policy/

American Speech-Language-Hearing Association. (2023). *Code of ethics* [Ethics]. http://www.asha.org/policy/

American Speech-Language Hearing Association, Special Interest Group 3. (2009). *Consensus Auditory-Perceptual Evaluation of Voice (CAPE-V).* https://www.asha.org/siteassets/uploadedFiles/ASHA/SIG/03/CAPE-V-Procedures-and-Form.pdf

Andrews, M. L., & Schmidt, C. P. (1997). Gender presentation: Perceptual and acoustical analyses of voice. *Journal of Voice, 11*, 307–313.

Baken, R. J., & Orlikoff, R. F. (2000). *Clinical measurement of speech and voice* (2nd ed.). Singular Publishing Group.

Bockting, W. (2008). Psychotherapy and the real-life experience: From gender dichotomy to gender diversity. *Sexologies, 17*(4), 211–224.

Byrne, L., Dacakis, G., & Douglas, J. (2003). Self-perceptions of pragmatic communication abilities in male-to-female transsexuals. *International Journal of Speech-Language Pathology, 5*(1), 15–25.

Carew, L., Dacakis, G., & Oates, J. (2007). The effectiveness of oral resonance therapy on the perception of femininity of voice in male-to-female transsexuals. *Journal of Voice, 21*, 591–603.

Cheshire, J., & Trudgill, P. (1998). Section 1: Introduction. In J. Cheshire & P. Trudgill (Eds.), *The sociolinguistics reader: Vol. 2. Gender and discourse* (pp. 1–6). Arnold.

Coates, J. (1997). *Language and gender: A reader.* Basil Blackwell.

Coleman, E., Radix, A. E., Bouman, W. P., Brown, G. R., de Vries, A. L. C., Deutsch, M. B., . . . Arcelus, J. (2022). Standards of care for the health of transgender and gender diverse people, Version 8. *International Journal of Transgender Health, 23*(Suppl. 1), S1–S260. https://doi.org/10.1080/26895269.2022.2100644

Dacakis, G., & Davies, S. (2012). *Trans Woman Voice Questionnaire.* https://www.latrobe.edu.au/communication-clinic/resources

Davies, S., & Goldberg, J. M. (2006). Clinical aspects of transgender speech feminization and masculinization. *International Journal of Transgenderism, 9*, 167–196.

Davies, S., Papp, V., & Antoni, C. (2015). Voice and communication change for gender nonconforming individuals: Giving voice to the person inside. *International Journal of Transgenderism, 16*(3), 117–159.

Deutschmann, M., & Steinvall, A. (2020). Combatting linguistic stereotyping and prejudice by evoking stereotypes. *Open Linguistics, 6*(1), 651–671.

Goldberg, A. C. (2021, June 25–26). *Holistic approaches; creating intentional spaces for gender voice modification.* Paper presented at Gender Affirming Voice Training: A Course for Voice Clinicians, Online Live Event.

Goldberg, J. M. (2006). *Recommended framework for training in speech feminization/masculinization.* http://www.vch.ca/transhealth/resources/library/tcpdocs/training-speech.pdf

Goldberg, J. M., & Lindenberg, M. (Eds.). (2001). *Transforming community: Resources for trans people and our families.* Transcend Transgender Support & Education Society.

Gorham-Rowan, M., & Morris, R. (2005). Aerodynamic analysis of male-to-female transgender voice. *Journal of Voice, 20,* 251–262.

Günzburger, D. (1995). Acoustic and perceptual implications of the transsexual voice. *Archives of Sexual Behavior, 24,* 339–348.

Hancock, A., Colton, L., & Douglas, F. (2014). Intonation and gender perception: Applications for transgender speakers. *Journal of Voice, 28*(2), 203–209.

Hancock, A., & Siegfriedt, L. (2020). *Transforming voice and communication for transgender and gender-diverse people: An evidence-based process.* Plural Publishing.

Hirsch, S., & Boonin, J. (2019). Nonverbal communication: Assessment and training consideration. In R. K. Adler, S. Hirsch, & J. Pickering (Eds.), *Voice and communication therapy for the transgender/gender diverse client: A comprehensive clinical guide* (3rd ed., pp. 249–280). Plural Publishing.

Hirsch, S., Pausewang Gelfer, M., & Boonin, J. (2019). The art and science of resonance, articulation, and volume. In R. K. Adler, S. Hirsch, & J. Pickering (Eds.), *Voice and communication therapy for the transgender/gender diverse client: A comprehensive clinical guide* (3rd ed., pp. 217–247). Plural Publishing.

Hooper, C. R. (2000). Voice treatment for the male-to-female transsexual. In J. C. Stemple (Ed.), *Voice therapy: Clinical studies* (2nd ed., pp. 274–284). Singular Publishing Group.

Hooper, C. R. (2012). Changing the speech and language of the male to female transsexual client: A case study. *Journal of the Kansas Speech-Language-Hearing Association, 25,* 1–6.

Hooper, C. R., Crutchley, S., & McCready, V. (2012). Syntax and semantics: A menu of communicative choices. In R. K. Adler, S. Hirsch, & M. Mordaunt (Eds.), *Voice and communication therapy for the transgender/transsexual client: A comprehensive clinical guide* (2nd ed., pp. 297–317). Plural Publishing.

Jefferson, L., Bloor, K., Birks, Y., Hewitt, C., & Bland, M. (2013). Effect of physicians' gender on communication and consultation length: A systematic review and meta analysis. *Journal of Health Services Research and Policy, 18*(4), 242–248.

Kayajian, D., Pickering, J. & Mordaunt, M. (2019). Group voice and communication training. In R. K. Adler, S. Hirsch, & J. Pickering (Eds.), *Voice and communication therapy for the transgender/gender diverse client: A comprehensive clinical guide* (3rd ed., pp. 281–290). Plural Publishing.

Knudson, G., De Cuypere, G., & Bockting, W. (2010). Recommendations for revision of the DSM diagnoses of gender identity disorders: Consensus statement of the World Professional Association for Transgender Health. *International Journal of Transgenderism, 12*(2), 115–118. https://doi.org/10.1080/15532739.2010.509215

Ladegaard, H. (2011). Doing power at work: Responding to male and female management styles in a global business corporation. *Journal of Pragmatics, 43*(1), 4–19.

Leaper, C., & Ayres, M. (2007). A meta-analytic review of gender variations in adults' language use: Talkativeness, affiliative speech, and assertive speech. *Personality and Social Psychology Review, 11*(4), 328–363. https://doi.org/10.1177/1088868307302221

Leung, Y, Oates, J., & Chan, S.-P. (2018). Voice, articulation, and prosody contribute to listener perceptions of speaker gender: A systematic review and meta-analysis. *Journal of Speech, Language, and Hearing Research, 61*(2), 266–297.

LGBTQ Nation. (2022). *What does it mean to be transfeminine?* https://www.lgbtqnation.com/2022/06/what-does-it-mean-to-be-transfeminine/

McCready, V., Campbell, M., Crutchley, S., & Edwards, C. (2011). Doris: Becoming who you are: A voice and communication group program for a male-to-female transgender client. In S. Chabon & E. Cohn (Eds.), *The communication disorders casebook: Learning by example* (pp. 518–532). Pearson Education.

McNeill, E. J. M. (2006). Management of the transgender voice. *The Journal of Laryngology & Otology, 120,* 521–523.

National Center for Transgender Equality. (2016). *Frequently asked questions about transgender people.*

https://transequality.org/issues/resources/frequently-asked-questions-about-transgender-people

Oates, J. (2019). Evidence-based practice in voice training for trans women. In R. K. Adler, S. Hirsch, & J. Pickering (Eds.), *Voice and communication therapy for the transgender/gender diverse client: A comprehensive clinical guide* (pp. 87–103). Plural Publishing.

Pausewang Gelfer, M., Pickering, J., & Mordaunt, M. (2019). Pitch and intonation. In R. K. Adler, S. Hirsch, & J. Pickering (Eds.), *Voice and communication therapy for the transgender/gender diverse client: A comprehensive clinical guide* (3rd ed., pp. 191–216). Plural Publishing.

Robinson, G., & Toliver-Smith, A. (2021). Sociopolitical implications to consider when working with the LGBTQIA+ community. In R. Horton (Ed.), *Critical perspectives on social justice in speech-language pathology* (pp. 18–38). IGI Global.

Simpson, A. (2001). Dynamic consequences of differences in male and female vocal tract dimension. *Journal of the Acoustical Society of America, 109*(5), 2153–2164.

Stemple, J., Glaze, L. E., & Klaben, B. G. (2000). *Clinical voice pathology* (3rd ed.). Singular Publishing Group.

Stemple, J., Lee, L., D'Amico, B., & Pickup, B. (1994). Efficacy of vocal function exercises as a method of improving voice production. *Journal of Voice, 8*(3), 271–278. https://doi.org/10.1016/s0892-1997(05)80299-1

Tannen, D. (1990). *You just don't understand.* Ballantine Books.

Titze, I., & Verdolini Abbott, K. (2012). *Vocology: The science and practice of voice habilitation.* National Center for Voice and Speech.

University of California, Davis, LGBTQIA Resource Center. (2020). *LGBTQIA Resource Center Glossary.* https://lgbtqia.ucdavis.edu/educated/glossary

Van Borsel, J., Janssens, J., & De Bodt, M. (2009). Breathiness as a feminine voice characteristic: A perceptual approach. *Journal of Voice, 23*(3), 291–294. https://doi.org/10.1016/j.jvoice.2007.08.002

Verdolini, K. (1998). Resonant voice therapy. In K. Verdolini (Ed.), *National Center for Voice and Speech's guide to vocology* (pp. 34–35). National Center for Voice and Speech.

Wolfe, V. I., Ratusnik, D. L., Smith, F. H., & Northrop, G. (1990). Intonation and fundamental frequency in male-to-female transexuals. *Journal of Speech & Hearing Disorders, 55*, 43–50. https://doi.org/10.1044/jshd.5501.43

Wood, J. T. (2009). *Gendered lives* (8th ed.). Wadsworth Cengage Learning.

VOICE
CASE 61
Teresa: Voice Therapy for an Elementary School Teacher With Vocal Fold Nodules
Judith Maige Wingate

Conceptual Knowledge Areas

Vocal nodules are benign lesions of the vocal folds, which may appear as small blisters or calluses, usually on both folds. They result from acute phonotrauma or hyperfunctional voice use (Karkos & McCormick, 2009). The lesions have a threefold effect on vocal fold mechanics. The weight of the nodules increases the mass of the vocal folds, resulting in slower vibration and a lowering of the fundamental frequency. The nodules increase the stiffness of the folds, making it harder to initiate quiet voice and interfering with vocal fold closure. This leads to air escape and an increasingly breathy voice quality. Other vocal characteristics include increased roughness, loss of flexibility and vocal range, and voice breaks (Mansuri et al., 2018; Sapienza & Hoffman, 2022). Teachers, with their high vocal demand, are at risk for developing vocal nodules.

Description of the Case

Background Information

The client, Teresa, was a 38-year-old Caucasian female teacher with a history of vocal problems that began when she started teaching and that had grown progressively worse over the last several years. She complained of hoarseness, increased effort to speak, difficulty being heard by her students, pitch breaks, and deterioration of voice quality throughout the day. She reported that her voice became increasingly hoarse as the week progressed and that she often lost her voice by the end of the week. Typically, her voice improved on Monday after a weekend of rest, and by Friday her voice was almost gone. She also noted improvement of her voice during summer vacation with voice loss occurring every year after the first week of school. She was seen by a laryngologist and was diagnosed with bilateral vocal fold nodules. The nodules were described as moderate in size with a typical hourglass closure pattern. There was also slight erythema of the vocal folds. The client was referred to the Speech and Hearing Clinic for voice therapy.

Reason for Referral

Further information was obtained from Teresa during her voice evaluation. She had been a kindergarten teacher for 15 years. Teresa recalled that she had had intermittent problems with her voice throughout her career but that they had become more persistent in the last 5 years. Her problems had become severe enough for her to consider a change to a job that did not require her to use her voice. Teresa was the mother of three children, ages 5, 7, and 12. The children were involved in a variety of sports, and Teresa described herself as their biggest fan. She admitted to yelling and screaming at their sporting events several times a week.

Teresa indicated that she wanted to improve her voice quality. She stated that she was willing to participate in therapy and to make any changes necessary to change her voice.

Findings of the Evaluation

Perceptual evaluation revealed a breathy, rough voice quality. Teresa was able to sustain phonation for a maximum of 6 seconds and was able to sustain exhalation for 25 seconds. Excessive tension of the strap muscles of the neck was noted during loud talking. Frequent throat clears were also noted, averaging two per 5 minutes. Harmonic-to-noise ratio was 1.25, consistent with a rough voice quality and incomplete vocal fold closure. Average fundamental frequency during speech was 145 Hz, significantly lower than the average fundamental for an adult female. Phonation frequency range was 15 semitones, less than the expected range of 24 semitones. Frequent pitch breaks were noted during pitch glides and conversational speech. All of these characteristics may occur with vocal fold nodules.

Teresa completed the Voice Handicap Index (Jacobson et al., 1997). This measure quantifies the impact of a voice problem on the client's quality of life. Her score on this measure was a 70 out of a possible 150, indicating that her voice problem had a severe impact on her quality of life.

Treatment Options Considered

Following completion of the voice evaluation, it was hypothesized that the vocal fold nodules occurred as a result of high vocal load and high vocal fold collision forces that occurred both on the job and while yelling at sports events. In order for Teresa to meet her vocal demands on the job, she needed to be able to produce a clear, audible voice in the classroom without undue strain and effort. However, in order to accomplish this, she first needed to reduce her loudness demand and vocal load to allow the vocal fold nodules to resolve. Several behavioral treatment options were considered, including the following:

- An exercise-based program utilizing vocal function exercises (Angadi et al., 2019). Exercises are easily learned by clients and offer a consistent program of home practice that is purported to

560 PART IV. ADULT CASES

strengthen the three subsystems of voice (respiration, phonation, and resonance).

■ Resonant voice therapy. This therapy method has been demonstrated to produce efficient voice production while reducing vocal fold collision forces (Salturk et al., 2019; Verdolini et al., 1998). The method is easy to learn and focuses on sensory feedback.

■ Classroom amplification. The use of amplification has been reported to reduce the perception of vocal strain for teachers (Gaskill et al., 2012). Additionally, the use of amplification reduces the amount of loudness the teacher must produce. Some clients do not want to consider amplification as they feel that it is artificial and cumbersome.

■ Confidential voice. Confidential voice, as described by Colton and Casper (1990), emphasizes gentle voice onset and use of a relaxed, quiet voice in conversation. Clients are instructed to speak as if they are in the library and don't want to be overheard or to speak in a way to not disturb a sleeping baby. This should not be a whisper, but the voice is breathy with reduced volume. This easily learned technique reduces medial compression of the vocal folds, resulting in a decrease in phonotraumatic behavior.

■ Projection exercises. In order for a teacher to be heard in the classroom without straining the voice, it is helpful to utilize projection exercises such as those used by actors. The emphasis is on open mouth, increased resonance, crisp production of consonants, and slight prolongation of vowels (Wingate et al., 2007).

■ Vocal hygiene instruction. Vocal hygiene instruction consists of targeting and eliminating behaviors that may contribute to vocal fold irritation. Environmental manipulation may also be undertaken in a vocal hygiene program. This is a useful adjunct to voice therapy techniques (Sapienza & Hoffman, 2022).

■ Voice rest. While often recommended for persons with voice problems, voice rest is not an option for a working professional. There are also compliance issues with vocal rest as well as possible detraining of muscle (Ishikawa & Thibeault, 2010). Although a short period of voice rest might serve to reduce vocal fold irritation, the client will not make any behavioral changes and would return to the work situation using the same vocal behaviors that led to the development of the vocal fold nodules. Therefore, voice rest was not recommended in this case.

Course of Treatment

For this teacher, an eclectic approach was selected utilizing all of the techniques listed above with the exception of voice rest.

Therapy Session 1

Teresa was seen weekly for voice therapy sessions over the course of 12 weeks. At the beginning of the session, basic vocal hygiene recommendations were reviewed. Two issues were targeted. The first was the need to reduce the amount of time that Teresa spent yelling at her children's sports events. She was encouraged to use a noisemaker to express her enthusiasm and allow her voice to rest. The frequent throat-clearing behavior was also targeted. It was suggested that Teresa take a sip of water instead of clearing her throat. This, in turn, would help to reduce vocal fold irritation and swelling. She expressed some concern about increasing her water intake as she had few bathroom breaks during the school day. Other alternatives to reduce throat clears were offered, including keeping a piece of hard candy in her mouth or using a silent cough in place of a throat clear. In a silent cough, air is forced through open vocal folds so there is no contact of the vocal fold edges. Teresa agreed to combine these techniques.

The client was given a demonstration of abdominal breathing with an emphasis on prolonged exhalation. This was practiced during sustained productions of /f/ and /sh/ as well as during the vowels /i/ and /a/. The concept of confidential voice was then introduced and practiced in words and sentences. The pitch glides from the vocal function exercises were demonstrated and practiced with the client. These consisted of glides up and down, which were repeated twice. The client was asked to practice all of the above during the next week.

Finally, a personal amplification system was introduced consisting of a speaker worn around the waist, which was connected to a headset microphone. The client was asked to wear this in the classroom at all times and to use a confidential voice with the microphone.

Therapy Session 2

During the second session, the remainder of the vocal function exercises was introduced. The client sustained a warm-up tone using a nasal /i/ sound on F above middle C. Then the upward and downward glides were produced twice each. Following this, the client sustained five pitches as softly and for as long as she could on the word "knoll." The pitches used were middle C-D-E-F-G. Each pitch was sustained twice. The client was instructed to practice these twice daily and to record the length of the sustained pitches on a record sheet.

Easy onset was reviewed and practiced. The client used the technique to answer questions and read short paragraphs. She was asked to continue practicing easy onset daily at home.

Therapy Session 3

The session was begun with a review of the week. Teresa reported some improvement in vocal quality and a reduction in vocal strain since using the personal amplifier. She reported that she had stopped clearing her throat after implementing the alternative behaviors suggested. Vocal function exercises were also reviewed and sustained phonation times were recorded. An increase in phonation time, especially in midrange pitch levels, was observed. Next the concept of increased resonance was introduced. An emphasis was placed on feeling increased sensation around the lips and nose during production of nasal sounds and a hum. The client was asked to try to maintain this feeling while reading sentences loaded with nasal sounds. Home practice combining resonance materials and easy onset materials was assigned.

Therapy Session 4

Vocal function exercises were practiced. The client also practiced resonant voice production using sentences containing both nasal and nonnasal words and responded to short questions using resonant voice.

During this session, Teresa was asked to describe her typical voice use in the classroom and then to brainstorm ways to change her activities to help her voice improve. For example, instead of using her voice to get attention, the teacher was able to realize that she could use a hand signal for quiet. She also decided that she could utilize parent volunteers to help give instructions during some activities. She was asked to continue to think of other ways to minimize any unnecessary talking that she might be doing. The clinician suggested that she look at her schedule and try to alternate quiet activities with those that required more talking. She was asked to begin incorporating some of her new vocal strategies at work for short periods of time.

Therapy Session 5

After reviewing vocal function exercises, the concept of projecting the voice was introduced. This was built on the concept of easy onset. The teacher was instructed to increase the rate of air being utilized while allowing the mouth and throat to be very open. She was then asked to slightly prolong the vowels in short phrases while maintaining the sensations experienced using resonant voice. Next, crisp articulation of consonants was emphasized. Portions of famous speeches (e.g., the speech by Martin Luther King Jr., "I Have a Dream") were used to practice projection. After a brief trial in which she gave her typical classroom directions while using a more projected voice, she was asked to continue this for at least two activities per day.

Therapy Session 6

As in previous sessions, vocal function exercises were reviewed. Practice was continued with resonant voice and projection. Fewer pitch breaks were noted during glides, and Teresa demonstrated longer phonation times. She reported that her voice was becoming clearer and that she noticed much less effort to speak at work. She no longer experienced voice loss at the end of the week. A follow-up session was scheduled in 2 weeks. Further instruction on incorporating her new vocal techniques in the classroom was given.

Therapy Session 7

Teresa reported that she utilized the techniques in the classroom but had to consciously think about using them and/or would forget to breathe. To assist with the transition, Teresa agreed to schedule two activities on the day following her therapy session in which she would use her new techniques. She was asked to double the number of activities on the following day and to continue in this manner. Further follow-up was scheduled at a 1-month interval.

Therapy Session 8

By this session, Teresa reported that she was able to incorporate the techniques in the classroom with little effort and that she felt they had become more habitual. She continued to use the amplifier, especially during noisier periods in the classroom. She reported no voice loss and significant reduction in effort to speak. However, there was some occasional hoarseness at the end of the day. Throat clearing was no longer observed. Repeat measures were taken, which revealed that Teresa was able to sustain phonation a maximum of 25 seconds across her modal pitch range. Her average fundamental frequency had increased to 185 Hz with phonational frequency range increased to 28 semitones. No pitch breaks were noted during pitch glides. Harmonic-to-noise ratio was .65. Her score on the VHI was 30 out of 150, indicating that her voice problems now had a very mild impact on her quality of life. Subsequent follow-up with the laryngologist revealed that the nodules were almost resolved with only a small amount of swelling visible.

Further Recommendations

Therapy was discontinued. It was recommended that Teresa continue using amplification in the classroom and continue to practice the vocal function exercises 2 to 3 days a week. A practice regimen for vocal conditioning was designed, which consisted of reading aloud, using her typical classroom voice, for an increased amount of time daily until she was able to read aloud for 15 to 20 minutes at a time with no vocal strain. She was asked to implement this regimen at least 3 weeks prior to the beginning of school to help condition her voice to meet the vocal demands of a new school year. She was urged to contact her clinician for assistance as needed.

Author's Note

This case is not based on an actual client but on a composite of cases seen in the author's clinical practice.

References

Angadi, V., Croake, D., & Stemple, J. (2019). Effects of vocal function exercises: A systematic review. *Journal of Voice, 33*(1), 124e13–124.e34. https://doi.org/10.1016/j.jvoice.2017.08.031

Colton, R. H., & Casper, J. K. (1990). *Understanding voice problems: A physiological perspective for diagnosis and treatment.* Williams & Wilkins.

Gaskill, C. S., O'Brien, S. G., & Tinter, S. R. (2012). The effect of voice amplification on occupational vocal dose in elementary school teachers. *Journal of Voice, 26*(5), e19–e27. https://doi.org/10.1016/j.jvoice.2011.10.010

Ishikawa, K., & Thibeault, S. (2010). Voice rest vs. voice exercise: A review of the literature. *Journal of Voice,*

24(4), 379–387. https://doi.org/10.1016/j.jvoice.2008.10.011

Jacobson, B. H., Johnson, A., Grywalski, C., Silbergleit, A., Jacobsen, G., & Benninger, M. S. (1997). The Voice Handicap Index (VHI): Development and validation. *American Journal of Speech-Language Pathology, 6*(3), 66–70.

Karkos, P. D., & McCormick, M. (2009). The etiology of vocal fold nodules in adults. *Current Opinion Otolaryngology & Head and Neck Surgery, 17*(6), 420–423. https://doi.org/10.1097/MOO.0b013e328331a7f8

Mansuri, B., Tohidist, S.A., Soltaninejad, N., Kamali, M., Ghelichi, L., & Azimi, H. (2018). Nonmedical treatments of vocal fold nodules: A systematic review. *Journal of Voice, 32*(5): 609–620. https://doi.org/10.1016/j.jvoice.2017.08.023

Salturk, Z., Ozdemir, E., Sari, H., Keten, S., Kumrat, L., Berkiten, G., . . . Uyar, Y. (2019). Assessment of resonant voice therapy in treatment of vocal fold nodules. *Journal of Voice, 33*(5), 810.e1–810-e.4. https://doi.org/10.1016/j.jvoice.2018.04.012

Sapienza, C., & Hoffman, B. (2022). *Voice disorders* (4th ed.). Plural Publishing.

Verdolini, K., Druker, D., Palmer, P., & Samawi, H. (1998). Laryngeal adduction in resonant voice. *Journal of Voice, 12*, 315–327. https://doi.org/10.1016/s0892-1997(98)80021-0

Wingate, J. M., Brown, W. S., Shrivastav, R., Davenport, P., & Sapienza, C. M. (2007). Treatment outcomes for professional voice users. *Journal of Voice, 21*, 433–449. https://doi.org/10.1016/j.jvoice.2006.01.001